ARCTIC OCEAN

ndinavia

Baltic Sea

Scandinavia

EUROPE

lps

Danube R.

Black Sea

Sicily

Anatolia

Mediterranean Sea

eb

Caspian Sea

Volga R.

Zagros Mts.

Southwest Asia

Tigris R.

Euphrates R.

Syrian
Desert

Ob R.

Yenisei R.

Siberia

Eurasian Steppe

L. Balkhash

Central
Asia

Lena R.

ASIA

L. Baikal

Tarim
Basin

Gobi Desert

Manchuria

Bering Sea

Sea of
Japan

Huang He

Yangzi R.

Yellow
Sea

East Asia

Himalaya Mountains

Persian Gulf

Strait of
Hormuz

Indus R.

Ganges R.

South
Asia

Deccan

h a r a

e l

Nile R.

Red Sea

Arabian
Desert

Bab al-Mandab

AFRICA

Ethiopian
Highlands

Central
Africa

Congo R.

L. Victoria

East
Africa

Zambezi R.

Arabian
Sea

Bay of
Bengal

Sri Lanka

Straits of
Malacca

Sumatra

Southeast
Asia

Mekong R.

South
China
Sea

Philippines

Borneo

Java

New
Guinea

PACIFIC OCEAN

INDIAN
OCEAN

Madagascar

Coral Sea

Southern
Africa

Cape of
Good Hope

Great Sandy
Desert

AUSTRALIA

Tasmania

New
Zealand

0   1,000   2,000 mi

0 1,000 2,000 km

ANTARCTICA

J. R. McNEILL

THE WEBS *of* HUMANKIND

A WORLD HISTORY

W. W. NORTON & COMPANY
Independent Publishers Since 1923

W. W. NORTON & COMPANY has been independent since its founding in 1923, when William Warder Norton and Mary D. Herter Norton first published lectures delivered at the People's Institute, the adult education division of New York City's Cooper Union. The firm soon expanded its program beyond the Institute, publishing books by celebrated academics from America and abroad. By midcentury, the two major pillars of Norton's publishing—trade books and college texts—were firmly established. In the 1950s, the Norton family transferred control of the company to its employees, and today—with a staff of five hundred and hundreds of trade, college, and professional titles published each year—W. W. Norton & Company stands as the largest and oldest publishing house owned wholly by its employees.

Editor: Steve Forman
Associate Managing Editor: Melissa Atkin
Manuscript Editor: Alice Vigliani
Senior Associate Editor: Gerra Goff
Assistant Editor: Lily Gellman
Cartographic Editor: Charlotte Miller
Copyeditor: Marne Evans
Managing Editor, College: Marian Johnson
Managing Editor, College Digital Media: Kim Yi
Director of Production, College: Jane Searle
Media Editor: Carson Russell
Media Project Editor: Rachel Mayer
Media Associate Editor: Alexander Lee
Media Assistant Editor: Alexandra Malakhoff
Photo Editor: Stephanie Romeo
Photo Researcher: Lynn Gadson
Associate Art Director: Jillian Burr
Permissions Manager: Bethany Salminen
Permissions Specialist: Josh Garvin
Layout Artist: Brad Walrod/Kenoza Type, Inc.
Cartographer and Illustrator: Mapping Specialists—Fitchburg, WI
Manufacturing: Transcontinental Interglobe Inc.—Beauceville, QC

ISBN 978-0-393-97911-4

Library of Congress Cataloging-in-Publication Data

Names: McNeill, John Robert, author.
Title: The webs of humankind : a world history / J. R. McNeill.
Description: First edition. | New York : W. W. Norton & Company, [2021] |
   Includes index.
Identifiers: LCCN 2019045123 | ISBN 9780393979114 (hardcover)
Subjects: LCSH: World history—Textbooks. | Human ecology—History—Textbooks. |
   Globalization—History—Textbooks.
Classification: LCC D20.M4843 2021 | DDC 909—dc23
LC record available at https://lccn.loc.gov/2019045123

W. W. Norton & Company, Inc., 500 Fifth Avenue, New York, NY 10110

wwnorton.com

W. W. Norton & Company Ltd., 15 Carlisle Street, London W1D 3BS

1 2 3 4 5 6 7 8 9 0

This book is dedicated to families: especially the one into which I was born, the one that Julie and I created, and the one that is the community of historians at Georgetown University—students and teachers, past and present.

ABOUT THE AUTHOR

J. R. MCNEILL studied at Swarthmore College and Duke University, where he completed a PhD in 1981. Since 1985 he has taught at Georgetown University, in the History Department and School of Foreign Service, where he held the Cinco Hermanos Chair in Environmental and International Affairs before becoming University Professor in 2006. He has taught roughly 3,000 Georgetown students in courses on world history, international relations history, and environmental history.

McNeill's books include: *The Atlantic Empires of France and Spain* (1985); *The Mountains of the Mediterranean World: An Environmental History* (1992); *Something New under the Sun: An Environmental History of the Twentieth-Century World* (2000), co-winner of the World History Association book prize and the Forest History Society book prize; *The Human Web: A Bird's-Eye View of World History* (2003), co-authored with his father, William McNeill; and *Mosquito Empires: Ecology and War in the Greater Caribbean, 1620–1914* (2010), which won the Beveridge Prize from the American Historical Association. His latest book, *The Great Acceleration: An Environmental History of the Anthropocene, 1945–2015*, appeared in 2016. He has edited or co-edited 15 other books, including two volumes of *The Cambridge World History* (2015).

In 2010, McNeill was awarded the Toynbee Prize for "academic and public contributions to humanity." In 2014, the World History Association awarded him its annual prize for achievement in that field; in 2019, the American Society for Environmental History presented him with its Distinguished Scholar Award. The Royal Netherlands Academy of Arts and Sciences awarded him the Heineken Prize for history in 2018. In 2011–2013, he served as President of the American Society for Environmental History, and in 2019 as President of the American Historical Association. He is a member of the American Academy of Arts and Sciences.

CONTENTS IN BRIEF

CONTENTS

8. The West End of the Old World Web: Carthage, Rome, and the Mediterranean World, 800 BCE to 200 CE   **207**

18. Cultural Upheavals: Religious and Intellectual Movements, 1500 to 1750   517

PART 5   REVOLUTIONS, 1640 TO 1920   604

MAPS

FEATURES

The Webs of Humankind offers three text features that reinforce and enrich the book's presentation of world history. They are meant to support student work with primary sources and strengthen their engagement with world history questions.

The first is a primary source feature called **Considering the Evidence**, which appears in every chapter. Authored by Daren Ray (Auburn University), **Considering the Evidence** presents text documents and images of art and artifacts for analysis by students. Each box includes a contextual headnote and study questions. The primary sources all shed light on the events and developments of each chapter.

The second feature, **Puzzles in World History**, comprises short essays by J. R. McNeill on compelling world history questions that emerge from the text discussions. There are seven **Puzzles** features integrated throughout the book. They can be used to key class discussion and/or student writing.

The third, **The Human Web**, is an infographic feature that combines images, text, and maps to illustrate webs of interaction at key periods. Each volume of the textbook offers three **Human Web** features. Each one is built around a central map of an important web, with images and text reflecting the goods, technology, beliefs, and material culture shared by peoples across the web. Each includes an introductory headnote by J. R. McNeill and study questions based on the feature and the chapter reading.

FEATURE CONTENTS

PEDAGOGY

The Webs of Humankind presents a set of pedagogical features intended to guide introductory students through the chapters and support their understanding of world history.

All chapters open with a list of **Focus Questions** that correspond to the major section headings in the chapter. These questions, which appear also in the relevant running heads at the tops of pages, are meant to alert students to the key developments in each section. All chapters also open with a **Chronology** of major events and an **immersive narrative vignette** to draw students into the reading.

The chapters end with a summary **Conclusion** and a **Chapter Review** page that includes **Review Questions**, a list of the **Key Terms** (with page references) that appear in bold in the chapter, and a **Further Reading** list compiled and annotated by J. R. McNeill. A **Glossary** at the end of the book includes definitions of all key terms and a pronunciation guide.

The author also collaborated on the art program, which includes more than 700 images, and on the more than 150 original maps, all with captions by the author.

DIGITAL RESOURCES FOR TEACHING AND LEARNING

W. W. Norton has a long history of delivering robust and carefully designed digital resource packages to support teaching and learning. The resources described here have been built from the ground up—with guidance and input from active world history instructors—specifically for use with *The Webs of Humankind* by J. R. McNeill.

Resources for Students

The following resources are available using the access card at the front of this text.

INQUIZITIVE

InQuizitive is Norton's award-winning adaptive learning tool that personalizes the learning experience for students and enhances their understanding of the key themes and objectives from each chapter. This new **InQuizitive** course, written for *The Webs of Humankind*, features hundreds of interactive questions tagged to each chapter's **Focus Questions**—including questions based on maps, historical images, and primary source documents—all of which are delivered in an engaging game-like environment with detailed, answer-specific feedback. InQuizitive can be integrated directly into your existing learning management system for easy student access.

▶ **Increased student scores by 16%**

In efficacy studies, when history students completed InQuizitive activities prior to taking a summative quiz, their quiz grades increased by an average of 16 percentage points. Go to www.wwnorton.com/inquizitive for more information.

xl

HISTORY SKILLS TUTORIALS

The History Skills Tutorials are interactive, online modules that support student development of key skills for the world history course—such as analysis and interpretation of primary source documents, images, and maps. With interactive practice assessments, helpful guiding feedback, and videos with John McNeill modeling source analysis, these tutorials teach students the critical analysis skills that they will put to use in their academic and professional careers. These tutorials can be integrated directly into your existing learning management system for easy student access.

PRIMARY SOURCE AND MAP EXERCISES

Building from the critical analysis skills developed in the History Skills Tutorials (above), a series of assignable Primary Source Exercises and Map Exercises provide students the opportunity to practice these skills in every week of the course. Each exercise includes 5 to 10 interactive questions based on documents, images, and maps found in the chapter reading. These exercises can be integrated directly into your existing learning management system for easy student access.

STUDENT SITE

The online Student Site offers additional study and review materials for students to use outside of class. Resources include:

- An **Online Reader** features dozens of additional primary source documents and images, with brief headnotes and sample questions for analysis.
- **Author videos** featuring John McNeill help students understand the webs of interaction that shape world history.

- **Flashcards** invite students to review the key terms from the textbook.
- **Chapter outlines** give students a detailed snapshot of the key topics of each chapter.

EBOOK

Norton Ebooks give students and instructors an enhanced reading experience at a fraction of the price of a print textbook. Students are able to have an active reading experience and can take notes, bookmark, search, highlight, and even read offline. Instructors can add notes for students to see as they read the text. Norton Ebooks can be viewed on—and synced among—all computers and mobile devices. Features in the ebook include:

- Enlargeable maps and art
- Embedded videos and animations
- Pop-up key term definitions

Resources for Instructors

All instructor resources are available for download after free registration at

wwnorton.com/catalog/instructor-resources

RESOURCES FOR YOUR LMS

Easily add high-quality Norton digital resources to your online, hybrid, or lecture courses. Get started building your course with our easy-to-use integrated resources; all activities can be accessed right within your existing learning management system. The downloadable file includes integration links to the following resources, organized by chapter:

- **Ebook**
- **InQuizitive**

- **History Skills Tutorials**
- **Primary Source Exercises & Map Exercises**
- **Student Site Resources**
- **Instructor-facing author videos**

TEST BANK

The Test Bank features more than 1,500 questions—including multiple choice, true/false, and short-answer questions—aligned with the chapter's Focus Questions. This bank of quiz and exam content provides multiple avenues for comprehension and skill assessment.

Norton Testmaker brings Norton's high-quality testing materials online. Create assessments from anywhere with an Internet connection, without downloading files or installing specialized software. Search and filter test bank questions by chapter, type, difficulty, learning objectives, and other criteria. You can also customize questions to fit your course. Then, easily export your tests to Microsoft Word or Common Cartridge files for import into your LMS.

INSTRUCTOR'S MANUAL

The Instructor's Manual contains:

- Detailed chapter summaries
- Chapter outlines
- Discussion/forum prompts
- Lecture ideas
- Sample responses to Questions for Analysis in the text, and more

LECTURE AND ART POWERPOINT SLIDES

The lecture PowerPoint slides combine chapter review, images, maps, and lecture notes, and are easily customizable. Art PowerPoint slides and JPEGs are available separately for every image and map in the text. Alt-text is provided for each item.

PREFACE

How did our world get to be the way it is? Why are some parts of the world so much richer than others? Is gender inequality universal, or have societies ever existed without it? Why are empires, so common throughout most of world history, so rare today? Why in both the Americas and Eurasia—which developed in isolation from each other—did many early cities feature monumental architecture, grid patterns, and open public spaces? When and why did slavery begin, and why, after thousands of years, was it abolished almost everywhere in the nineteenth century? What role has climate change played in history, and has that role changed in recent decades?

The study of world history can provide answers to big questions like these. Almost any variety of history can help explain how and why societies have changed over time. However, world history (or global history—I make no distinction between the two terms) is a special kind of history. It is not the sum of all history: it is in fact more than the sum of its parts.

What Is Distinctive about World History?

World history is comparative: it helps distinguish what is commonplace from what is distinctive about societies. In the early chapters of this book, we will notice that places where people raised crops that store well were much more likely to develop kingdoms, empires, and other states than places where people relied on crops that spoil too quickly to be stored and distributed. An important pattern like this would be harder to see if we were looking at the histories of China, India, Africa, and South America separately, without comparison. So too with several religious movements of the sixteenth and seventeenth centuries. The Protestant Reformation in Europe, the birth of the Sikh religion in India, and the Shi'a Islamic revival in seventeenth-century Iran all emphasized personal relationships with divinity, and valued intuition over institutions in matters of faith. Comparing these (as Chapter 18 does) suggests a common pattern despite the different contexts.

World history is also selective. Because the past is virtually infinite, all historians must choose what to include in their accounts and what to leave out. World historians must be more selective to avoid having their subject become a giant jumble of facts. World history tends to foreground parallels, contrasts, and connections among societies rather than the details of national history. So, for example, Chapter 9 considers the impact of iron working on both northern Europe and sub-Saharan Africa after 1000 BCE. In Africa, iron making and iron tools tended to bring societies closer through trade, but in northern Europe it had the opposite effect, weakening linkages. A world historical lens on international politics similarly shows that on every continent in the sixteenth and seventeenth centuries a handful of big empires grew much larger, eliminating hundreds of smaller states. In Chapter 19, we see that this was not an accident but a result of faster flows of new technologies and techniques of warfare through a globalizing world.

In the process of being selective, world history can also highlight the global trends that are distinctive across long stretches of time. For thousands of years, powerful states saw fit to build and maintain empires as long as their power lasted. But after 1960 or so, the idea of empire lost its appeal, and ever since the powerful have preferred to avoid formal empires. That is a historically unique development, although not necessarily a permanent change. On even longer time scales, we can see, as Chapter 29 explains, that the modern rise in greenhouse gas concentrations in the atmosphere has been faster—by far—than any other such rise in the historical or geological record. These two examples of distinctive, and even peculiar, aspects of our own period are best understood in the long sweep of world history.

The Approach of This Textbook

This book differs from most world history textbooks in a few ways. It has one author, not several, which has been hard on that author but might be good for the reader because it raises the odds of achieving a consistent viewpoint and framework. I hope I have achieved that because it might compensate for the chief disadvantage of a single-authored world history: no author can know everything. I do not have the same command of human evolution, ancient Chinese history, medieval Russian history, or modern U.S. history that specialists in these fields have. However, I have taught world history for decades and learned a fair bit along the way, not least from my students. I've also written global-scale histories before, mainly environmental histories. This book reflects my own background as a historian, giving frequent attention to matters of geography and environment.

This book features a particular framework for understanding world history. Having an effective framework is essential because it helps organize information and put it into a context—avoiding that giant jumble of facts. The framework here is based on the concept of webs of social interaction. It's an approach that, I hope, will provide readers with a strong sense of the connectedness, but also the contrasts, of world history—and in an easily accessible way.

The Webs of Humankind: An Overview

People always and everywhere have been connected to others. These connections have taken many forms, ranging from kinship and friendship to economic exchange and military confrontation. In all such relationships, people exchanged information and used it to guide their future behavior. They often also exchanged technologies, religious beliefs, artistic visions, trade goods, food crops, violent threats, lethal infections, and much else. These exchanges shaped what people could do and could imagine. When exchanges and connections became regular, I call them webs of interaction.

For most of human history—from the dawn of our species' existence some 300,000 years ago until roughly 13,000 years ago—our ancestors lived in a very loose, far-flung human web. Their communities were normally small migratory bands that only occasionally mixed with others. That way of life only rarely presented them with the stimulus of new ideas and objects to consider. By later standards, the pace of change in arenas such as technology or social organization was glacially slow. This doesn't mean nothing happened, though: this was the time when humans invented religion and language, and migrated from their place of origin in Africa to settle every habitable continent. These were momentous changes, even if they happened extremely slowly.

Beginning around 13,000 years ago (or roughly 11,000 BCE), a handful of changes occurred that encouraged the weaving of much tighter webs of interaction. While the loose and far-flung human web continued in the background, new, tighter webs developed where people began to settle into permanent, sedentary communities. Sedentary life in those times worked best beside a seashore with abundant edible marine life (as on the coasts of Japan, for example) or amid wild grasses that yielded reliable and nutritious seeds (as in what is now southeastern Turkey). Some of these now-sedentary people domesticated wild animals and plants, converting them genetically into livestock and crops, respectively. Farming, the first evidence of which comes from Southwest Asia, encouraged larger communities, denser populations, and more vibrant, if still local, interactive webs—"local" here means several villages and a few thousand people. Changes in technology and social organization now came more rapidly than before.

Around 5,500 years ago (3500 BCE), much bigger and tighter webs formed when people first clustered together into cities, and then built networks of cities linked by regular trade and communication. This too happened first in Southwest Asia, specifically in what is now southern Iraq. But it didn't take long—a thousand years at most—before cities and regional webs linking multiple cities emerged elsewhere—in northeast Africa, South Asia, and East Asia, and by 200 CE in the Americas, especially in Mesoamerica and the Andes region of South America. Each of these regional webs, between roughly 2500 BCE and 200 CE, would grow to contain a few million people, dozens of cities, and thousands of villages. Within these emerging webs, changes in ideas, technologies, and social structures came faster than before, and faster than among people not connected to webs. Cities—nodes in these larger webs where people with different outlooks, religions, skills, and technologies rubbed shoulders every day—became hothouses of innovation and adaptation.

Mainly through the expansion of long-distance trade, those urban-based webs gradually linked up to one another. The biggest one formed between the Nile and the Ganges, and the next biggest in East Asia. By roughly 200 CE, sprawling webs of interaction spanned continents. By far the biggest, called the Old World web in this book, was anchored at either end by China and Egypt, stretching over most of Eurasia and North Africa. (Scholars often refer to Eurasia and Africa as the Old World, a usage I adopt because human occupation of those continents predates that anywhere else.) In 200 CE, it encompassed tens of millions of people living in cities and villages especially along rivers such as the Huang He (Yellow River), the Yangzi, the Ganges, the Indus, the Tigris and Euphrates, and the Nile. All of these rivers served as sources of irrigation water and arteries of transport, permitting more productive farming, larger food supplies, more people, more trade—and more frequent and sustained interaction of all sorts. The Old World web eventually—by 1400 CE—grew to include almost everyone living within a space the edges of which were Japan and Java in the east, and Iceland and West Africa in the west. At the time, that area included at least three-quarters of humankind, or more than 200 million people.

Smaller but still sizeable regional webs grew up else-where. In Africa, the northeastern region along the Nile and the Red Sea coast was enmeshed in the Old World web early on—by 1500 BCE if not before. Elsewhere in Africa, much smaller webs developed, especially along the Niger River in West Africa. That one merged with the Old World web by about 800 CE, mainly through the trans-Saharan trade routes that linked North Africa and West Africa as never before.

In the Americas, local webs developed based around irri-gation agriculture, the first of them starting as early as 3000 BCE in the Andes. Bigger regional webs formed in the Andes by about 100 CE and another in Mesoamerica by about 200 CE. Both the Mesoamerican and Andean webs grew, but intermittently with many reversals. The outer threads of these two webs by 1450 CE extended far across the Amer-icas and linked both continents very loosely through trade and migrations.

In Oceania, as people sailed from what is now Indonesia out to remote Pacific islands, a process that began around 2000 BCE, they formed thin webs linking island communi-ties, bringing thousands of people into contact with one another over vast distances.

In character, these smaller webs bore many similarities to the Old World web: they were held together by trade, travel, and communication, and clusters of people—whether in cities or tightly packed villages—served as key nodes for the transmission of ideas, goods, and everything else. But in size, the Old World web, from its beginning around 200 CE, always outstripped all others.

A Global Web

Beginning in the fifteenth century, breakthroughs in trans-port and communication fused all these webs into a single global one. Breakthroughs in ship design and in informa-tion storage, especially printing technology, contributed to a bigger breakthrough: sailors accumulated enough infor-mation to crack the code of the planet's winds and cur-rents, enabling them to navigate the deep oceans much more securely than ever before. That launched an era of intercontinental navigation that wove the world's coastlands together into a global web. Beginning with Chapter 16, which overlaps both volumes of the text, this Global web is the main story of the book.

This new Global web triggered thorough-going and accelerating changes in the sixteenth through the eighteenth centuries, the first of which I call biological globalization. Infectious diseases such as measles and smallpox spread to populations with no acquired immunity, especially in the Americas and on Pacific islands, cutting populations by 50 to 95 percent. Sailors and ships also carried crops to new environments. Potatoes, for example, native to the Andes, gradually became part of the diet in northern Europe, and eventually in China and north India as well. Maize, originally from Mexico, became Africa's most important crop.

The Global web brought changes that extended far beyond biological transfers. New information and ideas from the four corners of the Earth led people to reconsider long-cherished beliefs, altering religious landscapes in Europe and Asia, as Chapter 18 details. The variety of political formats in which people lived diminished as small polities gave way to growing empires. The productive techniques and technologies that underpinned industrialization spread widely within decades after their introduction during the eighteenth and nineteenth centuries, reflecting the accelerating flow of information characteristic of the Global web. So too with new ideas about freedom, justice, and sovereignty that underlay political revolutions around the world, from the United States and France in the late eighteenth century to Mexico, Russia, and China in the early twentieth.

Throughout the last 150 years, with telegraphs, telephones, and networked computers, the Global web has grown tighter, its communications faster, its linkages stronger. Cities, which were home to about 10 percent of humankind in 1800, by 2010 accounted for more than half of the world's population. Today, almost everyone lives within a single, unified, global-scale web of interaction, competition, and cooperation. Different people experience this differently, but almost no one (aside from a few thousand people deep in rain forests) lives outside it.

Web Making: A Globalizing Process

The long process of web making over thousands of years is in effect a globalizing one. The first webs launched a long-term trend—with reversals—toward greater connectedness. In this sense, world history has a direction to it. Several motors drove the web-making process. Among them were the economic advantages of specialization and

exchange, which inspired trade. The desire of monarchs, whether Macedonian kings such as Alexander the Great or Chinese emperors such as Han Wudi, to expand their power and influence also extended the reach of webs. So did the ambition of missionaries to spread their religions. Merchants, monarchs, and missionaries weren't trying to extend webs—they didn't think in these terms at all. But their ambitions and actions had that effect. So did the routine movements of travelers, pilgrims, refugees, soldiers, sailors, pastoral nomads, and everyone else who moved around, interacted with strangers, and—unintentionally—helped to build sustained webs of interaction.

The long-term trend of webs growing, tightening, and consolidating was far from consistent. At times, when empires fell apart, plagues swept through, or trade routes shifted, contacts and connections might languish and webs unravel. This happened after the fifth century CE in western Europe when the Roman Empire fell. Webs might also fray as a result of deliberate choices, as in East Asia in the late eighth century CE when the rulers of China's Tang dynasty

MAJOR WEBS OF WORLD HISTORY

NAME AND EXPLANATION	LOCATION	APPROXIMATE DATES
Human web This refers to the faint and intermittent ties that have linked all, or almost all, humans throughout our species' entire career. But its connections were weak compared to the tighter local and regional webs, and to the Global web of the last five centuries.	Everywhere people have lived, except in the few cases where groups became genuinely isolated	From human origins ca. 300,000 years ago until today
Southwest Asian web This formed in the Tigris-Euphrates valley beginning about 5000 BCE. It extended into surrounding uplands by 3500 BCE, lasting until 2500 BCE when it was subsumed into the Nile-Indus web.	Mesopotamia and neighboring areas	5000 BCE to 2500 BCE
Nile-Indus web This was an expansion of the Southwest Asian web to both the east and the west.	From Egypt, and at times its southern neighbor Nubia, across Southwest Asia to the Indus valley	2500 BCE to 1500 BCE
Nile-Ganges web A further expansion across north India.	From Egypt across Southwest Asia and north India	1500 BCE to 200 CE
East Asian web Originated in China but extended to neighboring societies.	North and central China, with strands reaching into Korea, Japan, Central Asia, and northernmost Vietnam	1000 BCE to 200 CE
Old World web This is the fusion of the East Asian web and the Nile-Ganges web, with extensions into Europe and Africa.	From Senegal and Scotland in the west to Japan and Java in the east, including the Indian Ocean world	200 CE to 1500 CE
Andean web This formed in South America from the Moche and Tiwanaku cultures.	From the Altiplano in Bolivia to the coasts of Peru, straddling the high Andes	100 CE to 1500 CE
Mesoamerican web This developed with the interactions among the Maya, the Zapotecs, and Teotihuacán.	Central and southern Mexico and the Maya lands of Yucatán and northern Guatemala	200 CE to 1500 CE
Global web This is the fusion of the Old World web, the American webs, and all other local and regional webs.	Global, but tiny uncontacted communities deep in rain forests such as Amazonia remain outside it.	1500 CE to the present. It began to take shape with oceanic voyagers in the fifteenth and sixteenth centuries and is still tightening in the twenty-first.

decided to reduce foreign contacts of all sorts. The complete disappearance of webs occurred often on local scales, probably more often in the Americas than elsewhere. But bigger webs, although they often frayed or shrank, rarely disappeared altogether and normally rebounded within a century or two, as happened in East Asia after new dynasties replaced the Tang.

The expansion of webs was often a brutal process. It frequently involved warfare and epidemics. Both occurred at once in many cases—as, for example, after Christopher Columbus's voyages of the 1490s when the Americas were firmly linked to the Old World web. Newly introduced diseases in combination with warfare killed tens of millions of people in the Americas. Peoples who had lived outside of webs, such as the indigenous populations of the Americas, Australia, Polynesia, or Siberia, often suffered heavily for a century or more once they became entangled in webs.

As a rule, the expansion of webs, especially the Global web in recent centuries, has worked to reduce cultural diversity. The number of languages spoken has fallen by about half since 1500, while English, Spanish, Hindi, Arabic, Chinese, and a few others have acquired more speakers. The number of legal traditions too has declined: more and more people live under fewer and fewer legal systems, many of them now based on English common law or Islam's code of shari'a. Farmers' fields feature fewer strains of wheat, maize, and rice than they did 100 years ago, partly because farmers now have more information about which crop varieties yield best in their environments.

The table at left summarizes the main webs featured in this book. Many smaller ones that involved thousands, but not millions, of people are left out of the table. The dates are given in round numbers and are approximate because webs formed and merged gradually, with no sharp beginnings or end points.

Organization of the Book

With the globalizing process of web making at work throughout, this book takes a largely regional organization in Volume 1 and a largely global one in Volume 2. The schemes of regionalization it adopts change as the world changed, reflecting the formation, and occasional decay, of webs. So, for example, "Africa" in some periods is treated as a continental unit, but at other times regions of Africa appear as parts of larger maritime webs. In Chapter 13, the coasts of eastern Africa are presented as a key element of a region called the Indian Ocean world. In Chapter 21, parts of Africa appear as components of a different region, the Atlantic world, united by trade, travel, and exchanges among the coastlands of the Americas, Europe, and Africa. The book often avoids the vocabulary of regions as we typically see them today. A conventional regionalization of the world takes the continents as regions, with a few additions such as "Middle East" and lately "Asia-Pacific." In emphasizing webs of interaction, this book minimizes the projection onto the past of today's conventional regions. So there is no "Middle East" until the twentieth century here, and no "Latin America" until the nineteenth century. It is worth noting too that in this world history some of the most important regions are defined by water, not land. There is no perfect way to regionalize the globe for all time periods. The different regionalization schemes used in this book reflect the changing reality of web connections among people in the past.

Parts and Periods

This book is divided into six parts, each of which corresponds to a period of time.

Part 1 (Chapters 1–3) takes on the longest sweep of time, from human origins to about 1500 BCE. For most of this period, all people lived in Africa. When some migrated to other continents, beginning about 70,000 years ago, we follow them wherever they went, which included every habitable continent by 12,000 BCE. Part 1 is global in the sense that it considers the experience of the entire human population. The very thin and faint web uniting our entire species endured despite the inter-continental wanderings of peoples.

Part 2 (Chapters 4–10) deals mainly with the period between 3500 BCE and 200 CE and shifts to a regional scheme of organization. It addresses the emergence of regional webs in parts of Eurasia, Africa, and the Americas, as outlined in the table above. In so doing, it examines the rise of cities, states, organized religions, and stratified, hierarchical societies. In places such as China, India, or Egypt—among others—these millennia also saw the formation of durable cultural traditions anchored in religion. By 200 CE, several regional webs in Eurasia and North Africa had fused into the single, sprawling Old World web. Chapter 9 pairs two places not often drawn together for comparison: northern Europe and sub-Saharan Africa. They were similar in that they stood on the frontiers of the big webs in the millennia before 200 CE. Among the resulting commonalities were smaller polities, a slower pace of technological change, and better health than that of people living in the larger webs. Slowly, though, they too became entangled in the Nile-Ganges web and, eventually, the full Old World web. The Americas and Oceania, the focus of Chapter 10, remained autonomous, unaffected by the formation of the Old World web until well beyond 200 CE. So this chapter continues up to 1000 CE, by which time a big web linking both North and South America had taken shape.

Part 3 (Chapters 11–15) maintains a regional organization and takes up the centuries between 200 CE and 1400 CE—and in one chapter to 1500. Most of it is devoted to developments within the Old World web, in East and South Asia, Africa, and Europe. It deals with several aspects of the maturation of regional webs—such as improvements in transport and navigation, and the accelerated spread of cultural traditions such as Buddhism, Christianity, and Islam. The final chapter of Part 3 returns to the Americas and Oceania, each of them still standing apart with no significant links to the Old World web until 1492 in the Americas and about 1770 in Oceania. Both built, or extended, webs of their own, which developed in accordance with prevailing conditions: the vast distances of the Pacific, for example, rewarded the navigational skills that islanders developed, while the paucity of domesticable animals in the Americas encouraged agriculture that did not require plowing. Yet strong, thought-provoking parallels existed between the societies in the Old World web and those of the Americas—as, for example, in the relationships between religious and political power, or the prevalence of gender inequality.

With **Part 4** (Chapters 16–20), the book becomes global in scope again because the links connecting every large population strengthened so much between 1400 and 1800 with the weaving of the Global web. Chapter 16, a pivotal chapter that ends Volume 1 and begins Volume 2, focuses on the convergence of the world's webs into a single Global web and the wave of biological exchanges that followed. This biological globalization set some of the basic conditions for world history in the next centuries, mainly through major shifts in agriculture and population. The connections of the Global web meant that the oceans no longer separated peoples as much as before. The histories of Angola and Brazil, as we see in Chapter 17, were firmly linked by a slave trade that established African culture in much of Brazil. As we see in Chapter 19, the effective use of guns in sixteenth-century Japan illustrates the effects of the Global web in distributing techniques and technology around the world. In Chapter 20, we see that the histories of China and Mexico developed a tie through transpacific trades in silver, silk, and porcelain routed through the Philippines. Part 4 considers the comparatively sudden changes resulting from this surge of globalization in the realms of ecology, ideas and culture, economies, and political competition.

With one exception, the chapters of **Part 5** (21–25) are also global in scope and organized by theme. They span the centuries between 1620 and 1920. The exception is Chapter 21, which is devoted to political revolutions in the Atlantic world—Africa, Europe, and the Americas. Collectively, these Atlantic revolutions were momentous enough, and their legacies global enough, to merit treatment as a unit unto themselves. The balance of Part 5 considers fundamental changes such as industrialization, the near-elimination of slavery and other forms of forced labor, and the rise of such political trends as nationalism and imperialism. It also treats some major political revolutions—in part, efforts to resist imperialism and industrialization—in India, China, Mexico, and Russia. Its main theme is the many political and social realignments and revolutions encouraged by the formation, and tightening, of the Global web. It seeks to find some balance between global currents and local factors in explaining these turbulent times.

Part 6 (Chapters 26–29) takes on a mere century and a half, from 1870 to the present—an era of accelerating globalization and episodes of fierce resistance against it. Maintaining the pattern of chapters that are global in scope and focused on themes, it takes up international politics more than earlier parts do, including two world wars, the Cold War, and decolonization. It also explores the global economy, particularly the rapid rise of East Asia; global ecological shifts including recent climate change; and social and cultural transformations such as migration, urbanization, or the rise of globalized popular music and sport. The pace and scope of global integration in this last century and a half is extraordinary, and many peoples and communities found the rapidity of changes wrenching or the direction of change unwelcome. Part 6 explains why the pace was so fast and the process so disruptive.

Considering the Evidence of World History

One last point to bear in mind before the story begins. Understanding history is like assembling a challenging jigsaw puzzle. Some of the pieces clearly fit together in obvious ways. Most of them don't, and it is not easy to know

一对夫妇只生一个孩子

what to make of them. Many of the pieces are missing, hidden under the rugs of time. All this means that history is an exercise in creating plausible interpretations from incomplete evidence.

One needs to use imagination disciplined by evidence to arrive at a reliable reconstruction of the past. It is evidence—written texts, works of art, archeology, oral traditions, historical linguistics, and now also genetic analysis—that helps us figure out what is plausible and what isn't, what arguments to accept and what to reject. Among the skills history teaches are the abilities to assess evidence thoughtfully and to recognize when the evidence is insufficient or contradictory, making strong conclusions difficult.

When multiple pieces of evidence seem to be saying the same thing, and especially when different types of evidence harmonize, we can be more confident of our conclusions. So, for example, when linguistic evidence, genetic evidence, and pottery fragments all suggest that people from West Africa filtered into central and southern Africa beginning roughly 1500 BCE, we can be confident that something historians call the Bantu migration took place—even though there is not a single written document that says anything about it. If pottery were the only evidence, we could not be sure about the migration—people can trade pots over long distances, one person to the next, without migrating. If we had only the genetic or the linguistic evidence, we would have only the fuzziest idea about when the migration occurred.

For the deeper past, we have fewer written records, and none more than 5,000 years old. In some places—the Americas, Oceania, and most of sub-Saharan Africa, for example—written records are non-existent or at best extremely rare until 500 years ago. In these situations, other forms of evidence such as archeological remains or genetic analysis become much more important in underpinning interpretations of the past.

Keep in mind too that written documents almost always reflect the viewpoints of adults rather than children, men rather than women, rich rather than poor, powerful rather than weak, and literate rather than illiterate. In archeology, as well, we are likelier to find the remains of royal palaces built of stone than peasant huts made of thatched reeds. Historians (and other scholars) have shown some ingenuity in overcoming these inherent biases, "reading against the grain" as historians often put it. But these asymmetries of information remain, and it is important to remain aware of them.

Sifting, evaluating, and interpreting incomplete and sometimes contradictory evidence, and evidence of different types, are crucial intellectual skills. The study of history, and especially world history, hones those skills. As Ziauddin Barani, a scholar of the fourteenth century writing in Persian but working in India, said: "I have not observed such advantages from any branch of learning as I have from history." The branches of learning have changed since his day, as a grounding in history would lead you to expect, but he could still be right.

ACKNOWLEDGMENTS

During the years devoted to researching, writing, and revising this book, I have accumulated deep debts to many people. First to acknowledge are those to my former students who have read parts of the text and suggested improvements: Kwabenah Akuamoah-Boateng, Dan Brendtro, Adrienne Kates, Michelle Melton, Ani Muradyan, and Michael Samway. Then various classes of History 007 and History 008 in recent years, undergraduates who collectively made thousands of (anonymous) comments on a first draft of the book. Because the book is written for students, their feedback proved enormously valuable. I also wish to thank—enormously—Robynne Mellor and Javier Puente, who worked as teaching assistants in my world history classes and provided their own advice on drafts of the book. And Benan Grams, a PhD student who helped me with medieval Arabic passages.

I am fortunate to have family members willing to share their unvarnished opinions of my prose. These include Katriona McNeill and Patrick McNeill, Mairead MacRae, Leila Meymand, and especially my sister and brother-in-law Ruth McNeill and Bart Jones. They read every word of every chapter and were not stingy with their advice. My sister taught me to read before I went to school and ever since, it seems, has felt a responsibility to improve my facility with the English language. When she read my PhD dissertation, she wrote that it could be improved if I added 20 commas per page, and it would hardly matter where I put them. I must have taken her suggestion too strongly, because when she read this book she said I should remove most of its commas. My wife, Julie Billingsley, also read passages and suggested, tactfully, that I should try to make the book more amusing.

Another family member earned my deepest thanks although he never read a word of this book. In his final years my father, William McNeill, never failed to ask me when I would finish it, which spurred me along. Debating with him how best to present the big picture in our short, co-authored book, *The Human Web: A Bird's-Eye View of World History* (2003), influenced the thinking behind this book more strongly than anything else—other than my years teaching world history.

Several professional colleagues also earned my deep gratitude. Three experienced world history teachers helped shape my understanding of how to introduce the subject to students: Alan Karras of the University of California and Merry Wiesner-Hanks of the University of Wisconsin–Milwaukee, with both of whom I served for several years creating and vetting questions for the Advanced Placement world history examination; and the late Jerry Bentley of the University of Hawaii. Rick Potts of the American Museum of Natural History, an expert in human evolution, helped me avoid missteps in the first chapter. At the Foundation for Civic Space and Public Policy in Warsaw, Poland, professors Spasimir Domaradzki, Maciej Janowski, Dariusz Kołodziejczyk, and Jan Szemiński critiqued parts of the manuscript, correcting some of my misconceptions especially about central and eastern European history. My colleagues in the History Department and Walsh School of Foreign Service at Georgetown University have contributed to my education in countless ways over the past 30-plus years. Their insights, perspectives, knowledge, and encouragement have enabled me to come to grips with world history in ways unimaginable to me without their help.

I wish to acknowledge as well the superb work of a team of colleagues at W. W. Norton, beginning with Steve Forman, who has patiently supervised the entire project from start to finish, read multiple drafts, and made thousands of valuable suggestions—of which I probably should have taken more than I did. Lily Gellman was invaluable in her orchestration of myriad details in the publishing process. Alice Vigliani, the excellent manuscript editor, improved and tightened my prose and eliminated some of those extraneous commas to which I am now apparently prone. Charlotte Miller, our outstanding cartographer, created an ambitious map program with insight and vigor, and politely tolerated my endless suggestions for revisions. Gerra Goff and Stephanie Romeo were creative and resourceful in building the extensive illustrations program. Melissa Atkin brought order to the puzzle pieces of the book as project editor. Jillian Burr, our brilliant designer, created beautiful book and jacket designs. Sarah Bartley gave us timely advice from the perspectives of marketing and sales. Carson Russell, our media editor, planned and implemented the important digital resources that support the book; and Jane Searle, our production manager, kept this big train running on schedule.

Reviewers of the First Edition

Other professional colleagues, most of whom I have never met, have also worked wonders for this book. World history teachers and scholars from many colleges in the United States and abroad have read draft chapters and made useful suggestions:

Anthony Barbieri-Low, University of California, Santa Barbara
Hayden Bellenoit, United States Naval Academy
David Biggs, University of California, Riverside
Beau Bowers, Central Piedmont Community College—Levine
Kevin Brady, Tidewater Community College—Chesapeake Campus
Gary Burgess, United States Naval Academy
Annette Chamberlin, Virginia Western Community College
Stephen Chappell, James Madison University
Katy Clay, Shippensburg University
Sean C.D. Colbert-Lewis, Sr., North Carolina Central University
Phyllis Conn, St. John's University
Judith Davis, Three Rivers College
Peter De Rosa, Bridgewater State University
Eric Dursteler, Brigham Young University
Gregory Ference, Salisbury University
Allen Fromherz, Georgia State University
Denis Gainty, Georgia State University
Jessica Gerard, Ozarks Technical Community College
Rachael Goldman, Rutgers University
Noah Goode, Central Piedmont Community College—Levine
Andrew Goss, University of New Orleans
Candice Goucher, Washington State University
Hans Hägerdal, Linnaeus University
Sarah Hamilton, Auburn University
Ann Hardgrove, University of Texas at San Antonio
Matthew Herbst, University of California, San Diego
Carsten Hjort Lange, Aalborg University
Stephanie Holyfield, Wesley College
Paul Stephen Hudson, Georgia State Perimeter College

John Hyland, Newport University
Joanna Jury, Georgia State University
Sofia Laurein, San Diego City College
Jess LeVine, Brookdale Community College
Scott Lloyd, University of Arkansas
Anthony Makowski, Delaware County Community College—Marple Campus
Harold Marcuse, University of California, Santa Barbara
Matthew McCoy, University of Arkansas—Fort Smith Campus
Ian Miller, St John's University—Queens Campus
Elizabeth Milliken, Mount Hood Community College
Philip Misevich, St. John's University
Lance Nolde, California State University, Channel Islands
Hosok O, Dixie State University
Annette Palmer, Morgan State University
Alejandro Quintana, St John's University—Queens Campus
Daren Ray, Auburn University
Charles V. Reed, Elizabeth City State University
Thomas J. Rushford, Northern Virginia Community College—Annandale Campus
Ruma N. Salhi, Northern Virginia Community College—Annandale Campus
Christine Senecal, Shippensburg State University
Michael Seth, James Madison University
Emily Story, Salisbury University
Barbara Syrrakos, City College of New York
Peter Utgaard, Cuyamaca College
Evan Ward, Brigham Young University
Molly Warsh, University of Pittsburgh
James Webb, Colby College
Andre Wink, University of Wisconsin
Jennifer Winters, Northern Virginia Community College—Annandale Campus

In a book that aims to explore the history of the world from the origins of humans until today, there are sure to be more than a few lapses. Those are all my fault and no one else's.

J. R. McNeill, *Georgetown University*

PART 1

THE FIRST 99.93 PERCENT OF HUMAN HISTORY

Part I (Chapters 1 through 3) of this book deals with the history of humans and our hominin ancestors up until about 5,000 years ago. That means it covers about 97 percent of the history of our species, *Homo sapiens*, and about 99.93 percent of the history of hominins. (Hominins are our branch of the family of apes, which diverged from the ancestors of today's chimpanzees about 7 million years ago.) The two most important things to know about this long stretch of history are that nobody knows much about it because the evidence is so scanty, and that cultural and social changes came slowly by the

Lascaux Caves On the walls of caves at Lascaux in France, between 18,000 and 12,000 years ago, the semi-sedentary Magdalenian people made vivid paintings of the animals—deer, horses, bulls—that provided them with sustenance.

standard of more recent history. A third point, but a less important one, is that there is no satisfactory way to slice up the first 99.93 percent of human history into periods that fit the facts everywhere around the world.

SOURCES OF EVIDENCE

Here's how we know what we *think* we know about the long stretch of time, 7 million to 250,000 years ago, during which our hominin ancestors evolved into modern humans. Our information mainly comes from the study of very ancient bones and stone tools. Systematic archeological work in what may be the cradle of humankind, East Africa, began in the 1930s. Only a few thousand artifacts from that long period have been dug up and analyzed, and those artifacts are—inevitably—a biased sample. Bones, teeth, stone tools, and a few footprints survived, but no soft tissues, no wooden tools, let alone any evidence of our remote ancestors' mental world. Moreover, the artifacts all come from only a few sites where conditions were dry enough to allow preservation. Dating of these artifacts is imprecise, which makes for contentious debates among specialists.

Since 2004, a few remarkable new discoveries, explained in Chapter 1, have re-written the story of human evolution. And you should expect more discoveries in the years to come. Archeology for any period is a bit like a challenging jigsaw puzzle with most of the pieces missing. It can only provide fragments of the full picture. Fortunately, there are other ways to get at the remote human past.

Ever since the deciphering of the human genome began in the 1990s, a new form of evidence about human history has rapidly become available. The study of ancient genetic material is now known as paleogenomics. The distribution of certain varieties of genes can tell us much about human origins and migrations—for example, that the humans who left Africa about 100,000

years ago probably were few in number, probably only around 100 to 1,000 individuals. All non-Africans in the world are descended from those few.

A weak link in paleogenomics is chronology. Scientists make assumptions about the rate of genetic mutations over time in order to try to date events in the past, such as the exodus from Africa. But the margin of error in such estimates is considerable. Archeology is usually better than paleogenomics for dating things.

Another way to make inferences about what life was like among the earliest humans is to examine current societies that maintain the same general way of life followed by early humans: foraging, hunting, and (in places) fishing. Anthropologists have studied such groups carefully in recent decades to make educated guesses about the human condition 50,000 or 100,000 years ago. Their observations suggest, for example, that our ancient ancestors spent only a few hours each day foraging and hunting their food, and that they enjoyed a lot of leisure time. This anthropological approach is instructive, but it's also just as unreliable as any other because it's hard to know which social traits have changed the most and which the least over such long spans of time.

Archeology, paleogenomics, and inference based on current forager-hunters are the three main sources of information about early humans and other hominins. Even when used together, the three methods leave lots of interesting questions unanswered. So these chapters are—regrettably but necessarily—peppered with words such as *perhaps* and *probably*.

SLOW CHANGE

The second important thing to remember about this long span of history, beyond the uncertainty, is that change was slow in early human societies. The genetic evolution of our ancestors and our own species took place over thousands of generations, with only imperceptible change from one generation to the next. Cultural evolution was also slow. The record of changes in tools is the best evidence of this. As Chapter 1 explains, tools showed very little change until roughly 50,000 years ago. And even then, in what is sometimes called a cultural revolution, the pace of change remained glacial by today's standards. In thinking about history before about 15,000 years ago, we have to contemplate immense stretches of time that were marked by strong continuity in culture.

PROBLEMS OF PERIODIZATION

Scholars divide up this immensity of time in a few different ways, none of them truly satisfactory. Some scholars use the term *prehistory* to refer to the entire human past before the invention of writing (which occurred roughly 5,000 years ago). This book doesn't use the term on the grounds that there are now so many ways to learn about the human past that the invention of writing is no longer the watershed moment that it once seemed. The term *prehistory* is going out of fashion, and deservedly so.

Natural scientists generally use terms that come from geology, and they divide the last several million years into epochs such as the *Pliocene* (5.3 million years ago to 2.6 million years ago) and the *Pleistocene* (2.6 million years ago until 11,700 years ago). This book rarely uses these terms and confines them to discussion of matters such as climate shifts.

Other scholars, especially archeologists, divide up the distant past based on the materials used to make tools and weapons. Thus they refer to a *stone age*, eventually followed in some places by *bronze ages* and *iron ages*. This scheme emphasizes certain aspects of archaic peoples' lives—tool technology—over others. The main advantage of using this scheme is that evidence for tool technology shows up well in the archeological record. This book employs a version of this terminology in its early chapters and refers to the Paleolithic and Neolithic eras.

The Paleolithic literally means "old stone age" and in this book refers to the time span from the first appearance of stone tools anywhere until the first evidence of farming anywhere (about 2.6 million years ago until about 13,000 years ago). *The Neolithic* means "new stone age" and in this book refers to the time between the earliest sign of agriculture anywhere about 13,000

years ago and the first appearance of cities anywhere about 5,000 years ago. Note that specialists in archeology use these terms to mean different slices of time in different places, typically depending on local dates for the first tool use, agriculture, and cities. So, for example, the Neolithic began later in Southeast Asia than in Southwest Asia. This book will not use *Paleolithic* or *Neolithic* to mean different periods for different places.

This difficulty of terminology reflects the strong local and regional focus of archeologists and the weakness of global perspectives. Because they do painstaking local work, without which we would know almost nothing about the deep past, archeologists don't need terms for time periods that will work everywhere around the globe. That is why we don't have a satisfactory vocabulary for thinking about deep history in general and its periodization in particular.

Chapters 1 and 2 explore the ancestry and evolution of the human species, which took its—our—approximate shape about 250,000 years ago. They also cover our colonization of the globe from about 100,000 to about 13,000 years ago, and our cultural evolution along the way. Chapter 3 focuses on the more rapid cultural change that led some of our ancestors to settle down, farm, and—about 5,000 years ago—start to create cities, governments, writing, and other features of human societies that govern our lives today. In each chapter of Part 1, as throughout the book, we are concerned with the connections among human communities and how those grew to become webs of interaction.

CHRONOLOGY

ca. 50,000–30,000 years ago
Neanderthals, Denisovans, Flores Islands "Hobbits" go extinct

Between 2 million and 120,000 years ago
Language emerges

ca. 50,000–12,000 years ago
Massive megafauna extinctions

2.6 million years ago
Paleolithic period begins

ca. 75,000 years ago
Mount Toba erupts

ca. 66 million years ago
Asteroid hitting Yucatán
Peninsula causes massive
extinction event

ca. 100,000–65,000 years ago
Homo sapiens migrates out of Africa

ca. 400,000 years ago
Neanderthals emerge

ca. 190,000 years ago
Homo erectus
goes extinct

**ca. 6 million–
4.5 million years ago**
Bipedalism evolves

**ca. 2.5 million
years ago**
First evidence
of tool use

ca. 1.5 million years ago
Homo erectus emerges

ca. 300,000–200,000 years ago
Homo sapiens emerges

**ca. 45,000
years ago**
Homo sapiens
enters Europe

ca. 130,000 years ago
Last ice age begins

3.2 million years ago
Lifetime of the hominin Lucy

**Between 1.5 million and
500,000 years ago**
Hominins first control fire

ca. 90,000 years ago
Flores Island "Hobbits" appear; late
Paleolithic cultural revolution begins

1

12,000 years ago
Last ice age ends

13,000 years ago
Paleolithic period ends

ca. 30,000 years ago
Homo sapiens reaches
China and Japan

ca. 23,000–14,000 years ago
Homo sapiens reaches
the Americas

ca. 40,000 years ago
Homo sapiens reaches
Australia and Tasmania

Last Hominin Standing

BECOMING HUMAN

I n 1974 in Ethiopia, a pair of paleontologists (scientists who find and interpret fossil remains) decided to take an unusual route back to their camp.
Walking through a gully, they spied what looked like an arm bone resting
on the ground. A moment's inspection told them they had happened upon a
relative, perhaps an ancestor, of the human race. In camp that evening, the paleontologists celebrated the find with their French and American teammates, and
because the Beatles song "Lucy in the Sky with Diamonds" was playing on their
tape machine, they named the skeleton to which the arm bone belonged "Lucy."

Lucy was a marvelous discovery. Paleontologists and other specialists
hunting for early human remains generally count themselves lucky to find a
tooth or a finger bone. But after two weeks of digging and scratching, the
paleontologists who found Lucy's arm bone uncovered hundreds of bone fragments, amounting to about 40 percent of her skeleton.

Lucy was a young adult female who died of unknown causes about 3.2 million years ago. She stood about 3'7" (1.1 m) tall and weighed about 65 lbs. (30
kg). Her feet, pelvis, and spine were astonishingly human-like, but her cranium,

Human Culture A human hand outlined in red pigment decorates the wall of a cave in
France, alongside vivid images (not shown) of animals such as mammoths and rhinos.
Perhaps serving as the artist's signature, the hand image dates from 36,000 years ago—
evidence of the explosion in culture that humans throughout the world experienced during
the late Paleolithic period.

5

FOCUS QUESTIONS

1. What significant events led to the emergence of human ancestors?

2. What were the major traits and skills that distinguished our species, *Homo sapiens*?

3. What were the major characteristics of the hominin species most closely related to us?

4. How did the global migrations of *Homo sapiens* contribute to increasing cultural and genetic diversification?

5. In what ways did human culture change dramatically in the late Paleolithic period?

teeth, and jaw more ape-like. She walked upright and probably ate mostly fruits, vegetables, and leaves. Her hands suggest she was good at climbing trees. Her braincase was in the average range for modern chimps, only one-third the size of your brain. She is classified as an *Australopithecus afarensis*, a species of hominin that lived in what is now Ethiopia and Kenya about 4 million to 3 million years ago. (The term **hominins** refers to humans, all extinct branches of humans, and all our ape-like ancestors over the last 7 million years.) After touring the world's museums for several years, Lucy now makes her home in a climate-controlled vault in a museum in Ethiopia's capital city of Addis Ababa. Lucy's bones provided more new information about human origins and evolution than any previous find, but her skeleton contained only fragments of the human story.

It's disconcerting to admit it, but we are, all of us, descended from a very ancient mammal that looked something like a modern tree shrew—a small, slender, furry creature. And like all earthlings, our ancestry ultimately extends back to single-celled creatures resembling pond scum. It was highly unlikely that the course of biological evolution should have produced modern humans. If, somehow, the epic could start up again, it almost certainly would turn out differently—just as human history, if magically replayed, would almost certainly not produce Aztecs or Buddhism or the Constitution of the United States. Biological evolution, like human history, was and is full of chance. Nonetheless, biological evolution did produce us, and it's instructive to think about how that unlikely turn of events happened.

This chapter deals with the story of human origins, the migrations of people from their original African home to the far corners of the Earth, and the fabric of life during the period scholars call the Paleolithic. It ends with the burst of cultural change that occurred near the end of the Paleolithic, roughly 70,000 to 15,000 years ago. During the Paleolithic, even though people were few and widely scattered, they retained connections that spanned the inhabited world. As we will see, there is reason to suppose that even when transportation meant walking and communications technology consisted only of speech, a slender and faint web embraced all our ancestors.

LIFE ON EARTH

The human story goes back to the origins of our universe, which scientists now think happened in the **Big Bang** some 13.8 billion years ago. In this mysterious moment, time, space, and energy somehow began. The universe started out hot (trillions of degrees), dense, and smaller than an atom. Ever since that initial moment, the universe has been cooling and expanding. It reached the immense size of a galaxy in a fraction of a second. Protons, neutrons, and electrons—the building blocks of all matter, including our bodies—appeared in the first few minutes. Within the first 300,000 years after the Big Bang, most of these building blocks had formed into atoms of hydrogen and helium. Gravity collected these atoms into stars, and the stars into galaxies such as the Milky Way, which includes our sun and billions of neighboring stars.

The sun and our solar system, Earth included, took shape about 4.6 billion years ago. Then, in a process for which no consensus explanation yet exists, life emerged on Earth about 3.8 billion years ago, perhaps in the hot thermal vents under the oceans. For most of its career, life on Earth was dull, lived by single-celled organisms sloshing about in the seas. Not until about 1.2 billion years ago were there multi-celled organisms, and no sizeable animals until about 600 million years ago. Living things climbed onto dry land to stay some 440 million years ago, and by 240 million years ago dinosaurs and small mammals walked Earth. New forms of life were appearing faster now, because life on land evolved in response to more variable conditions than in the sea.

Life anywhere on Earth was risky business. Every now and then an asteroid, meteorite, or something else hurtling through space smashed into the planet. Volcanoes rumbled and belched forth fire and toxic gases. The continents slid here and there, slowly crunching into one another, opening and closing seas and raising mountain chains. As a result of these and other hazards, large proportions of life on Earth went extinct on five occasions. Whenever

Lucy The skull of Lucy, an early hominin, indicates a brain size comparable to that of modern chimpanzees.

this happened, biological evolution took new directions. On the last such occasion, when an asteroid slammed into the northwestern Yucatán Peninsula in Mexico about 66 million years ago, the shock from its impact opened a crater the size of Belgium or Maryland. It ignited fires that consumed much of the planet's vegetation, and it raised a veil of dust that blocked sunlight and chilled the Earth. All land animals bigger than a medium-sized dog went extinct, including all dinosaurs and most other reptiles. The meek inherited the Earth. Among the meek were small mammals, such as the ancient tree shrew that is our ancestor.

Within a few million years, there were many new kinds of mammals, creatures that couldn't have gotten their start had dinosaurs still trodden the Earth. The first primates (the extended family of primates comprises all monkeys and apes, including humans) soon emerged. By 35 million years ago, creatures that looked like modern monkeys had evolved, and some 15 million years later, ancient apes appeared. From genetic evidence, it now seems that the last common ancestor of humans and chimpanzees lived around 7 to 5 million years ago. Although we still share 98.4 percent of our genetic material with chimps, even 1.6 percent can make quite a difference. The chimpanzee ancestors stayed in forest habitats and eventually evolved into the two modern chimpanzee species. Human ancestors adapted to changing climate and ecology by fleeing

Chicxulub Crater This illustration depicts the magnitude of the impact on Mexico's Yucatán Peninsula caused by an asteroid collision about 66 million years ago. The effects of the collision caused the extinction of all dinosaurs and many other reptiles.

the forest for what was slowly becoming the East African savanna. This is now a land of plentiful grass, scarce water, and only occasional trees; but 5 million years ago, it was a mosaic of forest, shrubs, and grassland.

OUR HOMININ ANCESTORS

A bewildering variety of hominins roamed the African earth over the last 5 million years. Early hominins had brains, and probably habits, more like chimpanzees' than like ours today. Fossil hunters have found about 18 different species of hominin, each with a double-barreled, tongue-twisting name such as *Australopithecus afarensis*, Lucy's species.

Regrettably, we don't know much about how our own species evolved over the last 5 or 6 million years. We don't

African Vegetation and Hominin Fossil Sites The location of belts and patches of forest, grassland, and desert have changed considerably over the time in which humankind evolved. Hominin remains are mainly found in what were savanna zones, and it is likely that most of our hominin ancestors' history took place there.

know whether it happened gradually or in comparatively sudden leaps. We don't know when the various steps took place, and we don't know why it happened. The evidence is still too spotty. But there are a few things we can say with some assurance about the evolution of humans. It surely happened in Africa: the earliest remains of hominins have been found mainly in Chad, Ethiopia, and Kenya. Human evolution happened over hundreds of thousands of generations, until, by about 300,000 to 200,000 years ago, our species, **Homo sapiens**, had definitively emerged somewhere between the areas of modern-day Morocco and Tanzania. And the first big step toward the emergence of our species was standing upright.

BIPEDALISM

One of the crucial distinctions, and apparently the earliest, that separates our recent ancestors and ourselves from other apes is that we stand and walk upright. **Bipedalism** evolved about 6 to 4.5 million years ago. It may have been a result of climate change—drier conditions that expanded the savanna and made upright posture more rewarding by affording a better vantage point from which to see opportunities and dangers. It may have developed as a way of shedding heat more efficiently by reducing the amount of midday sunlight that falls on the body and exposing it to more wind. Bipedalism also freed the forelimbs (hands) to carry things or pick fruit from bushes and trees. For one or several of these reasons, **natural selection**—the process through which genetic traits helpful for survival and reproduction spread over many generations, enabling species to better adapt to their environment—favored bipedalism in hominins. It also favored the development of a fine sense of balance. The first bipedal hominins were short and small-brained, but successful enough as a species to survive for over 2 million years. The most famous among them is Lucy.

After hominins stood up on their hind legs, they eventually became good throwers, walkers, and runners. Anatomical changes, especially to the shoulder, gradually allowed our ancestors to throw hard and accurately. This new skill, which seems to have developed about 2 million years ago, brought many advantages, including the ability to attack edible animals from a safe distance by pelting them with rocks. Safer hunting easily translated into a meatier diet with more protein and fats. Bipedalism also allowed our ancestors to run better.

Many of the changes in our bodies after our ancestors came down from the trees resulted from selection for long-distance walking, trotting, and running prowess: loss of body fur, proliferation of sweat glands, longer legs, narrower waists, arched feet (which provide extra spring) with short toes, neck ligaments that keep our heavy heads from jolting, shoulders that allow our arms to swing free, knees and ankles that serve as shock absorbers.

Thanks to all these bodily changes, humans could (and can) jog long distances in warm weather better than any other animal. Good marathoners today can outrun a horse over 26 miles. While the fastest human sprinters are almost turtle-like over short distances compared to other animals of our African homeland, fit humans can outlast anything on the savanna, even antelopes, mainly because we can keep cool more efficiently by sweating.

As they became good distance walkers and runners, our ancestors could cover more ground; gather, hunt, and scavenge much more food; and sustain larger groups. Improved mobility brought new selective pressures for better memory of terrain, better communication, and better social coordination for actions like getting and sharing food and for defense against predators or rivals. Hominins that somehow were a little better at these tasks stood a much better chance, in the long run, of surviving and reproducing. In this way, bipedalism may have helped stimulate bigger and better brains even as better running and throwing allowed a richer diet that could feed such brains. In short, our bodies probably evolved primarily to jog for hours under the hot sun, while our brains probably evolved to handle complicated social situations.

BIG BRAINS

Our brains are big, complex, and capable. Lucy and her hominin kin had brains the same size as those of modern chimpanzees—much smaller than ours. For *Homo sapiens*, the ratio of brain size to body size is three times bigger than is normal in the animal kingdom. Our big brains are also amazingly complex, possibly the most complex structures in the universe, with 100 billion cells and perhaps 80,000 miles of pathways linking cells to one another. The neural connections in the brain of a 20-year-old, if laid end to end, could wrap around the Earth at least three times.

The size and complexity of our brains come at a cost. Our brains are energy guzzlers: we devote 20 to 25 percent of our metabolism to keeping them well supplied with oxygen and nutrients; other mammals use about 5 percent. Big-brained hominins needed lots of high-quality food rich in proteins and fats. Some small-brained apes can survive by foraging for fruits, roots, berries, and the like. But for big-brained hominins, this sort of diet was insufficient. Our ancestors had to take the risks associated with hunting animals or scavenging the kills of other predators for fats and protein, unless they lived somewhere with abundant fish and shellfish. They had to become hunters and scavengers as well as foragers.

Big brains also require more cooling. An overheated brain doesn't work properly, and a big one is more difficult to keep cool than a small one. Overheating was a real risk under the African sun, especially for those who needed to trot for hours on end after antelope, gazelle, or wildebeest. The evolutionary answer to this problem was nearly hairless skin with plenty of sweat glands, which had become standard equipment on some hominins by about 1.6 million years ago. Humans are by far the sweatiest of primates, and together with horses by far the sweatiest of creatures. The importance of sweat as the body's

Hominin Ancestors These *Australopithecus afarensis* footprints, preserved in volcanic ash over 3 million years ago, show that our ancestors had a foot structure like ours, enabling them to walk upright. These are the footprints of two adults and a child and, at right, an ancestor of the horse.

Lucy versus Modern Humans Lucy's skeleton (left, with shading for the discovered parts of the skeleton) compared to the skeleton of a modern human female (right). Note Lucy's shorter stature and smaller brain size.

equivalent of engine coolant meant that our ancestors needed to drink plenty of liquids, walk efficiently between water sources, and have a good sense of where to find water. Even so, they couldn't afford to venture far from water—a real constraint in many environments.

Big brains—or skulls big enough to house big brains—carry another cost as well: they make childbirth hazardous for mothers. Before modern medical interventions, about 1–3 percent of births killed the mother. That usually resulted in the death of the infant as well. With these costs, big brains had to offer great advantages; otherwise, natural selection would have made sure we don't have them. The greatest advantages of big brains were the ability to form larger social groups and the imagination to invent tools, harness fire, and develop language. All these achievements were related, but we'll look at them one at a time.

SOCIAL COOPERATION Bigger brains probably allowed our ancestors to capitalize on the advantages

of mobility and bipedalism by organizing tighter, more cooperative, and possibly larger groups. Individuals with brains that could recognize the rewards of cooperation and sharing, and organize more cohesive groups, enjoyed better survival chances. Through teamwork, they could reap benefits from more efficient foraging, scavenging, and hunting.

Improved teamwork made it possible to coordinate foraging strategically over larger territories, assigning specific roles to group members. Teamwork also enabled people to hunt bigger animals with greater safety by fixing a plan of attack. Better coordination raised the quantity of food available, and improved cooperation meant that less food went to waste. No single hunter, not even a team of hunters, could eat a two-ton hippo before its meat began to spoil. But if they shared it with others, confident the favor (or an equivalent) would one day be returned, no meat need go bad. Sharing food strategically—which other primates scarcely do at all, except mother to infant—radically improved everyone's survival chances, because even the best foragers and hunters have bad days. Moreover, keeping others who were inefficient foragers and hunters alive allowed the most efficient food-getters to concentrate on getting food rather than doing other chores. Early hominins figured out that a society could benefit collectively from specialization and exchange.

In short, bigger brains permitted greater social cooperation, and tighter social units in turn promoted bigger brains. Both processes allowed a dietary shift toward more meat—the proteins and fats that, in turn, fed bigger brains. Humans are by far the most cooperative of primates. Ants and bees cooperate intricately by instinct. We do it more as a result of culture—the collective habits, skills, and achievements that we transmit from one generation to the next, which only creatures with big brains can develop.

PAIR BONDING Bigger brains may also have complicated the hominin social scene—specifically, what scholars call mate selection. Chimpanzees live in small social groups in which dominant males keep a harem of several females and respond violently to any rival male's attention toward harem members. Male chimps are much larger than female chimps, a pattern that prevailed among early hominin species as well. To judge by the available skeletons, females on average weighed about 60 to 75 percent as much as males among our early forebears. Like chimps, these early hominins also probably lived in small hierarchical groups in which females reproduced with one dominant male and most males had no offspring.

But at some point a different pattern evolved. About 1.5 million years ago, one hominin species (early ***Homo erectus***, called by some scholars *Homo ergaster*) emerged in which males and females were closer in size. This may have signaled the beginning of male-female pair bonding, an arrangement in which couples enter into long-term partnerships. Today, pair bonding is characteristic in most human societies, in one species of small ape called gibbons, and in a few distantly related species, mainly birds. With pair bonding, all males have a good chance at securing a mate and reproducing. They can coexist less violently, live together in larger social groups, and find it rewarding to take a durable interest in one female and offspring—which male chimps decidedly do not.

To the extent that males cared for their children, they helped their species to prosper. Among other ape species today, mothers get comparatively little help and must breast-feed their offspring for six or seven years. They then cease providing for their young soon after the young are weaned. Hominins, however, gradually evolved a system in which the young were weaned earlier, and caring for toddlers was shared by mothers, grandmothers, aunts, older sisters—and even males who could be enticed into helping with the children. This evolving arrangement translated into higher fertility, because adult females who aren't breast-feeding are far more likely to conceive than those who are breast-feeding. This approach possibly led to higher infant and child survival rates, because the incapacitation or death of a mother didn't automatically doom her children. In this way—perhaps—hominins out-competed other less cooperative apes by helping mothers raise the young.

If comparative male-female body size is any guide, then early *Homo erectus* (or *Homo ergaster*), who lived 1.9 million to 1.4 million years ago in eastern and southern Africa, was the pioneer of greater sexual equality. Subsequent hominin species all showed narrower differences in size between males and females. Among humans today, males on average are 17 percent heavier and 8 percent taller than females. Greater physical and social equality between the sexes and pair bonding rewarded better brains, because navigating the social scene so as to get and keep a good mate, or to trade up for a better one, was—and remains—a mentally challenging process. Beyond

tracking social relations, there are three other crucial skills that our ancestors' outsized brains proved useful for: toolmaking, fire management, and language.

TOOLMAKING The first evidence of tool use dates to about 2.5 million years ago, before the hominin brain had grown much. Early tools were chipped from stone and used for cutting and smashing—actions that were probably helpful for getting at bone marrow, a rich source of protein. Toolmaking required imagination and dexterity, and perhaps over time toolmaking hominins developed these traits, stimulating further refinement of their mental capacities. (Incidentally, archeologists think most early toolmakers were right-handed, from patterns in the chipped stones. About 90 percent of humans are right-handed today.) Stone tools available more than 2 million years ago enabled hominins to cut meat better than a sharp-toothed lion and dig up roots and tubers better than a sharp-tusked warthog.

Once good stone tools were invented, tool technology stagnated. For nearly a million years, hominins used the same sorts of tools, made in the same ways. Then, around 1.6 million years ago, a new generation of tools was invented—notably, a double-sided hand axe, which was good for butchering large animals. These served, with virtually no modification, for another million years—until a mere 500,000 or 300,000 years ago. One variety of archaic humans, *Homo erectus*, wandered out of Africa all the way to Southeast Asia, but everywhere they went their hand axes looked just like the ones their distant cousins used

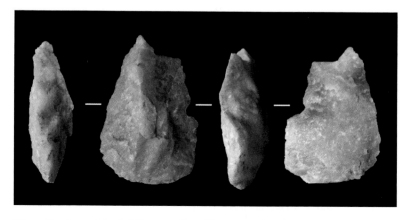

Stone Tools and Social Cooperation These handheld stone tools, unearthed at archeological sites in China, date from between 2 million and 500,000 years ago. The creation and likely use of these tools are evidence of social cooperation in early hominins.

Hand Axe Hand axes found in northern France were likely used by *Homo erectus* to butcher the carcasses of large animals. This one dates to 800,000 years ago.

in Africa. Archaic humans were conservative in their culture and technology.

After about 400,000 years ago, that conservatism slowly waned and a few innovative ideas spread. These included attaching wooden handles to stone tools, using projectiles as weapons, and applying pigments as decoration. The evolution of the hominin tool kit apparently came in occasional leaps more than in slow, steady modifications. If the links between tools and brains were strong (better brains, better tools; better tools, better food, better brains), then perhaps the evolution of the brain sometimes came in leaps as well.

CONTROL OF FIRE Other primates, notably chimpanzees, use primitive tools such as sticks to probe holes in the ground at spots that might contain tasty insects. But only hominins have ever controlled fire. Control of fire was probably more important as a cultural accomplishment than the invention of stone tools; but because it shows up poorly in the archeological record, we know much less about it. We have only the haziest idea when hominins first came to control fire. It may have been as recent as half a million years ago, or as long ago as 1.5 million years. Control of fire was so useful that it probably spread quickly. With fire, our ancestors could keep warm in colder climates, which opened higher latitudes and higher elevations to them. They could keep dangerous animals at bay—especially at night, when big cats, for example, had the advantages of keener smell and better night vision. They could brandish fire to scare carnivores away from their kills or to aid in their own hunting. They could burn whole landscapes, turning forests into grasslands to attract tasty herbivores—in effect, converting natural vegetation into good habitat for animals they could eat, and therefore, good habitat for themselves. And, perhaps most important, with fire our ancestors could cook.

Cooking increased the amount of food available. Scorching or smoking meat delays its decay. Cooking kills some bacteria, neutralizes some toxins, tenderizes tough fibers and meats, and alters the chemistry of molecules in ways that ease human digestion. Today's chimps and gorillas have much larger intestines than we have, and they can digest a wider range of raw organic materials than we can. They don't need to cook. But about 60 percent of their food intake is needed just to provide the energy for chewing and digesting. Cooking enabled our ancestors, in effect, to outsource and speed up digestion, thus requiring less elaborate stomachs and intestines. Thanks to cooking, they no longer needed big jaws and large teeth either.

The harnessing of fire probably had social consequences as well as dietary ones. Managing fire—finding fuel, stoking a flame, keeping it under control—required cooperation. It was a skill that had to be taught carefully to the young. Groups that managed fire probably developed a stronger solidarity because if they didn't cooperate successfully, they couldn't keep fire under control. Fire-wielders might even have sent rudimentary messages by smoke signals, even before speech emerged. The usefulness of fire is reflected in its universality: every human group, however remote, has used it—although some (generally, isolated groups confined to islands) could only preserve fire, not make it.

LANGUAGE If anything our remote ancestors did proved more important than harnessing fire, it was developing language. Other species have systems of communication: for example, bees transmit information by dancing, and ants do so by releasing chemical scents. Chimpanzees use about 30 different calls to communicate. Only humans have fully developed language, capable of communicating abstract meanings. The average American 20-year-old knows roughly 40,000 words, although most people regularly use only about 4,000 of them. They can combine those words to transmit an almost infinite number of meanings.

Language is a biological adaptation as well as a cultural one. In order to speak, our ancestors had to develop peculiar anatomical features, such as a long and low larynx, which is absent elsewhere in the animal kingdom. Our ancestors' brains, as well as their larynxes, evolved so as to permit us to speak and understand language. Indeed, this is partly what human brains are *for*, and why they're wired the way they are. Between ages one and four, healthy humans learn to understand and speak whatever languages surround them, without being taught. That is a large part of what makes us human; no other creatures can do it.

The ability to use language, even if it began as a simple code with minimal grammar or syntax, conferred great advantages. It allowed the sharing of practical information (e.g., "lion behind bush") that improved survival chances. As language evolved and improved, it permitted groups to plan hunts in detail, work out quarrels peacefully, and teach skills to youngsters with greater efficiency. Language, like fire, was so useful that those groups who had it, even in rudimentary form, enjoyed great advantages over those without. So those without language either acquired it or vanished.

No one knows when language emerged or how long it took to do so. Some skeletal evidence suggests it might have begun 2 million years ago. Many scholars think it developed only with our own species, *Homo sapiens*, between 200,000 and 120,000 years ago, and a few think it was more recent than that. We will probably never know when this most extraordinary of human achievements arose. But because all human groups around the world speak, it's safe to say that the capacity to do so arose before humans left Africa roughly 100,000 years ago.

Of the traits and skills that distinguish our species, bipedalism came first. After that, developments got more complicated. Bigger brains, bigger social groups, and toolmaking perhaps came together and reinforced one another. Fire management and language also favored the development of bigger brains and bigger groups. Although the chronology of these developments remains unclear, it is likely that the biological evolution of the traits and the cultural evolution of the skills that make us human overlapped in time and collectively encouraged one another.

OUR CLOSEST COUSINS

Of the 18 or so hominin species that at one time or another inhabited the Earth, only one remains. Our family tree is a bushy shrub with all but one of the branches now dead. Most of those extinct species lived and died out long ago in Africa. A few, like our own species, left Africa for Eurasia (the large landmass spanning Europe and Asia). But unlike *Homo sapiens*, the other hominins, including

Homo naledi (see page 15), went extinct. The last of our close relatives, the three varieties of humans known as Neanderthals, Denisovans, and Flores Island "Hobbits," disappeared between 50,000 and 30,000 years ago.

NEANDERTHALS

Neanderthals, so named because their remains were first found (in 1856) in the Neander River valley in Germany, lived from about 400,000 to about 40,000 years ago in Europe, Siberia, and southwestern Asia. They evolved from a hominin species, *Homo erectus*, that migrated out of Africa nearly 2 million years ago. We—*Homo sapiens*—also descend from *Homo erectus*, which went extinct only about 190,000 years ago and was one of the longer-lived branches of the human family. So we are remote cousins of Neanderthals.

Neanderthals flourished in an Ice Age environment, adapting to it both genetically and culturally: they were compact, heat-retaining, heavy-limbed, powerful creatures, on average about 30 percent heavier than modern-day people and with braincases larger than ours. Skeletons indicate that males on average stood about 5'5" (165 cm) and weighed about 145 lbs. (66 kg), and females about 5'1" (155 cm) and 120 lbs. (54 kg).

Neanderthal Culture A geometric pattern etched on the wall of a cave on Gibraltar, at the southern tip of Spain. It was probably created deliberately by a Neanderthal—perhaps as a map or a symbol of the people who lived in the cave, suggesting that Neanderthals were capable of abstract thought.

More is known about Neanderthals than any other extinct hominin, mainly because they lived in Europe, where far more archeological work has been done than in Africa or Asia. They hunted big game with stone-tipped spears and foraged for berries, nuts, roots, and fruits. They buried their dead, which may mean that they had religious beliefs. In 2014, archeologists found the first clear example of Neanderthal art: some scratchings on the wall of a cave in Gibraltar that are at least 39,000 years old. Neanderthals, it seems, were capable of abstract thought. Whether or not they had language, or how much they had, is controversial; but expert opinion currently is skeptical about their linguistic attainment. Almost all Neanderthal tools (among those found so far) remained close to where they were made, suggesting that the Neanderthals had only small trade networks—if any. Genetic evidence suggests their total population never exceeded a few thousand.

Neanderthal life was tough and cold: they lived out in the open when not in caves, and they didn't live long. To judge by surviving skeletons, none managed to last beyond age 45. Their skeletons show many broken bones and possible indications of cannibalism. DNA evidence suggests that they were highly inbred, which is perhaps not surprising since they lived in small bands and rarely encountered strangers. Ice Age life grew colder for them about 39,000 years ago, owing to a giant volcanic eruption in what is now southern Italy that darkened skies for about three years and may have nudged them closer to extinction.

The last of the true Neanderthals lived in what is now

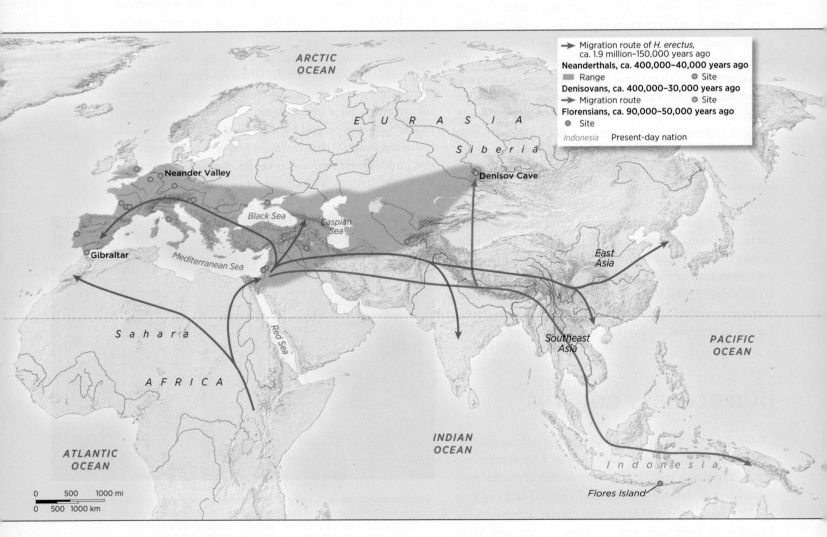

Our Closest Cousins, 400,000–30,000 Years Ago Among the closest relatives to our species are three hominins, the last ones to go extinct, known as Neanderthals, Denisovans, and Florensians or Flores Island "Hobbits." Just how they are related to us is unclear, but they and we might be descendants of *Homo erectus*, the first hominin species to migrate out of Africa.

CONSIDERING THE EVIDENCE

Our Cousin Neo

In 2013, paleontologists began excavating nineteen hominin skeletons from the Rising Star cave in South Africa. The reconstructed skull of the most complete skeleton, named Neo by the scientists, is shown here. At an estimated 100 lbs. (45 kg) and 4′10″ (1.2 m) in height, Neo was shorter than modern humans and had a much smaller brain—closer in size to the brains of *Australopithecus afarensis* like Lucy than hominins in our genus, *Homo*. Yet his brain was shaped more like ours, suggesting that he may have been able to use language. His hands, legs, and feet suggest that he was fully bipedal, but scientists usually link the shape of his hips and curved fingers with species from millions of years ago. So it was surprising when scientists confirmed that Neo lived 300,000 years ago, about the same time that our *Homo sapiens* ancestors first appeared in Africa. It's possible that Neo's species, *Homo naledi*, encountered early *Homo sapiens*, as our cousins the Neanderthals and Denisovans did.

QUESTIONS FOR ANALYSIS

1. Sequencing events in time helps historians to understand how people and communities influenced one other. Neo's skeleton dates to a time when *Homo sapiens* was one of several human species, including Neanderthals, Denisovans, and Flores Island "Hobbits." Most of our *Homo sapiens* ancestors lived far to the north of Neo's *Homo naledi* community. However, if they did happen to meet, do you think they would have recognized each other as human? Why or why not? How might they have cooperated and competed with each other?

2. Some scientists have suggested that the caves where Neo and other *Homo naledi* skeletons have been found were burial chambers because they required intentional effort to access. The scientists argue that such burials prove that *Homo naledi* was human, but others disagree because the caves contained no objects usually found in human burials. What does burial reveal about the way in which early humans likely imagined their world and their community? Assuming that *Homo naledi* communities did bury their dead, is that enough to consider them human? Explain your response.

3. Besides burial, what tools or other kinds of artifacts described in this chapter would help scientists to prove that *Homo naledi* possessed modern human behaviors?

Spain about 39,000 years ago, but Asians, Europeans, and Native Americans today are all, genetically speaking, about 1 to 4 percent Neanderthal. Africans carry a much smaller genetic inheritance from Neanderthals, well under 1 percent. (They acquired that via migrations of Eurasians back into Africa, starting about 8,000 years ago). Neanderthals vanished, but almost all of us are in small part Neanderthal.

DENISOVANS

We have other extinct cousins called Denisovans, named after a cave in Siberia where archeologists found some remains. Careful study of their genome (the full set of genes of an organism) suggests that the Denisovans were more closely related to Neanderthals than any other (known) species of hominin. Like Neanderthals, they were stocky and well suited to cold conditions. Denisovans probably lived in Siberia and throughout East Asia for a few hundred thousand years. They had enough culture to make bone needles as of about 41,000 years ago, before any other branch of humans started sewing. The human population today that is genetically closest to the Denisovans lives in East and Southeast Asia. The genetic overlap shows that somehow, somewhere, Denisovans and *Homo sapiens* encountered one another and interbred. So Denisovans, like Neanderthals, went extinct, but their genes live on in many humans today.

HOBBITS

The most remarkable of our recently extinct cousins is *Homo floriensis*, popularly called Hobbits after the imaginary creatures in J.R.R. Tolkien novels. They were tiny folk, a little over 3 ft. (1 m) tall on average. Their remains were discovered on a cave floor on an Indonesian island, Flores, in 2003. Only a single skull and parts of nine skeletons have been found, so generalizations remain questionable. But it seems likely that they were the last of a very old pre-human lineage, isolated from all other hominins for thousands of generations. They lived on Flores as early as 90,000 years ago and shrank to their small stature under the pressure of natural selection. (Miniature mammals of many sorts have evolved in island habitats, where lower food requirements are an advantage.) They went extinct about 50,000 years ago, perhaps without any contact with *Homo sapiens*, unlike Neanderthals and Denisovans. Once

the Flores "hobbits," Neanderthals, and Denisovans had disappeared, *Homo sapiens* was the last species of hominin standing anywhere on Earth, as far as we know now.

THE MIGRATIONS OF *HOMO SAPIENS*

We—the last of the hominins—are an upstart species. The fossil and genetic evidence suggests that our species appeared between 300,000 and 200,000 years ago in North and East Africa. We are also wanderers. Within Africa, groups of *Homo sapiens* migrated south, starting more than 80,000 years ago. Others went west a little later. These wandering groups had spread out over Africa by 25,000 years ago. In the thinly populated continent, some groups became isolated from the rest for thousands of years, which helps explain why African populations today exhibit greater genetic diversity than all other humans combined.

OUT OF AFRICA

At some point between 100,000 and 65,000 years ago, other wandering *Homo sapiens* trekked out of Africa and began to colonize parts of Eurasia. A run of dry weather in northeastern Africa about 74,000 to 60,000 years ago might have motivated them to try their luck further afield. There is as yet no archeological evidence speaking directly to this migration. But somehow they traveled, either on foot via Egypt and the Sinai Peninsula or by island-hopping across the southern Red Sea to the Arabian Peninsula. In those Ice Age days, sea level was much lower than today and the Red Sea less of a barrier. Once the wanderers crossed to Asia, they seem to have headed along the shorelines eastward toward India. They then split up and spread out.

One set of human migrants drifted eastward. They soon reached New Guinea and Australia, landmasses that were then united as a single continent owing to the lower sea level of the Ice Age. Getting there from the Asian mainland still required a sea journey of at least 60 miles (100 km). This voyage implies a considerable technological and logistical competence, as well as high tolerance for risk. The first Australians were surely a plucky

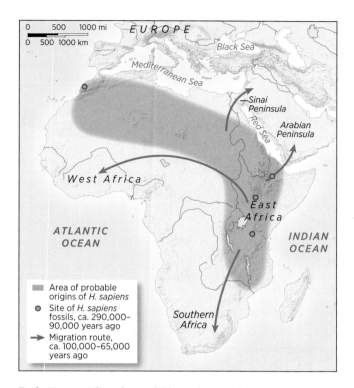

Early Human Migrations within and out of Africa, 300,000–65,000 Years Ago Our own species evolved somewhere in East or northern Africa by roughly 300,000 years ago. Tiny populations of early humans migrated into southern and West Africa as well as into Southwest Asia. Accurate dating of these migrations remains a challenge, but the evidence suggests that the exodus from Africa occurred between 100,000 and 65,000 years ago.

lot. They continued on southward to Tasmania by about 40,000 years ago, but stopped short of Antarctica, leaving it uninhabited.

Other *Homo sapiens* entered Europe from southwestern Asia around 45,000 years ago. These new Europeans, according to genetic evidence, are the ancestors of 75 to 85 percent of contemporary Europeans. They soon encountered the depths of the last ice age and—not unlike their more affluent descendants today—headed for Spain and southern France in search of balmier climes. Other human groups walked into the frigid expanse of Siberia, attracted by the abundance of large, tasty mammals such as woolly mammoths, whose hides were as useful as their meat. Groups of humans also headed into what is now China and Japan, arriving about 30,000 years ago.

Some people moved still further afield. The last chapter in these epic migrations brought people to the Americas—possibly as early as 23,000 years ago, certainly by 14,000 years ago. They came to Alaska from Siberia via a broad land bridge exposed by the lower sea levels. They might have walked across it, or perhaps paddled rafts along its southern coast. Once in the Americas, they apparently spread out quickly, reaching Chile no later than 12,000 years ago. The archeological, linguistic, and DNA evidence concerning the human discovery of America is not consistent, so arguments rage about its timing, the size of the founding population, and whether they came all at once or in several separate waves. It does seem that the first Americans are most closely related to peoples of southern Siberia, although rival interpretations maintain their cousins were from what is now Korea and northern China.

These long, slow migrations out of Africa and throughout the world no doubt experienced many setbacks. As of roughly 50,000 to 75,000 years ago, the total human population in all of Africa and Eurasia was probably only a few hundred thousand—fewer people than live today in Wyoming or Newfoundland. It was an uncrowded world in which people rarely encountered strangers. It was full of lethal risks too. Some migrating groups guessed wrong and found themselves in deserts. Others attempted what they thought was a short sea voyage and never saw land again. But slowly, in fits and starts, humankind colonized the globe.

THE ROLE OF CLIMATE

Human colonization of the globe took place during the last ice age, which lasted roughly from 130,000 to 12,000 years ago. Cold, dry, and fickle climate presented our ancestors with strong reasons to move around.

The Earth's climate has always been changing. For the past 3 million years or so, climate has periodically entered long cold spells that last on average 100,000 years or more. These ice ages were punctuated by brief interglacial periods lasting generally a mere 10,000 years. An ice age typically brought great expansions of polar ice sheets and mountain glaciers, colder temperatures everywhere, and dryer conditions in most places. The ice age that began around 130,000 years ago hit a particular cold snap starting about 24,000 years ago; today's Chicago and Glasgow were under ice sheets thicker than skyscrapers are tall. That big chill ended abruptly about 12,000 years ago.

The last ice age was not only much colder and dryer than modern climate, but also far more unstable. Periods of sudden cooling or warming might occur, with swings of 9 to 18 degrees Fahrenheit (5 or 10 degrees Celsius) over

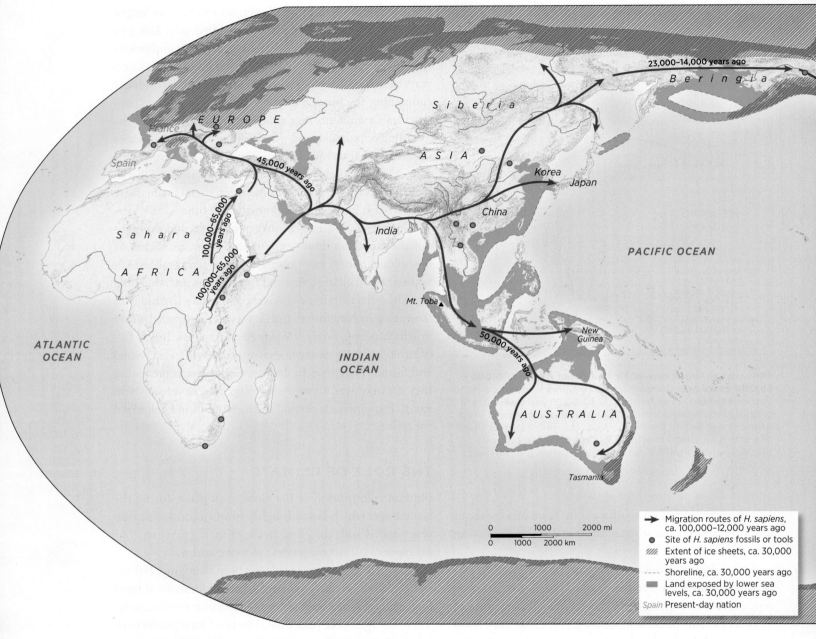

Early Human Migrations throughout the World, 100,000–12,000 Years Ago When humans first left Africa, they soon spread out in all directions, taking advantage of the lower sea levels during the last ice age. The voyages to Australia and New Guinea were the only ones that required rafts or boats, although it is possible that the rapid migrations along the western coasts of the Americas also took place by sea.

a few centuries. The slender evidence suggests these swings were smaller in Africa than elsewhere. But everywhere the incentives to migrate, either to avoid the worst of the cold and drought or to take advantage of warming and moisture, were often strong.

With so much water frozen into ice sheets, our wandering ancestors enjoyed the advantage of lower sea levels

during the Ice Age. This gave people more land to work with—the equivalent of a bonus continent the size of North America. It was possible to walk from Korea to Japan, from Britain to France, or, as we've seen, from Siberia to Alaska.

The most challenging moment of the last ice age came around 75,000 years ago when a giant eruption occurred at Mount Toba, a volcano in what is now Indonesia. The eruption spewed enough dust and ash into the skies to block sunlight for years, and it may have lowered global temperatures by 10 to 30 degrees Fahrenheit (5 to 15 degrees Celsius). It's likely that this catastrophe played havoc with plant and animal life, and it may have brought the human species close to extinction: DNA evidence suggests that at around this time our ancestors' numbers were reduced to 10,000 or so—only a little more than the populations of endangered species such as pandas or tigers today. The

Toba event was unique. But the last ice age contained numerous cold spells and severe droughts, a circumstance that surely rewarded migration, innovation, learning, and communication.

GENETIC AND CULTURAL DIVERSITY

The experience of migration to all the continents except Antarctica during a time of cold and fickle climate changed *Homo sapiens*. It made our ancestors more diverse, both genetically and culturally.

Recall that by moving around within Africa, the small populations of early *Homo sapiens* often separated themselves from one another. As with all species whose populations fragment into isolated groups, early *Homo sapiens* within Africa underwent considerable genetic diversification, with each small population adapting genetically to its local environment. That process of diversification continued in the small group or groups that left Africa for Asia and Europe. They also spread out, grew isolated from one another, and diversified enough genetically so that humans eventually developed a range of skin, hair, and eye colors. Their body shapes also diversified. People who lived in colder places benefited from being stockier (as had Neanderthals), because a stocky build retains heat more efficiently than a lean one. Others who lived at high elevations developed genetic adaptations to a low-oxygen environment.

The genetic diversity of the entire non-African human population, however, remains smaller than that among Africans themselves, a result of what in population genetics is called a founder effect. All non-African peoples of the world are descended from a few groups of African emigrants—probably (to judge by genetic evidence) between 600 and 10,000 people. So despite all the globe-trotting that took people to places as far apart as Europe, Australia, and the Americas, people of non-African descent today remain less genetically diverse than Africans.

The opposite proved true with respect to cultural evolution because culture can change faster than genomes. The variety of environments that those emigrants from Africa encountered stimulated changes in culture. By 30,000 years ago, people outside of Africa had developed more diverse behaviors and tool kits than were found within Africa. For example, people needed more clothing when they got to higher latitudes, so they learned how to use animal furs and skins to keep warm. They learned how to sew small bits of fur into big patchwork cloaks. They also found in most of Eurasia, especially its chillier parts, that there were fewer nutritious plants to gather than in warmer climates, but that hunting big game was far easier. The big animals in Africa had had time to evolve defenses against clever, fire-wielding, spear-throwing team players, because humans took so long to develop these skills. So animals there instinctively kept their distance from *Homo sapiens*. But outside of Africa, big animals had no such experience, so they naively allowed humans to approach and surround them. As a result, people outside of Africa often developed cultures with a larger role for big-game hunting and a smaller role for gathering roots, nuts, and berries. Artistic styles and the variety of languages spoken multiplied outside of Africa. So our ancestors' wanderings after leaving Africa led eventually to vast cultural diversity among peoples with only modest genetic diversity.

This saga of cultural, and to a lesser extent genetic, diversification as people spread out across the globe testifies to the weakness of webs of interconnection prior to 15,000 years ago. When people lived in small bands and rarely encountered other groups, they had limited opportunity to learn from and exchange with strangers. Over time, these groups grew apart. As we shall see, that trend eventually reversed itself as stronger webs multiplied the opportunities for exchanges.

PALEOLITHIC CULTURE

The word *Paleolithic* means "old stone age." It began 2.6 million years ago with the first stone tools and ended about 13,000 years ago. For most of that time, cultural change came very slowly compared to that of more recent times. People were few in number and rarely experienced the challenges of meeting strangers with different ways. Great uncertainties cloud our understanding of Paleolithic society and culture. Most of what we know comes from the last 50,000 years of the Paleolithic.

THE HAZARDS OF DAILY LIFE

One advantage of those uncrowded times, it seems, was that early *Homo sapiens* did not often indulge in

Early Art The geometric pattern on this 70,000-year-old ocher plaque, found in a cave in South Africa, is a very early example of art made by humans of the Paleolithic.

interpersonal violence: of the 6,000 skeletons available for examination from times before 20,000 years ago, only one betrays signs of death via weapons. One likely explanation for the sparse evidence of violence is that Paleolithic people didn't lose much by running away from a fight. Aside from bands that settled around a reliable resource, like a shellfish bed, people were normally on the move in search of food. They rarely had to fight to preserve access to food, and they probably had a weaker sense of territorial possession than do modern chimps.

But Paleolithic life had its hazards. Hunting big animals, probably exclusively a man's job, involved routine, if small, risks of injury or death. Childbirth brought larger, if less frequent, dangers for women. Anyone too big to carry and too feeble or injured to walk when it was time to move on was an encumbrance to a mobile group—and was presumably abandoned to a solitary and probably short life on his or her own. Small children, if too numerous or troublesome, often met the same fate, as they do in modern mobile hunting and foraging societies. But it's noteworthy that archeologists have found in what is now Pakistan the remains of one young woman with severe birth defects who could only have survived to young adulthood with constant care from others.

SOCIAL STRUCTURES

Paleolithic people lived in unstable bands of roughly 20 to 80 individuals, sometimes as many as 150—much larger than the social groups of chimpanzees or, in all probability, hominins of any other species but our own. These bands were composed of a few closely related families, and often a sprinkling of unrelated people as well. Groups could easily fragment as a result of quarrels. Stragglers normally would have wanted to join up with a band, especially in places where big-game hunting was the dominant way of life: it was much more efficient, and safer, to hunt in groups.

Like their hominin and probably pre-hominin ancestors, Paleolithic people had a very strong sense of who belonged to their group and who did not. Indeed, our species still has a powerful tendency to divide the human population into "us" and "them," and to build strong bonds with one's group—which helps explain the emotional satisfactions of activities such as team sports.

These small bands occasionally met up with other groups with whom they could swap goods, information, and young people of mating age. In this way, they created bonds of mutual obligation and kinship and also formed new families. Women tended to join their mates' bands, to judge from DNA evidence. Within and among small bands, people cultivated one another's good will by extending kindnesses, giving gifts, and doing favors. Individuals who did this cannily emerged as influential, and in this way they insured themselves against temporary misfortune. As one modern Inuit (Eskimo) put it, "The best place for [an Eskimo] to store his surplus is in someone else's stomach." The same attitudes and behaviors survive today; they can be observed in any workplace, residential neighborhood, or college dorm.

Late Paleolithic people lived a mobile but in many ways low-stress life. Those who roamed the grasslands of Eurasia or East Africa, thickly populated by large herbivores such as mammoths, deer, or gazelles, lived largely by hunting. People living by, or periodically visiting, seashores ate plenty of fish, mussels, crabs, clams, and seaweed. These groups were in the minority, however. In most places, Paleolithic people got most of their food by gathering fruits, berries, nuts, roots, and seeds, supplemented by hunting and scavenging. Everyone accumulated a refined understanding of their local ecosystems, learning the characteristics and habits of dozens of species of plants and animals. They generally didn't have to work hard to acquire all the food they needed—probably about four to six hours per day on average. This left plenty of time for talk, instruction of the young, song and dance, and sleep. Paleolithic people also lived healthy lives (at least, by the standards of later populations), having few infectious diseases and getting plenty of exercise through their daily activities.

A LATE PALEOLITHIC CULTURAL REVOLUTION

At some point late in the Paleolithic, technology and culture began to change a little faster. The sparse archeological remains found so far can support different conclusions, but it looks like the process began in Africa about 90,000 years ago and in Eurasia maybe 50,000 years ago.

DEMOGRAPHIC CHANGE Part of the reason for the technological and cultural revolution was likely demographic. Paleolithic people before about 50,000 years ago didn't live long by today's standards. Scanty evidence suggests the odds of making it to age 15 were about 60 percent. Judging from the evidence contained in fossil teeth, it seems that over the long haul, hominin and human populations lived longer, meaning that they contained larger proportions of people who survived to age 30 or so. But then about 50,000 to 15,000 years ago, the proportion of older people increased more than fourfold. With more "old" people (age 30 and up) around to help look

Paintings from the Cave of Altamira Dated some 38,000 years ago, these paintings from a cave in Spain feature vivid images of mammoths and deer, as well as human handprints.

after small children, women could bear more children and more babies survived, bringing a surge in population. Human population grew rapidly in the late Paleolithic, and perhaps an unprecedented abundance of helpful grandparents was part of the reason. At a guess, the world contained some half a million people as of 50,000 years ago, but perhaps 2 to 6 million people by 15,000 years ago. It remained an uncrowded world.

The lengthening of life expectancy added to the cultural dynamism of Paleolithic society. With more grandparents around to help teach the young, the efficiency of communication and learning increased, helping to account for the accelerated technological and cultural change evident in the archeological record.

Population growth had a similar effect. The mental horizons of people expanded through more frequent contacts with strangers. Living one's entire life within the same group of 20 to 80 people wasn't as stimulating as occasionally meeting up with other bands. The frequency of such encounters climbed with population growth. When people got the chance to learn from a wider array of strangers, new ideas were hatched at a faster rate. This helps to explain a pattern we saw earlier: the long conservatism in toolmaking followed by the sudden emergence of new styles of tool manufacture.

The Lion Human The first known representation of an animal or a human is in fact both: a 35,000- to 40,000-year-old ivory figurine with a human body and a lion's head (perhaps a representation of a deity), found in present-day Germany.

TECHNOLOGY AND ART After 50,000 years ago, not only did tools evolve more quickly than before, but entirely new inventions appeared faster. By 39,000 years ago, Paleolithic people—at least, those living in one cave in Germany—had a musical instrument, a pipe carved from a swan's bone. They sewed garments with needles by 30,000 years ago. The bow and arrow appeared about 30,000 to 25,000 years ago and spread almost everywhere by 20,000 years ago. People started making nets, probably for fishing, about 25,000 years ago. The first fishhooks, ropes, and knife blades appeared around the same time. People now made things out of bone and antler as well as of stone.

Further evidence for the idea of a cultural revolution at some point late in the Paleolithic comes from the world of art. In what is now South Africa, geometric patterns etched into a clay called ochre and beads made out of snail shells appeared at least 70,000 years ago. Some rock shelters in Namibia (in southern Africa) bear animal images that might be 30,000 years old. The first figurine of a human form with an animal's head, the so-called Lion Human (Löwenmensch) found in a cave in Germany, dates from 35,000 to 40,000 years ago. In southern France and northern Spain over 38,000 years ago, artists started decorating more than a hundred caves with paintings, mainly of hunted animals. In Indonesia, there's a stenciled image of a human hand that appears to be 40,000 years old. Paleolithic people seem to have engaged in cave and rock-shelter art in only a small part of the human realm in Europe, Africa, Indonesia, and Australia—although more might yet be found one day.

The first surviving evidence of humans depicting the human form, dug out of a cave in southern Germany in 2008, is a 40,000-year-old figurine of a woman carved from a mammoth tusk. These innovations in art—beads, painting, figurines—may signal big changes in human mental worlds: perhaps greater self-consciousness, greater abilities in language, a new sense of the supernatural.

All these changes—demographic, technological, and artistic—whenever and wherever they began, likely reinforced one another. Older and larger populations, organized in bigger groups, helped to bring more innovations to technology and art, while new technologies helped more people to live longer. The new art may have helped them to enjoy life more and may have reflected tighter social bonds formed around spiritual beliefs.

A SPIRIT WORLD: SHAMANISM The mental world of Paleolithic peoples is difficult to penetrate, but it's possible that during the late Paleolithic people began to extend their notions of kinship and reciprocity into a spirit world. They envisioned supernatural power not as abstract but as specific, located in important objects around them—certain trees, animals, or rocks. People forged connections with these supernatural agents through various rituals that probably featured music, dance, trances, and possibly mind-altering drugs. They reached out to spirits through gifts offered in the form of sacrifices. They also believed the dead were transported to a spirit realm, a notion powerfully reinforced by dreams, in which one can, after all, see the

Paleolithic Cultural Revolution A bone flute found in a cave in France, dating from about 30,000 years ago. Early musical instruments like this spread throughout human communities in the late Paleolithic period.

departed. People began to bury the dead with objects that were intended to help them in the next world. This loose set of religious beliefs and practices is often called **shamanism**. In some societies, including isolated indigenous peoples in Amazonia and Siberia, shamanism survives today, making it by far the most durable variety of religion in history.

It is worth pondering what religion did for Paleolithic human society. There is evidence that groups with religion were likelier to grow, sustain larger-scale cooperation, and withstand the risks of Paleolithic life slightly better than others. Religion enhanced group solidarity: those human groups with religion generally found it easier to act together toward a common goal than those without it. This improved their odds of survival and reproduction. It's even possible that over tens of thousands of years human brains adapted so as to become increasingly willing to believe in an unseen spirit world, just as our brains became adapted to enjoy group solidarity.

The emergence of religion also shows growing connections among people throughout Africa and Eurasia before 15,000 years ago—a modest tightening of the faint web binding all humankind. Shamanism existed in different forms, but many of its rituals and practices—dance, drugs, and sacrifices, for example—spread widely. The performance of such rituals held in common probably made it easier for strangers to mingle peacefully. So shamanistic religion both thickened the web of human interaction during the late Paleolithic and provides us with evidence of its workings.

One example of Paleolithic human connectivity in the spiritual realm comes from scholars who collect folk myths. Tales of hunters and animals turned into constellations of stars appear widely in Africa, Asia, and among Native Americans. There are at least 47 versions recorded featuring different animals and constellations but following the same storyline. As people migrated around the world with their myths and beliefs, they changed them gradually to make sense in new environments. Slowly, the myths diverged—as did languages, tool kits, and other

forms of culture. Yet the basic form of these myths, linking people with the heavens, remained a common human heritage.

The late Paleolithic cultural revolution strongly suggests heightened levels of interaction among our ancestors by 50,000 and especially by 15,000 years ago. The pace of change in tool design, art, and religion is likely the result of more frequent encounters with strangers whose ways were slightly different and inspired people to rethink their habits.

ENVIRONMENTAL IMPACTS With improved technology, greater numbers, and stronger social solidarity owing to the late Paleolithic cultural revolution, our species acquired additional power over the plants and animals with which they shared the Earth. Despite their belief in the supernatural qualities of living things, Paleolithic people devastated parts of their environment. Their most important environmental impact came in altering vegetation through repeated burning of landscapes, which people did wherever conditions were suitably dry, as in East Africa and Australia. The goal of burning was to promote populations of useful plants and animals that would re-colonize burnt ground—grasses with edible seeds, for example, or tasty grazing animals such as gazelles. The "natural" vegetation that has prevailed in Australia over the past 50,000 years is actually made up of fire-tolerant species that can flourish amid frequent burning. Paleolithic Australians relied on these species, and on the animals, such as wallabies and kangaroos, that thrived on the vegetation that sprang up in the aftermath of a burn.

The second great environmental impact of Paleolithic peoples was a surge in extinctions. One of the less pleasant facts about our ancestors is that when they first reached new lands, mass extinctions among large mammals and birds soon followed. Around the world, between 50,000 and 12,000 years ago, about 65 percent of the genera (families) of big mammals were swept into the dustbin of natural history. The biggest wave

"Venus of Hohle Fels" This three-inch-tall statue, recently discovered in Germany, is a stylized representation of a woman carved from a mammoth tusk. Its exaggerated proportions may indicate it was used as a fertility object.

Human Hands Red-stenciled outlines of hands appear on the wall of a cave in Indonesia. The images are dated to around 40,000 years ago.

of extinctions followed when humans first arrived in Australia, in the Americas, and on countless small islands. There were fewer extinctions in Eurasia, and fewer still in Africa. Most specialists think these extinctions resulted from human over-hunting: Paleolithic peoples were efficient hunters, and as they left Africa for different lands, they found many of the big mammals of Eurasia, Australia, and the Americas unsuspecting, easy prey. Climate change may also have contributed to some extinctions.

Mass extinctions had important long-term consequences, because in Australia and the Americas especially they reduced the number of potentially domesticable animals. With almost no wild animals that could be tamed, bred, and raised in captivity, the original human populations of Australia and the Americas had more limited food supplies and sources of muscle power than people elsewhere. As we will see in Chapters 3 and 4, peoples with domesticated animals such as horses, cattle, sheep, goats, and pigs enjoyed important advantages.

CONCLUSION

It is important to remember that we still know very little about the human history of the deeper past. For long stretches of that history, the useful fossils are so few that they would all fit in the back of a pickup truck, far outnumbered by the scholars studying them. A new find or two could generate radically new interpretations and drive some current ideas to extinction. The work on genetic evidence is still recent; in the years ahead, new findings will change prevailing understandings of our deep past.

All of our history until the last 100,000 years took place in Africa. Our remotest hominin ancestors lived in East and North Africa, in unstable environmental conditions that rewarded adaptability. Bipedalism, big brains, and culture helped make some species of hominins flexible enough in behavior to survive, and at

times to flourish. Those species that didn't have big brains and culture—tools, fire, and language especially—died out, although it is humbling to note that some of these extinct species lasted far longer than we have so far. Our own species, *Homo sapiens*, appeared about 300,000 to 200,000 years ago and gradually spread out across most of Africa. Following the path of some earlier hominins, a few of our own branch wandered out of Africa, opening a new chapter in human history perhaps as early as 100,000 years ago.

Homo sapiens is the only remaining hominin. All others went extinct more than 30,000 years ago. Our branch proved more adaptable to changing environments, better able to bear and raise plentiful children, and more imaginative in our culture than any other. As a result, we are the last hominin standing.

On the whole, the period from 100,000 to 15,000 years ago was one of expansion and differentiation in human history, and of accelerating cultural change. Our ancestors colonized almost the entire globe, braving deserts and rain forests, and even making short sea voyages. Their numbers increased, in large part because of this occupation of new regions and habitats. Those who colonized Eurasia continued to live in small groups, sometimes very isolated ones, so that their languages and cultures quickly diverged. Those who stayed in Africa also grew in number but—obliged to respond to fewer unfamiliar environments and somewhat less scattered geographically—maintained their old cultures more successfully.

All humans, wherever they lived, shared some cultural traits. They all used language and fire from the time our species originated. They made and used similar stone tools. They all developed, or acquired, religion and art by 40,000 years ago, and in some cases long before. Some of these similarities, such as the use of fire, merely represent the continuation of very ancient practices. Others, like the bow and arrow, were innovations, and their eventual use by almost all human communities is evidence of links among those communities.

At a more basic and biological level, *Homo sapiens* remained a single species. Even when humans were very few, living in small bands, and scattered thinly over most of the globe, sporadic interactions kept them loosely in contact with neighboring groups and indirectly in touch with the entire species. A faint and slender web connected all our Paleolithic ancestors.

CHAPTER REVIEW

KEY TERMS

Lucy (p. 5)
hominins (p. 6)
Big Bang (p. 6)
Homo sapiens (p. 8)

bipedalism (p. 8)
natural selection (p. 8)
Homo erectus (p. 11)
Neanderthals (p. 13)

Paleolithic (p. 20)
shamanism (p. 23)

Go to INQUIZITIVE to see what you've learned—and learn what you've missed—with personalized feedback along the way.

REVIEW QUESTIONS

1. How did the asteroid that hit the Yucatán Peninsula 66 million years ago facilitate the evolution of our ancestors?

2. What is the significance of bipedalism in hominins?

3. What were the main advantages of large brains?

4. Why was the control of fire so important to hominin development?

5. How does the development of language set *Homo sapiens* apart from other species?

6. What assumptions can we make about Neanderthal culture based on archeological evidence?

7. How did the unstable climate of the last ice age encourage human migration?

8. Why did the populations that moved out of Africa become culturally diverse?

9. In what sense was there a cultural revolution during the late Paleolithic period?

10. What changes in Paleolithic human societies did the emergence of religion bring?

11. What were the two biggest environmental impacts of Paleolithic humans?

12. What are the main reasons that *Homo sapiens* is the last hominin standing?

FURTHER READING

Robert BOYD and Joan SILK, *How Humans Evolved* (2014). A standard textbook on human evolution.

William C. BURGER, *Perfect Planet, Clever Species* (2003). A highly readable account of the origins and evolution of the solar system, Earth, life, and humanity, from a biologist's viewpoint.

William J. BURROUGHS, *Climate Change in Prehistory* (2008). An exploration of what climate shifts meant for early humans.

David CHRISTIAN, *Maps of Time: An Introduction to Big History* (2004). A historian's innovative look at the career of the human species in its fullest context.

Daniel EVERETT, *How Language Began: The Story of Humanity's Greatest Invention* (2017). A highly readable account that argues for a very gradual development of language beginning with *Homo erectus*.

Renée HETHERINGTON and Robert G. B. REID, *The Climate Connection: Climate Change and Modern Human Evolution* (2010). A look at how climate affected early humans from

the onset of the last ice age to the dawn of agriculture, with a few words about the future too.

Sarah B. HRDY, *Mothers and Others: The Evolutionary Origins of Mutual Understanding* (2011). Not an easy read, but a work that's worth the effort if you want to grasp how special humans are.

Jonathan KINGDON, *Lowly Origins: Where, When, and Why Our Ancestors First Stood Up* (2003). An interesting argument about the origins of bipedalism, grounded in geography and ecology.

Douglas PALMER, *Prehistoric Past Revealed* (2003). A geologist's perspective on the history of life on Earth, human included.

Rick POTTS and Chris SLOAN, *What Does It Mean to Be Human?* (2010). A lavishly illustrated work, very brief, a great starting point.

Chris STRINGER, *Lone Survivors: How We Came to Be the Only Humans on Earth* (2013). A study that's especially strong on the African background of human evolution.

CHRONOLOGY

ca. 15,000–9000 BCE
Magdalenian culture flourishes

ca. 12,500–9500 BCE
Natufians flourish

ca. 9000–7000 BCE
Göbekli Tepe

ca. 8500 BCE
First domestication
of pigs

ca. 11,000–9000 BCE
First domestication of
goats and sheep

ca. 7000 BCE
Jomon culture
settlements
in Japan

ca. 5000 BCE
Transition to
agriculture in
Southeast Asia

ca. 30,000–18,000 BCE
First domestication of dogs

ca. 11,000 BCE
First transition to agriculture and
plant domestication in the Levant

9700 BCE
Holocene begins

ca. 6000 BCE
Settlements in North
America; crop
domestication
begins in
Mesoamerica

ca. 25,000–10,000 BCE
Mammoth hunters flourish

10,700–9700 BCE
Younger Dryas

ca. 8000–7000 BCE
First domestication of
cattle; transitions to
agriculture in China's Yangzi
and Huang He river valleys

Settling Down

DOMESTICATION AND AGRICULTURE

30,000 to 6,000 years ago

ca. **4000** BCE
Domestication of llamas

ca. **4000–3000** BCE
Domestication of
potatoes and manioc

ca. **2500** BCE
Transition to agriculture
in North America

ca. **4500** BCE
First domestication
of chickens

ca. **3000** BCE
Transition to agriculture
in Africa

I n 2008, archeologists dug up the floor of Hilazon Tachtit cave in Israel. There they found the 12,000-year-old remains of a burial feast for a 45-year-old female shaman. She was buried in high style, with tortoise shells under her skull and pelvis, and gazelle horn, an eagle's wing tip, some chalk, and a human foot all placed around her. These and other burial objects led the archeologists to infer that she was a religious specialist of great reputation. The feast in her honor was a special occasion. The menu featured fish; meat from gazelles, foxes, and snakes; and no fewer than 80 roast tortoises—enough food for several dozen people. The guests tossed their leftovers over the body of the deceased woman. Someone then placed a big stone slab on top. No other burial from the time shows anything like the elaborate care lavished on this one.

The people who held the feast and buried the shaman are called **Natufians**. They flourished from about 12,500 to 9500 BCE. The Natufians lived in settled villages of 100 to 150 people with round houses dug into the ground. Their tool kit suggests they were in contact with people in northernmost Africa and acquired shells from Egypt's Nile valley. They used obsidian that came from

Natufian Burial A delicate shell and bone necklace found in a burial site in Mount Carmel, Israel. The necklace is dated ca. 11,000 BCE.

FOCUS QUESTIONS

1. How did the gradual emergence of a warmer, more stable climate contribute to changes in human life?

2. What factors contributed to the emergence of the earliest settled communities?

3. Why was domestication a major landmark in human history?

4. What were the major characteristics of the first transitions to agriculture around the world?

5. In what ways did agriculture spread from its points of origin to adoption throughout most of the world?

6. What were the main effects of the transition to agriculture on human life and culture?

hundreds of miles away in Anatolia (modern Turkey). They hunted gazelles and gathered wild cereals. They invented the world's first sickles for harvesting cereals, and they used bowls for grinding grain. At some point, they started sowing their favorite cereals and eventually became farmers, producing their food rather than finding it. They were among the pioneers of sedentary lifeways and—as far as we know—the world's pioneers of agriculture.

The pioneer of Natufian studies was Dorothy Garrod. Born in England in 1892, she earned an undergraduate degree in history from Cambridge University in 1916. After her three brothers and her sweetheart died in World War I, the despondent Garrod went to the Mediterranean island of Malta to figure out what to do with her life. There she became fascinated by ancient artifacts, and soon returned to England to study archeology. Garrod found some Neanderthal remains at Gibraltar in 1925, which at a stroke made her an accomplished archeologist of the Paleolithic. In 1929, she began digging at Shuqba Cave, 20 miles (30 km) northwest of Jerusalem. She

assembled a team of researchers, mostly women—a first in the history of archeology. Her team began the documentation of Natufian culture.

In 1939, much to her surprise, Garrod was appointed to a prestigious professorship in archeology at Cambridge University. She was the first woman ever to hold any professorship at the centuries-old university. Like her subject, the Natufians, Garrod was a pioneer in her own right.

Back in the Paleolithic, as we've seen, history unfolded at a leisurely pace. Over the first several tens of thousands of years of human history after the emergence of language, all people lived in approximately the same sorts of social units, and they all lived mobile lives focused on foraging, hunting, and, in places, fishing. Environment and culture changed with the onset of the Ice Age and its violent climatic fluctuations, with new tools, and with the invention of art. People spread out over the Earth. But the basics of their lives remained much the same.

As the last ice age waned and climate continued to warm, people who formerly wandered in search of food began in several sites to settle down. In multiple places they also began to domesticate animals. And in the final landmark transition considered in this chapter, people invented agriculture at many times in many places. Farming spread widely, changing the basics of life irrevocably. By our twenty-first-century standards, this sea change came slowly. By the standards of Paleolithic history, it came as suddenly as a tsunami.

THE END OF THE LAST ICE AGE

The coldest part of the last ice age came about 26,000 to 23,000 years ago. Then a slow global warming—a planetary defrosting—began. It coincided with the appearance in a few spots around the globe of settled communities and prepared the way for transitions to a new way of life: farming.

RETREATING ICE AND RISING SEA LEVELS

By 20,000 years ago, thanks to slow global warming, the great ice sheets covering northern Siberia, half of Europe, and a third of North America had begun to melt back. Vegetation crept northward into the soggy landscapes that were now free of ice. Wildlife and people followed. Almost everywhere, climate started slowly to improve from the human point of view. In Africa and South Asia, where aridity more than cold had constrained human endeavor during the Ice Age, conditions grew wetter as well as warmer. Deserts, like the northern ice sheets, retreated, opening new land for plants, animals, and humans. The changes took place too slowly for anyone to have noticed but were large enough to help human population to grow a little faster during the final stages of the Paleolithic.

Some ground was lost while climate warmed. Sea level rose because of melting glaciers, which drowned coastal plains and pushed people inland, if only by a few inches every year. Indonesia, Britain, and Japan eventually became the archipelagoes we know today, cut off from the Eurasian landmass. Rising seas separated Taiwan from mainland China, Tasmania and New Guinea from Australia, and Newfoundland from North America.

Usually, the rising seas claimed low-lying lands slowly; but whenever rising waters overtopped a ledge or broke through an ice-dam, epic floods resulted. According to one theory, the Black Sea, formerly an immense inland lake, filled up with Mediterranean seawater splashing over the sills of the Dardanelles and Bosporus with the force of 200 Niagara Falls. In the span of a single year (perhaps around 7400 BCE), the former shores of the inland lake were flooded and a larger, saltwater Black Sea was born. It's possible that the great flood sagas, such as those in the Epic of Gilgamesh (the first known story, written in Mesopotamia about 2100 BCE) or in the Bible's Book of Genesis, derive from folk memories of such events. But scholars don't know: the archeological evidence isn't conclusive, and the flood stories may have nothing at all to do with the forming of the Black Sea.

As of about 6000 BCE, the melting was almost over and sea level was close to where it is now. Over 15,000 years,

it had risen by 430 ft. (130 m)—about the height of a 25-story building. With these environmental changes, the human population expanded, spreading out into formerly ice-covered northern (and mountain) zones and into former deserts, even as people had to abandon former coastlines and retreat inland. Far more land had been gained than lost thanks to the defrosting.

THE YOUNGER DRYAS

The Ice Age had one last shiver in it. Between 12,900 and 11,700 years ago (10,900 to 9700 BCE), another brutally cold and dry spell hit the Northern Hemisphere. It is called the **Younger Dryas**, named for a tundra flower that turns up often in sediments from that time. It probably resulted from a massive outflow of fresh water from an ancient North American lake (Lake Agassiz, centered on what is now the Canadian province of Manitoba and larger than all the Great Lakes put together) that had formed from glacial meltwater during the warming. When those waters broke through into the North Atlantic, they suddenly made it less salty, changing the Atlantic Ocean's circulation pattern and plunging the Northern Hemisphere back into the deep freeze for more than a thousand years.

The Younger Dryas seems to have been coldest around the North Atlantic, in Europe especially. In Europe, the summers were 9 to 13 degrees Fahrenheit (5 to 7 degrees Celsius) cooler, and in winter more like 18 to 21 degrees F (10 to 12 degrees C) colder—the difference between sweatshirt weather and parka weather. The change apparently came on suddenly, within a decade or two, which is unusual in the annals of climate change, and made adjustment especially challenging. As during ice ages, in the Younger Dryas conditions were dry throughout the Northern Hemisphere as well as colder. In the tropics, so far as anyone can tell, the Younger Dryas was mainly drier. The Younger Dryas came as a catastrophe for people, animals, and plants that had been getting used to warmer and wetter conditions.

EMERGENCE OF A MORE STABLE CLIMATE

But when the Younger Dryas ended, the forecast was good: the warmth and wet returned, and more important still, the chaotic flickering so characteristic of the Ice

Age climate came to an end—or at least a long interlude. From the end of the Younger Dryas until now, a roughly 11,700-year period known as the **Holocene** (from ancient Greek meaning "wholly recent"), climate has been remarkably stable. We of course regard our weather as unstable and unpredictable, and over short time spans it is just that. But Holocene climate fluctuates much less than climate did during the last ice age. In particular, the probability of extremely cold winters far outside the statistical norm was significantly reduced after the Younger Dryas. This relative stability of climate made it much easier for people to settle down in one place and rely on the plants that grew there. When and where climate fluctuated chaotically, people had to stay on the move. With the stability of Holocene climate, they could become sedentary with less risk.

SEDENTARY SOCIETIES: THE FIRST PERMANENT SETTLEMENTS

Range of Human Settlement in Pacific Northwest Coastal Region, ca. 6000 BCE Among the best places in the world to pursue sedentary cultures were spots along the Northern Hemisphere rivers that salmon use on their annual migrations. Once people figured out how to preserve salmon by smoking or salting the fish, they had a year-round food supply.

While their cousins were still roaming the world, a few people began to settle down. In several places around the globe, they began to do so at roughly the same time. The first few formed settlements toward the end of the Ice Age, and then more followed after the end of the Younger Dryas. The best places to settle were along the migratory routes of nutritious beasts: let the food come to you, rather than chase after it.

FOOD SOURCES AND THE EARLIEST SETTLEMENTS

People could do this only in a few places—for example, alongside the salmon rivers of the North Atlantic and North Pacific. Salmon swim up rivers to spawn in seasonal mass migrations that allow anyone with a net, the appropriate knowledge, and hand-eye coordination as good as a grizzly bear's to stand beside a stream and harvest a year's food supply in just a few weeks. The salmon runs are reliable and abundant in certain rivers, especially those from Alaska to northern California. This Pacific coastal region provided an ideal environment for **sedentary** life, and by about 6000 BCE— to judge from archeological remains—people had begun to settle down along several salmon rivers in western North America. Salmon harvesting also played a large role in the food supply of early post-glacial settlers of Scandinavia and the British Isles, but Atlantic salmon rarely run in the same profusion as their Pacific cousins, and therefore provided a poorer basis for sedentary life.

Jomon Pottery The characteristic rope pattern is visible on this Jomon pot.

JOMON CULTURE On the western shores of the Pacific, in Japan, sedentary life also emerged in what archeologists call the **Jomon culture**. (In Japanese, the name refers to the rope-pattern decoration on pottery characteristic of this culture.) By about 7000 BCE, these people had found it possible to settle down, especially on the Pacific coast of east-central Japan, blessed with plenty of shellfish, fish, acorns, and chestnuts. They collected these foods but also hunted deer and other animals. The Jomon were among the first inventors of pottery in world history, even though they had no kilns or potter's wheels—they made their pots by hand and fired them in bonfires. Their earliest pottery seems to be about 13,000 years old, but they didn't make it in quantity until they became sedentary in their way of life. They lived in oval houses built over pits dug into the ground, and they used chestnut wood (among other types) to make dwellings, canoes, and shoes. They may even have planted chestnut trees. The Jomon attained an unusually high population density for a foraging people.

GÖBEKLI TEPE Recent archeology has turned up a curious case of sedentary or semi-sedentary life in

Göbekli Tepe Archeological excavations at Göbekli Tepe have revealed the monumental stone buildings that people built at the site.

southeastern Turkey at **Göbekli Tepe**. About 9000 BCE, semi-settled people (meaning they spent most but not all of each year in one spot) started doing something that no other pre-farming people anywhere on Earth did: building a large stone temple. Using only stone tools, they quarried blocks of stone weighing as much as 10 to 20 tons; dragged them several hundred yards; carved boars, ducks, snakes, and other wild animal shapes into them; and assembled them into a temple. These people had no draft animals. They needed at least 500 individuals working together to lug such big blocks of stone, and they fed themselves without agriculture. Göbekli Tepe is, as far as we know, a unique case of monumental architecture created by a hunting and foraging people.

The best guess is that Göbekli Tepe is a religious site and gathering place built by semi-settled villagers who inhabited a landscape abundant with wild wheat, the result in part of warm and lush conditions that prevailed following the Younger Dryas. The choice of the site may have had something to do with its location between the plains of Mesopotamia and the mountain passes that gave entry into Anatolia. It stood beside trade routes. But by 7000 BCE, the site was abandoned—indeed, purposely buried in rock and debris—until archeologists started scratching around in the twentieth century. Nobody knows why people abandoned it. The temple at Göbekli Tepe shows that semi-settled people could organize their efforts on a substantial scale. Since 95 percent of the site remains to be excavated, we should expect to learn much more in the years ahead.

MAMMOTH HUNTERS OF UKRAINE The best places to settle down were beside salmon rivers, along coastlines rich with shellfish, or on rare patches of land flush with edible wild plants. A more dangerous and less reliable environment for settlement was along the migration routes of big mammals, such as the now-extinct wooly mammoths. Huge, shaggy beasts related to elephants, mammoths could provide hunters with plenty of food as well as leather and wooly clothing—the height of Eurasian fashion during the depths of the Ice Age.

The earliest evidence of sedentary lifestyles anywhere comes from the mammoth hunters of Ukraine, the region to the north of the Black Sea. They may have been only semi-sedentary, spending a few months at a time in the same place—no one knows for sure.

Scholars use the term *mammoth steppe* to refer to the region south of the glaciers, from France to eastern Siberia, where during the Ice Age summer grasses sustained sprawling herds of mammoths. As the Ice Age waned, the mammoths drifted northward, allowing skilled mammoth hunters to follow and flourish in otherwise forbidding landscapes. Mammoths probably migrated with the seasons along well-worn paths, especially river valleys. This made them easy to find and enabled teams of spear-wielding hunters and their families to stay put, especially after they learned to dig pits in the autumn and freeze meat for later roasting during the bone-chilling winters.

The mammoth hunters ate mammoth meat to stay alive, and to stay warm they lived inside shelters made of

Mammoth Huts Archeologists in Ukraine excavated this characteristic hut made out of mammoth bones. Mammoth hunters began constructing dwellings of mammoth bones and hide around 27,000 years ago.

mammoth bones and skins. Around 27,000 years ago—during a cold phase of the last ice age—they began to build houses using mammoth tusks, ribs, and leg bones as the equivalent of construction timber. Carefully arranged and covered with hides, these materials made cozy dwellings against the cold. Archeologists have found about 70 of these mammoth-bone huts. The largest is over 190 ft. (60 m) long and 16 ft. (5 m) wide and must have housed scores of people. Whether people lived in this mammoth-mansion year-round is unclear. By 15,000 years ago along the Dnieper River in today's Ukraine, clusters of mammoth huts developed—perhaps history's first villages.

The mammoths died out 12,000 years ago. One likely explanation is that mammoth hunters were too skillful and killed off their favorite prey. It's also plausible that warmer climate opened habitats to other herbivores, such

as deer, that competed successfully against mammoths for edible vegetation. The huts of these inventive hunters were abandoned, to be discovered by archeologists only in the twentieth century.

MAGDALENIAN CULTURE The mammoth hunters weren't alone in settling down to make a living off of herds roaming the steppe. To their west between 18,000 and 12,000 years ago lived groups of reindeer hunters known to archeologists as the **Magdalenian culture**, named after a particular rock shelter in France—although the Magdalenians left archeological remains scattered between Portugal and Poland. These people hunted reindeer with the same general approach used by mammoth hunters: intercepting seasonal migrations. In staking out migration routes, they became at least semi-sedentary. Like the mammoth hunters, they varied their diet by hunting deer

Sedentary Cultures of Europe and Southwest Asia, 27,000–11,000 Years Ago Mammoth hunters and Magdalenians settled astride the migration routes of big game animals, a strategy analogous to that of people in the Pacific Northwest who settled along salmon rivers. The Natufians, in contrast, like the Jomon, found a location with abundant local food sources.

and wild horses too. They supplemented their meals with whatever nuts, fruits, and berries they could find in their chilly surroundings. Edible plants were rare, but the Magdalenians were clever and bold. They ate partially digested reindeer lichen (a small, bushy-looking fungus) scooped out of the stomachs of freshly killed reindeer.

Settled or semi-settled life allowed new possibilities unavailable to peoples constantly on the move. Some Magdalenians in what is now France and Spain spent at least part of their time in caves, including the famous ones at Lascaux, where they painted some of the most stirring images known to history. The salmon eaters of North America staged rituals known as potlatch, which included competitive feasting and gift giving in quests for social status. The mammoth hunters accumulated jewelry, statuettes, baskets, and needles, and they seem to have pioneered a society stratified by social class: burials as well as house sizes indicate that some people had far more accumulated wealth than others. In the several spots where settled life became feasible at the end of the Ice Age, cultural revolutions took place: people had more leisure time to create new art, tools, and rituals, and they no longer had to limit their possessions to an amount they could conveniently carry.

SEDENTARY COMMUNITIES AND CULTURAL CHANGE

The scattered sedentary or semi-sedentary communities were hubs of social and cultural activity, loosely

Lascaux Caves On the walls of caves at Lascaux in France, the semi-sedentary Magdalenian people made vivid paintings of the animals—deer, horses, bulls—that provided them with sustenance.

connected by the movements of mobile hunting and foraging peoples. In effect, the mobile peoples served as the threads on the very faint web of interaction that kept almost the entire human race in sporadic contact. The settled and semi-settled communities served as hubs of innovation. Their cultures grew more elaborate not only because they stayed put for all or most of the time, but also because they received influences from distant communities through contacts with mobile hunters and foragers. The mobile peoples—still the demographic majority even as recently as 8000 BCE—could serve as messengers, transmitting, for example, technologies such as the bow and arrow.

Sedentary life, paradoxically, spurred the mobility and exchange of objects. Before any groups had settled down, everyone had pretty much the same small set of tools and clothing, and more or less the same skills with which to make them. People didn't have much else. Nobody carried trade goods around because they didn't know when they might meet up with others, and they rarely met others who didn't already have the same few items. But with the advent of sedentary life, people created more, and more varied, objects—tools, ornaments, maybe different kinds of clothes. Mobile people of the late Paleolithic could count on finding food, water, shelter, and probably a warm welcome at fixed places, so they had good reason to carry around rare things that other people really wanted. Among those items were flints for making fire, shells for

The Spread of Technology A Spanish cave painting from about 14,000 to 10,000 years ago shows a hunter wielding a bow and arrow. Mobile peoples transmitted technology like the bow and arrow among settled communities.

decoration or cutting tools, and obsidian, a hard rock that can be fashioned into an excellent cutting edge.

These items often show up in archeological sites far from their points of origin, giving evidence of long-distance trade. For example, at an archeological site in Jordan (Kharaneh IV), where sedentary or near-sedentary people lived 19,000 years ago, scholars have found shells used as ornaments that came from the shores of the Indian Ocean, more than 1,200 miles (2,000 km) away. No doubt traders also carried more perishable goods that haven't lasted. In short, sedentary life created a class of mobile traders who built webs of communication and exchange among communities of settled folk.

DOMESTICATION

While some Ice Age foragers and hunters of Eurasia made long strides toward settled life, others achieved something equally momentous: the partnership between humans and dogs. We call it the domestication of dogs; but if they could think about such things, dogs might see it as the domestication of humans. In any case, it was the first domestication in history, a mutual accommodation.

Domestication is a complicated subject, with two main parts: the domestication of animals and the domestication of plants. Together, they represent a major landmark in human history: the transition between finding one's food and producing one's food.

THE PROCESS OF DOMESTICATION

The domestication of plants involves the genetic modification of cultivated plants through human selection. People can cultivate (i.e., sow and harvest) wild plants. But when they consciously select certain seeds over others to sow in order to harvest more plants with desired characteristics, and do this consistently for many years, inducing genetic changes in the plants, the process is called domestication. In some cases of domestication, plants evolve that depend on humans for their propagation because their seeds don't disperse on their own. A corn (maize) cob is one example, the result of genetic modification over thousands of years and now the world's third most important food crop.

The domestication of animals also involves genetic modification through human actions. People can sometimes keep wild animals as pets, although it doesn't work well for most adult animals. However, when people breed animals in order to achieve offspring with desired characteristics—for example, tameness or small size—and do this consistently across many generations, they are domesticating animals. They can create versions of animals that couldn't survive without human aid, such as poodles.

DOGS: HUMANKIND'S FIRST FRIEND

Dogs evolved from wolves over thousands of years. Just how, when, and where this began is unclear. All specialists think it happened somewhere in Eurasia. The latest genetic evidence suggests it occurred between 32,000 and 20,000 years ago. Dog skulls show up at mammoth-hunter settlement sites by 15,000 years ago.

No matter how it began, the dog-human partnership was a mutually profitable one. Dogs provided people with hunting help, compensating for our poor sense of smell. Unlike wolves, dogs bark upon the approach of unexpected animals, which gave people warning against surprise attackers. And dogs offered loyal companionship, including furry warmth on cold Ice Age nights. In dire circumstances, people could also eat their dogs.

In return, people provided dogs with food (or hunting help, as the dogs might see it), and sometimes protection and shelter. Dogs with cooperative people got a more reliable food supply, including access to big game such as mammoths that dogs could scarcely hope to bag by themselves. Over time, a genetic selection occurred for dogs that worked well with humans—dogs that showed loyalty, accepted human commands, and could read human gestures and expressions. At the same time, a cultural selection took place for human groups that worked well with dogs, training, breeding, and protecting them, and eating them only in times of need. Some specialists suggest that the dog-human partnership worked so well, and began so early, that the canine-human team out-competed Neanderthals, who didn't keep dogs. If so, "man's best friend" was among the Neanderthals' worst enemies.

By 14,000 years ago, people had grown fond enough of dogs to include them in human graves. Hunting peoples—especially those operating in forests, where sight is impeded and a good sense of smell is all the more

Domesticated Animals Dogs became closely integrated within human society. Engraved rock art from the northwestern Arabian Peninsula, from 9000 to 10,000 years ago, shows a person hunting with the aid of a pack of dogs.

useful—came to revere good hunting dogs. From Europe to Japan, some dogs were buried with full honors, which might consist of deer antlers, hunters' tools, or colorful stones.

The dog-human team spread rapidly and became nearly universal. The Ainu, a people in Japan's northernmost island of Hokkaido, even taught their dogs to catch salmon for them. When the first humans trekked into the Americas, their dogs trotted along too. Today, for every wolf on Earth, there are more than 3,000 dogs. For dogs, domestication has been a tremendous success. It's been a success for humans too.

GRASSES

The domestication of dogs was the first of many. Dozens of animals and hundreds of plants proved susceptible to domestication. Almost all these domestications took place in remote times before written records, but archeologists can often tell the difference between wild and domesticated species from the remains of seeds and bones, and geneticists can tell wild and domestic species apart.

Like dogs, certain grasses—wild ancestors of cereals such as wheat, barley, rye, rice, and maize—in effect took advantage of human needs to become much more biologically successful, and much more prevalent over the face of the Earth. Those grasses with seeds that didn't easily fly off the stalk were most likely to be gathered, stored, and then planted by humans. If we consider the process from the grasses' point of view, humans became domesticated animals toiling away to increase the domain of grasses. Let's look at some other crucial cases of domestication connected to the emergence of agriculture.

THE ORIGINS OF AGRICULTURE

As we've seen, the first settled societies appeared in scattered locations around the world, and the first domestication—of dogs—occurred somewhere in Eurasia. The first farming community—both sedentary and based on domestication—probably appeared in the Levant, along the eastern shore of the Mediterranean and its hinterland, about 13,000 years ago (11,000 BCE). The **Levant** forms the western edge of the Fertile Crescent, which encompasses a boomerang-shaped zone in Southwest Asia from the Red Sea northward along the Rift Valley and the Jordan River valley, curving around to the middle and southern reaches of the Tigris and Euphrates. The latest evidence suggests the possibility that several farming communities popped up here and there throughout the Fertile Crescent at roughly the same time. After farming got under way in the Fertile Crescent, agriculture soon emerged independently in several other parts of the world.

FAVORABLE CONDITIONS

As the Ice Age gave way to warmer and damper climate, both before and after the Younger Dryas, plant life flourished. Forests overgrew steppe and scrubland, deserts retreated, and rivers rose. In many locations, these were favorable trends for people, enabling some groups to settle down and live off newly abundant local plants and animals. In many spots in Southwest Asia, for example, there were now plenty of acorns, almonds,

Processing Food This 11,000-year-old mortar and pestle from the Natufian culture would have been used to grind seeds or grains into powdery, edible forms. Sedentary peoples had the time and could create the tools necessary to process foods that couldn't be eaten otherwise.

and grasses with edible and storable seeds. Grasses ancestral to wheat and barley spread like weeds with the changing climate, and their seeds provided 50 times more calories than a person burned in gathering them. Gazelles and other tasty herbivores provided meat. The scant evidence suggests that population across Eurasia rose, perhaps quintupling from 16,000 to 12,000 years ago, as climate warmed and foraging became easier. In a few favored locations, including the Levant, the locally abundant food made it possible for foragers to settle down.

SETTLED POPULATIONS Settled populations tended to grow far faster than mobile ones. Parents didn't have to lug children long distances and so were less inclined to try to prevent their birth or abandon babies. Where people collected the seeds of wild grasses, they could mash the seeds into gruel and feed it to babies, weaning infants from their mothers' milk at a younger age. Since lactating women are much less likely to conceive, early weaning meant that mothers became fertile again sooner. The intervals between births tended to be shorter among settled people than among mobile ones.

But population growth among the settled folk gradually caused difficulties. More hunting thinned the numbers of big animals. In the Levant, for example, archeologists have found that people were hunting smaller and smaller animals as time went on—fewer gazelles and more rabbits. In many parts of the world, the standard solution for food shortage remained practical: walk somewhere else. But for settled folk with accumulated possessions, lots of small children, and perhaps spiritual and emotional commitments to preferred places, this approach was less practical. Instead, people intensified their quest for food, especially in circumscribed places such as the Levant (located between a rising sea and a desert), the Nile valley in Egypt (surrounded by desert), and China's Yangzi valley (surrounded by steep hills). Rather than walk elsewhere, they foraged for a wider variety of plants,

Settled Peoples New artistic techniques, and more substantial forms of art and architecture, flourished among populations who became sedentary after the development of agriculture. The people who lived at 'Ain Ghazal in the Levant around 9,000 years ago made this statue, one of the first large-scale representations of a human.

hunted more kinds of animals, and began to work spreading the seeds of preferred plants such as wild wheat and rice. Such efforts probably took place elsewhere as well, but the archeological record is so spotty that no one knows for sure.

INTELLIGENCE AND CLIMATE Not long ago, scholars used to wonder why everyone didn't take up farming. Now scholars wonder why anyone did. Farming turns out to involve more work than foraging and hunting, and it

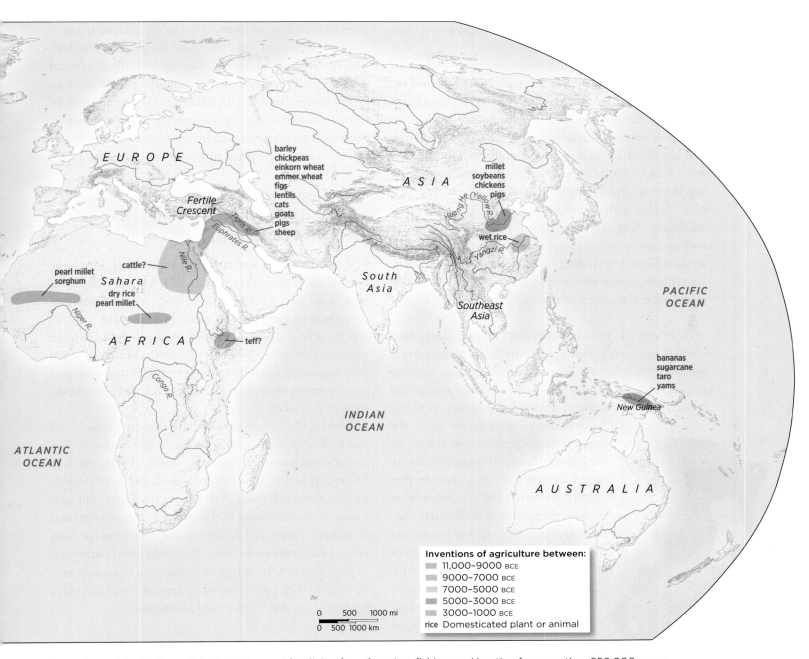

Inventions of agriculture between:
- 11,000–9000 BCE
- 9000–7000 BCE
- 7000–5000 BCE
- 5000–3000 BCE
- 3000–1000 BCE
- rice Domesticated plant or animal

0   500   1000 mi
0   500 1000 km

Inventions of Agriculture, 11,000–1000 BCE After living from foraging, fishing, and hunting for more than 250,000 years, humans invented agriculture at least seven times, and probably more, after the end of the last ice age. The earliest of these occurrences, as far as we know, took place in the Fertile Crescent of Southwest Asia.

usually results in worse nutrition and worse health. Yet after more than 200,000 years without bothering to farm, shortly after the end of the Ice Age humans undertook at least seven transitions to farming on four continents. This seems most unlikely to be a random turn of events. Two important factors may help bring us closer to an understanding of what triggered the change: intelligence and climate.

Turning to a way of life that brings poorer nutrition and health yet requires more work may not seem a hallmark of intelligence, yet it surely did take intelligence to notice which plants grow best in which sorts of places, which ones yield easily edible seeds, which seeds store well, and so forth. Developing this sort of knowledge required communication—language—as well as powers of observation, memory, and reason. So it couldn't have happened before modern, intelligent, language-wielding humans were on the scene.

Depending on when language emerged, there were either no or very few such humans around before the onset of the last ice age 130,000 years ago. During that ice age, conditions were too dry or too cold for agriculture outside of tropical locations, sharply reducing the chances that people would make a transition to farming successfully. And within tropical latitudes, the yield from foraging, hunting, and fishing was usually sufficient, so people didn't bother with domesticating plants. The existence of intelligent, language-bearing humans living outside of lush environments yet enjoying interglacial climate, then, seems a likely prerequisite for transitions to agriculture. That might explain why no transitions to agriculture took place before the retreat of the ice.

THE PIVOTAL ROLE OF WOMEN One thing most scholars agree on is that agriculture in its earliest stages was women's work. As far as we know, in most hunting and foraging societies women and children specialized in gathering useful plants for food, medicines, or fibers. Adult women presumably were the most knowledgeable about the habits of helpful plants. Although there's no direct evidence for this, women presumably pioneered the transition from merely collecting plants to deliberately sowing the seed of desirable types of plants, and the further transition to sowing the seed of specific, individual plants with desirable characteristics. It seems highly likely, then, that one of the hallmark transformations of the human condition began with a change in women's approach to the task of getting food for their families.

Women's Work A ca. 4000 BCE statue from the Negev Desert in present-day Israel shows a woman carrying a pot, reflecting the role women played in procuring food and water in sedentary communities.

OTHER CONDITIONS Two further conditions for the emergence of agriculture also seem sure. First, only sedentary people would try to farm. Roving bands had no good reason to plant seeds, or save seeds for next year, since they couldn't be sure they would come back to their plantings or that others might not reap their harvest first. The only other species that cultivate—those termites and ants that raise fungi—are also sedentary. Second, in every case, agriculture developed gradually over several centuries, and the people involved didn't know they were undertaking a momentous shift. They were tinkering, experimenting, trying to improve their food supplies or reliability, or perhaps just trying to hold on to what they had in worsening circumstances.

THE FIRST TRANSITION TO AGRICULTURE: THE FERTILE CRESCENT AND THE LEVANT

The **transition to agriculture** that scholars know the most about is probably the earliest. It occurred in Southwest Asia, somewhere in the Fertile Crescent, probably on its western edge in the Levant, just inland of the eastern shore of the Mediterranean. Archeological evidence suggests that the earliest plant domestications took place here beginning around 11,000 BCE. Thereafter, more and more humans increasingly relied for their food on specific sorts of grass seed.

The Fertile Crescent isn't really crescent-shaped, and much of it wasn't especially fertile in soil nutrients. But it supported potentially domesticable food plants such as wheat and barley, and several domesticable herd animals such as sheep and goats. And the region offered fine gradients of climate owing to the interplay of air masses and elevations. People didn't have to walk far to move from one microclimate to the next. This could have contributed to plant domestication by enabling people to go only a little ways to take a plant out of its natural range and place it where it needed human help to reproduce.

THE NATUFIANS: ENVIRONMENTAL REFUGEES After a few millennia in which climate grew warmer and wetter, the sudden shock of climate change in the form of the Younger Dryas cold snap hit around 10,700 BCE. For mobile people, this was a challenge, but one that they could meet by walking to warmer latitudes. For settled peoples, it was a crisis. One such people was the Natufians.

With the onset of the Younger Dryas, the 100 or so plants that the Natufians relied on became less reliable. The gazelles, sheep, horses, deer, and boar that they liked to eat grew rare because the grass and shrubs the animals fed on became scarcer. Populations of settled folk declined, and many of them became, in effect, environmental refugees, crowding into oases and river-beds where there was still enough moisture and warmth for plant growth. (Some Natufians became migratory, although they continued to return to old villages, which they used as cemeteries.) The refugees may have brought seeds with them and sowed them in new settings. In one such location, Abu Hureyra on the Euphrates River in what is now northern Syria, there is spotty archeological evidence of cereal cultivation—not yet domestication—undertaken by Natufians from as early as 11,000 BCE.

As climate cooled down and dried out with the Younger Dryas, food plants withered. Gazelles and other hunting targets grew scarce. The Natufians increasingly sowed einkorn, emmer, and barley—wild grasses that would still yield a harvest in dry conditions. Over generations, they chose to sow and harvest the plants that yielded best. They probably also selected for softer husks, which made getting at the seed easier. With their choices they were slowly creating new plant species, including what we now call wheat and rye.

FIGS, CATS, GOATS, AND SHEEP Soon after domesticating cereals, peoples of the Fertile Crescent began to cultivate and then domesticate figs, chickpeas, peas, and lentils. They also domesticated wild animals, with cats perhaps coming first. Genetic evidence suggests that Arabian wild cats are the ancestors of today's pet cats. Around 11,000 to 8000 BCE, when the Natufians were keeping piles of grain, they indirectly created paradises for mice. The lucky mice gorging themselves on

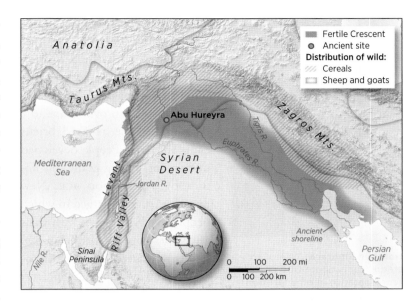

The Fertile Crescent The first transition to agriculture (as far as we know) took place somewhere in the boomerang-shaped region encompassing the valley of the Tigris and Euphrates Rivers and the coast of the eastern Mediterranean Sea. The earliest evidence of farming we have at present comes from Abu Hureyra.

stores of Natufian grain attracted wild cats, which ate the well-stuffed mice. Natufians connected the dots: more cats, fewer mice, more grain. Their protection of cats over centuries produced increasingly domesticated cats, comfortable with humans and good at protecting grain by catching mice.

The domestication of goats and sheep began between 11,000 and 9000 BCE, soon after the first plant domestications. People captured juveniles, raised them, and protected them from predators. Like dogs, wild goats and sheep had (and have) a social structure, and most animals follow a leader. Human herders in effect replaced the dominant rams as leaders of the flock. Once people controlled which animals reproduced and which ones did not, they could breed for desired characteristics such as docility, thick wool, and abundant milk. By killing the most defiant males and allowing only the more docile ones to breed, people gradually produced more submissive sheep and goats. They did the same with pigs starting around 8500 BCE, and cattle a few centuries later. The most important farm animals in most of the world—pigs, cattle, sheep, and goats—were created from wild ancestors through domestications undertaken between 11,000 and 7000 BCE in Southwest Asia or, in the case of cattle, possibly northeastern Africa.

Livestock The people who lived at Aşıklı Höyük in Anatolia (today's Turkey) about 10,000 years ago kept sheep and other animals in pens in between their mud-brick houses, one of the earliest known examples of the domestication of herd animals.

Natufian Embrace A Natufian statue from about 9000 BCE is representative of other art from the period in depicting themes of fertility and sexuality.

CULTURAL CHANGE Some fundamental cultural changes came along with the transition to agriculture in the Fertile Crescent. Settlement size grew. Houses changed from an oval shape to a rectangular one as mud bricks came into use. People developed pottery for storing grain and liquids by about 7000 BCE. New burial practices emerged in which people lived in houses with their ancestors buried underneath. Skulls were used for home decoration, perhaps implying some sort of ancestor worship. And people fashioned clay figurines that are interpreted as mother goddesses and presumed to represent a fascination with fertility and sexuality.

By 6000 BCE, farming had taken firm root in many places in the Fertile Crescent. People had transformed several wild species into domesticated ones. They had acquired and shared knowledge of how to manage these new species. They learned when to plant and reap, which types of soil to use, how to manage flocks and herds, use animals' manure to boost the growth of food plants, and discipline themselves to the daily and seasonal routines of farming. They may also have learned to share less widely and keep more within family units—that is, to consider crops, animals, tools, and so forth as private property. A new economic and cultural configuration had emerged, a blueprint of sorts for billions of people as yet unborn.

CHINA

So far as we know, the next transition to agriculture took place in China beginning about 7000 BCE. It happened entirely independent of developments in the Levant. There were actually two transitions to agriculture in China: one each in the basins of its two biggest rivers, the Yangzi and the Huang He (Yellow River). As elsewhere, the transition from wild plants to genuinely domesticated ones in China took thousands of years. It is still poorly reflected in the archeological record, so the chances are good that new finds will revise our understanding in the future.

THE YANGZI VALLEY In the valley of the **Yangzi River**, people began to domesticate rice by 7000 BCE if not before. Wild rice exists in many varieties, including some that grow in swampy terrain. These were the ancestors of many of the wet rice varieties cultivated in China today. They yield far more grain per plant, or per patch of ground, than the wheat or barley of Southwest Asia. But they also take much more work to cultivate. Rice shoots must be transplanted when only a few weeks old, and to achieve maximum yields they must be raised partly underwater. Natural seasonal flooding could do this in a few favored places, but elsewhere it required arduous labor. People had to level their land by building "terraces," divide it into small patches marked off by little ridges of earth, divert stream or lake water onto these terraced paddies (or padis) at certain times of year, and drain them at others.

Wet rice agriculture often required cooperation among large numbers of people. They had to share water somehow. The vast labor needed to terrace sloping land and prepare it for planting required many hands. These considerations offset the crop's enormous yields somewhat and slowed its spread. The first communities substantially dependent on rice farming appeared near the mouth of the Yangzi about 4500 BCE.

THE HUANG HE VALLEY In northern China, where rainfall was spotty and rice impractical, agriculture began with millet by 7000 BCE, then soybeans and a handful of other crops by about 6000 BCE. Millet, the most important crop, remained only a small part of people's diets until well after 5000 BCE. Wild food sources predominated until perhaps 3000 BCE. Many parts of northern China have highly fertile loess (windblown) soils that yield excellent crops if enough rain falls. When and where rain didn't fall, starvation threatened. This provided strong incentive to manage water carefully, as with rice cultivation along the Yangzi. Chickens and pigs were domesticated in northern

Chinese Pottery A red-clay pottery vessel (ca. 6000–5200 BCE) from a site in northern China rests on three legs, which might have allowed it to be placed over a cooking fire.

China by 4500 BCE if not before. This was the second domestication of pigs, after the first in Southwest Asia.

One of the distinctive features of the development of agriculture in both river basins of China is that pottery marked the first step in the long process. Some recent archeological finds suggest that pottery preceded the domestication of rice and millet by nearly 10,000 years. Pre-farming peoples in East Asia developed a tradition of boiling and steaming their food in pots. With good pots, the storage of rice and millet was easy and the logic of relying on them improved. The more people relied on these crops, the more likely they were to start down the path toward domestication.

SOUTHEAST AND SOUTH ASIA

Somewhere in Southeast Asia, another independent transition to agriculture took place. Good evidence suggests that people on the island of New Guinea domesticated sugarcane, bananas, and root crops such as yams and taro by at least 5000 BCE and probably earlier. They used wetlands and patches of surrounding forest in the eastern highlands in a form of agriculture often called swidden, which involves farming for a few seasons at one spot and then moving one's operation to another nearby. They didn't domesticate any animals but eventually acquired chickens and dogs from mainland Southeast Asia. New Guinea's may have been the only independent transition to agriculture in Southeast Asia, but we can't be sure.

On the Southeast Asian mainland, sedentary villages and pottery preceded farming, as in China. The first evidence of farming dates from about 2500 BCE, and it probably represents an introduction from South China rather than an independent transition. Pigs and chickens were the important animals domesticated, and rice was the central crop.

It's quite possible, however, that Southeast Asians made a transition to agriculture, or several, before the documented case in New Guinea, maybe even before it happened in China or the Levant. Some domesticable plants don't normally leave traces that last over millennia, unlike rice, wheat, and barley grains. So all we can say with assurance is that there was one transition to agriculture in Southeast Asia, on New Guinea, by 5000 BCE if not before—and that the odds are good that we know only a fraction of the truth of the matter.

In South Asia, people took up wheat farming as early as 7000 BCE and rice farming by 6000 BCE. The strongest evidence at the moment suggests that these were imported introductions of agriculture to South Asia rather than independent transitions.

AFRICA

The story of early agriculture in Africa is sketchy because archeologists have done much less work there than elsewhere. Africans probably domesticated cattle, perhaps in Egypt, as early as 6000 BCE. For a few millennia after that, they refined their cattle-keeping ways and spread the practice into suitable parts of the continent, but as far as we know they didn't yet domesticate plants. In this respect, Africa followed a different path from most parts of the world, where either the plants came first or both came more or less at the same time.

Then, beginning about 3000 BCE, another independent transition to agriculture took place in Africa. It apparently happened at about the same time in several spots on the southern edge of the Sahara. Millet, sorghum, and dry rice (different varieties from the rice grown in East Asia) were the chief crops. As in the Fertile Crescent, climate change was probably a key factor motivating the transition to agriculture in Africa. After 8000 BCE, the Sahara

African Sedentary Peoples Rock art found in present-day Algeria attests to humans settling at water sources near the Sahara. The art depicts the animals that would have congregated around the same water sources: giraffes and another animal, perhaps a zebra.

CONSIDERING THE EVIDENCE

Crocodiles in the Sahara

The Sahara desert might be the last place you'd expect to find a crocodile. Water has been scarce in the Sahara for thousands of years, but between 8000 and 4500 BCE it was a green place full of lakes and rivers. It attracted people who hunted hippos, elephants, and antelope, speared catfish with stone harpoons, and did their best to avoid the crocodiles. In addition to life-size paintings and carvings of animals and themselves, these people left behind ivory jewelry and pottery. The first humans to enter the Sahara eventually became sedentary hunters and fishers, living alongside lakes until the climate shifted again and forced them out. The crocodile engraving below is locatd in the Messale plateau in southwestern Libya and dates back at least 10,000 years.

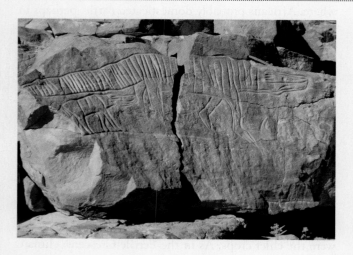

QUESTIONS FOR ANALYSIS

1. Carving such large images into rock faces would have taken much time and work. What do these efforts suggest about the role of large game animals in the culture of the people who created these images?
2. How did life in the "green" Sahara compare to that of the Magdalenians in Europe, who painted scenes of wildlife in caves like Lascaux during the last ice age?
3. Some scholars suggest that rock art served a religious purpose. Does this example give any evidence for that? Explain your response.

grew wetter with regular summer rains. It hosted grass and wildlife—even lakes and hippopotami. People lived among the lakes, fishing, foraging, and hunting. As in East Asia, they developed pottery before domesticating plants, perhaps by 9000 BCE. They tended to boil their food into stews and porridges, in contrast to the tradition that prevailed in Southwest Asia in which grains were ground up and baked into bread and meat was roasted.

The Sahara region began to dry out about 4500 BCE. Lakes and wetlands began to shrink, depriving Saharan peoples of some of their best environments for foraging and fishing. With less food to go around, they faced pressures similar to those in the Levant when the Younger Dryas hit. They crowded into the remaining lakeshores, just as the Natufians had sought refuge in oases and next to riverbeds. Since the Saharan lakes were all shallow, they expanded and shrank considerably with the rains, which made soils around their edges often moist and suitable for growing plants. It was on these lake edges that Africans first began to domesticate and raise millet, rice, and sorghum.

In what might have been yet another independent transition to agriculture, people in the highlands of Ethiopia began to raise different crops before 1000 BCE—maybe long before. The main one was a cereal called teff, still today grown mainly in Ethiopia. Teff does well at mile-high altitudes, in dry conditions, and provides a nutritious payload of minerals and protein. It is still uncertain whether the domestication of teff occurred independently or in imitation of one of the nearby earlier transitions to agriculture.

SOUTH AMERICA

The archeological record is also thin in South America, so we don't know much about the transition to agriculture there. Some scholars think it began with horticulture (the raising of vegetables or fruits in garden patches) in the lowland rain forests of what is now Colombia as early as 9000 BCE. Scattered evidence exists for domesticated plants in what is now Colombia, Ecuador, and Peru between 8000 and 4000 BCE. There is firmer evidence for squash and bean domestication, as well as the existence of small villages, along the coasts of Ecuador and Peru after about 3000 BCE. Squash and beans alone cannot support human populations, but on these coasts people lived next door to the Pacific's Humboldt Current, one of the world's richest marine provinces. Teeming with fish and offering a hunting ground for millions of seabirds, the Humboldt Current provided the coastal peoples of Peru with plenty of fish and birds' eggs to eat.

But the Humboldt Current sometimes flowed weakly, thinning the fish and bird populations. During El Niño years, the fishing was poor and the incentive to seek other food sources was strong. It could be that the revival of El Niño after about 3000 BCE, a response to a general warming trend in the Pacific, provided a climate-change trigger to the emergence of agriculture here, as other climate changes seem to have done in the Levant and in Africa.

Potatoes, first domesticated in highland Peru between 3000 and 2000 BCE, could serve as a staple crop, a staff of life like rice or wheat and unlike squash and beans. Potatoes yield well in terms of calories per acre and also provide a healthy variety of vitamins and minerals by themselves. When people in the Andes learned to freeze-dry potatoes to make an easily storable and portable foodstuff, called *chuño*, they acquired the basis for exchange and accumulation of foodstuffs that rice, wheat, or maize provided elsewhere in the world.

Manioc, also known as cassava, is a root crop native to South America that was first domesticated in the western part of Amazonia's rain forest no later than 4000 BCE. It provides plentiful calories but little else in the way of nutrition. But if raised by people who also fish, hunt, and forage, it could provide a reliable food supply. It fares well in poor soils and withstands drought better than most crops. So in South America at least one, and perhaps more, independent transition to farming took place.

MESOAMERICA AND NORTH AMERICA

In Mesoamerica—roughly the region between Costa Rica and northern Mexico—crop domestication began perhaps

as early as 6000 BCE. Squash, beans, and especially maize formed the basis of Mesoamerican agriculture. Thanks to human selection, maize evolved from a small wild plant called *teosinte* to become the staple of life in much of the Americas. Over thousands of years, maize farmers chose to plant those varieties of *teosinte* that grew bigger, matured faster, and had other desirable traits. Scholars debate just where the domestication of maize began, but most argue for western Mexico.

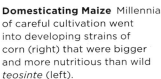

Domesticating Maize Millennia of careful cultivation went into developing strains of corn (right) that were bigger and more nutritious than wild *teosinte* (left).

We may never know just when and where maize was domesticated, but we know that it mattered for the societies that relied on it. Dried maize stores very well, making it—like rice, wheat, barley, and freeze-dried potatoes—a basis for accumulation and exchange. Maize also yields richly in calories, although it lacks niacin (a form of vitamin B and an essential human nutrient), so people who rely on it heavily often suffer from deficiency diseases. Farmers grew it widely in the Americas. It became a significant food in Peru by 2000 BCE at the latest, and in what is now the southwestern United States at about the same time. Farming spread across the North American continent, arriving as far as eastern Canada about 1,000 years ago.

Archeologists have also found evidence for an independent transition to agriculture in the heartland of North America. By about 2500 BCE, people living in river floodplains of what is now Ohio, Kentucky, Tennessee, and Illinois were raising plants such as sumpweed and goosefoot. These people are sometimes called mound builders because they piled up earth into mounds, presumably in connection with ceremonies of some sort. They lived in small villages until they acquired maize from Mexico (about 800 CE), which enabled their populations and the scale of their settlements to grow quickly. We'll return to them in a later chapter.

One important feature of the transitions to farming in the Americas is that animals hardly figured in the story. In the Andes, people domesticated llamas about 4000 BCE. But nowhere did they have animals they could use for traction, like the oxen and horses of Eurasia. People had to do all the work of farming themselves. And nowhere did domestic animals, or their milk, form a significant part of people's diets.

The archeological and genetic record concerning the transitions to agriculture elsewhere around the world is slender. We don't even know how many independent transitions there were, although the best guess is eight in all. But we do know that the turn to agriculture spread widely and began a sea change in the human condition.

THE SPREAD OF AGRICULTURE

From its several points of origin, agriculture spread far and wide. The cereal culture of the Fertile Crescent, the rice culture of China, and the maize and beans culture of Mesoamerica diffused farthest and gave rise to the world's most influential and widespread farming systems. The Fertile Crescent farming system spread along the northern shores of the Mediterranean into Anatolia and Greece. Between about 7000 and 4000 BCE, people carried it from Anatolia to the British Isles. It moved eastward too, into northwestern India by perhaps 7000 BCE. Meanwhile, on a small scale, the rice-based system of the Yangzi apparently spread westward into the Ganges valley of northeastern India by about 6000 BCE, although some scholars maintain that rice was independently domesticated there. The rice system also spread to mainland Southeast Asia after about 2500 BCE. Maize culture spread from its Mesoamerican home both northward and southward, and became the staple food of most farmers in the Americas by 1000 BCE.

While those three farming systems cast the longest shadow in world history, they weren't the only ones to spread. In Africa, the cultivation of millet and sorghum spread southward from its origins in the Sahel (the belt of semi-arid land on the southern edges of the Sahara) into parts of West and Central Africa. Highland Ethiopia's teff-based farming system, however, scarcely expanded beyond its homeland. The same was true of the high Andes tradition of potato farming, which (until after 1500 CE) barely spread at all. Manioc, however, first cultivated in the forests of Amazonia, proved a good traveler throughout the damp lowlands of South America and,

by 500 BCE, was raised in the small islands of the eastern Caribbean.

Farming spread in two main ways. First, farmers sometimes displaced foragers, pushed them off fertile lands, and extended their own domain. Second, the idea of agriculture sometimes spread: people who hadn't formerly practiced it learned about it and imitated the practice of others.

EXPANSION BY DISPLACEMENT

Farmers could often displace foragers through violence. Food production allowed greater densities of population. Bigger groups normally prevailed over smaller ones in violent contests. Moreover, the bigger social groups became, the more likely they could support specialists in weapon making and the arts of violence. People who had the skills to make good farming tools could also make good weapons. Foraging bands, even those that included skilled hunters, couldn't consistently withstand the collective pressure that farming peoples could bring to bear.

INFECTIOUS DISEASE Farmers could also displace foragers and hunters without even trying—through infectious disease. Because farming folk lived side by side with herd animals, their bodies gradually came to host microbes whose ancestor-microbes had routinely lived in sheep, goats, cattle, or dogs. Some of these species-jumping microbes caused deadly diseases among humans. Influenza comes from pigs and ducks. Smallpox may derive from some rodent-borne virus. Camels donated a common cold virus. In all, about 60 percent of the infections that human bodies host came originally from other animals. Over many generations, in what must have been a painful process with many mini-epidemics along the way, the immune systems of farming folk became increasingly resistant to these microbes. Indeed, when infectious diseases were constantly present, only those individuals with robust immune systems survived childhood. Their own children, in turn, would be likelier to have robust immune systems, or at least immune systems attuned to the risks posed by sedentary life among animals and animal-derived diseases. In effect, a new selection process was at work among farming peoples—selection for disease resistance.

Hunters and foragers didn't normally face this grim pressure. As long as they kept their distance from farmers, they stayed healthier than sons and daughters of the soil.

But if they came into prolonged contact with farmers, disaster routinely followed. Their immune systems hadn't built up resistance to the infections now common among farmers, and they sickened and died at appalling rates. This process has happened again and again in more recent times, and it's extremely likely that it happened early in the history of the expansion of farming too, although the archeological evidence for it is slender. It's highly probable that greater vulnerability to new human infections cost foragers and hunters terribly, clearing the way for further expansion of farming.

ENVIRONMENTAL CHANGE In some environments, farming probably spread because it indirectly ruined landscapes for hunters and foragers. The daily activities of farmers often depleted the nearby wild herds on which hunters depended. Farmers' own herds and flocks munched and trampled their way over the countryside, reducing the availability of forage plants for wildlife. Farmers often set fire to vegetation to prepare the ground for their own plantings. By pursuing their own subsistence methods, farmers often made it harder for anyone to make a living without farming.

EXPANSION BY IMITATION

Farming also spread through less destructive processes, as when the ideas of domestication and cultivation spread from one person to the next, without anyone killing or infecting anyone else. The early crops of Iberian (today's Spain and Portugal) farming, and all the animals that farmers raised, came from the Levant and its

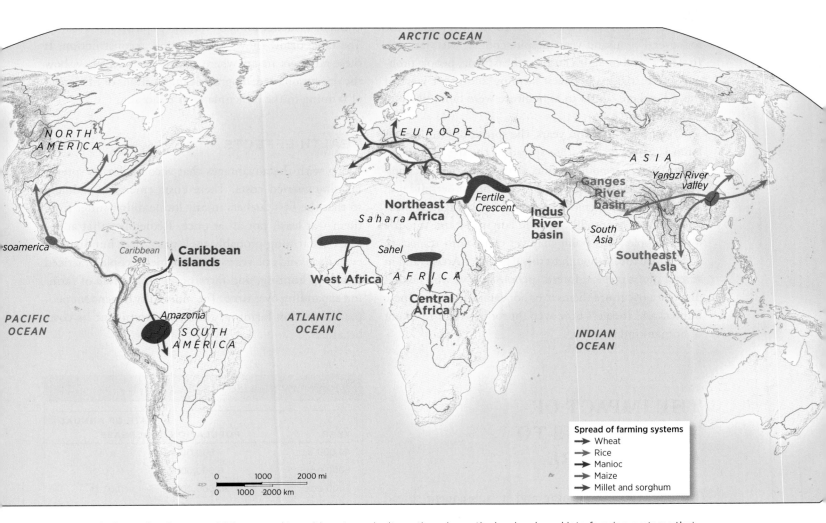

The Spread of Farming Systems Of the several transitions to agriculture, three in particular developed into farming systems that spread especially widely: those based on rice in East Asia, wheat in the Fertile Crescent, and maize in Mexico. Other crops and farming systems spread less widely. In every case, the spreading took thousands of years.

neighborhood. But genetic evidence shows clearly that Iberians did not, in the main, come from the Levant. The idea of farming spread to Iberians: they became farmers without being substantially replaced by immigrant farmers. Studies of the advent of farming to neighboring North Africa, and to the Baltic countries in northeastern Europe, show much the same thing. In short, examples abound of both ways in which farming spread—as a process of demographic displacement and as a process of inspiration and imitation.

THE FARMING REGIME

Not everyone took up farming. Some people either lived in or retreated to environments too dry, cold, or infertile for farming. Others, like the Jomon in Japan, found farming unappealing compared to the rewards of foraging and hunting, and they persisted in their way of life for several thousand years despite contact with farmers. In Africa, and in South and Southeast Asia, people probably often toggled between farming and other ways of life. Elsewhere, shifts to agriculture were more likely to be permanent.

Over the last 10,000 years, the spread of farming has almost matched the earlier spread of the use of fire and language. At one point in time, no one used these technologies. Then some people used them while others did not; and those who did, enjoyed great advantages against those who did not. Eventually, fire and language came into use by all people. This point may yet come with respect to agriculture too, although to this day in the Arctic, and in several moist tropical forests, people survive who neither practice agriculture themselves nor eat its products. These hunters and foragers now account for less than 1 percent of humankind.

THE IMPACT OF TRANSITIONS TO AGRICULTURE

The transitions to farming and its subsequent spread brought fundamental and durable consequences for human communities. Human populations increased even as people grew unhealthier. New expressions of culture in arenas such as religion, architecture, and pottery also emerged.

EFFECTS ON POPULATION

The most basic advantage of farming, and the reason for its widespread practice, is that it enabled far more people—10 to 100 times as many—to live on the same amount of land as did hunting and foraging. Farming women had more babies, at more frequent intervals, than the women of hunting and foraging peoples. Although those babies died in droves from infections, the number of children still grew. This conferred the advantages of superior numbers on farmer folk in any competitions with hunters and foragers.

No censuses were taken during the Paleolithic, and the available evidence for early human populations is scanty. The table below shows one plausible reconstruction. If these numbers are anywhere close to accurate, they show the revolutionary demographic implications of the spread of farming in the millennia after 8000 BCE.

HEALTH EFFECTS

Along with the advantages that account for its spread, farming carried costs. These costs emerged gradually so that the first farmers in any locale didn't suffer from them—at least, not all at once. Remember that adoptions of farming probably took place over hundreds or even thousands of years during which people practiced foraging, hunting, and farming, with the role of farming expanding over time. The more fully dependent people became on farming, the more prominent its costs became.

GLOBAL POPULATION ESTIMATES		
YEAR	POPULATION	RATE OF ANNUAL INCREASE
40,000 BCE	600,000	n/a
8000 BCE	6,000,000	0.003%
3000 BCE	20,000,000	0.014%
1500 BCE	100,000,000	0.053%

Source: M. Perrault, "85 milliards d'humains plus tard" (2003).

DIET AND STATURE Farming folk ate a narrower diet than foragers and hunters. Depending heavily on a few staple foods left them at greater risk for poor nutrition from a lack of key vitamins or minerals. They ate less meat and got less protein, which probably accounts for the smaller stature of farming people compared to their pre-farming ancestors. Skeletal remains from sites between Ukraine and North Africa indicate that late Paleolithic men on average stood 5'8" (177 cm) tall, and women 5'4" (166 cm). In the last thousand years before agriculture—the period when game was growing scarce and climate colder and dryer—their average stature shrank by 2 inches (5 cm). During the first millennium after the origins of farming, they shrank faster, by another 2 to 4 inches (5–10 cm).

DISEASE Farmers were sicker as well as smaller than their hunting and foraging ancestors. The shift to agriculture was a gigantic stride backward for human health. Among the reasons for this is that farming folk, like all sedentary people, lived amid their own garbage and wastes. Moreover, they often deliberately handled human and animal feces to use it as fertilizer. They suffered heavily from gastrointestinal diseases carried by worms and other parasites, which one might collectively call diseases of sedentism.

Farming communities also suffered from what one could call diseases of domestication. As we've seen, many human diseases derive from domesticated-animal diseases. Half of these come from dogs, cattle, sheep, and goats. Even chickens and cats have donated some of their infections to their human masters. As these infections evolved into human diseases, babies in farming communities in Eurasia and Africa (not in the Americas, which hardly had any domesticated animals) increasingly were born into hazardous microbial environments teeming with influenza, smallpox, mumps, tuberculosis, tetanus, and a host of other killing diseases.

Farming invited diseases from other sources as well. As we've seen, stored grain attracted rats and mice, putting farming communities at enhanced risk for hemorrhagic fevers and other nasty infections carried by rodents. There are about 35 human diseases derived from rats or from the fleas and ticks that live on rats. And where farmers cleared forest, and especially where they allowed water to accumulate, they created new habitat for malarial mosquitoes, another dangerous disease vector. Malaria, one of humankind's worst scourges, seems powerfully correlated with farming environments—at least, where climates are warm enough for the relevant mosquitoes. In Africa and Asia, it seems to have taken firm hold among humans soon after they took up farming, although it probably wasn't unknown before.

CHILDREN AND WOMEN All these diseases made life for farming folk, especially children, far more hazardous than for hunting and foraging peoples—at least, for those who could stay away from disease-bearing farmers. Farmers had far more babies than did hunters and foragers, but their disease environments also killed them faster. If anyone had known these facts of disease history, they would have avoided agriculture like the plague. But they didn't know.

Our old friends the Natufians show that some of the health costs of taking up farming fell mostly on women. The Natufians left more skeletons than most people, giving archeologists an opportunity to calculate life expectancies. After the Natufians shifted to agriculture, men lived longer than before but women less long. Two likely reasons for this gender difference are that death by violence and hunting accidents (more likely to befall men) decreased as people took up farming, but that death in the act of giving birth became more common as fertility rates rose. The routines of work among farmers also left telling marks on Natufian female skeletons. They show signs of stresses in their knees, wrists, and backs from the endless kneeling and bending required for grinding

Social Units Neolithic rock art found in present-day Algeria depicts a small group of people of different sizes, possibly adults and children within a larger farming community.

grain. In general, the transition to agriculture made people shorter, sicker, and more likely to suffer from acute malnutrition—and in most cases, the effects were worse for women than for men.

THE SELF-DOMESTICATION OF HUMANS

Here is a final reflection on what settling down and taking up farming meant for human bodies. At the same time that our ancestors were domesticating dogs, grasses, sheep, and goats, they were—equally unknowingly—domesticating themselves. Their bodies became smaller and weaker. Survival came to depend less on strength and physical courage, and more on the ability to get along with others and accept one's place in a hierarchy, the same sort of docility that humans appreciated in goats and sheep.

GRACIALIZATION In some respects, this process of self-domestication may go further back: **gracialization**—the evolutionary process by which skeletons became thinner, smaller, and lighter—began in Eurasia as early as 40,000 years ago. Earlier skeletons show much stronger legs among mobile hunters and foragers than among later farmers, and more powerful right arms on most males, perhaps a result of throwing rocks and spears. Gracialization suggests a gradual process of selection for traits other than brute strength.

Gracialization in recent millennia (since 40,000 years ago) has gone furthest among Africans and Asians. It has gone least far among the isolated populations of Tierra del Fuego at the southern tip of South America (they only arrived there 12,000 years ago at the earliest) and Australian Aborigines. This suggests gracialization is ongoing and recent, and connected to the emergence of bigger social groups. Survival and reproduction within the bigger groups made possible by sedentism and farming favors the sociable, the politically skilled, the good cooperators and clever deceivers—as well as those with strong immune systems. In short, sedentism and farming encouraged the evolution of a wily political animal no longer as reliant on strength and stamina.

SELECTION FOR DOCILITY So as our ancestors were domesticating other species, they were also domesticating themselves through genetic selection. Farming in particular selected for people who would accept both the repetitive routines of farming life and their place in a social order in which only a few could be near the top. Farming began a process that selected against defiance and for docility in humans as well as in farm animals. This process is still ongoing after 10,000 years.

At the same time that our bodies and minds evolved so as to fit the demands of the farming life, we created cultures that help us endure numbing routines and social subordination. Cultural adjustment to the demands of farming eased the pressures for genetic adjustment. And our cultures evolved quickly in response to the risks and rewards of farming, as much of the rest of this book will show. Even in the first few thousand years after the transitions to farming, major cultural shifts occurred. Let's look briefly at some of these.

CHANGES IN HUMAN CULTURE

The transition to agriculture is one of the great transformations in the history of the human species. Raising one's food as opposed to collecting or hunting it brought broad cultural changes. It required people to submit to laborious routines, but it allowed enormous expansions in cultural richness and diversity. Mobile hunters and foragers around the world had only a few, very similar tools, the same social structures just about everywhere, and—as far as we know—roughly the same sorts of ideas about nature and spirits. By later standards, there wasn't much cultural diversity during the Paleolithic, because mobile people had to carry their culture with them. With sedentary farming, all that changed.

ENERGY The most fundamental change brought by farming was an energy revolution. Like cooking long before it, or the harnessing of fossil fuels long afterward, farming vastly increased the amount of energy available to human communities. The added calories that farming made available brought a dramatic change in demography, as we have seen. Now people died at faster rates than before; but babies were born even faster, and populations grew more quickly than at any previous time, thanks to the fertility of farming families.

THE SOCIAL UNIT Transitions to agriculture also changed the basic social unit: from the mobile band of

Spiritual Practices A circle of stones at the Nabta Playa site in the Egyptian desert from around 5000 BCE may have been arranged to indicate the positions of the sun and stars at certain times of the year, perhaps related to religious observances.

perhaps 30 to 80 people, to farming families. These weren't necessarily nuclear families of just two parents and their children. Many agricultural societies recognized family units of three generations or groups of cousins. Bigger family units were useful for some kinds of farm work. Moreover, many farming societies clustered into villages where hundreds of people gathered together, forming another, larger, looser social unit. In global terms, until the rapid urbanization of the last 30 years, the farming village remained the characteristic human settlement and social environment.

DAILY ROUTINES Farming brought big and long-lasting changes in daily routines. Farming people normally had to work more days and longer hours every day than did hunters and foragers. Preparing the ground for sowing or planting was laborious, even with the help of fire and domestic animals. Planting, weeding, watering, and harvesting all required long hours of tedious work. So did threshing, preparing, and cooking grains. Grinding grain, where that was practiced, took even more time and effort. Farmers had far less free time than foragers and hunters did.

RELIGION Farming brought changes in religion too. Most farming communities placed an emphasis on fertility and found ways to revere it. They also came to locate their gods in the skies as much as in animals, trees, and rocks. This gave greater scope for religious specialists—priests—who could study the heavens and give advice about when to plant and harvest. Unlike migratory birds or flowering plants, humans have no innate sense of when in the year to perform certain tasks, but agriculture in most settings required that farmers act with a precise understanding of changing seasons. Religions acquired ever more features that connected them to the annual rhythms of farm life.

CULTURAL DIVERSIFICATION With farming came cultural elaboration in other areas as well. New styles of architecture emerged, owing in part to new materials such as bricks. Pottery became larger, more widespread, and more intricate in design. Art, tools, and weapons grew more diverse and elaborate. People could make these advances not because they had more time to spare but because they were staying put in one spot, and the efficiency of food production allowed a tiny minority to engage in creative activities.

A basic similarity in social structure underlay this cultural diversification. Agricultural society allowed social stratification of a sort unseen in mobile bands or even among sedentary foragers. Farming opened more opportunities for the accumulation of wealth, both through clever exchanges and through violent intimidation and seizure. This broad pattern of heightened stratification was fundamental to farming societies. It emerged in both Eurasia and the Americas, between which there was no contact during this period, as well as in Africa. Later chapters will explain the forms it took.

Honoring the Dead These tortoise shells were found in the grave of the Natufian shaman who was buried 12,000 years ago at Hilazon Tachtit. They are remains of the lavish feast held during her funerary rites. Religious practices were transformed by the transition to agriculture.

CONCLUSION

With the domestication of plants and animals, *Homo sapiens* for the first time became the dominant mammal on Earth. Over the four-billion-year history of life on our planet, several species (and groups of species such as the dinosaurs) have enjoyed their moments in the sun. Despite being well adapted to the conditions of their time, sooner or later they all went extinct, usually in consequence of some major environmental change to which other species adjusted more quickly and successfully. Is human dominance only the latest in this long line, or are we so clever that the pattern will change?

Given its tremendous importance in human history and its nearly universal adoption by human groups, the transition to agriculture may appear to be an inevitable stage in the progress of humankind. A century ago, most scholars who thought about such things believed just that. But it was not. Remember that the first transition didn't happen for more than 200,000 years of human history. It took place only after the climate changes at the end of the last ice age and the gradual growth in numbers of clever hunters. If big game had remained plentiful and foraging opportunities abundant, there probably would have been no incentive to experiment with the cultivation of plants.

The transitions to sedentism and agriculture are among the crucial turning points in human history, ranking with the harnessing of fire, the emergence of language, and (later) the adoption of fossil fuels. The big changes at the end of the Paleolithic are clearly momentous in their long-term consequences but hazy in their causes. Climate shifts probably played a role, and perhaps population pressure did too. What else might have been involved we just don't know. We do know that after the domestication of dogs more than 20,000 years ago, the first flurry of domestications and probably the first genuine transition to farming took place in the Levant, soon before 10,000 BCE. And we know that several other transitions to agriculture took place over the next few thousand years on every inhabited continent except Australia.

The development of sedentism and farming had important consequences. They included faster population growth, worse health, and new directions in religion and other forms of cultural expression. These trends all shaped farmers' lives, and those of non-farmers too, fairly soon after farming took root.

One other trend, slower to develop but with powerful long-term effects, is noteworthy. With farming, population grew more rapidly, communities became larger, and eventually the networks among communities grew denser than before. Farming communities formed nodes in the fragile and faint webs of humankind, connected to one another mainly by more mobile peoples such as foragers and hunters. After the transitions to farming, the world became more densely settled, with more well-worn routes among settlements and more regular contacts among communities. In a few places, such as the Fertile Crescent and the lower Yangzi valley, people, settlements, routes, and communication were much denser than elsewhere, and highly interactive local webs emerged. In most places, population was still sparse, settlements rare, routes and communication intermittent. It would be another 5,000 years after the first farming communities took shape before large-scale webs of interaction emerged with sustained long-distance linkages.

CHAPTER REVIEW

KEY TERMS

Natufians (p. 27)
Younger Dryas (p. 29)
Holocene (p. 30)
sedentary (p. 30)

Jomon culture (p. 30)
Göbekli Tepe (p. 31)
Magdalenian culture
  (p. 32)
domestication (p. 34)

Levant (p. 35)
transition to agriculture
  (p. 38)
Yangzi River (p. 40)
gracialization (p. 48)

Go to INQUIZITIVE to see what you've learned—and learn what you've missed—with personalized feedback along the way.

REVIEW QUESTIONS

1. Why was slow global warming after about 18,000 BCE a benefit for humans?

2. How did accessibility to food sources affect where the first sedentary and semi-sedentary people lived?

3. Why did sedentary life spur the development of tools and other objects?

4. Describe the process of domestication with examples of animals and plants.

5. What were the most important conditions for the first transition to agriculture?

6. Approximately where and when did the domestication of the most important farm animals occur?

7. Why do you think agriculture developed independently in different parts of the world?

8. What were the two main ways in which farming spread far and wide?

9. How did the transitions to agriculture impact human population and health?

10. In what sense was the development of farming an energy revolution?

11. Is the development of agriculture an inevitable stage in human progress? Explain why or why not.

FURTHER READING

Graeme BARKER, *The Agricultural Revolution in Prehistory: Why Did Foragers Become Farmers?* (2006). A general study by one of the foremost scholars of the subject.

Peter BELLWOOD, *First Farmers: The Origins of Agricultural Societies* (2005). An informative work by another major authority.

John L. BROOKE, *Climate Change and the Course of Human History: A Rough Journey* (2014). A scholarly synthesis, leaning toward the climatic determinist side.

Steven MITHEN, *After the Ice: A Global Human History, 20,000–5,000 BC* (2003). A breezy tour through the late Paleolithic and the transitions to settled farming.

James SCOTT, *Against the Grain: A Deep History of the Earliest States* (2017). A broad work whose early chapters provide a readable account of domestication, mainly in Asia.

David WENGROW, *What Makes Civilization*? (2018). A compact discussion of Egypt and Mesopotamia and their neighborhood.

Yoshinori YASUDA, ed., *The Origins of Pottery and Agriculture* (2002). A work that is strong on the pottery traditions of East Asia and their relation to early farming.

CHRONOLOGY

Between 8000 and 5000 BCE
Lactose-tolerance genetic
mutations occur in some
people in West Africa, East
Africa, northern Europe,
Southwest Asia

By ca. 7000 BCE
Jericho is home to
around 2,000 people

ca. 7000 BCE
Pottery appears in
the Fertile Crescent

ca. 7500 BCE
Çatalhöyük settlement begins

ca. 6000 BCE
Mesopotamians develop
the potter's wheel; large-
scale smelting operations
begin

ca. 4800 BCE
Domestication of horses

ca. 5000 BCE
Herding becomes a
full-time specialization

Between 3500 BCE and ca. 1500 BCE
Complex societies emerge in Mesopotamia,
Egypt, Indus valley, China, Mesoamerica, Andes

ca. 4500 BCE
Pottery appears in
North America

ca. 4000 BCE
Eurasia's Indo-
European migrations
begin

By ca. 3500 BCE
Steppe people ride horses

ca. 3500 BCE
Large-scale irrigation begins;
Mesopotamian smiths begin
making bronze; first wheels,
axles, plows, and donkey
caravans appear; pottery
appears in South America

ca. 3300 BCE
Lifetime of
"Ötzi the Iceman"

ca. 3000–2500 BCE
Bantu-speakers migrate within
West Central Africa

ca. 3000 BCE
People begin to use sails
efficiently

ca. 2000 BCE
Domestication
of camels

ca. 1500 BCE
Lapita migrations
begin

ca. 1500 BCE–500 CE
Bantu-speakers migrate into East and southern Africa

Building Complex Societies

9000 to 1500 BCE

I n 1991, hikers in the Ötz Valley near the mountainous border between Italy and Austria came upon a frozen corpse protruding from glacial ice. Medical examination revealed that "Ötzi the Iceman" was well preserved for his age: 5,300 years old. When he died, Ötzi was about 45 years old, elderly by the standards of his time. He stood 5'5" (160 cm) tall and weighed about 110 lbs. (50 kg). He was brown-eyed, wore his hair long, and sported a shaggy beard and tattoos of small dots.

Few corpses have aroused as much scientific interest as Ötzi's. The contents of his stomach showed that he had eaten two balanced meals within eight hours of his death: deer and mountain goat meat, roots, fruits, and wheat bran, perhaps eaten as bread. Pollen ingested with his last meals indicated that he died in the springtime. Clues in his fingernails suggested he had been sick three times in the six months before his death. Chemical analysis of his tooth enamel revealed he had grown up nearby, and slight deformations of his leg bones and pelvis indicated he did a lot of walking in hilly terrain. Genetic evidence showed he suffered from something similar to Lyme disease and was lactose intolerant (meaning he couldn't digest milk or dairy products). His

ca. 1200 CE
Polynesians reach New Zealand

ca. 500 CE
Polynesians reach Hawaii and Easter Island

The Wheel Mosaics from the Sumerian city of Ur show soldiers riding into battle in wheeled, horse-drawn wagons. The wheel gave Sumerian troops an advantage over rival armies. These panels, inlaid with lapis lazuli and dated to around 2500 BCE, were found in a royal tomb.

FOCUS QUESTIONS

1. What were the main characteristics of life in early farming villages?

2. What were the main characteristics of herder societies?

3. What was the significance of the major farmer migrations in Eurasia, Africa, and Polynesia?

4. How did the spread of farming and herding change human biology, culture, and the environment?

5. What characteristics did the first cities, states, and complex societies all share?

6. Why did the first faint webs of connection begin to develop at this time?

hands were smooth, suggesting he didn't regularly handle rough objects and may have been a trader or a shaman.

Ötzi the Iceman was a sharp dresser, sporting an array of animal skins. His boots—bearskin soles with deerskin uppers—were so elegant that many researchers suppose he came from a society with specialist cobblers. He wore a striped goatskin vest, a calf-leather belt, goatskin leggings, and goatskin underwear. He topped it all off with a bear-fur cap.

Ötzi carried an axe with a precision-crafted blade of almost pure copper, an expensive material. Like his elaborate dress, this suggested that Ötzi may have been prosperous. He also had with him a sewing kit, a fire-starter kit with fungi and flints, a modest medical kit including some natural antibiotics, a small dagger held in a sheath, a deerskin quiver with 14 arrows, and an unfinished bow.

Ötzi needed his weapons. He had bruises and cuts on his legs, hands, and chest, implying hand-to-hand combat. DNA analysis of blood found on his body and clothes indicates that others, whether friends or enemies, were wounded with him. The fight apparently took place shortly before his death. Someone shot an arrow into his back that sliced through his shoulder blade, severed an artery, and lodged under his armpit. Enfeebled by the wound and several bruises on his skull, he froze to death.

His murder remains a very cold case. Who killed Ötzi? Why was he walking near a mountain pass and carrying so much gear? How did he get into a fight, and why was he shot in the back? Was he a trader heading over the mountains? Was he a traveling shaman? Was he fleeing from someone? Despite the remarkable ingenuity of the many scientists who have pried into Ötzi's secrets, even locating some of his living relatives in Austria, we have no answers.

The first half of this chapter will focus on the world that Ötzi knew, one that developed after farming had begun to spread and before there were any cities—in other words, the millennia known as the Neolithic. In Southwest Asia, this world lasted from roughly 10,000 to 3500 BCE. But in sub-Saharan Africa and Polynesia, for example, it started later and comes forward much closer to the present, in some particulars to about 1000 CE. The second half of the chapter considers the emergence and character of cities, states, and complex society—defined when we get there—with special attention to some common features among early complex societies, including social hierarchy, writing, and metallurgy. The chapter concludes with observations on the enduring challenges to complex societies and the intriguing parallels among them.

EARLY FARMING VILLAGES

As we saw in Chapter 2, farming gradually spread from its several lands of origin. In most parts of the world, early farmers clustered together in villages. These weren't entirely new: a few favored locations had supported villages of hunter-foragers or fisherfolk before farming. With farming, villages soon became the new norm, the basic cell of human society, and the typical human habitat. Most of your ancestors over the past 8,000 years probably lived in farming villages.

VILLAGE SOCIETY

Farm villages usually contained several dozen to several hundred people. As a rough rule, most adult men worked preparing fields, planting, tending, and harvesting crops. Adult women often tended and harvested crops too, and took primary responsibility for grinding grain, fetching water and fuelwood, and minding small children. Recent studies of bones of women from farming villages in central Europe after 5000 BCE imply a strenuous work load: they had upper-arm strength equal to today's elite female rowers. Children by the age of five took part in farm routines, fetching wood and water, and weeding fields. These roles varied from place to place with the crops and technologies used and the prevailing cultural traditions and beliefs.

SOLIDARITY BEYOND KINFOLK Farm villages were made up partly of kinfolk. But some people lived close by others who weren't their kin, and a new social category—neighbor—acquired importance. People in villages had to find ways to live harmoniously with others unrelated to them, which until then hadn't been a large part of human experience. Forging bonds of solidarity with non-kin was especially important when big tasks needed doing, such as building a wall around one's village. Villages that were subject to attack by strangers depended on solidarity among neighbors for survival.

The earliest farm villages, it seems, were composed of near equals. Old social hierarchies continued, based on age and gender and inherited ultimately from the deep hominin past. As in all societies, some people were held in higher esteem than others for their abilities. And settled farmers could own more than mobile people. But the opportunities for accumulation of wealth remained modest in early villages. Most families enjoyed roughly the same standard of living as their neighbors. This rough equality narrowed the scope for envy and jealousy, which are never far below the surface in human societies. Customs and rituals that emphasized community over

Carnac The standing stones of Carnac in Brittany date roughly from 4500 to 3300 BCE and indicate a level of social solidarity.

individuals helped smooth over potential jealousies. Early villages developed festivals, often anchored by events in the agricultural calendar such as harvest time. Most villages today still have such celebrations.

MAXIMIZING FERTILITY One feature of village life—noted in Chapter 2—was large numbers of children. Whereas hunter-foragers contrived to limit their fertility, farmers usually tried to maximize it. Roughly half of all babies died before their fifth birthday in farming villages. Parents wanted to be sure of having adult children to help out as they aged, so they eagerly welcomed births. Analysis of burials around the world suggests that women in early farming villages, on average, had two more babies in their lifetimes than did their forager ancestors. Just about all farming peoples scorned or pitied childless men and women. This cultural preference for lots of children remains strong today where village life prevails, although it tends to vanish within two generations in the context of city life.

POTTERY AND ITS USES Another characteristic of settled village life was pottery. Mobile people rarely used pottery because pots are heavy and break easily in transport. Typically made of clay and baked, at first in bonfires and later in small ovens called kilns, pots became essential household items in farm villages. As we saw in Chapter 2, the first pottery predated farming in a few places

Jomon Pots and Potters

Pots, bowls, cups, and other vessels are so common today that it's difficult to appreciate how revolutionary pottery was at first for storing and preparing food and liquids. Farmers produced most of the pottery that archeologists find, but some of the earliest pots yet found were made about 15,000 years ago in Japan by foraging and fishing people whom we call the Jomon. These people used at least some of their pots to cook salmon that passed along the northwestern shore of Japan to spawn. The pots were formed by hand without the aid of a potter's wheel and were hardened in an open fire rather than inside a kiln. In later centuries, Jomon potters decorated their work with braided ropes (*jomon* in Japanese), but earlier vessels had more varied decorations, such as hatch marks, indentations, and bored holes. Most Jomon pots were left undecorated. Historians and archeologists often analyze variations in decoration, method of manufacture, and location of pottery fragments to trace movements of people and the expansion of material culture.

QUESTIONS FOR ANALYSIS

1. Like all tools, pottery improved humans' ability to manipulate the environment. What could they do with pots that was difficult to accomplish with animal skins, stone tools, or baskets made from reeds? In what ways was pottery an energy technology?
2. Do you think the Jomon people might have used the vessel pictured here for cooking or storing? Why or why not?
3. How can pottery help reveal the migration or expansion of cultural groups?

in East Asia, appearing as early as 18,000 BCE. Elsewhere, people generally settled down before taking up pottery. In the Fertile Crescent, for example, pottery appeared only around 7000 BCE, millennia after the first villages. It existed by 4500 BCE in North America, where the earliest finds are in Georgia and South Carolina, and by 3500 BCE in South America. Each of these inventions of pottery was independent of the others.

Pottery answered villagers' needs. Pots made it easier to store seeds, food, and liquids. They were useful for cooking, enabling people to make stews and soups with otherwise tough-to-digest foodstuffs. By boiling tough meat or fibrous beans all day, people could make meals that even toddlers and toothless elders could eat. So pottery expanded the range of potential foods, and in this way helped improve nutrition and life expectancy.

Pottery also served as a means of artistic expression. Although most pots were purpose-built and artistically

Potter's Wheels An Egyptian statuette from around 2450 BCE shows a potter squatting in front of a wheel. This key techno-logical advance had spread throughout many different cultures by this time.

bland, sometimes people lavished care on pottery. Certain styles were based on the shapes of objects, such as the rope-coiled pattern of Jomon pottery in Japan or the inverted bell-shaped pottery, called beakerware, in fashion in western Europe after 3000 BCE. Other styles became possible once pottery glaze was developed, allowing potters to use more colors and to paint designs on their pots.

Pots were extremely useful but hard to make in quantity until about 6000 BCE, when Mesopotamians developed the potter's wheel. (Mesopotamia encompasses the basin of the Tigris and Euphrates Rivers in modern Iraq.) By spinning wet clay, one can quickly fashion it into desired shapes. The potter's wheel was the Neolithic equivalent of the modern assembly line: using it, potters could make hundreds or thousands of nearly identical bowls.

THE RISKS OF VILLAGE LIFE

In Chapter 2, we saw that early farmers suffered from a handful of new diseases that were the result of settlement and farming. Village life, especially farming, also carried other risks, one of which was attack by strangers.

The core of the problem was that villagers, unlike foragers and hunters, had much to lose by running away from a fight. Farming folk used agricultural tools and storage vessels, usually pottery, and lived in carefully constructed dwellings. In some places, they had domesticated animals. They couldn't flee at a moment's notice without losing almost everything. So when raiders descended on them, they often chose to stand and fight. Many of the skeletons of men from early villages show fractures of the left forearm, an indication that they had parried blows from weapons such as clubs—although whether wielded by marauding strangers or irritated neighbors we cannot tell.

Fickle weather posed another risk. Village farmers couldn't gather up everything they valued at a moment's notice if floodwaters threatened to engulf them. Some of the early village walls—at Jericho in the Jordan River valley, for example—may have been built to deflect floods as much as to repel attackers.

In most locations, crop-killing drought was a more worrisome risk than flood. Villagers developed methods of ensuring water supplies when rains didn't suffice, typically by irrigation—diverting water from lakes, streams, and rivers to their fields and gardens. In long droughts, however, even irrigation channels might run dry, leading to hunger and perhaps starvation.

The risks and concerns of village life, whether from one's fellow humans or from the caprice of the weather, affected culture. To judge from art, architecture, burials, and other snippets of evidence, early villagers developed religious practices that emphasized fertility—of the soil, their animals, and themselves. In dry lands, rain deities became popular. Symbols of fertility—bulls or pregnant women, for example—decorated countless village homes. In a world where babies died so often, where crops withered without warning, it made sense to worship fertility in its various forms.

Some villagers also developed ancestor cults, a widespread practice wherever people lived in the same place over many generations. Villagers hoped their departed ancestors could intervene with

Death by Violence A reconstruction of the site in the Alps where Ötzi the Iceman was found. Not only was he carrying weapons, but his remains suggest that he had sustained battle wounds—evidence of the violence that could occur in farming villages.

supernatural powers and protect them against the hazards of their world. Worship of ancestors and attachment to their places of burial made villagers even more reluctant to flee in the event of attack, drought, or flood.

THE ADVANTAGES OF VILLAGE LIFE

Despite these risks, and the toll of disease discussed in Chapter 2, the populations of farming villages grew faster than those of hunters and foragers. In favorable spots, the village way of life could feed 100 times as many people per acre as could hunting and foraging. Clusters of villages formed in favored places such as the soft alluvial soils of riverbanks or deltas, or the light, windblown loess soils (loamy with small-grain clay or silt) of northern China and central Europe. The distribution of people over the face of the Earth, always uneven, became more so with the spread of farming villages. At a rough guess, the world contained 6 million people at the dawn of agriculture (or the start of the Neolithic, ca. 10,000 BCE) and 20 million by the time the first cities appeared (ca. 3200 BCE), most of them living along rivers. The spread of village farming was the main innovation that allowed such population growth.

JERICHO AND ÇATALHÖYÜK In ideal locations, villages could contain a few thousand people. Jericho, for example, located near a series of freshwater springs and a supply of salt—a commodity in great demand as a food preservative—seems to have been home to some 2,000 people by 7000 BCE. Larger still was Çatalhöyük, a village in south-central Anatolia. Founded around 7500 BCE, it attained a size of perhaps 6,000 or 8,000 residents. It was a well-watered site, with rich alluvial soils and a supply of obsidian. A black volcanic glass, obsidian made good, sharp edges for tools and weapons. It was also a valuable trade commodity: exports of obsidian contributed to Çatalhöyük's prosperity. The village houses were all similar, made of mud brick with no doors but with openings in their roofs, perhaps intended for better defense against enemies. Its people lived off their wheat and barley farming; sheep, goat, and cattle raising; and a little hunting. Men and women seem to have enjoyed similar nutrition, a sign of relative gender equality. Despite its size, Çatalhöyük was not a city: it had no public buildings or temples, no public spaces or plazas, and no signs of a ruling elite.

SHIFTING AGRICULTURE Most early farmers didn't live in large villages like Çatalhöyük, and some didn't live in settled villages at all. Especially in forest zones without good soils, shifting agriculture often made more sense than permanent village settlement. **Shifting agriculture**, also called slash-and-burn or swidden, involved cutting

Architectural Advances Both of these sites are indicative of the new kinds of architecture embraced by settled agricultural communities: The Tower of Jericho (left) was built around 8000 BCE and measures 30 feet (9 m) in diameter and nearly 28 feet (8.5 m) high. The foundations of the 9000-year-old village of Çatalhöyük (right) reveal how thousands of residents lived in houses and farmed over a fairly sizable area.

and burning a clearing, farming it for a few years (usually three to ten), and then moving on to start anew elsewhere. At first, swidden farmers obtained good yields because the ash from burned forest contained abundant nutrients for their crops. But as nutrient supplies dwindled and weeds grew up, it paid to head elsewhere and repeat the cycle. These people typically mixed their farming with a fair bit of hunting and foraging in surrounding forests. Shifting agriculture was the most practical way to farm in much of the world. In some places, it still is.

Once people became farming villagers, they tended not to change their ways. Dense populations required food production. The archeological record shows few cases in which farming communities reverted to hunting and foraging. In this respect, the history of early farming shows a clear tendency: many communities shifted from food collection to food production, and few shifted the other way, giving up farming. This did happen occasionally, though—probably more often in the forest zones of Africa and Southeast Asia than elsewhere—because farming in moist tropical forests with the crops available then was not clearly preferable to hunting and foraging.

HERDERS

Some environments, such as arid scrubland and semi-arid grasslands, couldn't support much in the way of food crops. To survive in these parts of the world, people had to live off animal products. Sheep, goats, cattle, donkeys, horses, camels, yaks, reindeer, llamas, and other domesticated grazing animals can turn grass or shrubby vegetation into meat, milk, wool, hides, horn, bone, and dung. With enough skill, people could make these animal products into food, clothing, tents, tools, weapons, and fuel. Domestic grazing animals expanded human reach into new environments and enriched human life.

People who live mainly off their animals are called **herders** or pastoralists, and their way of life is called pastoralism. How pastoralism originated is unclear, but it was probably an offshoot of early farming. Tending animals requires specialized skills, and herders at first were people who acquired these skills and used them on lands that were either temporarily or always unused for agriculture. Herding likely became a full-time specialization only

after 5000 BCE or so. Most scholars think herding arose first on the fringes of farming communities in Mesopotamia. It might also have evolved as a full-time specialization on the southern edges of the Sahara, in the belt of semi-arid land called the African Sahel, perhaps around 4500 BCE. Millions of people in Africa and Asia live as herders today.

It's convenient to divide people into fixed categories and to think of farmers and herders as separate groups, as we do here. But in practice, the line between the two was sometimes fuzzy. Farmers often kept animals and might take them out to graze on nearby grasslands for a few weeks. Herders might settle for a few months and grow some crops. People might shift back and forth between farming and herding, depending on weather or other factors. But more often than not, farmers and herders regarded themselves as fundamentally different and preferred their own company.

Anatolian Art A highly skilled craftsperson must have created this gold figure in the shape of a stag, found at Çatalhöyük. It is evidence of the prosperity that could exist even in farming villages.

HERDER LANDS AND LIVESTOCK

The domain of herders was primarily the grasslands and scrublands of Eurasia and Africa. In Australia and Oceania, there were no grazing animals capable of domestication, so there were no herders. In the Americas, herding as a way of life didn't exist because only llamas and alpacas could be domesticated among large animals, and since they were useful in farm work, farmers raised them. In sub-Saharan Africa, herders concentrated in the Sahel and grassy parts of eastern and southern Africa. In moister African lands, their range was restricted by a livestock disease carried by the tsetse fly. In the zone from northwestern Africa to northeastern China, pastoralism became a common way of life, especially on the broad grasslands known as the **Eurasian steppe**.

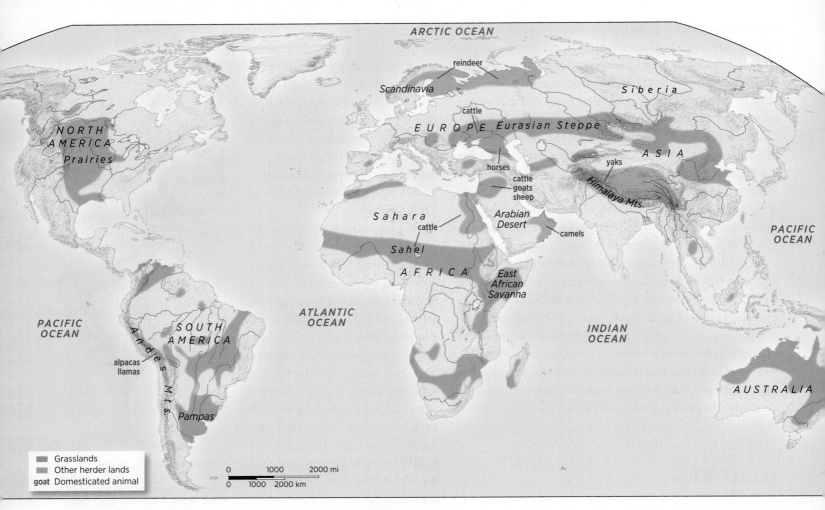

Grasslands and Pastoralist Lands, ca. 5000–1500 BCE Well after the domestication of herd animals, people in several parts of the world came to use natural grasslands for their herds and flocks as a full-time, and sometimes nomadic, way of life. Pastoralism was much more important in Eurasia and Africa than in the Americas or Australia, where suitable animals were rare or absent entirely.

Eight different animals supported herder societies. Some were found almost everywhere, but others had narrow ranges. Yaks, for example, were herded at high elevations in the Himalaya and the Tibetan Plateau but nowhere else. Reindeer herding has been confined mainly to Scandinavia and Siberia. Camels, first domesticated around 2000 BCE, were wondrously adapted to the arid conditions of North Africa as well as Southwest and Central Asia. In sub-Saharan Africa, most herders focused their attention on cattle, although they might keep sheep and goats as well. In Southwest and Central Asia, sheep and goats were the preferred livestock, but herders also raised cattle, donkeys, and eventually horses and camels. On the Eurasian steppe, herders kept sheep and goats

too, and sometimes cattle and Bactrian (Central Asian, two-humped) camels as well. On the broad steppe lands, herding came into its own only with horse domestication.

HERDER SOCIETIES

Herders routinely traded with farming folk. Farmers often wanted the hides, wool, and sometimes the meat or cheese that herders produced. By 2000 BCE, farmers, or at least their rulers, also wanted horses as weapons of war. Herders wanted grain and other foodstuffs, weapons, pots, baskets, and woven cloth. Many herder societies could make all these things for themselves, but often they found it advantageous to focus their efforts on raising animals and trading animal products for other items: economic specialization and exchange could work to everyone's advantage.

Herders spent all or part of their time on the move, seeking better grass and forage for their animals. Some were true nomads with no fixed homes. Most, however, followed defined routes and settled for a few weeks or months in familiar places when the grazing was good. Their movements were seasonal, aimed at getting the best food for their livestock. Like all human communities, they also liked to congregate with relatives for periodic festivals and ceremonies.

PROPERTY, STATUS, AND GENDER Like hunters and foragers, pastoralists had to limit their possessions to what they and their animals could carry. As a result of their mobility and limited material culture, herders typically didn't recognize private property in land; pastures generally belonged to groups such as lineages or tribes. This marked them off from farmers, who usually did eventually develop concepts of private property—individual or family property—in land. Even with less fixed property, herder society exhibited status hierarchies. Status among herders rested in part on individual and family achievements—feats of fertility, war, and endurance, for example. In part, it rested on the size of one's herds, the main form of wealth. It could also depend on ancestry: different families and clans enjoyed differing levels of prestige.

Herder societies normally observed sharp distinctions between male and female roles. Boys were raised to herd, fight, and if they had horses, ride. Courage, endurance, and defense of personal and family honor were highly

Herder Lifestyles Rock art from Tassili n'Ajjer in present-day Algeria vividly depicts life in a cattle-herding tribe. Women and children work close to huts and tethered animals at the left of the scene, while a few men tend cattle in the fields beyond.

prized male virtues. Girls were raised to do chores around tent or hut; to cook, sew, and mind babies and toddlers. Some women in Central Asia around 500 BCE were buried with weapons, perhaps an indication of warrior roles or of high social status. Women often handled commerce, especially when menfolk were away.

SMALL NUMBERS, LARGE IMPACT Herding supported much smaller, and more scattered, populations than farming. The reasons for this difference were, first, that farmers ate plants while herders ate animals that ate plants, giving them access to only about one-tenth of the energy per unit of area available to farmers. Second, herders' lands were normally less fertile to begin with, limiting the nutritional support for larger animals. Herder populations were limited by conditions, not preference. They revered fertility in soil, animals, men, and women no less than farmers did.

Despite their smaller numbers, herders often terrified farming folk. Where and when they mastered horses, their enhanced mobility gave them a great military advantage. They could attack when and where they pleased, and then fade away into the steppe or desert. They often operated what today we would call protection rackets—in effect, trading promises to forgo violence in exchange for grain or other goods. Conflict with farming communities

Nomadic Peoples A necklace of wood and leather created by nomadic peoples of the steppe around 400 BCE. Artifacts of perishable materials like this one rarely survive into the present day.

Equestrians A man rides a horse in a Mesopotamian clay relief dating from around 2000 to 1600 BCE. When people learned how to domesticate horses, cavalry became an increasingly important aspect of war.

usually took place on small scales, as raids rather than warfare.

Through their mobility, raiding, and trading, herders played an outsized role in world history, strengthening the strands of connection among settled folk in Eurasia and Africa, spinning additional threads of the world's webs. In the Americas and Australia, where pastoralism didn't develop until recent centuries, the process of web building was slower.

FARMING SOCIETIES ON THE MOVE

While herders played an outsized role in linking populations over long distances in Eurasia and Africa, migrating farmers occasionally had the same effect. Sometimes they moved into uninhabited spaces, but at other times they pushed other people off the lands they wanted. Either way, they spread the village way of life and, where villages became clustered together, built new and tighter, if local, webs of exchange.

Most of the farmer migrations of the period before

1000 BCE were small in scale and lost in the mists of time. To minimize the problem of scanty evidence, we will look at some farmer migrations that lasted for millennia and left comparatively good traces through archeology, genetics, or historical linguistics. This will take us momentarily into later periods of history.

EURASIA'S INDO-EUROPEAN MIGRATIONS

On occasion, farmers and their ways spread like slow-motion starbursts in multiple directions. There is linguistic evidence of such an event in the common roots of what became Germanic, Slavic, Romance, Celtic, Iranian, and several Indian languages. Migrations likely brought a single ancestral language into Iran, India, and Europe. Although there's no consensus, most specialists think such migrations began north of the Black Sea about 4000 BCE, when the onset of colder and drier climate may have triggered migrations.

The Indo-European migrations, which extended into westernmost China as well, seem in most cases connected to the spread of farming. Many words, notably for items related to agriculture, are sufficiently similar in Indian and European languages to indicate common origin. The word for "yoke," a wooden crosspiece fastening two oxen together so that they can pull a plow, is one example. In Sanskrit, a language of ancient India, it is *yuj*; in ancient Persian, *yog*; and in Latin, *iugum*. Similar variants exist in most other Indo-European languages. Archeological and genetic evidence supports the idea of a starburst migration of farmers into Europe and India.

As is often the case in migrations, young men seeking to establish themselves may have led the way. The Indo-European migrations were probably not ones in which men, women, and children all picked up and moved. Genetic evidence suggests that women were much less likely to have migrated. It also suggests that the immigrants to Europe and India had more success than local men in passing their genes on to future generations. This implies that the newcomers enjoyed higher status, supporting the notion they were farmers and more prosperous than other men.

Farming people from Southwest Asia also migrated into Africa. (This is how Africans acquired their tiny proportion of Neanderthal genes.) A 4,500-year-old male skeleton, called Mota after the Ethiopian cave in which it was found, tells us so. When compared to modern African populations, Mota's remains indicate considerable admixture of Eurasian DNA. The imported DNA reached all but the most isolated populations of East Africa, implying that immigrants from Southwest Asia were both numerous and highly successful in transmitting their genes to later generations. But the evidence from Mota's mortal remains cannot tell us how that happened.

Overall, the linguistic, archeological, and genetic evidence combine to suggest a starburst migration of farming people originating roughly 4000 BCE north of the Black Sea. Different groups moved in different directions—into India, Europe, and on a much smaller scale, northeastern Africa and westernmost China.

AFRICA'S BANTU MIGRATIONS

Later farmer migrations shaped African history much more deeply. **Bantu** is a language group of about 600 related tongues, now spoken widely in East, central, and southern Africa by hundreds of millions of people. Yet Bantu-speaking populations show the lowest genetic diversity within Africa, implying a small and comparatively recent founding population—another starburst that occurred around 3000 BCE.

Bantu-speakers originated in the Cameroon-Nigeria border region. In two main pulses they spread out, first within their region (ca. 3000–2500 BCE) and then into much of East and southern Africa (ca. 1500 BCE–500 CE). We know nothing about why they moved. They went slowly, reaching what is now South Africa about 1000 CE. Later Bantu migrants had better tools and weapons than the prior populations in central and southern Africa. They were skilled at cultivating yams and bananas, which do well in rainforest settings, and some of them became herders of cattle at some point along the way, probably in East Africa. With these skills they became increasingly successful colonizers, especially once they got south of central Africa's rain forests, which are challenging environments for farmers.

The migrants also had a secret weapon. They were more malaria-resistant than the pre-existing central and southern African populations. Genetic evidence shows that these local populations had minimal experience with malaria before Bantu-speakers trickled in.

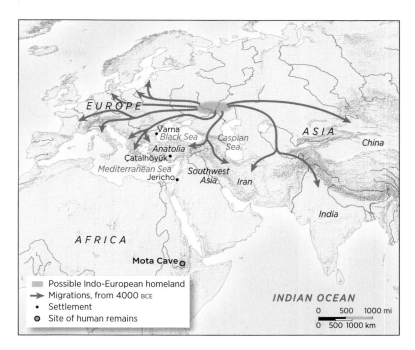

Indo-European Migrations, ca. 4000–1500 BCE Evidence from historical linguistics, archeology, and genetics indicates that farmers and herders originating somewhere north of the Black Sea spread out widely over western Eurasia. In most cases, they settled among foraging and hunting folk and either replaced them or absorbed them.

Bantu-speakers and their ancestors, in contrast, had lived in intense malaria environments for many generations in West Africa, an experience that had ruthlessly selected for malaria resistance. On top of that, their staple food, yams, included chemical compounds that fight malaria. When Bantu-speakers moved into central, East, and southern Africa, they brought malaria with them. The mosquitoes that transmit malaria, not suited to dense forest, thrived in the agricultural clearings. The Bantu-speakers—quite accidentally—created dangerous environments for others in which they themselves could survive more successfully than anyone else.

Genetic evidence suggests that Bantu-speakers both replaced and absorbed the existing populations of central, East, and southern Africa. More specifically, it implies that migrant men had great success in passing their genes on to future generations, whereas the indigenous male populations did not—and that women of all backgrounds increasingly had their children with Bantu-speaking men. This is similar to the pattern revealed in the Indo-European migrations into Europe and India.

Bantu Migrations, ca. 4000 BCE–1000 CE Speakers of Bantu languages, who originated somewhere near the border of today's Nigeria and Cameroon, spread out into central Africa's equatorial forests, East Africa's savanna lands, and southern Africa's woodland and grassland mosaics. The Bantu were farmers and either displaced or absorbed most of the people they encountered on their migrations.

POLYNESIAN MIGRATIONS IN THE PACIFIC

While Bantu-speaking farmers slowly made their way across a continent, Polynesians made their way across an ocean. Their distant ancestors came from islands of the westernmost Pacific such as Taiwan. Farmers, probably speaking a language ancestral to those of modern Southeast Asia, spread out from the Asian mainland into the islands of the western Pacific by 2000 BCE. Here they stayed put for a while, not venturing further out to sea—and with good reason. The Pacific covers about one-third of the globe and has only a few thousand habitable islands in it, most of them tiny. Those who sailed the open Pacific had to know what they were doing.

About 1500 BCE, the ancestors of today's Polynesians—

often called Lapita after their style of pottery—began to sail over immense distances and settle formerly uninhabited islands. By 1200 BCE, some had reached Samoa and Tonga. A thousand years later, Polynesians settled the Marquesas Islands in the central Pacific, and by 500 CE they had arrived in Hawaii and on Easter Island. It took until about 1200 CE before they settled New Zealand, the final frontier of Polynesian settlement.

Navigating the Pacific required skill and courage. Polynesians used big wooden dugout canoes with outriggers for stability. The largest could fit a hundred or more paddlers, but all canoes used sails on the open sea. They often sailed in fleets. The Polynesian voyagers learned to get their bearings from the stars, read the patterns of ocean waves and swells, and find land by watching the flight patterns of birds. They recorded geographic information on maps made of reeds and shells. Unlike the Indo-Europeans and the Bantu, the Polynesians couldn't simply walk to their new lands.

This extraordinary epic of exploration and colonization, like the Bantu and Indo-European migrations, was a movement of farmers. The Polynesians took their favorite crops—taro (a starchy root crop), and coconut and breadfruit (both tree crops)—wherever they went. They also brought their domesticated animals, mainly chickens, pigs, and dogs. These fellow passengers helped them colonize a few hundred Pacific islands, most of which didn't offer abundant food. On islands with coastal

Polynesian Canoe This model of an eighteenth-century sailing canoe from Tonga greatly resembles the exploratory vessels used by Polynesians navigating the Pacific around 1200 BCE.

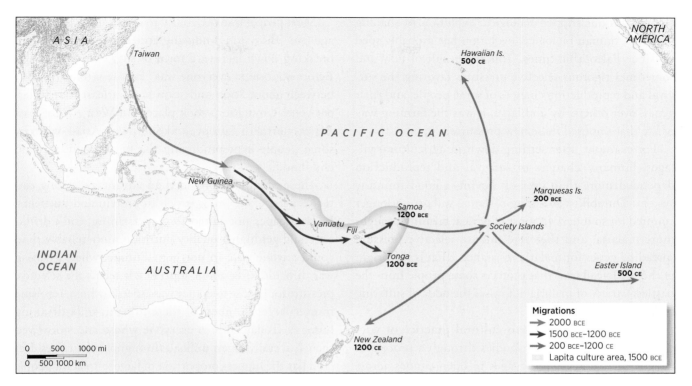

Pacific and Polynesian Migrations, ca. 2000 BCE–1200 CE Migrating in dugout canoes, small numbers of Pacific peoples spread out over immense distances, often heading out into the unknown, and settled hundreds of previously uninhabited islands. New Zealand acquired its first human population about 1200 CE, the last big place on Earth to be settled.

lagoons, Polynesians enjoyed an initial bonanza of fish and shellfish. After they depleted the lagoons, and where no lagoons were present, they farmed to survive.

THE DYNAMISM OF FARMING SOCIETY

The Indo-European, Bantu, and Polynesian migrations show the dynamism of farming populations. Their ways of life gave them certain characteristics that encouraged them to spread into lands that had no farmers or, in the case of the Polynesian islands, no people at all. First, their populations tended to grow and provide streams of young people seeking their futures. Second, at least in some cases such as the Bantu and malaria, they had disease resistance that others lacked, easing their migrations. Third, as farmers, they all had some combination of tools and skills that were previously absent in the lands to which they went. They had reasons to migrate and skills that enabled them to do so successfully.

It is also instructive to note that hunter-foragers did not migrate into terrain occupied by settled farming communities and somehow displace them. They didn't have the numbers and power to do so. Moreover, the Bantu speakers did not migrate into Egypt, which already had a dense network of farming villages; they moved into sparsely inhabited territory instead. The Polynesians didn't colonize the coasts of China, which already hosted farming communities; they risked voyages into the unknown instead. These farmer migrations thus extended the domain of farming into new lands and stretched the thin web of human interaction in new directions.

FARMING CULTURE AND HUMAN BIOLOGICAL EVOLUTION

One of the fascinating results of recent genetic research is evidence of just how fast the human animal has been evolving since the dawn of agriculture. While cultural change has outstripped biological evolution in shaping our lives, human biological evolution has probably sped up since Paleolithic times. This is a result of new and sometimes rigorous selective pressures favoring the survival and reproduction chances of some people, and their genes, over others. By and large, it was the farming way of life that imposed these new pressures.

For example, after settling down in agricultural villages, humans' chances of survival and reproduction depended more than ever on having a good immune system. Durability as a long-distance walker no longer counted for so much. In most of Africa, farming brought more malaria, and therefore intense selective pressure spreading genes for malaria resistance. That is the origin of the sickle-cell trait that protects some people from the nastiest variety of malaria but raises the odds of suffering from anemia.

Likewise, the Polynesian cultural practice of voyaging changed Polynesian bodies through a process of genetic selection. Long voyages in open canoes across empty ocean with little food may have favored those Polynesians with genes for thriftier metabolisms—more able to withstand the stresses of cold and hunger. This process of genetic selection may be connected to the high risk for diabetes among Polynesians today: a thrifty metabolism was useful for their ancestors but is no longer necessary now that food is easier to come by. The genetic adaptation carries costs without the former benefit.

Genes and culture affect one another: ever since the advent of farming, we have been remaking animals, ourselves, and our culture all at once, and faster than before. Geneticists now think there are hundreds of genetic mutations that spread in response to cultural shifts in the last 10,000 years. With village farming, people changed their environments and cultures, and indirectly changed themselves biologically. Let's look at some of the ways they did so.

CATTLE, MILK, AND LACTOSE TOLERANCE

Cattle domestication changed the human animal. It led to the emergence of the ability among some adult humans to digest animal milk. About one-third of the world's adults today can digest milk.

Most people lose the ability to digest milk after about age five. They stop producing an enzyme that assists in breaking down lactose, a form of sugar found in milk. Before 8000 BCE, everyone was "lactose intolerant." But between about 8000 and 5000 BCE, at least four different genetic mutations took place—in West Africa, East Africa, northern Europe, and Southwest Asia—whereby some people kept producing the key enzyme beyond childhood.

These mutations provided an advantage among cattle keepers. Cows' milk is rich in protein and nutrients. In landscapes not suited to crop farming, milk drinkers could get higher quality nutrition more reliably than could anyone else. In northern Europe, where farming was difficult, after about 3000 BCE it seems the selective pressure for lactose tolerance was especially high, resulting in ever larger numbers of these mutant, milk-drinking humans. Today, almost everyone whose ancestors lived there can easily digest milk all throughout their lives. Ireland has the highest proportion of lactose-tolerant people anywhere in the world.

Mutations among cattle keepers in Africa achieved the same effect. In parts of East Africa, most people whose ancestors had kept cattle can digest milk as adults. In West Africa's Sahel, some pastoral peoples also have high proportions of lactose-tolerant adults. In both East Africa and the West African Sahel, where water is often scarce, milk drinking was useful not only for nutrition but also for avoiding dehydration.

Raising Cattle A rock art painting from Somaliland in East Africa shows a person milking a cow. East Africa was one of the key regions where lactose tolerance and cattle keeping helped people to survive in challenging environments.

People who developed lactose tolerance avoided some nasty waterborne diseases too. Cattle, camels, sheep, and goats can absorb moisture from the grasses they eat, drink water swimming with microbes that would make humans sick, and then turn all that into a healthful liquid for humans. They are water purifiers.

The lactose-tolerance mutations were so advantageous that they spread everywhere people kept cattle, and to some extent where they kept camels, sheep, and goats. The most recent of the mutations permitting milk-drinking adults took place in Southwest Asia, perhaps Arabia, after 3000 BCE, and probably only after the domestication of camels (whose milk is also good to drink). People in Central Asia, where keeping sheep and goats was common, today show a moderate rate of lactose tolerance. Most of them can easily digest cheese and yogurt, which have less lactose than milk. But in East and Southeast Asia, southern Europe, and most parts of Africa, none of these mutations spread widely, so adults didn't drink milk. In the Americas, where early people had no domesticated animals other than dogs, there was no advantage to lactose tolerance at all.

The history of milk drinking is a case of ongoing genetic change in the human population in response to human culture. An innovation in culture—cattle keeping—opened the way to an innovation in the human genome, and each reinforced the other: the more lactose tolerant people became, the more likely people were to keep cattle and drink milk; and the more they kept cattle, the stronger the selection became for lactose-tolerance genes. By the standards of genetic shifts, this one swept through human populations very quickly—in just a few thousand years, suggesting strong advantages for milk drinkers in environments good for cattle.

Milk drinkers are not the only ones whose bodies adjusted to new dietary possibilities that resulted from cultural changes. At some time in the past 15,000 years, residents of the Arctic, people known as Inuit, developed a genetic mutation that allows them to metabolize quantities of whale, seal, and fish meat, which are rich with fatty acids, and yet keep their bloodstreams free of unhealthy levels of those fatty acids. Their migration into places such as northern Canada and Greenland, in which there was precious little to eat other than fish and whale blubber, created a strong selective pressure favoring the spread of

Herd Animals Different regions and peoples domesticated different animals, but all those animals could provide humans with milk, meat, skins, and other by-products. Here an illustration of a grazing goat decorates a Sumerian clay tablet from around 2500 BCE.

this adaption, which is rare in other human communities. Once again, cultural change dovetailed with biological change in human bodies.

HORSE DOMESTICATION

The domestication of horses, like the emergence of lactose tolerance, opened new spaces to denser human settlement. As with the earlier domestication of dogs, this one proved to be a durable partnership. Humans deliberately selected for preferred characteristics in horses. When they succeeded in genetically altering horses so as to make them useful to human societies, they—unintentionally—created a cultural selection for societies that were good at managing horses.

Wild horses live in small groups with one stallion, five to seven mares, and their young offspring. Mares routinely accept guidance from stallions or lead mares. Stallions, in contrast, are uncooperative and violent. Genetic evidence shows that today's tame horses are descended from many mares but from very few, perhaps only one, stallion. Taming mares wasn't so difficult: they usually accept human

Horse-Rider Partnership A fourth-millennium BCE cave painting found in present-day Algeria shows a confrontation between a swordsman on horseback and a spearman on foot. Societies that had horses held military advantages over those that did not.

guidance willingly. Taming a wild stallion took extreme courage and persistence.

Horse domestication probably happened somewhere on the grassy steppes between the Black and Caspian Seas around 4800 BCE. The reason people tried to tame horses initially was to eat them or to drink their milk and blood. People ensured that the most docile and obedient mares had the most offspring; and as a result, over hundreds of generations horses grew tamer and easier to control.

Horses are much better than cattle or sheep at surviving hard winters because they will paw at snow to find grass and will kick through ice to get water. On the chilly steppes, herds of horses were more reliable food sources than flocks of sheep or herds of cattle, which couldn't survive the winters if not carefully fed by humans. A cold snap on the steppe lasting a few centuries around the period 4200–3800 BCE might have helped spread the practice of domesticating horses.

Eating horses allowed people to survive cold winters, but riding horses allowed them to do much more. By 3500 BCE at the latest, people on the steppes had learned to ride horses, launching a partnership at least as important as the earlier one with dogs. The curious fact that horses and humans can sweat profusely, which no other animals can, meant they were made for each other. Horse and rider can exercise for hours on end without overheating, even in warm climates.

The advantages of riding for horsemen were tremendous. Horsemen could herd two or three times as many sheep or cattle as could someone on foot, and could also hunt much more efficiently. They could steal animals and abduct women and children from rival groups more easily. After 2500 BCE, where grass was abundant and horses thrived—which at this time meant much of western and central Eurasia—no human group could last long without becoming skilled riders and horse-breeders. People who exploited the economic and military potential of the horse managed to amass wealth and power on a scale formerly impossible. The rise of the horse-rider partnership led to the rise of greater social stratification, which is evident in changes in goods buried in the graves of prominent men.

The importance of horses goes further. Before horse domestication, the steppe grasslands posed a daunting challenge to people, like seas before sailboats. On foot, people could scarcely hope to find enough food and water to cross the sea of grass. Domesticated horses made the steppe accessible—indeed, they transformed it from a barrier to a highway, just as sailboats did to seas. Transport and travel on these grasslands ultimately brought all the cultures of Eurasia and North Africa into contact with one another, forming a giant web, as we shall see in some detail. So the genetic changes in horses as they became domesticated, and attendant cultural change in horse-using societies, altered the patterns of world history.

NEW ECOSYSTEMS, NEW SPECIES

In addition to changing the human genome and human culture, farming and herding changed the planet. Early farmers, we must remember, inherited environments already in flux. Their ancestors had used fire liberally to clear forest and had probably spearheaded the accidental extinction of many large mammals everywhere they went. On top of those human-induced environmental alterations, climate shifts led to vegetation changes. Thanks to the warming after the last ice age, early farmers faced a world of expanding forests, shrinking ice caps, and disappearing tundra—although all these changes came so slowly that no one understood what was afoot.

Against this background of both natural environmental change and the ongoing alterations caused by hunter-foragers, early farmers added their weight to the balance. Through domestication, they created several new species of plants and animals, as we've seen. Herding and farming meant spreading these chosen species far and wide at the expense of others, now considered weeds and pests.

In other words, farmers and herders created new ecosystems—pastures and farmlands—as well as new species. Tame cattle and sheep roamed over far greater spaces than their wild forerunners ever did. Maize, rice, and other cereals also covered far more space than their wild predecessors had.

Early farmers, without plows and draft animals, found grasslands too difficult to cultivate. They preferred riverbanks, lake edges, or cleared forestland. Across Eurasia, early farmers gradually cleared forests in river floodplains, using fire and axe. They also cleared patches here and there in deep forests. Once they harnessed strong animals, such as oxen or water buffalo, and invented plows (around 3800 BCE), farmers found it worthwhile to farm heavy or damp soils. Early farmers also assaulted forests in the Americas and sub-Saharan Africa. In both settings, they typically either practiced shifting cultivation in forest zones or used the soft soils of riverbanks.

The environmental impacts of early farmers were surely of greater scale than that of hunters and foragers in the vicinity of villages, where fields were cleared, fuelwood gathered, and domestic animals grazed. But the environmental consequences of early agriculture, before cities and states, were small compared to what was yet to come.

THE EMERGENCE OF CITIES, STATES, AND COMPLEX SOCIETIES AFTER 3500 BCE

The advent of farming also made possible the emergence of new political forms and much bigger social units, which brought still more radical changes in turn. This section explains the emergence of cities and states, first created during the fourth millennium BCE and still with us today. They became the social contexts in which more and more people lived, and which produced ever more ideas, technologies, and other forces shaping human history. Their emergence was simultaneous with what social scientists call complex society. The development of all

three—complex society, states, and cities—accelerated the building of larger webs of interconnection.

WHAT ARE CITIES, STATES, AND COMPLEX SOCIETIES?

These three related innovations in the structure of societies shaped world history from 3500 BCE onward. They require some definitions. **Complex society**, in the language of the social sciences, means a large-scale social unit with an elaborate division of labor, pronounced social hierarchy, hundreds of different social roles that people can fill, and institutions to regulate exchanges among individuals and among groups. Every society, even a hunting and foraging band, is *complicated*, with intricate networks of social relations; but in this specialized sense, not every society is *complex*. Complex societies usually developed together with states and cities.

A **state** is a territorial unit and political community with a formal government. States are easy to identify. They employ office-holders who govern according to set rules (bureaucrats), specialists in the administration of justice (judges), and masters of the arts of violence (soldiers). States claim for themselves a monopoly on the legitimate use of violence. They extract goods, labor, or money from a subject population through taxes and conscription. States, except for the most nakedly coercive, also have ideologies—sets of ideas that justify their existence and operations. State ideologies have typically been based in religion. An effective ideology can enable the rulers of a state to harness the willing support of their population, without frequent resort to coercion.

It's not easy to draw a sharp line separating a city from a town or big village. But in general, a **city** contains the elaborate division of labor and social hierarchy of complex society, and it is distinguished by dense living quarters, open public spaces, and imposing public buildings. Cities feature trade and exchange, and institutions—usually, markets—that bring buyers and sellers together. Villages, at least big ones, may have some of these features, but never all.

Cities are central to world history because they are hothouses of innovation and exchange. They are the densest parts of interactive webs. In cities, unlike villages, people regularly dealt with strangers, provoking adoption and diffusion of new techniques, technologies, and ways of thinking. The dense living quarters of cities also facilitated the faster exchange and evolution of disease organisms.

As we've seen, by 7000 BCE a world of farming, herding, and villages had begun to emerge in Eurasia and Africa. A parallel world would soon emerge in the Americas, although without herding. In all of these villages, scores or hundreds of people living side by side experienced life very much as their neighbors did. They all took part in the tasks of agricultural life. Aside from roles specified by age and gender, there was little economic specialization or social stratification. Exchanges took place, as in all societies, but were usually a matter of reciprocal gifts rather than market transactions. This was not complex society.

In 3500 BCE, the world had no cities. Then, in six places around the world, something new evolved: urban life and complex society. These six places were Mesopotamia, Egypt, the Indus valley, China, Mesoamerica, and the Andes. Two of these places, Egypt and the Indus valley, may have acquired some of the habits of complex society from neighbors—specifically, Mesopotamia. But for the most part, these were all autonomous transformations. Every other complex society in the history of the world derives, directly or indirectly, from one or more of these original six. By 1500 BCE, the world contained hundreds of cities. Only 1 to 2 percent of the human population lived in cities, but the most powerful people did.

In the chapters to come, we'll explore these complex societies in greater detail. Here let's consider three widely shared aspects of early complex societies: (1) their underlying economic base, especially irrigation agriculture; (2) the social and political implications of cities and states; and (3), two basic tools that shaped the development of cities and states—writing and metallurgy.

ECONOMIC BASES OF EARLY COMPLEX SOCIETIES

The development of complex societies depended on farmers growing more food than they needed so that other people—soldiers, artisans, bureaucrats, and priests who did not produce food—could eat.

PLOW AGRICULTURE Where people had domesticated strong animals, they could use them to pull heavy things. Oxen and water buffalo—the tractors of the pre-modern world—proved especially adept at pulling

Oxen and Plows A painting on the wall of an Egyptian tomb shows a farmer driving oxen, which pull a plow to till the soil—one of the many innovations that enabled Egyptians to practice agriculture in an arid climate.

plows through the soil. The earliest plows came into use soon after 3800 BCE in Mesopotamia. They quickly appeared in Egypt too, and possibly in China—estimated dates for the advent of **plow agriculture** in northern China range from 3000 to 500 BCE. Chinese plows differed enough in design from those used in Southwest Asia that many scholars think they were independently invented.

The first plows were made of wood, suitable only for soft ground. They scratched a shallow furrow in the soil, preparing it for planting. But they allowed farmers to cultivate up to five times as much land as they could without oxen and plows. Soon plows acquired metal tips, and later metal plowshares, which turned soil over, uprooted weeds, and brought deep-seated nutrients to the soil surface. These plows could work heavier soils, including ones moistened by irrigation. Whether by diffusion or by independent invention, between 3500 and 1500 BCE, plows became routine farm equipment in North Africa and Eurasia.

But in sub-Saharan Africa, Australia, and all of the Americas, there were no plows until much later—in most cases, because there were no animals suited to pulling them. Instead, farmers used hoes or digging sticks. On steep, rugged terrain, digging sticks worked better than plows. Without plow agriculture, it was harder for farmers to generate enough surplus food to support city life and complex society. Where this developed without plows, as in Mesoamerica, Peru, and along the bend in the Niger River in Africa, the needed surplus came from intensive human labor and irrigation.

IRRIGATION Among the perennial hazards of farming are drought and flood. Providing crops just the right amount of water at just the right times was at first a matter of luck. No doubt the earliest farmers quickly learned to carry water-filled skins or pots to their crops. But big fields required **irrigation**—that is, the construction of artificial channels to carry water from lakes, rivers, or streams to thirsty crops.

We don't know when or where irrigation began. Some patchy evidence from the Levant and northern Mesopotamia suggests the presence of small irrigation works before 7000 BCE. But irrigation remained small-scale until about 3500 BCE, after which it appeared, via diffusion and independent invention, in suitable zones throughout Eurasia and North Africa. In the Americas, it began around 1900 BCE. The technologies of canals, ditches, dikes, and dams were simple enough in principle even if laborious to build, so it's plausible that irrigation emerged independently in many places.

Irrigation had dramatic consequences. First, it raised per-acre yields by five or ten times. With this enormous expansion of farming productivity, the world's food now increasingly came from a few pockets of irrigated farmland, surrounded by much less productive zones of rain-fed farming and herding, and by even broader zones where people collected and hunted food rather than growing it. Lands suitable for irrigation became distinctive, a new sort of agro-ecology capable of feeding far more mouths than any other landscapes on Earth. Irrigated landscapes not only raised grain yields but also served as nutritious aquariums swimming with fish, frogs, snails, and other protein-packed delicacies. In particular, irrigation produced abundant *surplus* food, enabling societies to support far more people who specialized in other things, from pottery to philosophy.

Second, even as successful irrigation fed many more mouths, it also needed many hands. Digging and maintaining canals, ditches, and reservoirs, and building dikes and dams, took enormous coordinated effort on a scale beyond what families alone could provide. Families and neighbors had to band together to build irrigation systems and make collective decisions on who would do what and when. Most irrigation schemes began as grassroots efforts, but over time religious and political authorities, and also rich landowners, usually stepped in to coordinate the necessary tasks. The greater the degree of coordination achieved, the larger the scale irrigation could attain. So irrigation favored the emergence of religious and political leaders, and in turn, successful leaders favored the extension of irrigation. Where irrigation prevailed, it co-evolved with social complexity: neither was a necessary pre-condition for the other, but each encouraged the development of the other.

Everywhere it developed, irrigation farming raised yields, generating surplus food that supported denser populations and more specialists. These were the conditions for the emergence of cities. Almost every early city was fed by irrigation agriculture.

DRAWBACKS OF IRRIGATION FARMING Along with its role in shaping social development, irrigation brought great vulnerabilities. Enemy armies, even a band of brigands, could easily destroy dikes and dams, ruining fields and starving those dependent on their bounty. Moreover, large-scale irrigation rested on the sustained cooperation of thousands of laborers—a fragile thing. Whenever that cooperation broke down, irrigation systems fell to ruin in short order through lack of maintenance. Societies dependent on the food surpluses delivered by irrigation agriculture became vulnerable to interruptions in the production and delivery of that surplus. In a loose way, we can liken the adoption of irrigation to modern societies' adoption of oil as their principal fuel: both technologies allowed enormous expansion of economic activity, the production of more and cheaper food, and therefore larger populations. But both added new sources of vulnerability as well.

With respect to human health, irrigation carried additional risks. Irrigated landscapes invited certain diseases, such as schistosomiasis, which is spread by snails, and malaria, which is spread by anopheles mosquitoes. People who engaged in irrigation agriculture in Eurasia and Africa probably carried heavier parasite loads and hosted more infections than anyone else, and consequently often couldn't work at full strength. In the Americas, where neither schistosomiasis nor malaria existed until much later, any health penalty of irrigation was much smaller.

ENVIRONMENTAL IMPACTS The most significant environmental impact of plowing and irrigation was on the soil. Animal-drawn plows enabled people to slice deeper into the earth. Upturned and loosened soil eroded easily. Over centuries and millennia, wherever people engaged in plow farming they suffered problems of soil erosion and nutrient loss. The process of soil erosion was highly visible and could be combated to a degree by measures such as building terraces. Nutrient loss was invisible but sometimes happened fast enough that people could see the result in the form of lower yields within their lifetimes. They typically understood this as the land becoming "tired," which led ancient farmers to seek ways to renew soil fertility.

The most effective solution to nutrient loss was the use of manure on fields. Where farmers had livestock, they could graze their animals on nearby pastures, pen them at night, collect their manure, and spread it on fields. In effect, this strategy collected nutrients from a broad area and concentrated them where they did the most good for humans—one of the chief contributions to human welfare made by livestock. Where farmers didn't have animals, as in Mesoamerica, or had few, as in East Asia, they relied more on "night soil," or human excrement, as fertilizer. Another attempted solution was prayer: most early farmers, and most irrigation-based societies, worshipped earth deities whose portfolios included soil fertility. These were usually goddesses, such as Bhumi in India or Brigid in Ireland.

Irrigation agriculture brought damaging salinization of soils. Irrigation with poor drainage—which describes most irrigation—left soils waterlogged and brought dissolved salts up to the surface. As water evaporated from the soil surface, the salt content remained. Where waterlogging was common and evaporation intense, accumulated salt in topsoil layers eventually created white crusts. Only a few plants, and no useful crops, can flourish in salt-encrusted soils. In the *Epic of Gilgamesh*, a long narrative poem written around 2100 BCE in Mesopotamia, the gods turn soils white, perhaps a reference to salt encrustation.

The emergence of cities introduced a new peril to farm soils. In village agriculture, nutrients traveled from soil to plants to people and back to the soil again in a fairly closed system. Few nutrients disappeared altogether in the process. Cities, however, imported nutrients in food but didn't necessarily return them to farmers' fields. Most cities were built on rivers, which operated as convenient sewers carrying excrement and its soil nutrients to the sea. As a result, cities threatened to undermine the systems of agriculture and nutrient flows that supported urban life itself.

CITIES AND STATES AS SOCIAL SYSTEMS

Irrigation farming fed the growth of cities, and growing cities made new social orders possible. Where tens of thousands of people clustered together, they developed specialized skills and institutions that helped them live together in peace. Cities needed institutions to administer justice, oversee defense and war against outsiders, organize taxation, and manage other aspects of public affairs, often through organized religion.

SOCIAL INEQUALITY City life made social inequalities larger and more visible. In villages populated by farm families, status was based mainly on age, gender, individual achievement, and sometimes ancestry. In cities, there were added layers of stratification based on wealth, occupation, and social class.

Social Stratification City life led to a proliferation of social roles and hierarchies. A Mesopotamian stone carving from around 2600 to 2300 BCE shows many laborers preparing and serving a feast to some dignitaries, who eat while being entertained by musicians (bottom left).

Why Do Humans Behave Like Ants?

One of the puzzles of world history is why human beings put up with the demands of complex society when it's not in our nature—our genetic makeup—to live such regimented lives. Termites, bees, and ants live in complex societies. In fact, their societies are more complex than ours were for 99 percent of human history. Let's just consider ants, a biologically successful life form that currently accounts for about 10 percent of the animal biomass on Earth: until a few decades ago, the total ant population outweighed the total human population.

It is in the nature of ants to live regimented lives in hierarchical societies. Ants live in colonies of some 5 million inhabitants and cooperate in their social roles. They domesticate insects called aphids, which digest plants that ants cannot and produce "honeydew" (actually, aphid excreta), which ants eat. When a colony moves, it carries its aphid livestock with it. Ants even farm fungi for their own food supply. Ant colonies also display a division of labor. There are food-collector and food-producer ants, warrior ants, and ants responsible for raising the young. And there is one ant, the queen, whose job is to give birth.

Humans are programmed genetically to behave more or less like chimpanzees. But since the rise of complex societies 5,500 years ago, we have programmed ourselves culturally to behave more like ants. We started to live in big social groups that cooperate to achieve things no individual could. We began to specialize in chores such as producing food or fighting. We started to domesticate other species to expand our food supply. We grew to accept that most of us will labor long and hard for little reward, and will support a tiny minority who need not work.

We are not ants, but our social behavior since adopting farming and forming complex society is much more ant-like than chimp-like. Ants behave like ants naturally. Humans have adopted habits, ideologies, religions, rituals, and institutions—in a word, culture—that allow us to suppress our inner chimpanzee and behave instead like ants.

QUESTIONS FOR DISCUSSION

1. What's your view of the comparison of human social behavior to that of ants?
2. Give an example of how our culture prepares us to accept the social specialization and inequality of complex society.

Early cities typically had a ruling elite of specialists in government, religion, and commerce; they worked mainly with their thinking and communication skills, not with their hands. Beneath this elite stood a class of people who worked with skilled hands—smiths, carpenters, builders, stonemasons, potters, weavers, spinners, brewers, and musicians. Many in these latter occupations were women. Cities typically also had a class of unskilled male laborers who worked with their backs—stevedores, cart-pullers, animal drovers, water-carriers. Sharing the lower rungs of the social ladder were people who worked with disagreeable materials—handling manure or night soil, or tanning animal hides. Almost all early cities also had slaves, most of whom did manual labor. Some slaves had skills that enabled them to work as smiths or even scribes—specialists in writing, an honored occupation in mostly illiterate societies. Cities also normally had an underclass of people without regular work—beggars, thieves, and prostitutes. An elaborate social hierarchy like this posed

acute problems of social harmony, which officials in government and religion strove to solve.

DISEASE Early cities were also cesspools of filth and infection that killed people faster than others were born. Only continuing in-migration from villages kept cities from shrinking. Disposing of human and animal excrement, carcasses of dead animals, residues from tanneries, offal from butcher shops, and other unhealthy wastes threatened human health. Few cities had clean water supplies, and all teemed with pathogens preying on tightly packed human populations.

Crowd diseases in particular afflicted cities, and especially networks of interacting cities. These infections, mostly derived from diseases of herd animals, need big populations to stay in circulation because the pathogens provoke immunity in people who survive a bout. Crowd diseases such as the smallpox, mumps, and pertussis viruses became childhood diseases when circulating in large populations. Interconnected cities had enough people, in frequent enough face-to-face (to be more precise, breath-to-breath) contact, to maintain perpetual circulation of lethal infections. Everyone encountered these infections in childhood, and those who survived became immune or resistant. A society needed several hundred thousand people regularly breathing in one another's germs to make them endemic (always present) rather than epidemic (infrequently present). These diseases took a terrible toll on children.

Crowd diseases made cities, as well as complex societies of interlinked cities, extremely dangerous not only for their own children but also for adults who had grown up in more isolated places. In demographically smaller societies, with less breath-to-breath exchange of viruses, these infections were usually absent. That was good for the survival of children; but when these infections appeared as epidemics, they killed adults and children alike—a catastrophe. In this way, interacting networks of cities, if they contained enough people, were reservoirs of lethal infections that at any time could leak out into surrounding smaller communities and cause epidemics.

ENSLAVED LABOR These characteristics of cities meant that complex societies constantly needed more laborers. They needed them to toil in the fields that fed the cities and to do the most disagreeable jobs in the cities themselves. To meet the demand, the rulers of states normally resorted to enslaving people within reach who didn't have the means to defend themselves. Or they organized slave trades, buying people from more distant lands who had been captured to meet the need for labor. Most cities and states thus gave rise to violent slaving frontiers, either just beyond their own borders or farther afield. After the rise of cities and states, the hunting and foraging peoples of the world, and stateless farmers too, lived in greater fear of capture and enslavement. For self-defense, they retreated into mountain forests, deserts, and swamps, where slave raiders and slave traders would not easily find them.

THE EMERGENCE OF STATES AND RULERS

The world had no states before 3500 BCE but scores of them by 1500 BCE. Wherever dense populations existed—mainly in lands of irrigation agriculture—opportunistic, forceful, and charismatic people saw the chance to set themselves up as rulers. In order to succeed they needed the means to reward followers and intimidate others, and in order to stay successful they needed an ideology to convince people that it was right that some should toil while others did not. Effective ideologies normally consisted of claims to divine status for rulers or to their special power as intermediaries to the gods or ancestors.

Divine Kings A seal from Babylon, dated to around 900 BCE, shows the legendary Mesopotamian king Gilgamesh holding a lion above his head, testifying to the supernatural strength that the gods were said to have given him.

Most early states were monarchies. Kings, and occasionally queens, made the final decisions on important matters. Bureaucrats and soldiers carried out royal commands. To retain the loyalty of these agents of royal power, kings had to show themselves worthy of their thrones. They had to reward bureaucrats and soldiers with food, goods, war booty, or captives. They had to claim royal ancestry, because kingship was always hereditary. Kingship was also always sacred. Kings typically professed to be the sons of gods and always claimed divine support, if not divine powers. They officiated at religious rituals, which were often sacrifices (of animals or humans), emphasizing that sacred and political authority were one and the same. Kings and their households showed off their power and wealth through displays of stunning jewelry and art, fancy clothes, and magnificent palaces.

As of 1500 BCE, no more than 2 percent of the globe's land surface was controlled by states. But owing largely to irrigation agriculture, perhaps half of the world's population lived in areas controlled, or partly controlled, by states. Over time, more and more states emerged because people without a state needed one to protect them from conquest and enslavement by existing states.

THE DEVELOPMENT OF WRITING Almost all complex societies developed writing as a means of preserving and transmitting information. The development of

Early Writing One of the earliest known examples of writing for the purposes of accounting comes from Mesopotamia. This tablet, dated to around 3200 BCE, contains pictographic symbols that correspond to specific quantities of certain goods—including, perhaps, cereal grains such as wheat.

writing—a system of abstract images to represent either the countless ideas that can pass through human minds, or the many sounds that human voices can make—was a major human achievement. Yet people had managed without it for more than 200,000 years. Writing—like telephones, email, and Facebook—is a networked technology of little use to anyone until other people are using it too. So how and why did writing develop?

The answer lies in the demands of complex society. The first customers for information stored in writing were states and merchants. States that depended on thousands of inhabitants to pay taxes needed a way to monitor and record who had paid and who hadn't. Merchants needed writing to track their numerous transactions and debts.

Whatever the format and whatever its original purpose, writing proved to be fundamental to history over the past 5,000 years. Writing and reading made possible much faster accumulation of knowledge and, indeed, the creation of new knowledge and belief. A reasonable case can be made that writing is the second most important innovation, after agriculture, since the origins of language. In later chapters, we'll examine specific features of writing as it developed in Mesopotamia, Egypt, China, India, and Mesoamerica.

METALLURGY Another important tool that played a role in state making was **metallurgy**—the working of metal ores first into metals and then into useful objects. The important metals for this chapter are copper and bronze; iron had revolutionary effects in Eurasia and Africa, but only after 1500 BCE. In the Americas and Oceania, metallurgy remained of trivial importance until far later, after 1500 CE.

All metals come from the earth, and most are chemically or physically bound up with rock in ores. They require processing, often smelting with fire, to separate metal from rock. Smiths used high temperatures to make metals pliable enough to hammer into useful shapes. They applied even greater heat to melt metals into liquid that could be poured into molds. To generate heat, they burned wood or charcoal in enclosed spaces called forges. Smiths also learned how to combine metals into useful alloys. Smiths were highly skilled men—there is no evidence of female smiths until recent centuries.

The earliest evidence of metalworking comes from the Paleolithic, but metals weren't important anywhere until about 6000 BCE. The first smelting operations on a large scale occurred, remarkably, in southern Mesopotamia, a region with no useful ores and not much wood for fuel. Soon after 6000 BCE, smelting developed elsewhere in Southwest Asia and in southeastern Europe, mainly in upland regions where both ores and wood were abundant. Copper, tin, and lead were among the easiest metals to work. Ötzi the Iceman, to judge by chemical analysis of his hair, lived some of his life around copper smelters in the Alps.

Metallurgy acquired much greater importance at about 3500 BCE, when smiths in Mesopotamia started to make **bronze**, an alloy of copper and tin. Bronze was a harder metal than any yet in use, good for axes, armor, and weapons as well as ornamentation. Since tin and copper aren't generally found together, bronze making always involved long-distance trade of tin, much the rarer of the two metals. So bronze was always expensive and became a favorite ornament of the

Metalworking Ötzi the Iceman was found carrying a copper axe, evidence that the people he lived among used smelting techniques to process copper ore.

Using Bronze A display of bronze knives found in present-day Iran, and dated to around 2000 to 1000 BCE, represents only a small range of the many items that could be made from the versatile and durable material. Knives could serve as tools, as weapons, or as luxury items to signify status.

rich and powerful. By 2000 BCE, bronze-making skills had spread widely in Eurasia and North Africa.

Bronze quickly became important to states and rulers. It made much better weaponry than stone or any other available metal. Those who could control its supply held a military advantage over everyone else. Most early states in Eurasia struggled to acquire the tin and copper needed to make bronze weapons and armor. They set out either to conquer upland regions where the ores were found or to establish trade links. Few states without bronze could survive for long anywhere near others that had it. Bronze in Eurasia was a bit like fire, language, and farming everywhere: those with it enjoyed advantages over those without it, and those without it either acquired it, were conquered, or fled from those who had it.

THE TWIN CHALLENGES OF COMPLEX SOCIETY

In Chapter 2, we tried to account for the emergence of agriculture at least seven times between 11,000 and 4000 BCE after more than 200,000 years without it. The appearance of complex society presents a broadly similar problem. It arose independently in at least four places, and probably

six: Mesopotamia, Egypt, the Indus valley, China, Mesoamerica, and the Andes. In all these places, it came several thousand years after a transition to agriculture. And in each case, complex society shared many of the same features: irrigation agriculture, cities, markets, states, monumental architecture, armies, and bureaucracies. Almost all shared kingship, writing, and metallurgy too.

Could it be accidental that such a similar sociotechnological package evolved a few millennia after each transition to agriculture? It can't be inevitable: people practiced farming for millennia in most of sub-Saharan Africa and North America without proceeding to develop cities, states, or writing. But it's also not random—not by a long shot. Complex societies showed so much uniformity because they all faced two main challenges: attack by neighbors and civil strife within. They all had to develop practices, beliefs, technologies, and institutions to equip themselves to address these two problems.

THREATS FROM WITHOUT AND WITHIN Defense against unfriendly neighbors, whether skilled and violent horsemen or organized in a state with an army, was a matter of survival for complex societies. To create the means of protection, complex societies generally organized as states. Kingship, armies, metallurgy, and other practices—even writing—contributed directly to the goal of self-protection. Ideologies of social solidarity, religious emphasis on fertility, and technologies of irrigation agriculture contributed indirectly to a society's ability to defend itself.

The other main problem for complex societies was conspicuous social inequality. The quest for status may be innate among humans, as it is among chimpanzees; but simple human societies, as we've seen, are relatively egalitarian. In complex society, however, the difference between kings and slaves was much greater than the difference between leaders and followers in any hunting-foraging band or village—or chimpanzee troop. This chasm expanded the scope for envy, jealousy, rivalry, division, and conflict within any given society.

All complex societies that endured developed cultures that persuaded people to accept, even if only resentfully, enormous inequalities. (In later chapters, we'll examine some of these cultures in detail.) Religions played the leading role in convincing the toiling masses that it was proper that they should sweat and suffer while others lived in comfort. They justified kingship and elite power, keys to the survival of such unequal societies. To be sure, soldiers used violence (or threats of violence) when needed to keep the masses in line and societies stable. Architects designed awe-inspiring monuments to remind everyone of rulers' authority. Rituals and ceremonies of social solidarity, including examples of public generosity on the part of elites, also helped to keep the lid on.

The twin problems of complex societies were closely related. To be strong in the face of threats from neighbors required some measure of inequality because rulers needed to equip and train warriors—which, if it required expensive equipment, made for a social structure with warrior elites. But too much inequality could become a source of weakness and division: the downtrodden might welcome defeat at the hand of outsiders on the theory that nothing could be worse than the rulers they had. This helps to account for the unstable nature of politics in most examples of complex society: states and dynasties came and went even if the underlying structures of societies remained much the same. States lasted longest, by and large, when and where effective ideologies united elites and commoners and on those occasions when and where trade, technology, or conquest allowed a society to enjoy an expanding economic pie.

THE FIRST BIG, FAINT WEBS

By 5000 BCE, if not before, village farmers made up most of humanity. There were still hunter-foragers, of course, and in areas inhospitable to farming—deserts, steppes, and dense forest zones—they might well have outnumbered farmers at that time. But globally, farmers accounted for ever larger numbers and spread their ways with each passing century. As the world became dotted with farming villages and inhabited by ever more people, it knitted itself together into interactive webs faster than before.

TRADE AND TECHNOLOGY

Although villages could be self-sufficient for a time, producing their own food, fuel, and other basic commodities, most could not always do so. To acquire commodities beyond the basics, many villages linked to one another, and sometimes to distant sources of high-value goods, like the obsidian of Çatalhöyük or the salt of Jericho.

Precious goods might be traded, one village to the next, over distances of hundreds of miles. For example, a farming center in the lower Indus valley region, Mehrgargh, acquired shells from the Persian Gulf and turquoise from Central Asia as early as 6000 BCE.

Trading Luxury Goods The elephant shown here was carved of the rare stone lapis lazuli and mined in Afghanistan. The trade of this valuable commodity extended across Southwest Asia into North Africa.

WHEELED CARTS Trade in bulk goods was limited to easily navigable rivers and coastlines until someone invented the wheel. The earliest evidence of wheels and axles dates to around 3500 BCE and turns up in several places more or less at once—Poland, the Balkans, the Caucasus, and Mesopotamia. It's possible that people re-invented the wheel shortly after it was invented, or the technology may have spread quickly because it was so useful. Oxen pulling wheeled carts could move ten times the load that a beast of burden might carry. By 3000 BCE, people on the steppes of western Eurasia probably lived in animal-drawn wheeled carts—the first mobile homes. On flat land, oxcarts became a crucial technology, smoothing movement and exchange. In rugged lands, the wheel had little use. Its invention and spread, therefore, contributed to the unevenness of the Eurasian economy: a boon to level lands, especially the clusters of villages in the already well-populated floodplains of Mesopotamia, Egypt, and the Indus, but of no value in hilly country.

DONKEY CARAVANS At about the same time that the wheel made its debut, people in Southwest Asia and Egypt started transporting goods in donkey caravans. Although much less efficient on flat land than wheeled transport, strings of donkeys could navigate uneven terrain. They helped to link uplands, where timber and useful ores were more common, to the more densely populated lowlands. By and large, pack animal transport developed earlier and more fully in Southwest Asia than anywhere else. In East and Southeast Asia, river transport loomed larger. In Africa south of the Sahara, river transport and human porterage proved more practical than beasts of burden, which suffered heavily there from a livestock disease. In the Americas, there were no suitable beasts of burden outside the Andes, where llama caravans played much the same role that donkey caravans did in Southwest Asia.

Pack Animals A herd of llamas decorate the walls of a cave (ca. 2000 BCE) in the mountains of Chile. The art may have been created by the herders who domesticated llamas and used them as beasts of burden in the hilly terrain.

Beyond these economic links, villagers interacted with their neighbors in nearby settlements through regular festivals and ceremonies, and at times in efforts to defend themselves against invaders from afar. Families sought marriage partners for sons and daughters in neighboring communities—it was always prudent to have kinfolk a day or two away in case something went wrong in one's own village. So for social as well as economic reasons, villages formed ever tighter, if tiny, webs of interaction with neighboring villages.

THE FIRST REGIONAL WEBS

The first regional webs in Eurasia and North Africa began to appear by around 5000 BCE, even before cities and states. Rivers were central to this web-building process. Water transport, even on mere rafts or canoes, was far cheaper than on land. The frequency of interactions with distant villages was far greater for people living along navigable rivers. Where these rivers linked up to seaborne transport networks and to local overland routes, villages became especially interactive and interconnected. Examples of such locations include the mouth of the Nile in Egypt and the Tigris-Euphrates in southern Mesopotamia.

Two technological developments soon spurred on the development of regional webs in Eurasia and Egypt. The first was the combination of horse domestication and the wheel, which gradually made it easier to transit broad grasslands after 3500 BCE. The second occurred by roughly 3000 BCE, when people from the Persian Gulf to the Pacific began to learn how to use sails efficiently, making seaborne and upstream river-borne transport more practical. It took many more centuries for people to learn the best routes and the ideal ways to rig sailing vessels. These two technological changes eased human trade and travel in Eurasia and North Africa, and helped prepare the way for bigger, thicker, regional webs to form—as we will see in later chapters.

After 3000 BCE, writing as well as transport technologies eased the development of regional webs. Record keeping enabled merchants to operate more reliably over long distances by keeping track of who owed how many bolts of cloth or baskets of rice. And it enabled states to recruit, feed, and equip larger armies and extend their authority over larger territories.

WEB EXPANSION FROM THE TOP DOWN The expansion of these regional webs also derived from the wishes of people involved, especially powerful people. Village and rural elites benefited from involvement in larger networks. If they could get farmers or herders under their influence to produce goods that cities wanted such as grain or leather, then in exchange they could enjoy the fruits of urban craft production—fine clothing, dazzling jewelry, effective weaponry. Rulers normally sought to collect rents or taxes from more people to maximize their income. When they could, they spread the worship of their preferred gods widely. Such goals were attractive enough that rulers everywhere routinely used their armies, priests, and wealth to break down centers of resistance to their authority. They extended their states, founded new cities, and in so doing spread webs of interaction.

WEB EXPANSION FROM THE BOTTOM UP Web building, to a lesser extent, also resulted from the daily activities of petty traders, sailors plying unfamiliar seas, refugees escaping from wars, slaves taken from their homes, soldiers posted to faraway lands, and countless others who introduced their accustomed ways in new places. The metals that were traded over long distances were passed from trader to trader in little towns; after all, big trade networks consisted of lots of smaller networks. Sailors, soldiers, refugees, and slaves—anyone traveling or living far from home—occasionally introduced to their new communities novel ways of worshipping, cooking, dyeing cloth, decorating pots, or fletching arrows.

Without intending anything of the sort, they too brought communities into closer economic and cultural contact, simply by traveling or living away from home.

As a result of the routine activities of common people and the ambitions of the powerful, fewer villages retained the autonomy of earlier times. Instead, people found themselves entangled in larger webs, entranced by the culture of cities, enmeshed in complex society—and subject to the authority of states.

WEBS AND THE DURABILITY OF KNOWLEDGE

Although webs grew bigger and tighter, the whole process was fragile and occasionally reversed. Webs could break down under the impact of epidemics and famines that reduced population sharply. Pirates and brigands could stop traffic on seas or steppes. But usually these proved to be temporary interruptions, and patient effort guided by

the self-interest of elites and the daily routines of people traveling far from home normally rebuilt torn webs.

With the advent of dense populations, complex societies, cities, and states, the likelihood of a lasting breakdown in webs dwindled. During the Paleolithic, when people were few and spread out, disasters could eliminate skills and knowledge. An example is the case of the native Tasmanians. Tasmania, now an island the size of Indiana or Maine, was part of the Australian mainland until rising seas filled the Bass Strait about 10,000 years ago. At that time, fewer than 4,000 people lived on the new island. No one had boats capable of crossing the strait, so the Tasmanians were isolated. They gradually lost the capacity to make items such as fishhooks and sewing awls (big needles). They could no longer fish or make clothing. They even lost the ability to make fire.

This small story shows the penalty of small numbers. When those Tasmanians who knew how to make fishhooks died, they hadn't passed on their knowledge to

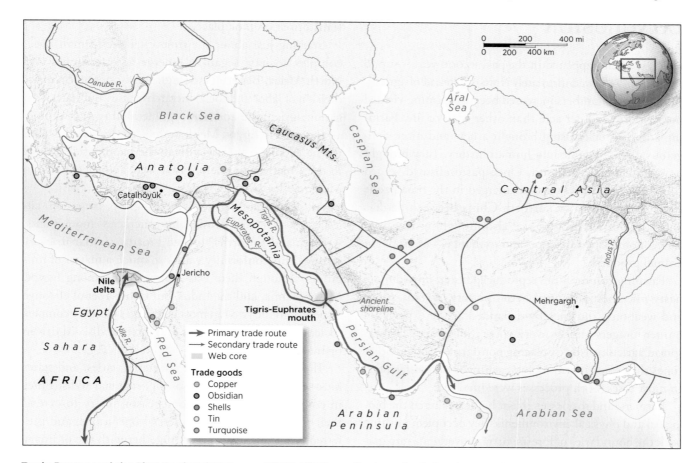

Trade Routes and the First Regional Webs, ca. 5000–3500 BCE Trade routes in Southwest Asia, especially those involving Mesopotamia, acquired more and more traffic after 5000 BCE, well before any cities or states emerged. Gradually thickening connections came to form a thin web that by 3500 BCE extended loosely to the Nile and to the Indus.

enough other people to ensure its perpetuation. Useful knowledge was lost because it wasn't stored in enough different brains.

In large regions such as Mesopotamia, Egypt, China, or Mesoamerica, however, once dense populations, complex societies, and regional webs were in place, such cultural losses couldn't happen. Population density meant that skills diffused readily to large numbers of people. Interactive webs enabled people far away to learn of every new skill or technology, and some of them would adopt it or alter it to fit their circumstances. With writing, information could survive outside of people's brains altogether, and live on beyond any individual's death. Innovation and learning became more cumulative inside the webs. The losses that Tasmanians experienced only happen among small, isolated populations—of which there were ever fewer as complex society, cities, states, and webs spread.

CONCLUSION

Much of what happened in the past 10,000 years—up to the present—flowed ultimately from the spread of agriculture. Human numbers increased because farming yielded much more food per acre than other ways of life. Farming and livestock raising brought a new and more dangerous disease regime into human history. They brought new emphases in religion. Once pastoralism diverged from farming, a new tension emerged in the broad zone from North Africa to northern China between herders and farmers. That divergence also brought a new basis for economic specialization and exchange—of crops for animal products.

Farming communities reproduced faster; hosted more nasty microbes; fashioned better pottery, textiles, tools, and weapons; and thereby expanded at the expense of hunter-foragers almost everywhere. Sometimes farmers spread agriculture by displacing non-farmers, but at other times they spread farming by teaching it to non-farmers. In most cases, both processes were involved.

Farmers, and to a lesser extent herders, altered the biological and physical environments they occupied, pushing back the boundaries of forests, turning wetlands into gardens, and exterminating wildlife. In doing all these things, they also changed humanity, creating environments that imposed new selective pressures on the human genome,

resulting in smaller people with stronger immune systems, and yielding some local adaptations such as the ability to digest milk in adulthood.

Perhaps the most important thing farmers did, although no one at the time recognized it, was to produce food efficiently enough to create a surplus. The surplus food could support smiths, potters, weavers, warriors, traders, and priests—specialists who concentrated their talents on single pursuits, and so developed new skills and, in turn, a greater economic surplus. This bigger surplus production permitted the creation of cities, states, and complex society.

History sped up and grew more complicated after the shifts to agriculture. For over 200,000 years, people had lived as hunters and foragers until, almost in a flash, they developed agriculture in several places between 11,000 and 4000 BCE. Once some people had taken up farming, population tended to grow faster and more people tended to live more closely together. This sped up interactions to the point where, again almost in a flash, another crucial transformation took place.

Starting just about the time Ötzi the Iceman lived, complex society began to emerge across Eurasia and North Africa. Between 3500 BCE and 1500 BCE, elaborate division of labor and social hierarchy, cities and states, irrigation agriculture and herding, metallurgy and writing, all appeared in Egypt, Mesopotamia, the Indus valley, and China. Complex society with all the trappings developed in the Americas too before 1500 BCE, and specifically in Mesoamerica and the Andes.

All these trappings—divine kingship, irrigation, cities, markets, states, armies, bureaucracies, monuments, writing, and so forth—looked broadly similar in every setting. This conformity wasn't so much a matter of imitation, although there was some of that among Egypt, Mesopotamia, and the Indus, but rather a set of effective responses to the two foremost challenges faced by complex societies: attack by strangers and internal discord driven by inequality.

The formation of complex societies, cities, and states kick-started the emergence of big, regional webs. Elites in complex societies had good reason to try to extend their political control, commercial operations, and preferred religions. By doing so, together with the ordinary activities of ordinary people, they extended the interactive webs to new territories and tightened the existing links of culture, trade, and politics.

CHAPTER REVIEW

KEY TERMS

shifting agriculture (p. 58)

herders (p. 59)

Eurasian steppe (p. 59)

Bantu (p. 63)

complex society (p. 69)

state (p. 69)

city (p. 69)

plow agriculture (p. 70)

irrigation (p. 71)

crowd diseases (p. 73)

metallurgy (p. 75)

bronze (p. 75)

Go to INQUIZITIVE to see what you've learned—and learn what you've missed—with personalized feedback along the way.

REVIEW QUESTIONS

1. How did the needs and desires of people in settled village societies differ from those of people in mobile societies?

2. What were the risks and advantages of village life?

3. Why did people turn to pastoralism for survival in arid scrubland and semi-arid grasslands?

4. What was the relationship between herder societies and farmers?

5. What characteristics of farming societies encourage migration?

6. Describe how culture and biology affected each other in the cases of cattle and horse domestication.

7. What were the three important features that complex societies often shared?

8. Why do complex societies often rely on plow agriculture and irrigation?

9. How did access to bronze confer military advantages?

10. Why do complex societies in different regions share many of the same traits?

11. What was typically the purpose of religion in complex societies?

12. What technologies spurred regional connections in Eurasia and Egypt?

FURTHER READING

David W. ANTHONY, *The Horse, the Wheel, and Language: How Bronze-Age Riders from the Eurasian Steppes Shaped the Modern World* (2007). A challenging mixture of historical linguistics and archeology concerning the origins of Indo-European speakers.

Eliza Wayland BARBER, *Women's Work: The First 20,000 Years* (1994). An accessible history of textiles and the women who made them.

Peter BELLWOOD, *The First Migrants: Ancient Migration in Global Perspective* (2013). A broad study whose later chapters are relevant here and detail some of the key farmer migrations.

Barry CUNLIFFE, *By Steppe, Desert and Ocean: The Birth of Eurasia* (2015). A masterful synthesis of the Neolithic in Eurasia.

Aalia GNANADESIKAN, *The Writing Revolution: Cuneiform to the Internet* (2009). A work that is very good on early scripts—their origins, development, and characteristics.

Ian HODDER, *Religion at Work in a Neolithic Society: Vital Matters* (2014). A detailed account of religion and everything else at Çatalhöyük.

Charles MAISELS, *The Archeology of Politics and Power: Where, When and Why the First States Formed* (2010). A searching exploration of the origins of states and complex society.

Susan MCCARTER, *Neolithic* (2007). A compact and readable work, mostly on the early Neolithic in Eurasia.

Hans NISSEN and Peter HEINE, *From Mesopotamia to Iraq: A Concise History* (2009). A book whose first five chapters deal expeditiously with the region from the dawn of farming to the formation of big states.

Bruce TRIGGER, *Understanding Early Civilizations* (2003). Challenging reading, but a revealing comparative study of its subject that takes on the Americas as well as Eurasia and Africa.

REGIONAL WEBS AND THEIR FUSION INTO THE OLD WORLD WEB

3500 BCE TO 200 CE

Unlike the first three chapters, which take on the development of humans and their early societies across the world as a whole, Chapters 4 through 10 approach world history regionally. They deal with similar themes in several different settings around the world. The most crucial themes include the formation of regional webs of interaction and the spread of complex and hierarchical societies and states. The web-making process, introduced here, will stay with us as the key impetus for globalization, weaving together localities, regions, and then the entire world.

Warring States Art This bronze from the period of the Warring States (771–256 BCE) depicts Chinese forces in battle in northern Yunnan.

Part 2 carries the human story up to 200 CE. The major exception comes in Chapter 10, which treats the history of the Americas and Oceania up to 1000 CE.

DEVELOPING WEBS

The logic behind choosing 200 CE is that by this date large parts of Eurasia and northern Africa had developed strong and steady enough connections so as to be considered a single, sprawling web of human interaction, called here the Old World web. Although patchy in places, and here or there unraveled for centuries, this web linked most of humankind—perhaps as much as 70 percent. It represents the fusion of earlier webs that developed first around Mesopotamia, then Mesopotamia together with Egypt, and the Indus and Ganges valleys in India. While those regions were growing in population and connectivity, in East Asia something similar was under way centered on northern China. An East Asian web was emerging, and by 200 CE it had linked up with those to its west to form the Old World web. This process was pushed along by the emergence of big, powerful states—notably Achaemenid Persia, the Han Empire in China, and the Roman Empire around the Mediterranean Sea. But millions of anonymous merchants, muleteers, and missionaries also helped this integration along by pursuing their daily routines. So did millions of silk spinners, silver miners, and shipbuilders whose labor created goods that inspired trade and travel.

REGIONS OUTSIDE THE WEB

The logic behind ending the chapter on the Americas and Oceania in 1000 CE (rather than 200 CE) is that these places followed their own traditions and trajectories outside the Old World web. The web fusion that took place in Eurasia and North Africa did not involve or affect them. Moreover, we know much less about their history because they had no writing before 200 CE and almost none as late as 1000 CE. Archeology, ancient DNA, and historical linguistics are all we have to go on here. In Oceania, people built seaborne webs over formidable distances, but those webs touched on thousands, not millions, of people. In the Americas, societies built mainly terrestrial webs over vast distances and rugged terrain, involving at most a few million people. As late as 1000 CE, the biggest and most influential of these societies remained smaller in scale than the big ones within the Old World web. So it's fair to say that over this period the Americas and Oceania remained isolated from the main centers of human population and interaction.

That was less true for most of Africa and Europe. Parts of those regions, such as Egypt, took part in big regional webs very early on, and by 200 CE sizeable parts of northeastern Africa and southern Europe had become deeply entangled in the Old World web. But at the same time, broad regions of Africa and Europe stood on the frontiers of the web. They weren't as isolated as the islands of Oceania or the plains of North America, but nonetheless they were unentangled, free to follow their own traditions and trajectories without much interaction with the cultures and empires of China, India, Southwest Asia, or Egypt.

REGIONAL VARIETY, COMMON THEMES

So in Part 2 we see how the most populated parts of the world, from Egypt to China, developed up to 200 CE and how they slowly forged links among themselves. We also see regions on the frontiers of this process—large parts of Africa and Europe—as they evolved up to 200 CE. And finally, we see other regions, the Americas and Oceania, that stood far outside this giant process of Old World fusion.

In the Indian folk tale about the blind men and the elephant, each man touches only part of an elephant and describes what he feels. One, who touches only the tail, says an elephant is like a rope. Another, who touches only the trunk, claims an elephant is like a tree branch. In approaching world history regionally, as we do here in Part 2 (and will again in Part 3), we risk the same confusion, failing to see the trends of human history as a whole because we focus on one part of it at a time.

So even though each chapter deals chiefly with one or at most two regions, most chapters also address some common themes to help keep the bigger picture in mind. We will be concerned with how societies organized themselves politically and how states expanded their territories. We'll look at the spread of big, multicultural empires. We'll examine how cultures structured social relations. And we will chart the formation and development of influential traditions such as religions and systems of thought. These chapters also address health and disease, military techniques and technologies, agriculture and animals. And all of these chapters address the slow and unsteady process of web building.

CHRONOLOGY

ca. 2300 BCE
Poem "Enki and the World Order" is written

By ca. 2300 BCE
Farmers use a water-lifting device, the *shaduf*;
Mesopotamia and Indus region are linked through contact

1792–1750 BCE
Reign of Hammurabi,
king of Babylon

**ca. 2200–
2100 BCE**
Prolonged
drought
occurs

By ca. 2600 BCE
Five main cities arise in Indus valley

ca. 3200 BCE
Signs of irrigation appear in lower Indus valley

ca. 2000 BCE
Salinization begins
to ruin fertile
Mesopotamian land

ca. 7000 BCE
Farming begins in upper Indus valley

ca. 3500–3000 BCE
City of Uruk emerges and flourishes

ca. 6000 BCE
rmers settle floodplain of
gris and Euphrates Rivers
gin small-scale irrigation

ca. 3400–3300 BCE
Writing begins in Uruk with cuneiform

**ca. 2340–
2150 BCE**
Rule of
Akkadian Empire

**ca. 1900–
1700 BCE**
Indus valley cities
fall apart and are
abandoned

By 3000 BCE
Mariners regularly sail the Indian Ocean

ca. 2100 BCE
Epic of Gilgamesh is written.
Warriors use chariots in Egypt, Mesopotamia, Iran, India, China.

By 1500 BCE

4

The Southwest Asian Web

MESOPOTAMIA AND THE INDUS VALLEY

3500 BCE to 200 BCE

Ancient **Sumer**, in today's southern Iraq, developed a lively literature of myths, poems, and epics. One poem, called "Enki and the World Order," details the feats of the god Enki as he arranges everything to suit Sumer. Written down around 2100 BCE, the poem celebrates Sumer's thriving trade with lands to the south on the Persian Gulf (Magan and Dilmun) and to the east in the Indus valley (Meluha).

> Let the lands of Meluha, Magan and Dilmun look upon me, upon Enki. Let the Dilmun boats be loaded with timber. Let the Magan boats be loaded sky-high. Let the boats of Meluha transport gold and silver and bring them to Enlil, king of all the lands....
>
> Sumer...land of heaven and earth, trailing glory, bestowing powers on the people from sunrise to sunset: your powers are superior powers, untouchable, and your heart is complex and inscrutable. Like heaven itself, your good creative force [?], in which gods too can be born, is beyond reach. Giving birth to kings...giving birth to lords who wear the crown on their heads....

Timber Trade A stone relief found in the palace of the Mesopotamian king Sargon II shows ships laden with cedar logs from Lebanon rowing through the seas off the coast of the Levant.

911–609 BCE
Height of Assyrian Empire

ca. 900 BCE
Solomon's temple in Jerusalem becomes center of Hebrew religion

By ca. 700 BCE
Slavery is widespread in Southwest Asia and Egypt

ca. 75 CE
Last use of cuneiform

ca. 1200 BCE
Advent of high-quality iron

ca. 1200–800 BCE
Mounted archers using composite bows become widespread

Then Enki proceeds to the land of Meluha and its rich resources:

> Black land, may your trees be great trees!... Chairs made from them will grace royal palaces! May your reeds be great reeds.... May your bulls be great bulls, may they be bulls of the mountains! May their bellowing be the bellowing of wild bulls of the mountains! The great powers of the gods shall be made perfect for you!... May your birds all be peacocks! May their cries grace royal palaces! ...Land, may all you possess be plentiful!

The poem celebrates the superiority that Sumerian rulers and subjects alike claimed for themselves. In this it resembled much of the art and literature from ancient Mesopotamia (and elsewhere), which consisted mainly of boasts about the greatness of rulers and gods.

In a more unusual vein, the poem details trade flows, suggesting that Sumer imported goods from the shores of the Persian Gulf and the Arabian Sea. It offers an inventory of products from Meluha, including bulls and peacocks, which prompts scholars to think Meluha was in the Indus valley. Meluha's big trees would have come from the flanks of the Himalaya and been floated down the Indus River before becoming furniture in Sumerian palaces. The gold and silver likely came from today's Afghanistan, north of the Indus valley.

This text is one of the clues that shows how interconnected the two river valleys—the Tigris-Euphrates of Mesopotamia and the Indus—had become by the late third millennium BCE. A handful of Indus valley products, unearthed by archeologists in Mesopotamia, confirm these links.

Each river valley was itself the central avenue of a system of trade and travel routes that extended hundreds of miles, linking farming areas to pasturelands, and to upland zones rich in timber and minerals. In the case of Mesopotamia, its links connected it to Anatolia, the Levant, Egypt, and the Iranian plateau. The Indus's tendrils extended into Central Asia, especially Afghanistan, and much of western India. These two riverine webs merged in the third millennium BCE to form the Southwest Asian web—the first big regional web in world history. The next chapter considers the extension of that web to the Nile valley in northeast Africa and the Ganges valley in northern India.

This chapter examines two of the core components of the Southwest Asian web, Mesopotamia and the Indus valley. Since we know far more about it than about the Indus valley culture, Mesopotamia draws more attention here. Mesopotamia also bequeathed more to the future than did the culture of the Indus. Firm bonds linked Mesopotamia and the Indus, but the complex societies they spawned differed in many respects, as we shall see.

THREADS OF CONNECTION IN SOUTHWEST ASIA

Because networks of trade and travel held the Southwest Asian web together, we will begin with geography focusing on Mesopotamia, the Indus valley, and their vicinity.

RIVERS

The life-giving rivers of Southwest Asia rise in mountain regions that served (and still serve today) as water towers for the whole region, reliably squeezing rain and snow out of passing clouds. The twin rivers of Mesopotamia, the Tigris and Euphrates, flooded every spring with snowmelt from the highlands of eastern Anatolia. The flood carried an annual gift of water and fertile silt to the lowlands—a gift that made farming and cities possible in central and southern Mesopotamia, which is mainly desert. Farther east, the Indus brought a similar gift as its spring flood tumbled down from the Tibetan Plateau and the western Himalaya. With ample sunshine and a fresh coating of nutrient-rich and well-moistened silt, the river valleys invited people to farm. Once people mastered the necessary irrigation techniques, the result was bountiful agriculture, and soon thereafter dense populations, urban life, and complex society.

CONNECTING UPLANDS AND LOWLANDS The highlands provided more than water and silt to the populations that crowded into the river valleys. Without nearby forests, the cities and villages in these valleys had to import wood from the nearest mountain ranges—the Taurus, Zagros, and Himalaya, all crowned with tall forests. Mesopotamia had to import most of its metals as well, from upland Anatolia, Iran, or farther afield. As a result, each valley's population had reason to build and maintain linkages to distant uplands—linkages that over time evolved into webs. By 3500 BCE, this binding of upland and lowland in Southwest Asia was well along, and Mesopotamia was the center of its own emerging web. That became true several centuries later of the Indus valley as well.

These developing webs stretched—tenuously—across dry scrub, steppe, and desert land in between the river valleys. The general lack of water confined the scattered farming settlements mainly to oases. Rainfall was sufficient, however, to support grazing animals and herders on lands of grass and scrub vegetation. The herders provided leather, meat, and other animal products to the cities and villages of the river valleys in exchange for grain, cloth, and other items the herders couldn't easily make themselves. During the fourth millennium BCE, trade links increasingly bound the sparsely populated steppe lands, like the uplands of Iran and Anatolia, to the dense

populations of Mesopotamia. A similar process occurred several centuries later along the Indus.

MARITIME THREADS AND THE MONSOON

Both of these nascent webs had maritime threads. People and goods moved not only along the rivers and donkey tracks, but on the sea as well. Mesopotamia stood at the head of the Persian Gulf, a body of water that was easy to navigate and that connected to the much larger Arabian Sea. The Indus valley lay adjacent to the Arabian Sea itself. Mariners took to these waters early, and by 3000 BCE were regularly sailing along the coasts and learning the patterns of the Indian Ocean monsoon.

The **Indian Ocean monsoon** is so important to world history that it merits a geophysical explanation. Eurasia is by far the biggest continent, so its interior, far from the moderating impact of oceans, gets very hot in summer and very cold in winter. This regular seasonal pattern generates

The Indian Ocean Monsoon Steady and predictable winds characterize the Indian Ocean north of the equator. This geographical and climatological feature helps explain the early development of sailing technology and maritime trade and travel involving people from Egypt to India.

Emerging Webs of Southwest Asia and Egypt, ca. 3500–3000 BCE The great rivers of the Indus, Tigris-Euphrates, and Nile valleys provided the geographic basis for growing webs of interaction by 3000 BCE. Donkey caravans and wheeled carts helped people to transport goods across the dry steppes and deserts between the rivers.

strong and reliable winds over South Asia and the Indian Ocean that blow northward in summer and southward in winter. The regularity of the monsoon made the Indian Ocean comparatively easy to sail. On its western side, the monsoon linked western India, Southwest Asia, and Egypt to the East African coast. On the ocean's eastern side, the winds linked Southeast Asian islands to the mainland. Essentially, the monsoon made the Indian Ocean into the first large, interactive seascape in the world.

No other region on Earth matched the corridor between the Indus and Mesopotamia for the combination of easy river and seaborne transport, and suitable animals and forage for land transport. This helps explain why people here were among the first to develop the systematic social and economic interactions of complex society, cities, and states, and the first to create regional webs. While occasional exchanges between the Indus and Mesopotamia date back at least to 6000 BCE, after 2500 BCE regular trade connections by river, land, and sea linked the two river valleys and their surroundings together as the Southwest Asian web.

ENVIRONMENTAL CHALLENGES: DROUGHT AND DISEASE

The complex societies of Mesopotamia and the Indus valley, and the big regional web that they were forming in the third millennium BCE, faced two great environmental challenges: drought and disease. Occasionally, the rain and snow didn't fall in the mountains and the rivers didn't rise. Without the annual flood, irrigation agriculture failed and the specter of starvation haunted these lands. The worst of these climate shocks, a prolonged drought lasting for about a century after 2200 BCE, drastically reduced population everywhere from the Indus to Mesopotamia to Egypt. Trade fell off, weakening or unraveling the threads that connected these regions. But, as with every such catastrophe, after the drought population and connections eventually recovered, even if specific kingdoms and cultures disappeared.

Epidemic disease was the second great enemy of peoples living in the fertile and populous river valleys. The problem lay in the density of human population, the prevalence of irrigation, and the frequent contact of people with herd animals. Working with, and often in, irrigation ditches promoted the spread of snail-borne diseases such as schistosomiasis and mosquito-borne ones such as malaria. Living in tight quarters eased the spread of breath-borne infections such as smallpox. The populations of Southwest Asian valleys gradually built up resistance to many communicable diseases, turning some infections into childhood (endemic) diseases to which adults carried resistance or full immunity. But this process—which no one at the time understood—took many centuries of recurrent epidemics to achieve.

Over time, the bounty of irrigation agriculture prevailed over droughts and epidemics, and population grew. In the Indus valley, archeologists have found over 1,000 settlements, including two major cities. Mesopotamia at times had dozens of cities with populations of 10,000 to 80,000. While estimates are rough, each river valley as of 2000 BCE held about 3 million people (and neighboring Egypt's Nile valley another 1 to 2 million). The dense population and urbanization of these river valleys made the region (including Egypt) the world's demographic center of gravity for a long time. From 3000 BCE until 500 BCE, it hosted between one-quarter and one-third of the global population.

MESOPOTAMIA

Mesopotamian history stretches over several millennia. Here we'll look closely at the early stages before 2000 BCE, when most basic patterns were formed. The availability of abundant ancient texts, inscriptions, and art allows a much more confident depiction of society and religion in **Mesopotamia** than has been possible for any other society to this point.

IRRIGATION AGRICULTURE

The emergence of complex society in Mesopotamia depended on the bounty of irrigation agriculture: grain farming, mainly wheat and barley.

The earliest evidence of irrigation in Mesopotamia suggests it began on a small scale at about 6000 BCE in the floodplain of the **Tigris and Euphrates Rivers**—at that time a mosaic of wetlands, braided river channels, and

shifting islands of silt. Snowmelt from the mountains of eastern Anatolia spurted through the river channels in springtime, briefly filling the floodplain with life-giving water. However, the water came at the wrong time of year for grain crops such as wheat and barley. To grow grain in Mesopotamia's dry climate, one had to plant it in the fall and harvest in the late spring. Summer was too hot and dry for plant growth. Farmers had to figure out how to store the floodwaters from springtime until just before fall planting.

Topography helped them out. The Euphrates normally runs at a higher elevation than the Tigris, so it was possible to cut channels in the east bank of the Euphrates and let gravity carry water to fields between the rivers, and then use the Tigris to drain off any excess water. But southernmost Mesopotamia is so nearly flat that directing water by gravity was a fine engineering art. Yet farmers mastered it and throughout the length of Mesopotamia produced enough grain to feed cities, armies, priests, and bureaucrats as well as themselves and their families.

Mesopotamians invented a water-lifting device, the *shaduf*, a bucket attached to the end of a pole that rests on a lever and has a counterweight on the other end. The device, in use by 2300 BCE, allowed irrigation of small areas at higher elevations than the local water source. It was useful for a grove of date palms, for example, but less so for grain farming.

In Mesopotamia, irrigation exacted its normal price. After several centuries of intensive farming, salinization

Irrigation In this stone carving dated to around 695 BCE from Nineveh, a city in Mesopotamia, workers use a *shaduf* to lift water out of a river.

forced farmers to abandon wheat in favor of barley, which is more salt-tolerant. But this adjustment didn't solve the basic problem. Beginning by 2000 BCE, if not before, salinization sapped the agricultural potential of much Mesopotamian land so that even barley yielded poorly, if at all. In a tragic irony, ancient Mesopotamians often fought wars over scraps of territory while salt ruined broad expanses of their otherwise fertile soils.

URUK AND THE CITY-STATES OF SUMER (3500–2500 BCE)

The Sumerian city of Uruk lay in what is today southern Iraq, where a channel of the Euphrates flowed across a flat plain just inland from the head of the Persian Gulf. It is here that archeologists have found the first evidence of urban life, state apparatus, monumental architecture, and writing. Uruk was the first of several Sumerian city-states. (A city-state was a small state consisting of a city and its surrounding farmland.)

SOCIETY AND ECONOMY Beginning around 3500 BCE, Uruk emerged among the smaller, mud-brick villages that dotted southern Mesopotamia. At first, its people grew barley, herded sheep and goats, and fished in nearby marshes. They traded with people to their south, on the shores of the Persian Gulf, and with others to their north, along the Euphrates. Uruk's merchants organized donkey caravans into the uplands of western Iran, where wood, metals, and other goods could be obtained. Uruk stood at the confluence of maritime, river-based, and land-based merchant networks and exerted economic sway over a growing region. Soon its people started building big structures out of imported limestone—first temples, then temple-palaces. Called **ziggurats**, and dedicated to local gods, they were visible for many miles around in the flat Sumerian landscape. (The tower of Babel described in the Bible was a ziggurat.) Uruk grew to be a full-fledged city in a century or two.

Uruk at its biggest, between 3400 and 3000 BCE, covered about half a square mile, the size of a small college campus. About 50,000 to 80,000 people huddled inside its walls, and most toiled in surrounding barley fields. They believed that their work fed gods, and that gods—if satisfied—protected them from bad weather, floods, sickness, plunderers, and other perils.

A remarkable surge of technological creativity helped make Uruk's growth possible. Between 3800 and 3100 BCE, plows came into use in Mesopotamia, multiplying the area farmers could till. Potters' wheels after 3500 BCE allowed the mass production of clay pots, one of Uruk's chief exports. Wheels and wagons were in use by 3100 BCE, extending the area from which it was practical to transport grain, pots, woolen cloth, and other bulky items. All these inventions advanced the social process of specialization and exchange, helping Sumerians—especially potters—refine their skills, create wealth, and extend their trade networks.

These potters, weavers, and hardworking farm families supported a priestly elite, specialists who claimed to know how to keep the gods happy. The priests accepted a share of the wheat, barley, dates, onions, beans, peas, and fish that Uruk's people produced. They kept it in temple storehouses, eating some of it themselves, using some in sacrifices to the gods, and saving the rest for feasts, for the poor, and eventually for an army. They also fed it to

Life in Uruk A limestone jug from early Uruk, dated to around 3000 BCE, is decorated with lions and with the sheep that Sumerians often herded.

Archeological Site of Uruk Uruk's impressive walls were first built around 3400 BCE.

potters and weavers, whose pots and cloth the priestly elite distributed and traded. Control of this surplus food, pottery, and cloth was a crucial source of priestly power, but ultimately that power rested on the popular belief that only the priests could keep the gods contented. As Uruk's temples became temple-palaces, its priests became priest-kings.

Religion helped ordinary Sumerians to accept their hard life. So did beer. Barley, which yielded abundantly on the soils of Sumer, could be brewed into beer. Women took responsibility for brewing, done in the home. Sumerians had some 70 varieties of beer and drank it day and night. It was healthier to drink beer than to drink the water around their fields and cities, which was normally contaminated by animal and human feces. As one Sumerian proverb had it, "He who does not know beer, does not know what is good."

WARRING CITY-STATES A few centuries after the emergence of Uruk, similar social, political, and religious arrangements prevailed in several other city-states elsewhere in Sumer. Each one had its own king and preferred gods. City-states often went to war with one another, obliging citizens to build walls and refine their fighting skills. They fought with bows and arrows, spears and shields, inventing new armor (such as metal helmets) and weapons (such as battle axes) at a remarkable rate. By 3000 BCE, Sumer had become a university of war. Peasant farmers did most of the fighting. Priest-kings led from the front and often died in battle. Nevertheless, a roster of Sumerian monarchs claims that an early one, Alalgar, king of Eridu, ruled for 36,000 years, later matched by Dumuzu, and topped by Enmen-lu-ana, who lasted 43,200 years on the throne. Perhaps the reigns seemed that long to their subjects.

CULTURE AND WRITING While Uruk and its neighbors were battling it out, Uruk's cultural influence spread far and wide. Its styles of architecture, bowls, and mosaics have turned up in archeological digs in Iran, Syria, and Egypt. Perhaps Uruk had colonies in all these lands; certainly, Uruk exported manufactured items in exchange for timber and metals. So far, only a small fraction of ancient settlements have yielded their treasures to the archeologists' trowels, and much more remains to be learned.

Appeasing the Gods A detail from a limestone vase from Uruk, dated to around 2900 BCE, shows people making offerings, including a valuable bull, to the fertility goddess Inanna, who they hoped would ensure the viability of their crops.

Uruk's most important cultural legacy was writing. As far as we know, writing began here. The earliest examples date from about 3400 to 3300 BCE. They are cuneiform: scratches made with dried reeds on wedge-shaped pieces of wet clay, which were then baked so as to become durable. Most early examples seem to be records of merchant accounts, a type of bookkeeping. They indicate quantities of goods, such as "14 sheep temple," which might mean that someone gave 14 sheep to a certain temple. There isn't much contextual information in early **cuneiform**—presumably, it was already known to writers and readers. As Uruk grew as a commercial economy and a city-state, the value of written records to merchants, rulers, and bureaucrats grew as well.

Early Sumerian cuneiform was both pictographic and logographic, meaning that the symbols were either pictures of things or representations of words. Sumerians used several hundred symbols, at times up to 1,200, and many surviving documents are the equivalent of spelling lists: guides to how to write things. It was hard to learn several hundred symbols, so only specialists—scribes—did so. Ordinary folks remained illiterate. So did most merchants and kings for whom written information was

Cuneiform This cuneiform tablet, dated to around 3000 BCE, records the allocation of beer to a workforce. The symbol for beer is the upright jar with a narrow, pointed base—in profile, as here, almost a triangle. Beer was the drink of choice in Mesopotamia; it was probably much healthier to drink than water from the lower Tigris-Euphrates. Brewing was done at home and was considered women's work, like baking.

highly useful. In Sumer in those days, it was so tedious to learn to read and write that it paid to hire someone to do it for you if you could.

Despite its imperfections, cuneiform worked well enough to serve for some 3,000 years. Early cuneiform was by later standards very rudimentary writing: it didn't include verb tenses or prepositions. You just had to know if the sheep had already gone or were still expected to go to or from the temple. It was almost like texting exclusively with emoji and no words. Like later forms of information technology, cuneiform got better over time, capable of communicating more efficiently by using more symbols for sounds and fewer for ideas or words.

Cuneiform spread widely among the neighbors of the Sumerians in Southwest Asia, who adapted it to their own languages. At least 15 languages were written in cuneiform throughout its long career, which lasted until around 75 CE (the last remaining tablet had to do with astronomy). And thousands of the inscribed clay tablets survive until this day, more than any other form of writing until printing. Modern scholars gradually figured out how to read cuneiform, enabling us, miraculously enough, to read words spoken and written nearly 200 human generations ago—even if we have no idea how the Sumerians pronounced them.

GILGAMESH The masterwork of cuneiform literature is the *Epic of Gilgamesh*, the oldest surviving epic poem in world history. According to Mesopotamian legend, one of Uruk's kings around 2600 BCE was named Gilgamesh. In the poem, Gilgamesh and his friend Enkidu decide to slay a ferocious monster guarding a cedar forest, in order to "establish forever a name eternal." They succeed in their quest, reduce "the forest to a wasteland," and return victorious. Gilgamesh wins the love of Ishtar, a Sumerian goddess of love, sex, and war, but spurns her, which together with the destruction of the forest earns him and his friend the anger of the gods. Their curse leads to Enkidu's death. Forlorn, Gilgamesh refuses to leave his friend's corpse for seven nights. When a worm falls out of Enkidu's nose, Gilgamesh gives up his vigil. After wandering the world in fruitless search of the secret of eternal life, Gilgamesh returns home to Uruk and concludes that he must be satisfied with the fate of mere mortals. He may not have established a name eternal, but at 4,600 years and counting, his renown is more long-lasting than most fame-seekers can expect.

The *Epic of Gilgamesh*, which covers 12 cuneiform tablets, was first written down around 2100 BCE, more than half a millennium after the king's supposed life. Although the characters resemble superheroes and monsters abound, the narrative illuminates some aspects of Sumerian life. It indicates the value of timber, gold, and silver. It refers to livestock and lawsuits, boats and baked bread. It also explores eternal human questions about the purpose of life, the nature of happiness, friendship, divine power, and the proper response to the fact of mortality. It is the mother of all literature, from Tolstoy to Tolkien and beyond, and its script, Sumerian cuneiform, was the most important information revolution since the emergence of speech.

THE WORLD'S FIRST EMPIRE (CA. 2340–2150 BCE)

The city-states of southern Mesopotamia came and went with the fortunes of war and the shifts in river channels. They were all monarchies, led by rulers who claimed divine authority. Few if any contained more than 100,000 people. They never united among themselves, but around 2340 BCE they were forcibly united by **Sargon of Akkad**. Sargon pioneered a new political format—empire—that became standard in Mesopotamia for millennia to come, and routine in world history.

SARGON OF AKKAD According to legend, Sargon was born to a priestess and an unknown father and, like Moses in the Bible, placed in a reed basket and put afloat on a river. A gardener found the abandoned infant and raised him to work in an orchard. Somehow (the legends invoke divine intervention) after this unpromising start, Sargon became king of a small city-state called Kish. He built the world's first professional army of full-time soldiers and conquered all of Mesopotamia from the shores of the Persian Gulf to the foothills of the Taurus Mountains. He reigned for about 56 years.

Mesopotamia in Sargon's day was culturally diverse. It was a land of two main languages—Sumerian-speakers in the south and Akkadian-speakers in the north. Each city had its favorite gods. Sargon founded a new capital, Akkad (also known as Agade), which archeologists haven't found but suspect might lie beneath modern Baghdad. It lay in the linguistic frontier zone between Sumerian-speakers and Akkadian-speakers. Sargon was tolerant on religion: he prayed to several gods. He based his approach on performance: he worshipped those gods who seemed to help him and ignored those who didn't deliver.

TRADE AND POWER Political power in Mesopotamian kingdoms hinged partly on access to trade goods, and Sargon was an architect of interaction who promoted long-distance trade. Inscriptions reveal that ships from the Indus valley ports and Oman (on the Arabian Peninsula) docked at Akkad in his time. Sargon expanded trade to the west and north, bringing timber from the Levant (Lebanon and Syria) and minerals from what is now southeastern Turkey under his control. Previous Mesopotamian states had relied exclusively on trade to procure timber and minerals. Sargon went further by establishing control over the territories from which they came. Thereafter, he could command his underlings to provide these essential materials.

It proved more difficult to obtain the luxury products such as lapis lazuli (a prized and striking blue stone) or gold that came from lands not under Sargon's control. Such items were important for displays of royal wealth and for the appropriate decoration of statues of the gods. Kings by Sargon's time also needed copper and tin, the

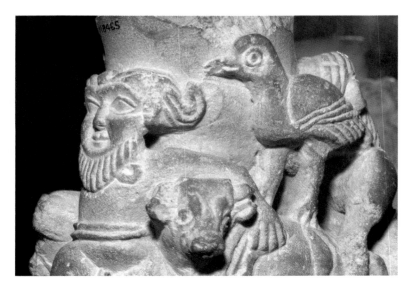

Gilgamesh A Sumerian vase from around 2000 BCE, which would have been used to pour out offerings to the gods, is decorated with animals and what is thought to be a representation of the mythic king Gilgamesh.

ingredients of bronze. These metals had become, like timber, strategic materials. Bronze made better weapons and armor than any other metal yet in use, and control of bronze supplies had helped make Sargon's army the scourge of Mesopotamia.

For the purpose of obtaining the trade goods on which royal power rested, Sargon built on a Mesopotamian tradition: weaving cloth. His royal workshops employed hundreds, maybe thousands, of women who wove linen and wool into garments valued in foreign markets from the Nile to the Indus. The wool came from steppe pasturelands good for raising sheep and goats. Herders, often children, and weavers, always women, working on the king's account helped to secure the luxury imports with which Sargon could buttress his authority. His was a commercial as well as a military empire. As one Mesopotamian text put it, "The houses of Agade [Akkad] were full of gold ... and silver, the city was full of music, and the quays where the boats docked bustled." His empire helped integrate larger and larger spaces, encompassing more and more people, into a broad web based on Mesopotamia.

THE EMPIRE'S COLLAPSE Sargon's empire did not long survive his death. His daughter, Enheduanna, an accomplished poet whom Sargon appointed as both governor and high priestess of the moon god in the conquered

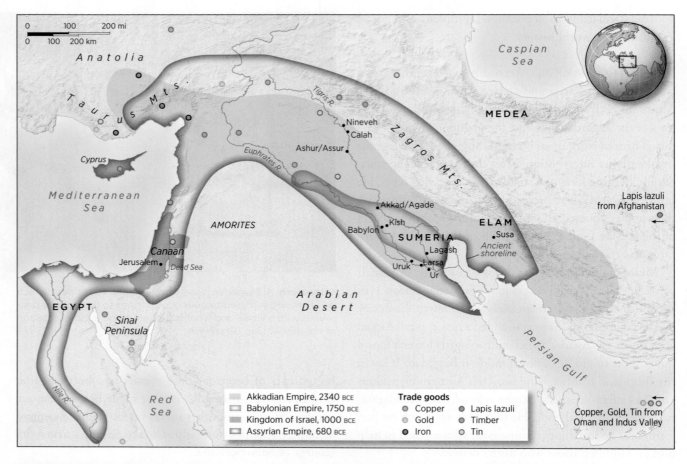

Empires of Mesopotamia after 2340 BCE The agricultural surpluses of Mesopotamian agriculture undergirded three main imperial states over the next 1,800 years. The Akkadian Empire was the first true empire in world history. The Assyrian Empire was the first to unite the rich farmlands of Egypt with those of Mesopotamia.

city of Ur, wrote an account of her city's fall to local rebels. She had to flee "like a swallow," which shook her faith in the moon god. More rebellions followed, and the empire crumbled. Sargon's grandson rebuilt it, but thereafter it all fell apart again—for reasons unknown.

The prolonged region-wide drought that began around 2200 BCE probably contributed to the collapse of Sargon's Akkadian Empire. Archeological evidence suggests that in neighboring Palestine the population fell by 80 percent. The water level in the Dead Sea, to the west of Akkad, fell by 110 yards (100 m) from 2200 to 2100 BCE. Lakes in Iran, to the east, dried up. Akkad's trading partners were suffering, no longer able to provide Sargon and his inner circle with the goods—tin and copper, for example—that underpinned their rule. Only the well-irrigated land in Mesopotamia remained productive, and there starving flocks driven by desperate herders clattered into the fields, damaging crops. One such pastoral group from northern

Syria, the Amorites, seems to have played a large role in dismantling the Akkadian Empire.

A Sumerian text titled "The Curse of Akkad," composed about a century after the abandonment of Sargon's capital, explicitly refers to a lack of rain.

> *For the first time since cities were built and founded,*
> *The great agricultural tracts produced no grain,*
> *The inundated tracts produced no fish,*
> *The irrigated orchards produced neither syrup nor wine,*
> *The gathered clouds did not rain, the masgurum* did*
>   *not grow.*
> *At that time, one shekel's worth of oil was only one-half*
>   *quart,*
> *One shekel's worth of grain was only one-half quart....*
> *These sold at such prices in the markets of all the cities!*

———————
*"Masgurum" is an as-yet-unidentified crop.

He who slept on the roof, died on the roof,
He who slept in the house, had no burial,
People were flailing at themselves from hunger.

The sharp and prolonged drought affected all of Southwest Asia and brought several states to ruin. In Mesopotamia, it helped to end the century-long interlude of political unification that Sargon and his family brought about. For the next 13 centuries, no one could unify Mesopotamia for long.

DISUNITY AFTER SARGON Sargon's short-lived achievement appealed to kings ever after. In Mesopotamia after 2100 BCE, as in Egypt after 2600 BCE and China after 200 BCE, rulers and many of their subjects considered unity to be natural and desirable. In Egypt and China, as we will see, unity was more consistently attained than in Mesopotamia.

That was not for lack of trying. Ambitious rulers of Mesopotamian city-states often made bids for empire and tried to pose as Sargon's natural successors. Their claims to power hinged on controlling the rich alluvial farmlands of Sumer and—because of Mesopotamia's lack of timber and minerals—the northern reaches of the Tigris and Euphrates where copper, silver, and other metals could be found. Ur, in Sumeria, flourished for a century, then was overrun. Other city-states such as Lagash, Kish, and Ashur conquered a few neighbors, made a brief run at empire under a lucky or skilled king, and then faded. As one Sumerian poet put it,

Ur was given kingship, but no eternal reign was she
　given,
From time out of mind, from the foundations of
　this land
and the multiplying of its people,
Who has ever seen a reign of kingship that endured
　uppermost for long?

BABYLON In the eighteenth century BCE, one city, Babylon, suddenly conquered north and south and formed another Mesopotamian empire under a king named Hammurabi. A master of both tactical alliance and treachery, **Hammurabi** (r. 1792–1750 BCE) made Babylon the center of power and trade, eclipsing the Sumerian cities to its south. The Babylonian Empire's control over the north was fragile and intermittent, but that didn't stop Hammurabi from proclaiming himself "the king who made the

four quarters of the world obey." His son, however, soon lost much of the empire to rebels and invaders, leaving Babylon once more merely a local kingdom, and Mesopotamia fragmented again.

At times, monarchs of Mesopotamia's divided states recognized the mutual advantages of peace. Through alliances and the exchange of princesses as brides, they managed to create temporary zones of peace and prosperity, especially in the period 1400–1300 BCE. Such comparatively peaceful interludes in the absence of any overarching power are rare in world history.

THE ASSYRIAN EMPIRE (911–609 BCE)

Disunity prevailed in Mesopotamia until the 300-year career of the **Assyrian Empire** (also known as the Neo-Assyrian Empire). A small kingdom, based at a stronghold on the upper Tigris called Assur, launched a spurt of local conquering as early as the fourteenth and thirteenth centuries BCE. Under a series of merciless kings (with merciless names such as Ashurnasirpal and Tiglath-pileser), the Assyrians assaulted their neighbors in all directions, and by the seventh century BCE they controlled everything from western Iran to southeast Anatolia to northern Egypt.

In their hilly homeland of upper Mesopotamia, the Assyrians lived off rain-fed farming, flocks, and a caravan trade connecting Mesopotamia with Syria and Mediterranean ports. Irrigation agriculture was less necessary for them than for Sumerians farther south in Mesopotamia. The Assyrians raised horses, which inhabitants of southern Mesopotamia did not, and this helped them develop a formidable army with cavalry and chariot corps as well as infantry. They had easy access to metal ores. Their economy was well suited to supporting their military.

IRON AND ASSYRIAN SUCCESS A large part of Assyrian military success came from the labor of countless ironsmiths. Bronze remained the most important metal to rulers and would-be rulers in Southwest Asia until the advent of high-quality **iron** about 1200 BCE. In Anatolia, people were working iron by 2000 BCE, but it took several centuries for them to make tools and weapons that anyone preferred to bronze. Iron ore is more common than copper and tin, the components of bronze, but it is harder to work. Ironsmiths had to heat, hammer, and re-heat ores at just the right temperatures to get good metal. They had

CONSIDERING THE EVIDENCE

The Banquet Stele of Ashurnasirpal II

When Ashurnasirpal II (r. 883–859 BCE) ascended the throne, the Assyrian Empire was only a few decades old, but his predecessors had ruled the city of Assur for around 1,700 years. In order to elevate his stature among generations of famous kings, he relocated the Assyrian capital from Assur to Calah (now Nimrud). The Banquet Stele, named for the 10-day feast that celebrated the city's renovations, announced his achievements to the empire.

Ashurnasirpal is the king whose fame is power!

I took over again the city of Calah...I heaped up a new terrace measuring from the water level to the upper edge 120 layers of bricks;...to proclaim my heroic deeds I painted on [the palace] walls with vivid blue paint how I have marched across the mountain ranges, the foreign countries and the seas, my conquests in all countries....

I brought in people from the countries over which I rule ...who were conquered by me personally...I settled them there in the city of Calah.

I dug a canal...straight through the mountains;...I provided the lowlands along the Tigris with irrigation;...

I collected and planted in my garden...the trees and plants raised from seeds from wherever I discovered them....

I erected...temples...which did not exist [in Calah] before; I rebuilt...temples of the great gods...[and] presented them with golden jewelry and many other precious objects which I had won as booty.

I organized the abandoned towns which during the rule of my fathers had become hills of rubble, and had many people settle therein; I rebuilt the old palaces across my entire country in due splendor; I stored in them barley and straw.

I killed 450 big lions; I killed 390 wild bulls from my open chariots in direct assault as befits a ruler....

I added land to the land of Assyria, many people to its people.

When I inaugurated the palace at Calah I treated for ten days with food and drink 47,074 persons, men and women, ...from across my entire country, also 5,000 important persons, delegates from [other] countr[ies], also 16,000 inhabitants of Calah from all ways of life, 1,500 officials of all my palaces, altogether 69,574 invited guests....

I did them due honors and sent them back, healthy and happy, to their countries.

Source: James B. Pritchard, *The Ancient Near East*, Vol. 2: *A New Anthology of Texts and Pictures* (Princeton: 1975).

QUESTIONS FOR ANALYSIS

1. The inscription on the stele claims that fame is power. What did Assyrian kings like Ashurnasirpal II do to ensure they were famous in their lifetimes and would be remembered by later generations?

2. The detailed numbers lend a sense of accuracy to the inscription. Do you think everything on the stele is an accurate portrayal of Ashurnasirpal II's deeds? Explain why you may have doubts about some parts but not others.

3. From your reading of the chapter, you know that trade was important to Assyria and other parts of Mesopotamia. Why do you think trade isn't mentioned in the Banquet Stele? What does this omission suggest about how Assyrian kings viewed their responsibilities as government leaders?

Iron Weapons Iron was widespread throughout Southwest Asia by 1200 BCE. Archeologists have found iron daggers like those at center throughout Iran, Mesopotamia, and Anatolia.

to build a furnace for each smelt, pack the ore just right amid layers of charcoal, and pump the right amount of air in with a bellows for hours on end. Iron requires much higher temperatures than bronze to smelt and shape. So the constraint on iron use wasn't the availability of ores, as with bronze, but of fuel and, above all, of specialized knowledge.

By 1200 BCE, well-wrought iron was far cheaper than bronze and for many purposes better, accounting for its widespread adoption in Southwest Asia and southeastern Europe. (Iron came into common use in India by 800 BCE, Egypt by 700 BCE, and China by 600 BCE.) It made good plowshares and sickles, improving the productivity of agriculture, especially of cereal crops. It also made good armor and weapons. With iron tools, states could feed more people. With iron weapons, they could field larger armies of well-armed men. The Assyrians, the first people to realize the potential of cheap iron, built their empire on iron, horses, and brute force.

THE ART OF INTIMIDATION In the process of building their empire, the Assyrians acquired a reputation for extreme brutality, partly because they boasted of it. Their atrocities may not have been unique, but their delight in recounting them in gruesome detail was. When Assurbanipal (r. 668–627 BCE) chose to teach a lesson to Elam, a state in western Iran that had supported a rebellion led by his brother, he flattened its capital and took the extra step of planting thorn bushes in Elam's fields. Sennacherib (r. 704–681), responding to a rebellion in Babylon, boasted

that he "completely destroyed it by flooding and left it like an open field," leaving no man, woman, or child alive. He even plundered its soil, carrying it away to Assur, his capital city. Other Assyrian kings proudly described the flaying of enemies, the bonfires of their captives, the piles of rebels' skulls, and so forth. They sometimes blinded captives and set them loose so they could spread the word of the horrors that resulted from resisting Assyrian power. Intimidation is always a component of governance; the Assyrians raised it to a fine art.

Even their artwork was intended to intimidate. Assyrian kings went to great lengths to get suitable stone to build grandiose cities, palaces, and defensive walls. They inscribed their monuments with terrifying boasts, part of a long tradition of Mesopotamian rulers. Assurbanipal, for example, referred to himself as "ferocious dragon, conqueror of cities . . . the king whose command disintegrates mountains and seas." He departed from tradition when he added boasts about his skill in solving mathematical problems and deciphering problematic texts in ancient languages.

The Assyrian Empire was much larger and more

Intimidating Art Assurbanipal's palace displayed stone reliefs like this one to boast of Assyria's military strength. Dated to around 645 BCE, this relief shows Assyrian soldiers attacking an Egyptian city, killing some of its inhabitants and taking others as captives.

multicultural than those built by Sargon or Hammurabi. To cope with the tensions that diversity brought, the Assyrians began systematically relocating populations. Millions of people had to uproot and move. Tribes were scattered in order to undermine their solidarity. Hill peoples were moved to the plains and deprived of their horses. Kings sought, with some success, to encourage an Assyrian identity among their diverse subjects and to inspire loyalty to the throne. Assurbanipal II, upon completion of a gargantuan palace, threw a 10-day party for (the sources claim) 69,574 guests. Assyrian kings also created a royal messenger service and built a system of guardhouses and wells along roads and tracks, all in the service of integrating a diverse empire.

Like every empire, the Assyrian one eventually declined and fell. In 612 BCE, the Medeans, originally a confederation of pastoralists from northwestern Iran, sacked Nineveh, the Assyrian capital, and together with their allies destroyed everything they could touch—Assyrian-style. With Assyrian power shattered by 609 BCE, the city of Babylon recovered its position and briefly became the dominant power in Mesopotamia—until the Persians arrived in 535 BCE.

PATTERNS OF MESOPOTAMIAN POLITICS

There were some underlying patterns to the repeated rising and falling of states and empires. The whole region of Mesopotamia alternated between periods of fragmentation and unity for a reason. Each arrangement had its beneficiaries and its advantages. Unity improved conditions for trade and usually helped repel invaders such as mobile pastoralists from the nearby steppe grasslands. Fragmentation allowed more men to enjoy the charms of being king. If foreign invaders loomed, the odds of Mesopotamian elites banding together and accepting an overlord improved. If there were no threatening invaders, elites preferred to go their own way, rebel against central authority, and set up their own smaller kingdoms. So, part of the rhythm of unification and fragmentation in Mesopotamia came from the action of foreigners in neighboring lands, mainly pastoral tribes from the steppe.

Another source of this cycle of unity and fragmentation was internal. It was hard to maintain unity because local chieftains were quick to start up their own states if they saw a chance. Even rulers as strong as Sargon or Hammurabi constantly had to repress rebellious subjects. Lesser kings failed to win over rebels and saw their empires fragment. But sooner or later, an ambitious, skilled, ruthless king would come to power somewhere and start conquering his less formidable neighbors. Thus the Mesopotamian region swung back and forth between unity and fragmentation, often briefly parked somewhere in between.

THE PREVALENCE OF WAR Throughout the centuries, from soon after the first establishment of Sumerian cities, violence frequently wracked Mesopotamia and nearby lands. Mesopotamian societies were often militaristic and dominated by army men. This was especially true after the time of Sargon, before which priests had often exerted more authority than soldiers. The prevalence of war and armed force resulted in part from the inability of anyone to dominate the entire region for long.

A second explanation for the pattern of routine violence and militarism, which contributed to the first, was the proximity of mobile pastoralists. On the Iranian plateau and in Syria, steppe grasslands supported herding peoples. They gradually mastered horsemanship and developed the skills to fight from the saddle. As we've seen, mounted pastoralists regularly traded with nearby farming peoples, but they could also make war when and where they chose. If they perceived weakness among the farming folk and their protectors, it often served as reason enough to attack. When herder groups were numerous, as after a string of years with good rains, they might like the odds of war. When they were desperate, as in times of drought, they might feel they had no choice but to attack, having nothing left to trade.

HORSE-DRAWN CHARIOTS Let's zoom out briefly to look at the bigger picture of which Mesopotamian politics was a part. Two technologies of war helped shape the balance between pastoralists and agrarian states throughout Eurasia. The first was the horse-drawn war chariot. It initially gave an edge to pastoralists, mainly because they had the skills and space to raise, manage, and train plenty of horses.

Chariots appeared in western Asia around 2100 BCE and spread quickly throughout Eurasia's suitable lands.

Mesopotamian Chariot Warfare This fragment of a stone relief from the palace of Assurbanipal in Nineveh, dated to around 645 BCE, depicts the Assyrian army's use of a chariot in battle.

By 1500 BCE, warriors in Egypt, Mesopotamia, Iran, India, and China, had adopted them. Chariots were difficult to build and use. The proper technique involved controlling horses with reins while standing on a mobile platform and hurling a javelin or loosing an arrow at one's enemy. When done well, it proved to be a formidable and intimidating way of warfare. Eventually, two- and three-man chariots appeared, allowing driver and warrior to specialize in their tasks.

Chariot warfare became an aristocratic way of war: only a few well-off people could afford the expense of good chariots and spare the time needed to master the skills. Pastoralists, although they had plenty of horses, usually lacked wood and skilled carpenters, so they could rarely field large numbers of chariots. But few were better than none, and pastoralists dominated militarily when and where no one else could deploy lots of chariots. Rulers of agrarian states, in contrast, usually found it hard to get enough horses. But since after 1500 BCE no ruler within reach of Eurasia's pastoralists could expect to survive long without a corps of charioteers; where possible, kings paid the price for horses and chariots in sufficient quantity to keep pastoralists at bay.

Chariots helped shape the politics of Eurasia from their invention until about 500 BCE. Agrarian states across Eurasia, from Egypt to China, either adopted chariot warfare quickly or were conquered by peoples who had mastered it. Chariots became standard burial goods for kings and grew prominent in the myths and religions of Indians, Persians, the ancient Hebrews, Egyptians, and Greeks.

THE COMPOSITE BOW The second important step in military technology was the adoption of the composite bow, made from pieces of wood, bone, and horn glued together. Like the chariot, it was hard to make and use. It required strong and flexible wood, horn from water buffalo or oryx (an antelope), sinew from antelope or deer, glue (also made from animals), and very precise craftsmanship. To shoot arrows with a composite bow required considerable muscular strength. Unlike the chariot, the composite bow was an innovation that pastoralists could easily make for themselves.

The composite bow's origins are hazy, but they probably date back to about 1500 BCE. Its importance came only after continual refinements made the bow better and better, tipping the military balance in favor of mounted archers from around 1200 to 800 BCE. The key to this shift lay in the bow itself, which was shorter but much more powerful than an ordinary bow. Composite bows enabled horsemen to shoot arrows at enemies hundreds of yards away and gallop out of range of ordinary bows while preparing for their next shot. As with chariots, agrarian states had to adopt the new technology or be overrun by pastoralist groups who mastered it.

The more formidable the pastoralists became, thanks in part first to chariots and then to composite bows, the stronger the incentive for agrarian peoples to band together for defense. This process of change in military technology and the power of pastoral peoples helps explain why agrarian states grew larger over time, culminating in giant empires in Persia and China, as we will see.

THE SCALE OF WARFARE Let's zoom back in on Mesopotamia. Farmers, increasingly, had to submit to rule by soldiers to avoid being plundered by steppe pastoralists. When not fighting off pastoralist raiders, brutal rulers such as Sargon and Sennacherib used their men and skills to amass more territory for themselves and crush rebellion by members of their own royal families or disaffected local leaders. The scale of warfare, like the scale of states, grew over time: Sumerian armies numbered in the thousands; Assyrian armies in the tens of thousands.

By the standards that prevailed in the Southwest Asian web, Mesopotamian political life was eccentric. It was unusually violent compared to life in the Indus valley or, as we will see in the next chapter, Egypt. It was more directly affected by the politics, fortunes, and military technologies of pastoral peoples in neighboring regions such as Iran or Syria. In Mesopotamia, it was a lucky peasant farmer who never heard the beating hooves of horses from the steppe or the clash of spear on shield.

GODS AND GODDESSES, PRIESTS AND PRIESTESSES

Everyone in Mesopotamia lived in an unpredictable world shaped by violent politics and forces of nature that worked in mysterious ways. They explained this unpredictability, as people elsewhere had done, in spiritual terms. Their version emphasized gods of the sun and moon, earth and sky, water and storm, as well as specialists in love and war. Sumerian gods, with a few alterations, made sense to Akkadians, Babylonians, Assyrians, and others in Mesopotamia. Conquerors, beginning with Sargon, found it made good politics to embrace these gods, so they gradually became standard throughout Mesopotamia.

THE ROSTER OF DEITIES Enlil/Ellil was in charge of choosing kings and decreeing the destinies of people and gods, as well as sharing responsibility for regulating floods. He was the father of several other gods but was ultimately subservient to An/Anu. The gods were all related in one way or another. The only female among the top gods was Inanna/Ishtar, perhaps the most popular of all. She was responsible for power, combat, love, sex, fertility, and beauty. She went in for casual sex, treated men and male gods as disposable, and enjoyed provoking them to combat. The gods all had their own personalities and tendencies, although quick temper and jealousy were a family trait.

A host of more-local gods joined this rowdy family of deities. Each city typically had its own god responsible for its protection. Marduk, for example, was the god of the city of Babylon. When Babylon built an empire, Marduk-worship expanded with it.

Inanna/Ishtar This relief from around 2000 BCE of the goddess Inanna/Ishtar holding a weapon comes from a Sumerian city later conquered by the Akkadians.

A TEMPLE ECONOMY According to Mesopotamian myths, the gods created humans because they were tired of the drudgery of doing farm work, grinding grain, and baking for Enlil. They were about to kill him when one of them had the bright idea of creating humans to do all the work. The main job of humans was to see to the care and feeding of the gods.

Temples, shrines, and statues of the gods served this purpose. Priests oversaw a temple economy that produced food for the priesthood and for sacrifices to the gods. Sacrifices of animals or food were typically burned before statues of gods, who drew nourishment from the smoke and smell of the burnt offering. Temples owned farmland: one Mesopotamian king granted 200 square miles (520 sq. km) for a temple to Inanna/Ishtar. Workers employed by temples—often enslaved war captives—raised crops, tended animals, baked bread, brewed beer, and carved statues. In return for their labor, they got a ration of bread or beer and a place to sleep.

THE PRIESTHOOD Priests and priestesses, or the laborers they commanded, kept temples and statues clean and properly guarded against thieves. They divined the will of the gods by examining the entrails, especially the

MESOPOTAMIAN GODS AND THEIR ASSOCIATIONS		
SUMERIAN NAME	**AKKADIAN NAME**	**RESPONSIBILITIES AND ASSOCIATIONS**
Utu	Shamash	Sun, justice
Nanna	Sin	Moon
An	Anu	Sky, creation
Ishkur	Adad	Storm, war
Enki	Ea	Water
Inanna	Ishtar	Love, sex, war
Enlil	Ellil	Fates of individuals

livers, of sacrificed animals and by watching the movements of heavenly bodies. They kept careful records of the shapes and sizes of animal livers and of shooting stars and eclipses. These divinations were of the utmost importance, because knowing the will of the gods helped one make the right choices in life—which crops to plant where, whom to marry one's children to, whether to launch a war or sue for peace.

At regular intervals, priests and priestesses organized festivals that often involved carrying the statue of a local god to a neighboring town in a gesture of friendship, sealed with feasting, dancing, and drinking. They also oversaw burials of important people and preparations for the afterworld, which in Mesopotamian texts was described as a grim, grimy place, full of dust: nothing to look forward to at all (unlike the Egyptian version, as we will see).

The priesthood enjoyed considerable authority, prestige, and wealth, especially in the early centuries in Sumer, before the militarization of Mesopotamia. Even in Assyrian times, however, the army chieftains had to share power with the priests. Kings had to build temples and worship devoutly, as publicly as possible, to shore up their legitimacy. And amid their boasts of greatness and brutality, they usually included a few phrases about being the favorites of the gods. Power in Mesopotamia—as would become common in world history—consisted of an alliance between throne and altar.

ASTRONOMY AND MATHEMATICS The prominence of divination in Mesopotamian religion led to the precocious development of astronomy and mathematics. Babylon acquired a particular reputation for math and science. Although the effort put into reading goat livers led to no practical applications, studying the heavens did. Babylonians learned how to predict eclipses and devised a lunar calendar. They used a base 60 system (ours is base 10) for mathematics and worked with fractions, square roots, and exponents. Babylonian math and astronomy improved over time and became impressive enough that foreigners from Egypt to India adopted much of it. Our minute, hour, and 360-degree circle are legacies of the Babylonians' base 60 system. They were good at calculating the area of irregularly shaped fields, and highly skilled at the architecture of monumental building—temples, palaces, and fortifications. Less useful, but very

Great Ziggurat of Ur This famous ziggurat, a temple-palace dating from around 2100 BCE and dedicated to the moon god Nanna, was almost 100 ft. (30 m) tall. The photograph was taken during archeological excavations in the 1930s that revealed the temple.

important to them, was astrology. Kings and commoners often believed that people's fates could be read in the stars, and they chose to schedule weddings, invasions, and other important events only after due consultation with astrologers. Generally, ordinary people, except those employed by priests, did their worshipping at home, with smaller statues of the gods they preferred, and left higher mathematics to the priestly class.

THE ANCIENT HEBREWS AND MONOTHEISM

One important cultural and religious innovation occurred on the edges of the Mesopotamian world: the emergence of a novel spiritual outlook among a then-obscure tribe we know as the ancient Hebrews or Israelites. Throughout Southwest Asia, gods were numerous, resembled humans, and behaved more or less like elite humans with superpowers. They competed for power, status, honor, love, and sex. They didn't care much about human fates, but they used humans to advance their own agendas. And they were best approached through the intervention of priests, who knew the arcane rituals—usually involving sacrifices of animals or food—that improved the chances of a successful appeal to divine power.

The ancient Hebrews, although surrounded by this general understanding of spirituality, came to see divinity differently. They created a dissident, minority tradition within the larger Southwest Asian, and mainly Mesopotamian, religious sphere.

House of David The words "House of David" are inscribed on a victory stele honoring the military triumphs of a king in the late ninth century BCE. The tablet features the earliest known mention of the Davidic dynasty—which emerged from the kingdom formed by the ancient Hebrews—outside the Bible.

MONOTHEISM According to traditions written down about 450 BCE in scriptures that were compiled into the Hebrew Bible, the ancient Hebrews were led out of bondage in Egypt, wandered in the Sinai, and settled in the land of Canaan (the southern Levant). Along the way, they accepted a vision in which there was only one supreme god, Yahweh, who was concerned that justice and morality should prevail among humans—at least, among his chosen people. If the Israelites followed his rules in their everyday lives, he would protect them; protection was a role expected of all gods everywhere. However, this pact between a *solitary* god and believers constrained by religious laws was a new departure in world religion, and the first lasting example of **monotheism**.

Once in Canaan, the ancient Hebrew tribe gradually formed a kingdom. It conquered the settlement of Jerusalem, where one king, Solomon, built a temple that became the focal point of Hebrew religion in the late tenth century BCE. It was here, in particular, that Hebrew religion became fully monotheistic and its variety of rituals and practices more or less standardized.

THE ANCIENT HEBREWS AND THEIR GOD The ancient Hebrews were few, poor, and weak and often buffeted about by the great Mesopotamian powers of the day. An Assyrian ruler deported thousands of them in the mid-eighth century BCE. Babylonians sacked the temple in Jerusalem in 586 BCE and carried off Jewish leaders to Babylon in imitation of the Assyrian policy for undermining the identity of unreliable groups. Yet through it all, the ancient Hebrews retained Yahweh as their god.

Yahweh was all-knowing and all-powerful, generous to his people when they behaved according to his instructions, but spiteful and jealous when they did not. In fact, the ancient Hebrews had great difficulty living up to Yahweh's standards and often worshipped Babylonian gods—called idols in the Hebrew Bible. Their leaders sometimes found it expedient to cooperate with the earthly powers in Babylon or Assyria. These failings gave rise to a tradition of prophets, priests, and scribes who railed against the shortcomings of other priests, kings, and people in general. Uncompromising scolds, the prophets were unloved in their day. But they shaped the tradition of Hebrew religion and sharpened its emphasis on ethical conduct as an overriding human responsibility.

Yahweh's commitment and his terms (the basis for Jewish law) were revealed in scriptures so complex and contradictory that experts might argue endlessly over points of interpretation. Expertise in the understanding and explanation of scripture became a point of honor for the ancient Hebrews—among men and boys, at least. Weekly gatherings to observe rituals and discuss textual interpretation became routine. This weekly observance is the root of our weekend.

Judaism, as we now call it, marked a significant departure from prevailing religious practice in Southwest Asia. It not only insisted on monotheism and strongly linked the ethics of daily life to religion, but it held that a single divinity ruled Earth, with no tie to a certain city. The ancient Hebrews' religious vision endured, and large parts of it, especially its core of ethical monotheism, proved sufficiently attractive to survive the ages and inform the belief and practice of Christians and Muslims—in other words, about one-third of the world's population today.

SOCIETY, FAMILY, AND LAW

Ancient Mesopotamia is the earliest society for which we have abundant evidence of social life and daily affairs. Like all complex societies, Mesopotamia had social hierarchies. These generally became more pronounced over time as the division of labor grew more refined and militarism more entrenched. By Hammurabi's day (eighteenth century BCE), a tripartite social structure was enshrined in law. At the top stood the landowning class, and at its apex were the rulers and priests. In the middle were free but landless, and usually poor, people—artisans, scribes, petty merchants, and ordinary farmers. At the bottom were slaves. The hierarchy had some flexibility, as class structures normally do. If one had to sell off one's land, one's status slipped with the transaction. Slaves could be freed and acquire property. The free, when desperate, might sell themselves or their children into slavery. A man could also legally sell his wife into slavery, but she could not sell him.

SLAVERY AND PEASANT LABOR While slavery on a small scale had existed in most agricultural societies for thousands of years, it became common first in Mesopotamia. Mentions of it appear in early Sumerian texts. Law codes from the time of Hammurabi refer to slavery. Enslavement was often punishment for unpaid debts. It was the usual fate of war captives. But one could also be born a slave: the status was hereditary. Over the centuries, slavery became more common, a result of both the demand for routine labor in fields and workshops and the supply of captives in ceaseless raids and conquests. Terms for "slave" in Mesopotamian languages implied foreign-ness. Slavery became widespread by the eighth century BCE, when large-scale conquests by the Assyrians generated streams of captives.

All that slaves produced belonged to their owners. Most slaves worked in households. Female slaves spun, wove, and served as concubines for prosperous men. Male slaves performed manual labor too and were sometimes trained as craftsmen—cobblers, carpenters, or smiths, for example. A lucky few who were skilled in cuneiform kept accounts for merchants. On occasion, masters might permit loyal and clever slaves to go into business for themselves, accumulate money, buy other slaves, and perhaps buy their own freedom.

Landless peasants, the largest class by far, did most of the farm work. A good chunk of what they produced went, as rent and taxes, to the landowners, temples, and states. Their precise status is unclear: they weren't slaves, but not entirely free either. They normally met their obligations in kind, with grain, fish, wool, dates, and so forth,

Unfree Labor A stone relief from the palace of the Assyrian king Sennacherib at Nineveh shows how that palace was likely built: dozens of forced prison laborers, guarded by soldiers, chisel stone from a quarry and carry it to the construction site.

but might instead perform military service or labor on irrigation works, fortifications, palaces, or temples. The urban population included all manner of craft workers, unskilled laborers, and peddlers.

MARRIAGE AND THE FAMILY The surviving evidence is long on the legal aspects of marriage, most of it drawn from the reign of Hammurabi in the eighteenth century BCE. People of all classes expected to marry as teenagers. As in most societies, in ancient Mesopotamia marriage, normally monogamous, was an alliance between two families for the purpose of having children, including a legal heir. There was often a formal contract between families concerning property arrangements. This contract specified "gifts"—both the bride-price (a sum given by the groom's family to the bride's) and the dowry (a sum paid by the bride's family to the groom's). Breaking a marriage engagement brought big fines. If a groom died before his wedding, his bride would ordinarily be married to one of his brothers. If a wife died, her husband expected a refund of the bride-price or else a sister of the wife as a substitute bride. Widows normally continued to live with their husband's family, supported by their children. A husband might divorce a wife who bore no children, but he had to negotiate with his wife's family to do it. However, wives who neglected their household duties or insulted their husbands might be divorced more freely. Adultery was a serious offense: women, and in some societies men, if judged guilty might be killed for it. By Assyrian times, brides and married women wore veils, which unmarried women were prohibited from doing.

Some poems and artwork reveal that passion and love occasionally blossomed within marriage. Babylonian love poetry (sometimes relating to marriage) could be unabashedly romantic and shamelessly explicit. A stanza from a twenty-first-century BCE poem, the earliest surviving love poem in history, gives some sense of a bride's passion:

> *Bridegroom, let me caress you,*
> *My precious caress is more savory than honey,*
> *In the bedchamber, honey-filled,*
> *Let me enjoy your goodly beauty,*
> *Lion, let me caress you*

A later Sumerian poem speaks of an enduring passion: "Though she has already borne me eight sons, she is still ready to make love." Throughout ancient Mesopotamian history, figurines of erotic scenes were popular artwork displayed in temples and homes, and placed in graves to accompany the departed.

Not all marriages were happy. A Sumerian text includes a husband's lament: "My wife is down at the temple. My mother is down at the river. Here I am starving. Whoever has not supported a wife and child does not know what it's like to have a leash through one's nose." One Assyrian woman wrote to her husband, presumably a traveling cloth merchant: "Why do you keep writing me that the textiles I send you are no good? I'm the one who makes every effort to produce and send you textiles so that with each caravan you make at least ten shekels [a unit of money] of silver." Money worries divided many a Mesopotamian couple.

The point of marriage was to have children—ideally, sons, and lots of them. Many infants and mothers died in childbirth, and perhaps half of all children never made it to age five. So parents who wanted someone to look

Veiled Woman This Sumerian statue from the third century BCE was found in a temple of Ishtar in the region of present-day Syria. A seated woman wears a headdress with a veil, as many brides and married women did—especially by Assyrian times.

after them when they grew feeble needed many children. A woman who had many sons enjoyed a boost in status. But fathers enjoyed full legal rights over children. Raising children was a married woman's main job. Most kids, especially girls, had no schooling but learned their skills within their family.

For the elite, formal schooling existed from at least 2500 BCE. Its chief goal was to teach writing and reading. A cache of clay tablets from the eighteenth century BCE tells us almost all we know about Mesopotamian schooling. Most students were boys, probably ages 10 to 15, the sons of scribes, rich businessmen, or government and temple officials. Families had to pay for their sons' schooling. Teachers specialized in subjects such as math, writing, music, or field surveying. A specialist in discipline beat the students with canes for offenses such as speaking out of turn. After Sargon's time, students had to learn cuneiform in both Akkadian and Sumerian, which would take several years. They did it by rote memorization and endless copying on clay tablets. Records indicate a few female scribes—very few—in the long history of Mesopotamia, but how they learned to read and write is unknown.

LAW AND HAMMURABI Mesopotamian kings claimed special powers bestowed by gods and took responsibility for administering divine justice on Earth and enforcing laws. The earliest laws known to history are Sumerian, set forth by kings and no one else, on behalf of the gods. Some date to the twenty-fourth century BCE. The fullest picture of Mesopotamian law comes from a black stone stele (a tall slab used as a monument) erected by Hammurabi in the eighteenth century BCE. It is often described as a law code, although its 282 laws are a disorganized jumble, not comprehensive, and may merely be intended to show that the king took his duty as purveyor of justice seriously.

Sumerian and Babylonian laws dealt with crime and punishment, but also with wages and prices, inheritance, and other economic matters. They do not advance principles but are invariably specific, following a regular format: if such-and-such happens, then the penalty will be such-and-such. If a doctor blinds a patient, the doctor shall have his hand cut off. If a boatman loses a cargo, he must pay for the cargo and the boat. If a wife is a spendthrift, she will be thrown into the river.

Penalties were strict: either fines or bodily harm. There was no imprisonment. The early Sumerian laws usually prescribed fines, such as 60 shekels (maybe four years' wages for a commoner) for breaking someone's leg. Hammurabi and the Assyrians especially went in for mutilation as punishment. Stealing, burglary, or adultery earned the death penalty. A priestess who entered a tavern would be burned alive. A son who struck his father would lose his hand. A man who kissed another man's wife, Assyrian law prescribed, would have his lower lip sliced off with an axe.

Hammurabi's laws show how the tripartite class division of Mesopotamian society worked in practice. People were far from equal before the law. Punishment not only fit the crime, but also fit the relative status of the victim and criminal. It was a more serious offense to cause injury to a social superior than to a social inferior. If you stole from the palace or temple, you had to pay back 30 times the goods heisted. If you stole from a commoner, the fine was one-third as much; and if you couldn't pay, you were put to death. At the same time, fines were bigger for the landed class than for the poor. In the prologue to his list of laws, Hammurabi claims his purpose is to "protect the weak from the strong." Perhaps in prescribing these penalties he was preventing harsher ones. But it looks like the main purpose of his laws, as of those promulgated by other kings, was to uphold the authority of fathers within families, protect the property of those who had any, and maintain social hierarchy.

There were judges in Mesopotamia, but no lawyers or juries. One represented oneself in Sumerian, Babylonian, or Assyrian courts. In villages, respected elders would serve as judges whenever a case came up. In the cities, and for serious cases, royal appointees who specialized in justice would preside. When a panel of judges couldn't come to a verdict, they sometimes referred cases to a higher power. The accused would be thrown into a river: if he or she drowned, or seemed sure to, that indicated guilt. If the accused bobbed to the surface and made it to shore, that revealed innocence.

Some traces of Mesopotamian law, as well as astronomy, religion, technology, art, and literature, remain with us today. The practices and culture of Sumer, Babylon,

Hammurabi's Laws On this eighteenth-century BCE stele on which Hammurabi's laws are written, the most prominent aspect is the frieze in which the king (left) receives the laws from the god Shamash, asserting Babylonian justice to be divinely inspired. The laws themselves are written in cuneiform below.

and Assyria proved highly influential in their time and spread along the routes of the Southwest Asian web and eventually beyond. Today, our concepts of marriage, kingship, and calendrical time, as well as our habit of writing—even certain board games such as checkers—are all echoes of ancient Mesopotamian culture.

THE MYSTERIOUS INDUS VALLEY SOCIETIES, CA. 2600–1700 BCE

One of the places touched by Mesopotamian culture was the Indus valley and its complex urban society. Its history is one of the compelling mysteries of the ancient world. No one can read the writing it left behind, and no one knows why urban society along the Indus River vanished—although theories abound.

The **Indus River** runs nearly 2,000 miles (more than 3,000 km) from Himalayan glaciers to the Arabian Sea. It splashes through deep gorges in the mountains, then slows down in the Punjab (meaning "Five Rivers"), acquiring the water of tributaries before weaving through the arid region, called Sind, near the sea. Even the summer monsoons bring almost no rain to Sind because it's flat and the rain clouds push farther north, piling up against the Himalaya and dumping torrential rains on the mountain slopes. The Indus carries a tremendous silt load, twice that of the Nile. Eons of silt deposits have built up the river's banks so that in Sind it flows above the level of the surrounding plain. Like the Huang He (Yellow River) in northern China, the Indus changes its course now and then during big floods. The river stays in its bed and is easily navigable in winter, but not in summer when monsoon and snowmelt floodwaters swell the flow five- or tenfold.

The annual flood of the Indus and its burden of fertile silt made its floodplain and valley a good place for farming. In Punjab, people could farm in a limited way without irrigation. Farming in the upper Indus valley, with barley and wheat, began about 7000 BCE. Subsequently, farming and villages spread out over the Indus basin. Most experts believe that farming techniques were transplanted to the Indus valley from the Fertile Crescent.

In the lower Indus valley—in Sind—farmers needed to irrigate. Signs of irrigation appear in the archeological record starting around 3200 BCE. We have no way of knowing whether Indus farmers developed irrigation on their own or learned of it from somewhere else. They raised wheat and barley, as Mesopotamian farmers did, and on approximately the same annual rhythm. As elsewhere, the development of cities and complex society along the Indus rested on the high yields of irrigation agriculture.

CITIES OF THE INDUS, CA. 2600–1900 BCE

By about 2600 BCE, five main cities had arisen in the Indus valley. The largest, Mohenjo Daro and Harappa, housed perhaps 20,000 people (some archeologists say 50,000 for Mohenjo Daro) at their height a few centuries later. Each site covered around 200 to 250 acres (80 to 100 hectares), or the equivalent of 200 football fields. Unlike the higgledy-piggledy layout of cities of Mesopotamia, those in the Indus valley had a regular design on a grid pattern. These were the first planned cities in world history. The main thoroughfares were laid out almost precisely north-south and east-west. The cities' buildings were made of baked mud brick. New, painstaking, and highly standardized styles of pottery, bead making, and metalworking appeared. The Indus cities developed a strong craft tradition, especially in stoneworking. Their artisans knew how to make bronze but rarely did so, perhaps because copper had to come from afar. A system of writing emerged, used for inscriptions on seals made of a soapstone called steatite. This was a sudden transition to complex, urban society, similar to Uruk's in Sumer 500 years before.

CULTURAL UNITY The cultural unity visible in the archeological remains is remarkable, considering that the five big cities stood far apart. The nearest pair were separated by 175 miles (280 km), roughly the distance between Cleveland and Detroit or Houston and San Antonio. Sumerian cities, by contrast, were often only a long day's walk from one another.

Each Indus valley city had a lower town, divided into rectangular blocks; an elevated inner city, built on a mound and surrounded by walls; and a sprawling warehouse or granary complex adjacent to the river by which the city sat. Houses typically had bathrooms with sit-down toilets, and earthenware drainpipes encased in brick walls. Mohenjo Daro had a water tank, perhaps used for ritual bathing, about half the size of an Olympic swimming pool and an average of one well for every three houses. The **Harappans**, as the Indus River populations are often called, paid more attention to the problem of clean water—separating wastewater from drinking water—than any urban population anywhere until about 170 years ago. The Indus cities all used the same script, the same weights and measures, and the same shells and beads for ornamentation. Even their bricks were the same size.

TRANSPORT AND TRADE This cultural unity rested on a regional network of transport and communications. There is archeological evidence of riverboats, which would have moved up and down the navigable waters of the Indus. A second crucial component of this network was wooden ox-carts, which do not survive in the archeological record except as models or toys made of durable clay. Mesopotamian societies used ox-carts, and it's highly likely that those along the Indus did as well. The invention or refinement of ox-carts was probably necessary for urban development along the Indus, because it allowed more efficient hauling of harvested crops from farm to riverbank, and from there to the granaries and storehouses of the cities.

As in Sumer, this local network of overland transport was linked both to a riverine system and to a maritime one—in fact, to the same maritime system, that of the Arabian Sea and its monsoon winds. Mesopotamian texts mention Indus traders and trade goods such as timber, stone, animals, and ivory. Mesopotamian archeological sites yield Indus seals, as well as lapis lazuli. Lapis lazuli came from Afghanistan, probably via the Indus and sea routes. A city that archeologists regard as an outpost of Harappan culture existed in Afghanistan, near the main supply of lapis lazuli. Some copper came from Oman on the Arabian Peninsula. Ivory and other goods came from the western shores of India. For luxury items at least, the Indus peoples traded far and wide, and funneled some of what they acquired to Mesopotamia. Unfortunately, neither texts nor archeology can tell us what the Indus traders accepted in exchange from Mesopotamia, but woven cloth is a strong candidate.

Indus Valley Settlements, ca. 2600–1900 BCE In and around the Indus River, urban societies developed after 2600 BCE with growing overland and maritime links to Mesopotamia. No one can read the script used in these cities, so much about them remains mysterious despite a century of archeological work.

THE MYSTERIES OF HARAPPAN CULTURE Just how the integrated urban society of the Indus originated is entirely unclear. Most of the archeological sites show evidence that previous settlements were burned and rebuilt in a grander, more orderly style. Could this mean that warfare and conquest brought complex society to the Indus? Could it instead represent the arrival of some new ideology, to which gridded cities and sanitation were important? No one knows.

There are other mysteries concerning Harappan culture. All other complex societies of the ancient world show traces of a ruling class in palace architecture, big statues, luxury grave goods, or boastful inscriptions, and usually all of the above. None of this existed—or has yet been found—for the Indus. The biggest statue so far discovered is the size of a flashlight. Could Harappan culture, unlike

Indus Valley Cities The regular grid pattern on which Indus valley cities were organized is evident in this view of Mohenjo Daro. The large rectangular area with a deep recess in the middle, visible in the background, held a water tank and may have been used for bathing; beyond it lies the granary.

almost all the others, have had no sharp social hierarchy and no ruling elite? No kings? Was there a remarkably unified culture with no overarching state? Were the cities linked in some empire, in a confederation, or were they fully independent politically? The archeological traces suggest an unusually egalitarian society.

Harappan culture also shows no signs of organized religion. In sharp contrast to the archeological record of Mesopotamia, Egypt, and Mesoamerica, nothing has been found in the Indus cities that was clearly a temple. Perhaps the water reservoirs were used for religious rites and indicate an emphasis on cleanliness and purity, which were important in later Indian religions. Perhaps the presence of figurines of animals and trees means they were objects of worship. No one knows.

Something else is missing from Harappan archeological sites: signs of violence or warfare. There are no chariots, weapons, or armor. The walls seem built for defense against floods rather than human foes. Indus valley art includes no scenes of warriors, in dramatic contrast to that of Egypt, Mesopotamia, China, and Mesoamerica. Could the complex society of the Indus have been peaceful, unlike all other ancient societies? This seems unlikely. Some 60 years ago, scholars thought that the ancient

Maya (in Mesoamerica) was a peaceful culture; but when they cracked the code of Maya writing, they found many bloodthirsty boasts about battles and conquests.

If you seek undying fame, you might try decoding the Indus valley writing system and unlocking its secrets. The Indus valley script appears on stone seals, pots, bits of bone and ivory, and a few copper and bronze items. Unlike the hieroglyphs of Egypt and the cuneiform of Mesopotamia, it wasn't written on walls, statues, clay tablets, or tombs—although at one Harappan site, there is an example of writing with stones affixed to what was probably a wooden signboard. Some 3,700 inscriptions have been found so far, but about 40 percent of them are duplicates. It could be that most writing was done on perishable surfaces—palm fronds, for example, or wood slabs—that have decayed over the centuries. The inscriptions often appear together with images of big animals: rhinos, elephants, tigers, cattle, and even imaginary ones such as unicorns—but never horses, which people of the Indus didn't have, although their trading partners in Afghanistan surely did. Most scholars think there are about 400 symbols in all. People have been working hard on the Indus script for about 80 years now, but Indus writing may remain a mystery for some time to come.

THE DISAPPEARANCE OF THE INDUS CITIES, 1900–1700 BCE

The greatest Indus valley mystery of all is what happened to its urban society. Around 1900 BCE, after thriving for seven or eight centuries, it fell apart. By 1700 BCE, the cities were abandoned, the writing stopped, the oceanic trade dried up, the careful and standardized craftsmanship of jewelry, pots, and tools vanished. Village life persisted, and settlements grew more numerous to the south and east of the most urbanized districts of the Indus. But something happened to make city life either impossible or unappealing. At Mohenjo Daro, it seems to have happened suddenly. Dead bodies were hastily buried. Caches of valuables were left by their owners. What happened to cause this collapse?

Maybe it was disease. The carefully laid out drains, the countless bathrooms, the systems of water tanks and wells in Indus cities all testify to skillful hydraulic engineering and unrivaled attention to sanitation. Maybe this somehow broke down, and cholera, typhoid, or some other

Indus Seals A seal from Mohenjo Daro, dated to around 2500 to 2000 BCE, bears the image of an elephant as well as symbols in the Indus script, which scholars are still unable to decipher.

Piled-up silt formed deltas and marshes in the lower Indus, inhibiting waterborne trade and improving habitat for malarial mosquitoes. But the evidence for massive flooding is poor, and people living in the Indus were used to periodic flooding.

Maybe outsiders caused the decline. Generations ago, most archeologists believed an invasion from the north ended Indus civilization amid a blaze of destruction. This almost certainly did not happen—although a couple of centuries after the end of Harappan city life, migrants from the north did pass through.

Maybe trade with Mesopotamia fell off as a result of the strife that followed the collapse of Sargon's empire, and people from Gujarat (a region to the southeast of the Indus) took over the maritime trade. Beginning around 2000 BCE, drought-resistant African millets were grown in Gujarat, making it possible to harvest two crops annually there. The new crops raised its ceiling for population, wealth, and power and enabled elites there to dominate

waterborne diseases got into the drinking water and ravaged city populations. Perhaps malaria, spread by mosquitoes that flourish amid stagnant water, swept through. Some of the skeletons from the last days of Mohenjo Daro show signs of malaria.

There is good geo-archeological evidence for earthquakes and shifts in river channels. This might have separated the cities from their hinterlands and trade routes, making it expensive and impractical to transport food from farm to city. City dwellers may have migrated elsewhere rather than starve, leading perhaps to the increase in the number of villages.

Climate change likely was involved. After 2200 BCE, the whole region of Southwest Asia grew more arid for a century or more, and the summer monsoon over South Asia weakened—as it does from time to time over the millennia, owing mainly to solar cycles. Soil samples imply that vegetation patterns were changing, and perhaps agriculture became less rewarding as water grew scarce and the silt-bearing floods became unreliable.

Maybe deforestation and greater flooding took a toll. Baking all those bricks required fuelwood, and so did metalworking and pottery. Perhaps the Punjab region lost much of its former forest cover, leading to increased erosion. Soils and vegetation that had formerly absorbed floodwaters were lost, so floods became more violent.

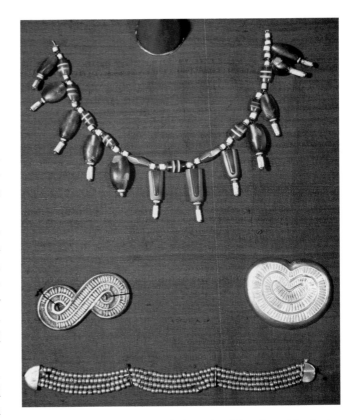

Indus Jewelry The characteristic style of jewelry of the Indus valley culture featured geometric patterns and materials including gold, silver, and polished stones—as is evident in these examples from around 3000 BCE.

Water Sanitation This large well in the residential area of Mohenjo Daro was part of the city's elaborate system of irrigation and water supply.

long-distance trade that had formerly sustained the Indus cities. (How African crops got there is another, smaller mystery, but an indication that the trade and travel links of the Southwest Asian web could extend to East African shores.)

Maybe all these things occurred, or maybe it was something else entirely that the experts haven't thought of yet. In the unlikely event that the decline of Harappan culture had a single cause, the best bet would probably be disease. But to judge by the decline of every other culture, city, or state that we know anything about, the likelihood is that several things came together at the same time, or one immediately after another; probably none of these alone could explain the decline, but several taken together may have overwhelmed the resilience of urban society in the Indus valley.

In any case, the disappearance of urban culture and complex society in the Indus valley remains mysterious. Something similar happened in Peru and in the Maya lands of Mesoamerica, as we'll see later. In general, complex society and urban culture, once developed, usually stay intact. In Mesopotamia, Egypt, and China, for example, the tradition of complex society lasted, uninterrupted,

from its origin until today. That is the rule; the fate of the Indus valley cities is the exception.

FORMATION OF THE SOUTHWEST ASIAN WEB

Links between Mesopotamia and the Indus region began by at least 6000 BCE. Their farm tools and crops are similar. Both regions had a long tradition of baking grains into bread and roasting meat, as opposed to the cooking traditions prevalent in most of China and Africa, in which foods were more often boiled and prepared in porridges and stews. Long-distance trade in luxury goods intermittently connected the two regions too. But the volume and velocity of exchanges increased in the mid-third millennium BCE after cities emerged in both settings. Both valleys hosted complex urban societies with their own trade networks, their own riverine webs that extended tendrils in all directions. Those tendrils intertwined by 2500 BCE and quickly grew to form a trunk route across

Mesopotamian Food and Drink In a relief from the palace of Assurbanipal, from around 645 BCE, the queen (left) and king are shown in a garden, feasting on the region's particularly luxurious foodstuffs of fruit and wine.

the Arabian Sea with its predictable winds so beloved of sailors. As the poem "Enki and the World Order" suggests, by the end of the third millennium BCE the twin rivers of Mesopotamia—the Tigris and Euphrates—and the Indus River had become linked in a single sustained web of contact, trade, and cultural influence.

TRADE

Trade links left the strongest evidence of these connections, both in texts and in archeological sites. The Indus valley exported timber from the Himalayan foothills above Harappa to the treeless cities and villages of southern Mesopotamia. Indus merchants also traded stone beads, gold dust, and Central Asian lapis lazuli. In exchange, the Indus cities must have imported perishable things—perhaps cloth or food—because the archeological record shows no sign of Mesopotamian objects, with the possible exception of silver items. Most of this Indus-Mesopotamian trade probably went through middlemen based in ports along the Persian Gulf in places such as Oman, where Indus weights and measures were used, and Bahrain. But inscriptions from the time of Sargon show that Indus ships also docked in Akkad in the twenty-fourth century BCE. The Mesopotamia-Indus web presumably included many other dimensions. Surely they exchanged diseases, for example, something about which archeology and surviving texts have nothing to say.

LAND AND WATER

Several features of the entire region between the Indus and the Levant proved especially helpful in promoting this sort of connectivity, both on land and on water. First, the region supported good beasts of burden for land-based transport. Donkeys, and later horses and camels, could carry heavy loads. Moreover, the floodplains along the Indus, Tigris, Euphrates, and lesser rivers could provide forage for caravans with animals. Caravans could also carry a day or two's supply of grain and some water for pack animals, allowing them to get from one grassy spot to the next across an intervening desert.

Second, the rivers themselves were easy to sail, with minimal rapids and few waterfalls. The Indus, Tigris, and Euphrates all offered seasons in which the winds were strong enough and currents weak enough to enable boats to move upstream as well as down. Once sailing vessels existed, these rivers became inexpensive two-way highways. Third, the surrounding seas—the eastern Mediterranean, the Persian Gulf, and the broad Arabian Sea—offered favorable conditions to sailors. Their winds were remarkably predictable, thanks mainly to the annual monsoon pattern. These geographical features help to explain why the world's first big regional web formed in Southwest Asia.

Indus Weights and Measures Standardized weights and measures enabled traders from the Indus valley to exchange consistent quantities and values of goods, allowing for the efficient operation of the trade network.

CONCLUSION

Mesopotamia developed complex society first and maintained it far longer than the Indus valley. Archeology and textual evidence is much richer for Mesopotamia than for the Indus valley; in particular, some of the languages of Mesopotamia can be read by modern scholars, while that of the Indus cannot.

Mesopotamia's political history featured a series of mainly short-lived states and empires. All were agrarian and, until the Assyrians, based on the irrigation agriculture of the Tigris-Euphrates floodplain. All were hierarchical, led by elites who were either religious or military specialists, and sometimes both at once. Over the centuries, Mesopotamian societies became more militaristic. Soldiers increasingly wielded more power than priests and played a larger role than in most other early complex societies. As they became more militaristic, Mesopotamian states relied more heavily on slavery for labor. They were the first societies in world history in which slavery played a substantial role. Usually Mesopotamia was politically fragmented, and often its cities engaged in warfare with one another. But under Sargon in the mid-third millennium BCE, Hammurabi 500 years later, and under the Assyrians in the early first millennium, the whole region attained a temporary unity.

Mesopotamian culture and religion spread among its

neighbors. The power of its states lent a certain prestige to its languages, literature, art, science, and religion. Everywhere from Egypt and the eastern Mediterranean all the way to the Indus valley felt Mesopotamian influence.

The Indus valley cities of Harappa and Mohenjo Daro remain mysterious compared to the cities of Mesopotamia. But diligent archeological work has revealed some extraordinary features. First is the high degree of cultural unity among the various settlements, demonstrated by artistic and architectural styles. We don't know if that unity was politically imposed or, more likely, voluntary. Second is the obsession with water and its cleanliness, unique for the time. Indus cities achieved a standard of

urban water supply and wastewater management that wouldn't be matched until as recently as 170 years ago.

The biggest mystery surrounding the Indus valley cities is their disappearance. The interpretation that best fits the scanty evidence is that their populations migrated to the east as other centers took over the long-distance trade routes. Epidemics, river channel shifts, and adverse climate change could have provoked such a migration.

The Indus cities and those of Mesopotamia formed the urbanized core of the Southwest Asian web. The societies on its western and eastern frontiers, anchored in two other river valleys, the Nile and the Ganges, were much less urbanized. But they too became nodes in the web.

CHAPTER REVIEW

KEY TERMS

Sumer (p. 85)

Indian Ocean monsoon (p. 87)

Mesopotamia (p. 89)

Tigris and Euphrates Rivers (p. 89)

ziggurats (p. 90)

cuneiform (p. 91)

Epic of Gilgamesh (p. 92)

Sargon of Akkad (p. 92)

Hammurabi (p. 95)

Assyrian Empire (p. 95)

iron (p. 95)

chariot (p. 98)

monotheism (p. 102)

Indus River (p. 106)

Harappans (p. 107)

Go to INQUIZITIVE to see what you've learned—and learn what you've missed—with personalized feedback along the way.

REVIEW QUESTIONS

1. Which natural features of the Tigris, Euphrates, and Indus River valleys made them attractive for human settlement?

2. Why were drought and disease sometimes disastrous for river valley populations?

3. What were the costs and benefits of irrigation agriculture?

4. What needs spurred the invention of writing?

5. In what way was Sargon of Akkad a trailblazer?

6. What are the advantages and disadvantages of bronze in comparison to iron?

7. Describe how chariots and composite bows impacted the balance of power between Eurasian agrarian states and pastoralists.

8. How did early Judaism differ from prevailing religious beliefs and practices in Southwest Asia?

9. How did Hammurabi's law codes reflect the social structure of Babylon?

10. In what ways do remnants of the Harappan culture reflect a society much different from other societies of its time?

11. What are the two most extraordinary features of Harappan culture?

12. What three big geographical features promoted connection between Mesopotamian and Indus valley societies?

FURTHER READING

Burjor AVARI, *India: The Ancient Past* (2007). A compact survey of the subcontinent from the earliest times to around 1200 CE.

Jean BOTTERO, *The Oldest Cuisine in the World: Cooking in Mesopotamia* (2004). A discussion of food and drink, with lots of recipes.

Glenn S. HOLLAND, *Gods in the Desert: Religions of the Ancient Near East* (2009). A handy history of a complicated subject.

Jane MCINTOSH, *The Ancient Indus Valley* (2007). An accessible synthesis of Indus valley archeology

Amanda PODANY, *Brotherhood of Kings: How International Relations Shaped the Ancient Near East* (2010). An analysis of war and peace in Mesopotamia, Syria, Egypt, and Anatolia from around 2300 to 1300 BCE.

Andrew ROBINSON, *The Indus: Lost Civilizations* (2015). A compact, popular history that touches on just about everything to do with Harappan culture.

Rita P. WRIGHT, *The Ancient Indus: Urbanism, Economy, and Society* (2010). An authoritative scholarly synthesis of the evidence.

CHRONOLOGY

ca. 500 BCE
Jainism takes shape

2575–2125 BCE
Egyptian Old Kingdom

1539–1069 BCE
Egyptian New Kingdom

After 800 BCE
Small kingdoms emerge
in Ganges basin

ca. 500–400 BCE
Siddhartha Gautama,
the Buddha, is born

ca. 3000 BCE
Development of
heiroglyphics

2010–1630 BCE
Egyptian
Middle Kingdom

**ca. 1700–
1500 BCE**
Hyksos rule
of Egypt

ca. 1100 BCE
Rig Veda is written down

ca. 712–664 BCE
Kush controls
most of Upper
Egypt

ca. 2500 BCE
Reign of Khufu;
construction of Great
Pyramid at Giza

ca. 1700 BCE
First use of Chinese rice in Ganges basin

ca. 1000 BCE
Caste system takes shape
in Ganges basin

ca. 664 BCE
Egypt becomes
Assyrian vassal
kingdom

525 BCE
Persians
conquer
Egypt

ca. 2950 BCE
Narmer/Menes unifies
Egypt through conquest

ca. 1500 BCE
Complex society emerges in Ganges valley

ca. 1000–800 BCE
Inhabitants of Ganges
basin acquire iron tools

From Nile to Ganges

AN EXPANDING WEB

3000 BCE to 200 BCE

A text known as the Lansing Papyrus (ca. 1800 BCE) surveys the occupations of ancient Egyptian society and offers advice for young men:

Love writing, shun dancing; then you become a worthy official.... Befriend the scroll.... It pleases more than wine. Writing... is better than all other professions. It pleases more than bread and beer, more than clothing.... It is worth more than an inheritance.... Young fellow, how conceited you are! You do not listen when I speak....

See for yourself with your own eye. The occupations lie before you. The washerman's... limbs are weak, [from] whitening his neighbors' clothes every day.... The maker of pots is smeared with soil.... His hands, his feet are full of clay; he is like one who lives in the bog. The cobbler mingles with vats. His odor is penetrating.... The merchants travel downstream and upstream. They are as busy as can be, carrying goods from one town to another.... The scribe, he alone, records the output of all of them. By day [the peasant] cuts his farming tools; by night he twists rope. Even

On the Nile In this New Kingdom mural (ca. 1567–1320 BCE) from the Tomb of Sennefer, Egyptian boatmen ply the waters of the Nile River.

ca. 268–230 BCE
Reign of Ashoka

321–230 BCE
Height of Mauryan Empire

By 400 BCE
Classic Hinduism evolves

400 CE
Last use of hieroglyphs in Egypt

FOCUS QUESTIONS

1. What features of Egyptian life account for its high levels of political and cultural unity?

2. What do the religious texts of the Ganges basin peoples tell us about their society, culture, and politics?

his midday hour he spends on farm labor....He does three plowings with borrowed grain....Now the scribe...surveys the harvest. Attendants are behind him with staffs....One says [to the peasant]: "Give grain." "There is none." He is beaten savagely. If you have learned about the peasant, you will not be able to be one.

Come, [let me tell] you the woes of the soldier, and how many are his superiors: the general, the troop-commander, the officer who leads, the standard-bearer, the lieutenant, the scribe, the commander of fifty, and the garrison-captain.... He is hungry, his belly hurts;...He is called up for Syria....There are no clothes, no sandals....His march is uphill through mountains. He drinks water every third day; it is smelly and tastes of salt. His body is ravaged by illness. The enemy comes, surrounds him....He is told: "Quick, forward, valiant soldier! Win for yourself a good name!" His body is weak, his legs fail him....His wife and children are in their village; he dies and does not reach it. ...Be a scribe, and be spared from soldiering!

The author, no doubt a scribe himself, disdains hardworking washermen, cobblers, potters, merchants, peasants, and soldiers. Only the scribe has it easy. The text lays bare the division of labor in Egyptian society, something of the hierarchy among social classes, and delivers a full dose of condescension directed against everyone who is not part of the literate bureaucratic elite. The author addresses only men, taking it for granted that the profession of scribe would not include women.

Literacy was rare everywhere 4,000 years ago, and much rarer among women than men. Along the Ganges River after about 1000 BCE, the literate were mainly male religious specialists known as Brahmins. Most of them, like the author of the Lansing Papyrus in Egypt, looked down on everyone who lacked education and refinement. Like him, they sometimes served as bureaucrats, and their standing and authority came from their position within a state as well as within a religion. The precise nature of social stratification differed from one society to the next. But in all the complex societies, from the Nile to the Ganges, stratification and inequality were dominant facts of social life. All societies had to develop ways to deal with the tensions they brought.

This chapter considers the complex societies that emerged in the valleys of the Ganges and the Nile. It dwells on social structure, religion, and state and empire building. In the case of Egypt, where the textual record and the harvest of archeology are far richer, it also reflects on foreign relations, the economy, and health.

The chapter also considers these societies as components of the world's first big web. The Southwest Asian web formed initially in Mesopotamia and surrounding lands. As we saw in Chapter 4, seaborne trade to the Indus expanded and thickened it. The societies of the Southwest Asian web also had connections farther afield—with Central Asia, some coastlands and islands of the eastern Mediterranean, and Egypt. As these links solidified over time, the Southwest Asian web by 2500 BCE became something larger: a Nile-Indus web. It incorporated the societies along the Nile and Indus river basins as they became ever more connected to the circuits of Southwest Asia and the Arabian Sea.

Gradually, over the next thousand years, as new settlement and new linkages developed in northern India, the Nile-Indus web expanded into a Nile-Ganges web. Integral parts of this enlarged web, the societies of the Nile and Ganges were also frontier regions. To the east, south, and north of the Ganges, and to the west and south of Egypt, the web shaded off into more thinly populated lands with societies that, as of 200 BCE, remained only intermittently affected by the trends within the Nile-Ganges web.

EGYPT, 3000–200 BCE

Herodotus, the renowned fifth-century BCE Greek historian, wrote: "I will speak at length about Egypt because there is no other land like it." Egypt had several distinctive geographical features. For the last 5,000 years, Egypt has consisted of broad expanses of sandy and rocky desert where almost no one could live, split by the narrow river valley of the Nile and its lush, muddy delta, where almost every Egyptian lived. Rainfall was negligible. The **Nile River** flows more than 4,000 miles (nearly 7,000 km) northward from its source at today's Lake Victoria, in East Africa, to its delta near the Mediterranean Sea. The Nile has several shallow rapids, called cataracts, that posed obstacles to navigation. Yet, despite climatic and geographical constraints, Egyptians were among the first people anywhere to create cities, states, and writing. As far as we know, only Sumerians preceded them—and not by much.

Egypt had a political peculiarity too. After about 3000 BCE, Egypt was usually a unified state—in sharp contrast to Mesopotamia, the Ganges valley, probably the Indus valley too, the Chinese river valleys, and almost every other center of population in the ancient world until 200 BCE.

The Nile itself helped shape this political peculiarity. Its annual flood with loads of fertile silt from the Ethiopian highlands made its banks and delta the most durably productive farmland anywhere in the ancient world. The

Nile also served as a two-way highway. Its current flows north, while for most of the year winds blow south: boat traffic could move either up or down the river easily north of the First Cataract. Water transport was so cheap and efficient that Egypt didn't need roads. Once people figured out how to exploit the annual flood, farming with the same techniques and crops worked well throughout Egypt. These characteristics of the Nile made Egypt easier to unify than most other lands, and when it fell apart, it was easier to re-unify. Herodotus called Egypt, with some justice, the "gift of the Nile."

Whether it was politically united or not, Egyptians conceived of their country as divided into two parts. The southern part—the Nile valley—was a narrow ribbon of life only 4 to 20 miles (6 to 30 km) wide and 600 miles (900 km) long, roughly the area of New Jersey. The northern part—the delta—was twice as large. In 4000 BCE, it

The Nile Valley An aerial photograph shows the small extent of the arable land in Egypt, narrowly clinging to the banks of the Nile River and only widening at the river delta as it flows into the Mediterranean. The river valley is surrounded by desert. To the east lies the Red Sea and the wedge-shaped Sinai Peninsula.

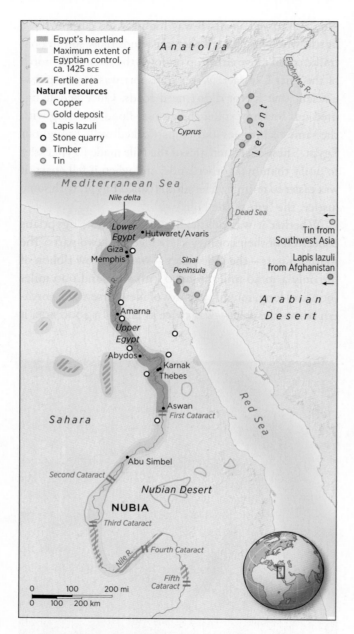

Ancient Egypt, ca. 2575–1069 BCE Ancient Egypt, a united kingdom more often than not after 2950 BCE, was simultaneously part of Africa and the Mediterranean world. A narrow ribbon of life, villages, towns, and cities in one of the driest parts of the world, Egypt was the "gift of the Nile." In most years, Egypt produced surplus food that it exchanged for metals, timber, and other items that were hard to come by in Egypt.

was a triangle of shifting river channels, mud banks, and reed beds teeming with geese, ducks, herons, and other wildfowl, and home to crocodiles and hippos. It was, however, undergoing transformation into a cultivated and irrigated landscape. As we'll see, the extent of southern Egypt

varied, as its rulers enjoyed fluctuating success in conquering territory upriver. But Egypt's heart remained the Nile delta and valley north of the First Cataract. Scholars refer to southern Egypt as Upper Egypt; northern Egypt, the region of the delta, is called Lower Egypt.

Egypt was politically distinctive in another way that geography helps to explain. Whereas people living along the other big rivers hosting complex societies—the Tigris-Euphrates, Indus, Ganges, or Huang He—often had much to worry about from invaders sweeping into their valleys, Egyptians were comparatively secure. The surrounding desert provided a formidable barrier against outsiders, so there were only two practical ways into Egypt: from the north or northeast either by sea or across the Sinai desert; or from the south along the middle reaches of the Nile and the land called **Nubia**. Egypt suffered comparatively few invasions and devoted far less of its wealth and effort to self-defense than did other parts of the ancient world. Political unity meant that Egyptians were rarely fighting one another, and geographical barriers meant that they rarely had to fight invaders. This combination of unusually fertile soil and unusually low defense requirements is unique in world history. It made Egypt a wonderful country to live in—at least, for the 1 percent of society who commanded the labor of all the rest.

UNIFICATION

People lived along the Nile for thousands of years before complex society took shape. From about 9000 BCE to 5500 BCE, wetter climate enabled people to live among lakes and rivers, grasslands and forests in what is now the Sahara desert. After 5500 BCE, climate grew dryer, the Sahara slowly became desert, and people crowded into the Nile valley. At first, they hunted abundant fish and wildlife and collected edible plants. To judge from the few skeletons of this era, these were violent times in the Nile basin. By 5500 BCE, wheat, barley, peas, and lentils were prominent crops. By 3500 BCE, Egyptians had mastered the art of irrigation along the Nile, had built farming villages, and were harvesting enough surplus food to support a social elite. Elaborate burials with precious lapis lazuli imported from Afghanistan and gold from Nubia testify to the existence of a dominant class.

By 3300 BCE, a few villages had grown into towns. Each town identified with an animal deity and presumably prized its independence. But independence didn't last. A process of consolidation, probably violent, quickly followed. Soon there were only two or three polities. At around 3100 BCE, rulers of a city in Upper Egypt called Abydos managed to unite all the towns and countryside from the Nile delta in the north to Aswan, a city near the First Cataract, in the south. Thereafter, the kings of Egypt, eventually called **pharaohs**, wore a double crown symbolizing Upper and Lower Egypt. The Egyptian kings chose Memphis, near today's Cairo, where the delta and the Nile valley meet, for their capital.

NARMER AND HIS SUCCESSORS From then on, Egypt was usually unified, and for Egyptians it became normal to think that it *should* be unified. The first ruler of all Egypt, known as both **Narmer** and Menes, probably completed unification through conquest around 2950 BCE. (Incidentally, he was the only ruler in world history to be mauled to death by a hippo.) No texts illuminate this early period of Egyptian history, so scholars rely on archeology and artwork such as the so-called Narmer Palette, which seems to show the king about to bash someone's skull. It's unclear whether that was intended to represent historical events or to establish the principle that Narmer would deal harshly with enemies. Beneath Narmer stand two long-necked animals, perhaps lionesses, whose intertwined necks, bound by leashes, may represent the union of Upper and Lower Egypt and Narmer's control over

King Narmer The Narmer Palette features scenes of battle with mythical creatures and an illustration of Narmer (large figure at left) as the warrior king who conquered and unified all of Egypt.

both. The motif imitates a Sumerian cylinder seal, providing evidence of cultural links between Egypt and Mesopotamia. Narmer's successors ruled Egypt for nearly 3,000 years.

This long era is conventionally divided into three periods of political unity—the Old Kingdom, the Middle Kingdom, and the New Kingdom (see Table 5.2). Each of these is subdivided into dynasties following a scheme invented by a third-century BCE Egyptian historian-priest named Manetho. In between the three kingdoms are the Intermediate Periods, when unity broke down. There were about 33 dynasties and roughly 170 pharaohs in all. One could create chronologies of Egyptian history based on pottery styles or climate shifts, but Manetho's scheme, which emphasizes the significance of Egyptian unification, is still preferred by experts despite its uncertainties.

The Egyptians created the world's first stable monarchy and more or less invented hereditary kingship. The first kings, of the Early Dynastic Period, were understood as both divine and human, children of Ra, one of the sun gods. The kings cruised up and down the Nile every other year, dispensing justice, conducting an agricultural census, and extracting grain and other goods from every community. Little is left of their legacy except their mud-brick tombs at Abydos, and for the last king, Djoser, a small

PERIODIZATION OF ANCIENT EGYPT	
PERIOD	**DATES**
Pre-dynastic Period	to 2950 BCE
Early Dynastic Period	2950–2575
Old Kingdom	2575–2125
First Intermediate Period	2125–2010
Middle Kingdom	2010–1630
Second Intermediate Period	1630–1539
New Kingdom	1539–1069
Third Intermediate Period	1069–664
Late Period (Assyrian, Kushite, Persian rule)	664–332
Macedonian and Ptolemaic Period	332–30 BCE

Source: The dates before 664 BCE are approximate, and some are disputed. Those used here follow Toby Wilkinson, *The Rise and Fall of Ancient Egypt* (2010), xiv–xxiii.

pyramid. We know next to nothing about the first kings or of Egypt in their time. However, beginning with the Old Kingdom, around 2575 BCE, we know a surprising amount.

AGRICULTURE AND THE ECONOMY

Ancient Egypt was one of the most densely populated places on Earth. Most people lived in the delta in farming villages.

FARMING AND IRRIGATION The foundation of ancient Egypt was farming. Every year, upward of 90 percent of the population took part in the sowing and harvesting of barley, wheat, and a few vegetable crops. They also raised flax, from which linen cloth was made, sesame (for its oil), and eventually a variety of fruits and grapes. All these crops came originally from Southwest Asia. The delta region also specialized in livestock, especially oxen used for traction.

Irrigation, annual silt deposits, and ceaseless toil made ancient Egypt the richest agricultural land anywhere in the world. No fallow period was needed to restore fertility to soils because the annual summer flood brought a coating of rich silt. The technologies and methods of Egyptian farming changed little over 3,000 years, once

Egyptian Agriculture Paintings on the wall of an Egyptian tomb (ca. 1290 BCE) show workers engaged in the daily tasks of agriculture: using oxen to plow a field, and sowing and reaping crops such as flax, wheat, and fruit growing on trees.

the techniques of irrigation were mastered. Basin irrigation, used along the Nile, involved capturing part of the floodwaters behind earthen berms, or embankments, and releasing water to crops as needed over the following months. During the New Kingdom, an irrigation device called the *shaduf* was developed to help in the watering of gardens and vegetable plots. Later, waterwheels called *saqia* improved irrigation efficiency and added 10 to 15 percent to Egypt's cropland. But in general, under Egyptian conditions, little incentive existed to experiment and innovate in agriculture. Tried and true routines brought huge surpluses in most years.

All land belonged, in name at least, to the pharaoh. His agents took a share of the harvest in kind (Egyptians didn't use money before 300 BCE) and shipped it to central distribution points. From there grain went to the court, the bureaucracy, temples, far-flung garrisons, and royal enterprises such as mines. Large parts of the economy were state-run. Markets played only a small role in Egypt compared to Mesopotamia. Transport was by boat or donkey until camels came into use around 200 BCE. Egyptians didn't need wheeled carts much because riverboats and barges could go just about anywhere goods had to go except around the cataracts. Nile shipping made the transport of grain easy in normal times, so local famines were rare. Moreover, pharaohs typically kept a reserve of grain to use against hunger where needed. Nine years out of ten, the river's flood was neither too low nor too high, grain ripened, pharaohs took their cut, and the people still had enough to eat.

LOW NILES AND FAMINES Big famines were also rare in Egypt, but impossible to prevent if harvests failed throughout the country. Royal granaries might hold a reserve good for a few months—maybe enough to get most of the population through one bad harvest. But consecutive bad harvests brought starvation. There was nowhere else to turn to for food. Importing it from Mesopotamia would require overland travel and be too costly. Nubia and other lands dependent on the Nile would themselves have too little food in years when Egypt's harvest was poor.

The most frequent cause of a bad harvest was a low Nile flood that brought too little water and silt to Egypt and Nubia alike. Periods of sustained drought in Ethiopia's mountains brought repeated "low Niles," which spelled disaster for Egypt. Around 2300 to 2200 BCE, several low

Niles helped to bring the Old Kingdom to an end: without surplus grain, the pharaohs had nothing to distribute to their followers, their moral authority evaporated, and support for the state withered away amid starvation and chaos.

About 1210 to 1100 BCE, recurrent low Niles helped to bring down the New Kingdom. On both these occasions of dynastic change, searing droughts afflicted the whole of northeastern Africa and Southwest Asia, making it unlikely that people whose crops failed could get food from elsewhere. This misfortune spanned the entire web from the Nile to the Indus, brought about by a large-scale disturbance in climate patterns that lasted for decades. But when the gifts of the Nile began to flow once more, agricultural abundance and re-unification of Egypt soon followed.

Hieroglyphs This excerpt from The Book of the Dead attests to the quantity of pictographic symbols a scribe would need to memorize and interpret—even in papyrus manuscripts, such as this, which usually employed a more simplified form of hieroglyphs than that used for stone inscriptions.

SCRIBES AND SMITHS Ancient Egypt had crafts and industries as well as farms. In the desert outside the Nile valley, there were copper and gold mines and stone quarries, where unlucky men toiled in miserable conditions. Potters, weavers, smiths, and boatmen worked in many villages and every town. Women in most rural households spun linen cloth out of flax. In bigger towns, there were also stonemasons and scribes.

Only 1 to 2 percent of the population could read or write, almost all males. The few who mastered writing were professional scribes, most of whom worked at the court in service of pharaohs, who were usually illiterate. It was great work if you could get it, as the Lansing Papyrus made clear. But learning to write took five to ten years of hard study. The Egyptian writing system, called **hieroglyphs** ("sacred carvings"), developed beginning about 3000 BCE, possibly influenced by the Sumerian cuneiforms. It reached full complexity by 1500 BCE, when it comprised some 1,000 symbols—a lot to memorize.

Hieroglyphs can represent either sounds or words, and they can be written left to right, right to left, or top to bottom. Simplified versions developed, but even they were hard to learn. Priests used an easier version called hieratic script, for example, and after 700 BCE an even easier one, called demotic script, served for daily transactions. Hieratic and demotic were often used for the less formal texts—letters, bills of sale, poetry—that were written on papyrus, a thick and absorbent paper made from the stems of a reedy plant that grew in the Nile delta swamps. Stone inscriptions used the more formal hieroglyphs. The last use of hieroglyphs in Egypt came around 400 CE, by which time Egyptians had turned to alphabets.

Smiths were comparatively rare in Egypt. The techniques and technologies of metallurgy changed only slowly, as with agriculture, and Egypt had some copper and gold but little else in the way of useful ores. Egyptians adopted bronze for some weapons and tools beginning around 1600 BCE. They were late turning to iron, which they used sparingly before 670 BCE, perhaps because working iron requires much charcoal or fuelwood, always scarce in Egypt. Neighbors in Southwest Asia and to the south in Nubia used iron in greater quantities at earlier dates than Egyptians did.

TRADE Egypt was normally self-sufficient in food and in most other necessary items—but not all. With few sturdy trees, Egyptians had to trade for timber, which came mainly from the shores of the Levant. With the advent of bronze weaponry, Egypt had to import tin, also from Southwest Asia. Perhaps its most important import was gold, that favorite metal of ancient monarchs. Egypt had its own gold mines in the desert east of the Nile, but imported plenty from Nubia, to the south, and perhaps from elsewhere in Africa. The pharaohs' desire to secure access to timber and metals from abroad shaped their foreign policy.

EGYPT AND ITS NEIGHBORS

Egypt's most important trading partners were its near neighbors. To the south, upstream along the Nile, was Nubia. To the northeast, across a stretch of desert, stood the societies of the Levant and Mesopotamia.

NUBIA AND THE LEVANT South of the First Cataract lay the land called Nubia. Nubians were farmers, cattle herders, and fisherfolk living along the Nile. When pharaohs were strong, they sought to control Nubia, pushing Egypt's frontiers south. From the time of the Old Kingdom if not before, they occasionally mounted expeditions to seize Nubian slaves, ivory, ebony wood, cattle, animal skins, and above all, gold. During the Middle Kingdom, Egyptians managed to drag riverboats around the Nile's cataracts to launch assaults on Nubian towns and conquer parts of the country. But Nubia always reasserted its power south of the Second Cataract, if not all the way north to the First. Nubians often worked for Egypt as mercenary soldiers (they were renowned for their archery skills), especially during the Middle Kingdom.

When Nubian kings were strong and pharaohs were weak, they traded for Nubia's ivory and gold. And when Egypt was divided and at its weakest, Nubian rulers pushed out Egyptian garrisons and traders, and took control of the fortified posts at the First Cataract. Once, around 712–664 BCE, a Nubian state called Kush controlled most of Upper Egypt for half a century and Kushite kings became Egypt's pharaohs.

But that was exceptional. Most of the time, Egypt exploited Nubia through greater military power and better knowledge of the value of goods in the wider world. Pharaohs frequently boasted of their savage treatment of Nubians: Senusret III, in the nineteenth century BCE, for example, wanted people to believe he had "carried off their women . . . poisoned their wells, driven off their bulls, ripped up their barley and set fire to it." Pharaohs preferred reputations as brutal rather than merciful rulers—at least, as far as Nubians were concerned.

Over the millennia, through war and peace, Nubia provided vast quantities of goods that helped sustain the refined tastes of Egypt's elite. At the same time, Nubia's elite, especially the royal houses of Kush, took on attributes of Egyptian culture. They came to speak the Egyptian language and use Egyptian hieroglyphs in inscriptions. They adopted the worship of Egyptian gods—especially Amun, a major god in Thebes and eventually in all of Egypt, and built temples to him in the Egyptian style. They wanted to be buried with Egyptian-style funerary goods, and after 750 BCE or so, Nubian rulers began to build small pyramids.

Surplus grain and Nubian gold enabled Egypt to trade for timber and minerals from the Levant and elsewhere in Southwest Asia. Here too, exceptionally strong pharaohs occasionally preferred to exercise control over territory, installing garrisons in Palestine and Syria and sometimes as far afield as Mesopotamia in order to secure access to timber and metals. Weaker pharaohs might make peace with the dominant power in Southwest Asia, hoping to ensure access to trade goods. When Egypt was truly weak or divided, it couldn't keep "miserable Asiatics" (as one Egyptian text put it) from infiltrating the northeastern delta or perhaps even invading Egypt—as in the case of the Hyksos.

Nubia Depictions of Nubians speak to their relationship with their Egyptian neighbors. In this frieze from an Egyptian temple (ca. 1490 BCE), a group of Nubians are shown as mercenary soldiers whose archery skills could aid the Egyptian army.

THE HYKSOS Starting in the eighteenth century BCE, the **Hyksos** either invaded Egypt militarily or infiltrated as peaceful migrants. They probably came from what is now Lebanon, spoke a different language than Egyptians did, and worshipped different gods. The Hyksos were skilled in the latest military technique, chariot warfare (unknown in Egypt), and the arts of horsemanship. They also had bronze weapons, composite bows, and body armor, all new to Egypt. So armed invasion is plausible, but so is a peaceful movement into an Egypt suffering from famines and divisions. Soon after 1700 BCE, the Hyksos took the Egyptian capital of Memphis.

Hyksos rule (ca.1700–1500 BCE) brought Egypt stronger connections to the trading world of the eastern Mediterranean. They built a large port in the northeast delta—Hutwaret (also called Avaris)—to handle the trade with Southwest Asia and the islands of Cyprus and Crete. Wine, olive oil, copper, and timber flowed into Egypt from Cyprus and the Levant. Egyptian artwork began to show—for a few decades, at least—influence from the Minoan kingdom on the island of Crete. Egyptian technologies, especially of war, came to resemble those in use in Mesopotamia. As Egypt became more tightly integrated with Southwest Asia after 1700 BCE, the linkages of the western edge of the Nile-Indus web thickened—not long after those of the eastern edge, the Indus valley itself, had weakened.

While the Hyksos dominated the delta, and at times as far south as Thebes in Upper Egypt, Nubians made incursions from the south. Egypt seemed about to disappear, gobbled up by neighbors. But soon, and surprisingly quickly, Egyptian pharaohs based in Thebes turned the tables first on the Nubians and then on the Hyksos, and drove them out of Egypt. Perhaps a string of good harvests lifted their fortunes to the point where they could finance bigger armies. Perhaps they learned the arts of chariot warfare and the making of bronze weapons well enough to oust their neighbors. In any case, the tighter links to Southwest Asia remained.

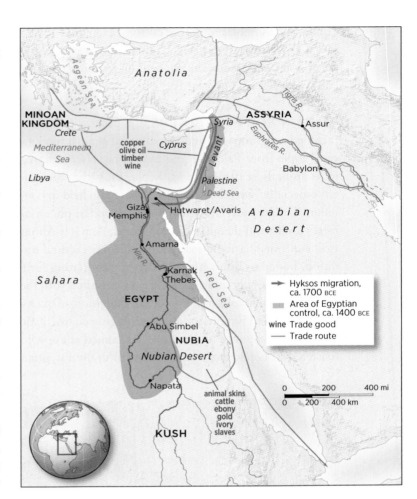

Egypt and Its Neighbors, ca. 1700–600 BCE In addition to trade links, Egypt after 1700 BCE was increasingly involved in politics and war both in Nubia to the south and in the Levant. Politically speaking, after the Hyksos intrusion, Egypt was tightly enmeshed in a web of interactions with its nearest neighbors and occasionally further afield.

Hyksos Scarab This Egyptian scarab, or beetle-shaped ornament, is dated to around 1620–1581 BCE and is decorated with the name of the Hyksos king Khayan. During this period, scarabs were symbolic of divine manifestation and were commonly used for seals and amulets, as well as in funerary rites. Through trade, many scarabs were spread throughout the eastern Mediterranean and to Mesopotamia.

A REGIONAL POWER During the Middle and New Kingdoms, when Egypt was usually strong, it was often a major player in the international relations of Southwest Asia, raiding and invading rather than suffering raid and invasion. Pharaohs fought the various powers of Mesopotamia and Syria from time to time. One, Tutmose III, campaigned annually in the Levant for nearly 20 years running. The pharaohs' aims, in addition to looting and ensuring access to metals and timber in Southwest Asia, included making names for themselves as glorious leaders. The ideal career for a pharaoh of the Middle or New Kingdom featured victories in both Nubia and Syria, followed by peace and a spree of monument building. Warfare and diplomacy, as well as trade and cultural exchange, linked Egypt to Southwest Asia, as to Nubia, more strongly after 2000 BCE than before and, by and large, more strongly still with each passing century.

DISDAIN FOR FOREIGNERS Egyptian elite culture included a vigorous chauvinism directed against foreigners. People from Palestine and Syria were often referred to as animals or disdained as shepherds. Other foreigners, especially "wretched Kushites," were also held in contempt. Unlike most monarchies, the Egyptian pharaohs rarely used royal daughters as tools of diplomacy. About 1500 BCE, one Mesopotamian king, following cultural tradition, hoped to boost his standing by negotiating for a pharaoh's daughter in marriage. He was rebuffed with the remark that pharaohs never sent their daughters to marry foreigners. Elite Egyptians, although highly chauvinistic about their language and culture, welcomed those who mastered it. Foreigners who became culturally Egyptian

Race in Egypt A relief from around 1250 BCE of the pharaoh Ramses II conquering other peoples shows the range of skin tones that Egyptians used to visually represent foreign peoples.

married freely with native Egyptians and had as good a chance of enjoying high status and power as anyone else. A few foreigners did rise into the elite.

In the nineteenth and twentieth centuries CE, some scholars of ancient Egypt tried hard to prove that Egyptians were representatives of either a white or a black race. Either argument would have puzzled ancient Egyptians. In their art, they depict four different shades of human: Libyans (from Mediterranean coastlands west of Egypt) were the fairest; people from Palestine and Syria a yellowish-brown; Egyptians a reddish-brown; and Nubians black. Women were always portrayed a few shades lighter than men, perhaps indicating that they either were, or should be, less often outdoors in the sun. In their texts, ancient Egyptians took no interest in skin color or physiognomy. The variations among humankind that mattered to them were cultural.

Egyptian disdain for foreigners grew harder to maintain as Egypt's power waned. After the eighth century BCE, Egypt was more often weak than strong in comparison to its neighbors. We've seen that Nubian kings ruled Egypt for half a century. They were driven out not by Egyptians but by Assyrian invaders from northern Mesopotamia, whose iron weapons and mass armies made them masters of much of Southwest Asia. Egypt, dependent on distant sources for iron and without a reliable supply of horses, had no military answer for Assyrian power. After 664 BCE, for half a century Egypt lost its autonomy and became an Assyrian vassal kingdom. And in the sixth century BCE, a new power arose, Persia, which in 525 BCE ended Egyptian self-rule for many centuries to come. More invasions and rule by foreign elites followed.

PHARAOHS AND MONUMENTS

Of the roughly 170 pharaohs from Narmer's time onward, two were women. The female pharaoh we know most about, Hatshepsut, came to power by marrying a pharaoh—her half-brother—who died a few years afterward. She at first served as regent for her infant son, but then claimed full powers for herself. Hatshepsut proved to be a highly competent pharaoh for 20 years until her death about 1458 BCE. She often had herself depicted in official artwork as a muscular man with a beard and referred to as "son of Amun," an indication of ancient Egyptian expectations of pharaohs.

MAAT The main duties of pharaohs were to oversee Egypt's irrigation system and ensure a good harvest, defeat Nubians and other neighbors when necessary, and keep the temples properly supplied and the gods satisfied. As Egyptians saw it, the pharaohs' primary role was to maintain *maat*, a concept that embraced justice and truth as well as order. Pharaohs could fulfill this responsibility only through proper mediation with the gods—a crucial duty of almost every ancient monarch anywhere. There were two final duties: to have a son suitable for succession and to build monuments to oneself. To achieve the former, pharaohs usually married several women, frequently including their sisters, and most pharaohs had liaisons on the side. To build monuments, they conscripted labor and materials in gargantuan quantities. Suitable monuments included temples with boastful inscriptions recounting their achievements in life and above all an impressive tomb worthy of a divine, or at least semi-divine, king. Egyptian religion, as we'll see shortly, took the concept of an afterlife to heart, much more so than Mesopotamian peoples did.

Hatshepsut A statue of Hatshepsut created during her reign depicts the pharaoh with a masculine body and a beard. In her hands, she carries vessels for making offerings to the gods.

PYRAMIDS For tombs, pharaohs of the Old Kingdom came to prefer **pyramids**. In the Old Kingdom, Egyptians believed that only pharaohs would experience an afterlife. Since afterlife was eternal, preparations for it were exacting. Early pharaohs arranged to have servants, pets, and dwarves (they had a fascination with dwarves) killed by strangulation and buried with them. One king had 600 people sacrificed to keep him properly attended in the afterlife. By 2600 BCE, pharaohs had stopped human sacrifice and instead stocked their tombs with *shabti*, or miniature statues of people, and things they might need in the afterlife. And they started conscripting thousands upon thousands of peasants to build giant pyramids to serve as pharaonic tombs.

Khufu, also known as Cheops, reigned for 20 years around 2500 BCE. He oversaw the construction of a pyramid that, at 481 ft. (147 m), remained the world's tallest building for 4,300 years, until completion of the Eiffel Tower in Paris in 1889. The Great Pyramid at Giza—just outside of today's Cairo—is built of 2.5 million blocks of stone weighing about 2 tons each. It took a minimum of 10,000 men—some say 25,000—working day and night to satisfy Khufu's megalomania. If his labor force worked every single day of his 20-year reign, they would have had to place a block of stone every 4 minutes. They worked with great precision under the direction of skilled engineers: the base is nearly perfectly flat, and its four sides are within 1/20 of a degree of alignment with the four points of the compass.

Scholars used to think that legions of slaves built the pyramids. But it seems that slavery was rare in Egypt before the New Kingdom, and the unlucky army of laborers was made up of conscripted peasants. If, as experts believe, Egypt as a whole contained about 1 to 2 million people during the Old Kingdom, and only males above age 14 were conscripted, then during Khufu's reign 2 to 10 percent of adult male Egyptians were drafted to build pyramids. The few skeletons that survive show evidence of many accidents and arthritis of the joints. What these men thought about pushing and pulling huge blocks of limestone up ramps to ensure a suitable afterlife for the pharaoh is unrecorded.

Pyramids at Giza The pyramids Khufu built—with the Great Pyramid in the center—loom over the people and horse in the foreground of this nineteenth-century photograph, giving an indication of the pyramids' vast scale.

Pharaonic Monuments The pharaoh Ramses II built this monument to his own greatness as part of a temple complex in southern Egypt around 1250 BCE. The enormous statues of Ramses emphasize his status, likening him to a god.

After the Old Kingdom, pyramids gradually went out of style, in part because of the expense. The last of the pyramids, a mere 2 percent the size of Khufu's, was built in 1745 BCE. Later pharaohs devoted their subjects' labor to erecting other kinds of monuments, temples, obelisks, stelae, and statues of themselves; these far outnumber pyramids. Some involved moving stone blocks weighing 1,000 tons—using only muscle power. The pharaohs employed stonemasons to carve messages into these monuments, most of which record their great deeds. These were platforms for pharaonic propaganda rather than launching pads for the afterlife. In this respect, the pharaohs' behavior grew less distinctive and more like that of rulers elsewhere.

Every pharaoh wanted to undertake a program of monument building, but not all could afford it. The biggest programs occurred during periods of peace, especially during the Old Kingdom. In effect, pharaohs had to choose between foreign wars and monument building; doing both at once was usually too costly in manpower terms. But during the Middle and New Kingdoms, several pharaohs began their reigns with wars in Nubia or the Levant. When these wars went well for Egypt, they burnished royal reputations and brought home loot that made it easier to finish pharaonic careers with magnificent monuments. When foreign wars went badly for Egypt, pharaohs built fewer monuments.

RELIGION

The fundamental purpose of religious practice in Egypt, as in Mesopotamia, was to win the favor of the gods. They, after all, were believed to control the elemental forces of the universe. Careful attention to rituals was needed to ensure that they would continue to bestow blessings—the warmth of the sun, the life-giving waters of the Nile—upon those who honored them properly. As it did in all ancient states, religion also underpinned the power of Egypt's rulers. The pharaohs claimed to have unique access to the gods, and some of them claimed to be gods themselves. Most Egyptians probably accepted these claims—at least, when order prevailed and the Nile's flood didn't fail.

GODS What we know about Egyptian religion comes from a handful of texts and a lot of archeology, almost all of which speaks only to the experience of the elite. In the Old Kingdom, every Egyptian village and town had its own gods, usually associated with a particular animal and represented by a stylized image of that animal or the animal's head on a human body: for example, a falcon (Horus, associated with kings and the sky), a wolf or jackal (Anubis, associated with preparation for the afterlife), a cat (Bastet, originally a goddess of warfare, later the protector of cats). Some peasants honored gods who specialized in helping people through trials such as childbirth. Many relied heavily on Isis, goddess of the home and fertility, at least by the time of the New Kingdom. Magic and charms surely played a big role in popular religion. Humble folk often carried amulets, small pieces of jewelry thought to ward off evil spirits.

By and large, ancient Egyptian deities were benign and helpful, bringing warmth, water, fertility, and other blessings. However, one, called Set or Seth, eventually became associated with chaos and deserts. A popular myth held that he killed his brother Osiris and chopped up the body to prevent anyone from carrying out the

MAJOR EGYPTIAN GODS	
NAME	**IDENTITIES, RESPONSIBILITIES, AND ASSOCIATIONS**
Ra	Sun; pharaohs
Amun	Patron god of city of Thebes
Amun-Ra	Sun, air; a fusion of Ra and Amun, considered the most powerful of gods during the New Kingdom
Hathor	Kindness, motherhood, love; Nile flood; often considered mother of Ra
Isis	Motherhood; mother of kings; originally associated with Hathor
Osiris	God of the afterlife; husband of Isis
Anubis	Death, embalming, underworld
Thoth	Writing, mathematics, wisdom, magic, the moon; patron of scribes and priests

appropriate funeral rites. Another, Hathor, was goddess of joy and erotic love, fate and divine vengeance, and drunkenness. In one myth, the sun god Ra grew irritated with humankind's evil conduct and assigned Hathor the job of punishment. She took to it with relish and by the end of the day had killed half of the people on Earth. Ra managed to trick Hathor and save humankind, and Egyptians eventually associated Hathor with motherhood and childbirth.

Over the centuries, gods could change their responsibilities, merge with one another, or disappear—just as in the pantheons of Mesopotamia or, as we'll see, the Ganges basin. Egyptians had no formal scripture, no holy texts invested with divine authority. Their religious texts were more like guidebooks, with instructions on how to perform rituals and how to ensure an afterlife. Theirs was a living, evolving religion, less constrained in its mutations than many others for which sacred scriptures exist.

With the arrival of the Hyksos in the eighteenth century BCE, Egyptian religion acquired features borrowed from the Levant. Some Egyptians, especially in the delta, began to worship Baal, a Semitic god. A cult developed devoted to Astarte, a goddess based on the Babylonian Ishtar who in Egypt became a war goddess. Egyptians in the delta started to bury dead infants in clay jars (called amphora) from Palestine. In religion, as in trade, the Hyksos occupation brought Egypt closer to Southwest Asia, tightening the Nile-Indus web.

THE AFTERLIFE Elite Egyptians placed great stock in the afterlife. At first, only pharaohs could attain it. To arrive in good condition, one needed to be mummified and provided with all manner of grave goods, tools, weapons, and servants. Mummification alone took up to 10 weeks and required skilled morticians who removed a corpse's organs (except the heart) through narrow incisions. They took brains out in small pieces through the nasal cavity. After this, they had to dry the body with salts and wrap it in linens. Egyptians believed that elaborate funerary rituals had to be carefully carried out to ensure passage into the afterlife.

During the First Intermediate Period, just after the Old Kingdom, a democratization of the afterlife took place, associated with an emphasis on Osiris as lord of the afterlife (he had formerly been a god of farming).

Egyptians came to believe that anyone who followed the necessary procedures was eligible to make the journey to Osiris's domain, not just pharaohs. It was beyond the means of ordinary folk, but those who could afford it normally took the necessary steps, and understandably so. The afterlife was eternal, one was always young and healthy there, and food, drink, and sex were always available. If you took the precaution of including a ***shabti*** of a human laborer among your grave goods, in the land of Osiris it would do all the manual labor that might be needed, ensuring an afterlife of leisure.

Hathor A relief of the goddess Hathor, with allusions to her association with sex and fertility.

During the Middle Kingdom, Egyptians developed a concept of the final judgment: you could only gain entry to the land of Osiris with a good moral transcript. The dead, including pharaohs, could plead their case to a panel of gods, but that wouldn't help if they flunked the real test: their heart, which contained all the evil they had done in their lives, was weighed in a scale against the feather of *maat*—the concept of truth, justice, and order. Only those with minimal evil in their hearts could pass to the land of Osiris. Others, whose hearts outweighed the feather of *maat,* had their beings forever destroyed by the

Shabti Important people were buried with dozens of *shabti* figurines—like this troop, found in a tomb from 500 BCE—who would perform all necessary domestic labor for the dead person in the afterlife.

Final Judgment In this scene from the Book of the Dead, dated to around 1275 BCE, a heart is weighed in a scale against *maat*'s feather of truth to determine its bearer's eternal fate.

goddess Ammut, devourer of the dead. Whether this new concept constrained immoral behavior or not is uncertain, but it placed responsibility for one's eternal fate squarely upon the individual.

An important text, the Book of the Dead—a collection of magic spells and religious recommendations in use by 1500 BCE—offers some guidelines on how to pass the ultimate test. All would go well if one lived so as to be able to make a declaration to Anubis like this:

> I have not done falsehood against men, I have not impoverished my associates, I have done no wrong in the Place of Truth, I have not learnt that which is not, I have done no evil, I have not daily required labor in excess of what was to be done for me, my name has not reached the offices of those who control slaves, I have not deprived the orphan of his property, I have not done what the gods detest, I have not slandered a servant to his master, I have not caused pain, I have not made hungry, I have not made to weep, I have not killed, I have not turned anyone over to a killer, I have not caused anyone's suffering.

Like every durable faith, Egyptian religion evolved over the centuries, absorbing foreign influences and adapting to changes in society.

AKHENATEN In the fourteenth century BCE, a pharaoh of the New Kingdom, Amenhotep IV, tried to change Egyptian religion by using his authority to impose monotheism. After a few years on the throne, he led a religious revolution, forbidding worship of gods other than his favorite, Aten, the sun disk and a manifestation of the sun god Ra. He had references to other gods scratched out of Egypt's temples, and he diverted resources from all other cults to that of Aten. He changed his own name to Akhenaten ("living spirit of Aten") and founded a new city, today's Amarna, dedicated to Aten.

Just what lay behind this radical departure in Egyptian religion is unclear. Akhenaten had himself depicted differently from all previous pharaohs, who always appear as young, athletically built, and serene. Akhenaten's physique is less imposing, and he and his wife, Nefertiti, are shown in homely scenes. Nefertiti in some representations appears with the trappings of a pharaoh, leading scholars to suppose that she may have been a co-regent with Akhenaten. All this novelty proved unpopular with the priesthood and did not long outlive Akhenaten himself. Most of his monuments were torn down, defaced, and re-used by his successors. A few scholars suggest that Akhenaten's religious revolution provided the basis for the monotheism that infuses Judaism and Christianity (the first evidence of Judaic monotheism came about two centuries after Akhenaten, as we saw in Chapter 4). Akhenaten's son, incidentally, was Tutankamun, the famous King Tut, an insignificant pharaoh who died as a teenager and whose only distinction was that his tomb

Akhenaten A wall relief depicts Akhenaten and Nefertiti playing with their three daughters while the sun's rays shine Aten's blessings on them.

was among the very few never robbed before archeologists got to it in 1922.

Egyptian religion had the effect of justifying pharaonic rule. The great mass of Egyptians led lives of unremitting toil that supported an opulent and often slothful courtly life for pharaohs and their families. The fact that Egyptians rarely rose up in revolt against this arrangement suggests that the ideology of divine kingship convinced almost all Egyptians almost all the time that things were as they should be. The common folk may have been intimidated—that was part of the purpose of monumental architecture—but they were more ideologically intimidated than physically. There is little evidence within Egypt (as opposed to lands that Egyptians conquered) of the sort of apparatus of repression used by Assyrian kings, for example.

After a long and successful career, Egyptian religion faded away—but it didn't vanish without a trace. After 300 BCE, Egyptian beliefs and rituals were influenced by Greek and Roman religion. Later, most Egyptians became Christians and then later still, Muslims. But even today, modern Egyptians observe festivals originally offered in honor of Osiris.

HEALTH AND SOCIETY

At the time of the unification of Egypt around 3100 BCE, the entire country contained perhaps 300,000 people. During the Old Kingdom, population reached 1 to 2 million and in prosperous moments of the New Kingdom, about 3 million. People's lives were short by our standards, filled with suffering and disease. Few reached age 40, and the average life expectancy for those who made it past toddlerhood was about 30 years. A large proportion died between ages 2 and 4. With high death rates, Egyptians, like all ancient farming peoples, tried to have big families. Some texts refer to contraceptives, including honey and crocodile dung, but few Egyptians used them.

DISEASE Disease lay at the heart of life for ancient Egyptians at least as much as for other ancient peoples. Since the Nile, like other rivers along which people clustered, served as both a sewer and a source of drinking water, gastrointestinal ailments were common. Peasants who waded for long hours in irrigated fields usually had schistosomiasis, a debilitating illness spread by worms that are carried by snails. Skeletons testify to the existence of tuberculosis in perhaps a quarter of all Egyptians. No doubt ancient Egyptians hosted some crowd diseases—infections such as smallpox that can circulate indefinitely among large enough populations. Many skeletons show evidence of malaria, probably widespread in Egypt, or of hookworm. Malnutrition was routine among the masses. A celebrated pharaoh of the thirteenth century BCE, Ramses II, in contrast, suffered from hardening of the arteries, likely reflecting a meat-rich diet. Pharaohs, according to texts, ate meat often, including such delicacies as cranes, antelopes, and hyenas. Hatshepsut, the female pharaoh of the New Kingdom, who died at about 50 years of age, was obese. She, like most Egyptians, had worn-down teeth, a result of eating food containing dust and sand.

Ancient Egypt had doctors and a number of detailed medical texts. Egyptian doctors specialized in the treatment of specific diseases and parts of the body. Specialists in eye ailments were in demand, as one would expect in a population subject to windblown Saharan dust and sand. Surviving Egyptian texts suggest doctors could deal with wounds and broken limbs fairly well, but—like everyone else—had no clue what to do with malaria or tuberculosis. In any case, doctors only treated the top 1 percent in

Care of the Body A tomb painting (ca. 1400 BCE) shows two specialists tending to the physical needs of a group of people: the one on the left is giving the seated man a haircut, while the one on the right is treating an eye problem.

Egypt; everyone else trusted to luck, the gods, and home remedies.

SOCIAL HIERARCHY Egyptian society was as hierarchical and unequal as human societies get. Pharaohs enjoyed a degree of authority rarely equaled elsewhere. The main threats to their position came from provincial elites and their own extended families, which often included several wives eager to see their sons on the throne and many sons and nephews hankering for a turn as pharaoh. So palace intrigues and occasional coups d'état were the essence of court politics.

An elite of powerful families surrounded the king and court, together making up perhaps 1 percent of Egyptian society. Provincial elites ran temples and estates throughout the country. Some of them amassed great wealth. Most were literate and took part in the high culture of Egypt. Artisans, normally illiterate, made up another small percentage of the population. Cities such as Memphis, Thebes, and Abydos were home to many artisans, scribes, temple priests, construction workers, beggars, and thieves; city residents accounted for less than 5 percent of the population. Close to 95 percent of Egyptians worked the land.

In one sense, Egypt was a society of immigrants. Its first settlers had wandered in from the Sahara. From the Old Kingdom onward, Egypt absorbed Nubians from the south, as slaves, mercenaries, laborers, and—as we've

seen—as conquerors of the southern part of the country. After the New Kingdom, foreigners referred to as Libyans drifted in to the delta from the west, dominated some areas, and set up their own dynasties. Others came from Southwest Asia, sometimes as shepherds hoping their herds might nibble on the Nile delta's lush vegetation, sometimes as conquerors like the Assyrians. Egyptian texts indicate a few ancient Hebrews migrated to Egypt too, although they left no archeological trace. Almost all of these immigrants were "Egyptianized": they or their children learned the local tongue, came to worship the local gods, and conformed to the conventions of Egyptian culture and society. And, as immigrants generally do, they changed Egypt a little by bringing their own traditions, beliefs, artistic styles, and cooking habits with them.

The Nile valley and delta, like Mesopotamia and—as we'll see—the Ganges, was a magnet for people looking for work, food, and opportunity. All neighboring lands were poor compared to these river valleys. And the river valley environments were so unhealthy that societies in Egypt, Mesopotamia, and the Ganges often needed immigrants to take the place of the sick and the dead. The newcomers probably died at even faster rates than the native-born, but they kept coming, sometimes willingly, sometimes as slaves.

FAMILY LIFE Family life in Egypt was similar to that in other ancient agrarian societies. As usual, the available

Immigrants A group of warriors dressed in the tunics and sandals of Semitic nomads asks permission to enter Egypt in a tomb painting from the nineteenth century BCE. This evidence may indicate the presence of ancient Hebrews in Egypt during the period.

evidence overwhelmingly concerns elite families and largely comes from texts authored by men until after 300 BCE. Elite women took responsibility for the domestic sphere and supervised squadrons of servants. Some texts remind men not to criticize or interfere with their wives' conduct of a household. Arranged marriage was the norm, typically around ages 12 to 14 for females and 18 to 21 for males. Divorce was possible. Women could own property and conduct trade on their own accounts. By and large, elite women didn't work outside their homes, although a very few served as priestesses. None seem to have worked in the state bureaucracy. By the seventh century BCE, marriages often included contracts that safeguarded the property of individuals, both men and women.

Children were numerous and often sickly. When healthy, they played with dice, knucklebones, dolls, and board games. They swam in the Nile, wrestled, and boxed. By age five or six, they spent much of their time working alongside their parents and older siblings. Children were beloved, regarded as gifts from the gods, but discipline could be tough: parents often beat their children to improve their behavior. That apparently didn't always work. One lad studying to be a scribe earned this report card: "[Y]ou neglect your studies and think only of pleasure. You wander through the streets, stinking of beer." Inheritance was typically equal among all children, male and female. One document from the New Kingdom shows a mother named Naunakht playing favorites among her offspring, cutting out of her will those who she felt had treated her poorly.

GENDER AND CLASS Most Egyptian women spent their adult lives tending to children, weaving cloth, baking bread, and preparing other foods. They and their families lived in humble mud-brick houses. Artwork from the Old Kingdom shows women winnowing grain—although later art shows only men doing this chore. Other images suggest that women also harvested flax and gleaned fields (gleaning involves picking up loose seeds or kernels after a harvest). Some women worked as domestic servants in elite households. Almost no women, even members of the elite, could read or write.

Class trumped gender in some respects. Elite women could command male servants, but lower-class males couldn't command elite women. Texts suggest that occasionally lower-class men could rise in government service and join the elite. Beautiful lower-class women might be recruited for the royal harem. But the great majority of people died in roughly the same circumstances into which they were born— again, much as in other agrarian societies.

Women's Work This statue of a woman grinding grain on a stone mill from around 2500 BCE provides a vivid example of the daily labor that Egyptian women performed at home.

There is one last point to consider about social class in ancient Egypt, one that will come up again in other contexts. The written sources about Egyptian life indicate a strong preference for social stability and order. They portray the Intermediate Periods as dark ages. From the point of view of toiling peasants, however, periods when the state was weak might have been the best of times, not the worst. After all, the state when weak had less power to extract a share of the harvest from peasant families. And fewer men were conscripted for foreign wars or building sprees.

Egyptian society developed in a context of tightening links to its neighbors. The whole Nile valley north of the Fifth Cataract formed something of its own web by 2500 BCE, thanks to the ease of transport along the river. The Nile's links to Mesopotamia and indirectly to the Indus meant that a far larger Nile-Indus web was under construction by 2500 BCE and was firmly in place after Hyksos rule around 1500 BCE. By that time, people along the Ganges were beginning to build another complex society in northern India—in effect, another eastern expansion of the web.

THE GANGES BASIN, THE VEDAS, AND EARLY INDIA, 2000–200 BCE

Before their collapse, the Indus valley cities had stood at the easternmost edge of the web that stretched from the Nile to the Indus. As they declined, a slow frontier movement of people wafted across northern India. Many settled in the forested plains of the **Ganges basin**. These rich alluvial lands could support dense populations and numerous urban centers, provided farmers had suitable crops, tools, skills, and sufficient organization to undertake irrigation.

Most of what we know about the people of the Ganges basin (or the Gangetic plain) comes from religious texts—in sharp contrast to what we know of people in the ancient Indus, Egyptian, or Mesopotamian societies. As we've seen, the material remains of Indus valley, Egyptian, or Mesopotamian cities and villages allow us to make strong inferences about agriculture, trade, crafts, art, and architecture. With respect to the early history of the societies of the Ganges, scholars working from Sanskrit texts can reconstruct something of the spiritual and social world, but less of ancient economic life along the Ganges.

INDO-ARYAN MIGRATIONS AND VEDIC PEOPLES

From around 1500 BCE, the Ganges valley became the cradle of a new Indian culture and complex society. Just how this happened, and the degree to which it involved migrant populations from outside India, are fiercely contested among specialists and political partisans in India today. The textual, archeological, linguistic, and genetic evidence is not consistent. But it looks as if pastoralist migrants from Central Asia and Iran, mainly men, filtered through mountain passes and into Punjab and the upper Ganges beginning around 2000 BCE. They spoke an Indo-European language, closely related to Iranian tongues, that evolved into Sanskrit, the sacred language of Hindu religion. The migrants called themselves *arya*, which originally meant "people from Iran" but in Sanskrit came to mean "noble." Scholars generally call them Indo-Aryans or Vedic peoples.

The newcomers to north India were herders, skilled in cattle raising and equestrian warfare. The migrants brought horses and war chariots to India, as well as new gods and rituals, often built around fire and animal sacrifice. They merged with people departing the declining settlements of the Indus valley, and together they forged a new culture, one often called Vedic after the religious texts they created—the **Vedas**.

The Gangetic plain to which Indo-Aryans and early Vedic culture came had a scattered population of foragers, hunters, and shifting cultivators as of 1500 BCE. They

Indo-Aryan Equestrians These stone figurines, dated to around 2000 BCE, suggest the importance of horses to the early Vedic peoples.

used mainly stone tools. Dense forests, nourished by the monsoon rains, covered most of the land.

By 1200 to 800 BCE, archeology suggests, incoming migrants had occupied the upper Ganges. They practiced their traditional cattle raising and, increasingly, settled agriculture. They gradually expanded eastward to the middle and lower Ganges, taking up rice farming as they went. The further east they moved, the more their language, Sanskrit, incorporated features of existing north Indian languages. Their communities were led by religious specialists; kings and states came only after about 800 BCE. What held them together was a sense of kinship, of superiority over local folk, and a high culture encapsulated in songs and poems—the Vedas.

THE VEDAS

The four Vedas are the earliest extant examples of literature in Sanskrit and the oldest sacred texts of the Hindu religion. The Vedas—*veda* means "wisdom"—say they were composed by sages just "as a skilled craftsman makes a chariot." Modern scholarship says they were oral traditions recited for many centuries before being written down and may have originated as early as 1800 BCE. Memorizing the *vedas*, which include many thousand verses, required deep devotion. Their contents include hymns, myths, magic spells, and rules for carrying out rituals properly.

The earliest, the *Rig Veda*, probably dates from about 1500 to 1200 BCE as an oral tradition. People wrote it down no earlier than 1100 BCE. It shares similarities with a sacred Iranian epic, the *Avesta*, both in language and in the stories it tells. Much of its dialogue is spoken by women. It recounts the exploits of some 33 gods, most of whom were responsible for features of nature such as the sun or rivers. To stay on their good side, people had to offer them sacrifices, usually of animals ranging from bees to elephants but most often livestock. The gods in the *Rig Veda* undertake heroic and violent deeds, prize horses and cattle, and indulge in drinking, gambling, and sex. Their behavior reflected the values and self-image of a male warrior elite. In these respects, the gods of the *Rig Veda* bore strong similarities to the gods of Iran and Mesopotamia and contrasted with those of Egypt.

The early Vedas depict pastoral peoples in the process of taking up farming. Cattle raiding, horse racing, and sheep and goat herding figure prominently, but there are references to plows and fields as well. They portray a society without much specialization in the division of labor (beyond age and gender) and without villages or towns. The later Vedas (and other Sanskrit texts), composed after 800 BCE when farming loomed larger and settlement of the Ganges valley was moving eastward, show a more complex society with the first hints of urbanization.

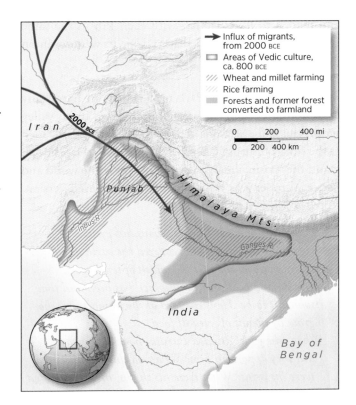

Ancient North India, ca. 2000–800 BCE Like certain other river basins before it, the Ganges came to host an interactive web of thousands of villages engaged in irrigated farming of grain crops—typically wheat, millet, or rice—in the millennium after 2000 BCE. People in these villages developed a distinctive religious tradition involving elements of ritual practice brought by migrants from Central Asia and Iran. That tradition evolved into Hinduism.

GENDER AND FAMILY LIFE From the Vedas and other texts, we can get some idea of family and gender relations in ancient north India. Women have speaking roles in some early Vedic hymns, and in one a young wife is invited to speak publicly. Another refers to a "learned daughter," implying that education wasn't entirely limited to males. Women could take part in religious rituals. They could boast unblushingly about their sexual prowess. Nonetheless, the Vedas also contain plenty of misogynistic views, and over time it seems the situation of women deteriorated. Later texts connect women with evil. One from the eighth to sixth century BCE, the *Shatapatha Brahmana*, declares: "The woman, the Sudra, the dog and the crow are falsehood." (A Sudra was a low-status person in the Hindu caste system, as we'll see shortly.) The *Law of Manu*, from about the third century BCE, portrays women as in all things dependent on fathers, husbands, and sons. The north Indian case is one of several in which the independence of women diminished as pastoral societies took up farming and created states.

Households were normally composed of multiple generations all under the authority of one senior male—a father or grandfather. Sons took part in farm work and religious rituals. Daughters took responsibility for preparing food and other household chores. All women were expected to marry, subordinate themselves to their husbands, and ideally produce sons who could perform proper funeral rites and sacrifices. Husbands were urged to honor wives and give them specific clothing and foods as gifts on holidays. Widows could not remarry (widowers could). Marriage was usually monogamous, but polygamy was not unknown. Property was held by families and perhaps by large extended families—clans—but not by individuals. Later Vedic texts sometimes consider wives as their husbands' property. Families belonged to clans and tended to live together with their kin in the same villages. Most of these social arrangements were common in ancient agrarian societies.

SOCIAL DIVISIONS Parts of the Vedas are hardly any easier to understand than the undeciphered Indus valley script. But some sections are more straightforward, such as the story of Purusa (also spelled Purusha), the primeval giant, the "cosmic man" from whose body the world and its social order was built. Here is a condensed version, from the *Rig Veda*.

> *Thousand-headed is Purusa, thousand-eyed, thousand-footed. Having covered the earth on all sides, he stood above it the width of ten fingers.*
> *Only Purusa is all this, that which has been and that which is to be. He is the lord of the immortals, who grow by means of [ritual] food.*
> *When [the gods] divided Purusa, how many ways did they apportion him? What was his mouth? What were his arms? What were his thighs, his feet declared to be?*
> *His mouth was the Brahman [caste], his arms were the Rajanaya [Ksatriya caste], his thighs the Vaisya [caste]; from his feet the Sudra [caste] was born.*
> *The moon was born from his mind; from his eye the sun was born; from his mouth both Indra [war] and Agni [fire]; from his breath Vayu [wind] was born.*
> *From his navel arose the air; from his head the heaven evolved; from his feet the earth; the [four] directions from his ear. Thus, they fashioned the worlds.*

This excerpt allows a glimpse into the social divisions of ancient India. The most basic division, as ancient Indians saw it, was among the various castes—a social hierarchy created and sanctioned, like the moon, the sun, and the earth, by the gods.

CASTE, HIERARCHY, AND EARLY HINDUISM

The early migrants who drifted into the Ganges basin divided society loosely into rulers, priests, and producers. But they apparently had no rigid distinctions. Once settled, they gradually developed a four-tier hierarchy, the basis of the **caste system** that was taking shape around 1000 BCE.

EARLY CASTE SYSTEM At the top stood priests, or Brahmins; next came rulers and soldiers, or Kshatriya; then peasants and traders, or Vaishya; and at the bottom of the hierarchy, slaves and artisans, or Sudra. Caste status was hereditary: your caste was the same as your parents' caste. It's notable that genetic admixture from Central Asia is found much more frequently among people of the Brahmin caste than among other Indians. This suggests that the migrating newcomers became religious specialists above all else—and that Brahmins generally obeyed the religious law that they should marry only fellow Brahmins. By 500 BCE, north Indian society was far different than that of a millennium before: more complex, more hierarchical, more agricultural—and more like that which already existed in Mesopotamia and Egypt.

Brahmins were held to be the most ritually pure, the least "polluted," and were expected to wear white clothing. The Sudras' black garb symbolized their impurity. But there were people who ranked even lower, people who had no caste at all, such as those who worked with hides and leather, which were considered ritually impure. They were called untouchables (and today are often known as *dalits*). Brahmins in particular tried hard to avoid them. Dozens of sub-castes eventually evolved within this four-tier structure. Doctrines and habits emerged that prohibited different castes from intermarrying or even eating together.

The Vedas and later texts spelled out the duties and privileges of all castes and provided justifications for the system as a whole. Brahmins preserved—and altered—the Vedas as oral traditions long before they were written down. It's reasonable to suppose that the position of Brahmins improved over time thanks to their role as custodians of the Vedas. All ancient agrarian societies, including those of Mesopotamia and Egypt, had systems of social rank based on birth. The north Indian caste system, embedded in the texts and laws of early Hinduism, made social rank unusually explicit. The system proved more durable than most. It still matters in India today.

CLASSIC HINDUISM By 400 BCE, Vedic religion, with its emphasis on caste, ritual, and sacrifice, evolved into **classic** (or Brahminical) **Hinduism**. Its character is known to us partly through sacred texts such as the Upanishads, some 200 densely philosophical treatises probably composed between 800 and 100 BCE. Believers

Shiva A bronze statue from present-day Pakistan depicts a sixth-century BCE religious leader as an incarnation of Shiva, a popular Hindu deity.

understood the tangible world to be illusion, a mere reflection of an eternal, pure, spiritual world. Ascetic meditation on this hidden but eternal world joined, and in cases replaced, animal sacrifice as the mark of religious specialists.

To the core Vedic beliefs, classic Hinduism added a powerful moral idea, the doctrine of the endless migration of souls: one's soul persists through cycles of birth and death, re-birth and re-death, and appears as living flesh in incarnations determined by one's moral conduct, or *karma*. As the *Chandogya Upanishad* put it, "Those who are of pleasant conduct here will enter a pleasant womb, that of a Brahmin, Kshatriya, or a Vaisya. But those who are of stinking conduct here will enter the womb of a dog, a pig, or an untouchable." Release from these cycles of re-birth and suffering is possible only if one performs one's duties consistently and attains true self-knowledge. (Different traditions within Hinduism understand this concept of release, *moksha* in Sanskrit, differently.) Brahmins stood closer to release than anyone else, owing to their accumulated moral record through previous incarnations.

Hindu believers also developed a notion of time that was as central to their faith as the moral code and cycle of re-birth and re-death. Like many peoples, Hindus came to believe in a golden past in which people had carried out religious obligations carefully and had behaved more ethically. They believed that time divided into four ages, in each of which morality, virtue, and religious observance (*dharma*) successively declined by a quarter. The present age, called Kali ("discord" in Sanskrit), is the worst, in which wickedness, ignorance, and conflict flourish. The Kali age precedes the destruction of the world, after which the cycle will begin again with another golden age. The current Kali age, according to conventional calculations, began on January 23, 3102 BCE, and has about 427,000 years left to run. That may seem a long time, but it's nothing compared to the time elapsed since the current cycle began, according to Hindu texts, a little over 155 trillion years ago. Hindu theology required formidable arithmetic skills to calculate the immensities of time.

Like the moral codes of other enduring religions, Hinduism provided a potent logic for accepting one's circumstances. One could hope for a better future life if one fulfilled one's duties and accumulated good karma. It was a religious idea that made social inequality and personal suffering easier to bear. Almost all complex societies with stark social hierarchy developed ideas that blunted envy and soothed suffering.

Ordinary people took comfort in several routines of worship. Anyone could appeal to any god at any time if feeling the need. On a daily basis, parents (normally fathers officiated) performed small sacrifices of rice, barley, or ghee (a form of butter) to one or more gods preferred in their household. Households also observed carefully prescribed rituals at key moments in life: birth, naming, first exposure to sunlight, first food, puberty, marriage, and above all, death. More publicly, male Brahmin priests undertook ritual sacrifices at holidays and festivals under the open sky (only after about 300 CE did temples become common). In addition, Hindu believers expressed their devotion by visiting pilgrimage sites associated with various gods, most of which lay along the banks of the Ganges. Eventually, the most important of these sites became Varanasi, where one could wash away one's sins in the river.

The Hindu pantheon was (and is) a crowded one, especially because each deity had many manifestations and equivalents. For example, Vishnu, preserver of the universe and humankind, had alternate forms as Rama or Krishna. Different traditions within Hinduism saw (and see) divinity differently, so depending on how you count there are only one, dozens, or thousands of gods and goddesses. In the early texts such as the *Rig Veda*, the most frequently mentioned are Indra, responsible for storms and warfare, and Agni, god of fire. The more popular deities of later Hinduism, such as Vishnu and Shiva, didn't figure prominently in the early Vedas. Each deity could help with specific problems, so if you needed an obstacle to some enterprise removed, you appealed to Ganesh, the

Vishnu A sixth-century CE relief from a Hindu temple in what is now Karnataka, southwest India, depicts the popular god Vishnu in the form of a boar.

elephant-headed son of Shiva; if your father was dying, you prayed to Rama; and if you wanted to enjoy good fortune, you turned to the goddess Lakshmi.

Hinduism took its enduring shape along the Ganges between 1000 BCE and 400 BCE. It is a particularly rich and variegated religious tradition, partly because it has had time to evolve in multiple directions, and partly because it has had few formal institutions to enforce conformity. Hinduism is today one of the world's great religions, accounting for about one-sixth of humankind.

RICE, POWER, AND THE MAURYAN EMPIRE

The people who developed Hinduism found, along the Ganges, fertile soil for the creation of complex society, states, and cities. As along the Tigris-Euphrates and the Nile, religion and politics were intertwined here.

By 1000 BCE, the inhabitants of the Gangetic plain followed a mixed economy of herding and farming. The *Rig*

Veda has more references to pastoralism than to agriculture, but it includes mentions of plows, oxen, irrigation, rice, lentils, and more. The upper reaches of the Ganges could support wheat and millet cultivation. The lower (and more easterly) section of the Gangetic plain suited rice.

Growing rice required different knowledge and skills from those needed for wheat, and the beginning of rice farming in India presumably indicates contacts with China, the homeland of rice cultivation. Texts are silent on this point, but genetic evidence from rice suggests that Ganges rice farmers began using seeds from China about 1700 BCE.

Everywhere along the Ganges, farmers faced two obstacles. The first was the dense forest that they had to cut and burn. Their acquisition of iron tools, beginning around 1000 to 800 BCE, eased the task of clearing forests. The second obstacle was the management of water. The Ganges swelled with summer rains brought by the Indian Ocean monsoon. The river's floodplain had many swamps. The rains came at inconvenient times for wheat and barley, the leading crops of northwest India. Farmers along the upper and middle Ganges needed to drain swamps and build irrigation networks, comparable to what had been done along the Nile, Indus, or the Tigris-Euphrates, for the benefit of agriculture. The same was true on the lower Ganges: rice farming required careful water management too.

SMALL KINGDOMS After 800 BCE or so, the farming communities of the Gangetic plain were numerous enough and produced enough surplus food that a more specialized division of labor emerged, and with it, cities. Riverside markets grew into river port towns. Clusters of smiths and carpenters grew into manufacturing centers.

Charismatic leaders used surplus wealth—mainly foodstuffs that stored well, such as rice—to attract and reward followers. Specialists in politics and violence, usually of the Kshatri caste, successfully challenged the priestly caste for social leadership, even as they depended on the endorsement of priests to establish their authority. Small kingdoms, the first states in the Ganges valley, began to sprout when chiefs and rulers converted moral and spiritual authority into territorial control. The many new kingdoms fought one another frequently and rose and fell rapidly, often within the lifetime of a single warlord.

MAGADHA Then, in the fifth century BCE, a warlord managed to conquer far and wide and create a much larger state in the Ganges basin. This state was called Magadha. The scanty evidence suggests that Magadha's power rested on the spread of iron tools and rice farming in the Ganges basin, which produced enough surplus food to support a professional army, religious specialists, literate bureaucrats, artisans, and all the skilled personnel a state needs. Its rulers were not from the Kshatri caste, an obstacle to legitimacy that they overcame with military prowess.

Magadha's expansion rested in part on military innovations involving coordination of the "four-limbed" army, consisting of infantry, horse cavalry, chariot corps, and war elephants. The first mention of war elephants—uniquely important in South Asian history—comes in fourth-century BCE texts. Pachyderm power (which involved capturing elephants in forests, taming them, and training them to trample enemies) became a crucial component of political success in India. Even the most experienced and best-trained foot soldiers felt helpless (and

The Mauryan Empire, 321–230 BCE The Mauryan Empire rose and fell quickly, lasting roughly a century. It was the first state in South Asia to unify both productive river basins, the Ganges and the Indus. Its leaders welcomed religious diversity, while ruthlessly commanding surplus grain and other tribute from much of South Asia.

War Elephants Soldiers mounted on an elephant are ready to throw spears down upon their enemies in this statue from the first century BCE. War elephants first came into use in South Asia during the fourth century BCE.

rightly so) when faced with charging elephants. One indication of their value is that a Central Asian king traded the entire region of today's southern Afghanistan plus much of what is now Pakistan and eastern Iran, as well as one of his daughters in marriage, to an Indian prince for 500 war elephants.

CHANDRAGUPTA MAURYA That Indian prince was Chandragupta Maurya. He was a soldier of fortune of obscure origins, allegedly from a family of peacock tamers. He managed to overthrow the Magadha rulers, conquer neighboring states, and unite all of north India into the **Mauryan Empire**. By 321 BCE, for the first time, the valleys of the Indus and the Ganges were under the same rule, enabling a great expansion of trade and specialization in the division of labor.

A foreign diplomat, Megasthenes, left a portrait of the Mauryan Empire as of about 298 BCE. It survives today only in fragments quoted or paraphrased by other authors. Some of it was fanciful—men who could outrun horses, women who gave birth by age six, men with ears so large they used them as blankets. Some of it is overly optimistic—no famines, no slavery, almost no theft. But much of it is plausible. The Mauryan state had a powerful professional military that included an elite imperial body-guard composed of women archers. The state controlled the supplies of horses, imported from Central Asia, and elephants. It maintained a sizeable bureaucracy and tax collection unit, and controlled trade up and down both the Indus and the Ganges. Its population was composed mainly of farmers growing rice, wheat, barley, and other crops. Its society, according to Megasthenes, was organized into seven occupation-based castes (Megasthenes included herders, artisans, bureaucrats, and judges as separate castes). This was a society far more elaborate than that described in the early Vedas and as complex as that of Mesopotamia or Egypt.

KAUTILYA

The Mauryan Empire in Chandragupta's day (he died in 297 BCE) also had one of the cagiest political advisers ever to walk the Earth: Kautilya, whose book of advice for kings and princes, *The Arthashastra*, was found inscribed on palm fronds just over a century ago. Kautilya wrote in a most practical vein with little reference to the supernatural. His manual of statecraft contains practical advice on everything a king might need to survive and prosper in a world of pitiless political competition. He advised his boss on how to out-maneuver rivals, relying on spies, deceit, and ruthlessness as needed. He made recommendations for coping with potential assassins within one's family. Some of his advice for kings is useful for students today: cultivate the intellect by association with learned elders; avoid daydreaming and addiction to drink, lust, or gambling; schedule 90 minutes a day for recreation and contemplation. However, Kautilya also imprudently recommended only four and one-half hours sleep per night.

ASHOKA

The Mauryan Empire conquered far and wide under Chandragupta's son and grandson. Ashoka, the grandson, was one of world history's most unusual rulers. He took the reins in about 268 BCE and added territory through conquests in eastern India. When his armies slaughtered thousands upon thousands of one tribal people, the Kalingas, Ashoka, full of remorse, suffered a spiritual crisis. When walking through a corpse-strewn battlefield, he allegedly said:

> What have I done? Is this a victory? What's a defeat then? Is this justice or injustice? Is this gallantry or a rout? Is it valor to kill innocent children and women? Did I do it to widen the empire or for prosperity or to destroy the other's kingdom or splendor? Someone has lost her husband, someone a father, someone a child, someone an unborn infant.... What's this debris of

Pillar of Ashoka Topped with the royal emblem of a lion, this example of the many pillars Ashoka erected is covered in writing (right) that outlines his religious edicts.

CONSIDERING THE EVIDENCE

Death and Taxes in the Mauryan Empire

Megasthenes was a Greek diplomat who visited India during the expansion of the Mauryan Empire. His original writings, like many historical texts, have been lost, but later writers had preserved fragments of his observations as quotations in their own works. Besides describing India's caste system, Megasthenes reported on the administration of justice, geography, and the training of war elephants. In the following excerpt, he describes the work of India's royal officials in their capital city.

Some superintend the rivers, measure the land, as is done in Egypt, and inspect the sluices . . . so that every one [*sic*] may have an equal supply of it. The same persons have charge also of the huntsmen, and are entrusted with the power of rewarding or punishing them. . . . They collect the taxes, and superintend . . . the woodcutters, the carpenters, the blacksmiths, and the miners. . . . Those who have charge of the city are divided into six bodies of five each. The members of the first look after everything relating to the industrial arts. Those of the second attend to the entertainment of foreigners. . . . They escort them on the way when they leave the country, or, in the event of their dying, forward their property to their relatives. . . . The third body consists of those who inquire when and how births and deaths occur, with the view not only of levying a tax, but also in order that births and deaths among both high and low may not escape the cognizance of Government. The fourth class superintends trade and commerce. Its members have charge of weights and measures, and see that the products in their season are sold by public notice. No one is allowed to deal in more than one kind of commodity unless he pays a double tax. The fifth class supervises manufactured articles, which they sell by public notice. What is new is sold separately from what is old, and there is a fine for mixing the two together. The sixth and last class consists of those who collect the tenths of the prices of the articles sold. Fraud in the payment of this tax is punished with death.

Source: J. W. McCrindle, *Ancient India: As Described by Megasthenes and Arrian* (London, 1877).

QUESTIONS FOR ANALYSIS

1. What sorts of activities did the government of the Mauryan Empire keep track of, and why? For which offense was the death penalty reserved?
2. What similarities did Megasthenes notice between India and Egypt? What similarities do you notice, both in this excerpt and in the chapter?
3. Does Megasthenes's status as an outsider make it more or less likely that his description of India's society is accurate? Who do you suppose he got his information from?

the corpses? Are these marks of victory or defeat? Are these vultures, crows, eagles the messengers of death or evil? What have I done!

We know about Ashoka's anxieties because he had dozens of inscriptions carved on rocks and pillars scattered around India. Ashoka's spiritual crisis—probably a quest for self-purification—took the form of deepened commitment to the tenets of Buddhism, a new religion with a strong ascetic streak. His rock and pillar edicts urge his people to avoid animal sacrifice, practice non-violence toward all people and animals, respect all faiths, and love justice and fairness. Ashoka had roads built, wells dug, shade trees planted, and in general sought to promote the welfare of people under his rule. He renounced wars of expansion—although in one of his edicts he warned a forest people not to resist his authority. His principles, after his conqueror's remorse, were about as far from those of Kautilya as a ruler can get. Like most people, he didn't always live up to his principles, and in one of his rock edicts he admitted that despite his efforts his palace kitchen still killed two peacocks a day and often a deer as well. It's a rare ruler who inscribes his own moral failings in stone.

Ashoka's pillars were erected all over India except for the far south. But he probably didn't fully control all that territory. The Mauryan Empire was more likely a collection of cities and rich agrarian hinterlands under direct imperial rule, with stretches of uncontrolled mountainous and forested land in between. When Ashoka died around 230 BCE, the Mauryan Empire soon fragmented. Its last remnant disappeared in 187 BCE, after which India once again became an arena of small states, often at war among themselves.

NEW INDIAN RELIGIONS

While Chandragupta Maurya, Ashoka, and their successors were gaining and losing empires, a religious revolution was overtaking India. The Vedic traditions that had evolved into Hinduism acquired new rivals. In the middle of the first millennium BCE, many people in north India were experimenting with novel approaches to faith and ritual. They found some aspects of Hindu practice unappealing.

DISSENT AND SOCIAL CHANGE The most enduring of these spiritual experiments were Buddhism and Jainism. Like Hinduism, from which they are offshoots, both were (and are) religions of renunciation, in the sense that their doctrines emphasize the rejection of earthly desire. If one could abandon desire and cease all actions harmful to other life forms, one might achieve release from the endless cycle of re-birth and re-death, and attain a state of infinite understanding and bliss that Buddhists call *nirvana* (akin to the Hindu *moksha*). This ideal required pious Jains to follow a path of non-violence, truthfulness, non-acquisitiveness, and, for monks and nuns, celibacy. Pious Jains will not knowingly kill even a mosquito. Hindu sacrifice of animals and other Vedic rituals offended Jains and Buddhists alike. They had no use for Brahmins, nor for caste.

An even more radical departure from Hindu belief arose at the same time. Charvaka was a school of thought that rejected all spirituality including soul, afterlife, and karma, denied the authority of all sacred texts and priests, and claimed that the only reality is the one people can perceive.

Buddhism and Jainism, and other creeds and philosophies that didn't last as long, such as Charvaka, arose as dissent from Vedic religion and revolts against the social order. That order was changing after 500 BCE as iron tools and rice cultivation spread in north India. Larger food surpluses encouraged the emergence of more and bigger cities, mainly along the Ganges. Kaushambi (also spelled Kosambi), for example, a commercial center on a tributary of the Ganges, attained a population of roughly 36,000 by 500 BCE. River trade burgeoned, and people were accumulating more wealth, including some for whom their caste status was an irritating constraint. Many felt that Brahmins and Kshatriyas didn't deserve their exalted position and that animal sacrifice was wasteful and cruel. City life generally inspires people to question the established social order. Cities along the Ganges had that effect.

ROOTS OF JAINISM The slender textual and archeological evidence suggests that Jainism took shape after the sixth century BCE. One of its great proponents, Varhamana (also known as Mahavira), starting at age 30 wandered for 13 years as a naked beggar before achieving enlightenment and spreading his wisdom throughout the Ganges plain. He took his ascetic principles so seriously that he starved himself to death. Jainism, despite its demands on believers, acquired many followers in the early years of the Mauryan Empire. Chandragupta himself took an interest in Jainism, supported its monasteries, and by some accounts late in life devoted himself to that religion. Jainism, like Buddhism, appealed to merchants and artisans,

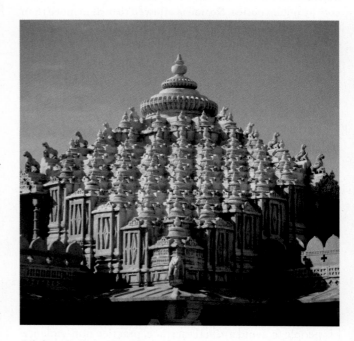

Jainism Built in the fifteenth century CE, the Jain temple at Ranakpur in western India is one of Jainism's most important religious sites.

who didn't enjoy high status in Hindu culture. Its rejection of all forms of killing made it unsuitable for farmers, hunters, fisherfolk—indeed, anyone inclined to squash a bug. A demanding faith, it remained a minority creed in India, confined mainly to cities and towns, and never spread much beyond India. But it continues to be influential among modern India's business and financial elite.

ROOTS OF BUDDHISM Buddhism in many ways offered a more accessible, less demanding path than Jainism. **Siddhartha Gautama**, the Buddha (the Enlightened One), was born a Kshatri caste prince in what is now lowland Nepal sometime in the sixth or fifth century BCE, a rough contemporary of Varhamana. Spurning his privileged inheritance, he wandered for years, including a visit to the city of Kaushambi, trying to understand the sorrows and sufferings of the world. According to tradition, enlightenment came to him after he sat for 49 days beneath a pipal tree (a variety of fig) in Bodh Gaya, a village in north India. Sorrow and disappointment, he realized, spring from desire; and if one could abandon all desire, one could find a path to wisdom and contentment, escape the endless cycle of re-birth and re-death, and achieve nirvana.

INSTITUTIONS AND BELIEFS Buddhist doctrine is recorded in several texts, some purported to be the words of the Buddha himself, others to be writings of his followers. These began as oral traditions, like the Vedas, but eventually were written down in a language called Pali, similar to Sanskrit but more in use by common people. Unlike Hinduism, Buddhism built an institutional framework with monks and monasteries at the center. Monks took primary responsibility for maintaining, and modifying, Buddhism's spiritual heritage. Buddhism probably invented monasteries: communities set apart from society as a whole in which monastic membership replaced family and other social ties, and everyone devoted themselves to religious exercises. Monasteries also trained missionaries who could explain the insights of the Buddha to anyone willing to listen. This formed another contrast with Hinduism, in which there was little missionary work. Supporting monasteries financially was good for anyone's moral balance sheet, and dozens of them flourished.

Buddhism, like Jainism, held particular appeal for merchants and entrepreneurs. It didn't recognize the caste privileges of priests and warriors. While its doctrines encouraged asceticism and begging among monks, it also legitimated the quest for riches. One text credits the Buddha with these words:

> Whoso is virtuous and intelligent,
> Shines like fire that blazes,
> To him amassing wealth, like a roving bee
> Its honey gathering,
> Riches mount up as an ant-heap growing high.
> When the good layman wealth has so amassed
> Able is he to benefit his clan.

The layman who has amassed wealth can support not only his clan, but his local monastery as well.

The core beliefs of Buddhism evolved over time. Although for most Buddhists there is no god, some of the Buddha's followers eventually awarded him divine status—against his wishes. Within four or five centuries of his death, Buddhism split into two main doctrinal camps, called Mahayana (or the Greater Vehicle) and Theravada (the Lesser Vehicle). They differ on just what is required for enlightenment. The Mahayana view holds that anyone can attain nirvana and can do so in one lifetime if one tries hard enough. Theravada Buddhists believe that only monks and nuns can achieve enlightenment; everyone else first has to be re-born as monk or nun. Mahayana became the majority sect and today is dominant in Tibet, China, Japan, and Korea. The Theravada school is more important in Southeast Asia and Sri Lanka. Each is by now subdivided into many smaller sects.

Buddhism and Jainism weren't for everyone. Pastoralists needed to kill animals. Anyone who cherished fire rituals, animal sacrifices, the Vedas, or caste privileges wouldn't admire Buddhism or Jainism. They emphasized an ethical commitment to all humankind rather than privileges and constraints based on caste status.

Buddhists and Jains found the question of whether or not women could achieve enlightenment a divisive one. The voices recorded in the relevant texts are all men's. The Buddha himself at first thought women should stay at home, but later he decided they could become devotees as nuns, if always subordinate to monks. Remarks attributed to him (although perhaps the work of his followers) castigate women as by nature envious, greedy, unwise, and sensual—common notions at the time. Buddhist sects differed as to whether women could attain enlightenment

The Nile-Ganges Web

200 BCE

POLYBIUS (CA. 200–CA. 118 BCE), a Greek historian, recognized some of the globalizing changes under way in his time. But the integration he observed was only part of a longer trend that extended to larger spaces. Beginning with the exchanges among Mesopotamian cities going back at least to 3000 BCE, a slow process of web building took hold that eventually spanned the entire area between the Nile and the Ganges river valleys.

Countless people spun this web through their actions. Traders trudged, rode, or sailed from city to city, carrying food, cloth, salt, and hides. Soldiers and refugees streamed across territories. Monks and sages spread religions such as Zoroastrianism and Buddhism far and wide. Travelers also transferred technologies and pathogens along routes that by their actions they were fusing into the first large-scale web in human history.

The regions of this web were in at least intermittent and indirect contact with one another by 200 BCE, and often in sustained and direct contact. Egyptian artwork made of lapis lazuli, a turquoise stone imported from Afghanistan, had become a sought-after luxury among prosperous Egyptians before Polybius was born. War elephants, first developed for military advantage in India, had come into use in Greece by Polybius's time. History, as Polybius observed, had become an organic whole throughout the Nile-Ganges web.

Questions for Analysis

Based on this feature and your chapter reading, consider the following questions:

1. What were the key processes that built a web of connections over the Nile-Ganges region?
2. How do you think this connective web affected the everyday lives of people living in the Nile-Ganges area?

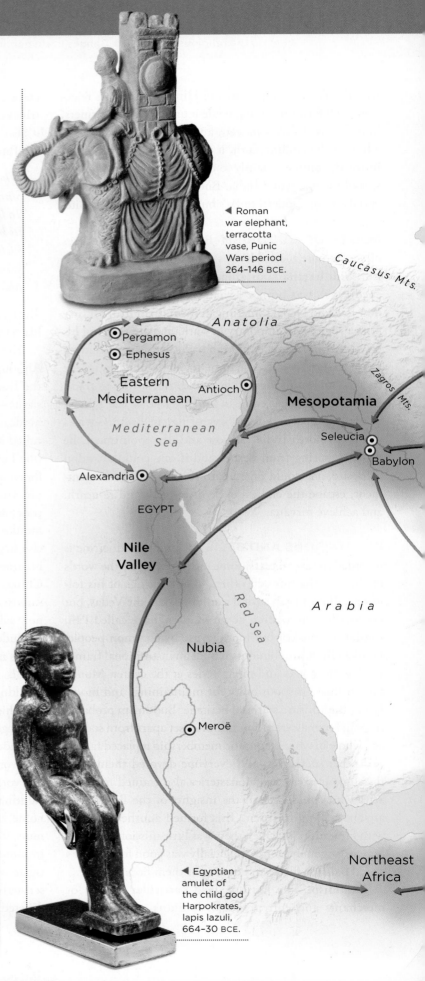

◀ Roman war elephant, terracotta vase, Punic Wars period 264–146 BCE.

Caucasus Mts.

Anatolia

Pergamon
Ephesus

Eastern Mediterranean

Antioch

Zagros Mts.

Mesopotamia

Mediterranean Sea

Seleucia

Babylon

Alexandria

EGYPT

Nile Valley

Red Sea

Arabia

Nubia

Meroë

◀ Egyptian amulet of the child god Harpokrates, lapis lazuli, 664–30 BCE.

Northeast Africa

> NOW IN EARLIER TIMES THE WORLD'S HISTORY HAS CONSISTED, SO TO SPEAK, OF A SERIES OF UNRELATED EPISODES, THE ORIGINS AND RESULTS OF EACH BEING AS WIDELY SEPARATED AS THEIR LOCALITIES BUT FROM THIS POINT ONWARD HISTORY BECOMES AN ORGANIC WHOLE: THE DAILY AFFAIRS OF ITALY AND AFRICA ARE CONNECTED WITH THOSE OF ASIA AND GREECE, AND ALL EVENTS BEAR A RELATIONSHIP AND CONTRIBUTE TO A SINGLE END.

POLYBIUS, CA. 146 BCE

Core area
City
Web connection

▲ Ur (southern Mesopotamian) lyre with bull's head, lapis lazuli inlay, 2600–2400 BCE.

Merv

Central Asia

lapis lazuli

Iran

Taxila

Indus Valley

Persian Gulf

Himalaya Mountains

Ganges Valley

Pataliputra

India

◄ Indian elephant sculpture, first millennium BCE–second century BCE.

INDIAN OCEAN

as women, or whether they first must be reincarnated as males. None of the Buddha's 547 past lives, as recorded in Buddhist tradition, were lived as a female, even those he lived as an animal. Jains, for their part, debated for 1,500 years whether women could attain enlightenment, an issue that turned on whether or not life as a naked beggar was required; all parties agreed that was out of the question for women.

RELIGIOUS PLURALISM Hinduism, Buddhism, and Jainism (and some less prominent creeds) competed for followers in the Mauryan era and beyond. Competition among religions usually breeds innovations—often, ones that make a creed more accessible and appealing, and so it was in north India. Hinduism and Buddhism evolved forms that emphasized devotion to *bodhisattvas*, who achieved enough enlightenment to attain moksha or nirvana but by choice stayed in the human realm to help others on their way. Many Indians came to believe that some deities could grant release from suffering directly, freeing people from the slow ascent via reincarnations. This notion of a faster track to release had obvious appeal, but for some people the more arduous route seemed the only true one.

These three religions, with their literature, art, architecture, and moral codes, all spread widely throughout India and a little beyond—along some but not all the strands of a growing web. Sometimes they spread with the assistance of rulers such as Ashoka, but often without, propelled by the power of moral example. Except for Buddhism, they did not have missionaries. In the early centuries CE, as we'll see, maritime connections took Indian religion, art, and architecture to newly forming royal courts in Southeast Asia. Trans-Himalayan routes followed by traders and the occasional missionary carried Buddhism to Tibet and eventually to China. Indian religions didn't make much of an imprint in Southwest Asia. Although more strongly connected to India than almost anyone else, people there found their own gods satisfactory. The existence of strong web connections did not guarantee the movement of religious ideas and culture.

Political fragmentation after the end of the Mauryan Empire encouraged cultural and religious diversity. No king could enforce any orthodoxy over the Ganges basin, let alone the whole Indian subcontinent. Over the centuries, India experienced a few brief moments of unification—the Mauryan Empire and, as we'll see, the Gupta and the Moghuls. But more often than not it was politically divided, helping to explain the rich religious pluralism of India. Yet, at the same time, owing to the steady spread of Hinduism, Buddhism, and Jainism, all India shared broad cultural similarities.

THE GANGES BASIN AND THE DEVELOPING WEB

As complex society, cities, and states developed along the Ganges after 1000 BCE, the region deepened its ties to the wider world. Its strongest links, by far, extended to the northwest, toward Iran and Southwest Asia. To the northeast, the Himalaya posed a formidable barrier. The developments along the Ganges in effect extended what had been a Nile-Indus web into a Nile-Ganges web beginning faintly around 1500 BCE and firmly in place by 300 BCE with the Mauryan state.

BIOLOGICAL LINKS The connections between the Gangetic plain and the wider world took many forms. On a biological level, north India acquired several crops from elsewhere. Wheat and barley had come long ago from Southwest Asia, and rice came from China by 1700 BCE. Millets and sorghums came from northeast Africa, presumably by maritime trade routes, and were in use by 1000 BCE. North India acquired horses from Iran and Central Asia by 2000 BCE and sustained a horse import trade ever after. There's evidence of Indian cattle breeds as far west as Syria by 1500 BCE, and by Mauryan times India exported war elephants to kings in Southwest Asia. Beyond these biological links for which good evidence exists, there was also the almost certain exchange of pathogens such as smallpox, which arrived in north India after 1000 BCE from Central and Southwest Asia.

CULTURE, TRADE, AND CONFLICT On a cultural level, as we've seen, north India imported language and religious practices from Iran, and over time melded that

Bodhisattvas A first-century CE stone depiction of a *bodhisattva*, arm raised in greeting or blessing, found in northern India.

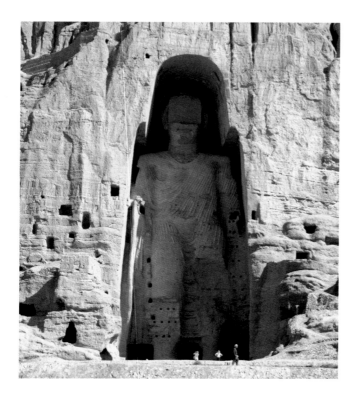

Buddha of Bamyan An enormous stone Buddha carved into the side of a mountain in Afghanistan in 554 CE testifies to the spread of Buddhism beyond India. It was destroyed by the Taliban in 2001.

with local forms into Sanskrit and Hinduism. Two of the early Hindu epics contain a flood story that resembles the Mesopotamian one and that of the Hebrew Bible. By the time of the Mauryans, artistic motifs flowed back and forth between north India and Iran: capitals on columns of the Mauryan palace in Pataliputra resemble Iranian and Greek capitals. Elephant sculpture appeared in Iran and Syria after 300 BCE.

In terms of trade and technology, north India's links to Southwest Asia were especially strong. Chariots came from Iran. Iron working came from either Southwest or Central Asia. North India imported jade and horses from Central Asia, and woolen cloth from Mesopotamia. It exported gold, elephant ivory, honey, indigo (for making dyes), and wood to Mesopotamia and Persian Gulf ports. The Mauryan Empire maintained flourishing caravan routes to the northwest by land and maritime routes across the Arabian Sea. It had weaker trade connections to the east, into the Bay of Bengal, and to southernmost India.

Finally, on a political level, Mauryan armies fought frontier wars with various powers in Southwest Asia.

In addition, Ashoka sent diplomatic embassies to Syria, Anatolia, and as far as northwest Greece in search of allies. The Mauryans introduced to India a new element of statecraft—minted coins, a practice borrowed from Southwest Asia.

CONCLUSION

In this chapter, we've seen two expansions of world history's first big web, which had initially formed around a core area of Mesopotamia and the Indus valley. Connections with Egypt, although they began long ago, took hold around 2500 BCE and solidified with the arrival there of the Hyksos (1700–1500 BCE). As those links were firming up, new ones with north India were developing. Migrations into the Ganges valley paved the way for stronger connections between north India and Southwest Asia after 1500 BCE, and the rise of the Mauryan state by 300 BCE solidified those links, consolidating what was now a Nile-Ganges web.

The complex societies that formed along the Nile and the Ganges lay on the frontiers of this newly expanded web. To the east of the Ganges, and to the west and south of Egypt and Nubia, populations were sparser and their connections to the wider world weaker. So it makes sense to see the region from the Nile to the Ganges as a giant web in full operation by 300 BCE. It extended threads—intermittent links—into the adjacent parts of Africa and Asia, and as later chapters will show, into Mediterranean Europe.

The two frontiers of the Nile and Ganges showed contrasts and commonalities. Along the Nile after 3100 BCE, unity was frequent and came to be regarded as natural. Along the Ganges, political disunity was the rule. In both places—as in all complex societies—sharp social and political hierarchies prevailed. Along the Ganges, but not the Nile, these hierarchies became formalized in a caste system.

Religion underpinned both social systems. Although pharaohs liked to boast of their brutality against foreigners, there is little evidence of systematic resort to violence as a tool of government within Egypt. India's Mauryan emperors likewise did not shrink from slaughtering foreigners, but rarely found it necessary to butcher their subjects. Along both the Nile and the Ganges, rulers generally succeeded in winning moral authority through religion and, in effect, alliance with priests—a pattern we've seen before in Mesopotamia and will see again elsewhere.

The underlying philosophies of Egyptian and Indian religion were quite different. Egyptian religion had no endless cycle of re-birth from which one could only find release by fulfilling one's duties meticulously. The pantheons of Hinduism and of Egyptian religion bore only passing resemblance to one another, although both had many gods with specific responsibilities and powers. Both had loose connections to Mesopotamian religion, in one case by way of the Levant and in the other through Iran. Despite the differences in detail, religious life along the Ganges and the Nile both served to ease the suffering and salve the resentment of the poor and downtrodden—the great majority of the population in both places.

CHAPTER REVIEW

KEY TERMS

Nile River (p. 117)
Nubia (p. 118)
pharaohs (p. 119)
Narmer (p. 119)
hieroglyphs (p. 121)

Hyksos (p. 122)
pyramids (p. 125)
shabti (p. 127)
Ganges basin (p. 131)
Vedas (p. 132)

caste system (p. 134)
classic Hinduism (p. 134)
Mauryan Empire (p. 137)
Siddhartha Gautama
 (p. 141)

Go to INQUIZITIVE to see what you've learned—and learn what you've missed—with personalized feedback along the way.

REVIEW QUESTIONS

1. How did the Nile contribute to Egypt's political unification?

2. Explain "low Niles" and their social and political consequences.

3. Describe Egypt's relationship with Nubia when Egyptian pharaohs were strong, and when Nubian kings were strong.

4. What was *maat*, and how did the pharaohs maintain it?

5. How did the Egyptian understanding of the afterlife change over time?

6. Why did Egypt both attract and need many immigrants?

7. Define the four primary tiers of the early caste system in India.

8. In what key ways did classic Hinduism evolve from Vedic religion?

9. What were the two biggest obstacles facing farmers in the Gangetic plain?

10. How were Jainism and Buddhism linked to dissent and social change?

11. How was the Ganges valley linked biologically, culturally, politically, and through trade to Mesopotamia?

12. What were the main similarities between the complex societies that emerged along the Nile and the Ganges?

FURTHER READING

Nayanjot LAHIRI, *Ashoka in Ancient India* (2015). A highly readable work by an archeologist, who sorts out the strange story of the Mauryan emperor who regretted his conquests.

Barbara MEERTZ, *Red Land, Black Land: Daily Life in Ancient Egypt* (2008). A delightfully quirky look at every aspect of life in ancient Egypt.

Ian SHAW, ed., *The Oxford History of Ancient Egypt* (2000). Mainly political history, with detailed essays on every period.

Romila THAPAR, *Early India* (2004). An authoritative guide to the thickets of ancient Indian history, written by the leading scholar on the subject.

Thomas TRAUTMANN, *India* (2011). A very compact survey by a major scholar of early India.

Marc Van De MIEROOP, *A History of Ancient Egypt* (2010). A detailed survey up through the fourth century CE; more compact than Wilkinson.

Toby WILKINSON, *The Rise and Fall of Ancient Egypt* (2010). A narrative synthesis that will make you glad you don't live under the pharaohs.

CHRONOLOGY

ca. 2500–1400 BCE
Minoan palace culture of Crete

ca. 1900 BCE
Earliest example of
alphabetic writing

ca. 1400 BCE
Mycenaeans occupy Crete

ca. 700 BCE
Song-poem *Iliad* is written down;
Greeks develop the *polis*

ca. 559–330 BCE
Achaemenid imperial rule

427–348 BCE
Lifetime of Plato

ca. 470–399 BCE
Lifetime of Socrates

490–480 BCE
Persian Wars

508/7–322 BCE
Athenian use of
democracy

By 2000 BCE
Introduction of sailing boats
in eastern Mediterranean

ca. 1500–1200 BCE
First traces of Greek
language and culture

ca. 1000 BCE
Phoenicians begin
writing with alphabet

ca. 1000–900 BCE
Founding of Sparta

559–530 BCE
Reign of Cyrus II

522–486 BCE
Reign of Darius

486–465 BCE
Reign of Xerxes

431–404 BCE
Peloponnesian War

6

Building the Old World Web

PERSIA, GREECE, AND THE HELLENISTIC WORLD

600 BCE to 200 CE

Webs of connection are sometimes visible in images. A coin (see p. 150) from what is now eastern Afghanistan, in the second century BCE, displays an image of Hercules, a hero from Greek myth, with his club and lionskin. One side of the coin shows Greek writing that says "of King Demetrius," and the other shows a profile of the king. He seems to be wearing an elephant head, complete with tusks and trunk, as a hat.

Another image (see p. 150) comes from eastern Pakistan and was carved in stone during the first or second century CE. It shows the Buddha in human form, wearing a halo and a toga-like garment draped over both shoulders. This is striking: the earliest Buddhist art usually depicts the Buddha abstractly, and when he's shown in human form, he's wearing a loincloth, not a toga. Every fold and wrinkle of the toga is carved with great skill. How should we understand this?

These are examples of Greco-Buddhist art. As we will see, armies that were culturally Greek invaded Central Asia in the fourth century BCE, led by a young Macedonian king, Alexander the Great. Over the next several centuries, Greek language, culture, religion, and artistic styles spread in and among cities in what

356–323 BCE
Lifetime of Alexander the Great

323–31 BCE
Hellenistic age

311 BCE
Seleucid dynasty emerges

247 BCE– 224 CE
Height of Parthian dynasty

331 BCE
Alexander the Great founds Alexandria

384–322 BCE
Lifetime of Aristotle

Achaemenid Power Darius's palace featured many images of the mythical griffin, such as this multicolored frieze found on a wall in the palace, to project an image of his royalty and might.

149

FOCUS QUESTIONS

1. In what ways was multiculturalism a strength of the Achaemenid Empire?

2. How did political fragmentation contribute to the dynamism of Greek culture?

3. How was Alexander the Great able to establish a vast empire?

4. How did a developing market culture connect people within the Nile-Ganges web during the Hellenistic age?

The Hellenistic World A coin issued by the ruler of Bactria (located in what is now Afghanistan) features an image of Hercules and the king's name in Greek, indicating the far-reaching spread of Greek language and culture.

intellectual, and commercial traditions of the ancient Greeks, which the conquests of Alexander the Great spread throughout this vast region.

is now northern Pakistan, Afghanistan, and westernmost China. Local people, who were mainly Buddhist, adopted these styles. They built new Buddhist temples with columns that would have looked at home in a Greek temple. They carved reliefs of bodhisattvas surrounded by Greek gods or figures from Greek myth. They fused Greek and Buddhist traditions, myths, and styles. And they continued to do so for about a thousand years after Alexander the Great's invasion.

Greco-Buddhist art allows us, in effect, to see the formation of a bigger, thicker web of interaction extending from the Mediterranean through Central Asia and into China. This chapter explains how the process happened. It presents the history of the first superpower in world history—a Persian state that stretched from India to Egypt and for two centuries pursued policies that helped to integrate that vast space economically and culturally. And it recounts the political,

Greco-Buddhist Art Trade and communication links could lead to the fusion of Mediterranean and Asian cultures: here, a representation of the Buddha from first- or second-century Central Asia depicts him wearing a toga with folds like those that appear on Greek statuary.

THE ACHAEMENIDS OF PERSIA

For 3,000 years after the emergence of complex societies in Southwest Asia, the broad region from Egypt to north India remained a political patchwork. Even the Assyrians with their giant armies and iron weapons couldn't conquer so vast a space. Then, in an astonishing shift in pattern, an obscure dynasty from what is now southwestern Iran managed to unify the whole region in just a few decades in the middle of the sixth century BCE. This dynasty is called the **Achaemenids** (or Achaemenians). At their height, they ruled over about 20 to 30 million people—roughly 20 to 30 percent of humankind. Only one state in world history—China's Ming dynasty (1368–1644 CE)—ever ruled a higher proportion of the human race.

Compared to the Assyrians or Egyptians, we don't know much about the Achaemenids. Greek historians such as Herodotus, whose home city of Halicarnassus was controlled by the Achaemenids, are among our best sources. His *Histories* is mainly a narrative account of the empire. But Herodotus included tall tales for entertainment value, and he knew only the western part of the empire well. He depicted the Achaemenids as a decadent, despotic foil against which to highlight the virtues of the Greeks. The Achaemenids themselves left royal inscriptions and tens of thousands of cuneiform tablets in several languages. They shed light mainly on economic and social issues. Archeology supplements these written sources.

THE RISE OF THE ACHAEMENID DYNASTY

The Achaemenids arose from a people called Persians, who hailed from the foothills of the Zagros Mountains and the western Iranian plateau. Before they acquired an empire, their language—an Indo-European tongue—was not written, and they had scant urban tradition and no monumental architecture. Starting in 559 BCE, however, under a king named Cyrus II, they built an imperial state that eclipsed any previous ones in size and power. This imperial state conquered all the major powers from Egypt to northwestern India. It was the first superpower in world history.

Cyrus II must have been both a lucky and a skilled military commander. He toppled local monarchs, then swung west into Anatolia (Asia Minor) and conquered Lydia, a kingdom that pioneered the use of coins and was known for its wealth. In 539 BCE, Cyrus took over Babylonia and all of Mesopotamia, cagily presenting himself as the chosen instrument of Marduk—the god of the city of Babylon—for the liberation of oppressed peoples. He is warmly remembered in the Old Testament's books of Ezra and Isaiah for ending the Babylonian captivity of the ancient Hebrews and restoring them to Jerusalem. In a public inscription, he boasted of his respect for religious traditions. Whatever his other merits, Cyrus had a shrewd cultural policy—not unlike Sargon's 1,500 years before—by which he embraced the religions of the people he conquered, encouraging the defeated to adopt him as their rightful king. He died on campaign in Central Asia in 530 BCE.

Territory under Achaemenid Control, 559–486 BCE A Persian dynasty that took the name Achaemenid became the world's first superpower in the sixth and fifth centuries BCE, uniting the oases of Central Asia with the riverine societies of Mesopotamia and Egypt. Its borders stretched from the Nile to the Indus, but through imperial policies and the daily routines of merchants, travelers, soldiers, and many others, the Achaemenid Empire consolidated and extended the web stretching from the Nile to India.

CONSIDERING THE EVIDENCE

Herodotus on the Persians

Like other Greek writers, Herodotus intended his *Histories* for performance. He interrupted detailed accounts of wars and revolts by sharing with his Greek audiences odd tales and other information about customs among Persians, Egyptians, and other people. Later writers accused him of making things up for entertainment. Yet, in his description of Persian customs below, Herodotus carefully distinguishes between what he saw and what others told him during his travels around the Mediterranean Sea and along the Nile in Egypt.

131. The customs which I know the Persians to observe are the following. They have no images of the gods, no temples nor altars, and consider the use of them a sign of folly. This comes, I think, from their not believing the gods to have the same nature with men, as the Greeks imagine....

132. To these gods the Persians offer sacrifice in the following manner: they raise no altar, light no fire, pour no libations; there is no sound of the flute, no putting on of chaplets, no consecrated barley-cake; but the man who wishes to sacrifice brings his victim to a spot of ground which is pure from pollution, and there calls upon the name of the god to whom he intends to offer.... The sacrificer is not allowed to pray for blessings on himself alone, but he prays for the welfare of the king, and of the whole Persian people, among whom he is of necessity included.... When all is ready, one of the Magi comes forward and chants a hymn, which they say recounts the origin of the gods. It is not lawful to offer sacrifice unless there is a Magus present.

...

135. There is no nation which so readily adopts foreign customs as the Persians. Thus, they have taken the dress of the Medes, considering it superior to their own; and in war they wear the Egyptian breastplate. As soon as they hear of any luxury, they instantly make it their own....

...

140. Thus much I can declare of the Persians with entire certainty, from my own actual knowledge. There is another custom which is spoken of with reserve, and not openly, concerning their dead. It is said that the body of a male Persian is never buried, until it has been torn either by a dog or a bird of prey. That the Magi have this custom is beyond a doubt, for they practise it without any concealment.

Source: *The History of Herodotus*, Vol. 1, ed. and trans. George Rawlinson (New York: 1861).

QUESTIONS FOR ANALYSIS

1. Herodotus is careful to note the lack of fire, music, and altars in Persian worship. How does he explain the differences between Greek and Persian religious practices?
2. How did adopting customs from other people help the Persians to strengthen their empire?
3. Herodotus suggests that the burial custom he describes may be a rumor. Should historians include information that they think may be untrue? Why or why not?

Cyrus's son, Cambyses II, continued the Persian expansion. He conquered Egypt in 525 BCE and made himself pharaoh. Like many an earlier pharaoh, he tried to conquer Nubia but failed. Like his father, he ruled through local elites and folded local religion into his ruling ideology. With their conquests, the Persians held the two richest regions in the world at this time: Mesopotamia and Egypt. They also nominally controlled many other lands from Anatolia to Central Asia, although much of the region was pasture, home to nomads who rarely paid tribute to anyone. The empire of Cyrus and Cambyses was a loose one. Its size made it a hard empire to rule.

THE ACHAEMENID EMPIRE (CA. 550–330 BCE)

The empire contained farmers, herders, and city-dwellers of many ethnicities and religions. It included peoples accustomed to ruling themselves, and many who regarded the Persians—plausibly enough—as upstarts. Stitching together all these constituencies was a challenge. Revolts popped up in Cambyses's time, during one of which he died in mysterious circumstances. A few months later, in 522 BCE, his lance-bearer, **Darius**, then about 27 years old, pulled off a coup d'état. He claimed descent from a Persian king named Achaemenes, and from this point forward the Persian kings were called Achaemenids.

THE STATE An empire this large required good communications, bureaucracy, and armed forces. Darius, whose talent lay as much in consolidation as in conquest, was equal to the challenge. Early in his long reign (r. 522–486 BCE), he had to put down revolts left and right. He then added new territory along the Indus River and the North African coast as far west as Libya, and chased a nomadic confederation, the Scythians, north of the Black Sea. To project power over such distances, Darius adopted a system of mounted couriers and post stations, pioneered on a smaller scale by the Assyrians. His system made it possible to carry information quickly throughout his empire from the banks of the Nile to those of the Indus. (Herodotus found this especially impressive and wrote, "Neither snow, nor rain, nor heat, nor dark of night prevents these couriers" from their appointed rounds, a phrase adopted over 2,000 years later by the U.S. Post Office as its motto.) To make the courier system fully effective, Darius had roads and bridges built throughout the empire. One of the important routes was a "royal road" connecting the cities of Sardis in western Anatolia and Susa in western Iran. Horsemen clattering along this road could transmit messages over 1,500 miles (2,500 km) in about 12 days. The Achaemenids even developed a system of mountaintop bonfires to send information faster still.

Darius supplemented his communications system with a carefully crafted bureaucracy. He solidified his rule by building on an inherited structure of provinces (called satrapies) with hand-picked governors (satraps) who were usually ethnic Persians. Each satrap had to furnish a specified amount of gold or silver, extracted from conquered peoples, to the Achaemenids. Satraps had to maintain roads and provide soldiers when Darius wanted to launch a campaign. Persians, although liable for military service, paid no taxes. The Achaemenids allowed local traditions to continue and local elites to retain some power—as long as they supported the dynasty.

Darius also organized his army crisply, forging a tight hierarchical force integrating infantry and both light and heavy cavalry. Many rulers before Darius had fielded infantry and light cavalry, meaning horsemen typically armed with bow and arrow. Darius's **heavy cavalry** was an innovation: big, strong horses able to carry riders, weaponry, and armor—precursors to the steeds of medieval European knights, almost as terrifying as Indian war elephants, and capable of charging and often trampling anyone in their way. Darius's army, like his bureaucracy, was multiethnic but Persian at the top. According to Herodotus, Darius's elite unit, known optimistically as the "The Immortals," numbered exactly 10,000. When a man was killed, another instantly was promoted to take his place.

Darius was an innovative ruler. However, governing such a big empire also required reliance on tried-and-true methods. He included in his imperial management playbook techniques such as the construction of monumental architecture and the use of religion as political ideology. In the grand tradition of Mesopotamian monarchs, Darius built a new ceremonial city, Persepolis, in southwestern Iran. His minions leveled a sloping hillside and erected palaces and temples made of precisely cut stone, all behind a triple wall, the height of which reached 40 ft. (12 m) according to ancient authors. Persepolis also had an elevated water storage tank and sewage tunnels dug through rock. Darius spared no expense to make Persepolis an awe-inspiring monument to his rule. He used artistic motifs, such as griffins—mythical beasts with the head of an eagle and the body of a lion—that symbolized strength, power, kingship, and perhaps the fusion of cultures.

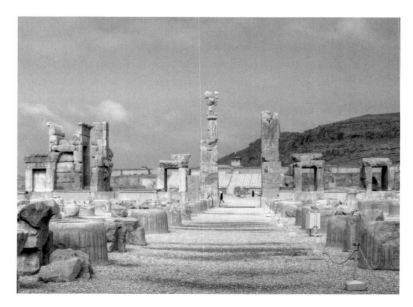

Persepolis A wide avenue ran down the center of Darius's capital at Persepolis, lined with rows of large stone buildings that included temples, palaces, and other public and monumental structures.

Since no clear rule of succession existed, palace intrigues and power struggles among royal sons were routine. According to Herodotus, royal wives maneuvered to get their sons into power—their political conniving struck Herodotus as a sign of Persian decadence. Aspirants to the throne and newly installed kings often killed their brothers to consolidate their position. All this was normal for monarchies without fixed rules of succession, and although it led to frequent political crises and occasional civil wars, it was a system that ensured no weaklings came to power.

Achaemenid kings had to prove themselves as politically ruthless and militarily capable. They led their troops into battle personally. They increasingly relied on mercenaries: soldiers of shifting loyalties who fought for whoever paid best. Mercenaries—many of them Arabs, Indians, Central Asians, and Greeks—were hired from the edges of the empire. These hired soldiers played something of the same role with respect to Persia as Nubians did to pharaonic Egypt: they provided military manpower but occasionally, when their loyalty strayed, proved to be a thorn in the imperial side.

ACHAEMENID RELIGION Like all other monarchs, Darius found ways to use religion to secure his power. Cyrus had enlisted the Babylonian deity Marduk on his behalf, and Cambyses exploited Egyptian divine kingship in his own interest. Darius and later Achaemenids linked their regime with the worship of a god named **Ahura Mazda**, an all-knowing and benevolent creator who with human help would eventually vanquish evil and darkness. The Ahura Mazda rituals were similar to those described in the *Rig Veda*, involving fire ceremonies and sacrifices conducted outdoors. Unlike the practices of earlier religions in Southwest Asia, temples played no major role in Ahura Mazda worship.

The creed of Ahura Mazda was only one of several in circulation in the Achaemenid Empire, but in Darius's time its priesthood, called the Magi, came to occupy a privileged position. Darius supported the priesthood and it supported him. Thereafter, Ahura Mazda, in the official version, selected the ruler from the Achaemenid clan, and that ruler served as the god's regent on Earth, responsible for embodying and enforcing morality and truth. (Herodotus wrote that the Persian elite trained their sons in only three things: archery, horsemanship, and truth telling).

Darius and his son Xerxes (r. 486–465 BCE) each left inscriptions claiming that they punished people who worshipped other gods. Xerxes boasted of murdering them. But if they did persecute people who didn't revere Ahura Mazda, it had little effect. The old Mesopotamian and Egyptian gods retained their followers. Scattered documents mention at least a dozen gods other than Ahura Mazda invoked by Achaemenid kings. So, Persia remained a multireligious society, and the Achaemenids, like Mesopotamian rulers before them, adapted to religious practice in lands they conquered, even if they preferred Ahura Mazda over all other deities.

Techniques of government both new and old enabled Darius, and his son Xerxes, to preside over a stable order and growing prosperity in Persia. Revolts were few and always suppressed. With the exception of a few decades in the fourth century BCE when they lost hold of Egypt, the emperors maintained control over the richest agricultural heartlands, Egypt and Mesopotamia.

AGRICULTURE AND TRADE The Persian Empire grew stronger still, thanks to improvements in agriculture. Rice from India joined the crop mix, allowing higher yields than other grains could provide, especially in the swampy settings of, for example, Mesopotamia. Darius and Xerxes expanded the networks of irrigation, particularly *qanats,* the underground irrigation tunnels that are still in use in parts of Iran. They extended the cultivation of alfalfa, useful especially as nutritious feed for horses

Qanat Throughout Persia, extensive systems of irrigation tunnels known as *qanats* ran underground, conveying water from underground wells to points where farmers could access it. Designing, building, and maintaining such systems required considerable engineering skill.

and indispensable to the big steeds of the Persian heavy cavalry. Alfalfa was also good for fixing nitrogen from the air into the soil, which improves crop yields of all sorts; planting a field one year to alfalfa and the next year to wheat raised the food supply. With more *qanats* and more alfalfa, the Achaemenids addressed two of the problems that most constrained farming: shortages of both water and soil nitrogen (although no one at the time knew of the existence of nitrogen).

Beyond improvements to agriculture, the stability of the Achaemenids encouraged trade. Darius completed a canal begun by a pharaoh to connect the Red and Mediterranean Seas. The road system helped drive down the cost of transport for merchandise and information. Control of port cities of the eastern Mediterranean such as Tyre and Sidon opened the commerce of the entire Mediterranean to Persia, and control over desert oases in the east did the same for trade to India and Central Asia. The expanded use of Arabian dromedaries, thirst-resistant camels, allowed direct travel from upper Mesopotamia to the Mediterranean across the Syrian desert. The increased circulation of coin reduced another obstacle to commerce, because money exchanges are so much more efficient than barter. But above all, it was the political unification of the entire region from the Nile to the Indus that promoted trade. The economic integration of so many ecologically and culturally different regions inspired specialization and exchange, which for a few centuries under Achaemenid rule encountered minimal political barriers.

The Achaemenids reveled in the diversity of their empire and didn't try to homogenize it. The empire's population of 15 to 30 million remained multiethnic, multireligious, and multilingual. Darius celebrated the varying origins of materials and artisans assembled in his building program at the city of Susa: cedar from Lebanon, gold from Sardis and Bactria, lapis lazuli from Sogdiana (Central Asia), silver and ebony from Egypt, ivory from Ethiopia and Sind; stonecutters from Ionia (western Anatolia), goldsmiths from Egypt and Medea (western Persia), brickmakers from Babylonia. Their inscriptions usually appeared in three languages: Akkadian, used in central Mesopotamia, and Elamite and Old Persian, both from western Iran. Their administration was often conducted in a fourth language, Aramaic, spoken in Syria. The Achaemenids made multiculturalism a strength of their empire.

Multicultural Empire A life-sized relief carved on a hillside in Behistun (located in what is now Iran) commemorates the reign of Darius the Great. He holds a bow, signifying his kingship, and faces shorter figures that stand for conquered peoples. Beneath the frame of the image, the story of Darius's reign is written in the three primary languages of the Persian Empire: Old Persian, Elamite, and Akkadian. In this way, even official royal proclamations embraced linguistic and cultural diversity.

The basic structure of the empire remained in place for 135 years after the reigns of Darius and Xerxes. Achaemenid Persia continued to stand as the lone superpower for nearly two centuries.

THE GREEK WORLD TO 338 BCE

In many accounts of human history, the ancient Greeks loom large. Here they will too. Although many people ringed the Achaemenid Empire—including Scythians to the north and Arabs to the south—the one we'll discuss at this stage will be the Greeks. There are two reasons for this. First, unlike other peoples on the frontiers of the Nile-Ganges web, the Greeks burst out of their homeland, conquered Persia, and spread aspects of their culture throughout the region. Therefore, they were important in their own time. Second, they are important to our time as well. Certain of their distinctive cultural traits, detailed below, while almost forgotten for more than a thousand years, resurfaced in later times and became widely admired among European elites in the fifteenth and sixteenth centuries CE, just as those elites were embarking upon a world-girdling spurt of imperialism. Thus ideals of democracy and rationalism, for example, articulated in what was an obscure corner of the world in the fifth century BCE, profoundly affect almost everyone today. But as a starting point, it's useful to remember that in the fifth century BCE the Greeks were few in number and just one of the many peoples on the fringes of a Persian-dominated world.

CRETE AND MYCENAE

The first traces of Greek language and culture date back to around 1500 to 1200 BCE. On the island of Crete, and later in the Peloponnese (the southernmost part of mainland Greece), a palace culture arose that owed something to the examples of Egypt, Anatolia, and Mesopotamia. The introduction of sailing boats into the eastern Mediterranean, soon before 2000 BCE, improved communications. The palaces at Knossos, on Crete, and at Mycenae, in the Peloponnese, organized artisan workshops, stored grain for distribution to loyal followers, and hosted ceremonies to underscore the majesty of kings, in the same general manner as the rulers of Egypt or Babylonia.

The palace culture of Crete is now called Minoan, after the mythical King Minos. It developed slowly, beginning as far back as 2500 BCE, when the Old Kingdom was taking shape in Egypt and urban centers were appearing along the Indus. Scanty evidence suggests its people spoke a language that was not Indo-European. Clay tablets with hieroglyphs, and a later partly syllabic writing system, called Linear A, are as yet undeciphered. The Minoans' religion, to judge by surviving artwork, featured goddesses far more than gods. Minoan art, mainly pottery and frescoes, proved appealing enough to be imitated in Egypt and in mainland Greece. Some of it, such as the possibly female acrobats risking their lives somersaulting over bulls, can be interpreted to mean that women enjoyed unusually high status in Minoan society.

Linear A This tablet from around 1500 to 1400 BCE was found in the palace at Knossos. It is inscribed with the syllabic Linear A script in which the Minoan language was written, which scholars have yet to decipher.

Cretan Palace Culture A fresco from the Cretan royal palace at Knossos shows athletes (who may be women) competing in the dangerous sport of vaulting over bulls.

Minoan Crete's prosperity, which peaked around 1600 to 1450 BCE, was based on agriculture but to an unusual extent also on seaborne trade. Crete exported olive oil to Egypt and probably enjoyed a strong position in the trade of bronze goods. Crete took part in an interactive eastern Mediterranean network linking Egypt, the Levant ports, and Anatolia. Minoan Crete suffered from earthquakes, and around 1550 BCE its northern coasts were flooded by a tsunami caused by a gigantic eruption on a nearby volcanic island.

After 1450, more calamities struck (perhaps more earthquakes), and by 1400 BCE or so Mycenaean invaders from the Greek mainland had taken over the palaces of Crete. They brought their own language, which they soon wrote in an adapted version of the Minoan script known as Linear B. Thousands of Linear B tablets dug up in Crete and in Mycenae have been decoded since the first decipherment of the script in 1952. They reveal that the writing served to record administrative business and that only a few dozen hands did all the writing. The earliest evidence of a Greek language comes from Linear B and dates to about 1500 BCE.

Greece in the next three centuries was a thinly populated region dominated by a warrior aristocracy using bronze weaponry and organized into small kingdoms. The outlook of these aristocrats is reflected in the *Iliad*, a song-poem that recounts events during the Trojan War, which occurred in the thirteenth or twelfth century BCE. (The *Iliad* was recited and sung for centuries before being written down in the eighth century BCE. Along with the

Minoan and Mycenaean Greece, ca. 2500–1100 BCE The first inklings of Greek culture emerged on the island of Crete as early as 2500 BCE but flourished only after 1600 BCE. Its royal courts and its merchants maintained links with Egypt, the Levant, and Anatolia. On the mainland, another palace culture developed somewhat later, named for the citadel of Mycenae. Both specialized in olive oil production, and both used bronze goods and a language ancestral to Greek.

Odyssey, it is attributed to the Greek writer Homer.) That aristocratic outlook bears comparison to the *Rig Veda*: the *Iliad*'s heroes—Achilles, Agamemnon, and dozens of others—were obsessed with honor, quick to violence, disdainful of social inferiors, and respectful of their gods.

After 1100 BCE, bigger kingdoms, including that of Mycenae, fell to ruin. Small-scale polities prevailed for the next several centuries. No one could build a big one in Greece, where rugged terrain worked against centralization—unlike in Egypt or Mesopotamia, where big states now were the rule.

THE *POLIS* AND GREEK POLITICAL CULTURE

Instead, the Greeks, starting around 700 BCE, developed a distinctive political institution called the **polis**, a word often translated as "city-state." Sumer had had city-states, but some of the Greek ones veered onto an unusual path. Instead of a king, some Greek *poleis* had magistrates who governed for a set period of time (often, no more than one year) and were selected by citizens. Sometimes they were chosen by lot. Only adult males of the *polis* could be citizens—no women, slaves, or foreigners. This left perhaps 10 to 20 percent of the population with political rights—far more than anywhere else. Magistrates served at the citizens' pleasure and could not stay in office if they displeased a majority. So magistrates struggled to find policies acceptable to majorities rather than acting solely in their own interests, those of a royal family, or those of a few families. Self-government, even by only a subset of the total population, was abnormal among settled agricultural societies. Even among tribal societies without formal political institutions, the norm was rule by chieftains.

The sense of collective interest and identity that underlay the *polis* rested in part on the military requirements of the day. The Greek city-states, like the Sumerian ones, were often at war with one another. By the end of the seventh century BCE, the cutting edge in warfare in Greece was a formation of citizen-soldiers called the phalanx. In a phalanx, each citizen-soldier, called a hoplite, stood shoulder-to-shoulder with his neighbor and wielded his long spear and shield so as to protect men around him. This tactical unit was far more effective than the individual, aristocratic combat duels celebrated in the *Iliad*. Now weapons were cheaper (they were iron, not bronze), and each citizen had to own a set. Political rights came with doing one's duty in the phalanx with one's fellow hoplites.

Each *polis* had a powerful interest in enabling citizens to equip themselves for war, which meant not letting the divide between rich and poor grow too wide. Some of the city-states, most prominently Athens, also developed navies that enrolled the poorest classes—men who couldn't afford shield and spear. Yet they too could be citizens. This system gave even the poorest a stake in politics and at times a pride in the achievements of their *polis*. The tactical advantages of the Greek phalanx (at least, on level ground), and the political allegiances generated by the Greek *polis* were sufficient to keep the tiny Greek city-states independent for centuries. Some of them, notably Athens, conducted the brand of citizen politics that Greeks called democracy.

The connection between self-defense and self-government helped to justify the exclusion of women, even free native-born women. Beyond that, most Greeks held to the view that women were unsuited to public life.

Hoplites An illustration on a Greek vase shows a phalanx of spear-wielding hoplites, standing close together to protect their fellow soldiers with their shields.

They were, it was thought, easily influenced by unruly passions and intellectually inferior to men. An Athenian playwright of the fifth century BCE, Euripides, may have recognized the illogic of the prevailing view: one of his characters says, "Of all living, thinking beings, we women are the most unlucky." Plato (ca. 427–348 BCE), the great Athenian political philosopher, suggested that women might be fit to receive the same education as males and—this was scandalous in the Athens of his day—to fight and rule. But such views were rare and never prevailed. The more common view was expressed by the Athenian political leader Pericles, who thought that a woman's reputation stood highest when no one spoke of her at all. In this respect, the ancient Greeks' outlook was conventional, broadly similar to views expressed in the later Vedas or, as we'll see, in Chinese texts of the same era.

About 30 Greek city-states founded colonies on the shores of the Mediterranean and Black Seas, beginning as early as 900 BCE but for the most part after 650 BCE. The purpose of these colonies was primarily to enhance the trade and wealth of their founding city (or "metropolis"). The colonies generally maintained cordial relations with their metropolises, sending delegations to take part in religious festivals, for example. Some of them became self-governing *poleis* in their own right while maintaining

ties of trade and sentiment with their ancestral home cities. Among the most important colonies were Syracuse, in Sicily, a Corinthian outpost; Cyrene, on the coast of Libya; and Massalia, where the French city of Marseilles stands today. The colonies numbered several hundred in all, stretching from the easternmost Black Sea to the coasts of Spain. Collectively, they created an archipelago of Greek culture far beyond the Aegean, a culture that included the self-governing *polis*, Greek religion and language, and a way of life that emphasized maritime trade.

SPARTA Greeks such as Herodotus prided themselves on their distinctive democracy, but democracy held sway in only a few hundred of the roughly 1,000 Greek city-states. Sparta, for example, was an oligarchy, meaning a state run by a handful of ruling families, led by kings. Founded in the eleventh or tenth century BCE, Sparta eventually ruled by far the largest territory of all Greek city-states.

Sparta was a militaristic society that held other Greeks in bondage. In the eighth century, its warriors conquered a neighboring land, Messenia, and turned its inhabitants into *helots*, a word that meant "captives" but in practice meant "slaves." Helots did the agricultural work in the lands Sparta controlled, handing over a share of the grain, olive oil, and wine they produced to the Spartans. Some also served as artisans and servants. Female helots often bore children of Spartan fathers in an officially encouraged effort to top up the supply of potential soldiers. Girl babies produced in this way were probably killed.

All Spartan males at age 7 left their families to reside in a communal barracks, where they trained, at public expense, in the martial arts until age 18. As part of their preparation, the best of them were encouraged to sneak up on helots and murder them. Spartans used terror to keep helots in their place. But Spartans lived in fear that the more numerous helots (Herodotus wrote that for each Spartan there were seven helots) might rise against them, so they carried weapons at all times. They suppressed the occasional helot uprisings with unrestrained brutality. Adult male Spartans lived in barracks, even if married, until age 30. They remained on active military duty until 60, an age that few attained.

Their social system made Spartans more formidable in war than any other Greek polity. Sparta built no city walls, relying for defense on its army and its fierce reputation.

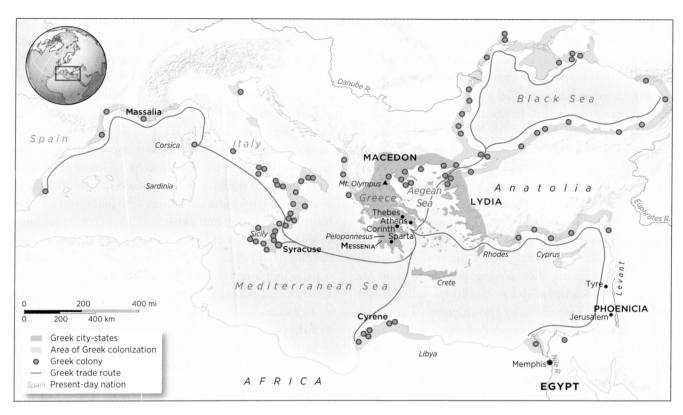

Greek Colonization, ca. 900–500 BCE Greeks were among the peoples who took advantage of the favorable conditions for sailing on the Mediterranean Sea. Greek city-states established hundreds of colonies on the shores of the Mediterranean and Black Seas, creating a tight network of trading communities by 500 BCE.

That was practical partly because of the extreme training and commitment of their soldiers, and partly because every male was a warrior. Sparta had ancient Greece's only genuinely professional army. In other Greek states, the cost of armor and weaponry was such that only about one-third of the male population could afford to take part in the phalanx. Other Greeks regarded Spartan men as unusually pious, overly attuned to omens, and inhumanly restrained in their approach to wine. Spartans, who felt that real men exercised self-control, routinely humiliated helots by forcing them to drink too much wine. The highest honor for a Spartan male was glory in warfare.

For a Spartan woman, the highest honor was having sons who attained glory in warfare. Ancient authors (none of them Spartan, however) often wrote that Spartan mothers taunted and even killed their own sons if they showed cowardice in battle. Spartan girls underwent obligatory physical training too, which included running, wrestling, and javelin- and discus-throwing; they also practiced dancing and singing. In their late teens, they typically

married and soon began begetting the next generation of warriors. They might accomplish this with their husbands or with other men—uniquely for ancient Greece, adultery for women was no crime in Sparta. They did no housework, nor the disagreeable parts of child rearing,

Greek Colonies The Temple of Zeus at Cyrene in Libya was built in a size and style similar to that of the Parthenon in Athens, reflecting Cyrene's importance as a Greek outpost on the southern coast of the Mediterranean.

which fell to helot women. They could own property in their own right, unlike Greek women elsewhere. And they had a reputation as promiscuous among other Greeks—but we should bear in mind that Greek women elsewhere typically lived in seclusion after puberty.

Spartan men launched the practice of exercising naked, their bodies coated in olive oil. As this habit spread to other Greek city-states, a cult of naked male beauty evolved, emphasizing the chiseled, muscular physiques we see in Greek statuary from this period. Greeks occasionally denigrated foreign men as being too scrawny or tubby to appear in public without clothing.

Sparta's political system was, as we've seen, an oligarchy. Its constitution stipulated that two hereditary kings would rule together, serving as a check upon one another. They worked with five executives, called *ephors,* elected for one-year terms by the citizenry. The constitution also included a select council that could veto any decisions taken by its assembly, a check upon the wishes of the citizenry. The council consisted of 28 males over the age of 60 who were elected for life by the assembly, plus the two kings. It served as a high court as well as the key lawmaking body for Sparta. The assembly could accept or reject proposed laws and policies, but it could not initiate any. Ultimately, a total of 35 men directed Spartan public life.

Like Sparta, most of the Greek *poleis* were not democratic. Some, like Corinth or Thebes on the Greek mainland or Syracuse and Rhodes on islands, were run at least from time to time by kings or upstart dictators called tyrants. But at times they also practiced a form of democracy, which Sparta never did. Because taking part in politics and debates is time consuming, those with more leisure time—both the idle rich and the unemployed—were more likely to be active citizens, while those who needed to work to feed their families often neglected their responsibilities as citizens. Where democracy went the furthest, poor men and rich men had, at least in principle, equal rights and equal voice.

ATHENS AND DEMOCRACY Only a few Greek city-states experimented with democracy, and none took it further than Athens in the fifth century BCE. Under a written constitution drafted by Cleisthenes in 508–07 BCE, the Athenians created a political system, eventually termed ***demokratia***, based on equal rights for all citizens.

Cleisthenes, an aristocrat and brother-in-law of the last tyrant of Athens, wanted to break old allegiances based on kinship and locality, and focus everyone's loyalty narrowly on the Athenian *polis*. He did this by creating new political units of the city, the coasts, and the hinterlands of Athens, and according them rights to supply members to a ruling council of 500 that met to do the business of the state every day. This council was responsible to a larger assembly, in which all male citizens age 18 or older who had completed military training could sit, but only those 30 and over could speak. No man who had thrown down his shield and run from battle was allowed to speak, nor could anyone convicted of prostitution or failing to support his parents properly. The assembly of citizens, which usually met a few times a month to discuss policy, was the unit that passed legislation.

In Athens in the mid-fifth century BCE, slaves made up half the population and foreigners one-tenth. Among free Athenians, citizens—males age 18 or older—numbered some 25,000 to 40,000. About 6,000 could fit into the space dedicated to the assembly at any one time. One needed a loud voice, and it was easy for dozens of men to shout down any single speaker whom they didn't like. A show of hands served as the voting system, so everyone knew how others voted. The assembly also elected the city's military commanders, of whom there were normally 10, which led to some hapless generalship. It was an unwieldy system, often swayed by silver-tongued demagogues who promised favors or cash for support. The assembly was quick to vote for war: in the fifth century BCE, Athens was at war more often than not. Greek cities not under Athenian sway—Corinth or Thebes, for example—did not choose to imitate this constitution.

To improve it, Athenians imposed a fine on proposed legislation that didn't pass, discouraging frivolous proposals. The assembly could also vote to ostracize—that is, ban from Athens for 10 years—any individual. Men who seemed dangerously or selfishly ambitious could find themselves in exile under this system. Surviving records indicate 13 ostracisms between 487 and 416 BCE.

THE PERSIAN WARS Athenian democracy in one form or another lasted for nearly two centuries. Its greatest peril came in wars against Persia and then against Sparta. Athens in 490 BCE had taken the gamble of supporting a rebellion against Persian rule mounted by a few

Greek cities in Ionia on the coast of Asia Minor. Darius responded with a punitive expedition against Athens in 490, but Athenian skill and valor at the Battle of Marathon convinced the Persians to give up and go home. Darius died in 486 while preparing another expedition against Greece.

His son Xerxes carried it out and initially had better luck. He enjoyed the support of several Greek cities and defeated those who resisted in battle. His forces occupied Athens briefly, burning the temples of the Acropolis, the citadel of the city. But his fleet lost a key naval battle at Salamis in 480 BCE, and he soon withdrew. From the Greek point of view, tiny Athens had defeated the superpower of the day, Achaemenid Persia, and preserved its experiment in democracy.

These events loom large in ancient Greek history, partly through the magic of Herodotus's storytelling. From the Persian point of view, they were merely rebuffs at the edge of the empire, costly in manpower and embarrassing in terms of prestige but far from vital concerns. In comparison, when Egypt and Mesopotamia rebelled in 485–484 BCE, Xerxes prevailed against the rebels and preserved core areas of his empire. Greece was a relatively poor land despite its mines and maritime trade, worth far less than Mesopotamia or Egypt. Failure to conquer Greece posed no threat to Persia. Even though Greece was a low priority after 480 BCE, Persian kings kept a hand in Greek affairs. They financially supported one city-state against another in a developing rivalry of alliances surrounding Athens and Sparta, and they tried to enlist both as client states of the Achaemenid dynasty.

The Persian Wars, 490–480 BCE By banding together, several Greek city-states managed to resist invasion attempts mounted by Achaemenid Persia, the great power of the day. For Persia, this conflict was merely one of many on the fringes of its empire. For the Greeks, it was a matter of political and cultural survival. Persian-Greek warfare continued intermittently until 449 BCE.

THE PELOPONNESIAN WAR Athens used the prestige it won in the rebuff of Persia and the wealth it acquired from silver mines to create a small Athenian empire, composed mostly of island states that couldn't resist the Athenian navy. Athens grew richer by taxing these states ruthlessly, forming in effect an Athenian maritime empire in and around the Aegean. The apparent rise of Athenian power distressed Spartan rulers, who judged it wise to attack Athens rather than allow Athenian strength to build further. The Peloponnesian War (431–404 BCE) involved most of the Greek world. Thanks in part to Persian aid, Sparta won in the end by destroying the Athenian navy.

In victory, the Spartans resisted their allies' suggestions

to destroy Athens and enslave its entire population. After a brief interruption—a repressive oligarchic government subservient to Sparta—Athenians restored their democracy. But in 322 BCE, an invasion of Macedonians from the north brought this experiment in self-government to an end. A few democracies elsewhere in Greece survived a bit longer, until they were finally extinguished by the Roman conquest of 146 BCE.

Although they died out, the Athenian and other Greek experiments in democracy eventually became the touchstone for democratic movements many centuries later, and they loom large today wherever people consider democracy to be a suitable form of government. This continuing resonance is a result of the intellectual legacy of ancient Greece. Its historians and philosophers left a detailed account of Greek democracy and political thought, part of an extraordinarily influential culture.

GREEK CULTURE

To the ancient Greeks themselves, the gods and the rituals of worship were the most important aspects of their culture. Greek religion carried influences from Mesopotamia and Egypt and, like religion everywhere, was tied up with politics.

RELIGION All of Greece shared the same pantheon of gods, a big quarrelsome family believed to live among the clouds of Mount Olympus. Zeus ruled the heavens with his thunderbolts. Poseidon's domain was the sea. Others took responsibility not for places but for concepts—for example, Aphrodite was the goddess of love and beauty, Athena of wisdom.

These deities often struggled with one another and meddled in human affairs, as the Greek myths recount in entertaining detail. They displayed human failings such as lust, jealousy, and anger, rather like the gods of the *Rig Veda* or of Mesopotamia. The Greeks believed in an afterlife, overseen by a brother of Zeus named Hades. They eventually came to understand the afterlife as taking one's soul to a specific place, the realm of Hades, which included agreeable destinations such as Elysium for those who had led virtuous lives, and a place of eternal torment called Tartarus, reserved for the wicked.

Greek religion contained an ethical component. Throughout the Greek world, including the scattered colonies, the gods expected humans to submit to the discipline of regular worship, pay proper respect to their elders, and extend hospitality to strangers. Worship of the gods usually involved sacrifices of sheep or other livestock intended to win the goodwill of one or another deity.

Beyond these widely held beliefs, each *polis* had its own religious identity, rituals, and bonds to specific deities. Atop the Acropolis and visible across Athens, the Parthenon was a temple to Athena, the city's favored god. Corinth esteemed Aphrodite above all others. Frequent festivals not only reinforced the bonds of gods and city, but also helped to forge a distinct identity for each *polis*. Festivals often featured athletic contests and large

Misbehaving Gods Many Greek gods behaved unethically and harmfully. A large pot from around 400 BCE features such a scene from mythology: Aphrodite, the goddess of love (seated in the center of the top panel), watches approvingly as the semi-divine twins Kastor and Polydeukes abduct two young women.

processions ending at a city's main temple. They offered prominent roles to women, lesser ones to children, and sometimes even to foreigners and slaves. By allowing members of those social classes with no political rights to take part in the public life of the *polis* and feel a commitment to it, religious festivals sustained social bonds within each *polis*.

Religion helped shape everyday life in the Greek world, and through the work of Greek playwrights, poets, and scholars it filtered into the broader intellectual life of literature and philosophy. As we will see, Greek religious ideas informed the world in which Christianity arose, and its intellectual culture had a lasting influence on thinkers in western Eurasia and Africa's Mediterranean lands.

ALPHABETS AND INFLUENCE The intellectual achievement of Greece between about 500 and 330 BCE isn't easy to account for. In part, it may derive from the use of an alphabet, which made literacy easier to acquire than in most parts of the world, where scripts were more complicated. The invention and spread of alphabetic writing in Greece merits a brief detour in our discussion.

The earliest example of alphabetic writing dates to about 1900 BCE in Egypt. Representing a language spoken in Southwest Asia, probably Canaanite, this form of writing had 22 symbols that stood for consonant sounds rather than words or ideas as in all previous scripts. If Egyptian scribes saw it, they probably thought it was inelegant and inefficient: it required many symbols—what we call letters—to record just one word.

But over the centuries that followed, alphabets proved to be an appealing alternative to logographic script (in which symbols represent words) and ideographic script (in which symbols represent ideas) because readers only had to memorize a small number of symbols. By 1000 BCE or so, a trading people called the Phoenicians, based in the merchant cities of the Levant, were writing with an alphabet. From there, the idea of alphabetic writing spread westward to the Greeks, who were the first to use letters to represent both consonant and vowel sounds. That system spread in many directions as people adapted it to different tongues. The alphabet stands among the most important cultural innovations that circulated within the world's webs. The concept of alphabetic writing, although adopted in hundreds of cultures, was invented only once. Today, other than in Chinese and Japanese, alphabets of about 20 to 35 symbols are the building blocks of written language everywhere, all of them adapted from or inspired by the Phoenician alphabet.

After about 700 BCE, the use of an alphabet enabled larger numbers of people to read and write Greek. The Greeks began to write down their myths, and soon their histories and philosophy, rather than merely recording merchants' transactions and royal feats. With more people writing, the odds of brilliant thoughts being written down improved. With more people taking part in intellectual exchanges through writing, the chances of brilliant thoughts occurring to anyone improved. That can't be the whole of the explanation for the Greek achievement, however, because Phoenician cities used an alphabet and left nothing comparable to the Greek intellectual legacy.

Another part of the explanation probably lies in the combination of cultural unity and political disunity. The Greek cities shared a written language, although their inhabitants spoke several different dialects. They shared the same set of gods, military tactics, marriage customs, farming routines, poetic and dramatic forms, architectural styles, and much else. The whole of the Greek world took part in certain rituals such as the Olympic Games, begun in the eighth century BCE. It was a culturally unified space, if politically fragmented. This situation helps to explain (although nothing fully explains) the extraordinary Greek intellectual flowering in the century and a half after the Persians' retreat in 480 BCE.

Political fragmentation meant that no single king, no priesthood, no authority of any sort could stamp out experimental thinking among the Greeks. Poets, playwrights, and philosophers were often at liberty to disagree and to compete with one another for influence. New ideas flourished. Just as the laws of the *polis* guided the behavior of society, some Greeks supposed that there might be laws governing the behavior of nature. Philosophers (which meant deep thinkers of all sorts) increasingly disregarded the older explanations in which just about everything represented the will of the gods. Eventually, they crafted a much more rational explanation of human affairs.

HISTORY, PHILOSOPHY, AND RATIONALITY

That progression is illustrated by accounts of Greek wars over several centuries. In Homer's *Iliad*, written down in the eighth century BCE (although recited and sung earlier), the struggles between Greeks and Trojans are manipulated by rival Greek gods. Herodotus, the Greek historian, writing in the 440s about the Greco-Persian Wars of a few decades before, gathered evidence, sifted it, formed hypotheses, but in the end also often attributed outcomes to divine wills. However, Thucydides, an Athenian general-turned-historian, in his account of the conflict between Athens and Sparta composed late in the fifth century BCE, explained events quite differently. In his work, the gods have virtually no role and people make their own history, as individuals or in groups. Thucydides sought purely human, not supernatural, explanations for the events in his history.

The rationalism exemplified by Thucydides appeared in other spheres of Greek intellectual life as well. Socrates, an Athenian philosopher and son of a stonemason, proclaimed that reasoned arguments could produce answers to life's most vexing questions about virtue, honor, and the meaning of existence. He had the misfortune to make his case just after Sparta's defeat of Athens and a brief civil war in which one of his students led the losing

Philosophical Life An illustration from an Athenian drinking cup shows two young men sharing a couch at a symposium, a gathering centered around wine drinking and conversation. The image also suggests an erotic relationship between the men common among the educated elite.

(pro-Spartan) faction—all of which left Athenians anxious. For Socrates's insistent moral questioning and his supposed neglect of the gods, Athenian authorities put him on trial, despite his record as a minor war hero. Socrates, charged with corrupting Athenian youth, argued that his relentless rationalism provided Athens a service, but to no avail. He was sentenced to death. A different man would have avoided this fate by leaving Athens for another city. But Socrates drank the prescribed poison and died in 399 BCE.

A flock of more fortunate philosophers made respectable livings by teaching the arts of reasoned argument. Citizens found that skill essential if they wished to be effective in politics or to defend themselves in lawsuits. In fact, the political format of the *polis* with its citizen assembly and the skillful use of argument reinforced one another. The philosophers with the most enduring and widespread influence were Plato (427–348 BCE) and Aristotle (384–322 BCE).

Plato came from the upper ranks of Athenian society and was the star student of Socrates. He lectured on, discussed, and wrote about philosophy for more than 40 years in and around Athens, where he created an academy for reflection on philosophical and practical problems.

Having grown up in Athens as it was losing the Peloponnesian War, and having seen what the Athenian assembly did to his teacher, Plato was no friend of democracy. He recommended that the best people—meaning those with self-discipline and unmoved by luxury, dedicated to virtue, and educated in philosophy and mathematics—should rule over everyone else. He considered women worthy of education, and felt that those who mastered philosophy and math, and whose souls were suitably aggressive, could also fight and rule. He argued for dissolving the family and encouraging the best men and the best women to have sex for the purpose of producing the best offspring.

Plato was concerned by questions that ran deeper than politics. He was absorbed by the relationship between appearances, which anyone could perceive, and true reality, which he thought only those with years of systematic philosophical study could detect. He had a mystical bent too, arguing for the existence of a human soul, distinct from the body, that lived on after death. Indeed, his concept of the soul had overtones of Hindu belief in which one's ethical record held consequences for one's future existence, which might include being reborn in another body. Later religions such as Christianity and Islam carried on some of Plato's ideas on these subjects. He was a firm believer in the value of religion, and late in life he recommended that anyone spreading atheism should be put to death. Plato had an obsession with discipline, order, and virtue.

Aristotle was Plato's star pupil. He came from northern Greece but studied in Athens, in Plato's Academy, from age 17 to 37, before making his career as a teacher throughout the Greek world. He was more interested than Plato in the empirical study of reality, and he delighted in classifying objects and pointing out exceptions to rules, including his own. He pursued an extraordinarily wide set of interests, writing on ethics, botany, zoology, weather, logic, drama, music, and poetry as well as politics, law, and constitutions. He held more charitable views of his fellow Greek citizens than Plato, and thought that farmers and soldiers, for example, were worthy of political rights and capable of reasoned judgment, without the extended training that Plato recommended.

But Aristotle drew the line at uneducated tradesmen, foreigners (meaning non-Greek speakers), and women, none of whom he considered equal to the demands of citizenship. He explicitly objected to Plato's notion that women might be suited to rule. He also thought that some people, mainly foreigners, were by nature suited to be slaves because they lacked the discipline and judgment to direct their own lives. At age 40, he took a job at the court of Philip, the king of Macedon, and for seven years labored as the tutor for Philip's son Alexander. Aristotle stands among the most influential thinkers who ever lived.

Greek poets and playwrights also flourished in the world of competitive city-states. Some dramatists, especially in Athens, commented on current politics, even mocking the authorities. Such expression was dangerous in Athens but would have been impossible in a monarchy. The best example may be the bawdy comedy *Lysistrata*, written by Aristophanes and produced in Athens in 411 BCE in the middle of the Peloponnesian War against Sparta. It challenges the wisdom of the war by supposing what might happen if all the married women of Athens and Sparta refused to have sex with their husbands and lovers until the men stopped the war. In the play, the men, desperate for sex, give in and negotiate peace. (In reality, the war went on and on.) Most Greek poetry and drama, however, dealt indirectly with political events through the exploration of timeless themes of love and longing, ambition and revenge, honor and justice—often enacted in conflicts of the gods.

The emphasis on rationalism, debate, and quests for truth also affected inquiry into nature—what we now call science. Ancient Greeks developed a theory of matter based on atoms. Aristotle systematically pursued scientific truth, painstakingly gathering observations about plants, animals, astronomy, and so forth. His portrayal of the natural world was based on evidence and logic. His worldview had little room for the gods, although he allowed that something supernatural could account for the origins of the universe.

After Aristotle, who died in 322 BCE, Greek creativity ebbed somewhat, although it continued to hum for another century or more in mathematics and science, and especially in Alexandria, a culturally Greek city in Egypt. In mainland Greece, the extinction of the independent *polis* by Macedonian conquest (338 BCE) soon narrowed the scope for speculative and irreverent thought. So, perhaps, did the achievement of Aristotle, who seemed to have had the last word on so many subjects. The intellectual golden age of the Greeks did not last long, although its impact is still with us today.

GREEK INTELLECTUAL CULTURE Political fragmentation in the Greek world encouraged this intellectual flowering by making thinkers feel freer. As Chapter 7 will show, a similar efflorescence in Chinese thought accompanied a period of political fragmentation in ancient China. Such moments are rare. Rulers typically regard ideas as too dangerous to be free, and they use their power to constrain if not thought, at least expression. But where a common language and culture exist over a politically fragmented space, as for a while in ancient Greece and China, thinkers can speculate, argue, and interact without careful self-censorship.

The Greek philosophical tradition also answered a growing need felt far and wide in Eurasia during these centuries. Greece, like Mesopotamia in Hammurabi's time, badly needed strong ethical codes. With population growth, the rise of trade and markets, and especially the emergence of urban living with its daily encounters with strangers, Greek societies needed rules. In village settings, where everyone knew everyone else and their families, bad behavior was noticed quickly. But in the city, where people often interacted with others they didn't know, the chances of avoiding retribution for theft or violence were greater.

In the anonymous city, ethical codes carried special appeal. That helps to explain the rise of religions such as Buddhism and Jainism, which offered ethical codes and flourished among commercial communities in north India. In Greece, however, the gods didn't require, model, or even suggest responsible behavior. Indeed, in Greek myth, the gods ran amok, deceiving, tricking, cheating, and raping without remorse. Greek philosophers by the late fifth century BCE felt a need for ethical codes to help navigate the social terrain of the city, above and beyond what religion provided.

Socrates, Plato, Aristotle, and a later school of thinkers known as the Stoics—founded in Athens about 300 BCE—all offered guides to ethical conduct that had appeal in their time and in later centuries

Greek Sculpture This Roman copy of a Greek statue—which would have been cast in bronze in its original fifth-century BCE form—shows every muscle and tendon of the discus-throwing athlete's body, evidence of the sophisticated Greek understanding of anatomy.

too. The Stoics emphasized virtue as the key to happiness and recommended seeking contentment through rational contemplation rather than questing after pleasures. All this is not to say, however, that carpenters, fruit sellers, slaves, sea captains, or priests behaved any more ethically after Greek philosophers wrote their treatises. Ordinary folks had at best the vaguest idea of what philosophers recommended. Rather, it is to say only that Greek thinkers found ethical questions in need of answer as never before, and some of their answers seemed so persuasive as to appeal to reflective minds from their day to ours.

GREEK MARKET CULTURE

In addition to the unique *polis* and the remarkable intellectual outpouring, there is a third notable distinction of the ancient Greeks: the unusual role of markets and money in their society. Their rocky lands suited grain poorly, but olive groves and vineyards thrived. Greek city-states often had to import grain by exporting olive oil and wine, and sometimes wool, honey, pottery, weaponry, and silver too. Their proximity to the sea encouraged trade and specialization, and enabled them to rely on Egypt, Sicily, and their own colonies on the coastlands of the Black Sea for grain. Athens took this commercial orientation furthest. Its foremost marketplace, the agora, adjacent to the citadel of the Acropolis, symbolized the importance of trade and merchants in Athenian life with its location. Its arcades of shops and warehouses, clustered together, eased transactions.

The invention of coinage in Lydia (western Anatolia) sped the development of commerce from the late sixth century BCE. The prominence of commerce and especially risky sea ventures in Greek economic life led to the invention of financial instruments and contracts for loans and insurance. Ports often had rudimentary banks, and cities—especially Rhodes, off the southwest coast of Anatolia—adopted maritime and commercial legal codes that dealt with issues such as liability in the event of a shipwreck. By Plato's time, money and markets had grown so prominent that he argued states ought to control them.

Money and markets changed the way people thought and behaved. Money connected people with total strangers through multiple social networks. Its use weakened the older bonds of kinship and patronage based on social rank. Soon after money was introduced, some priests came to prefer cash contributions for temples and gods over the

blood of a firstborn lamb or the first fruits of the harvest. Families quickly put money into the balance when arranging marriages, so that dowries and bride-prices were paid in cash as well as in sheep or bolts of cloth. Money provided a common denominator that encouraged people to think in terms of equivalences: a goat was worth 3 weeks' rent, or 16 poems, or half a slave, or 3 amphorae of olive oil—because all were worth the same amount of money. Sparta, incidentally, resisted the use of money into the third century BCE, clinging to the concepts of honor, valor, and ancestry after the rest of Greek society had accepted the values of the marketplace.

The combination of networks of colonies, a common culture embracing both popular religion and rational philosophy, combined with an unusually market-driven economy, made the ancient Greek world into a densely interconnected extension of the Nile-Ganges web. Ship traffic on the Mediterranean and Black Seas held it all together and linked the Greeks to neighboring communities, such as the equally maritime and mobile Carthaginians (whom we'll encounter in a later chapter).

Ancient Greece contained only 3 to 4 million people, maybe 15 to 20 percent as many as in Achaemenid Persia. That population was divided among more than a thousand small polities, none of them—not even Athens at its imperial height—powerful or rich compared to the kingdoms of Egypt or Southwest Asia. Just one of several cultures on the fringes of the Persian world, the Greeks would ordinarily not count for much. But because Greek market culture spread throughout the Nile-Ganges web in the fourth century BCE, because Greek philosophy influenced enduring religious traditions, and because of the rediscovery of Greek ideas of democracy and rationalism in later times, ancient Greece deserves an outsized place in world history. The first step in the spread of Greek influence was the fusion of Greek and Persian culture and power that took place under the command of Alexander the Great.

ALEXANDER THE GREAT AS PERSIAN KING

The politically fragmented world of the many Greek *poleis* came to an end in 338 BCE. Macedonians, led by King Philip II and his son, **Alexander the Great**, conquered almost all of the Greek world. The Achaemenid dynasty came to an end in 330 BCE when Alexander routed Persian forces. But in a way, Alexander himself became the last of the Achaemenids and consciously tried to fuse Greek and Persian cultural heritage and military power.

RAISED TO RULE

Alexander was born in 356 BCE. He was raised to rule by his father, Philip of Macedon, and his mother, Olympias, a princess from Epirus in northwestern Greece. Macedon was not a city-state but a small regional kingdom, not Greek but with a Hellenized elite culture—that is, one modeled on Greek ways. It was a client state of Achaemenid Persia that rose in power with the long decline of Athens and Sparta (ca. 400–350 BCE). Philip was a political and military innovator, highly successful in kingly pursuits. He introduced the Greek phalanx formation to his army with great effect. He and Olympias saw to it that their son was prepared to follow in his footsteps.

They retained a disciplinarian tutor, Leonidas, whose idea of a good breakfast (claimed Alexander) was a long night's march. Olympias hired a second, gentler tutor who taught Alexander to read, write, and play music. When Alexander was 12 or 13 years old, Philip announced a competition for the post of tutor to the prince. The winner, an old crony from Philip's childhood, was Aristotle, a Macedonian himself, fresh from 20 years in Plato's Academy. Just what Aristotle taught Alexander is uncertain, but he likely emphasized politics, medicine (always of interest to Alexander), mathematics, philosophy, rhetoric, and poetry. By some accounts, he urged Alexander to see himself as champion of the Greeks and to treat barbarians, in which category he included Persians, as "beasts or plants." While Alexander absorbed Aristotle's wisdom, he continued to pursue the arts of horsemanship and hand-to-hand combat, in which any Macedonian king needed to excel. Then Philip in effect gave his 16-year-old son an internship as governor of part of Macedon and commander of a military campaign.

BUILDING AN EMPIRE

Alexander helped his father acquire a small empire, incorporating most of the territory of Greece by 338 BCE. When a disgruntled bodyguard murdered Philip in 336 BCE, Alexander became king of Macedon. Power went to his head—as might be expected when a 20-year-old inherits

Alexander the Great A mosaic from the first century CE depicts Alexander at the head of a conquering army. The armor reflects Roman motifs.

a mighty army. Some of Aristotle's influence, however, stayed with Alexander. He carried a copy of the *Iliad*, annotated by Aristotle, with him on all his campaigns, and seems to have modeled himself on the hero Achilles in his quest for glory. When he oversaw the sack of Thebes (335 BCE) and ordered the slaughter of its adult males and enslavement of its women and children, he arranged that the house of the poet Pindar, whose verses he had learned to admire, should be spared.

Alexander had faith in his talents, no end of ambition, and an army grown accustomed to victory, glory, and loot—still the standard form of payment for ancient soldiers. Macedon's new empire, although it enfolded almost all of Greece, was still a modest state on the fringe of the Persian world. That wasn't enough for Alexander. In 336 BCE, at age 21, he chose to invade Anatolia and attack the world's lone superpower with about 38,000 men, mostly Macedonian and Greek infantry. The full-time soldiers of the Macedonian phalanx, intensively drilled in maneuvers, served as the cutting edge of Alexander's military machine just as they had for Philip. Alexander refined his father's military methods, in particular combining cavalry with infantry phalanxes. Like Cyrus, the founder of the Persian Empire, he invited cities to surrender peacefully and to support him, which many chose to do. Those that resisted he treated with savage violence and calculated cruelty. His improbable successes in battle after battle, often when heavily outnumbered, led retreating Persians to murder their king, Darius III, who was not performing up to expectations.

Alexander then claimed succession to the Achaemenid throne. He hunted down and killed Persians who claimed to be Darius's successor, and then accorded Darius III full funereal honors. In effect, Alexander was another usurper, like the first Darius, except he had no claim to be of the Persian royal lineage. He did marry two Achaemenid wives (one a daughter of Darius), dressed in the Persian style, and conducted himself—after razing the Achaemenid ceremonial city of Persepolis—as a Persian king.

Having captured the Persian treasury with many tons of silver and gold, he could buy, support, and hire all the mercenaries a king might want. He had coins enough to equal the budget of the Athenian empire for 200 years. He was, surely, the richest man in the world. Like a good Achaemenid king, Alexander busied himself with suppressing rebellions and fighting frontier wars. He won over Egypt easily and, like Cambyses before him, arranged to be made pharaoh. But he struggled in anti-guerrilla campaigns in Bactria, roughly modern-day Afghanistan, where he married a local chieftain's daughter, Roxanne (allegedly the second most beautiful woman in Asia), improving his political position in Central Asia. In 324 BCE, Alexander oversaw a mass marriage of his Macedonian veterans with elite Persian women, which he hoped would strengthen his political position in western Asia.

A FLAWED LEADER

As for many people, a steady diet of success proved hard for Alexander to digest. He was growing more mercurial, grandiose, and intolerant. He named at least a dozen new cities for himself, as Macedonian kings tended to do. (They include modern Kandahar and Herat in Afghanistan, and Alexandria in Egypt). He required everyone

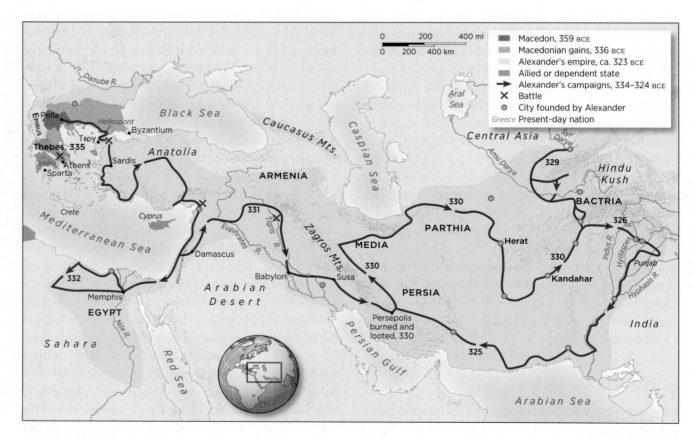

Alexander the Great's Empire, 323 BCE In a span of 15 years, a small kingdom, Macedon, conquered the Greek mainland and then, under Alexander, took over Achaemenid Persia. Alexander briefly united a space from Greece to India, but he died of fever before he could consolidate his empire. It fell apart soon after his death, but he had laid a foundation for a tighter web and more cultural integration among societies from Central Asia to the Mediterranean.

to fling themselves to the ground upon entering into his presence, following the Persian royal custom. He boasted of descent, through his mother, from the mythical heroes Achilles and Hercules. He claimed to be a god himself and the son of Zeus. He killed several old comrades, including advisors and generals, either for subversion or for speaking truth to power, on one occasion in a drunken rage.

For his army veterans, some of whom had known him since he was a boy asking their advice and help, his petulance and self-importance were tough to take. Over eight years, they had walked 12,000 miles (19,000 km) across deserts and over snowy mountains, forded raging rivers, climbed icy cliffs, and had watched their comrades die of combat and disease. Now they had had enough conquering to burnish Alexander's legend. Many of them resented his promotion of Persians into positions of authority. In Punjab in 326 BCE, his remaining Macedonian officers finally balked. So Alexander had to skip the chance to add India to his empire, and instead he set about consolidating his rule. While Alexander still lived, the whole region from the Nile to the Indus remained united, as under the Achaemenids, although he, like them, never stopped fighting rebellions.

When, after his military successes, Alexander began to claim divine status, his former teacher, Aristotle, now back in Athens, objected. Alexander had arranged for the imprisonment of Aristotle's great-nephew, who was working as a historian of the campaigns in Asia. He threatened bodily harm to his former tutor. But before he could silence one of the most rigorous intellects in history, Alexander, one of the greatest commanders in history, veteran of eight combat wounds, died of fever in Babylonia in 323 BCE. He was not yet 33 years old.

Alexander's legend in one form or another turns up in literature and myth from Egypt to China. He appears in the Bible and the Qur'an. His body, snatched by one of his old friends and veteran commanders, Ptolemy, ended up somewhere in Egypt. Many archeological quests have tried and failed to find it. For world history, his chief importance lies in the fact that he and his successors spread a Greco-Persian culture and more commercial ways of life throughout the vast space from the Mediterranean to the Himalaya—an area with nearly half the world's population at the time. This wasn't their purpose; it was an unintended result of their strategies to amass wealth and power.

Soon after Alexander's death, his generals quarreled over who would succeed him. Together, they took the precaution of murdering Alexander's mother, Olympias (a formidable veteran of lethal palace politics in the Macedonian court), his wife Roxanne and her infant son, and a few other members of his family. But the generals agreed on nothing else, and none managed to eliminate all rivals. In the end, they divided the empire: Ptolemy took Egypt, Antigonus got Macedon and Greece, and Seleucus claimed the Persian and Mesopotamian heartland.

WEAVING THE OLD WORLD WEB IN THE HELLENISTIC AGE

Historians use the term ***Hellenistic age*** to refer to the centuries of Greek and Macedonian rule in Greece, Egypt, and Southwest Asia following Alexander's death. Culturally and commercially, Alexander's successors expanded the networks of linkages they inherited, inaugurating an Old World web that embraced peoples and lands from the shores of the Mediterranean all the way to China. (The "Old World" refers to Eurasia and Africa, as opposed to the "New World" of the Americas.)

THE SELEUCIDS, THE PARTHIANS, AND TRADE

From 311 BCE, a new dynasty, the Seleucids, the descendants of Alexander's general Seleucus, ruled Persia. In their early years, they ruled over about 14 to 18 million people. Although much diminished compared to the realms of Alexander or Darius, the Seleucid kingdom was for a time the most powerful polity in the world. It ruled first from a capital on the Tigris (at today's Baghdad) and then from Antioch in Syria.

The Seleucids, as Macedonians and Greeks governing Persia and Mesopotamia, had a legitimacy problem they could never solve. They lost some territory in India to Chandragupta, the founder of the Mauryan Empire, and faced continual rebellion in numerous corners of their kingdom. Fully 13 of 15 Seleucid kings died by violence. But, like the Ptolemies, the dynasty that succeeded Alexander's rule in Egypt, they presided over a remarkable

Hercules This statue of Hercules at Mount Behistun, located in what is present-day Iran, dates to around 153 BCE and was constructed during the time of the Seleucid Empire. Hercules was and is among the most celebrated of the Greek mythological heroes.

economic upturn and participated in a historic commercial integration of the entire Eurasian corridor.

The Seleucids sought to Hellenize their realm—that is, install Greek ways—and they succeeded in several respects. They built new cities, Antioch chief among them, with Greek features such as amphitheaters and gymnasia. They introduced Greek styles of coinage and statuary. They continued Alexander's policy, adopted from Greek tradition, of sponsoring athletic contests. They welcomed tens of thousands of Greek and Macedonian immigrants to their cities. With Seleucid patronage, Persian clergy adopted some aspects of Greek religion, and for some people Ahura Mazda merged with Zeus. The Greek language appeared on some public inscriptions.

But Hellenization could only go so far. As foreigners, the Seleucids had to conform to Persian traditions in order to win support from local elites. Even with their best efforts, frequent rebellions obliged them to rely on armed force more than the Achaemenids had needed to do. The Seleucids were often equal to that task. They combined the Macedonian phalanx with Achaemenid heavy cavalry (i.e., big horses capable of carrying armor) and added Indian war elephants to the mix. Thus their military technique was a hybrid, like the religious fusions they promoted, and probably more central to their rule.

Less obvious, but ultimately even more significant than cultural Hellenization, was the Seleucids' success in promoting commercial activity and markets—a Hellenization

of sorts. The Seleucids, both by accident and by design, furthered the use of coins and markets in the economy of regions they controlled. They nurtured the linkages of long-distance trade. Chinese silks, for example, made their first appearance in Southwest Asia in Seleucid times.

The Seleucids deliberately developed the infrastructure of commerce. They built ports along the Mediterranean shore of the Levant and on the Tigris. They subsidized overland caravans by maintaining way stations (caravanserais) at regular intervals along trade routes. They adopted a uniform coinage throughout their realm, based on Athenian standards. Long-distance trade and cities such as Antioch boomed.

THE PARTHIANS The Seleucid dynastic line lasted for two and half centuries, but Seleucid power did not. Rebels and rival kingdoms nibbled away at Seleucid territory, and by 100 BCE there was little left. But their most successful successors, the **Parthians**, formerly a group of mobile pastoralists, continued the economic and political traditions of the Seleucids and in particular nurtured long-distance connections. They set up a new Iranian state, stretching

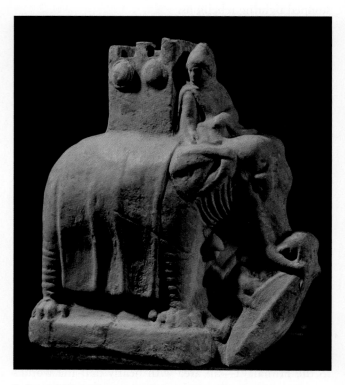

Seleucid War Elephants A terracotta figurine from Greece, dated to around 150 BCE, shows a Seleucid soldier mounted on an Indian elephant trampling an enemy—evidence of how the Seleucids adopted technologies and tactics from foreign lands.

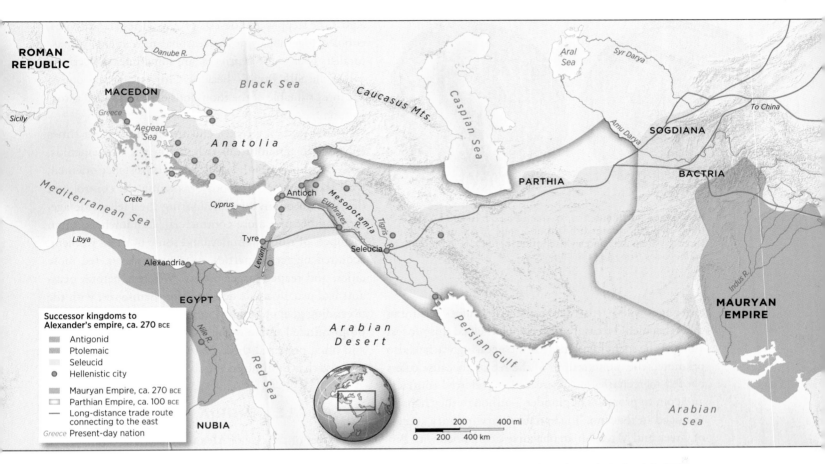

Hellenistic States, the Mauryan Empire, and the Rise of the Parthian Empire, 311–30 BCE Soon after Alexander's death in 323 BCE, his empire fragmented and three main kingdoms resulted: the Ptolemies centered in Egypt, the Seleucids in Mesopotamia and the Persian heartland, and the Antigonids in Macedon and Greece. Ptolemaic Egypt became a center for science and literature, and together with the Seleucids built on Alexander's effort to establish Greek culture from the Nile to the Indus, a program in which creating new cities featured prominently. After the Seleucid decline, the Parthians built an empire that stretched from Mesopotamia to Bactria and the western end of India's Mauryan Empire. Like the Seleucids, the Parthians promoted trade links that stretched to India and China, the first inklings of the Silk Road.

from Mesopotamia to Bactria, that lasted until 224 CE, and they maintained their end of the new long-distance caravan trade that linked China, Central Asia, India, and the Mediterranean.

The Parthians, like the Seleucids before them, relied upon heavy cavalry and religion to keep their subjects under control, and upon commerce and Mesopotamian agriculture for their revenues. Parthian kings supported Greek urban elites throughout their domain, especially traders whose money could easily be taxed. They found it prudent to cooperate with urban commercial elites, often Greek in outlook: many of their kings put the word *philhellenos*, meaning "friend of the Greeks," on their coins.

Over several centuries, the Seleucids and Parthians built something fundamental to world history that was a legacy both of the Achaemenids and of Alexander: a commercialized quickening of interconnections within the Nile-Ganges web and new systematic, sustained contacts with China. This was the—faint—beginning of an Old World web.

MONEY AND TRADE The commercial awakening sponsored by the Seleucids and Parthians rested partly on transport improvements such as navigation canals and domesticated camels, and partly on cultural common denominators such as the spread of Greek as a trading language, Greek weights and measures, and Greek commercial law. Perhaps more fundamentally, it resulted from the spreading use of coined money, adopted by rulers who saw its advantages over barter especially in cross-cultural

Philhellene Parthians The reverse of a coin issued by the Parthian king Mithridates II bears an image of a Greek goddess (possibly Demeter) and an inscription identifying Mithridates as *philhellenos* (friend of the Greeks).

across the steppes and deserts of Asia. These land routes, cobbled together from the seasonal movements of pastoralists over many centuries, are sometimes collectively called the **Silk Road**—because Chinese silk was one of the most valuable of the thousands of items traded across Eurasia.

The spread of market culture in Hellenistic times extended to agriculture as well. Before the Achaemenids, most farming in Southwest Asia was subsistence oriented, with states and priesthoods organizing the control and distribution of any surplus. During the Hellenistic age, farming became more commercial. Landowners, often members of ruling families (and some of them women), acquired bigger properties, used more slaves, fed more cities, and reaped larger profits. Whereas before, peasants had usually made decisions for themselves, with the overriding goal of avoiding crop failure and famine, now profit-minded estate owners chose which crops to sow and often preferred those that would fetch a good price to those that minimized the risk of famine.

GREEK ALEXANDRIA

The career of the city of **Alexandria** in Egypt under the Ptolemies—another of Alexander's successor dynasties—exemplifies these changes in commerce and culture. The city was founded by Alexander in 331 BCE as a Mediterranean seaport, far from the former centers of power in Egypt that were along the Nile to the south. Alexandria attracted a lively merchant class, largely Greek, and other immigrant groups as well, perhaps most prominently Jews from the Levant. Its trade tightened old links between the economies of Egypt and northeastern Africa and those of the Mediterranean and Southwest Asia. Alexandria also became a manufacturing center and by 200 BCE had perhaps half a million citizens, the biggest city of its time. Its hinterland, the fertile farmland of the Nile delta, became ever more commercialized. Alexandria's merchants directed the grain surplus of the Nile delta toward urban markets of the eastern Mediterranean. They traded gold from Nubia to Seleucid (and later Parthian) Persia, where it was exchanged for Chinese silk. To judge from dozens of surviving letters written by (or for) elite women in Ptolemaic Egypt, they too occasionally took part in the commerce in goods and property, although for most of them childbirth, child rearing, and household management loomed larger among their concerns. Alexandria

exchanges where trust was scarce. Alexander's seizure of the Achaemenid treasury in Persepolis helped this process along, as he spent his coins freely. Unceasing warfare also promoted the monetization of the region, because rulers needed mercenaries and mercenaries preferred contracts and coin to promises of plunder—although they happily indulged in that too. The extraordinary military success of Greek and Macedonian phalanxes, combined with Persian heavy cavalry, enabled mercenaries experienced in those two ways of war to command large sums: rulers who would not or could not pay in coin did not stay in power long.

Another reason behind the growing scale of commerce was the new availability of Chinese silk. Silk was a luxury good, much esteemed by urban upper classes. At the time, it came only from China. Women in western Asia competed in wearing the best silk, and men competed in adorning their wives and daughters in it. The Seleucids and later the Parthians controlled the routes over which most silk came to the Hellenistic world and had every reason to support the trade. Tolls and taxes helped provide their revenues. As the next chapter will explain, China was simultaneously building an East Asian web, which quickened the commercial economy in Seleucid and later Parthian lands.

The trade in silk, Greek market culture, and Seleucid and Parthian policy drew the hubs of Eurasia and northern Africa, from China to Egypt, into regular contact. The connecting links were made via relay trades in which goods passed from one merchant to another, along sea routes through the Indian Ocean and caravan routes

Ptolemaic Egypt A gold relief shows King Ptolemy VI, who ruled Egypt from Alexandria during the period 180–145 BCE. He is wearing the double crown of the pharaohs to make a symbolic connection to the previous rulers of Egypt.

became a byword for wealth. One rich citizen built a lighthouse 500 ft. (120 m) tall that lasted 16 centuries before earthquakes brought it down. Its last remnants were recycled into fortifications in 1480 CE.

Like other Hellenistic kings, Alexandria's rulers patronized the arts and sciences. They built a library that housed every manuscript its directors could buy. It served as an institute for advanced study, where teams of scholars worked away at public expense. One team of 70 Hebrew linguists translated holy texts of the Jews into Greek for inclusion in Alexandria's library. Known as the Septuagint, their work is the basis of later translations of much of the Hebrew Bible. Alexandria also became a center for medical and mathematical training. One of its scholars, Eratosthenes, director of the library, calculated the Earth's circumference and was accurate within 2 percent. The Ptolemies turned Hellenistic Alexandria into a commercial engine, cultural hothouse, and cosmopolitan magnet for talent from near and far.

Alexandria was exceptional, but a market culture spread throughout the Nile-Ganges web. It radiated out from the cities and trade routes to thousands of villages and farms. Migrants and mercenaries moved about in ever greater numbers. So did captives sold into slavery. Scientific and religious ideas circulated a bit faster. The web of Southwest Asia and Egypt thickened and, through the contacts of the Silk Road, connected to a newly forming web of East and Southeast Asia (discussed in the next chapter) that fused into an Old World web. No record exists of any person traveling all the way from China to the Mediterranean or vice versa until a millennium after Hellenistic times. But now goods, ideas, technologies, crops, and infections, among other things, were carried the length of Eurasia far more often—and far faster—than ever before. This was among the legacies of the Achaemenids, Alexander, and

Greek market culture, transplanted to Southwest Asia and Egypt in the Hellenistic age.

The political unity that Cyrus and Persian rule had brought to the region had vanished, and there was no superpower anymore. Alexander's successors couldn't hold together what Cyrus had built. But the commercial connections strengthened by Achaemenid unification and the expansion of market life under Alexander, the Seleucids, the Parthians, and the Ptolemies lived on.

CONCLUSION

The stories of the Persians and the Greeks were quite different: one featured a great state that unified a broad space, and the other involved many small states that quarreled constantly among themselves. Drawn together in the Hellenistic regimes that followed Alexander's conquests, they contributed to a cultural and political blend that proved to be influential from the rocky shores of the Mediterranean to the snowy mountains of Central Asia. That blend helped to tighten, and extend, existing webs and begin the process of making a more comprehensive Old World web.

Achaemenid Persia was the first superpower in world history, ruling over nearly a third of humankind. The scale of its state created new challenges for its rulers, who refined or invented technologies and techniques of power. These ranged from heavy cavalry to multicultural symbols such as griffins, a common royal motif everywhere in Southwest Asia. Like Ashoka in India, who found Buddhism a helpful way to legitimate his rule, the Achaemenids deployed Ahura Mazda worship as their core ideology while permitting other faiths. Religions that were in effect portable, not tied to any local city, rock, or tree, were much more useful to big multiethnic states such as Persia.

The tiny states of the Greek world competed ruthlessly with one another in every sense. They fought militarily. Several of them tried to amass commercial wealth, partly to be able to fight effectively. And many competed to host the most glorious thinkers, artists, and dramatists they could attract. This situation was highly unusual in world history. More often, a given region united by language and culture is ruled by a single state, which for reasons of its own power and survival limits the freedom of merchants and thinkers. The Greek city-states' stubborn disunity before Alexander's conquests in 338 BCE helps to explain the remarkable development of both commerce and culture for two centuries in Greek lands. Neither merchants nor philosophers were consistently beholden to kings. Of course, there's more to it, because not every case of political fragmentation gives rise to the equivalent of Socrates, Plato, and Aristotle.

It took the combination of Persia and Greece—brought together by the conquests of Alexander and his followers—to Hellenize and tighten links among most landscapes of Southwest Asia and Egypt. Alexander's successors, in power from Epirus and Egypt to Bactria and Sogdiana, admired Greek culture and found ways to meld it with local traditions to support their authority. Greco-Buddhist art, with which this chapter began, is an example of this cultural melding. Alexander's successors also favored the development of commerce and commercial agriculture because it helped expand their tax base. Trade, cities, crafts, and agriculture all flourished in the Hellenistic world, quickening the pace of economic life and linking cities and farms into tighter webs. Trade in the gold of Nubia and the silk of China connected these commercial webs with both Africa and East Asia. Hellenized culture did so too, as widespread artistic motifs such as the halo show. By 200 CE, a new and bigger web, an Old World web, was under construction, thanks in large part to the Achaemenids, the Greeks, Alexander, and Alexander's successors. The new trade contacts with China were links to another big web, an East Asian web, one that had been developing for thousands of years—as we will see in the next chapter.

CHAPTER REVIEW

KEY TERMS

Achaemenids (p. 150)

Darius (p. 152)

heavy cavalry (p. 153)

Ahura Mazda (p. 154)

polis (p. 157)

demokratia (p. 160)

Alexander the Great
    (p. 166)

Hellenistic age (p. 169)

Parthians (p. 170)

Silk Road (p. 172)

Alexandria (p. 172)

Go to INQUIZITIVE to see what you've learned—and learn what you've missed—with personalized feedback along the way.

REVIEW QUESTIONS

1. How did Achaemenid rulers regard the cultural practices of peoples they conquered?

2. How did Darius project power across the expanse of his empire?

3. In what ways did the stability of the Achaemenid Empire encourage trade?

4. What were the main characteristics of the Minoan and Mycenaean cultures?

5. Why was the Greek *polis* such a distinctive and important political institution?

6. Describe the social system that made the Spartans particularly formidable in war.

7. Why was Greek culture so rich and dynamic?

8. What was the impact of money and markets in ancient Greece?

9. What was Alexander the Great's chief importance for world history?

10. How did the Seleucids and the Parthians Hellenize their realm, both culturally as well as through money and markets?

11. How did Chinese silk contribute to the growing scale of commerce in western Asia?

12. What does it mean that Ahura Mazda worship was portable, and why was that an important feature for the Persian Empire?

FURTHER READING

Lindsay ALLEN, *The Persian Empire* (2005). Developed to accompany a museum exhibit, this survey is strong on material culture, well illustrated, and readable.

Paul CARTLEDGE, *Ancient Greece: A Very Short Introduction* (2011). Clear and quirky, a work by one of the world's foremost authorities on ancient Greece.

Angelos CHANIOTIS, *The Age of Conquests: The Greek World from Alexander to Hadrian* (2018). A survey of the sprawling Hellenistic world into the second century CE.

Charles FREEMAN, *Egypt, Greece, and Rome: Civilizations of the Ancient Mediterranean* (2004). The best combined overview of these three societies.

P. J. RHODES, *A History of the Classical Greek World* (2010). The best overview of the subject up to the death of Alexander.

Carol G. THOMAS, *Alexander the Great in His World* (2007). An examination of how his circumstances shaped Alexander's behavior.

Matt WATERS, *Ancient Persia: A Concise History of the Achaemenid Empire, 550–330 BCE* (2013). A survey that is especially good at explaining how we know what we think we know about the subject.

CHRONOLOGY

ca. 13,000 BCE
Earliest use of pottery in Japan

By 5000 BCE
Farming exists in New Guinea

ca. 1800–1500 BCE
First large, walled sites emerge along Huang He River; Erlitou is largest East Asian population center

ca. 1500 BCE
Korean bronze working and dolmen building begin

By 1000 BCE
Japan acquires millet, yams, taro from East Asian mainland

771–256 BCE
Eastern Zhou rule; Warring States period

ca. 551–479 BCE
Lifetime of Confucius (Kong Qiu)

ca. 3500 BCE
Shift toward complex society in China

By 3500 BCE
Farming begins in Korea

ca. 8000 BCE
Pottery emerges in Korea

ca. 1200–1050 BCE
First writing in China

ca. 1450 BCE
Copper smelting begins in central Thailand

1045–256 BCE
Zhou dynasty

ca. 1600–1046 BCE
Shang dynasty

ca. 800–700 BCE
Introduction of iron in China

ca. 700 BCE
Rice is introduced in Korea

ca. 500 BCE
Lifetime of Laozi; *Daodejing* is written down

Weaving an East Asian Web

5000 BCE to 200 CE

Things ended badly for the Trung sisters in 43 CE. They were among the millions of people who tried to resist the expansion of China at a time when the gap between Chinese power and that of China's neighbors was widening fast.

Trung Trac and Trung Nhi were daughters of a prominent family in the Red River delta of what is now northern Vietnam. Chinese armies had conquered the Red River delta in 111 BCE, and it soon became the biggest population center in East Asia south of the Yangzi River. China controlled it very loosely. Its people lived by fishing, hunting, and farming, often using swidden techniques—cutting and burning forests before planting—or "farming with fire" as Chinese authors put it. The Viet, as these people are called, seemed exotic to Chinese observers: they ate strange foods, tattooed their skin, married only after a couple's first baby was born, and expected women to share in property and in family decision making. Upon marriage, men usually moved in with their wives' families, and so adult sisters often lived together. The Trung sisters both married the same man, a minor local lord.

In time, the potential of the Red River delta and adjacent lands became too great for China to allow it to remain loosely governed. Its ports gave access to

ca. 300–400 CE
Korea and Japan adopt writing

221–207 BCE
Qin dynasty

ca. 1 CE
Chinese governors try to control the Viet; wet rice production spreads into Southeast Asia from China

39–43 CE
Trung sisters revolt and rule

By 100 BCE
Silk roads link China and the Mediterranean

206 BCE–220 CE
Han dynasty

259–210 BCE
Lifetime of Shi Huangdi

Imperial Burial The Qin emperor, Shi Huangdi, had a giant mausoleum built for himself that was guarded by more than 7,000 terra-cotta warriors and 100 horses. The emperor died in 210 BCE.

FOCUS QUESTIONS

1. What were the most important features of East Asia's geography and ecology?

2. What were the main features of early complex societies in East Asia?

3. What accounts for the spread of Chinese cultural influence across East Asia?

4. What were the major shared features of peoples living in the emerging East Asian web?

lucrative trade with peoples farther south, in what is now Indonesia and Malaysia. The delta itself was perfect for irrigated rice cultivation. Beginning about 1 CE, Chinese governors took a more active policy with respect to the Viet, trying to "civilize the barbarians," as they put it. This policy included building roads, developing ports, introducing iron tools and plows, and imposing higher taxes. It also involved requiring the use of Chinese language and Chinese hairstyles, and welcoming thousands of Chinese settlers. Moreover, the Chinese overlords wanted to "correct" the Viet's "betrothal and marriage procedures"—in particular, to ensure that males were masters of their own houses and that women no longer could inherit property.

When a Chinese governor executed the Trung sisters' husband for objecting to taxes in 39 CE, they raised a revolt. Rather than secluding themselves in mourning, as the Chinese thought proper, the sisters gathered thousands of Viet, organized them into armies, and captured 65 cities. The Chinese governor retreated, leaving the Trung sisters in charge of what is now northern Vietnam and a sizeable chunk of southern China. Trung Trac declared herself a queen.

Word of the rebellion led by women soon reached the Chinese capital in Luoyang. A large army descended on the Viet in 41 CE, and although it lost half its men to combat and disease, by 43 it had captured the Trung sisters. Together with several thousand leading families of the Viet, the sisters were beheaded and their skulls delivered to the Chinese emperor. The Chinese then got on with the business of "civilizing" the Viet, settling more Chinese in Viet lands, and converting the Red River delta into a productive rice bowl. For the next 900 years, northern Vietnam was, except for brief intervals, part of China.

The term *East Asia* for the purposes of this chapter means the sprawling region including all of modern China, Korea, Japan, and parts of Southeast Asia (mainly Vietnam). For the last 3,000 years, this East Asian region has been home to something like one-quarter to one-third of humankind. This chapter shows how in the millennia before 200 CE, the region of East Asia slowly knit itself together into a vast web of interaction—the East Asian web—broadly comparable to the process afoot in the region between the Nile and the Ganges at the same time.

As it did between the Nile and the Ganges, the process of integration in East Asia involved trade links, the spread of farming, the appeal of certain religions and cultures, and plenty of military conquest—Chinese armies eventually became as ruthlessly efficient as the Assyrians. However, here in East Asia, the role of one political and cultural tradition—the rich and ever-changing one we call Chinese—was much larger than that of Sumerians, Babylonians, Assyrians, Egyptians, Harappans, Persians, or Greeks, or anyone else in between the Nile and the Ganges.

EVOLVING ENVIRONMENTS IN EAST ASIA

Before getting into the particulars of East Asian history, let's examine how its geography and ecology helped to shape the region before 200 CE.

MONSOONS

East Asian climate is powerfully influenced by seasonal monsoon winds that in summer months carry warm, moist air from the tropical Pacific, and to a lesser extent the Indian Ocean, bringing plentiful rain. The southern coasts of China, for example, where mountains intercept monsoon winds every summer, get a reliable soaking of about 60 inches (1,500 mm) of rain almost every year. Inland regions of East Asia are drier. In winter, the monsoon winds reverse direction, bringing cold, dry air from Central Asia and Siberia over almost all of East Asia. Although not fully reliable, the monsoon pattern, apparently in place for the last 20 million years or so, became the foundation of East Asian agriculture. When it failed, crops withered and people starved. Many of the earliest surviving writings from East Asia express anxiety that spring rains might be too little or summer rains too strong for a good harvest.

One reason monsoons sometimes failed was the irregular shift in currents of the tropical Pacific called El Niño. For reasons no one fully understands, every few years currents of warm water that usually flow from east to west across the Pacific instead stay put near South America. This keeps water in the western Pacific cooler than usual, and the air above it both cooler and drier. When this happens, the monsoon winds bring much less moisture to East Asia. A strong El Niño spells drought for most of Southeast Asia and sometimes southern parts of China. In the past, it meant not only more fires, but also more hunger.

RIVERS AND SEAS

Monsoon rainfall fed a series of rivers that formed another environmental feature important for East Asian history. Several of the world's biggest rivers flow across the region, most of them rising in the Tibetan Plateau or the Himalayas and traversing thousands of miles en route to the sea. The Huang He (or Yellow River), the Yangzi, Mekong, Chao Phraya, Irrawaddy, and Salween served as sources of drinking water, irrigation water, and fish, and as arteries of transportation.

All these rivers had dozens of tributaries, making for a gigantic network potentially available for boat traffic. The combination of navigable rivers and the adjacent seas made East Asia a strong candidate for early development of

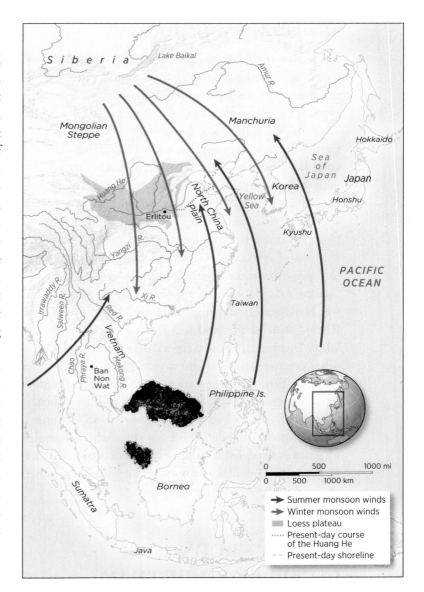

East and Southeast Asia, ca. 1800–1000 BCE The agricultural potential of East Asia depended in part on the seasonal monsoon winds that brought spring and summer rains. Some of the richest soils, important to the development of early Chinese states, lay in the loess region along the Huang He. The monsoon winds aided navigation especially in the South China Sea, helping to tie China to Southeast Asia. (Note that the lower course of the Huang He has shifted over time, and the shoreline of the sea it empties into has also moved. All maps of East Asia will show the river course and shoreline as of the date of the map.)

long-distance trade and transport networks—in short, for webs of human interaction. The combination also made it all the more rewarding to build yet more waterways—canals linking the rivers together.

ENVIRONMENTAL DANGERS

East Asia's environment also featured earthquakes, tsunamis, typhoons, volcanic eruptions, and floods. The offshore islands, from Japan to the Philippines, are especially exposed to typhoons—tropical cyclones with high winds. They also lie across geologically unstable cracks in the Earth's crust, so they're often rocked by earthquakes and volcanic explosions. East Asians have had to learn to live with this dynamic, unpredictable, and at times dangerous environment. In Southwest Asia, by contrast, drought was a frequent risk, and earthquakes an occasional one, but tropical storms, tsunamis, floods, and volcanic eruptions were rare. East Asian societies had to organize themselves to cope with a more diverse array of risks.

East Asia 5,000 years ago was growing warmer and wetter. Alligators slithered along the Huang He (Yellow River). Most of the land was forested and dotted with lakes. Elephants, rhinos, tigers, deer, black bears, and other creatures roamed the woods. Wild water buffalo splashed through the swamps. In most of the region, human population was sparse. But here and there clusters of farming villages had formed, as we saw in Chapter 3. These clusters provided the basis from which complex societies evolved. Eventually, networks of complex societies established regular communication with one another, the beginnings of an East Asian web.

THE EMERGENCE OF COMPLEX SOCIETY IN EAST ASIA TO 1000 BCE

According to later Chinese traditions, most every component of complex society in East Asia is attributable to the Yellow Emperor, Huang Di. Both god and ruler, he taught people to build shelters, grow grain, and tame animals. He invented boats, carts, the calendar, and clothing. He also instructed an associate to invent writing and wrote the first medical text. His chief wife taught people to weave silk. He reigned for a hundred years (it took some time to get everything done), and all Chinese are descended from him.

Archeologists regard matters differently. As we've seen, rice farming began in the Yangzi valley at least 9,000 years ago, and cultivation of soybeans and millet began along the Huang He at least 8,000 years ago. People living in the floodplains of these two river systems were probably loosely linked even before they started farming. After farming began, it spread from these centers, along both big rivers and into the landscapes in between, where rice and millet were raised. The emergence of complex society began along the Huang He where the river leaves the mountains for the plains.

GROWING SOCIAL STRATIFICATION

To judge by burials, the early villages in East Asia were egalitarian in social structure. Remains found in grave sites imply the recognition of nuclear families within larger lineages or clans—kinship groups that might contain hundreds or even thousands of people. Chemical analysis of a few skeletons (from ca. 5000 to 3000 BCE) in the lower Huang He valley shows that males and females ate the same diet, heavy on millet but with plenty of animal protein. But we should bear in mind that new archeological finds could overturn prevailing interpretations.

Evidence from genetics and historical linguistics suggests that these villagers in what is now China were a diverse lot. They spoke a cluster of languages, many of them ancestral to a language family called Austronesian, which today is spoken mainly in Southeast Asia. The languages that we now call Chinese—Mandarin, Cantonese, and others—acquired some of their characteristics, such as tones, from these early Austronesian languages. What we now sometimes call China proper, the zone inhabited by ethnically Han Chinese, was a culturally, linguistically, and genetically diverse region.

The archeological record suggests that around 3500 BCE a shift took place toward more complex society—at roughly the same time as in Southwest Asia. Bigger settlements and more social stratification emerged in several centers between the Huang He and the Yangzi. Skeletons show evidence of more anemia and shorter life spans than in earlier eras, and more signs of violence, perhaps including human sacrifice. Over a dozen walled towns have been unearthed, several with palace-type architecture.

One cemetery shows how far stratification had developed by 2000 BCE. Most graves contain only one or two objects interred with the dead, and few contain none at all. But one, of an adult female, includes nearly 200 burial objects—ceramics, decorative stones, rings, bracelets, and pendants. Some of the graves contain goblets and pig skulls, perhaps meaning that elites confirmed their status by throwing parties and feasts for lesser folk. Ritual displays of generosity are in many cultures a way for elites to show off their status and reward their supporters.

Early Chinese grave sites also seem to show great awareness of rank and kinship, which if true would be consistent with values held in later East Asian societies. In what is now southern China, elites amassed objects of jade (a lustrous green stone), such as carved masks, taken to signify refinement and symbolize continuity across the generations.

In short, it seems that over time elites got richer and their followers more numerous. Social units were growing larger. A hefty dose of compulsion and intimidation may have been involved: centers built ever-larger fortifications—walls of packed earth—perhaps to shield elites from rebellious commoners.

Even in these early times, communities in East Asia forged long-distance links and networks. Pottery is our best evidence of these trends. Millet and rice were boiled or steamed, not ground into flour and baked like the grains of Southwest Asia, so early Chinese families had incentives to make durable pots. The earliest yet found, in the Yangzi valley, are nearly 20,000 years old.

Cooking pots acquired symbolic importance: handed down from one generation to the next, they connected the living with their ancestors. Similarities in pottery styles show that as early as 4000 BCE villages in China hundreds of miles apart were in contact. Decorative styles in jade ornaments also testify to early long-distance exchanges. Such connections grew far stronger after East Asian communities began to build states.

EARLY STATES

The earliest states in East Asia appeared in northern China. How this happened is unclear. Perhaps states arose from cooperative arrangements intended to manage irrigation and flood control. Rain-fed agriculture is feasible in much of northern China, including the loess region along the Huang He. But the silt load of the Huang He was so great that on its lower reaches it gradually built its bed up above the elevation of the surrounding plains (like the Indus River) and thus was prone to devastating floods. Chinese villagers constructed levees and dams to keep floodwaters from washing away their crops and homes.

Early Chinese Society Our first evidence of complex society in China includes grave goods like these intricate jade ornaments, discovered in burials across China dating between 2500 and 2000 BCE. The presence of such luxury objects indicates the emergence of money, trade, and social hierarchy.

Flood control infrastructure could also be used for irrigation. Chinese legends maintain that kings (now generally considered mythical) directed water control, but the scant evidence suggests that it began, as in Egypt and Mesopotamia, at the village level.

The emergence of cities in China is also a hazy story. Settlements in the loess region along the Huang He had existed for millennia before the first large, walled sites emerged around 1800 to 1500 BCE. Thereafter, cities dotted the landscape wherever irrigation allowed surplus food production. Still, two millennia later in 200 CE, under 5 percent of Chinese lived in cities. Most people lived in farming villages.

The first clear evidence of a state in East Asia is a site called Erlitou, just south of the Huang He in what is now China's Henan province. It dates to somewhere around 1800 to 1500 BCE. The site appears to have housed as many as 30,000 people, by far the largest population center in East Asia at the time. It had eight palaces for ruling elites, royal tombs

Erlitou Bronze With its tripod legs and elongated spout, this bronze pitcher dated to around 1600 BCE is characteristic of the vessels used for ritual offerings. Traces of gold and red lacquer paint are visible on the side of the vessel.

crammed with expensive grave goods of turquoise and jade, paved wagon roads, and workshops for the manufacture of bronze objects.

Bronze working probably arrived in East Asia from Mesopotamia or Iran across the Eurasian steppe. The first East Asian bronze objects date from around 3000 BCE. Mass production seems to have begun at Erlitou. Bronze making became a hallmark of ancient China, not only for weaponry—as in Southwest Asia—but especially for ritual vessels used for making offerings to ancestors. The great majority of Chinese bronze work served this religious purpose, at Erlitou and elsewhere.

THE SHANG DYNASTY IN NORTH CHINA (CA. 1600–1046 BCE)

Erlitou might have been its own city-state, or perhaps the capital city of an early dynasty called the Xia. It's more likely that the Xia are mythical and that Erlitou was built under the **Shang dynasty** (ca. 1600–1046 BCE). The base of the Shang dynasty stood in the lower reaches of the Huang He. At times, the dynasty seems to have controlled people almost as far south as the Yangzi basin, but more often its domain was much smaller, closer to the size of a middling New England state, and the edges of its control usually fuzzy.

The Shang were likely one of dozens of states in East Asia, and in their time no more important than several others. Chinese tradition regards the Shang as the precursor of all things Chinese—because they had writing that evolved into the later Chinese scripts. All accounts of early East Asian history over-emphasize the Shang because we know more about them than any of their contemporaries.

WRITING The first authors of Egyptian hieroglyphs probably drew inspiration from Sumerian writing, but in Shang China writing was invented entirely anew. Although there are a few earlier pottery fragments with what might be meaningful scratches on them, the first clear-cut writing in China dates from about 1200 to 1050 BCE—the twilight years of the Shang dynasty. The Shang writing, now called **oracle bone inscriptions**, consisted of markings made on turtle shells or cattle scapulae (shoulder blades). Most of these were questions put to the gods about big decisions—what and when to plant, whom to marry one's child to, or whether to launch a war. With questions inscribed on them, the shells and

bones were heated until they cracked. Then specialist diviners read the cracks as revealing the gods' answers, so people would know whether or not to proceed with their plans. No doubt this left plenty of room for artful interpretation.

The principles of Shang writing are the same as those of modern Chinese script, although all the symbols have changed. It was mainly logographic, like cuneiform and hieroglyphs, in that most symbols represented a word or idea, but a few implied a specific sound. The oracle bone writers used about 4,500 characters, one-third of which modern scholars have deciphered. Subsequent dynasties used modified scripts for purposes of state bureaucracy, literature, and the writing of history. Little survived, because they wrote on strips of bamboo rather than shell or bone. Later Chinese writers used cloth, often silk, on which they wrote with brushes and ink.

Around 100 BCE, the Chinese invented paper, making writing easier than ever before. By mashing rags and plant fibers, such as mulberry bark, in a watery solution and then drying it, papermakers created a cheap material

Shang Writing A turtle shell dated to around 1050 BCE is covered in writing in the logographic Shang script. It asks the gods for guidance on a military campaign.

that preserved ink markings indefinitely. Chinese scribes developed standardized lists of characters used over wider and wider territories. Because the script was logographic, it could represent words that were pronounced in very different ways, so even though there were (and still are) several different and mutually incomprehensible languages in China, all were written in the same script. This helped keep Chinese culture cohesive and helped Chinese dynasties keep diverse linguistic regions politically unified for thousands of years—despite the continuing evolution of the Chinese script.

Like cuneiform and hieroglyphs, the Chinese writing system invented in Shang times has lasted about 3,000 years; but unlike them, it still has a future ahead of it. It's the only ancient writing system still in use. First-year university students in China today are required to know 4,500 characters, about the same number as used by Shang oracle bone writers.

SOCIETY AND ECONOMY The oracle bones and archeology reveal a stratified society. Like all complex societies, the Shang needed an agricultural surplus to support city-dwellers and elites. Although based in the dry north of China, they didn't use irrigation on a significant scale. Instead, they developed something of a plantation system, with gangs of laborers cultivating millet. They also raised wheat, the preferred food of the upper classes, and barley; both crops had been introduced to the region from Southwest Asia. Beer brewed from barley dates back 5,000 years in China. Beans and peas appeared on the menu in ordinary homes. Villagers also raised pigs, sheep, horses, and oxen.

The Shang elite was ruthless in controlling the food surplus. They ran a very hierarchical, stratified, and militarized society. Kings moved around a good deal, checking up on their domains. The oracle bones show a constant concern with warfare, especially against "horse barbarians," presumably pastoralists to the north and west of the Shang heartland. By 1200 BCE, the elite used chariots, another import from Southwest Asia introduced to the Shang by neighboring peoples from the steppe. The Shang employed chariots both as fighting vehicles and as show pieces. Every male aristocrat wanted to be buried with one.

Bronze was central to Shang religious and economic life. A giant bronze foundry at one Shang center near the modern city of Anyang covered about 2.5 acres (1 hectare) in extent. The Shang bronze workers produced enormous quantities of weaponry and even more artistic objects—chiefly, cups for ritual offerings to the ancestors. One piece weighed almost a ton (862 kg, to be precise), the weight of a good-size bull or half of an average American car. Shang bronze production was a state business. Officials organized every step: copper and tin mining, smelting, transport, and casting. To judge by grave sites, only the top rung of society owned bronzes. Common people made offerings to their ancestors with wooden or clay vessels. Shang bronzes were imitated far and wide in their time, and they still attract admiration for their craftsmanship.

Shang Bronze The upper echelons of Shang society owned intricately molded bronze art objects, such as this jug in the shape of an owl from roughly the period 1600–1027 BCE.

THE TOMB OF FU HAO Powerful evidence for the extreme stratification of Shang society comes from the tomb of Fu Hao, who lived around 1300 to 1250 BCE. She is mentioned on about 180 oracle bones. She was a king's consort and a military general—a very unusual role for a woman in ancient East Asia or anywhere else. She organized military campaigns and ran her own agricultural estates. She also handled some divination ceremonies, an honor usually reserved for kings. She had at least one son, revealed in oracle bones that express anxiety about her health at childbirth. Of the thousands of Shang tombs excavated, hers is the only one that was never looted. Here's what looters missed:

Shang cultural area, ca. 1200 BCE
Bronze-working site

Huang He

Anyang

Erlitou

Sanxingdui

Yangzi R.

Xi R.

Red R.

South China Sea

0   250   500 mi
0   250   500 km

The Cultural Area of the Shang Dynasty, ca 1200 BCE The Shang dynasty (ca. 1600–1046 BCE) controlled varying parts of the north China plain with its reliable agricultural surplus. Its artisans raised bronze working to a high art.

- her skeleton
- 16 other human skeletons
- remains of 6 dogs
- 468 bronze objects—weapons, bells, knives, tiger heads, mirrors, and more
- 755 jade items
- 564 bone objects, mainly hairpins
- 63 stone objects
- 11 pieces of pottery
- 5 ivory items
- nearly 7,000 fragments of cowrie shells

Fu Hao's Tomb The luxury goods found in Fu Hao's tomb include ornaments like this jade bird and elephant—two of the 755 jade items with which Fu Hao was buried.

Her tomb shows the reverence accorded to high-ranking individuals, women included. It also attests to long-distance trade, because cowrie shells (used as money) come from warm oceans thousands of miles away.

In life, Fu Hao was exceptional as a woman exercising military and religious authority in a society that, according to oracle bones, regarded the birth of a daughter as a misfortune for parents. But in death she was less exceptional: lavish burials were normal for members of the Shang elite.

The aristocracy ruled through both intimidation and ideology. Human sacrifice figured prominently in keeping the masses in line. On occasions such as the inauguration of a palace or a temple, or the funeral of a king, hundreds of captives and slaves might be killed at a time to keep gods and ancestors happy. Several sacrificial victims joined Fu Hao in her tomb. On balance, it seems the Shang relied on intimidation more heavily than most ancient states, such as Egypt or Babylonia.

ANCESTORS AND THE FAMILY The Shang kings, like their counterparts in ancient Mesopotamia or Egypt, also relied on ideology in the form of religion. They claimed special access to divine power and presided over divination ceremonies personally. They honored a supreme god known as Di, accessible only through esteemed ancestors. Only the king could ask the favor of Di. Lesser mortals, through their lesser ancestors, approached lesser gods. The Shang, and probably their neighbors too, believed that ancestors resided in heaven and took an active interest in the affairs of their descendants. So a family's fortunes depended on keeping its ancestors content through ritual sacrifices and offerings. Commoners paid taxes or tribute to the Shang elite, and in a sense paid taxes to their ancestors too.

Family life in Shang China emphasized hierarchy. Children and wives owed deference to fathers and husbands. Women upon marriage left their homes and surrendered membership in the lineage of their birth to join the household and lineage of their husbands. If they gave birth to sons, however, they could expect to be venerated for it—after death. Elite men could marry several wives. Shang kings often married into many important lineages, and their wives sometimes played political roles in the Shang court, as the career of Fu Hao shows. The slender evidence suggests that women of the court figured more prominently in royal politics under the Shang than in most later Chinese dynasties.

LONG-DISTANCE TRADE The presence of chariots and cowries shows that the Shang interacted with people far away. They probably did so indirectly: goods and ideas were relayed from one people to their neighbors over long distances. As we've seen, by 100 CE a Silk Road linked China and the Mediterranean; but long before that there was, it seems, a chariot or cowrie road, intermittently connecting Southwest Asia and India to China. (Recall also that Chinese rice was transplanted to India, and West Asian wheat reached China.) During the fourth and third millennia BCE, the steppe lands of Eurasia were apparently a bit warmer and wetter than they are now, and more conducive to farming. That may have eased occasional long-distance trade across Asia.

SANXINGDUI AND OTHER STATES According to the official chronology, the Shang dynasty was overrun in 1046 BCE. Their successors contended that the Shang kings had grown corrupt and lost the favor of the gods. It could be that their relentless exactions and cruelties provoked more frequent peasant uprisings, giving their enemies an opening. Drier, colder weather after 1100 BCE may have undercut their agricultural surplus. Later chronicles say the Shang fell in part because the Huang He temporarily dried up.

While the Shang were building their state in north China, other states developed elsewhere in what is now China. No writing illustrates the career of Sanxingdui, a walled city to the southwest of modern Chengdu, in Sichuan province. But recently uncovered archeological evidence shows that Sanxingdui, at its height around 1500 to 1100 BCE, featured a fortified city with thick walls and moats, irrigation agriculture, and artisan workshops especially for bronze work.

Sanxingdui's bronze artifacts were made with a different process from those of the Shang foundries, in entirely different styles, but with equal skill. The oldest extant life-size human statue was found here, and an elegant 10-foot-tall tree of bronze. Ivory found here seems to have come from Southeast Asia, implying some long-distance trade links. Future archeology is likely to show the existence of other centers of complex society in China beyond the Shang and Sanxingdui.

SOUTHEAST ASIA, KOREA, AND JAPAN

In Southeast Asia, the Korean Peninsula, and the Japanese archipelago, no major urban centers, states, or complex societies appear in the archeological record before 1000 BCE. Long after life in parts of China had come to feature states, taxes, and wars, people living elsewhere in East Asia remained mobile foragers and small-scale village farmers.

SOUTHEAST ASIA As we saw in Chapter 2, Southeast Asia, if perhaps only highland New Guinea, was an early site of crop domestication. Farming existed by at least 5000 BCE in New Guinea and perhaps as early as 8000 BCE. In mainland Southeast Asia, some people had turned to farming by 2500 BCE. But populations remained very sparse.

After 3000 BCE, Southeast Asia received small streams of migrant farmers from what is now southern China. They extended the domain of agriculture, as Indo-European-speakers were doing in Europe, as Bantu-speakers were beginning to do in central Africa, and as other farming folk were starting to do on islands of the western Pacific. This was another example of a farmer

migration of the sort we saw in Chapter 3. These people were speakers of Austroasiatic languages that in time evolved into Vietnamese, Khmer (spoken in Cambodia), and several other tongues. They drifted south along river valleys such as the Red, Mekong, and Chao Phraya. They substantially replaced the sparse indigenous populations and also went by sea to the Philippine and Indonesian archipelagoes. The great majority of Southeast Asians today are descended biologically from these migrants. The migrants probably brought bronze-working technology with them. Recent archeology also indicates large-scale copper smelting, in central Thailand, beginning around 1450 BCE. In all likelihood, the mining, smelting, and casting techniques came with the migrants from what would later become southern China.

The scale and consequences of farming and metallurgy in Southeast Asia remained modest. Only one archeological site, Ban Non Wat in Thailand, shows any significant social stratification. As of 1000 BCE, Southeast Asians had taken a different path from peoples in northern and central China, or Southwest Asia, with minimal social hierarchy, no state structures, and no cities.

KOREA On the Korean Peninsula, complex society and social stratification also came well after 1000 BCE. Korean tradition holds that Koreans descend from the marriage of a god and a bear who had taken human female form after spending 100 days secluded in her cave eating only garlic and mugwort. Their marriage, the tradition goes, produced a son who founded a Korean kingdom around 2300 BCE.

Archeology and genetics, however, tell a less colorful tale. Koreans themselves came from Manchuria (now northeastern-most China) and the Lake Baikal region of Siberia. Most early inhabitants of the peninsula lived in

Sanxingdui Among the artifacts found at Sanxingdui in southwestern China was this life-size bronze statue of a man wearing an elaborately decorated robe. The statue dates to the eleventh or twelfth century BCE.

small communities near the sea, harvesting fish and shell-fish. The western coast of Korea features a broad intertidal zone and is one of the world's best places to find clams, mussels, and crabs. Some of these coastal dwellers were settled, some mobile. People began making pottery by 8000 BCE and were farming by 3500 BCE. Pottery styles suggest connections to both China and Japan.

After 1500 BCE, most people moved inland to fertile patches of lowland amid Korea's mountains. There they raised millet and soybeans, and lived in bigger communities, including walled towns. Farmers gradually colonized most of Korea's low-lying land, accelerating their pace after the introduction of rice from China around 700 BCE.

Korean bronze working began in the north around 1500 BCE, also introduced from China. It spread to southernmost Korea by about 700 BCE. That slow pace of diffusion, and the modest amount of bronze found by archeologists, suggests that most ancient Koreans found pottery satisfactory for their tastes and saw no reason to go to the trouble of making bronze. Jade also turns up in the archeological record, a luxury item that implies the emergence of elites.

After 1500 BCE, elaborate burials, called **dolmens**, dotted the Korean landscape. Dolmens are stacks of carefully arranged big stones, usually with three or more upright and one flat capstone, erected over burial sites. Dolmens existed in many parts of Eurasia, from western France and Ireland to Korea and Japan. Korea has nearly half the world's dolmens, erected mainly between 1500 and 500 BCE. Nobody knows why people started building them, or why they stopped, or if the structures have any connection to the dolmens of Europe, India, and the Levant. The effort required to place heavy stones above ground and the valuable bronze or jade items in the burials below are indications of social stratification. Not everyone rated a dolmen burial.

Korean Dolmens A dolmen erected approximately during the years 1500 to 500 BCE, with two upright stones and one large flat capstone, still stands in a park in present-day North Korea.

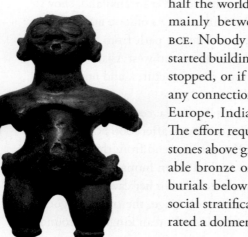

Japanese Fertility Worship Figurines of plump women like this one, dated to around 1500 BCE, may indicate that ancient Japanese peoples venerated fertility.

JAPAN The Japanese archipelago, like the Korean Peninsula, is mountainous and in ancient times was well forested. Its first inhabitants walked there from Korea 35,000 years ago when sea level was down. As we've seen, some of the world's earliest pottery appeared in Japan, perhaps as long as 15,000 years ago. Japan, like Korea, did not adopt writing until after 300 CE, so for early periods archeology provides almost all the evidence.

Japan had few people before 5000 BCE. Most of them lived in caves and practiced hunting, fishing, and gathering. After 5000 BCE, some built shelters, fished well out to sea on boats with harpoons and fishhooks, and traded a little with Korea. Their skeletons indicate they were unusually short for non-farming people: women on average under 5 feet (1.5 m) tall, and men only a little taller. There might have been a quarter-million inhabitants scattered throughout the archipelago by 3000 BCE.

After about 2500 BCE, population grew faster, villages and buildings sprang up, and more and more people took up farming, presumably introduced via Korea. Remains of houses suggest these people lived in extended, not nuclear, families. After 1500 BCE, they produced lots of clay figurines, often of plump women. These led scholars to suppose they had developed a religion with an emphasis on fertility—almost all ancient peoples worshipped fertility. As of 1000 BCE, Japan had acquired millet, yams, and taro from the East Asian mainland, and the farming way of life was spreading to most lowland regions.

At the same time, similarities among pottery styles throughout the islands imply more and more contact within the archipelago. Japan was knitting itself together, slowly, and linking to the mainland via Korea. As of 1000 BCE, it still had no rice, no writing, no metallurgy, no cities, and only modest social hierarchy. But all that was soon to come: Japan, like Korea and Southeast Asia, was too close to China to persevere for long without the trappings of complex society.

EAST ASIA TRANSFORMED, 1000 BCE TO 200 CE

In the centuries before 1000 BCE, farming, pottery, social hierarchy, cities, and states had cropped up in several places in China. These habits and institutions would continue to spread in the centuries to come with a slow, almost irresistible logic. In the presence of complex society, other societies had to become complex themselves or risk being subsumed, conquered, and perhaps exterminated. As elsewhere in the world, the nodes of dense population and interaction in East Asia—such as the Shang cities—were also nodes of wealth and power, more formidable than other agricultural regions.

This formidability, as elsewhere, consisted of cultural, military, economic, demographic, and epidemiological power. Chinese elites developed cultural traits such as writing and bronzes that elites elsewhere admired and often adopted. Chinese states (those that lasted) created efficient armies that generally swept enemies aside. Chinese agriculture, with its crop mix and irrigation techniques, produced abundant food for growing populations. And growing populations could sustain crowd diseases such as smallpox as endemic infections, dangerous to children but not to adults who had survived them.

Taken together, appealing culture, powerful armies, productive farming, and unseen biological weapons help to explain the expansion of Chinese influence in East Asia—just as they did the expansion of Mesopotamian influence in Southwest Asia.

THE SPREAD OF CHINESE INFLUENCE AND ITS LIMITS

The history of East Asia after 1000 BCE features two powerful dynamics at the center of which stood north China. The first was the political and military competition that led to the unification of large spaces. The earliest example was the gradual creation of what we today call China. Later and smaller versions of similar political-military competition yielded increasingly unified political and cultural zones we can fairly call Korea and Japan. In Southeast Asia, however, nothing of the sort happened. While there was no shortage of political competition, polities remained small and no single state or handful of states succeeded in imposing rule over broad regions. This difference helps explain why cultural and linguistic diversity remained stronger in Southeast Asia than in Japan, Korea, or China.

The second dynamic was the forging of a cultural synthesis, one that formed first in north China and then spread throughout most of East Asia. In some places, Chinese culture spread when local people were wiped out by violence or disease (or both) and replaced by migrants from northern or central China. In other cases, local people over many generations adopted piecemeal those features of the Chinese culture—writing and bronze making, for example—that they liked or felt they required. Of course, local people altered what they borrowed to fit local circumstances; for example, Korean bronzes looked different from Chinese ones. But overall through demographic replacement and cultural change East Asia became less

Chinese Writing Found on the Chinese cultural periphery in northwestern China, these wooden slips from 22 CE bear writing that lists a government official's expenses—indicating the spread of both the Chinese writing system and the Chinese state bureaucracy.

culturally diverse, more Chinese in its traditions and technologies, and more politically centralized.

Before seeing how these processes worked in practice, it's important to recognize their limits. First, they worked only where sedentary agriculture was practical. On the grasslands of Mongolia, in the deserts of what is now Xinjiang, on the icy plateau of Tibet, people—although few in number and vulnerable to epidemics—found it possible to retain their political and cultural autonomy. Indeed, those on the grasslands often found they could trade and raid on favorable terms, because horses and horsemanship gave them mobility and a military formidability all their own.

To the south, in the mountainous terrain of what is now southern China, local people also found it easier to retain their autonomy if they kept to the mountains. Until well after 500 CE, these southerners usually resisted Chinese expansion successfully. Up in the hills they could stay safe; keep their own languages, gods, and traditions; and usually choose the times, places, and terms on which they dealt with lowlanders who were gradually becoming Chinese in culture, language, and political loyalty. Unlike the horse pastoralists of the northern grasslands, these hill peoples, despite sometimes legendary ferocity (according to Chinese authors), posed minimal military threat to the settled farmers of East Asia and the expansion of Chinese culture and power. They could raid from time to time, but they could not conquer.

Malaria was another check to the expansion of Chinese settlement to the south. Malaria probably entered Southeast Asia and what is now southern China with the first human migrants during the Paleolithic. It probably intensified with agriculture, because cultivated landscapes are good ones for the mosquitoes that carry the disease. Like smallpox, it killed children in droves; but for those who lived to adulthood, it posed a smaller threat. Malaria doesn't confer full immunity on survivors, but repeated bouts of the disease build up one's resistance to subsequent infection. So people who grew up in Southeast Asia or southern China had greater resistance to the disease than did those who came from the north, where colder conditions reduced the populations of relevant mosquitoes and therefore the frequency of malaria. In effect, in East Asia, malaria served as something of a shield for southern peoples against northerners.

The slow expansion of Chinese power and culture, almost irresistible in large parts of East Asia for more than a thousand years, reached its limits on the grasslands to the north and west, and in the mountains and malarial forests and clearings of the south. But within these limits, the big story in mainland East Asia between 1000 BCE and 200 CE was Chinese expansion.

THE ZHOU (1045–256 BCE)

The spread of Chinese cultural influence throughout East Asia was accompanied by the formation of a large state. For the last 2,000 years there has been, more often than not, a very big country we call China. The long process of building a large, durable, and unified China began with the **Zhou dynasty** in the eleventh century BCE.

CONSOLIDATING POWER   In what would become a formula for dynastic successions, Zhou traditions depict the Shang rulers as debauched and cruel, providing just cause for the restoration of order and righteousness by the Zhou. More likely, the Zhou were the most successful of many lineages making alliances, attacking enemies, and struggling for survival and power, enabling them to push aside the ailing Shang state. The conventional dates for Zhou rule are 1045 to 256 BCE, but after the eighth century BCE they controlled only a fraction of China.

Once in control of the rich loess soils of the middle and lower Huang He, the Zhou set about consolidating their power. They supported the development of irrigation works and agriculture, enormously expanding the food production capacity of Zhou lands. The adoption of iron farm tools, which spread after the introduction of iron-working techniques from Central Asia in the ninth or eighth century BCE, had a similar effect. Irrigation and iron proved to be a powerful boon to agriculture in north China, as in Mesopotamia and north India. With more to eat, population in north China grew more quickly than before.

Like many early dynasties, the Zhou ran something like a franchising operation, allowing local leaders considerable leeway as long as they handed a chunk of their revenues, generally in grain, to the Zhou leadership. Some evidence suggests that farming under the Zhou was more a matter of family units than work gangs as under the Shang. In the idealized version, square fields were subdivided into nine smaller squares, and one-ninth of the harvest went to landowners, who forwarded some of that to their overlords. The rest belonged to those who worked the land. Rarely were things as smooth as that, though. One song recorded from the time suggests how peasants felt about their landlords:

> *Big rat, big rat*
> *Do not gobble our millet!*
> *Three years we have slaved for you,*
> *Yet you take no notice of us.*

Peasant happiness wasn't foremost among Zhou concerns. As long as enough surplus worked its way up the social hierarchy into the hands of the Zhou kings, they could maintain a military that intimidated any local lords who might be thinking about not paying up. And they could fight border wars with other states and fend off raids from the equestrian tribes of the steppe grasslands. At times, the Zhou exacted tribute from farming folk nearly as far south as the Yangzi.

The Zhou Dynasty, 1045–ca. 600 BCE While the Zhou officially lasted until 256 BCE, the dynasty controlled a large part of the north China plain only until the eighth century BCE, after which political fragmentation prevailed for several centuries. Under the Zhou, the use of iron tools and of irrigation expanded markedly.

THE MANDATE OF HEAVEN As the Zhou solidified their power, they supported a cultural elite, scholars called *shi* who consolidated much of what is now considered Chinese culture. Some members of this cultural elite held bureaucratic positions in government for Zhou lords. Others had to work as teachers, roving from town to town instructing boys and young men in the literary arts. Collectively, this class of scholars crystallized the cultural formula often called the **Mandate of Heaven**, whereby rulers owed their position to the favor of heaven and styled themselves as sons of heaven.

Supernatural power for the Zhou did not reside in a god (like the Shang's Di), but in a more abstract entity, *tian*, usually translated as "heaven." Ancestors remained important intermediaries between the living and heaven. But human sacrifice, common under the Shang, became rare under the Zhou.

The idea of the Mandate of Heaven, which took shape under the Zhou, was the Chinese version of the widespread tendency for rulers to claim legitimacy from their special relationships with the supernatural rulers of the universe. We've encountered it in Mesopotamia and Egypt, for example. But in the Chinese variant of

that claim, the support of supernatural authorities was provisional, not permanent. This provided a measure of dynastic performance that made cultural power and political symbolism all the more important: rulers had to convince everyone that they retained the Mandate of Heaven. If floods, plagues, droughts, or rebellions seemed excessive, supporters might begin to think that a given ruler or dynasty had lost the Mandate of Heaven. If their army commanders came to that conclusion, rulers were in deep trouble.

WARFARE In the realm of warfare, the Zhou sponsored some important innovations. The Zhou mastered the complex tasks of integrating chariots with infantry and maintaining disciplined formations on the battlefield. By some accounts, their final defeat of the Shang featured 300 chariots. These skills made them hard to beat on the plains of northern China, although uneven terrain—common in China—negated any advantages that disciplined charioteers enjoyed. Unlike the states of Southwest Asia or north India, the Zhou did not use cavalry.

Zhou Chariots The remains of horses and chariots interred with the dead in a burial pit in present-day Henan demonstrate the centrality of chariots to Zhou society.

The Zhou maintained their military edge until the eighth century BCE. Then local lords began to rebel and rival states grew stronger. The Zhou had reached an equilibrium of sorts. Their state had grown big enough that it had long borders to defend, and many ambitious local leaders inside their borders to co-opt or intimidate. Newly conquered lands to distribute to followers grew harder to come by, and rebellions more common. The Zhou responded with assertions of power—grander rituals, bigger bronzes, and more frequent demands for displays of loyalty. On one occasion in 860 BCE, a King Yi, fed up with lack of cooperation from a local lord, captured him and boiled him alive in a cauldron. Even this demonstration of determination couldn't solve the Zhou's problem of disunity, and by 771 they were overrun by horse pastoralists from the west. Only a remnant of their kingdom survived, called the Eastern Zhou. Later ages held up the early Zhou as a Chinese golden age of order, virtue, prosperity, and power.

THE UNIVERSITY OF WAR: WARRING STATES (771–256 BCE)

For 500 years after the Zhou decline, no single state could dominate China. Specialists use different designations for parts of the entire period (771–256 BCE) when the Eastern Zhou and many other kingdoms competed against one another, but the term *Warring States* captures the reality most clearly.

ECONOMIC AND SOCIAL CHANGE With the decline of the Zhou, China became a university of war. States got good at it or were swallowed up by their neighbors. The survivors were highly inventive. They developed to a high art the technology of crossbows, which were more powerful than ordinary bows, and perfected the interplay of infantry and cavalry formations, which replaced chariots in the fifth or fourth century BCE. States relied less on hereditary rulers and more on technocratic elites, men who had proven themselves as military leaders or logistical wizards. The *shi* now became both scholars and practitioners of war.

States also needed strong economies and streams of revenue to pay for wars. Kings introduced coin money beginning in the seventh century BCE—about the same time that coins first appeared in Southwest Asia. The use of money made commerce and tax collection more

Chinese Currency Early Chinese coins were made of bronze and cast in a shape that resembled agricultural implements—in this image, mostly spades, although there is also a knife-shaped coin at top right. Such coins circulated widely from around 600 BCE.

efficient. Iron weaponry and farm tools spread as fast as coin money. So did the use of draft animals, such as water buffalo, and irrigation technology. Some states even allowed families to own and work their own land, and to sell it, hoping to harness private self-interest for the purpose of raising state revenues.

At the same time, some states sought to boost production themselves. Around 600 BCE, Sunshu Ao, a minister of a small state along the Yangzi River in central China, oversaw construction of what was probably the largest single irrigation operation in ancient times. The Peony Dam and reservoir irrigated about 9,300 square miles of farmland (24,000 sq. km, an area bigger than the state of New Jersey).

Despite violence and political instability, China's economy was growing more commercial and prosperous through the use of money, expanded irrigation, and experiments with private ownership of land. A sage from the third century BCE, Xunzi, took notice of the interlocking trade networks of his time:

> In the far north there are fast horses and howling dogs; the central states acquire and breed them and put them to work. In the far south there are feathers, tusks, hides, pure copper, and cinnabar; the central states acquire them and use them in their manufactures. In the far east are plants with purple dye, coarse hemp, fish, and salt; the central states acquire them for their food and clothing. In the far west there are skins and colored yaks' tails; the central states acquire them for their needs.

Xunzi portrayed a world in which the peripheral regions sent their wares to the heartlands of China between the Yangzi and the Huang He. In return, cloth, bronzes, tools, weapons, and grain presumably flowed from the center of China to the peripheries. In ways that recall fifth-century BCE Greece, but on a larger scale, commercial vitality and political strife went hand in hand in China during the Warring States period.

The university of war promoted social change too. As rulers came to depend increasingly on experts in politics, war, and tax collection, young men of talent and ambition were able to overcome humble birth and rise to positions of power and prestige, bringing their families up the social ladder with them. The authority of aristocrats eroded, and many held their positions at the pleasure of their nominal social inferiors, the *shi*. Improvements in iron-making technology brought cheaper weaponry, so that it became possible to fit out huge armies of peasants with spears, swords, shields—even armor. The old aristocratic warriors with their expensive bronze weapons and their chariots were now—after 500 BCE or so—relics of a time gone by.

The Warring States period, and indeed the preceding several centuries, witnessed a deepening of gender inequality in China. Whereas skeletons from before 3000 BCE showed that males and females ate the same diet, later bones tell us that by 500 BCE women ate far less meat than men. Women on average now were shorter than their foremothers a few millennia before, whereas men's average heights stayed the same. Parents were now investing more in their sons than their daughters.

The university of war and the advent of iron weaponry bear some comparison to developments we've seen in Mesopotamia, north India, and Greece. Aristocracies declined in all of these regions. The geopolitical impacts in China

Trade Expansion This beautiful cinnabar-dyed bowl, dated to around 200 BCE, is characteristic of the manufactured goods produced in central China that began to be traded for raw materials from the peripheries during the Warring States period.

were, however, unlike those in Mesopotamia, where one state, Assyria, took fuller advantage of the potential of mass armies and iron weaponry than all rivals and built a sprawling empire. China during the Warring States centuries was more like Greece—but on a bigger scale—with continual warfare among states and with alliance systems of roughly equal power.

SUN TZU The bloody chaos of the Warring States centuries suggested that the Zhou, unable to prevent mayhem and chaos, no longer enjoyed the Mandate of Heaven. But why did heaven not award its support to another ruling house that could restore peace and order? Texts from the period explored this issue and others as a new spirit of questioning—of philosophy—took root amid the destruction and gore. In this respect, too, Warring States China bore some resemblance to Greece of the fifth and fourth centuries BCE.

Among the remarkable works written during China's Warring States period was a classic of strategy attributed to **Sun Tzu** (also known as Sunzi), *The Art of War*. By tradition, Sun Tzu was a general active in the sixth century BCE, but modern scholars aren't sure he really existed. Clues in the text such as descriptions of giant battles suggest that it was written in the fifth century BCE or even later, and perhaps by several authors.

Whatever its authorship, *The Art of War* has shown extraordinary staying power and is widely read today in military and business circles. It not only explains points of military strategy and tactics, but offers insight on public administration, diplomacy, espionage, and statecraft generally. It emphasizes the importance of deception, patience, and humility in military leadership:

Warring States Art This bronze from the period of the Warring States (771–256 BCE) depicts Chinese forces in battle in northern Yunnan.

All warfare is based on deception.... For to win one hundred victories in one hundred battles is not the acme of skill. To subdue the enemy without fighting is the acme of skill.... A good commander is benevolent and unconcerned with fame.

CONFUCIUS Less widely read by business and military figures, but more influential overall, was another scholar and strategist for hire, Kong Qiu (also Kong Fuzi), or **Confucius** (ca. 551–479 BCE). He came from a down-on-its-luck military family based about 300 miles (500 km) south of today's Beijing in what is now Shandong province. As a youth, he reportedly worked odd jobs as a herdsman, clerk, and accountant. He married at age 19 and became a father a year later. He made his career as a political adviser, one of the legions of *shi*. Like Aristotle who tutored Alexander, Confucius helped train young princes. He also shared his wisdom with older ones. According to some sources, he worked many years for one warlord, but then left him and traveled around north and central China, giving advice about how rulers should run their kingdoms. As the students of Socrates had done, the followers of Confucius eventually collected some of his ideas into a book; this one was called the *Analects*.

Confucius's advice could hardly have been more different than that recorded in *The Art of War*. Confucius admitted he was "unversed in military affairs" and couldn't tell rulers how to win battles. Instead, he argued that in order to prosper and succeed, rulers needed to behave ethically toward both their ancestors and their living followers. He emphasized morality, the proper exercise of ritual (especially the reverence for ancestors), and careful study of ancient wisdom. He imagined the past, especially the early years of the Zhou dynasty, to be a better age when rulers had behaved honorably, greed had been less rampant, and sages like himself had carried more influence. In his emphasis on ethical conduct, ritual, social hierarchy, and the proper status of scholars, his views resembled those of north India's Brahmins.

Confucius saw the family as a suitable model for the state. Just as a responsible adult male ruled a family, so a king ruled a state. Unlike Sun Tzu, he insisted on truthfulness in speech, even in facial expressions. He wanted rulers to inspire their subjects through ethical, dignified conduct, rather than to rely on laws or, worse yet, bribery, deception, and intimidation. All members of society had a duty to fulfill, hierarchies to recognize, deference to pay—to fathers, husbands, elders, sages, officials, and above all the ruler. Confucius thought women had no place in public life. He mentions women only once in the *Analects*, saying they are "unpleasant" to have to deal with.

At a time when market forces were growing in China, Confucius held money-grubbing merchants in contempt. Philosophers and scholars, in contrast, merited admiration. As he put it: "The mind of the superior man is conversant with righteousness; the mind of the inferior man is conversant with profit."

Confucius died in 479 BCE, still an obscure political adviser. For the next few centuries, his thinking went in and out of fashion in China. In the second century CE, as we'll see below, a dynasty called the Han made

Confucius's Legacy A portrait of Confucius, from around the seventh century CE, indicates the lasting influence Confucius had on Chinese society centuries after his death.

CONSIDERING THE EVIDENCE

The Great Learning

"The Great Learning" is from the *Book of Rites,* a compendium of Confucian teachings about ethics and rituals collected in the third century BCE. Aspiring scholars would memorize the "The Great Learning," along with a commentary attributed to Confucius's disciple Zeng Shen, before moving on to more complicated texts like the *Analects* of Confucius. "The Great Learning" encourages learners to set their politics in order by regulating their families and mastering themselves. The following excerpt is the final section of Zeng's commentary in which he discusses the proper way for rulers to acquire and manage wealth.

There is a great course also for the production of wealth. Let the producers be many and the consumers few. Let there be activity in the production, and economy in the expenditure. Then the wealth will always be sufficient.

The virtuous ruler, by means of his wealth, makes himself more distinguished. The vicious ruler accumulates wealth, at the expense of his life.

Never has there been a case of the sovereign loving benevolence, and the people not loving righteousness. Never has there been a case where the people have loved righteousness, and the affairs of the sovereign have not been carried to completion. And never has there been a case where the wealth in such a State, collected in the treasuries and arsenals, did not continue in the sovereign's possession.

. . .

When he who presides over a State or a family makes his revenues his chief business, he must be under the influence of some small, mean, man. He may consider this man to be good; but when such a person is employed in the administration of a State or family, calamities from Heaven, and injuries from men, will befall it together, and, though a good man may take his place, he will not be able to remedy the evil. This illustrates again the saying, "In a State, gain is not to be considered prosperity, but its prosperity will be found in righteousness."

Source: *The Chinese Classics: With a Translation, Critical and Exegetical Notes, Prolegomena, and Copious Indexes*, Vol. I, ed. and trans. James Legge (London: 1861).

QUESTIONS FOR ANALYSIS

1. What is the primary difference between the way a virtuous ruler and a vicious ruler use wealth?
2. Although this document doesn't mention merchants directly, what insights does it offer about why Confucian scholars held merchants in contempt?
3. In Confucian philosophy, what is the relationship between the righteousness of a ruler and the prosperity of the state?

---

his works the standard canon that all aspiring officials had to study. His influence has permeated the Chinese state and society ever since, and has seeped into Korea, Japan, and Vietnam as well.

LEGALISM The five centuries of war and political chaos after 771 BCE proved to be intellectually creative in other respects too. Several other philosophers offered ideas—some thoroughly at odds with Confucianism—that resonated ever after. One group advanced a grim set of principles known as **Legalism**, according to which stern laws and punishments were the only basis for a sound society, and loyalty to the state and ruler was everyone's highest obligation. As a political philosophy, Legalism put the power of the state above all other considerations and advocated a ruthless approach to building and maintaining power.

In a book compiled by his followers, Lord Shang (390–338 BCE), one of the great exponents of Legalism, maintained that "in applying punishments, light offenses should be punished heavily; if light offenses do not appear, heavy offenses will not come." In its extreme regimentation of society and idolization of the military, Legalism loosely resembled the ideology of the Greek city-state of Sparta.

Legalism took shape in the fourth and third centuries, partly in opposition to the influence of Confucian scholars—whom Lord Shang called vermin. The *Book of Lord Shang* lists "six parasites":

...rites and music, odes and history, cultivation and goodness, filial devotion and brotherly love, sincerity and trustworthiness, uprightness and integrity, humaneness and rightness, criticism of the army and being ashamed of fighting.

That's actually 16 parasites in all, most of them Confucian virtues. Legalism scorned the past and any rituals that glorified it. It urged statesmen to maximize state power without respect for tradition. Lord Shang recommended intimidation as a better tool than exemplary virtue. Citizens should be rewarded for killing the state's enemies, while those who didn't report crimes committed by their neighbors should be sliced in half at the waist. Many punishments recommended in Legalist texts involved mutilation or disfigurement—a special disgrace for Chinese, who believed their bodies were a gift from their parents and should be respected as such. Tattoos, for example, were regarded as a punishment. Unlike Hammurabi in Babylonia, for whom appropriate punishments of crimes varied with the social status of victim and perpetrator, Lord Shang insisted that all be treated equally harshly before the law, even aristocrats. This principle seems to have hastened his own end: according to most traditions, vengeful aristocrats had him fastened to five chariots and torn limb from limb.

The legacy of Lord Shang and Legalism did not match that of Confucianism in China. It appealed only to China's most authoritarian and heartless rulers, although the Qin dynasty relied upon it. Unlike other schools of thought that took shape during the Warring States period, Chinese Legalism had no appeal outside of China.

Daoism A bronze vessel dated to the third century BCE is decorated with mountains and animals significant in Daoism.

DAOISM Daoism (or Taoism) is another intellectual tradition that crystallized during the dark years of the Warring States. Like Confucianism, it has remained influential for more than 2,000 years. It draws on centuries of folk religion and Chinese philosophy, assembled into key texts such as the *Daodejing* (or *Tao Te Ching*, sometimes translated as *The Classic of the Way of Virtue*). By tradition, this text is held to be the work of Laozi, who is placed in the sixth century BCE and sometimes referred to as a teacher of Confucius. But, as with Sun Tzu, it's uncertain if there ever was a Laozi.

The heart of Daoism is the three "jewels": compassion, moderation, and humility. Daoism is full of indirection and analogy, not easily pinned down to a single set of meanings. A sample of its slipperiness appears in the first phrases of the *Daodejing*: "The Way that can be described is not the true way. The Name that can be named is not the constant name." Paradox is at its core: "Do nothing and everything is done." It has, then, multiple meanings and is easily re-interpreted at any time, which is part of the reason for its durability. At its heart, however, are messages of simplicity, humility, renunciation, and restraint—not unlike its Indian contemporary, Buddhism. Daoism had limited appeal to rulers, for whom the justifications for hierarchy found in Legalism or Confucianism seemed to provide better guidance. But educated people often found its puzzles and mysteries attractive. Daoism found eager audiences outside of China, especially in Korea, Japan, and parts of Southeast Asia.

Warring States Symbols This jade pendant in the shape of a dragon is an example of the cultural creativity of the Warring States period.

For ordinary Chinese in these centuries, the majority of whom were illiterate peasant villagers, the doctrines of Confucianism, Legalism, or Daoism provided little direct guidance. Instead, they took their inspiration from traditions of ancestor worship mixed with combinations of local gods. For them, the centuries after the decline of the Zhou were times of violent chaos rather than intellectual achievement.

DISUNITY AND CREATIVITY The university of war was also a university of the mind. The Warring States period was a dismal one in most respects, but its disunity and competition created situations in which no overarching authority could impose conformity in thought or art. China as a cultural space was so politically fragmented that rival schools of thought and styles of expression could easily co-exist. Art and music showed much more diversity than they had under the Zhou. So did medical thought and other forms of science—according to some experts, acupuncture made its debut at this time.

In some respects, Warring States China paralleled the nearly simultaneous political disunity and creative cultural explosion of both the ancient Greek world and that of north India before the Mauryan Empire. In all three cases, a community shared a language and a culture but lived amid political rivalry and chaos in which no single ruler could enforce a single creed, philosophy, or way of thought. As the sages recognized, these were terrible times to live in but wonderful times to think in.

THE QIN (221–207 BCE)

In the chaos following 771 BCE, hundreds of little states flourished in the north China plain between the Huang He and the Yangzi. Within 200 years, there were only half a dozen left standing. They continued their wars until one state, the **Qin**, managed to gain control of the rich rice lands of Sichuan, in the middle Yangzi region, and tip the scales in its favor. Its rulers followed the ruthless path recommended by Lord Shang and often slaughtered entire populations whose armies had been defeated. In the late 230s BCE, the 22-year-old King Zheng launched a series of campaigns lasting 16 years and put an end to the Warring States period by conquering the Qin's last rivals in quick succession. Judging that "king" was no longer title enough, he proclaimed himself First August Emperor, or **Shi Huangdi**. For most of its history from this time forward, China was an empire.

The early career of Shi Huangdi bears comparison with that of Alexander the Great, born a century before. Both men were heirs to power in royal families and masterminded wars of imperial conquest when still young. Both met with extraordinary success, although only Alexander led troops in the field. Within nine years, Alexander had created a Greco-Macedonian empire that stretched from the Adriatic Sea to the Indus River. Shi Huangdi in 16 years conquered an area ranging from Sichuan to the mouth of the Yangzi to Manchuria.

Upon unifying most of China by 221 BCE, Shi Huangdi (also known as Qin Shi Huang, Qin being the name of his dynasty) wasted no time expanding his domain at the expense of "barbarians," meaning all people who weren't culturally Chinese. After choosing Chang'an (part of

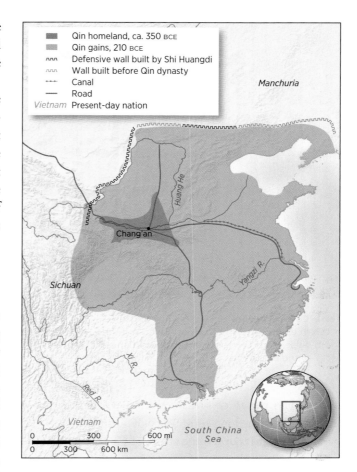

The Qin Dynasty, 221–207 BCE The Qin state, ruled for most of its duration by Shi Huangdi, was the first real empire in Chinese history. Although short-lived, it established the precedent of a large and unified China. Among its legacies was a much-enhanced infrastructure of roads and canals and a simplified written language.

today's city of Xi'an) as his capital, he launched campaigns in the south against peoples in what is now Vietnam. He built walls in the north to keep steppe raiders out and his people in—walls that later dynasties would extend and strengthen to the point they became known as the Great Wall of China.

Within his borders, Shi Huangdi worked to unify China in every way possible. He standardized weights and measures, coins, and even axle lengths for carts. He built canals and nearly 4,000 miles (roughly 7,000 km) of roads. He tore down city walls and melted down weapons not needed in his arsenals so that no local leaders could resist him. He simplified the written language, a useful reform when conquering linguistically diverse peoples. The Chinese characters required in his reign remained standard for almost 2,000 years until another reform

Terra-Cotta Warriors Here are a few of the 7,000 soldiers and 100 horses made from terra-cotta who guarded Shi Huangdi's tomb near Xi'an. The tomb is considered one of the great artifacts of ancient China.

occurred in the 1950s. This common written language helped ensure the long-term unity of China.

Shi Huangdi scorned the ethics of Confucianism. He tried to destroy all copies of Confucian texts and imposed Legalism as the only acceptable school of political thought. The court historian of the next dynasty, Sima Qian, wrote that Shi Huangdi took a special delight in killing off sages by burying them alive, although that could be exaggeration. In short, he consolidated his power with vigor and ruthlessness second to none, doing his best to live up to the brutal principles of Lord Shang and Legalism.

Shi Huangdi was by all accounts obsessed with immortality and feared his empire would not outlast him. When he died at age 48 or 49, in 210 BCE (perhaps of mercury poisoning from the elixirs of immortality he liked to drink), his fears were confirmed when the Qin Empire fell apart, just as Alexander's disintegrated after his death. His followers engaged in civil wars, subjects rebelled, and China seemed once more bound for disunity and perpetual war. But Shi Huangdi, although not immortal himself, had laid a firm foundation for imperial Chinese unity.

Before his death, Shi Huangdi arranged a giant mausoleum for himself. It stood roughly half the height of the tallest of ancient Egypt's pyramids. According to the historian Sima Qian, all his concubines were buried with him, as were the legions of workers who built the tomb.

It was guarded by 7,000 statues of warriors, made of terra cotta, together with about 100 chariots. His mausoleum fell to ruin and remained buried and unknown until well diggers accidentally discovered it in 1974. Shi Huangdi's legacy was not his tomb, but a large and united China.

THE HAN (206 BCE–220 CE) AND THE CONSOLIDATION OF EMPIRE

In short order, a warlord of peasant origin defeated rivals and re-assembled the empire, calling himself Emperor Gaozu. He founded a dynasty in 206 BCE called the **Han**. It lasted until 221 CE, a golden age according to many subsequent Chinese. Nowadays, ethnic Chinese refer to themselves as Han Chinese.

For the Han dynasty, the number, variety, and value of written sources is much greater than for earlier periods. One of the most valuable texts, *Shiji*, translated as *The Records of the Grand Historian*, was completed in 91 BCE by Sima Qian. More than a mere tale of the exploits of emperors (although there's plenty of that), it is an insightful and analytical history, commenting on motives, social forces and conditions, causation, and other matters still of concern to historians today. In these respects, it's like the history of Thucydides—analytical as well as narrative, and still read after two millennia. Thanks to Sima Qian and other authors, we have a firmer sense of the Han dynasty than any earlier ones in East Asian history.

The Han dynasties were keen expansionists. With their capital at Chang'an (today's Xi'an), they pushed the frontiers of the reconstructed Qin state in almost all directions, south into what is now Vietnam, east into what is now North Korea, and west to the Tarim basin. Han Wudi, who reigned from 141 to 87 BCE, enjoyed tremendous success in military matters. At times he prevailed even against the pastoral peoples to the north and west, known at this time as the Xiongnu and increasingly organized in large and formidable confederations. His successes stabilized Han rule, for which he is remembered among China's greatest emperors. China was now a true empire, a gigantic state, and it approximated the borders of what we call China today.

The historian Sima Qian worked—uneasily—for Han Wudi. As a boy, Sima Qian studied ancient texts with his father, the librarian of the Han state. As a young man, he took part in imperial inspection tours with Han Wudi, who made him a senior official and adviser. As an adviser,

The Han Empire, 206 BCE–220 CE The Han dynasty quickly rebuilt the empire of the Qin and then, especially under Han Wudi, extended Chinese rule westward into Central Asia and to the southwest into rugged highlands. This expansion laid the groundwork for sustained contacts with western Asia and India, the basis of the Old World web.

Sima Qian became entangled in a controversy over a general who had surrendered to "barbarians." Sima Qian defended the general, provoking Han Wudi to sentence him to a fine, if Sima Qian could pay, or castration if he could not. Sima Qian could not pay and suffered the consequences. He was not kind in his judgments about Han Wudi, and as a historian he got the last word.

POPULATION AND ECONOMY China's population grew rapidly under the Han dynasty. According to a census taken in 2 CE (the oldest surviving one in the history of the world), the Han domains included more than 57 million people living in 12 million households. The world's population at this point came to roughly 200 to 250 million, so Han subjects accounted for perhaps one in four people on Earth. The biggest city, Luoyang, in the center of the north China plain and the Han capital after 25 CE, had about half a million people.

The economy also grew rapidly under the Han, thanks to the infrastructure built by the Qin and long years of internal peace. The Han fought endless border wars, and in both the dynasty's first and final years they faced several rebellions. But in many decades in between, and in comparison to the bloody centuries that preceded them, theirs was a peaceful time, which helped make it a prosperous time.

A small part of Han prosperity came from trade with their neighbors. As they had done for at least 1,500 years, Chinese merchants swapped grain and crafts to the northern pastoralists in exchange for horses, hides, furs, and other items. Now, however, they expanded their commercial horizons, especially as the emperors and their armies extended the empire. Trade thrived along the caravan routes of the Eurasian steppe and deserts, collectively called the Silk Road, linking China to Iran and the Mediterranean via Central Asia. When Han China gained

The Silk Road Thanks to the Silk Road, Chinese silk was known as far away as Rome. A fresco from Pompeii (79 CE) shows a woman wearing a silk dress.

control of several Central Asian oases, trade to Central Asia's Hellenized kingdoms in Bactria and Sogdiana—also Silk Road trade—flourished. Chinese silk brought big war horses, much prized by Han Wudi, from Central Asia. Precious cargoes of all sorts traveled the Silk Road routes: gems, gold, silver, salt, ivory, spices, pepper, porcelain, slaves, and much more.

Maritime trade also flourished during the Han period, expanding with Korea and Japan and extending further afield into the lands facing the South China Sea. By the first century BCE, Chinese gold and silk appeared as far south as Thailand's shores, exchanged for pearl and jade, among other goods.

The Silk Road and maritime trade of Han times helped keep the craftsmen and women (silk production was mainly women's work) gainfully employed, gave them incentives to refine their skills, and provided an easily taxable source of revenue for the emperors to fund wars and build palaces. With the expansion of traffic across Central Asia, the gigantic space from Japan to Spain was

becoming a single interactive Old World web—woven in no small part by the fingers of Chinese women and girls who raised silkworms, spun thread, and made silk.

Han prosperity rested only partly on long-distance trade. The state created government monopolies over salt and iron production. When well run, they proved beneficial not only to the state treasury but to the population as well. State monopolies also controlled the making of bronze and a popular alcoholic drink. The Han tried to keep prices for important goods stable, by hoarding when prices were low and selling when prices were high, which moderated the normal price swings of markets.

Outside of a few industries, the Han encouraged production for markets and private enterprise. Paper, for writing, and porcelain, for high-end pottery, were developed as private industries. The Han required that some taxes be paid in money, motivating ordinary people to take part in a growing cash economy. By 5 CE, the treasury minted upward of 200 million coins annually. In a sense, the 500 years of internal warfare preceding the Qin and Han made China an excellent candidate for rapid economic growth once peace prevailed. Merely providing more peace and infrastructure, as the Qin and Han did, unleashed pent-up potential from which society and state both profited.

The large government role in the economy provoked frequent opposition. In 86 BCE, the government organized a review of the empire's economic situation, which soon led to debates among learned advisers that were recorded decades later as *The Salt and Iron Debates*. Confucian scholars regarded all commerce as suspect, an unproductive temptation to dishonesty. They felt that government officials, especially, shouldn't taint themselves with mercantile pursuits. Their notions of virtue drove them to advocate an economy based on local self-sufficiency with minimal production for market. In particular, the Confucian thinkers objected to trade with the Xiongnu, the steppe nomads to the north and Han China's most formidable military threat. However, an eloquent opponent, a minister of state, explained the advantages of trade with foreigners:

[A] piece of Chinese plain silk can be exchanged with the Xiongnu for articles worth several pieces of gold and thereby reduce the resources of our enemy. Mules, donkeys, and camels enter the frontier in unbroken lines; horses . . . come into our possession. The furs of sables, marmots, foxes, and badgers, colored rugs and decorated carpets fill the Imperial Treasury.... [F]oreign products keep flowing in, while our wealth is not dissipated.

This interpretation, reminiscent of Xunzi's two centuries before, won the day. Policies favoring commerce, and state monopolies in key industries, remained in place.

CONFUCIAN IDEOLOGY Despite their statist economic policy, the Han emperors also sealed the triumph of Confucian doctrine over all rivals as the official state ideology. The Confucian emphasis on obedience and hierarchy suited emperors just fine. Indeed, Han Wudi began the practice of recruiting technocrats and bureaucrats based on their scholarly mastery of Confucian and other texts, rather than their family background. While this practice went in and out of fashion after Han Wudi's death, the Han rulers did open government careers to men (not women) of humble origins but scholarly talent. At one point, the imperial compound contained 50,000 young men studying at its Confucian academy.

Confucian education became a requirement for high office. The gradual adoption of Confucian principles as the leading ideology of the state, and the emphasis placed on mastery of Confucian texts as the best education for a government career, gave rise to one of China's distinctive characteristics: an imperial bureaucracy made up of humanistic scholars. This scholar-bureaucrat tradition, begun under the Han although formalized later, lasted until 1905 and helped to define Chinese culture.

SOCIAL CHANGE AND GENDER Under the Qin and the Han, Chinese social structure gradually grew more complex. In part, this was the result of Qin and Han conquests of non-Chinese peoples. Some of these peoples assimilated to Chinese culture, but others remained ethnic and cultural minorities. A more important source of social change was the economic development discussed above. In earlier ages, China's main social divide was simple: privileged, aristocratic, and educated landowning classes above the toiling peasantry. With the emergence of more and more craft work, industry, and trade, new classes emerged.

Like the caste system in India, Confucian ideology recognized four main groups within society. But Confucianism arranged them in a different hierarchy: gentlemen-scholars (often now called literati, the class suited for government office), peasants, artisans, and merchants. This ordering reflected Confucian scorn for traders, who produced nothing. It didn't reflect the distribution of wealth or real social status. Most merchants were richer than almost all peasants, and often richer than the literati. And there were groups unrecognized in the Confucian scheme: slaves (who might have accounted for 1 percent of the population in ancient China), priests, soldiers, and women. The Confucian scheme applied to men. Women took on the status of their fathers or husbands.

Women could look forward to neither government careers nor formal education. Daughters, wives, and mothers were expected to exemplify the "Three Obediences"—to their fathers, husbands, and sons if they had any. Yet a few maneuvered their way to the center of power in the Han court. As wives or concubines of top officials, women could acquire influence. Should one of their sons attain high office, mothers might wield considerable power. When the first Han emperor died, one of his wives, known as Empress Lü, ruled as regent for 10 years, deftly engineering a succession of infants to the throne so that she might continue in power until her death in 180 BCE.

She wasn't the only woman to wield power behind the scenes. Han Wudi's mother was effectively empress during his early years on the throne. She was a commoner, called Wang Zhi, who divorced an undistinguished husband and became concubine to a prince who soon became emperor. Wang Zhi promptly bore a son, the future Han Wudi. Skilled in palace intrigue, she managed to prepare the way for her son to succeed to the throne. For several years thereafter, she exercised indirect power through the teenage emperor.

More customarily, women followed the general advice of Ban Zhao (45–116 CE) in her book *Lessons for Women*. She came from an elite family of extraordinary

Han Lady This figurine from the Han dynasty, 206 BCE–24 CE, depicts the traditional court lady modestly dressed in flowing silk robes. Han women were expected to be obedient and domestic, though royal women occasionally wielded significant political power.

Why Is Patriarchy So Widespread in World History?

Hatshepsut reigned for 20 years as pharaoh in Egypt. Fu Hao took a leading part in political and military affairs of China's Shang Dynasty. The Trung sisters ruled part of Vietnam for four years. But they are exceptions. Few women wielded political power in the societies we've seen so far, from Mesopotamia and Egypt to India, Persia, Greece, and China.

In fact, all large-scale societies that we know much about have been patriarchal: men dominated at all levels, from the family to religious institutions to political power, even the afterlife. Why?

Explanations tend to be either biological or historical. Biological explanations hold that adult males are on average larger and stronger than females, and that males are inherently more aggressive or genetically programmed for power-wielding behavior. But our closest living ancestors, chimpanzees and bonobos (African ape species in which males are larger and stronger than females), show contrasting behavior: chimps are patriarchal, and bonobos are matriarchal. And our previous puzzle feature on the ant-like behavior of humans in complex society (Chapter 3) indicated that cultural training can sometimes override genetic programming. Does that mean biological explanations are wrong?

Historical explanations argue that in the distant past, usually among foraging and hunting cultures, human societies either were matriarchal or exhibited gender parity. Societies then developed patriarchy as a result of one or more innovations: the development of private property, agriculture, plow agriculture, or states. These societal inventions, the argument goes, diminished the standing of women and elevated men into privileged positions. When societies developed concepts of private property, they normally understood it as belonging to males and passing from fathers to sons. Agriculture, especially with plows and draft animals, made property out of land and rewarded muscular strength. Settled life reduced opportunities for foraging, often a female specialization. These changes, the argument goes, made women more economically dependent on men. States reinforced patriarchy through laws governing property and family relations, and public offices that were almost always open only to men. Patriarchy on this argument was a societal choice, but one constrained by prior choices such as adopting plow agriculture.

But if patriarchy was a societal choice, even one constrained by prior economic and social decisions, it seems unlikely that every society we know much about should make roughly the same choice. None that we've encountered so far or that we'll encounter later appears to have organized itself as a matriarchy. Even in societies where women have more frequently held political power—chiefly in Southeast Asia—female power never became a lasting part of their culture. Does that mean historical explanations are wrong?

QUESTIONS FOR DISCUSSION

1. How best can we account for the prevalence of patriarchy in world history?
2. How different in this respect is our world from the ancient societies in which men ruled families and empires?

accomplishment. Her father and brother were historians, and she became one herself. They lived at the Han court. In a highly unusual violation of social norms, her family arranged an education for her. She wrote poetry, the mark of an educated person, and dabbled in mathematics and astronomy. But her advice to women was orthodox in China, and broadly consistent with what Pericles had recommended for Athenian women centuries earlier. She wrote that women should be modest, obey their parents, husband, and in-laws, speak sparingly, weave, sew, cook, and keep themselves and their homes clean. She included in her book an argument for the education of girls, which she said was important so that they might better serve their future husbands. Her manual for womanly conduct remained influential for centuries.

Family life during the Han dynasty generally conformed to Ban Zhao's recommendations, although not the one about educating girls. According to the census of 2 CE, households averaged 4.7 people, implying nuclear family households. Men arranged their children's marriages, and family property was divided among sons and not daughters. Women wove, cooked, and cleaned and were expected to obey male kin. But the rapid rise of silk production gave families new opportunities to make money from female labor, which may have reduced the regret Chinese parents felt at the birth of daughters.

THE FALL OF THE HAN Sima Qian's study of history led him to suppose that all dynasties were subject to laws of rise and fall, and the experience of the Han bore him out. After the reign of Han Wudi, successes against the Xiongnu nomads grew rare. After about 90 CE, peasant rebellions became more numerous, as mounting tax and military conscription demands became harder to bear. The Han's economic policies, helpful to the dynasty for a century or more, in the longer run allowed a few lucky and shrewd people to buy up land from less successful peasants, creating a new economic elite. That elite acquired enough political influence to avoid taxes and military service—a common pattern in world history.

As normally happens when affairs of state go poorly, court politics became more quarrelsome. Advisers, concubines, and palace eunuchs (castrated male attendants) struggled ever more fiercely for advantage, defaming and poisoning rivals—even the occasional emperor. Beginning in the Qin, China's rulers employed eunuchs in their royal households and the bureaucracy on the theory that men who couldn't have children would serve the emperor with undivided loyalty. Court eunuchs became more influential in the later years of the Han. After 184 CE, the court lost control of most of China, and in 220 CE the empire split into three warring parts.

Despite the dynasty's inglorious end, the Han, in consolidating and extending the work of the Qin emperor Shi Huangdi, left a legacy of a strong, unified, and morally legitimate state. This ideal helps explain why in centuries to come China's periods of fragmentation were comparatively brief interruptions. One dynasty followed another for the next two millennia. These dynasties oversaw the crystallization of a society and culture, based on peasant toil and ruled by educated, landed families, that we now call classical China. Its ideals remain influential in China today, and in their own time appealed powerfully to elites in neighboring lands.

SOUTHEAST ASIA, KOREA, AND JAPAN

The lands adjacent to China could not escape its political power and alluring cultural example. The geopolitical expansion of the Qin and Han came at the expense of non-Chinese peoples about whom we know little. In what is now southern China, indigenous peoples retreated southward or took to the hills when faced with Qin and Han expansion. Many were killed, by violence or unfamiliar diseases, and their lands settled by Chinese. Many who survived adopted the Chinese language, assimilating to the dominant culture within a generation or two. In this way, lands that are now southern China began to become culturally Chinese under the Qin and Han. The process continued long after.

SOUTHEAST ASIA Under the Han, the spread of Chinese power and culture extended into what is now Vietnam. The fertile Red River basin became a major Chinese center for 900 years after the Han took it over in the first century CE, crushing the Trung sisters' rebellion.

Before 200 BCE, all of Southeast Asia—islands and mainland—was sparsely populated. Widespread malaria was partially responsible. Villagers lived by fishing and farming. There were no cities or states of any size. As in much of Africa, political power consisted of control over people, who were scarce, not over land. It was normally a matter of charismatic individuals temporarily winning many followers whose labor they could then direct. Slavery and other forms of servitude and obligation to elites were widespread. Free women enjoyed more equal status to men in Southeast Asia than in most parts of the world, and often handled matters connected to trade and money.

A slow transformation overtook Southeast Asia when, beginning about 1 CE, irrigated rice production spread from China to lowland river valleys and deltas elsewhere. Wet rice cultivation yielded far more food per acre than any technique used before, undergirding faster growth

Wet Rice Cultivation A brick frieze dated to the period 200 BCE–200 CE illustrates the new model of irrigated agriculture in China. Farmers guide an ox and plow through a swampy field, allowing for more efficient sowing of seeds and thus more productive cultivation.

The Beginnings of the Old World Web, ca. 220 CE In the early centuries CE, thanks in part to the political consolidation and expansion undertaken by Shi Huangdi and Han Wudi, the East Asian web both grew and began to fuse with its counterpart that had stretched from the Nile to the Ganges. This fusion created a single interactive web from the Mediterranean to the East China Sea, extending as far south as the Horn of Africa and the Molucca Islands in Southeast Asia, all held together loosely by trade routes on land and sea.

in population. When and where people had tamed water buffalo to pull their plows through swamp and mud, wet rice cultivation was all the more productive.

More revolutionary still, rice as a grain is easily stored, transported, and hoarded. This is markedly different from the foods previously eaten by hunters, gatherers, and fishers, or by the root-crop farmers of Southeast Asia. Their foods didn't store well. If one had surplus, the best thing to do with it was throw a party, invite one's neighbors, and enjoy the prestige and good will that resulted. But with rice, people in Southeast Asia could trade food over longer distances and keep it longer. Canny people could amass food, distribute it to loyal followers, and withhold it from enemies. Priests and warriors could demand a share of the rice harvest in exchange for protection from dangers both supernatural and human. Rice raised the odds of complex society and full-blown states developing in Southeast Asia.

The emergence of wet rice cultivation was even more revolutionary in Southeast Asia than in China. Substantial centers of grain production had already existed in China

before irrigated rice. In Southeast Asia, irrigated rice supported the first elaboration of states and courts, extensive artisan and craft work, temples and formal religious specialists. This process was just getting going by 200 CE.

With the Han expansion, Chinese trade and culture also shaped Southeast Asia more than it had previously. Connections between China and Southeast Asia extended further south. For example, cloves from the Molucca Islands, an archipelago in today's Indonesia, reached Chinese markets by the second century BCE. Other spices from Southeast Asia came to season Chinese food as well, establishing a lasting connection that shaped Chinese cooking ever after. Vietnamese began to write their language in Chinese characters in the first century CE.

KOREA Proximity to China and the emergence of irrigated rice production also changed Korea between 200 BCE and 200 CE. As in Vietnam, the northern part of Korea was conquered by the Han and substantially sinicized (i.e., drawn into China's cultural orbit). Settlers trickled in. The techniques of irrigated rice production came with them, leading to new centers of dense population. Like Vietnamese, the Korean language was first written down in Han times, in Chinese characters—even though Korean and Chinese are unrelated languages. The prestige of Chinese culture was so great that educated Koreans preferred to write in Chinese—as in the Hellenistic world educated people often used Greek in writing rather than their native tongue. The Chinese brought more refined artisanal skills, especially iron working, and helped generate more wealth, luxuries, and growing social stratification. The first evidence of slavery in Korea dates from this period (although the practice might have existed earlier). Elite burials grew more elaborate.

Koreans outside of Han control increasingly organized themselves in large clans. The clans fought among themselves, the strong devouring the weak—which helps to account for the popularity of a handful of family names in Korea such as Lee, Park, Kim, and Cho, which derive from the victors among these clans. When Han power receded from Korea at the end of the second century CE, three main kingdoms emerged, providing Korea's political framework for the next several centuries. In addition to technologies and crops from China, according to DNA studies, Koreans also acquired malaria and tuberculosis from their western neighbors at this time, further evidence of tightening linkages between Korea and the rest of East Asia.

JAPAN Most of the innovations that made it to Japan before 200 CE came via Korea. Around 300 BCE, bands of refugees from Korea's wars settled in Japan's southernmost big island, Kyushu. They brought bronze and iron-working skills, and irrigated rice techniques too, all of which Koreans had learned from China. Japan now began to conform more to general East Asian patterns. Population grew faster, thanks to rice and iron farm tools. Steeper social hierarchy followed, states proliferated, and wars broke out. Soon Japan acquired coinage, the potter's wheel, and much of the technology that underlay the economic growth and military prowess of the Qin and the Han, although not wheeled transport. Chinese made great use of carts and wheelbarrows, but wheeled vehicles didn't catch on in Japan until the nineteenth century CE.

Cities popped up, such as **Yoshinogari** on the southern island of Kyushu, where archeologists have found indications of weaving, bronze casting, and other crafts. Before long, Japanese states were building roads and small ships,

and trading throughout their archipelago. Tighter links to mainland Asia also developed, as trade goods such as Korean-made bronze daggers and Chinese bronze mirrors uncovered at Yoshinogari attest. Chinese texts refer to "tribute" missions from small states in Japan in 57 and 107 CE, which the Japanese would have regarded as trade, not tribute, expeditions. As elsewhere, people with states victimized those without. The hunting, gathering, and fishing populations that remained in Japan were driven to the mountains and to the northern, less hospitable, island of Hokkaido.

Japan didn't develop writing until the fourth century CE, so what we know of it before 200 CE comes from archeology and writing by Japan's neighbors. Bigger and bigger tombs indicate growing social stratification. Grave goods attest to Korean influence, and also suggest some of the rituals of what would become the Japanese religion of Shinto. One Chinese text, from 297 CE, describes extreme forms of hierarchy and deference to high-ranking persons. The poor had to bow and scrape when their social betters passed by. From the Chinese point of view, however, women had it better in Japan. They were accorded more respect and could more easily enjoy leadership positions within clans. That might have been so, but it might merely reflect the Chinese author's angle of vision.

Korea and Japan, still sparsely populated lands in 500 BCE, underwent rapid changes in the centuries to 200 CE. The introduction of intensive rice techniques led to population growth and state formation. A brutal winnowing followed, whereby many states became few. In the Korean case, where iron weaponry had something of the same democratizing effect upon warfare as it had in China, by the early centuries CE three states divided the peninsula. In Japan, according to the Chinese text of 297 CE, some 30 states shared the archipelago. Meanwhile, in cultural terms, influence from China flowed into Korea and Japan, a trend that would continue for centuries. Both lands became economically linked to the ports of coastal China, an arrangement that lasts to this day.

WEAVING THE EAST ASIAN WEB

Long before the Qin and Han dynasties, sustained interactions within what is now China marked the beginnings of an East Asian web. During the Han, this web extended into Southeast Asia, especially the northern part of Vietnam, as well as Korea and, less firmly, Japan. The most important feature of this East Asian web was the spread of intensive rice cultivation from China into Korea, Japan, and Southeast Asia, where it came to support dense settlement and more complex societies. Other parts of Chinese culture, from bronze bells to Confucian ideology, also appealed to people throughout East Asia and accordingly traveled along the threads of the web. The consolidation of this web, like all others, took place slowly and normally went unrecognized. But when ordinary people reaped wheat in north China, suffered from smallpox in Vietnam, cast bronze statues in Korea, or watched their social superiors ride horseback in Japan, they were experiencing life as shaped by the East Asian web—and increasingly its broader networks.

In 3500 BCE, the world's webs were mainly local, involving clusters of villages. Long-distance linkages were rare. But by 1000 BCE, traders and travelers had spun the Nile-Ganges web, and by 100 BCE a large East Asian web was in place. The rest of the world, as yet, had built only much smaller and thinner webs, involving far fewer people and less frequent interactions.

These two big webs, centered on Mesopotamia and China, were starting to connect while they were still forming. Among the earliest evidence for this is the movement of food crops. Crops of Chinese origin such as buckwheat, broomcorn millet, and foxtail millet turned up in Central and western Asia by 2000 BCE, and perhaps much earlier. Wheat from Southwest Asia arrived in China by about the same time, and barley well before. Chinese fruit trees—peaches, for instance—had taken root on the shores of the Mediterranean by 600 BCE.

Skills and technologies also spread across Eurasia. By 1200 BCE, the use of chariots—a Southwest Asian invention—had reached China. Bronze- and iron-working skills, also pioneered in Southwest Asia, extended over most of Eurasia by 800 BCE. Merchant caravans passed goods to one another in relay trade all the way from the Levant to north China and back again, using the series of routes now known as the Silk Road.

Meanwhile, slender connections linked China to northern India by 500 BCE. Chinese varieties of rice were brought to India long before, but now became well established. Traders began to carry Buddhist doctrines on trans-Himalayan routes from northern India into China

by the first century CE, with consequences we'll encounter in later chapters. By 200 CE, a huge transcontinental web—the Old World web—long in the making, still thin and vulnerable, had formed spanning much of Eurasia from Morocco and Spain to Korea and Vietnam. The Silk Road was its longest thread, but only one of many land routes. Sea routes linking the South China Sea, the Indian Ocean, and the Mediterranean also bound this space together.

CONCLUSION

By 200 CE, the East Asian region had a population of approximately 75 million, more than three-fourths of it in China. Japan had perhaps 3 million, the Korean peninsula half that. Southeast Asia, from New Guinea to Thailand, contained roughly 10 million people. Some 90 percent of East Asians lived within the orbit of states, paying taxes, tribute, or providing labor services to elites who in turn served a lord or monarch. Monarchs lived in splendor, but in constant danger too. Bureaucratic elites lived comfortably, often in royal or imperial courts, and enjoyed some modest authority. The vast majority of people lived hand-to-mouth, often hungry, never secure, despite long hours of toil in the fields and, in the case of women, often with looms and needles too.

The toiling masses feared the agents of the state but sometimes respected them too. They rebelled from time to time, but more often delivered up their grain, coins, or labor as required. Practicing the rituals of ancestor worship, they knew nothing of the extraordinary intellectual efflorescence centered in northern China from around 400 BCE onward, the crystallization of philosophical, political, and religious thought that would remain influential among East Asian elites for more than 2,000 years. They also knew nothing of the increasing scale of interaction over long distances that characterized East Asia, and indeed connected East Asia to wider worlds. Yet the East Asian web shaped their lives in ways great and small, from basic features of life such as rice as a dietary staple to trivial ones such as the bronze daggers wielded by their social superiors. To some small extent, they were experiencing life as influenced by the Old World web, just taking shape in 200 CE.

CHAPTER REVIEW

KEY TERMS

Shang dynasty (p. 182)

oracle bone inscriptions
    (p. 182)

dolmens (p. 186)

Zhou dynasty (p. 188)

shi (p. 189)

Mandate of Heaven
    (p. 189)

Sun Tzu (p. 191)

Confucius (p. 192)

Legalism (p. 193)

Qin (p. 195)

Shi Huangdi (p. 195)

Han (p. 196)

Yoshinogari (p. 203)

Go to INQUIZITIVE
to see what you've
learned—and learn what
you've missed—with
personalized feedback
along the way.

REVIEW QUESTIONS

1. What geographical and environmental features made East Asia a strong candidate for early development of long-distance trade and complex societal organization?

2. What key shifts among East Asian societies took place around 3500 BCE?

3. What is the early Shang writing called, and what was its purpose?

4. How were Southeast Asian, Korean, and Japanese societies different from those in northern and central China around 1000 BCE?

5. What two powerful dynamics defined the history of East Asia after 1000 BCE?

6. How did the Chinese Mandate of Heaven differ from rulers' claims to supernatural legitimacy in Mesopotamia and Egypt?

7. In what ways did the Warring States period trigger military innovation, prosperity, commercial activity, and social change?

8. Name and describe the three principal doctrines that arose during the Warring States period.

9. What measures did Shi Huangdi introduce to unify China?

10. What was the scholar-bureaucrat tradition introduced during the Han?

11. How did the geopolitical expansion under the Qin and the Han affect non-Chinese peoples in surrounding lands?

12. What changes occurred in Korea and Japan between 500 BCE and 200 CE, and what was the Chinese contribution to these changes?

FURTHER READING

Gina BARNES, *Archaeology of East Asia: The Rise of Civilization in China, Korea, and Japan* (2015). A fine synopsis of the region.

Valerie HANSEN, *The Open Empire: A History of China to 1800* (2015, 2nd ed.). A valuable summary of early Chinese history.

Charles HIGHAM, *Bronze Age Southeast Asia* (2010). An overview by a leading archeologist.

Thomas HÖLLMANN, *Chinese Script: History, Characters, Calligraphy* (2017). A good look at the origins and mechanics of Chinese writing.

Mark Edward LEWIS, *The Early Chinese Empires: Qin and Han* (2007). The handiest place to go for information on the first imperial dynasties.

Li LIU and Xingcan CHEN, *State Formation in Early China* (2003). A guide to a controversial field.

Koji MIZOGUCHI, *The Archaeology of Japan: From the Earliest Rice Farming Villages to the Rise of the State* (2018). A study that covers roughly 600 BCE to about 700 CE in detail.

Sarah M. NELSON, *The Archeology of Korea* (2007). Still the best general study of the subject.

CHRONOLOGY

ca. 1100–1000 BCE
Tyre begins to flourish

ca. 800–700 BCE
Tyre's merchants
expand operations in
western Mediterranean

ca. 800 BCE
Carthage is founded

ca. 500–450 BCE
Beginning of Roman Republic

ca. 600–500 BCE
Babylonians and then Achaemenid
Persians conquer Tyre and Phoenicia

ca. 1000–900 BCE
First settlements in Rome

ca. 300 BCE
Introduction of Roman coinage system;
start of Roman road building

ca. 350 BCE
Rome stops selling slaves
and has them work on farms

260 BCE
Rome starts building a navy

218–201 BCE
Second Punic War

264–241 BCE
First
Punic War

247–ca. 182 BCE
Life of Hannibal Barca

31 BCE
Marc Antony and Cleopatra kill themselves

49 BCE
Caesar wins victory over
Pompey and the Senate;
rules as dictator for the
rest of his life

100–44 BCE
Lifetime of
Julius Caesar

149–146 BCE
Third Punic
War

73–71 BCE
Spartacus leads
largest slave
revolt in Roman
history

The West End of the Old World Web

CARTHAGE, ROME, AND
THE MEDITERRANEAN WORLD

800 BCE to 200 CE

About 390 BCE, before Rome was much of a city, a band of marauders nearly cooked its goose. The marauders were a tribe of Gauls, originally from what is now France but recently settled in northern Italy. They probably were on the way home from a job as mercenaries in southern Italy when they defeated a Roman army just north of the city. The surviving Romans, the story goes, scurried back into their walled city so hastily that no one closed the gates behind them. The able-bodied among them retreated to the citadel, the Capitoline Hill, and prepared for a siege. They had with them a flock of geese, sacred to the goddess Juno. Some Romans complained that the geese were better fed than they were.

The Gauls sacked and burned most of the outer city while the Romans cowered in their citadel. Then one night the attackers discovered a path up to the Capitoline Hill. As they scaled the walls of the citadel, Romans and their watchdogs slumbered unaware. But before the Gauls could murder the last of the Romans in their sleep, the well-fed sacred geese of Juno started to cackle. The

27 BCE
Rome transitions from republic to empire
27–14 BCE
Rule of Augustus (Octavian)

60–61 CE
Queen Boudica leads uprising in Britain

161–180 BCE
Reign of Marcus Aurelius

ca. 30–33 CE
Jesus of Nazareth is crucified

132–135 CE
Jewish revolt and the destruction of Jerusalem

Commerce and Empire A relief depicting the Roman port of Ostia during the reign of Emperor Trajan (98–117 CE) depicts it as a hub of activity, full of ships, traders, soldiers, animals, temples, and other monumental buildings—all watched over by gods such as Neptune, standing in the foreground with his trident.

FOCUS QUESTIONS

1. What made the Phoenician cities important players in the Mediterranean world?

2. How did Carthage rise as a sea power in the Mediterranean?

3. Why was the Roman Republic strong and stable for so long?

4. What were the major sources of stability in the Roman Empire?

Romans awoke just in time, repelled the assault, and saved their city and themselves from annihilation.

That, at least, is how Roman historians told the story. Perhaps, as some modern historians claim, the Romans saved themselves only by agreeing to turn over to the Gauls all their gold and treasure. Either way, the survival of Rome was a close-run thing. Had the geese not cackled, or the Gauls not accepted gold, Rome would have been obliterated long before it could become one of history's great empires. Without Rome, perhaps Carthage would have ruled the Mediterranean world and its legacy would loom large over the past two millennia. Little things can make a big difference in history.

This chapter follows the fortunes of two great Mediterranean empires that stood on the far western fringe of the Old World web: Carthage and Rome. Carthage, on the Mediterranean's North African coast, was founded as a Phoenician colony about 800 BCE. But within two centuries it had dozens of its own merchant colonies around the Mediterranean and soon would establish more on Atlantic coasts. As its own colonies grew more numerous and larger, Carthage gradually became something we can call an empire, held together by religion, language, trade, and the most formidable navy the world had yet seen.

Unlike the empires of Sargon or Cyrus or Shi Huangdi, this one was based not on conquest of contiguous territories but on commerce and ships. It was the first seaborne empire in world history. Its traders and sailors went far toward integrating the western Mediterranean, from Sicily to Spain, with the more populous eastern Mediterranean—specifically, the Levant and Egypt.

Historians of Rome call that polity a republic from its origins up to 27 BCE, and only after that date do they refer to it as an empire. But it was an empire from early on. At first it was a land empire in Italy, but eventually it became, like Carthage, a Mediterranean seaborne empire, held together by religion, language, a concept of citizenship, and an army as well as a navy. Rome in time acquired territories in northwestern Europe and Southwest Asia, but the empire's heartlands—Italy, Egypt, North Africa, Spain—all lay around the Mediterranean Sea. For most of its history, 90 percent of the population of the Roman Empire lived within a day's walk of the sea, just as Carthage's did. It turned out that the Mediterranean wasn't big enough for the two of them.

Carthage was like Cyrus's land-based Persian Empire in one respect, however: much of what we know about it comes from its enemies. If Carthaginians wrote any works of history, none have survived. Texts in Punic, as the Carthaginian language is known, mainly consist of prayers and thank-you notes to the gods. Instead, the history of Carthage comes down to us primarily through the prejudiced eye of Roman historians, who tended to see Carthage as dangerous and most Carthaginians as dishonest, corrupt, and cowardly. To a lesser extent our knowledge of Carthage derives from Greek writers, including Herodotus and Aristotle. Fortunately, archeology complements the several texts, and in recent decades it has yielded much of interest, corroborating some claims of the ancient authors and casting strong doubt on others.

Rome, in contrast, produced many histories. The

textual record is extremely rich, at least on politics, wars, and religion. As usual, information about the lives of ordinary people, women especially, turns up only now and again in the written record. Archeologists have found troves of stones and bones that also illuminate the history of Rome.

So the information available is both more abundant and more reliable for Rome than for Carthage. But we shouldn't let the spotlights that historians and archeologists shine on Rome blind us to the significance of Carthage: even if often in the shadows, it lasted 700 years as a state, 1,000 years as a culture, and helped make the Mediterranean a hive of trade and cultural exchange. Indeed, by 200 CE the Mediterranean zone, thanks to Carthage and Rome, was as tightly integrated as anywhere in the world. Rome, moreover, helped to link the Mediterranean world—although thinly—to the East Asian web, creating the Old World web that encompassed North Africa and much of Eurasia, from Morocco and Spain to Japan and Java.

PHOENICIAN CITIES

The history of Carthage begins with the prosperity of the Levantine trading city of **Tyre**, and the prosperity of Tyre began with snail mucus. Tyre was one a handful of port cities along the Phoenician coast of the eastern Mediterranean. (*Phoenicia*, the Greek term for the cities of this coast, is derived from the Greek word for "purple." It's the root of the word *Punic* used to describe things Carthaginian.) Tyre flourished after the eleventh century BCE. Its merchants served as middlemen linking Egypt, northern Mesopotamia, Syria, and Anatolia. Its neighboring city, Byblos, specialized in importing papyrus from Egypt for scribes of the Levant and gave its name to books generally—and thereby to the Bible. Tyre itself specialized in the export of a maroon-purple dye extracted from the mucus of a particular mollusk, a sea snail native to eastern Mediterranean waters. The dye, used for fine cloth, was a

Phoenician Ships This image of a Phoenician (sixth to fifth century BCE) sailing vessel with its characteristic rounded hull appears on a sarcophagus from the Levant.

brilliant color, didn't fade easily, and was cherished far and wide, so much so that some accounts claim it was worth 15 times its weight in gold. Its shade of purple became a symbol of royalty in parts of the Mediterranean.

Tyre, Byblos, and other Phoenician cities were part of the same cultural world as the ancient Hebrews, who called them Canaanites. They all spoke Semitic languages. The Phoenicians worshipped gods that the ancient Hebrews considered idols, but this didn't prevent business or political alliances between Tyre and the kingdom of Israel. In fact, Israel's King Solomon sold dominion over several cities to the merchants of Tyre.

The Phoenician cities were trade hubs. Phoenician sailors were among the first to recognize that you can always find north by sighting the Pole Star at night (if you're in the Northern Hemisphere). They pioneered a round-bottomed ship design that did well in rough seas and were the first to coat ship hulls in tar, making them more seaworthy. These innovations, combined with their purple dye monopoly, helped the Phoenicians win a dominant position in Mediterranean trade after the tenth century BCE. In addition to purple dye, they specialized in trading metals to the metal-hungry Mesopotamian states of Assyria, Babylon, and Persia.

In the eighth century BCE, under pressure from Assyria to provide still more metals, Tyre's merchants were driven to expand their operations in the western Mediterranean—especially Spain, which was rich in tin,

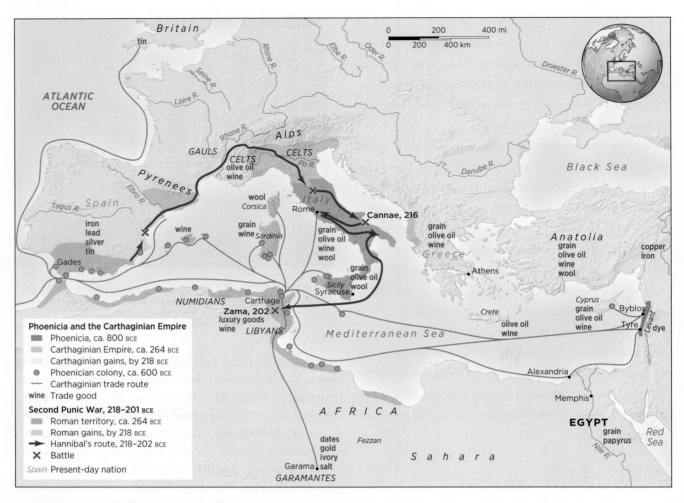

Carthage and the Mediterranean, ca. 800–200 BCE Carthage, itself originally a colony of the Phoenician city of Tyre, proved remarkably successful in colonizing the coasts of the central and western Mediterranean for more than 500 years. Although chiefly a commercial empire, it spread its cultural influence widely, especially in Spain. The rise of Roman power after 300 BCE eventually spelled the end for the Carthaginian Empire, which was finally destroyed in 146 BCE.

lead, iron, and silver deposits. Expeditions to Spain, at the other end of the Mediterranean Sea, took months. To establish a few safe havens in between, Tyre set up little colonies around the Mediterranean. One of these, established about 800 (the ancient texts imply 814), was Carthage.

CARTHAGE

Carthage had a fine harbor and looked to the sea. But it stood firmly on land, in what is now Tunisia, among thinly scattered populations called by the ancient writers Libyans and Numidians. Somehow, Carthaginians seized

or otherwise acquired land and recruited local Libyans to work those lands as sharecroppers. No doubt early Carthaginians intermarried with Libyans too. Carthage lay just a few days' sail from central Mediterranean islands such as Sicily and Sardinia, and soon its traders were active in circuits of exchange involving Greek colonies on these islands and various peoples in Italy. Carthage prospered by working these trade circuits of the central Mediterranean.

The Carthaginians also traded with a people of the central Sahara, the Garamantes, based at oases around Fezzan, in today's southwestern Libya. The Garamantes flourished from about 900 BCE to about 500 CE, living off of oasis agriculture using refined irrigation techniques, and holding a tight grip on the modest Saharan trade.

Garamantes Ruins of the Garamantes city of Germa, with walls built of stone and mud, still stand in the desert environment of present-day Libya. The city flourished between 900 BCE and 500 CE.

Carthage probably imported gold, ivory, dates, salt, and a few slaves from the Sahara, exchanging ceramics and bronze artifacts from Mediterranean workshops. Like Egypt, Carthage and Fezzan served as funnels through which Mediterranean and African goods and influences flowed. Rock art in Garamantes centers includes images of chariots and ox-carts, implying at least knowledge, and maybe use, of these technologies. But the absence of domesticated camels, still rare in these parts until after 300 CE, severely limited the scale of trade into and out of Fezzan. These Saharan contacts with the Garamantes, all evidence suggests, were dwarfed by Carthage's links to the seaborne world of the Mediterranean, especially Italy, Sicily, Greece, the Levant, and Egypt.

A RISING CITY

By 650 BCE, Carthage's population reached 30,000 or so—a sizeable city for that time, although probably only one-quarter the size of Nineveh or Babylon, or Luoyang, the Zhou capital in China. At least half of Carthage's food came from overseas. It depended on trade and the grain that its merchants could get for the pottery, jewelry, ivory carvings, and bronze statuettes that poured forth from its workshops. Burial goods show that Carthage imported not just food but wool, slaves, metals, and other goods from Egypt, the Phoenician cities, Greece, Sicily, and Sardinia, among other Mediterranean lands. Carthage's artistic styles reveal the cultural influence of Egypt and Greece above all.

Despite its cosmopolitan flavor, during its first three

centuries Carthage remained firmly tied to Tyre. Every year it sent representatives to make sacrifices in Tyre's temples. It retained the Phoenician language and alphabet and an enduring attachment to Phoenician names for the sons and daughters of Carthage.

Carthaginians worshipped Phoenician gods, eventually preferring above all others the pair known as Baal Hammon and Tanit. Baal Hammon was a male fertility god associated with the ram, while Tanit, his consort, was a goddess of war and, like almost every other female deity, of fertility as well. Archeological findings suggest that Carthage supported a large priesthood with numerous temples. Public worship was closely coordinated with the state—as was normal wherever states existed. Carthaginian worship, as in all Semitic religions, involved frequent animal sacrifice. Before any major endeavor such as a trading voyage, sacrifices had to be made to ensure divine favor.

Greek and Roman authors accused Carthaginians of practicing child sacrifice. In fact, the Hebrew Bible contains many references to child sacrifice among the Semitic peoples from whom Carthaginians derived their religious practices. Recent archeology has unearthed funeral urns (big pots) containing the remains of babies and toddlers,

Carthaginian Art Some Carthaginian art, such as this fourth-century BCE statue of a woman playing a flute (left), displays the influence of Greek artistic styles; other art, such as this sixth-century BCE bust (right), combines an Egyptian headdress with almond-shaped Greek eyes.

Carthaginian Religion A first-century CE Carthaginian statue depicts the fertility god Baal Hammon wearing a crown and seated on a throne.

some of them intermixed with animal bones. It seems that in difficult times the Carthaginian elite sometimes sacrificed their firstborn sons to Baal Hammon. Occasionally, they sacrificed multiple children from a single family.

Carthage was ruled by magistrates who held office for a fixed period. They were selected from among a handful of elite families. If Carthage ever had a monarchy, as Greek and Roman authors claim, it didn't last long. A council and an assembly worked with the magistrates, which led Aristotle to conclude that Carthage enjoyed the best possible system of government. Modern scholars regard it as an undemocratic oligarchy dominated by the merchant elite, an unusual feature in the ancient world where most elites were landowners, not traders.

State power rested, as so often, on religion and armed force. Carthage's military consisted mainly of a navy of several hundred warships, the Mediterranean's most formidable. Until the Romans built a navy, starting in 260 BCE, the main duties of the Carthaginian fleet were intimidating the Greek city-states of Sicily and attending to the endless chore of piracy suppression. The Mediterranean, with all its islands and capes to hide behind, and all its shipping to attack, was a playground for pirates except at times when someone had a strong navy. The Carthaginian navy employed loyal Carthaginian subjects, and for centuries each adult male was expected to serve in it. The army, much smaller until the later third century, consisted mainly of subject peoples and mercenaries from North Africa or Spain, men either compelled or paid to fight Carthage's wars.

A SEA POWER, SIXTH TO THIRD CENTURIES BCE

Carthage's fortunes rose when those of Tyre fell. In the sixth century BCE, first the Babylonians and then the Achaemenid Persians conquered Tyre and all Phoenicia. In 332 BCE, Alexander the Great took Tyre and sold into slavery

those of its people he didn't slaughter. Tyre's misfortunes, from the 570s BCE onward, allowed Carthage to take over the trade in metals from Spain and build its own trading empire in the western Mediterranean.

Spanish silver sustained Carthaginian power. Carthage's rulers inherited Tyre's colonies, including the settlement of Gades (today's Cadiz, on Spain's Atlantic coast), through which increasing amounts of silver flowed. At Gades and other Spanish ports, Carthaginians traded luxury goods from their workshops to local chiefs for silver. People in southwestern Spain didn't always know how valuable silver could be in the far-away eastern Mediterranean, but the Carthaginians did. Carthaginian merchants also traded along Atlantic coasts as far north as Britain, where they acquired tin. They founded settlements on Morocco's Atlantic coast. According to one Greek text, a fifth-century BCE Carthaginian navigator named Hanno

Carthage and Spain Archeologists discovered this fourth-century BCE bust of a woman wearing an elaborate headdress and jewelry in southeastern Spain. It is believed to represent the Carthaginian goddess Tanit, indicative of Spain's close connections to Carthage.

managed a round trip to the mouth of the Niger River in West Africa. Whether that tale is true or not, the Carthaginians profited handsomely from western Mediterranean trade. Like all successful trading states, their fortunes rested in part in information advantages: knowing what prices certain goods might fetch in distant markets.

Carthage buttressed its financial and military strength with soft power. It spread some of its religious beliefs and practices to the western Mediterranean. In particular, its alphabet, the Phoenician one that was comparatively easy to learn and use, appealed to people without writing. The Phoenician alphabet could be adapted for any language, as the Greeks had adapted it to theirs.

In some respects, the Carthaginians' state by the fifth and fourth centuries was a larger version of Athens: a seaborne empire sustained by a strong navy, a network of colonies and clients, financed in large part by control of silver mines and advantages in market knowledge. Carthage, like Athens, also fostered an elite culture that other peoples found attractive. But, as we've just seen, their silver came from Spain—not, as was the case for Athens, from their own backyard. So naval power was even more essential for Carthage than for Athens.

The Carthaginian economy wasn't all overseas trade and minerals. At home they developed new agricultural lands worked by Libyan sharecroppers. They specialized in fruit orchards, olives, and vines but also raised wheat and barley. They exported wine, particularly a raisin wine much admired in Italy. They must have drunk a fair bit of it themselves, because there are records of laws against the consumption of wine by slaves, soldiers, and, when on the job, judges, magistrates, and harbor pilots. Carthage's hinterland was moderately fertile but had rainfall barely adequate for most crops. So farmers raised irrigation to a high art. One Carthaginian author, Mago, probably of the fifth century BCE, wrote a detailed handbook on agriculture, unfortunately lost to us now but cited and used by later Roman authors who appreciated his insights on viniculture. By the fourth century BCE, Carthaginians occupied the northern half of modern Tunisia, and more and more of their land was worked by slaves captured in war. While Carthage is properly remembered as a seaborne trading empire, its agricultural sector was technically sophisticated and highly productive.

The Carthaginians meantime used their commercial wealth to deepen their involvement in the central Mediterranean. Their enclaves expanded in Sicily and Sardinia,

bringing frictions with Greek colonies, especially the Greek city of Syracuse. To bolster its position on the Italian mainland, Carthage made a deal with the small and undistinguished city of Rome, in 509 BCE, to stay out of one another's commercial business.

CARTHAGE IN THE PUNIC WARS, 264–146 BCE

Carthage and Rome coexisted and indeed cooperated during the fifth and fourth centuries, but that happy arrangement broke apart in the 260s BCE. The former allies eyed each other warily, each seeing the other's growing strength in Sicily as a threat. The first of the three **Punic Wars** between Carthage and Rome broke out in 264 BCE and was mainly fought at sea. Remarkably, the Romans, who had no navy of their own in 264, were routinely besting the Carthaginians in naval battles by the war's end in 241 BCE. Carthage had to sue for peace and agree to unfavorable terms.

One particular Carthaginian elite family, the Barcas, found defeat and the peace terms an affront. Men of the Barca clan (their name meant "thunderbolt") went to Spain in 237 BCE, where they led a Carthaginian conquest of local tribes. They converted the loose trading system of Carthage in Spain into a true empire—of the Barca family as much as of Carthage. In particular, they re-organized the silver mines to increase output. One Carthaginian who went to Spain was nine-year-old **Hannibal Barca**.

Hannibal's father led the subjugation of Spain. When he drowned and his heir was assassinated, it fell to Hannibal,

Hannibal Barca A Carthaginian coin from around the years 213 to 210 BCE celebrates Hannibal's feats as a military commander. One side bears his portrait, and the other an image of an elephant, his legendary weapon of war.

then age 26, to command Carthaginian efforts in Spain in 221 BCE. After consolidating his personal authority, he laid siege to a client city of Rome's, inviting renewal of war. In the Second Punic War (218–201 BCE), Hannibal acquired everlasting fame as a brilliant commander.

His opening gambit was to march an army of 50,000 men and a few war elephants—small Moroccan ones, less formidable than those used in India—over the Pyrenees and the Alps and into northern Italy. Carthage no longer had the sea power to convey an army to Italy; Rome now had the stronger navy. Hannibal lost half his men on his two-month-long march, but in what is now northern Italy he recruited many warriors hostile to Rome, mostly Gauls and Celts. In a series of battles Hannibal repeatedly routed Roman armies, a feat as remarkable as the newly created Roman navy's sea victories over Carthage in the previous war. On one occasion, at Cannae in 216 BCE, his men slaughtered 46,000 Roman soldiers, the largest death toll in a single day of European warfare—ever.

The Romans, however, had more men to take the place of the fallen. Hannibal did not, and he began to lose some of his allies in Italy. Roman armies seized Carthaginian holdings in Spain, including the main sources of silver. A Roman commander then carried the war to Carthage's backyard, where Hannibal lost a climactic battle at Zama, near Carthage, in 202 BCE, which effectively ended the Second Punic War. In defeat, Carthage had to agree to pay Rome large sums of silver for the next 50 years, limit its navy to 10 ships, and disband its war elephant corps.

Hannibal, for his part, escaped the usual fate of Carthaginian generals defeated by Rome—crucifixion—and fled into exile in Anatolia, where he took refuge with Rome's enemies. There he was credited with inventing the "snakes on a boat" tactic: catapulting brittle clay jars stuffed with poisonous serpents onto the decks of Roman warships. When locals betrayed him to Roman authorities, he poisoned himself, probably in 182 BCE. His battle tactics—mobility and envelopment, but not snake launching—are still in the curriculum in military academies today.

The defeated Carthaginians returned to their trading and farming ways. They never developed the disdain for commerce that elite Romans, Assyrians, and Chinese paraded. Their success brought renewed prosperity, and by the 150s BCE they seemed, to some Romans at least, to be a potential threat once more. Rome launched the Third Punic War (149–146 BCE), which climaxed in a thorough sack of Carthage. Roman forces burned and obliterated the city, ending Carthage's career as a Mediterranean power and as a state. Most of the 700,000 people in Carthage's home territory were killed, sold into slavery, or fled, never to return. Contrary to popular myth, the Romans did not spread salt on the city and its fields to prevent anything from growing again; salt was too valuable for that.

Carthage remained deserted for a century and then became the site of a new Roman colony. Yet Carthaginian culture lived on in North Africa. In dozens of towns and

Roman Colonization The Roman amphitheater in El Jem, Tunisia, built in 238 CE, provides evidence of the Roman colonial presence on the site of a former Carthaginian settlement.

hamlets in the western Mediterranean, people who were culturally Carthaginian survived despite the destruction of Carthage. The Punic language coexisted with Latin and other tongues in North Africa up until that region became Arabized in the seventh century CE. The Carthaginian alphabet, originally Phoenician, in revised forms became the basis for all writing systems around the Mediterranean.

Over the six-century career of their city and state, the Carthaginians extended and consolidated trade networks in the western Mediterranean and ratcheted up silver production in Spain. They pioneered the connections between Britain and the Mediterranean, and inaugurated seaborne contacts between the Atlantic coast of Africa and Mediterranean peoples. To judge by the number of shipwrecks found by underwater archeologists, Mediterranean trade grew fivefold between 500 and 100 BCE. Traders from many ports took part in this intensification of commerce, but Carthage (together with Alexandria) was among the leaders. The Carthaginians, in effect, created a Mediterranean world with trade links spanning from North Africa to southern Europe and Spain to Syria.

ROME FROM ITS BEGINNINGS TO THE TIME OF AUGUSTUS, CA. 500 BCE TO 14 CE

For several hundred years, Romans told a story about their origins as descendants of Romulus. The legend, in short, is that in the aftermath of a few murders within the family, Romulus and his twin brother, Remus, were born when Mars, a god of war, raped a priestess renowned for her chastity, Rhea Silvia, who became their mother. Their great uncle tried to have the babies killed, but instead they were abandoned, suckled by a she-wolf, and raised by shepherds. Once grown up, they killed their great-uncle and then quarreled, which led Romulus to murder Remus. Romulus and his followers, feeling the need for wives, invited neighbors to a feast and at a prearranged signal abducted the guests' daughters. This story, one of several versions of Rome's origins, was written down by the fourth century BCE.

Rome's own foundation myths featured murder, rape, child abandonment, attempted infanticide, more murder,

sibling rivalry, and fratricide, followed by mass kidnapping of young women. The archeological and historical record is only a little kinder to the Romans than they were to themselves. We will look at that record in some detail, because Rome proved so influential to later ages.

ROMAN EXPANSION IN ITALY TO 264 BCE

In its early centuries, Rome was a town of no particular account. The earliest archeological evidence of settlements at Rome date from the tenth century BCE, and the first texts to mention the city are from the eighth. When the Assyrians in Mesopotamia and the Zhou dynasty in China were at their height, Rome was still a small settlement on the fringe of Etruria, the land of the Etruscans. Etruscan building styles, art, and political institutions, notably its army, influenced Rome considerably.

But in the fifth century BCE, as the power of other trading peoples—mainly Carthage and the Greeks based in Sicily—began to grow, the Etruscan towns declined. Etruscan misfortune elevated Rome in the balance, and by 450 or so Rome obliged some Etruscan towns to become Roman clients. Etruscans gradually lost their political independence to Romans, but their language and culture, like that of Carthage after its fall, survived for several centuries longer.

After subsuming the Etruscans, Rome frequently fought neighboring peoples in central and southern Italy. If the ancient authors can be trusted, Rome was at war in about 90 percent of the years between 500 and 300 BCE. Rome's fortunes in warfare improved over time for two main reasons connected to manpower: slavery and citizenship. When the Romans defeated a people, they enslaved their captives, as was normal everywhere from Central Asia to Spain. But increasingly, after 350 BCE or so, instead of selling slaves abroad for cash, they kept them at home and put them to work on Roman farms. This arrangement freed adult male Romans for warfare, and indeed the rights of Roman citizenship

Etruscans An Etruscan oil jar from the fourth or third century BCE is covered in Etruscan writing, an ancestor of the Latin (and thus our) alphabet.

required all men age 17 to 46 to serve in the army when called. With abundant slaves doing the farming, Rome, like Sparta with its helots, could put a higher proportion of its manpower into its military than did other peoples who, upon victory, couldn't resist the temptation to turn war captives into cash.

The other innovation in Rome's approach to foreign relations was to extend the rights of citizenship to some neighbors, adding further military manpower. It often came as an offer the neighbors couldn't refuse: become Roman citizens or be conquered and either slaughtered or enslaved. Roman citizenship often included exemption from taxes as well as the obligation to serve in the army, so it was an appealing offer by itself. Compared to the alternative, the offer was often irresistible, so more and more peoples of Italy became Romans.

With these sources of manpower, Rome almost always had the biggest armies and could recover faster from losses than any rivals in Italy. Each success made Rome stronger

and the next victory more likely. Between 340 and 290 BCE, just about everyone in Italy south of the Po valley had accepted Roman rule, either by conquest, by intimidation, or by negotiation.

Rome's political and military system proved its effectiveness in a spurt of conquests of the Greek cities of southern Italy between 280 and 272 BCE. These cities, collectively known as Magna Graeca, were originally Greek colonies founded during the seventh through the fifth centuries. Over time they had grown rich, powerful, and independent. When threatened by Rome and Carthage both, some wished to knuckle under, but others hired the able King Pyrrhus of Epirus to defend them. With a large army and a few war elephants, not yet encountered in Italy, Pyrrhus defeated both Carthaginian and Roman forces, becoming master of Sicily. Subsequently, he developed ambitions to match the empire of his distant kinsman, Alexander the Great. But together Carthaginians and Romans defeated Pyrrhus's forces in 272. According to one Roman author,

Roman Expansion, ca. 450 BCE–14 CE From its beginnings as just one of several polities on the Italian Peninsula, Rome steadily expanded. Its conquests within the peninsula were substantially complete by the 260s, when it undertook the first of three major wars against Carthage. Known as the Punic Wars, these conflicts ended with Rome in control of most of the central and western Mediterranean coastlands. Later conquests, especially in Anatolia, Syria, and Egypt, contributed mightily to the empire's wealth and population by the time Augustus took power in 27 BCE.

the Romans learned that elephants were afraid of pigs and managed to panic Pyrrhus's pachyderms. He died soon thereafter when hit on the head by a roof tile hurled by an elderly woman in the Greek town of Argos—an ignoble end for a man deemed by Hannibal the greatest of all war commanders. With Pyrrhus out of the picture, the stage was set for the First Punic War, discussed above.

By the third century BCE, Rome was a large city with perhaps 100,000 people. It had begun to build a network of roads and a system of aqueducts to provide the city with clean water. The aqueducts, by reducing the toll of waterborne disease in a filthy city, helped Rome sustain its manpower advantage. And it was now in full control of almost all Italy south of the Po River, Sicily and the rich cities of Magna Graeca included, and poised for expansion overseas.

THE ROMAN REPUBLIC

For hundreds of years following the rise of Rome in the fifth century BCE, its powerful and expanding state took the form of a republic. The institutions and politics of the Roman Republic proved remarkably resilient over those centuries, until they foundered in the crisis of the second century BCE.

GODS AND RITUALS As in all ancient states, religion played an important role in Roman life under the Republic. Romans worshipped many gods, some of whom were based on Etruscan deities that acquired Greek overlays over time. Jupiter, modeled on Zeus, and Mars, the Roman equivalent of Ares and god of war, stood in the front rank of the Roman pantheon. Quirinus, god of the Roman people, had no Greek counterpart but ranked third in importance after Jupiter and Mars. Poor people were especially attentive to Ceres, goddess of grain, fertility, and growth, who corresponded to the Greek Demeter. Romans even had a god for manure (Sterculinus) and a goddess for the city's main sewer (Cloacina). Romans, like Greeks, expected their gods to meddle enthusiastically in human affairs, so they sacrificed to them frequently and put great faith in omens.

Romans built an elaborate set of rituals and institutions around their gods. Part of being Roman consisted of following these rituals. Male heads of households saw to religious observance in the home, making offerings of grapes, grain, or wine to a statue of a Lar, a guardian god. Every city, neighborhood, and household, not to mention roads

Religious Ritual Priestesses offer sacrifices to Vesta at a temple dedicated to the goddess in a relief from first- or second-century CE Rome.

and ships, travelers and seafarers, had a Lar. Public rituals were the responsibility of official priests and priestesses, such as the Vestal Virgins. Girls selected from prominent families at ages 6 to 10 were taught how to maintain the cult of Vesta, goddess of the hearth. As Vestal Virgins they kept the sacred flame at Vesta's temple, fetched water from a sacred spring, and held places of honor in religious ceremonies. After 30 years on the job they retired, unless first found not to be a virgin, in which case they were buried alive. No major undertaking, least of all wars, could proceed without priests checking the omens and procuring appropriate blessings. All the important religious offices were the preserve of the social elite.

Like every religious community, the Romans adopted a few new practices now and then, but none that seemed to threaten the fabric of Roman religion and society were tolerated for long. One such, the cult of Bacchus, god of wine and ecstasy, introduced from the Greek cities of southern Italy, involved secret meetings (originally attended only by women) at which all manner of crime and political conspiracy was allegedly hatched. Seeming to get out of hand, the Bacchus cult was outlawed in 186 BCE. Roman religion helped unite Romans culturally and helped keep the elite in control.

ROMAN LAW AND CITIZENSHIP All powerful societies find a way to manage social conflict. Religion alone is rarely enough. Confucian ideology served this purpose in China, as did the democratic assembly in Athens. Like all complex societies, Rome had sharp cleavages between rich and poor, and division threatened any and all common purpose. The Roman Republic developed a series of practices and institutions that kept class conflict and civil war to a minimum until 91 BCE and checked the power-lust of successful politicians.

The first of these practices and institutions was the rule of law. Sometime about 450 BCE, Romans drew up a code of law called the Twelve Tables (it was written on 12 tablets). Its main concerns were marriage, property, debt, and the procedures of law. It also prescribed punishments for various offenses. Killing, for example, was illegal outside one's family except in cases of thieves caught in the night. Within families, the male head of household, called *paterfamilias*, technically had the legal right to kill any member of his family, a right rarely exercised. Like the Qin dynasty's laws in China but unlike the Babylonian laws of Hammurabi, Roman laws applied equally to rich and poor. The other important feature of this code was that it was written down (although schoolboys were expected to memorize it anyway). Both features helped it to endure as the basis for a tradition of law that Romans came to think was part of what made them Romans—and better than anyone else.

Another important practice in the Roman Republic was the political use of citizenship. There were several gradations of citizenship with different rights, but full citizens—always male—enjoyed the right to hold office and vote in assemblies, and freedom from most taxes. Romans used citizenship tactically to defuse social conflict and, as we saw above, to enroll defeated peoples in their legions. Citizenship could be offered in negotiations with unruly groups, as occurred repeatedly in the early years of the Roman Republic. It was used in desperation

and on a large scale after a major revolt during the years 91 to 89 BCE: to avoid another war, Rome tripled the number of citizens. Since citizenship often came with exemption from taxes, Romans didn't bestow the honor casually. The forms of partial citizenship served in situations where full citizenship seemed too much to concede. Their caution notwithstanding, the Romans were much freer with the extension of citizenship than, for example, the Greek poleis or, in all likelihood, Carthage. Citizenship meant the right to take part in politics too, and it gave people a stake in the fate of Rome—even if in practice one had to live within a day's walk of the city to be politically active, because all deliberations took place there.

A FLEXIBLE POLITICS The third major source of Roman power and stability was the political system of the Republic, an oligarchy with just enough flexibility to bend when needed. The Greek historian Polybius of the second century BCE thought the Roman system of government, which he and others called the Roman constitution, combined the best elements of monarchy (rule of one), oligarchy (rule of the few), and democracy (rule of the many)—just what Aristotle had written about Carthage. Rome had no written constitution, but it did have institutions, laws, and traditions that for a few centuries commanded respect among its citizens and admiration among many foreigners.

Roman mythology held that their ancestors had overthrown a tyrannous Etruscan king in 509 BCE and thereafter established the consulate. True or not, sometime about 500 and no later than 450 BCE, Rome was governed by a pair of consuls, each serving for only one year—a variation on the practice of temporary rulership present also in Greek democracies and Carthage. The consuls' main duty was to lead armies in the field, and success brought glory, influence, and war booty. With two consuls always in office, the system checked the ambitions of Rome's politicians. The consuls were the most powerful men in Rome, superior to the scores of lesser magistrates charged with administrative duties.

Consuls didn't enjoy absolute power, though: former consuls and magistrates of the higher echelons, and other elite men too, sat in the Senate. Senators held office for life and weren't paid, so the Senate was full of men rich enough not to need to work. It began as a forum of 100 men who typically came from the same elite families and knew one another, and one another's families, by the time they held office. By the mid-first century BCE, the Senate had ballooned to nearly 800 members and included able and ambitious men from lesser families. Like all exclusive clubs, the Senate was a cauldron of personal ambition for status, honors, and power. Its official concerns included religious rites, issues of war and peace, and finances. The Senate's role was nominally advisory, but when it agreed on anything it was very hard for consuls not to accede to its wishes—until about 100 BCE.

The political system of the Roman Republic also included larger assemblies that approved or rejected legislation and elected high magistrates. As Rome grew larger, more offices were created: praetors, quaestors, censors, and tribunes. They too checked the power of the consuls, especially the tribunes, some of whom represented the lower classes and had the power to veto laws. The assemblies enrolled all citizens, even the poor, although through complex arrangements their voice was limited and that of the rich amplified. The system as a whole—the Roman constitution—included checks and balances and encouraged compromise. It allowed an oligarchy to remain in power but gave the ruling families the flexibility to appear to be bowing to the will of the people when that seemed prudent.

THE ARMY The final institution that ensured the power and stability of the Republic until 91 BCE was the army. It was occasionally called on to put down revolts. But its more important function was as a plunder machine that kept most Roman citizen-soldiers happy most of the time, even if army duty led to the early deaths of countless young men. All citizens had to serve, and the ambitious among them eagerly sought war and victory in order to advance their careers and achieve renown. (It didn't always work: at the monumental defeat of Cannae, Hannibal's forces killed 80 senators serving in the Roman army.) Roman citizens typically served in the legions—heavily armed and highly disciplined infantry units of about 5,000 men. The army also included auxiliaries, typically non-citizens, organized as both infantry and cavalry.

The poor were often needed to fill out the legions. This worked to their advantage in two ways. First, if they fought and Rome won, as it usually did, and if they survived their term of service (about a 60 percent chance), they could expect a small share of the resulting booty and perhaps some land taken from the conquered—instant advancement and a very attractive gamble for poor young

The Forum The ruins of the Forum—the traditional seat of government in Rome during the Republic—still stand today in the center of Rome. In the left foreground stands the Temple of Saturn, built in 497 BCE.

men. Second, if the poor could band together and decline to serve in the army, the magistrates and senate might make political concessions. Five times between 494 and 287 BCE, Rome's poorer classes refused to work or fight, winning cancellation of debts or expanded political rights in the negotiations that followed.

With these practices and institutions, Rome managed to remain stable and become ever more powerful in the centuries after 350 BCE. However, the system began to break down shortly before 100 BCE, partly because Rome became too successful as an empire.

THE CRISIS OF THE REPUBLIC

The Roman Republic's political system worked well, and eventually too well. After winning the Second Punic War (218–201 BCE), Rome dove deeply into the affairs of the Greek peninsula. In 146 BCE, the year of Rome's final destruction of Carthage, it also crushed the city of Corinth, ringleader of Greek resistance to Roman expansion. Roman aristocrats found much to admire in Greek culture, including theater, philosophy, religion, athletic competitions, marble statuary, and architecture. As a later poet, Horace, who had studied in Athens, put it, "Conquered Greece conquered in turn the uncultivated victor." The upper ranks of Roman society gradually learned to read and speak Greek, and increasingly Rome came to resemble a Hellenistic state—although not yet a monarchy.

Further Roman conquests followed in Anatolia. The quantities of war booty now available dwarfed what earlier consuls had won in wars within Italy. Successful generals became fabulously rich overnight, and their power swelled in comparison to that of the Senate—and the law. They found it easy to bribe officials, even the whole Senate, and to put on displays that won them public adulation.

RISING PERSONAL POWER Now Roman politics became more personalized. Charismatic military heroes competed more fiercely for pre-eminence. Some aristocrats sought to mobilize the masses in their own struggles for honor and power, such as the brothers Tiberius and Gaius Gracchus. The two men, serving as tribunes, pursued radical reforms such as redistributing land and extending citizenship to large numbers of poorer Romans in hopes of gaining popular support for their quest to restore the political standing of their family. Both were murdered for their political proposals (in 133 and 123 BCE, respectively). Respect for tradition and law ebbed. Observers complained about corruption and money in politics.

After 107 BCE, a consul of humble origin, Marius, managed to get himself elected consul seven times by citing military necessity—in violation of law and tradition. Marius enacted various reforms of the army, including allowing landless men to join up, and proved remarkably successful in wars in North Africa and northern Italy. Thereafter, his armies increasingly owed their allegiance to him, not to Rome. His soldiers had less of a stake in—and probably less knowledge of—the traditions, institutions, and practices of the Roman Republic than had earlier generations. They knew their chances of getting land and a wife were better if Marius won his battles in both war and politics.

This tendency toward the transformation of Roman armies into private forces serving personal ambition was soon confirmed. Another consul, an aristocrat named Sulla, won glory and booty in wars in Anatolia. When a potentially lucrative command was awarded to a rival, he marched his army upon Rome in 88 BCE. Thus began six decades of political chaos and frequent civil war. Sulla became dictator, stuffed the Senate with his supporters, and became the law unto himself, protected by a 10,000-man bodyguard. His troops slaughtered thousands of his political enemies and confiscated property from many more. Sulla distributed land and money to his loyal soldiers.

After Sulla's power grab, there was no limit to what a successful general might seek. Sulla retired just before his death in 78 BCE. In 73, the largest slave revolt in Roman history erupted, involving tens of thousands of slaves led by a former gladiator, Spartacus. It took eight legions two years to kill or capture the rebels. Two of the generals who took part, Crassus and Pompey, used their glory to launch political careers. Soon they were joined by another military hero, **Julius Caesar** (100–44 BCE), and in a private arrangement the three divided the sprawling Republic—whose borders their legions had extended—among themselves. Quarrels followed, leading to civil wars among armies loyal to their commanders, not to the Republic.

CIVIL WAR The Republic soon collapsed. Crassus died on campaign in 53 BCE. Pompey, supported by the Senate, and Caesar, supported only by his soldiers, dueled for ultimate power. Caesar was an aristocrat from a down-on-its luck family who had joined the army at age 15 and served widely. He won glory, a reputation as a brilliant commander, and the loyalty of his legions by crushing tribes in Gaul during the years 58 to 52 BCE. In 50 BCE, the Senate summoned Caesar to Rome and instructed him to disband his army. Caesar, like Sulla before him, defied the Senate and chose to bring his troops with him.

Caesar's decision provoked civil war on the grand scale. He won in battle against forces loyal to Pompey and the Senate in 48 BCE, by which time he had a quarter-million legionnaires under his command. Chasing Pompey around the Mediterranean brought him to Alexandria, the domain of Cleopatra, last of the Ptolemies to rule Egypt. She was then a 21-year-old queen engaged in a power struggle in which she wanted Caesar's help. She got it, according to the ancient authors, after being smuggled into Caesar's quarters in a rolled-up carpet. Caesar had planned to annex Egypt to the Roman Empire, but Cleopatra changed his mind. A young woman in a

Cleopatra VII This bust of Cleopatra was created in the first century BCE and depicts her Grecian features. She was the last ruling monarch of the Ptolemaic dynasty.

hurry, she soon bore Caesar a son and moved with him to Rome, despite the fact that the 52-year-old Caesar already had a wife there.

Undeterred by scandal, Caesar after 49 BCE helped himself to all offices he didn't already hold and installed his friends in the Senate. He ruled as dictator for five years, taking good care of his army veterans, extending citizenship to a few Celtic chiefs and rich foreigners who supported him, and reforming the calendar to give it 365 ¼ days through the device of leap years (which he had probably learned from Alexandria's astronomers). To accommodate calendar reform, the year 46 BCE had a total of 445 days in it, which must have puzzled ordinary folks. Caesar generously named a warm month after his clan, July. In 44 BCE he unwisely thought his situation secure enough to attend a meeting of the Senate without a bodyguard. Members of that august body, including his own brother-in-law, stabbed him to death. He was 55 years old.

Caesar ranks among the great military commanders. Those who heard him described him as a brilliant orator. He used his skills to further his own power, create a cult of personality for himself, and undermine the institutions of the Roman Republic. His supporters proclaimed him a god.

Another 13 years of on-and-off civil war followed Caesar's death. His will named a teenaged grand-nephew, **Octavian**, as his adopted son and heir. Despite a law stipulating that men had to be 42 years old to become consul, Octavian took the office when still 19. He and Caesar's fellow consul, Marc Antony, led troops against Caesar's assassins and destroyed them at Philippi, in Greece.

Octavian and Marc Antony, who were brothers-in-law, worked together for a few years but soon fell out. Antony—like Caesar before him—made a political and personal alliance with Cleopatra, who had returned home to Alexandria upon Caesar's assassination. She and Antony had three children, whom she hoped to see become rulers of the Roman world. Yet even her political skills did not suffice, and Octavian's commanders crushed their forces in 31 BCE, driving Antony and Cleopatra to suicide. Octavian added Egypt, the richest region of the world, to Roman lands.

AN EMPIRE BORN Octavian was now the most powerful and richest man in the world, with the possible exception of his contemporary, the Han emperor of China.

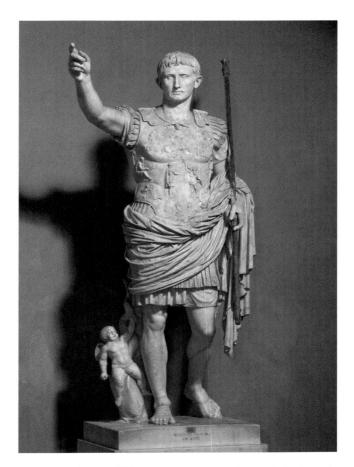

Augustus Caesar This statue, a copy of an original made to honor Augustus during his lifetime, ca. 20 BCE, shows the emperor as the commander in chief of Rome, wearing armor covered in insignia that illustrate his military conquests.

He took the name Augustus ("the revered") and ruled from 27 BCE until his death in 14 CE. His power lay in his immense wealth, his position as Julius Caesar's heir, the loyalty of many legions, and the prestige accorded by the offices that a cowed Senate heaped upon him. Augustus too had a warm month named for him. He styled himself a son of a god (because of the deification of Julius Caesar) and the "first citizen" of Rome.

The Roman Empire was born in blood, the result of quests for personal power and public adulation on the part of Marius, Sulla, and, above all others, Julius Caesar. The checks and balances of the Republic failed when several successful Roman conquests of rich lands enabled some generals to become spectacularly rich and famous. Several of them used their riches and fame to corrupt the institutions of the Republic, make politics a matter of personal loyalties, and undermine the Roman constitution.

CONSIDERING THE EVIDENCE

Hortensia's Speech

Following Julius Caesar's assassination in 44 BCE, his allies Octavian and Marc Antony seized control. They "proscribed" their enemies by executing them, seizing their property, and banning their relatives from political office. Those who escaped launched a civil war for control of Rome. Two years later, as war expenses mounted, the new leaders violated custom by taxing the wealthiest 1,400 women of Rome. Many of the targeted women—including Hortensia, their spokesperson—stormed the floor of the Roman Senate to protest the tax. The following excerpt is from Hortensia's speech. Original Latin transcriptions did not survive, but the historian Appian (ca. 95–165 CE) made a Greek translation of her speech in his history of Rome a few centuries later.

You have already deprived us of our fathers, our sons, our husbands, and our brothers, whom you accused of having wronged you; if you take away our property also, you reduce us to a condition unbecoming our birth, our manners, our sex. If we have done you wrong, as you say our husbands have, proscribe us as you do them. But if we women have not voted any of you public enemies, have not torn down your houses, destroyed your army, or led another one against you; if we have not hindered you in obtaining offices and honours,—why do we share the penalty when we did not share the guilt?

Why should we pay taxes when we have no part in the honours, the commands, the state-craft, for which you contend against each other with such harmful results? "Because this is a time of war," do you say? When have there not been wars, and when have taxes ever been imposed on women, who are exempted by their sex among all mankind? Our mothers did once rise superior to their sex and made contributions when you were in danger of losing the whole empire and the city itself through the conflict with the Carthaginians. But then they contributed voluntarily, not from their landed property, their fields, their dowries, or their houses, without which life is not possible to free women, but only from their own jewellery, and . . . not by force and violence, but what they themselves were willing to give. What alarm is there now for the empire or the country? Let war with the Gauls or the Parthians come, and we shall not be inferior to our mothers in zeal for the common safety; but for civil wars may we never contribute, nor ever assist you against each other!

Source: *Appian's Roman History IV*, trans. Horace White, Loeb Classical Library, eds. T. E. Page, M. A. Rouse, and W. H. D. Rouse (New York: 1913).

QUESTIONS FOR ANALYSIS

1. What kind of property could free Roman women control independently of their male relatives?
2. How did Hortensia use the official exclusion of women from politics to argue for their property rights?
3. In Hortensia's view, what is the difference between the historical contributions of Rome's women to the war against Carthage and the taxes against which she is protesting?

THE ROMAN EMPIRE FROM AUGUSTUS TO 200 CE

The Roman Empire, born from political chaos, proved remarkably stable for two centuries. Augustus built on the legacy of the Republic and established enduring structures that enabled Rome to survive periods of spectacularly bad leadership for a long time. The end came slowly: a few centuries of stagnation, teetering, and slow collapse in the central and western Mediterranean. In the eastern Mediterranean, Roman rule survived in the form of the Byzantine Empire until 1453. The remainder of this chapter will explain why the Roman Empire lasted as long as it did and will carry the story up to about 200 CE.

Despite chronic bad health, Augustus lived and ruled until the age of 76, which gave him 40 years to get things done. He was among the most ruthless and conniving of Rome's rulers (a very high standard, that) and among the few to die peacefully in his bed. He arranged the murder of more political opponents than the next 20 emperors combined. He used his boundless wealth, and his two marriages, for political purposes. By the standards of monarchs he lived modestly himself, insisting publicly that he was just another Roman citizen. Indeed, he was offended by the excesses and loose morality of his fellow aristocrats and even had his daughter and granddaughter exiled for their wanton ways.

THE STATE AND THE EMPERORS

The remarkable endurance of the Roman Empire is partly the result of Augustus's political and administrative legacy. If you want to learn how to wield near-absolute power over a gigantic organization for most of your adult life, you can do no better than to study Augustus.

CONSOLIDATION UNDER AUGUSTUS Augustus ruled with an iron fist in a velvet glove. He maintained, or restored, the fiction of Senate power, and he permitted aristocrats enough in the way of political roles and personal wealth that they almost entirely went along with his rule. He had already killed off those most likely to resist, leaving him with a more docile flock. He rebuilt temples and theaters, making Rome an awe-inspiring architectural spectacle. In one of his rare boasts (rare by the standards of pharaohs or Assyrian kings), he said he had found Rome a city of bricks and left it a city of marble. He used his immense personal wealth, much of it derived from the annexation of Egypt, to fund public construction, including more aqueducts and fountains. He also perfected the tradition, followed by most Roman emperors, of sponsoring athletic games, religious festivals, and periodic distribution of free grain to the poor—a successful strategy for keeping a population content.

Augustus also reorganized the state administration and the army. The main thrust was to make officeholders and army commanders more dependent on the emperor's favor, a continuation of a trend begun under consuls Marius and Sulla. He re-established the census, which hadn't been taken in 40 years. He often paid soldiers out of his personal coffers to remind them where their loyalties should lie. He worked tirelessly to make sure no commander outside his family won too much military glory. He also added the so-called **praetorian guard**, an elite corps of 4,500 men, paid three times a soldier's wage, whose job was to protect the emperor. They did their job in the case of Augustus. But before they were disbanded in 312 CE, the praetorian guard had murdered five other

Praetorian Guard Soldiers in the uniform of the emperor's elite bodyguard look armed and watchful in a relief from the second century CE.

emperors and, on one occasion, auctioned off the emperorship to the highest bidder—who offered 10 tons of gold.

The strongest testimony to Augustus's work in consolidating the Roman state is that it survived two challenges: uncertain successions and the reigns of several bungling emperors. The emperorship was not nominally a hereditary position, but most emperors tried to put a son or nephew in a position to follow in the family business. The uncertainty of succession encouraged frequent conspiracies, murders, and poisonings in the extended imperial family. Only about 30 percent of emperors died of natural causes.

SUCCESSORS, BAD AND GOOD The strong foundation Augustus laid enabled Rome to withstand the reigns of less skilled and dutiful successors. Caligula (r. 37–41 CE) squandered a full treasury in record time; insisted on being worshipped as a god; acquired a reputation for wanton cruelty and creatively perverse sexuality, often involving his sisters; opened a government-run brothel, also involving his sisters; and tried to make his favorite horse a consul. The praetorian guard killed him in 41 CE. They put in his place his uncle Claudius (r. 41–54 CE), a political wallflower who to this point had kept busy meekly writing histories. He proved to be an effective emperor, no doubt helped by his knowledge of history, until he was poisoned by his wife, who was also his niece. Much worse followed.

The track record of bad emperors was so discouraging that after 98 CE rulers often adopted promising young men as their sons, and in some cases made them co-emperors, in order to get better successors. Three formidably competent emperors, Trajan (r. 98–117), Hadrian (r. 117–138), and Marcus Aurelius (r. 161–180), came to power this way. Each was a military man who proved his worth in a long apprenticeship in the army and politics before succeeding to the emperorship in middle age; each enjoyed the support and respect of the legions; and each met with success in expanding or defending the empire's frontiers. A few capable emperors attained power through civil war or military coup—Vespasian (r. 69–79) and Diocletian (r. 284–305), for example. Both were military men who as emperors enacted effective reforms strengthening the empire.

Some emperors, like Marcus Aurelius, were paragons of self-discipline and duty. Others were not, such as the licentious teenager and religious zealot Elagabalus (r. 218–222), who came to power at age 14 thanks to the influence of his grandmother. Four years later, having witnessed his escapades and abuses of power, she then arranged his murder. Rome survived the likes of Caligula and Elagabalus in part because the praetorian guard, responsible for their safety, murdered them promptly and didn't give them the chance to reign for long.

Something of the traditions, offices, and bureaucracy of the Republic survived, although debased and personalized by consuls and emperors. Following Augustus, emperors developed a bureaucratic layer staffed by slaves and former slaves, loyal to the emperor and often of high administrative skill. The rule of law, although watered down by emperors' decrees and frequent illegality, survived in principle. So did the tradition whereby elite Romans competed for honor in the service of the state. All this helped the empire to bounce back from the frequent disastrous emperors and occasional military defeat.

In addition, bad emperors didn't make much difference in the provincial world of villages and towns. Emperors might either persecute and kill fellow aristocrats or plumb the depths of moral depravity in their not-so-private lives, and thereby earn the undying hostility of the literate classes. But that made no difference to Egyptian peasants, Spanish miners, or Sicilian shepherds. As long as they worked, paid taxes, and performed military service (as auxiliaries, because they were unlikely to be citizens), and Roman legions won most wars, Rome could survive.

COINS, ROADS, SOLDIERS Another source of the coherence and durability of Rome was the coinage system. Beginning under the Republic about 300 BCE and continuing under the empire, Rome's mints stamped out millions of coins, using gold, silver, copper, bronze, and other metals. Although occasionally debased (by using alloys with less precious metal per coin) to pay for wars, Roman coins were accepted far and wide, even beyond the empire's borders, especially after Augustus imposed a standardization. Reasonably reliable money spurred economic growth and commercial exchange, binding the Roman world together.

Superb infrastructure also helps explain the longevity of Rome. The road system, begun before 300 BCE, spread its tendrils under the empire. Its overall length by 200 CE stretched to 52,000 miles (83,000 km), a little more than the current US Interstate Highway System. Its main arteries were about 25 feet (8 m) wide, made of paving stones, and usually straighter than an arrow. Some of the roadbeds, and numerous stone bridges, remain in use 20 centuries later. These main roads, and many more gravel ones, sped the movement of armies and official information. Couriers could cover 50 miles (80 km) a day. Important news from the farthest corners of the empire could make it to Rome in a month or less. The Romans also built hundreds of aqueducts and sewers, which kept their cities healthier than most. Urban life on the scale it attained during the first through the third centuries CE would have been impossible without the provision of clean water. Roman engineers designed water systems that in some cases required cutting tunnels through mountain rock. Rome itself had a water system that provided about 200 gallons (800 L) per person per day, a more lavish water supply than any other big city enjoyed until recent times. Aqueducts also served to

Roman Coin A silver coin minted in 49 or 48 BCE bears an image of an elephant and the word *CAESAR*, indicating that it was issued under Julius Caesar's authority.

Roman Roads (Left) A section of paved Roman road built between 312 and 264 BCE in Italy testifies to the longevity of Roman material culture. (Right) As this first-century relief from Rome shows, countless laborers worked with hand tools to construct the thousands of miles of paved roads that connected the far-flung regions of the Roman Empire.

deliver irrigation water to thirsty fields. Like the Achaemenid Persian Empire, Rome lasted as long as it did partly due to investment in durable infrastructure.

The army held the empire together at least as much as did the roads and coins. The imperial army was somewhat different from that of the Republic. Under the Republic, the state raised legions as needed to make war and promised them land for their service. Augustus built a standing, professional army, paid in money. It numbered nearly 300,000 by his death. The imperial army took about 40 percent of the state's budget, rising later to 60 percent—normal or below normal for pre-modern states. Army service lasted for 20 years, and for 25 after about 90 CE. Soldiers earned approximately 80 percent of a laborer's wage. After about 50 CE, the recruits included more and more Spaniards, Gauls, Syrians, and others from outside Italy. If they survived long enough (well under half did so), they could acquire citizenship upon retirement.

Imperial Rome also had a professional navy, created under Augustus. It cruised the Mediterranean and patrolled navigable rivers such as the Danube and Rhine, important for the defense of Rome's northern frontiers. Sailors had to serve for 26 years, after which they earned a handsome bonus and citizenship. The Roman navy stamped out Mediterranean piracy for two centuries, a feat not matched until modern times.

EARLY REVOLTS

The army's job included suppressing revolts. By the standards of most empires, these were few in Rome. Part of the reason was the brutal force that legions brought to bear against them. The Roman historian Tacitus, writing in about 98 CE, credited a Scottish chieftain with this apt summary of Roman policy toward rebellious tribes: "they make a desert and call it peace." Another reason that revolts were rare was that Rome usually found a way to make submission appealing to local elites, including allowing them cultural and religious autonomy, or perhaps Roman citizenship, if they didn't threaten Roman rule.

REVOLTS OF THE JEWS But on the edges of the empire, peoples sometimes found the imposition of Roman rule grounds for revolt. Among the most threatening uprisings were those of the Jews, who amounted to perhaps 5 percent of the Roman Empire's population. The first sizeable revolt came in 66 CE in Judaea, a Roman province that included a recently created client kingdom of the Jews centered on Jerusalem. Many Jews resented Roman taxation, disrespect for Jewish tradition, and the pro-Roman policies of their Roman-appointed king. The revolt was provoked in part by a Jewish political group,

Roman Triumph A relief from the Arch of Titus (built in 82 CE) in the Forum in Rome celebrates the conquest of Jerusalem, showing soldiers with a menorah looted from the temple and prisoners captured during the destruction of the city.

the zealots, among whom extremists discouraged opposition by stabbing those Jews who seemed sympathetic to Rome. The conflict evolved into a war among Jewish factions. Its suppression required 60,000 Roman troops. Some 220,000 Jews died in a Roman siege of Jerusalem. The temple in Jerusalem, the center of Jewish community life, was destroyed in 70 CE, never to rise again.

A bigger Jewish revolt came in the years 132 to 135 CE, during the reign of Hadrian. It led to the death of hundreds of thousands of Jews, the enslavement and exile of many more, the destruction of Jerusalem, and the end of all Jewish political authority in the Roman Empire. Hadrian forbade Jews to return to their sacred city of Jerusalem and changed its name to Aelia Capitolina. He executed Jewish scholars and tried to eradicate Judaism in the empire.

These revolts, sometimes called the Roman-Jewish Wars, aimed to win autonomy for the Jewish kingdom and shield Jews from Roman power. Their suppression, and the exile of a major population of the Roman Empire, temporarily shook the Roman political landscape but ever after loomed large in the history of the Jewish people, who were scattered to the winds.

QUEEN BOUDICA Another uprising occurred in Britain in the years 60 to 61 CE, shortly after Roman legions conquered it. **Queen Boudica**, whose succession to a local throne wasn't recognized by Roman authorities, organized an assault on all things Roman in southeastern Britain. According to one Roman historian, Boudica, "tall, with flashing eyes, menacing voice, and yellow hair falling to her waist," inspired her followers to slaughter tens of thousands of Rome's supporters. The story of Queen Boudica recalls that of the Trung sisters on the edge of China's Han Empire only 20 years before. Roman troops eventually defeated Boudica, and Roman rule in Britain, like the Chinese in Vietnam, survived for centuries. Under the empire there were no massive slave revolts like that of Spartacus during the Republic.

The army itself mutinied from time to time. Frequent campaigns, sometimes in unforgiving environments such as the Syrian desert in summer, or tedious garrison duty in remote outposts, with no chance of glory, booty, or promotion, led some soldiers to think treasonous thoughts. Bad food and harsh discipline, the fate of most soldiers in pre-modern times, did nothing to change their minds. Every mutiny, however, was suppressed by loyal legions. The Romans held their army to high expectations: units showing insufficient resolve were sometimes decimated, meaning every tenth man was executed to persuade the others to shape up.

EXPANSION AND FRONTIERS

When not employed crushing the occasional revolt or rare mutiny, the army's main job was extending or holding the empire's frontiers. As we've seen, from about 300 BCE the Roman polity had expanded rapidly. Even during the tumultuous era of civil wars at the end of the Republic,

Frontier Campaigns A column erected by the emperor Trajan in Rome in 113 CE features detailed carvings of Trajan's victories against the Dacians in southeastern Europe, such as this one of Roman troops in a fortress fending off a Dacian rebellion.

generals such as Pompey and Julius Caesar added or consolidated new territories.

The expansionary trend continued under Augustus. His annexation of Egypt brought rich farmland under Roman control, giving emperors surplus grain to use as a political tool. He also firmed up Roman control of the Alps and Spain, where state-run silver mines formed another crucial component of imperial power. After Augustus, the pace of expansion slowed. Emperors sometimes sought new conquests to acquire prestige and strengthen their grip on power, as Claudius did in seizing Britain in the years 43 to 44 CE, and as Trajan did along the Danube early in his distinguished reign. Trajan also extended Roman power into Mesopotamia, but his successor, Hadrian, judged it too costly to keep.

After Trajan's time, the frontiers remained more or less stable for two centuries. Most emperors had to fight little wars around the edges of the empire. Ambitious tribal leaders too might feel the need for glory and choose to attack Roman outposts. Or whole peoples might need to flee their neighbors and calculate that fighting their way into Roman terrain was their least bad option. The most violent frontiers were, first, in Europe in the neighborhood of the Rhine and the Danube Rivers, to the east and north of which Germanic and other tribes such as the Dacians and Sarmatians roamed free. And, second, in the east along the Euphrates River, where the Parthians, an Iranian dynasty (247 BCE–224 CE) that had overthrown the Seleucids, presented a formidable foe. Roman forces tried on at least five occasions to best the Parthian Empire, but never did. Twice they captured the Parthian capital of Ctesiphon, but each time the Parthians soon recovered it.

The Roman Empire, 14–180 CE After the consolidation undertaken by Augustus, who died in 14 CE, later emperors extended the frontiers especially in Britain, northwest Africa, and the eastern Mediterranean. But they often found it hard to hold what they took, and they faced frequent frontier warfare and occasional revolts.

Frontier warfare, like the suppression of revolts, was always brutal and frequently genocidal. Under the Republic, Roman generals had often enough killed all males among conquered foes, a practice far from peculiar to Rome. Allegedly Scipio Africanus, who defeated Carthage in the Second Punic War, killed all males and dogs of both genders after taking New Carthage (Cartagena in Spain) in 209 BCE. The Romans were no gentler after the establishment of their empire. Campaigns against Germanic tribes routinely featured scorched-earth policies. The emperor Domitian (r. 81–96 CE) officially forbade the existence of one North African tribe that he found especially irksome. No mercy accompanied the suppression of the Jewish revolts, as we have seen. Rome's enemies rarely behaved any more generously. In 9 CE Germanic tribes completely obliterated three Roman legions, roughly 10 percent of the Roman army. As on the frontiers of the Mauryan Empire, or Qin and Han China, politics often took the form of savage violence.

Not all was blood and gore, though: frontier policy included diplomacy and political seduction as well. Roman commanders had much to offer tribal chieftains or petty kings if they agreed to become clients of Rome, willingly accepted formal Roman rule, or merely promised to refrain from assaults. One incentive was trade goods such as wine or silver. Another was Roman support against rival tribes or petty kingdoms. A shrewd Roman frontier commander, if not fixated on military glory, could achieve a lot with bribes and diplomacy. Several emperors encouraged peace and diplomacy on the frontiers, aware that war was expensive and that war heroes were politically dangerous for sitting emperors.

The stability of the frontiers also reflected economic geography. After Augustus secured Egypt and Spain, there was much less left that was worth conquering. Neither the Sahara nor northern Europe had much to offer. The enormous bonanzas that had come with the capture of the Macedonian treasury (167 BCE), Pergamum (130 BCE), Syria (67 BCE), or Egypt (30 BCE) could no longer be found anywhere except perhaps in Parthia (Iran), and Parthia was too distant and too formidable. In addition, anywhere that couldn't be reached by water transport was a remote and expensive place to send an army and supplies. So lands beyond the Mediterranean coastlands were costly to conquer and costly to keep, despite the Roman roads and the navigability of the Rhine and Danube. Thus there were good reasons for the stability of frontiers from the time of Trajan onward.

THE ECONOMY

As a state, the Roman Empire, like the Republic, was a plunder machine. Conquests topped up the treasury, despite the lavish spending by some emperors. But the stability of the empire's frontiers after the time of Trajan paradoxically undermined Rome—slowly.

When expansion ceased, the flow of land, war booty, and slaves slowed to a trickle. Only through improvements in the efficiency of agriculture, mining, or better terms of trade with foreigners could the Romans now expand the economic pie that needed to be divided. They succeeded only modestly in these respects. A state and society built for over 400 years on periodic windfalls, in the form of rich provinces conquered or enemy treasuries seized, ran out of windfalls.

Now the state had to rely for revenue on taxes, rent on public land, and the minting of new coins. Good evidence that all this was insufficient comes in the form of the falling silver and gold content of Roman coins. Beginning in the late first century, but quickening in the late second, the official mints used less and less precious metal in each coin, enabling them to mint far more coins. This trick enhanced government revenues in the short run but invited currency inflation over the long haul. Eventually, the state refused to accept its own coins for tax payments. Taxation was inefficient and haphazard: there was little before 6 CE, more thereafter, but nothing as reliable as in Han China. Some Roman cities taxed nails, others taxed prostitutes. Sometimes officials just confiscated wealth.

FARMING While the state often struggled to acquire enough revenues, ordinary people working the land often struggled to survive. In the first and second centuries CE, the empire's total population reached around 50 to 70 million, comparable to the population of Han China at the same time. Roughly 90 percent of these people lived in the countryside and followed the rhythms of farming life. These rhythms varied considerably from Egypt to England. Every province grew grain. Egypt normally harvested more than Egyptians ate, leaving a substantial reserve used for the Roman military or for distribution to the hungry; but when Egypt's crops failed, hunger stalked Roman cities. Mediterranean lands provided olive oil and wine in quantities sufficient for consumers all over the empire, from Egypt to distant Britain. Cattle, sheep, and goats grazed on lands not suited to grain, olives, or grapes.

Although Roman authors complained about the spread of latifundia, or big estates, in fact almost everywhere small farms prevailed. (This is an example of archeology correcting a bias in the textual record.) Even small farms often produced for sale as well as subsistence, conforming to the pattern—the commercialization of agriculture—of the Hellenistic world. Under the empire, farms had to pay tax in money, so they needed to sell something to meet their obligations. The Romans made few technical improvements in agriculture, certainly nothing as helpful as the Achaemenid Empire's adoption of alfalfa. Once all the good lands were in use, it was close to impossible to expand output. Soil erosion and soil nutrient loss nibbled away at agricultural yields.

MINING Mining was ancient Rome's most important industry. Spain provided the bulk of the empire's gold, silver, and lead, and a good bit of its iron too. Britain, the Balkans, and Anatolia contributed heavily as well. Italy itself had less in the way of useful ores. Roman mines achieved remarkable levels of production in the early empire. Lead mines yielded nearly 80,000 tons per year

The Economy of the Roman Empire, ca. 200 CE At its height, the Roman Empire was a highly integrated economic space. Specialists produced a wide variety of goods for market exchange, and merchants shuttled around the empire, especially on its sea routes. Mining, mints, and coinage smoothed commercial transactions. For some goods, routes extended beyond the frontiers to the Sahara, the Baltic, the steppe, Persia, and even to India and China.

Miner's Lamps A Roman miner's workday lasted as long as the oil in his lamp, about 11 hours. Mines in Spain were as much as 450 feet (137 m) deep. Some miners were free men who worked for wages, some were slaves. These Roman clay lamps were unearthed in present-day Spain and date to between the third and first centuries BCE.

in Augustus's time, more than the whole world would produce again for 1,700 years. Lead was used for water and sewer pipes and in pottery. Iron production outstripped that of Han China by perhaps 16-fold. But, as in agriculture, the Romans scarcely improved technologies and yields, perhaps because the plentiful supply of slaves ensured that labor in the mines was rarely short. The only notable technical improvement was a water-powered hammer for crushing ore, mentioned in one text from about 75 CE and probably not widely used.

Without technical advances, Roman mining inevitably ran into the law of diminishing returns. Lead production peaked before 50 CE, and silver about 150 CE. Gold production, most of which took place at a single mining complex in northwestern Spain called Las Médulas, tailed off by 200 CE. Reduced output of silver and gold made it hard for Roman rulers to resist debasing coinage.

TRADE Trade within the empire boosted the Roman economy. Mediterranean agriculture had long been highly commercial, with some zones specializing in grain and others in olive oil or wine. The Romans continued in this tradition and expanded its scale, reaching into almost every corner of the Mediterranean. They built on the Carthaginian trade networks in the western Mediterranean, organizing even larger exports of Spanish metals. Ships

bearing olive oil, wine, textiles, timber, ceramics, slaves, and more crisscrossed the Mediterranean in Roman times, shuttling among hundreds of ports large and small—as hundreds of shipwrecks attest. The pace of Mediterranean trade quickened after about 200 BCE and again with Augustus's acquisition of Egypt. Rome took part in the gradual process of commercialization that characterized the Hellenistic world, as we saw in Chapter 6.

Foreign trade mattered less to the Roman economy than farming, mining, or internal trade did. After Augustus's time, everything it truly needed came from within its broad territories. Imports consisted mainly of slaves and luxury goods. Trade links connected Rome to distant lands including Scandinavia, Russia, Arabia, India, even China and Korea. Amber, ivory, spices, and silks trickled in. They were taxed heavily (at about 25 percent), perhaps because officials sought to stem the tide of silver flowing out of the empire. Rome exported wine and pottery to northern Europe for slaves and amber, but in trade with Arabia, India, and China it had little to offer except silver.

Roman coins have turned up from Korea in the east to Ireland in the west, and as far south as Mali in West Africa. That distribution shows that the whole Eurasian world, and northern Africa too, took part in a giant web by 200 CE—the Old World web. By that time, however, as we have seen, the plunder machine and the mining that fueled the state and the economy had peaked. Thereafter, despite some energetic attempts at reform and economic stimulus, the Roman economy lurched, chugged, and slowed, never to recover its momentum.

RELIGION AND CULTURE

The core of Roman religion under the empire remained the same pagan gods, rituals, and offices inherited from the days of the Republic. However, in a space as large as the Roman Empire, inevitably there were many competing religious concepts. The connectedness of the empire—the result of roads, military campaigns, shipping, and so forth—ensured that millions of people encountered novel beliefs and rituals.

NEW BELIEFS AND PRACTICES The first change to take hold involved the divine status of rulers, a familiar belief in Egypt and Mesopotamia. From Augustus onward, Roman emperors were regarded as gods in the empire except in Italy, where they were deified upon their death—provided they enjoyed good approval ratings. Unpopular emperors were denied deification.

Other new practices crept in as more and more people with different gods were enrolled in the Roman Empire. Some Romans, mainly women, followed a new cult of Isis, the Egyptian goddess whom they hoped would protect home, hearth, and family, and especially women in the dangerous moment of childbirth. From Persia and Mesopotamia came a mysterious religion devoted to a god named Mithra, about whom we know very little because no scriptures or revealing texts survive. But Mithraism acquired many followers in the army. A Celtic water goddess was absorbed into Roman circles in Britain and given a Roman-style temple at the hot springs near Bath, England. Emperor Elagabalus tried to convert Romans to the worship of the Semitic god Baal, but that failed to catch on. The geographical expansion of the empire brought a modest expansion to its pantheon, thanks to Roman exposure to the religions of peoples they conquered.

CHRISTIANITY One of the religious innovations that arose in the Roman Empire would eventually attain world historical importance: Christianity. Jesus of Nazareth was born in an Aramaic-speaking Jewish community during the reign of Augustus. As a young man he began to preach in the tradition of the Hebrew prophets, upbraiding the rich and powerful for their neglect of the poor and of God. His view, reported in the gospels, that it is easier for a camel to pass through the eye of a needle than for a rich man to enter the kingdom of heaven wasn't calculated to win friends in high places. His followers cast him in the role of messiah, the fulfillment of predictions concerning a liberator made centuries before by ancient Hebrew prophets. Gradually, the concept of messiah came to include the idea that Jesus was the son of God, put on Earth to show humankind the way to righteousness and salvation. Jesus's irreverent preaching irritated many influential people, who urged Roman authorities to kill him. The Roman prefect, who saw Jesus as a source of political instability, ordered his execution using a standard Roman method, crucifixion, in either 30 or 33 CE. Jesus's followers claimed he would return to oversee a reign of peace and justice that would last for all eternity. But at his death he had only about 120 followers.

That might have been the end of it, but for the relentless work of Paul (ca. 5–ca. 65 CE), a Greek-speaking Jew and

The Travels of Paul, ca. 46–62 CE After a conversion experience, Paul devoted his life to spreading the Christian faith. His itinerary reflected the existing infrastructure of roads and ports of the eastern Roman Empire of his day. He was executed in Rome around 65 CE.

Roman citizen from Tarsus, a Mediterranean port city in Anatolia. Sent to Jerusalem for his education, he vigorously persecuted Christians there until—on the road to Damascus, according to Christian tradition—a vision of Jesus changed his outlook. Thereafter, he began to preach as a Christian, enduring the beatings and persecution he had formerly dealt out. His innovation was to preach not just to fellow Jews, as Jesus had done, but to pagans, who by and large proved more receptive than Jews.

Paul also diverged from Jewish tradition by arguing that anyone could achieve salvation through faith alone, without adhering to the rituals and rules of Judaism. No elaborate dietary restrictions, no male circumcision, no adherence to Jewish law was required—just faith in God and Jesus. This amounted to a re-negotiated covenant between God and the faithful. Paul traveled about 12,000 miles (20,000 km) from town to town between approximately 46 and 62 CE, preaching his faith and founding churches. He couldn't have done it without Roman roads and shipping networks. He absorbed endless harassment from Jewish leaders, who eventually arranged his arrest by Roman authorities in Jerusalem. He insisted on being taken to Rome for trial, the right of any Roman citizen. After a two-year delay, he was tried and beheaded. His writings, recorded in the Bible's New Testament, helped to establish the traditions of Christianity.

Roman religious policy, as under the Republic, remained one of toleration except where political challenges emerged. Christianity, from the Roman point of view, seemed an obscure and curious Jewish heresy with strange beliefs and perplexing rituals that brought cannibalism to mind. Emperor Nero found it convenient to have Paul executed and to throw a few Christians to wild dogs in attempts to divert attention from his own failings. Local authorities in Roman Carthage condemned a young mother to death for converting to Christianity. The woman, Perpetua, was mauled by wild beasts in the amphitheater before being killed by a soldier in about 203 CE. But for the most part, Roman authorities found little to worry them in Christianity. While the empire remained strong, Christians remained few and unthreatening,

perhaps 200,000 of the total population of 50 to 70 million as of 200 CE. They were mostly urban, petty traders and artisans. Later, when the empire began to teeter in the middle of the third century, and Christians grew more numerous, more systematic persecution would begin.

LITERATURE, ARCHITECTURE, SPORT Elite culture in imperial Rome began with religion but did not end there. Literature and architecture flourished, both influenced by Greek precedents. Poetry, satires, and histories remained the preferred modes of expression in literary high culture, as in previous centuries. Ovid's often saucy love poems, still read today, were too ribald for Augustus, who had him exiled. Martial, a satirist of the first century CE, specialized in quips, including one at the expense of a droning teacher whose lectures took place too early in the morning:

> We next door wish to doze during some of the night
>   hours.
> Total lack of sleep makes us ill.
> Let them out; what they pay you for screeching
> We will pay if only you keep still.

Imperial Aqueducts A Roman aqueduct in Segovia, Spain, is one of many that the Romans built to transport clean water to cities throughout the empire. This one is 11 miles (17 km) long and was built around 100 CE.

The empire, like the Republic before it, also produced notable historians, political commentators, and—more than any other ancient society—agricultural writers. All writers unless rich themselves needed patrons, a role that emperors often filled. As a result, much writing was drivel meant to flatter the powerful. But the best flirted with the indistinct line of what was permitted and occasionally, like Ovid's poetry, stepped over.

Roman architecture has proved to be as enduring as Roman literature. In addition to their roads, bridges, and aqueducts, Roman engineers and architects sprinkled the landscape with temples, theaters, amphitheaters, and triumphal arches, many of which survive to this day. The precision, design, and craftsmanship involved have attracted wonder for 2,000 years. The heavy lifting, of course, was done by slaves and laborers.

Rome provided its full share of popular culture, enjoyed by rich and poor alike, and sometimes deliberately sponsored by the rich to keep the poor amused and distracted. Chariot races were the most popular sport, held in amphitheaters all over the empire. The largest, the Circus Maximus in the heart of Rome, could hold crowds of 250,000 people. (Ovid said it was a good place to meet members of the opposite sex.) Charioteers were full-time professionals, usually slaves of wealthy men who took pride in their athletic teams' achievements. Supporters bet on the races and often brawled with other fans, just like modern soccer hooligans. The crowds attracted

by Roman chariot racing count as the largest for sporting events in world history to date.

Gladiatorial combat, an Etruscan tradition, was another favorite entertainment in imperial Rome. It took several forms. Professional gladiators (again, often slaves) might battle one another to the death. Their careers were normally short; one, however, a certain Publius Ostorius, allegedly won 51 bouts in a row. Sometimes amateurs, often convicts, fought one another. People fought animals. Animals fought animals. Trajan celebrated his conquests with combats in which 11,000 animals were killed, hastening the extinction of North Africa's elephants and hippos as well as Mesopotamia's lions. The emperor Domitian arranged combats in which women battled dwarves.

These and other entertainments—comic theater, poetry readings, footraces—helped keep the populace amused. Together with frequent handouts of grain, they formed the combination of "bread and circuses" that the satirist Juvenal mockingly identified as the main concern of Romans of his day (ca. 100 CE.)

SOCIETY AND FAMILY

The available literary texts tell us far more about Roman aristocrats (well under 1 percent of the population) than about the lower classes. Archeological sites such as Pompeii—a city in southern Italy frozen in time by smothering volcanic ash in 79 CE—or several in Rome itself help fill the gaps.

Circus Maximus Charioteers race around the track at the Circus Maximus and spectators cheer from the sidelines in a relief from first-century CE Rome.

SLAVERY Slaves stood at the bottom of the social pyramid. Under the empire they accounted for perhaps 12 to 18 percent of the population, more in the earlier centuries and less later when conquests slowed down. Whereas in the time of the Republic most slaves were war captives taken in Italy or Greece, now they mainly came as trade goods from lands north of the Danube and east of the Rhine. Some came from Nubia via Egypt, and others from the Black Sea shores. Rural slaves worked as farm laborers or shepherds. Urban slaves toiled as artisans, construction workers, cooks, nurses, domestics, messengers, and in some cases secretaries and tutors. The least fortunate worked in mines, where life expectancy was short, or as gladiators. Rich people owned slaves as much for the prestige it conferred as for the profit their labor might provide.

Manumission of slaves was common, more so than elsewhere in the Old World web, and too common for Augustus, who restricted it. Former slaves, or freedmen, still owed allegiance to their former masters, who owed some measure of protection to their freedmen. Freedmen became the clients of rich patrons and fit tidily into Roman social structure that way. Augustus employed some as middling officials. Freedmen often made a living through commerce, which was beneath the dignity of noble Romans. A few freedmen became wealthy businessmen, and if male they could become citizens. Normally there were limits on the social mobility of freedmen. They couldn't hold high office and couldn't marry aristocrats. The children of freedmen, however, were citizens: one emperor, Pertinax, who reigned for three months in 193 after a brilliant army career, was the son of a freedman. In time, some senators counted slaves among their ancestors.

PLEBEIANS The majority of the people were commoners—or **plebeians**, meaning citizens not from elite families. Plebeians performed many of the same jobs that slaves did; but unlike slaves, the plebeians were paid for their work. In the city of Rome, they lived in flimsy multi-story wooden tenements. Most lived hand-to-mouth, and the emperors' periodic handouts of free grain were important to their survival. In the countryside, plebeians worked as farm laborers, often alongside slaves, sometimes as supervisors of slaves. Women specialized in spinning and weaving cloth, often done on country estates (latifundia) as well as in towns. Some plebeians grew wealthy, however—either as clients of rich patrons or, for some few, on their own.

MARRIAGE AND THE FAMILY Marriage remained, as in the Republic, a property contract and, in political families, an alliance. Elite Roman men had long viewed wives, like children and slaves, as a human form of property. The senator Cato the Elder (234–149 BCE) found it shocking that women might lobby for the repeal of a law restricting lavish display of jewelry and finery, and he complained that "We rule the world and our wives rule us." He lost; the law was repealed. But that didn't change the patriarchal nature of marriage.

Toward the end of the Republic, a shift took place in marriage law and practice that allowed women to remain under the authority of their fathers even after marriage, rather than of their husbands. They could now inherit

Women at Home A richly colored fresco preserved at Pompeii in 79 CE shows elite women in the home, making preparations for a religious ritual.

from their parents without turning property over to their husbands. This enabled families to keep their property intact even if several daughters married, and it reduced the incentive to kill baby girls. Child abandonment remained commonplace, however, as many babies were unwanted. Divorce was legal and routine among the upper classes, for whom shifting political winds might make an old alliance unhelpful and a new one desirable. Affectionate marriage was considered remarkable among the upper classes. Girls married at 13 to 16 years of age, usually to much older men.

Girls prepared for marriage from an early age. But by the second century CE, urban girls sometimes received formal education as well, learning basic literacy before marriage, when their schooling stopped. A very few women managed to participate in the lively intellectual world of Rome. Graffiti from Pompeii show that while women couldn't hold office and had no political rights, they occasionally endorsed candidates for office. Women moved about in public and didn't remain in seclusion at home, unlike women in many eastern Mediterranean cities. They attended sporting events and spectacles, although at gladiatorial combats they were confined to the topmost seats farthest from the action.

The Roman authors of the early empire complain bitterly about the slipping moral standards of the elite. There was too little traditional virtue, too many childless marriages, and too much adultery, abortion, divorce, and vice. Women spent too much money on clothing—such as Chinese silks—that concealed too little. Augustus agreed and, like many before and after him, tried to legislate

Women in Public A first-century BCE marble relief shows two women working as butchers in a market stall, dressing and selling poultry, pigs, and rabbit.

virtue and increase population. He offered tax breaks for big families and more legal rights for women with three or more children. (Augustus himself had only one child, a daughter whose scandalous adultery earned her exile.) He penalized widows for not re-marrying quickly and criminalized adultery, imposing tougher penalties for women than for men. As usual, class and rank mattered: married men could blithely have sexual relationships with women of low birth, slaves, or prostitutes. Several later emperors, not just Caligula and Egalabalus, gleefully broke all Roman sexual taboos. To what extent the masses and provincials imitated the elite in these respects is unclear, but early Christian writers found no shortage of licentiousness to rail against.

THE BEGINNING OF THE END

Licentious or not, under rulers good and bad, the Roman Empire lasted for centuries after these complaints. Few emperors were better than Marcus Aurelius (r. 161–180). He came from a prominent family in southern Spain, allied to the emperor Hadrian. Young Marcus studied too much for his health, according to his biographer. He excelled in literature, oratory, and philosophy; and like Alexander the Great, he had a particular fondness for Homer's epics. Under Hadrian's patronage he began a public career, worked his way up the ladder, became consul at age 23, married well, and fathered 13 children. He was adopted by Hadrian's successor and groomed for the top job.

As emperor he was disciplined, diligent, calm, and modest. At one point he sold his palace furniture to help balance the imperial budget. He led the army in person on campaigns along the Danube and in Anatolia. His greatest character flaw was that he wrote repetitive and unoriginal philosophical treatises—a harmless defect by any standards, let alone those of Roman emperors.

But even a stalwart emperor such as Marcus Aurelius couldn't overcome the problems that now beset the Roman Empire. In 165 CE troops returning from war with the Parthians brought back an epidemic—perhaps smallpox, perhaps multiple diseases—that killed possibly 10 to 15 percent of the empire's population. The epidemic reached as far as Gaul and legions on the Rhine. The very success of the empire in building connections among far-flung places, by land and sea, created the conditions for epidemics to sear through entire populations quickly. Marcus Aurelius had to call off planned offensives against tribes along the Danube. He couldn't prevent Germanic tribes from marauding through northern Italy in 167. Italy had been safe from foreign invasion since Hannibal nearly 400 years before, so this failure came as a shock. Marcus Aurelius was reduced to the expedient of inviting some 10,000 Germanic tribesmen to settle inside Roman territory, hoping they would prove loyal to him and fight for Rome against other tribes. Rome, which had enjoyed a manpower advantage in its wars for seven centuries, now depended on the kindness of strangers.

That was the very beginning of the end for the empire. As we will see, it was mostly downhill after the travails of Marcus Aurelius. He died without adopting a promising young man as heir and left the empire to his biological son, a disastrous choice. In a few more years Roman coins were nearly worthless, almost every general tried to make himself emperor, and civil war was as routine as in the dying days of the Republic. In 260 CE Iranian forces (under a new dynasty called Sasanians) managed to capture an emperor and treated him as a living footstool before killing and skinning him. Things had changed since the time of Augustus. And still Rome limped on.

CONCLUSION

Indeed, much had changed since the time when Phoenician settlers sailed forth to plant a new colony at Carthage roughly a millennium before Marcus Aurelius's death. The little colony became a seaborne empire, pioneering trade routes throughout the western Mediterranean and into the Atlantic Ocean. In the Punic Wars it lost its dominant position to a rapidly rising Rome. Colonists, traders, travelers, scholars, slaves, and soldiers now crisscrossed the Mediterranean, linking Spain to Syria and Egypt to Italy. As Polybius put it, soon after the final destruction of Carthage in 146 BCE:

> Now in earlier times the world's history has consisted, so to speak, of a series of unrelated episodes, the origins and results of each being as widely separated as their localities, but from this point onward history becomes an organic whole: the daily affairs of Italy and Africa are connected with those of Asia and Greece, and all events bear a relationship and contribute to a single end.

For Polybius, Africa meant North Africa only, and Asia meant only Southwest Asia. He was witnessing the effect of centuries of Carthaginian, Greek, and Roman integration of the Mediterranean world. By 200 CE it had become the most tightly integrated large space in the world, a Mediterranean-centered web held together by the power, economy, and culture of the Roman Empire.

But Rome did not stop there. Its soldiers, diplomats, traders, and colonists extended its political, cultural, and economic connections well beyond the Mediterranean, to the banks of the Thames, Rhine, Danube, and Euphrates. And its neighbors in Persia and Arabia sporadically carried its silver—if little else—to India. Through relay trade, its silver, and again little else, went as far as the East Asian web. Together, the Roman world and the Chinese-centered East Asian world made up the nodes of the Old World web.

CHAPTER REVIEW

KEY TERMS

Tyre (p. 209)
Phoenicia (p. 209)
Carthage (p. 210)
Punic Wars (p. 213)

Hannibal Barca (p. 213)
Julius Caesar (p. 220)
Octavian (p. 221)
praetorian guard (p. 223)

Queen Boudica (p. 226)
plebeians (p. 234)

Go to INQUIZITIVE to see what you've learned—and learn what you've missed—with personalized feedback along the way.

REVIEW QUESTIONS

1. How was the basis of the Carthaginians' empire different from that of the empires of Sargon, Cyrus, and Shi Huangdi?

2. What seafaring innovations did the Phoenicians pioneer?

3. What prompted the merchants of Tyre to found Carthage?

4. In what ways was Carthage like Athens?

5. How did the Barca clan change the Carthaginian presence in Spain?

6. What was the legacy of the Carthaginians' empire for trade and commerce?

7. How did slavery and citizenship contribute to Rome's military success?

8. What practices and institutions minimized the outbreak of conflict and civil war in Rome prior to 91 BCE?

9. In what ways did the success of the Roman Republic's political system change Roman politics following the Second Punic War?

10. What measures did Augustus institute in the Senate, the army, the state, and for the public to ensure his power?

11. Why did Rome's frontiers stabilize, and how did this stabilization undermine Rome's economy?

12. What was Rome's response to Christianity prior to 200 CE?

FURTHER READING

Mary BEARD, *SPQR: A History of Ancient Rome* (2016). A prominent classicist's coverage of both the Republic and the empire in accessible prose.

Brian CAMPBELL, *The Romans and Their World* (2011). A recent and compact survey, emphasizing the military dimensions.

Nick CONSTABLE, *Historical Atlas of Ancient Rome* (2003). An overview that's great for maps and illustrations and very quick treatments of major events and themes.

Robin Lane FOX, *The Classical World* (2006). A readable survey of the Greeks and Romans through the mid-second century CE.

Robert GARLAND, *Hannibal* (2010). A very short and readable biography of the Carthaginian commander.

Dexter HOYOS, *Mastering the West: Rome and Carthage at War* (2015). Perhaps the best study of the Punic Wars.

Serge LANCEL, *Carthage: A History* (1995). An overview by the leading archeologist of Carthage.

Richard MILES, *Carthage Must Be Destroyed: The Rise and Fall of an Ancient Civilization* (2011). Now the most authoritative study, and easy to read.

CHRONOLOGY

by ca. 18,000 BCE
People occupy entire African continent

ca. 9000–3000 BCE
Sahara is mostly grassland with lakes and rivers

ca. 7500–6000 BCE
Farming and farmers arrive in mainland Greece

ca. 6500–5500 BCE
Farming emerges in Danube River basin and loess zones of Europe; menhirs appear

ca. 7000 BCE
Domestication of cattle in Africa; people occupy every area of Europe

ca. 6000 BCE
Pastoralism becomes dominant way of life in the Sahara

ca. 4500–2000 BCE
Group burials and stone monuments spread widely within western Europe

ca. 3000 BCE
Pastoralism spreads to East Africa

ca. 2900 BCE
Bell beaker ware appears

ca. 2500 BCE
Agriculture begins in Africa; Stonehenge is built

ca. 2200 BCE
Bronze making begins in Europe

ca. 1800 BCE
Iron working appears in Anatolia

ca. 1300–700 BCE
Emergence of Celts

ca. 1100–1000 BCE
Iron working appears in Europe

ca. 900–800 BCE
Cimmerians migrate westward into Europe

ca. 800–500 BCE
Iron working reaches parts of East and West Africa

by 800 BCE
Iron working is well established in eastern and central Europe

ca. 1000 BCE
Rice cultivation begins in Africa; earliest uncontested evidence of iron working in Africa; states and kings emerge in Nubia

after 600 BCE
Mediterranean luxury goods flow northward into central Europe

ca. 500–200 BCE
Mass migration of Celts

ca. 300 BCE– 100 CE
Meröe thrives

9

On the Frontiers of the Old World Web

AFRICA AND EUROPE TO 200 CE

by 100–450 CE
Jenne thrives

ca. 300 CE
Camel caravans
across the
Sahara begin

ca. 300–500 CE
Aksum thrives

Around 2900 BCE a new fashion craze took Europe and North Africa by storm. **Bell beaker ware**—clay vessels shaped like an upside-down bell and developed many centuries before—became all the rage. The first examples came from (today's) Portugal, and within a few centuries everyone from Morocco to Poland and Hungary to Ireland wanted the new pots.

In most cases, bell beaker ware spread because people valued it and learned how to make it. In most of Europe, it's found mainly along trade routes, especially those along rivers and shorelines. But in the British Isles, genetic evidence suggests that arriving peoples came with the pots. The appearance of beaker ware in the archeological record coincides with the appearance in the genetic record of a new population, apparently from what is now the Netherlands. There was, it seems, an invasion of Britain by people bringing new pottery. There is no sign of violence or conquest.

Beaker ware had several uses. For families, it could hold the ashes of cremated relatives for burial. In metallurgy, it could contain super-hot molten

Cities of Africa The Temple of Amun rises above the ruins of the city of Naqa, part of the prosperous kingdom of Meroë that flourished in the area of present-day Sudan between the fourth century BCE and the fourth century CE. The temple is dedicated to the Egyptian god Amun, reflecting one of many ways in which Egyptian culture influenced Meroitic culture.

FOCUS QUESTIONS

1. What commonalities were shared by Africans and Europeans living outside the Nile-Ganges web?

2. What was distinctive about Africa's environments and early transitions to agriculture?

3. Why did Africans organize themselves into more fluid societies than peoples elsewhere?

4. What was distinctive about Europe's environments and early transitions to agriculture?

5. How was the impact of iron technology different in Europe than in Africa?

6. How did the development of Mediterranean Europe affect people in northern and eastern Europe?

(liquid) copper. But the primary purpose of beaker ware is evident in the many pots dug up by archeologists that retain chemical residues of beer. The introduction of beaker ware to new lands often coincided with an upsurge in the cultivation of barley—a key ingredient of beer. Indeed, it seems that the invention and spread of beaker ware is associated with the first use of alcohol in European culture.

The bell beaker ware phenomenon shows that by 2000 BCE something of a commercial and cultural web-in-the-making existed among elites in Europe. People in Poland may have been unaware of people

in Portugal, but they made the same kinds of pots and used them for the same purposes. About 1800 BCE, people stopped making bell beaker ware. Beer drinking continued, but the connections among Europe's elites eventually weakened by 1000 BCE: the web-in-the-making frayed, only to be rewoven.

In Africa, as we'll see below, the invention of iron working after 1000 BCE had a broadly similar web-building effect. African communities developed a loose network of ironsmiths, as well as more long-distance trade in iron goods such as farming tools, weapons, and ornaments. Iron-bladed hoes made it easier to prepare ground for planting. The few faint webs of interaction that developed in sub-Saharan Africa were, as in Europe, fragile and far from permanent. Sustaining webs was always easier and likelier where complex hierarchical society and states existed, such as in Southwest Asia or East Asia. However, Europe and Africa stood on the edges of the robust web uniting the lands between Egypt and the Indus. They built their own smaller and more fragile webs by 200 CE, and became increasingly linked to the more populous, more durable, and bigger web linking Egypt to India.

In many presentations of world history, Europe is not on the margins but at the center. In every account of human origins and evolution, Africa is at the center. But in this chapter, which deals with Africa south of the Sahara and Europe outside the Roman Empire, they are both at the frontiers. In the millennia between the end of the last ice age (say 12,000 BCE) and 200 CE, Africa and Europe stood in the wings, not at center stage. And they had a lot in common.

COMMONALITIES OF AFRICANS AND EUROPEANS

People in Europe and Africa were few in number. Before farming came to Europe, its population is estimated at

Bell Beaker Ware Culture By 2000 BCE, the same type of clay pots, shaped like inverted bells, were being used from eastern to western Europe. These beakers were found (left to right) in Spain, England, and Hungary.

below 200,000 for the entire sub-continent from the Atlantic to the Ural Mountains. As almost everywhere, agriculture allowed higher population densities than did hunting and foraging. So by 3000 BCE, when farming villages dotted the landscape, Europeans numbered perhaps 1 to 2 million; and by 1000 BCE, perhaps 5 to 10 million.

For early Africa, we can only guess at population totals due to the paucity of archeological work. Even after the emergence of irrigation agriculture in Egypt, the entire continent in 1000 BCE had under 7 million people. In 200 CE, when Egypt had 3 to 5 million people and the Han Empire in China perhaps 50 million, Africa beyond Egypt had roughly 10 million. The population density of Han China was dozens of times greater than that of (non-Egyptian) Africa or (non-Roman) Europe.

Africans and Europeans, in addition to being few and scattered, lived in small-scale polities outside Mediterranean lands. Low population densities meant plenty of open space. People could wander off rather than accept the discipline and subordination required of all but a privileged few in the hierarchies of complex societies and states. Most people lived in chiefdoms or smaller units, and very few, even at 200 CE, lived within states. Their societies exhibited little of the hierarchy so pronounced in China, India, Mesopotamia, or Egypt after 2000 BCE. While the roles of men and women were clearly defined in early Africa and Europe, gender inequality was probably less sharp in most communities than in the great centers of population such as Mesopotamia or China. African and European technologies, and probably religious ideas too, changed more slowly than did those of peoples within the webs of West and East Asia.

The basic reason behind the similarities of Africans and Europeans in this period is that both regions were on the margins of the Nile-Ganges web and, to greater or lesser extent, removed from the upheavals and innovations underway there. The peoples closest to this web, in the middle Nile region or the middle and lower Danube, for example, felt powerful influences coming from Egypt and Southwest Asia—both as examples to emulate and as pressures that they wished to avoid.

Africans and Europeans were vulnerable to enslavement. Egypt, Mesopotamia, and the Roman Mediterranean—the western end of the Old World web—imported people as slaves to perform unpleasant work and to make up for the high death rates that urban life and irrigation agriculture entailed. So people close to the web, and sometimes those not so close, suffered routinely from slave raiding. Sometimes their leaders took part in slave trading to buttress their own wealth. Among Africans, those living in the upper Nile and Horn of Africa region probably ran the highest risks of enslavement and export to the cities and fields of the Old World web. Among Europeans, those around the shores of the Black Sea probably suffered most at the hands of slavers.

Europeans and Africans living farthest from the web, in Scandinavia or southern Africa, remained substantially isolated and more at liberty to chart their own course than peoples in the web. Africans and Europeans were, in general, taller, healthier, and freer than the subordinated peasants of Egypt, Mesopotamia, or China. But their societies were less militarily formidable, less resistant to many deadly diseases, and less organized for the production of surplus than those of complex societies within the world's webs.

Sub-Saharan Africa and northern Europe stood semi-isolated from the world's big webs. As we have seen, between 3500 BCE and 200 CE big webs of interaction developed between Egypt and India, and another in East Asia, with dense populations at many places and great social complexity. Taking these two big webs together, they probably accounted for two-thirds, maybe even three-quarters, of humankind at 200 CE. Everywhere else in the world was peripheral both in demographic terms and with respect to the pace of technological change and the overall volume of intersocietal and intercultural contacts. Sub-Saharan Africa and non-Roman Europe weren't fully isolated from the great webs stretching between India and the Mediterranean, but they weren't part of those webs either. They were on the frontiers, the far reaches of the interactive world. And people there were probably better off for it—at least, in terms of health and freedom from taxes and conscription.

AFRICA TO 1000 BCE

Africa accounts for one-fifth of the world's land area. It is 4,000 miles (7,000 km) from the Cape of Good Hope to the Mediterranean Sea, and almost as far from the coasts of Senegal to Somalia's. Africa stands astride the equator: most of it lies within the tropics, and none of it extends further than 37 degrees north or south. So except at altitude, it is usually warm or hot. The great ice sheets of the last ice age never touched Africa.

EVOLVING ENVIRONMENTS

About 40 percent of Africa is now desert. The Sahara accounts for most of that, but smaller deserts exist, especially in the southwest of the continent. This proportion has varied considerably with climate change over the millennia, as we'll see shortly. Rain forest accounts for another 8 percent or so of the continent, mostly in West and Central Africa. This proportion, too, has fluctuated over the long haul with climate change, and it has shrunk in recent decades through forest burning and logging. Most of Africa is, and usually has been, savanna grassland. A broad belt runs across the continent south of the Sahara, and most of East and southern Africa is also

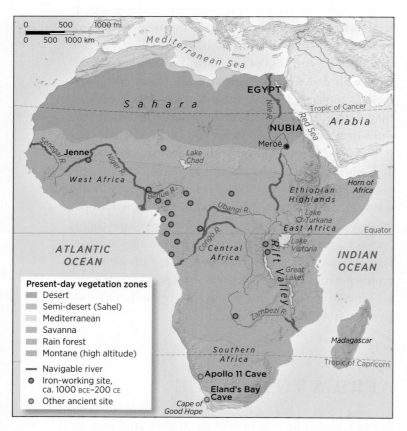

Ecological Zones of Africa Rainfall is the primary determinant of ecological zones in Africa. More falls around the equator than elsewhere. Well-watered areas supported forests, where abundant wood supplied fuel for early iron making. Over the centuries, rainfall patterns have shifted somewhat, so this current map provides only an approximation of the ecological zones in the distant past.

mainly savanna or mixed savanna and parkland (meaning grassland with occasional clumps of trees).

The most important variable determining the land cover is rainfall: the more rain, the thicker the vegetation. Climate changes in Africa have raised and lowered temperatures, but rarely enough to matter for human occupation. What has mattered, tremendously, are variations in rainfall. Rainfall shifts that endured for decades or centuries obliged societies to move or change their ways.

Africa is an old continent geologically, with soils that are for the most part weathered and low in nutrients. Its native plants and animals, having evolved in this environment, use nutrients sparingly. But still the agricultural potential of most African landscapes is limited by their soils. The main exceptions lie in and around the geological rift running through East Africa from the Great Lakes northward through Ethiopia. Here young rock from volcanic eruptions has weathered into rich soils.

It is important to remember one other feature of African geography: the avenues of, and obstacles to, transport. Three big African rivers are well suited for boat traffic: the Nile, the Niger, and the Congo. They all have waterfalls or rapids here and there, as most rivers do, so it was hard to travel their entire length. But long stretches were navigable by dugout canoe. Other rivers, however, were less useful in this respect, and in the drier parts of the continent there was no alternative to walking.

Africa's coastlines are mostly sand beaches, frequently pounded by surf. With few natural harbors, bays, offshore islands, and archipelagoes to protect vessels from ocean wind and surf, there was little chance for maritime cultures to develop in Africa. People were sailing to Australia from New Guinea some 50,000 years ago, and others almost surely sailing or paddling from Siberia to Alaska, and southward along the Pacific coast of Canada some 15,000 years ago. As we've seen, Polynesians sailed the open Pacific thousands of years ago. But no such precocious maritime culture existed in early African history, except along the Red Sea linking Egypt with the Horn of Africa.

AFRICA BEFORE FARMING AND HERDING

When small bands of humans left Africa about 100,000 years ago and started to occupy the rest of the globe, Africans who stayed behind were doing something similar at home. They, too, were highly mobile hunters and foragers, often settling in for a few months at one place or another, but rarely for longer periods. By 20,000 years ago, if not before, they had occupied the entire continent. Africans improved their hunting and fishing toolkits, to judge by the surviving stone evidence. They took up art, using a red ochre to decorate some rock shelters and making beads from ostrich egg shells in southern Africa. A rock painting in Apollo 11 Cave, in today's Namibia, dates to about 20,000 years ago and shows what appear to be a giraffe, a rhinoceros, and some sort of wild cat.

Like most hunting and foraging people, Africans lived in small bands connected mainly by kinship. Population density and birth rates were low, as among all hunting and foraging peoples. So they rarely encountered other human groups. When they did so, sometimes it was by design—a gathering of a clan to exchange gifts, information, and young people in marriages. Their ways of life changed only slowly. They didn't have to change quickly: Africans knew how to exploit their environments and were too few in number to imperil those environments.

Climate change—specifically, dry periods—made life harder at times. Some genetic evidence suggests that African populations fell during dry millennia such as 25,000 to 12,000 years ago. This was the last stage of the last ice age, when most of Africa was a little cooler and much drier. Lake Victoria, today the world's largest lake, vanished entirely around 11,000 BCE, and sand dunes blocked the flow of the Niger River. The Sahara crept southward about 300 miles (500 km). The savanna grasslands in West Africa shifted southward, and West Africa's rain forests shrank to a narrow coastal strip.

These were hard times. People had to move off the dried-out savannas, to forest edges, river banks, or sea-shores, where food supplies were more reliable. For example, at around 12,500 BCE in Elands Bay Cave in southern Africa, near the ocean, people found tortoises, mussels, seals, flamingoes, pelicans, cormorants, gulls, rock lobsters, and a variety of fish to eat. Fortunately, they failed to tidy up after themselves, leaving shells and bones galore for archeologists to study. The climate improved (for humans, at least) after about 10,000 BCE, bringing more rain more often over more of Africa.

Although they all lived by hunting, fishing, and foraging before 2500 BCE, in some ways these Africans were highly diverse. As we saw in Chapter 1, the genetic diversity among Africans today is greater than that among all other humans. That would have been true 50,000 and 10,000 years ago as well. Africans also spoke a great variety of languages. Linguists lump modern African languages into broad families but estimate that perhaps 700 to 1,000 languages are spoken today. Low population density, low levels of interaction, and lots of opportunity for isolation produce a condition favorable to the development of both genetic and language diversity.

Four language families in particular seem to have prospered and spread when the long dry spell ended and conditions improved. In northeast Africa, Afro-Asiatic-speakers lived along the Red Sea coast and by 10,000 BCE were harvesting wild grains. Nilo-Saharan-speakers, based in the upper reaches of the Nile in today's Sudan, made their living mainly by hunting and fishing. In West Africa, a group called Niger-Congo-speakers coalesced, living by collecting yams, hunting, and fishing. Last, in East Africa lived a group called Khoisan-speakers, also hunters and foragers. Today, most African languages fall into one of these four families.

EARLY PASTORALISM

With so much savanna grassland, Africa offered good habitat for grass-eating animals such as gazelles, wildebeest, zebra, and, in places, cattle. For thousands of years, Africans had hunted them and had scavenged kills made by big cats and other carnivores. As it happens, few of

Pastoralism This small terra-cotta model of a bull from the area of present-day Sudan dates to between 2300 and 1600 BCE. Cattle herding was central to the structure of many African societies by the late millennia BCE.

Africa's grazing animals can be domesticated. They're just too feisty. But, as we've seen, one of the earliest and most important animal domestications probably took place in Africa: cattle. It probably happened about 7000 BCE somewhere in what is now Sudan or southern Egypt. And it launched a new way of life for some Africans.

From about 9000 to 3000 BCE, the Sahara, far wetter than today, was mostly grassland dotted with lakes and threaded with rivers. In the millennia after 8000 BCE, a pastoral way of life gradually took hold over much of northern Africa, based on cattle and, probably no later than 6000 BCE, also on sheep and goats introduced from Southwest Asia. These three animals would become the basis of African pastoralism ever after.

Before going any further, we must pause and reflect upon the term *pastoralist* in the African context. Evidence both modern and archeological indicates that people might practice herding as an exclusive way of life or might mix it with hunting; with hunting, fishing, and foraging; or with seasonal agriculture. Moreover, people changed their chosen mix over time, depending on climate, new technologies that made one or another pursuit more appealing, and a host of other factors. The Khoisan-speakers of southernmost Africa, for example, shifted in and out of pastoralism in response to climate shifts and other factors. So pastoralist is a fuzzy term and not a category in which people conveniently stayed put forever. While that is true elsewhere too, the category is probably more fluid in African history than, for example, in the steppe lands of Asia.

When the Sahara was grassland speckled with lakes, pastoralism proved appealing there. After 6000 BCE it was the predominant way of life, replacing an earlier one in which fishing featured prominently. Rock art and artifacts such as pottery show remarkable similarity in styles throughout the Sahara both before and after the shift to pastoralism, which implies high mobility and regular interaction among the Saharan peoples. Pastoralism spread into East Africa by 3000 BCE and into southern Africa around 1 CE. Throughout Africa, pastoralists kept female animals for milking. They kept a few males around to ensure the future of their flocks and herds, but they didn't for the most part castrate bulls and use them as oxen, as was often done in Asia and Egypt. Instead, most young male animals were killed for their meat. In some pastoralist societies, people also often drank the blood of

Pastoralist Society Numerous pendants and earrings were found among the remains of hundreds of sheep herders buried in the rock near Lake Turkana, in present-day Kenya, about 5,300 years ago. The items indicate the level of modest prosperity this society enjoyed.

their animals or mixed it with milk. Some African pastoralists (as we've seen) underwent genetic changes enabling adults to digest milk, but others did not.

Animal diseases or drought might ravage herds suddenly, so resilience was always on pastoralists' minds. It was crucial to take good care of females of breeding age. In times of drought, herders might have to move long distances. They might have to encroach on other groups' grass and water, risking conflict. They might trade or eat some of their animals, but they always tried to keep possession of some breeding stock. Although we have no evidence about it, the adoption of pastoralism by hunters and foragers must have changed ideas and practices about property and ownership in much of Africa.

The best evidence we have of social conditions among early African pastoralists comes from the area around Lake Turkana in northern Kenya. Around 3000 or 2500 BCE, sheep herders there began to bury their dead in pits carved into bedrock. This took a lot of work, and no one knows why they did it or why after 700 years they stopped. They buried some 600 to 1,000 people: men, women, and children together, carefully arranged, with modest ornamentation including, in one case, a necklace of gerbil teeth. It was apparently a rather egalitarian society, but one with a considerable capacity for working together toward a common purpose.

EARLY AGRICULTURE

Chapter 2 explained the general circumstances surrounding the transition to farming in Africa. It occurred as the Sahara was getting dryer, its lakes and rivers shrinking, and its inhabitants inclined to experiment because business as usual—gathering, fishing, and hunting—was getting less rewarding. It might have occurred in several places along what is now the southern fringe of the Sahara, or it might have happened only once and spread to other environments with the same pressures. It probably began around 2500 BCE, long after pastoralism had taken hold in Africa. The first crops were sorghums and millets, which prospered in savanna conditions and withstood drought fairly well. Rice later joined the mix in West Africa, perhaps by 1000 BCE.

As with pastoralism, a few cautionary points are in order about our understanding of farming and farmers in African history. First of all, as usual, there's a great deal

Women and Agriculture Reliefs on a pot made in the West African Nok culture during the sixth century BCE show women, carrying children on their backs, harvesting crops.

we don't know and probably never will know about it. The archeological record is so spotty that, for example, native African crops (pearl millet, sorghum, cowpeas) turn up in South Asian archeological sites around 2000 BCE, long before they do in East African ones—where they must have been in use before being carried to India.

Second, the transitions to farming in Africa were less decisive and important for Africans than such transitions were for most people elsewhere. Unlike wheat or rice, African crops by and large didn't store well, so they were less suited for hoarding and trading and harder to convert into political power. This made them less practical as a basis for state making or long-distance exchanges. It also reduced the incentive to produce surplus crops. Thus Africans had less interest in spreading agriculture to every available patch of ground than did people in rice or wheat lands.

Third, African agriculture was normally women's work. Partly because of thin soils but mainly because of the absence of oxen or water buffalo, Africans outside of Egypt and Ethiopia didn't use plows. Farmers scratched the earth with digging sticks to plant their crops. It was arduous work but didn't require much physical strength, unlike handling a plow harnessed to a powerful animal.

Fourth, as with pastoralism, Africans moved in and out of farming as climate change, migrations, or other forces and factors directed. In the river valleys from Egypt to China, once people turned to agriculture their populations surged and they couldn't turn back to their former ways. They lived on ribbons of irrigated ground surrounded by desert or steppe and couldn't easily wander off to new lands. They were in an ecological cul-de-sac, committed to irrigation agriculture and its tremendous yields, with no going back. Africans lived differently, with more geographic mobility, and more fluidity and flexibility in their ways of life.

For most Africans, over many millennia, farming wasn't an attractive option. Hunting, foraging, and fishing were preferable, and there was always more room in which to do it. Farming was more work without any more reward. And it required people to stay put and defend their land against attackers, whereas foragers and hunters could walk away from conflict at little cost.

So it took quite some time for farming to spread throughout the continent. It remained rare in the Great Lakes region of east-central Africa until 1000 BCE. From there, sorghum and millets spread southward, reaching South Africa about 300 CE. In West Africa, the first archeological dates for sorghum, rice, okra, and cowpeas are around 500 BCE, although cultivation, especially of yams, might have begun much earlier without leaving a trace. By 1000 BCE, most Africans north of the equator lived as farmers or pastoralists or some mix of the two. South of the equator, hunting and foraging prevailed. Everywhere (except Egypt and Nubia), Africans lived in small groups with no states, no cities, minimal hierarchy, and unusual freedom to live as they pleased.

AFRICA, 1000 BCE TO 200 CE

After 1000 BCE, farming and pastoralism, and various combinations of the two, continued to spread in Africa. Part of the reason for the expansion of farming was iron.

IRON WORKING

Before 1000 BCE, almost all Africans used tools and weapons of stone and wood, not metal. Although copper smelting appeared in Nubia by 2600 BCE and in the central Sahara by 1000 BCE, Africa has no equivalent eras to those in Mesopotamia or China when bronze was widely important for weaponry and art. Iron, however, made a big difference in Africa.

Iron making, as we've seen, is technically difficult work. It's even harder to do it if there's no tradition of working bronze, an easier process that in Asia preceded and probably led to **iron working**. In the pre-Columbian Americas, no one ever figured out how to make useful metal out of iron ore, which isn't surprising. The surprise is that anyone in the ancient world did figure it out. The earliest iron working in world history appears to be in Anatolia, begun about 1800 BCE and reaching a large scale by 1200 BCE.

Archeologists cannot agree on how, where, and when iron working arose in Africa. The raw material, iron ore, is widespread throughout the continent. The earliest uncontested archeological evidence dates from about 1000 BCE and comes from the Great Lakes region. Early African ironsmiths used different technologies from those of Anatolia, and archeologists have found no signs of iron working prior to 1000 BCE in the lands between Egypt (where, in any case, there was virtually no iron ore) and the African Great Lakes. So it's unlikely that iron working originally entered sub-Saharan Africa from Egypt. The best guess at the moment is that iron working developed independently somewhere in Africa, perhaps at more than one place, around 1000 BCE.

No matter how it arose, iron making—always men's work—spread into the easily traversed savanna zones of East and West Africa, probably by around 800 to 500 BCE, although its adoption remained spotty. Smiths carried the secrets of iron working along river routes in central and West Africa, reaching the coastal forests there no later than 500 CE. Iron working usually remained not only the preserve of men, but the preserve of certain men acting as a guild and keeping their techniques secret from others. The sons of ironworkers tended to marry daughters of other ironworkers; and especially in West Africa, iron making became associated with certain clans, in effect forming a hereditary caste. They encouraged the view that iron working involved magic powers, a belief reflected in many African oral traditions.

African ironsmiths mainly made tools such as hoes and axes. No iron weapons have turned up in early archeological sites. This forms a sharp contrast to the work of early Anatolian smiths, who made large quantities of weapons that helped the Assyrians conquer far and wide. Early Chinese bronze workers also mass-produced weaponry. In Africa, the demand was for tools, not weapons, perhaps because stone-edged weapons were lethal enough, or perhaps because there were no big states to organize and pay for mass production.

In the forest zones of West and Central Africa, iron tools opened new possibilities. Felling trees to create a forest clearing for planting is extremely slow work when done with stone axes—so slow that almost no one bothered to do it. Iron axes, sharper and more durable than stone ones, made it sufficiently rewarding that frontier farmers increasingly slipped into the forests and hacked out clearings to plant yams. In southeastern and southern Africa there was very little agriculture at all before iron tools made it easier to clear forest and break sod.

Early Iron Working This object, made of forged iron, was found in 2018 in the Irougou Cave in Gabon in West-Central Africa, along with hundreds of human bones and many other metallic objects. It is about 2 feet (70 cm) long and might have been used as a form of money.

Everywhere, iron was the enemy of trees. To make enough iron for three hoe blades took one ton of charcoal, which required about four tons of fuelwood. (Charcoal is made by heating firewood and limiting oxygen to prevent full combustion.) Iron-bladed axes allowed the felling of trees for charcoal making and the clearing of ground for farming. Open ground permitted cattle and goats to graze, which prevented saplings from growing into trees. So where iron spread, forests and woodlands disappeared, replaced by fields and pastures.

MEROË The biggest single center of iron production in ancient Africa was at **Meroë**, on the Nile in the land of Kush (today's northern Sudan). It was known to Achaemenid Persian emperors and referred to by the Greek historian Herodotus as a "great city" whose people worshipped Egyptian gods such as Amun and Osiris. Meroë stood astride the river route between Egypt and sub-Saharan Africa. It occupied about one square mile and had avenues and monumental architecture in the Egyptian style. Its prosperity rested on commerce, and at its height around the first century BCE Meroë exerted a chokehold on the export of African goods (ostrich feathers, tortoise shells, ivory, elephants, and slaves) to Egypt. Meroites gave their kings fancy burials, including pyramids, and had sizeable merchant and artisan classes—a pattern of social structure unusual in Africa outside of Egypt. They wrote in the

Meroë The prosperity brought about by iron and other trading commodities allowed Meroë to build monuments such as these pyramids and temples, dated to between 800 BCE and 350 CE. The Egyptian influence on Meroite culture is evident in their architectural style.

Meroitic Script A stone altar on which offerings would be placed in a Meroite temple is decorated with images of vases and bread (representing the offerings) and inscriptions in Meroitic script, dated to between 700 and 300 BCE. Scholars have not been able to fully decipher the Meroites' script.

Egyptian language until about 200 BCE and adopted some features of Egyptian religion. But they were not Egyptians. They traced descent through mothers (matrilineal descent), a social trait unknown in Egypt but common among peoples of the central and upper Nile. And they had their own language, Meroitic. Around 200 BCE their scholars invented a Meroitic script, using an alphabet of 23 characters, which no one today knows how to read.

Meroë also had abundant iron ore and woodlands. Its artisans learned the techniques of iron making from Egyptians. Meroë's iron technologies were Mediterranean and different from those used in East or West Africa. By 300 BCE—well after iron working had independently emerged farther south in Africa—Meroë was exporting iron to Egypt and other destinations. For 400 years Meroë was Africa's chief iron-making center. According to a recent estimate, it produced 5 to 20 tons of iron per year for centuries, much of which went to Egypt. By 250 CE Meroë's iron industry was a spent force, perhaps the result of a shortage of wood for charcoal. Elsewhere, especially in East and West Africa, smiths continued to make iron tools for local use. They, more than the ironsmiths of Meroë, spread iron working within Africa and opened new landscapes to hoe agriculture.

FARMING AND HERDING FRONTIERS

Iron tools helped to reduce forest and spread farming and pastoralism in Africa, but iron was only part of the story.

Two other factors assisted in this transition, especially in the moist tropical forest zones.

The first, which we encountered in Chapter 3, was malaria. When people brought farming to forest zones and opened holes in forest canopies, they unwittingly created good conditions for malaria outbreaks. These proved devastating to populations that lacked malaria resistance. Migrating farmers, already experienced with and resistant to malaria, inadvertently thinned the ranks of peoples who hadn't previously practiced farming, making more space for themselves and their descendants.

Bananas and other Southeast Asian crops such as taro, sugarcane, and Asian yams also sped the spread of farming, especially in East and central Africa. These crops all do well in moist climates, better than sorghum and millets. They probably arrived in Africa somewhere around 1 CE. Bananas yield abundantly and pack a lot of nutrition. They have no calcium or iron, and little protein or fat, but if eaten with a little meat now and then they provide most of what a human needs. And once a banana grove is mature, it requires little work. Women probably welcomed and encouraged the spread of bananas because they require no pounding or grinding to prepare, unlike grains and most root crops. Today, Africa grows one third of the world's bananas, and the average African eats 500 lbs. (250 kilos) of bananas per year, 25 times as much as the average American.

Plantains, another tree crop from Southeast Asia, were just as useful. They grow well in very rainy areas, such as equatorial Africa, and unlike yams don't require a forest clearing and prepared ground. They out-yield yams by ten to one. One woman tending plantains or bananas could easily feed a large family.

With these new crops, as well as iron tools, farmers in moist tropical zones of Africa could reliably produce surplus food for the first time. Opportunities for long-distance trade by canoe along the rivers developed. Bananas wouldn't store for years, liked dried rice, but could keep long enough to be transported a few hundred miles along rivers. In the rain forests, farmers and ironsmiths built trade connections with hunters and foragers, who developed specializations as providers of honey, ivory, monkey meat, leopard skins, and other high-end goods. Population centers gradually emerged in places such as the shores of Lake Victoria.

Just how the Southeast Asian crops arrived in Africa is unclear. Linguistic evidence implies that they first arrived on the East African mainland at roughly 1 CE, presumably via coasting voyages around the Indian Ocean. Speakers of Austronesian languages, characteristic of Southeast Asia, settled the previously uninhabited island of Madagascar around the same time. Perhaps the Austronesians brought bananas, plantains, and other crops with them on deliberate voyages of colonization, as Polynesians did in the Pacific at roughly the same time. No matter how it happened, the addition of bananas and other Southeast Asian crops to the African farmers' repertoire paved the way for agricultural expansion and population growth, especially in moist forest zones.

Bananas and plantains didn't thrive in dry or cool areas, but cattle did. Throughout much of East Africa's savanna lands, elevations are high enough that nights are cool. Cattle keepers filled these landscapes, bringing languages and culture from the Nilotic Sudan into East Africa's savannas. Gradually, cattle herders pushed farther south, bringing pastoralism all the way to South Africa. By 200 CE, farmers and herders occupied almost the entire African continent that wasn't desert. But they remained mobile except in the most fertile areas, and their numbers probably didn't exceed 10 million.

LONG-DISTANCE TRADE

Like almost everyone else, Africans traded goods over considerable distances several thousand years ago. Archeologists have unearthed especially valuable stone, such as obsidian, which holds a sharp edge well, as much as 500 miles (300 km) from where it had been quarried. But logistics constrained trade in Africa. Except on river routes, people had to carry just about everything because there were no horses or mules, no donkeys except in northeast Africa, and no domesticated camels until about 200 CE. Heavy or bulky objects—rock salt, pottery, or ivory, for example—could only be transported in small quantities and locally, on people's heads or backs. Rivers and lakes (at least, after the development of boats) provided better options. The oldest dugout canoe yet found dates from about 4400 BCE, and it's plausible that by that time people were routinely gliding along the many rivers of Africa's well-watered zones. In the savannas and deserts, however, they had to walk, carrying trade items on their heads.

Metallurgy and then bananas improved the logic of long-distance trade from 500 BCE onward. Every man trying to carve out a forest clearing wanted an iron axe, and

CONSIDERING THE EVIDENCE

The Periplus of the Erythraean Sea

In the middle of the first century CE, an anonymous, Greek-speaking merchant who lived in Egypt wrote *The Periplus of the Erythraean Sea*. A *periplus* is basically a travel itinerary for sailors, and the Erythraean Sea is what Greek-speakers of the time called the western parts of the Indian Ocean, including the Red Sea. Though written by an outsider, the descriptive notes on sailing distances, friendly ports, products, local diets, and politics offer a fairly objective view of what people were buying and selling, as well as how they used these items. The following excerpt describes how towns controlled by Aksum, such as Coloe and Adulis in modern Eritrea, attracted merchants who brought goods from as far away as Italy, Anatolia, Egypt, Sudan, and India. As merchants traded iron and cloth for ivory, tortoise shell, and other products, they drew Aksum's modest web of exchange in northeast Africa into the expanding Old World web.

On the mainland ... lies Adulis, a fair-sized village, from which there is a three-days' journey to Coloe, an inland town and the first market for ivory. From that place to the city of the people called Auxumites [i.e., Aksumites] there is a five days' journey more; to that place all the ivory is brought from the country beyond the Nile through the district called Cyeneum [Kush], and thence to Adulis. Practically the whole number of elephants and rhinoceros that are killed live in the places inland, although at rare intervals they are hunted on the seacoast even near Adulis....

There are imported into these places, undressed [unfinished] cloth made in Egypt for the Berbers; robes from Arsinoe [near Suez in Egypt]; cloaks of poor quality dyed in colors; double-fringed linen mantles; many articles of flint glass, and others of murrhine [delicately carved stone or glass], made in Diospolis [Thebes in Egypt]; and brass, which is used for ornament and in cut pieces instead of coin; sheets of soft copper, used for cooking-utensils and cut up for bracelets and anklets for the women; iron, which is made into spears used against the elephants and other wild beasts, and in their wars. Besides these, small axes are imported, and adzes and swords; copper drinking-cups, round and large; a little coin for those coming to the market; wine of Laodicea [in Anatolia] and Italy, not much; olive oil, not much; for the king, gold and silver plate made after the fashion of the country, and for clothing, military cloaks, and

thin coats of skin, of no great value. Likewise from the district of Ariaca [in coastal northwest India] across this sea, there are imported Indian iron, and steel, and Indian cotton cloth; ... and girdles, and coats of skin and mallow-colored cloth, and a few muslins, and colored lac [resin]. There are exported from these places ivory, and tortoiseshell and rhinoceros-horn.

Source: W. H. Schoff, ed. and trans., *The Periplus of the Erythraean Sea: Travel and Trade in the Indian Ocean by a Merchant of the First Century* (London, Bombay, and Calcutta, 1912).

QUESTIONS FOR ANALYSIS

1. Why would merchants be concerned about the time it takes to travel between towns or the origins of the products available at different markets?

2. How does the writer use origin, value, quantity, material, and purpose to sort the products that are available to buy and sell in northeast Africa?

3. Given Aksum's trading contacts with merchants from India and Sudan, would you consider Aksum to be part of the Old World web or some other web? Why?

every woman digging the earth wanted an iron hoe. But iron goods were made only where ore and fuelwood, and the jealously guarded iron-making expertise, existed. As a result, many communities had to trade for iron goods. In the warm and wet parts of Africa, bananas made that easier. As noted above, they yielded so well that surplus food production became more common, and they could travel for a few weeks before rotting. All evidence, which isn't

much, suggests that trade quickened throughout much of Africa after 500 BCE. The reason the evidence is sparse is that most trade goods—cloth, food, animals—decayed in the humid and acidic soils of Africa long before archeologists could find them.

JENNE A major exception to our ignorance about ancient trade is the region of the interior delta of the Niger

Jenne and the Niger Trade System, ca. 250 BCE The Niger River was one of the best in Africa for navigation. Canoes laden with goods glided upstream and downstream, connecting people in rainforest, savanna, and Sahelian zones. At Jenne, trade routes converged with good conditions for farming, leading to dense clusters of settlement and early development of artisan crafts.

in today's Mali—specifically, the archeological site of **Jenne** (also known as Djenne and Jenne-jeno). Here clusters of settlement developed by 250 BCE. As the Sahara and West African savanna dried out and the Niger's seasonal floods grew tamer, people, probably migrants from the Sahara itself, found the alluvial lands and braided river channels around Jenne appealing. They grew rice, sorghum, and millet in the rich riverbank soils. Nearby savanna offered grass for livestock, and the river channels yielded fish. People also made tools and jewelry from iron, although there is no iron ore nearby. It had to come by canoe along the Niger. A sprawling regional trade network developed, with merchants and markets, using the river for transport. In addition to iron wares, markets offered livestock, leather, dried fish, rice, copper, and other items. Two Roman beads are tantalizing evidence of a cross-Saharan connection as well, although there is no further evidence of this. The days of trans-Saharan camel caravans lay a few centuries in the future.

By 100 CE, Jenne had as many as 2,000 inhabitants and social complexity in the form of a division of labor among specialists in metallurgy, leather working, and other crafts. By 450 CE, Jenne had grown to cover 60 acres (25 hectares). Some scholars call it a city, others a cluster of villages. There is no archeological evidence of pronounced social hierarchy. In any case, archeology at Jenne provides a rare glimpse into a vanished world of long-distance trade and markets along the Niger River.

FLUID SOCIETIES

Over the millennium before 200 CE, Africa was developing more commerce, greater specialization, and bigger, more numerous settlements. Its population was surely growing. But outside of the northeast, the region in close

touch with Egypt, it retained its small-scale political and social structures. It's possible that around 200 BCE some of the iron-producing villages southeast of Lake Victoria banded together to form a state—the evidence is ambiguous at best; but if so, it lasted a few centuries and faded away. Most Africans organized themselves into more fluid societies, built on kinship, without the formal institutions and complex hierarchies of states.

In its minimal development of states, Africa resembled Europe outside the Roman lands and differed from the prevailing pattern of the river valleys and steppe lands of Egypt and the Asian webs. The simplest explanation for this divergence is sparse population. In Africa and Europe low population density, even after the spread of farming, allowed people to move whenever they wanted. Chiefs had trouble exerting authority over people in these circumstances, especially where foodstuffs were hard to store, trade, and hoard. People had better options than submitting to political hierarchy.

African agriculture, as well as low population density, encouraged fluid societies more than state building. Africans outside of the Nile Valley didn't need major irrigation works. They built small ones here and there, but usually chose adequately rain-fed lands for their fields. This, too, helped Africans remain free of overarching authority—unlike the peasants of Egypt, Mesopotamia, or China, who found priests and bureaucrats organizing their labor on irrigation canals and dikes, and making decisions about when and what to plant.

Finally, Africans didn't need to band together in large numbers for protection against equestrian raiders. As we've seen, after pastoralists mastered the arts of horsemanship and bowmanship (roughly 2000 BCE), everyone between the Levant and Korea needed organized armed forces to resist steppe horsemen. In most of Africa south of the Sahara, a disease called trypanosomiasis, carried by tsetse flies, made it almost impossible for horses to survive. So Africans, free from the threat of equestrian raiders, had less incentive than Asians to submit to rulers, taxes, and conscription and more opportunity to live in small communities of their own making.

SOCIAL VIOLENCE African life was often violent, but not because of states, armies, and farming. Cemeteries in Africa are packed with ancient skeletons that show signs of weapon wounds. At one graveyard in northern Sudan from

12,000 BCE, fully 40 percent of the skeletons betray signs of violent deaths. An attack at a lakeshore in what is now northern Kenya in about 8000 BCE left 27 people dead. Among hunter-forager people worldwide, violent death at the hand of one's fellow man (rarely one's fellow woman) amounted to about 15 percent of all deaths and about 25 percent for adult males. Such rates of violent death probably also prevailed among African hunter-foragers, and perhaps pastoralists, before 200 CE. (For comparison, in the United States and among Americans overseas from 2001 to 2017, murders and warfare accounted for well under 1 percent of all deaths.) Pastoralists fought over water or pasture and raided one another's herds. Archeological evidence suggests that deadly encounters were usually ambushes or massacres of unarmed victims.

In the absence of states, mobile farmers in Africa often lived more peacefully than pastoralists. Battles among armed parties of adult men took place, according to some rock shelter art, but they were probably rare. In Africa, fleeing was often a viable option for anyone likely to lose a fight—even farmers, who would have to leave their crops behind. By contrast, in the river valleys of Asia and Egypt surrounded by deserts, one had to stand and fight because there was nowhere to go where refugees wouldn't die of thirst or hunger. Moreover, fleeing on foot when one's enemies rode horses scarcely improved one's chances of survival. And because there were states, people had to fight wars to satisfy the ambitions of kings. In Africa, until states emerged, farmers had no kings to obey; and with empty land at hand, they could walk away from a fight peacefully and start farming somewhere else.

SOCIAL IDENTITY AND HIERARCHY In most of Africa, circumstances worked against the accumulation of personal wealth and power and its conversion into political strength and state formation. Small-scale politics prevailed, based on family and clan. People normally affiliated with others whom they knew or believed were their kinfolk. Clans traced their descent from a common ancestor, often awarded supernatural powers by descendants. Language groups, too, provided some basis for social identity, as did ways of life: farmers tended to regard themselves as different from, and of course better than, hunters, fisherfolk, and foragers—and vice-versa.

Social hierarchy existed, but also on a small scale. Women who worked as farmers or produced large numbers of children earned respect and status. Men who were especially good at hunting, or at raiding strangers' cattle, were admired and perhaps feared. They might acquire more wives than ordinary men, more children, and more dependents—a word that Africanist historians use to refer to people who voluntarily or otherwise attach themselves to a successful man (or more rarely, woman) for survival or perhaps a chance at betterment. Dependents might or might not be considered slaves, often an inexact category in African history. In any case, they owed deference and labor, and in the case of women perhaps sexual services as well, to someone more successful than they were. Men counted themselves rich and powerful when they had many wives, children, and dependents, and in pastoral societies when they had many cattle too. Africans generally took ancestry seriously, so that status, whether high or low, could be inherited from parents.

In Africa, as in non-Roman Europe, land was abundant and people scarce. So social power and economic wealth came in the form of control over people and livestock, rather than control over land. In China or Egypt, by contrast, land was the scarcer resource, not people, so wealth and power were expressed in the form of control over land. Africa didn't have landlords, as China, Mesopotamia, and Roman lands had; instead, it had what could be called labor-lords. Very successful Africans might have hundreds or even thousands of followers, but they normally didn't seek to convert that power into territorial states—at least, not until later periods of African history.

EARLY STATES: KUSH AND AKSUM

In northeastern Africa, however, states developed earlier thanks to proximity to Egypt and the ease with which rulers could control traffic on the Nile. As we saw in Chapter 5, states and kings emerged in Nubia, just south of Egypt, much influenced by the pharaonic model. They built pyramids and used Egyptian hieroglyphs. In the eighth century BCE a unified Nubian state, called Kush by Egyptians, managed to conquer and rule Egypt for about 60 years. Subsequent kingdoms of Kush rose and fell, one of them, mentioned above, based at Meroë. The strength of these kingdoms was based in control of north-south trade routes in and out of Egypt, as well as land well suited to cattle raising along the Nile and its tributaries. Kings of Kush frequently provided Egypt with slaves. According to Roman authors and some images carved into stone, by 170 BCE Kush had queens either ruling in their own right or as co-regents. Meroë, which declined after 250 CE, was the last powerful Kushitic kingdom, although smaller states survived until the fifth or sixth century CE.

The final eclipse of Kush came at the hands of another northeast African state, **Aksum** (sometimes spelled Axum), in the fourth to the fifth centuries CE. Based well to the south of Kush, Aksum arose in what is now northern Ethiopia and Eritrea, lands where plow agriculture had existed since perhaps 3000 BCE and several types of grain were cultivated on rich, volcanic soils. It was a pocket of unusually high population density. Towns sprang up by the fifth century BCE. A few centuries of higher-than-average rainfall helped Aksum to flourish. Some migrants from the Arabian Peninsula, perhaps mainly merchants, added to the cultural mix. Aksum began to specialize in the export of gold, frankincense, and myrrh, as well as rhino horn and elephant ivory. Frankincense and myrrh, featured in the gospel stories of the birth of Jesus, are fragrances derived from trees that grew in Arabia, Yemen, and Ethiopia.

Like the kingdoms of Kush before it, Aksum grew prosperous trading African products —ivory, hippopotamus hides, and slaves, to judge by the ancient authors— to Egypt, the Mediterranean world, Mesopotamia, and beyond. The dramatic surge in Egyptian population and wealth under the Ptolemies and Romans helped Aksum.

Aksum Once standing 79 feet (24 m) tall, the now broken Great Stele of Aksum was that state's equivalent of a pyramid—a burial monument that also attested to the might of a ruler. The extensively decorated stele indicates the wealth of Aksum in the fourth and fifth centuries CE.

Its trading towns grew, and by about 50 CE it was a genuine territorial empire controlling, perhaps loosely, lands in what are now northern Ethiopia, Eritrea, and Sudan, and at times across the Red Sea in Arabia. It also developed a naval force on the Red Sea. The narrow shape of the Red Sea made it comparatively easy for Aksum's rulers to dominate seaborne trade between Egypt and India, and the export of African goods, especially ivory, to India.

As Red Sea commerce mounted, so did the wealth and power of Aksum. Its sailors went at least as far as Sri Lanka just south of India. It minted its own coins, probably based on Roman models. Even more than Meroë or Kush, its fortunes rose with the strengthening of linkages—seaborne linkages, for the most part—of the Old World web. A Persian sage of the early third century CE referred to Aksum as one of the four great powers of the time, together with the Roman Empire, Persia, and China. One of Aksum's rulers, according to an ancient Greek author, was conversant with Greek literature. A later king, Ezana, embraced Christianity about 325 CE, and gradually most of the kingdom's subjects did as well, which is why so many Ethiopians are Christians today. In the fourth and fifth centuries CE, Aksum enjoyed its fullest flowering. Aksum declined and fell in the sixth and seventh centuries under the impact of war with Byzantine and Arab powers, and perhaps declining rains as well.

By the time of Aksum's ascendance in northeastern Africa, Africans were developing stronger links throughout the continent. The slow transmission of farming and

Kushitic Kingdoms Carvings on a first-century CE temple at Meroë picture King Natakamani and Queen Aminatore as joint rulers, both wearing crowns and carrying swords and other symbols of their authority.

cattle keeping all the way to southern Africa was fully under way. Iron working was well established and had already spread widely throughout the midsection of the continent. And the domestication of the dromedary in Arabia had given rise to the ship of the desert—the camel, capable of crossing the now-desiccated Sahara. Prior to 6000 BCE, the wetter Sahara hadn't been much of a barrier to human movement and communication. As it dried out over the following millennia, though, the Sahara became a rocky and sandy wasteland separating the Mediterranean world from sub-Saharan Africa. The Nile valley pierced that barrier, and routes along the Red Sea and the East African coast also reduced the isolation of Africa from the Old World web. But as late as 200 CE that isolation remained considerable: least so for Aksum and Kush, more so for societies farther south, and almost total for southern Africa. Camel caravans across the Sahara, which

started around 300 CE, would provide a new link between the emerging Old World web and Africa, bringing new commerce, new religion, new animals, and much else besides—as we will see.

EUROPE TO 1300 BCE

Like sub-Saharan Africa, Europe stood beyond the dynamic Nile-Ganges web until the expansion of Carthage and Rome. Even then, only Mediterranean Europe became entangled in any webs until Rome conquered Gaul and Britain. And even after Rome's empire reached its fullest extent, Europe north of the Danube and east of the Rhine remained outside what was now the Old World web, sparsely populated and poor.

EVOLVING ENVIRONMENTS

Just as Egypt was the gift of the Nile, Europe—best understood geographically as a subcontinent of Eurasia comparable to India—is the gift of the **Gulf Stream**. For the last 11,000 years or so, the counterclockwise movement of ocean currents in the North Atlantic has reliably brought warm waters, and warm humid air above them, to the coasts from Portugal to Norway. The sun-splashed Bordeaux wine country of southwestern France is at the same latitude as northern Maine. Scotland, where palm trees grow on the western coast, is as far north as Hudson Bay. The reason these European lands aren't as frosty as their counterparts in North America is that warmth wafted northeastward from the Gulf of Mexico across the Atlantic, to Europe. When, as has happened over geological time, the Gulf Stream shuts down, Europe goes into a deep freeze. The Gulf Stream conditioned life in the European subcontinent just as much as the monsoon did in the Indian subcontinent.

During the last ice age, the Gulf Stream stopped and the northern third of Europe lay under great ice sheets. Temperatures were 10 to 16 degrees Fahrenheit (6–10 degrees Celsius) colder than today. Sea level stood 400 feet (120 m) lower than it does now. As the ice began to melt after 20,000 BCE, sea level crept up. By 8000 BCE, Ireland was an island, and Britain too by 6500 BCE. Europe had acquired its present shorelines, or very close to them, by 4000 BCE. After about 7500 BCE, its climate remained fairly stable by the standards of the past.

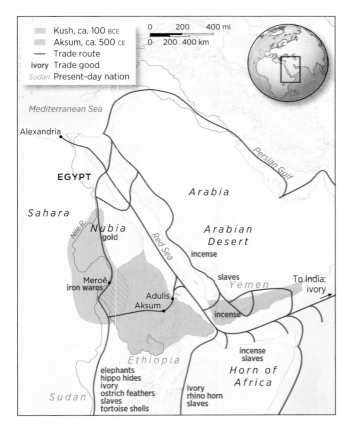

Kush and Aksum, ca. 100 BCE–500 CE Proximity to Egypt and north-south trade routes along the Nile and the Red Sea helped to spur settlement, prosperity, and social complexity in northeast African polities such as Kush and Aksum. They formed part of a trade web extending from Mediterranean shores to India, but they were cattle-raising societies as well. Aksum was also part of a political and cultural cluster including Persia and Rome, and in the fourth century CE its inhabitants began to adopt Christianity.

Vegetation belts moved northward as climate warmed. Oak and beech forest, previously confined to southern Europe, inched northward into what had been steppe and soggy tundra, reaching as far as southern Scandinavia. Coniferous forest—pines, spruce, and fir—grew farther north still. The large herds of steppe-grazing mammals, which had sustained the hunters and foragers who left us the Lascaux cave paintings, dwindled. Forest creatures, such as deer, replaced them. By 6000 BCE, forests covered most of Europe except the farthest north. Whereas in Africa the key component of climate change was precipitation, accounting for the waxing and waning of the Sahara as well as the rain forests, in Europe it was temperature.

The landscape that emerged as the ice melted back had four important features that shaped Europe's history ever after. The oldest, which had been there long before the ice, were the mountains. Europe was broken up by mountain chains that posed real challenges to the movement of people and goods. There is one broad plain across northern Europe, stretching from the Netherlands to Russia, but otherwise its mountain chains fragment Europe.

The second key feature is the river system that emerged from under the ice. Fairly reliable rain and snowfall for the last 9,000 years has fed a series of rivers suited for navigation because they flowed year-round and often had estuaries that served as harbors—examples include the Po, Garonne, Seine, Rhine, Vistula, and Danube. Most were flat for long stretches, with few waterfalls or rapids. As in Africa, one could get around in the forest most easily by following the rivers. Unlike much of Africa, the density of rivers in Europe is high, making a large proportion of it accessible by river. Good river routes spanned Europe in a north-south direction, connecting the Mediterranean to the North Sea and Baltic Sea with only short land portages.

Europe's third defining geographical feature is the coastline that took shape with the rise of sea levels. Partly because of glaciations, Europe's coastline has countless indentations, fjords, estuaries, and bays that make good harbors. If Europe's coastline were straightened out, it would reach all the way around the world. One is never more than 200 miles (300 km) from the sea in western Europe, and never more than twice that in eastern Europe. The combination of a dense river network and a long, irregular coastline made Europe one of the best places in the world for water transport.

The fourth feature is the soil. In Mediterranean Europe there are pockets of good soil, but in central and northern Europe there is much more. The grinding of the ice sheets crushed masses of rock and released minerals that enriched soils. Farther south, from France to Russia, lies a band of loess soils created by the deposition of windblown dust off the ice sheets. These soils are fertile, lightweight, and easy to work, and they drain well. Early farmers, as we'll see, preferred them, as did their counterparts in the loess region of northern China.

HUNTERS AND FORAGERS, 10,000 BCE TO 4000 BCE

After the retreat of the ice, as forest spread over the landscape and the big herbivores disappeared, Europeans had to change their ways. Hunting in thick woodlands was far harder than on open steppe because one can't shoot arrows through thickets. And the forest animals—wild boars and deer, for example—carried less meat on them than some of the grassy steppe's gargantuan grazers had carried, so hunting became less rewarding even when it was successful. In the winters, although much milder now, there were no fruits and berries, so bad luck in the hunt meant hunger or starvation. In response, some Europeans migrated northward, following waning herds of reindeer. Others kept on the move, migrating seasonally to spots where they expected to find berries, nuts, fruits, edible roots, or animals to hunt.

By 7000 BCE, people lived just about everywhere in Europe, although they usually didn't stay still for long. Reliable food supplies were hard to find. Total population probably fell markedly after 10,000 BCE, to judge by the reduced number of archeological sites found to date. Europe's forests, like Africa's, supported very sparse populations, and more forest meant fewer people.

Scandinavian Settlements Artifacts that attest to the presence of coastal settlements in Scandinavia include these combs made from bone in the area of present-day Denmark around 5000 to 4500 BCE.

The best solution to this food crisis, archeological evidence suggests, was to head for the coast. Europe's abundant and irregular coasts, especially river estuaries such as the Garonne's or the Rhine's, were teeming with edible life. The ambitious could hunt seals and seabirds on coastal rocks and cliffs. Fish were easier to catch, especially the salmon that made annual runs up many northern European rivers. Anyone, including small children, could pick up oysters, mussels, cockles, birds' eggs, or seaweed. At some places, the seafood harvest was so abundant and reliable that clusters of people lived year-round. At one spot in Denmark, generations of people munched away on shellfish for at least 800 years (4600–3800 BCE), leaving behind a trash pile (politely called a midden by archeologists) about the size of 75 school buses. From giant dugout canoes, these people also fished and harpooned sea mammals in the narrows between Denmark and Sweden. They, and other seaside dwellers, probably also used boats, made of animal skins stretched over wooden frames, for exploring estuaries and bays. They probably didn't venture onto the open sea. In addition to food, the seaside offered abundant salt and iodine, important for human health. As in Japan, where the Jomon culture prospered in year-round seaside settlements, so in Europe life by the sea was one of comparative ease.

Inland there were far fewer sites where permanent settlement made sense. Most appeared along rivers such as the Rhine or Danube, where trapping big fish was feasible. Perhaps the biggest inland settlement was along the Danube, at a point in today's Serbia where the river passes swiftly through a gorge called the Iron Gates. By 6500 BCE, permanent villages had sprouted here, with houses built of stone and timber. To judge by the rubbish left behind, the inhabitants ate beluga and other fish from the Danube, deer from the surrounding forest, and the occasional migratory duck or goose so unfortunate as to land in the neighborhood.

With permanent settlements inland being rare, the normal habit was to stay on the move, stopping for weeks here and there to exploit a food source—berries or acorns, for example—when it was in season. Lakes or wetlands attracted immense flocks of migratory birds such as ducks and geese in spring and fall, and consequently attracted hungry humans too. It was a precarious existence.

In this mobile world, social organization remained simple—mainly, bands of kinfolk. Opportunities for the accumulation of wealth, prestige, and power were limited, although at the Iron Gates on the Danube grave goods indicate modest social differentiation. Infants buried with precious goods such as flints or amber suggest that, as in Africa, high status could be inherited as well as earned. (Amber is fossil tree resin, good for making jewelry and scents.) Bands of loosely related kin probably gathered at regular intervals for festivals, gift exchange, and marriages—as almost everywhere among hunting and foraging peoples. Some goods also moved around a lot, whether as trade items, gifts, or possessions carried by wandering peoples. Some flints have turned up nearly 250 miles (400 km) from their places of origin.

River Communities Peoples living along the Danube in the area of present-day Serbia ate fish and other river produce—as suggested by this sandstone carving of a fish, which decorated a house in the region around 5600 to 4300 BCE.

As everywhere else, European bands sometimes ran across one another and exchanged blows rather than gifts. Perhaps 20 to 40 percent of skeletons from Europe (ca. 10,000 to 4000 BCE) show traumatic fractures and arrow wounds. The rates of violent death were comparable to those suggested by the skeletons unearthed in Africa. At one site in Bavaria (southern Germany), 37 skeletons of men, women, and children were dug up in 1908. All had their skulls bludgeoned and their heads cut off. This massacre took place about 6400 BCE.

Archeology can tell us little about the spiritual life of these mobile Europeans. A few group burials and several tiny wooden carved figurines have been found, but there is no clear idea what to make of them. Just about everything else these peoples made of wood has long since rotted away. The evidence grows far richer after 4000 BCE, when more Europeans settled down to farm and created much more in the way of durable artifacts for future archeologists to dig up.

FARMING COMES TO EUROPE

Europeans did not invent farming. To some extent, they learned it from their neighbors in Anatolia. But to a larger extent, Europe acquired agriculture because farmers from Anatolia migrated into Europe. The migrants out-competed and substantially replaced indigenous hunter-forager Europeans, just as Bantu farmers out-competed the indigenous Khoisan-speaking populations of southern Africa, and Chinese farmers out-competed hunter-foragers in what is now southern China. The precise mix of migration, replacement, and learning varies for different parts of Europe. The farther northwest one goes, apparently, the larger the role of cultural learning and the smaller the role of migration.

SOUTHEASTERN AND CENTRAL EUROPE Farming came to Europe as part of a package consisting of the same cereals cultivated in the Levant—wheat and barley—together with domesticated animals such as cattle, sheep, goats, and pigs. It also included something not normally found in the Levant, square houses made from timber. All these things show up easily in archeology, so the chronology of the spread of farming in Europe is known with remarkable precision, far more so than the comparable process in Africa.

Farming folk migrated to mainland Greece between about 7500 and 6000 BCE. They, and their practices, moved north into the Danube basin by 6500 to 5500 BCE, by which time the process involved less migration and more imitation. By 5500 BCE, people in the loess zones of central Europe, especially Hungary, had begun to shift to farming and found it so rewarding that it spread westward at roughly 2 miles (about 3 km) per year. The loess zones quickly became a world of tiny villages amid shrinking forests. Their middens show that people had almost given up hunting by 5000 BCE. The villagers lived in multi-family longhouses as much as 100 feet (30 m) long and developed great skill as carpenters. They raised grains, peas, and livestock. The villagers of the loess regions set the pattern—farming villages every few miles—that would eventually prevail throughout most of Europe until industrialization 7,000 years later.

As farming was catching on in southeastern and central Europe, it was also spreading by sea along Mediterranean coasts. By 5400 BCE, farmsteads dotted the shores from Greece to Spain and had begun to sprout in the river estuaries of Portugal. This movement consisted mainly of tiny seaborne colonization efforts by young men who carved out farms and tried to attract or capture local women for their wives. Farming spread inland more by imitation, as in central Europe, and by 4000 BCE people had adopted it all along the Atlantic shores of Europe. The British Isles were among the last to switch to farming, but inhabitants there did so quickly between 4100 and 3800 BCE.

THE BALTIC As far as we can tell, the only groups stubbornly opposed to farming lived on the shores of the Baltic. As early as 5100 BCE they borrowed pottery and some tool designs from farmers to their south. But they didn't switch to farming and weren't replaced by farmers for over a millennium, which is a puzzle given the record elsewhere in Europe. Perhaps the seafood of the Baltic was so good and plentiful that no one wanted to work hard in order to eat porridge and gruel. Skeletons show this was a time of heightened violence, so perhaps the resistance to farming took the form of military resistance to invading farmers. About 3900 BCE something—we don't

Stonehenge The most famous of the stone monuments erected in northern Europe is Stonehenge in England, built with remarkable skill and effort around 2500 BCE.

know what—changed, and within a century the whole Baltic region took up farming and the raising of livestock. So between 8000 and 3800 BCE farming had spread throughout Europe, from Greece all the way to the shores of the Atlantic. That transition led to a flood of changes in Europe, just as farming's spread did in Africa.

MENHIRS Mysterious changes took place in the realm of spiritual life, indicated by the practice of setting up **menhirs**—big oblong stones set to stand upright. They began to appear at about 5500 BCE in western France. The heavy stones—one of them weighs 350 tons—must have required the coordinated effort of hundreds of people to put up.

Stone monuments followed elsewhere, most famously at Stonehenge in southern England, built about 2500 BCE. People dragged or rolled its stone blocks some 140 miles (225 km) from Wales before standing them upright in southern England, suggesting a society with the capacity to organize many people around a single task. The blocks, which weigh up to 40 tons, are carefully lined up with the positions of the sun, moon, and certain stars at the summer solstice. Stonehenge stayed in use for 800 years, though what it was used for, beyond celestial observation, is unclear. Some scholars say it was a healing center, others a burial ground, still others a center for religious rites involving human sacrifice. Perhaps it was all of the above. By the time Stonehenge went up, large stone structures had sprouted throughout Atlantic Europe, from Sweden to northern Spain. Some of these, like those of Carnac in France, are dolmens, eerily similar to those erected several centuries later in Korea. But there is no evidence of contact between these dolmen-raising peoples.

In addition to stone monuments, Europe's early farmers practiced group burials, another indication of changing attitudes toward the spirit world. Gravesites tended to become fancier over time, eventually housing treasure troves of ornaments and weapons. Some had deep shafts dug into the earth. Others had sprawling mounds on top. The habits of group burials and stone monuments spread widely within western Europe between 4500 and 2000 BCE.

Other practices were spreading too, reflecting new local webs that arose in Europe after farming took root. For example, one particular mine in Brittany, in northwestern France, yielded the stone for some 2 million hand axes, used roughly between 4000 and 2200 BCE, which

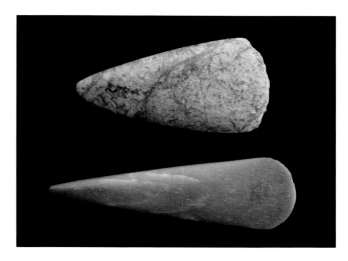

Luxury Goods Weapons made from precious materials could be exchanged as gifts and could also symbolize prestige. These highly polished hand axes made from jade sometime between 5500 and 1800 BCE were found in northern France.

archeologists have found all over France, Belgium, and southern Britain. Axe-heads of a type made from jade found in the western Alps, mainly between about 4300 and 4100 BCE, have turned up from Italy to Scotland. In eastern Europe, copper ornaments from a particular mine in today's Bulgaria have been found from the Alps to the Volga. The pottery style called bell beaker ware came into vogue throughout Europe and northwest Africa after 2900 BCE. All these goods were probably not traded in the sense we understand that word today; rather, elites of neighboring societies likely exchanged them as gifts until lost, broken, or carefully buried in someone's grave.

THE FIRST LOCAL WEBS IN EUROPE

Farming favored the development of networks of exchange in Europe just as it did in Africa and everywhere else. First of all, farmers could have, and needed to have, more material culture—more stuff—than did mobile hunters and foragers. Second, the efficiency of food production allowed some people to work as craft specialists, so skills in pottery, tool making, and weapon making improved rapidly. Improved quality made it more desirable to have such items, so the number of people making them and exchanging them grew. Third, with farming the total number of people swelled, and it was easier to know where to find them. If you wanted to secure the friendship of a powerful man, in the olden days of mobile hunting and

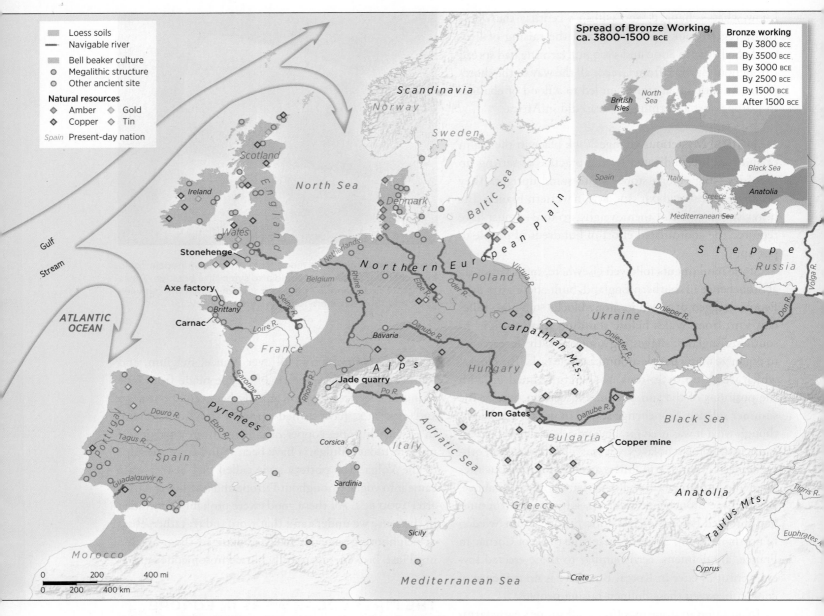

Europe, ca. 7500–1000 BCE Most of Europe is well equipped with navigable rivers that facilitated local and regional trade. With the advent of bronze artwork and weaponry after about 2200 BCE, European elites organized more frequent long-distance exchanges, binding together much of the subcontinent in its own web. The decline of bronze and the rise of iron weakened those ties.

foraging you had to locate him first, which could take months. And if you succeeded and gave him a gift in order to win his good will, he might be on the other side of a mountain range when you needed his help. In stable agricultural settings, however, you could send a messenger to a known location, invite a powerful man and his friends to a pig roast, drink beer together, and give him a nice jade hand-axe. When you needed his help, you knew where to find him.

After 2200 BCE or so, yet another factor favored the formation of webs of exchange in Europe: bronze. Recall that bronze is made from tin and copper. Tin is found only in a few places, so where bronze goods became popular long-distance networks of exchange always arose, in Europe as in Southwest Asia and China. Bronze appealed strongly to everyone, although only elites could afford it. Bronze weapons were far better than copper, stone, or wooden ones. Bronze made for handsome jewelry and ornaments because it shone brightly and could be worked into precise shapes.

Bronze goods were in such demand that new items in far greater quantities entered into Europe's circuits of exchange after 2000 BCE. These included furs from the northern forests; amber from the shores of the Baltic; horses from the steppe lands of today's Ukraine and Russia; and gold from Bulgaria, Spain, and elsewhere. Young women, too, were increasingly given as gifts to important men, either as wives or as concubines. Transactions included not only items and people, but also understandings of future obligations owed by the receiver to the giver. Gifts were investments. Poor and weak people surrendered small shares of what they could raise, often including their daughters, to more powerful men in exchange for future protection. Although no money was used, the pace of exchanges quickened over time. Sailing ships came into use, first in the Mediterranean but eventually along Atlantic shores as well. River routes became highways. Ox-carts creaked along overland tracks. With farming, most people stayed put; but with farming and bronze, European goods were on the move. Europe was knitting itself, or at least its elites, together.

Like Africa outside Egypt's orbit, Europe was knitting itself together in partial isolation from the much more populated, and more interactive, Nile-Ganges web. Before 1000 BCE, most Europeans, like most Africans, remained unaffected by the priests, soldiers, microbes, and other forces of complex society shaping the history of the Nile-Ganges web.

A TIME OF TRANSITION, 1300 TO 800 BCE

In many respects, European integration reached a plateau in the five centuries after 1300 BCE. The pervasive presence of bronze weaponry and ornamentation helped give shape to a pan-European elite culture. One component of it was the cult of the warrior, expressed in art. Bronze figurines of warriors wearing horned helmets were in style from Scandinavia to Sardinia. Weapons increasingly became works of art, with lovingly fashioned sword hilts and hand axes. Although not an especially warlike period, it was one of glorification of young male warriors.

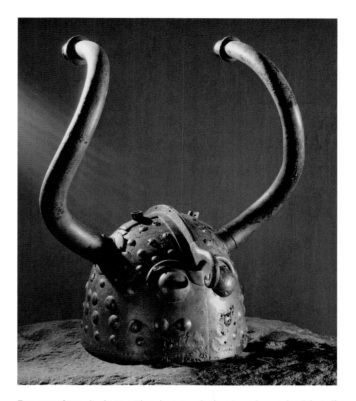

Bronze Age A decorative bronze helmet—adorned with tall horns—from Denmark, dated to between 800 and 400 BCE, is indicative of bronze goods that were exchanged in European trade networks, and the connection of high status for men with warfare.

The pre-eminent symbol of high social status for males was possession of fine bronze weaponry. And for females it was bronze jewelry.

Religious life took on a new character after 1300 BCE. Cremation increasingly took the place of burial of the dead. All over Europe, the dead were burned on funeral pyres—as in Homer's *Iliad*—and ashes buried in urns. Often, the urns were carefully arranged in cemeteries. This may indicate new ideas about death and afterlife, perhaps a transition in the location of eternal spirits from an underworld to the heavens. The sun also was featured more prominently in artwork. This transition was common across Europe.

THE IMPACT OF IRON TECHNOLOGY

In the eleventh century BCE, Europeans began to work with iron as well as bronze. The technology came from Anatolia and first took hold in southeastern Europe. Iron was no better for weapons and tools than bronze, and

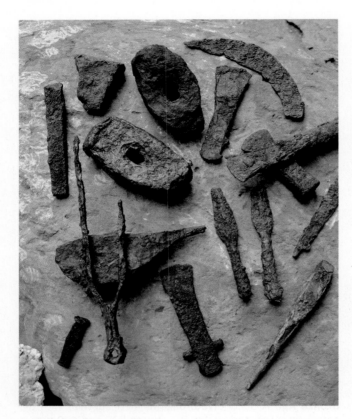

Iron Working Iron began to supplant bronze as the metal of choice in Europe starting around 800 BCE. Spearheads, axes, and blacksmith's tools dated to around 500 BCE from eastern Europe indicate the variety of iron objects.

inferior (in most eyes) for ornamentation. But iron ore was widespread and much cheaper. In eastern and central Europe, iron working was well established by 800 BCE. Its adoption in western and northernmost Europe came several centuries later.

In Europe, the spread of iron technology had sharply different implications from those it had in Africa. In Europe, long-distance exchange networks had already emerged, built upon the elite's enthusiasm for bronze and the wide diffusion of farming. Iron did nothing to build these networks, and if anything, it weakened them. Iron ore could be found widely, as could wood for charcoal, so once people learned how to smelt ore and make iron, almost any community could do it. The logic of long-distance exchange, both of raw materials such as tin and of finished products such as swords or statuettes, diminished when and where iron replaced bronze. In Africa, where bronze had never mattered as much, iron working helped to build long-distance exchange networks. Moreover, in Africa the techniques of iron

working remained jealously guarded secrets, whereas in Europe, as in Southwest Asia and China, prior experience with bronze meant that metalworking skills were more widely diffused. Eventually, every village had its blacksmith, and the need for long-distance exchange declined accordingly. The advent of iron in Europe shows that the expansion and thickening of webs is far from inevitable. It also shows that the same metal can have sharply different consequences in different historical contexts.

HORSE NOMADS FROM THE STEPPE

This transitional half-millennium saw two other important developments in Europe. One was the migration westward, as far as the Hungarian plain, of horse nomads from the Russian and Ukrainian steppe. A group known as **Cimmerians** rode in beginning in the ninth century BCE. Although domesticated horses had been in use for many centuries already, the arrival of the Cimmerians marked a new emphasis on equestrian life and a new infusion of steppe customs into the heart of Europe. In Hungary, artifacts associated with mounted warfare and horse-themed art became more common. Pottery, however, didn't change much, probably because horse nomads didn't bring much in the way of potters' skills with them. Time and again after the Cimmerians, new groups of equestrian nomads or semi-nomads would drift into eastern Europe from the steppe, each time using their military strength to gain a foothold in, and occasionally a chokehold on, societies in and around the grasslands of Hungary. As in northern China and everywhere in Southwest Asia, in eastern Europe after the Cimmerians periodic incursions by mounted peoples helped to shape politics and culture.

THE CELTS

The second development to note was the emergence of a loose language group in Atlantic Europe called the **Celts** (pronounced "kelts"). Celtic is part of the Indo-European language family. Just when and where it arose is controversial among specialists, but it seems to have emerged between about 1300 and 700 BCE in both central and western Europe. Whatever its origins, its speakers became more and more numerous in these and later centuries as new crops (peas, lentils, and so-called celtic beans), and increased use of livestock manure as fertilizer, improved farm yields and boosted population. In the northern reaches of Europe, the domestication of rye and oats, cereal grains that do well in chilly climes, improved the fortunes of everyone, Celts included. As we shall see, the Celts became so numerous that they soon could overrun large parts of Europe and small parts of Asia.

TRADE AND INSTABILITY, 800 BCE TO 200 CE

In the millennium after 800 BCE, the dominant historical development in Europe was the rise of Mediterranean societies, culminating in the Roman Empire. As we've seen, by 200 BCE Roman trade and cultural influence extended into western and central Europe. By 100 CE, the Romans extended their frontier into Britain and controlled Europe west of the Rhine and south of the Danube. The rise of Roman power and culture changed things for almost everyone in Europe. The fate of people throughout Europe was increasingly shaped by their interactions with the Mediterranean societies.

CHANGES IN EXCHANGE NETWORKS

The nature of trade itself changed with Europe's increased contact with the Mediterranean. Europe's exchange networks, like those in Africa, had long been confined to the exchange of gifts by elites. Powerful men swapped prestige items with one another, such as the jade axes or bronze swords we have encountered already, forming obligations to and alliances with one another. But by 300 BCE or so, the nature of exchange in Europe had begun to shift, perhaps first on the northern shores of the Black Sea. At the same time as Alexander and his Seleucid successors were monetizing the economy of Southwest Asia, a smaller-scale version of the same process was affecting Europe. Coins—at first Greek and Etruscan, then mainly Roman—came into use, spreading the concept of purchase with no social obligations attached. As in Southwest Asia and the Mediterranean world itself, this monetization helped generate economic growth and social change, notably a richer class of rich.

In contemplating the changes in Europe, it is important to remember that available evidence steers us toward Rome and the Mediterranean. For the first time we have written texts, including carefully composed histories by Greek and Roman authors as well as inscriptions on coins and the odd piece of graffiti on pots or walls. These texts, overwhelmingly, are written by, and in the languages of, the Mediterranean peoples—mainly, Greeks and Romans. The peoples of northern and eastern Europe at this time didn't use writing. In addition, the archeological evidence is slanted toward the Mediterranean, even though plenty of archeological work has been done in northern Europe. The artifacts that have survived the last twenty centuries tend to be durable goods, especially ceramic and metal ones, which Mediterranean peoples manufactured in bulk. The slaves, horses, cattle, leather, furs, and so forth traded within northern, central, and eastern Europe have left a much smaller trace in the archeological record. Genetic and linguistic evidence, so far, has not done much to redress this imbalance.

After 800 BCE in northern Europe, from the British Isles to the Baltic, the exchange networks forged in earlier millennia decayed. The abundance of local iron reduced the demand for distant supplies of bronze goods. Populations grew, in part because of the efficiency of iron farming tools and the continued spread of livestock, the new cereals oats and rye, and the practice of manuring. The British Isles, for example, had about 1 million people at the advent of iron, and 2 to 4 million by the time of Roman conquest (43 BCE). Despite this population growth, a certain localization, or disintegration, occurred in Europe before the Romans came, visible in the elaboration of more regional and local styles of pottery and weaponry, and perhaps also in the differentiation of the various forms of Celtic speech. Northern Europeans lived in greater isolation between 800 and 100 BCE. To some degree, the Celts were like the Khoisan of southern Africa in this period, geographically removed from the centers of innovation and disruption, more left to themselves than others of their continent.

EXPANDING TRADE WITHIN EUROPE

Elsewhere, connections to the Mediterranean world generated new and unstable social patterns that rested on long-distance trade. After 600 BCE or so, a trickle of Mediterranean luxury goods flowed northward into central Europe. Meanwhile, close interactions on the Black Sea coasts between Greek cities and local nomads (called Scythians by Herodotus) brought similar goods into

European Slave Trade A first-century relief from a Roman sarcophagus shows Roman soldiers taking European men, women, and children as captives. This was a common circumstance during the height of Roman power, when Europeans might be enslaved either as prisoners of war or as an export commodity.

eastern Europe through Scythian migrations and trading expeditions.

Gradually, access to Mediterranean goods became essential for leaders in the heart of Europe. Their position depended on being able to distribute to their followers the beautiful jewelry, sturdy weaponry, and other goods manufactured on the Italian Peninsula or in Greek colonies. They also hosted feasts with plenty of wine to solidify their prestige and leadership. Elaborate drinking cups were an important trade item linking the Mediterranean with the European heartland, and so was drink itself. By one estimate, the quantity of Italian wine shipped to Gaul (as the Romans called what is now France) reached 2 million gallons per year in the first century BCE. The historian Diodorus of Sicily remarked at the time:

> [The Gauls] are exceedingly fond of wine. Their desire for it makes them drink greedily and fall into a stupor. Italian merchants . . . look upon the Gallic craving for wine as a treasure. They receive for wine an incredibly high price, for one amphora [jug] they get in return a slave: a servant in exchange for a drink.

Of course, the Gauls probably thought they were robbing the Roman merchants blind, giving up only one slave, of which they could always get more, for an entire amphora of wine, of which they could produce none.

To get the trade goods they wanted, European elites had to accumulate slaves, cattle, hides, furs, and other northern goods. They could sell these to Roman merchants for silver coin, which they might then use to buy their wine, weapons, and jewelry. The reach of this commercial system by 100 CE extended throughout lands under Roman control (west of the Rhine and south of the Danube) and into what is now Poland. Scattered Roman objects have been found far beyond Roman borders, in Ireland, Scotland, Scandinavia, and northern Russia; but these remote and poor lands produced little of commercial interest beyond slaves. So they remained on the outside, both beyond Roman borders and beyond the trade circuits routinely dispersing Mediterranean goods. They were the most isolated regions of Europe.

This new situation, in which trade goods from the Mediterranean and the Greco-Scythian Black Sea region loomed large, produced more than the normal political upheaval. Ambitious European chiefs competed for access to trade goods and the influence over people it brought. Securing slaves was a big part of success, so slave raiding in northern, central, and eastern Europe became increasingly popular as both a business and a political strategy. This is one of the reasons for the increasing resort to fortification and hilltop villages among Europeans, which shows up strongly in the archeological record after 500 BCE.

Commerce without personal obligation was inherently unstable, so depending on it was a risky strategy—in effect, feast or famine for chiefs. A shift in trade patterns could quickly bring the rise of one and the fall of another chief. A bad grape harvest near the mouth of the Rhone, a rash of banditry discouraging merchants—any such event—might interrupt the flow of needed goods and ruin the standing of a given chief or a cluster of them. Lest they see their followers desert them for someone else, they would make desperate efforts to seize more slaves, horses, or furs to secure the needed Mediterranean goods. Rulers in Kush, south of Egypt, faced a similar situation during the same centuries: their position hinged on control of trade goods to and from Egypt; and if trade patterns shifted, they lost the basis of their authority over supporters.

THE CELTIC MIGRATIONS

A second source of political unrest, which might have been linked to the instability of commerce, was the folk migrations of the Celts—movements of men, women, and children beginning in the fifth century BCE. The Roman historian Livy thought that population growth drove the Celts of central and western Europe to expand their territory. There is good archeological evidence for continued population growth almost everywhere in Europe from 800 BCE to about 160 CE. Some regions, such as what are now Poland, southern Ukraine, and southern Germany, seemed to pump out people in this period. So Livy could have been right.

But the Celtic migrations might also have been a response to the uncertainties of the new trade regime, which produced desperation as well as prosperity and power. They might also have been propelled by a social system in which young men, if they wished to distinguish themselves, win glory, and marry well, could do no better than to assault strangers, steal their cattle and perhaps women and children, and build new communities.

Whatever their motives, bands of Celts poured over the Alpine passes into northern Italy during the fourth and third centuries BCE, settling down in the rich Po valley to a life of farming and raiding their neighbors. As we saw in Chapter 8, a party of Celts managed to sack the city of Rome and came close to killing off the Roman population. The Celts remained active in northern Italy until around 200 BCE, by which time Roman power had magnified to the point where Roman armies crushed Celtic independence, sent many Celts back north to their ancestral homelands, and settled the Po valley with Roman colonies.

At the same time, other bands of Celts migrated—forcefully—southward from the Danube region. By 279 BCE some had raided as far south as central Greece. Others crossed into Anatolia, setting up a kingdom near today's Ankara. Wherever they found ill-defended cities or country estates, the Celts raided and traded for the prestige goods they had come to prize. The scale of this population movement was unprecedented in European history. Romans and Greeks retained a lasting disdain for the uncouth, unlettered, undisciplined people they called barbarians—of whom the Celts were but one.

CONCLUSION

In (sub-Saharan) Africa and (pre-Roman and non-Roman) Europe before 200 CE, people lived on the frontiers or beyond the big webs that were developing around the Mediterranean. Their lands were less thickly populated, and people had more room to roam. Unlike the populations of the narrow river valleys in Egypt, Mesopotamia, and China, they could walk away from men seeking to convert them into forced labor. They didn't need irrigation. With rare exception, they didn't face militarily formidable mounted nomads. So they did not need states, did not organize themselves into elaborate social hierarchies, and did not readily submit to ambitious men hoping to live like kings and pharaohs.

Africans and Europeans were, as a result, usually less constrained by taxation, conscription, and forced labor than the peoples of the webs in Egypt or Asia. But when and where populations grew and links to Egypt or Rome developed, Africans or Europeans might find themselves bartered as slaves by chiefs eager for prestige goods from the workshops of complex societies. This risk of enslavement eventually extended to almost all Europeans by the height of the Roman Empire, but in Africa not far beyond the northeastern quarter of the continent, closest to Egypt.

Although partly isolated from the world's big webs, Africans and Europeans built their own networks of trade, often along river routes. In Africa, this process accelerated with the rise of iron and the spread of new crops from Southeast Asia. In Europe, it accelerated with the rise of bronze and probably weakened—certainly in northern Europe—when after 800 BCE iron came into use, a case in which an existing web decayed.

Both Africa and Europe slowly entered more and more into the tangle of the Nile-Indus web and by 100 CE the Old World web. The distant reaches of each, southern Africa and northernmost Europe, remained but little affected. But those regions closest to Egypt, the Mediterranean, and Mesopotamia slowly changed their ways under the influence of opportunities and risks emanating from the Nile-Indus web. This process began very slowly and was certainly imperceptible to people then alive. But by 200 CE trade, artistic styles, military techniques, food crops, and diseases long in circulation in Egypt, the eastern Mediterranean, and Southwest Asia had clearly made their imprint on most of Europe and parts of Africa.

Although their circumstances and social worlds had much in common at the end of the last ice age, by 200 CE Africa and Europe increasingly differed. More of Europe showed the effects of interaction with the Mediterranean and with Asian steppe people. Its incorporation into the larger webs of humankind, although far from complete, was fuller than Africa's. It was swept up in more sustained exchanges than was Africa, outside of Kush and Aksum.

While there were several reasons for this diverging fate between Europe and Africa, the simplest ones are geographical. First, Africa is much larger than Europe, and more of it is a long way from the Mediterranean or Mesopotamia. Northeast Africa interacted regularly with the web links of the Mediterranean and Indian Ocean,

and both East and West Africa were in occasional contact with the wider world. But central and southern Africa remained, before 200 CE, more isolated. Second, the Sahara, after it dried out, made a more effective barrier to communication than did the Alps or any obstacles in Europe. In time, as we shall see, geography came to matter less, and human ambition came to matter more in forming and sustaining connections among human communities.

CHAPTER REVIEW

KEY TERMS

bell beaker ware (p. 239)
iron working (p. 246)
Meroë (p. 247)

Jenne (p. 250)
Aksum (p. 252)
Gulf Stream (p. 253)

menhirs (p. 257)
Cimmerians (p. 259)
Celts (p. 260)

Go to INQUIZITIVE to see what you've learned—and learn what you've missed—with personalized feedback along the way.

REVIEW QUESTIONS

1. What significant commonalities did Africa and Europe share between the end of the last ice age and 200 CE?

2. Explain the importance of variations in rainfall, the geological age of the African continent, and the features of African rivers for the continent's history.

3. Why were African ways of life—both pastoralism and farming—more fluid and less permanent than those of people living in river valleys between Egypt and China?

4. What three factors were essential for the spread of agriculture and pastoralism in Africa, and why?

5. What did social power and economic wealth look like in Africa and non-Roman Europe in comparison to Egypt and China?

6. Why did states develop earlier in northeastern Africa than in sub-Saharan Africa?

7. What are the four important landscape features that shaped Europe's history, and how did they do so?

8. What were the different processes by which farming spread across Europe?

9. What important cultural elements did Europeans share in the 500 years following 1300 BCE?

10. What were the effects of iron working on trade in Africa versus Europe, and why did they differ?

11. In what ways did the nature of exchange in Europe change around 300 BCE?

12. How did sub-Saharan Africans and non-Roman Europeans avoid hierarchical rule, conscription, and taxation before 200 CE?

FURTHER READING

Peter BOGUCKI, *The Origins of Human Society* (1999). A work that is especially useful on human society in Europe.

Stanley BURSTEIN, *Ancient African Civilizations: Kush and Axum* (2009). The most accessible recent overview.

Barry CUNLIFFE, *Europe between the Oceans* (2009). A comprehensive overview of European archeology and history from 9000 BCE.

Barry CUNLIFFE, *On the Ocean: The Mediterranean and the Atlantic from Prehistory to AD 1500* (2017). A handy and well-illustrated survey of (mainly) archeology.

Christopher EHRET, *The Civilizations of Africa: A History to 1800* (2002). The most comprehensive survey of early Africa; based heavily on historical linguistics, the book is often controversial with archeologists who prefer other methods.

Philip KOHL, *The Making of Bronze Age Eurasia* (2007). A study that is interesting on the steppe lands of eastern Europe and Central Asia, with especially rich archeological detail.

Ann Brower STAHL, ed., *African Archeology* (2005). A smorgasbord of interesting chapters, written mainly for fellow archeologists.

CHRONOLOGY

ca. 48,000 BCE
First migrants arrive in Australia

ca. 11,000–9000 BCE
Mass extinctions of large
mammals in the Americas

ca. 23,000 BCE
First migrants
arrive in the
Solomon Islands

ca. 38,000 BCE
First migrants arrive
in New Guinea

ca. 21,000–13,000 BCE
First migrants arrive in the Americas

ca. 12,000–11,000 BCE
Clovis points are widely used in North America

ca. 9000 BCE
First signs of
farming in the
Americas

ca. 7000–6000 BCE
Transition to agriculture
in New Guinea

By 6000 BCE
Australian aborigines
begin to use weirs to
trap eels and fish

ca. 4000 BCE
First migrants reach
Remote Oceania; a
new wave of migrants
from Taiwan settle
in Near Oceania

ca. 3000 BCE
Aleuts and Inuit
cross the Bering Strait

From ca. 1800 BCE
Large villages develop
in the Pacific Northwest

ca. 1600–300 BCE
Olmecs flourish

ca. 1300 BCE
Lapita culture begins
to settle Remote Oceania

ca. 200 BCE–700 CE
Moche flourish

ca. 900–200 BCE
Chavín culture flourishes

ca. 100–1100 CE
Tiwanaku rises and falls

ca. 100–700 CE
Teotihuacán flourishes

10

The Americas and Oceania

BEFORE 1000 CE

ca. 700 CE
Amerindians in New England and
the Canadian Maritimes acquire
the bow and arrow; first migrants
reach Easter Island

ca. 200–750 CE
Zapotecs flourish
ca. 200–900 CE
Maya flourish

ca. 600 CE
First migrants
arrive in Hawaii

O ne summer evening in the 590s CE, the 200 villagers of Cerén, in today's El Salvador, ran for their lives. Their village stood at the foot of a volcano, which erupted and buried the surrounding landscape under 20 feet (6 m) of ash. Cerén was frozen in time until a bulldozer sliced into it in 1976. Archeologists followed and found about 70 buildings, including homes, a communal sweat bath, and a presumed religious edifice. In their fields the villagers left maize, manioc, beans, squash, agave, cacao, guava, cotton, and other crops. In their kitchens they left clay jars full of beans, and chili peppers hanging from the rafters. No skeletons remain: all the villagers, apparently, got away in time. Culturally, Cerén was a Maya village. The Maya, as we shall see, flourished from about 200 to 900 CE in the Yucatán Peninsula of Mexico and adjacent lands.

Cerén provides detailed information about villages and households in ancient America. There's nothing like it elsewhere in the Americas, nor in

Mesoamerican Knowledge The Maya used a calendrical system known as the Long Count that enabled religious leaders to calculate, based on the movements of celestial bodies, the most auspicious days for religious, political, and agricultural events and ceremonies. The stone medallion seen here commemorates the date of one such festivity. These calendars are evidence of the complexity of Mesoamerican culture and knowledge, especially in mathematics.

267

FOCUS QUESTIONS

1. How did early Amerindians adapt to their distinctive environments?

2. Where and how did complex society develop in the Americas?

3. What was distinctive about the early cultures of Australia and Oceania?

Oceania. It compares, perhaps, only to Pompeii and Herculaneum in southern Italy, the Roman towns buried by volcanic ash in 79 CE. Cerén was characteristic of village life in the Americas in that it was a farming community and its inhabitants raised most of the crops important in the Americas.

This chapter begins with the earliest human migrations into the Americas at least 15,000 years ago and takes the story beyond 200 CE (in contrast to Chapters 6 through 9) all the way to 1000 CE. In some respects, 1000 CE is an arbitrary end point, but it also represents a few important transitions in the history of the Americas and Oceania. First, it roughly matches the temporary end of urbanized society in the Maya world. Second, it matches another temporary end point of urban, complex society in the Andes. Third, 1000 CE marks the point when the spread of maize cultivation in North America reached its geographic limit—and few other things in North American history mattered as much as maize. Fourth, it is when Europeans, specifically Vikings, crossed the Atlantic and dented the isolation of the Americas. And fifth, it is—again roughly—the time by which the settlement of the Pacific Islands was complete.

The Americas and Oceania are together a sprawling space. The two American continents make up 28 percent of the Earth's land surface, half again as much as Africa and almost as much as Asia. There is

no clear definition of "**Oceania**." Here we include Australia with Oceania. If one counts only the land and not the water between islands, Oceania amounts to less than 1 percent of the Earth's land surface—if one excludes Australia—or 6 percent if one includes it.

At first glance, the Americas and Oceania may seem an odd couple. What links them is that they represent the farthest frontiers of settlement, the last big places on Earth to acquire human populations. Beginning about 50,000 years ago, people from Asia migrated into Australia, and later into the Americas and Oceania, and for the most part never looked back. People living in these regions were, with small exception, isolated from other, larger human populations.

In a rough way, the human colonizations of the Americas, Australia, and the Pacific Islands resemble the first exodus from Africa about 100,000 years ago. In that case, people left Africa for Eurasia, entering worlds where *Homo sapiens* had never trod before. In these latter cases, people left Eurasia for new worlds that neither humans nor hominids had ever visited. In all these cases, people entered novel environments that offered food and other resources for the taking and that filtered out diseases that couldn't survive the new conditions. As soon as these migrants learned enough about their new lands, they prospered, grew in numbers, spread out thinly over huge spaces, and diversified culturally.

The Americas and Oceania were also worlds unto themselves. As we've seen, the large populations that lived in China, India, Southwest Asia, and around the Mediterranean were in ever greater contact with one another, so that by 200 CE they formed the Old World web. The sparse populations of southernmost Africa, northernmost Europe, and Siberia took little part in this giant network. But the populations of the Americas and Oceania stood more fully apart. They had only the most slender connections, if any, to Eurasia and Africa. Thus their histories, up to 1000 CE, followed independent tracks.

In the case of the Americas, that track showed remarkable parallels to the general trajectory of history in the lands of the Old World web. People made transitions to agriculture; developed cities and states run by priests and warriors; built monumental architecture; invented pottery, textiles, writing, calendars, and mathematics; evolved religions that emphasized concepts of sacrifice to gods and temples with elaborate rituals; created roughly the same pattern of gendered division of labor; and built up networks of long-distance trade and exchange. Indeed, by 1000 CE they had woven two substantial webs of interaction in large regions of the Americas, one in Mesoamerica and one in the Andes.

In Oceania, this broad pattern did not prevail. People either didn't need agriculture, as in Australia, or they brought it with them when they migrated from Southeast Asia. They did not invent it. They built no cities and no states until after 1000 CE. These societies and populations remained modest in scale compared to those of the centers in the Americas—and tiny compared to those of China, India, or the Mediterranean world. The peoples of Oceania followed historical trajectories of their own making. Their trajectories were different from those of complex societies in the Americas or the Old World web, not incomplete versions of those elsewhere.

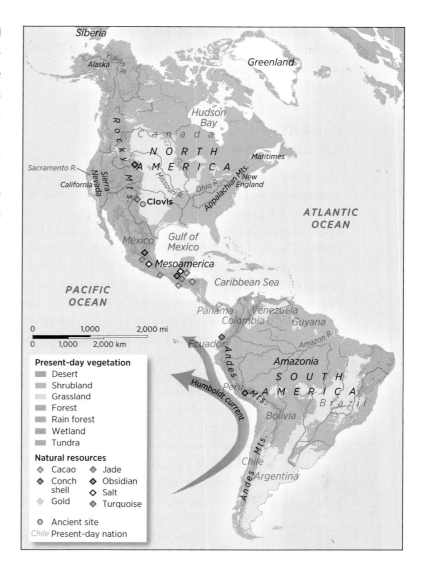

The Americas The natural vegetation zones of the Americas reflect rainfall, temperature, and soil variations. Those shown here indicate today's conditions but have been approximately the same for the past 6,000 years. The chief centers of population, Mesoamerica and the Andes, featured high ecological diversity due in large part to mountainous terrain. Because of the lack of domesticated grazing animals, grasslands in the Americas had none of the importance they carried in Eurasia and Africa.

THE AMERICAS: ENVIRONMENTS AND ECONOMIES

The first migrants to America, had they been more considerate of later generations, would have left big trash heaps of easily dateable rubbish for future archeologists. As it is, we have scraps of evidence and many puzzles. The best current hypothesis is that the first

Americans—Amerindians*—came from Asia, somewhere in southern Siberia, and crossed to Alaska between 23,000 and 15,000 years ago. They then spread quickly along the Pacific coasts of the Americas as far south as Chile. The

*There are many terms in use for the peoples who lived in the Americas before 1492 CE: *Native Americans, First Americans, First Nations, Aboriginal Americans, Amerindians, Indians, Paleoindians, Paleoamericans,* among others. Some terms are used only for one time period or region. All have supporters and critics. I will use just one term, *Amerindians.*

migration probably occurred in one or two early spurts, followed many thousands of years later by a third. The last one brought the peoples known as Inuits (or Eskimos) and Aleuts from Arctic Asia to Arctic America.

MIGRATION AND ENVIRONMENTAL CHANGE

This epic migration took place while North America was undergoing two major transformations. The first was the retreat of the great ice sheets that, as late as 25,000 years ago, had extended as far south as the Missouri and Ohio Rivers. The ice sheets probably obliged the earliest Amerindian migrants to go by sea as they headed south from Alaska. As the ice melted, it formed a giant lake in the heart of North America from 11,000 to 6000 BCE. The lake drained to the sea in several pulses, raising sea level by several feet each time and changing global climate. So the first migrants to North America came at a time of rapid climate change, just as the continent was defrosting.

The second transformation of this period was the extinction of many of the big mammals of North America. Some 90 genera (families) of animals went extinct around 11,000 to 9000 BCE, including mammoths, mastodons, giant beavers, and saber-toothed tigers. Possible explanations include overhunting by the first people to arrive in North America, climate change, and animal diseases. Whatever the causes, these mass extinctions fundamentally altered the ecosystems of North America. Simultaneous mass extinctions took place in South America.

In South America some 25,000 years ago, ice sheets covered the southern third of Chile and Argentina and all the Andes—about 20 percent of the continent. When the first people arrived, the ice sheets were melting back. Sea level was still rising until 3000 BCE, and Amazonia's rain forest was growing bigger—most of it had been savanna grassland during the last ice age.

Clovis Points Archeologists have found the spearheads called Clovis points, dated from between 13,200 and 12,900 years ago, all across North America and in a few places in Central America. The nearly identical style of all these weapons suggests that one hunting culture diffused across the continent.

THE KELP HIGHWAY Underwater forests of seaweed called kelp probably lured the first Amerindians south to Chile. The kelp beds of the Pacific coast, rich with seals, otters, shellfish, and other seafood, attracted people like magnets. Moreover, big rivers along the Pacific coast, from the Yukon to the Sacramento, were (and still are) highways for migratory salmon, chutes of high-protein food for anyone with a net. Exploiting kelp beds and salmon rivers is something people had already been doing along the North Pacific coasts from Japan to Alaska. So, the first arrivals in the Americas already had knowledge and skills that suited the American Pacific coastline, making it easy for them to traverse the kelp highway en route to Chile as early as 12,000 BCE.

CLOVIS CULTURE By 11,000 BCE, people had traveled almost everywhere in North America. The evidence for this is the distribution of stone spearheads called **Clovis points**, in wide use in North America (and in a few places in Central America) by 11,300 BCE. The points are nearly identical wherever they are found, indicating an early case of rapid diffusion of a useful technology—and of remarkable cultural homogeneity. Many Clovis points were discovered hundreds of miles away from the site where they were quarried. So either Clovis points were exchanged over long distances, or their users were mobile hunters—or both. Since many points are found together with mastodon and mammoth remains, it seems likely that Clovis culture included mobile hunters. Strikingly, people stopped making Clovis points only about 600 years after they started. Perhaps big game in North America had already grown scarce.

South America never had Clovis points, nor did it ever have the cultural homogeneity or the reliance on hunting that Clovis points imply for North America. People reached the southern tip of South America by 9000 BCE. The first settlers seem to have stuck to the coasts, both Pacific and Atlantic. It took longer to colonize the entire continent than in North America.

ECONOMIC LIFE

When people exited the kelp highway and headed inland, it took them a while to learn which plants, berries, fruits, and nuts were good to eat. Early on, away from the shorelines, the best option was to follow the big game animals.

But, over centuries and millennia, early Amerindians learned in great detail how best to live in dozens of different environments. Let's see how they did it in a few places.

FORAGING, FISHING, AND HUNTING At first, their options consisted of foraging, fishing, and hunting. In North America for the first several centuries, hunting probably played a major role in subsistence. By 8000 BCE, indications are that hunting had waned in significance, partly because most of the big game animals—mammoths, mastodons, giant beaver, horses—were gone. Foraging and fishing took up the slack.

One of the best places for foraging and fishing was California, which by 5000 BCE was the most densely populated region of North America. It offered fish, sea mammals, nuts, seeds, and acorns. California was more ecologically diverse than any similar-sized region in North America, offering plenty of food and many different types, so that if one source failed people could turn to others. People especially clustered around San Francisco Bay, which was still filling with seawater until 3000 BCE, and along the coast around today's Santa Barbara. After 3000 BCE, groups took up acorn harvesting amid the oak groves on the flanks of the Sierra Nevada.

As every squirrel knows, acorns store well and can provide calories all winter long when other foods are hard to find. Acorns are highly nutritious but require grinding, leaching, and boiling before humans can eat them, because they contain toxic tannins. The tedious labor of acorn processing was almost surely women's work. California's acorn foragers built year-round camps and even sedentary villages, some with more than a thousand people. Eventually, they were harvesting 60,000 tons of acorns per year, creating a food surplus that they could exchange for decorative shells from the Pacific coast and inland obsidian, the black, volcanic stone that holds a sharp edge.

Foraging for acorns and settling down led early Californians to have more children. When babies could eat acorn mush instead of drinking their mothers' milk, mothers became fertile again sooner after childbirth. Skeletons show shorter intervals between births, but also higher mortality among infants, children, and women of child-bearing age. Both birth and death rates climbed. California's acorn eaters established a reliable source of subsistence that led to social and health changes, and

commercial networks, comparable to those that followed transitions to agriculture around the world.

Amerindians in the Pacific Northwest also evolved a settled way of life without farming. This is a land of rugged mountains, jagged coastlines, tall forests, moderate temperatures, and frequent rain. The economic base here was the extraordinary abundance of migratory fish, mainly salmon, in rivers from northern California to Alaska. Permanent settlements developed by about 4400 BCE, and large villages from 1800 BCE. People also gathered berries, nuts, and fruits when the season permitted. But the key was the abundance of fish, which provided a food surplus. Smoked fish lasted for months before going bad.

This way of life permitted some people to accumulate power and wealth in the Pacific Northwest. Those who harvested more fish than others could accumulate followers and, in the case of men, have more wives and children. Elaborate burials show the rise of status differentiation. Elites were buried with spear-points, beads, carvings, and copper items. At some point, warfare and slavery became commonplace. At one cemetery site in northern British Columbia, the majority of male skeletons show signs of violence, either skull fractures or broken forearms. By 200 CE, villages built defensive fortifications, suggesting routine conflict. Population along this coast peaked around 1150 CE, after which it sharply declined for reasons unknown.

Across the continent in what is now New England and the Canadian Maritimes, Amerindians lived a more mobile and precarious existence. People first arrived here around 10,000 BCE, as the ice sheets were retreating. As in post-glacial Europe, they at first found hunting the most rewarding option. But as forests colonized the landscapes, hunting became harder and foraging for berries and nuts easier. By 7000 BCE, some people had begun seasonal migrations, congregating along rivers in the spring to exploit runs of migrating fish, and dispersing in summer for berry and nut picking. They huddled together in the hungry winter months when food often ran short. By 1000 BCE, they had cooking pots used for a wide variety of nuts, berries, roots, and seeds. They became more efficient hunters after 700 CE when they acquired the bow and arrow.

In early South America, big-game hunting was rarely if ever the main way of life. Most early archeological sites are near the coasts or along rivers. They reveal that Amerindians in these regions followed mobile lifestyles until about 3500 BCE, with great variation in subsistence strategies from place to place. On the Peruvian coast by 5000 to 4000 BCE, people learned how to fish in the rich waters of the Humboldt Current, one of the planet's great reservoirs of seafood. Along the coasts of southern Brazil, people harvested shellfish, leaving behind giant middens.

In California, the Pacific Northwest, New England, Peru, and Brazil, early Amerindians figured out ways to make a living from their varied environments. Some created settled ways of life, with fish or acorns prominent on the menu. Most moved seasonally in search of edible plants and animals. In both North and South America, coastal landscapes usually sustained the densest populations because they allowed people access to the resources of both land and sea. Within a few thousand years of their arrival in the Americas, people on both continents began to domesticate plants and turn to farming.

FARMING, AMERICAS-STYLE The first signs of farming in the Americas come from South American lowlands, around 9000 BCE. There is firmer evidence of agriculture in Mexico by 5000 BCE, the Andes by 3000 BCE, and the eastern woodlands of North America by 2000 BCE. In every case, these transitions were slow and unsteady. People used garden crops as just another food

source together with what they might gather and hunt. Groups often farmed for a few centuries and then gave it up for reasons we can only guess at—perhaps droughts, soil exhaustion, or warfare. So the distinction between farmers on the one hand and forager-hunters on the other was fuzzy in the Americas, as in Africa, and much more so than in most parts of Eurasia.

Farming in the Americas had a few distinctive characteristics. First, it involved a completely different set of crops from those grown in Eurasia or Africa, featuring maize, squash, beans, potatoes, quinoa, and a few others. There was no rice, wheat, barley, millet, or sorghum. We'll see some of the consequences of these crops shortly.

Second, all farming work was done by human hand. Amerindians had very few domesticated animals, and in North America none of significance except dogs. In the high Andes, people herded llamas from 3500 BCE. But llamas carried loads as pack animals and didn't pull carts or plows. With no oxen, horses, or water buffalo, farmers in the Americas had no plows. They used digging sticks, as farmers did in sub-Saharan Africa, to prepare ground for planting.

Third, in many locations, people labored long and hard to improve soil and terrain for farming. In swampy lowlands, from today's Bolivia to Mexico, farmers developed **raised-field agriculture**, one of the world's most ingenious and productive farming systems. The idea is to pile up mud, muck, and organic matter into small islands in swamps or along shallow lakeshores, and then plant crops on the raised fields. This practice ensures adequate moisture even in a dry season, keeps many pesky nibbling animals away from crops, and even provides a little climate control: the surrounding wetlands moderate extremes of heat and cold, reducing the risk of crop loss. Modern experiments show that raised-field agriculture—amphibious farming, one might say—offers bountiful yield per acre. But it was a lot of work to build and maintain the raised fields—as it was in amphibious farming of the rice padis of East and Southeast Asia.

Another important, and labor-intensive, modification of farmland was the building of terraces on mountain slopes. Terracing began by 2000 BCE and was done on a huge scale in the Andes after 500 CE. The Andes are often steep, but terracing and irrigation water from melting mountain snows converted mountain slopes into fertile farmland. By 1000 CE, Andean farmers had carved out about 600 square miles (1,500 sq km) of terraced fields.

Terraced Agriculture This photo, from Písac in present-day Peru, shows agricultural terraces carved into the Andes nearly 10,000 feet (ca. 3,000 m) above sea level. Farmers who worked steeply sloping land on all continents engaged in terracing, despite the enormous effort involved in both creating and maintaining terraces, because it helped prevent soil erosion and allowed easier water control. These terraces are probably from the fifteenth century, but Andean farmers built others beginning no later than 500 CE and likely before.

A Spaniard who arrived several centuries later said the Andes looked like staircases.

Another way to improve the soil was to create patches of so-called black earth. In Amazonia, where soils are usually poor, archeologists have recently found black earth soils deliberately enhanced by careful addition of organic matter—mainly charcoal, animal and fish bones, and manure. Far more fertile than surrounding soils, black earth allowed people from about 500 BCE onward to farm productively in landscapes that otherwise would yield little. By 1 CE, Amazonian farmers had built settled villages around their black earth patches.

INTENSIVE FARMING IN THE ANDES AND MESOAMERICA

In the Andes and Mesoamerica, combinations of crops eventually proved so productive, nutritious, and easy to store that they served as the basis for complex hierarchical societies and states, just as rice and wheat did in Eurasia and Egypt. These two locations became the great centers of population in the Americas.

THE ANDEAN FARMING SYSTEM The heart of the Andean farming system consisted of quinoa, maize, and potatoes. Quinoa, a grain native to the Andes, does well at high elevations and yields superbly nutritious seeds. Its cultivation began around 2000 BCE. Maize is an import to the region from Mexico, but somehow it arrived as early as 5000 BCE. Andean farmers grew it on mountain terraces up to 7,000 feet (2,000 m) in altitude and down on the desert coast with irrigation water from the mountains. The most important crop was potatoes, indigenous to the Andes, grown as high up as 13,000 feet (4,000 m). Potato farming began around 3500 BCE.

This farming system formed the foundation of complex society in the Andes for three main reasons. First was its reliability. In the Andes, irrigation water came from high glaciers, which melted in the tropical sun in dry and wet years alike, reducing the impact of droughts. Moreover, farmers had three different crops they could grow at different elevations in the mountains, so if one failed for any reason, they had a backup plan.

The second important feature of Andean farming was the nutritional value of its staple crops. Quinoa and potatoes are unusually nourishing foods, with a wide variety of vitamins, minerals, and proteins.

The third and most important characteristic of the Andean farming system was that all three staple crops stored well, especially in the dry and chill mountain air. As we've seen, storable food surpluses that can be hoarded, traded, and distributed formed the basis of political power in complex societies around the world. Quinoa and maize kernels can last for months. Potatoes cannot; but at some point probably well before 1000 CE, Andean farmers learned to make *chuño* by freezing small potatoes at night, heating them up in the midday sun, and then crushing them into a pasty, tasty meal. *Chuño* can last for years without spoiling—it's among the most durable foods ever invented.

Staple Crops Indentations resembling those found on potatoes are featured on this vase, from the Andes and dating to between the second and fifth centuries CE. The sculpture indicates the importance of the nutritious crop to Andean farming communities.

Andean people also made freeze-dried llama meat, called *charqui* (from which our word *jerky* derives), which also stores well. So with these storable and portable foodstuffs, Andean farmers provided an essential requirement for states, cities, and complex societies.

THE MESOAMERICAN FARMING SYSTEM In Mesoamerica, farmers developed a different intensive farming system, centered on maize, squash, and beans. As we've seen, maize—or corn, as it is also known—is the domesticated form of the Mexican grass *teosinte*. Starting at the latest by 5000 BCE, farmers produced bigger grains and taller stalks through genetic modification achieved by careful human selection. Maize lacks important nutrients but is very efficient at turning sunshine into edible calories.

Maize, squash, and beans—sometimes called the Three Sisters—seemed made for one another. Bean plants used maize stalks to climb upward. Beans (or, to be precise, microbes attached to their roots) fixed nitrogen in the soil, compensating for maize's big nitrogen requirement. Squashes helped out by spreading over the ground, denying sunlight to weeds and holding moisture in the soil. As food, beans provide the niacin and proteins that maize lacks, so they not only grow well together but also complement one another in the human diet. For more than 4,000 years, this trinity of crops has formed the heart of Mesoamerican agriculture. People in Oaxaca, in south-central Mexico, acknowledge this when they say they are *hombres de maiz*.

The Three Sisters traveled well. Like many plants, maize takes its cues about when to flower from changing day length. Mexican varieties can't grow properly in Minnesota, for example. It took millennia to develop maize varieties that would grow well at different latitudes, but Amerindian farmers gradually did it. By 1000 CE, most farmers in the Americas, from Argentina to Canada, raised maize among their crops, usually together with beans and squashes, and many made it their staple food.

In raised fields in the Maya lowlands and central Mexico, the Mesoamerican farming system, like that of the Andes, provided enough storable, portable surplus food to support the formation of states, cities, and complex societies.

MANUFACTURING AND TRADE

We've explored the subsistence strategies—ways of life— and farming systems in the Americas before 1000 CE. It remains to consider realms we can loosely call manufacturing and trade.

TEXTILES AND METALLURGY The most important item of manufacture throughout most of the Americas was clothing. In the Andes, the most common material was alpaca wool, but cotton and even cactus fiber were used too. Andean weavers by 1000 BCE had invented on their own just about every technique in use worldwide. Men apparently sometimes wove cloth in the Andes, but everywhere else in the Americas all evidence suggests it was exclusively women's work, often done in outdoor courtyards and in the company of others. Maya weavers used hemp for everyday cloth, and cotton only for luxury. In Mesoamerica and the Andes, cloth makers found excellent dyestuffs—indigo (blue) and cochineal (red)—that yielded vivid and durable colors. They even had a purple dye made from the mucus of a snail that was a distant cousin of the mollusk so important to the merchant cities of Phoenicia.

Metallurgy mattered little in the Americas, in contrast to Africa and Eurasia. In the Andes, smiths worked copper and gold by 1800 BCE, mostly for ornamental purposes. Metal ornaments helped high-ranking people show off their importance, both in life and in death. Some burials

in Peru include farm implements made of bronze or silver, too heavy to be useful as tools but just right to demonstrate one's social status. The Maya scarcely worked metals at all. Since no one worked iron, the Americas didn't experience the revolutionary impacts of that metal on farming, warfare, and politics that it wrought in Africa and Eurasia.

TRADE, CULTURAL EXCHANGE, AND AMERICAN WEBS In the Americas, especially within Mesoamerica and the Andean region, people and goods were constantly on the move, creating arenas of interaction that developed into American webs.

The earliest exchanges involved food crops. As we've seen, maize spread from Mesoamerica both north and south so that by 1000 CE farmers from Quebec to Argentina raised it. People also carried sweet potatoes both north and south from their origin in Colombia or Panama, so that by 2000 BCE they flourished in warm, humid lands on both continents.

People also exchanged shells and stone over long distances. By 800 CE, the Ecuador coast, for example, hosted a thriving export business in conch shells, a luxury good. The big shells were hard to get—one had to dive 60 feet (18 m) beneath the sea—and served as ornaments for the wealthy. Traders, probably navigating coastal waters on rafts, took them as far afield as Mexico. In a world with no iron goods, obsidian had high value. Amerindians in the Ohio River valley acquired obsidian quarried in what is now Wyoming. The Maya got it from central Mexico. Jade, a stone more prized for decorative than practical purposes, was also traded over long distances, especially in Mesoamerica. Another trade good that was prized enough to be traded over long distances was cacao: in the 770s CE, people in Utah were eating chocolate made from Mesoamerican cacao beans. Conch shells and obsidian were high-value products, like tin in ancient Europe or lapis lazuli in Asia, and they provided the necessary incentives for people to knit networks of long-distance exchange.

The two centers of trade and exchange, unsurprisingly, were the two centers of population: Mesoamerica and the Andes. In the Maya world, trade and tribute involved not only obsidian but also feathers, cotton cloth, pottery, jewelry, and especially salt. The cities of northern Yucatán were well situated to produce sea salt and to trade it throughout Mesoamerica. In return they acquired goods from far and wide, such as gold from Panama and turquoise from New

Cacao Traded over long distances, cacao beans were a luxury good and status symbol across the Americas. The god depicted in this Maya statue from between 600 and 900 CE wears a cacao pod at his waist.

Mexico. In Mesoamerica, people used cacao beans as currency, an unusual choice because they don't last well. All goods went by raft, canoe, or human porter in the absence of beasts of burden and wheeled vehicles.

In the Andes, economic exchange was also common from 2500 BCE onward, but it proceeded differently. First, llamas could carry loads of up to 110 lbs. (50 kg), and to judge by artwork, they did so regularly in caravans by 200 BCE. Second, unlike in Mesoamerica, in the Andes markets and merchants played a small role. Instead, economic exchange was in the hands of political leaders, who organized llama caravans along regular routes. They bartered—there is no evidence of money—for cotton, salt, obsidian, and coca leaf. Coca leaf, from a bush that grows only in the Andes, served as medicine, aphrodisiac, and in religious ceremonies. People chewed wads of leaf to fend off fatigue, hunger, and thirst. People rarely traded for basic necessities in the Andes.

These trade patterns were part of broader webs of cultural exchange. In the lowlands of eastern South America, pottery styles were very similar over huge spaces, and new styles spread quickly. That suggests a large zone of interaction, presumably along the many navigable rivers. The practice of building mounds was even more widespread. Amerindians in California, Ohio, Venezuela, Guyana, and many points in between piled up earth to create ceremonial centers for religious rites. From Alaska to the Maya region, people used sweat baths for ritual cleansing. A team game played on special courts (discussed below) spread from southern Mexico to Arizona. So at least in a loose way, all peoples in the Americas were linked to one another—because they were linked to either Mesoamerica or the Andes.

Each of these centers of population had its own orbit, its own web. There were connections between the two—somehow maize, manioc, and the bow and arrow spread to both—but they were still slender as of 1000 CE.

HEALTH, SOCIETY, AND CULTURE

No one knows how many Amerindians were alive in 1000 CE, let alone in earlier times. The Americas contained perhaps 5 million people in 1000 BCE, 15 million in 1 CE, and 40 million in 1000. Even by the earliest date, the Andes and Mesoamerica held the biggest concentrations of population, home to as much as two-thirds of the hemisphere's population—thanks to the bounty of intensive farming systems.

HEALTH What we know about the health of Amerindians before 1000 CE comes mainly from the study of skeletons, and to a lesser extent from analysis of DNA. In global terms, people in the Americas had two great health advantages. Since they didn't live cheek by jowl with herd animals, they had none of the infections that humans elsewhere acquired from their flocks and herds. And because their ancestors had crossed to America through very cold environments, they left behind those pathogens that need warmth to survive, such as malaria. But, like everyone else, their health suffered when they settled down, took up farming, and built cities.

Health varied greatly from place to place and over time. The healthiest peoples tended to live near abundant seafood resources—for example, along the coasts of southern Brazil. Mobile peoples were also among the healthiest. The unhealthiest were sedentary farmers and—once cities developed—city folk.

Before 500 BCE, the average life expectancy in the

Americas was around 34 years—high by world standards of the time. People in urbanized areas, however, lived on average only 21 to 22 years. Over time, as farming and city life spread, fertility climbed and health nosedived. Between 1 CE and 1000 CE, life expectancy averaged only about 23 to 25 years for the hemisphere as a whole. As in Eurasia, the spread of farming generally made people shorter in stature as well as shorter-lived. The main reason, probably, was a decline in animal protein in the diet as people depended more on maize and beans, and less on meat and fish.

In the eastern woodlands of North America, populations remained comparatively healthy until the arrival of maize after 500 CE, especially those living near the fishing grounds of the Great Lakes. There was an unusual decline in stature here even before the transition to farming, perhaps a reflection of diminishing game supplies. Average height shrank by 3 inches (6 cm) from 6000 BCE to 1000 BCE, more for males than females. To judge from their skeletons (ca. 600–1000 CE), peoples of the desert Southwest suffered frequent malnutrition but low rates of infectious disease.

Risks of violence, as well as malnutrition and disease, varied tremendously across time and place. Mesoamerican skeletons show violent trauma in about 6 percent of cases, low by world standards of pre-modern times. In Ecuador, rates of violence in general were also low, but higher among farming people than among others. In some Ecuadorian burials, only female skeletons show signs of violence. In the eastern woodlands of North America, rates of violence were lower still, and similar for males and females. In California, violence spiked after the introduction of the bow and arrow around 400 CE: over the next eight centuries, 10 percent of adults appear to have suffered arrow wounds. As noted above, extremely high rates of violence prevailed among males in the Pacific Northwest in the centuries before 1100 CE. As a general rule, violence became more common over time, as more people lived in permanent settlements and adopted new technologies such as the bow and arrow that enabled people to maim and kill others at lower risk to themselves.

FAMILY AND GENDER For the first 10,000 years of human history in the Americas, we have scant evidence of the nature of family life or the roles of men and women. Judging from the archeological record since 1000 BCE, we can say that in most respects, gender history in the Americas looked a lot like gender history elsewhere. The best evidence available comes from artwork, burials, and skeletons.

Family arrangements ranged from small nuclear households to big extended ones. Most Amerindian societies practiced monogamy, even for elite males. The exceptions came mainly in the case of conquering states, in which successful warriors might acquire multiple wives from among the conquered. Maya kings had multiple wives, usually as a means of political alliance.

In foraging and hunting societies, women spent most of their time collecting and preparing food, raising children, and perhaps making stone tools. Social groups remained small in most cases, kin-based, and with little formal hierarchy. Some scholars surmise that because women's food collecting provided most of the sustenance for their societies, they enjoyed comparatively higher status. Among the acorn harvesters of California, for example, women probably had some say in the choice of settlement sites. Their health and life expectancy, to judge from skeletons, was equal to that of men if one discounts high mortality among women of child-bearing age.

After 1000 BCE, most women lived in farming societies. They typically made pots and jars, spun and wove textiles, collected wild foods, took some part in the work of farming, spent long hours in food preparation, and raised children. Wherever maize was the staple, women ground kernels into flour to make either tortillas or maize porridge. Their skeletons show enormous wear and tear on wrist joints, something absent in male skeletons. In maize-based farming societies, men planted crops, harvested them, hunted, and built homes and other buildings. They might also roam far and wide for purposes of trade or warfare.

Gender arrangements varied from place to place. Artwork from New Mexico (ca. 200–1000 CE) shows men and women in conventional roles, but in a few cases also shows women hunting with traps and sticks, while men hunted with spears and bows and arrows. In many cases, including New Mexico and Peru after 600 CE, artwork shows women taking part in religious ceremonies—as women did in most other parts of the world. Peruvian art also implies that men sometimes joined in textile work; and elsewhere in the Andes men were buried with spinning implements, which was rare by world standards. According to glyphs—the writing system of the Maya—a woman named Sak'k'uk ruled a city for three years (612–615 CE) until her son attained the age of 12. But women in the Americas, as elsewhere, only rarely held positions of political power.

RELIGION AND LANGUAGE Amerindians followed a variety of religious practices, but some beliefs and rituals enjoyed wide currency. Amerindians overall accepted the existence of numerous spirits and the notion of a supreme deity. The spirits were generally associated with animals, plants, rivers, mountains, fertility, death, celestial bodies, and other aspects of nature. Appeals to the spirits could be made through departed ancestors, who now lived in the spirit world, or through shamans.

The closest thing to a universal in Amerindian religious practice was shamanism. A shaman—as we've seen—is someone with special knowledge of, and access to, the spirit world. Amerindians generally communicated with the spirit world through visions, which might come through dreams, trances, or hallucinations. They often placed great importance on dreams, which might reveal the future or allow conversation with the dead.

Many Amerindian cultures also sought access to the spirit world through hallucinogenic drugs derived from plants. These might be eaten, drunk in a potion, snorted, or smoked, often together with tobacco. Peyote, a kind of cactus native to northern Mexico and the southwestern United States, provided a psychoactive drug used by shamans from at least 3000 BCE. Central American mushrooms and the Amazonian vine product *ayahuasca* also helped shamans explore the unseen. Siberian shamans had long used drugs to enhance access to the spirit world, so this practice probably came with the first arrival of people in the Americas, although the plants employed differed from place to place.

From Central America to Amazonia, shamans were often associated with jaguars. The big, powerful cats moved in the night, normally unseen. They hunted in the trees and the water, moving from one world to another, as shamans did. In some traditions, jaguars protected shamans as they approached the spirit world. Artistic motifs often put shamans and jaguars together, and sometimes show shamans becoming jaguars.

Amerindian religions, like those of most other parts of the world, also emphasized the practice of sacrifice as a means of gaining the good will of spiritual forces. Amerindians were unusual in that they rarely sacrificed crops, beverages, or—aside from llamas in the Andes—livestock.

Human Sacrifice A Maya stone relief shows a priest holding the head of a sacrificial victim he has beheaded. The carving was created during the first millennium CE.

Sometimes they used humans for religious sacrifice. The Moche, who lived in coastal Peru around 200 to 600 CE, apparently sacrificed teenagers. The Maya sacrificed people by throwing them into *cenotes*, water-filled sinkholes common in Yucatán. They also decapitated people whose blood was expected to sustain the gods. It's likely that war captives provided many of the victims for human sacrifice. Maya rulers often made sacrifices of their own blood, piercing themselves with sharp tools. They hoped this would ensure good fortune for newborns or for a newly enthroned king.

Mesoamerican religion also emphasized the measurement of cosmic time. Mesoamericans developed several

CONSIDERING THE EVIDENCE

A Maya Bowl for Cocoa

Mayan glyph carvers toiled continually to record the births, deaths, ceremonies, and conquests of their kings and queens on the surfaces of their temples, plazas, and monuments. Scholars have also deciphered glyphs about lesser nobles on seemingly mundane objects that offer insights into their personal lives. Pictured here, for instance, is an inscribed, white stone vessel just over six inches (15 cm) in diameter and around four inches (10 cm) tall. The three glyphs along its rim record that the carving was completed on (by our calendar) August 18, 731 CE, for a "guardian-priest" named Yiban who served the "holy lord of [the land of] K'an." The carver also labeled the bowl as "cup for *ixiimte*-flavored cocoa," a potent concoction that Yiban would have prepared for his lord as part of ceremonies for communicating with the gods.

The carvings on the side of the bowl depict Yiban and his deceased parents. In the close-up reproduction below, Yiban's mother (center) carries the image of a god in her right arm. Her name is inscribed in smaller glyphs near her forehead as Ix-Mo', or Lady Macaw. Although Maya-carved jade made its way throughout Mesoamerica, white stone bowls were rare, prized possessions often entombed with their owners. For Yiban, this cup not only connected him to his lord and his gods, it also memorialized his parents.

Cocoa bowl of Yiban, 731 CE

QUESTIONS FOR ANALYSIS

1. Why was this bowl important to Yiban and his lord? Why were similar bowls important to Maya society in general?
2. Search the Maya glyphs below for numbers. (Hint: small circles equal one and bars equal five.) Why do you think scholars could translate number glyphs before any of the other glyphs?
3. What can historians learn from personal objects like this bowl that may not be evident from the carvings on Maya monuments designed for everyone to see?

Rollout of inscriptions on the bowl This presentation of the bowl's full exterior in two dimensions shows Yiban (left), Ix-mo' (center), and his unnamed father (right). The glyphs are traced in black ink for greater readability.

remarkably accurate calendars based on the perceived movements of the sun, moon, Venus, and Mars, and one, a calendar with a 260-day cycle, based—perhaps—on the human gestation period. Some calendars were used to help figure out the best days for religious rituals or coronations of new rulers. Others served to organize the agricultural years.

Shamanism, visions, and sacrifice were widespread in Amerindian religion. The sophisticated calendrics were confined to Mesoamerica.

All Amerindian languages are derived from tongues spoken in Northeast Asia long ago. Migrants from Asia may have brought one or several languages with them. As early Americans then spread out over the two continents, their contacts with one another diminished and gradually their speech evolved into a few thousand different languages. California alone had at least 74 Amerindian languages.

After thousands of years of language diversification, however, the trend reversed. By 500 CE and probably well before, certain languages such as Qechua in South America and Mayan in Central America, spread at the expense of local ones. Just as Latin spread with the growth of the Roman Empire or Chinese with the conquests of the Qin and Han, so Qechua and Mayan spread because of the political strength of people who spoke those tongues. There was nothing inherently better about these languages than the ones they replaced—just as there was nothing intrinsically better about Latin than Etruscan. This process of the spread of imperial languages was slow, and by 1000 CE thousands of languages still remained in the Americas.

STATES AND COMPLEX SOCIETIES IN THE AMERICAS

In the Americas, as elsewhere, the development of states, cities, and complex society depended on the availability of foods that would store and travel well. As we've seen, maize and potatoes fit the bill, and that is probably why the Americas' earliest and most extensive centers of political and military power, urban life, and hierarchical society developed in the homelands of these crops, Mesoamerica and the Andes.

MESOAMERICA: OLMECS AND MAYA

By 2000 BCE, farming villages dotted Mesoamerica. By 1000 BCE, the first signs of monumental architecture and urban life appeared, and writing evolved by about 500 BCE. As far as we can tell, most of these developments began with the Olmecs and reached a mysterious climax with the Maya.

THE OLMECS, CA. 1600–300 BCE At around 1600 BCE, in the steamy lowlands of southern Mexico at a place now called San Lorenzo, people now called **Olmecs** ("people from the land of rubber") began to build large structures such as temples, limestone-paved plazas, earthen mounds, and ball courts. The Olmecs farmed maize, beans, squash, gourds, and avocadoes in the floodplains of local rivers, gathered food including turtle eggs, and hunted for peccaries, deer, turtles, and other animals. Bones in their garbage heaps suggest that their main source of animal protein, however, was domestic dogs.

San Lorenzo had urban features such as monuments and public spaces, but its population probably never exceeded 3,000. To what extent, if any, it dominated a hinterland is unclear, but Olmec artistic motifs appeared in villages for many miles around. There is no trace of an army or a priestly caste. But something—perhaps control of trade and prestige goods such as jade and obsidian—allowed some families to dominate the rest, claim special access to the spirit realm, and become rulers. By roughly 900 BCE, San Lorenzo was abandoned. Many monuments appear intentionally smashed, so archeologists suspect organized violence, a revolution, or an invasion.

A new center of Olmec culture called La Venta, about 50 miles (80 km) away, arose around 900 BCE. It is nearer the coast than San Lorenzo and is situated in swampy terrain. Its great earthen pyramid, the first in the Americas, stands tall above a flat landscape and served as a ceremonial site.

The most remarkable feature of Olmec culture is a series of giant basalt heads, usually assumed to represent rulers of San Lorenzo and La Venta. Seventeen have been found, the biggest of which is nearly the size of an elephant. The Olmecs somehow moved stones, as large as any at Stonehenge, far from where they were quarried. This must have required the coordinated effort of thousands of people, a key sign of the degree of complexity

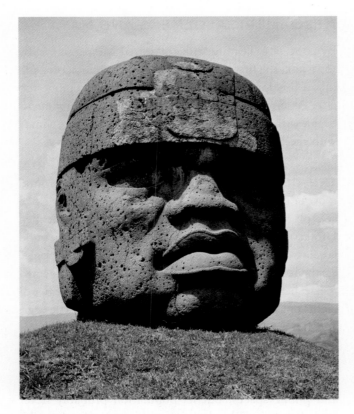

Colossal Heads Dating from between 1200 and 300 BCE, this is one of the seventeen remaining basalt human heads that the Olmec culture created. It took considerable labor and ingenuity to erect these massive sculptures.

and organization among the Olmecs. But we haven't a clue how it happened. The scraps of Olmec writing found so far, which date to about 650 BCE, shed little light. The most revealing fragment, a stone inscription deciphered only in 1993, explains that a certain "King Harvest Mountain" cut off the head of his rival.

By 300 BCE, the Olmec centers were empty. Once again, no one knows why. Village farming persisted in the region, but urban life and complex hierarchical society disappeared.

The Olmecs were the first people in Mesoamerica to develop complex hierarchical society. But some of their neighbors, such as the Maya and the Zapotecs, were moving in similar directions at almost the same time, and they all interacted through trade and perhaps military competition. The art, architecture, religion, and calendars in use throughout Mesoamerica overlapped. So it is perhaps reasonable to see the whole region together evolving toward social complexity over many centuries from 1600 BCE.

THE MAYA, CA. 600 BCE–900 CE People lived in the Maya lands—Yucatán and its neighborhood—for thousands of years and had taken up farming by 1100 BCE if not before. Chronically short of fresh water, the Maya landscape required a lot of work to become productive. But with enough wisely invested labor, it could be enormously productive, as it was from about 200 to nearly 900 CE.

In their origin myth, the **Maya** are made of maize, which is not far wrong. Farmers raised peppers, tomatoes, sweet potato, manioc, cotton, and cacao as well as the Mesoamerican Three Sisters. The indispensable crop for the Maya, as for the Olmecs, was maize. The Maya created a variation of Mesoamerica's amphibious agriculture with systems of ditches, drains, canals, and reservoirs to cope with seasonal water shortage and flooding. The Maya built raised fields amid their canals, replenishing fertility by piling muck from canal floors atop their fields. In hilly terrain, they also cut thousands of terraces to keep soil in place. They grew crops year-round. Maya agriculture was enormously labor-intensive.

Beyond farming, the Maya secured a little more food by hunting deer, turkeys, monkeys, crocodiles, and manatees, and collecting fruits and berries. Like the Olmec, they raised dogs for food. Those living near the coast fished and collected mollusks. Inland Maya probably stocked their canals with fish.

The Maya developed some industries that helped enrich and empower their leaders. In the northern Yucatán, Maya perfected the art of salt making by the evaporation of seawater held in ponds. They exported high-quality salt throughout Mesoamerica. Maya artisans excelled in jade carving. Harder than steel, jade isn't an easy stone to work. Maya artisans used obsidian blades and stone drills—they had no metal tools—to carve, scrape, and polish jade into works of art. They exported jade items throughout Mesoamerica, much as bronze smiths in ancient China or Mesopotamia did in their regions. Anyone claiming elite status in Mesoamerica wanted Maya jade.

Maya trade networks contributed to the wealth and power of the elite families who dominated Maya societies. Trade links involving salt, jade, and obsidian extended to the Pacific coast of Central America and to the region around today's Mexico City—the Valley of Mexico, an excellent obsidian source.

Through extensive archeology and advances in deciphering Maya glyphs, we know much more about Maya

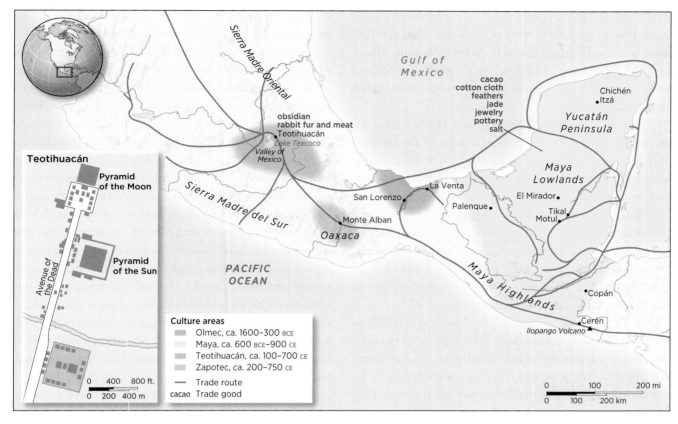

Mesoamerican Cultures, ca. 1600 BCE–900 CE Beginning with the Olmec, a succession of Mesoamerican cultures arose all based on intensive irrigated farming, often in wetlands. Some built substantial cities, none greater than Teotihuacán. Despite a lack of beasts of burden, long-distance trade and cultural exchange networks grew up, binding the entire region into its own web of interaction.

society and politics than about the Olmecs. It seems that the Maya had Mesoamerica's most complete writing system and could write anything that they could speak. Maya scribes were at work by 250 BCE, and perhaps by 600 BCE.

By 600 BCE the Maya were also building pyramids, indicating that someone had the power to direct the labor of many others. Pyramids served as temples for religious rituals, often involving sacrifices of food, tobacco, and human life. The pyramids stood in the heart of genuine cities, which by 500 CE might hold tens of thousands of people. These cities—Tikal, El Mirador, Palenque, Copán to name a few—exercised some control over surrounding landscapes. They were territorial states, although small ones compared to what came later in Mesoamerica.

Despite common culture and language, these cities never united politically. Instead, they competed fiercely with one another. In 679 CE, for example, the city of Tikal, which might have had 50,000 people, overran a rival city, Motul. The victors composed a glyph that summarized the war: "the skulls of Motul people were piled into mountains." The Maya cities, like the fifth-century BCE Greek *poleis* or the even more ancient Sumerian city-states, competed politically, militarily, and probably commercially. That competition made the surviving polities extremely formidable with respect to neighboring villages and communities, which the bigger cities easily dominated.

The glyphs and archeology also offer a sense of the Maya social order. It was a sharply hierarchical society, at least after 200 CE, in which kings and royal lineages lorded it over everyone else. Kings and queens performed religious rituals and lived at the ceremonial temples. As with monarchs elsewhere, authority rested in part on expert access to supernatural power. Maya royalty eventually claimed to be descended from the gods. Authority also rested on prowess and leadership in war, often undertaken to acquire captives needed for sacrifices. Maya rulers were shaman-rulers, just as rulers of early complex societies almost everywhere were priest-kings. Elite families from non-royal lineages shared in power by holding offices such as judge, general, or priest. Some commoners became prosperous, either as merchants or artisans, or as artists employed by rulers.

The vast majority of Maya labored in the fields. All owed tribute to the ruler, paid as a share of the harvest, or in goods, or as labor on temples, roads, or other public works. At the bottom rung of society were slaves, often war captives who, for the moment at least, escaped being sacrificed. Orphans usually were enslaved too. We can't tell what percentage of Maya were enslaved, but considerable evidence suggests a lively slave trade throughout Maya lands. The glyphs have plenty to say about the glorious deeds and distinguished ancestry of Maya rulers, but not a syllable about slaves or commoners.

More than anyone else in the Americas, the Maya refined their mathematical skills. For them, as for the Babylonians, math was the servant of religion. With multiple calendars, the Maya needed dexterity with numbers to figure out the right day to perform a particular ritual. They used a base 20 system that included the concept of zero (also invented independently in India) and could perform calculations in the millions. By the second century CE, the Maya had devised another calendar, the so-called Long Count, which marked consecutive days beginning August 8, 3114 BCE (by our calendar), which they reckoned was the fourth beginning of creation. Their calendar even had a word (*alautun*) for periods of 23,040,000,000 days—a

little over 63 million years. You couldn't be a good Maya priest without strong quantitative skills.

The Maya also elaborated the ball game that seems first to have appeared among the Olmecs and became a hallmark of Mesoamerican culture. We don't know exactly how the game was played, but it was a team game played on an outdoor court involving a hard rubber ball about the size of a grapefruit. The biggest court, at Chichén Itzá, a northern Yucatán city that had 13 ball courts, is nearly twice the size of a football field. Teams of as many as six per side wore uniforms and tried to put the ball through a stone ring, mounted vertically high up on the court's wall. They used fists, elbows, and hips, or maybe paddles—but not their open hands. Goals must have been as rare as in soccer. Some scholars think the game was part of divination ceremonies, used to foretell the outcome of some venture, perhaps a planned attack on enemies. Some think the game was played by captives, and the losers sacrificed. Artwork suggests rivulets of blood commonly flowed in the course of a match. Rulers perhaps encouraged the ball game as a distraction for the masses, like chariot races in ancient Rome. Archeologists have found about 1,500 ball courts so far in Mexico, Arizona, and Cuba.

The Maya flourished from about 200 CE. They suffered a devastating setback in the late 530s when the Ilopango volcano erupted, raining down ash and pumice waist-deep over much of the southern fringe of the Maya world. Within 50 to 75 miles (80–120 km) of the volcano, farming ceased for 200 years. Survivors of the blast fled north and east, toward the center of the Maya lands. But

Maya Sport The Ball Game Court at the Maya city of Chichén Itzá is over 180 yards (165 m) long. The stone rings used as goals appear midway down the court, near the top of the high stone walls surrounding it.

by 750 CE people had resettled the buried region, and population in the Maya region as a whole approached its maximum, perhaps 10 million—far higher than the Olmecs'.

Then beginning late in the ninth century CE monumental building and inscriptions stopped. Cities emptied, and population declined by at least three-quarters over the next 150 years. As with the Olmecs a millennium earlier, no one knows why this collapse of urban life occurred—although drought probably was part of the equation. Late in the ninth century a long searing drought, the worst in many centuries, afflicted the region. Perhaps soil erosion and nutrient loss undermined agriculture in some areas. Stepped-up warfare was likely involved. All these problems could have combined in a deadly downward spiral. The collapse of urban, complex society among the Maya is one of the great mysteries of the history of the American hemisphere, parallel in some respects to the disappearance of urban society along the Indus River 2,000 years before.

Zapotec Culture Funerary urns buried with Zapotec dead between 200 BCE and 800 CE featured images meant to evoke dead ancestors: here, a woman (left) and a man (right).

MESOAMERICA: ZAPOTECS AND TEOTIHUACÁN

Alongside the Maya, but well to their west, two other complex societies rose and fell in Mesoamerica: the Zapotecs of the Oaxaca region, and the urban population of Teotihuacán. We know less about these societies than about the Maya, mainly because they left little writing. But they interacted regularly with Maya centers, forming a lively Mesoamerican web by 200 or 300 CE.

ZAPOTECS IN OAXACA, CA. 200–750 CE The Zapotecs lived—as their descendants do today—in a region of southern Mexico called Oaxaca. This is mountainous terrain, but with frost-free valleys it is ideal for maize cultivation. Farming and villages appeared by 1500 BCE here, even earlier than in the Maya lands. Most villages had defensive palisades, an indication of regular warfare. Writing emerged by 700 or 600 BCE. Their language, a descendant of which is still spoken, was different from Mayan. Scholars have yet to decipher Zapotec writing securely. What they think they can read is mainly about the heroic slaughter and mutilation of enemies by rulers, very much in the tradition of Mayan—and for that matter, Assyrian—literature. But Zapotec art shows no kings trumpeting their great deeds, and the architecture suggests a more egalitarian society than the Maya.

By 100 BCE the people of the Valley of Oaxaca had begun a successful expansion and built a city, today called Monte Alban. At its height it might have housed 15,000 to 20,000 people, rivaling most Maya centers. Its centerpiece was a leveled ridge with palaces, tombs, ball courts, and plazas. The ridge, although lacking in water, is a good defensive location, a citadel with long views in every direction. The entire Valley of Oaxaca was dotted with maize-growing villages—the Zapotecs too considered themselves children of maize—and by 500 CE may have held 100,000 people. If you like tortillas, you're in their debt, because this is the society that invented the maize tortilla.

By 750 CE, the grand buildings at Monte Alban had begun to crumble, and the city shrank in population to the size of a village, with about 2,000 residents. People dispersed to other settlements in the Oaxaca valley, and perhaps farther afield. Once again, no one knows why.

TEOTIHUACÁN, CA. 100–700 CE The last of the Mesoamerican societies we will consider, Teotihuacán, was distinctive in several ways. It was located in the Valley of Mexico, where today's Mexico City stands, at an elevation of 7,500 feet (2,300 m) and surrounded by mountains. Rain was scarce, but the Valley had several small lakes. In this environment a giant city grew up. Unlike other Mesoamerican societies, it left no evidence of real writing, ball courts, or elaborate calendars.

Why Were Complex Societies in the Americas More Fragile Than Those in Eurasia and Egypt?

The formation of complex hierarchical societies in the Americas began about 3100 BCE in Peru and 1600 BCE in Mesoamerica. Thereafter, several complex societies rose and fell across the two American continents. These generally shared the same features we've seen in complex hierarchical societies in Eurasia and Africa: cities, public buildings, public spaces, monumental architecture, bureaucratic states, armies, irrigation agriculture, and writing. Not every example had all these characteristics—none of the Peruvian cases used writing, for example. Yet the broad similarity in pattern is striking, especially since we have no evidence of meaningful contact across the oceans before about 1000 CE. One puzzle, then, is why societies evolved on such parallel tracks when they had no contact with one another.

There's a second puzzle as well. When complex societies in the Americas fell, people in most cases did not re-create this social format for centuries. There's nothing like the long-term continuity of complex society exhibited in the history of north China, Mesopotamia, or Egypt. In those lands, once people organized complex society, they never departed from it. Particular dynasties, states, and cultures came and went, but the basic format endured.

In the Americas, however, the pattern resembles that of the Indus valley, repeated several times over: complex society develops, flourishes for a few centuries, and then disappears, generally for unknown reasons. When it recurs, it is usually somewhere else nearby. In Peru, after the end of Norte Chico around 1600 BCE, it took 700 years for complex society to return in the form of the Chavín culture, and it reappeared up in the mountains rather than along the coast. It took about 1,500 years after the fall of the Norte Chico society before complex hierarchical society recurred on the coast, in the form of the Moche culture.

In Mesoamerica, the Olmecs, Maya, Zapotecs, and people of Teotihuacán forged complex hierarchical societies, with similar features, that lasted for five or fifteen centuries. In every case, the people involved abandoned that social format for smaller-scale, simpler, village society. We don't know why.

For some reason, complex society in the Americas was more fragile than in Eurasia and Egypt. Perhaps rulers found it harder to monopolize organized violence without war horses or weapons of bronze and iron. Perhaps without steppe nomads to worry about, people thought it less urgent to rebuild states once they had collapsed. Perhaps the environmental shocks, such as droughts and floods associated with El Niño, were more severe or more frequent. Perhaps the religious ideologies justifying inequality and hierarchy were less convincing. The explanation may draw on all of these factors, or it may be something else altogether. One of the virtues of world history is that it invites comparative questions like this. The study of a single culture—for example, the Maya or Egyptians alone—does not.

It does seem clear that for the peoples of the Americas, life in complex society held some appeal, especially for rulers. But life without taxes, tribute, forced labor, military conscription, and human sacrifice apparently had its advantages too.

QUESTIONS FOR DISCUSSION

1. What do you make of the similarities in complex society as it developed in Eurasia, Africa, and the Americas?
2. Which explanations of the fragility of complex society in the Americas do you find most convincing, and why?

Around 100 BCE to 100 CE, the population of the Valley of Mexico, previously huddled around the shores of the lakes, started gathering at Teotihuacán. Soon 100,000 people, almost everyone in the Valley, crowded into the city. Careful control of a freshwater spring allowed leading families to create a big swamp with raised fields, called *chinampas*, where maize, beans, and squash thrived. The people of Teotihuacán also raised rabbits for food and fur, and they traded both to surrounding communities.

Teotihuacán had another basis of wealth: obsidian. The city lay close to the sources of the best obsidian in Mesoamerica and organized the stone's quarrying and export. Perhaps because of its obsidian business, Teotihuacán had a bigger role in long-distance trade and diplomacy than any other community in the Americas. In 378 CE, one of its leaders mounted a military expedition that dethroned the ruling house in the Maya city of Tikal, one of the two most powerful Maya centers. By 400 CE, Teotihuacán's population approached 150,000, by far the biggest city in the Americas.

Uncharacteristically for Mesoamerica, Teotihuacán had a regular grid plan, carefully laid out to awe visitors. At the heart of the city was the so-called Avenue of the Dead, with adjacent tall pyramids. The tallest, the Pyramid of the Sun, served as the main ceremonial center, atop which stood a temple used for sacrifices. The city had a sewage system, like ancient Rome and the cities of the ancient Indus. Some of the residential quarters seem to have been organized ethnically, with sections of the city housing immigrants from Oaxaca, Guatemala, and other nearby regions. It was the multicultural metropolis of Mesoamerica, drawing in people from far and wide.

Although the lack of writing limits our knowledge of religion at Teotihuacán, artwork, mainly wall paintings, shows that the residents believed in the usefulness of human sacrifice. It also implies an unusual feature—the worship of a female deity, one of eight main gods. Sometimes called (by modern scholars) the Great Goddess of Teotihuacán, she is usually pictured with a bird headdress and a nose pendant with fangs. She often appears with spiders, which may associate her with the underworld. Her image appears only in Teotihuacán and places where natives of that city settled, whereas most Mesoamerican deities had followers throughout the region. Other artistic styles of Teotihuacán spread widely, and its influence stretched from Honduras to the south as far north as northern Mexico.

Then, perhaps in the 530s, the metropolis of Mesoamerica suddenly and mysteriously crashed. Central buildings burned. Its population fell to 20,000 or 30,000, still the equivalent of a big city anywhere else. A new hypothesis explains this by emphasizing cold and drought resulting from a volcanic dust veil—well documented around the Northern Hemisphere for the years 535–536. But some scholars think the city's fires and collapse came later, perhaps as late as 700, and instead see evidence of a social uprising and overthrow of the rulers.

A MESOAMERICAN WEB These four societies—the Olmecs, Maya, Zapotecs, and Teotihuacán—show a host of strong similarities that reflect growing interaction among peoples throughout Mesoamerica. Religion,

Teotihuacán The Avenue of the Dead runs through the center of Teotihuacán. The Pyramid of the Moon, constructed between 100 and 450 CE, is the city's second-largest pyramid and part of the temple complex; it appears in this present-day photo of Teotihuacán.

culture, farming, technology, diet, and much else give evidence of an intensely interactive web in Mesoamerica, already forming by 500 BCE and at its height around 500 CE. It survived, in attenuated form, the disasters—if they were disasters—that shrank or eliminated urban centers at Teotihuacán, Monte Alban, and throughout the Maya world.

The word *collapse* is often used to describe the sudden decline of Teotihuacán, Monte Alban, and the Maya cities. But from the point of view of survivors who didn't enjoy elite status, the word *liberation* might be more appropriate. With the end of cities and states, ordinary Mesoamerican families no longer had to sweat building pyramids and temples, pay tribute to kings, surrender sons for military conscription, and offer up victims for human sacrifice when a king's supply of war captives ran low. Instead, after the disappearance of cities, states, writing, and kings, they dispersed into the forests, farmed, hunted, and collected their food, made pottery, wove clothing—and left little trace.

THE ANDEAN WORLD

The other great center of population and complex society in the Americas was centered in the Andes, mainly in what is now Peru and Bolivia. We know less about the people and cultures of the Andes prior to 1000 CE than we do about Mesoamericans, mainly because some Mesoamericans left writing and Andean peoples did not. Pockets of population existed here from very early on, both on the coast and up on the Altiplano, or high plateau, at 13,000 feet (4,000 m). The steep and snow-packed mountains next door to the fish-rich waters of the Humboldt Current made this a distinctive environment. It meant that people living on the western side of the mountains could move quickly from one ecological zone to another by hiking up or downhill. It was also a precarious environment because of the periodic El Niños—as we saw in Chapter 2. The biggest El Niños, which occur every few centuries, bring devastating floods that could annihilate towns.

NORTE CHICO AND CHAVÍN, CA. 3100–200 BCE

The earliest signs of complex society in the Andes region appeared about 3100 BCE—by coincidence, about the same time as in Mesopotamia and Egypt. The Peruvian coast is perpetually foggy but almost completely without rain. About 50 rivers slice through it, tumbling out of the Andes onto the coastal plain. Between 3100 and 1600 BCE, along four of these rivers, people clustered into roughly 25 settlements, collectively known as **Norte Chico**.

One of these, called Caral, contained perhaps 3,000 people. Caral and towns like it had pyramids and earthen theaters large enough to hold several hundred people, possibly for religious ceremonies. But they had no defensive walls or any signs of war. They lived off a combination of irrigation agriculture—the only possible kind here—and fishing. Their crops featured beans and squash, but not maize. Their middens show that they ate plenty of clams, mussels, anchovies, and sardines. The Norte Chico people played music with pipes made from pelican and condor bones, but they seem to have left behind no art, statuary, carvings, or pottery.

Norte Chico is a curious case of a complex society with monumental architecture based not on a storable grain but, apparently, on dried fish. Somehow, it seems, an elite managed to control the food supply and use that power to coerce or persuade thousands of others to build pyramids, mounds, and theaters. The total population, at its height between 2600 and 2000 BCE, came to a few tens of thousands of people. By 1600 BCE, complex society here had vanished, and people had moved away for reasons unknown.

After the decline of Norte Chico, Andean people lived in small-scale communities until the rise of the so-called

Cultures of the Andes, ca. 3100 BCE–1100 CE Complex societies developed in the Andes region based on irrigation, both on the coastal plain and at elevations up to 11,000 feet (3,300 m). Most of them exploited opportunities of steep inclines, which when terraced enabled them to raise a wide variety of crops at different altitudes. After 200 BCE if not before, llama-based transport helped bind the region into an Andean interactive web.

Chavín culture several centuries later. It lasted from about 900 to 200 BCE. Chavín people used irrigation to grow potatoes, quinoa, and, in smaller quantities, maize. They raised llamas for food. The main population center, Chavín de Huántar, unlike Norte Chico, stood high on the western slope of the Andes at an elevation of around 10,000 feet (3,100 m). Its central town housed about 3,000 people and included a temple complex and a big outdoor U-shaped theater. People came to Chavín from all over the Andes, presumably for religious purposes. Archeological finds suggest the religious rites included music played on trumpets made from conch shells, the use of hallucinogenic plants, and feasting on llama and guinea pig meat washed down with maize beer.

Chavín's influence stretched far and wide, to judge by the presence of its artistic motifs—snakes and jaguar heads figure prominently—on pottery and textiles occurring throughout the Andes. Chavín stone carvings show animals found only on the eastern side of the Andes, such as caimans, monkeys, and anacondas. Some obsidian tools at Chavín came from 300 miles (500 km) away in southern Peru.

The temple at Chavín de Huántar was built of limestone and granite brought from afar. That implies the coordinated labor of many people, and probably hierarchical society. Chavín burials confirm an extreme gulf between rich and poor. As with Norte Chico, there is no sign of warfare in Chavín sites.

MOCHE AND TIWANAKU, CA. 200 BCE–700 CE

About the same time that the Chavín culture fell into obscurity, roughly 200 BCE, another Peruvian people on the coast were beginning to build small cities: the Moche (or Mochicas). Like the Norte Chico people before them, the Moche combined irrigated farming—maize, squash, beans, and cotton—with the harvesting of seafood. They traded for potatoes grown in the mountains.

From about 200 CE to 600 CE, the Moche invested heavily in religious buildings, including earthen pyramids, and ceremonial objects. Political power here rested even more squarely than usual on religious authority. Graves of the elite were stuffed with precious objects, gold, silver, and items used in religious ceremonies. The poor, whose skeletons imply protein deficiency, were buried with little more than the rags they wore. The average height for adult Moche males was 5′3″ and for females 4′7″—the elite were a few inches taller, evidence of better diet.

Moche artwork, of which a good deal has survived in the form of pottery and wall paintings, emphasized religious power. Much of it shows ceremonial scenes of human sacrifice, dismemberment, and the drinking of blood. Moche sites show little evidence of war, so sacrificial victims probably weren't war captives. Perhaps the authority of the shaman-rulers was sufficient that they could sacrifice members of the Moche population. Unusually for ancient America, Moche art also shows human faces in realistic fashion. Uniquely for ancient America, much of it depicts explicit sex.

Moche centers were residential as well as ceremonial, and perhaps contained a few thousand people each at their height. The largest of them attained about 10,000 inhabitants. They all shared the same architecture, pottery, and burial styles, but probably were never politically united. By 550 CE or so they had begun to decline, and by

700 complex society here had disappeared—once again, mysteriously.

About the same time that the Moche were getting started on the coast of northern Peru, another urban society got under way. **Tiwanaku** (also spelled Tiahuanaco) was a city and an empire, connected to the Andean traditions but distinct in several ways, especially in its innovative, bountiful agriculture.

The city lay near the shores of Lake Titicaca, high on the Altiplano in what is now Bolivia. For most of the year, it's a dry, dusty, windy landscape, sunny and warm by day but chilly by night. Most rain falls in downpours between December and March. People were farming and raising llamas in the abundant grasslands before 1500 BCE. But large-scale intensive farming and city life date from about 100 CE. Early Tiwanaku shows some signs of Chavín influence in religion, and of coastal Peruvian traditions in art, but nothing from farther afield. By 500 CE, the city contained perhaps 15,000 to 30,000 people, the largest yet in the Andes.

Tiwanaku's economic basis differed from that of previous Andean centers. Llama herding was important, and control over the supply of llamas probably helped undergird the position of Tiwanaku's elite, approximately as control over supplies of horses helped some peoples in Eurasia to dominate others. Llamas weren't war animals like horses, but pack animals and a source of food and wool. Their dung was burned as fuel in a wood-short land and used as fertilizer especially for maize farming. Llamas

Moche Art Painted earthenware vases created between 300 and 800 CE illustrate the Moche culture's characteristically realistic representation of faces. These particular examples may be portraits of high-status individuals.

were also important to religion and were sacrificed on important occasions. Long-distance trade, conducted in llama caravans, also supported the Tiwanaku elite. Fishing in Lake Titicaca helped feed everyone. But most important of all was the system of raised-field agriculture.

Farmers figured out how to cope with the frequent killing frosts, lack of moisture, and nutrient-poor soils by creating raised fields in the shallows along the marshy banks of Lake Titicaca. Their techniques resembled those of the amphibious agriculture of Mesoamerica. They piled up mud and muck to create rectangular islands on which they planted quinoa and potatoes. Yields were 10 to 20 times higher than farmers could get elsewhere in the Altiplano. Tiwanaku farmers maintained canals, stocked with fish, among these islands. The canal waters absorbed sunshine and warmth all day long and released it at night, keeping the immediate environment warmer and normally preventing the Altiplano's night frost from killing the crops. Recent experiments show that this form of farming in Lake Titicaca is more efficient, measured by yield per acre, than modern high-tech farming, and much more frost-proof. But, like similar systems in Mesoamerica, it took tremendous labor to create and maintain.

Tiwanaku These stone walls surround the city of Tiwanaku, which flourished between around 500 and 700 CE. The anthropomorphic statue under the arch at the center of this image may have had religious significance. The heads of sacred animals and ancestors adorn the wall in the foreground.

And it depended on rain to keep the lake's water level up. Good rains after 200 CE helped float Tiwanaku farming for centuries, providing enough food for tens of thousands.

Tiwanaku, like Chavín, was a religious center. People came from near and far to take part in rituals and make their appeals to the gods in the presence of gargantuan statuary and altars. With no obvious economic or military reasons for its location, Tiwanaku's site was probably selected for its significance in some spiritual geography now invisible to us. Its monumental architecture impressed visitors and underscored the authority of its rulers. Some buildings include huge blocks of stone weighing 40 to 140 tons (bigger than the Olmec heads or pieces of Stonehenge), which were somehow transported from quarries across the lake and then dragged—without any help from animal power—several miles to sacred sites. Plenty of hard work also went into a ceremonial mound of packed earth about 430 feet (130 m) high, and stone statues nearly 22 feet (7 m) tall. The city's elite quarters also had a water and sewer system. The city was built for display, like a combination of Vatican City and Disney World, as one scholar put it.

Ordinary people must have thought highly of their priests and gods to build all this—unless they were forced to work on religious architecture and sewer drains. Residents of Tiwanaku worshipped several deities, the main one being a sun god. Priests from the elite families took responsibility for ensuring the good will of the spiritual forces, which required proper attention to rituals and ancestors. Rituals prominently featured sacrifices involving food and drink, animal and human blood; at times they required decapitating llamas or humans. As elsewhere in South America, psychedelic drugs played a big role in religious life, helping people see into the world of spirits. In this way, the shaman-rulers tried to safeguard the community against calamity and ensure the fertility of the raised fields, llama herds, and human families. Tiwanaku religion spread far and wide in the Andes and influenced subsequent Andean peoples.

At its height around 500 to 700 CE, Tiwanaku's power and economic influence reached northern Chile, lowland Bolivia, and throughout the Peruvian Andes. Its elite families had forged a fully fledged state, even an empire. There is evidence of colonization projects. The ruling class, a set of families interlocked by marriage, managed to control most long-distance trade, artisan production, and much of the food supply. Warehouses collected goods, including storable food, for distribution to those who showed sufficient loyalty to the rulers. Families produced food, ceramics, and textiles and shared them among kinfolk. There is no evidence of markets or marketplaces: political and religious authorities directed economic life beyond families and households. Tiwanaku's workshops churned out pottery and textiles for distribution throughout the region. The city imported obsidian from 200 miles (300 km) away in Peru and psychotropic drug plants from the eastern slopes of the Andes.

By 1100 CE, ancient Tiwanaku was empty. Population dispersed to small villages around the Altiplano and beyond. The leading explanation for Tiwanaku's end is protracted drought. Ice cores from nearby glaciers show reduced precipitation after 900 CE. By 1300, water levels of Lake Titicaca fell by about 40 to 50 feet (12–15 m), playing havoc with both agriculture and llama herding. With less food to distribute, the elites lost influence. Their rituals and sacrifices now seemed ineffective at bringing rain, fertility, and security, further undermining their legitimacy. Other factors too, invisible to archeology, might have played a role in the abandonment of Tiwanaku and the disappearance, for three centuries at least, of complex society on the Altiplano.

THE AMERICAN WEBS

Farming peoples in Mesoamerica and the Andes built cities, states, and webs of interaction that by 1000 CE had attained considerable proportions. Of course, there were settlements and centers elsewhere in the Americas too. Mound builders toiled away in northern South America and southern North America. Irrigation agriculture communities developed in Bolivian Amazonia and in what is now Arizona. Some of these peoples also built substantial trade or exchange networks. Throughout lowland South America, from the Guyanas to Argentina, people on the region's rivers used the same kinds of pottery, implying sustained interaction. The mound builders of eastern North America, especially those of the Hopewell cultural tradition (ca. 100 BCE–400 CE), exchanged obsidian, sharks' teeth, copper, and silver from Canada to the Caribbean shores. Compared to Mesoamerica or the Andes, these were thin, sparse webs of interaction, involving fewer people and no great centers of wealth and power. Some were probably fully independent webs, at least at

first. Others were the farthest extensions of the larger and thicker webs centered on Mesoamerica and the Andes, as the spread of maize, ball courts, human sacrifice, and mound building indicate.

The two large webs shared many features, such as intensive agriculture and long-distance trade. They had some slender links between them, evidenced by the spread of maize, bows and arrows, and probably some techniques of copper working that in Ecuador and Mexico used similar techniques. Neither had iron working, deep-sea sailing craft, or crowd diseases—all widespread in Eurasia and northern Africa by 1000 CE, indeed by 1 CE. The Andes had livestock (llamas, alpacas) and metallurgy on a scale unknown in Mesoamerica. Mesoamerica had writing, which Andean societies did not.

AUSTRALIA AND OCEANIA

Australia and Oceania were just as isolated from the big Eurasian centers of population as were the Americas. But they were smaller spaces, with few good spots for settlement. They lacked some of the environmental features, such as domesticable large animals, that underpinned most complex societies elsewhere. More important, they were cut off from the major circuits of knowledge and innovation in the Americas and the Old World.

AUSTRALIA

By the time groups of Northeast Asians had begun to migrate to North America, some Southeast Asians had already crossed open water to settle in Australia. We know even less about this colonization than about the first settlement of the Americas, but it happened at least 50,000 years ago. Sea level then was 400 feet (120 m) lower. People could walk to what is now the island of Bali. Beyond that, they had to take to the sea for about 100 miles (150 km) to reach Australia.

The first Australians, often called Aborigines, must have found their new home a strange one. They met kangaroos that were 10 feet (3 m) tall, lizards longer than canoes, carnivorous snakes that weighed as much as a man, wombats the size of rhinos, and flightless birds as heavy as a bear. Most of the big animals went extinct soon after people arrived in Australia, likely a result of hunting

Australia The natural vegetation zones of Australia reflect rainfall and soil quality. Those shown here match today's conditions but approximate those of the last 8,000 years. Despite the challenge of aridity and the absence of pack animals, aboriginal Australians crisscrossed the continent with trade routes, carrying all goods themselves. They were almost fully isolated from human communities elsewhere in the world until 1788 CE.

pressure and an increase in fire. Early Australians used fire to clear paths in the bush and to encourage the growth of species they could eat. Skillful use of fire increased the human food supply.

Soon after setting foot on Australia, people headed inland. About 50,000 years ago some had camped at Lake Mungo, now a dry lakebed. The oldest cremated human remains—Mungo Lady, as she's known to archeologists—were found here, dating to 40,000 years ago. Lake Mungo offered fish, shellfish, and waterfowl until it dried up about 20,000 years ago.

Life was hard in Australia during the depths of the last ice age. Temperatures averaged about 11 degrees Fahrenheit (6 degrees Celsius) cooler than today, and conditions were much drier. By 35,000 years ago, people had explored every corner of Australia and had made camps in

all the appealing places. The end of the last ice age, about 10,000 years ago, brought wetter climate, more springs, lakes, and rivers—much better conditions for humans.

Better climate led to more people and more interaction, which helped spark a cultural revolution. It is dimly visible to us through art and archeology. Upon arrival, the first Australians had a tool kit similar to that prevailing in Eurasia 60,000 years ago. Their art consisted mainly of handprints and modest geometric designs, some of which are still faintly visible on the walls of rock shelters. For 40,000 years they made only a few changes to their tool kit and artistic repertoire. But after about 10,000 BCE, their art shows new subjects, including hunters armed with spears and boomerangs, images of animals, and even pictures of warfare. They invented new blades and spear-points.

This cultural revolution extended to the economy. People turned more and more to strategic use of fire, sometimes called **firestick farming**. It wasn't farming in the sense of planting and domesticating species and didn't involve settlement. Australia had few plants or animals that could be domesticated. Rather, firestick farming meant the deliberate burning of landscape to promote the growth of edible plants. The purpose was to attract wild animals, especially kangaroos, that people could hunt. In addition, by about 6000 BCE in suitable places such as Gunditjmara—western Victoria today—people started to pile up stones creating weirs to trap eels and fish. They didn't domesticate eels, but they in effect raised them as one raises fish in a fishpond. The role of long-distance exchange also expanded. Pearls, flints, and quartz were valuable enough to be traded over distances of a few hundred miles.

Without texts—there was no writing in Australia—our knowledge of early Australians' culture and religion is sketchy. Some 200 to 250 related languages evolved, implying some separation among groups. But aboriginal Australian religion seems remarkably consistent. It featured numerous nature spirits and a "**dreamtime**"—a distant past when the world was born, accessible only to a fortunate few. According to this worldview, great spirits roamed Australia, creating everything one can see. Their paths are "songlines," crisscrossing the continent. All that one sees existed in spirit before it existed physically, and it will continue to exist in spirit after it is physically gone. Song, dance, ritual, stories, and law transmitted this knowledge over the generations. The animist beliefs of Australian aboriginals, like the shamanist core to religion in ancient North America, showed strong similarity across the continent.

Part of the explanation for this consistency in religion may lie in the mobility of **aboriginal Australians**. Once population reached sufficient levels, they were always bumping into one another. While it's impossible to know their numbers with any precision, a reasonable guess is that by 1000 CE there were 200,000 or 300,000 people in Australia. They moved continually, setting up camp for days or weeks in plush locations, and moving on when food grew scarce or other problems arose. They migrated seasonally to avoid the worst of wet and dry seasons, especially in eastern Australia where—over the last 5,000 years or so—El Niño cycles have often heightened the effects of flood and drought. Nowhere, it seems, did they build permanent settlements. This mobility, perhaps, helped to check the diversity of aboriginal culture and to encourage strong commonalities. It also discouraged the elaboration of material culture, because people had to carry everything with them on their migrations. They didn't bother with pottery, for example.

In some respects, we ought to consider ancient aboriginal Australians as the intellectual aristocracy of hunter-forager peoples. They survived for tens of thousands of years in a harsh land, much harsher than today, with the aid of only stone tools and fire. This required an exquisite knowledge of their environment, plants, animals, and weather.

It also required a canny knowledge of human nature and social relations, because no one could survive for long alone. Everyone had to navigate the currents of group life, securing help and cooperation through judicious use of reciprocity or threat. And all this knowledge had to be transmitted from old to young with each passing generation.

Ancient Australians acquired the necessary knowledge without help from overseas. Some evidence exists of occasional contacts with peoples of what is now Indonesia, but only one outcome of this interaction was consequential. About 2000 BCE someone brought dogs, or perhaps just one pregnant female dog, to Australia. These were the ancestors of wild dogs, called dingoes, that joined humans as top predators in Australian ecosystems and still roam the continent. Dingoes figure in aboriginal art and lore. Some were domesticated and helped people hunt and stay

The First Australians Cave art created in southeast Australia around 13,000 BCE depicts a dingo (right). Some dingoes were domesticated by ancient Australians.

warm at night. Up to and beyond 1000 CE, Australians forged their own societies and cultures, based on mobile foraging and hunting underpinned by detailed knowledge of their continent's ecosystems. Other than the import of the dingo, Australians' contact with outsiders had no discernible impact either on Australia or on the rest of the world.

NEAR AND REMOTE OCEANIA

Southeast Asians and their descendants also first settled those parts of Oceania commonly called Melanesia, Micronesia, and Polynesia. A more useful division of the vast Pacific for present purposes emphasizes their position with respect to Southeast Asia: Near Oceania and Remote Oceania. Near Oceania consists of New Guinea, the Bismarck Archipelago, and the Solomon Islands. Remote Oceania extends as far as Hawaii and Easter Island. The biggest difference between Near and Remote Oceania is that people arrived in the former about 40,000 years ago and in the latter only 6,000 years ago.

The early history of Oceania is a history of pioneering by sea. People first arrived in New Guinea about 40,000 years ago and had settled in the Solomons by 15,000 years later. Then voyaging stopped. In Near Oceania, people could see the mountain tops of the next closest island.

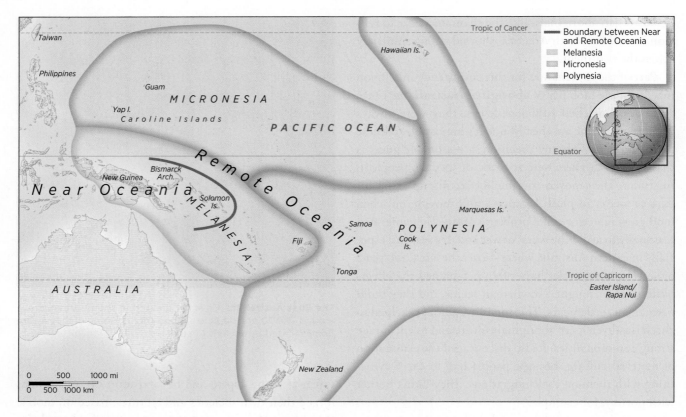

Oceania Immense distances separated the thousands of islands of Oceania, encouraging inhabitants to develop maritime skills and culture. Fishing and farming underpinned life on most islands. The division into Near and Remote Oceania more accurately reflects cultural differences and settlement history than do the older categories of Melanesia, Micronesia, and Polynesia.

Once they reached the end of the Solomons chain, they couldn't see any more land and—prudently—called a halt.

After tens of thousands of years as hunters and foragers, people in New Guinea—as we've seen—made a transition to agriculture, perhaps 8,000 or 9,000 years ago. They developed irrigation and crop rotations that could support dense populations. The rugged topography of the New Guinea highlands discouraged interaction, and tremendous linguistic diversity emerged. Today, several hundred languages are spoken in New Guinea, and dozens more in the nearby Bismarcks and Solomons, where New Guinea voyagers went about 30,000 years ago. In time, New Guinea's styles of farming also spread to the Bismarcks and Solomons.

Farming in Near Oceania was always only one subsistence strategy among many. People also hunted, foraged, and fished. Outside of the cool New Guinea highlands, populations remained scattered and sparse, partly because

of widespread malaria. Farming relied on root crops such as yams or taro. Most of the harvest didn't keep well, which made it hard for anyone to amass food, give it to supporters, and deny it to enemies. Instead, people used food politically by throwing big parties and making conspicuous displays of their generosity, winning friends and supporters.

Scattered population and perishable harvests meant that in Near Oceania it was highly unlikely that any state or complex society would develop. The feast approach to cultivating political support works fine on a small scale, but it has much less potential reach than the ability to store, hoard, trade, distribute, or deny grain or any storable food. In any case, for this and perhaps other reasons, polities in Near Oceania remained small, and social complexity modest.

About 4000 BCE, a new wave of pioneers came to Near Oceania. They were Austronesian speakers and originated in Taiwan. (They were not Chinese—Taiwan had an indigenous population before it became Chinese.) The Austronesians developed seaworthy craft including 100-foot-long outrigger canoes. They acquired navigational skills far beyond those of anyone else of their time. They visited the coasts of New Guinea, the Bismarcks, and the Solomons, and some of them settled there.

About 1300 BCE, one group in the Bismarck Archipelago took things further. Known as the **Lapita** culture, and distinguished by their pottery style, they began to sail out into the open Pacific. Over the next several centuries, they settled island archipelagoes such as Fiji, Tonga, and Samoa, thousands of miles away. These were the first of the great Polynesian migrations, sketched in Chapter 3. Just about all of Remote Oceania was settled by peoples whose ancestry traced back to the Lapita culture. The island of Guam is a likely exception, however, as people there raised rice, which suggests that its settlers came from the Philippines.

Wherever they went, Pacific Islanders brought their life-support system, consisting of a handful of plants and animals. Their food crops were of Southeast Asian origin, notably yams, taro, bananas, breadfruit, and coconuts. They also brought chickens, dogs, and pigs. These were deliberate colonization attempts in which people were bringing resources with them rather than moving in hopes of finding new resources.

When settling a new island, voyagers usually found most of its natural features familiar. Reefs and lagoons offered abundant seafood. Tall islands, which in the Pacific means islands with the remnant of a volcano as opposed to low atolls, usually had flowing water suitable for irrigation. Colonization efforts typically thrived after initial adjustments, and populations rose quickly.

Many tall islands eventually supported dense populations of farming folk. For them, as for their Austronesian forebears, the central purpose in life was farming land, having lots of descendants, starting or continuing a lineage, and honoring one's ancestors. On formerly uninhabited islands, this was comparatively easy: there was no one already there to contest claims to land. In Remote Oceania, moreover, there was no malaria, the main limit to population growth in Near Oceania. (The reason is simple: the mosquitoes that carry malaria hadn't made it to the distant islands of Remote Oceania.) So populations in the Marquesas, Hawaii, and the other outposts were comparatively healthy.

Sooner or later, and it came sooner on atolls where water was often in short supply, population growth dwindled as it approached the limits of what an island could support. People quarreled over land and food, and some of them chose—or were obliged to choose—emigration as a solution. So people left, and with luck found a new island on which to settle.

Population growth encouraged not only migration but also political complexity. Especially on bigger islands such as Tonga or Hawaii, ambitious leaders with large followings found more scope to organize irrigation projects or the terracing of mountain slopes. They thereby acquired more authority and prestige, and their innovations helped to sustain, or re-start, population growth. States eventually evolved, the most notable being a kingdom on Hawaii—but only after 1500 CE.

PACIFIC WEBS AND ISOLATED WORLDS

In those parts of Remote Oceania where islands were clustered together, networks of communication and exchange sometimes developed. By 300 CE, for example, inhabitants of the small island of Yap, in the Caroline chain, had forged links with many other islands of the western Pacific. Yapese pottery shows up in archeology on dozens of islands, and genetic data from today's populations indicate that women on other islands often had children by Yapese men. Whether these flows of pottery and genes

South Pacific Religion These stone statues, called tikis, are from the island of Hiva Oa in the Marquesas. Statues like these are found in many South Pacific cultures and are believed to represent deified ancestors.

represent a seaborne empire, a trading network, or something else entirely remains uncertain. These links centering on Yap persisted until well after 1000 CE.

Other parts of the vast Pacific, however, became isolated worlds unto themselves. Voyagers first arrived in Hawaii about 600 CE and eventually lost touch with everyone else. On Easter Island, or Rapa Nui, where settlers arrived about 700 CE, they not only lost touch with the wider world but forgot about it too: they believed they were the only people in existence.

Some tantalizing tidbits suggest that Pacific Islanders and South Americans somehow made contact long ago. The best evidence is the case of the sweet potato, a South American food crop that by 1000 CE was being cultivated in the Cook Islands, half an ocean away from the coast of Peru. Sweet potatoes cannot float or fly, and they don't have seeds that could be carried by birds. No one has ever suggested a plausible way for sweet potatoes to turn up in the Cook Islands except deliberate human action. Since the peoples of Peru used only reed boats and left no traces on islands out of sight from their beaches, the best guess is that Pacific Islanders visited South America and returned with sweet potatoes in the hulls of their giant canoes.

At the northernmost latitudes, evidence for ongoing connections between the Americas and Siberia is abundant. The Aleuts and Inuit arrived across the Bering Strait only about 3000 BCE. They stayed in touch with their Asian cousins, eventually bringing iron working, Asian-style pottery, the bow and arrow, and acupuncture to Arctic America. The bow and arrow, as we've seen, proved so useful that it spread throughout the Americas. Arctic America, in fact, was at least as connected to Arctic Asia as it was to more southerly parts of America. People moved back and forth freely from Siberia to Alaska in a circum-Arctic web based on sea voyages. Population in these frosty lands, however, remained extremely sparse.

So Pacific Islanders probably visited South America at least once, and Arctic peoples paddled back and forth between Siberia and North America. These linkages were small-scale, one-off or intermittent exchanges, nothing we could call webs of interaction, but they carried some consequences nonetheless. The sweet potato became an important crop on many islands, especially New Zealand (where it is called kumara), and the bow and arrow became an important technology for hunters and warriors in the Americas.

CONCLUSION

The Americas, Australia, and Oceania were the last sizable places on Earth settled by humankind. People migrated there, but their descendants had little or no contact with the rest of the world. They remained isolated from the big, dense, and interconnected populations that developed between China and Egypt until well after 1000 CE.

Nonetheless, in some places where population growth encouraged it, people in the Americas and Oceania developed their own webs of interaction. These were much larger scale in the Americas than in Oceania, involving millions rather than merely thousands of people. In the Americas, people also built their own forms of complex society. Nothing we could call complex society emerged in Australia or in Oceania until after 1000 CE. But in both Mesoamerica and the Andes, dense and hierarchical societies developed. They were founded upon distinct and highly productive farming systems that generated food surpluses that elites came to control.

People in both Mesopotamia and the Andes also created states and cities. These bore strong resemblances to states and cities elsewhere, with interlocking religious and political elites, armies, bureaucracies, and monumental architecture. But, for whatever reasons, unlike much of Asia, before 1000 CE the states and cities of the Americas rose and fell without much durable tradition. In Egypt, north India, or China, once states and cities emerged, that format of society never disappeared, even if specific cities or dynasties did. In the Americas, both complex society and webs of interaction flickered in and out of existence. In Oceania, thin webs flickered to life and then died away. In Australia, only the thinnest of webs existed. Only a few centuries later, as we shall see, all that changed.

CHAPTER REVIEW

KEY TERMS

Oceania (p. 268)
Clovis points (p. 270)
raised-field agriculture (p. 272)
Olmecs (p. 279)

Maya (p. 280)
Norte Chico (p. 286)
Tiwanaku (p. 287)
firestick farming (p. 290)

dreamtime (p. 290)
aboriginal Australians (p. 291)
Lapita (p. 293)

Go to INQUIZITIVE to see what you've learned—and learn what you've missed—with personalized feedback along the way.

REVIEW QUESTIONS

1. What parallels did the Americas share with centers of trade and connection in Eurasia and Africa? How was Oceania different?

2. Which two large transformations were occurring in the Americas when the first migrants arrived?

3. What features supported settled life in California and the Pacific Northwest?

4. What were the three main characteristics of farming in the Americas that made it distinctive?

5. In terms of the development of societies, why is it significant that Mesoamerica was the home of maize and the Andes region was the home of the potato?

6. In what ways were the Olmecs, Maya, Zapotecs, and Teotihuacán connected?

7. Describe the subsistence strategies of the Norte Chico, Chavín, Moche, and Tiwanaku peoples.

8. What caused the Australian cultural revolution around 10,000 BCE, and in what ways did it affect the Australian economy?

9. How did the mobility of ancient aboriginal Australians affect their religion and material culture?

10. What were the subsistence strategies of the inhabitants of Near Oceania, and how did the type of food they grew affect the development of complex society there?

11. What main trends did population growth on the islands of Oceania encourage?

12. How did the size and scope of linkages in the Americas compare to those in Oceania?

FURTHER READING

Karen Olsen BRUHNS and Karen E. STOTHERT, *Women in Ancient America* (1999). An overview based on archeology and ethnography, a fair bit of which deals with more recent times than does this chapter.

Craig CHILDS, *Atlas of a Lost World* (2018). A breezy, journalistic travelogue focusing on the early settlement of the Americas.

Susan Toby EVANS, *Ancient Mexico and Central America* (2004). A comprehensive archeological history of Mesoamerica.

Josephine FLOOD, *The Original Australians: Story of the Aboriginal People* (2006). A study that includes an excellent and readable chapter on early Australia.

Lynn V. FOSTER, *Handbook to Life in the Ancient Maya World* (2002). An excellent source of information on almost any Maya subject.

John W. JANUSEK, *Ancient Tiwanaku* (2008). A general synthesis of the archeology and history of Tiwanaku.

Charles C. MANN, *1491: New Revelations of the Americas before Columbus* (2005). A popular account of the controversies in pre-Columbian archeology, perhaps the best starting point.

Timothy R. PAUKETAT, ed., *The Oxford Handbook of North American Archaeology* (2012). A handy overview of its subject from first settlement to 1500 CE, with thematic chapters.

Dean SNOW, *Archaeology of Native North America* (2010). A survey by a major figure in the field; includes Mesoamerica.

PART 3

MATURING WEBS

200 TO 1400 CE

Part 3 of this book, Chapters 11–15, traces changes in world history between about 200 CE, when durable links were first established all the way from China to the Mediterranean Sea (the Old World web), and 1400 CE, when the world's oceans were opened to routine navigation. The trans-Eurasian links of the Old World web weakened, but did not disappear, in the centuries after the Han dynasty fell in 220 CE and the Roman Empire declined. Then, in the seventh and eighth centuries, trans-Eurasian connections grew stronger again, by both land and sea, and in the thirteenth through fourteenth centuries

Piracy A detail from a fifteenth-century manuscript shows pirates attacking a merchant ship in the Indian Ocean. The pirates board the ship and kill its crew, throwing their bodies into the sea below.

stronger still. Although the Old World web contained perhaps 70 percent or more of humankind, it wasn't yet a truly global web. Millions of people in the Americas, southern and central Africa, and Oceania lived in smaller webs of their own making, which would link up with the Old World web, and with one another, only after 1450.

KEY THEMES

Several important—and interlinked—themes crop up time and again in these next five chapters. One, of central importance to the building of the world's webs, is transport and navigation. Sailors mastered the monsoon winds of the Indian Ocean as never before. Camel drivers learned how to cross the Sahara safely. The invention of the compass in the eleventh to twelfth centuries allowed people, especially at sea, to find their destinations more reliably than before.

A second theme, for which the invention of the compass also serves as an example, is technological change. People figured out how to make windmills, gunpowder, and paper during this period, and how to print texts on paper. These technologies changed the lives of ordinary people and the power of kings. Thousands learned these skills and adapted these technologies—from camel management to gunpowder to printing—as they spread throughout the Old World web.

A third theme, one to which technological change contributed, is agricultural improvement. In China, Southwest Asia, and Europe above all, diverse new farming practices after 900 CE raised yields substantially, enabling higher levels of population and bigger cities. Human numbers nearly doubled in this period, from about 200 to 250 million in the third century to about 375 to 425 million by 1450, of whom about 20 million (5 percent) lived in cities. Most of that demographic growth happened in a dynamic burst after 900 CE thanks to agricultural improvements, making the world more crowded, more urban, and more connected than ever before—especially but not only inside the Old World web.

That growth in population took place despite horrific epidemics and some disastrous climate events—a fourth theme. In the 540s, a sudden turn to cold conditions destroyed a few years of harvests. In some places, such as Southwest Asia, this climate shock was compounded by an epidemic of plague that killed millions. Seven centuries later, around 1250 a long cold spell set in

that historians call the Little Ice Age—"little" compared to the ice ages of millions of years ago. It lasted until about 1850. Average temperatures fell by about 1.5 degrees Fahrenheit (1 degree Celsius) during the Little Ice Age, enough to bring more frequent harvest failures in northern lands and more searing droughts in arid ones. Then in the 1340s, bubonic plague erupted into a giant epidemic, now known as the Black Death, killing several tens of millions of people in one of humankind's most gruesome encounters with disease. The density of Eurasia's connections by the 1340s enabled the plague to spread more thoroughly, and faster, than would have been possible at any earlier time. This string of calamities—climate shocks and plague outbreaks—checked population growth temporarily, slowed the consolidation of the world's webs, and brought great suffering to millions.

A fifth theme is the simultaneous spread of certain cultural patterns—notably religions such as Buddhism, Christianity, and Islam—over sprawling spaces of the globe, mainly in Eurasia and the northern half of Africa. The strengthening connections of the Old World web enabled these religions to acquire more followers. As they did so the diversity of human religion, measured by the number of distinct religions, declined somewhat. If human cultural diversity could be reduced to a single index number (it can't!), it would show a slow increase from the dawn of humankind, as people spread out and went their separate ways, until some point between 200 and 1400 CE. Since that peak point, cultural diversity has declined. The success of a handful of religions in attracting most of humankind is the most conspicuous respect in which cultural diversity has dwindled in recent centuries.

FROM REGIONAL TO GLOBAL

The chapters in Part 3 explore these five themes, and more, primarily in regional contexts. Like Part 2, this one is organized mainly by region, though with the globalizing process of web integration ongoing. The chapters covering periods after 1450 are organized globally by time period and by theme. After 1450, the interactivity of the world reached such a level that an era of true global history had begun.

CHRONOLOGY

ca. 150–200
Start of shift to cooler, drier, unstable climate in Roman territory

306–337
Reign of Constantine

541
Outbreak of Justinianic Plague

324
Constantine establishes second Roman capital at Constantinople (Byzantium)

622
Muhammad's flight from Mecca to Medina; year 1 in Muslim calendar

249–260
Epidemic devastates Mediterranean populations

409
Romans lose control of Britain

476
End of western Roman Empire

165
Start of Antonine Plague

224–651
Sassanid Iran

370s
Start of Hun migrations

439
Romans lose control of Spain; Vandals take North Africa

527–565
Reign of Justinian

570–632
Lifetime of Muhammad

ca. 216–276
Lifetime of Mani

284–305
Reign of Diocletian

354–430
Lifetime of Augustine

637–638
Arabs conquer
Ctesiphon and
Jerusalem

750–1258
Abbasid caliphate

656–661
Civil war under
Ali, fourth caliph

661–750
Umayyad caliphate

639–646
Arabs conquer Egypt

The West End of the Old World Web

NEW PATTERNS OF POWER AND FAITH

200 to 800

I n the sixth and seventh centuries CE, two buildings capped by soaring domes rose over the landscapes of the eastern Mediterranean. Each stood as a monument to an ascendant faith and the power of a confident empire. One was Christian and Byzantine, the other Islamic and Umayyad. Christianity evolved from a fringe faith to a major religion largely through its adoption by rulers of the Roman Empire and Rome's successor state, the Byzantine Empire. Islam, a new religion forged in the seventh century, prospered in part through the efforts of the **Umayyad caliphate**, the first Muslim empire. The intertwined fates of these religions and empires form a central thread in this chapter.

The church of Hagia Sophia—Greek for "Holy Wisdom"—built between 532 and 537 CE, dominated Constantinople (today's Istanbul), the seat of the Byzantine Empire. The Hagia Sophia was at the time the world's largest building, and it remained the largest church or cathedral for a millennium. It stood on the site of earlier churches but exceeded them in every respect. Some 10,000 laborers and skilled craftsmen sweated to build the Hagia Sophia. It was an engineering and architectural marvel. Its daring dome, 182 feet (55 m) tall,

Islamic Architecture The Dome of the Rock was completed in 691 and stands as a testament to the power and grandeur of the Umayyad caliphate. The structure was likely built to outshine the Byzantine churches that influenced it stylistically.

FOCUS QUESTIONS

1. How did climate change and disease affect the Sassanian and Roman Empires in this period?

2. What were the major shifts in the political landscape of the western Old World web between 200 and 800 CE?

3. How did Christianity and Islam emerge as major religions during this period?

4. What were the major economic and social changes across the Old World web in this period?

seemed almost to float on air thanks to 40 arched windows that filled the church with light. Its airy interior featured towering columns of marble, hewn from quarries all over the empire. Glittering golden mosaics were soon added to the walls.

The emperor who oversaw the construction of the Hagia Sophia, Justinian (r. 527–565), built the church to symbolize the empire's unshakeable Christian faith and to demonstrate his own wealth and might. It was, like most examples of monumental architecture, an exercise in soft power, intended to inspire awe.

Hagia Sophia The magnificent Hagia Sophia church that Justinian built in 532–537 still stands in present-day Istanbul. Converted to a mosque in 1453, it is now a museum.

Gazing upon the completed church, Justinian said he had outdone Solomon—a reference to the first Jewish temple in Jerusalem, which had been destroyed a thousand years before.

The Dome of the Rock stands on Temple Rock in Jerusalem—the site of the Jewish Second Temple, which replaced Solomon's temple and was itself destroyed by the Romans in 70 CE. The oldest surviving example of Islamic architecture, the Dome of the Rock was built during the years 687–691. Its base is octagonal, perhaps to reflect the Muslim belief that paradise has eight openings. Its wooden dome—the gold leaf was added later—looms 67 feet (20 m) tall, just a bit larger than that of the Church of the Holy Sepulchre in Jerusalem, built by the Roman emperor Constantine in the fourth century. Its architectural style reflected that of Byzantine churches and represented a radical departure from the spare simplicity that earlier Muslim builders had preferred. Legions of laborers from all over the Levant toiled on it, and the cost equaled seven years of tax receipts from Egypt.

The Dome of the Rock is not a mosque, and its original purpose remains unclear. The Umayyad caliph chiefly responsible for building it, Abd al-Malik (r. 685–705), surely intended to put Christian churches of Jerusalem in the shade, especially the Holy Sepulchre. He had it decorated with verses from Muslim scripture chosen to emphasize that Islam was the fullest and finest revelation of God's word. Its décor included crowns and other symbols of earthly power, a motif common in Persian and Byzantine artistic traditions. Everyone, whether Muslim, Jewish, or Christian, was supposed to conclude that Islam took precedence over other religions and that the Umayyad caliphate had replaced earlier dynasties.

This chapter concerns the tumultuous history of the western region of the Old World web, from Persia to Spain, from about 200 until about 800. It was a time when change outpaced continuity. The great empires of Rome and Persia teetered and, in most places, collapsed. Christianity spread around the Mediterranean, and then, after 630, Islam spread even faster. Politics, religion, and culture changed almost beyond recognition. Even the bedrock of societies—family life, farming routines—shifted a little.

We will consider Rome and Persia together. Their fates were closely connected, and contacts between the two empires were commonplace. Similarly, we will pair the spread of Christianity and the rise of Islam, as twin examples of the same phenomenon—the emergence of a monotheistic world religion. By now, the western region of the Old World web had become such an interactive space that it makes sense to try to see it whole.

In this period, the terms *Roman Empire* and *Persia* need some explanation. The Roman Empire split into eastern and western halves in the fourth century. Historians call the eastern Roman Empire by the late fifth century the Byzantine Empire, or Byzantium for short. Its rulers considered themselves Romans nonetheless. The term *Roman Empire* here refers to the whole empire until 324 CE. After that date, I specify either eastern or western when using the term. But by 480, I use *Byzantine Empire* for the east, which was all that remained of the empire. This procedure may seem complicated, but it's the least confusing option. *Persia* means the Parthian Empire until 224 CE and thereafter the Sassanian Empire, led by a dynasty called the Sassanids. The Sassanids popularized the term *Iran* to refer to Persia. So, I will normally use *Iran* for times after 224.

ROME AND PERSIA: FARMING, CLIMATE, AND DISEASE

In 200 CE, the western region of the Old World web held between a quarter and a third of the world's population. The Roman Empire counted about 45 million people,

down from perhaps 60 million before a nasty epidemic of the 160s called the Antonine Plague. Another 5 to 8 million lived in Persia. Neighboring lands under neither Roman nor Persian control were sparsely populated, so the grand total for the western region stood around 65 to 75 million of a global total of perhaps 200 million. As always with population figures from the pre-modern world, these estimates could be well off the mark.

In Roman territory at 200 CE, about 8 to 10 percent of the people lived in cities. Rome itself had housed 1 million residents before the Antonine Plague, maybe 750,000 in 200, and 500,000 in 400. Alexandria, in Egypt, was the empire's second-largest city, less than half the size of Rome. In Persia, the **Sassanid dynasty** founded several new cities after 224, and their Mesopotamian breadbasket contained many old ones, but even so it's unlikely that more than 10 percent of the population lived in cities.

FARMING

In both empires, farming remained the staff of life. The Sassanids invested heavily in the irrigation works of Mesopotamia and encouraged farming everywhere. Archeological surveys suggest their efforts expanded farmland by 50 percent. Farmers relied on traditional crops, mainly the cereal grains of wheat, barley, and rye, supplemented by chickpeas and lentils, and orchard crops such as figs, dates, and grapes. But under Sassanid rule, some new and useful crops were introduced: apricots, olives, cotton, and sugarcane—the latter two coming from India. Rice, already grown in southernmost Mesopotamia, spread more widely in Sassanian times.

The most significant innovation in farming was the widespread use of irrigation to support alfalfa (lucerne). Alfalfa is a forage crop, highly nutritious for cattle and horses. It is probably native to Iran. It does not need irrigation but yields much better with it. Like other legumes, its roots harbor microbes that can take nitrogen from the air and lodge it in the soil, improving soil fertility for other plants. So alfalfa was grown in rotation with cereals or vegetables, and this practice raised their yields. More alfalfa meant more and better animal feed, and indirectly (via nitrogen fixation) more human food. The latter made it easier to supply cities as bulwarks of Sassanid power and culture. The former made it easier to maintain cavalry.

Roman farming stayed prosperous in most places, but less innovative than Persia's. The gradual spread of markets

Commercial Agriculture Third-century mosaics from Roman Gaul (modern France) show laborers working to harvest olives and then to press them into olive oil. New and improved trade networks enabled farmers to make a living by exclusively farming this hardy tree crop.

and transport, a legacy from classical Greece and Carthage, encouraged ever-greater specialization. This commercialization of agriculture enabled people to make a living in stony hill country where only olives would grow. During the third and fourth centuries CE, this process was still advancing, and Roman agricultural output was still growing, especially in the farther reaches of the empire: Syria, North Africa, and Britain. In Italy itself, by contrast, food production slumped—perhaps due to loss of tax exemptions, perhaps to adverse climate change.

In Egypt, Rome's primary breadbasket, the Nile floods became less reliable in the late second century because of climate shifts. The empire's cities and armies became more reliant on food supplies from places other than Egypt and Italy. The most important agricultural innovation took place in the eastern empire, in the sixth century if not before, when Byzantine villagers in northern Syria began to raise silkworms. These changes in Roman and Byzantine agriculture had smaller impacts than those in Sassanian Iran. The growing specialization inadvertently deepened a vulnerability for Italy and the city of Rome: if Rome's empire lost access to its distant provinces, the city of Rome and Roman armies would starve.

DISEASE OUTBREAKS AND CLIMATE CHANGE

Just about everyone, whether in Roman or Persian territory, became more vulnerable to epidemics. This resulted from both denser settlement and continuing urbanization on the one hand, and further development of long-distance connections on the other. One of the consequences of the tightening Old World web was faster and wider circulation of infections. Beginning in 165, as we've seen, the Antonine Plague (possibly an outbreak

of smallpox) killed off 10 to 15 percent of the Roman Empire's population. During the years 249–260, another epidemic ripped through the Mediterranean. Cyprian, a bishop in Carthage at the time, observed that "the human race is wasted by the desolation of pestilence." Such disease disasters, long a feature of life in densely settled parts of the world, came more frequently to the Roman (and probably Persian) realms, and on bigger scales, after the late second century. The tighter networks of transport put in place mainly by Rome helped spread the outbreaks, and they, more than anything else, held population in check.

Climate shifts and shocks also weakened Rome after 150 CE. Through the last century of the Republic and the early years of the empire, most Roman regions prospered in part because of an unusually stable, warm, and moist climate. Those conditions were especially favorable for Rome's northern provinces: vineyards thrived in Britain. The Nile floods were consistently good, rarely too low or too high, so Egypt pumped out grain to the empire. But after 150 CE, and especially after 200, a cooler, dryer, and more unstable climate brought disappointing harvests. Climate change led to more hunger, less tax revenue, and less military manpower, all of which contributed to the fiscal and military crises the empire endured in the third century CE. Climate conditions improved for Roman agriculture in the fourth and fifth centuries, although never achieving the stability enjoyed during the early empire.

Unruly nature brought unprecedented calamities in the sixth century. Beginning in 535 or 536, the whole Northern Hemisphere experienced the sharpest climate shock in the previous 2,000 years. Written accounts from Ireland, Byzantium, and China speak of dark sky at noon and snow in midsummer. A Byzantine chronicler wrote that "the sun became dark and its darkness lasted for one and a half years." Temperatures plummeted, and rainfall diminished. Tree rings show that until 551, trees in Eurasia scarcely grew at all. The likely cause was a cluster of big volcanic eruptions in Alaska and Mesoamerica, between 535 and 539, that filled the sky with tiny dust particles (sulphate aerosols), partially blocking sunshine in the Northern Hemisphere. The likely consequences included repeated harvest failures and, in places such as Ireland and northern Italy, famine. In Sweden, more vulnerable than most places to deep cold, three-quarters of all villages were abandoned about this time.

Just as the dust veils were lifting, another calamity hit.

Plague, an extremely lethal disease, broke out in Egypt in 541. The Justinianic Plague, named after Justinian, the Byzantine emperor at the time, probably originated in Central Asia or northwest China, where plague had long circulated among wild rodents. Travelers and traders unwittingly brought it to Egypt along the threads of the Old World web, probably over both land and sea. Once loose in the lands of the eastern Mediterranean, it killed about a quarter of the population (some experts say half) within a few years. This was more severe than the Antonine Plague, or indeed any other epidemic in prior recorded history. One eyewitness, a historian named Procopius, wrote that it killed up to 10,000 people a day in the Byzantine capital of Constantinople, that bodies piled up in the streets like stacks of hay, and that it threatened to extinguish humankind.

This last claim was exaggeration. Plague affected people living in port cities (such as Constantinople) more than anyone else, because plague-carrying rats swarm to ships and cities, attracted by stored grain. Cities in general suffered more than villages, and villagers more than mobile herders. The urbanized societies, such as Byzantium and Sassanian Iran, suffered more than others. Plague appears also to have hit Italy hard. Pope Gregory in Rome, then a town of maybe 50,000 people, was sure the world was coming to an end shortly. The Justinianic Plague receded after a few years, but plague bouts kept flaring up every decade or so until about 750. An outbreak in 745 killed 25 to 35 percent of the population of several Arab cities.

The twin disasters—climate shocks and plague— together cast a long shadow. The enormous loss of life in the more urbanized societies tipped the military balance in favor of tribal and nomadic peoples, probably assisting in the demise of Sassanian Iran and the decline of Byzantium. The plague surely contributed to the decay of urban life from 540 to 750, especially around the Mediterranean, and to two centuries of extremely bad health.

POLITICS AND WAR IN IRAN AND ROME

Between 200 and 800 CE, some big political changes unfolded in the western region of the Old World web. A short version might be this: The Sassanian Empire rose and fell; the Roman Empire shifted to the east; and new dynasties professing a new religion, Islam, overshadowed them both.

SASSANID IRAN, 224–651

The Sassanid dynasty started its political career as a tribe from southwestern Iran. We know far less about them than the Romans, because fewer texts survive and recent politics in the region has limited archeological work.

In the second century CE, Parthian power had weakened owing in part to Roman military pressure. The Sassanids finished off the Parthian dynasty and proclaimed their own in 224. They consciously modeled themselves on the Achaemenids, the dynasty of Cyrus and Darius, imitating their artwork. Explicitly anti-Greek, they opposed the Hellenization under way in Persia since Alexander five centuries before.

The Sassanian Empire, 224–651 CE Like the Achaemenids and Parthians before them, the Sassanid dynasts built a formidable state by controlling both the fertile farmlands of Mesopotamia and the Iranian plateau, which was well suited for grazing and specifically raising horses. The Sassanian Empire's military strength posed a stern challenge to the Roman—and later, Byzantine—Empire. Its relations with India were more peaceful, featuring much cultural exchange.

The Sassanids made Persia—or Iran, as they called it—into a great power, as Cyrus had done long before. Their rulers considered themselves the "king of kings," equaled only by the emperors of Rome and China. Their investments in agriculture, especially the irrigation canals of Mesopotamia, paid off in enhanced revenues. So did their encouragement of long-distance trade on land and sea. Their merchants sailed the Indian Ocean world, from East Africa to India. Sassanid coins turn up as far away as China, implying linkages all across Eurasia. Like every empire, Sassanian Iran converted economic wealth into military power, and did it successfully enough to endure for more than 400 years.

The Sassanian military had to face diverse threats, from Roman infantry to Central Asian horsemen. Beginning in 230, they fought several wars against Roman armies and enjoyed frequent success. They almost always held on to their Mesopotamian provinces, which were by far their richest and home to their capital, Ctesiphon (near today's Baghdad). Their heavily armored cataphracts—armored riders on armored horses—equipped with lances (an innovation) and supported by war elephants imported from India, proved highly formidable against anyone's infantry. Sassanian armies also developed expertise in laying siege to enemy fortifications. Mainly learned from their Roman enemies, siege craft helped Sassanian forces hold key cities and occasionally take Roman ones in Syria. At times, they extorted large sums of gold from the Romans in exchange for peace. When most successful in war they extended their rule to Egypt, eastern Anatolia, and parts of Central Asia. The high-water marks of Sassanian political success came in the late third, the late fourth, and the very early seventh centuries.

In addition to fighting frequent wars on its western frontier, Sassanian Iran had to keep nomadic tribes from the Eurasian steppe in check. Like China and northern India, Iran and Mesopotamia often looked tempting to the horse nomads. When they were desperate or they sensed weakness, the nomads used their superior mobility to swoop in and pillage. The Sassanians usually fared well in protecting their population and wealth, but a big exception came in 469, when a group of steppe raiders (often called the Hephthalite Huns) captured an emperor and his harem, demanding both gold and territory before returning them. Luckily for Iran, the Central Asian tribes and the Romans could not easily coordinate simultaneous campaigns. Sassanian diplomats could play one pastoral

Sassanian Power The Sassanian rulers used art to represent their military and political strength. This rock relief, made at the height of Sassanian power in the mid-third century, shows the Roman emperor Valerian surrendering to the Sassanid emperor Shapur I in 260 CE.

tribe against another, a practice at which they, like the Achaemenids before them, excelled.

The Sassanid dynasty's luck ran out in the seventh century. After a spurt of conquests and near-total destruction of their enemies, wars in the west went badly for them in the 620s, and their richest lands were devastated by Byzantine armies. Revenues plummeted, and internal quarrels turned to assassinations, civil war, and instability. In one four-year span, the empire had five rulers. By 632, what remained was governed by a boy-emperor who failed to command allegiance. Arab warriors fighting under the banner of a new faith, Islam (see below), proved irresistible. Sassanid authority crumbled. By the 640s, Sassanid forces, such as they were, scampered off toward Central Asia. The last king of kings was murdered for money by a miller in an oasis town in 651, an inglorious end to the long career of the Sassanids. His sons fled to China.

THE FALL OF ROME IN THE WEST, 200–476

The fate of the Roman Empire took a different course. Half of it fell, and the other half lasted another thousand years. Let's start with the fall. Few subjects have fascinated scholars as much as the fall of Rome. They have come up with hundreds of explanations, ranging from the poisoning of the elite from lead-lined aqueducts to a loss of martial vigor brought on by Christianity. In fact, the western part of the Roman Empire was accidentally toppled by people trying to take it over and preserve it for their own benefit.

CRISIS IN THE THIRD CENTURY As we've seen, in 200 CE the Roman Empire sprawled from Britain to Iraq, a powerful state matched only by China of the Han dynasty (206 BCE–220 CE). But its fortunes quickly decayed. For two centuries, Rome had been victorious in its wars, which proved reliable sources of loot, glory, and captive slaves. But by the 230s, Rome's enemies, especially in Iran, were stronger. The early Sassanids proved much more formidable than their Parthian predecessors. And the Germanic tribes north of the Danube and east of the Rhine—undisciplined barbarians in Roman eyes—had become much more dangerous neighbors.

In effect, these tribes had become less egalitarian and fragmented, more cohesive and hierarchical, than before. In large part, it was contact with the Romans that brought these changes about. Roman trade goods helped to create or strengthen political elites among the tribes, and so did Roman diplomacy, which always sought individual leaders to bargain with. Over time, the **Germanic tribes**—Goths, Vandals, and Franks, among others—organized in larger confederations with more effective top-down command, and perhaps a stronger sense of ethnic identity as well. So their ability to mount effective attacks across the frontiers improved.

These military challenges required a vigorous Roman response. But the mines of Spain ran low on silver and gold, and emperors inflated the value of the coinage. Military manpower became harder to pay for. Bandit gangs roamed some provinces, especially Gaul, destroying property and siphoning revenue away from the state. Unpaid troops became unruly. Many army commanders tried to make themselves emperor, and some succeeded. From 235 to 284, Rome had 51 emperors or co-emperors. Almost all died violently, many of them murdered by their own troops. Civil war became the normal condition, further emboldening Rome's enemies.

Rome's military helped the empire to recover from this deep political crisis. Its navy remained supreme on the Mediterranean and along the Danube and the Rhine. Neither the Sassanians nor the Germanic tribes could contest Roman naval power. Its fortifications on the European frontiers, if amply supplied, could still hold out indefinitely. Rome's infrastructure of roads and harbors was so well built that even if poorly maintained it could still serve its purpose. The empire still had a weapons industry, and when revenues sufficed it could still churn out disciplined, trained, and well-equipped armies. By the 270s, the worst of the crisis had passed. In 283, an emperor even managed to sack the Sassanian capital of Ctesiphon—whereupon he was killed by a lightning bolt. His would-be successors launched another round of civil war.

DIOCLETIAN AND CONSTANTINE That instability ended when a military man, Diocletian, became emperor (r. 284–305) and managed to re-impose unity and order with a spate of reforms. An upstart of humble background, he re-fashioned and expanded the army and bureaucracy to lower the odds of someone else seizing power (as he had done), making both institutions more obedient to him. He reformed the empire's tax system and coinage. He considered rampant greed a source of weakness and tried to fix prices for everything from silk underwear and lions to the salaries of teachers of rhetoric. (One hundred lines of writing by a scribe, decreed Diocletian, was worth the same as 12 haircuts, or one-tenth of a fattened pheasant.)

Although the price fixing did not work well, Diocletian achieved some stability during his long reign, helped by a favorable peace with the Sassanians. Unlike most of his fellow emperors, he was not murdered on the job but retired to raise cabbages at his villa. The empire, in better health than at any time in the previous 150 years, still stretched from the Sahara to Scotland, and from Syria to Spain.

Only one subsequent emperor, **Constantine** (r. 306–337), was able to hold the empire together. Born into the military and political elite, Constantine rose rapidly to positions close to Diocletian. Upon the latter's retirement, the inevitable succession struggles began. After winning glory in campaigns on the empire's frontiers, in 324

Constantine Under the emperor Constantine, the Roman Empire split into eastern and western halves and began a gradual transition to Christianity. This bust of Constantine was made toward the beginning of his reign, around 312 to 315 CE.

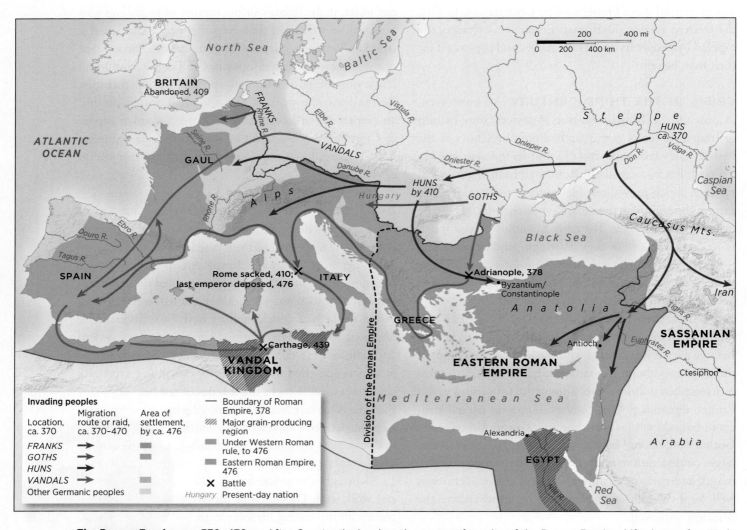

Invading peoples

Location, ca. 370	Migration route or raid, ca. 370–470	Area of settlement, by ca. 476
FRANKS	→	▬
GOTHS	→	▬
HUNS	→	
VANDALS	→	▬
Other Germanic peoples		▬

— Boundary of Roman Empire, 378
▨ Major grain-producing region
▬ Under Western Roman rule, to 476
▬ Eastern Roman Empire, 476
✕ Battle
Hungary Present-day nation

The Roman Empire, ca. 370–476 CE After Constantine's reign, the center of gravity of the Roman Empire shifted away from Italy to the east, and Constantinople gradually became more important than the city of Rome. In the west, Germanic peoples by the fifth century had acquired sufficient skills and numbers to take over much of what had been Roman territory. Rome could no longer muster the money and manpower to defend itself.

Constantine emerged triumphant in civil wars against rival would-be emperors.

He judged the empire too large to govern solely from Rome—a place Diocletian had scarcely visited—and created a second capital in the Greek city of Byzantium, thereafter called Constantinople (today's Istanbul). It lay closer than Rome to the Iranian and Danube frontiers, where an emperor most needed to be. Thereafter, the Roman Empire had two halves, one mainly Latin-speaking and governed from Italy, and the other increasingly Greek-speaking and ruled from Constantinople. Both halves slowly became Christian. As we will soon see, Constantine himself accepted the faith during his wars.

ECONOMIC AND MILITARY DECLINE Upon Constantine's death in 337, his sons fought for power, launching a long period of intermittent civil war spiced by religious turmoil. A campaign against Iran ended badly for the Romans, and in 378 a battle against the Goths, one of the Christianized Germanic tribes, ended worse: two-thirds of the army was killed in Rome's worst defeat since the time of Hannibal 590 years earlier. The eastern and western halves of the empire often feuded and sometimes fought. Gradually, it became too costly to maintain garrisons in the distant provinces, and the empire began to shrink. Britain was cut loose first in 409. By 439, Rome had lost control of Spain and the breadbasket region of

North Africa, overrun by Vandals, another originally Germanic tribe.

The fundamental weakness of the empire at this point was the same as during its third-century crisis: it lacked the money to pay enough men to defend its borders. Despite the economic and fiscal reforms of Diocletian and Constantine, poorer harvests, reduced trade, and renewed inflation all hampered the empire's ability to pay its army. As security weakened around the edges and in rebellious regions, trade declined further, and the fragile economic benefits of specialization and exchange crumbled. For centuries, the Roman Empire had enjoyed the fruits of a commercial economy in which farmers raised the crops that suited their lands best, and craftsmen developed specialized skills. Everyone came together through money and markets to exchange what they had for what they wanted. But this arrangement hinged on peace and order; and when disorder prevailed, the economy shrank and imperial revenues plummeted. The economic strength of the empire for so many centuries—its commercial complexity, which had sustained its formidable military against so many challenges—now became a source of weakness.

The money problem was a military problem because imperial armies depended directly on tax revenues. There were no central banks from which to borrow. There were virtually no other branches of government to starve in order to feed the military; it already accounted for the great bulk of government spending. Each year's tax haul determined how big the next year's army could be. So economic decline translated into military weakness within months.

THE HUNS AND THE GERMANIC TRIBES The borders became harder to defend after the 370s because the Germanic tribes were desperate to cross the Rhine and Danube to get away from formidable bands of horsemen known as the Huns. The Huns migrated from somewhere east of the Volga River. They soon began to attack everyone they could reach in Iran, and in central and southeastern Europe. Goths, Vandals, and Franks fled in fear, infiltrating or invading Roman territory sometimes as refugees, sometimes as plunderers. The movements of the Huns upset the geopolitical balance in western Eurasia, just as the rise of Achaemenid Persia, or of Rome, had done centuries before.

The migration of the Huns formed the first large-scale example of a pattern that would last a thousand years: the westward migration of mostly Turkic-speaking peoples of the steppe. (Turkic is a language group that includes modern Turkish, Uzbek, Kazakh, Tatar, and a dozen other languages.) Turkic-speakers also rode into China and India at times, often as invaders. Sometimes they were escaping long-term drought cycles, sometimes political violence—and probably in many cases both at once. They paused if they found good pasture or some opportunity for trade or plunder. Their movements were a bit like a bus: at every stop, some people got off and others joined, sometimes Turkic-speakers, sometimes not. So the farther west they went, the more polyglot and multicultural their society became. But their political core was always horsemen skilled in the arts of mounted warfare.

The Huns and other mobile pastoralists preferred grasslands in the western steppe, today's Ukraine and southern Russia. At times they kept going as far west as Hungary, where the grassland ended. Farther west the land was a patchwork of forests and fields, not suited to herders and their animals. The Huns were unusual not only for being the first of many peoples to make this trip, but also for raiding far into western and southern Europe.

When not fleeing the Huns, the Germanic tribes were often invited into Roman territory. Roman governors might hire them to fight for Rome against other tribes, or for one set of Romans against another in civil wars. Each such invitation was a rational, cost-cutting example of outsourcing. The tribesmen were cheaper than Roman legions. Collectively, however, these invitations were self-defeating. The Germanic peoples could not easily be controlled, and often they took by force what they were not freely given. Unlike previous generations of foreigners recruited into the Roman military and eventually Romanized, encouraged to marry (poor) Roman women, and granted citizenship, the Goths, Vandals, and Franks were allowed to maintain their own communities and were often discouraged from embracing Roman ways. Their rough-and-tumble conduct further eroded security within the empire and undercut its economic base. The tribes had no intention of destroying the western Roman Empire. To the contrary, they wanted to enjoy the comforts and relative safety it afforded. But in helping themselves to land and its revenues, they gradually killed the geese that laid the golden eggs.

In the early fifth century, Germanic tribes settled here and there throughout the western empire. They set up little states, demanding protection money from Roman authorities and fighting among themselves just as regularly as did the Romans. Other tribes accepted Roman gold to stay away. In 410, one group of Goths sacked the city of Rome itself, which had been free from foreign attack for 800 years. Roman slaves poured out of the city to help the Goths.

When Vandals took over North Africa and captured a Roman fleet in the harbor of Carthage in 439, the western empire lost both a crucial source of surplus grain and the inestimable advantage of peaceful seaborne trade. The Mediterranean Sea after Pompey had suppressed piracy in 67 BCE had been a tranquil Roman lake, a highway for commerce in all directions. Now the sea became a no-man's-land. The benefits of a commercial economy became still harder to reap, and increasingly each little region depended on its own resources—disastrous for areas that did not grow much food.

In the 450s, Rome's death spiral sped up when one of the Huns' chieftains, Attila, united several factions. He instantly launched a campaign of looting, sacking, and pillaging that took him to the walls of Constantinople, where an emperor bribed him to go elsewhere. In 451–452, he contemplated taking Rome itself and was dissuaded only when summer malaria savaged his forces and the Christian pope offered him all the gold he could muster. After Attila's death in 453, his confederation promptly

splintered and ceased to terrorize Europe. So while the Huns battered the remaining dregs of the Roman Empire, they did not end it. When the end of the western empire finally came, traditionally dated 476, at the hands of a group of Goths, hardly anyone noticed. There was virtually nothing left to fall. Rome ended with a century of whimpers, not a bang.

The eastern empire survived, despite repeated hammerings by Goths and Huns. It had the advantages of great walls around its capital of Constantinople. Its navy kept open the routes to and from Egypt, the source of grain for cities and armies. Its revenues shrank, but modestly compared to the western empire's fiscal collapse. And eastern emperors wisely limited the degree to which they outsourced defense to Germanic tribes—especially after 399, when one tribe briefly threatened the capital. The eastern Roman Empire, known to historians as the Byzantine Empire, lasted until 1453. Its inhabitants called themselves Romans to the end.

THE BYZANTINE EMPIRE, 500–800

The **Byzantine Empire** included Egypt, the Levant, Anatolia, and the Balkans. In 500 CE, its population numbered about 20 million. Its cities were many and prosperous, concentrated in Egypt, Syria, Palestine, and western Anatolia. As long as it could rely on the surplus grain of Egypt and, to a lesser extent, Syria, it could maintain cities and armies. Its capital, Constantinople, sat astride the route that links the Black Sea to the Mediterranean, one of the most strategic locations on Earth. The city's gigantic walls (portions are still visible today) kept it safe from many assaults. It could be supplied by sea, so no sieges could starve it out as long as the Byzantine navy remained strong. Indeed, it outlasted a dozen sieges.

Constantinople had symbolic strengths too. Earlier emperors had built it up into a great city, with monumental architecture, streets, cisterns and water systems, and a hippodrome for chariot racing that rivaled Rome's. The emperors in Constantinople considered themselves the champions of Christianity and heirs to the entire Roman Empire. They thought the western part only temporarily escaped their control, and they sought to re-conquer it. They had no luck in that quest until the reign of **Justinian** (r. 527–565).

Justinian came from a peasant family in the Balkans but as a child was brought to the capital and received an

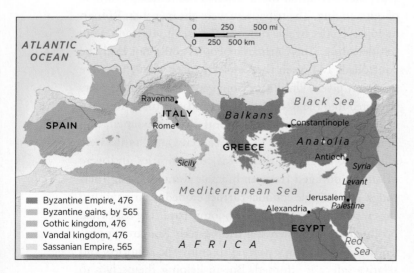

The Byzantine Empire, 476–565 CE After the final eclipse of the western Roman Empire, its successor state, the (mainly) Greek-speaking Byzantine Empire based in Constantinople, carried on Roman traditions for another millennium. Under vigorous leadership in the sixth century it recovered territories in Italy and North Africa, but its strength lay in Egypt, the Levant, Anatolia, and the Balkans.

Theodora and Justinian These sixth-century Italian mosaics in luminous colors celebrate the Byzantine empress Theodora (left) and emperor Justinian (right), who both rose from modest origins to expand and consolidate Byzantine power.

education, including the study of Roman history and the Greek language. He spent much of his youth following the chariot races at the hippodrome, but at age 36 he helped vault one of his uncles from the imperial guard to the emperor's throne. Justinian quickly showed himself adept in palace politics and military affairs. That came in handy, because his elderly uncle soon died.

Despite a scandalous marriage to Theodora, a dancer and actress, Justinian became emperor himself in 527. He needed and got exemption from a law prohibiting marriage between high officials and actresses. Justinian and Theodora shared low origins and high ambition. Although holding opposing views about which sort of Christianity was the right one, they made a strong team. They were far from popular and barely survived riots in 532, perhaps only through the resolve and street smarts of Theodora. According to one account, she kept her head under pressure when Justinian wanted to flee the rioters. His mind changed by her advice, Justinian's troops massacred thousands of his opponents and he kept his throne.

In 533, Justinian launched a series of conquests that nearly re-constituted the old empire. His good fortune included the services of a magnificent general, Belisarius, who led Byzantine armies in the field and had organized the massacre of rioters in the capital the year before. He conquered (or re-conquered, as Justinian saw it) the North African kingdom of the Vandals. He added several large Mediterranean islands to that, and eventually all of Italy. For good measure, Belisarius drove marauding tribes back across the Danube, consolidating the empire's northern frontier in the Balkans. Byzantine (re)conquests almost ended then, although in Justinian's later years his armies also brought southern Spain back into the empire. Belisarius and Justinian both died in 565.

Justinian's ambition had strained the treasury. In addition to his wars, he built his great church in Constantinople, the Hagia Sophia, and employed teams of scholars to codify Roman law. He did all this in a time of diminishing resources (remember the natural disasters that began in 536), leaving his successors less to work with. They gradually lost North Africa, Italy, and southern Spain. They fought back-and-forth campaigns in the Balkans against tribes invading from the north. And they fought on the eastern front against Sassanid Iran, which they helped to bring down. After the 640s, the Byzantine Empire fought a rising power in Southwest Asia—the Arabs, of whom more shortly.

The Byzantines lost Egypt to Arab conquerors in 642, a critical defeat. Without Egypt's grain and revenues, the Byzantines were often on the defensive. Arab armies pushed into Anatolia and besieged Constantinople twice, in 674–678 and 717–718. On the latter occasion, the Byzantines survived thanks to a new military invention of theirs, Greek fire (flaming liquid squirted at enemy ships), and a storm that sank the Arab fleet. After the loss of Egypt's grain surplus in 642, the eastern empire was lucky not to follow the path of the western empire after it lost North Africa in 439.

The empire teetered on the brink of collapse, revived, and teetered again in the centuries ahead. Its army

Greek Fire An illustration from a history of the Byzantine Empire shows ninth-century Byzantine sailors using Greek fire (a mixture of quicklime, sulphur, and petroleum) to attack an enemy ship.

remained formidable, especially its cataphract units, modeled on the Iranians'. So did its navy. But deprived of Egypt after 642, the emperors had trouble paying troops and suffered recurrent mutinies and rebellions to go along with frequent religious schisms, palace intrigues, and usurpations. Every emperor lost territory, population, and revenue. In 800, Byzantium's empire consisted of no more than Anatolia, bits of Greece, the island of Sicily, and the southernmost tip of Italy. In 540, it had been the greatest power in western Eurasia and northern Africa, with roughly twice the population and resources of its nearest rival, Sassanid Iran. By 800, it was one of several middling powers, beset by marauding tribes and upstart neighboring kingdoms.

RELIGIONS ON THE RISE

The western end of Eurasia, specifically the Levant and Arabia, spawned two of the world's most successful and enduring religions—Christianity and Islam. Each now has more than a billion followers. Only north India, which gave rise to both Hinduism and Buddhism, can offer a parallel in world history. Both Christianity and Islam followed in the traditions of earlier monotheisms.

ZOROASTRIANISM AND MANICHAEISM

Zorastrianism's origins are obscure. It arose around the prophecies of Zoroaster, who lived in eastern Iran sometime between the tenth and sixth centuries BCE, and

sacred texts such as the *Avesta*, which had parallels to the early Vedas. Its popularity rose under the Achaemenid emperors, some of whom supported it. **Zoroastrianism** was a monotheistic religion, and many scholars think it and early Judaism influenced one another. It included concepts of a single creator-god (Ahura Mazda), angels, and the existence of human choice between good and evil. Its texts forecast a savior, born to a virgin, who would have the power to resurrect the dead. It added notions of heaven and hell, and divine judgment. After Achaemenid Persia conquered Egypt in the sixth century BCE, Zoroastrianism borrowed the concept of final judgment—one of several respects in which Egyptian culture influenced Persia. Of all world religions, Zoroastrianism was distinctive in that its priests and texts endorsed sex and marriage among siblings and between nieces and uncles, elsewhere normally regarded as incest and repugnant. The practice seems to have died out in the ninth or tenth century CE.

The Zoroastrian creed was one of several in circulation in the Achaemenid Empire, but its priesthood, the magi, enjoyed royal support. It became a genuine state religion under the Sassanids, who championed all things native to Iran and held Christianity and other creeds in contempt. Although almost eliminated in Iran in the centuries after the Sassanids' fall, Zoroastrianism still survives, with about 200,000 adherents worldwide today. The largest group, the Parsis, live in western India.

Manichaeism once rivaled Christianity and Zoroastrianism for the allegiance of millions. It derived from the preaching of Mani, born in Iran (probably in 216 CE) just before the Sassanids took power. His parents were members of an obscure Christian cult. Starting at age 12 he had visions and within a few years had begun to preach an innovative blend of Christianity, Zoroastrianism, and Buddhism. Mani's teachings emphasized a code of conduct of restraint, non-violence, honesty, fasting, weekly confessions, and chastity if at all possible. Manichaeism's theology featured a permanent struggle between good and evil, light and darkness, in which everything good was spiritual and abstract, and everything evil was material and worldly. Mani seemed to have a particular loathing for human bodies and sex. In his view the only route to salvation, knowledge of the light, involved escape from the endless cycle of reincarnation—as in Buddhism—and freedom from the body.

Mani hoped his creed might become the state religion of Iran, and a Sassanid emperor, Shapur I, provided early

Zoroastrianism A Persian rock relief dated to around 235 CE shows the Zoroastrian god Ahura Mazda (right) assenting to the coronation of the Sassanian king Ardashir I by giving him a symbolic ring.

support. A few years after Shapur died, another emperor took a different view about religion and had Mani imprisoned. He died in chains about 276, but his religion lived on. Despite vigorous persecution, Manichaeism won converts throughout the Roman Empire as far as Britain and North Africa. It did so among Zoroastrians in Iran and Buddhists in India too, and flourished along the Central Asian Silk Roads. It even spread to China, where it lasted until about 1400. In its homeland of Iran, it endured for a few hundred years, but underground and overshadowed by Zoroastrianism. Manichaeism ultimately lost out nearly everywhere to state-sponsored religions, chiefly Christianity and Islam, but not before leaving its imprint upon them both.

THE SPREAD OF CHRISTIANITY, 200–800

In 200 CE, Christianity remained a minor religion in the Roman Empire and even more marginal outside it. Despite the efforts of Paul and his allies to spread the faith, its followers were few, scattered among dozens of cities and worshipping in homes or makeshift churches. It had only rickety organization, partly because most believers expected the material world to come to an end soon, so building durable institutions did not seem urgent. Christians were fewer in number than adherents of the Isis or Osiris cults emanating from Roman Egypt, or worshippers of the Persian deity Mithras. In the 270s, an emperor

considered making Mithraism the state religion of the Roman Empire, which would have changed history's course, but he died before doing it. Christian population, while growing, still came to well under 1 percent of the empire's total. Roman authorities occasionally threw a few to the lions but by and large let them be, considering them an insignificant Jewish heretical cult. As of 300, nothing suggested Christianity would ever become the dominant religion of the Roman Empire.

FAVORABLE CONDITIONS But it did. Christianity held some appeal to the Roman masses. Pagan religions offered few specifics about any afterlife, and nothing more attractive than endless ghostly wanderings. But Christianity promised eternal salvation for those who could keep the faith. This resonated with the millions whose earthly lives included heavy doses of suffering and humiliation. In Christian belief, the poor and downtrodden had just as good a chance at heaven, if not better, than the rich and powerful. Christianity embraced sinners and offered them a fresh start.

Plagues, violence, and chaos helped Christianity on its way. As we've seen, beginning in the 160s repeated epidemics ravaged the empire. Christians distinguished themselves by their reaction, which included often selflessly caring for fellow Christians regardless of risk. As a result, they probably survived in slightly higher proportion than non-Christians, and their charitable conduct attracted admiration.

Political chaos, which peaked in the third century, helped to create Christians too. Against the backdrop of civil war, reckless ambition, and boundless greed, conscientious Christian behavior looked noble in comparison. For the many who grew discouraged by the duplicity, savagery, and sin of the visible world, an alternative universe of the spirit held strong attractions. The remarkable courage of some Christians in the face of mortal peril also provided inspiration: in Gaul about 180 CE, for instance, a slave woman named Blandina withstood days of torture with stoic calm, proclaiming her attachment to Christianity.

Like Manichaeans, Christians objected strenuously to Roman practices such as infanticide, abortion, homosexuality, and indeed sex for any purpose beyond procreation, so they might have had larger-than-average families. By 300, roughly 10 percent of the Roman Empire's population was Christian.

Monasteries St. Catherine's Monastery still stands in the desert at the foot of Mount Sinai today. Its high walls, built in 557, emphasize its inhabitants' desire to withdraw from the outside world.

This modest demographic success began to worry some Roman officials. More systematic persecutions began in 250, involving confiscation of property, exile, and occasional torture and execution. Diocletian took it to another level, feeling that religious tension undermined the empire's cohesion. Seeking to use religion to bind the empire together, he had himself recognized as semi-divine and an object of worship. He banned Manichaeism for its associations with Iran, and then attacked Christianity in the final years of his rule. Romans were required to demonstrate that they sacrificed to Roman gods. Many Christians complied, but many others preferred to accept the penalties, including death. Such steadfast Christian commitment again attracted admiration. According to Christian traditions, some eagerly sought martyrdom, even if it meant a grisly death nailed to a cross or in the jaws of hungry lions, confident it would earn them a place in heaven. Diocletian retired before his persecutions had reached more than a few thousand Christians, and his successors wavered in their policy. So the Christian community easily survived, still a small minority, mainly confined to the cities.

That changed with Emperor Constantine. During the civil wars that ultimately made him emperor, he chose to become a Christian. Just how it happened is uncertain: he apparently saw visions, entrusted his fate to Christ, won several battles, and was a changed man. In any case, during the period 310–313 Constantine ended persecutions of all religions, including Christianity, in those lands he controlled.

When he assumed command of the entire empire in 324, Constantine had already become a patron of Christianity. He built churches, donated land, extended tax breaks, and otherwise supported his fellow Christians. The formerly rickety church organization became a solid edifice with institutionalized hierarchy based chiefly on regional leaders called bishops, each of whom had a specific territory (now called a diocese) to administer. He also supported Christian communities outside the Roman Empire—in Iran, for example. (That support deepened their persecution by the Sassanids.) Christianity was, suddenly, an imperial religion with the weight of the Roman Empire behind it. Without Constantine's conversion, it is hard to see how Christianity would have transcended its prior status as one among several minority religions in Roman lands.

STRUCTURE AND SCHISM With success came both structure and **schism**. By the time of Constantine's death, there were a few hundred bishops; and the most important, in cities such as Constantinople, Antioch, and Alexandria, came to be called patriarchs. The bishop in Rome came to be called the Pope in the late fourth century and claimed primacy within the church. Bishops enjoyed power over their human flocks, church personnel, and doctrines. The other great institution of the early church was **monasticism**, which took shape first in Egypt in the third through fifth centuries. For those who sought a perfect Christian existence, free from the corruption of daily life, self-exile made good sense. Soon like-minded men and women clustered together, forming monastic communities devoted to spiritual rigor. Desert terrain was especially suitable for such conscious attempts at withdrawal. One of the first major monasteries grew up at the foot of Mount Sinai, where Christians and Jews believe Moses saw the burning bush.

At first, although Christian communities had had their arguments, by and large they were cohesive, small, and intensely loyal to one another. As they flourished, they lost some of that cohesion—as is normal with successful social movements. Rival bishops competed for authority. Points of doctrine became divisive. Most of these had to do with the precise nature of Christ, whether he was man, God, or somehow both.

In 325, Constantine summoned all the bishops he could gather to Nicaea (Iznik in modern Turkey) to sort out these questions. The prevailing view became the so-called Nicene Creed, the classic formulation of Christian belief endorsed by most churches around the world today. It required that Christians declare their faith in God, Christ, and the Holy Spirit—the Trinity of Christianity, the three forms of the same divine essence. The losing argument, that of a churchman named Arius, became a heresy. Arianism denied the Trinity, holding that Christ was the son of God but not a co-equal form of God. Although proscribed by the church, Arianism retained many followers within Christendom, including one Byzantine emperor, and lasted until the mid-sixth century.

Arianism was only the first big schism. Another arose in the mid-fifth century when a bishop, Nestorius, complained that priests and bishops ought not to refer to Mary, who in his view did not have a divine nature, as Mother of God. Another council of bishops met, argued, and then ruled in 431 that Nestorianism was a heresy. It too, however, survived official condemnation, especially outside Roman borders, and became the primary expression of Christianity in Iran and Central Asia. In fact, the bishops' ruling helped Christians in Sassanian Iran, because as disloyal heretics in Roman eyes the Nestorians were no longer suspect as enemy agents.

Yet another unorthodox view, called Monophysitism, arose in the fifth and sixth centuries. It held that Christ had only a single and divine nature. Ruled a heresy in 451, it thrived nonetheless in the eastern reaches of Christianity. Empress Theodora was a Monophysite (Justinian was not). The Coptic Church of Egypt and Ethiopia is Monophysite today. These and other doctrinal disputes preoccupied bishops and theologians and threatened to divide Christianity and Byzantium, which is why emperors needed rulings to define orthodoxy.

Fishmongers and washerwomen probably worried less about doctrine. A fourth-century bishop claimed that on the streets of Constantinople if he asked the price of bread he would hear that God the Father was greater than God the Son. But surely most ordinary folk only occasionally spared a thought for the precise nature of divinity and found the priests' theological arguments and vocabulary bewildering. They accepted Christianity because their leaders told them to, because their friends and family did, or because the simpler teachings of the church—charity, community, love, redemption—appealed to them.

By the fourth century, the experience of Christian worship and community had evolved in new directions.

Christians worshipped under the guidance of trained priests (clergy), who handled the reading of sacred texts, and conducted rituals that took the place of communal meals. As the church got larger, more bureaucratic (as all state religions must), and more remote, Christians embraced local saints to provide personal, local, and intensely emotional attachments. Saints' biographies provided exemplary role models, and saints could serve as intermediaries if God or Christ seemed as remote as the emperor.

SPREADING BEYOND ROME By the 450s, Christianity had become the majority religion within Roman borders—which still held up in the east. Tens of millions now professed the faith in one form or another. Monks, who had sought isolation at first but eventually sought converts as well, carried it far and wide. The Byzantine state promoted it in its orthodox form, both at home and

The Spread of Christianity, 300–600 CE Thanks in large part to the efforts of the Roman, and then Byzantine, Empire, Christianity gradually became the dominant religion over broad swaths of the Mediterranean world and Europe. The kings of Aksum promoted the Christian faith in what is now Ethiopia. Many Christians, mainly Nestorians, also lived in Iran and cities of Central Asia stretching (by 635) to China. Southwest India also had a small Christian community.

abroad, while cracking down as best it could on heresies. Monarchs elsewhere in the western end of Eurasia took an interest, sometimes from curiosity, sometimes out of political calculation. In the fourth and fifth centuries, kings in Armenia, Georgia, Ethiopia, and Nubia all became Christian—and so, over many generations, did their populations. A king in what would become France followed suit in the sixth century. These were top-down conversions, like Constantine's, linking the power of the state to the fortunes of the faith. After the fourth century, this was the primary way in which Christianity spread.

Top-down conversion prevailed even in some lands that did not have kings. In the British Isles, for example, missionary monks spread Christianity to peoples with minimal political structure such as the Irish and Scots. But the monks focused their efforts on local elites—chieftains or landowners whose example would attract imitation. Beginning in the sixth century, with backing from the Pope, their efforts met gradual success.

Missionary monks, mainly Nestorians, took Christianity along the Silk Road and the Indian Ocean trade routes as far as China and India. They made converts in the oases of Central Asia and a few in China, India, and Sri Lanka. In the third and fourth centuries, Greek-speaking Christians from Egypt brought the faith to southern India, and Christians from Iran carried it to northwest India. Christianity has survived as a minority religion ever since in India. In China, Christian monks arrived by the early seventh century, a favorable time because the ruling Tang dynasty then welcomed foreigners and unfamiliar ideas. The court sponsored translations of Christian scripture into Chinese. An imperial decree referred to the "Iranian religion"—Christianity—as "mysterious, wonderful, and calm" and judged it "right that it should spread through the empire." But none of the emperors became Christians, and it did not spread widely within China.

In the absence of any overarching authority, Christianity took many forms. A king in Ethiopia or Armenia might try to root out all but his preferred form of the faith, but political fragmentation allowed multiple religions and sects to survive. In Latin-speaking Europe, despite plenty of political fragmentation, increasingly the intellectual heft of a North African bishop and the institutional power of popes forged a more consistent, if not quite uniform, Christianity we call Catholicism. More and more of the Germanic tribes adopted it, slowly abandoning paganism or Arianism, both of which went extinct in Europe by 600 or so.

AUGUSTINE   The North African bishop was **Augustine** (354–430). In his youth a shameless libertine, in his maturity a prolific author and strict moralist, and always a deep thinker, he wrestled candidly with his unruly passions. No one other than Christ had a stronger influence upon Christianity.

Born in today's Algeria and raised by Monica, his devoutly Christian mother, Augustine left the faith and became a Manichaean for a decade, absorbing some of Mani's stern morals (although he did not live up to them, fathering a child by a slave woman) and his theology. Augustine found much to admire in Platonic thought. Then, dazzled by the intellect and arguments of a bishop in Italy, he agreed to be baptized at age 33. He abandoned his child (and its mother) and became a bishop soon thereafter in the North African town of Hippo, in the years when Roman North Africa was crumbling under Vandal assault. Somehow, he found time to write numerous books that have helped shape Christian theology ever since.

Some of his works, such as his *Confessions*, were deeply introspective, concerned with doubt, unworthiness, and sin—he was obsessed with having once stolen a pear just for fun. He renounced the waywardness of his youth and demonized the Manichaean faith he had long professed. From it, nonetheless, he took Mani's ungenerous view of womankind as a distraction from sacred pursuits. Augustine's other works, especially those of his final years, took on more political themes. The sack of Rome in 410 made a deep impact on his outlook, inspiring a long meditation (translated as *The City of God*) on the relation between faith and the material world, and between church and state. Others saw Rome's misfortune at the hand of pagan Goths as evidence that casting off traditional gods in favor of Christianity was a mistake. Augustine assured Christians that what really counted was the kingdom of heaven and one's own inner being. As he put it, "The Heavenly City outshines Rome, beyond comparison. There, instead of victory, is

Augustine of Hippo Augustine appears on the right in this small seventh-century painting on ivory. St. Jerome, another influential thinker and leader of the early church, is depicted on the left.

truth; instead of high rank, holiness; instead of peace, felicity; instead of life, eternity."

Augustine's writings helped to establish doctrines of original sin, the Holy Trinity, and the indispensability of God's grace to human freedom, all touchstones of Western Christian philosophy. He also helped to inject a neo-Platonism into Christian thought. Augustine laid the intellectual foundation for a more unified Christianity—Catholicism—in the Latin-speaking west. His ideas carried little weight in the Greek-speaking east.

MUHAMMAD AND ISLAM

The second monotheistic faith to spread over the western reaches of the Old World web was **Islam**. Its founder, **Muhammad** (570–632), was born to a lesser family of a ruling tribe in Mecca, an oasis and crossroads in western Arabia. Arabia was a dry, dusty, rocky land dotted with oases and coastal ports, a hard place to make a living. Its few inhabitants, organized mainly in tribes, survived by herding, trading, and raiding others' herds and trade caravans. Their main export was leather. Except for those living at the biggest oases or in the more welcoming districts of the far south such as Yemen, where there was a small kingdom, the **Arabs** were either nomadic or close to it. Despite a long tradition of oral poetry, almost nothing as yet was written in their language, Arabic (the earliest surviving inscription dates from 512). The Arabs were polytheistic, with dozens of nature deities and gods specific to individual tribes, although behind them all was a more general god, referred to as Allah.

These Arabian tribes lived on a southern fringe of the Iranian and Byzantine world, and because of trade links they often knew something of it. They also knew something of the monotheistic religions—Judaism, Zoroastrianism, Christianity—and the dualistic faith of Manichaeism through contact with the more populous lands to the north, and with Christian Ethiopia. As Arabia was drawn more tightly into the Old World web, its religious options multiplied, and Muhammad added one more.

MUHAMMAD His father died before Muhammad was born, and his mother died when he was six. The grandfather to whom he turned soon died as well, and from the age of eight he was raised by an uncle. Little else is known of his youth, but he somehow got work helping merchants in Mecca. At age 25, he married one of them, Khadija, a prosperous widow 15 years his senior. They had at least six children, of whom only three daughters survived childhood. By his 30s, he was well acquainted with the sorrows of this world but also a respected businessman in Mecca, known for his judgment and wisdom. At age 40, while visiting a desert cave for peace and contemplation, as Arab men regularly did, he had visions and heard a voice telling him that he, Muhammad, was the messenger of God. At first confused and frightened, he ran from the cave thinking perhaps devils had possessed him. But his wife, Khadija, and his cousin, a Christian, helped him come to terms with his vision and to see it as the revelation of God.

His closest family and friends endorsed this understanding of Muhammad as a prophet. Soon many others in Mecca did as well, but, in a common response to prophets, some thought he had lost his mind. The ruling elite, especially the merchant clans, objected to his preaching. They feared that his uncompromising denunciation of idols and paganism would be bad for business.

When he was about 50, Khadija died, as did a powerful uncle who had helped protect him. The Mecca elite now harassed him and his followers, many of whom he sent to Christian Ethiopia for safety. All seemed bleak. But one night while sleeping—as Muslim tradition has it—he was transported by an archangel to Jerusalem and then to heaven, where the sum of God's wisdom was entrusted to him. This journey, known as *Mi'raj* in Arabic, is sometimes regarded as a spiritual journey through the various levels of existence, and sometimes as an actual physical journey.

THE BIRTH OF ISLAM In any case, Muhammad's earthly fortunes soon changed. A town a few days' walk to the north, Medina, where his reputation for sagacity had spread, asked him to become its judge and leader. In 622, he left Mecca just before his enemies attacked his house, and he fled to Medina. There he set up the first mosque and formed a community of followers called Muslims, a word that means "people who submit to the will of God." Muslims use this date, 622 CE, the year of the flight to Medina, as the year 1 in their calendar (a lunar calendar with 354 days to the year).

Muhammad and his followers still faced a rocky road. They took to preying upon Meccan traders returning from Syria. His enemies in Mecca, who regarded this as outright banditry, launched expeditions against him and wounded him in one fracas. He struggled to keep

The Spread of Islam, 632–750 CE In one of the more remarkable cultural transformations of world history, the Islamic religion became the majority faith over broad areas in little more than a century. Muhammad's followers found populations weary of Sassanian and Byzantine rule willing to accept Arab leaders instead, and often ready to convert from Zoroastrian or Christian belief to Islam.

his community whole, losing many men in skirmishes (and often marrying their widows, routine conduct for an Arab political chieftain). But military successes boosted his standing, and by 630 he had won over the population of Mecca. Although he generally showed mercy to those he defeated, on one occasion he either ordered or acquiesced in the execution of the males, and enslavement of the females, of a Jewish tribe that had sided against him. Many tribes of the Arabian Peninsula found it prudent to join him and become Muslims. He even invited emperors and kings of all the nearby great powers—Iran, Byzantium, Ethiopia—to join his faith, but there is no record of any response. Some of the Jews, Christians, and Zoroastrians of Arabia accepted his political authority while retaining their religions. Muhammad specifically granted them that right as "People of the Book"—a phrase that meant they had scripture.

Muhammad died in 632 after a brief illness. His

political achievement, beyond defeating the Meccans in battle, was to forge a community of Arabs that transcended their strong tribal identities and bonded them together in a common faith. Their political power extended throughout the western half of Arabia.

Like the several People of the Book, Islam itself had scripture, which Muslims regard as a fuller and finer—indeed, final—version of God's message. Islam's scripture, the Qur'an ("recitation"), was the text of the revelations from God as Muhammad spoke them. To believers, they are the words of God himself. The Qur'an includes a history of Jewish, Christian, and Arab prophets, exhortations to Muslims to follow only one god and to form a community of the faithful, some harsh words for unbelievers, and moral and legal guidelines for Muslims. These form the basis of divinely sanctioned law and ethics in Islam, known as **shari'a** ("the path"). The Qur'an has many echoes of the Bible, including the expectation that the day of reckoning will soon be at hand. Muhammad regarded the Qur'an, together with his family, as his most precious gifts to Muslims. He regarded himself, and was regarded by Muslims, as the last in the line of prophets stretching back to Abraham, Moses, and Jesus—just as Mani had seen himself four centuries before. Muhammad considered himself a reformer, restoring the religion of Abraham that Jews and Christians had corrupted, rather than the founder of a new religion. But a founder, in the end, is what he was.

He was the only founder of a major new religion to exercise political power directly. Jesus and the Buddha never directed armies and never had to delve far into the grimy compromises of politics. Muhammad, in contrast, left a political record that has served as one of the guides to political behavior for Muslims ever after.

THE ARAB CONQUESTS The career of Islam as a political and religious movement after 632 forms one of the more remarkable stories in world history. At first, as word of Muhammad's death spread, tribes broke away, showing that their allegiance to Islam had been merely pragmatic. But soon his kin and closest companions, men such as Abu Bakr, Umar, and Uthman, forged the community of Muslims into an effective military force and broke out of the Arabian Peninsula into the richer lands then ruled by the Sassanids and Byzantines. Those great powers had just expended legions of manpower and vast fortunes in decades of pitiless warfare against one another, and at first they could not see the Arabs—mere camel herders and petty traders to them—as a threat. Many Arabs had fought as auxiliaries for both powers and had learned something of their strengths and weaknesses. They also had learned of the Byzantines' doctrine of Christian holy war and its emphasis on the importance of capturing Jerusalem.

Before the emperors knew what they were up against, the Arabs had conquered the Iranian capital of Ctesiphon (637) and the Byzantine city of Jerusalem (638). By 646, they ruled Egypt. They built navies, a new enterprise for Arabs, and seized the island of Cyprus in 649. The peoples they conquered sometimes resisted fiercely, but often they welcomed the Muslim Arabs as an improvement on their current rulers. In Byzantine Syria and Egypt, religious schism again came into play: local elites preferred a different brand of Christianity to the one championed in Constantinople, and felt only a weak loyalty, if any, to Byzantine emperors. Islamic rule appeared to offer them greater freedom of religion. Similarly, the Jews of Egypt generally welcomed Muslim conquest, having suffered under Byzantine rule.

When they did fight, the Arabs proved remarkably formidable for men with no tradition of siege craft, infantry tactics, or naval operations. They had mastered the art of camel management, an advantage in desert environments. More decisively, they had a tremendous solidarity born of religious conviction. Their leaders convinced them that death in battle earned a ticket to paradise, a belief hardly unique to Muslims. And military campaigns promised booty and plunder beyond all imagination for poor men raised in the oases and deserts of Arabia. By 650, the Sassanian Empire was finished, Byzantium had lost its richest provinces, and the first pulse of Arab Muslim conquests was essentially complete.

In conquering Iran and Mesopotamia, Muhammad's successors echoed the conquests of Alexander the Great nearly a thousand years before. He too had molded a formidable fighting force out of an originally small and unsophisticated population, the Macedonians, and brought low the great power of Persia.

TENSIONS WITHIN ISLAM Dividing the plunder from such conquests caused quarrels among Muhammad's followers, as it had among Alexander's. So did competition for recognition as the true successor to Muhammad, or caliph ("deputy of God"). Within just a few years of the Prophet's death, the Muslim community fractured. Should the caliph be of the Prophet's family—perhaps his closest male relative Ali, his cousin and son-in-law? Patrilineal descent was extremely important to Arab tribes. Or should the caliph be the best Muslim or the best leader—a man like Umar, a cultured and charismatic companion of Muhammad?

Discord prevailed. As it happened, the first three caliphs were not from Muhammad's family, but close companions of the Prophet who had shown their resolve and piety in many a stern test. They proved remarkably successful winning battles and converting people to Islam in Egypt, Iran, and Mesopotamia. Then, when Ali became the fourth caliph (r. 656–661), civil war resulted. The winners defeated Ali and in 661 formed the first genuine Islamic state, the Umayyad caliphate, with its capital at Damascus. Ali was murdered in prayer the following year. Here and there the partisans of Ali (known as Shi'a or Shi'ites) rose in rebellion, climaxing in a pitched battle in 680 at Karbala (in Iraq), a defeat at the hands of the

CONSIDERING THE EVIDENCE

The Succession to Muhammad

Muhammad, the Prophet of Islam, died in 632 CE. His close friend Abu Bakr was helping to prepare the Prophet's body for burial when he was interrupted by an urgent message. At that very moment, the people of Medina were assembling to proclaim one of their own as Muhammad's successor. Although the people of Medina were called the Helpers, they actually formed the majority of the Muslim army. They had not included Muhammad's earliest converts from Mecca, known as the Migrants, in their gathering. Abu Bakr rushed to the meeting with two of Muhammad's earliest supporters. By the end of the meeting, and without consulting Muhammad's family, the assembly pledged allegiance to Abu Bakr as the first caliph, or successor to Muhammad. The following excerpt is from a compilation of recollections about the meeting that the Arab historian al-Tabari assembled around 915 CE.

When the Prophet of God...died, the (Medinese) Helpers assembled...and said, "Let us give this authority, after Muhammad...to Sa'd ibn Ubada [a native of Medina]."... Sa'd said..."O company of Helpers! You have precedence in religion and merit in Islam possessed by no other Arab tribe. Muhammad remained for more than ten years (here in Medina) among his people....But among his own people (in Mecca) only a few men believed in him, and they were not able to protect the Prophet of God or glorify his religion.... Therefore keep this authority for yourselves alone....

. . .

[After Abu Bakr arrived at the meeting, he said:] "God singled out the first Migrants of his people by allowing them to recognize the truth and believe in him. They consoled him and shared in his suffering.... They were the first in the land to worship God and to believe in God and the Prophet. They were his friends and his clan and the best entitled of all men to this authority after him.... Here is Umar and here is Abu Bayda [of Mecca]. Swear allegiance to whomever of them you choose." The two of them then objected: "No, by God, we will not accept this authority above you.... Give us your hand so that we may swear allegiance to you."

Source: F. E. Peters, *A Reader on Classical Islam* (Princeton, 1994).

QUESTIONS FOR ANALYSIS

1. What reasons did the Helpers and the Migrants present to claim leadership of the Muslim community after the death of Muhammad?
2. Why did the Helpers rush to proclaim a successor to Muhammad?
3. What were the consequences of deciding on a successor without consulting Muhammad's family, especially his son-in-law Ali?

Umayyads. The Shi'a champion, Hussein, a grandson of the Prophet, was killed and humiliated, and his martyrdom remains a rallying cry for Shi'a Muslims to this day. Shi'a Muslims have always been a minority within the Islamic population, and they've usually been regarded as heretics by the majority, known as Sunni Muslims.

Young religions are especially prone to schism, as the early careers of Christianity and Islam both show. Without the weight of tradition, much remains to be settled. Rival doctrines and factions compete for dominance—often violently, even in religions that preach peace. When religions acquire the powers of a state, as with Constantine's adoption of Christianity or the establishment of the Umayyads, the stakes only grow. Winners define the losers as heretics, persecute them, and if they have the means, perhaps try to exterminate them. When religions become international, as Christianity and Islam did early on, and no single state can control believers, then stamping out heresy becomes more difficult. Schisms can last for centuries or even millennia, and new ones can always develop.

Despite schism and struggle, in the first few decades of Islam the Muslim community set its rules. The most important are called the Five Pillars of Islam, which hold that a Muslim must: (1) profess that there is but one God, Allah, and that Muhammad is his messenger, (2) pray five times daily, (3) give alms to the needy, (4) fast during daylight hours during the month of Ramadan, and (5) make a pilgrimage to Mecca at least once if financially possible. On these five rules, all pious Muslims agree.

THE UMAYYAD CALIPHATE Over the next century and a half, from 650 to 800, Islam became a state religion of a sort. Caliphs claimed to be both successors of the Prophet and leaders of a political community. The Umayyad caliphs in Damascus echoed the traditions of Mesopotamian kingship and Roman emperorship. They formed no church, and by and large left the selection of religious authorities to the community of the faithful (the *umma* in Arabic). They permitted Christians, Jews, and Zoroastrians to run their own affairs, as long as they did not challenge the authority of the caliphs or denigrate Islam. They taxed non-Muslims at a higher rate than Muslims, which created an economic incentive for people to convert, and one for rulers to discourage conversion. Christianity and Judaism survived throughout the caliphate, faring better than paganism in the Christianized Roman Empire. It took centuries for Iran, Syria, and Egypt to become Muslim-majority lands.

Meanwhile, the Umayyads expanded their empire geographically. Another pulse of conquests (705–715) took Arabs and Islam into northwest India and across North Africa to Morocco, where again the Jewish population welcomed the invaders, and across the Mediterranean into Spain. Small Muslim forces raided as far north as the Loire valley in France by 732.

Governing a state with several religions, dozens of ethnicities, and newly conquered peoples was a new challenge

Arab Conquest A painting on the ceiling of a lavishly decorated, early eighth-century Umayyad palace shows a man leading a camel. Because the Arabs' skill in camel management gave them an advantage in desert warfare, these animals helped Arab Muslims to control Iran and Mesopotamia.

for the Arabs. The first Umayyads relied on Arab tribes to make their wishes felt throughout their domain. As the community of Muslims grew in size and the ranks who had known the Prophet and stood with him in his struggles thinned, the loyalty of tribesmen grew less reliable. Umayyad caliphs by 680 or so, half a century after Muhammad's death, needed new sources of legitimacy.

To bolster their authority, they relied in part on "soft power" exerted in forms such as monumental architecture. The magnificent Dome of the Rock, begun in 681 on the site of the Jewish Second Temple in Jerusalem, offered an awe-inspiring reminder of Umayyad wealth and power. The Umayyads also relied on the expertise of the conquered. Like the Goths who overran the western Roman Empire or the Macedonians who conquered Persia, victorious Arabs recruited experienced specialists to sustain technical aspects of their state, such as finance, large-scale irrigation, and monumental architecture. The Dome of the Rock was built under the guidance of Greek architects and consequently shows some decorative features borrowed from Byzantine churches. Some Greeks and Iranians enjoyed considerable power and amassed fortunes working for the caliphate, which irked many Arabs and Muslims.

Managing the tribal, religious, and ethnic divisions within the Umayyad state required great skill on the part of caliphs. In time, as in the Roman Empire, some rulers came to power for whom the glitter of evenings at court outshone the allure of long days spent governing—a great liability in a state based on an ideology of piety and

Dome of the Rock The Umayyad caliph Abd Al-Malik oversaw the construction of this grand edifice, completed in 691–692. The site is sacred to Muslims, as it is believed to be the place where Muhammad's journey to heaven began.

Abbasid Power Abbasid emirs signaled the reach of their authority across the Mediterranean by building, starting in 793, a grand mosque at Córdoba (left) in what is now Spain. Its characteristic rounded arches echo the style of the early eighth-century Umayyad mosque at Damascus (right).

righteousness. By the 740s, the Umayyads were barely holding onto power.

THE ABBASID CALIPHATE A rebellious faction from Iran, called the Abbasids, overthrew the Umayyads and established a new caliphate in 750. Based in a new city, Baghdad (in Iraq), the **Abbasid caliphate** boasted luxurious palaces and all the trappings of the Persian/Iranian imperial tradition. Islam was losing more and more of its original tight-knit character and becoming increasingly a religion of power—a path Christianity had followed as well. The Abbasids consolidated power over most of the Islamic world, although southern Spain became an independent Muslim state, led by the last of the Umayyad dynasts.

The Abbasids flourished for roughly a century (ca. 750–850). They rebuilt the irrigation infrastructure of the Tigris-Euphrates, which, combined with the grain surplus from Egypt, provided them with a powerful economic base. The Abbasids also tapped into the growing trade network of the Indian Ocean world, another source of prosperity. Arab and Iranian merchants roamed as far as China. And, like all Iranian or Persian states for a thousand years before them, they profited from overland trade along the Silk Roads.

The early Abbasids invested not only in palaces and military power, but in supporting scholars and artists. They took to heart the saying of Muhammad that "a scholar's ink is more precious than the martyr's blood." Jurists sorted out the finer points of Islamic law and organized various schools of jurisprudence, most of which survive

today. The Abbasids underwrote translations of learned works from Chinese, Sanskrit, Hebrew, Greek, and Latin into Arabic and Persian. They patronized poetry and science on an unprecedented scale, and Baghdad became the greatest center of learning in the Old World web.

Their lesser rival within the world of Islam, the emirate based in Córdoba (southern Spain), flourished as well. By 800, its armies controlled most of Iberia. Arab immigrants developed irrigated agriculture there to new heights. They also reinvigorated mining. The court sponsored scholars and scientists, just as in Baghdad, and beginning in 793 successive emirs built the sprawling Córdoba mosque modeled on the Umayyad one in Damascus. Parts of Spain would remain under Muslim authority until 1492.

With establishment of the Abbasid caliphate and the survival of the Byzantine Empire, the western end of the Old World web once again featured two superpowers, as in the days of Rome and Persia. Byzantium and the Abbasids served as champions of two great religions. They often fought, like their predecessors, and generally saw themselves in implacable opposition to one another. But they were also something of a unit. Together, they housed almost all the great cities of western Eurasia and northern Africa, all the great concentrations of wealth, all the important seats of culture and learning. Together, they preserved the science and learning developed in the ancient worlds of Babylon, Persia, Egypt, Greece, and Rome. As of 800, the zones of western Eurasia that they did not control, such as Russia and almost all of Europe, were backwaters in comparison, home to petty kingdoms and wandering tribes.

RE-CENTERING THE OLD WORLD WEB

The biggest economic and social changes in the western region of the Old World web, during the period 200–800 CE, were associated with the breakup of Roman imperial unity and the re-unification of much of the Romano-Persian world under the banners of Islam.

Both processes were terribly violent. Warfare was commonplace in the days when the Roman and Parthian empires were intact, but it took place in frontier zones and involved military specialists. Parthian and Roman subjects not in the army and not living along the frontiers could expect to live in peace. Their cities needed no walls. But that security disappeared with the breakdown of the Parthian state and the incursions of Germanic tribes into Roman lands in the third century, followed by the nearly incessant civil wars among Roman generals. Pillaging armies and raiding tribesmen overran towns and farmsteads frequently, killing, raping, and enslaving as they went. Roman cities began to build walls in the third century, and by the fifth century almost every remaining city had walls. The Byzantine-Sassanid wars, especially that of 603–630, brought horrific violence to non-military populations as armies campaigned back and forth. The ideology of religious righteousness may have added extra intensity to the bloodletting in those contests. The Arab conquests too brought violence, although in the early decades the scale of their warfare was much smaller than that of the Byzantine-Sassanid struggles, which had opened the door to those Arab conquests.

The crumbling of powerful states—the western Roman Empire after 370 and the Byzantine and Sassanian empires in the 640s—allowed civil violence to spike. Brigands and gangs caused as much grief as armies did. For the millions caught in the maelstrom, this breakdown of public order was disastrous—probably more so for young women than anyone else. The scale of civil and military violence lowered population at times, although famines and epidemics normally did more damage.

UNRAVELING AT THE WESTERN EDGE

On the westernmost fringes of the Old World web—in North Africa, Iberia, Gaul, and Britain, but also in Italy and the Balkans—the end of Roman rule brought a distinct simplification of economic and social life. With heightened violence, political chaos, and the loss of security, long-distance trade withered. With it went specialized production, honed artisan skills, and the markets for both luxury goods and trade staples such as olive oil. The working of both copper and lead almost ceased. Pottery and housing styles became much more basic. Literacy declined. Money almost disappeared. Economic life became much more local and self-sufficient. By the 570s, several centuries of vibrant trade linking Mediterranean and Atlantic ports had come to an end.

Cities shriveled to little more than castles and outbuildings. In Britain, the former city of York reverted to marshland. In Italy, Rome itself became just a small town. Its population fell from nearly 1 million in 350 to 50,000 or so in 550. In Greece, by 600 or so, complex society almost vanished, after more than a thousand years. From about 400 to roughly 700 (in North Africa) or 750 (in Europe), the Old World web unraveled at its western edge.

Let's pause for a moment to consider what this unraveling meant. As with the disappearance of urban life after the Maya collapse noted in Chapter 10, this trend struck elites as the end of everything they treasured. Some Romans tried to sell their expertise to new rulers who needed bureaucratic skills. Others became beggars or brigands. For people living in the path of violent bands, the loss of organized complex society often meant the end of life.

For those lucky enough to avoid violent hordes, the breakdown of Roman networks and social complexity might have seemed a liberation, worth the price of never seeing fine buildings or good pottery again. No more taxes to pay; no more haughty aristocrats flaunting their power, wealth, and education. The average heights of ordinary people in formerly Roman lands grew in the fifth and sixth centuries, suggesting that poor people got more or better food. Falling production and trade made it harder to get rich and left almost everyone, even kings and bishops, more equal.

Like the economy, culture in the far west, and indeed almost all of Europe, became more local. Fewer people spoke Latin, and more spoke versions of Gothic languages. Over generations, these tongues melded with Latin to produce new languages. In the Balkans after 400, Slavic languages began to replace Latin.

In 200 CE the same language, Latin, had been understood from England to Egypt, and the same Roman coins accepted. Public buildings, city layouts, roads, and aqueducts looked the same. But by 600 Europe was fragmented, and no one built roads and aqueducts. It would remain culturally and politically fragmented forever after—despite the ambitions of later conquerors such as Charlemagne, Napoleon, and Hitler.

In a sense, however, the conquered Romans won the cultural battle in Europe. Most of the evolving languages, at least in western Europe, were based on Latin. The prevailing religion, after Arianism disappeared, was Catholic Christianity as formulated in Rome. The victorious Vandals in North Africa quickly opted for Roman comfort and sophistication—hot baths and silk robes, Latin speech and Christian spirituality. This outcome in Europe and North Africa resembled what typically happened when steppe people conquered China: they gradually became Chinese culturally.

It forms a sharp contrast with the Arab expansion into Iran, Syria, and Egypt—lands of wealth, power, and social complexity. The conquering Arabs, unlike Vandals and Goths, did not take up the religion of the conquered. Nor did they come to speak Persian, Syriac, Greek, or Coptic (the majority language in Egypt before 640). Instead, over time most of the conquered peoples became Muslim and, outside of Iran, shifted to speaking Arabic. One explanation for this divergent pattern is that in Europe the language of religion remained Latin, but in the newly conquered Arab lands the language of religion became the language of the conquerors, the Arabs.

RESILIENCE IN SOUTHWEST ASIA

In the Byzantine, Iranian, and Arab lands, things worked out very differently from the way they unfolded in Europe after 400. Social complexity and market society survived, partly because it had deeper roots going back millennia. Imperial control broke down now and again but always revived. Urban life and economic specialization endured. Byzantine pottery retained artistic flourishes. In Byzantine Syria, villages in rocky hill country could become prosperous by producing only olive oil and trading it for all else they needed. Cities, by and large, grew. After the Arab conquests, most of the conquered cities revived, and the Arabs built new ones, such as Baghdad, soon to be among the world's biggest. In 800 the population of Baghdad topped 1 million.

Córdoba in Spain, Basra in Iraq, and dozens of other cities grew from small towns into big cities. The parts of the Old World web controlled by the caliphs and Byzantine emperors did not unravel.

The volume of trade probably grew under Islamic and Byzantine rule, although we have no reliable numbers. The new Islamic caliphates provided fertile ground for the spread of ethnic trade networks, especially of Jews and Armenians. These traders formed neighborhoods in every big city and took advantage of the heightened trust that minority status usually brings within a group to conduct business with their fellows from other cities. By 800, Jewish trade networks extended from Muslim Spain to India and beyond. Armenian traders were active over almost as broad a span, and some minority sects of Islam built similar networks. Some Christian monasteries became economic centers too, specializing in skills such as wine making and beer brewing, a niche open because alcohol is forbidden to Muslims by the Qur'an. Muslim rulers were often delighted to welcome prosperous Jews and Christians, who by law were taxed at higher rates than Muslims.

The prosperity of the lands of Islam after 680 opened up new markets and trade routes, and thickened traffic on older ones. For their ambitious building projects the caliphs needed supplies of timber, which their lands largely lacked. It came from the headwaters of the Tigris and Euphrates Rivers, India, and the shores of the Adriatic Sea. Their subjects also needed fuelwood for expanding glassworks, sugar refining, and metallurgy. Damascus became a center for high-quality steelmaking, which required many tons of charcoal. The Islamic lands also needed more metals than their own mines could provide, so they imported gold from parts of Africa and Central Asia, iron from East Africa, and steel ingots from India.

The caliphates drew their slave labor from afar, because by law Muslims cannot enslave other Muslims, and the Qur'an afforded protection to People of the Book (Christians, Jews, Zoroastrians, Hindus, Buddhists, and others). That left pagans from Russia, Central Asia, or Africa as the nearest target populations legally suitable for enslavement. The Byzantines and Sassanians had had slavery and slave trades too, but on a smaller scale than the new caliphates. The intense warfare of the seventh century, and the repeated bouts of urban plague during the sixth through the eighth centuries, sharpened the demand for slaves in cities, especially women and children for textile work. The establishment of Abbasid sugar and date palm plantations in southern Iraq led to the large-scale import of male slaves from East Africa.

Islamic states also pioneered the use of slave soldiers, especially as palace guards and elite cavalry units. Called *mamluks* in Arabic, slave soldiers were common in the Muslim world until the nineteenth century. Sold or captured as boys, they underwent grueling training. Survivors of proven merit often earned privileges unavailable to other slaves or soldiers, in exchange for unstinting loyalty to their commanders. A steady supply of male slaves became important to the security of many Islamic rulers. At first, Russians and Central Asian Turks formed the largest sources of slave populations, but by 800 most slaves entering Abbasid lands came from East Africa. These slave trades strengthened some threads of the Old World web, north along Russian rivers, and south both by sea and up the Nile into East Africa.

The comparative political unity and security of life in the new caliphates encouraged urbanization, commerce, and development of new trade routes. So did the cultural unity that Islam extended from Spain to Iran. After 680, Arabs, Iranians, and other Muslims built a thicker network of trade links than the one they had inherited, integrating old sea routes with traffic on land.

Growing networks of exchange favored the accumulation of wealth and growing social inequality, as rapid economic expansion normally does. Pre-Islamic Arab society, already attuned to markets and trade, had had its inequalities. But Arabia had so little wealth in total that few could amass fortunes. On the wider Islamic canvas, which by 750 stretched from northwest India to Spain, lucky and skilled traders could become extremely wealthy. So did rulers and their financiers. This rising inequality did not sit well with Arabs who felt left behind, despite prestigious ancestry or Islamic piety. At the same time, many Iranians considered their new rulers unfit to govern a great and ancient land such as theirs. So uprisings threatened the caliphates. Securing religious legitimacy, therefore, was all the more important for caliphs. So was maintaining control over the trade routes that brought the timber, metals, and slaves to the Islamic heartlands. When the Abbasid caliphate lost its grip on those routes after the 870s (when Egypt acquired autonomy), it became a shadow of its earlier self.

POWER MOVING EAST, 200–800

In general terms, we can see an eastward drift in the center of gravity of the entire region—indeed, in all of Eurasia—with the fall of the western Roman Empire and the rise of Islam. Linkages, networks, prosperity, and centers of power in the far west weakened. The networks, merchants, and rulers in Byzantium (until the 640s) grew stronger, and those in Egypt, Iraq, and the Muslim lands generally also strengthened, especially after 660. The great isthmus of land connecting the seaborne networks of the Indian Ocean world and those of the Mediterranean once again became the leading center of wealth and power in western Eurasia—as it had been, on smaller scales, in the time of the Achaemenids, Assyrians, and pharaohs. Broad trends contributed to this, such as the rise of Indian Ocean commerce discussed in a later chapter. That was an economic tide that raised all boats, as was the expansion of caravan commerce in desert and steppe lands.

The breakdown of authority, security, and social complexity in the western Roman Empire also played a big part in this re-centering. The re-direction of the grain surpluses of Egypt, North Africa, and Syria confirmed it. From 212 BCE, when Roman forces added Sicily to their republic, the flow of overseas grain had sustained Rome, its cities, and its armies. Its acquisition of North Africa with the defeat of Carthage, and then of Egypt, allowed enormous expansion of urban life and military power, enough to sustain an empire. With the loss of North Africa (430), and then of Syria and Egypt (640s), Rome and its successor state in the east, Byzantium, could not

Gold Coin of Mercia Reflecting the shift of trade and power away from Rome toward the Arab world, this gold coin, minted by an English kingdom in the eighth century, was designed in the style of Arab coins in order to ease commercial exchange.

so easily support elaborate urban life or big armies. Those regions, instead, pumped grain into the cities and armies of the Umayyad and Abbasid caliphates. Only a few regions in the western part of the Old World web could produce vast surpluses of food, and by 710 the caliphs controlled them all.

That breakdown of authority and complexity was part of a remarkable fraying of the western edge of the Old World web. The general trend throughout history has been for webs to grow and tighten. But exceptions exist, and one of the larger ones was the experience of post-Roman Europe and Vandal North Africa. In those regions, at least at most times after 450, the linkages to the wider world withered, and life became more local, simpler, poorer, and less hierarchical—until after 800.

SOCIAL CHANGE ACROSS THE WEB

Big social changes followed on the spread of Christianity and the rise of Islam. Both were moralizing, ethical religions in contrast to the paganism of the Greeks and Romans. The pagan gods rewarded humans not for ethical behavior but for making sacrifices to them. Christianity and Islam, in contrast, preached moral codes of conduct required of believers and recommended for all humankind. These codes emphasized charity to the poor, kindness to one's neighbor, and peace (in most circumstances), as well as keeping faith with one's God. Penalties for greed, lying, and civil violence ranged from fines to eternal damnation.

On balance, both religions probably improved the lot of women and children—with plenty of exceptions—given what had preceded them. In pagan Rome, women had been legally the property of husbands and fathers, although that condition softened in the early second century. In Zoroastrian Iran, women could legally be killed for refusing to marry. Zoroastrianism explicitly associated women with evil, sin, and temptation, and it encouraged social policies that constrained the damage they might do. Sexuality outside the context of procreation invited penalties in Zoroastrian society, especially for women. Christian and Muslim women had more hope of carving out safe or independent spheres for themselves than did women in pagan Rome or Zoroastrian Iran.

Christianity and Islam offered women new opportunities. Both included women in sacred roles, notably Mary

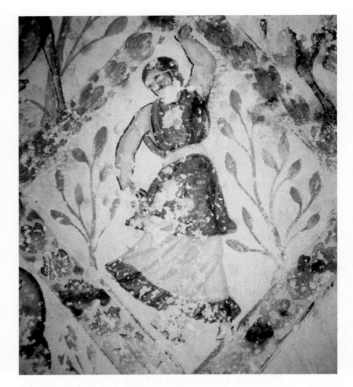

Women and the New Religions A woman dances in a fresco illustration from the ceiling of the baths in an Umayyad castle, Qasr Amra, dated to the early eighth century. Christianity and Islam both provided space for women to take on a variety of social roles and achieve a level of relative safety and security.

in Christianity and the Prophet's daughter, Fatimah, in Islam (especially important to Shi'a Muslims). Both insisted that marriage should be consensual, although reality often departed from this ideal. Their sacred texts included rules about the proper treatment of women and wives.

The Qur'an made it clear that husbands must support their wives, and in polygamous marriages—a long tradition in Arabia—treat all wives equally. It further specified that wives should obey their husband and that females should inherit a share of their parents' property, although only half as much as their brothers. The societal expectation remained that all girls should marry, and ideally before age 18. Such provisions were probably improvements for women in Arabia, Iran, Syria, and much of the rest of the region to which Islam spread.

As for Christianity, in Rome and the Byzantine Empire, girls were also expected to marry as teenagers. Wives in Byzantine lands could inherit and own property, although sometimes there were restrictions on landed property. Theodora, once in power, tried to eliminate prostitution in Constantinople and devoted state funds to help prostitutes find husbands. A few Christian women managed to become wealthy in their own right—such as a certain Scholastica, who paid to build the public baths of the city of Ephesus in the late fourth century. By the fifth century, Christianity was making room for women who preferred female society, or sought refuge from the wider world, with the institution of convents. In the early church women had been active preachers, and many became saints for their pious or courageous conduct. Eventually the church denied all but nuns any formal religious role.

So for most women, the advent of Christianity and Islam improved their position and allowed them a little more room for maneuver in their lives. The new religions probably also improved the lot of children slightly. Both religions condemned infanticide, and Muhammad made special provisions for orphans.

None of this would likely have cheered the hundreds of thousands (perhaps millions) of women and children shipped as slaves from Africa and what is now Ukraine and Russia. The Islamic heartlands of Arabia, Egypt, Syria, Iraq, and Iran imported far more women than men in slavery, perhaps 2:1 in ratio. Most of these women were held in domestic slavery, which typically required housework, textile work, child care, and concubinage.

Christian Byzantium acquired far fewer slaves in all, mainly Slavs from the Balkans, again mostly women. For these women, the codes and norms of Christianity and Islam probably offered cold comfort. Males were not thrilled to become agricultural or military slaves either.

The success of the monotheistic religions also changed entertainments and education. Constantine banned gladiatorial combats, mock battles, and athletics, where the problem was nudity. Neither he nor later Christian emperors dared to ban chariot racing, though. The Hippodrome was the most important meeting place in Byzantine Constantinople, a place of entertainment and politics. Emperors opened the season's racing in person, just as U.S. presidents today sometimes throw out the first ball of the baseball season. Theater of the sort admired by ancient Greeks and Romans declined, but a tradition of bawdy performances (where Theodora got her start) took its place, to the dismay of the pious. Islamic societies often tried to ban alcohol, prostitution, and gambling, occasionally with success, but often without. Abbasid Baghdad apparently failed utterly in this regard.

Classical education of the sort pioneered in Athens in the fifth century BCE, with its emphasis on restless inquiry, vanished gradually after 400 CE. Learning became increasingly allied with religion, whether Christianity or Islam. In Byzantium, scholars studied the Greek of the New Testament rather than the Greek of pagans such as Homer or Herodotus. The main purpose of literacy was now to acquaint one with scripture and prevailing truths, rather than to debate with Socrates or Cicero. A Byzantine theologian of the early eighth century, promoting his own book, boasted that it had nothing new in it.

In the caliphates, education also centered on religion. Formal education featured memorization of the Qur'an and mastery of a growing body of commentaries. In taking over Iran, Iraq, and Byzantine Syria, Muslims inherited proud traditions of philosophy, mathematics, medicine, and other fields of knowledge. Reconciling them with Islamic scripture required generations of intellectual effort. Learned men enjoyed high status in Muslim societies, so many families wanted their sons to wrestle with these texts. Girls had less incentive and opportunity to do so.

The new emphasis on sacred learning meant that many ancient pagan texts were lost for good. Those that survived often lingered, little-read, in monasteries, convents, or the libraries of Islamic schools called madrassas. In later centuries, Byzantine and Islamic scholars would take a renewed interest in ancient wisdom.

All these social changes were gradual. They affected those closest to state and religious authority first, and peasants in mountain villages least of all. But in time, they affected everyone. Belief, culture, social norms, and law traveled, if slowly and irregularly, along the threads of the Old World web, leaving almost no one in Western Eurasia or North Africa untouched by 800 CE.

CONCLUSION

The clashes of politics, the inspiration of prophets, and the catastrophes of plague and climate change reorganized the western edge of the Old World web between 200 and 800.

Rome's empire first shrank and then vanished west of the Adriatic Sea, but it survived in the east as the Byzantine Empire, with its capital at Constantinople. The city of Rome and urban life more broadly in Europe dwindled. The Sassanian Empire vanished altogether, replaced by Islamic caliphates based in Damascus and then Baghdad. Both Christianity and Islam spread rapidly, at the expense of paganism, Zoroastrianism, and other religions. The center of the entire western end of the Old World web shifted east, to Constantinople, Damascus, and

Baghdad. These became the new seats of power, wealth, and learning.

Ordinary farmers, shepherds, smiths, and weavers scarcely recognized these broad and gradual trends. They knew what was going on in their village and its neighborhood, but usually little else. Few could have named the emperor or caliph in whose name taxes were collected. Fewer still could have explained the schisms within Christianity or Islam. Nonetheless, over the generations, these big shifts altered the lives of almost everyone.

CHAPTER REVIEW

KEY TERMS

Umayyad caliphate (p. 299)

Sassanid dynasty (p. 301)

Germanic tribes (p. 305)

Constantine (p. 305)

Byzantine Empire (p. 308)

Justinian (p. 308)

Zoroastrianism (p. 310)

Manichaeism (p. 310)

schism (p. 312)

monasticism (p. 312)

Augustine (p. 314)

Islam (p. 315)

Muhammad (p. 315)

Arabs (p. 315)

shari'a (p. 316)

Abbasid caliphate (p. 320)

Go to INQUIZITIVE to see what you've learned—and learn what you've missed—with personalized feedback along the way.

REVIEW QUESTIONS

1. What were the twin disasters that affected the Roman and Persian Empires during the third to the eighth centuries?

2. What two military threats did the Sassanids face?

3. Explain the causes and effects of the fundamental weakness of the Roman Empire in both the third and the fifth centuries.

4. How did the movements of the Huns upset the geopolitical balance in western Eurasia?

5. In what ways did the power, population, prosperity, and territory of the Byzantine Empire change between 500 and 800?

6. What were the main features of Manichaean theology?

7. Why and in what ways did the status of Christianity in the Roman Empire change between the third and fourth centuries?

8. What was Muhammad's chief political achievement, and how did he differ from Jesus and the Buddha in terms of political power?

9. What military advantages did Arab armies have over the Sassanids and the Byzantines?

10. How did the Umayyad caliphs' sources of legitimacy shift between 650 and 680?

11. In what ways were the Abbasids and Byzantines in opposition to one another, and how were they part of a greater unit?

12. What factors drove the eastward shift of power and trade into Southwest Asia between 200 and 800?

13. How did the spread of Christianity and Islam affect women, forms of entertainment, and education?

FURTHER READING

G. W. BOWERSOCK, *The Crucible of Islam* (2017). A brief but thoroughly scholarly account of the context, in Arabia and beyond, in which Islam first appeared.

Touraj DARYAEE, *Sasanian Persia: The Rise and Fall of an Empire* (2009). The best work in English on the subject.

Beate DIGNAS and Engelbert WINTER, *Rome and Persia in Late Antiquity* (2007). A work that makes a compelling case for the importance of seeing these two empires together.

Fred DONNER, *Muhammad and the Believers at the Origins of Islam* (2010). An accessible account of Arabia and Islam up to about 700 CE.

Judith HERRIN, *Byzantium: The Surprising Life of a Medieval Empire* (2007). A readable overview, with in-depth looks at select subjects, including Greek fire.

Robert HOYLAND, *In God's Path: The Arab Conquests and the Creation of an Islamic Empire* (2015). A compact treatment of the first century of Islam, with good maps.

Matthew INNES, *Introduction to Early Medieval Western Europe, 300–900: The Sword, the Plough, and the Book* (2007). Useful depth on many subjects.

Robert Louis WILKEN, *The First Thousand Years: A Global History of Christianity* (2012). A brilliant overview with an appreciation of the role of Islam in the evolution of Christianity.

CHRONOLOGY

ca. 100–600
Funan emerges in Vietnam

220
End of Han dynasty in China

ca. 370–380
Elite Koreans begin to
study Confucian classics

ca. 500–700
Buddhism arrives in Japan

581–618
Sui dynasty in China

ca. 618–842
Tibetan Empire

618–907
Tang dynasty in China

ca. 670–1300
Srivijaya flourishes

Shinto first appears in written documents

676–892
Silla dynasty flourishes
in Korea

ca. 700–800

ca. 700–902
Nanzhao flourishes

730
Smallpox
first appears
in Japan

755–763
An Lushan rebellion in China

794–1185
Heian Japan

918–1392
Koryo kingdom

926–1125
Liao dynasty
in north China

ca. 800–900
Migrants from
Tibet form a
state in Burma

ca. 802–1431
Khmer Empire
in Southeast
Asia

The East End of the Old World Web

CHINA AND ITS NEIGHBORS

200 to 1400

960–1279
Song dynasty in China

1279–1368
Yuan dynasty in China

ca. 1250
Little Ice Age begins

1198
Largest Koryo
slave revolt

1209–1279
Mongol conquests
in Eurasia

ca. 990
Paper money appears in China

I n the fourteenth century, a Chinese author, Wang Li, commented on what he saw as a new development in the history of Eurasia:

> …the land within the Four Seas had become the territory of one family, civilization had spread everywhere and no more barriers existed. For people in search of fame and wealth in north and south, a journey of a thousand *li* [about 300 miles, or 500 km] was like a trip next door, while a journey of ten thousand *li* constituted just a neighborly jaunt. Hence, among people of the Western Regions [meaning Central Asia and Iran, mainly] who served at court, or who studied in our south-land, many forgot the region of their birth and took delight in living among our rivers and lakes. As they settled down in China for a long time, some became advanced in years, their families grew, and being far from home, they had no desire to be buried in their fatherland. Brotherhood among peoples has certainly reached a new plane.

China as World Power In a seventh-century wall mural from a Tang dynasty tomb, representatives of the cosmopolitan Tang court receive foreign visitors: an emissary from Korea in an elaborate robe and headdress stands to the right, alongside a brown-robed European traveler.

FOCUS QUESTIONS

1. Why was China so prosperous and stable during the Tang period?

2. How did developments in China under the Song affect the rest of East Asia?

3. How did the Mongols become the most powerful political force in East Asia?

What Wang Li noticed was the effect of political conquests that united broad regions of Eurasia. People moved long distances more freely owing to this political unification. Merchants could travel safely across Central Asia from China to Iran along the routes of the Silk Roads. In earlier times, such voyages had been more perilous because of bandits and local rulers who would help themselves to a share of any merchant's goods.

Paradoxically, the brutal conquests of much of Eurasia by the Mongols in the thirteenth century created these peaceful and prosperous conditions—one of the major themes of this chapter. By 1300, the Old World web was humming with activity as never before. This growth in the Old World web was grafted onto the rapid intensification of web connections in East Asia that occurred especially when China was both strong and most open to foreign trade. Those moments came especially under the early Tang dynasty and the Song dynasty. The ups and downs of China's wealth and power, and how they influenced developments throughout East Asia, constitute the other main theme of this chapter.

In the course of the period from 200 to 1400 CE, all of East Asia became increasingly connected, although in fits and starts with several rollbacks. Military expansions, cultural exchanges, and diplomatic contacts all helped push this process of integration along. The rollbacks came when China grew weaker or its leaders chose to restrict foreign contact. More than anything else, it was trade that linked the regions of East Asia.

EAST ASIA, 200–907

Merchant networks and webs of exchange develop only when and where people see opportunities that justify the risks of trade and travel. Political frameworks always matter in these calculations. Where large states keep the peace, risks are smaller and trade likelier to grow. Where they keep the peace and actively encourage commerce, which is what Wang Li observed, trade networks almost always grow. So we begin with political frameworks.

There are three related themes to note about East Asian politics in this period: China always carried the most weight in East Asian affairs; China stayed politically unified more consistently than any other country in world history; and the rhythms of unification and disunity in China tended to be mirrored in neighboring lands.

As we saw in Chapter 7, by 200 CE China dominated East Asia demographically and exerted considerable sway politically, economically, and culturally with its neighbors. That trend continued after 200, sometimes strengthening, sometimes weakening, depending mainly on the degree to which China stayed unified. The historical unity of China is so remarkable, as well as so important for the broader region of East Asia, that it deserves a closer look.

CYCLES OF UNITY AND DISUNITY

During the roughly 2,200 years since the formation of the Qin and Han dynasties until today, a large contiguous China, ruled by an emperor (or lately by the Chinese Communist Party), has existed about 70 to 75 percent of the time. China has been fragmented into multiple states about 25 to 30 percent of the time. No other country in world history, except for some small island states, shows anything like China's record of unity. It exceeds that of Egypt, the closest comparable case. In the first 2,200 years after Egypt's initial unification (ca. 2600–400 BCE), pharaohs ruled the entire country, or close to it, about 65 percent of the time. The durability and resilience of unity in Chinese political history are very peculiar by the standards of world history—even if today everyone takes it for granted. It is all the more remarkable given that China normally accounted for a quarter to a third of humankind, as shown in the table on this page.

The irregular rhythms of China's periods of unity and disunity helped to shape a larger East Asian pattern that prevailed between 200 and 1400. From the end of the Han dynasty in 220 CE until the seventh century, disunity was the rule both in China and throughout East Asia. There followed an era of centralized states, anchored by China's Tang dynasty (618–907). As the Tang weakened, the pendulum shifted back toward disunity, although more briefly this time. By the mid-tenth century, unity returned again until the mid-twelfth century. Then steppe nomad confederacies conquered most of East Asia piecemeal. That brought another era of fragmentation until one nomad confederacy, under the Mongols, conquered so widely as to open another period of centralized power in China from the 1280s to the 1350s and 1360s. Broadly speaking, then, periods of consolidation and fragmentation of state power came and went in East Asia, and tended to follow similar rhythms throughout the region.

What accounts for this cyclical pattern? Climate change might have had something to do with it. The centuries from 900 to 1200 were, on average, times of better rains, fewer droughts, and more reliable rice harvests—conditions that favored stable rule. More irregular climate prevailed in the thirteenth century in East Asia, with some sharp droughts, cold spells, and unreliable harvests—conditions conducive to conflict, rebellion, and the breakdown of states. Climate change, however, at most explains only part of the story.

The demographic and economic weight of China powerfully shaped the incentives for unity and disunity in its neighborhood. When China was united, the odds improved that kingdoms elsewhere in the region would grow and centralize. If neighboring peoples wished to resist China's power, they needed to band together. Alternatively, if one faction in a neighboring country could gain the support of China, its chances of crushing its rivals improved. As we shall see, the Silla dynasty came to dominate Korea because it enjoyed the support of the Tang, and a modest amount of China's support could make a huge difference in a small country such as Korea.

ESTIMATED POPULATIONS (IN MILLIONS) OF CHINA AND THE WORLD

200–1400 CE

YEAR CE	CHINA	WORLD	CHINA'S PROPORTION
200	55	230	24%
400	50	200	25%
600	46	200	23%
800	53	220	24%
1000	90	275	33%
1100	125	300	42%
1200	115	400	29%
1300	85	360	24%
1400	60	350	17%

Source: Robert Marks, *China: An Environmental History* (2012), 170; Joel Cohen, *How Many People Can the Earth Support?* (1995), appendix 2, 400–401.

Conversely, when China was disunited, the countries in its orbit tended to be disunited too. The defensive logic of sticking together to resist Chinese power did not apply. And China, when fragmented itself, could not easily vault one or another faction in Korea or Tibet or anywhere else into a dominant position. Thus the numerous rises and falls of states and dynasties in East Asian history between 200 and 1400, while confusing on the surface, conform to a general pattern.

CHINA, 220–618

As we saw in Chapter 7, the Han dynasty teetered for decades and collapsed in 220 CE. A 360-year period of disunity and warfare followed, opening the door to two important shifts. The first was the establishment of Buddhism as a major cultural and religious feature in China. The second was the rise of the south, meaning the Yangzi River valley and points south.

BUDDHISM The collapse of the Han and the warfare that followed shook many people's faith in the value of Confucian precepts, such as the obligation of the best-educated men to serve the state. With small rival kingdoms fighting continually, bureaucrats and officials sought to withdraw from the turbulence of political life in favor of peaceful contemplation. Daoism, which had developed within China several centuries earlier (see

Early Buddhism A leaded bronze Buddhist monk, dated to the late sixth century, depicts the simple robes worn by devotees of the newly popular religion.

Chapter 7), endorsed this choice with its emphases on meditation and quests for health and longevity. Meanwhile, beginning in the last decades of Han rule, monks from northern India crossed the Himalaya mountains bringing Buddhism to China via Central Asia. In the following centuries, Buddhism blended into the Daoist tradition in China. Both emphasized the virtues of contemplation and self-discipline. Like Daoism, Buddhism urged people to withdraw from the clamor of politics and worldly struggle in favor of the inner life. Unlike Daoism, it put high value on monasticism and celibacy—alien concepts in China, where individuals were expected to identify powerfully with their families. But many women who chafed under the Confucian expectation of submission to fathers, brothers, and husbands found Buddhism appealing. Its doctrines placed less emphasis on the authority of males over females than did Confucian tradition. Political chaos and chronic warfare in China, not to mention a brutal famine of the late 530s, invited people to reconsider their outlooks, and in this setting both Daoism and Buddhism prospered.

Buddhism already took many forms by the time it was carried to China, but it was the Mahayana school that traveled best. One reason for that was the translations by a Mahayana Buddhist monk named Kumarajiva, who was captured by Chinese forces and in 401 CE removed to a court in Chang'an, where he rendered the Buddhist sutras into elegant, philosophical Chinese texts. Although its followers initially centered around the eastern ends of the Silk Roads, Buddhism also attracted converts in southern China. It is possible that it spread by sea routes as well as overland. In China, the Zen tradition developed from the fifth century onward, one in which mastery of texts took a back seat to person-to-person teachings that emphasized meditation, self-control, and contemplation of the deeper nature of things. As we shall see, Buddhism in China continued to prosper with the advent of the Tang dynasty after 618.

SILK AND THE SOUTH The breakdown of central control in China after the Han collapse also led to the rise of the south. Without a unified state to oversee the production and transfers of food, people often migrated to lands where food was easier to grow and restrictions on trade were fewer. Millions moved from north China to the Yangzi River valley and farther south. The rich soils of Sichuan, on the middle Yangzi, rewarded farmers more generously than did the dusty plains of north China. Sichuan became a rice-basket, yielding vast quantities of marketable grain. Soon, Sichuan and even Tibet were linked, via the Yangzi, to seaborne trade for the first time. The river became an artery of commerce. The lower Yangzi and adjacent regions on the coast of the East China Sea became one of the world's foremost centers of wealth and population.

The warmer climate of the Yangzi valley, and of regions farther south, suited silkworms as well as people. As we've seen, the Han dynasty had promoted silk trade to India, southwestern Asia, and the Mediterranean along trans-Asian Silk Roads. Silk exports thrived when production shifted southward to warmer climes, where the white mulberry grew well and people could raise more silkworms.

These fussy creatures, a kind of caterpillar, strongly prefer to dine on the leaves of white mulberry trees. Domesticated **silkworms** have been raised in China for 5,000 years. As they progress from larva to pupa, they secrete through their salivary glands a fine silk thread, up to a mile long, with which they build cocoons. Patient people can unspool the thread from cocoons and weave it into a lustrous and sheer cloth—silk. Silk making remained an East Asian secret for many centuries. The techniques spread to Japan in the fourth century CE and to Southwest Asia in the sixth century, but the Chinese still made more and better silk than anyone else.

Extremely laborious and requiring nimble fingers, silk making was the work of women and girls. The rise of the silk industry allowed thousands of females to produce for the market. When political unity returned to China under the Sui dynasty (581–618), the country was richer than in the time of the Han; more integrated into long-distance circuits of trade; and less centered, in demographic and economic terms, on the north—thanks in part to the nature of silkworms and the labor of Chinese women.

RE-UNIFICATION UNDER THE SUI DYNASTY, 581-618 The Sui dynasty, like the Qin, was short-lived but left a lasting legacy. The Sui's founder was a general from a northern regional kingdom. He overthrew the royal family, and—taking no chances—proceeded to murder 59 males of the royal lineage. In the 580s, he conquered the rest of China's many kingdoms and by 589 declared himself emperor, taking the reign-name of Sui Wendi. He launched reforms of coinage and land tenure that boosted the economy, already energized by the booming silk market. Before his death, he started work on a new canal that would link the southern rice-producing regions with the northern frontier, where the bulk the Sui army stood guard against steppe raiders.

His son, Emperor Yang—or Yangdi—had a grandiose streak to match that of Alexander the Great, Qin Shi Huang, or any pharaoh. He launched a disastrous invasion of Korea. To supply his army, he ordered the extension of his father's canal starting in 605. Up to 5 million men and women worked as conscripts on this massive project, which opened in 609. The canal eventually stretched nearly 1,200 miles (2,000 km), linking fertile regions south of the Yangzi to the Huang He basin in the north.

The **Grand Canal**, as it is now called, stands among the world's most important public works projects ever built. It enabled the emperor—and his successors for 1,300 years—to move troops around the empire cheaply and quickly, countering rebellions. Rice from the lower Yangzi and the rich basin of Sichuan could be shipped reliably to northern frontier garrisons. China could now support bigger armies on its northern border, by far its most vulnerable.

The Grand Canal had a unifying effect in China. It was, in essence, a Nile made by human hands, binding north and south together politically. Economically, it provided merchants with a safe route for north-south trade, avoiding the open sea with its risks from storms and pirates. Easier rice transport on the Grand Canal also enabled China to support bigger cities and reduced the severity of famines. Less helpfully, the canal obliged the Chinese state to keep it dredged and in good working order ever after, because without it the northern cities and frontier armies would starve.

Yangdi also improved China's northern defenses by investing in walls. Earlier dynasties, particularly the Qin, had built walls along the northern frontiers to check the raids and invasions of **steppe nomads**. The walls stood in disrepair when the Sui came to power, but the prosperity brought by their economic reforms enabled them to extend the barriers and link segments together into what is now called the Great Wall of China. The Great Wall was a long-term project, begun long before the Sui and

The Sui Dynasty, 581–618 CE The Sui dynasty lasted less than four decades, but it left China with two crucial legacies that affected its fortunes ever after. Both were infrastructure projects. The Grand Canal linked the Yangzi and Huang He (Yellow River) basins, allowing reliable and cheap transport between the two great centers of the Chinese economy. The walls along the northern frontier, which together ultimately became known as the Great Wall, helped protect China from its most fearsome enemies, steppe horsemen.

continued long after, but they were among the dynasties that tried hardest to keep nomads at bay by building walls.

Hundreds of thousands died while toiling on Yangdi's public works projects, and he over-strained the treasury. His legendary excess irritated his generals to the point where they engineered his murder in a royal bath. Few lamented his death and the end of the dynasty. But Yangdi left China with the Grand Canal.

THE TANG DYNASTY, 618–750

The general who orchestrated the splashy assassination of Yangdi proclaimed a new dynasty in 618: the Tang. It took ten years to crush rebellions and consolidate power. Soon after, the Tang emperors set to work building the most powerful state in the world, one that later Chinese would regard as an ideal.

EARLY TANG GOVERNANCE AND REFORMS The early Tang inherited an economically robust China. These were times of reliable monsoon rains and rich harvests. The Grand Canal boosted trade and improved imperial finances. The Tang built upon this inheritance. They firmed up their borders and conquered small states and tribes in Central Asia, putting all Silk Road routes as far as Afghanistan under their power by 650. Thereafter, they kept wars to a minimum.

The Tang emperors reformed the machinery of the state. Their measures included reasserting the "rule of avoidance" whereby officials could not serve in their home districts, which reduced corruption and favoritism. They organized a state postal service for official communications, with roughly 20,000 miles (30,000 km) of post roads and canal routes. They enacted a detailed legal code in 653 that served as the basis for Chinese law until the twentieth century. It applied to all the emperor's subjects, rich and poor, male and female, ethnic Han and ethnic minority alike. Punishments for infractions, however, varied depending on the social status of the transgressor—a principle of law that was routine in the deep past and is found, for example, in Hammurabi's laws. The code solidified Confucian principles: fathers might strike children or servants with little to fear, but if children struck fathers—or teachers—they courted trouble.

THE EXAMINATION SYSTEM Another important and long-lasting measure was the Tang's use of **civil service examinations** as a means of selecting government officials. Earlier dynasties had pioneered this practice. The Tang extended it and created academies to teach Confucian principles. They published authorized editions of preferred Confucian texts to make sure their administrators were steeped in the right ideology. Reliance on examinations ensured that the Tang bureaucracy included legions of very clever men. Under this system, talented and bookish youths from the provinces with no family connections might occasionally win government appointments, rise through the ranks, and exercise great power. The Tang thereby encouraged the development of a social and political elite that esteemed learning and refinement above raw courage, swordsmanship, and other military virtues—a sharp contrast to the ruling elites most everywhere else in Eurasia. Like the Grand Canal, the examination system also helped preserve Chinese unity, because officials who mastered Confucian ideology typically embraced it, including its emphasis on loyalty and subservience to the emperor. No other states in the world—except those under Tang sway—would recruit administrators through written examination for another thousand years.

WU ZETIAN, THE MOST POWERFUL WOMAN IN THE WORLD The Tang was unique among Chinese dynasties in another respect: one emperor was a woman. To most Chinese, both men and women, the notion that a woman might rule a state seemed unnatural—like "hens crowing," as they often put it. Women account for about 1.5 percent of all rulers recorded in world history, and less than that in China.

Only one woman has ever ruled China in her own name. Born in 624, **Wu Zetian** (also known as Wu Zhao) came from a prosperous and well-connected family. Her parents encouraged her to educate herself, a rarity for girls of the time. Family connections enabled her to become part of the royal household at age 13, perhaps as a concubine of the emperor Taizong (r. 626–649). Life in the imperial harem provided a political education for those keen to learn. Wu Zetian was more than keen and absorbed the evident lessons in political intrigue. She became concubine and then wife of the next emperor (Gaozong, r. 650–683), and by 655 as his health faded she came to exercise more and more power. She proved highly capable,

Wu Zetian The face of this colossal statue of the Buddha carved into a rock face in present-day Henan, China, was allegedly modeled after that of the empress Wu Zetian, the great patron of Buddhism in the empire.

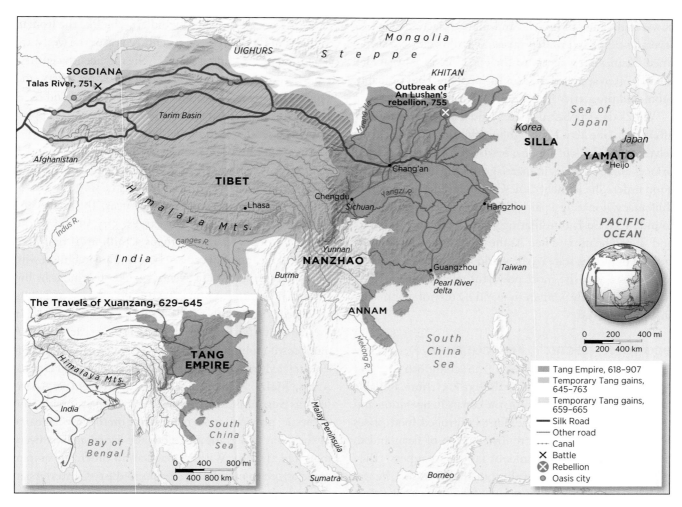

The Tang Dynasty, 618–907 CE Regarded as one of China's most effective dynasties, especially in its first century, the Tang strengthened Chinese influence in all neighboring kingdoms and in Central Asia. Traffic along the Silk Roads reached one of its peaks during Tang rule. The monk Xuanzang traveled these routes extensively, seeking out Buddhist wisdom in India to bring back to China.

drawing deftly on literature and history in her rulings, as was expected of an emperor. When Gaozong died in 683, she became regent for her son and then ruled in her own right from 690, proclaiming a short-lived dynasty called the Zhou. She was overthrown shortly before her death in 705. Her career was controversial, to put it mildly.

Confucian historians, aghast at the idea of a female in authority, credited her with poisoning some of her children for political purposes. They claimed she was a bewitching beauty who slept and murdered her way to the top and kept at it when in power. How much of this is true is open to question. She was surely a masterful manipulator and politician within the court. Her rivals regularly turned up dead or exiled. Her underlings operated a reign of terror, torturing anyone who might pose a challenge to her.

Wu Zetian was also the greatest patron of Buddhism in Chinese history. She supported Buddhist monasteries, commissioned Buddhist art, and encouraged the import of Buddhist texts from India. In her later years, she tried to require vegetarianism within her empire. Buddhists rewarded her efforts. They found it easier to accept a female ruler than did conscientious Confucians. Dutiful Buddhist scholars conveniently justified Wu Zetian's rule and extolled her virtues. Craven ones creatively edited sacred texts to serve her propaganda needs. The alliance between ruler and religion, important since the first states in Sumer and commonplace ever since, was fully in evidence in Wu Zetian's reign.

Wu Zetian also encouraged commerce. A merchant's daughter and an opponent of the Confucian educated elite, she felt none of their disdain for business. She had new canals dug, and docks and marketplaces erected in several cities. She lowered taxes. She allowed rich, unrefined businessmen access to the corridors of power. Her policies often appalled the Confucian literati but probably promoted prosperity in the empire.

Wu Zetian's political talents paid dividends in foreign affairs too. She kept her neighbors fighting among themselves. She doled out money, bestowed titles, and offered princes and princesses in marriage to keep her alliances in good order. She launched the Chinese tradition of panda diplomacy, donating a pair of bears to a ruler in Japan. She found ingeniously humiliating ways to execute diplomats and allies who crossed her. As the ruler of the most powerful and populous state in the world for a quarter-century, Wu Zetian was the most powerful person on Earth in her day—the only woman in world history of whom that statement is true.

ECONOMY, SOCIETY, AND CULTURE Despite sordid intrigues at court, the years from about 630 to about 750 proved a prosperous and stable era for China. Reliable monsoons continued, keeping the canals in operation and the harvests bountiful. The Tang controlled food prices and oversaw the periodic re-distribution of farmland to families, reducing the ranks of landless paupers. They regulated agriculture carefully, but trade less so. The rise of the south continued: a census of 742 showed that half the population of the empire lived south of the Yangzi, whereas in 618 only a quarter did. Tea, grown in the south, became a national drink. It probably improved health in the empire: boiling tea water killed many unhealthful bacteria. Although smallpox had arrived in China (from Southwest Asia, perhaps via India) by 500 CE or so, no spectacular epidemics reversed population growth, as happened repeatedly, for example, in the Mediterranean world after the 540s. With good harvests and few epidemics, it was easier for the Tang to claim the Mandate of Heaven. (As we saw in Chapter 7, since the Zhou dynasty, rulers showed they enjoyed the Mandate of Heaven by governing well, and were shown to have lost it by disorder, natural disasters, and poverty in their realm.)

During the Tang era, Chinese families continued the settlement of the rich basin of Sichuan. Han Chinese also settled the Pearl River delta, in the far south adjacent to the South China Sea. This region provided new crops such as sugar and cotton, both introduced from India. The settlement and colonization of Sichuan and the far south

were for Tang China a huge windfall, a bit like the Roman conquest of Egypt in the first century BCE or the westward expansion of the United States in the nineteenth century: a destination for people in search of better prospects, and a source of new resources and wealth for society and state. The expansion came at the expense of indigenous peoples, who had to move onto poorer lands.

The frontier settlement to the south and the expanded commerce everywhere in China during the seventh through the eighth centuries supported a surge of urbanization and a buildup of the armed forces. The main Tang capital, Chang'an, easily the largest city in the world, attained a population of perhaps 2 million. It had been the Qin, Han, and Sui capital, but the Tang rebuilt it with a grid pattern and wide avenues—like Teotihuacán but far larger. Dozens of other sizeable cities, such as Hangzhou near the mouth of the Yangzi and Guangzhou in the far south, sprang up along riverine trade routes. A more cosmopolitan urban culture developed. Market cities attracted traders from near and far, including Persians, Arabs, Malays, Japanese, Koreans, and Central Asians such as Sogdians and Uighurs. Trade, both foreign and domestic, provided more tax revenue on top of what came in the form of a grain and cloth tax levied against every male age 21 to 59. With its finances in order, the empire could afford to maintain garrisons in dusty Central Asian towns and all along the northern frontiers. Those garrisons, in turn, kept the peace and made life safe for traders. The economy and the military, in effect, supported one another.

The Tang promotion of Buddhism also helped stimulate trade. Buddhist monasteries were commercial centers: they lent money at interest, operated flour mills, owned farmland, ran inns, conducted auctions, accepted donations, and sold what we would now call tourist trinkets, especially religious icons. Until the ninth century, monasteries enjoyed special tax breaks, strengthening their commercial position. Some of the goods that China imported along the Silk Roads—gems, incense—were used in Buddhist worship rituals. Tang control of the oasis towns around the Tarim Basin, now in western China, helped foster trade with Central Asia and beyond. The city of Chang'an became the eastern terminus of the emerging camel caravan networks that made up the Silk Roads.

Tang prosperity underwrote high culture. Emperors encouraged additional translations of Buddhist texts from Sanskrit and celebrated a well-traveled monk, Xuanzang,

Printed Books The earliest known printed book, a Buddhist text called the Diamond Sutra, was printed in 868 CE. It included texts and illustrations printed with wooden blocks.

who in 645 returned to China after fifteen years spent gathering Buddhist books and wisdom in India. Xuanzang was one of several seekers who journeyed across the forbidding Himalaya, demonstrating Chinese interest in India—that mysterious land (as Chinese saw it) of spiritual truths, magic, and medicine. The Tang, after Wu Zetian died, also established new Confucian academies and institutes of poetry.

Under the influence of Buddhism, Tang poetry and painting turned to scenes of nature, especially remote mountainous landscapes. Every literate person aspired to write poetry, even members of the imperial family. Tang poetry acquired great prestige at the time, and educated Chinese ever since have memorized its outstanding passages. Du Fu, for example, an eighth-century poet who twice failed the civil service exam, is regarded as the greatest poet-sage of the Chinese language, his lines savored for their poignancy on themes such as friendship and political turmoil. His contemporary, Li Bai, acquired an equally towering reputation as a romantic poet, reflecting on nature, loneliness, and the appeal of wine. The earliest printing, done by hand-carving into woodblocks, originated in China in the seventh and eighth centuries, and made texts more readily available and reading more popular. Tang woodblock printers specialized in poetry, agricultural and medical texts, and Buddhist scriptures.

Tang high culture was famously cosmopolitan. Foreign influences, especially from India, came in the saddlebags of sojourners on the Silk Roads. Many Tang emperors showed interest in India's longevity potions, and a few are thought to have died from overdoses of Indian elixirs.

One Indian envoy in the seventh century brought sugar-cane and sugar-making technology to China. The sport of polo and a new lute from Persia became popular. Camels became a new artistic motif. Foreign merchants brought new religions—Islam, Judaism, Zoroastrianism, and the form of Christianity known as Nestorianism—all of which the Tang tolerated. Foreign students from Korea and Japan flocked to Tang China.

The sphere of women expanded under the Tang, as under the Sui before them—at least, for the upper classes. Since the fall of the Han, elite women had taken larger roles in public life, and under the Sui and the early Tang this reached its height. Some women of the imperial family engaged fully in politics and exercised real power. Others, in arranged marriages to steppe chieftains or Tibetan kings, served as de facto diplomats for the Tang dynasty. Tang artwork shows elite women enjoying archery, playing polo, dancing, and doing things never depicted, and rarely done, by Chinese women under earlier dynasties. This liberty was mainly a result of the Tang rulers' descent from peoples of northwest China, among whom women typically enjoyed wider latitude.

Under the Sui and early Tang, families from prestigious lineages welcomed the birth of daughters. As brides, they could bring large gifts (brideprice) from rich families eager to boost their social standing. As one aristocrat, Yan Zhitui (d. 591) complained, "In the present age, when marriages are arranged, some people sell their daughters for the betrothal gift or buy a wife by making a payment

Tang Sportswoman The Tang noblewoman in this statuette, dated to the eighth century, once held a polo mallet. Polo was one of the many high-culture pursuits that Tang elites enjoyed.

of silk. They compare ancestry [of the two families], calculate down to the smallest sum, demand much and offer little, exactly like bargaining in a market place." Their "market" value gave young women from prestigious families some negotiating power with their parents and brothers.

However, the practice of brideprice vanished in the late Tang, and elite families once again came to prefer sons over daughters. Property and family name were transmitted through sons; women could not easily own property. Less distinguished families—of whom we know very little—normally shared the preference for sons, although in silk-producing areas hard-working daughters could bring their families useful income and enjoyed more esteem as a result.

Peasant women during the Tang worked at home much as their foremothers had done, but on average spent more time feeding mulberry leaves to silkworms, fashioning silk thread, and weaving silk cloth. Although the Tang taxed only men, a large share of tax obligations took the form of cloth, which women and girls produced. The Tang era saw an expansion not only in the market for women's work, but also for young women—as concubines whom prosperous men bought and sold. Poor families sometimes found it necessary to sell daughters to make ends meet.

EAST ASIA AT THE HEIGHT OF THE TANG, 618–750

In foreign affairs, the Tang dominated their neighborhood. By and large, the Tang managed to prevent the rise of large nomad confederacies by playing one group off against another and bribing chieftains judiciously—much as Romans, Byzantines, and Sassanids did in western Eurasia. Small sums for the Tang would buy, or at least rent, a lot of allegiance from nomads. In this way, the Tang extended their power far into the oases of Central Asia. Sometimes they controlled these directly, although more often through local rulers whom they bribed or intimidated as necessary. They even marched an army into north India in 649, sacking the Buddha's birthplace and bringing back 2,000 slaves. Satisfactory relations with their northern and western neighbors helped boost Silk Road trade, filling state coffers and providing a steady stream of horses for Tang armies. China itself lacked enough good grassland to raise horses cheaply.

TIBET AND YUNNAN In the southwest, flourishing exports—in metals and animal products, for example—contributed to the rise of a **Tibetan Empire** (ca. 618–842) centered on the high, chilly plateau just north of the Himalaya. A dynasty, sometimes called Yarlung for the valley in which Tibet's capital of Lhasa is located, exerted influence from northern India to Mongolia. (See map on page 335.) Tibet's new rulers embraced Buddhism and worked to share it with their subjects, a substantial minority of whom were Christians. The Tibetans competed with the Tang and other powers in Central Asia in a geopolitical great game—with remarkable success, given the paltry population and resources of their homeland. When rebellion weakened China, Tibetan forces even occupied the Tang capital of Chang'an for two weeks in 763. Their success in war and diplomacy diminished after 830, and soon internal divisions brought an end to imperial Tibet. Never again would Tibet compete as a regional power in Asia.

A smaller kingdom, called Nanzhao, emerged in the eighth and ninth centuries in what is now China's southwestern Yunnan province. Its leadership also followed Buddhist traditions, especially Tantric Buddhism, a novel variant emphasizing faster routes to nirvana (the release from all suffering promised to those who follow the proper way) through mastery of special rituals. Brought by Indian monks, in Nanzhao it became a state religion. Nanzhao often resisted Tang China, occasionally in alliance with Tibet. At one point, Nanzhao took control of much of the rich basin of Sichuan, including its capital of Chengdu, and extended its sway southward to Burma. It dissolved in 902, just as the Tang dynasty was collapsing.

KOREA, JAPAN, VIETNAM China's neighbors to the east and south flourished partly through Tang influences. In Korea, Japan, and Vietnam, states usually recognized the Tang as overlords, although their subservience to China varied and sometimes was merely a polite fiction. (See map on page 335.)

In Korea, the Tang helped to install the Silla dynasty in 676. With Tang help, Silla conquests ended a long era of fractious politics among rival Korean kings. In cultural terms, however, China virtually conquered Korea. Elite Koreans had studied Confucian classics since the 370s. Buddhism came to Korea at about the same time, mainly via Chinese monks, and in the northern part of

ESTIMATED POPULATIONS (IN MILLIONS) OF EAST AND SOUTHEAST ASIA					
200–1400 CE					
YEAR CE	JAPAN	KOREA	MAINLAND SOUTHEAST ASIA[1]	ISLAND SOUTHEAST ASIA[2]	CHINA
200	0.7	0.3	2.5	2.0	55
600	3.0	1.0	3.5	3.0	46
1000	5.0	2.5	5.0	4.0	90
1400	12.0	3.0	9.0	7.5	60

Source: Colin McEvedy and Richard Jones, *Atlas of World Population History* (1978), 166–81, 190–203.

1. Modern Burma, Thailand, Laos, Cambodia, Vietnam
2. Modern Indonesia, Philippines

the peninsula (a kingdom called Kogurgo) it became the state religion. A few Korean monks went to India to study at the birthplace of Buddhism. While Buddhism appealed strongly to elites, the masses of Korean society still found shamanism—the oldest Eurasian form of spirit worship—satisfactory. Chinese script, fashion, art, and music attracted elites in Korea too, and for a brief while in the eighth century the Silla kingdom even adopted the examination system of the Tang to select officials. Many Korean men went to China to study, and some learned Chinese and Confucian ideology so well that they passed the examinations in China and served in the Tang administration. Many more wrote Chinese poetry, or Korean-language poems in Chinese characters. Korean women were especially prized as slaves and concubines in elite Tang households.

Even as Korea absorbed more and more Chinese influences under the Silla, it retained political independence. The Tang were satisfied with the Silla rulers, who regularly had to declare their loyalty to the Tang. But the Silla elite, a formidable military class, helped preserve Korean autonomy. For them, the greatest honor was to have a son die in battle—a very different outlook from that of the Chinese literati, who raised their sons to be scholars.

Tang China also influenced Japan. Our evidence for Japanese history before 500 CE is spotty. Tiny states existed in rice-growing regions, but in much of the archipelago people continued hunting and foraging in preference to farming. Rice, iron, and horses all had been introduced from the mainland, via Korea, before 500. As elsewhere, these innovations favored state building. By the early 600s,

one state in the southeast—the **Yamato region**—began to assert control over most of the populous rice-growing areas. Buddhism arrived in the sixth to seventh centuries, providing the Yamato rulers with an additional source of prestige as they mastered its rituals and knowledge. As in China, Buddhism's success provoked a nativist reaction among people who thought it threatened cherished traditions. The Yamato imported Tang city planning—they modeled their capital on Chang'an's grid pattern—temple architecture, writing, and, to some extent, laws. Yamato law codes, however, were more generous to women than the Tang's had become. Japanese women could own land, for example.

Japanese political culture retained some distinctive features. Despite an aristocratic ethos built around warfare, some of the Yamato rulers were women. Japan never adopted the Chinese notion of the Mandate of Heaven—the Yamato clan could never lose the right to rule, no matter how many earthquakes or epidemics hit Japan. No examination system was ever used, and men of learning never rivaled military men in prestige. Chronic warfare plagued Japan even after the rise of the Yamato state, keeping a premium on military skills. After crushing potential rivals within Japan, the Yamato tried to invade Korea in the early 660s. That effort failed—it was the last overseas attack Japan would launch for more than 900 years.

Vietnam felt the power of Tang China more than did Korea or Japan. Recall that the Han dynasty had conquered northern Vietnam (called Annam) but could

Southeast Asian Trade A carving of a ship on the wall of the Buddhist Borobudur Temple in Java, dated around 825 CE, suggests the importance of maritime trade in Southeast Asian waters.

not hold it. The Tang re-conquered Annam, and thereafter Vietnam increasingly adopted Confucian ideals, Daoism, Chinese script, and Chinese versions of Buddhism. Nonetheless, Chinese settlers never overwhelmed Vietnam—as they did what is now south China. The trickle of Chinese immigrants was absorbed and over time became Vietnamese, and the language and identity of Vietnam survived.

THE MEKONG DELTA AND SRIVIJAYA The other lands of Southeast Asia remained essentially outside the sphere of Tang power. Small states grew up where river valleys allowed rice farming. They quickly formed their own seaborne trading webs, especially among Vietnam, the Malay Peninsula, and Java. In the Mekong delta of southern Vietnam, a state called (in Chinese texts) Funan arose around 100 to 600 CE, more influenced by India and Brahmin traditions than by China. Archeologists have found Roman coins and ceramics from Persia there, showing the reach of its seaborne connections. The script used for Sanskrit, the north Indian language of the Vedas, was used to write several Southeast Asian tongues by 500 CE. Until the fourteenth century, Indian culture, carried across the Bay of Bengal by traders and missionaries, made a stronger impression in Southeast Asia than did Chinese culture, except in the northern half of Vietnam.

The most durable of these Southeast Asian states was the Buddhist kingdom of **Srivijaya**, centered on the island of Sumatra. It emerged in the 670s and lasted until the thirteenth century. Its territory waxed and waned through the centuries, sometimes extending to the Malay Peninsula and the island of Java. Its fortunes rose and fell with tax receipts from trade with China and India, and especially from shipping passing through the straits between Sumatra and Malaya. The Straits of Malacca, like the straits of the Bosporus and Dardanelles where the Mediterranean and Black Seas meet, was one of the premier choke points on the map of world trade for the last 2,000 years. Control of the Straits ensured streams of revenue. Srivijaya's rulers also controlled gold exports from inland Sumatra and at times tin exports from Malaya, some of which they traded to India. For centuries, its Buddhist shrines, such as Borobudur in Java, the world's largest Buddhist temple, attracted pilgrims from as far away as India.

The Tang created something of a sinosphere in East

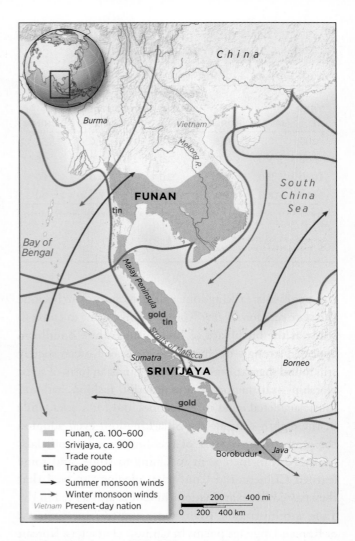

Southeast Asia, ca. 200–900 CE In the early centuries CE, Southeast Asians exploited the potential of irrigated rice production and revenues from maritime trade to build new and larger states, the greatest of which was Srivijaya. Monsoon winds allowed comparatively easy sailing to India and China, each of which exerted strong cultural influence in parts of Southeast Asia.

Asia. Politically, economically, and culturally they dominated the entire region, despite frequent military defeats at the hands of Koreans, steppe raiders, Nanzhao, and Tibetans. Their script, poetry, architecture, dress, food, and religions carried prestige that rulers everywhere admired. The Tang did more than any other factor to make East Asia into a political, cultural, and economic web—or more precisely, the eastern end of the Eurasian web.

The root of Tang influence lay in relative size and strength: the Tang ruled 45 to 60 million people and had revenues to match, while other polities of the region were far smaller.

The Tang ruled parts of the sinosphere directly, and other parts they influenced through puppets and intermediaries. Some of the lands that they ruled directly, such as Annam, did not in the long run become part of China. Yunnan, the seat of Nanzhao, however, is today a southwestern province of China. But in all these lands, the cultural influence of Tang China was profound and enduring, carried by merchants, students, monks, soldiers, officials, and settlers. Chinese took up residence in many port towns of East and Southeast Asia. To this day, the Chinese word for overseas Chinatowns is *Tangrenjie*, or "streets where the Tang people live."

THE DECLINE OF THE TANG, 750–907

Although the Tang dynasty lasted until 907, it teetered for most of its last 150 years. The biggest shock came in the 750s with the An Lushan rebellion, a civil war from which the Tang never recovered.

One of Wu Zetian's reforms had been to station army garrisons permanently on the northern frontier to check steppe nomad incursions. This backfired on later emperors when a general named An Lushan, himself probably of Central Asian origin, rose in revolt in 755. He had enjoyed great success keeping northern "barbarians" in line; but when he sensed court politics shifting against him, he decided, like Julius Caesar in the last days of the Roman Republic, to overthrow the state rather than lose his position. He led several hundred thousand soldiers on a rampage across north China, taking the Tang capital and forcing the emperor to flee. Emperor Xuanzong escaped toward Sichuan with his favorite consort, Yang Guifei, one of the fabled beauties of China; but on the road his imperial guard refused to protect him unless he strangled her, which he did. Their unhappy love remains one of China's favorite stories. After writing a few sad poems, Emperor Xuanzong died in 763.

An Lushan could not keep his forces united. With the rebels divided, the Tang dynasty survived, if just barely, by inviting Central Asian forces, mostly Turkic and Tibetan warriors, to help them—a strategy not so different from the one Rome had employed 400 years previously. This cost them their leading position in Central Asia, already weakened in 751 when a Tang army was crushed by Arab,

Persian, and Turkic forces at the battle of the Talas River. For the next thousand years after the An Lushan uprising ended in 763, neither the Tang nor later Chinese dynasties controlled any of Central Asia.

The Tang dynasty never recovered from the An Lushan uprising. They lost a quarter of their territory and a large proportion, some say up to half, of their population. They abandoned their cosmopolitan outlook. Now they tried to undermine Buddhism as a foreign import and sought to restore what they saw as a more Chinese, more traditional, more Confucian culture that would—they hoped—restore a golden age. In the years 841 to 845 this nativist outlook, as well as ordinary greed, inspired the Tang rulers to assault Buddhist institutions, destroying 4,600 monasteries, dismissing 250,000 monks and nuns, and seizing the enormous wealth amassed by monks over the centuries—including 150,000 slaves.

Although the later Tang won some military successes, their political prestige and practical power dwindled. Without their Central Asian garrisons, the Tang lost much of their lucrative Silk Road trade. They ceased their periodic redistribution of farmland in China. They abandoned supervision of urban markets, allowing market culture to thrive but disappointing traditional Confucians who regarded unbridled pursuit of wealth through commerce as unseemly. They relied for their revenues on a new salt tax, which after the An Lushan rebellion provided more than half of the revenue. By abandoning supervision of the economy in favor of unregulated markets, the Tang inadvertently fostered an increase in wealthy merchants and landlords—as well as countless landless peasants who would provide manpower for future rebellions.

After about 820, the emperors frequently lost their hold on the palace to bands of eunuchs. These were usually men of humble origin, often sold to the court as boys by desperate parents. Once castrated, they worked as low-ranking servants to the many thousands of women in the emperor's harem. During the late Tang, about 5,000 eunuchs lived and worked in the palace. Clever and ambitious ones sometimes became bureaucrats and advisers. They used their privileged access to the imperial family to build their own networks of power, extending to influence over the palace guard. One eunuch grew so rich he could donate a billion copper coins to a monastery. At times, eunuchs ran the state through puppet emperors, executing ministers who opposed them.

Eunuchs A large group of eunuchs appear in a mural of palace life painted on the wall of the tomb of a Tang prince in 706 CE.

The eunuchs often governed better than emperors, and Tang China enjoyed a modest revival of fortunes in the mid-ninth century.

After 860, however, rebellions flared up more frequently. Rebel leaders found willing foot soldiers in the masses who had been impoverished by the Tang's liberation of the economy. Popular resentment against wealthy merchants, especially foreign ones, led to massacres. On one occasion in the 870s, according to an Arab author, an army of rebels opposed to the Tang slaughtered over 120,000 foreigners—Arabs, Persians, Jews—in Guangzhou. The rebels, led by a revenge-seeker who had failed the civil service examination, went on to take the capital, Chang'an. When someone posted a mocking poem about them, they rounded up 3,000 people deemed capable of writing clever poetry and killed them all. By 907, the shell of the Tang state shattered and China splintered.

Chinese intellectuals tended to regard times when China was unified and powerful, as during the early Tang, as a golden age. Periods of disunity and weakness at the center seemed to them the unfortunate results of bad governance. For ordinary people, however, if civil wars and bandit gangs stayed away, a weak state with limited power to tax families and conscript young men could seem a liberation. As with the collapse of urban states in the tenth-century Maya world, in tenth-century China

the breakdown of the state seemed a crisis to those who depended on it but may have been a boon to those whose taxes and labor supported it. China's population grew faster after the rebellion of An Lushan, despite the frequent political chaos, than it had during the glory years of the Tang, suggesting improved conditions for the masses.

EAST ASIA IN THE TIME OF THE NOMADS, CA. 900–1400

With brief exceptions, the Tang had kept their northern borders under control before 750. But as their strength waned, the relative power of the nomadic tribes of Manchuria and Mongolia grew. From time to time, charismatic leaders arose among these nomads and built confederations that could exploit China's vulnerability. In the centuries following the Tang, one pastoralist group after another conquered northern China, established a dynasty, and found enough collaborators among the Chinese literati to help them rule. Southern China usually eluded their grasp and remained independent, but typically had to pay large sums to the nomads to stay that way.

As the Tang weakened, China and East Asia fragmented politically: the Chinese call this era the period of Five Dynasties and Ten Kingdoms. Fragmentation was contagious. The Tibetans' empire had already fallen apart by 842. The Silla kingdom in Korea did so by 892, and Nanzhao in Yunnan followed suit in 902. Vietnam again won its independence from China.

As warlords, kings, and would-be emperors battled it out, new powers arose to the north. One of these, a band of nomads from Manchuria known as the Khitan, outmaneuvered rivals and built a state in north China in the early tenth century. The Khitan were true nomads. They lived in tents and on horseback, and they chose their leaders every three years—until an especially ambitious one canceled further elections. When he died in 926, his lieutenants suggested his wife ought to pay her respects by joining him in the grave, as hundreds of his warriors were obliged to do. She declined, citing a mother's obligations to small children, but offered to cut off her arm and place it in her husband's coffin as a sign of wifely respect. Negotiations continued, and in the end she sliced off only one hand. She then ruled the Khitans herself with an iron fist, led the conquest of Chinese territory around Beijing,

CONSIDERING THE EVIDENCE

Tang Poetry

When the An Lushan rebellion reached the Tang capital of Chang'an in 755, Du Fu was forced from his hard-won position as an official. He returned a few years later, first as a prisoner of the rebels and then as a minor official in the restored dynasty. But he left again when he was demoted to work as a provincial Commissioner of Education. His travels during and after the rebellion inspired an unusually wide range of subjects for his poetry, which is often amusingly personal. In one poem, he described his drunken fall from a horse; in another, he complained about endless paperwork. Like other Tang officials who took poetry seriously, Du Fu wrote verses critical of the hardships that the government imposed on commoners. He wrote the following poem about forced labor recruitment in 759, about halfway through the An Lushan crisis.

The Recruiting Officers at the Village of the Stone Moat

I sought a lodging for the night, at sunset, in the Stone
   Moat Village.
Recruiting Officers, who seize people by night, were
   there.
A venerable old man climbed over the wall and fled.
An old woman came out of the door and peered.
What rage in the shouts of the Recruiting Officers!
What bitterness in the weeping of the old woman!
I heard the words of the woman as she pled her cause
   before them:
"My three sons are with the frontier guard at Yeh Ch'eng.
From one son I have received a letter.
A little while ago, two sons died in battle.
He who remains has stolen a temporary lease of life.
The dead are finished forever.
In the house, there is still no grown man,
Only my grandson at the breast.
The mother of my grandson has not gone,
Going out, coming in, she has not a single whole skirt.
I am an old woman, old woman, and my strength is failing,

But I beg to go with the Recruiting Officers when they
   return this night.
I will eagerly agree to act as a servant at Ho Yang;
I am still able to prepare the early morning meal."
The sound of words ceased in the long night,
It was as though I heard the darkness choke with tears.
At daybreak, I went on my way,
Only the venerable old man was left.

Source: Shihao li, 石壕吏, The Recruiting Officers at the Village of the Stone Moat. Poem by Du Fu, 杜甫, trans. Amy Lowell and Florence Ayscough, in *Fir-Flower Tablets: Poems* (Boston: 1921).

QUESTIONS FOR ANALYSIS

1. How did the official activities of the Chinese state impact commoners during the Tang dynasty?
2. Which parts of the poem suggest that Du Fu drew on a personal experience when he wrote it?
3. What do the old woman's words and actions reveal about relationships among generations and between men and women at this time?

and under the reign name Shulü (also known as Chunqin) oversaw the formation of the Liao dynasty, which dominated northeast China for two centuries (926–1125).

THE SONG COME TO POWER

Another military force from the north formed around a general whose innovative battle tactics enabled him to conquer all rivals, unify much of China, and proclaim the Song dynasty (traditionally 960–1279), taking as his reign name Song Taizu.

From their capital at Kaifeng, near the Huang He in the north China plain, the Song ruled a much smaller empire than had the Tang or Han. They could not dominate their frontiers and frequently fought a new power in Vietnam, the Ly dynasty, which arose soon after 1000. In the northwest, another state, called Xi Xia, comprising only 3 million people (called Tanguts) posed further problems. But the most formidable neighbor was the Liao, with their seemingly endless supply of horses and horsemen. When not fighting the Liao, the Song were usually paying them protection money in silk and silver—if the Song didn't want to fight, they had to pay. They often paid off the Tanguts too. In the 1120s, another pastoralist

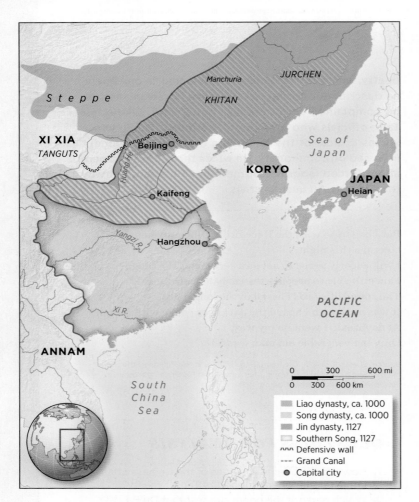

The Liao and Song Dynasties, 926–1279 CE After 900, a series of peoples from the north established ruling dynasties in northern China, a pattern that would continue for many centuries to come. The most important dynasty, however, the Song, was established by a Chinese general who re-unified China after the fragmentation that followed the Tang collapse. After 1127, the Song ruled only the southern half of the country, but its record stands out in Chinese history for the development of commerce, the arts, and science.

economically and demographically, they oversaw tremendous expansions despite the compromises this required in Confucian principles. They let businessmen profit, however distasteful that felt, in order to maximize their tax revenue and pay for their military. They deftly combined state ownership and high taxation in some sectors of the economy with unregulated markets in others. To oversee their nuanced policies, the Song needed a reliable and skilled bureaucracy, which drove them to promote Confucian ideology.

The Song relied heavily on examinations to fill the ranks of officialdom. Some 100,000 men took the civil service exam in 1150, and in 1250 about 400,000 did—maybe 0.1 to 0.3 percent of the total population. Aspirants had to study for a minimum of 300 days, and most chose to prepare far longer. The average age of an exam taker was about 30. After reforms to combat grade inflation in 1009, the pass rate varied from around 1 to 3 percent. In the entire population, about 1 in 10,000 held the qualification needed to work in the bureaucracy. Only the top-graded exam takers could enter the civil service—most of the rest became teachers. The Song's reliance on examinations resulted in a more talented cadre of administrators than existed under the Tang, who at times had accepted aristocratic birth as a qualification.

The Song's social policy was inconsistently Confucian. A revival of orthodoxy constrained women's roles, but not dramatically. Manuals of proper behavior for girls and women emphasized deference to males and to their elders. Girls were expected to learn to cook, clean, care for children, make silk, embroider, and sew. Upon marriage, they moved in with their husband's family and took orders from

group called the Jurchen, whose homeland was Manchuria, overran the north, eliminated the Liao, built an even bigger state, and confined the Song to the region south of the Yangzi. The Southern Song, as they are called, had to pay the Jurchen even more to leave them in peace.

REFORMS This embattled situation gave the Song rulers every incentive to maintain an efficient state, economy, and war machine. Internally, the rulers insisted on civilian rule to prevent regional generals, like the dynasty's own founder, from seizing power. Compared to the early Tang, the Song were politically and militarily weak. But

Song Society The artistically inclined Song emperor Huizong is said to have created this painting of ladies treating newly woven silk—one of the main forms of work that Song society envisioned for women—in the early twelfth century.

Foot Binding The practice of female foot binding became widespread during the Song dynasty. The shoes shown here are 3.5 inches (9 cm) long, and from the nineteenth century.

ping small girls' feet so that, as they grew, the bones broke, leaving women to hobble through life. Printed evidence of foot binding begins to appear in texts in the 1140s, and objections to it a hundred years later. Tiny, stunted feet became regarded as dainty and erotic, especially in the upper classes. A hobbled wife who couldn't work in the fields or roam away from home became a status symbol for a husband. Paradoxically, mothers often imposed this practice (usually overseen by grandmothers or elderly women who worked as foot-binding specialists) on their daughters in hopes of improving their marriage prospects. It also became a mark of Chinese identity, something that foreign barbarians did not do but cultured Chinese did. Foot binding lasted into the twentieth century in China, and between 900 and 1900 hundreds of millions of Chinese girls underwent the ordeal.

The Confucian revival during the Song contained a mixed legacy for Chinese women. They could own property, and older women exercised some authority within families. In wealthy families, girls were often encouraged to study history and literature, as well as manuals of good comportment. Some found it possible to take on a more public role through writing—most enduringly perhaps Li Qingzhao (ca. 1080–1150), a poet and scholar whose verses remain admired today for their emotional intensity. She got her start writing poetry as a teenager, grew fond of books and ancient artifacts, but lost her collections when the Jurchen overran her home. She and her husband fled to the south, where he soon died, and she lived out her days modestly, writing taut verses often on the theme of loss.

ECONOMY The Song needed a robust economy. Military costs ate up about three-fourths of their budget. Theirs was the first state in East Asia to create a standing

their in-laws. Widows found it nearly impossible to remarry.

The distinctively Chinese custom of foot binding became widespread during the Song. It first arose among elite women during the late Tang, around 900. This painful practice involved tightly wrapping

navy, always an expensive undertaking, which they deployed chiefly on rivers and canals against the Liao and other northern foes. For their army, which reached 1.25 million men at times, they spent fortunes on armor and arrowheads.

To meet their military requirements, the Song built the world's first military-industrial complex. After 1020, they developed iron-mining, mainly in government-owned mines. The mines yielded 10,000 to 20,000 tons of iron per year, mainly for weapons. This was more iron than the entire world produced as late as 1700. To smelt it (to extract metal from surrounding rock), they first used charcoal; but because the mines were mainly in the north where trees were scant, the Song soon turned to coal—the first major use of fossil fuels in world history. In the 1070s, when iron production peaked, they also mined more than 13,000 tons of copper—more than the whole world mined as late as 1800. Gold and silver mining increased too. Taken as a whole, the Song mining and metallurgy complex was of an entirely different order of magnitude than anything achieved anywhere before in world history. As we shall see, it did not last.

Agriculture almost kept pace with mining and metallurgy. Under the Song, a new variety of rice called champa entered China from Vietnam. **Champa rice** had spread in Southeast Asia in the eighth through the tenth centuries, helping to sustain the trading state of Srivijaya. In the early eleventh century, a Song emperor fostered its spread, first into southern China and then the Yangzi basin. Champa rice matured quickly, allowing two or even three harvests per year. It also resisted drought well and could ripen at higher and cooler elevations. It soon became the standard crop in most of China's rice-growing regions. Champa rice is probably the first instance in world history of a government promoting an improved crop variety.

Combined with an extension of irrigation systems under the Song, champa rice proved an enormous windfall that translated into rapid population growth. The capital, Kaifeng, swelled to 1.4 million people by 1100. Hangzhou held 2 million. Before the Jurchen conquests of the 1120s, the Song realm held perhaps 125 million people, China's largest population to this point.

Foreign trade matched the booms in mining and agriculture. By 1130, half of state revenues came from taxes on trade—a much higher proportion than under the Tang. The Song deliberately fostered markets and commerce, despite the irritation of Confucian traditionalists who resented uncouth, upstart tycoons. With overland trade to western and South Asia difficult because of hostile powers on China's western and northern frontiers, the Song turned to the sea. One emperor, Gaozong (r. 1127–1162), explained Song trade policy: "The profit of maritime trade contributes much to the national income. Therefore, pursuing the former custom [perhaps referring to the early Tang] the people of faraway countries should be encouraged to come and sell an abundant supply of foreign goods."

Foreigners did come. Languages such as Arabic, Persian, Tamil, and Malay were again heard in the streets of south China's cities. A dramatic expansion of trade to the Indian Ocean world took place after 1200 or so. China exported porcelain, an invention of the Tang era that the Song mass-produced, and, as usual, silk. China imported pearls, elephants, ivory, and precious metals. Shipbuilding boomed, and ship technology improved. Chinese shipwrights invented bulkheads—watertight compartments of a ship's hull that allowed it to sustain damage without the vessel sinking. Chinese ships also started using a rudimentary compass no later than 1117. Overseas trade networks, which had prospered under the early Tang but withered after the 750s, recovered in Song times. The Song lacked the tendrils of trade and power reaching into Central Asia that had distinguished the Tang, but after 1200 China's seaborne links to Southeast Asian and Indian Ocean coastlands strengthened.

The Song also allowed new forms of business and new forms of money. Merchant groups found ways to spread their risk in far-flung operations, combining assets, selling shares, and insuring voyages. Primitive banks popped up, issuing promises of payment called flying money. Paper money appeared about 990, first made from the bark of mulberry trees. This was another revolutionary development. The Song economy grew so fast that they could not mint enough iron, copper, silver, and gold coins to grease the wheels of commerce. Besides, they needed all the iron and copper they could get for military production. The solution was paper money. Because of high demand for the books that prepared men for the exams, the Chinese already had good woodblock printing technology that could mass-produce images on paper. With paper money, merchants no longer had to carry heavy strings of iron coins on long voyages. Song currency notes were as large as a shoebox top, but still a major step forward in convenience. They included helpful notices to the effect that counterfeiters would be beheaded. For two centuries, paper money helped nourish the Song economic boom and the creation of a true market society. This market revolution confirmed China's place as the center of East Asia's economic webs, and indeed Eurasia's. Paper money was not used in Japan until the 1330s and in Europe until the 1660s.

The needs and incentives of a market society helped to generate several technological advances of economic importance. In addition to the compass and paper money, Song China witnessed the development of printing with moveable type, astronomical clocks, and, for doing calculations quickly, the abacus. Shipping improved with the bulkhead and the sternpost rudder, which enabled captains to steer their vessels more easily. Silk manufacture now featured looms with 1,800 moving parts. Of less economic importance, but ultimately of great consequence for world history, Chinese of the Song also invented gunpowder weapons. For the millions of tax-paying peasant families on whom Song power and prosperity largely depended, none of these innovations mattered as much as champa rice. More reliable food supply, not paper money or clocks, was the biggest change the Song brought to the masses.

Despite these successes in business, the economy, and technology, the Song proved militarily inferior to the Jurchen. The Jurchen were hunters, farmers, and horse breeders in Manchuria who had been vassals of the Liao. Early in the 1100s, they asserted their independence by making a deal with the Song to attack the Liao. That worked well, but the Jurchen then turned on their ally and overran much of north China. The Song retreated south of the Yangzi and made Hangzhou their new capital. The Jurchen, now called the Jin dynasty, ruled from Kaifeng, dividing China uneasily with the Southern Song. The Jin dynasty lasted in north China until it was demolished by a Mongol confederation in 1234.

Song Economy Advanced woodblock-printing technology enabled the Song to produce the world's first paper money. This banknote, dated to the eleventh century, would have been about a foot (30 cm) long and 8 inches (20 cm) wide.

THE SONG'S NEIGHBORHOOD, CA. 960–1240

From the early eleventh century on, the rise of market society and of steppe nomad power in the form of the Khitans and Jurchen affected almost all of East Asia. Korea, perhaps, felt these developments most because it stood on the doorstep of the steppe peoples' homeland.

KOREA After the Silla kingdom fell apart in 892, Korea remained divided for a generation. But the rise of the Khitans inspired some Koreans to put aside their differences and join forces behind a single warlord. He forged a new kingdom, called **Koryo** (or Goryeo, 918–1392), from which our word *Korea* comes. The new state quickly extended its sway over the whole peninsula. It consisted of a de facto alliance of aristocratic families—called *yangban* in Korean—who spearheaded successful resistance to Khitan and Jurchen attacks. After 1170, the state weakened and the alliance frayed under the impact of revolts by soldiers, slaves, and Buddhist monks. Local warrior-aristocrats grabbed more power, and the central state held less. The Mongols (see below) began occasional attacks on Korea in 1217.

In its first century, Koryo was more isolated from the wider world than the Silla kingdom had been. Relations with the Khitans and Jurchen were often violent, although Korea did trade iron and grain to the Khitans for horses. With Song China less devoted to Buddhism than the early Tang dynasts, cultural relations between Korea and China diminished somewhat. But by the late eleventh century, when Koryo was firmly established and Song China was booming economically, commerce revived. Koreans imported horses from the steppe and Chinese goods, both for their own use and for re-export to Japan. Muslim traders from Southwest Asia came to Korea too. During the Koryo dynasty, despite the social dominance of old *yangban* families, Korea, like China, gradually grew more market oriented.

Korean society evolved in response to the changing political and economic environment. After 1100 or so, aristocratic families enhanced their influence, Korea's class structure rigidified, and slavery increased in importance. Nowhere else in East Asia was slavery as prevalent as in Korea. In late Koryo times, perhaps a third of the population were slaves. Most were farm laborers, often working on estates owned by *yangban* families. Some were in effect household servants. Several slave revolts broke out, the largest in 1198. Despite sharp class cleavages, Korea became more linguistically and ethnically uniform in Koryo times, in part through the frequent struggles against foreign invaders.

In the early years of the Koryo dynasty, Korean society allowed freedoms to women that shocked Chinese visitors. Korean women not only owned and inherited property, but they could mingle freely with men in public spaces and were not confined to households. Upon marriage, a husband usually moved in with his wife's family—the opposite of Chinese practice. Widows could remarry. Prosperous women might even take more than one husband, a rare custom in world history. However, as contacts with the Song expanded, Confucian influence seeped into Korea. After 958, Koryo used Confucian examinations to recruit bureaucrats, helping to promote Confucian ideals in high places, which narrowed the opportunities open to women.

Koryo Pottery These characteristic examples of Koryo celadon pottery, dated to around 1150, are decorated with engraved illustrations of flowers and leaves and, on the large wine jug, boys picking grapes.

Chinese influence appeared also in the most iconic product of Koryo culture, a type of glazed pottery called celadon. It first developed in China, but Korean potters refined the technique and produced a blue-green glaze that elites throughout East Asia, and collectors to this day, came to prize.

While Korean culture grew more Confucian in some respects, Korean religion remained Buddhist on the top rungs of society. Lower classes often retained their attachment to shamanist beliefs and practices, disdained by the elite as unsophisticated and akin to the religion of the Khitans, Jurchen, and other enemies.

JAPAN In Japan, no steppe nomads battered at the door. China was farther away. So the incentives to cooperate against foreign enemies were weaker, and the costs of disunity among Japanese were smaller than for Koreans. The Yamato state only slowly consolidated its rule. The capital was shifted to Heian (modern Kyoto) around 794, so historians refer to the following centuries as **Heian Japan** (794–1185). Its politics were dominated by struggles between the center (meaning the imperial court and the Fujiwara clan that served as the power behind the throne) and landowning aristocratic families in the countryside. The Fujiwara family provided all the wives to emperors; and since children were raised in their mother's families, the Fujiwara clan nurtured child emperors and influenced adult ones.

The Japanese elite had long promoted foreign religions from China such as Buddhism and Daoism. But after the power of the Tang waned, the influence of China fell accordingly, and Japanese culture became more distinctive. Japan's elites proved skillful at melding revived indigenous religious traditions, notably Shinto, with imported ones to create an ideology that undergirded their dominance. **Shinto** ("the way of the gods") was, and is, a bundle of practices and beliefs that extols ancient traditions—and supposed traditions—and emphasizes folklore, shrines, and monuments. Shinto followers diligently performed rituals honoring a multitude of gods or spirits and linking the present to the past. Gods were often associated with natural features such as rocks, streams, or trees. Shinto appeared first in written documents in the eighth century, although its practices must surely be much older. Its followers often practiced Buddhism as well, and the two religions swapped features back and forth.

The result was a tremendous religious creativity in Heian Japan, with new sects popping up all the time. Charismatic religious leaders, often women, competed for followers, often by offering easier routes to nirvana—a belief adopted in many versions of Shinto.

These evolving religious ideologies convincingly supported and justified social hierarchy. The aristocratic social order in Japan remained remarkably stable despite frequent civil wars and the slow rise of a class of swordsmen-for-hire who in later times loomed large in Japanese politics—the samurai.

Courtly life in Heian Japan featured leisure and refinement that later ages admired. A few thousand residents of the Heian court lived insulated lives of privilege, devoting themselves to poetry, parties, and pleasure. They honed the arts of bodily beautification to novel heights that included silk costumes, plucked eyebrows, and carefully blackened teeth—the epitome of elegance. Courtiers spent their nights in romantic intrigues and their days in literary idylls. Men aspired to write poetry in Chinese. Women typically wrote in Japanese, using a syllabic script called *kana*, which made their work appealing to nationalistic Japanese in modern times.

The Tale of Genji An illustration from a Heian-era edition of Murasaki Shikibu's famous novel shows Prince Genji visiting his wife, both clad in clothing characteristic of Japanese elites.

The first substantial body of literature written by women anywhere in world history comes from the Heian court. The most famous female Japanese author of any age is Murasaki Shikibu (a pseudonym—her real name is unknown), an aristocrat of the early eleventh century. She wrote the *Tale of Genji*, a story of a handsome and chivalrous prince with a varied and troubled love life. Much of it is devoted to the complicated protocols and manners of the Heian court. Today, many Japanese regard it as the high point of their national literature, much as the English see Shakespeare's plays. Several other women wrote novels or memoirs. It is mainly through such literature that we get glimpses of social life in Heian Japan, and it refers only to the courtly elites.

In one respect, Japan decisively joined the East Asian web in the eighth century. Until then, its island location had kept it safe from many epidemics. Moreover, its small and dispersed population could not sustain crowd diseases. But with denser population and urban growth, and more frequent contact with mainland Asia, Japan both received and sustained more lethal infections. Smallpox made its first appearance in 730, killing perhaps a quarter of the archipelago's population. The emperor's response was to commission a giant Buddha statue, 60 feet (18 m) tall and coated in gold. That did not suffice: wave after wave of epidemics followed. Other crowd diseases ravaged Japan as well (measles arrived in the 990s), an unhappy consequence of its closer ties with China and Korea.

This sharp change in Japan's disease environment

contributed to the religious experimentation of the Heian period. Everyone wanted supernatural protection, and none of the established practices seemed to deliver it. The new fear of epidemics may have helped motivate the exquisite culture of the court: escapism was a normal response to anxiety. A woman in the Heian court remarked on a measles outbreak of 998 that claimed "victims of all ages and classes" and left survivors feeling "depressed and uneasy." Not until about 1200 did the spate of epidemics abate, and diseases such as smallpox become endemic, childhood diseases.

SOUTHEAST ASIA, 900–1400

The surplus production of rice by farming families in river valleys supported several Southeast Asian states. Migrants from Tibet formed a state in Burma in the ninth century along the Irrawaddy River. People moving south from China to the Chao Phraya Basin created a Thai state in the eighth to the tenth centuries. Seaborne links between these states and India proved powerful: kings and courts adopted Buddhist and Hindu beliefs, rituals, and trappings and often declared themselves incarnations of the Hindu god Shiva or, if they preferred, Buddhist bodhisattvas. They hired Brahmin priests, advisers, and astrologers to help them to behave prudently and to impress their subjects and neighbors—exercising a type of soft power.

Ordinary folks, as usual, were more concerned with rain, crops, food, and social relations in their

Angkor Wat This temple in Angkor Thom, built in the twelfth century as a Hindu temple before being converted for Buddhist worship, is the largest religious complex in the world. Building it required the labor of some 70,000 stonemasons.

family and village than with kingdoms. In most Southeast Asian settings, men worked the fields. Buying and selling was often the work of women. They could own property, and some got rich enough to endow monasteries. Women could also divorce unsatisfactory husbands. Southeast Asian women before the fifteenth century lived less constrained lives than did women in those parts of East Asia more attached to Confucian ideals.

In terms of territory and probably population, the largest Southeast Asian state was the Khmer Empire of the ninth through the fifteenth centuries. At its height, it held sway in most of mainland Southeast Asia. It relied on efficient rice production, taking advantage both of the champa strain of rice and of innovative irrigation techniques. Chinese visitors reported that much of the farm work was done by forced labor and that prominent families might own as many as 100 slaves.

At first, the kings of the Khmer state were Hindu in religion. Early in the twelfth century, they employed some 70,000 stonemasons to build the sprawling temple complex of Angkor Wat, the carvings on which follow Hindu artistic motifs and styles. But by 1200 or so, Buddhism had superseded Hinduism and the temples became Buddhist places of worship (as they are today), showing a religious fluidity common in Southeast Asian history.

The capital city of the Khmer, Angkor Thom, contained a few hundred thousand people in the fourteenth century. Its surrounding irrigation network of reservoirs

Southeast Asia, ca. 900–1400 CE Southeast Asian rulers extended their power after 900, building larger states such as that of the Khmer, which flourished from the ninth through the fifteenth century. Irrigated rice production underpinned every Southeast Asian kingdom. So did the support of either Hindu or Buddhist priests.

and canals covered about 400 square miles (1,000 sq. km). The liberty accorded women in Angkor Thom offended Chinese visitors, one of whom noted with disdain that here "it is women who are concerned with commerce." Women also took part in the poetry and musical performances at the Khmer court, and in rare cases even served as Buddhist sages.

The Khmer state fell apart early in the fifteenth century for reasons that remain obscure. A recent hypothesis is that a deep drought deprived the Khmer of the water needed for irrigated rice, provoking widespread famine and political disorder. There is strong evidence from tree rings for such droughts, especially around the years 1345–1360 and 1400–1430. Whether that ended the Khmer Empire or not remains uncertain, but it could not have helped.

THE MONGOLS, CA. 1200–1368

The most powerful political force in East Asia by 1220 was not the elegant aesthetes of the Heian court or the master farmers of Angkor or even the mighty Jin or Song, but illiterate, unschooled Mongol herders. How did that happen?

Over the centuries, the Tang and Song dynasties had improved their frontier defenses, mastered the craft of fortification (including ditches that horses couldn't cross), and the subtle art of setting one group of steppe people against another. So in the centuries before the Khitans' success, by and large the Chinese enjoyed the upper hand with respect to northern "barbarians." By the tenth century, the wheel of geopolitical fortune had turned once more. The Khitans were learning a lot from the Chinese. They drove hard bargains for the horses they sold for iron weapons, helmets, and other armor. They mastered siegecraft—the techniques of laying siege to fortified cities. And they learned the subtle art of pitting one group of Chinese, some unhappy generals perhaps, against another. The Jurchen and the Mongols learned all this too.

So from the tenth century through the fourteenth, the Khitan, Jurchen, Mongols, and others enjoyed frequent success in their military struggles with China, conquering north China three times, all of China once, and making life anxious for the Song all the time. They also posed recurrent threats to Korean security.

The Mongols, who numbered about 1 million in 1200, conquered almost all of East Asia—indeed, about half of Eurasia. At first glance, their feats seem impossible, considering that over 250 million people dwelt in Eurasia then. Let's look at the Mongols more closely.

MONGOL WAYS OF LIFE

The Mongols lived as mobile pastoralists on the steppe grasslands to the north of China. They raised horses, sheep, and goats, keeping on the move in search of lush grass and good water for their herds. Warm and wet spring seasons, good for grass and grazing animals, suited them perfectly. Drought, deep snowfalls, or long spells of extreme cold threatened their animals and themselves. The Mongols took great pride in their riding skills. Women as well as men learned to ride horseback from childhood. Mongols conducted periodic hunts involving the coordinated movements of thousands of riders, honing skills they would use in warfare.

As with all mobile peoples, Mongol material culture was spare. They had to carry everything with them and be ready to break camp and move within minutes when enemies galloped over the horizon. Just about everything they needed they made from animal hide, bone, or sinew. But they also traded animals for iron and grain from Koreans and Chinese. Their religion was no more elaborate than their material culture. Although some had begun to experiment with Buddhism, most preferred shamanism, revering a sky god and lesser gods of rivers, rocks, and other landscape features. Shamans had neither temples nor sacred texts—indeed, no texts at all. The Mongolian tongue was not a written language until the thirteenth century.

Mongol politics consisted of the constant struggles among charismatic men seeking to build bigger followings. They succeeded by promising their followers protection against rivals and loot from successful raids. Mongol chieftains, if they wished to remain chieftains, needed to hand out the spoils of war—normally women and livestock—frequently. In a sense, it was an informal democratic system for males: men gave their allegiance to the leaders they chose. Women and children followed husbands and fathers. Family and clan mattered for survival. Everyone needed the protection of adult males, and among adult males the most admired were those most skilled in the military arts.

GENGHIS KHAN AND THE MONGOL CONQUESTS

Genghis Khan, or Temujin as he was called in his youth, was born into this rough society about 1165. Little is known of his early life. His father, apparently, was a minor chieftain who arranged for nine-year-old Temujin's marriage to a girl from a related clan—a political match. Before the marriage took place (Mongols married as teenagers), Temujin's father was poisoned. Since no one wished to give allegiance to a mere boy, Temujin, his mother, and his several siblings were abandoned to fend for themselves. Keeping a family alive without an adult male and without a larger kin network was an unusual feat, but his mother had what it took. Temujin and his siblings learned all there was to know about charming strangers, stealing horses, and living off roots, fruits, berries, and small game.

Temujin was a difficult child with burning ambition. He killed one of his half-brothers in a quarrel and allegedly refused to apologize to his mother. He aimed to re-capture his dead father's stature as a chief. In his teenage years, Temujin managed to acquire support among blood brothers of his father, as well as from the clan of his betrothed, whom he married when he was about 16. He acquired a reputation for luck, skill, cunning, and cruelty to his enemies—just the sort of man Mongols wanted to follow.

In his 20s, Temujin kept defeating rivals and attracting more followers. By 1206, he had brought most Mongols into his fold and led them against neighboring peoples. Recognizing the importance of clans and kin in Mongol society, and its potential to undermine loyalty to him, he re-organized his fighting forces. Men no longer rode and fought with their kinsmen, but in units of tens, hundreds, and thousands—a decimal system of military organization he borrowed from the Khitans and the Jurchen. This helped focus Mongols' allegiance on their commanders, men chosen for their loyalty to the man now known as a "supreme leader," or *khan*—Genghis Khan.

Genghis led his armies to victory after victory, first on the steppe, and then against the Tanguts—the Tibetan-speaking people of the Xia state northwest of China. By 1215, the Mongols had crushed the Jurchen and dominated north China. They then headed west to Central Asia, where by 1220 they had taken the Silk Road cities of Bukhara and Samarkand. For another five years, Genghis and his generals campaigned in Central Asia,

northern India, Iran, the Caucasus, Russia, and Ukraine. They won almost every battle and conquered every city they assaulted.

Mongolia enjoyed a favorable climate during Genghis Khan's years of conquest. From 1211 to 1225, Mongolia experienced an unprecedented run of wet and warm years, allowing grass and herds to flourish. With more animals there was more food, and with more food, more Mongols. Simultaneous surges in population growth of sheep, goats, horses, and humans helped propel Mongol expansion.

Genghis Khan Dated to the fourteenth century, a Chinese series of portraits of powerful historical rulers included this image of Genghis as he might have appeared later in life.

Genghis commanded 70,000 to 130,000 Mongol men on his campaigns of the 1210s and 1220s. They brought their families with them, which meant that if they lost a battle their wives and children would be killed or enslaved. That probably sharpened their motivation. Their mobility and military skills, especially as bowmen, brought consistent success.

So too did the Mongols' justified reputation for ruthlessness. A Persian historian of the thirteenth century wrote that in their conquest of Herat, in today's Afghanistan, the Mongols killed every person, cat, and dog, and flattened the city. As a matter of policy, Genghis and his generals committed legendary acts of cruelty, routinely ordering the slaughter of all adult males in conquered populations. Their goal was to acquire a bloodthirsty reputation that would tempt people to surrender without a fight. Those who did so often met lenient treatment if they offered up their horses, young women, skilled artisans, and treasure to the Mongols. Genetic evidence strongly suggests that the Mongols engaged in wholesale rape of captive women: today, roughly 8 percent of the population of Inner Asia, and 0.5 percent of all humans, are descended from a single male ancestor, probably someone from Mongolia who lived about 1,000 years ago.

When it came to religious politics, the Mongols employed a more tolerant approach. They felt no need to force anyone to adopt their gods. Peoples who submitted to Mongol authority were left free to worship as they pleased, provided they gave the Mongols what they wanted. In his sunset years, Genghis Khan took an interest in Daoism, especially its promised avenues to immortality. In the 1250s, one Mongol khan, Mongke, a grandson of Genghis, invited wise men of several faiths to his tents to make their cases for Buddhism, Islam, Daoism, or Christianity. In the end, he and his advisers concluded that God had given different people different religions just as he had given people hands with multiple fingers. Some khans supported Buddhism, and grateful Buddhist sages found ways to justify the Mongol khans' rule. Showing remarkable intellectual flexibility, some sages declared generous khans to be reincarnations of the Buddha.

THE MONGOL EMPIRE After Genghis died on campaign in 1227, his sons, nephews, and grandsons continued the family business. They raided and conquered from Korea and Vietnam in the east to Palestine and Poland in the west. The Mongols controlled half the world's horse population— perhaps 20 million beasts. Their success extended wherever their horses could find nutritious grass. When they reached forested landscapes in Central Europe or Russia, they lost their edge, although they could still move with astonishing speed in winter on frozen rivers. (Several brutally cold winters in the mid-thirteenth

Mongol Campaigns and Empire, 1206–1260 CE Genghis Khan, his sons, and grandsons mounted extraordinarily successful assaults on most of the richest societies in Eurasia, creating a giant, if short-lived, land empire. Its influence included flourishing trade and cultural exchanges along the Silk Roads, as Mongol authority, once established, kept the peace and discouraged brigands.

century made their campaigning a little easier in this respect.) Their campaigns amid the tropical forests of north India, Burma, and Southeast Asia were beset by unfamiliar diseases, probably malaria chief among them. By about 1260, their run of conquests in Central and West Asia was coming to an end. They had built the largest empire in world history, conquering north China, the Abbasid caliphate, and nearly everything in between. Now, however, the descendants of Genghis Khan increasingly fought among themselves.

One grandson of Genghis, Khubilai, after emerging victorious in struggles within his family, needed more loot to reward his followers. Out of appealing options in western Eurasia, he turned the Mongol war machine back east. Beginning in 1260, he oversaw the Mongol conquest of China's Southern Song state. Mongol cavalry struggled in Chinese terrain with its rivers, canals, and mountains. Song officials had come to rely upon the Yangzi River as their Great Wall, too wide for Mongol ponies to cross. But the Mongols showed great capacity to innovate militarily, developing naval skills to fight along the Yangzi and other rivers. By 1276 the last Song resistance flickered out, and three years later Khubilai Khan declared himself the Son of Heaven, emperor of all China, and founder of a new dynasty, the Yuan.

Khubilai Khan A painting on silk—made in China in the thirteenth or fourteenth century, sometime after Khubilai's death—shows the ruler hunting with members of his court.

THE MONGOLS AS CHINESE EMPERORS: THE YUAN DYNASTY, 1279–1368

Like other steppe conquerors of other agrarian empires, Khubilai faced one big problem. He had several thousand Mongols at his back, almost all illiterate, almost all expecting regular handouts of war plunder, and none prepared for the desk work necessary to administer a sprawling empire. He needed to rule perhaps 75 million Chinese subjects who regarded him and his men as barbarians. Khubilai almost solved the problem.

GOVERNING STRATEGIES Khubilai moved his center of operations south, out of Mongolia to Beijing, which he made into China's capital. He hired Chinese literati to handle the routine paperwork of governing, but he eliminated the practice of staffing top posts with men selected by written examination. He prized loyalty over literary skill, so the highest offices went to Mongols. He occasionally appointed other foreigners such as Tibetans

and Persians—men with administrative skills but without Chinese loyalties.

Khubilai did, however, wish to benefit from Confucian ideology with its emphases on duty and deference. He patronized Chinese sages and painters. He promoted Buddhism too. Having nothing in their religious tradition that demanded conformity, the Mongols in China, as elsewhere, allowed all religions free rein. In short, Khubilai did all he could to win over the Chinese elite while keeping it from the highest rungs of power. He found enough educated Chinese willing to collaborate with "barbarians" to govern effectively.

Nonetheless, the **Yuan dynasty** was short-lived. Khubilai spent fortunes on palaces and wars, including two unsuccessful invasions of Japan, three of Vietnam, and one of the distant island of Java. These failures damaged Mongol prestige and drained their resources. Khubilai managed to conquer Korea, but at great cost. Moreover, the Yuan had to spend immense sums to extend the Grand Canal north to Beijing, to ensure that the new capital got enough rice. With the Yuan in financial straits, in 1294 the world's "mightiest man," as the Venetian trader Marco Polo called him, now an obese alcoholic, having long lost the hardy self-discipline so esteemed among Mongols, died peacefully.

POWER STRUGGLES, REBELLIONS, EPIDEMICS After Khubilai's death, violent power struggles divided his family. Whereas in the Chinese tradition the imperial throne normally went to the eldest son, the Mongols expected sons, brothers, and nephews of a dead leader to fight for power. This principle was common among steppe and Central Asian peoples. It ensured that no weaklings came to power—but it carried the cost of intermittent civil war. Khubilai's successors, like all Mongol chiefs, were distinguished by their military competence and political cunning more than bureaucratic skills.

As Chinese emperors, the Mongol leaders faced continued financial struggles and frequent rebellions. They printed too much paper money too fast, inflating the currency to the point where no one would voluntarily accept it. When troops and canal laborers were paid with paper money, they often rebelled. As foreign "barbarians" in Chinese eyes, the Yuan had trouble convincing people that they enjoyed the Mandate of Heaven.

The Yuan emperors, unlike their ancestor Genghis, also suffered from bad climate luck. Not only did storms sink their two invasion fleets of Japan, but in the thirteenth century big volcanoes around the world were erupting like popcorn, spewing sulfate particles into the upper atmosphere and blocking out some of the sun's warmth. Six major eruptions took place between 1227 and 1284, and a gigantic one in either 1257 or 1258 ejected more sulfates than any other eruption in the previous 7,000 years. The climate impacts—cooler and dryer weather—were global in scope. Crops failed here and there around the world, and people starved. In China, natural disasters were political—evidence that rulers, first the late Song and then the Yuan, had lost the Mandate of Heaven.

By the 1270s, just when the Yuan were finishing their conquest of China, cold weather set in with a vengeance. It was the beginning of the Little Ice Age, a worldwide shift to cooler temperatures that lasted for 600 years (ca. 1250–1850). The 1290s were particularly frigid. The cold itself reduced harvests, and in north China cold years were usually also drought years. They also coincided with outbreaks of locust swarms, a frequent danger to crops in China. To make matters still worse, the freezing of rivers and canals paralyzed most commerce for much of the year, making it harder to transport food to famine areas. While cold and dry years became normal after the 1270s, in rare wet years monsoon rains were often extra strong, as in 1295–1297, years of torrential flooding. Often flood soaked one part of China while drought parched another.

By the 1330s, a wave of epidemics compounded the Yuan's difficulties. China had long suffered from occasional epidemics, but especially devastating ones burned through the country in 1331, 1344–1345, and 1356–1360. No one knows for sure what diseases were involved, but one (much disputed) possibility is that the bubonic plague was among them. In western Eurasia, as we shall see, a plague pandemic killed off about one-third of the population between 1346 and 1352. In China, population plummeted as well, whether from plague or other infections. Before the Mongol conquest, the total population stood around 100 to 120 million. By 1350, it had dropped to 70 million; by 1400, to perhaps as little as 60 million. Certainly, the Mongol conquest killed many, but famines and epidemics played larger roles in what was by far the worst population crash in Chinese history.

CULTURE, SOCIETY, AND ECONOMY Under these strains, Chinese culture and society changed considerably. With the elimination of the civil service exams, even brilliant literati could not look forward to careers in high office. When the exams were restored in 1315, they were given in two versions, an easy one for Mongols and a harder one for Chinese. Most Chinese literati abandoned the hope of a government career and sought other ways to make a living and demonstrate their distinction. Some turned to playwriting, leading to an outpouring of popular drama including works that remain among China's most popular, such as the irreverent love comedy *Romance of the Western Chamber* written by Wang Shifu. Others took up mathematics, medicine, or philosophy. Arabic numerals came into use under the Yuan (about the same time they took root in Europe). Persian and Arab astronomers were appointed to a state-sponsored observatory. Religious thought flourished in the absence of persecutions, and many new Buddhist texts were translated into Chinese. The Yuan dynasty was a time of troubles for China, but a time of scientific and cultural creativity as well.

The adverse climate, epidemics, and other trials may have contributed to an upturn in female infanticide and a resulting shortage of women. In most Chinese families, only males could perform religious rituals honoring the ancestors, and every family desperately wanted at least one male heir. Female children were valued less for this reason, and for economic ones as well: upon marriage, women's labor would be lost to their parents and would serve their new in-laws. In Yuan times, the imbalance between male and female in the population reached about 20 percent, implying widespread female infanticide and meaning that about a fifth of all males could not marry. For Chinese men, failure to marry and produce male heirs was a crushing disappointment. The cultural prohibition on widows remarrying (in Confucian tradition, a wife should serve only one husband) weakened because of the bride shortage.

The Chinese economy reflected the demographic and social stresses of the Yuan era but also the opportunities presented by enforced peace along the Silk Roads. The Yuan oversaw a continued commercialization of Chinese society except for seaborne trade, which they banned from time to time. They relied on tax farmers—entrepreneurs who paid the emperor for the right to collect taxes—and on forced labor for major engineering works such as the extension of the Grand Canal to Beijing. In these circumstances, economic inequality expanded. Fortunes were rapidly made and lost. The iron and coal industries of early Song times, in sharp decline after 1100, nearly disappeared. Social mobility increased, and what remained of the grand old aristocratic families of Tang times vanished altogether. Chinese society became more entrepreneurial, unstable, and unequal. The goods produced—rice, millet, wheat, silk, porcelain—remained much the same as before, but everything else was changing.

THE MONGOLS AND THE WEBS OF EAST ASIA

Mongol rule in China encouraged trade and cultural exchange all across East Asia. With their conquests, not only were China, Mongolia, Korea, Burma, and Tibet brought under the same rule, but regions farther afield—including Japan, Vietnam, Java, and the Khmer Empire of mainland Southeast Asia—were drawn into the commercial and cultural orbit of Yuan China. When the Mongols were strongest (ca. 1250–1350), the East Asian web grew both larger and tighter than ever before.

More broadly, the Mongols' conquests and promotion of trade throughout lands they controlled brought the East Asian web into more regular contact with the rest of Eurasia. The Han-Rome linkages, the first Old World web, had weakened after 200 CE, to be strengthened during the early Tang. But the Mongols took the Old World web to another level, speeding up the movement of religious ideas, crops, technologies, and disease pathogens, among other things, throughout Eurasia. They oversaw trade and travel along the Silk Roads directly, encouraging it as best

they could. Genghis Khan and his successors turned the Silk Roads into silk superhighways.

After their conquests, the Mongols intimidated almost all of Asia into peace, sometimes called the Pax Mongolica. Peace reduced risk and cost for merchants and travelers. Whereas Chinese rulers usually regarded exports as bad for the economy (after all, useful goods left the country), Mongols deliberately encouraged foreign trade. Part of the appeal of controlling China was the ease with which the Mongols could amass silk and other Chinese manufactures for trade to Central Asia and points west. In the case of porcelain, the Yuan invested in large government-sponsored factories that churned out the blue-on-white styles that today we call china. The style was originally Persian.

Yuan Porcelain This rectangular wine flask from the Yuan dynasty (1279–1368), decorated with cobalt-blue mythical creatures, was manufactured in one of many government-sponsored porcelain factories.

As Indians, Iranians, and Arabs acquired more knowledge of China and Korea, and more interest in East Asian silk and porcelain, sea links along the shores of the Indian Ocean grew as well—as we will see. The Mongols had no direct impact on the Indian Ocean trade networks, but they helped them grow tighter nonetheless by stimulating demand for goods from exotic places. In this way, the Silk Road traffic provoked Indian Ocean traffic. Together, they formed the main connecting strands of the bigger and tighter Old World web, stretching by 1280 from Japan and Java to Spain and North Africa.

These trade networks helped make some Chinese cities into metropolises. According to the Venetian merchant Marco Polo, the Chinese city of Hangzhou, not far from modern Shanghai, was the world's most magnificent city. He marveled at the countless canals and bridges, and the sprawling market squares where one might buy "game of all kinds, such as roebucks, stags, fallow deer, hares and rabbits . . . partridges, pheasants, francolins, quails, common fowls, capons, and such numbers of ducks and geese as can scarcely be expressed." He also remarked upon the prostitutes "who are here in such numbers as I dare not venture to report."

Yet Mongol power in East Asia proved fleeting. By

the 1350s, the Yuan had lost control of most of China and Korea. Various native rebellions arose and easily found recruits among young men facing dismal marriage prospects. Violent chaos prevailed until new dynasties managed to crush all rivals. These were the Ming in China (founded 1368) and the Choson in Korea (1392). We will meet them again in later chapters.

The legacy of Mongol rule in China and East Asia was strong. Their violence left a trail of ruin. Their rough manners, illiteracy, and disdain for calligraphy, poetry, and other refinements left the Chinese elite more convinced than ever that they were culturally superior to everyone else—and that elegant literary and artistic expression was the highest form of human endeavor.

Beyond that, Mongol rule brought new foreign influences into Chinese culture. It had long been Mongol practice to capture artisans in warfare and bring them back to Mongolia, so skills and styles from India and Southwest Asia—such as Persian styles in porcelain—filtered into China. So did a few new crops, such as carrots, almonds, and pistachios, and administrative techniques, such as a courier system. The Mongols also invited Muslims, Christians, and others into their realms, including Yuan China, adding to East Asia's cultural diversity. Mongol rule in China left a legacy of religious toleration and experimentation. Finally, some of their customs allowing a wider sphere for elite women lingered on, to the dismay of proper Confucians. The Ming emperors, as we shall see, found little of this legacy to their taste and tried to undo foreign influences on China.

CONCLUSION

When the Han Empire fell apart after 220 CE and China fragmented, long-distance trade and travel in East Asia temporarily diminished. But by the time of the Sui dynasty, Buddhist monks were bringing new ideas from India. Buddhist outlooks and institutions favored commerce. By the time of the Tang dynasty, connections between China and its neighbors had grown much stronger. Goods, merchants, missionaries, monks, armies, students, and microbes were on the move by land and sea. This heightened interconnectedness, combined with a unified China, favored the emergence of unified states in Korea, Tibet, Japan, and, less directly, Southeast Asia. By 750, Tang China presided over a humming East Asian web, with strong threads tied deep into Central Asia, revitalizing the Old World web.

After the horrors of the An Lushan rebellion (755), the Tang rulers turned their backs on the outside world. Their xenophobia extended to Buddhism and foreign trade. The power, prestige, and unity of the Tang dynasty faded; and as it did so, part of the logic of unity in Korea, Tibet, and elsewhere disappeared—with no threat from the Tang, political division more often prevailed in other East Asian societies. At the same time, connections among societies weakened as a result of the Tang's nativist policy after 755.

The tempo of interaction in East Asia revived with the arrival of the Song dynasty in China and the economic boom it fostered. Japan, Korea, Vietnam, and other East Asian societies such as Srivijaya and Angkor were again more connected to China, and to one another. The East Asian web was again growing thicker.

The nomadic invasions that began with the Khitan in the early tenth century heralded a new era for East Asia. Indeed, for most of the following millennium, most Chinese were ruled most of the time by dynasties from the steppe. At first, with the Khitans, the impacts seemed confined to north China and Korea. But as steppe peoples learned more and more from their neighbors—one of the results of heightened interaction—they tipped the balance of power in their favor. This was most conspicuous with the Mongols under Genghis Khan and his offspring.

The Mongols' Eurasian Empire strengthened the Old World web and in so doing tightened trade and cultural connections both within East Asia and between East Asia and other lands. Despite the vast destruction and loss of life in a half-century of Mongol conquests, the peace they later imposed, and their support for trade and cultural exchanges, left East Asia resurgent.

CHAPTER REVIEW

KEY TERMS

silkworms (p. 332)
Grand Canal (p. 333)
steppe nomads (p. 333)
civil service
    examinations (p. 334)

Wu Zetian (p. 334)
Tibetan Empire (p. 338)
Yamato region (p. 339)
Srivijaya (p. 340)
champa rice (p. 345)

Koryo (p. 347)
Heian Japan (p. 347)
Shinto (p. 348)
Genghis Khan (p. 351)
Yuan dynasty (p. 353)

Go to INQUIZITIVE to see what you've learned—and learn what you've missed—with personalized feedback along the way.

REVIEW QUESTIONS

1. What were the two important shifts that followed the collapse of the Han, and why did they occur?

2. In what ways did early Tang rulers reform the state?

3. In what ways did the Tang dominate the regions in the sinosphere?

4. What cultural influence prevailed in Southeast Asia to 500, and what form did this influence take?

5. When did the Tang dynasty begin to fall, and what were its main hardships?

6. Identify the forms of business, economic measures, and technologies that the Song introduced, and their effects.

7. What impacts did the relationship between the Song and the steppe nomads have on Korean and Japanese religion, culture, and politics?

8. Why and how did the Chinese relationship with steppe nomads shift around the tenth century?

9. What environmental factors, motivations, and military tactics facilitated the Mongols' successes in warfare?

10. What were the main reasons that the Yuan dynasty was short-lived?

11. How did the strength of foreign connections change from the Tang to the Song to the Yuan?

12. Explain how and why both unity and disunity in China influenced the politics of its neighbors.

FURTHER READING

Timothy BROOK, *The Troubled Empire: China in the Yuan and Ming Dynasties* (2010). A readable survey of the thirteenth through the seventeenth centuries by one of the major historians of China.

Valerie HANSEN, *The Open Empire: A History of China to 1800* (2015). An insightful interpretative survey that emphasizes China's links to the world.

Dieter KUHN, *The Age of Confucian Rule: The Song Transformation of China* (2009). An authoritative account of the tenth through the thirteenth centuries, emphasizing economic changes.

Soyoung LEE and Denise Patry LEIDY, *Silla: Korea's Golden Kingdom* (2013). A lavishly illustrated look at the history, archeology, and art of Korea.

Mark Edward LEWIS, *China between Empires: The Northern and Southern Dynasties* (2009). A general account of the period from around 200 to 600 CE.

Timothy MAY, *The Mongol Empire* (2018). A compact and excellent general study.

Morris ROSSABI, *The Mongols and Global History* (2010). A useful overview with translations of relevant documents.

N. Harry ROTHSCHILD, *Wu Zhao: China's only Woman Emperor* (2008). A brief, readable account of the extraordinary life of Wu Zetian.

Edward SEIDENSTICKER, ed., *The Gossamer Years: The Diary of a Noblewoman of Heian Japan* (1989). A short, frank account of a woman struggling as a second wife in an unhappy marriage in tenth-century Japan. The author is unknown, referred to only as the "mother of Michitsuna."

Michael SETH, *A History of Korea* (2011). A survey that places Korea in a world context.

Zhenping WANG, *Tang China in Multi-Polar Asia: A History of Diplomacy and War* (2013). A systematic presentation of China's relations with its neighbors.

CHRONOLOGY

13

Forging an Indian Ocean World

SOUTH ASIA, SOUTHEAST ASIA, AND EAST AFRICA

ca. 200 to 1400

ca. 1175
Mapungubwe arises
in southern Africa

1304–1368
Lifetime of
Ibn Battuta

ca. 1275
First large stone
structures are
erected at
Great Zimbabwe

ca. 1250–1450
Great Zimbabwe
flourishes in
southern Africa

ca. 1300
Main mosque at Kilwa
on Swahili coast is built

ca. 1206–1400
Delhi sultanate rises
and falls in India

I n 1325, a 21-year-old Moroccan from a family of Islamic scholars, Abū ʻAbd Allāh Muhammad ibn ʻAbd Allāh al-Lawātī al-Ṭanjī ibn Batūtah (1304–1368)—Ibn Battuta for short—set out on one of the longest road trips of all time. He left his family "as a bird forsakes its nest," as he put it, intending to make the pilgrimage to Mecca that is expected of Muslims. He took detours that lasted 22 years. In the course of his journey, he visited Egypt, Arabia, Southwest and Central Asia, East Africa, India, Southeast Asia, and China. In middle age in the 1350s, he decided to cross the Sahara from Morocco and visit West Africa. In all he walked, sailed, or rode about 75,000 miles (121,000 km), equivalent to almost three times around the Earth. When he got home, he dictated an account of his experiences and claimed, with some justice, to be the greatest traveler of the age.

Just about everywhere he went, Ibn Battuta found Muslims happy to host him and sometimes to employ him. He visited out-of-the-way islands such as the

Tales from a Maritime World This painting of a seagoing ship comes from a 1237 manuscript, a collection of stories written by al-Hariri, a poet and linguist based in Basra. The image, one of 96 in the manuscript depicting life in thirteenth-century Iraq, is the work of Yahya ibn Mahmud al-Wasiti and is based on the painter's knowledge of ships of the Persian Gulf and Arabian Sea. It illustrates a humorous tale of a voyage to a market city in Oman on the Arabian Peninsula.

359

1. Why does it make sense to define this region by water—the Indian Ocean—rather than land?

2. What major social, cultural, and political changes occurred in India between 200 and 1400?

3. What were the major components of trade in the Indian Ocean world?

4. How did the connections of trade foster a cosmopolitan culture across the Indian Ocean world?

Maldives (off the western coast of India), where a local ruler kept him against his will while employing him as a judge. He went to great capitals—such as Constantinople, where he met a Byzantine emperor, and Delhi, where he also worked as a judge. His employer there, a sultan, asked him to head an embassy to China, where he arrived in 1345 during the final decades of Yuan rule. He didn't care for China much but admired Hangzhou, the Chinese city that 60 years before had so impressed Marco Polo. Ibn Battuta said it was the biggest city he had seen, noting with admiration the sails and ships filling the canals and the thriving community of Muslim merchants. He stayed with a family of Egyptian origin.

On his journeys he was robbed by brigands, hit by an arrow, and shipwrecked several times. But despite his mishaps and his mileage, Ibn Battuta was no trailblazer: he was following the beaten path. By the middle of the fourteenth century, the lands he visited were all part of a series of trade circuits, linked inside the Old World web.

This chapter tells the story of how the lands on Ibn Battuta's itinerary came to be connected in a single web during the millennium before his birth. It deals with the southernmost, and most maritime, parts of the Old World web. It says more about India than any other land, because India stood at the center of the watery web built on Indian Ocean travel and trade.

THE INDIAN OCEAN WORLD: AN OVERVIEW

We normally understand the world as divided into continents and regions within continents. But there are times when regions can, with equal or better logic, be understood differently—not as lumps of land, but as lands situated around a body of water. Historians habitually refer to the "Mediterranean world," for example. In recent decades, historians have seen a similar connectedness in the lands, economies, and cultures surrounding the Indian Ocean, at least after about 100 CE.

MASTERING THE MONSOON

The key reason the Indian Ocean world could become a coherent region after 100 CE is the accumulation of knowledge about the monsoon. Chapter 4 described the seasonal alternation of the monsoon winds and the geophysics behind it. Only gradually did mariners come to understand how to use that alternation for sailing purposes. That understanding was first codified about 45 CE by a Greek sea captain who probably lived in an Egyptian port along the Red Sea. His text, the *Periplus of the Erythraean Sea*, describes coasts and ports from East Africa to India. It explains that the winds reliably blow in a northeasterly direction across the Arabian Sea in the summer months and in a southwesterly direction in the winter. With this knowledge, sea captains could schedule their voyages so as to lose little time waiting for favorable winds. In addition, they could sail from East Africa or Arabia directly to India (and back) without having to hew close to the coastline. Sailing out in the open sea was rare before 100 CE, but it cut time from voyages and reduced risks of pirate attack.

The regularity of winds in the Arabian Sea was mirrored by those of the Bay of Bengal. The strength of the monsoon petered out below the equator, so the connected space of the Indian Ocean world extended only to northern Mozambique on the African coast and Java in Southeast

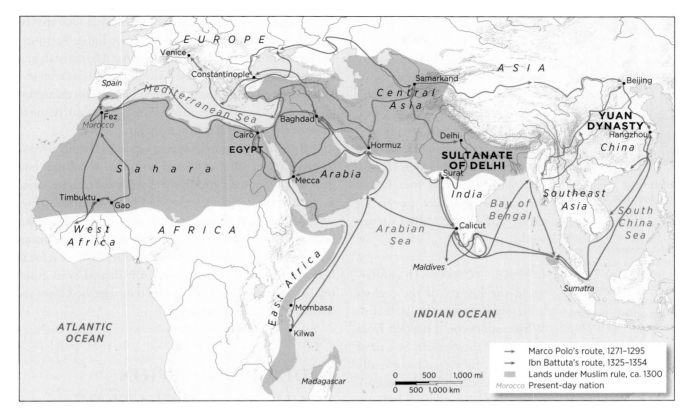

The Routes of Marco Polo and Ibn Battuta Marco Polo and Ibn Battuta never crossed paths because they were travelers of different generations. But their routes intersected in places such as Samarkand, Hangzhou, Calicut, and Constantinople. Both men crisscrossed the expanding Old World web of the thirteenth and fourteenth centuries, and together their routes give a good idea of the overland and maritime connections that held the web together.

Asia. After the first century CE, sailors, traders, travelers, missionaries, navies, and armies increasingly knit together the coastlands and hinterlands of the Indian Ocean world, building ties bound by the monsoon winds. The strength of the Asian monsoon made the Indian Ocean fundamentally different as a sailing sea from the Atlantic and the Pacific. Only the Indian Ocean (and the South China Sea) has winds that make direct back-and-forth journeys, as opposed to long circuitous routes, simple. Once the monsoon knowledge became widespread, the costs and dangers of sailing in the Indian Ocean world plummeted.

Although easier to sail in than the Atlantic or the Pacific, the Indian Ocean presented its share of challenges to mariners. The powerful monsoon wind itself posed dangers for the unwary. Any ship caught on the western coast of India in summer was likely to be dashed on reefs or rocks. Storms in the Bay of Bengal could swallow up a ship in a minute. Many warm-water coasts had coral reefs, which could punch a hole in a ship's hull. The characteristic ship design of the Indian Ocean was the

dhow, with slanting, triangular sails and planks sewn together with coir, or coconut fiber, rather than nailed together. This made hulls a bit more flexible and less likely to be crushed on a reef. The Indian Ocean was easy to sail only if you knew what you were doing, and when to do it. Dozens of authors helpfully wrote treatises on winds, currents, harbors, reefs, and stars to aid with navigation.

TRADE IN THE INDIAN OCEAN WORLD

Above all else, trade defined the Indian Ocean world after 200 CE. Reduced costs and dangers encouraged an enduring boom in seaborne trade from South China to East Africa. The goods traded were mostly luxuries—silks, porcelain, spices, ivory, gems, gold, horses, slaves—used only by social elites. But they were extremely important to the identity, and indeed the formation, of elites. In the Indian Ocean world, as everywhere else, to be a king you had to live like a king, showing off your wealth and power with luxury goods.

Dhows This boat type, the dhow of the Arabian Sea, has been in use for at least 1,000 years. Small dhows, like the one pictured here, carried coastal trade from port to port. Larger ones crossed the sea linking East Africa, Arabia, the Persian Gulf, and India. Carrying one or two masts, usually rigged with triangular sails well suited to the reliable monsoon winds, the bigger dhows required crews of 12 to 30 sailors.

Undergirding the long-distance trade in luxuries was a set of more local trades linking nearby ports—called **cabotage**. This trade involved goods for daily use such as salt, rice, mangrove poles, leather, cotton cloth, or pottery. Such items almost never traveled the breadth of the Indian Ocean. But they sustained merchants, ports, and ordinary people in every part of the Indian Ocean world.

CHOKE POINTS To understand the history of the region, a bit more geography is useful. While sailors could make it from one side of the Arabian Sea, or of the Bay of Bengal, to the other, they could not easily cross the whole Indian Ocean—5,000 miles (8,000 km). Everyone had to pause somewhere in southern India or Sri Lanka for water and food if they wanted to reap the rewards of trading from one half of the Indian Ocean world to the other. Thus the ocean had two halves, and India divided it. India's southernmost tip and Sri Lanka formed a **choke point** for long-distance navigation.

Along the eastern edge of the Indian Ocean stood another choke point for long-distance trade, the Straits of Malacca. Anyone aiming to trade between China and the Indian Ocean almost necessarily had to pass through the waters between Sumatra and the Malay Peninsula. The other options were slow and costly: either trans-shipping across the neck of the Malay Peninsula, or sailing to the south of Sumatra before heading north again. When and where catching the monsoon was involved, days and weeks lost could easily dictate a wait of many months.

The Indian Ocean world as a whole, counting the South China Sea as well as the Bay of Bengal and Arabian Sea, had three parts, with south India and the Straits of Malacca as the two main hinges. The bigger the trade grew, the more was at stake in controlling the good harbors of southern India and the Straits of Malacca.

INDIA AND AFRICA AS REGIONS Now a word or two about India and Africa as regions. India, historically, encompassed the subcontinent of South Asia, not just the part that forms the modern country of India. At times, the term *India* has included what is now Afghanistan and adjacent lands of Central Asia. The heart of India after 500 BCE was always the Ganges basin, with its cheap transport, good soils, easy irrigation, and dense population, home to most of the powerful states in Indian history.

Africa, in the centuries before 1400, was highly diverse in every respect and exhibited no unity of culture, language, politics, or anything else. I will treat eastern Africa as part of the Indian Ocean world. West Africa, as we shall see, was a world apart, although increasingly influenced by its trans-Saharan contacts with the Mediterranean world and Egypt. So, like East Africa, West Africa's history after 800 or so was powerfully shaped by its growing participation in the giant web that stretched from the Mediterranean to Japan.

INDIA: POPULATION, SOCIETY, AND CULTURE

India stood at the center of the Indian Ocean world not only in terms of geography, but in demography as well. The texts from the centuries before 1400 say next to nothing about population, so archeology is our best guide.

POPULATION AND HEALTH

India was the population heavyweight of the whole region, excluding China. The table on page 363 presents some estimates of the evolution of population in parts of the Indian Ocean world, with China included for comparison. Sub-Saharan Africa, for which population figures in this period are sheer guesswork, might have had 10 to 12 million people in 200 CE and 30 to 35 million in 1400.

These population figures, even for 1600, are only 10 to 15 percent of today's figures. Much land remained sparsely inhabited. More than half of India in 1400 was forest. The population was also growing much, much more slowly than today. Between 1000 and 1600, for example, India's population grew by only 0.1 percent per year, and China's by 0.085 percent. China's population showed the most dramatic fluctuations, a reflection of the havoc caused by steppe invaders—the Mongols above all—as well as a spate of epidemics and adverse climate change.

POPULATION (IN MILLIONS) IN THE INDIAN OCEAN WORLD				
200-1600 CE				
YEAR CE	INDIA	EAST AFRICA[1]	SOUTHEAST ASIA[2]	CHINA
200	40	0.5	3.5	55
600	51	1.0	5.0	46
1000	75	3.5	7.0	90
1400	94	6.5	12.0	60
1600	125	8.0	14.0	150

Sources: Colin McEvedy & Richard Jones, *Atlas of World Population History* (1978), 182–203, 250–53; Irfan Habib, *Man and Environment: The Ecological History of India* (2010), 88; Tim Dyson, *A Population History of India* (2018), 43–44, 61–62.

1. Modern Tanzania, Kenya, Somalia, Uganda; not just the Swahili coast
2. Modern Malaysia, Indonesia, Thailand, Cambodia, Laos, Vietnam

As everywhere, famines and epidemics kept population growth in check. Sanskrit texts first mention what appears to be smallpox in the seventh century, although it likely afflicted India well before. Other deadly infections, such as malaria and cholera, were probably also widespread. In the case of malaria, genetic evidence offers a powerful clue: many South Asian populations have a high rate of sickle-cell trait, a genetic adaptation to the presence of malaria, implying that their ancestors for many generations lived in the presence of the disease. We still don't know if the Black Death, the plague pandemic of the mid-fourteenth century, affected India.

FAMILY, MARRIAGE, AND SOCIETY

In Chapter 5, we considered family life in ancient India as revealed by the Vedic texts. Marriage was nearly universal, arranged by families, begun at or before puberty, and ended only by death. It took place within caste groups and frequently between close relatives. Cousin marriage was common in India, as in many rural societies. Uncle-niece marriage, taboo almost everywhere else, was acceptable. (There are often health disadvantages to children of marriages between close relatives, but it's a good practice for keeping property in the family.) Females lived under the authority of fathers, then husbands, then, if widowed, of their sons. Family property was held jointly by adult males.

None of that changed much in the centuries after 200 CE, but a little more variety is evident from the greater number of sources. For example, in parts of south India, the customary practice was to trace descent matrilineally—through the female line. Among one aristocratic group, the Nayar, women routinely had multiple husbands at the same time, none of whom was expected to take an interest in children. In other parts of India— Orissa and Kashmir, for example—women served as rulers, of which there is no hint in earlier times. One custom associated with Hinduism, *sati*, arose by the fifth century and spread throughout India by the tenth. Sati (or suttee) refers to the practice of widows leaping onto their dead husbands' funeral pyres and burning themselves to death. It was understood as a show of respect to the deceased and his family, and as a way to cancel his sins and improve his standing in the afterlife. The arrival of Islam in India (of which more later) brought further changes in marriage and family, such as the expectation that married women should seclude themselves behind veils. Muslim rulers from the fourteenth century also sought to suppress the practice of sati and held no objections to widows remarrying.

In most Hindu communities, caste remained the central social institution. It was, as before, a hierarchy of social groups based on their ritual purity and mainly rooted in men's occupations. But the broad fourfold categorization explained in Chapter 5 (Brahmins, Kshatriya, Vaishya, and Sudra), which Sanskrit texts presented as unchanging since the dawn of time, grew more elaborate. Sub-castes merged, others split, and new ones were created in response to the absorption of new peoples or the emergence of new professions. Tribals (to use the Indian term) from rain forests or mountainous landscapes were increasingly brought into the caste system as their forests were burned and turned to farmland. Even foreign raiders and invaders were folded into the caste system. Caste proved remarkably flexible, adjusting to changing times.

A further social change came with the rise of slavery in India after the twelfth century. As far as we know, slavery was rare in early Indian history. But with the arrival of Islam it became more common, although still less so than in Korea, Egypt, or West Africa, for example. In India, slaves came most often from Central Asia, but some from as far afield as Ethiopia and the coasts of the Black Sea. They worked as servants in court or aristocratic households, or as soldiers—we will soon return to the curious case of India's military slaves. One sultan of Delhi apparently owned 180,000 slaves.

RELIGION, CULTURE, AND SCIENCE

As we saw in Chapter 5, in the twilight of the Mauryan dynasty (321–187 BCE), India in the second century BCE was a land of multiple religions. Hinduism, with its Vedic texts and traditions of fire sacrifice, had begun to take shape. Buddhism and Jainism, with their emphasis on renunciation and the endless cycle of death and rebirth, had spread widely partly in reaction to unpopular features of Hindu lore and practice. In the centuries between 200 CE and 1400, religion in India changed dramatically. Buddhism almost went extinct. Islam became a major faith and Zoroastrianism a minor one.

Remember that in India, unlike many other lands, authorities rarely tried to suppress novelties in religious belief or practice. Rulers tended to support all versions of faiths, rather than to suppose that only one represented the truth. Hinduism had no institutional structure to enforce orthodoxy, so new innovations within it popped up frequently and sometimes caught on. Yoga, the practice of meditation aiming at tranquility, enlightenment, and health, provides a good example. It existed in Mauryan times but became more important and took many new forms, some influenced by Buddhist and Jain traditions that were folded into Hindu practice, in the second to the eighth centuries. Variety, cross-fertilization, and change prevailed in Indian religion.

THE BHAKTI MOVEMENT The biggest change in Hinduism came with the rise of intense, emotional cults of the **Bhakti movement**. Between the seventh and the twelfth centuries, first in the south of India, people began to practice personal dedication to one god, such as Shiva or Vishnu, or increasingly Devi, a composite of all female divinity. There was no need for learned Brahmin priests or Buddhist austerity—just intense devotion. The Bhakti movement was spread by charismatic "preachers" who disregarded caste, often discarded the learning of Brahmins, and taught their truths in local languages such as Tamil and Tegulu rather than Sanskrit, the language of

Bhakti Saints Sambandar was a seventh-century Bhakti child saint devoted to the god Shiva. He performed miracles and wrote devotional hymns, and is said to have attained *moksha*, or final release from the cycle of death and re-birth, at age 16. He is depicted here in a figurine from the eleventh century.

the Vedas. Many of these "saints" were of humble origin, low-caste by birth, and scorned by Brahmins. At least one, named Andal, was a woman—unthinkable to those steeped in Vedic tradition, in which women could not become religious specialists. Like India's Muslims, Bhakti followers opposed sati, a perspective that probably appealed to women. The Bhakti message found a wide audience, altering and reinvigorating Hinduism.

The Bhakti revival helped to drive Buddhism to the margins of Indian society. Its innovations enabled Hinduism to appeal to a broader slice of the population, including women and downtrodden low-caste men. Rich merchants found more justification for their wheeling and dealing, something that mercantile classes had formerly found more often in Buddhism. Fewer and fewer rulers supported Buddhist monasteries and monks. By the twelfth century, Buddhism was confined to pockets of eastern India; and with the rise of Islam, it soon lost most of its remaining foothold there too. Where it survived, it took forms increasingly similar to Hinduism. Ironically, Buddhism in these centuries was thriving in Southeast Asia and surviving in East Asia, while all but disappearing in the land of its birth.

Jainism survived a bit better, especially among traders and in the highly commercialized region of Gujarat (northwest India). But it too lost followers. In one case, a ruler of a small southern kingdom decided to abandon Jainism for the cult of Shiva; and following the advice of his spiritual counselor, he demonstrated his new commitment by impaling on stakes the heads of 8,000 Jain teachers. Evidently, the rule of religious toleration in India had its exceptions.

India acquired new religions from abroad as well. A community of Zoroastrians migrated from Persia during the seventh through the tenth centuries, fleeing persecutions by newly Islamized rulers there. They clustered in western India, where they are called Parsis (meaning "Persians"). A community of Christians emerged in southwest India, called St. Thomas Christians, who believed that St. Thomas the Apostle had visited their shores in the first century CE. (Firm evidence suggests Christianity was practiced there by about 300 CE.) Jews from Iraq and Arabia took up residence in west India's ports as well.

Starting in the early eighth century, Islam joined India's portfolio of religions. Arab traders had brought Islam to western Indian ports in the mid-seventh century. Then in 711, the same year that Arab armies crossed into Spain, forces of the Damascus-based Umayyad caliphate

Christianity in India St. Mary's Jacobite Syrian Church, built around 1400 CE, is one of the churches associated with the St. Thomas Christian movement that survives in present-day Kerala in southwest India.

conquered the region of Sind in what is now southern Pakistan. They got no further, owing to deserts and formidable foes, but in short order they managed to Islamize Sind.

THE SPREAD OF ISLAM IN INDIA A more powerful force for the **Islamization** of India came from Central Asia beginning around 1000. With the weakening of China's Tang dynasty and the Abbasid caliphate in the eighth and ninth centuries, Turkic peoples in Central Asia acquired more power. Some of them also adopted Islam. A group of slave soldiers, from a part of Afghanistan called Ghazna, began a program of conquest in Iran and India. Under a warlord named Mahmoud, they launched 17 raids into northern India, plundering cities and temples. The Ghaznavids were skilled horsemen and indiscriminate plunderers, sacking Hindu and Buddhist temples alike and assaulting Shi'a Muslims whenever an opportunity arose. An eleventh-century Central Asian scholar, al-Biruni, wrote of Mahmoud that he "utterly destroyed" northern India. That was exaggeration, but the long history of friction between Hindu and Muslim in India dates chiefly from the raids of Mahmoud and his fellow horsemen.

As we shall see below, other Turkic horsemen followed the Ghaznavids and set up durable states in northern India. Usually, the rulers of these new states were Muslim. But the villagers remained overwhelmingly Hindu except in two regions, the Punjab and Bengal. In the Punjab, Muslims enjoyed especially high prestige because they led the battle against Mongol invaders—descendants of Genghis Khan who after 1240 tried and failed several times to add India to their empire. In Bengal, which was a thinly populated frontier forest region, Islam became dominant because rulers granted land to Muslims who would clear forests and start up new farming communities.

By and large, despite the occasional massacre of Buddhists or Hindus, the new Muslim overlords preferred not to interfere in their subjects' religious affairs. Muslim doctrine and law afford respect and protection to Peoples of the Book, which until this time had meant Jews, Zoroastrians, and Christians. But the Turkic sultans found it easy enough to extend this special status (called *dhimmi* in Arabic and Islamic law) to Hindus, Buddhists, and Jains. They had financial incentives not to press conversion to Islam, because by Islamic law Muslims were taxed at lower rates than non-Muslims. Although Hindus and Buddhists, conversely, had financial incentives to become Muslims, over the centuries of Muslim rule in north India (i.e., 1206–1857) only about a quarter of the population did so, and far less than that outside of the Punjab and Bengal.

The changes in religion encouraged linguistic change in India. The rise of Bhakti worship involved the use of local languages rather than Sanskrit. Tamil, Telugu, Bengali, Gujarati, and Marathi became literary languages and tongues used in religious ritual. They gradually became major regional languages of India, as they remain today. Sanskrit lost some of its prestige and market share. Although still spoken by small numbers of Indians, Sanskrit's fate is a bit like Latin's in Europe: it is an ancestor of many living tongues but now survives mainly as a language of priestly ritual and ancient literature.

SCIENCE AND LEARNING IN INDIA The centuries between about 500 and 1000 CE proved especially fertile in several areas of learning. One was linguistics, the study of language itself. For Hindu rituals in which certain prayers had to be said in just the right way, detailed knowledge of Sanskrit was helpful. Science in India, as almost everywhere at the time, was part of religion. So was medicine, an active area of scientific work. Indian medical thought—the ayurvedic tradition, as it is known—dealt with everything from toxicology to sexual potency. It typically explained illness in spiritual terms but sought cures both in that realm and through drugs extracted from plants, including opium. Animal fats also served as salves. Ayurvedic medicine has ancient roots, but between 500 and 1200 CE it became codified. It has followers around the world today, attracted by its holistic approach.

Another vibrant field of science was astronomy and astrology, which in distant times were united, not only in India but in Mesopotamia, China, Europe, and elsewhere too. Indian astronomers figured out that eclipses are shadows cast by the Earth and moon upon each other.

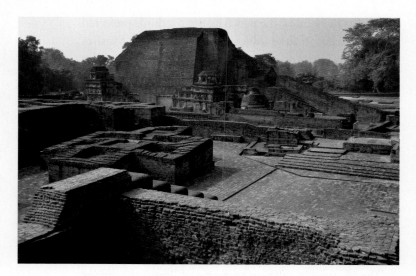

Nalanda The scale of the ruins of the monastery at Nalanda, which flourished between the sixth and ninth centuries CE, speaks to the site's importance as a center of knowledge and learning.

Astronomy and astrology were closely linked to mathematics in India, as in ancient Sumer and among the Maya. Indian texts from the fifth through the eighth centuries show a growing experimentation with new concepts in mathematics. They pioneered algebra, or at least basic quadratic equations. Indian mathematicians also explored trigonometry and developed the concept of zero and the first base 10 numerical notation. They calculated π as far as 3.1416—as far as you need to go for practical purposes. Indian math had drawn on Mesopotamian and Greek precedents, and in turn it would later influence Arab mathematics, which in turn influenced European math and eventually became globalized. Indian math texts were typically written as poems, a practice that sadly did not translate into other cultures.

Indian science and learning were concentrated in royal courts and in the remaining Buddhist monasteries. The greatest of these monasteries was **Nalanda** (in northeast India), which attracted students from China, Korea, Tibet, Southeast Asia, and Persia. According to one Chinese visitor in the seventh century, it had 1,500 instructors and its towers and temples "soared above the mists in the sky." Some 200 villages devoted their surplus food to supporting the monks and 10,000 hungry students at Nalanda in its heyday, which extended from the sixth through the ninth centuries. Its curriculum emphasized both Buddhist and Hindu philosophy, logic, linguistics, and medicine. When in 1193 Turkic Muslims sacked it,

three months were needed to burn all the manuscripts kept at Nalanda. Today, the governments of India, China, Japan, and Singapore are spending vast sums to create a new university there.

GREAT POWERS IN INDIA

In the aftermath of the Mauryan Empire in 187 BCE, most of India fragmented politically into tiny kingdoms or loose states dominated by a handful of adult males. But over time, kingdoms became both more common and larger, a pattern found in many places around the world. In India this trend was reinforced by the Vedic texts, which present kingship as the best political format. Kings in India were in theory responsible only to the gods. But in practice, like kings everywhere, they had to tread carefully. The councils of elders that ran the affairs of castes, for example, could not be disregarded lightly. Kings could pronounce edicts carrying the force of law, but human law, even kingly law, always carried less prestige than dharma, the righteous path in Hindu belief.

Most Indian kingdoms were in effect franchises. A successful king would leave matters such as justice and policing to lesser rulers, treated as vassals. He demanded tribute from them in the forms of money, war elephants, or soldiers, and required formal declarations of obedience. In exchange, he would protect them from attack. Hundreds of states rose and fell in India in the centuries between 200 and 1400. The three most important for world history are the Gupta, the Chola, and the Delhi sultanate.

THE GUPTA, CA. 330-550 The most successful kings in India after the Mauryans were those of the **Gupta dynasty**. Like most big powers in Indian history before and since, they got their start in the Ganges basin. Through astute marriages they expanded their domain. Via warfare they forced rulers throughout north India to pay them tribute in their capital, Pataliputra (present-day Patna). Samudragupta reigned for four decades (r. 335–375) and conquered at least 14 other kings, a record comparable to that of Alexander the Great or Qin Shi Huangdi. His successor, Chandragupta II (r. 375–415), ruled just as long and conquered almost as widely, even into Central Asia. As one of his boosters delicately put it, "he unburdened the sacred earth of the barbarians." The Gupta kings managed no enduring conquests in south India, but they enjoyed authority throughout the north. Although smaller than the Mauryan Empire, the Gupta state was probably the largest and most populous in the world by the end of Chandragupta's reign. (China at the time was divided among several states, and the Roman Empire was a shell of its former self.)

The Gupta kings claimed semi-divine status and enjoyed strong support from the Brahmins. They were, by all accounts, pious Hindus, but nonetheless patronized Buddhist and Jain monasteries and temples. The Guptas often granted religious leaders forest land to clear and till, accepting one-sixth of the religious merit earned by holy men instead of taxes. Taking a cut of religious merit earned by specialists in virtue allowed the kings the moral latitude to use violence, trickery, and other routine tools of statecraft without unduly jeopardizing their own souls. These deals, granted for "as long as the sun and moon endure," served both rulers and religious leaders, and cemented the alliance between them.

In addition to religious institutions, the Gupta kings supported the math and science noted above, and the work of artists and poets as well. The court hosted literary lions called the Nine Jewels, who wrote poetry that later ages came to regard as the best in the Sanskrit language. The most famous and widely translated literary work of

The Gupta State, ca. 330–550 The Gupta state grew by leaps and bounds in the late fourth and early fifth centuries, ultimately holding sway over half of the Indian subcontinent. Like the Mauryans a few centuries before, its kings controlled the two richest river basins, the Ganges and the Indus, and the surplus rice and wheat that peasants produced. The Gupta state was, for a while, the most powerful in the world. Its patronage of art and science brought creative results still admired inside and outside India.

Gupta Diversity A fresco from a Gupta palace, dated to the period 320–600 CE, shows a crowd of people of different ethnic groups and castes. Their social distinctions are symbolized through their clothing, jewelry, and tools.

the Gupta age (early drafts probably date to the first or second century) is the *Kama Sutra*, a guide to refined living that includes one of the most thorough and unabashed studies of human sexual conduct ever written. Faxian, a Chinese Buddhist monk, visited Gupta lands in Chandragupta II's time and found what he thought was a happy and satisfied kingdom, populated by vegetarians and teetotalers. Perhaps he had some difficulty interpreting what he saw: he also reported venomous dragons that spat out snow in the Himalayas. But the work of Gupta sculptors and architects, as well as of writers and scientists, inspired modern Indians to regard the fourth and fifth centuries as a golden age.

The Gupta kings, however golden their legacy, soon ran into trouble. Despite their military strength, based on war elephants and archers, by the 450s they could

The Chola Kingdom, 1044
- Territory under direct control
- Temporary gains

The Sultanate of Delhi
- Territory, 1206
- Gains, by 1316
- Timur's empire, ca. 1400
- ○ City sacked
- *Afghanistan* Present-day nation

The Chola Kingdom and the Delhi Sultanate, 1044–1400 The Chola kingdom was a maritime empire, supported by revenues from seaborne trade. The Delhi sultanate was a terrestrial empire, held together by cavalry forces. While neither one dominated India to the extent that the Mauryans or the Gupta had centuries before them, each was the greatest Indian state of its day.

no longer reliably defend their northern frontiers against Central Asian horsemen. One charismatic warlord, named Oprah, built a large following and in the 480s broke through Gupta defenses. After that, Gupta vassal rulers increasingly defected, declaring their allegiance to Oprah and other Central Asian chieftains. Soon almost no one was paying tribute to the Gupta anymore, and with lower revenues they could no longer defend their remaining vassals against anyone. Like most other agrarian states adjacent to the steppe lands, the Gupta eventually faced an enemy too mobile, militaristic, organized, and formidable for them. By 550, the Gupta dynasty ruled only a tiny kingdom, and north India was once again a patchwork of rival polities.

After the decline of the Gupta, many kings struggled for power, but none succeeded in re-uniting the rich Ganges basin. With its dense population, fertile farmland, iron and copper mines, and good riverine transport network, it remained the grand prize in Indian geopolitics. Small powers took shape in Bengal and, in the form of invading Arabs, in Sind (today's southern Pakistan). But in the absence of a great power in the north, India after 550—rather like China—experienced a slow rise of the south. Major new centers of wealth and power arose in the Deccan (west-central India) and the southeast, the Tamil-speaking region of India. The greatest of these was the Chola kingdom.

THE CHOLA KINGDOM, CA. 970–CA. 1300 For centuries merely a local dynasty in the Kaveri River basin of southeastern India, the **Chola kingdom** after 970 burst forth to become a transcontinental power. They sponsored new irrigation techniques that improved harvests. In the 980s, their kings started gobbling up neighboring lands on both the Coromandel (southeastern) and Malabar (southwestern) coasts. They built a navy and gradually took the islands of Sri Lanka and the Maldives.

More than any other major state in Indian history, the Chola drew their revenues from seaborne trade. Once they controlled the south Indian coasts and Sri Lanka, all shipping in transit across the Indian Ocean had to stop in their harbors—and pay for the privilege. Larger trends around the Indian Ocean world helped make the Chola rich and powerful. The rise of the Song in China and their commercial orientation buoyed long-distance trade, as did the simultaneous rise of a powerful and prosperous dynasty in Egypt, the Fatimids. The burgeoning trade helped rulers throughout the Indian Ocean world, but especially those situated at its choke points, such as the Chola.

The Chola state was in part an alliance of **merchant trading guilds**, not so different from the merchant families that many centuries earlier had dominated Carthage and its seaborne empire of the Mediterranean. Sea traders banded together to pool resources and share risk. The big guilds included hundreds of merchants. As their wealth grew, they used it to influence kings who needed their money. An inscription from 1055 gives a sense of the role of one of the merchant guilds and their pride in themselves:

Famed throughout the world, adorned with many good qualities, truth purity...and prudence, born to be wanderers over many countries...; ...by land and sea penetrating into the regions of the six continents, with superior elephants, well-bred horses, large sapphires, moonstones, pearls, rubies, diamonds...cloves, sandalwood, camphor musk, saffron, and other perfumes and drugs; by selling wholesale or hawking about on their shoulders, preventing the loss

Chola Art Under the sponsorship of Chola rulers, art and architecture flourished—ranging from immense Hindu temples such as this one in present-day Tamil Nadu, built around 1010 CE, to smaller-scale ornate bronzes such as this sculpture of the god Shiva, made in the same period.

by custom duties, they fill up the emperor's treasury of gold, his treasury of jewels, and his armory of weapons.

Under Rajendra I (r. 1012–1044), the Chola grew yet more ambitious. They enhanced their position in maritime trade by taking Indian ports to the north as far as Bengal. Rajendra allegedly arranged to have some holy water from the Ganges brought south to his kingdom. Next he started sending trade missions to China in 1016, bringing ivory, rhino horn, brocade, glassware, and other goods the Chola merchants expected Chinese markets to value.

In 1025 the Chola launched a naval expedition across 2,500 miles (4,000 km) of open ocean against the state of Srivijaya, the maritime powerhouse controlling the Straits of Malacca (see Chapter 12). No one had ever done anything like this in world history, and no one would do it again for centuries. We don't know exactly why Rajendra I chose this gamble. His motives probably included trying for better terms of access to the China trade. Srivijaya's sea captains were traders if you abided by their terms and pirates if you didn't, so perhaps the Chola understood their mission as pirate control. In any case, Rajendra's navy sacked a dozen or more Srivijayan cities but did not attempt to impose enduring control. He wasn't interested in building, or perhaps knew he was unable to build, a seaborne empire of the sort that Carthage had created in the Mediterranean. Soon Srivijaya was back in business, sending additional trade missions to China by 1028. The long-term impact of the Chola naval attack was nil.

The Chola stayed with their formula of commercial and naval activity, remaining prosperous and formidable until after 1100. They patronized the arts, especially literature and architecture. Some Tamil and Telugu literary classics, and versions of Sanskrit epics regarded as central to Hinduism, date from their reign. Chola kings and merchants paid for new temples, often dedicated to Shiva, such as that at Thanjavur, in its day the biggest in India. Chola bronze statuary earned the admiration of future ages.

Chola power slipped in the late twelfth century. But the merchant guilds of southeastern India remained active in overseas trade. The Chinese city of Guangzhou features a Hindu temple in the Chola style, with a Tamil-language inscription from 1281, implying a substantial resident Tamil population. One of the Chola ports had a Chinese pagoda, built in 1267. The commercial and cultural connections between south India and Southeast Asia waned somewhat in the fourteenth century, but never disappeared.

THE SULTANATE OF DELHI, CA. 1206–CA. 1400

Like China and Persia, India stood adjacent to the steppe corridor of Eurasia. It too experienced its share of nomad incursions, including those who helped bring low the Gupta state in the sixth century, and the Ghaznavids who brought Islam into the heart of India around 1000 CE. Other Turkic peoples from the steppe followed, drawn by the prospect of loot. As horsemen, they enjoyed a great advantage operating in north India, which for lack of

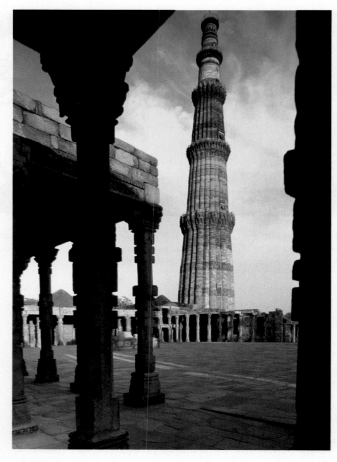

Islam in Delhi Successive Delhi sultans in the twelfth to the fourteenth centuries contributed building projects to the Qutb mosque complex in Delhi, taking their architectural inspiration from the Islamic world. The Qutb Minar, a 240-foot (73 m) minaret, still towers above the mosque's ruins.

good grasslands could not raise powerful steeds. Increasingly, these Turkic horsemen chose to settle in north India, where they could hope to live well off of taxes gathered from peasants.

The Turkic invaders brought with them the peculiar institution of slave soldiery. In Central Asia, families often sold excess boys to the armies of caliphs and sultans. No shame was attached to this form of slavery. Most of these boys lived out their lives as cavalrymen or in a palace guard. Occasionally, they used their military skills to overthrow their masters and install themselves on thrones. But most died anonymously—as unknown **slave soldiers**.

In the 1190s, a new band of Turkic soldiers from Central Asia began raiding north India. Like the Ghaznavids before them, most were nominally slaves. The various princes of north India could never unite against the invaders. They also lacked the horses to match their enemies' cavalry. Soon the entire Ganges basin as far east as Bengal was paying tribute to new masters, who set up a capital in Delhi, formerly a backwater town. In 1206 these Turkic horsemen established the sultanate of Delhi.

The new sultans became a new military aristocracy. Indians called their new overlords *ashvapati,* or "lords of the horses." The sultans of Delhi tried to monopolize the importation of horses in order to field cavalry in a land where no one else had enough horses. The sultans' forces clustered in garrison towns and left the villages alone, as long as they turned over taxes and conscripts. In that respect, their rule was ordinary.

In other respects, it was not. After the 1220s, when the Mongols had begun their assaults on Iran, many educated and skilled Persians fled either to Delhi or to Egypt, the main states still under Muslim rule. The language of administration and high culture in Delhi gradually became Persian, and art and architecture reflected powerful Persian influences. A new Indo-Islamic culture evolved, fusing elements of Indian tradition with Turkic, Persian, and Arabic contributions. Its most enduring features were palace and mosque architecture and poetry in the Urdu language, a blend of Hindi and Persian.

The **Delhi sultanate** was distinctive in another respect: one of its early rulers was a woman, Rayiza, whose father, a slave soldier who became sultan, judged her to be the most fit to rule among his offspring. Her brothers disagreed, and others in high places found the concept of a woman ruler too much to bear. So she faced continual rebellion—against which she sometimes led her troops on horseback—and was killed fleeing her enemies after four difficult years on the job (r. 1236–1240).

The Delhi sultanate endured despite political instability. It featured five dynasties in rapid succession, with a heavy dose of poisonings, assassinations, and coups d'état. Slave soldiers often seized power. The competition for succession among brothers, sons, and nephews of dying sultans resembled that of the Mongol and Central Asian world from which they came. To complicate matters, the Mongols themselves kept attacking through Afghanistan into the Punjab from the 1240s onward. Against the odds, the Delhi sultanate survived and prospered.

The sultanate's good fortune rested on its ability to loot temples and palaces to its south, in the Deccan and central India. This enabled it to buy new horses, pay Turkic cavalry, and hire Persian bureaucrats. Sultans ruled the

Ganges heartland directly and extorted payment from princes elsewhere. Powerful sultans could make this formula work and keep the Mongols at bay. Lesser or less lucky ones found Indian princes inclined to rebel rather than pay up, sapping the sultans' financial strength and diverting their military efforts. On one occasion, the sultanate was too weak to prevent the Mongols from sacking Lahore, a rich city in the Punjab. On other occasions, the productive lands of Bengal slipped from the sultans' control.

After 1306 the Mongol onslaught on north India slackened, and the sultanate reached the pinnacle of its power. It expanded its control of surrounding regions, notably under Alauddin Khalji, who murdered his way into the top job in 1296. He led winning campaigns against large Mongol attacks, inspiring him to compare his own record to Alexander the Great's. Unlike Alexander, and unlike his own contemporaries in Yuan China, Alauddin embarked on a program of direct state control over the economy. He curtailed the role of markets, fixing prices for everything from needles to horses. This worked as a short-term strategy to maximize revenue and the sultan's military power. After beating back the Mongols, Alauddin turned his well-tuned war machine against his neighbors, expanding the sultanate's frontiers in India. He earned a fearsome reputation for demolishing temples and wreaking homicidal vengeance upon his enemies and their families, especially anyone bold enough to question the justice of his rule.

The majority of Indians under the Delhi sultanate remained Hindu. Many temples were destroyed or converted into mosques. But the sultans could not afford to see all Hindus become Muslims, because by Islamic law non-Muslims paid twice the tax of Muslims. When one faction of zealous Muslim clerics asked a sultan's permission to force Hindus to convert to Islam, they were rebuked by the sultan with political arithmetic. We Muslims, he said, are only like the salt on a dish of food. By and large, outside of Bengal and the Punjab, only garrison towns became predominantly Muslim.

The sultanate's fortunes turned after Alauddin's death in 1316. Less skilled, if no less ruthless, sultans followed. Ibn Battuta described one of them, his boss, as addicted to both gift giving and the shedding of blood. The stream of plunder slowed, and sultans had to raise taxes, inviting internal revolts and banditry. By 1350, the Delhi sultanate was only one state among several in north India. Yet

another Central Asian conqueror, Timur, swooped in to sack Delhi in 1398, slaughter thousands, and carry off its treasures and skilled craftsmen to his own capital, Samarkand, in today's Uzbekistan. The Delhi sultanate limped on until finally extinguished in 1526—by yet another troop of Central Asian horsemen, the Mughals, whom we shall save for another chapter.

For toiling peasants hovering just above starvation, the advent and decline of the sultanate of Delhi didn't mean much: someone else collected their taxes. For Brahmins, the sultanate was a disaster: they lost their positions as advisers and ministers to upstart Persians and other foreigners—including Ibn Battuta, who worked as a high judge in Delhi despite not knowing Persian or Hindi. For Buddhists, too, the sultanate was bad news: its forces sacked their temples and monasteries and drove Buddhism to the verge of extinction in India. For elite women, it meant further restrictions upon their conduct and appearance, Rayiza's example notwithstanding. More broadly, the sultanate meant the integration of northern India into the world of Islam, which by 1400 stretched from Morocco, the home of Ibn Battuta, to Java.

THE INDIAN OCEAN WORLD, 200–1400

In 1944, in the Wessel Islands off the northern coast of Australia, a World War II radar team found a handful of old coins. The coins were well worn but still carried faint Arabic inscriptions. It turned out the coins had been minted sometime between 1000 and 1300 (old coins rarely had dates on them) in Kilwa, an island off Africa's eastern coast. In the same year of 1944, on the island of Zanzibar—not far north of Kilwa—a hoard of 250 Chinese copper coins was unearthed. Four of them dated to the Tang dynasty (618–907), and the newest was from the reign of a Song emperor who died in 1275. Just how and when East African coins got to islands off the coast of Australia, and Chinese coins got to islands off of East Africa, is unknown. But they are tangible evidence of a web of interaction connecting the shores of the Indian Ocean.

The Indian Ocean world for many centuries was one of the main arenas of interaction in world history, beginning no later than 2000 BCE. By 100 CE, together with

THE HUMAN WEB

The Indian Ocean World

CA. 1400

BY THE EIGHTH CENTURY, the Abbasid caliph al-Mansur was able to boast of the bounty of goods that traveled the sea connections joining Baghdad, his future capital, to faraway China. The maritime networks of the Indian Ocean world had become at least as important as the centuries-old overland Silk Roads.

The East African coast (or Swahili coast by ca. 800 CE) illustrates the region's growing web links. Sailors from Arabia, Iran, India, and East Africa traded throughout the western Indian Ocean. The Swahili coast exported elephant ivory, mangrove poles, animal skins, slaves, and, by 1250, gold. Its main import was cloth from India. Traders brought more than cloth, however, to East Africa. Arabic and Persian combined with Bantu tongues to form a new language, Swahili. Simplified trading languages that blended several linguistic traditions developed at all the crossroads of the Indian Ocean world.

Along with the goods and languages of trade, four great religions spread along the pathways of the Indian Ocean world—Hinduism, Buddhism, Christianity, and Islam. Hinduism and Buddhism moved into East and Southeast Asia. Coptic Christianity expanded its footprint in northeast Africa. Islam filtered into East and West Africa, parts of India, and Southeast Asia. Local religions retreated as these major ones spread and developed new variations suited to new locations. Nonetheless, the larger pattern of web building held for the Indian Ocean world: increased contacts meant decreased cultural variety overall.

Questions for Analysis

Based on this feature and your chapter reading, consider the following questions:

1. What geographical factors help explain the prominent role of the Indian Ocean world in making and maintaining web connections across Eurasia?

2. How did the web connections of the Indian Ocean world change religious life on the East African coast and in Southeast Asia?

EUROPE

Venice ⊙

Mediterranean Basin

porcelain, silk pepper, ivory spices

al-Andalus

Córdoba ⊙

ATLANTIC OCEAN

⊙ Fez

S a h a r a

AFRICA

Timbuktu ⊙ ⊙ Gao

West Africa

Niger R.

Danube R.

CHRISTIANITY

CHRISTIANITY

ISLAM

▶ From an Ethiopian manuscript of the Christian gospel, fourteenth or fifteenth century.

> HERE IS THE RIVER TIGRIS, WITH NOTHING BETWEEN US AND CHINA. ALL THAT IS CARRIED ON THE SEAS CAN COME TO US ON THE RIVER. "

ABU JA'FAR ABDALLAH IBN MUHAMMAD AL-MANSUR, ABBASID CALIPH (R. 754–775)

▲ Islamic textile fragment, Gujarat, India, thirteenth or fourteenth century.

◄ Buddhist-Hindu line of demons, Angkor Thom, Cambodia, twelfth century.

**Map labels:**

Black Sea
Constantinople
Caspian Sea
Samarkand
Merv
Central Asia
Iraq
Damascus
Baghdad
Basra
Iran
Persian Gulf
Hormuz
Strait of Hormuz
Arabia
Mecca
Red Sea
Aksum
Aden
Ethiopia
East Africa
Swahili Coast
Zanzibar
Kilwa
Great Zimbabwe
Madagascar
Zambezi R.
Cairo
Nile R.
Delhi
Indus R.
Ganges R.
Himalaya Mountains
Tibet
ASIA
Huang He
Beijing
Korea
Japan
Kaifeng
China
Hangzhou
Yangzi R.
Guangzhou
PACIFIC OCEAN
Gujarat
Cambay
India
Goa
Calicut
Quilon
Sri Lanka
Bay of Bengal
Angkor
Mekong R.
South China Sea
Philippines
Malay Peninsula
Southeast Asia
Straits of Malacca
Sumatra
Borneo
Java
Arabian Sea
INDIAN OCEAN

Trade/religion route labels:

CHRISTIANITY
CHRISTIANITY, ISLAM — horses, silver, gold
BUDDHISM
silk
CHRISTIANITY, ISLAM — silver, gold
silk
ISLAM
BUDDHISM
BUDDHISM, HINDUISM — cotton cloth
BUDDHISM — pepper, spices
BUDDHISM — cotton cloth
porcelain, silk — pepper, spices, slaves, ivory
porcelain, silk
coins
pepper, spices, slaves
CHRISTIANITY — coins
CHRISTIANITY — horses
CHRISTIANITY
ivory
porcelain, silk
porcelain, silk
ISLAM — ARABIC
PERSIAN — cotton cloth
BANTU
gold
ISLAM — cotton cloth
ISLAM
cotton cloth, pepper, spices
porcelain, silk

Currency and Trade These copper coins—minted in Kilwa in East Africa sometime between the eleventh and the sixteenth centuries—bear inscriptions in Arabic, the common language of the educated classes of the Islamic world, including Kilwa.

the Silk Road traffic across the steppe, its routes helped to weave together the existing (yet still developing) webs of East Asia and Southwest Asia, in effect creating the Old World web. So, after 100 CE, it was, at the same time, its own watery web and a sub-unit of the larger Old World web. The Indian Ocean world became a cosmopolitan space, an archipelago of interacting ports and, to varying degrees, their hinterlands. Although trade and cultural exchange were linked processes, here we will treat them one at a time.

TRADE AND POWER

It is unlikely that the Kilwa coins were carried by a single ship to the Wessel Islands. Despite the occasional long-distance voyage, most trade around the Indian Ocean, as everywhere, was local. Traders, essentially seagoing peddlers, carried sacks of rice and bolts of cloth from one port to the next in small vessels. Local trade from port to port—cabotage—outstripped long-distance trade several times over by volume and value. But long-distance voyages were of outsized importance culturally and politically. They brought people into contact with strangers whose languages, religions, and customs were alien— sometimes provoking imitation and sometimes disgust. Long-distance trade brought exotic luxury goods that served rulers' need to flaunt their power and wealth. Kings also sometimes found imported religions and customs useful to underscore their right to rule. Long-distance voyages occasionally brought crops and pathogens to new places. Cabotage did none of these things, so although

larger in quantitative terms, it did less to affect the cultural and political history of the Indian Ocean shores—or world history.

Component circuits of the Indian Ocean world had grown up over millennia. As we've seen, trade had linked ancient Mesopotamia and the Indus valley societies as early as 2500 BCE. An ancient Greek author, Strabo, wrote that in his day (the early first century CE) some 120 ships annually sailed from a single Egyptian Red Sea port to India. Austronesians from Borneo had traveled the breadth of the Indian Ocean bringing their food crops and language to Madagascar before 400 CE. This remarkable feat (an accident, so far as we can tell) did not give rise to sustained interaction between Indonesia and Madagascar. But to some degree, at least, the Indian Ocean shores already formed a loosely connected world by the first centuries CE.

Sustained long-distance traffic from one end of the Indian Ocean world to the other waxed and waned with political conditions. It ramped up in the time of the Abbasid and early Tang Empires (ca. 600–750). Persian Gulf traders sailed to southern Chinese ports, a trip of at least six months each way. A round-trip normally took two years, including time waiting for favorable monsoon winds. The Arab geographer al-Maqdisi, writing in the 980s, described Aden and Basra—southwest Asian ports—as gateways to China.

In the tenth to the eleventh centuries, however, through traffic was already becoming rare, even while total trade climbed. The naval forces of the Chola and the Srivijaya kings insisted that ships dock at their ports and part with a share of their cargoes. In these circumstances, Indian Ocean traders came to specialize in shorter round-trips. Rather than wait weeks for the winds to change, one could schedule these shorter voyages to minimize port time—just sail for a few weeks and on arrival sell one's wares, and then head home.

The eventual decline of Chola and Srivijayan power encouraged through voyages once again after about 1250. One merchant from Aleppo (in Syria) made five sea trips from Yemen to China in the early fourteenth century. Marco Polo, probably in 1290, took ship in South China for Iran on a voyage with 600 fellow travelers, including a 17-year-old "extremely handsome and accomplished" Mongol (Yuan) princess named Kogatin. The point of the expedition was political: to give her in marriage to an elderly Mongol khan in Iran. They were held up for months in Sumatra, waiting for the monsoon to shift, and by the time they made it to Iran the khan had inconveniently died. So she, perhaps feeling relieved, was given to the dead man's son. In 1290 at least, the best-informed people in China judged a sea voyage safer and cheaper than a land one.

We don't have enough quantitative evidence to chart the ups and downs of the Indian Ocean trade reliably. But textual evidence and archeology suggest that it peaked three times: around the years 600–800, 1000–1150, and 1250–1350. In the first and last of these three periods, through voyages took place regularly. In the 1000–1150 upturn, they did not, owing to the power of the Chola and Srivijaya. The ups and downs reflected the demand for exotic goods around the Indian Ocean, which in turn reflected political developments. New states and ambitious rulers wanted exotic goods to bolster their claims to power.

The occasional downturns in Indian Ocean trade differed from the fraying of the Old World web in western Europe after 450 CE or in the Maya lowlands after 900 CE. Urban life and long-distance exchanges around the Indian Ocean survived these downturns, even if diminished in quantity, and the pace resumed after a century or two. In this respect, the Indian Ocean world's web connections were more resilient, based as they were on the vast populations and economies of China, India, and Egypt.

That resilience also reflected the enduring infrastructure of ports and ships and the knowledge behind them. Most ships in the Indian Ocean trade were built to carry a dozen or two sailors and a few tons of merchandise. The biggest known, a Gujarati ship used in the early sixteenth century to ferry pilgrims to Jiddah (the port nearest Mecca), weighed about 800 tons. This was roughly eight times the size of Columbus's biggest ship, the *Santa María*, but smaller than Chinese ships that sailed the Indian Ocean in the early fifteenth century. Both Marco Polo and Ibn Battuta wrote of ships that could carry more than 500 passengers. As noted above, these ships' hulls were built for Indian Ocean conditions. Everything else about Indian Ocean sailing, from the technical sophistication of rigging and sails to the navigational skills of sea captains, was highly developed and in wide circulation. Skills and technologies could survive a commercial downturn.

To some extent, the maritime traders competed with the caravan masters of the Silk Roads, and often at an advantage. Even a small vessel such as the dhow of the Arabian Sea could travel three times as fast as a camel caravan, carry 1,000 times as much as a single camel, and needed fewer men to manage it than did a caravan—camels are stubborn beasts. And camel transport was the most efficient land transport going.

There was risk to consider as well as cost. An Egyptian merchant hoping to sell goods in India or China had to guess whether pirates at sea or brigands on land posed the greater threat, using information that was weeks or months old. Marco Polo and his shipmates made similar calculations when escorting Kogatin to her wedding.

But sea and land routes were not always in competition. The arrival of exotic goods by one route could provoke envy and stimulate demand for more such goods coming via any route. When trade was brisk, both camels and ships were busy. Moreover, different routes presented different commercial opportunities. If you wanted to add cinnamon to your inventory, you would take a sea route and stop in Sri Lanka. If you thought you could do better dealing turquoise, you would take a land route and buy some in Central Asia.

Indian Ocean Trade This thirteenth-century painting of a voyage to a market city in Oman is a colorful representation of the Indian Ocean world's brisk maritime trade.

GOODS AND ROUTES

Archeology and the surviving texts tell us a lot about the goods traded in the Indian Ocean world. The prosperity of Roman Egypt gave rise to a flurry of exchange with India in luxury goods during the first century CE. Romans sent silver, Mediterranean wine, and Greek slave women to India in exchange for pearls and pepper. Roman authors such as Pliny complained that the empire was squandering its wealth so patrician women could wear pearls. By 200 CE this trade had fallen off, but other routes in the Indian Ocean soon carried increasing traffic, which reached a plateau after 600.

While changes took place in particulars of production and trade, some basic patterns held for the whole period from 600 to 1400. Only western India and southern China offered important manufactures to the marketplaces of the Indian Ocean world. People elsewhere contributed mainly raw materials. China's main exports were porcelain and silk, although al-Idrisi, a Moroccan-born scholar, reported in the 1150s that Chinese ships carried leather, iron, swords, and glassware to Indian Ocean ports.

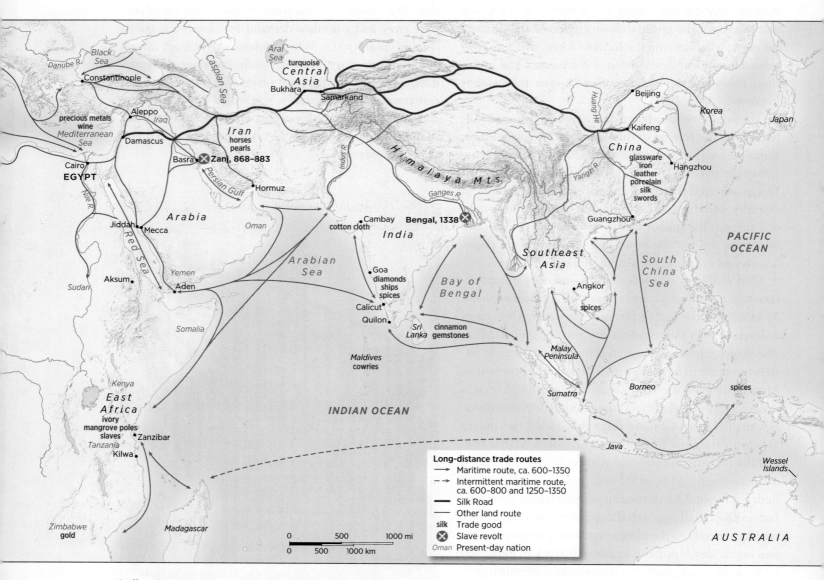

Indian Ocean Trade, ca. 600–1350 Sailing ships and camel caravans carried goods and people—and therefore ideas, artistic styles, pathogens, and much more—throughout the Old World web. Only luxury goods could justify the cost of transport over thousands of miles, and most trade was local. But the longer journeys were more important for world history because they did more to stimulate new ways of thinking, building, cooking, writing poetry, doing mathematics, weaving cloth, and so forth.

Porcelain from the Tang and Song dynasties has turned up all around Indian Ocean shores, including East Africa. Western India sold ships, made from its once-plentiful teak forests, and Gujaratis (in northwest India) marketed colorful cotton clothing, worn from Kilwa to Java. Thousands upon thousands of spinners and weavers turned Gujarati raw cotton into commercial gold. Gujarat was, in effect, the workshop of the Indian Ocean world.

Among raw materials traded around the Indian Ocean, **spices**—the taste that launched a thousand ships—took pride of place, as silk did on the Silk Roads. Most spices, like nutmeg, cloves, cinnamon, and a variety of peppers, came from Southeast Asia or southern India. They added welcome flavor to dull dishes. According to Marco Polo, for every shipment of spices that reached Europe, either 10 or 100 shipments went to China (he offers conflicting figures at different points in his book). Egypt, Arabia, and Iran also imported boatloads of spices. At times, merchant families in southern Arabia—Oman and Aden especially—held leading positions in the western Indian Ocean spice trade.

But the spice trade was not the half of it. India also sold precious stones, notably diamonds. Sri Lanka traded rubies, emeralds, sapphires, and more cinnamon than anywhere else. Iran sold pearls, gathered by specialist slave divers, and horses, which India always needed. According to Marco Polo, one Coromandel port purchased 5,000 horses annually from Iran, of which 4,700 would die within a year. And according to Ibn Battuta, horses in India cost 200 times as much as they did in Central Asia, inspiring a steady trade. The Mediterranean world, as in Roman times, contributed wine and precious metals, often in the form of coins. East Africa exported mangrove poles to Iraq (where wood was scarce), elephant ivory everywhere but to India above all, and iron and slaves to Egypt, Iraq, and India.

INDIAN OCEAN SLAVERY

The slave trade from East Africa is first mentioned in written sources in the seventh century, but it existed earlier. Most captives came from what are now Ethiopia, Sudan, and Somalia, but some were from Kenya and Tanzania. A few even hailed from Madagascar, where according to one book of sailors' tales (the *Kitab Ajab al-Hind*) Arab traders "never stopped swindling the natives, stealing their children, buying them from their fellows with . . . trinkets

and dates." One Chinese chronicle of the thirteenth century refers to "thousands and tens of thousands" of slaves sold on the East African coast, but it is impossible to know the true magnitude of the trade in this period.

Slaves performed all kinds of work. Among males, a few became slave soldiers. Some worked as pearl divers in the Persian Gulf, a dangerous job that exposed them to shark attacks. In the ninth century, the majority of slaves exported from East Africa toiled in southern Iraq, extending and maintaining irrigation systems, scraping salt crusts from abandoned farmland, and working on date and sugar plantations. Females, who at most times probably amounted to two-thirds of the slaves imported into Southwest Asia, worked mainly as domestic servants and concubines.

Plantation slavery on a large scale existed only in southern Iraq and only in the ninth century. It led to results no one wanted to see again. Working conditions on the date and sugar plantations, often carved out of swamps, were miserable. Africans encountered systematic prejudice, judging from the writings of al-Jihaz of Basra, a scholar born of an African mother. Several small slave rebellions broke out in the eighth and early ninth centuries, all crushed. A massive one, sometimes called the **Zanj revolt** for the word Arabs used to describe Africans,

East African Slave Trade This image from a thirteenth-century Yemeni manuscript shows a transaction in a slave market in which two Arab merchants negotiate a price for an African youth. From the seventh century to the early twentieth, the Arabian peninsula, like Egypt and Iraq, imported slaves from East Africa, roughly two-thirds of whom were female. Slave trades were a common feature of the Old World web.

shook the Abbasid caliphate during the years 868–883. It involved tens of thousands of slaves led by an Arab said to be "eloquent...a natural poet." The slaves managed to form their own army, control Basra and southern Iraq, kill hordes of their oppressors, sell thousands of captured Arab and Iranian women to slave merchants, carry the revolt into Arabia, and even mint coins—the privilege of a sovereign ruler—before their final military defeat.

As slave rebellions go, this ranks among the largest in world history, on the scale of Spartacus's uprising in Roman Italy but much longer-lasting. By some accounts more than a million people lost their lives in it, although no figures are trustworthy. The damage to southern Iraq, combined with the simultaneous massacres of Iranian and Arab merchants in South China's ports, severed the link between the Persian Gulf and China. Thereafter, the economic engine of the Islamic world shifted to Egypt. The revolt brought an end to large-scale plantation slavery in the Indian Ocean world until the nineteenth century.

The Delhi sultanate also imported African slaves into India, usually for military duty. Some managed to take over Bengal in 1338. Rich merchants in southern China during the Tang and Song also purchased slaves from East Africa. Some Arab and Chinese texts even suggest merchants came to East Africa all the way from Indonesia to buy slaves in the eighth century. A different and more localized slave trade existed in Southeast Asia in which captives were traded from one island to another, but almost never outside the region.

COMMERCIAL CULTURE

Trade around the Indian Ocean, whether for slaves, cotton, horses, or ceramics, usually used money rather than barter. Often, the currency involved took the form of cowrie shells, the preferred variety of which came from the Maldive Islands. Cowries made a good currency: they are durable, lightweight, and appealing to the eye. The Maldives traded millions of them for rice and other necessities. Silver money often came from Mediterranean lands via Egypt. Gold, after the tenth century at least, came above all from the Zimbabwe plateau in southern Africa, but also from West Africa via Egypt. Copper coins came from almost everywhere.

The merchants operating around the Indian Ocean hailed from certain places more than others. In the western region, Persians and later Arabs and Gujaratis were

Trade and Currency Currencies that facilitated the Indian Ocean trade included terra-cotta coins (above) and cowrie shells (below)—both these sets were found in present-day Thailand and date from the seventh through the thirteenth centuries.

prominent. In the eastern reaches, Malays, Tamils, and later, Bengalis, were notably active, as were Chinese. They typically worked within social networks of kinfolk, people from their home village or clan, or their co-religionists. Sometimes, as in the Chola kingdom, they organized formal merchant guilds. In the case of Indians, these networks involved people from the same caste—although normally not Brahmins, who had religious objections to travel across the sea. Successful traders had to know whom to trust; and the more people they could safely trust, the better their chances of making profits. So they had every reason to try to maintain their ties to kin and co-religionists, and to join every network that would admit them. For them, an ethnic identity as Persian or Arab or Tamil probably mattered less than other identities of kin, religion, or guild.

As a result of the need for trustworthy trading partners, much of the trade took place within commercial colonies. Faxian, the Chinese monk, noted Yemenis living in Sri Lanka in 414. By the seventh to the eighth centuries, the Malabar Coast in India hosted Jewish and Arab trading communities. Documents from a Cairo synagogue show Jewish traders operating in family networks in India after 950. Benjamin of Tudela, a Spanish rabbi of the twelfth century, found Jewish communities everywhere he traveled on his 12-year trek to India and back, and he claimed that 23,000 Jews lived in Sri Lanka (which he did not visit). Persians took up residence on the East African coast and throughout Indonesia—although we can probably discount Ibn al-Faqih's claim that even the parrots spoke Persian in Indonesia. Chinese traders settled in Sumatra, Java, and Indian ports, but almost never further west.

These merchant communities then served as brokers, helping their countrymen with languages, customs, loans, and legal complexities. Commercial agents were typically men. They often married local women, producing bilingual or multilingual children whose cross-cultural skills greased the wheels of commerce. One Persian author noted the "Chinese children" of India's Malabar Coast, for example. Traders riding the monsoon winds needed local agents to handle their business, because they had, in effect, a dated return ticket. Without local partners, they would grow desperate to sell their goods before the winds changed—and everyone knew it. In this way, the monsoon helped shape the social context and business procedures of Indian Ocean trade.

By and large, ports welcomed long-distance traders. Ports had to earn reputations as hospitable cities if they wanted merchants to return. In Calicut, in southwestern India, the ruler made foreign traders his guests for up to 90 days while they waited for favorable winds. His guards prevented looting from any merchant vessel, even shipwrecks. Other rulers took the trouble to enforce fair dealing in the marketplace or provide free warehouse space. Cheating or robbing foreign traders, however tempting, yielded only short-term rewards. The same was true of high taxes on trade, which would propel sea captains elsewhere.

The table on this page gives an idea of the population in 1400 of some of the seaports and riverports involved in commerce around the Indian Ocean. Cairo and Chinese ports outstripped the rest.

Ports competing with one another to welcome traffic sometimes had to restrain their overlords' rapacious instincts. In 912, for example, a Jewish trader returned home to Oman after 30 years away, bringing a rich cargo of Chinese goods. At first the caliph, in faraway Baghdad, ordered the cargo confiscated and the trader arrested. This promised a nice windfall for the caliph's treasury. But Omani merchants and the local governor protested vigorously, pointing out the costs to Oman of such heavy-handed seizure. They argued that continued trade promised more revenue in the long run. Ultimately, the caliph reversed himself. But not all rulers could be equally far-sighted: many exceptions to the rule of port city hospitality occurred where political authority was weak or rebellions were under way—as in the massacres of Muslims in South China in the late ninth century.

Port cities also catered to sailors' interest in women. Like port cities everywhere, those around the Indian Ocean hosted brothels, usually illegal. Most Muslim

ESTIMATED POPULATION OF INDIAN OCEAN WORLD PORT CITIES, 1400 CE	
CITY (BY REGION)	**POPULATION**
NORTH AND EAST AFRICA	
Kilwa	30,000
Aksum	30,000
Cairo	360,000
SOUTHWEST ASIA	
Mecca	35,000
Basra	60,000
Hormuz	50,000
INDIA	
Cambay	60,000
Goa	40,000
Calicut	50,000
Quilon	60,000
SOUTHEAST ASIA AND CHINA	
Angkor	40,000
Guangzhou	150,000
Hangzhou	240,000

Source: Tertius Chandler, *Four Thousand Years of Urban Growth* (1987), 266, 269, 286, 313–14, 317, 321, 358–59, 369, 387–88, 406, 418, 425–26.

communities allowed the practice of short-term marriages that visiting merchants might enjoy for a few weeks or a few years. Port traders also sold slave girls to merchants embarking on sea voyages. (Ibn Battuta repeatedly took advantage of both of these traditions.) The Islamic legal custom that a man might have up to four wives at a time suited sailors nicely. Some no doubt exceeded the quota. In the collection of stories called *Sinbad the Sailor*, set in the eighth century, the hero has no trouble finding a new wife whenever he wants one on the shores of the Indian Ocean.

Surviving texts imply an unusually peaceful world of commerce in the Indian Ocean, with refreshingly little in the way of massacres of minorities, sacking of cities, and naval warfare. Rulers had to enforce law and security, and treat traders well if they wanted to enjoy the rewards that commerce afforded them—wealth and power they needed to fight neighboring kings and overawe subjects when necessary. In effect, peace and prosperity at sea enabled kings to invest more heavily in war and destruction on land.

Merchant Solidarity in the Indian Ocean World

The Abbasid caliphate in the tenth century CE included Oman on the southeast coast of Arabia. The caliphs appointed a governor there to collect taxes and customs dues from merchants. Most of Oman's merchants remained in the western part of the Indian Ocean world. However, a few of them attempted the treacherous two-year journey to China, including a Jewish merchant named Ishaq. Buzurg ibn Shahriyār recorded the story of Ishaq's return to Oman in *Kitab Ajab al-Hind (The Book of the Marvels of India)*, a collection of true and fanciful sailors' stories about the Indian Ocean that he completed around 953 CE.

Ishaq, son of the Jew . . . came back to Oman . . . from China. . . . In order to avoid the customs and the payment of the tithe, he came to an arrangement with the Governor of Oman . . . which involved a sum of more than a million *dirhems*. . . . Such a prodigious fortune made a noise about the country, and roused the envious. A mischievous person . . . went to Bag[h]dad and [told the Caliph that the Governor] had levied a toll on him of [only] five hundred thousand *dinars* worth of merchandise. . . . The Caliph [sent his eunuch to arrest the] Jew. . . .

[The Governor of Oman] commanded that the Jew was to be seized, meanwhile secretly warning the merchants of it. . . . [T]hereupon, the markets closed. Papers of protest were signed by the people of the town and by strangers, declaring that, after the Jew had been arrested, ships would no longer put in at Oman, the merchants would leave, and that they would advise others by no means to land on the coast of [Abbasid] Iraq, where a man's property was not safe. . . . The merchants made an uproar in the city. . . . [They] brought their ships to the quay-side [the port] and put on board their goods, with the purpose of removing them, and [they exclaimed]: "We shall be deprived of all means of livelihood, when ships put in here no more; Oman is a place, whose citizens get everything from the sea. Sultans are like fires, which eat up all they touch. We can't resist them, and our best plan is to take ourselves out of their way." The eunuch and his men squeezed [just] two thousand *dinars* from the Jew, and then retired [back to Baghdad].

Source: Buzurg ibn Shahriyār, trans. L. Marcel Devic and Peter Courtney Quennell, *The Book of the Marvels of India* (London, 1928).

QUESTIONS FOR ANALYSIS

1. Why did the merchants of Oman think Ishaq's arrest would threaten their livelihood?
2. What specific actions did the merchants take to protest the arrest of a fellow merchant?
3. Why did the governor of Oman, an appointee of the caliph, secretly inform the merchants of the order to arrest Ishaq?

PIRACY AND PIRATES

Of course, life at sea was not always peaceful. The flourishing trade of the Indian Ocean world invited piracy. It was essentially another business practice, normally pursued by full-time specialists but sometimes by part-timers who found cabotage or fishing insufficiently rewarding. Few states had much in the way of naval power to suppress pirates. And the predictability of merchants' sailing routes, thanks to the winds and the geography of the Indian Ocean, made piracy tempting to those with ships, weapons, and fearless seafaring men at their disposal.

Merchant ships, therefore, had to be prepared to defend themselves. The Roman author Pliny noted that ships on the Red Sea in the first century CE carried archers to fend off pirates. The Chinese monk Faxian, while en route from Sri Lanka to Java in 413 CE, feared pirates in the Bay of Bengal (his ship encountered violent storms but no pirates). Eight centuries later, Marco Polo described how pirates plied their trade off southwestern India's Malabar Coast. They placed their ships in a line, reaching many miles out to sea, and used fires and smoke signals to alert their fellows when they spied a merchant vessel. Polo, like Pliny, noted that merchants had to arm their ships to fend off pirates, as did our friend Ibn Battuta.

Marco Polo also explained the cozy deals occasionally made between pirate chiefs and landlubber princes. In one case on the Malabar Coast, the local prince gave pirates free rein provided they gave him all the horses they captured. Since this deal ensured that no traders would

Piracy An image from a fifteenth-century manuscript shows pirates attacking a merchant ship in the Indian Ocean. The pirates board the ship and kill its crew, throwing their bodies into the sea below.

voluntarily visit the prince's domain, it shows how precious horses were in southern India.

Pirates lurked at the choke points, where merchants had to go: the Straits of Malacca, where as we have seen local traders functioned as pirates when it suited them; the seas around southern India; and the entrances to the Persian Gulf and the Red Sea. Ibn Battuta ran afoul of pirates several times on his Indian Ocean voyages. Only storms outranked pirates among the worries of seagoing merchants. Other thriving commercial seas, such as the Mediterranean or the South China Sea, also had active pirate populations.

RELIGION AND POWER IN THE INDIAN OCEAN WORLD

Overseas traders always brought more than merchandise with them. They and other travelers brought ideas and beliefs, some of which they communicated to people in the lands they visited. The chief exports in this category were Hinduism, Buddhism, and Islam, and the languages and culture that went with them.

The monsoon and its sailing routines helped to encourage a cosmopolitan culture around the Indian Ocean. Few voyages allowed quick turnarounds. In most cases, crews spent weeks or months waiting for the winds to change, which obliged them to interact with local people. They learned languages, made friends, sought romance, married, told stories, played chess (which originated in India around 500 CE), and talked about the weather, politics, or religion. Arab or Persian sailors going to the East African coast, for example, rode the monsoon winds south in December or January, but they had to wait until April to go home again. Many of them did it year after year.

THE SPREAD OF INDIAN RELIGIONS IN SOUTHEAST ASIA

India, the center of the Indian Ocean world demographically and geographically, was a primary exporter of culture and religions. Its cultural exports went east more than west. As we've seen, Buddhism was India's main cultural gift to China. Buddhism, together with Indian ideas of kingship, astronomy, and medicine, also took root in Central Asia and Tibet.

Neither Buddhism nor Hinduism, however, had much impact along the western shores of the Indian Ocean. Neither religion fit well with political circumstances in Southwest Asia, where rulers already had longstanding partnerships with religious authorities dating back to ancient Mesopotamia and pharaonic Egypt. At no time were either rulers or populations there eager for imported religions. In East Africa, the failure of Buddhism and Hinduism to take root was probably more a matter of timing. In the early centuries before 1000 CE, contact between India and the African coast remained sporadic. By the time that contact had grown into more sustained exchanges, sultanates had formed with Islam as the religion of rulers and traders. Religion and power were already in firm alliance.

Southeast Asia, however, proved a fertile field for Buddhism and Hinduism both. Seaborne contacts with India existed from the first century CE at the latest. Evidence of Indian cultural influences date from the fourth century. The intensity of interactions with India grew large enough, early enough, that Buddhism and Hinduism

Borobudur Borobudur is an Indonesian Buddhist temple built in the ninth century. Its distinctive, dome-shaped stupas show the influence of Indian architecture and religion in Southeast Asia during this period.

both had become entrenched before Islam reached the region—the opposite of the sequence in East Africa. The political condition of Southeast Asia in the first few centuries CE made it more receptive to novel religions. States and kingship were new concepts, and ambitious rulers needed ideologies and rituals that would help undergird their power. Therefore, Indian examples (and in Vietnam, Chinese ones) served as useful models to be borrowed and adjusted to local conditions.

The young kingdoms of Southeast Asia, forming where river valleys and irrigation allowed surplus rice production, lapped up Indian culture. Rulers enhanced their power by controlling the distribution of Indian cloth, and they bolstered their prestige by adopting Indian religions, court rituals, architecture, art, and dance styles. Indian-style monumental architecture was especially useful in this regard. Rulers relished Sanskrit texts that justified kingship, and they supported Indian scholars who copied, interpreted, and taught such texts. Sanskrit's alphabet became the basis for several Southeast Asian scripts such as those used for Thai and Cambodian.

In some respects, the spread of Indian culture to the courts of Southeast Asia was merely an overseas extension of the prior spread of the Vedic culture of northern India to southern India. The remarkable spread of Indian influence to Southeast Asia peaked from the eighth to the thirteenth centuries.

As always, those doing the adopting made a few changes to suit themselves. Southeast Asian kings such as the Khmer (based at Angkor Wat in today's Cambodia) claimed divinity for themselves, something that kings in India almost never tried. In India, Hindu Brahmins and Buddhist scholars had firm ideas about distinctions between gods and kings. The best a king could do was claim to be the most devoted follower of Buddha, Vishnu, or Shiva. In Southeast Asia, Brahmins were few and kings supported and selected the religious scholars, making it easier to blur the distinctions and promote kings to divine status.

The partial Indianization of Southeast Asian states was based on contact and emulation rather than conquest and settlement. This process stands in sharp contrast to the Hellenization of Southwest Asia that followed Alexander's phalanxes, or the spread of Chinese language and culture that came with the military expansion of the Qin, Han, and Tang dynasties. Even Vedic culture within India itself had often spread by war, conquest, and the colonization of hill and forest districts. Aside from the brief Chola expedition of 1025, no Indian state projected its power into Southeast Asia. No large-scale settlement took place, although a few traders and scholars did take up residence in Southeast Asian towns and courts. Instead, Southeast Asians, their rulers above all, wanted culture fit for newly centralized and hierarchical societies—and, except in Vietnam, Indian models were the ones at hand. Scholars, missionaries, and traders, as much as soldiers and kings, could extend and tighten the world's webs—especially when riding reliable monsoon winds.

TRADE AND ISLAM ON THE SWAHILI COAST

Another momentous cultural shift promoted by Indian Ocean trade and travel webs was the Islamization of coastal East Africa. In the centuries before 1400, a distinctive cosmopolitan culture developed along the East African coast, tightly linked to the Indian Ocean trade, if also connected to the East African interior. *Swahili* in Arabic means "people of the shore," so scholars use the term **Swahili coast**, at least for periods after 1000 CE.

Traders from the Red Sea shores had sailed the waters of the Swahili coast since at least the first century CE. The *Periplus* noted that sailors were familiar with this region, learned its languages, and married local women. Mariners had learned how far south they could go without being marooned for months waiting for the monsoon to change. The southern limit for a quick round-trip voyage was Zanzibar, or at most Kilwa. More northerly ports such as Mombasa, Malindi, or Lamu were more convenient for sailors, but their sparse hinterlands made them less attractive to merchants. By and large, the long-distance voyages from East Africa to Arabia, the Persian Gulf, and India were undertaken by traders from those latter lands, while the port-to-port cabotage on the Swahili coast was handled by East Africans. The scale of trade before the seventh century remained modest, but archeologists have found pre-Islamic ceramics from Arabia and Iran as far south as northern Mozambique.

The scale of commerce along the Swahili coast expanded in the ninth century, especially in slaves and ivory. The Abbasid caliphate's intensive agricultural development of southern Iraq relied on slave labor, leading to the slave trade described above. By the tenth century, rising prosperity in Fatimid Egypt, southern India, Song China, and elsewhere spurred demand for African ivory statuettes and jewelry. African elephant tusks are both bigger and easier to carve than those of Asian elephants, and so commanded higher prices. In India, brides from respectable families needed ivory bangles for their wedding ceremonies, ensuring a steady export market for East African ivory.

By the eleventh century, gold came to rival ivory as a magnet for foreign traders. Gold, gathered from streambeds, came only from the hilly country south of the Zambezi River. Local traders brought it to the coast at Sofala, in today's Mozambique. That was too far south for Arab and Persian Gulf sailors. So Kilwa and Zanzibar grew up as seaports connecting the long-distance trade with a cabotage trade between Sofala and Kilwa. The volume and value of the Swahili trade continued to grow during the twelfth through the fifteenth centuries, fed by the flow of African gold.

Arab and Persian men settled in the trading towns from Somalia south to Kilwa. They married local women and learned local Bantu languages, and local Africans learned theirs. The interplay of African languages and Arabic, and to a lesser extent Persian, over centuries produced a new tongue, Swahili, originally mainly a trading language. It gradually became the native tongue for almost all who lived along the coast, and (since about 1800) the second language of many inland Africans as well. Swahili, a living artifact of the Indian Ocean's web,

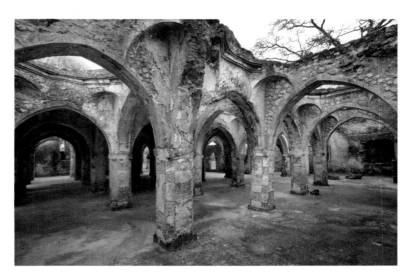

Islam on the Swahili Coast Built from coral, the Kilwa mosque was completed by the end of the thirteenth century. It represents the mounting influence of Arab and Persian merchants and the growing popularity of Islam among the Africans on the Swahili coast.

was written in the Arabic alphabet until the twentieth century.

Arab and Persian traders who settled along the Swahili coast also encouraged the practice of Islam. Many Swahili rulers wanted to burnish their Islamic credentials to help legitimate their rule—just as Southeast Asian monarchs found Hinduism or Buddhism politically useful. Swahili rulers always claimed descent from Arabia and Persia, sometimes from the Prophet himself. They supported religious scholars and architects who brought skills still rare along the Swahili coast. The earliest mosques in East Africa date from the eighth century, but big ones were built only after 1200. The main mosque at Kilwa, built of coral, dates to 1300 or so.

Conversion to Islam on the Swahili coast peaked between 1050 and 1250. When the Arab traveler and geographer al-Masudi visited in the early tenth century, he thought the local Africans "have no religious law . . . every man worships what he pleases, be it a plant, an animal, or a mineral." By the time Ibn Battuta turned up in the 1330s, all the rulers and elites along the Swahili coast were Muslims. Their Islam incorporated prior religious practices of the coast, such as veneration of local ancestors and use of the local agricultural calendar, which survived side-by-side with the Muslim one. The process of religious conversion here, as in most cases, was a melding of old and new.

The Swahili Coast, ca. 1000–1400
Between 1000 and 1400 the trading cities of the Swahili coast became more enmeshed in the Indian Ocean's commercial circuits. Swahili merchants funneled ivory, mangrove poles, slaves, animal skins and other trade items to markets in India and Southwest Asia, often dealing with Arab and Persian merchants. Among the results of these commercial connections was the consolidation of Islam as the majority religion on the Swahili coast.

Along the Swahili coast, as elsewhere throughout the Indian Ocean, trade promoted Islam and Islam promoted trade. At the heart of the equation were trust and law. Where commerce involved different languages and cultures, the umbrella of Islamic law permitted a degree of trust that fostered long-distance trade.

Of course, Africans on the Swahili coast accepted Islam for many reasons, not merely for commercial advantage. Rulers—usually big traders themselves—had other calculated reasons to become Muslim. But they, like many others, sometimes found the doctrines of Islam more satisfying than the religious practices of their ancestors. Religious conversion here, as everywhere, proceeded from a handful of motives and inspirations.

As in India, the filtration of Islam into East African society had geographical limits. No evidence exists for mosques or Islam except along the coast until well after 1400. The African traders who supplied ivory, slaves, mangrove poles, and iron to Swahili cities were local operators, active in cabotage and in the immediate hinterlands of the cities. The ocean-going merchants from the Red Sea, Persian Gulf, or Gujarat—the vehicles of Islamization—left the hinterland alone. The residents of the coastal cities treated the interior as a source of goods and slaves, but otherwise unworthy of their attention.

The spread of Islam and Swahili culture also reached Madagascar—but just barely. The Malagasy language contains many Bantu and a few Arabic words grafted onto its Austronesian base. Archeology reveals beads and pottery from Arab lands. These items were probably brought mainly by Swahili merchants. Madagascar was too far south for Arab and Persian Gulf traders unless they wanted to invest two years in their voyage. The few texts that say anything at all about the linkages between Madagascar and the Swahili coast refer to Malagasy slave

raiding on the mainland and enclaves of Swahili traders in northernmost Madagascar. Madagascar, like Borneo in Southeast Asia, was at the southernmost fringe of the Indian Ocean web.

The extension of Islam into East Africa, like that of Hinduism into Southeast Asia, narrowed the scope somewhat for local religions. Like the contemporaneous spread of Christianity into Europe or Buddhism into Central Asia, these amount to expansions of the world's great religions at the expense of smaller, more local ones. The networks of trade and power around the Indian Ocean promoted a form of cultural homogenization, reducing slightly the region's—and the world's—cultural diversity.

GREAT ZIMBABWE AND SOUTHEASTERN AFRICA

After 800, another thread of the Indian Ocean web reached into the interior of Africa, to the goldfields of the Zimbabwe plateau. Iron tools and farming had spread to southern Africa by 400 CE, but population remained sparse and social hierarchy simple. By the period 500–600, more and more people were taking up cattle raising, well suited to the region's semi-arid grasslands. With cattle as a form of storable food, like cereals elsewhere, the first signs of social hierarchies beyond those of age and gender appeared. In southern Africa, where farming brought inconsistent rewards due to unreliable rains, cattle assumed great importance in economic and political life. People with cattle could exert power over people without by providing or withholding meat in times of need. Cattle keeping led not only to greater status hierarchy, but also to the first efforts at state building. These efforts brought modest results: aspiring rulers could control only a few hundred people because there was too much empty space into which unhappy subjects might wander off.

The slow build-up of population over the centuries made it harder to wander off to empty land and easier for ambitious men to extend their authority over larger numbers. (Remember that in most of Africa, political power consisted of control over people more than over territory.) Continued growth in the cattle population meant more opportunity to amass power and wealth, more reason to struggle over access to good pastureland, more conflict, and a more male-dominated social order.

Ingenious historical linguists have inferred the emergence after about 800 CE of an expanded vocabulary for things having to do with cattle, such as 6 new terms for various shapes of cattle horns, and at least 17 new words for colors of cattle hide. Clearly, people were taking a deep interest in cattle.

Meanwhile, traders had extended the Indian Ocean web to the coasts of Mozambique and, weakly, up the river valleys of the Limpopo and Zambezi. The first signs of these trade links appeared about the period 700–800. Gold production began about this time too. In 916, al-Masudi, wrote—rather imaginatively—of "meadows of gold" in the Zambezi basin. The Zimbabwe plateau also developed iron mines and, like most parts of Africa, an ivory trade. Slowly but surely the economy and population grew, and with growth came better opportunities to amass political power.

The first sizeable state in southern Africa, called Mapungubwe, arose about 1175. Its rulers derived their authority from cattle keeping. But it also produced gold for export and imported beads made in India and Egypt. Mapungubwe did not last long, but the links to the wider world did.

A new power center arose about 1250 in a reasonably well-watered area good for cattle and better for controlling gold exports. **Great Zimbabwe** (*Zimbabwe* means "stone houses" in the Shona language) was based on cattle wealth, but with an international twist. Leaders who owned large herds let poor people eat if they gathered gold dust. Great Zimbabwe's ruling lineages traded that gold down to the coast for prestige items, including beads, cowries, and ceramics from as far away as China. They must have exercised unusual authority because starting about 1275 they erected stone buildings larger than anything else in sub-Saharan Africa for many centuries to come. The two biggest of these granite structures stand about 33 feet (10 m) tall, and their walls are up to 16 feet (5 m) thick. Someone put over a million flat stones into position

to build them. About 300 smaller stone buildings are scattered around the nearby plateau.

At its peak from 1300 to 1350, as many as 18,000 people lived in one cluster at Great Zimbabwe. (Kilwa at the time had perhaps 30,000 inhabitants, and the world's biggest cities roughly 400,000 or 500,000.) The gold trade reached as much as 1 ton (907 kg) per year, partly in gold dust collected from streambeds but, as the pickings grew sparser, increasingly from mines. Some mineshafts went down 100 feet (30 m), which testifies to considerable technical skill as well as determination. Skeletons indicate that women and children did much of the dangerous underground work.

These were happy times for the ruling lineages. Soapstone statues of birds suggest they exercised some form of spiritual power. Judging by the chemistry of bones left behind, the elite at Great Zimbabwe feasted on prime beef. Everyone else was lucky to get mutton or stringy beef.

Early States of Southern Africa, ca. 1175–1450 Cattle keeping and gold production distinguished the first states to arise in southern Africa. Great Zimbabwe in particular took part in the commercial exchanges of the Indian Ocean world, supplying a goodly portion of the gold in circulation there. These polities formed the southernmost frontier of the Indian Ocean world.

Great Zimbabwe Massive stone walls—up to 16 feet (5 m) thick—remain on a hillside at Great Zimbabwe, probably built during the city's heyday between 1275 and 1350. Artifacts found at the Great Zimbabwe site include this wooden sculpture of a human form from the same period.

Climate change deepened the plight of the poor and confirmed the power of the rulers. Cooler and dryer climate after 1290 or so made agriculture less rewarding. It aided cattle keepers because it reduced the domain of the tsetse fly, which carried a cattle-killing disease. Poor farmers grew more dependent on the cattle kings. When the rains failed altogether—perhaps one out of every four or five years—they had to come up with gold, iron, or ivory to swap for a cow if they were to eat.

By 1450, the stone buildings at Great Zimbabwe were abandoned. No one knows why. Trade routes seem to have shifted to the north. New gold strikes closer to the Zambezi drew people away. Better rains might have made it possible for poor people to scratch out a living as farmers at a safe remove from the cattle kings. Some evidence suggests that 150 years of comparatively dense population and intensive land use led to rapid soil erosion and, eventually, poor pasturage for cattle. Shona oral tradition has it that Great Zimbabwe was abandoned when people there ran out of salt, essential to the human diet. Whatever the truth of the matter, although Great Zimbabwe vanished as a center of power and population, the principle of complex, hierarchical society dominated by men who hoarded cattle lived on. And so did the gold trade. In 1497, when the first European to visit the shores of Mozambique sailed to the mouth of the Zambezi, he found Arab dhows loading up on gold dust.

CONCLUSION

Everywhere around the Indian Ocean from 200 to 1400 CE, the broad trend was much the same. Ports grew bigger, richer, more numerous, more active, more commercially sophisticated, and more culturally cosmopolitan. They served as the crossroads of cultural exchange, where people rubbed shoulders and swapped goods, ideas, and infections with strangers from other lands. At times, patches of this Indian Ocean web might fray for a century or two, overall volumes of trade and exchange might decline, but urban life and long-distance linkages never vanished.

India stood at the center of this watery web. Its religious and political landscapes evolved partly in response to challenges and opportunities emanating from around the Indian Ocean, but from Central Asia and its horsemen too.

New centers of political power emerged where none had existed before, especially in Southeast Asia and southern Africa. Rice and cattle, respectively, helped make this happen, serving as the storable surplus that enabled the haves to control the have-nots more efficiently than before. So did trade. Whatever their attitudes toward money-driven merchants, rulers everywhere could see that the extension of markets and long-distance trade offered them a chance to fill their treasuries, display exotic prestige goods, and build their power.

Long-distance seaborne trade transformed the Indian Ocean world culturally as well as economically. Buddhism and Hinduism colonized Southeast Asian kingdoms, and Islam spread to the Swahili coast and parts of India. Local religions continued to give way to the world's dominant religions, although Hinduism, Buddhism, and Islam (like Christianity) continued to fragment and evolve as they had done since their beginnings. This process of religious change reduced the world's cultural diversity somewhat and made it a bit easier for traders and travelers to interact peaceably with one another.

These religious changes were part and parcel of the formation of cosmopolitan cultures around the Indian Ocean shore, especially in the bigger port cities. People in Mombasa and Cambay, 3,000 miles apart, had more in common by 1400 than did Mombasans and the people living three days' walk into the interior of Africa. Now connected to island Southeast Asia and to East Africa, the Old World web had become bigger and tighter than ever before.

CHAPTER REVIEW

KEY TERMS

dhow (p. 361)
cabotage (p. 362)
choke point (p. 362)
Bhakti movement (p. 364)
Islamization (p. 365)

Nalanda (p. 366)
Gupta dynasty (p. 366)
Chola kingdom (p. 368)
merchant trading guilds (p. 368)
Delhi sultanate (p. 370)

slave soldiers (p. 370)
spices (p. 377)
Zanj revolt (p. 377)
Swahili coast (p. 382)
Great Zimbabwe (p. 385)

Go to INQUIZITIVE to see what you've learned—and learn what you've missed—with personalized feedback along the way.

REVIEW QUESTIONS

1. What constituted the Indian Ocean world, and what was the key reason it became a coherent region around 100 CE?

2. How did sailing in the Indian Ocean differ from sailing in the Atlantic and the Pacific?

3. In what ways did the rise of the Bhakti movement affect Indian religion?

4. What were the economic bases of the Gupta dynasty, the Chola kingdom, and the Delhi sultanate?

5. What was the largest impact of Delhi sultanate rule?

6. Compare and contrast the volume, value, frequency, and wares of long-distance trade versus cabotage.

7. What were the major contributing factors to the three peaks of sustained, long-distance trade in the Indian Ocean world between 600 and 1350?

8. Why were networks of kinfolk and hospitable port cities important for Indian Ocean traders?

9. What were the main reasons that some areas in Southeast Asia adopted Indian religions and the Swahili coast adopted Islam?

10. Why and how did cattle assume importance in economic and political life in southern Africa at this time?

11. How did Great Zimbabwe's gold trade function?

12. What were the broad trends around the Indian Ocean world from 200 to 1400?

FURTHER READING

Catherine ASHER and Cynthia TALBOT, *India before Europe* (2006). Good on the twelfth through the eighteenth centuries, and attentive to cross-cultural interaction.

Satish CHANDRA, *History of Medieval India* (2007). The first ten chapters deal with the years 800–1400 CE in detail.

K. N. CHAUDHURI, *Trade and Civilisation in the Indian Ocean: An Economic History from the Rise of Islam to 1750* (1985). A classic that did much to define the Indian Ocean as a unit of study and that is still useful on commerce.

Innocent PIKIRAYI, *The Zimbabwe Culture: Origins and Decline in Southern Zambezian States* (2001). A careful study of Great Zimbabwe and its contexts.

Patricia RISSO, *Merchants and Faith: Muslim Commerce and Culture in the Indian Ocean* (1995). A compact introduction to a complex subject.

Abdul SHERIFF, *Dhow Cultures of the Indian Ocean: Cosmopolitanism, Commerce and Islam* (2010). An excellent, thorough treatment of the western Indian Ocean.

CHRONOLOGY

ca. 300
Berber-speaking people in and around the Sahara acquire camels

ca. 700–1050
Ancient Ghana flourishes

ca. 700–900
Khazaria flourishes

by ca. 700
Berbers regularly cross the Sahara

ca. 750–843
Rise and division of Carolingian rule

750–1258
Rise and fragmentation of Abbasid caliphate
Fatimids, Almoravids, and Almohads conquer land in North Africa, Spain, and Egypt

ca. 800–1050
Height of Viking pillaging, conquering, and expansion

ca. 800–1100
Agricultural revolution in northern Europe

890–900
Magyars cross into grasslands of modern-day Hungary

ca. 900–1170

929–1031
Rise and fall of the Córdoba caliphate

ca. 980–1090
Formation and dissolution of Seljuk Turk Empire

1096–1231
Waves of Crusades

1204–1261
Crusaders rule Constantinople

ca. 1200–1500
Height of the spread of Sufism

1219–1260
Mongol western campaigns

ca. 1240–1450
Mali kingdom emerges and falls

1260–1350
Pax Mongolica

ca. 1250
Start of Little Ice Age

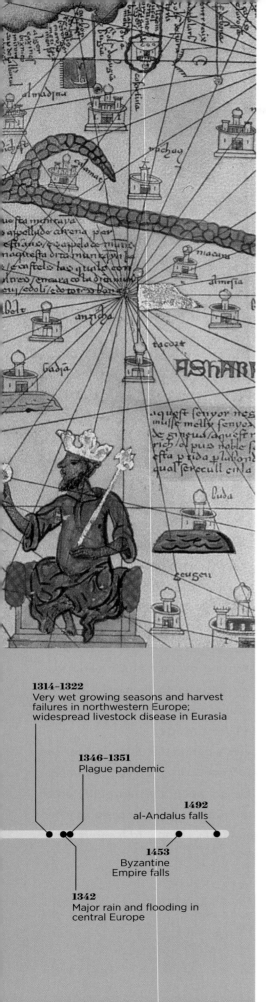

1314–1322
Very wet growing seasons and harvest failures in northwestern Europe; widespread livestock disease in Eurasia

1346–1351
Plague pandemic

1492
al-Andalus falls

1453
Byzantine Empire falls

1342
Major rain and flooding in central Europe

14

The West End of Eurasia and West Africa

800 to 1400

Around 960, Hasdai ibn Shaprut, a Jewish physician, foreign minister, and adviser to a Muslim emir of Córdoba, in southern Spain, wrote a letter. Curious about a Jewish kingdom he had heard about in what is now southern Russia, he wrote to the king in question. Several merchants conveyed the letter to a *kagan*, or king, named Joseph, who wrote back explaining that indeed there was a Jewish kingdom—**Khazaria**, as it is now known.

Khazaria arose in the 640s in the grasslands between the Volga and the Dniepr Rivers. It reached its height in the eighth and ninth centuries and lasted until about 970. Mainly Turkic-speaking, the Khazars were farmers, herders, smiths, and traders. Their merchants made connections along the Silk Roads to China and Byzantium, and along water routes such as the Caspian Sea and Russian rivers north to the Baltic Sea and south to Mesopotamia. Archeological digs in the region have turned up belt buckles with Chinese dragons and amber beads from Sweden. The Khazars had a formidable cavalry and fought

A Fourteenth-Century Worldview The Catalan Atlas (1375) mapped what its Spanish-Jewish illustrator understood as the known world, stretching from the Iberian Peninsula all the way to East Asia. This detail shows southern Spain and northwestern Africa, with numerous ports labeled and illustrations indicating the kingdoms of the Sahel. The Malian ruler Mansa Musa holds up a nugget of gold at lower right.

389

FOCUS QUESTIONS

1. In what major ways did material conditions improve in western Eurasia roughly from 800 to 1300?

2. Why were the great empires that dominated the region for a time so fragile?

3. Why were the settled societies of western Eurasia subject to invasion during this period?

4. For what reasons did this period of turmoil also experience economic and cultural growth?

5. Why was the fourteenth century such a calamity in western Eurasia?

wars with Byzantine emperors and Arab caliphs. Many Khazars were Muslims, some Christians, some sky-worshipping shamans—and a growing number of them were Jews, often refugees from persecution in Byzantine towns. By most accounts, the leadership of the Khazars embraced Judaism in the ninth century; thus Joseph described his multireligious kingdom as Jewish when writing to Hasdai ibn Shaprut in Spain.

In the same centuries, Spain too contained a swirling multicultural mix of Muslims, Christians, and Jews. At times they were ruled by one Muslim polity, the emirate (after 929, the caliphate) of Córdoba, but at others they were divided into several emirates and kingdoms, none of them led by Jews. Those ruled by Muslims made up the region known as **al-Andalus**. Thus by 750 the western region of the Old World web contained societies, such as al-Andalus and Khazaria, in which Muslims, Christians, and Jews lived and worked together.

Like Chapter 11, this chapter treats the western region of the Old World web, from Iran and Russia all the way to the Atlantic shores of Europe and West Africa. Many places were Christian at some times and

Muslim at others, such as Anatolia, Sicily, and Spain. Most Islamic lands were home to many Christians and Jews, and some Christian-ruled lands had Muslim minorities. So any distinction between Muslim and Christian lands is fuzzy.

It is conventional to divide Christendom and Islamdom on the grounds that their dominant religions make them distinct. However, there are better reasons to see them together within the western region of the Old World web, especially during this period. Each experienced an agricultural revolution that improved the food supply and helped spur population growth. Both enjoyed a cultural flowering, which in fact depended on contacts between Muslims and Christians. Both were terrorized by invaders. And both simultaneously suffered the worst epidemic in human history.

Five main themes run through this chapter. First is the heightened instability of population and ecology, as the west end of the Old World web underwent demographic growth until the fourteenth century and then catastrophe. Second is the political fragmentation that overcame giant empires such as those of Charlemagne and the Abbasids. Third is the mobilization of conquerors and migrants who helped undermine the giant empires, people such as the Vikings, Turks, and Mongols. Fourth is the economic quickening and cultural flowering of the ninth to early thirteenth centuries. And fifth, tying them all together, is the further expansion of the Old World web into northern Europe and West Africa.

The chapter covers a period that historians, drawing on European tradition, conventionally call medieval. Because specialists apply the term differently in various regions of Eurasia (and occasionally for Africa), I will use the term sparingly to mean roughly the period 500–1400.

POPULATION, ECOLOGY, AND AGRICULTURE

From 800 to the early fourteenth century, on average, the human condition improved in the western region of the Old World web. There were exceptions, of course, in some places and at certain times. But until 1315 the trend was broadly favorable.

POPULATION GROWTH

One strong indication of improving conditions was that more people survived longer and reproduced. In the region as a whole, population almost doubled between 800 and 1300, from about 60 million to roughly 120 million. By far the fastest growth took place in regions of western, central, and northeastern Europe, places that had hitherto been thinly populated. The table below shows the regional variation in estimated population size in selected places. The main reason that population climbed between 800 and 1300 was improvements in agriculture.

AGRICULTURAL REVOLUTIONS

Until recently, farmers usually did the same things year in, year out. But the late medieval centuries included some exceptions, times and places where many farmers experimented with new crops and technologies. After 800, the Old World web spawned three agricultural revolutions: one in China, a second in the Mediterranean and Mesopotamia, and a third one in northern Europe. In Chapter 12, we saw how Chinese farmers doubled their yields by planting champa rice from the eleventh century onward. In both the second and third cases, as this chapter will show, farmers figured out how to grow more crops on old fields and bring new lands under the plow.

MEDITERRANEAN AND MESOPOTAMIA In the Mediterranean and Mesopotamia, important new crops from South and Southeast Asia came via Indian Ocean networks. Some were food crops, such as spinach, eggplant, watermelon, coconut, bananas, oranges, and perhaps most important, sugarcane. Others, such as cotton, provided a new fiber for clothing. All were established by 1000. The food crops brought a small improvement in nutrition, but nothing dramatic. Sugar and cotton, however, stimulated industry. Because both crops require processing, they inspired businesses dedicated to sugar refining and cotton spinning. The main markets for sugar and cotton cloth were urban populations, often located far from the fields. So the sugar and cotton businesses stimulated long-distance trade and the cultural exchange that always goes with it. The most important consequence of the agricultural revolution in Mesopotamia and the Mediterranean was more commerce and exchange. Population growth and better nutrition, while real, were secondary.

The agricultural revolution in these lands was closely linked to irrigation and to slavery. Most of the new crops required irrigation to yield well. From southern Spain to Iran, old irrigation systems were revived and new ones built. The best technologies, such as *qanats* and waterwheels, spread throughout. With efficient irrigation, farmers could harvest four crops of eggplant or spinach annually.

Building and maintaining irrigation systems was hard and hazardous. It often involved draining swamps and converting them into date palm or sugar plantations. Everywhere it increased the risk of malaria, carried by mosquitos that thrive around stagnant water. As so often

ESTIMATED POPULATION (IN MILLIONS) IN SELECTED LANDS OF NORTH AFRICA AND WESTERN EURASIA

YEARS	IRAN	ANATOLIA	EGYPT	ITALY	IBERIA	BRITAIN AND IRELAND	RUSSIA	TOTAL: WESTERN EURASIA AND NORTH AFRICA
800	4	6	4	4	4	1	3.5	60
1000	4.5	7	5	6	4.5	3	4	85
1300	3.5	7	4.5	12	9	7	9	120

Source: Colin McEvedy and Richard Jones, *Atlas of World Population History* (1978), 41–49, 78–82, 99–109, 133–35, 152–54, 226–29; Paolo Malanima, "Energy and Population in Europe" (2010) at: www.paolomalanima.it/default_file/Papers/MEDIEVAL_GROWTH.pdf

occurred in world history, dangerous work fell to slaves. Scholars estimate that between 700 and 1500, perhaps 5 to 10 million slaves—mainly from Africa, Central Asia, and Russia—were sold to markets in North Africa and Southwest Asia, chiefly Iraq and Egypt. Perhaps a quarter of them worked in agriculture.

NORTHERN EUROPE The other agricultural revolution of this period occurred in northern Europe, from Britain to today's Poland. Before 800, farming in northern Europe took place in patches amid forests and swamps. Yields were low and surplus small, which is why no sizable cities existed after the Roman trade networks disintegrated. But between 800 and 1100, crucial changes took place that more than doubled farm output.

New technologies were part of the turnaround. Although oxen still pulled most plows, the horse collar, perhaps acquired from China, allowed horses to pull with all their might without choking themselves. That made plowing more efficient. So did the widespread adoption of the moldboard plow with a curved iron plowshare, which turned a deep furrow and permitted fruitful use of heavy, clayey, wet soils. A new crop rotation was just as important. European farmers replaced a two-field rotation, in which half their farmland stood fallow in any given year, with a three-field rotation often involving rye or barley as a winter crop and oats in summer. Under this system, only one-third of farmland stood fallow. Rye did well in the chilly north, especially along the Baltic shores.

Livestock also contributed to northern Europe's farming revolution. Since the arrival of Neolithic farming over 6,000 years before, European farmers had raised cattle and other farm animals. With the turn to oats, and with the new horse collar, they had good reason to raise more horses than before. They were creating a system of mixed farming in which livestock grazed in pastures and, after harvest time, on the stubble in grain fields. Animal manure helped to offset the depletion of soil nutrients.

In addition to making farming more productive, northern Europeans extended farming over a broader area. Between 1100 and 1300, they increased the cultivated area by one-third. An order of Catholic monks, the Cistercians, specialized in opening up new farmlands. Along the shores of the Baltic, German-speakers pushed east, cutting forests, draining swamps, and planting fields. In what is now the Netherlands, long years of toil created new land by building sea walls and draining the

Agricultural Innovation This twelfth-century Italian manuscript shows farmers using a moldboard plow drawn by oxen. The curved blades lift and turn aside the soil, creating a central furrow that enables farmers to plant seeds more efficiently and successfully.

soggy earth behind them. Europe's rising population both required new farmland and made it possible to do the work necessary to create it.

The surge in grain production created incentive to adopt watermills and windmills (an invention acquired from Iran) to grind grain into flour. Formerly this was women's work, done by hand. In England in 1086 (when an inventory called the Domesday Book was made), there were more than 5,000 mills. This technological shift freed women from some drudgery and made flour cheaper. It also opened the door to using water power in other ways, such as in sawmills.

COMPARING THE AGRICULTURAL REVOLUTIONS A comparison of the agricultural revolutions in northern Europe and in the Mediterranean and Mesopotamia points to three contrasts, one in causes and two in consequences. One of the contributing causes to the greater success of farming in northern Europe after 900 was better weather. Warmer and wetter climate bathed northern Europe from around 900 until about 1300. It became possible to grow rye in northern Norway and to raise grapes in England. Farmers could use higher elevations by as much as 200 feet (60 m). In the Mediterranean and Mesopotamia, however, while climate warmed it also became dryer, making agriculture more difficult and irrigation more necessary.

Whereas the agricultural revolution in the Arab and Persian lands led to more commerce and industry, it didn't generate much population growth. While the data are poor, it seems that population grew until 1150 or 1200 and then fell. In northern Europe, where the data are better, the new farming methods did boost population, as well as industry and commerce. The European agricultural revolution did not entail slave labor on any significant scale. It relied more on animal power and both wage laborers and serfs, peasants legally bound to a specific land or landowner.

A comparison also shows some characteristics that the two agricultural revolutions shared. Both extended the area of cultivation, and both involved supreme efforts to control water. In Europe, this usually involved drainage—getting excess water out of the fields. In Mesopotamia, Egypt, and the Mediterranean, it meant drainage but also irrigation—getting sufficient water onto the fields. When and where people could control water and land, whether in the wetlands of Mesoamerica or in the rice paddies of East Asia, they could grow much more food. In 1400, there were only a few landscapes around the world in which people had the expertise and labor power to regulate land and water so as to maximize farm output.

FLEETING EMPIRES

In 800, the west end of the Old World web contained great monarchies: the Abbasid caliphate based in Baghdad, the Byzantine Empire with its capital at Constantinople, and—much less imposing in terms of power and wealth—Charlemagne's kingdom, sometimes known as the Carolingian Empire in Europe, and the state of Ghana in West Africa. By 1400, little of them remained.

THE ABBASID CALIPHATE

As we saw in Chapter 11, the Abbasids overthrew the Umayyad caliphate in 750 and set up their own based in Baghdad. They hunted down and killed every member of the Umayyad clan except one, who slipped away to Spain. For roughly a century after 750, most of the Islamic world except southern Spain was under loose Abbasid control. The first few Abbasid caliphs fared well, using wealth from reinvigorated irrigation agriculture in Mesopotamia and Egypt. After a clash with Tang armies in Central Asia in 751, they forged good relations with China, enhancing revenues from Silk Road trade. As we will see, they also oversaw a magnificent flowering of arts and sciences.

Later caliphs could not hold the sprawling state together,

although it nominally lasted to 1258. The Abbasids originally counted both Arabs and Iranians among their supporters, and both Sunni and Shi'a Muslims. Soon after taking power, however, they endorsed orthodox Sunni theology, alienating Shi'a supporters. The Abbasids also consciously modeled their state upon the pre-Islamic Sassanids of Iran, choosing showy grandeur over pious simplicity. This too irritated some followers. Like the Sassanids, they relied on a chief minister, called a vizier, to run the day-to-day business of government. He, in turn, relied on provincial governors whose loyalty to the Abbasid clan proved flexible.

Soon provincial governors were setting up their own smaller states, pretending loyalty to the Abbasids when they had to, ignoring them when possible. Morocco broke away first, under a clan called the Idrisids in 793. Others followed in rapid succession during the ninth century, in Afghanistan, eastern Iran, Egypt, and Sicily. Soon the Abbasids controlled little but the neighborhood of Baghdad.

And they scarcely controlled that after the 840s. More and more they relied on slave soldiers from Central Asia, most of them Turkic-speakers, for their military and palace guard. Outsourcing defense in this way put them at the mercy of their slaves. Beginning in 842, military slaves killed or blinded several caliphs. The power behind the Abbasid throne now consisted of rough horsemen from Central Asia—whose broader role in the history of Eurasia we will consider again below.

The Abbasid caliphate illustrates a recurrent pattern in Islamic history. Its political elite was raised in a multicultural, multilingual, and multireligious environment, by no means strictly Arab and Muslim. Elite males could afford not only up to four wives (the legal maximum) but many concubines as well. Concubines were often Greek, Ethiopian, or Armenian in language, and Christian or sometimes Jewish in religion. They bore and raised many of the children of the Abbasid political elite, including most of the caliphs. A similar pattern held for other Islamic dynasties discussed in this chapter, such as the Fatimids. Among the common people, however, no men could afford multiple wives and concubines, so the likelihood of multicultural upbringing was minimal. This pattern opened the possibility of cultural chasms between elites and commoners, and it invited religious reformers to denounce caliphs and emirs as bad Muslims unfit to rule.

After Abbasid authority fell apart in the early ninth century, the Islamic world remained politically fragmented—as it remains today. Roughly 200 regional dynasties rose and fell over the next millennium, most of them aspiring, all unsuccessfully, to restore Islamic unity of the sort presided over by the first Abbasids.

THE BYZANTINE EMPIRE AND AL-ANDALUS

The Byzantines, as explained in Chapter 11, had lost the Levant and their richest province, Egypt, by the 640s. They held on to Anatolia, most Aegean islands, and Greece, but little else. Steppe peoples threatened from the north. Their eastern neighbors, the Umayyads, almost annihilated them in 717–718. The Byzantine state barely survived. In the ninth through the tenth centuries, the

Byzantines won back some lost territories during the reign of the all-too-aptly named Basil the Bulgar-Slayer, who oversaw successful military campaigns against the Khazars, neighboring Muslim dynasties, and the small Bulgarian Empire in southeastern Europe.

But over the next 400 years, Byzantine fortunes turned for the worse. Attacks by Russians, Turks, and Latin Crusader knights (of whom more below) took their toll. The Byzantine Empire shrank until all that remained was the capital, a few walled ports, and a scattering of islands. In 1453, a new group of Turks, the Ottomans, besieged and took Constantinople; with that final blow, the imperial tradition tracing back to Justinian, Constantine, and Augustus came to an end.

A similar fate befell a younger empire based in Córdoba and later Granada in Spain. Founded by the last of the Umayyads, it flourished in the tenth century, controlling

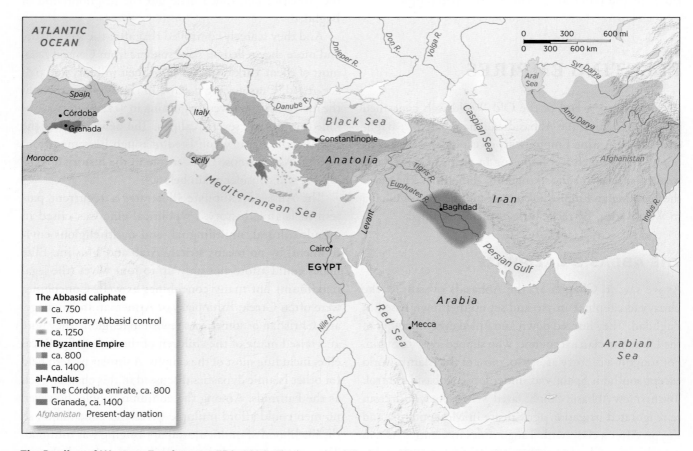

The Abbasid caliphate
- ca. 750
- Temporary Abbasid control
- ca. 1250

The Byzantine Empire
- ca. 800
- ca. 1400

al-Andalus
- The Córdoba emirate, ca. 800
- Granada, ca. 1400
- *Afghanistan* Present-day nation

The Decline of Western Empires, ca. 750–1400 The broad political trend in the west end of the Old World web in the centuries between 750 and 1400 was one of fragmentation. Big, populous states such as the Abbasid caliphate, the Byzantine Empire, and the emirate of Córdoba (a caliphate after 929) dominated politics for centuries. But provinces broke away while bands of mounted raiders assaulted the frontiers. These three empires shrank and then vanished altogether, replaced by new and smaller monarchies.

almost all of Spain, the northern tip of Morocco, and some offshore islands. It became known as the Córdoba caliphate because in 929 one of its leaders, much to Abbasid dismay, claimed to be the rightful caliph. Like the Byzantine emperors and the Abbasids, the caliphs of Córdoba presided over a sophisticated cultural and intellectual scene, funded by a lucrative combination of irrigation agriculture and long-distance trade. Córdoba's mosque, which featured Roman, Byzantine, and especially Syrian motifs, could hold 40,000 worshippers. But as a united empire the Córdoba caliphate lasted only a century, splintering by 1031 into a handful of lesser kingdoms, never long at peace with one another.

Fragmented authority enabled the Christians of northwestern Spain to begin what Spaniards call the Reconquista, the slow restoration of Christian rule. The Reconquista featured shifting coalitions of Christians and Muslims, often mercenaries, fighting under petty kings who were allies one year and enemies the next. By 1250, Muslim rule ebbed quickly, ultimately confined to the southeast of Spain and based in the city of Granada. The end for al-Andalus came in 1492, when Granada succumbed to Christian armies—just four decades after Byzantine Constantinople fell to Muslim ones.

CHARLEMAGNE'S EMPIRE

The Abbasids, Byzantium, and al-Andalus were based on centuries of urban refinement, court culture, and underneath it all, rich farmlands and bustling trade. In contrast, Charlemagne's empire was a crude upstart. But it met a similar fate: external pressures brought internal fragmentation.

After the dissolution of the Roman Empire in western Europe in the fifth century, a handful of small kingdoms slowly emerged. One of them, known as the kingdom of the Franks—one of the Germanic tribes that contributed to Rome's end—came under the control of a dynasty called the **Carolingians** by 750. Theirs was a petty monarchy with no real cities, no fixed capital, and no great sway over local elites.

The Carolingians helped to solidify a social order in western Europe that some historians call feudalism. The backbone of this order was hierarchical linkages among males in which those lower on the chain got access to land in exchange for labor or other services owed to someone higher up. At the bottom stood peasants, often called

The Frankish Kingdoms, 483–843 The Carolingian dynasty built the most powerful state in western Europe by 800. It proved fleeting, however, confirming the long-term pattern in Europe of political fragmentation. Charlemagne's grandsons divided the empire as shown in the 840s.

The expansion of Frankish lands
- 483
- 768
- 814
- Areas of loose control, 814
- Boundaries of the division of Charlemagne's empire, 840s
- Under Byzantine control, 814

serfs, who actually farmed the land. To do that, they had to pay dues (often, a share of their harvest) and swear loyalty to landowning aristocrats, generally called lords. Serfs were unfree in that they could not (legally) leave the lands or the service of their lord without his permission. Lords, in turn, were subordinates, or vassals, of a king. Legally, they enjoyed their lands through the king's generosity. As vassals, they swore loyalty and owed military service to their king. This social system took shape in the eighth and ninth centuries, mainly in what are now France, the Low Countries, England, and northern Germany, with variations from place to place. It was codified into law and embraced by the church. Kings, including the Carolingians, always had to keep an eye on ambitious lords who might wish to become kings.

Compared to the caliphates or Byzantium, the Carolingian state was poor and simple in structure—and yet it was the most powerful polity in western Europe. In 768, a young man came to the throne who would become known as Charles the Great, or Charlemagne. Born in the mid-740s, he was clever, devious, aggressive, and imposingly tall. He rode, hunted, drank, and womanized as elite males were expected to do. But at the same time, he took pains to try to learn Latin and was a devout Christian.

In the early decades of his long reign (r. 768–814), Charlemagne built his kingdom into an empire, conquering much of central Europe and Italy. He forced Christianity on pagans with calculated brutality and became the political protector of the Pope. His steadfast efforts on behalf of the church were rewarded on Christmas Day in the year 800, when the Pope crowned him emperor of a renewed Roman Empire—to the irritation of Byzantine emperors, who considered themselves the sole heirs of the Roman tradition.

Building an empire was, as usual, easier than holding it together. Charlemagne's expanded state remained a rural kingdom, consisting of hundreds of farming villages overseen by local lords who handled the administration of justice, tax collection, and other state functions. It had little in the way of urban life, long-distance trade, or sophisticated manufacturing. Its tax revenue consisted of what loyal lords could provide. Charlemagne built a capital, Aachen in today's Germany, but preferred to stay on the move, keeping up his ties to his lords and campaigning on his frontiers. He had the skill and prestige to maintain such a flimsy state, but his grandsons divvied it up in the 840s, and by the 870s lords everywhere went their own ways. The first European union lasted only two generations.

EMPIRES OF THE SAHEL: GHANA AND MALI

Far to the south of the Carolingian lands, a more durable empire arose in West Africa. The western **Sahel** is a strip of semi-arid grassland between the Sahara's southern edge and the forest belt further south (*Sahel* means "shore" in Arabic). The Sahel climate undergoes swings of dryer or wetter spells that can last decades. By and large the soils are poor for farming, but in the floodplains of the rivers—the big ones are the Senegal and the Niger—soils are rich. Centers of population grew up along the rivers.

In an environment as unstable as the Sahel's, everyone needed friends who would help in time of drought and hunger. Ideally, that included friends far away whose crops and animals might survive when those close by withered. People of the Sahel built a social order that emphasized kinship, lineage, reciprocity, and obligation—in effect, a social safety net. The people of the Andes and the Altiplano, as we've seen, did something similar. In the Andes, people had to walk everywhere they went. In the Sahel, sometimes they could go by boat. The Niger River was excellent for big canoes and sailing boats. It was an artery of exchange and travel for millennia, like the Nile or the Ganges, giving people access to broad networks of kin and friends.

Permanent settlements along the Niger began as early as 250 BCE. People raised millet, sorghum, and rice and kept cattle, sheep, and goats. Some people focused on

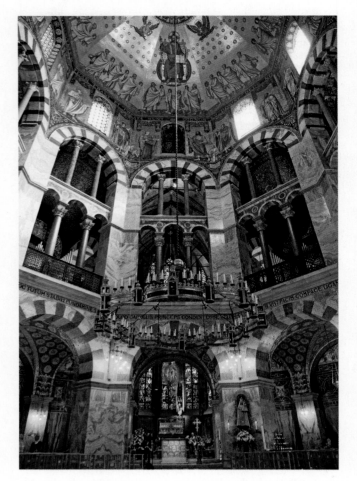

Christian Empire The cathedral at Charlemagne's capital, located in Aachen, celebrates his power and devotion to Christianity. But its curved arches display the influence of Islamic architecture, echoing the design of great mosques such as those at Córdoba and Damascus.

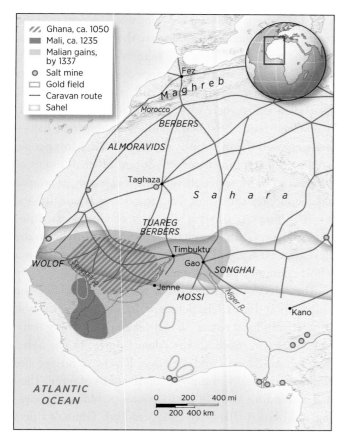

Ghana and Mali, ca. 1050–1337 The first big states in West Africa were Ghana and Mali. Both relied on combinations of river-basin farming, pastoralism, and long-distance trade. Controlling river ports along the Niger and the Senegal Rivers, as well as desert ports—the southern ends of trans-Saharan trade routes—enabled rulers of both states to amass wealth and power on a scale previously unknown in West Africa.

fishing or iron working. After 700 CE, a few centuries of wetter climate brought better harvests, more fish, and expanding human populations. A considerable tradition of urban life developed along the Niger valley, especially at Gao, which thrived after 700. It was in these circumstances that the first large monarchy in West African history, Ghana, emerged.

ANCIENT GHANA, CA. 700–1200 Ancient Ghana lay in the Sahel between the Senegal and the Niger Rivers (far from today's country of Ghana). We gather what we know of ancient Ghana from oral traditions, from written accounts by Arab authors who based their work on reports by visitors to Ghana, and from scattered archeological remains.

A key step in the emergence of ancient Ghana came

with a transport revolution in the Sahara based on camels. Berber-speaking peoples living in and around the Sahara acquired camels by 300 CE, enabling them to colonize the desert's oases and live as semi-nomads. As they gradually mastered the arts of camel breeding and camel management, they acquired a mobility in the desert that made them both formidable raiders and traders. It took centuries to learn the best routes between oases across 1,000 miles (1,600 km) of desert. Errors were often fatal. But just as sailors gradually mastered the monsoon system of the Indian Ocean, so Berbers learned to navigate the Sahara. By 700 or so, they regularly crossed the Sahara between the Maghreb and the Sahel. Like the maritime incorporation of East African coastlands into the Indian Ocean world, this trans-Saharan link brought more of Africa into the Old World web.

To understand how camel drivers connected West Africa to the Old World web, you need to know something about camels—one of world history's most important beasts, and one of the animal kingdom's most persnickety. Camels are distant cousins of llamas, which we encountered in the Andes. They come in two main varieties, one native to Central Asia (Bactrian camels, with two humps) and one to Arabia and northern Africa (dromedaries, with one hump).

Healthy adult dromedaries weigh over 1,000 pounds (450 kg) and can carry twice the load of oxen at twice the pace. They can walk over rough terrain and can cover 40 to 60 miles (65 to 95 km) per day. They can drink 25 gallons of water (95 L) at a time and then not drink anything for a week. They can binge on huge meals and then go weeks without food. Part of their secret is they don't regulate their body temperature as much as most mammals do; instead, they allow it to rise and fall so they don't need to sweat water. And they have enzymes no other mammal has that enable them to metabolize their fat (that's what the hump is made of) without losing any muscle. The camel is justly called the ship of the desert.

Camel-riding raiders and traders from the Sahara brought new incentives for state formation in the Sahel. Ancient Ghana took shape around 700 or 800 as heads of kin groups (lineages) negotiated alliances. United, they stood a better chance of repelling camel-riding raiders, just as Chinese elites did when confronting horse nomads of the steppe. These lineage heads also found that they could monopolize lucrative trans-Saharan trades, providing wealth they could then distribute to followers

Transport Revolution These camels were drawn in the thirteenth century by the Iraqi artist, al-Wasiti. Although camels were first used to navigate deserts in Southwest Asia, by the fourth or fifth century CE camel drivers had begun to cross the Sahara, linking Africa's Mediterranean shores with West and Central Africa. Trans-Saharan caravans were rare until the eighth or ninth century, and the desert crossing always remained perilous.

in exchange for loyalty. Whether their state should be considered an empire, a kingdom, or something else—a confederation of allied linages, perhaps—is the subject of scholarly debate.

One of those lucrative trades was in gold, which was found in several spots in West Africa. Arab authors wrote that gold grew "like carrots in the sand" in Ghana. As early as 804, North African states minted coins using Sahelian gold. Ibn Haukal, writing in the 970s, said the king of Ghana was the richest man in the world (almost surely wrong), and al-Bakri, a century later, claimed the Ghanaian king had a 40 pound (18 kg) golden knob on a post to which he hitched animals. In addition to gold, Ghanaian rulers sold a few thousand slaves taken annually from the Sahel to North African markets.

The most valued import to Ghana was salt, allegedly sometimes exchanged for gold on a pound-for-pound basis. In the middle of the Sahara, at Taghaza, sat a dried-up salt lake. There slaves—with miserably short life expectancies—dug out rock salt, which camels then carried south to the Sahel. Ibn Battuta spent a long week in Taghaza in 1352 and complained that its water tasted bad, that its dwellings and mosque were made of rock salt and roofed with camel hide, and that it had more flies than any place he'd ever seen—and he had been around. West Africa has little salt of its own and has a climate in which people need lots of salt to replace what they sweat out. Like bolts of silk in Central Asia, the salt of the Sahara

served as currency because everyone would accept it. If the trade routes of Central Asia deserve the name Silk Roads, then the trans-Saharan routes were salt roads.

The trans-Saharan routes tapped into a lively world of farming, fishing, herding, and trade in the Sahel. As almost everywhere else, most trade here was local. It involved foodstuffs—especially rice and dried fish—leather, jewelry, iron, copper, slaves, and salt. Most people lived in villages, but there were dozens of small towns of a thousand or more people. The most carefully excavated city, Jenne, on the Niger, had 20,000 or 25,000 inhabitants in 800. At times it was part of Ghana, at times independent. Ghana's capital, according to al-Bakri in the eleventh century, had 15,000 people. Ancient Ghana as a whole contained perhaps a million people.

The rulers of ancient Ghana were overlords, like the Gupta in India or Charlemagne in Europe, who took tribute from local rulers. When Ghana was strong, central rulers controlled all the "desert ports" in the Sahel between the Senegal and the Niger Rivers, so no one else could amass wealth and power on the basis of trade. They had a standing army of up to 200,000 soldiers, according to al-Bakri (likely an exaggeration). Ghana's rulers enjoyed religious authority too, although just how this worked is uncertain. Like pharaohs, when they died many slaves were buried with them.

Islam filtered into Ghana across the Sahara starting in the eighth century. It offered an alternative to local religions based mainly on spirits and gods connected to features of nature. Ghana's rulers did not immediately take to Islam (they wanted their subjects to consider them divine), but other members of the social elite found it attractive. The state could use the literacy and numeracy skills that came with becoming an educated Muslim. Some traditions were incompatible with Islamic customs. In Ghana, a ruler was succeeded by his sister's son, whereas Muslim societies normally trace descent through fathers, not mothers. By 1000 or so, Ghana's merchant elite generally practiced Islam, although in its own ways, melding it to local religious traditions and cultural norms. But the ruling families, and the common folk, preferred the religions of their ancestors.

The Ghanaian state reached its apex in the early eleventh century, but its wealth attracted enemies. In the 1070s, a Muslim dynasty of western Morocco, the Almoravids, either infiltrated and influenced—or perhaps attacked—Ghana from across the Sahara. The Almoravids hoped to secure the trans-Saharan salt and gold trade for themselves. Perhaps they were also offended by the standard of Islam practiced in Ghana. By 1076, most of Ghana's elite, including its rulers, accepted an Almoravid style of Islam. The Almoravids held several of Ghana's towns into the 1080s before withdrawing to Morocco. Recent archeology tells us that Ghana's population, and that of the Sahel region generally, fell after about 1100.

Ghana survived, now a more orthodox Islamic polity, but less powerful than before. Lineages and local rulers peeled off. By 1200, political authority in the Sahel was fragmented once again.

ANCIENT MALI, CA. 1240–1450 The political fragmentation of the West African Sahel did not last long. By the 1240s, a kingdom was forming in the region of the Niger bend. It would develop into a genuine empire, much larger and more centralized than Ghana. Thanks to archeology, oral traditions, and the texts of many Arab authors (including the ubiquitous Ibn Battuta, who visited in 1352–1353), we know a fair bit about ancient Mali.

Unlike Ghana, Mali was a conquest state built by a charismatic military figure. Sundiata, like his near-contemporary Genghis Khan, had a difficult childhood. He was born to an elite family, but political enemies killed all 11 of his siblings, trying to extinguish his lineage and its claim to a minor kingdom. He was spared, perhaps because he was unable to walk and seemed harmless. However, he grew into a vigorous and vengeful teenager and claimed his royal right, probably in 1230. By 1235, he had won a series of battles and was king of an expanding state along the upper Niger with access to the trans-Saharan trade routes. His story is still told as an oral tradition in modern Mali.

Mali's economic base resembled Ghana's but with a larger role for slave trading. Most people worked as farmers, herders, or fisherfolk, but many also fashioned iron and some mined gold. Under Sundiata, Mali acquired access to new goldfields on the upper Niger. North African merchants crossed the Sahara to get the gold, which in turn they traded to Egypt, and eventually shipped an increasing share across the Mediterranean to Europe, where states such as Florence (Italy), France, and England started minting gold coins in the 1250s. From 1250 to 1500, West Africa accounted for about half or two-thirds of the

ESTIMATED POPULATION OF CITIES OF WEST AFRICAN SAHEL IN 1400	
Gao	40,000
Kano	30,000
Timbuktu	20,000

world's gold mining. Until about 1400, most of that went through Mali.

In addition to gold, Mali exported slaves, probably several thousand per year on average. Most were female. When Ibn Battuta returned from Mali to Morocco in 1353, he traveled with 600 slave women destined for North African markets. Mali's slave dealers, chief of whom was its king, raided neighboring peoples for captives to sell across the Sahara.

In exchange for gold and slaves, Mali imported salt, which everyone in West Africa needed, and big horses, which Mali's kings needed to enforce their rule and raid for slaves. As the table above shows, Mali's "desert ports" by 1400 flourished as substantial cities, buoyed by the salt, gold, and slave trades.

Politically, Mali was built on horse power. Its kings relied on a cavalry corps, perhaps 10,000 strong. Malian cavalry rode powerful horses, capable of carrying armor and a rider. It was nearly impossible to raise big horses in West Africa because of disease carried by tsetse flies, so Malian kings bought their horses from Morocco. Like the sultans of Delhi, Mali's kings sought to monopolize horse imports, and thereby the political power that came from fielding cavalry when no one else had any.

Like Ghana in its later years, Mali was a Muslim state. Sundiata considered himself a Muslim. Most of the population in the "desert port" cities was Muslim. As in Ghana, the skills that came with a Muslim education, literacy first and foremost, were useful in running a bureaucracy. Kings always sought the

Malian Horseman A statue from the kingdom of Mali shows an elite man riding a horse, a symbol of the kingdom's military might. The man's status is also indicated by the heavy jewelry around his neck and the ornamentation on his horse's head.

Mansa Musa A map in the Catalan Atlas of 1375 illustrates Mali with an image of its most renowned ruler, Mansa Musa. He holds out a gold nugget, the source of his empire's wealth.

approval of Muslim clerics, which conferred a firmer legitimacy in the eyes of the elite. In rural villages, however, Muslims were a small minority and everyone else followed local religions.

Sundiata died about 1255, but Mali continued to thrive. In the next century, it doubled or tripled the lands under its sway. Its apex of power came under Mansa Musa (r. ca. 1312–1337), a grandson of one of Sundiata's half-brothers. Mansa Musa was more devout than earlier Malian kings, and in 1324–1326 he undertook a religious pilgrimage to Mecca (*hajj* in Arabic). Arab chronicles claim, with some exaggeration no doubt, that he brought along 60,000 companions. Ibn Battuta, who interviewed some of the companions 30 years after the fact, wrote that the royal party brought 12,000 slave women. In Cairo, apparently, Mansa Musa spent so much gold that its value sank for a decade.

On his return from Mecca in 1326, Mansa Musa brought architects and scholars with him. He funded young Malians eager to study Islam in North Africa's centers of learning. His imported architects built grand mosques and palaces. His building spree focused on Timbuktu, a modest town on the Niger bend. After 1326, it became a growing metropolis and a center of Islamic scholarship. Timbuktu eclipsed the other cities of Mali in both trade and cultural influence, becoming the chief desert port and link to North Africa. By 1352, according to Ibn Battuta, Timbuktu welcomed several trans-Saharan caravans weekly, and ordinary people wore Egyptian cloth.

Ibn Battuta also admired the standard of justice and security, writing that Malians "are seldom unjust and have a greater abhorrence of injustice than any other people. There is complete security in their country. Neither traveler nor inhabitant in it has anything to fear from robbers or men of violence." This remark suggests the authority of the state was powerful indeed, even 15 years after the death of Mansa Musa.

Not long after Ibn Battuta's visit, Mali's fortunes began to fade. The state lost control over some of the desert trade. With less salt and fewer horses, Mansa Musa's successors found people re-calculating their loyalties to Mali. By the 1430s, the cities of Gao and Timbuktu slipped away. Peoples to the east, the Mossi and Songhai, pressed attacks that the kings could not repel. In the west, Wolof and Tuareg groups seized towns and trade.

Archeological evidence suggests that population throughout the Sahel continued to fall. Perhaps the trans-Saharan traffic brought new diseases that became raging epidemics. A few statues show human bodies covered with what might be the pustules of smallpox or even the buboes of bubonic plague. Other evidence suggests that moister climate after 1400 favored the tsetse fly at the expense of horses, undercutting Malian military power. In any case, Mali by 1450 was just one of many states in West Africa.

But the Sahel, thanks to sustained trans-Saharan trade links, had joined the Old World web during the reign of the kings of Ghana and Mali. Even a breakdown of imperial authority would not change that.

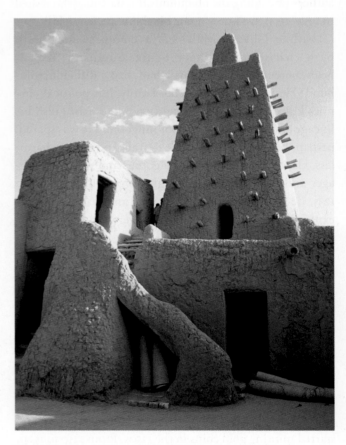

Timbuktu Mansa Musa paid for the construction of this mosque in his capital, Timbuktu. Built around 1327, the mosque became a center of Islamic scholarship.

MARAUDERS AND INVADERS, 850–1260

The decline or collapse of big states such as those of the Abbasids, Byzantines, Carolingians, the caliphs of Córdoba, Ghana, and Mali derived partly from the inherent difficulty of retaining the loyalties of ambitious governors, generals, and vassals. This problem spelled trouble for less forceful rulers. In most of these states, a second threat added more trouble: the arrival of formidable tribes or bands from steppes, deserts, or the far north—people accustomed to hardship and eager to plunder wealthier lands.

In earlier chapters, we saw that in the tenth and eleventh centuries tribes of horse nomads such as the Khitans and Ghaznavids took over the northern parts of China and India. They had learned enough about agrarian societies to besiege cities, outfox diplomats, and use their mobility to trade and fight on their own terms. Their equivalents on the western steppe did similar things to agrarian kingdoms in Mesopotamia and eastern Europe. So did Berber tribes from the Moroccan desert. And, in a variation on this theme, the Vikings of Scandinavia, using ships rather than horses, pillaged and conquered far and wide as well. Between about 850 and 1260, the settled agrarian societies of western Eurasia, like those of China and India, regularly faced raid or invasion from more mobile peoples in poorer lands.

TURKS AND MAGYARS FROM THE EAST

Turkic-speakers of Central Asia began to put their stamp on world history in the ninth century, but they began inauspiciously as slaves. Muslim polities, including the Abbasid caliphate from the 830s, started purchasing captured Turkic boys, often ages 10 through 12, by which time they already knew riding and archery. As slaves, they usually converted to Islam and trained to become elite troops. A ninth-century Iraqi scholar, al-Jahiz, wrote that Central Asian Turks were to warfare what Greeks were to philosophy and Chinese to craftsmanship. A tenth-century Arab geographer, Ibn Hawqal, wrote that Turkic boys and girls brought the highest prices of any slaves.

These slave soldiers often used their skills to promote themselves to general or governor. As we saw, by the mid-ninth century Turkic soldiers had become the power behind the throne in Baghdad, killing and selecting caliphs as they saw fit. In some cases, they set up dynasties, ruling directly as the Ghaznavids and the Delhi sultans did in India, or as one group, the Mamluks, did in Egypt after 1250. Thus a few tens of thousands of enslaved Turkic warriors, and their descendants, became rulers in several Muslim states of India, Iran, and Egypt.

A different form of Turkic power came with the arrival en masse of the **Seljuk Turks** from Central Asia. They were a pastoral people whose leaders embraced Sunni Islam in the 980s. They began to raid successfully—against fellow Muslims—in eastern and northern Iran, gathering people to their banners as they went and slowly adopting Iranian culture. Their growing numbers and military skills enabled them to take Baghdad (1055) and to smash Byzantine armies in eastern Anatolia (1071). They even formed a loose empire for a few decades, but by the 1090s it split up into petty kingdoms.

Perhaps a million Seljuk Turks, men, women, and children, walked and rode into Anatolia over the next 200 years, setting their herds loose on pastures and fields. Slowly, they occupied most of the peninsula, pushing Byzantine frontiers back to the vicinity of Constantinople. This was more than the ebb and flow of frontiers between Christian and Muslim powers. It was an enduring change, a Turkification and Islamization of a major region of the eastern Mediterranean. Greek and Armenian Christian populations remained, sometimes under Byzantine authority but increasingly under one or another Seljuk ruler. Turks, Greeks, Armenians, and others mingled in Anatolia until the twentieth century, often peacefully, sometimes violently. It became, together with Spain, Sicily, Syria, and others, one of the lands in which Muslim and Christian lived side-by-side for many generations, sometimes intermarrying, always learning from one another's ways.

The Magyars, the ancestors of today's ethnic Hungarians, were yet another pagan and pastoralist tribe from southern Siberia and Central Asia pushing westward from the sixth century onward. In the 890s, they crossed into the broad grasslands of today's central and eastern Hungary, a good landscape for flocks and herds. They displaced or absorbed the small existing population and mounted destructive raids on nearby lands, ranging from today's Denmark to Spain, for the next few generations. They pillaged southward, into the Balkans, until the 970s. But their leaders, like so many others before and since,

Seljuk Cavalry Two Seljuk horsemen joust in this plaque from twelfth- or thirteenth-century Iran. They are practicing the cavalry skills that were key to Seljuk expansion from Iran into the eastern Mediterranean.

gradually found that the charms of settled life surpassed the rewards of spreading terror on horseback. By 1000, they had converted to Christianity and set up a kingdom, one of the larger ones in Europe, and given up roaming and raiding in favor of taxing.

FATIMIDS, ALMORAVIDS, AND ALMOHADS FROM THE WEST

Horsemen from the steppe overran and conquered the settled societies of Iran, Anatolia, and east-central Europe in the centuries after 850. Horsemen from the desert edge of the Moroccan Sahara did the same to North Africa, Spain, and Egypt starting about 900, and Ghana soon after.

First came the Fatimids. They began as exiled Shi'a Muslims who took refuge in Morocco's oasis town of Sijilmassa. They gathered followers from other Shi'a populations throughout the Maghreb and formed a state based in today's Tunisia. They won victory upon victory in North Africa and in 969 took Egypt. For a few generations, their empire, now based in Cairo, stretched from Arabia to Morocco and included the island of Sicily. Like the Seljuks or the Khitans, they went from inconsequential tribe to imperial dynasty in less than a century. From Cairo their

ocean-going merchants roamed as far as China. Theirs was generally a tolerant and multicultural Shi'a state in which Christian and Jewish populations prospered. But within a few generations, dynastic quarrels, combined with terrible droughts and harvest failures along the Nile, brought down the Fatimids.

The Almoravids and Almohads also came from the Moroccan margins of the Sahara. The Almoravids promoted Islam with the zeal of new converts and practiced desert warfare with the skill of long-time inhabitants of the Sahara. In 1086, the Almoravids accepted an invitation from Muslim kings in Spain to help battle Christian armies, and soon they took control of the southern half of Iberia. At its height around 1100, their state also included almost all the Maghreb too. Over the generations, their rulers became more sedentary, urbanized, and worldly, and like the Magyars they gave up the strenuous life on horseback.

The Almohads, a collection of Berber tribesmen convinced that Almoravid rule had degenerated into sinful luxury, burst out of the mountains of Morocco in the 1130s, conquering Almoravid territory in North Africa by 1147 and ruling Islamic Iberia by 1172. Like the Almoravids before them, they intended to spread their righteous Islam to the degenerates and to do battle with infidels

CONSIDERING THE EVIDENCE

Religion and Diplomacy in Khazaria

As Turkic-speakers entered the western region of the Old World web, their leaders often converted to Christianity or Islam. Sharing the religion of their neighbors did not guarantee peace, but it could strengthen diplomatic ties and improve their access to wider networks of commerce and communication. Conversely, Muslim and Christian rulers promoted their religion to the conquerors and migrants who threatened to overwhelm their countries.

This chapter's opening mentioned a remarkable correspondence between a Jew who served as a royal advisor to a Muslim ruler in Spain and King Joseph of Khazaria, a Jewish kingdom located near the Caspian Sea between the Volga and the Dniepr Rivers. In his 960 CE letter, King Joseph explains the surprising decision of his ancestor to reject the entreaties of Muslim Arabs and Christian Byzantines in favor of Judaism.

[King Bulan] was a wise and God-fearing man... [who] expelled the wizards and idolaters from the land.... The kings of the Byzantines[,] and the Arabs ... sent their envoys and ambassadors with great riches and many great presents to the King as well as some of their wise men with the object of converting him to their own religion. But the King ... [also] sent for a learned Israelite....

[H]e called all the sages together and said to them: "Speak and argue with one another and make clear to me which is the best religion." They began to dispute with one another without arriving at any results until the King said to the Christian priest: "What do you think? Of the religion of the Jews and the Moslims, which is to be preferred?" The priest answered: "The religion of the Israelites is better than that of the Moslims."

The King then asked the [Muslim qadi]: "What do you say? Is the religion of the Israelites, or that of the Christians preferable?" The kadi answered: "The religion of the Israelites is preferable."

Upon this the King said: "If this is so, you both have admitted with your own mouths that the religion of the

Israelites is better. Wherefore, trusting in the mercies of God and the power of the Almighty, I choose the religion of Israel, that is, the religion of Abraham. If that God ... will aid me, He can give me without labor the money, the gold, and the silver which you have promised me. As for you all, go now in peace to your land."

Source: *The Jew in the Medieval World: A Sourcebook, 315–1791*, 2nd printing (New York, 1972).

QUESTIONS FOR ANALYSIS

1. Why did the Byzantines and the Arabs send ambassadors to try to convert the Khazar king to their respective religions?
2. What reason did King Bulan give for choosing Judaism?
3. Considering Khazaria's location, what unstated political factors may have motivated King Bulan to avoid choosing Islam or Christianity?

---

wherever they could be found—which in practice chiefly meant Spain. For a while, the Almohads united the fractured Muslim societies of southern Spain and mounted effective resistance to the several Christian kingdoms of the north.

Deteriorating climate as well as religious fervor and opportunism drove the peoples of Central Asia and the Moroccan Sahara to become conquerors. The same re-arrangement of the Earth's climate system that brought warmer and wetter weather to northern Europe led to more drought elsewhere. From the 950s, it appears, the frequency and duration of droughts in both the Maghreb and Southwest Asia increased markedly. Herders living

in semi-arid lands more frequently found only withered grasses, putting herds and herders at risk of starvation. Desperation drove them to attack neighboring cultivated and populated landscapes.

At the same time, dryer climate after 950 weakened neighboring agrarian states. Smaller harvests meant less revenue with which to pay their bureaucrats and soldiers, and thus less loyalty and more rebellion. In the eastern Mediterranean, the key, as usual, was Egypt. Its water came from rains in Ethiopia delivered by the annual monsoon, a different climate system from that of the Mediterranean. Egypt's water supply, the Nile, almost never failed for more than a year or two at a time. So

Egypt, since the time of the pharaohs, had served as insurance against famine for cities and armies throughout the region. But after 950, Nile floods failed more often, just when droughts afflicted the eastern Mediterranean. Starvation resulted in villages and cities alike. Food became so scarce in the 950s in Iraq, according to the Armenian chronicler Matthew of Edessa, that "Many went mad, attacking one another mercilessly and savagely, devouring each other.... Many villages and regions became uninhabited." Drought and famine peaked in the years 1051–1072, when Nile floods failed half the time. The Seljuks, whose victories over the Abbasids and Byzantines came in these decades, were emboldened by desperation borne of drought, which simultaneously weakened their enemies.

VIKINGS FROM THE NORTH

Neither religious zeal nor adverse climate propelled the **Vikings** out of their farmsteads in the few patches of good land in Scandinavia. Before 790, the Norse (as stay-at-home Vikings are called) society was growing more complex, with more trade opportunities emerging from the slow restoration of commerce in post-Roman northern Europe. A few ambitious Norse were trying to set up kingdoms. Losers in these struggles sometimes preferred to leave home rather than submit to the winners. They became merchants and pirates, trading, looting, conquering, and settling widely in Europe in the ninth to the eleventh centuries. The Norse Sagas, oral epics written down a couple of centuries after the events they describe, are full of family feuds leading to emigration.

In addition, the Vikings may have felt overcrowded. According to a Christian chronicler writing about 1020,

> [Viking males] live in outrageous unions with many women and then in shameless and unlawful intercourse breed innumerable progeny.... The young quarrel with their fathers and grandfathers, or with each other, about property, and if they increase too greatly in number...a large group is selected by the drawing of lots according to ancient custom, who are driven away to foreign peoples and realms.

The account depicts the Vikings as voyaging to new lands when population growth made resources scarce, much as Polynesian Islanders did.

The Vikings enjoyed certain advantages as pirates and

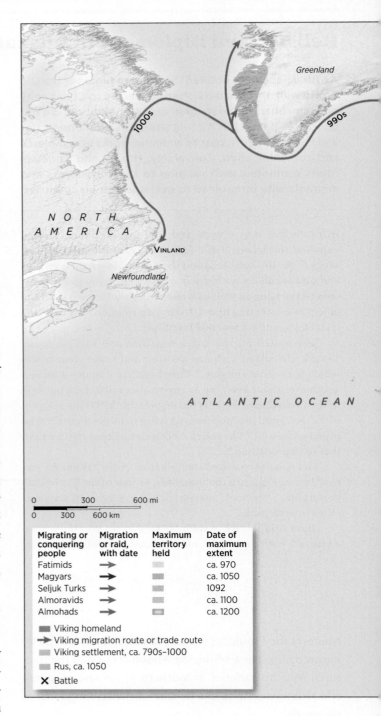

looters. They could forge weapons, armor, and helmets (alas, the horned Viking helmet is a modern myth) from the plentiful iron in Scandinavia's bogs. Their longships proved sturdy in heavy weather, maneuverable under sail or oars, and could sail up shallow rivers. They could sail from Norway to Iceland in three days, as fast as any vessel

Mobile Conquerors and Political Changes, 700–1200 Over the 500 years between 700 and 1200, the settled agrarian states in the west end of the Old World web came under intense pressure from highly mobile warrior bands. Several of these—Almoravids, Almohads, Magyars, and Seljuk Turks among them—became conquerors, typically using horses or camels to achieve superior mobility. Another warrior band, the Vikings, used ships. The successful conquerors set up their own states, or in the case of the Vikings took part in the creation of one, called Rus. The Fatimids, never a warrior band but a religious minority (Shi'a Muslims), also used superior mobility to take over existing states.

before the age of steam. Their ships were like the horses of the steppe and desert tribes. Like the Khitans, Magyars, or Almoravids, Viking raiders could appear without warning and, if necessary, flee just as quickly.

RAIDING AND SLAVING Starting in the 790s, Vikings began their reign of terror with attacks on the east coast of Britain. They specialized in pillaging gold and silver from Christian churches and monasteries. Burgeoning trade connections enabled them to sell all the valuables they could steal in order to get things they really wanted. (Looting and piracy make more sense as a business strategy where there are markets nearby; otherwise you can end up with piles of useless goblets and chalices.) The Vikings also learned that slaves brought good prices in distant markets, so they organized a business based on kidnapping women in Britain and Ireland. They founded Dublin as their main port for slave exports.

The Vikings quickly expanded their enterprise, looting and slaving along the coasts of Atlantic France and inland as far as Paris. By 859, they had sailed into the Mediterranean. They sold slaves as far afield as Córdoba, Constantinople, and Baghdad. Simultaneously they raided and traded eastward, along the Russian rivers well suited to their longships, and in 860 even attacked Constantinople, the capital of the Byzantine Empire.

SETTLEMENTS AND TRADE By the late ninth century, Viking chiefs had become rulers in parts of Britain and in northern France (Normandy is named for Norse settlers). In the 870s, they began to settle Iceland, previously uninhabited. Genomic evidence has recently revealed that almost all the early generations of females in Iceland came from the British Isles and the males from Norway, which strongly suggests that mass abductions (or purchases) of British women were part of the settlement scheme. In the 990s, a few Vikings also established small colonies on the giant island of Greenland, where a warming climate brought a few green patches around the edges of its thick glaciers.

The Greenland settlements served as the springboard for a brief effort to settle on Newfoundland, the northeastern edge of North America, around 1000 CE. Within a year or two, violent encounters with the local Amerindians caused the Vikings to abandon the colony, called Vinland. But before they did, Snorri Karlsefnisson was born—the first baby in the Americas not descended from Asian migrants. He would also be the last for nearly 500 years.

The Greenland Norse, never more than a few thousand in number, were linked to the Old World web although they were situated on its farthest fringes. They traded walrus ivory to Europe for centuries, became Christians, and even sent the Pope a polar bear in the 1050s. But as the Little Ice Age took hold after 1250, their lives grew ever grimmer and their connections to Scandinavia ever weaker. Elephant ivory from Africa replaced Greenland's chief

Viking Invaders A tenth-century Norse manuscript shows a fleet of Vikings disembarking from their ships, on one of their many raids along the east coast of England.

export to Europe, leaving the Greenland Norse destitute, victims of both climate change and economic integration. The last of them either packed up or died out in the 1420s. The Old World web no longer included Greenland.

But elsewhere the Vikings, like the Turks, Fatimids, and others, thickened the Old World web. Their traders enduringly linked Scandinavia to Russia, Byzantium, and the Arab world along the river routes between the Baltic and Black Seas. Some Viking graves include coins minted in Afghanistan, Iran, and Iraq. An Arab traveler, Ibn Fadlan, visited a settlement on the Volga River (in today's Russia) in 921 and found the people tall "like palm trees, fair and reddish" but "the filthiest of Allah's creatures." These were probably Vikings. To judge by Ibn Fadlan's account, a large part of their economy consisted of selling female slaves. Some Vikings helped set up the first state in the region, based at Kiev, called Rus, in the tenth century. Others became mercenaries for Byzantine emperors. Through their work as merchants, warriors, and pirates, the Vikings helped to extend the Old World web into the Atlantic and Russia, and to tighten it elsewhere.

Everywhere they settled, from Russia to Greenland, the Vikings gradually came to prefer Christianity to their Norse gods. Frequently, Christian wives converted kings who then encouraged or obliged their subjects to take up Christianity. By 1050, the Vikings were almost all Christians. Like the Magyars, Almoravids, and others, the Vikings gradually found the dangerous life as raiders less appealing than steadier work as farmers, soldiers, businessmen, and, in some cases, rulers.

WOMEN AND SOCIAL HIERARCHY With male mortality especially high among warriors and pirates, women far outnumbered men in Viking societies. The Viking Sagas show us women as merchants, missionaries, and occasionally warriors. There is also a grave site in Sweden with a woman's skeleton surrounded by weapons and armor.

Women in Viking society had no political rights and were barred from assemblies and courts. But in domestic life they enjoyed some power, managing money and choosing their husbands for themselves. They could own property and sue for divorce. In the sagas, a grandmother named Aud the Deep-Minded led a settlement expedition from Scotland to Iceland, building and commanding a longship. Another grave in Sweden includes among a woman's funeral objects some scales and weights used in market transactions. A woman of Viking extraction, Olga of Kiev, ruled the polity of Rus in the mid-tenth century, negotiating effectively with foreign powers including the Byzantine Empire. One chronicle records her rejecting a marriage proposal by burying alive the emissaries who brought it.

Viking society showed sharp inequalities of social class. Leaders enjoyed plenty of food and drink, decorative objects from afar, piles of silver and gold, and many slaves. One tenth-century household owned a Buddha figurine from India. But most people in Viking Scandinavia were poor farmers, and many were slaves. A thirteenth-century law from an island in what is now Sweden captures some of this hierarchy. It assessed penalties for murder: 10.6 pounds (4.8 kg) of silver if the victim was a freeborn local; 4.4 pounds (2 kg) of silver in the case of freeborn foreigners; and a tenth of that for slaves. As in Hammurabi's laws from ancient Mesopotamia or those of Tang China, murder penalties varied with the status of the victim.

CRUSADERS FROM THE WEST

Beginning in the 1090s, at the same time that Christian warriors in Spain were pushing against the frontiers of al-Andalus and re-taking Sicily from Muslim rule, Christian knights from western Europe launched the first of several waves of invasions of the Levant. These invasions were part pilgrimage to the Holy Land and part military campaign. Their motives included both religious merit, to be earned by taking Jerusalem from Muslim rule, and plunder. The undertaking is called the **Crusades**, part of the larger Mediterranean tug-of-war between Muslim and Christian rulers taking place in Spain, Sicily, and Anatolia.

The immediate origins of the Crusades lay with a response to the Seljuk Turks, who, as we've seen, threatened Christian Byzantium when they drifted into Anatolia after 1071. A Byzantine emperor asked the Pope for help. In 1095, the Pope, Urban II, called for volunteers from the length and breadth of Christendom to wrest the Holy Land from Muslims. In response, Christians flocked to Crusader banners, driven by religious zeal and attracted by the hope of rewards in this life and the next.

The Pope's recruiters promised that all who died in the venture would have their sins washed away and a clear path to Heaven. Popes had used this recruiting device since about 850 to inspire Christian warriors fighting against Muslims in Spain, against pagan Vikings, and on occasion against fellow Christians at odds with the Papacy. The Muslim caliphs had used similar promises too.

It is important to grasp that the Crusades, as a whole, were not a titanic struggle between a united Christianity and a united Islam—although they are often remembered as such. Rather, they amounted to a series of small-scale

Crusader Castles Crusaders built settlements and fortresses in the Levant, like this castle, Krak des Chevaliers, near Homs in present-day Syria. It was constructed over the course of the twelfth and thirteenth centuries.

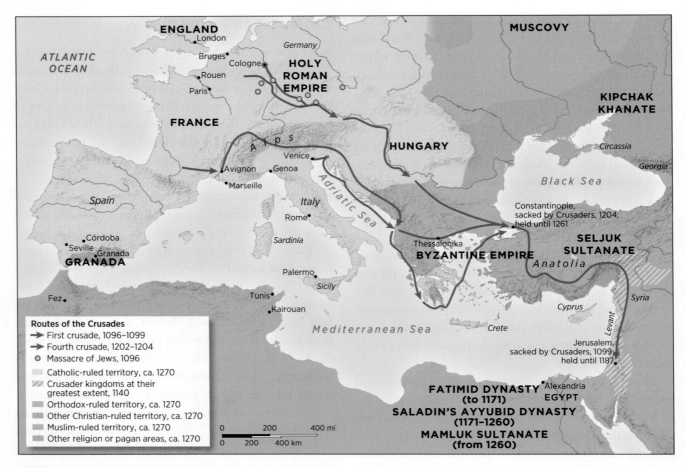

The Crusades, 1096–1291 Over two centuries, some 200,000 European Christians went to the Levant on crusades, hoping to take Jerusalem and the Holy Land from Muslim rulers and claim them for Latin Christendom. The map shows the routes of two crusades, revealing the multiple motives behind them. Along the way Crusaders sometimes assaulted Jewish communities in Europe and in 1204 sacked the Greek Orthodox Christian city of Constantinople. Once in the Levant, Crusaders met with initial success, set up small kingdoms, but soon quarreled among themselves and eventually faced foes, such as Egypt's Mamluks, who proved far too strong for them.

wars, often raids or sieges. Christians fought Christians and Muslims fought Muslims, and all parties sought allies where they could find them.

Crusaders—mainly French, Germans, and English—began arriving in the Levant by land and sea in 1097. Some paused en route to plunder the Jewish quarters of European towns. Once arrived, they stepped into a fragmented political world in which all major powers—Seljuk Turks, Fatimid dynasts in Egypt—were warring among themselves. None took much notice of the Crusaders for more than 50 years.

Meanwhile, the Crusaders redeemed Jerusalem for their faith in 1099. Indeed, they sacked it, massacring thousands of its Muslim, Jewish, and eastern (Greek Orthodox) Christian inhabitants and looting its treasures. As one Christian scribe described it:

Our men rushed around the whole city, seizing gold and silver, horses and mules, and houses full of all sorts of goods, and they all came rejoicing and weeping from gladness to worship at the Sepulchre of our Savior Jesus.... Next morning they went cautiously up on the Temple roof [where locals had been granted protection by some knights] and attacked the Saracens [Muslims], both men and women, cutting off their heads.... No one has ever seen or heard of such a slaughter of pagans, for they were burned on pyres like pyramids, and God alone knows how many there were.

Ambitious Crusaders built castles, recruited followers, and called themselves kings. They declined to accept papal control or recognize Byzantine authority. Fortunately for them, they seemed too insignificant to the warring Turks and Fatimids to be worth expelling.

The several waves of Crusaders brought some 200,000 Europeans to the Levant over a two-century period (1096–1291), mostly adult males, but also many women and children. This migration paled next to that of Turks from Central Asia flowing into the same general region. And mortality among the Europeans, from violence and disease, ran high. Soon the Crusader kingdoms quarreled among themselves and began to seek allies among the Muslim powers.

When Fatimid Egypt looked like it might fall apart and Crusaders seemed keen to grab it, a Sunni Muslim warlord, Ṣalāḥ al-Dīn Yūsuf ibn Ayyūb, known as Saladin, conquered Egypt for himself by 1171. He soon added parts of Syria. To firm up his hold over these lands, he launched a holy war against the Crusader kingdoms, crushing several and taking Jerusalem in 1187. Part of Saladin's success came from division among the Crusaders, just as their initial success had derived from division among Muslims. He noted in a letter to an Abbasid caliph that among Italian Crusaders "not a single one of them does not [sell] us weapons." Those Crusader states that survived Saladin, who died in 1193, were much weakened. His dynasty, the Ayyubids, based in Egypt and Syria, thrived until shattered by Mongol armies in 1260.

After Saladin's campaigns, a new wave of Crusaders in 1204 chose to skip the Holy Land altogether and pillage Constantinople, the Christian world's richest city. This was the first time since the city had erected its defensive walls 900 years before that it had fallen to attack. Its defenders had not expected an attack by their fellow Christians. In 1261, Greek Christians managed to oust the Crusaders and re-establish Constantinople as the capital of what remained of the Byzantine Empire.

Greek and other eastern Christians were attacked by all sides during the Crusades. After decades of persecution under Crusader rule, many (perhaps most) of them chose to convert to Islam when the Crusaders left—an ironic unintended consequence of the whole enterprise.

Later Crusaders often targeted Egypt rather than the Holy Land but met with only fleeting success. Slave soldiers, called Mamluks, took over Egypt by about 1250. The Mamluks, when not preoccupied with greater threats, carved up Crusader forces.

The Crusader kingdoms teetered from the time of Saladin but did not fall until the mid- and late thirteenth century. The geopolitical situation turned briefly in their favor when Mongol armies clattered into the region, bent on destroying all Muslim powers. The Mongols, in effect, briefly served as protectors of Crusader kingdoms, helping them to hang on until 1291, when the last one fell—to Mongol and Mamluk forces. Ultimately, the Crusaders were too few and too divided to survive if the locals ever united against them.

MONGOLS FROM THE EAST

The Mongols, as we saw in Chapter 12, built a confederacy of pastoralist peoples on the Mongolian and Central Asian steppes under the command of Genghis Khan in the early thirteenth century. Soon after, they rode west.

Mongol western campaigns began in the years 1219–1222, led by Genghis Khan and sons. They ventured into India, the Caucasus (the lands between the Black and the Caspian Seas), and Russia before Genghis decided to go

Mongol Conquests An illustration from a fourteenth-century Persian book depicts the Mongol invasion of Baghdad in 1258. The Mongols are shown using sophisticated siege tactics, including a bridge made out of boats and the trebuchet (for hurling heavy objects) at bottom left.

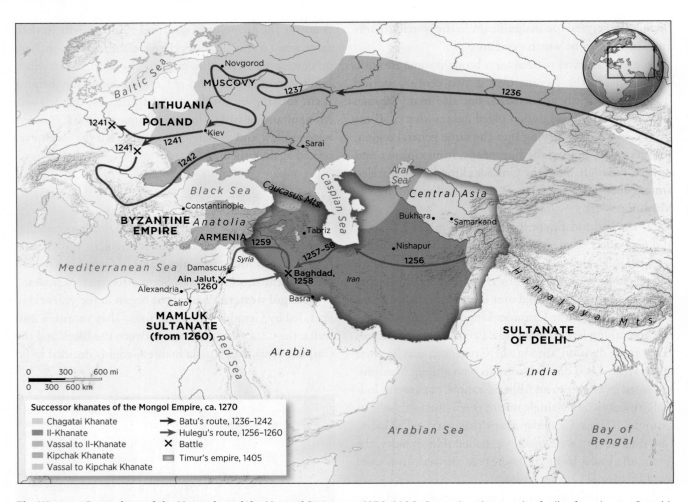

The Western Campaigns of the Mongols and the Mongol States, ca. 1236–1400 Operating thousands of miles from home, Genghis Khan's descendants, especially his grandsons Batu and Hulegu, led campaigns of conquest in Central and western Asia and into eastern Europe. Their mobile style of warfare suited the grasslands of the steppe but proved less effective in forested landscapes. The resulting Mongol Empire quickly fragmented into three khanates: Chagatai, Kipchak, and Il-Khanate. After the Mongol conquest of China, it became a fourth khanate in 1279.

back to Mongolia. His grandson, Batu, led another campaign in 1236–1241 against Russia, Poland, and Hungary, before he scurried home to defend his interests when one Great Khan died and another was to be chosen. Many of his soldiers stayed behind and settled on the grasslands north of the Black and the Caspian Seas. The third and last campaign, led by another grandson, Hulegu (probably a Buddhist), came in 1256–1260 against Iran and Syria, where Mongols briefly helped Crusader kingdoms. Like Batu, Hulegu had to head home to deal with a change of Great Khans. A remnant of his army lost a battle to the Mamluks in 1260, in Palestine. The Mongols went no further in the west.

As in East and Central Asia, in western Asia the

Mongols sowed terror. Their skills as mounted archers impressed even Turks and Hungarians, who came from the same steppe tradition. They had learned siege warfare in their struggles against China. Their habit was to demand that cities surrender and to starve out or assault those bold enough to refuse. They then killed all the men, perhaps excepting skilled craftsmen, and enslaved the women and children. Many cities—indeed, entire kingdoms such as Armenia—preferred to submit without a fight. The Mongols let them be as long as they handed over enough treasure, horses, and young women. Their conquest of Baghdad in 1258, still legendary in the Arab world, left several hundred thousand people dead and reduced a once-great city to the status of provincial market town. This calculated use of terror worked. By 1260, Mongol power extended from the Black Sea and Russia all the way to Mongolia.

Like the Abbasids and Carolingians, the Mongols could not hold their empire together for long. The world's largest land empire, by the end of the 1260s, had fractured into four parts. China, not yet fully under Mongol control, was the richest and most populous fragment of the empire. The Chagatai Khanate, in Central Asia, much weaker and poorer, struggled to survive between China and another strong Mongol state in Iran, called the Il-Khanate. The last of the four, called the Kipchak Khanate or the Golden Horde, was based in the steppe lands north of the Black and the Caspian Seas, where Batu's men had settled in the 1240s. It was almost always at war with the Il-Khanate.

Mongol warriors in the west, as in China, were vastly outnumbered by the peoples they conquered. They often married Iranian or Turkic women, and after about two generations they had largely assimilated to local culture. In Iran, the Il-Khanids, like Alexander's Macedonians and the Seljuk Turks, soon settled into roles as overlords, living luxuriously and governing through intermediaries. Beginning in the 1290s, they converted (from Buddhism in some cases, shamanism in others) to Islam and adopted the trappings of Muslim culture.

On the western steppe, the Golden Horde's leaders embraced Islam, starting in the 1320s, and over the generations became more Turkic and less Mongol. But here, unlike in Iran, there was no elaborate urbanized culture to seduce them, and they remained closer to their nomadic heritage.

The Mongol successor states suffered their own political troubles, usually in the form of succession crises abetted by outside enemies. By 1307, the Chagatai Khanate was falling apart, and the Il-Khanate by 1335. The Kipchak Khans (the Golden Horde) lasted longer, but by the 1330s were losing the allegiance of local lords in Muscovy (the area around Moscow), Poland, and Lithuania. The fragmentation of Mongol successor states, and the assimilation of Mongols into local populations, gathered pace.

Then a new Genghis Khan arose. A sheep rustler and petty brigand from Central Asia, more Turk than Mongol, Timur (also known as Tamerlane) fought his way to local power by 1380. Although a Muslim, he modeled himself on Genghis Khan and married a descendant of

Timur's Empire An illustration in a fifteenth-century Persian book shows Timur's army employing the ingenious military tactics for which they were renowned. They lower soldiers in a gondola down a cliff to surprise enemy soldiers hiding in a cave.

Genghis to bolster his prestige. Like his idol, he must have been a political and military genius, because over the next 23 years he gathered legions of followers—Turks, Mongols, Arabs, Bulgars, and many others—and forged them into a formidable fighting machine. He and his polyglot armies conquered far and wide, from India to Anatolia. He in effect re-united the fractured Chagatai, Kipchak, and Il-khanates, creating a new empire. By some calculations, his campaigns reduced world population by 5 percent, though this is hard to verify. In 1405, he died while on his way to attack China. So he fell short of re-creating the Mongol empire at its height.

ECONOMY AND CULTURE

Crumbling empires and rampaging invaders brought frequent turmoil to the western end of the Old World web from 800 to 1400. In such circumstances, you would not expect economic growth or cultural flowering. But economic growth and cultural efflorescence occurred in spite of turmoil, and perhaps also because of it.

COMMERCE AND ECONOMIC GROWTH

The economic quickening began shortly before 800, at different rates in different places. To a large extent, the quickening followed from the population growth and agricultural revolutions discussed at the start of this chapter. But state and religious policies, new technologies, more coin and credit in circulation, and greater exchange and specialization all contributed.

We can't forget, however, the tremendous economic destruction wrought by wars and invasions. The Vikings, Turks, Magyars, Almoravids, Crusaders, and Mongols and others like them at first were bad for business. They burned cities and destroyed irrigation systems. In the wake of the Mongol invasions in Southwest Asia, ceramic and metal production fell for decades because workshops were destroyed, raw material supply chains disrupted, and artisans killed or taken to Mongolia.

People who lived through such destruction felt only misfortune. But in the longer run, the brutal conquests of Vikings, Mongols, and others promoted commerce. At first, the conquering peoples needed to nurture markets in order to dispose of loot and captives. But in time they learned to live off taxing trade. The biggest boost to trade came from the Mongols. Their empire became a huge free-trade zone extending across almost all of Eurasia from the Black Sea to the Yellow Sea. Historians use the term ***Pax Mongolica*** (the "Mongolian Peace") to refer to this situation, on the analogy of the Pax Romana in the Mediterranean during the high point of Roman power. The Pax Mongolica was not entirely peaceful, but Mongol power and intimidation made the period 1260–1350 more peaceful along the Silk Roads than usual.

Throughout their realm, the Mongols built a system of **caravanserais**—rest stops for caravans—to support commerce. The Silk Roads became, more so than ever, a superhighway system for caravans laden with silks, furs, brocades, ceramics, and fine metalwares. Mongol khans and their Russian underlings extended the trade networks north to the Baltic, where iron, amber, slaves, and other goods entered circulation. Even after the Mongol Empire broke up, its four successor states tried to maintain trade networks. The Il-Khanids in 1320 negotiated a commercial treaty with Venice, a trade-oriented Italian city-state. So while extremely destructive in the short run, in the long run the Mongols helped propel commercial and economic growth throughout Eurasia.

Other peoples also played important roles in promoting commercial growth. In eastern Europe, for example, Jews and Armenians accelerated the monetization of economic life. Their religio-cultural emphasis on literacy made them good candidates for merchant and estate-managing duties, roles into which a small minority of each people moved. They helped to mobilize grain exports via the Baltic Sea ports and long-distance trade along the east European rivers. In the fourteenth and fifteenth centuries, many Jews from German lands chose to move east into what is now Poland and Ukraine. By 1500, Jews made up less than 1 percent of the population there, but every big town had dozens of Jewish families, a few of which did well in commerce.

Technological changes also favored growth. The most important ones came in agriculture—the horse collar, the moldboard plow, and crop rotations. Improved ship design, especially on the shores of northwestern Europe, helped trade. Mechanical clocks, building on water clocks in use in both China and Iran, were becoming routine in the fourteenth century and enabled people to coordinate their lives a little better.

Financial innovations spurred commerce too. In the Mediterranean, merchant guilds—mutual aid associations—developed forms of marine insurance. Primitive banking emerged too, with various subterfuges created to get around the moral and sometimes legal prohibitions against usury (lending at interest) found in both Christian and Islamic societies. Where Jews were permitted to follow their own laws and regulate their own affairs, they sometimes took up banking—many other economic roles such as landownership were prohibited to them—because lending at interest was acceptable practice in their communities. Big cities with Jewish populations eventually became financially linked through networks of family banking houses.

Silk Road Travel This thirteenth-century medallion functioned as a passport for travel on the Silk Road routes within Mongol lands. Its inscription, written in the Mongolian language, reads, "By the strength of Eternal Heaven, an edict of the Emperor. He who has not respect [for this pass] shall be guilty."

Why Were Most Old World Web Empires So Fragile?

Empires built quickly by charismatic, violent warlords—whether Timur, Genghis, Charlemagne, or Alexander—rarely lasted longer than a few decades. However durable their cultural impacts, they typically lacked institutions, loyal bureaucrats, and ideology beyond attachment to a forceful leader. The personal qualities needed to hold such an empire together were rare. The heirs to the founding generation of conquerors almost always surrendered to the delights of wealth and power, and as rulers they lacked the necessary commitment even if they had the native qualities. So empires without enough institutionalization and ideology fractured quickly and, once fractured, easily fell to enemies from without or within. The skills needed to run a plunder machine did not equip anyone to administer an empire.

A loot deficit often compounded the problem. Ruling an empire normally did not provide the windfalls that came with conquering. Conquests enabled warlords to secure their followers' loyalty by distributing looted property such as precious metals, lands, and livestock, as well as captives and slaves. But once conquests slowed, squeezing taxes or grain out of peasant communities offered less in the way of easily distributed riches, weakening the allegiance of followers.

A horse deficit often contributed as well to the fragility of empires in the Old World web, especially between 800 and 1600. Most rulers, from Manchuria to Mali, required a formidable cavalry to rise to power and then to keep their thrones. The rulers often came from pastoral, horse-rich societies but conquered agrarian, horse-poor lands such as China, India, or the Sahel of West Africa. When their personal connections to pastoral societies withered after a generation or two, rulers had to buy horses from peoples living on grasslands such as Mongols, Central Asian Turks, or Moroccans. If their suppliers didn't cooperate—and the Mongols at times strategically prohibited the export of horses—rulers without access to horses soon lost the cutting edge of their military power.

To survive for long in the lands of the Old World web, imperial dynasties needed to: ensure reliable access to horse-surplus lands; find ways to retain their followers' loyalty after the flows of conquest loot dwindled; raise their sons to ride and fight, but also to read and write administrative documents, rather than enjoy the luxuries of courtly life. These were difficult tasks, and dynasties often failed at one or more. Failing at one was often all it took to end a dynasty, because there was always someone else—an ambitious general, a band of hungry horsemen—eager to seize power. Fleeting dynasties vastly outnumber the more famous and durable examples of the Roman Empire, the Byzantine Empire, or the Tang dynasty in China.

QUESTIONS FOR ANALYSIS

1. Which explanations of the fragility of empires within the Old World web do you find most persuasive, and why?
2. From your reading of the chapter, why do you think Genghis and Charlemagne were successful as empire builders?

In addition to greater credit through banks, commerce quickened because it acquired more coin. Mining techniques spread to Central Asian lands previously unexploited, raising the silver supply. New technologies permitted older silver mines in central Europe to raise production levels. Egyptian links south of the Sahara brought more West African, Nubian, and Ethiopian gold into circulation. By 1400, roughly half the gold lubricating commerce in the Old World web came from West Africa.

URBAN GROWTH The quickening of commerce spurred urban growth, and urban markets in turn stimulated commerce. Cities could grow big only where farming

Caravanserais Built in 1114 in what is now Iran, this caravanserai stood in the middle of the desert as a resting place and trading post for travelers on the Silk Roads.

produced a surplus and transport costs were low. In 1000, the big cities of western Eurasia lay in Byzantine and Arab lands (including al-Andalus). Baghdad, as we have seen, may have attained a population of 1 million under the early Abbasids. It was smaller, but still a sizeable city when the Mongols burned it in 1258. Cairo probably had half a million inhabitants in 1300, and Constantinople about 200,000. By 1300 western Europe was urbanizing fast, creating new cities and expanding older ones.

New cities, albeit small ones, sprang up in lands that previously never had any, such as Russia, Scandinavia, Scotland, and Ireland. Starting in the thirteenth century, around the Baltic and the North Seas, a group of cities led by Lübeck and Hamburg banded together as the Hanseatic League to preserve their independence and merchants' privileges against kings and dukes eager to tax them. Their political success ensured flourishing maritime trade across northern European waters.

The Hanseatic cities also helped develop oceanic fisheries as never before. In 900, almost all fish eaten in northern Europe came from lakes and rivers; by 1300, it almost all came from the sea, and dozens of towns and cities specialized in harvesting cod, herring, and other marine fish. Here climate change played a role too: as the North Atlantic cooled, cold-loving fish were able to

Mongol Art Produced in the Il-Khanate in the early fourteenth century, this circular piece of silk is embroidered in cotton and gold thread with iconography celebrating the khan, seated at the center.

migrate south, closer to the urban markets of Europe. Where oceanic fishing thrived, cities depended less on agricultural surpluses.

The most rapidly urbanizing lands of all after 1300 were the formerly swampy plains of the Low Countries (Belgium and Holland) and the Po valley in northern Italy. Successful drainage opened the way to bountiful farming and cheap transport, making urban life more feasible. Perhaps 30 percent of the population in these formerly sodden landscapes lived in cities such as Bruges or Venice. In southern Spain, the urban proportion might have reached 20 percent. Elsewhere in Europe and Southwest Asia, 5 to 10 percent was normal.

WEB BUILDING The single biggest factor behind the commercial growth and urbanization in the western region of the Old World web was the extension and tightening—in some places, re-tightening—of networks of transport, trade, and communications. By 1300, northern Europe from Ireland to Russia joined larger trade circuits as never before. Trans-Saharan links to West Africa strengthened. And thanks to the Pax Mongolica, trans-Asian links tightened, bringing the Chinese and Indian economies into closer contact with those of western Eurasia. Moreover, many regions within western Eurasia, such as northern Italy, southern Spain, and the Low Countries, developed intensive networks of specialization and exchange to match, or nearly match, the older ones in Egypt and Iraq. So, economically speaking, the western end of the Old World web grew both tighter and bigger through 1300 and a little beyond.

It is important to note how uneven this web-building process was. Invaders (and routine warfare) wrought greater destruction on Southwest Asia than on Europe, at least after about 950 when the Vikings and Magyars settled down. And because European societies were poorer, with less in the way of elaborate infrastructure such as irrigation systems, they could rebound a bit more quickly from destruction. In 1100, European lands were still poorer, their populations less skilled, than those of Egypt, Syria, or Byzantium; the Crusaders were awed by the sophistication, especially the artisans' skills, they encountered around the eastern Mediterranean.

But by 1340, European societies, especially in Italy and the Low Countries, were growing rapidly. In population and productivity, skill and sophistication, they were growing much faster than the Islamic heartlands,

The Arab World The Arab geographer Muhammad al-Idrisi made this map in 1154 for the king of Sicily. It is oriented with North at the bottom and shows all of Europe, Asia, and North Africa. The map demonstrates awareness of the whole Indian Ocean world and even China.

Byzantium, or anywhere else in the western region of the Old World web.

Step back for a moment and think of the entire Old World web, from Japan to Morocco. In 800, the great centers of population, wealth, and power lay in northern China, northern India, Mesopotamia, and the eastern Mediterranean. By 1250, although that remained the case, now southern China under the Song and western Europe (under many kings) were the most dynamic regions of the Old World web, powered by agricultural revolutions and commercialization.

CULTURAL FLOWERING

Here and there throughout the western regions of the Old World web, especially in cities, courts, madrassas, and monasteries, high culture flourished despite all the violence and destruction. Thousands of leisured men, and a few women too, created lasting monuments to human ingenuity and wisdom in poetry, architecture, astronomy, mathematics, law, and other fields. Almost all of this cultural growth took place under the intellectual umbrella of either Islam or Christianity, stretching these traditions in new directions. A great deal of it took place because migrations, commerce, or refugee flows exposed thinkers to new ideas and practices and shook their faith in inherited ways. And it could take place because in some locations some people amassed enough wealth to sponsor art and science.

BAGHDAD One example was Baghdad under the early Abbasids, where Muslims, Jews, and Christians of many sects interacted. It was one of several courts competing for prestige in the Islamic world. The Abbasid court, especially under the caliph Harun al-Rashid (r. 786–809), gathered sages, artisans, and artists together. Silk Road connections to China brought exposure to Tang-dynasty porcelain, which Baghdad craftsmen adapted. Paper, also from China, helped the literary arts to prosper. Baghdad became a center of translation of philosophical and scientific texts from Greek, Sanskrit, Syriac, Persian, and other languages into Arabic. Arabs had little in the way of their own science and thus proved especially open to the mix of new ideas. The slave trades from Africa, Russia, and Central Asia brought new cultural influences. Connections to India led to the importation of mathematical concepts such as decimal notation and the use of zero.

The great scholar al-Farabi (ca. 872–951), for example, came from somewhere in Central Asia but lived most of his adult life in Baghdad. He learned several languages, including ancient Greek, and studied Aristotle with a Christian theologian. Al-Farabi wrote over a hundred treatises, including influential commentaries on logic and science, melding Aristotle with other philosophical strains and seeking to reconcile it all with Islamic principles. He wrote on sociology, math, psychology, and music too. He allegedly played music so well he could move people to tears at will. Islamic philosophers regarded him as the "second teacher"—with Aristotle being the first.

When the Seljuks (1055) and then the Mongols (1258) took Baghdad, many of its intellectuals fled. Some found sanctuary at courts in Cairo or Delhi, bolstering those cities as centers of literature and science.

CÓRDOBA Córdoba, and al-Andalus generally, was another creative melting pot of culture. It was less hospitable to Christians than Baghdad was, but welcoming to Jews. Hasdai ibn Shaprut, whom we encountered at the outset of this chapter, oversaw the collaboration of Byzantine Greek, Arab, and Jewish scholars on medical texts. The court gathered intellectuals from all over and employed translators and copyists. A tenth-century emir allegedly had 400,000 books. The city had 70 libraries and innumerable booksellers, which startled Christian visitors unaccustomed to such devotion to literature. Alvaro de Córdoba, a Jewish convert to Christianity in the ninth century, lamented:

> My fellow Christians delight in the poems and romances of the Arabs. They study the works of Muslim theologians and philosophers, not to refute them, but to acquire a correct and elegant Arabic style. Alas! The young Christians who are most conspicuous for their talents have no knowledge of literature save Arabic: they read and study Arabic books avidly.

Even after the fall of the Córdoba caliphate in 1031, the city hosted great scholars who blended philosophical traditions from far and wide. Ibn Rushd (also known as Averroes), a twelfth-century scholar, was born in Córdoba and served courts there, in Seville, and in Morocco. Like al-Farabi, he was a polymath and an interpreter of Aristotle. He was perhaps the pre-eminent philosopher of al-Andalus, a champion of rationalist thought who occasionally got himself into trouble with religious authorities. Maimonides, also born and educated in Córdoba, wrote in Arabic and became the most influential Jewish philosopher of his time. He melded Aristotle's logic with Jewish teachings. The learning of both Ibn Rushd and Maimonides would soon become influential in intellectual circles in Christian as well as Islamic lands.

MONGOL AND IL-KHANID COURT CULTURE The Mongols, for all their destruction, also stirred up a tasty intellectual stew of diverse ingredients. Like the early Arabs, they had minimal formal intellectual traditions of their own to defend, and readily adopted bits and pieces from China, India, Iran, and elsewhere. The Mongols sponsored scholars, artisans, artists, and poets but didn't indulge in the fine arts much themselves until they settled down. They liked to assemble religious scholars of all traditions and hear them debate. They encouraged the transfer of technology, techniques, and scientific knowledge from China to Iran (e.g., acupuncture) and Iran to China (e.g., astronomy) and throughout their domains. The cobalt blue dye that distinguishes Chinese porcelain came from Iranian artisans about 1325.

Maimonides In an illustration from a 1347 Hebrew translation of the Jewish philosopher's *Guide for the Perplexed*, Maimonides (dressed in blue and seated on the right) explains the "measure of men." Maimonides was born and educated in Córdoba.

Court Culture A Persian miniature showing touches of Chinese influence. It is one of several that illustrate a 1249 copy of the Persian poet al-Ferdawsi's epic poem *Book of Kings*.

The courts of the Mongol successor states, especially the Il-Khanids based in Tabriz in Iran, became important sponsors of the arts and sciences. Their court artists refined the tradition of miniature painting, incorporating Chinese influences. They (and their successors) supported astronomers and poets, including some of the Persian-language poets foundational to Iranian literature. Medieval Iran spawned generations of fabulous poets who blended Islamic themes with secular ones, with a notable emphasis on love and wine. Some lived shortly before the Mongol invasions, such as al-Firdawsi and Omar Khayyam, some such as Sa'di during the Mongol storm, and others such as Hafez afterward.

Sa'di (ca. 1210–1291) spent most of his adult life as a wandering refugee fleeing Mongols, which gave him a chance to experience the diversity of peoples, including Muslims, Jews, Christians, Buddhists, and Hindus of dozens of small sects. A translation of his verse celebrating the underlying unity of humankind is now inscribed on the United Nations building in New York:

> Human beings are members of a whole,
> In creation of one essence and soul.
> If one member is afflicted with pain,
> Other members uneasy will remain.
> If you've no sympathy for human pain,
> The name of human you cannot retain!

MEDIEVAL PARIS Like Tabriz, medieval Paris was a capital of culture. In Carolingian times, monasteries had served as preserves of the high culture of Roman antiquity, employing scribes whose only innovations were copying errors. But in the eleventh and twelfth centuries, with translations of Arab scholars from Spain reaching western Europe, a more creative era followed. Thomas Aquinas (ca. 1225–1274), an Italian churchman, studied and taught in Paris. Despite failing his first theological exams, he became one of Catholicism's great philosophers, drawing on translations of Ibn Rushd (Averroes) to write commentaries on Aristotle. Just as al-Farabi and Ibn Rushd tried to reconcile Aristotle and Islam, so Aquinas sought to build bridges between Aristotle and Christianity. He did it so artfully, defending Christian tenets against possible logical objections, that the church made him a saint half a century after his death.

A century later, Christine de Pizan (ca. 1363–1429), another Italian from an educated family, made her intellectual career in Paris. Widowed at age 25 and beset by grasping lawyers, she turned to writing love poems and ballads to earn her keep and feed her children. She was among the first women ever to make a living as a writer. Wealthy patrons paid her to write about their exploits—usually, daring deeds demonstrating religious piety and chivalry toward women. These poems and songs formed part of an oral culture as well, recited by professionals called troubadours. She soon

Christine de Pizan An early fifteenth-century French miniature shows the author at work in her study, accompanied by a canine friend.

got involved in literary controversies and began to write more serious works about politics and society, including law, statecraft, and military affairs. She was especially interested in the proper role of women. She argued that male writers demeaned women and took the biblical story of Eve as temptress too much to heart, and that in fact women typically have greater nobility of character than men. In her early work she too was (indirectly) heir to Islamic culture, not the interpreters of Aristotle so much as the Persian poets whose tales of love and adventure helped advance the tradition of troubadour balladry in Europe.

UNIVERSITIES Aquinas worked at the University of Paris and Christine de Pizan at the French royal court. Courts had long housed intellectuals and artists all around the world. Universities, however, were new. Al-Azhar opened in tenth-century Cairo. European ones opened in the twelfth century—Bologna, Paris, and Oxford were among the earliest—and by 1400 Europe had more than 40. They all used Latin even though it was no one's native tongue. At first, they operated under the authority of the Pope; but by 1241 through teachers' strikes they had become more independent and self-governing. Bologna, uniquely, was run by students, who could fine professors who turned up late for their own lectures.

European **universities** taught theology, law, medicine, and philosophy, a broader approach to learning than that which had prevailed in monasteries. A degree in philosophy required one to two years' study, and one in medicine six or eight. Theology was the least popular subject. No women were allowed in universities. They had to seek education elsewhere, typically in their homes, as Christine de Pizan did.

Universities firmly established the principle of debate and dispute as the avenue to knowledge and wisdom. Professors and students followed ideas where logic and inclination took them, sometimes clashing with the official positions of the church. That led to trouble at times, but the mobility of scholars made it harder for any bishop or king to clamp down on unorthodox thought. The comparative freedom of universities helped Christian Europe to attain a sophistication in science and the arts that previously had been scarce. Their debt to the intellectual production of Islamic centers of learning—Baghdad, Córdoba, Cairo, and many others—was enormous. Italian

Medieval Students A philosopher teaches his students in this illustration from the *Grandes Chroniques de France*, a vernacular history of France written during the years 1375–1379.

universities also benefited from contact with Greek scholars in Byzantine centers.

The intellectual and artistic awakening of western Europe in the thirteenth century was remarkable. Leonardo Fibonacci (ca. 1170–1250) traveled from Pisa in Italy to North Africa as a boy and later studied math in the Arab world. He did more than anyone else to introduce Arabic numerals to Europe. He sparked an explosion of work in mathematics that never would have happened had Europeans stuck with Roman numerals. Math helped make it easier to build the magnificent cathedrals that after 1150 dominated the skyline of dozens of cities. To build a structure 160 feet (50 m) tall like Beauvais Cathedral in northern France (begun 1225), you need reliable calculations about load-bearing columns.

By 1400, European mathematicians, architects, jurists, poets, accountants, mining engineers, and shipbuilders had learned enough, much of it from Muslim Spain or Greek Byzantium, that they no longer felt awed when exposed to the sophistication of Granada, Cairo, or Constantinople.

NEW CURRENTS IN RELIGION

After 800, religion remained the main framework for intellectual and cultural life in the western end of Eurasia as elsewhere. In the centuries after 800, both Islam and Christianity expanded geographically and attracted many new converts. Islam stretched into Central Asia and southern Russia, along the East African coast, and across the Sahara into West Africa's Sahel. Christianity reached into Scandinavia, eastern Europe, and Russia. In Spain, Sicily, Syria, Anatolia, the Levant, and elsewhere, the two religions shared space—often smoothly, sometimes not.

As both religions expanded and intermingled, their followers incorporated new features. Some West African Islamic practices, such as women's dress, offended Ibn Battuta in the 1350s. Christians were horrified by paganism in the conduct of Celtic harvest festivals in Ireland such as Samhain, the root of Halloween when witches and other spirits cavort after dark.

In response to challenges from popular religion and the educated elites who embraced the teachings of Aristotle and Plato, both the Catholic Church and the Byzantine (Greek Orthodox) Church took pains to defend dogmas and standardize rituals. The two churches had split officially in 1054 and drifted apart when the Crusaders sacked Constantinople in 1204. But both employed missionaries and monasteries to try to spread approved belief and behavior. The increasingly assertive Papacy waded deeply into European politics to try to impose its views. Non-conformists, increasingly, became defined as heretics, suitable for persecution or execution. The church often permitted, and at times encouraged, assaults on Jews, notably in fourteenth-century Spain.

In Islamic domains, many rulers and the religious scholars they allied with also sought to enforce orthodoxies. Although in Islam there was no church, no Pope, no patriarch, and thus no strong institutional base from which to promote standardization within the community of Muslims, any ruler could try to do it. Many did. Sunni caliphs, emirs, and sultans energetically persecuted Shi'a communities. Shi'a states, such as Fatimid Egypt, sometimes returned the favor. The Il-Khanids, after accepting Islam, ruthlessly purged their domains in Iran and Central Asia of Buddhist influences, turning temples into mosques and driving out those suspected of Buddhist persuasions. In the West African Sahel, reformers periodically tried to enforce orthodox forms of Islam beginning with the Almoravids in the 1070s.

But religious clampdown was a losing game. As authorities tried to establish their preferred versions of Islam

and Christianity, they lost the allegiance of millions. The worldly compromises (such as accumulation of wealth and power) made by the church and Islamic leaders offended many true believers for whom the attraction of religion was its other-worldliness and (in the Christian case) its embrace of poverty. Thus many new heresies arose and older ones found new followers, especially among people eager for a direct, emotional link to God. Religious refugees took their beliefs to new ground. Islamic persecution drove Zoroastrians to India and Manichaeans deep into Asia. Splinter faiths within Shi'a Islam, such as the Druze (whose origins date to the tenth century), found refuge in mountain areas of the Levant.

THE SUFI MOVEMENT The **Sufi movement** in Islam is one example of popular religion defying official control.

Sufism Followers of the Sufi movement perform an expressive dance of spiritual ecstasy during a religious service in this illustration by a fifteenth-century Persian artist.

It took shape in the ninth century among people who preferred a more mystical, personal, intense form of religious devotion to the scholarly, legalistic, and ritualized traditions of Islam. Sufis, typically from the poorer classes, scorned finery: *suf* means "wool" in Arabic, and the first Sufis wore woolen garments, not the cottons and silks of scholars and rulers. Sufism spread via missionaries and refugees throughout the world of Islam especially in the thirteenth through the fifteenth centuries—indeed, Sufi missionaries helped Islam win converts especially in India and Africa. Sufis involved song, poetry, and dance in their rituals, and frequently found that only metaphors of first love or drunkenness could express the rapture of their encounters with God. They were normally regarded as heretics by more sedate Muslim authorities, and often persecuted.

WALDENSIANS AND CATHARS Within Christendom, new currents arose condemning the greed and power-mongering of the Papacy and church. Waldensians cropped up in France in the late twelfth century, urging a return to Jesus's gospel and the embrace of poverty. Cathars, in Italy, France, and Spain, regarded themselves as proper Christians and the church as the work of Satan—and so were branded as heretics. They survived in mountain regions where the power of bishops and kings barely reached. Dissent, cults, and heresy moved the church to ever-sterner efforts to enforce orthodoxy. In 1229, the Pope established the office of the Inquisition, organized to destroy all heresy by launching investigations and holding trials before church officials. Religious dissent was part of the intellectual tumult of the age, inspired both by exchanges within the Old World web and by the worldly compromises of established religions.

That tumult, whether in Baghdad in the ninth to tenth centuries, Spain in the tenth to eleventh, Iran or western Europe in the thirteenth to fourteenth, owed its existence above all to two developments. One was the economic vitality that allowed more people more leisurely lives and supported richer institutions, whether courts or universities, in which intellectual and artistic activity might flourish. The other was the constant friction of ideas among people on the move, the gathering pace of cross-cultural encounters that resulted from trade, pilgrimages, invasions, and refugee flows. This friction took place everywhere, but most heatedly on the geographic frontiers of culture zones, above all where Muslims and Christians mixed.

THE CALAMITOUS FOURTEENTH CENTURY

No amount of philosophical, scientific, and religious study could prepare people to cope with the ecological turmoil of the fourteenth century, a miserable one in the western region of the Old World web. Despite the agricultural revolutions, many people were getting too little to eat; some places experienced catastrophic flooding; and a **plague pandemic** hammered almost every community.

A STARVING TIME

In northwestern Europe, beginning in 1314, a series of very wet growing seasons waterlogged fields and damaged harvests for eight years. Moreover, a nasty livestock disease—recorded in documents from Ireland to Mongolia—swept through, killing 60 percent of cattle and many sheep. People without reserves of food or money starved. Population in northwestern Europe fell by 5 to 10 percent, and by up to 18 percent in England. After 1322, the bad weather ceased and the animal disease abated. European population rebounded within a few decades.

Then warm, wet weather returned with a vengeance in the summer of 1342. In central Europe, half the average annual rainfall fell in one storm. The Rhine, Danube, and all their tributaries flooded, in some cases rising 30 feet (9 m) above normal. Roiling torrents washed away stone bridges, homes, and livestock. The rain came after four centuries of forest clearance in central Europe had opened the soil to erosion. It took three years for harvests to recover, during which time many people starved. Half the soil erosion of the last millennium in central Europe took place during that one flood.

THE PLAGUE

Then the plague hit. Its ravages extended much further than those of the 1342 flood or the harvest failures of 1314–1322. In western Eurasia and North Africa, population fell by 30 to 50 percent in the years 1346–1351. Perhaps other infections contributed, but recent genetic evidence gives a diagnosis of plague. Typically hosted by rodents and their fleas, bubonic plague is highly lethal to humans, killing 60 percent of those it infects, while another form, pneumonic (breath-borne) plague, kills nearly 100 percent. (Today, plague is treatable with antibiotics.)

The plague bacillus (a kind of bacterium) probably came to the western region of the Old World web from wild rodent burrows in Central Asia. Silk Road caravans carried it west. (It might also have moved east into China, and south into India, although we can't be sure.) It arrived on Black Sea shores by 1346 and soon spread throughout Syria, Egypt, and almost all of Europe by 1348. A few spots, especially Finland and regions in Poland, somehow avoided it.

Death and dying were everywhere. Ibn Khaldun, a North African scholar who lost both parents to the plague, wrote in retrospect, "Civilization [he meant the Islamic world] both in the East and the West was visited by a destructive plague which devastated nations and caused populations to vanish." A scholar in Cairo, al-Maqrizi, wrote that funeral processions could not help but collide in the streets. (Cairo probably lost about 40 percent of its population over three years.) In Florence, Italy, the author Giovanni Boccaccio described the gruesome scene:

> Such was the multitude of corpses brought to the churches every day and almost every hour that there was not enough consecrated ground to give them burial. . . . Although the cemeteries were full they were forced to dig huge trenches, where they buried the bodies by hundreds.

The small kingdom of Sweden lost 50 to 75 percent of its population. The havoc stretched from Egypt to England, and from Spain to Central Asia and perhaps beyond.

No one could cure plague. Many doctors believed it resulted from poisoned air, perhaps from exhalations of the Earth during earthquakes. Some thought bad air from butchered pigs caused it. Ibn Khaldun, who was not a doctor, thought overpopulation poisoned the air.

Most people didn't think in medical terms but saw the plague as divine punishment. Muslims normally believed such a major event must represent Allah's will, and they took Muhammad's sayings as evidence that pious Muslims killed by plague would be assured a place in paradise. In Christian Europe, those who didn't see it as God's wrath usually blamed witches, lepers, or Jews for the plague. In many European towns and cities, Christians who survived the plague massacred those Jews whom the plague had spared. In Islamic societies, there is no evidence of such

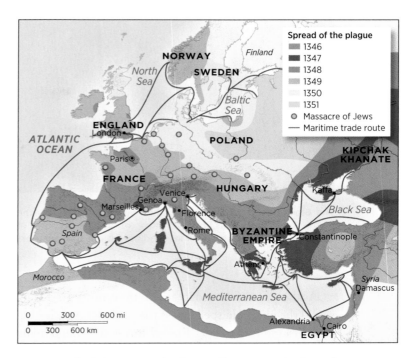

The Spread of the Plague in the Mediterranean Basin and Europe, 1346–1351 By the middle of the fourteenth century, the Old World web was sufficiently well connected and well traveled that routine movements of traders, armies, refugees, and pilgrims could efficiently spread infectious disease. Caravans and ships brought plague from Central Asia to the Mediterranean and then to northern Europe, killing tens of millions within five years.

scapegoating, perhaps because of the strength of the belief that only Allah's will could explain it.

The pandemic of 1346–1351 was only the beginning. For centuries the plague kept returning, carrying off millions more. The recurrence of plague helps explain why population in Europe did not recover until perhaps 1500 or 1550, and in Egypt, not until about 1800. This was a golden age for pathogens and a dismal one for humans.

In many places, the great calamity of the plague, piled on the earlier food crises, was a turning point economically. In Egypt and Iraq, where irrigation systems needed massive manpower, the demographic losses led to spirals of economic decline. Too few laborers meant too little water control and less food. The demand for slaves climbed.

Elsewhere, plague survivors enjoyed improved economic conditions. Scarcity of people in much of Europe, for example, pushed wages higher and rents lower. The changes were important enough that elites tried to legislate lower wages and prevent formerly poor people from dressing in fancy clothes. A spate of popular revolts resulted.

The Black Death Whole communities were devastated by the plague, as shown in this French manuscript of 1349. A crowd of survivors, bowed down with illness and grief, bury large numbers of the dead.

As the plague fastened its grip in the century after 1346, so did the long cold spell called the Little Ice Age, lasting from around 1250 to 1850. Europe shivered through many brutally cold winters, although the average temperature fell only about 1 degree Celsius (1.8 F) from the average of the tenth through the thirteenth centuries. The growing season shortened by about three weeks, and farmers had to abandon cultivation at higher elevations and latitudes. In the worst stretches, summers were too cold for crops to ripen. Climate-related harvest shortfalls occurred frequently, especially in the 1360s, 1410s, and 1430s, bringing widespread hunger and sporadic starvation. Never again would nature—harvest failures, floods, disease—treat the peoples of western Eurasia so brutally as it did between 1315 and 1440.

CONCLUSION

Between 800 and 1400, the west end of the Old World web—the lands from West Africa to Russia and from Iran to Iceland—survived some harrowing trials. Waves of invaders from the fringes—from deserts, steppes, and the far north—repeatedly assaulted the centers of population and wealth. The damage they inflicted, on property and people, was probably greatest in Iran, Iraq, and Syria. By 1260, the worst of the violence was over. But the plague followed in 1346–1351 and, like waves of invaders, kept coming back. The plague proved far deadlier than invaders, killing a third to a half of the entire region's population within five years. It was the worst demographic

catastrophe in world history. Unlike invaders, it did not destroy property, only people, which meant that in some settings survivors were—in economic terms at least—better off than before.

These terrible trials preoccupied everyone who lived through them. They scarcely noticed some happier trends, such as improved efficiency in agriculture. The changes came too slowly to register, but between 800 and 1400 farmers learned how to grow more food per acre with new technologies, crops, and crop rotations. Farmers also brought new land under cultivation, especially by draining swampy lowlands. These agricultural changes, loosely parallel to others going on at the same time in China, helped population to grow, especially in Europe, despite the ravages of war. The devastation of the plague, however, overwhelmed all population growth for at least a century after 1350.

The agricultural revolutions underpinned rising prosperity, commerce, and cities. Revitalized irrigation permitted the emergence of large cities such as Baghdad and Córdoba. A surge of urbanization in Europe, centered on the Low Countries and northern Italy, also rested on improved farming. New ship technology, new financial instruments, and other advances led to humming trade circuits. Those circuits also extended into new terrain, across the Sahara or into Scandinavia. The relative peacefulness of Mongol rule after 1260 provided another boost to commerce.

The new prosperity combined with the faster pulse of cross-cultural interaction brought an intellectual and cultural awakening. The Pax Mongolica helped here too. But even more important was the ongoing dialogue between Muslim and Christian scholars in places such as Spain, Sicily, and Syria. In Europe, the formation of universities provided an encouraging environment for inquiry, usually more free than monasteries or madrassas or royal courts.

By 1400, the Old World web had extended to new lands such as the West African Sahel, Russia, Scandinavia, Iceland, even Greenland (although not for long). Its threads were longer and stronger than in 800. The spread of Christianity and Islam played a large role in tightening far-flung connections, as did refugees and traveling merchants. The world was in effect getting smaller because of these growing links within the Old World web. But the web itself, in 1400 stretching from Japan to Morocco, would soon encompass the world.

CHAPTER REVIEW

KEY TERMS

Khazaria (p. 389)
al-Andalus (p. 390)
Carolingians (p. 395)
Sahel (p. 396)
Seljuk Turks (p. 401)

Vikings (p. 404)
Crusades (p. 407)
Mongol western
   campaigns (p. 409)
Pax Mongolica (p. 412)

caravanserais (p. 412)
universities (p. 418)
Sufi movement (p. 419)
plague pandemic
   (p. 420)

Go to INQUIZITIVE to see what you've learned—and learn what you've missed—with personalized feedback along the way.

REVIEW QUESTIONS

1. Why is it best to view Christendom and Islamdom as part of a greater whole?

2. What were the main similarities and differences between the agricultural revolutions in the Mediterranean and Mesopotamia and in northern Europe?

3. What is the pattern in Islamic history that the Abbasid caliphate represents?

4. How did the fall of the Córdoba caliphate lay the foundation for the end of Muslim Spain?

5. What common political problem did the fleeting empires face?

6. How did the successful navigation of the Sahara change the cultural and economic connections of West Africa?

7. In what ways was Mali's state formation and economic base different from Ghana's?

8. What were the main types of Turkification that occurred during this period?

9. Compare and contrast the reasons for mobilization of the Vikings, Crusaders, and horsemen from the steppe and Moroccan desert.

10. What were the main technologies, innovations, and shifts in trade connections that led to economic growth and urbanization?

11. How did wealth, diversity, and mobility spur cultural flowering?

12. What is the connection between the imposition of religious orthodoxy and religious dissent?

13. What were the calamities of the fourteenth century and their effects?

FURTHER READING

Robert BARTLETT, *The Making of Europe, 950–1350* (1993). An excellent synthesis.

Amira BENNISON, *The Great Caliphs* (2009). A work focusing mainly on the early Abbasids.

Michael GOMEZ, *African Dominion: A New History of Empire in Early and Medieval West Africa* (2018). The latest synthesis of the history of ancient Ghana and Mali; attentive to questions of slavery, race, gender, and religion.

Gwyn JONES, *A History of the Vikings* (2001). A classic that stands out among the dozens of Viking books.

Hugh KENNEDY, *Mongols, Huns, and Vikings* (2002). Brief but beautifully illustrated chapters on several of the peoples discussed here, including Arabs and Turks as well as those of Kennedy's title.

Janet MARTIN, *Medieval Russia, 980–1534* (2008). A detailed and authoritative study.

W. Montgomery WATT and Pierre CACHIA, *A History of Islamic Spain* (2006). A brief, readable overview.

CHRONOLOGY

ca. 800–1300
Settlement of
Hawaiian archipelago

ca. 1000–1350
Cahokia arises and empties

ca. 1000–1500
Thousands of settlements
arise in Amazonia

ca. 1090–1130
Drought and collapse of
Chaco Canyon society

1325
Aztecs "found" Tenochtitlán

ca. 1300–1500
Aztec state arises

ca. 1280
Settlement of New Zealand

By ca. 1200
Hawaiians begin to build
irrigation systems

ca. 1000
Chamorro begin erecting latte stones in Guam;
dependence on salmon increases on Pacific
Northwest coast

ca. 1000–1300
Profusion of Polynesian voyages in South Pacific

ca. 1100–1200
Sweet potato arrives
in Polynesia

ca. 1150–1300
Pacific Northwest
coastal population drops

ca. 1275–1300
Mesa Verde and Four Corners
region empty out

ca. 1400–1532
Inka Empire

The Americas and Oceania

1000 to 1500

1428
Aztecs join Triple Alliance

ca. 1450–1500
Oahu unifies into a single kingdom; bird extinction, seal scarcity, and cooling climate in New Zealand

ca. 1450–1700
Etzanoa in American Midwest emerges and disappears; Hawaiian chiefs make themselves kings

ca. 1460
Inkas begin building cities and monumental architecture

ca. 1438
Pachakuti organizes resistance against Chanka people and becomes Inka chief

From the earliest times, part of the standard equipment for states—especially imperial states with big, complex territories and population—was a system of writing. Storage of information was just as essential as storable food. The Inka, a giant imperial state in the Andean region of South America, is highly unusual among imperial states in world history in that it did not use writing.

The Inkas used something else for information storage and retrieval, a system of knotted and colored cords or strings, called a *quipu* (which means "knot" in the Qechua language). The Inkas did not invent *quipus*. They originated centuries before the Inkas organized their state in the fourteenth century. But the Inkas used them more than any of their predecessors.

Today, some 923 *quipus* survive, mainly in museums around the world. Each one includes several cords of llama or alpaca wool, dyed various colors, with knots of different numbers, sizes, and placements. Modern scholars still struggle to figure out exactly what they mean, as they did with Egyptian hieroglyphs,

Administrative Records This Inka *quipu* made from dyed cotton dates from around 1450–1532, but scholars have been unable fully to decode the system of knots that recorded inventories of goods and people.

FOCUS QUESTIONS

1. What major empires and cultures developed in the Americas between 1000 and 1500?

2. What were the main developments in the Pacific islands of Oceania between 1000 and 1700?

Mayan glyphs, and (unsuccessfully so far) the Indus valley script.

Most of the information kept with *quipus* was of direct interest to the imperial state and was quantitative. *Quipus* recorded population throughout the Inka realm. They also recorded transactions of goods, amounts of tribute paid to the Inkas, and some highlights of the annual calendar. Some *quipus* have up to 2,000 knots. They used a decimal system based on the placement of specific knots, and so could represent large numbers easily. According to persuasive interpretations published recently by an undergraduate, the colors of some *quipus* correspond to the names of individuals and the position of some knots records their social rank.

Those 923 surviving *quipus* illuminate the Inka Empire from within, showing us what the state officials considered important to record and something of the society they ruled. The *quipus* aren't writing and can't represent everything that writing can. But it is amazing what they did do. And future work may reveal that the *quipus* contain even more information than we now imagine.

This chapter, like Chapter 10, presents the American hemisphere together with the island world of Oceania. They were the last two big regions of the world to acquire human population. In this chapter, the saga of human occupation of the Earth reaches its conclusion with the settlement of New Zealand about 1280. The chapter deals with the indigenous histories of these regions before they came into sustained contact with people from other continents. In the case of the Americas, that means before 1492 (in the Caribbean), or 1519 (central Mexico), or the 1770s (Pacific Northwest coast). In Oceania, at least the parts considered here, it means before the 1760s. So, in a few places, the story will continue beyond 1500.

Some common themes unite the Americas and Oceania in the centuries after 1000 CE. Almost everywhere there are signs of population growth; in many cases there is evidence of state building, and in a few cases the creation of large multiethnic empires. In the Americas, there are also signs of growing and tightening interactive webs of trade and cultural exchange, although not on the same scale as in Eurasia and North Africa, which in this period were well integrated as the Old World web. In Oceania the pattern was different from that in the Americas. People spread out, settling distant new islands, and then in many cases became isolated from the rest of humanity. They formed their own tiny webs in places such as New Zealand, Hawaii, and the Mariana Islands, involving tens of thousands of people and eventually in Hawaii hundreds of thousands. But until the 1760s, when European mariners streamed into the Pacific, the islanders remained outside any and all larger webs, where most of humankind resided. They were extremely isolated from other peoples.

That extreme isolation was not quite total, however. After the migrations from Siberia into the Americas across Beringia (beginning at least 15,000 years ago), communication between the Americas and Asia languished. But some people continued to move back and forth across the Bering Strait. After their first settlement, the Pacific Islands and Australia seem to have had even less connection with Asia—and in the period treated in this chapter, none of any consequence. As we shall see, however, evidence exists to suggest—strongly—that Polynesians visited the coast of South America at least once. Otherwise, it appears the Americas and Oceania remained isolated from one another too, distinct worlds, evolving in their own directions free—for the time being—from influences and impacts of the world's largest societies, most powerful states, and most lethal diseases, those of the Old World web.

In the Americas, the absence of wheeled transport and the near-absence of pack animals (the llama in the Andes was the exception) made web building difficult in comparison to Eurasia. There was no analogue for the steppe grasslands easily traversed by horses and camels that served to bring communities together in sustained interaction. In Oceania, huge distances inhibited web building, keeping it to the archipelago scale. Most island chains, except New Zealand, had little variety within them, little complementarity that would stimulate exchange. The limited scale and pace of web building during this period in the Americas and Oceania did not reflect any lack of ambition on the part of elites, but rather greater obstacles in the form of costs, risks, and difficulties of long-distance transport.

In this chapter we will look at some societies, such as the Inka, that built sprawling states, and others that avoided state formation altogether, as in New Zealand and western North America. The state-builders left an outsized imprint on history, partly because of the power that the state apparatus conferred upon their leaders. It could be that by the end of this period, more people in the Americas and Oceania lived inside states than did not—the population history is too hazy to allow a confident judgment. But it is important not to be so dazzled by the Inkas and Aztecs as to ignore the millions who lived in petty chiefdoms, tribes, and other political structures, and who left a less visible mark behind.

THE AMERICAS

Three related trends stand out in the history of the Americas between 1000 and 1500. The first is the continued, and probably faster, growth of population. In 1000, the hemisphere had at most 50 million people, and by 1500 perhaps 70 million. These estimates are supported by archeological evidence of wider and denser settlement, spurred by the continued spread of farming and irrigation. Where populations took to farming as their main way of life, their numbers grew while their stature and health deteriorated—as happened in most other such cases in world history.

The second trend is one of increased vulnerability to climate change or military assault. Foraging and hunting peoples could walk elsewhere in search of food or run away from danger. People who had fully committed to agriculture, however, had to stay put in times of drought or brutal cold and hope for better weather in the years ahead. And they had to stand and fight rather than flee in the face of danger, lest they lose everything—lands, homes, tools, seed, and so forth. Evidence from New Zealand to British Columbia to Peru suggests increases in violence during this period, and some unexplained fluctuations in population that might indicate climate crises.

The third trend was toward larger states. The outstanding examples came in the fourteenth and fifteenth centuries: the Inkas and the Aztecs. Their careers should be seen as in parallel, but not as connected. There was nothing in the Americas like the dynamic along the steppe belts of Eurasia where agrarian states and nomad confederacies spurred one another to grow in size and power. What contact existed between Inkas and Aztecs has left next to no trace and was probably entirely trivial. Sometimes similar developments take place at the same time without any connection between them.

THE INKAS

In the span of little more than a century, the **Inkas**[1] built a sprawling empire, the largest in the Americas before European settlement. The Inka state arose in the fourteenth or fifteenth century (precise dates are elusive in

---

[1] Also spelled *Incas*, although people in the Andes tend to prefer *Inkas*.

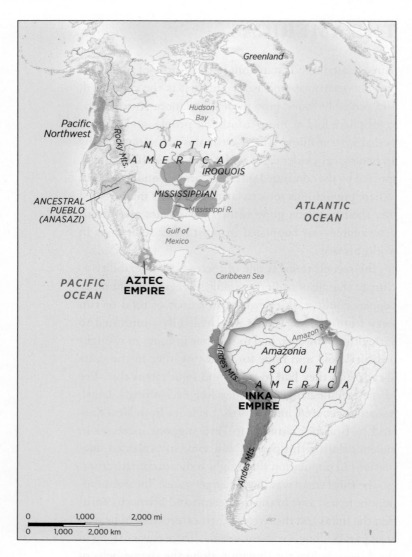

The Americas, ca. 1000–1500 This map shows the locations of peoples and cultures of the Americas considered closely in this chapter. Two of them, the Inka and the Aztec cultures, developed fully fledged empires with many millions of subjects each. Elsewhere, smaller-scale polities were the rule.

snow-capped peaks of the world's second-tallest mountain range. Andean people developed intensive farming, including potatoes that could be freeze-dried into *chuño*, a food that stored well over years. Andean peoples also had to get used to natural disasters: earthquakes, landslides, and floods are common there.

The Inkas built on prior traditions and knowledge of how to use the environment. In their region, the seacoast and mountain crests are often less than 70 miles (112 km) apart. In the span of a day or two, one could walk through several ecosystems at different elevations. The equatorial sun made it possible to live at very high altitude, where the air temperature is usually chilly. Nowhere else in the world did so many people live so high up, well over 10,000 feet (3,050 m). A warm spell that lasted from around 1000 until about 1500 probably made it a little easier for the Inkas to produce food surpluses and build a large empire.

Andean social organization generally featured lineages, called *ayllus*, which elsewhere might be called clans or tribes. Andeans exploited the region's "verticality" by placing people from a given lineage in communities at every elevation. Thus every *ayllu* could hope to draw from the rich fisheries of the coast, the irrigated farming of the lowlands and foothills, and the llama and alpaca pastures of the highlands. This arrangement is sometimes called the **vertical archipelago**. Although it predated the Inkas, they developed it on a larger scale than any of their Andean predecessors because, at the apex of their power, they controlled much more territory. At its height, the Inka Empire stretched over 32 degrees of latitude, equal to the distance from Mexico City to Juneau, Alaska, in North American terms. In total area, it was among the world's largest empires in 1500.

RISE OF THE INKAS The early career of the Inkas is murky. Their oral traditions suggest that they migrated, perhaps from the Lake Titicaca region, to what became their capital at Cuzco, about 1200. It was then no more than a village, and the Inkas a people of no great importance, one of many in the region. But at some point, perhaps in the 1430s, they began their remarkable imperial expansion. Oral traditions say that a neighboring people, the Chanka, attacked them. The Inka leaders fled, except for a younger son who organized fierce and successful resistance. Outmaneuvering the rest of his family, he

Inka history because they didn't reckon time in years, not even for people's ages) and lasted until 1532, when Spanish conquerors took it over. At its height, it contained about 10 to 18 million people. As we saw in Chapter 10, people developed complex societies very early in the Andes and along the Pacific coast of South America. The largest was that called Tiwanaku, which fell into decline before 1000 CE. All the Andean societies exploited the unique ecology of the region, with its teeming marine fisheries, its coastal deserts sliced by icy rivers, its steep slopes soaring up to the became the next chief (or Sapa Inka) perhaps in 1438. He took the name Pachakuti, which in Qechua—the main language of the Inkas and the Andes—means "shaker of the world."

Under Pachakuti and the next two rulers, the empire underwent a lightning rise, comparable to the instant empires of the Mongols or the Arabs. The Inkas, however, built theirs in much more challenging terrain and by different methods. Unlike the Mongols and the Arabs, they had no cavalry, for example, and no way to travel a hundred miles in a day.

For 30 years or more, until his death about 1472, Pachakuti oversaw the expansion of his authority through conquest, intimidation, and diplomacy. He or his sons approached local elites with offers they could not easily refuse. They offered the elites prestige goods, young women, and positions of honor within the growing Inka Empire, in exchange for a regular flow of whatever their region could produce—cloth, fish, potatoes—and laborers for the Inka elite. Local elites usually saw an advantage to themselves in these arrangements, especially because the alternative was war and likely defeat and death. Over a generation or two, most local leaders in effect swapped their independence and sovereignty for prosperous roles as protected vassals of the Inkas.

Their subjects paid a price. The flow of cloth, fish, potatoes, and labor to the Inkas required thousands of men and women to work for them, often far from home. This labor service requirement seems to have grown with time; by 1500, it often amounted to several months' work each year. The common folk got little out of these arrangements, whereas their lords, now vassals of the Inkas, got something in return for their subservience. Maintaining the allegiance of these vassals required the Inkas to dole out vast quantities of gifts, which in turn required constant production of fine clothing, jewelry, ceramics, and whatever the local lords valued. That included young women, some of whom the Inkas gathered together in special homes, called *aqllawasi*, where they were obliged to weave cloth and brew maize beer until the right political moment arose. Then they might be given to a local lord in exchange for his submission or continued loyalty.

The price of resistance to Inka expansion could be greater still. Andean chronicles tell of a coastal people, the Guarcos, who held out for three or four years until

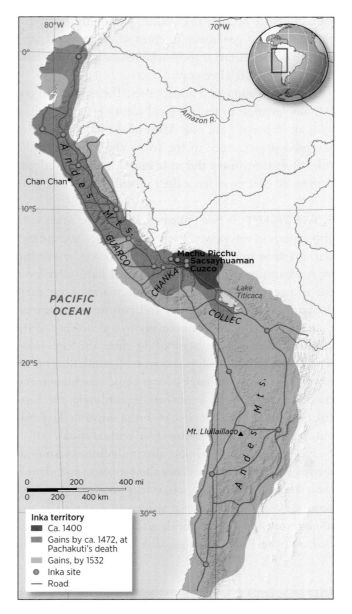

M15.2 The Inka Empire, ca. 1400–1532 The Inkas came from the area around Lake Titicaca but made Cuzco, high in the Andes, their center around 1200. This map shows their political expansion into an empire in the fifteenth and early sixteenth centuries.

tricked into abandoning their fortifications, whereupon Inka warriors seized them. Many of the Guarcos were hanged—in the Qechua language, *guarcona* now means "hanging." Their valley was colonized by people loyal to the Inkas. Another coastal people who tried to resist Inka power and were defeated, the Collec, met a sterner fate: the Inkas killed their entire adult male population. A few such bloody conquests convinced the majority of local leaders to become Inka vassals peacefully. With this combination of generosity to elites who submitted, and brutal violence aimed at those who resisted, the Inka state expanded quickly after 1440.

Rebellions abounded nonetheless. The empire did not last long enough to replace local identities and loyalties with an imperial Inka one. Most of the local elites who accepted subservience to the Inkas chafed under Inka rule. Over time, more did so because the Inka overlords demanded ever more from their vassals.

STATECRAFT While skilled at violence, the Inkas were also experts in soft power. Pachakuti and his descendants claimed to be sons of the sun, long the object of worship by Andean peoples. The Inkas worked hard to enforce the use of their language, Qechua, throughout their domains. Religion, language, and culture underpinned their power, reducing the necessity to use violence. They constructed an elaborate cult of the ruler, the Sapa Inka, who commanded worship as a god. His underlings tried to ensure that no ordinary person could touch anything that the Sapa Inka had touched. Accordingly, the Sapa Inka's clothing, food scraps, even the saliva he had spat out, were collected and burnt in an annual ritual.

From the 1460s, the Inkas also built cities and monumental architecture to overawe their subjects and express their religious devotion. Cuzco, at 11,000 feet (3,400 m), acquired a giant ceremonial space, a rectangle the size of eight or nine football fields and covered in sand carried up from Pacific beaches. The Inkas used this plaza for ritual meals and big festivals where with food and drink they publicly demonstrated their generosity to those who showed them loyalty. Somehow, without draft animals, Inka engineers and laborers erected walls with giant blocks of stone cut so precisely they needed no mortar. According to one sixteenth-century Spanish visitor, the head of a pin could not fit between blocks of stone on one temple. Some 20,000 laborers worked for 20 years to build the Inka capital city. The Inkas built several other cities, usually with large plazas for ceremonial events. Their architecture tended to be simple and somber, with occasional friezes carved into the stone blocks; but unlike other Andean peoples, they used no statuary. The buildings themselves, their geometry and their settings, were impressive enough.

City building and monumental architecture were part of the program for just about every empire in world history. But Inka statecraft included a less common practice, called *mitmaq*. This amounted to the forced migration of peoples in the interest of the state. The Inkas routinely moved loyal populations into areas where they could counterbalance others with suspect allegiances; they also transplanted rebellious groups to lands where they would be surrounded by reliably loyal subjects. The Guarcos lost their valley to settlers brought in this fashion. Few if any other empires pushed people around like this as regular policy, although many, such as the Assyrians, did it from time to time.

In addition to cities and monumental architecture, the Inkas constructed a remarkable system of roads. Previous

Inka Architecture Monumental Inka buildings include the palace complex at Machu Picchu (left), built for the emperor Pachakuti in the fifteenth century; and the thirteenth-century citadel at Sacsayhuaman (right), near the Inka capital of Cuzco, constructed from enormous boulders.

societies had built local roads and bridges in the rugged terrain of the Andes. But the Inkas built many more and unified them all into a single network. This enabled them to move goods around their domain more rapidly, essential for the politics of generosity they practiced. And, when necessary, their armies could march swiftly to any corner of the realm where generosity did not bring the compliance the Inkas wanted. The road network also helped with the frequent transfers of population the Inkas engineered. Ordinary people not on state business were not to use the roads. In all, the Inka road system stretched 20,000 to 30,000 miles (32,000 to 48,000 km)—about half the length of the Roman road network at its maximum extent—including two grand north-south trunk routes extending most of the length of the empire, one in the mountains and one below on the coastal plain. Many shorter roads ran east-west, linking the two trunk routes, often following the routes of river valleys.

Enormous labor went into building and maintaining these roads. Some were equipped with drainage ditches, and many were paved with stone. Often, the roads had to cross over rivers and gorges. Log bridges and, for long spans, rope bridges (with ropes made of vines and twigs woven together—"as thick as a leg" as one Spaniard put it) numbered in the hundreds and often had to be rebuilt after floods. The Inkas also built inns at intervals along the roads and kept them supplied with all that official travelers might need—a system similar to the state-sponsored caravanserais of Central and Southwest Asia. Theirs was an elaborate infrastructure of empire.

The Inkas used all these devices—the *quipus* we encountered at the beginning of this chapter, roads, the Qechua language, the relocation of peoples, the cult of the Sapa Inka, their "generosity," and as a last resort their army—to build and maintain their enormous empire.

Like most monarchies, the Inkas often had succession struggles that could escalate into civil war. They traced descent mainly through maternal ancestry, and Andean rulers traditionally chose a successor from among their sisters' sons, as was done in the West African kingdom of Ghana. But some rulers died before selecting a successor, leaving the field open to all his nephews and perhaps his sons as well—who could number in the dozens. Perhaps as a response to this problem, Pachakuti's successor, Thupa Inka, initiated a tradition by which the ruler married his sister (as many Egyptian pharaohs had done). This practice invited genetic defects in one's children, but it had

Transportation Networks Sophisticated paved roads, along with other infrastructure such as bridges and inns, enabled Inka rulers to unify and control their empire. The durability of these roads is such that many still exist today.

the advantage of making some of the Sapa Inka's offspring doubly royal, and it enabled rulers to pass the throne to their own sons rather than their nephews. Thupa Inka had many wives and more than 60 sons. Succession struggles continued, playing a central role in the end of the empire beginning in 1532.

ECONOMY AND RELIGION The Inka economy was bound up with the reciprocity principles of the empire's statecraft. The Inkas did not use money, and markets played only a tiny role in their economy. The Inka state organized production to a remarkable degree, requiring local lords and lineages to provide legions of male laborers for months at a time in a system called the *mita*. They might work as road builders, soldiers, miners, fishermen—whatever the government wanted and wherever it wanted them. The state also commandeered some farmland from local lords, and herds of llamas from highland peoples. This arrangement allowed the Inka state to collect all the goods it needed to keep its storehouses brimming with foodstuffs, clothing, weaponry, and everything else required to supply its armies and convince almost every local lord to accept the Sapa Inka's generosity in return for submission. But the state showed an insatiable appetite for goods and labor. The Inka rulers felt enormous pressure to squeeze more production out of their population, to make people build more terraces and grow more maize and potatoes, brew more beer, raise more llamas, weave more cloth, and when this was not enough, to conquer new lands.

Spiritual life revolved around worship of a sun god, Inti, and an earth and fertility goddess, Pachamama—both of which were important throughout the Andes. Several other deities resonated locally, sometimes in a single valley or even a single household. Like many empires, the Inkas typically incorporated gods or other features of the religion of conquered peoples into their own. But they also tried to make sure conquered peoples followed Inka religious traditions—notably, worship of the Sapa Inka. Ten elite families that could claim royal ancestry oversaw proper observances of rituals and ceremonies. Religious practice included the Andean tradition of occasional sacrifice of children and llamas. Andean peoples regarded children as especially suited to intervene with ancestral spirits, and in difficult moments sometimes ritually slaughtered them. One site on the Peruvian coast near the city of Chan Chan, the capital of a polity called Chimú, yielded remains of 140 children ages 5 to 14, together with 200 llamas, killed around 1425 CE, probably at the time of a giant El Niño event. Inka child sacrifices also occurred on smaller scales involving a few youngsters, usually 4 to 10 years old, who were left on mountaintops to die after being fortified with maize beer. It was, apparently, an honor to be sacrificed in this way.

The Inka Empire was one of the two largest polities in the Americas before 1492. It formed quickly, and in extremely difficult terrain, but exerted great power from the 1430s to 1532. Then, as we shall see in a later chapter, its tendency to civil wars over succession to the throne became its undoing.

AMAZONIA

Large populations existed in South America outside the reach of the Inka Empire. They did not leave behind grand temples or networks of roads, nor did they develop writing. So we don't know as much about them. But they were numerous even if less visible than the Inkas.

In the rain forest of Amazonia, for example, a space as large as the lower 48 states of the United States, millions of people scratched livings from the thin, acid, and leached soils, raising crops amid the trees. Most of their domesticated plants, of which they had more than 100, were tree crops, but their staple was the root crop bitter manioc, or cassava. They also fished in Amazonia's many rivers and harvested fruits, nuts, and berries from its wide variety of wild trees.

People had lived in Amazonia already for thousands of years when, perhaps in the first few centuries CE, they began to create their own soils by intentionally gathering wastes of all sorts—the equivalent of compost piles—to enrich the naturally infertile soils. Archeologists have a name for these patches of enhanced soil: **dark earth**. They are chock full of nutrients. On these soils, people could raise crops of maize and so-called sweet manioc, a variety that cannot prosper in ordinary Amazonian soils. This technique made farming more rewarding in Amazonia and food supply less of a constraint on population growth. In the five centuries between 1000 and 1500, archeological evidence—charcoal—shows great frequency of fire, which means people were burning forest in order to plant crops. Archeology also shows a remarkable extent of dark earth, most of it on bluffs overlooking major rivers, where people lived in order to fish and use the water as their highways (as they still do in Amazonia today). In all, dark earth might cover 3 to 10 percent of Amazonia, which doesn't sound like much, but 10 percent would be about the size of France or Texas.

Scholars used to think that Amazonia was almost empty of people until modern times and that its forests were a pristine wilderness. What few people existed, scholars thought, were mobile, either hunter-gatherers or slash-and-burn farmers. But recent archeology shows how misguided that view was. By the period 1000–1500, the people of Amazonia had founded thousands of enduring settlements numbering up to 2,500 people each—large villages or small towns by global standards—in all, home to perhaps 5 to 10 million people. The first outsider to sail down the Amazon, a Spaniard in 1541, wrote that he saw many villages "less than a crossbow shot" apart on the river's banks. Thousands of villages were connected to one another, mainly by river-going canoes. Amazonia had its own loose web of connections. Much more loosely, these villages were also connected to societies outside of Amazonia, including the Inkas over the passes of the Andes.

MESOAMERICA: TOLTECS AND AZTECS

In the fourteenth and fifteenth centuries, the Aztecs of central Mexico formed what would become the second-largest empire in pre-Columbian America. Like the Inka Empire, it lasted until Spaniards turned up in the early sixteenth century.

In Chapter 10 we saw how central Mexico had hosted

CONSIDERING THE EVIDENCE

Aztec Wealth

Members of the Aztec confederation and other Nahuatl-speakers shared a myth that their people had migrated to the Basin of Mexico from Tollan (modern Tula), a city in Hidalgo, Mexico, built by Toltecs in the tenth century. The Aztecs not only imitated Toltec art but also dismantled sculptures and looted ceramics from Tula to bring back home. In the Aztec myths recorded in the *Florentine Codex* after the Spanish conquest, Nahuatl-speakers described the Toltec government, economy, and religion as ideal.

This Quetzalcoatl they considered as a god.... He was prayed to in olden times there at Tula....

And the Tolteca [Toltecs], his vassals, were highly skilled. Nothing was difficult when they did it, when they cut the green stone and cast gold, and made still other works of the craftsman of the feather worker.... [N]owhere was [too] distant ... so very quickly they went that they were called "those who walked the whole day without tiring." And there was a hill [where] the crier mounted ...; everywhere was heard what he said.... [T]hey knew what Quetzalcoatl had commanded the people....

Of no value was food.... It is said that the gourds [squash] were each exceedingly huge; some were quite round. And the ears of maize [corn] ... could only be embraced in one's arms.... And also the varicolored cotton grew: chili-red, yellow, pink, brown, green blue, verdigris color, dark brown, ripening brown, dark blue, fine yellow, [and] coyote colored cotton.... All of these came forth exactly so; they did not dye them.

And there dwelt all [varieties] of birds of precious feather: the lovely cotinga, the resplendent trogon, the troupial, the roseate spoonbill. And all the various birds sang very well.... And all the green stones, the gold were not costly.... In very many places there was chocolate.... They lacked nothing in their homes. Never was there famine.

... And this Quetzalcoatl also did penances. He bled the calf of his leg to stain thorns with blood. And he bathed at midnight.... [T]he offering priests took their manner of conduct from [his] life. By it they established the law of Tula. Thus were the customs established here in Mexico.

Source: *Florentine Codex: Book 3, The Origin of the Gods*, Second Edition, trans. Arthur J. O. Anderson and Charles E. Dibble. Monographs for the School of American Research (Salt Lake City, 1978).

QUESTIONS FOR ANALYSIS

1. Besides gold, what did the Nahuatl-speakers who told this story associate with wealth?
2. What did they admire about Quetzalcoatl's mythical rule?
3. What does this myth about the Toltecs reveal about the things that Nahuatl-speakers valued?

complex urban society based at Teotihuacán. After its collapse in the mid-first millennium CE, urban culture diminished until the rise of the Toltecs in the tenth century. They were migrants from the north who built a city of perhaps 40,000 people, Tollan (modern Tula), including pyramids, palaces, and ball courts—squarely in the Mesoamerican tradition. Their wealth, decorative arts, military prowess, and religious devotion apparently commanded respect among neighboring peoples. The Aztecs used to say of people who excelled in every domain that they "had a Toltec heart." For unknown reasons, Tollan collapsed in the mid-twelfth century. The remaining Toltecs migrated once more, to the shores of Lake Texcoco in the Basin of Mexico, where they soon acquired the Aztecs as neighbors.

ORIGINS The legends of the Aztecs, or Mexica, say they came from a place called Aztlan.[2] Their language, Nahuatl (or Nahua), is closest to languages spoken in northern Mexico and the southwestern United States, so it's likely that they migrated from there southward to the Basin of Mexico. The Basin—the region around today's Mexico City—is saucer-shaped, sits about 7,500 feet (2,250 m) above sea level, and is surrounded, except to the north, by much taller volcanic peaks. When the Aztecs arrived in the thirteenth to the fourteenth centuries, several interconnected lakes and swamps lay in

---

2 The term *Aztec* was invented in the nineteenth century by a German geographer, Alexander von Humboldt. I use it because of its familiarity, although modern scholars sometimes prefer the term *Mexica*.

the Basin. The Basin had fish in its waters, wildlife on its slopes, and obsidian rock everywhere, which for people relying on stone tools was a vital resource. At first, the newcomers had to accept dominion by other peoples and usually lived in the swamps and other undesirable areas on the shores of Lake Texcoco.

The Aztecs struggled for position among people already around the lake and its main island; but through war, diplomacy, and clever marriage alliances, they did well in the fierce politics of the Basin of Mexico. In 1325, they "founded" their capital city, **Tenochtitlán**—which was actually already inhabited. Until 1428, they were subordinate to other peoples in the Basin of Mexico, but in that year they joined with two other vassal peoples to create a triple alliance and turned the tables on their overlords. Thereafter, the Aztecs were the political leaders of the region. By 1440, the Triple Alliance had begun to make conquests outside the Basin of Mexico. By 1500, they controlled most of central Mexico, and almost everyone else had to pay them tribute.

STATECRAFT A series of vigorous leaders led the Aztec conquests. Their empire grew quickly, like that of the Inkas, especially under kings guided by a political genius called **Tlacélel** (ca. 1398–1480). He was a successful advisor and general, and a brilliant propagandist. He ordered that the Aztecs destroy their enemies' historical records, which was standard practice among victors, but also their own, which was unique. That history, he felt, needed more heroic deeds and prestigious ancestry. So he invented a new past for the Aztecs—one with glorious ancestors, mainly the lords of the ancient city of Teotihuacán and the Toltec city of Tollan. He declared the Aztecs to be the linchpin of the cosmic order, responsible for its smooth working.

Toltec Gods A stele found at the Tula archeological site in central Mexico dates from the period of the Toltec society's height in the tenth through twelfth centuries. It is carved with an image of a Toltec god, some of whom were the same as those later worshipped by the Aztecs.

In particular, he recast Aztec religion so that the Aztecs alone had the sacred duty of providing the reigning sun god (that job rotated among deities) with *chalchihuatl*, the mysterious force of life, without which the sun would not continue to shine and all would soon go dark. That force of life came in the form of flowers, the first fruits of the harvest, and sacrificed human beings. So the continued harmony of the cosmos required that the Aztecs, as the people of the sun, obtain a steady supply of victims. Human sacrifice featured in many ancient cultures around the world, including all the large-scale ones of the Americas. In Mesoamerica, the tradition of sacrifice went back thousands of years. Men, women, and children of all ranks of life could be sacrificed (and some volunteered for it), but in practice the Aztecs needed prisoners of war, some of whom—the numbers are unclear—became sacrificial victims. The welfare of the world depended on continual conquests by the Aztecs and their allies: for the sun to continue to deliver its bounty, the Aztecs would have to continue to secure prisoners for sacrifice. Their religious worldview made the Aztecs militaristic.

Religion was only part of the spur to conquest. Further

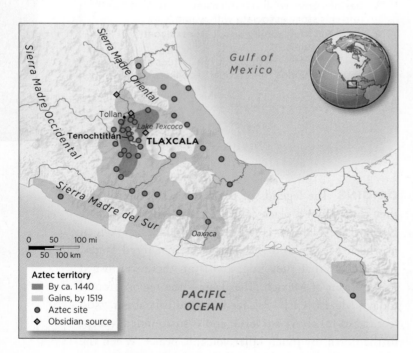

The Aztec Empire, ca. 1440–1519 The Aztecs, or Mexica, arrived in the Basin of Mexico from the north and by 1440 had begun an expansion into neighboring lands. By 1500, they ruled over 4 to 7 million people from their capital at Tenochtitlán. They dominated Mesoamerica and its 15 to 20 million inhabitants but never subdued one neighboring people, the Tlaxcalans. Obsidian, quarried at sites in the Basin of Mexico, was used for weapons and sharp-edged tools and was a major export of the Aztecs.

motivation came with a terrible drought and famine in the years 1450–1453. Aztec rulers responded by extending their domain over broader landscapes, lowlands as well as highlands, reducing the drought risk. By 1502, their reach extended throughout Mesoamerica, from Atlantic to Pacific coasts, and south to Oaxaca. One people in what is now Guatemala also paid them tribute.

The Aztecs could not dominate everyone, and like most conquerors they usually preferred to prevail without fighting. If local elites agreed to pay enough tribute, the Aztecs left them in peace. Their empire was less intrusive and meddlesome than the Inkas'. But from 1470 onward, the Aztecs were usually at war. They were mired in a stalemate with their neighbors to the west, and frequently they were fighting the people of Tlaxcala, a Nahuatl-speaking group like the Aztecs, who held out although surrounded by an Aztec-led alliance.

The formidability of the Aztecs rested on a robust economy, a large population, an efficient military, and an impressive culture.

Human Sacrifice A page from a 1530 pictographic history of the Aztec people offers a vivid rendering of a human victim being sacrificed to the sun god—right down to the victim's bloody body parts tumbling down the temple steps.

ECONOMIC LIFE Agriculture formed the heart of the economy. Maize, beans, and squash—the Three Sisters of North American farming—were the main crops, but the Aztecs raised peppers, tomatoes, and avocados too. The wetlands provided fish, turtles, and wildfowl. The Aztecs had only dogs and turkeys as domesticated animals. Fortunately for them, earlier peoples had developed the highly productive and reliable raised field agriculture, in which farmers piled up muck from the swamps into islands on which to plant their crops (see Chapter 10 for details). The Aztecs, who called the raised fields *chinampas*, refined this technique and extended it to many more lakes and swamps, multiplying the size of harvests in the Basin of Mexico. Only the deepest droughts could bring food shortages thanks to this system. Canoes, and porters using causeways, carried food into the capital city, Tenochtitlán. Human wastes, to be used as fertilizer, made the reverse trip from city to *chinampa*.

With improved food supply, especially after the droughts of the early 1450s were behind them, the Basin of Mexico was a hothouse of population growth. That provided Aztec rulers with plenty of male labor for the construction of temples, pyramids, causeways, and more *chinampas*—and with more soldiers. It also led to a larger female labor force and to growing quantities of cloth, spun by women and surrendered as tribute, which Aztec rulers

used to pay for whatever they required. Cloth and cacao beans served as money in the Aztec economy.

The Aztecs built on the market traditions of Mesoamerica. Most major settlements had an outdoor marketplace open once a week (the Aztecs used a five-day week). The biggest, at Tlatelolco in the capital, was open every day and attracted 25,000 people daily. One could find cotton cloth, copper axes, aromatic woods, maguey syrup, obsidian knives, salt, turkeys, tortillas, bird feathers, rabbit fur, and—one of Mesoamerica's gifts to the world—chocolate. Tlatelolco's market must have offered a swirl of colors, sounds, and smells. Although Aztec society had a guild of long-distance merchants, most items in the markets came from nearby. Within the Basin of Mexico, goods could often move by canoe. Elsewhere, porters carried them, often over rugged terrain. The Aztecs had neither wheeled vehicles nor beasts of burden.

Aztec society included plenty of craft specialists whose work supplied these markets. With time and imperial expansion, the division of labor and degree of specialization increased. Preparing feathers and obsidian blades, for example, became full-time specializations. Cloth making was a part-time job. Men (who spent most of their time farming) prepared thread from cotton or agave (cactus), and women wove it into fabric. By 1500, the Aztecs had built one of the world's most market-oriented societies.

Imperial Tribute A 1553 Aztec book recorded quantities of luxury commodities—feathers, leopard skins, cocoa beans—paid in tribute to Aztec rulers. The quantities are recorded both in pictograms and (for the benefit of the king of Spain, which had conquered Mexico some 30 years before) in Spanish translation.

The Aztec economy, like those of most complex societies in world history, supported a few people lavishly and a lot of people in misery. Aztec social structure, comparatively straightforward, featured a two-fold division: a small ruling elite responsible for administration, and a mass of common people who did all the manual labor. Life was short. Evidence from skeletons implies that death rates and birth rates were very high by global standards.

The capital city of Tenochtitlán ranked as one of the world's great cities, much larger as of 1500 than Rome or the Inka capital of Cuzco. It held 150,000 to 300,000 people, which made it larger than any city in China but Beijing. A Spaniard who saw the city in 1519 wrote:

> We were struck with the number of canoes, passing to and from the mainland, loaded with provisions and merchandise.... The noise and bustle of the marketplace below us could be heard almost a league off [a league is about 3 miles], and those who had been at Rome and at Constantinople said, that for convenience, regularity, and population, they had never seen the like.

The Aztec Empire, as of 1500, contained some 4 to 7 million people. The whole region of Mesoamerica, including peoples outside of Aztec control but connected to them by links of trade, politics, and culture, held perhaps 15 to 20 million people.

CULTURE In many cases, Aztec power came down to the ability to utilize organized violence. Their population and economy enabled the Aztecs to field a large military. The Aztec army had the advantages of numbers and weapons, especially obsidian-edged weapons such as spears, swords, and bows and arrows. Every male owed military service to the state. The Aztecs sponsored military academies, where males ages 15 to 20 learned how to handle weapons, build their endurance, and withstand acute pain. Successful warriors were those who captured many enemies: captives became candidates for sacrifice. These warriors moved up the social hierarchy quickly. They were rewarded with goods, deference, and fame that transferred to their descendants. They were entitled to wear distinctive clothing so everyone would know of their valor. Aztec art and literature lionized brave warriors, many of whom embraced the ideology according to which their success was essential to the survival of the cosmos—a good motivational tool.

In addition to markets, the Aztec economy involved obligatory tribute paid by conquered peoples to the Aztec ruling aristocracy. Each province had a different obligation. Some provided laborers. Some, near the frontiers of the empire, provided war captives. Others, close to the capital, sent foodstuffs. The Aztec elite apparently had a sweet tooth, taking as tribute 15,000 jars of honey annually. Most provinces provided mainly cloth. Aztec documents show that 22 of 30 provinces also sent bird feathers as tribute to Tenochtitlán.

Archeological digs reveal that the lives of ordinary people worsened as the Aztec Empire grew. More and more production went to the urban elite and the army, leaving less and less for common folk. Houses, made of adobe brick, typically had a few ceramics, obsidian tools, and grinding stones. Earlier ones had often had some jewelry and perhaps bronze tools as well.

While force was often necessary to expand the empire, religion could help hold it together. Like every other empire, the Aztecs sought to persuade subject peoples of their power, their justice, and their status as favorites of the gods. The Aztecs developed a highly complex cosmology that only well-educated priests could have mastered. The sky had 13 levels to it and the underworld 9, while the Earth stood in between. All intersected at the site of a great temple in the heart of Tenochtitlán. The Earth, itself a giant toad, rested on the back of a sea monster. A series of myths helped to explain how this cosmos evolved, as well as important questions such as the origins of the Aztec people, of maize, and of an alcoholic drink made of agave cactus sap, called *pulque*—still popular today in central Mexico. Rituals and sacrifices, done in the proper way at the proper times and regulated by priests and emperors,

Religious Art This ceramic urn, buried in a fifteenth-century Aztec grave in Tenochtitlán, depicts the rain god Tlaloc.

were expected to keep the cosmos in balance.

The Aztec pantheon was packed with gods and goddesses, and it expanded in ways that helped the empire to grow. Every town, neighborhood, and lineage had at least one god, and like Hindu gods they all could appear in different guises, often as animals. The god most venerated by the state—in effect, the tribal god of the Aztec people—was Huitzilopochtli, whose responsibilities included the sun, fire, war, and human sacrifice. Aztec gods, like ancient Greek ones, had kinfolk, suffered from jealousy and temper tantrums, and could be spiteful as well as kindly toward humans. Scholars have identified 144 gods, about two-thirds of them male. In addition to some conventional deities, such as a maize god, a moon goddess, and a god of the underworld, the Aztec pantheon included some distinctive ones, such as a god of feather workers and one who protected drunk people.

The Aztec elite oversaw the construction of monumental architecture worthy of a powerful empire. As elsewhere, such display was useful for religious rituals and for reminding ordinary people of the power of priests and rulers. Aztec ceremonial centers had stone temples decorated with elaborate carvings, often using jaguar, serpent, or eagle motifs to invoke supernatural power. The vicinity of Tenochtitlán included several large pyramids used in religious rituals that helped buttress the political order. Aztec artisans also specialized in ceramics, jade statuettes, wood carving, and colorful feather arrangements that were often used as headdresses. Art and architecture, from the layout of temples to the sequences of feathers, had religious and political meaning, and helped to legitimate the state and elite rule. The last of the Aztec rulers, Moctezuma, had a palace that accommodated about 1,000 people.

The Aztecs developed an extensive literature that built on Mesoamerican traditions. They wrote on paper made from fig tree bark. Their books, long folded sheets of animal skin, are conventionally called codices (sing. codex). Some 61 Mesoamerican codices survive, written by Aztecs or their neighbors. Nowhere else in the Americas

Aztec Daily Life The sixteenth-century *Florentine Codex* features numerous illustrations of Aztec daily life, such as these images of peasants harvesting, processing, and storing wheat. The text is in Nahuatl, in a writing system developed by a Spanish priest using the Roman alphabet.

produced books, so far as we know. Aztec books contained information on history and deeds of emperors, on tribute and laws, on rituals and gods, on medicine, botany, and poetry. The most important source for Aztec history and culture, the so-called **Florentine Codex**, compiled by a Spanish priest and his Aztec students after the fall of the Aztec Empire, is a comprehensive catalogue of some 1,200 pages.

The earliest Aztec writings used symbols that were either pictures of what they were intended to represent (pictographic) or pictures of things whose names included sounds in Nahuatl that if combined properly conveyed the intended meaning (logographic). So, to convey the sound of the name Ken, an Aztec scribe might draw a pot to indicate the *k* sounds, because the Nahuatl word for "pot" is pronounced ko-mit-el, followed by a bean and then a human head for the next sounds. It was not an easy system to learn, and only a tiny fraction of Aztecs could read. Nonetheless, in the capital, or at least its elite precincts, people recited and wrote poetry. Favorite themes included flowers, death, and the glory of Tenochtitlán.

Aztec science built on Mesoamerican traditions too. Like every pre-modern culture, they used plants as healing agents: the *Florentine Codex* lists 149 and the ailments against which they were used. Modern tests show that about 70 percent of these are actually helpful. The Aztecs were keen astronomers with a special interest in eclipses. Their most sophisticated scientific achievements lay in mathematics. They used a base 20 system and had names for numbers, formed with strings of suffixes, up to 64,000,000. They could perform complex calculations with large numbers.

SOCIETY A fair amount of textual and archeological evidence sheds light on family dynamics in Aztec society. It reveals that the broad patterns resembled those found in complex farming societies around the world, but the details were often unique. Aztec families could be simple nuclear families or joint families with several relatives living together, such as the nuclear families of two brothers. Men typically married around age 20 or 22, to brides of about age 12 to 16. Rich men could marry many wives. Divorce was legal in instances when men beat their wives or wives failed either to keep house satisfactorily or to produce children. Adultery invited stern penalties: strangling for women, and crushed skulls for men.

Parents raised children with tough love. That included

Aztec Children A page from a 1541–1542 Aztec codex shows boys and girls being educated in the social roles of Aztec culture: at top, boys learn to become priests or soldiers; the center image depicts a marriage scene.

plenty of lectures about the importance of honesty, industry, and proper conduct. Children who slipped up might expect to be lashed with cactus spines or forced to inhale smoke from sizzling chili peppers. Small children learned their roles and skills from their parents. But at age 15 or so, they began to attend school. Elite families sent their children to the priests' school (*calmecac*) to learn about religion and administration. Everyone else went to a *telpochcalli* ("house of youth") to learn about war (boys) or handicrafts and child care (girls). Obligatory formal education for everyone is extremely rare in world history, and the Aztecs were among the first to require it.

Gender roles were also typical for complex agrarian societies, although women took part in marketplace culture more than in most places. At birth, baby girls received a broom, a basket, a spindle, and a bowl. Boy babies got tools or weapons. Women were expected to work in the home and its courtyard, spending long hours grinding maize, making tortillas, and weaving cloth. They raised turkeys and gathered the cactus sap needed for *pulque*. A woman's most important role was as mother, and women who died in childbirth were celebrated like fallen warriors. Aztec women did, however, venture into the marketplace and transact business on their own accounts. Some became administrators of marketplaces, responsible for seeing that everyone played fair. They could own property. Women who survived past age 50 or so (female life expectancy seems to have been about 35) retired from active work and could expect to be respectfully treated as sources of wisdom and advice; they were also permitted to drink *pulque* day and night.

The more committed to conquest the Aztec Empire became, the more its rulers needed to extoll men's military virtue and extract cloth from women. Aztec mythology and art often portrayed women as sources of discord, disrupters of cosmic harmony whose bad deeds required men to fight and die to put things right. In this respect, the Aztec culture of gender resembled that of many warrior-aristocracies in world history, including, for example, the one Homer described in the *Iliad* or that of the *Rig Veda* in India.

The Social Order In a fifteenth-century image with Spanish annotations, Aztec men and women venerate their elders—including an old woman who is shown reclining and drinking *pulque*.

Like the Inka state, the Aztec Empire lasted roughly a century, using all the tools of power typical of big states everywhere in the pre-modern world. And like the Inkas, the Aztecs shared their continent with diverse peoples who lived without states and who left fewer clues about their lives. Let's look at a few examples from North America.

THE ANCESTRAL PUEBLO (ANASAZI)

The **Ancestral Pueblo**[3] lived not too far from the ancestral lands of the Aztecs, in the Four Corners area where Arizona, New Mexico, Colorado, and Utah meet today. The whole region that is now northwestern Mexico and the southwestern United States is mainly desert, much of it at high elevations. Oases and river valleys, the only hospitable landscapes where trees or crops might grow, are few. People had lived there for thousands of years, and in the few locations with enough water they had begun to raise irrigated maize by 2000 BCE. By 500 BCE, the Three Sisters—maize, beans, and squash—formed the heart of the farming system. Population ebbed and flowed with climate changes. Spring snowmelt flowing down from the mountains and high plateaus played the largest role in determining the success of irrigation farming. If the snowpack was thin and spring water scarce, crops failed and people had to live off of food reserves, survive on foraging and hunting, or migrate elsewhere.

Between 700 and 1100 or so, the Ancestral Pueblo population swelled. Wetter climate allowed more farming, food, and people, and a more sedentary existence. In a few spots they even farmed without irrigation for a while, relying on summer rains, which are often local thunderstorms. In effect, the Ancestral Pueblo placed a huge bet on agriculture, starting more than 10,000 new farmsteads between 850 and 1000. They cultivated just about every promising patch of land, hoping enough rain would fall to make the effort worthwhile. This was frontier farming, loosely analogous to expansions of agriculture into dry lands that took place in northern China or the North African Maghreb. The scattered distribution of Ancestral Pueblo farming increased the probability that rain would fall on someone's fields and gardens. Networks of kinship and reciprocity encouraged the lucky to share with the unlucky in the knowledge that the next year their roles

---

3 The *Ancestral Pueblo* are also known as *Anasazi*, a term today's Pueblo generally do not prefer. It means "ancestors of our enemies" in the Navajo language.

might be reversed. Rain didn't have to fall on everyone's crops for everyone to survive.

Since maize and beans store well, the Ancestral Pueblo could move food around as needed or keep it where the hungry could find it. An elite developed that oversaw the distribution of stored food. Its authority was probably more religious than military: there is no evidence of armies among the Ancestral Pueblo, nor of fortification. This elite also took responsibility for the rituals that the Ancestral Pueblo credited with bringing summer rain.

For centuries, this big bet on agriculture paid off. Rains in the region proved unusually good from about 1020 to 1130, according to tree ring evidence. Food was plentiful. Ancestral Pueblo women began to bear more children, and people migrated into the region as well. The Ancestral Pueblo started to carve elaborate houses into the sides of cliffs, accessible sometimes only by ladders. Their settlements also had larger ceremonial spaces, called *kivas*, often dug into the floors of buildings but sometimes at the foot of their cliff dwellings. In places such as Chaco Canyon, Mesa Verde, and Bandelier, you can still see their distinctive architecture. In the eleventh and twelfth centuries, they also built some 400 miles (650 km) of roads across the high plateau, perhaps for economic reasons— they had to drag timber a long way to their settlements— but perhaps for spiritual reasons too.

Almost all the roads led to the settlement at **Chaco Canyon** in northern New Mexico, suggesting it was the center of the Ancestral Pueblo world. Some Chaco

Canyon buildings served as food storehouses. Religious and political leaders probably lived there, although no more than 2,500 of them at any one time. Several thousand other people came for ceremonies and to trade or work for food in lean times.

This pattern of dispersed farming settlements, ceremonial centers, and mutual aid worked well enough most years. It could not always prevent seasonal hunger (evident from skeletal remains) and—if rains failed widely—temporary catastrophe. But the network of settlements, trade links, and kin obligations connected the whole region in ways that safeguarded against starvation as long as enough summer rain fell somewhere on Ancestral Pueblo crops. Most years it did.

But not all years. A few hundred skeletons tell another side of the Ancestral Pueblo story. Roughly half of those born died by age 18, most of them in their early years from malnutrition and disease. In the eleventh century in Chaco Canyon, four out of five children had acute iron-deficiency anemia. Many women died in their late teens and twenties, presumably most in childbirth. Men lived on average seven years longer than women. Those who made it to old age usually showed signs of arthritis and osteoporosis, indicating lives of hard work. Elite Chacoans fared somewhat better. They were on average nearly 2 inches (5 cm) taller than common folk, and their children more than three times as likely to make it past age five. The elite ate more deer and antelope meat, consequently suffering far less from iron deficiency.

At its height, Ancestral Pueblo society supported some 50,000 to 150,000 people, 10,000 to 20,000 farmsteads, and 120 of their distinctive cliffside apartment complexes. The Ancestral Pueblo had energetically taken advantage of two or three centuries of above-average rainfall, and naturally enough presumed it was normal. But a cycle of drought began in the 1090s, and after a few better decades during which the Ancestral Pueblo built *kivas* and roads as never before, it returned with a vengeance around 1130. Deep drought endured for decades. Building ground to a halt. Storehouses emptied. Some people starved. Others migrated away. Few people wanted to support the elite, whose rainmaking rituals seemed to have lost their power. Chaco Canyon and its neighborhood lost most of its population.

Pottery and architectural evidence imply that some people moved north into Colorado. One settlement there, Mesa Verde, thrived until 1250 or so. Searing droughts

Ancestral Pueblo Architecture The site of a major Ancestral Pueblo settlement at Mesa Verde includes a number of the round *kiva* rooms used for religious ceremonies.

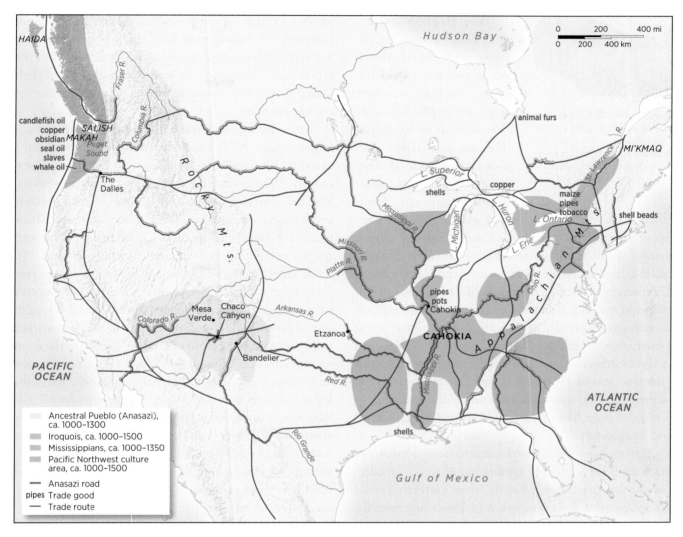

North American Cultures, ca. 1000–1500 This map shows the location of the North American cultures discussed in this chapter, together with some major long-distance trade routes. Altogether, perhaps 5 to 10 million people lived in North America in these centuries, loosely linked by trade. In the absence of pack animals or wheeled vehicles, seacoast, river, and lake transport were especially important.

reappeared about 1275 to 1300, by which time all the big settlements of the entire region had emptied out, and the network among them, the links of trade and power, had withered away. Fewer people remained in fewer major settlements, and the Ancestral Pueblo were less able to coordinate social action over long distances. Here the human web came and went with the rains.

PEOPLES OF THE PACIFIC NORTHWEST COAST

While the Ancestral Pueblo found ways to cope with water scarcity, the peoples of the Pacific Northwest coast—from the Alaska panhandle south to Oregon—learned to exploit water's abundance. Rain and snow fell reliably along the coast and on the west-facing slopes of inland mountains, feeding hundreds of rivers. Tasty and nutritious salmon swam up these rivers to their breeding grounds in shallow streams every summer. In a good year, 10 to 20 million salmon swam up the mighty Columbia and Fraser Rivers, and millions more up the smaller rivers

The ancestors of the Coast Salish, the Haida, and many other native peoples have lived here for 10,000 years at least, and likely more. By 1000 CE, about 30 distinct languages were spoken along the coast, but the cultures in question bore broad similarities.

Pacific Northwest Peoples Haida art often featured animals that bore cultural and religious significance. This wooden dish is carved to look like both an eagle (left) and a whale (right), with the central panel serving as both the whale's fin and the eagle's wing.

They lived in permanent settlements—big villages with hundreds of people—yet they did not farm. Their homes were large cedar-plank houses that held 20 to 80 people. The sea and rivers provided abundant food. They hunted seals and other marine mammals. Some of them, like the Makah, hunted whales. Above all they fished, using weirs, baskets, and nets to capture a small share of the migratory salmon and several other fish species that frequented the coastal waters and rushing rivers. They hunted deer and gathered shellfish, berries, and edible plants too. But after 1000 CE, they relied increasingly on salmon—especially dried and smoked salmon in the winter when other foods were hard to find. The peoples of the Northwest coast also conducted commerce with groups far inland, trading in slaves, copper, obsidian, and oil from whales, seals, and the candlefish (euchalon, so oily it can burn like a candle). Oil helped preserve dried and smoked fish.

These peoples lived amidst a temperate rain forest and made much of what they needed out of wood. In addition to constructing big houses, they routinely carved canoes, paddles, tools, weapons, and decorations from the abundant fir and cedar. They had no metal tools, carving instead with shells, stones, and beaver teeth. Their most distinctive decorative carvings, often done on poles or house-beams, represent sacred beings and family legends, and sometimes served to mark property. After 1800, when metal carving tools became available, this tradition gave rise to towering totem poles.

SOCIAL STRUCTURE Three main ranks existed in this hierarchical society: slaves, commoners, and chiefs. Slaves accounted for 20 to 40 percent of the population in some villages—broadly similar to the proportion in the ancient Roman world in the first century CE. Slaves were captives taken in raids or warfare, or the descendants of captives—slave status was hereditary. Free commoners composed the bulk of society, and a small percentage were chiefs. Chiefs could own and command slaves; indeed, they held power of life and death over slaves. A prominent chief might own dozens, partly for their labor and

partly as a mark of chiefly status. But chiefs could not command free commoners. They led by persuasion. They had to be charismatic, and it helped to be skilled in the arts of war. Their authority rested in large part on their ability to distribute goods to others, often in ceremonies called potlatches.

Slaves did much of the hard and dirty work, which might include felling mighty cedar trunks, carving out a canoe with beaver teeth, or cleaning piles of fish. Commoners might specialize as carpenters, carvers, or weavers. Men fished and hunted. Women cleaned fish, wove baskets and blankets, prepared meals, and tended children. Chiefs focused on resolving disputes, conducting diplomacy with neighbors, fighting enemies, and rewarding followers. To do so, chiefs claimed ownership of fishing grounds, cranberry bogs, timber forests, and even intellectual property such as songs, stories, and dances. Commoners, who might own their own clothing, fishing tackle, and canoes but little else, gained access to other forms of property and to natural resources through the generosity of chiefs. A chief with enough property to dole out might command the loyalty of hundreds of followers. A chief who couldn't or wouldn't compete with his rivals in generosity did not long remain a chief. There was, then, considerable specialization and division of labor both among the different ranks and within the ranks of commoners—even if everyone pitched in with nets and traps during the brief summer weeks when the salmon swam past.

WARFARE In the centuries after 1000, as dependence on salmon deepened, a plague of violence haunted the Northwest coast, especially its northern stretch. War, raiding, and fortification had existed for centuries here, as we saw in Chapter 10. But now villagers built more elaborate fortifications of wood and stone atop bluffs and cliffs. They increasingly located their villages in places chosen for defense. Population dipped severely around 1150 to 1300, perhaps partly a result of heightened violence and slaving—although an unusually dry climate for two centuries might have posed an even greater problem. Small streams where salmon breed could dry up in extreme drought. In any case, after 1300, reliable rains returned and population recovered, but the scourge of warfare, like the deepened dependence on salmon, lasted.

A LOCAL WEB Peoples along the Pacific coast lived in their own local web, aided by smooth sailing and paddling on the many bays, inlets, and straits from Alaska to Puget Sound. The rivers too were navigable for stretches, and one, the Columbia, hosted a big annual gathering at The Dalles (located 100 miles east of today's Portland) where coastal people mingled with their inland counterparts at festivals and fairs. The peoples of the coast had suitable trade goods to justify long voyages. They attacked enemies and raided for slaves hundreds of miles away at times. They stood apart from the wider world outside of North America until the 1770s, when European ships arrived.

CAHOKIA

The American Midwest, in 1000 CE, contained several dozen settled peoples who, unlike those of the Pacific Northwest coast, took up farming. Together they are sometimes called Moundbuilders, sometimes Mississippians. What they called themselves and one another, we do not know. Indeed, we know tantalizingly little about them, almost all of it through bones, stones, and shards of pottery. For centuries, they lived in hundreds of small villages. Then in the eleventh century, something strange happened at a place called **Cahokia**, in Illinois just across the Mississippi River from today's St. Louis. An Amerindian city sprang up.

Cahokia lay in the floodplain of the Mississippi River, which held two advantages. Its alluvial soils were fertile, and transportation along the river was easy. It also seems to have been an unusually peaceful place: the skeletons there from before 1000 CE show much lower rates of violence than those elsewhere in the American Midwest.

Cahokia, along with the rest of the American Midwest, was undergoing something of an agricultural revolution, loosely parallel to those in medieval China and northern Europe noted in earlier chapters, that dramatically boosted food supplies. The change probably had something to do with the warmer climate and longer growing season that set in around the period 900–1250 CE. It certainly had a lot to

do with the development of a new form of maize: **flint maize** (*maiz de ocho*), which yielded bigger, juicier kernels and grew to maturity faster than other varieties.

With flint maize, North Americans could take fuller advantage of the nutritious combination of maize, beans, and squashes. For millennia, they had raised these crops in gardens to supplement their hunting and foraging. Now, after 800 or 900, they could become true farmers, needing little food beyond what their plots produced. Cahokia's alluvium provided excellent soils for intensive maize farming. And the timing was good too: the Mississippi experienced no huge floods between about 600 and about 1200, so Cahokia was unusually free from disaster.

In 1000, Cahokia was still just another modest settlement with a population of about 1,000 people. But by 1050, about 15,000 to 20,000 people lived at Cahokia. It became a genuine city, the largest settlement north of the Rio Grande. Pottery styles of humble cooking pots indicate that people migrated to Cahokia from what is now Missouri, Indiana, Wisconsin, and throughout Illinois. Why they came to Cahokia is unclear. Once they got there, they built ceremonial plazas and the biggest mounds in North America.

They did their building in spurts, apparently in coordinated, disciplined efforts. There are more than 100 mounds at Cahokia, of varying sizes and shapes. The largest, Monks Mound, is about 100 ft (30m) high and covers 14 acres (6 hectares—roughly 12 football fields). Archeologists reckon it would have taken 1,000 laborers about a year to pile up that much dirt. Their bosses' motivations were probably religious. Monks Mound stood next to a ceremonial space and presumably was the setting for religious rituals. Most

Cahokian Objects A Cahokian statue shows a woman performing a religious ceremony celebrating the corn harvest.

Cahokia, ca. 1050–1250 Cahokia, in today's southwestern Illinois near the Mississippi River, developed into a city of perhaps 20,000 people in the eleventh century, the largest settlement north of the Rio Grande. This map shows Cahokia's defensive wooden palisade, some of its 120 mounds, and Monks Mound, the biggest earthen structure in the Americas before 1500.

mounds were used for sacrifices and burials. Most of those sacrificed were young women.

Cahokia was a city in the sense that many people clustered together. But most of them remained farmers. Some people specialized in craft production such as pottery and probably cloth as well. A very few might have been religious specialists and political leaders, although the political structure of Cahokia remains unclear. Burials, some of which include precious objects, indicate that the city had social hierarchy and a small elite. One man's corpse was carefully buried on 20,000 shell beads arranged in the shape of a bird and was accompanied by 53 young women apparently killed in his honor. Their skeletons imply they were poorly nourished and came from afar, perhaps as slaves. Despite its social hierarchy, Cahokia was not a state. As in Amazonia, among the Anasazi, and the peoples of the Northwest coast, Cahokia had elites but no king, no bureaucracy, and no army.

The new cultural configuration created by the surge of immigration to Cahokia proved attractive far and wide. Cahokian objects (pipes, pots, etc.) and imagery have been found as far away as Oklahoma and Minnesota, and were common in settlements that were in easy communication with the city along the Mississippi River. Shells from the Gulf coast and copper from the Lake Superior region have been unearthed at Cahokia. Evidently, Cahokia exerted some sort of power, perhaps partly economic, partly religious, that helped it spin its own thin and faint web in the heartland of North America—but only briefly.

By 1150, Cahokia was in trouble. Like people along the Northwest coast at the same time, Cahokians built fortifications of wooden walls (palisades) around the core settlement. Outer villages were abandoned. Both of these shifts suggest fear of attack—perhaps by strangers, perhaps by people unhappy about being at the bottom of the social hierarchy. Cahokians just about stopped building mounds and public buildings. Whatever central authority they had had was now too weak to organize collective undertakings. Unlike the villages of the Northwest coast, which recovered after 1300, by 1350 Cahokia was almost deserted.

Cahokia's fall remains a mystery. However, increased flooding, always a risk in the Mississippi floodplain, looks to be part of the riddle. Archeologists have found at the site much more sediment dating from around the period 1150–1250 than from either before or after. In the early 1200s an earthquake hit, knocking down part of Monks Mound. Charcoal deposits suggest parts of Cahokia burned. Droughts apparently became more common. No doubt many other things happened that contributed to the downfall of Cahokia; but however it happened, the city emptied, and the surrounding villages nearly did. No Amerindian settlement in North America since has equaled it in size. (Indeed, probably no city in North America surpassed its population until the late eighteenth century.) None of the surviving oral traditions of any Amerindian people mention anything about Cahokia.

Perhaps, however, Cahokia was not unique as a sizeable settlement in the heart of North America. Recent archeology suggests that from about 1450 to 1700 in south-central Kansas another community of perhaps 10,000 or even 20,000 people thrived as farmers, foragers, and hunters. They are probably ancestors of the Wichita, an Amerindian people. Their settlement, called Etzanoa, had vanished by 1700.

THE IROQUOIS

In the eastern woodlands of North America, people had been foraging, fishing, and hunting since at least 10,000 BCE. Their numbers were small and grew only slowly. After 1000 BCE, some of them dabbled in horticulture, raising plants such as goosefoot and sunflowers (see Chapter 10). Then, perhaps as early as 500 CE, some groups began to experiment with maize, a new crop transmitted from one people to the next all the way from its homeland in Mexico. One such group was the Iroquois, living in what is now upstate New York, southwestern Quebec, and southeastern Ontario. Their influence extended south to Virginia and west to Ohio. The term *Iroquois* refers to a broad Amerindian language group but also to a narrower set of peoples, made up of five (after 1722, six) so-called nations—popularly known as tribes. The word *Iroquois* itself, in the Mi'kmaq language, means "killer people," which says something about how their neighbors came to regard the Iroquois.

FARMING AND SETTLEMENT As the Iroquois gradually took up maize farming, they became more sedentary, more numerous, and more inclined to violence among themselves and against neighboring peoples. They did not forsake hunting and foraging, and still got 40 percent of their food that way in 1400. But maize became their mainstay, as it did in Cahokia and among most Amerindians of the eastern woodlands. The shift to maize, and later beans as well, increased the food supply and boosted population. The number and size of settlements seems to have grown quickly in the thirteenth and fourteenth centuries, while Cahokia underwent decline. Population growth also made the Iroquois and their neighbors more likely to compete with one another over hunting grounds. Their investment in settlements made them less willing to flee trouble and more inclined to stand and fight in the event of conflict. This suite of changes is common in world history when peoples turn to sedentary agriculture. Whereas in 1000 the Iroquois were dispersed among hundreds of small hamlets, by 1350 they lived in larger—and fortified—settlements.

At some point before 1450 (some scholars say the mid-twelfth century), the Iroquois managed to forge a confederacy, the **League of Peace and Power**. Iroquois legend attributed this to an outsider from the north, a prince of peace born of a virgin girl. He had a speech impediment and spoke through an interpreter. Nonetheless, he persuaded the leaders of all the Iroquois to give up warfare among themselves and to unite, the better to exert power over others. Legends notwithstanding, it likely took long negotiations to create the League.

Thereafter, the Iroquois generally stuck together, and their less organized, less numerous, less powerful neighbors came to fear their raiders and war parties. Some neighbors migrated away out of reach, some sought to negotiate their way to safety, and others fought—usually unsuccessfully. Like many peoples, the Iroquois usually absorbed war captives into their own clans, and indeed sometimes set out to capture people to replace their own people lost to capture or death. They needed people, mainly women, to grow and grind maize.

GENDER AND FAMILY The Iroquois liked to say that the forest was the world of men and the village the domain of women. Like most peoples, they organized social life by gender, but they did it in a distinctive way. Men hunted, fished, raided, traded, and conducted diplomacy. They were often away from their villages for days or weeks at a time. Women farmed, ground maize, cooked, fetched water and firewood, and raised children—and stayed in their village almost all the time, except when butchering deer in seasonal hunting camps.

This sexual division of labor resembled that of most other North American Amerindians and, aside from women doing all the farming, resembled the arrangements

followed by many agricultural societies around the world. But among the Iroquois, women also ran the affairs of their village. By the eighteenth century (for which there is plentiful documentary evidence), and probably well before that, women—or more precisely, some women—selected the chiefs of the Iroquois nations.

Life as an Iroquois woman had its struggles. After the introduction of maize, their daily routines grew tougher because grinding maize took much more effort than foraging or processing pumpkins, nuts, roots, or berries. Their skeletons show evidence of stronger musculature and more

Iroquois Ceremony This 1704 engraving by a French traveler depicts several Iroquois dances and ceremonial pipes. Such pipes were used in the context of peace and war, commerce, politics, and religious rituals.

arthritis after 800 or 900 CE, when maize became the staff of life. Skeletal remains also show much higher rates of violence, which specialists see as an indication that women were commonly captured from neighboring peoples, partly in order to work grinding maize. As captives, they were sometimes roughly treated. Life expectancy for females was lower than for males. In effect, the turn to maize raised the demand for female labor, making women a scarce resource. For some women, that translated into captivity, which might resemble adoption or might resemble slavery. For other women, especially those of respected lineages, it meant power.

The turn to maize, and to sedentary ways of life in which males were often absent, encouraged the Iroquois to develop a distinctive society with a matrilineal and matrilocal tradition. Upon marriage, a husband moved in with his wife's extended family, including her sisters, mother, and aunts and their families. The Iroquois normally lived in wooden longhouses, on average 60 by 25 feet (18 by 7 m), although some were as much as 400 feet (120 m) long. Longhouses were also horizontal silos, with room for storage of maize, beans, and smoked fish or venison. As more sisters married, brought in more husbands, and families grew, the Iroquois would build additions on their longhouses. Giant pots found by archeologists indicate women cooked for many families at once.

Some scholars think the Iroquois preferred female babies over males, because upon marriage sons would contribute to another family's welfare. If true, this was an unusual preference in world history. Even if not true, the matriarchs of Iroquois society—women who by dint of ancestry, age, and personality led their longhouse or a cluster of longhouses—exerted real power and enjoyed wide respect. They helped to impose an ethic of negotiation and peace within Iroquois society, while encouraging young men to distinguish themselves by violence against other peoples. The Iroquois evolved into a society that struck its neighbors as particularly aggressive and violent but at the same time accorded women unusual authority.

RELIGION In religion, the Iroquois were less innovative and more conventional. Like all their neighbors, they practiced a variety of shamanism that found spirituality in nature. Their rituals included trances, tobacco and other psychoactive drugs, and large roles for dancing that would test one's stamina—all of which helped people see and communicate with the spirit world (the tobacco they smoked was stronger stuff than that sold today and could induce hallucinations). They liked to leave offerings of tobacco at choice locations, such as waterfalls and cliffs, where spirits were believed to reside. Like other Amerindian peoples from Mexico on north, they connected blood with crop fertility and thus ceremonially shed their own blood, or that of captives, to improve the harvest.

The similarity of Iroquois religion to that of other eastern woodland peoples, and indeed other Amerindians, is evidence of routine contacts among the many Amerindian peoples. The flows of migrants and captives strengthened these contacts and connections. The Iroquois did not build mounds like the Amerindians of the Midwest and Deep South, a major difference. But some of their rituals, especially those involving the sacrifice of captives, resembled practices in faraway Mesoamerica. In spiritual matters as well as in cropping patterns, Amerindians of North America showed some broad similarities, probably of Mexican origin, that indicate a loose web of interaction spanning most of the continent, especially the lands suited to maize, in the centuries after 1000 CE.

A LOOSE WEB That loose web included trade networks in which the Iroquois took part. They swapped extra maize or tobacco to their northern neighbors in exchange for animal furs and to Amerindians in New England in exchange for shell beads (wampum). They received copper objects that originated in the upper Great Lakes region, several hundred miles away. They traded clay pipes with all their neighbors. Their trade took the form of ritual exchanges of gifts that took place now and again. They did not use money or markets.

OCEANIA

In the centuries between 1000 and 1700, many of the societies on Pacific islands changed under the pressures of their own success. As islanders learned how best to wring a living from their lands and lagoons, their populations grew. Their prospects improved further when some intrepid sailors ventured to South America and returned with a new crop, sweet potato. Recent genetic studies indicate that sweet potato first came to Polynesia between 1100 and 1200, from the Peru/Ecuador region, and quickly was carried to many different Polynesian islands. The sweet potato in Polynesia, like champa rice in Song China,

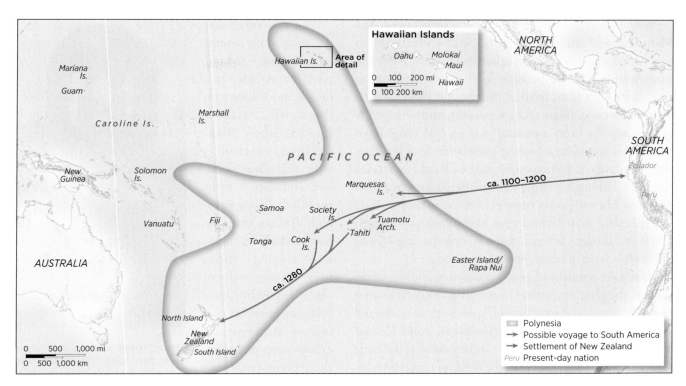

Oceania, ca. 1000–1500 Oceania in these centuries witnessed widespread population growth, a major episode of frontier expansion, and another of political development. The population growth in Oceania drew in part upon the acquisition of a new crop, sweet potato, which came from South America in the twelfth century along the routes depicted here. The frontier expansion took the form of the colonization of New Zealand after 1280, dramatically expanding the domain of Polynesian people and culture. The most notable political development was the evolution of kingship and kingdoms in Hawaii after about 1450.

brought about another agricultural revolution—but on a smaller scale than in China, more like maize among the Iroquois. Sweet potato yielded well in most of Oceania.

But by 1500 in most cases, abundance had given way to renewed scarcity. People organized themselves in order to defend their interests and compete for control of the best fishing grounds and farmlands. Partly in response to scarcity, several island societies took up abortion, infanticide, and celibacy and came to glory in war. In most regions of the Pacific, long-distance voyaging diminished, and isolation increased—in contrast to the situation in the Americas and in most of the world.

NEW ZEALAND: THE LAST FRONTIER

In 1000 CE, no humans lived in New Zealand. Its plants and animals were mainly remnants of the Cretaceous period (155 to 65 million years ago), almost completely isolated from the rest of life on Earth. The first people to arrive came in sailing canoes from central or eastern Polynesia, probably about 1280. They carried their

distinctive biological baggage with them, as Polynesians always did when seeking new islands. The most important animals they brought in their canoes were dogs and rats. They might have set out with pigs and chickens too, as Polynesians normally did, but they must have sailed for months and perhaps ate their tastiest animals en route. They brought Polynesian food crops too, although most would not grow in the chillier climates of New Zealand. The two that did best were taro and sweet potato (called *kumara* in New Zealand—from *kumar,* a Qechua word).

The first colonists, probably about 200 in number, found a paradise of Pacific protein. New Zealand's Cretaceous creatures included the moa, a flightless bird as tall as a horse and as heavy as a pig. Dozens of other species of flightless birds flapped around too. The coasts teemed with fur seals and shellfish. New Zealand's plants were less nutritious, although the **Maori**—as the Polynesians of New Zealand are called—found a fern whose roots they turned into an edible paste. Early Maori lived where the seals and moa were, especially on the eastern coast of the South Island, usually in villages of 50 to 200 people.

While the big birds and blubbery seals lasted, the Maori ate well and flourished. Skeletal evidence shows that Maori stood taller than other Polynesians. Very few adult women did not become mothers—an indication that diet didn't limit fertility. Infant and child mortality rates came to about 20 to 35 percent, and average life expectancy for both men and women was roughly 30 years. This counts as a healthy population by world history standards. Children apparently suffered few serious beatings, although many people suffered broken bones as adults. Hunting seals among the rocks in slippery surf might explain that. Archeologists have found few weapons of war and no signs of fortification among the early Maori. Their tools were of stone, bone, and wood.

After two centuries of peace, prosperity, and abundant protein, the good times came to an end in the decades after 1450. The moas, and 30 other bird species, grew scarce and went extinct. Seals became rare. The Maori worked harder at raising garden crops, but their climate cooled as the Little Ice Age set in, which restricted the range of taro especially. Still, by 1500, garden crops accounted for half of their food because the yields from hunting and foraging had tailed off. The population, now a few tens of thousands strong, began to compete more keenly for food.

Families and lineages banded together into larger units for defense. Weapons and warfare became routine. Like chiefs on the Pacific Northwest coast a few centuries before, Maori leaders began to build elaborate earth-and-wood fortifications (called *pa* in the Maori language) behind which their supporters huddled in times of danger. Maori chiefs eventually built about 6,000 *pa* sites, and no one could remain a successful leader without one. As elsewhere in Polynesia (and the Americas), warfare included spiritual dimensions that encouraged victors to eat parts of the vanquished, whereas the first two centuries of Maori settlement betray no signs of cannibalism. New Zealand's population between 1500 and 1750 probably grew only a little, reaching maybe 100,000 or 150,000.

New Zealand Wildlife A nineteenth-century biologist poses with a moa skeleton to indicate the size of the flightless bird, which Maori hunted to extinction.

The late Polynesian voyaging in the South Pacific (ca. 1000–1300) bears comparison to the Vikings in the North Atlantic (ca. 850–1100). Both required extraordinary maritime skills and resolute courage. Both Polynesians and Vikings seem to have sailed to America, staying there only briefly, affecting it negligibly, and bringing away nothing of consequence except sweet potato in the Polynesian case. With the settlement of Iceland after 874 by Vikings and New Zealand after 1280 by Polynesians, all the world's large inhabitable spaces were populated. The long saga of migration and human colonization of the Earth that had begun on African savannas about 300,000 years ago ended on a New Zealand beach.

Maori Tribal Life A ceremonial arch decorates the entrance to a traditional *pa* (a Maori fortified village), its spiked fence a defense against would-be invaders.

HAWAII

Some 5,000 miles north in the central Pacific, a similar story unfolded on the islands of the Hawaiian archipelago. There the first human settlers arrived about 800 to 1300 CE—the most recent archeological evidence suggests between 1220 and 1260. Genetic evidence implies a tiny founding population, maybe 100 people—only two or three full canoes. They came from central Polynesia, like the first New Zealanders. They brought the standard Polynesian biological baggage, which was well suited to Hawaii's warm climate, and soon located the best fishing grounds and garden spots for their crops (only about 5 to 10 percent of the islands' area is good for farming).

For a few centuries Hawaiians prospered, thanks mainly to seafood. Population grew quickly. They began to build irrigation systems to get higher yields in their taro and yam gardens, and to settle in larger numbers inland.

They maintained contact with other parts of Polynesia via long voyages in sailing canoes. By 1300 or so, they added fishponds to their economy, especially on Oahu. Some fishponds were nearly a mile long. The earliest Hawaiians lived in small villages. Like all Polynesian peoples, they were intensely aware of their ancestry and organized themselves into lineages or clans, led by chiefs, as was normal throughout the Pacific.

By 1400, Hawaii was starting to look less and less like a Pacific paradise. As in New Zealand, abundance gave way to scarcity once every patch of good land and every rich fishing ground was in use. Chiefs began to compete to control the good lagoons and irrigable plains. Population growth slowed, and perhaps ceased about 1450–1500. Hawaiians lost touch with other Polynesian islands and were thereafter among the world's most isolated populations, fully dependent on their own resources. To 1400, Hawaii's trajectory looked a lot like New Zealand's.

But something strange happened between 1450 and 1700 in Hawaii—well, strange by Pacific standards but normal in world history. Some of the chiefs made themselves into kings. Archeology and oral tradition agree that by the late fifteenth century Oahu was unified into a single kingdom. Soon Maui, Molokai, and most of the big island (called Hawaii) became kingdoms too. Each island now had a ruling class, organized into a bureaucracy with professional administrators. The kings organized the common people to work on monumental architecture, building bigger palaces and larger temples, and adjusted religious belief to make themselves divine or semi-divine. They encouraged royal cults, making religion into a state ideology legitimating the ruler. Kings claimed (although in practice did not easily exert) absolute power, including that of life and death over their subjects. Hawaiians could be executed for sneezing at a king's court.

With the rise of rival kings and kingdoms, Hawaii became a more violent place. The **Hawaiian kings** of the four main islands competed for power over the archipelago, resulting in continual warfare. When a king died, war for succession to the throne normally followed. Hawaiian society became more male-dominated and more martial in culture—just like New Zealand's. But Hawaii was the only one of roughly 30 Polynesian societies around the Pacific to develop kingdoms.

Hawaii's population stood at an estimated 400,000 to 500,000 in the period 1500–1750. Other islands in the Pacific had much smaller populations. Almost all followed a similar trajectory of early expansion and plenty, followed by scarcity and conflict, and painful adjustments to the stern realities of limited space.

Once again, it is instructive to compare the Polynesian and Viking experience. The inhabitants of islands, whether Hawaii or Iceland, sooner or later faced starkly limited resources. Hawaiians and Icelanders responded by limiting their population, achieved through a combination of later marriages and increased abortion or infanticide. Icelanders, however, also maintained long-distance seaborne connections, which Hawaiians—who had much longer distances to travel to the nearest populated places—lost by about 1300. So Icelanders could benefit economically from participation in trade networks. This enabled them to specialize in certain activities and exchange what they were good at producing (sealskins, fish) for what they were bad at producing (grain). The benefits of specialization and exchange, for Hawaiians, were available only within their archipelago. This was a much more limited field of operation, mainly because the Hawaiian islanders produced similar things. Hawaii may have been warmer and sunnier than Iceland, with tasty tropical fruits, but when it was isolated from the rest of humankind, its population lived with stricter limits.

GUAM

The first people arrived on Guam, an island in the Mariana chain in the western Pacific, about 4,000 years ago. Their descendants, the Chamorro, like most peoples in the Americas and Oceania, had no writing, so our understanding of their history is uncertain and relies mainly on archeology. The imperfect evidence implies that between 1000 and 1500 they were growing more numerous and more hierarchical, and were interacting culturally with far-flung people more frequently.

After about 1000 CE, the Chamorro began to erect pillars with semi-spherical caps on top, like mushrooms with the caps inverted. Called **latte stones**, they were quarried out of limestone, sandstone, or basalt, although sometimes the caps were of coral. Big ones, more common as time went on, stood 15 feet (5 m) tall and weighed 20 tons (18,000 kg).

Nobody knows for sure why the Chamorro went to the considerable trouble of quarrying and erecting latte stones. As we've seen, in ancient times from Korea to England, and in Mesoamerica as well, people found reasons to put up megaliths—dolmens, Stonehenge, the

Olmec heads—even if we today can't be sure what those reasons were. The leading hypothesis for the latte stones is that they served as the corner-posts or bases of buildings. They normally exist in pairs framing a rectangular space, and some sixteenth-century Spanish texts (Spanish sailors visited Guam in 1521) refer to buildings atop stone pillars. Some of the rectangles included as many as 20 latte stones and probably represent either a community building—maybe a structure for storing boats—or more likely the home of someone of especially high rank. The presence of latte stones and their rectangles in all sizes suggests that Chamorro society after 1000 was developing a new status hierarchy or finding a new way to mark social status. Spaniards wrote about a Guamanian society with three classes, living in communities segregated by social rank.

Latte stones also exist on several other islands in the Marianas, despite the hundreds of miles of ocean dividing them. This tells us that these islands, between about 1000 and 1521, hosted an interacting cultural community. Although almost entirely isolated from the larger world, the people of the Marianas were building their own modest, seaborne web like the Hawaiians—but on a smaller scale. Similar patterns were evolving on other Pacific archipelagoes, without the telltale latte stones.

Latte Stones Latte stones, such as these on the island of Guam, were erected on several of the Mariana Islands—but nowhere else—after about 1000 CE. They probably served as foundation posts for public buildings or homes of the highest-ranking community members.

CONCLUSION

Before 1492, the peoples of the Americas lived almost entirely isolated from the rest of humankind. Peoples of Oceania did as well, until an even later date. To some extent they forged their own webs of interaction, especially in the Andes and Mesoamerica, although always smaller and usually less integrated than those of Eurasia and North Africa. The main reason for that was the absence of suitable transport in the Americas, and in Oceania the tremendous distances and dangers of sailing in canoes.

Amerindians and Pacific Islanders found their own solutions to the problems of subsistence, social life, and dealing with the spirit world. In some instances, their solutions were unique to themselves. The Amerindian Three Sisters of agriculture existed nowhere outside the Americas. *Chinampas* existed only in Mesoamerica. Amazonian dark earths, the Iroquois League, and Polynesian sailing canoes were, if not unique solutions, then highly distinctive ones.

But many of the practices adopted in the Americas and Oceania resembled ones arrived at by peoples in China, India, Africa, or Europe, especially where leaders created states and empires. They made pots of clay, like people almost everywhere. They worshipped gods associated with nature, like many (by no means all) people. They divided work into male and female spheres. They irrigated their crops to improve yields. Imperial leaders in Mexico and the Andes used religion, architecture, and brute force to maintain their power. Amerindians and Pacific islanders arrived at these commonplace solutions quite independently, with no significant interactions with Africa or Eurasia. It is interesting to ponder the parallels among peoples who, thus far, were not in contact with one another.

After 1492, a new era in world history commenced. No longer would big regions such as the Americas or Oceania follow their own courses, nearly free from influence from further afield. In the next few chapters, Part 4 of this book, we will see how the breakdown of isolation and the formation of a single worldwide human web would affect the different people and places of the planet.

CHAPTER REVIEW

KEY TERMS

Inka (p. 427)
vertical archipelago (p. 428)
dark earth (p. 432)
Tenochtitlán (p. 434)
Tlacélel (p. 434)

Florentine Codex (p. 438)
Ancestral Pueblo (p. 439)
Chaco Canyon (p. 440)
Cahokia (p. 443)
flint maize (p. 443)

League of Peace and Power (p. 445)
Maori (p. 447)
Hawaiian kings (p. 449)
latte stones (p. 450)

Go to INQUIZITIVE to see what you've learned—and learn what you've missed—with personalized feedback along the way.

REVIEW QUESTIONS

1. How did *quipus* convey information, and what did they record?

2. How and why did the connections among people in the Americas and Oceania differ from those in Eurasia and North Africa?

3. What were the three important and related trends in the histories of the Americas?

4. What were the main forms of soft and hard power that supported Inka rule?

5. How did the people of Amazonia make a living?

6. How did the Aztec religious worldview underpin its militaristic society?

7. Describe and compare the economic bases of the Inkas and the Aztecs.

8. What were the subsistence methods of the Anasazi and the peoples of the Pacific Northwest coast?

9. In what ways did flint maize change societies in North America?

10. What did the Pacific Northwest coast, Cahokia, and the Four Corners region look like in the year 1300, and why?

11. How and why was the role of women in Iroquois society distinctive?

12. Identify the causes and effects of societal change in New Zealand at the end of the fifteenth century.

13. What was the common trajectory of many islands in the Pacific?

14. What do latte stones tell us about cultural exchange in the Marianas?

FURTHER READING

Manuel AGUILAR-MORENO, *Handbook to Life in the Aztec World* (2006). A reference work more than a narrative, with chapters on just about every aspect of Aztec life.

William ENGELBRECHT, *Iroquioa: The Development of a Native World* (2005). A brief and readable overview of the archeology.

Patrick KIRCH, *How Chiefs Became Kings* (2010). An anthropological and archeological history of Hawaii up to the time of European contact.

Craig MORRIS and Adriana von HAGEN, *The Incas: Lords of the Four Quarters* (2011). A recent overview and amply illustrated.

Maria Rostworowski de Diez CANSECO, *History of the Inca Realm* (1999). A brief overview by one of the great authorities, although a bit dated now.

David STUART, *Anasazi America* (2014). A handy overview, mainly of the Chaco Canyon Anasazi.

Camilla TOWNSEND, *Fifth Sun: A New History of the Aztecs* (2019). The latest overview by a top authority in the field.

Dirk van TUERENHOUT, *The Aztecs* (2005). A very accessible survey, perhaps the best starting point on the subject.

Gary URTON, *Inka History in Knots: Reading Khipus as Primary Sources* (2017). Ingenious interpretations of what can be gleaned from the Inka information storage system.

WEAVING THE GLOBAL WEB

1400 TO 1800

Chapters 16 through 20 cover world history between 1400 and 1800. During that period, human history became genuinely global for the first time. Events in South America, such as a discovery of silver, affected China, and changes in Chinese tax policies affected silver miners in South America. The regional webs featured in Part 3 fused into a single global web.

The great economist Adam Smith in his famous work, *The Wealth of Nations* (1776), wrote that:

The Cantino Planisphere This Portuguese map was drawn by hand in 1502. Its rendering of the African coastline is especially detailed, an indication of how quickly and how well Portuguese mapmakers and navigators accumulated geographical information.

The discovery of America, and that of a passage to the East Indies by the Cape of Good Hope, are the two greatest and most important events recorded in the history of mankind.... By uniting, in some measure, the most distant parts of the world, by enabling them to relieve one another's wants, to increase one another's enjoyments, and to encourage one another's industry, their general tendency would seem to be beneficial.

Now, two and half centuries after Adam Smith, it's a bit easier to see the full significance of "uniting, in some measure, the most distant parts of the world." In Part 4 we focus on just how this "uniting" happened, and its consequences—economic, political, intellectual, social, and biological. From here on in the book, as history became more globalized, our portrayal of it also becomes more global in scope.

THE FIRST PULSE OF GLOBALIZATION

Before starting in, one further point is worth establishing. Although Smith refers to the discovery of America, in fact America—the Western Hemisphere—already had tens of millions of people in it, and neither the Vikings nor Columbus actually discovered it. What Columbus did discover was a practical route between Europe and America. What he and dozens of other mariners collectively discovered was how to sail the world's oceans by exploiting the prevailing winds and currents. Before the fifteenth century, almost all sailors except Polynesians and Vikings hugged the shorelines. Polynesians in the tropical Pacific, and Vikings in the North Atlantic, had learned how to navigate and survive at sea for many weeks without sighting land. But even they did not establish enduring routes over the seas they sailed.

Between 1400 and 1800, mariners traversed all the world's seas and linked all the world's inhabited coastlines and hinterlands. They discovered oceanic routes, unlocked the secrets of the globe's wind patterns, and, armed with this knowledge, spun the first genuinely global web of humankind. That was the first pulse of true globalization, and its events belong—just as Smith said—among the most important in history.

NEW CROSSROADS

One aspect of the new global connections deserves underlining at the start. For thousands of years before the 1490s, the best place on Earth in which to learn about other places was Southwest Asia. Its connections, by land and sea, brought its peoples into at least intermittent touch with others in Africa, Europe, South Asia, and to a lesser extent Southeast and East Asia as well. Southwest Asian societies enjoyed access to the Mediterranean, Black, and Red Seas, the Indian Ocean world, and the overland routes of the Eurasian steppe. Southwest Asia was the land bridge connecting world regions, the closest thing to a center of the Old World web. This geographical position put Southwest Asian societies in a situation that was sometimes dangerous but often advantageous. Their position exposed them at times to more epidemics and perhaps more invasions than most peoples elsewhere. But it also enabled them to learn more from more places, and this they could turn to their advantage.

Southwest Asia gradually lost this dangerous but privileged position after the 1490s. Seaborne communications and trade enabled Atlantic Europeans gradually to take over this role. Increasingly they, rather than Southwest Asians, learned more about technologies in use around the world. Atlantic Europeans could now adopt useful technologies from a larger menu of options than others had done. And now they, rather than Arabs, Armenians, and Persians, knew more about relative prices in different markets, enabling them to make money in trade more reliably, buying low and selling high in different parts of the world.

GLOBAL HISTORY

In Part 3, the chapters each addressed a separate region, but they shared common themes. Here, in Part 4, with the world drawing together into a single web, the chapters address separate themes with a global scope. Chapter 16 explores the navigation advances that wove the world together and the biological exchanges among regions that resulted. Chapter 17 considers the impacts of the newly formed global web on societies previously enmeshed in smaller webs. All of these societies faced severe challenges that some survived but others did not. Chapters 18 through 20 deal with the cultural, political, and economic implications, respectively, of weaving a global web.

So how did all this weaving start? The answer lies with sailors.

CHRONOLOGY

1291
Italian sailors attempt
to circumnavigate Africa

1368–1644
Ming dynasty in China

ca. 1300–1400
European and Moroccan
sailors reach the Canary
Islands

1415
Portuguese army
captures Moroccan
port of Ceuta

1405–1433
Zheng He
organizes and
leads seven
maritime voyages

1497
Vasco da Gama embarks on expedition to
India; John Cabot makes round trip from
England to Newfoundland

1494
Spain and Portugal sign
the Treaty of Tordesillas

ca. 1480
Knowledge of how to make great
ships is lost in China; Portuguese
sailors establish a fort in
West Africa

By 1570
The Pacific Ocean wind
system is deciphered

ca. 1550–1750
Maize becomes a food
staple in Atlantic Africa

1402–1424
Reign of Yongle Emperor

1402–1496
Spanish conquest of the Guanches
in the Canary Islands

ca. 1430–1440
Henry the Navigator organizes systematic
voyaging along the coasts of Atlantic Africa

1492
Christopher Columbus
lands in the Bahamas

1492–1650
Populations in the Americas
fall by 70 to 95 percent

1500
Pedro de Cabral claims
Brazil for Portugal

1519–1522
Ferdinand Magellan's
surviving crew members
circumnavigate the globe

16

Convergence

THE DISCOVERY OF THE OCEANS AND BIOLOGICAL GLOBALIZATION

1400 to 1800

O n the morning of October 11, 1492, Amerindians living on an island in the Bahamas (probably Watlings Island) walked to the beach and, to their astonishment, discovered Christopher Columbus. Few if any Bahamians had ever seen men wearing clothes, which was not done in their islands, let alone men in metal armor. None had ever seen ships. Columbus's ships far eclipsed the dugout canoes that plied Bahamian waters. What those astonished people made of the strangers on their shores we will never know, although it's a reasonable guess that some were curious and some were terrified. Columbus, for his part, thought he stood on an island off the coast of China.

Nearly six years later, in 1498, residents of the Indian port city of Calicut, strolling along the harbor-front, were almost as astonished to discover Portuguese ships approaching. They had seen Europeans before, although not many. But they had never seen European ships anywhere in the Indian Ocean,

ca. 1670
Military expansion
of Asante kingdom
begins

ca. 1650
Population of the
Americas begins
to recover

Maize Comes to Asia This Japanese screen from the mid-seventeenth century was probably produced in Kyoto, where aristocrats valued finely detailed ink drawings of exotic plants. It shows the Mesoamerican food crop of maize, which together with potatoes and cassava spread from the Americas to the rest of the world in a surge of biological globalization after 1492. The screen is among the earliest evidence of maize in Japan.

FOCUS QUESTIONS

1. What were the major contours of world history in 1400, as shown in the regional webs of the time?

2. What were the main differences in oceanic voyaging conducted by China's Ming dynasty and the Atlantic Europeans?

3. What were the most important effects of the biological globalization initiated by the oceanic voyaging of Atlantic Europeans?

4. Why was the first global web to extend across the world a significant development?

nor any ships carrying big cannon as these did. The ships' commander, Vasco da Gama, soon found occasion to use the big cannon.

These two encounters in the 1490s symbolize the opening of a new era in world history. Before the 1490s, the Americas and Afro-Eurasia remained essentially separate hemispheres. Before the 1490s, the Old World web relied heavily on overland connections together with the maritime links centered on the Indian Ocean. After the 1490s, the world's coastlands quickly (well, over two centuries) became integrated as never before, thanks to seaborne trade. Indeed, the world's populated coasts, with scant exceptions, came to form the first genuinely global web of human interaction, channeling the flow of ideas, technologies, goods, crops, diseases, and much else.

But before we get to the story of several sailors and the seven seas, let's pause and look at the lands on which people lived as of the fifteenth century, and specifically, the webs of interaction within which they lived. Before examining the formation of a global web, it helps to remember its constituent parts.

THE WORLD'S WEBS IN THE FIFTEENTH CENTURY

As of 1400, the 350 to 450 million people on Earth spoke several thousand languages, followed several hundred religions, and recognized several hundred political rulers. (A few tens of millions of them recognized no rulers at all, although with each passing year fewer and fewer lived in so-called stateless societies.) Despite nearly 5,000 years of states, cities, and empires, and some 2,000 years of expanding, proselytizing religions, the human race remained politically and culturally fragmented. It was in no deep sense a community. Even within the Old World web, spectacular diversity prevailed—from the refined world of Confucian scholars in urban China, with its leisured philosophy and gorgeous calligraphy, to the austere and dangerous world of illiterate fisherfolk on the coasts of Scotland.

THE OLD WORLD WEB

That diversity resulted partly from the sheer size of the Old World web. Its frontiers, in 1400, stretched from Greenland to Japan and from Indonesia to West Africa. Three-fourths of humanity lived within it. Thousands of caravan tracks, navigable rivers, and sea routes held the web together. It included hubs or nodes, such as Malacca, Calicut, Hormuz, Cairo, Constantinople, or Venice, where people heard many languages and where the silks of China crossed paths with the ivory of East Africa or the amber of Scandinavia. But it also included spaces where people kept to themselves, deep in the forests of Siberia or high in the Himalaya mountains, minimally connected to empires, trade routes, or major religions. These people, comparatively few in number, lived within the Old World web's frontiers, but they were not part of its fabric—at least, not yet in 1400.

INTERACTIONS WITHIN THE OLD WORLD WEB
The Old World web had two main trunk routes. The overland caravan routes, collectively known as the Silk Road, linked eastern and western Eurasia. The caravan routes flourished in times of peace, when strong empires kept brigands in check and prevented dozens of local rulers from demanding payment from traders in exchange for safe passage. The best example is the Pax

Overland and Seaborne Trade These two fifteenth-century images show contrasting sides of the long-distance trade circuits of the Old World web. The image at left shows overland transport of Chinese ceramics to Southwest Asia; the image at right shows the seaborne spice trade from Southeast or South Asia as imagined by a French painter. Only high-value items could justify the costs and risks of transport, whether by land or sea, over thousands of miles.

Mongolica (ca. 1260–1350), when the short-lived Mongol Empire stamped out brigandage almost everywhere along routes between Korea and Iraq, making travel safer for merchants.

The second main trunk route, also in reality a series of connected routes, was by sea. It extended from the East Asian ports through the waters of Southeast Asia and into the Indian Ocean, as far west as the coasts of Africa. Via a short overland passage in Egypt, these routes connected to the Mediterranean. Mastery of the monsoon winds had opened this trunk route in ancient times.

The traffic within the Old World web, along these trunk routes and countless lesser ones, served as a homogenizing force. Cultural interaction and political conquests reduced the number of different languages spoken. Meanwhile, more and more people chose (sometimes under duress) to follow fewer and fewer religions, and so Buddhism, Hinduism, Christianity, and Islam (some people would include Confucianism as a religion too) each acquired tens of millions of believers, while many other religions disappeared. Of course, at the same time, the big religions fractured, developing internal splits such as the Sunni–Shi'a divide in Islam or the Orthodox–Catholic schism in Christianity. And the big languages fractured too, although slowly. They developed dialects, so the Arabic spoken in Morocco gradually came to seem strange to Arabs in Iraq because it sounded so different from their own. So the process of homogenization in the Old World web had its limits and counter-currents.

A THICKENING WEB During the fifteenth century, the eastern and western edges of the Old World web were rapidly consolidating and thickening as a result of maritime trade. In earlier centuries, mastery of the arts of camel management had boosted the connectivity of the central regions of the Old World web, making desert crossings in Central Asia, Arabia, and Africa much more practical. Mastery of the monsoon winds had given sea traders in the Indian Ocean world a precocious start in developing long-distance networks. But now, from at least 1200 onward, improving ship design and navigational skill in both western Europe and eastern Asia were fast accumulating, reducing the risks of sea travel and making trade and economic specialization yet more rewarding. Sailing the western Pacific waters from Japan to Java, or the eastern Atlantic from Scandinavia to Spain, was dangerous indeed. Both seas featured frequent, furious storms, not to mention (especially in the western Pacific) bold, enterprising pirates. But bigger and better ships helped sailors overcome their understandable fears of these hazards.

The rewards to risking one's life and cargo at sea were genuine and growing. Both western Europe and eastern Asia produced a wide diversity of resources and goods. Markets had sprung up offering tempting prices at which to sell scarce goods from afar, whether Spanish wine in the Netherlands or Moluccan spices in China. At times, even bulk goods such as rice, salt, and timber could justify voyages in these two sea rooms.

Comparing Currencies Strange as it seems, both these images show money. The coins at left come from the Southeast Asian kingdom of Srivijaya (seventh to thirteenth centuries) and look a good deal like money in circulation across the Old World web, where several centuries previously millions of people came to agree that small discs of gold, silver, or copper were valuable. The giant limestone disc at right served as money in the Caroline Islands of the western Pacific, especially the island of Yap, where money was used only for major transactions. The stones themselves, which might weigh a few tons, did not need to move. Instead, everyone agreed the stones had new owners after a transaction. Srivijayan society was much more trade- and market-oriented than Yap's.

Both these emerging maritime worlds drew additional traffic from networks of navigable rivers. In Europe, the big rivers flow fairly evenly throughout the year and permit ship or barge traffic well inland. In East and Southeast Asia, the big rivers are more seasonal because of the pattern of summer monsoon rain. But with painstaking construction of canals, dikes, and dams, these rivers too served as reliable avenues of commerce, linking interior regions with the sea.

So, in 1400, the eastern and western edges of the Old World web were humming with riverine and seaborne trade. Knowledge of geography, winds, and currents, of ship design, cartography, and navigation, of goods, markets, and prices was growing at ever faster rates. Both regions were developing a more maritime and commercial culture. Populations were recovering from the disease and climate disasters of the fourteenth century, and cities were expanding rapidly.

LOCAL WEBS

In 1400, some 60 to 120 million people in Oceania, the Americas, and the southern third of Africa lived outside the Old World web altogether. They too, of course, took part in trade networks, military conquests, and the same sorts of activities as people in the Old World web. But their scales of operations were smaller. In Oceania, people in Polynesia and Micronesia had built their own small webs of interaction. Archipelagoes like that of Hawaii,

or Tonga and Fiji, hosted constant interactions among hundreds of thousands of people. In the Caroline Islands of Micronesia by 1400 or 1450, a well-integrated exchange network had grown up, using big stone discs as money—some of them heavier than a car. But this little web probably involved at most tens of thousands of people. In demographic terms, these Oceanic networks were tiny compared to the Old World web.

WEBS IN THE AMERICAS

In the Americas, as we saw in Chapter 15, much larger webs had developed around the dense populations in the Andes and in Mesoamerica. In 1400, perhaps 40 to 70 million people lived in the Americas, and about half were in either the Andes or Mesoamerica. Most Amerindians, and all those in the Andes or Mesoamerica, took part in interactive webs. In the absence of pack animals (outside of llamas and alpacas in the high Andes), goods could travel only by watercraft or human porters in the American webs. Canoes and rafts linked peoples on riverbanks and shorelines. Elsewhere, people had to carry everything themselves.

So the character of the American webs was slightly different from that of the Old World web, with less bulk commerce in transit. Crops such as maize diffused widely within this web, and so did some cultural practices such as ball games and mound building. But the volume and intensity of the exchanges of goods over long distances were modest compared to what occurred in the Old World web with its caravans and shipping. Buzzing markets did exist, but mainly on the local level—as in the Basin of Mexico, the region around today's Mexico City. As in the Old World web, those societies enmeshed in the American web featured more specialization and exchange, greater wealth, greater inequality, greater military power, than those societies outside the web.

Like its counterparts, the American webs left some people out entirely. In the far south of South America and in the northern reaches of North America, scattered populations lived essentially subsistence lives. In pockets of Central American or Amazonian rain forest too, there were some people living substantially in isolation.

WEBS IN AFRICA

Most of the northern half of Africa, by 1400, lay within the Old World web. Egypt had long been one of its linchpins. Trade and cultural exchange, most notably the spread of Islam, tied the East African coast as far south as Kilwa and Sofala, the Mediterranean lands, and the West African Sahel firmly to the rest of the Old World web. Where rivers made travel easy, as along the Nile and Niger, tendrils of the Old World web reached further still.

But the southern third of Africa, like sizeable parts of the Americas, or Siberia, stood apart from any big web. People there were not importing shiploads of luxury goods from Egypt or India; they were not sending young men to study Islam in Cairo or Baghdad. They were not experimenting with Indian Ocean world technology such as sugar mills or lateen-rigged sails. Instead, they were producing food and clothing for themselves or for local use, they were following their own religions, and they were using the same technologies—perhaps with minor alterations—that their ancestors had employed for many generations. They lived outside the Old World web, but within much smaller webs of their own making.

As in the Americas, these little webs in southern Africa were better for circulating ideas than goods. Without pack animals, wheeled vehicles, or ships, people here had to move everything on their backs, on their heads, or in canoes.

So in 1400 the world included one giant interactive web in Eurasia and the northern half of Africa, a large one in the Americas, and small, local ones elsewhere. The Old World web was home to most of the world's people,

and to its most formidable states and societies. It alone had sailing ships capable of carrying hundreds of tons of cargo. It alone had many kinds of pack animals suited to almost any terrain. It alone had wheeled vehicles. By 1400, it had fewer obstacles to interaction, especially to trade, than did the other, smaller webs around the world.

The Old World web was not necessarily a pleasant place to live—certainly not if life expectancy or social equality are the measures—but it is where people had built the most powerful militaries, the most efficient communications networks, and the most sophisticated technologies. Therefore, it comes as no surprise that the people who brought the world's webs together, who forged the first truly global web, came from the edges of the Old World web.

THE DISCOVERY OF THE OPEN SEA

Before 1400, as earlier chapters explained, several peoples had developed maritime cultures. The most extraordinary of these was the Polynesian, which carried colonists throughout the archipelagoes of the tropical Pacific and as far south as New Zealand. However, by 1400 its farthest outposts had become cut off and sea traffic took place mainly within archipelagoes. The Vikings, too, had a seafaring history several centuries long, although by 1400 they had stopped exploring the North Atlantic and their Greenland colony was on the verge of extinction. Many other peoples sailed routinely on more protected seas, such as the Mediterranean, the Arabian Gulf, the Bay of Bengal, the South China Sea, or the Sea of Japan. The islands of Indonesia, and adjacent coasts of Southeast Asia, hosted sizeable regular traffic by 1000 CE. The traffic in all these seas was much thicker and more regular than in the Polynesian Pacific or the Viking North Atlantic. The vessels were often larger, and some could carry hundreds of tons of cargo. The routes were well established and studded with commercial seaports. Those who plied these routes usually hugged the shores, although certain passages, such as from East Africa to India and back, took sailors far from land for a week or two.

Sailors had accumulated a considerable, if fragmented, knowledge of winds and currents. Polynesians knew how to ride the currents and the trade winds of the Pacific. People all around the Indian Ocean knew how to use

Prevailing Winds and Ocean Currents Mariners of the fifteenth and sixteenth centuries figured out the global system of winds and ocean currents, enabling them to plot the routes of sailing ships that tied the Global web together.

the monsoon to sail north in the summer and south in the winter. Everywhere, sailors had mastered the local tides, currents, and winds for the short voyages that made up the great majority of seafaring. But no one knew the overall pattern of the planet's winds. No one knew how it might be possible, in the Atlantic and Pacific as well as the Indian Ocean, to find winds that would reliably take ships far out to sea, thousands of miles from land, and then safely home again. In the fifteenth and sixteenth centuries, people learned where to find these winds, unlocking the secrets of oceanic navigation.

The ocean winds form gigantic merry-go-rounds. In the North Atlantic, for example, the prevailing winds spin in a clockwise fashion. Its westerlies (winds are named for the direction *from* which they blow, unlike ocean currents; so a westerly wind and an easterly current are going the same way) whip across from North America to Europe. Further south, the trade winds blow along the northwestern coasts of Africa and then whistle across to the Caribbean. In the South Atlantic, the merry-go-round spins counterclockwise, so the westerlies lie far to the south and the trade winds cross from Angola to Brazil. The North and South Pacific have their own spinning wheels, as does the southern Indian Ocean. (The winds of the northern part of the Indian Ocean are governed by the monsoon.) The whole system slides north by a few hundred miles from April to August and slips back south from September to March. Thus there is a general pattern to the world's winds. But nobody knew that in 1400.

THE MING VOYAGES, 1405–1433

In 1400, the biggest ships and perhaps the best navigators were Chinese. Under the Song, the Yuan, and then the Ming (1368–1644) dynasties, the Chinese had rapidly developed ship and navigation technology, and Chinese merchants had taken a large role in the booming trade between East and Southeast Asia. The Ming maintained a state shipyard that employed between 20,000 and 30,000 workers. Their ships were by far the biggest in the world, capable of carrying a thousand people. Chinese tinkerers had invented the compass, and Chinese sailors used it more than sailors elsewhere. Their maritime culture was developing rapidly, thanks to constant voyaging to the islands of Southeast Asia, to Japan, and to every coast in between. By 1400, that maritime culture and Ming finances had reached a point at which they could support large, expensive, showy voyages to overawe just about everyone from Vietnam to East Africa.

Two crucial components of that maturing maritime culture were ship design and navigational tools. Chinese mariners had long used sternpost rudders and double-hulled construction. Rudders improved the steering of ships, and double hulls saved them from sinking if rammed or smashed on rocks. Chinese sailors also used the space between hulls to carry fresh water. During the Song dynasty, their seaborne trade links to the Indian Ocean acquainted them with new rigging and sails—particularly the lateen sail common in Arab shipping, good for sailing into the wind. Shipbuilders used these features, old and new, to design seagoing ships of 2,500 tons. They also put small cannon on these huge ships. As for navigation, Chinese sailors were already using the compass and printed sea manuals with star charts during the Song dynasty. A new emperor soon put Chinese maritime culture to new uses.

In 1402, a crafty uncle organized a military rebellion, overthrowing his nephew and becoming emperor of Ming China. Like all Chinese emperors, he took a reign name upon ascending the throne: the Yongle Emperor. To help consolidate his position, he promoted loyal eunuchs into positions of power. Eunuchs had minimal family connections of their own and therefore depended entirely on the emperor, making them highly reliable administrators. One of these eunuchs, **Zheng He**, became Yongle's indispensable adviser and political fixer. Ruling with an iron fist, Yongle moved the capital from the south to Beijing, launched campaigns against the Mongols (in which Zheng He distinguished himself), invaded and annexed part of Vietnam, and chased down and executed everyone loyal to his nephew.

Yongle also made his devoted aide Zheng He an admiral. Even though he had probably never smelled the sea, Zheng He organized a massive maritime expedition the likes of which China—and the world—had never seen. His official errand was to find and capture Yongle's nephew, who according to rumor had escaped his uncle's extermination campaign. But the scale of

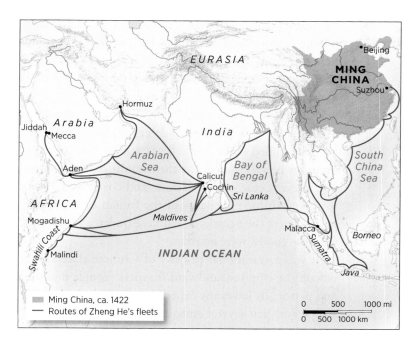

Voyages of Zheng He, 1405–1433 The Chinese admiral Zheng He led seven massive fleets into the Indian Ocean, following routes long familiar to merchants in these waters. Zheng He and his captains knew how to ride the monsoon winds, navigate with star charts, and find safe harbors. His routes extended to the far edges of the Indian Ocean world, the Swahili coast, the Arabian Peninsula, Java, and his home, China.

the undertaking indicates that Yongle had additional motives. In 1405, Zheng He set sail from Suzhou with roughly 300 ships, newly built in the shipyards of Nanjing along the Yangzi. They carried 28,000 men, both sailors and soldiers, a crew larger than the population of any city they would visit. His biggest ships, if we can believe the Chinese sources, were gigantic, about 400 feet (125 m) by 160 feet (50 m) and displacing 20,000 tons—far larger than any yet built anywhere and 10 times the size of Columbus's flagship. They were the largest wooden ships ever built.

Zheng He sailed well-traveled seas from China into the Indian Ocean. He used persuasion, intimidation, and military power to oust unfriendly rulers in Sumatra, Sri Lanka, and elsewhere, and install replacements more willing to acknowledge Yongle's overlordship and pay him tribute. In Sri Lanka he deposited a giant stone slab with inscriptions in Chinese, Persian, and Tamíl (a South Asian language in use in Sri Lanka after 1000 CE) commemorating his visit as an emissary of "the supreme overlord of kings"—lest anyone fail to appreciate Yongle's stature. Zheng He annihilated pirates—or maybe just

Ming Voyages As this artist's impression illustrates, the largest ships in Zheng He's fleet were 10 times the size of Columbus's flagship. The size of Ming ships was symbolic, enabling the emperor to advertise his power widely.

merchant princes who failed to show proper enthusiasm for the emperor and so earned the title "pirate" in Chinese accounts. Perhaps Zheng He was also looking for allies against steppe nomads, almost always the Ming's main enemies.

Whatever his purposes, Zheng He was not attempting to find new routes. On his first six expeditions (1405–1424) he commanded similar-sized fleets, and on more than one occasion he sailed as far as the Swahili coast of Kenya. But in every case he visited ports and coasts well known to the maritime merchants of the Indian Ocean world, places where the occasional Chinese trader, and certainly Chinese goods, were familiar.

It was a traditional priority of Chinese statecraft to defend the empire's landward frontiers. Yongle mounted and personally led many expeditions into the Mongolian steppe and sent several embassies to Central Asia trying to improve the political situation on his frontiers. Overawing distant foreigners by sea ranked well behind this priority, so the logic of doing it again and again came into question. Zheng He himself was an outsider in Chinese politics, a Muslim, a eunuch, and not even Chinese (he came from an ethnic minority population and had Persian ancestry as well). His career hinged entirely on the emperor's favor. When Yongle died in 1424, factions

came to power that did not favor overseas voyaging.

Those factions eventually prevailed. Voyaging was costly and did not contribute to the security or virtue of the empire, nor much to its prosperity. Repairs to the Grand Canal, finished in 1411, made seafaring less important to the Ming state and Chinese society, since shipping could flow more safely on the canal than on the sea. Yongle's successor judged the oceanic voyaging wasteful and ended it in 1424. Under a later emperor, Zheng He and the eunuch faction prevailed one last time and launched a seventh voyage (1431–1433), again reaching Africa. But Zheng He died en route home, and his remaining supporters lost influence. The Ming eventually broke up the great fleet and sold it for fuelwood. By 1480, the skills needed to build such great ships had vanished.

Ming Giraffe Giraffes are native to Africa, but here one appears as an illustration in a Ming manuscript, indicating the reach of Chinese maritime voyaging during the Ming period. Like other luxury goods, exotic animals could be brought back from voyages as status objects and prizes.

The geographical and other knowledge accumulated on Zheng He's voyages found its way into Chinese charts, maps, and books. But it did not vastly expand, or fundamentally alter, Chinese understanding of the world. It temporarily lubricated the wheels of commerce that connected China to the Indian Ocean trading ports, but only for a few decades. The **Ming voyages** left scant enduring legacy.

The scale of the Ming maritime effort before 1433 suggests that the Chinese had the ships and skills to sail around Africa to Europe, or south to Australia, or across the Pacific to the Americas. But they had no good reason to try to reach Europe. They didn't yet know Australia or the Americas existed. So, instead, they sailed familiar waters in grand style with enormous government support. Then, in 1433, they stopped.

Chinese Geographical Knowledge This map made by the cartographer Wang Qi in 1607 indicates the extent, by then, of Chinese knowledge of the wider world. Centered on China and the Pacific Ocean, it offers a remarkably accurate depiction of Eurasia, Africa, the Americas, and Antarctica.

EUROPEAN VOYAGING, 1400–1700

At the same time that the Ming were gliding into the Indian Ocean, western Europeans were probing the Atlantic. Some of them dreamed of sailing to the Indian Ocean too. They lacked the massive state support that Zheng He had enjoyed, and the states that helped them could mobilize only a tiny fraction of the resources the Ming could. These mariners were lucky if they could cobble together a tiny flotilla.

But European mariners usually had a good idea where they were heading. Navigational skill had accumulated slowly but surely over the centuries in Atlantic Europe. In Iberia especially, the practical experience of sailors combined with Arab mathematics and astronomy to create a more reliable—if by no means fully reliable—art of navigation. European sailors used the compass by the thirteenth century to find direction on cloudy days. By the fourteenth, they had translated Arabic texts on the use of astrolabes to help determine latitude. Soon they were authoring their own manuals on astrolabes—the English writer Geoffrey Chaucer penned one—and building the devices themselves. But even perfect navigational skill would have meant little without seaworthy ships.

Like the Chinese, Atlantic Europeans for a century or more had been rapidly refining their ship designs. More frequent connections in the fourteenth and fifteenth centuries between sailors in the North Atlantic and the Mediterranean yielded a hybrid in hull design and rigging. Shipbuilders combined the economical hull structure typical of Mediterranean ships—in which planks were nailed

Portuguese Caravel Caravels like this one were the relatively small sailing ships used by Portuguese and other European explorers on long-distance voyages. This mosaic appears near a sixteenth-century villa outside Lisbon, the Portuguese capital.

to ribs rather than to one another—with the sternpost rudder invented in the Baltic. This led to stronger, cheaper, and more maneuverable vessels. In addition, mariners supplemented square sails typical of northern waters with lateen sails characteristic of Arab seas to create the so-called fully rigged ship, which could sail swiftly before the wind

Portolan Charts This innovation in cartography helped explorers to navigate the routes between ports. A 1571 Portolan chart of West Africa shows numerous ports along the coastline, with crests indicating the powers—especially Portugal, the red and white shield—that controlled them.

and tack close to the wind. With these advances, European sailors could dispense with oars and oarsmen and rely entirely on the wind. Ships became cheaper to operate because much less was needed in the way of food, water, and wages to mount a voyage. So by the early fifteenth century, European shipwrights knew how to make sturdy, swift, and cheap ships, capable of carrying lightweight cannon and sailing anywhere in the world even in heavy weather. Their ships were far smaller than those of Zheng He, but no less seaworthy. And by 1500, they built ships large enough to carry heavy cannon capable of battering down walls or sinking any ship afloat.

Atlantic European mariners also had incentives to gamble on sailing the open seas. They, rather than the Chinese, began to unlock the secrets of the world's winds. And once they started, unlike the Ming they did not stop.

EUROPEAN MARINERS' MOTIVES Atlantic Europeans launched onto the high seas primarily in quest of wealth, fame, and the greater glory of their God. They started by sailing south into unfamiliar waters, looking for a practical route to African gold or Asian spices and silks, the most valuable trade goods they knew of. Merchants from Italian city-states such as Venice and Genoa had tapped into these trades, acquiring gold in Morocco

Iberian Art A wooden sculpture decorating a late-fifteenth-century altarpiece in the Cathedral of Granada shows the last Muslim king leaving Granada with his followers, after the Spanish Reconquista in 1492.

or Tunisia and spices in Egypt or Syria, after the goods had changed hands many times. Merchants who could get these goods closer to the source could buy them for less and make a fortune by cutting out several middlemen.

The search for glory and fame also propelled European navigators. Fifteenth-century Europeans, especially Iberians, were steeped in a culture of adventure and chivalry as proper male pursuits. Owing in part to the centuries-long **Reconquista**—in which Christians retook Iberia from Muslim rulers—Iberian books, songs, poems, and folk tales celebrated the deeds of heroes who took daunting risks and either triumphed or, if they died young, at least won lasting fame. Young males eager to vault several rungs up the social ladder learned that they could do so through acts of reckless heroism.

The Atlantic Europeans' third reason for taking the risks of oceanic seafaring was simultaneously religious and political. It appealed especially to Christian rulers, for whom victories against Muslim states meant more glory, political legitimacy, and support from the Pope. European voyagers who could find Christian allies in Africa or Asia against Muslim foes might tip the balance of power in favor of Christian kingdoms. Helping to find sea routes that deprived Muslim states of their trade revenues served the same purposes. If successful, quests for Christian allies might set the stage for renewed conquest of the Holy Land, in the tradition of the Crusaders of a few centuries before. For Iberians, voyaging south along

the African Atlantic coast seemed an extension of the Reconquista and the loot and glory it provided. Although the last Muslim rulers in Spain were ousted in 1492, there were more targets nearby in North Africa. Indeed, the Portuguese had already begun to attack Muslim strongholds in Morocco as early as 1415.

LEARNING THE ATLANTIC After about 1200, European and Moroccan mariners sailed hundreds of miles west into the uncharted Atlantic. By the fourteenth century, if not before, some stumbled across the Canary Islands, Madeira, and the Azores. The Canaries' population, called the **Guanches**, descended from North African Berber settlers who had arrived about 1000 BCE. Madeira and the Azores were uninhabited.

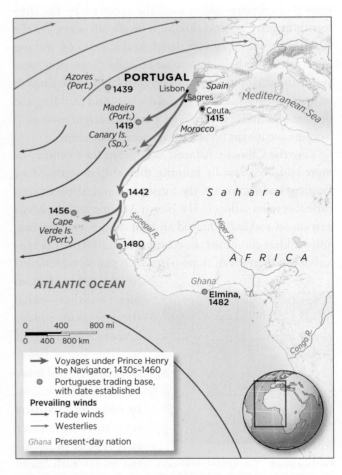

Early Exploration of the Atlantic, 1400–1480 In the fifteenth century, Iberian mariners figured out how to use the winds to venture far out into the Atlantic and get home safely. This accomplishment took navigation well beyond the familiar practice of hugging coastlines, and eventually led to successful crossings of the Atlantic and the discovery of routes linking the Atlantic and Indian Oceans.

By the early fifteenth century, Europeans were attempting settlement of these islands, which in the Canaries required Spain to undertake military conquest of the Guanches. They fought fiercely, but their long isolation meant the Guanches had never acquired metallurgy: they used only stone, bone, and wooden weapons. Moreover, with no experience of infectious diseases by now familiar to Spaniards, they suffered repeated epidemics. The conquest of the Guanches, begun in 1402, ended in 1496. Many isolated peoples around the world would soon share their fate.

Shuttling to and from these little archipelagoes helped European sailors grow accustomed to the open Atlantic. The Canaries were crucial because they served as the entrance ramp to the northeast trade winds, which would prove to be the highway to the Americas.

At the same time as they were learning about, and starting to settle, these archipelagoes, European sailors were also edging down the coast of Africa. A pair of Italian brothers, the Vivaldis, tried to circumnavigate Africa in 1291—but they were never heard from again. Others, mainly Portuguese, followed more cautiously. The northwest coast of Africa offered little fresh water, and the northeast trade winds, which made outbound journeys simple, made it hard to get back home to Portugal. Improved ship design helped with that problem, as did the gradual discovery that sailors could follow the trade winds as far south as the Canaries and then swing north to the latitude of the Azores and catch the prevailing westerlies to get home. This was the first step in deciphering the code of the oceanic wind pattern.

AFRICAN COASTS Portuguese efforts along the African coast quickened when in 1415 an army captured the Moroccan port of Ceuta. One of the leaders of that expedition, a prince known generously as Henry the Navigator, began to organize and support systematic voyaging along the coasts of Atlantic Africa in the 1430s. Henry was a seeker after honor and fame, which he once said were life's highest goals after salvation. He had strong religious convictions, influenced by chivalric notions of crusades against infidels. He also took astrology to heart and interpreted it to mean he was destined for great deeds. Henry the Navigator only put to sea two or three times in his life, but he siphoned off some of the modest resources of a threadbare dynasty in a poor country to pay for sea voyages along the northwest African coast, hoping to get at the source of West African gold.

The Portuguese voyages along the northwest coasts of Africa formed part of a larger, haphazard program that was full of failures. Several Portuguese sailors tried heading west from the Azores, out into the Atlantic, but either were pushed back by the westerly winds or lost at sea. Others tried to cross the Sahara on foot, but none returned. Henry encouraged various assaults on strongholds in Morocco, most of which failed.

All these efforts were dwarfed by the simultaneous voyaging of Zheng He, who commanded far greater resources than any Portuguese sea captain ever did. The tiny size of its investment, perhaps, explains why the Portuguese Crown did not give up and put a stop to the whole enterprise, as the Ming did with Zheng He's journeys. In any case, the Portuguese kept at it, even after Henry's death in 1460, despite meager returns on their investment for half a century.

By the 1480s, their efforts began to pay off. Sailors reached the West African coast of what is now Ghana and established a fort—called Elmina—through which they

Henry the Navigator A fifteenth-century painting depicts Henry the Navigator, the prince who sponsored Portuguese voyages along the coast of northwest Africa and to Atlantic islands.

Elmina Castle The basement of the Portuguese fort of Elmina, in present-day Ghana, was originally built as a pen to hold the enslaved people who were traded on the West African coast.

The Cantino Planisphere This Portuguese map was drawn by hand in 1502. Its rendering of the African coastline is especially detailed, an indication of how quickly and how well Portuguese mapmakers and navigators accumulated geographical information.

traded for gold. Soon they found they could buy slaves on the coast and export them from Elmina to Iberia, or the sugar plantations of the Canaries or Madeira in a lucrative supplement to the gold trade. After nearly a century of meager returns, the Portuguese monarchy now had a profitable toehold in African trade. Soon every kingdom in Atlantic Europe would be sponsoring sea captains trying to get in on African commerce. One captain would also try, as several luckless Portuguese had before, to sail to China by heading west across the Atlantic.

COLUMBUS CROSSES THE ATLANTIC In 1477, a ship broke up in a storm off the southern coast of Portugal. Almost everyone aboard drowned, but a 23-year-old sailor swam ashore. That sailor was **Christopher Columbus**.

Columbus was the son of a weaver from Genoa in northern Italy. He was a bit of a dreamer, easily lost in popular literature with its tales of adventure. He turned to the sea as a teenager, escaping the narrow horizons of an artisan's life in Genoa. As a sailor, he first roamed the Mediterranean and then made forays into the Atlantic. He became a trader too, and sometimes made lush profits in walrus tusk, whale blubber, and other items of Atlantic trade. After he washed up in Portugal in 1477, he went to Lisbon, where he had a brother working as a mapmaker. Through his brother, Columbus began to meet people with all sorts of tall tales about what lay over the western horizon.

Columbus was working in the sugar trade, shuttling between the eastern Mediterranean and the eastern Atlantic, when in the 1480s he began to peddle schemes for a voyage further west. Sometimes he said he would find new islands, as profitable as the Canaries or Madeira. Sometimes he said he would sail to China, which he claimed was a "few days" away. He had learned of the equatorial trade winds blowing to the west from Africa's northwest shores, and of the westerlies (blowing to the east) at higher latitudes. These prevailing winds, he figured, would allow a round-trip voyage to China. They would also allow him, the weaver's son, to join the titled aristocracy, which seems to have been his primary ambition. Columbus was at heart a social climber, willing to take great risks in his quest for status, wealth, and glory. But to get anywhere, he needed backers.

Like any would-be entrepreneur, Columbus pitched his schemes to anyone who would listen. He failed to convince the Portuguese monarchy to invest in his plans, so he went next door to Spain, where he proved more persuasive. Funded by Italian bankers residing in Spain, he secured permission from Ferdinand and Isabella, the king and queen of Castile (the largest region of Spain), to sail under their flag. The story that Queen Isabella pawned her jewels to finance the voyage is, sadly, mere whimsy. Some of her courtiers did invest in the voyage, using funds confiscated from Jews recently expelled from Castile.

Columbus promised the investors that he would forge a route to and from China by sailing west with the trade winds and then back home with the westerlies. He figured that Japan, which he had read about in Marco Polo's book of travels, lay about 2,500 miles (4,000 km) west of Spain. His estimate was off by about 10,000 miles. Had he calculated correctly, he surely would have stayed home.

Instead, he gathered sailors in the small Spanish port of Palos, acquired three little ships, and set out on the well-worn route to the Canary Islands. From there he ventured west into the open sea, seeing no land for 35 days before bumping into an island, perhaps Watlings Island in the Bahamas.

What he found looked nothing like Japan or China. Far from sporting silken robes, the locals stood stark naked and seemed unashamed of it. They had dugout canoes but no ships, and huts instead of palaces. Still hopeful, Columbus quickly moved on and in two weeks was in Cuba. He later stopped at the island of Hispaniola, where he met the more familiar trappings of complex society—dense populations, intensive agriculture, trade networks, and rumors of great kings. On Hispaniola, someone presented him with a few lumps of gold, something he could bring back for his investors. Upon his return home, he insisted to his backers that he had found a direct route to islands off the coast of Asia—and he probably believed it.

The Spanish Crown rewarded him with the title Admiral of the Ocean Sea and granted him broad powers to operate as he saw fit on subsequent voyages. He returned three more times to the Caribbean, even reaching the mainland shores of South and Central America. He engaged in slave trading (of Amerindians native to the Caribbean), bloody reprisals, and several sorts of atrocity in his eagerness for gold. His conduct met with rebukes among his followers and back in Spain. He hanged several Spaniards who defied his authority. A Spanish woman who reminded everyone that the Admiral of the Ocean Sea was the son of a weaver had her tongue cut out.

Columbus's final years were filled with recriminations, lawsuits, bankruptcy, imprisonment, and bitter disappointment that he had found few riches and had not made it to China. He died in 1506, still convinced he had reached the doorstep of the Great Khan. No one else in history has had so many streets, squares, schools, and hotels named after him for making such a big mistake.

Columbus was wrong and he was brutal, but he was nonetheless a central historical figure. His voyages inaugurated a new age of connection among worlds long separate.

Soon after Columbus returned from the second of his four transatlantic voyages, another Italian, Giovani Caboto, was proposing voyages to China across the Atlantic. John Cabot, as he is known, approached merchants in Bristol, England, who were growing rich on the

Columbus's Landfall In this 1493 engraving from *La lettera dell'isole*, Columbus's first account of his voyage, King Ferdinand observes from afar as Columbus and his crew land on an island in the Caribbean. The island's native inhabitants appear to flee.

whale and walrus trade of the North Atlantic. Cabot also enlisted support from the English court, and in 1497 he made it across the Atlantic to Newfoundland and back in a tiny ship, about 3 percent the size of Zheng He's flagship. His crew numbered about 18. Among the treasures Cabot reported, mostly fanciful, were the very real and stupendously rich cod fisheries off of Newfoundland. Like Columbus, he recruited more investors, fitted out more and bigger ships, and set sail across the Atlantic a second time. Unlike Columbus, he never came back. Nevertheless, from soon after Cabot's time, Europeans would sail regularly to the fishing grounds off of Newfoundland, creating an enduring link—something the Viking voyaging to Newfoundland, some 500 years before, had not done.

DA GAMA SAILS TO INDIA In 1497, the same year that Cabot sailed, the Portuguese court fitted out an expedition of four ships and 170 men under the command of a low-ranking provincial noble named **Vasco da Gama**. Just a few years before, a Portuguese captain, Bartholomew Dias, had sailed from Lisbon to the shores of South Africa and returned safely. Dias discovered the belt of westerly winds in the Southern Hemisphere that enabled ships to sidestep adverse currents and ride into the Indian Ocean from the South Atlantic. Counting on this information, da Gama sailed way out into the South Atlantic to catch the westerlies and made it safely to the tip of South Africa and into the Indian Ocean. He worked his way up Africa's southeast coast and soon found evidence, in the form of Indian cloth and glassware, that he was where he hoped to be—in the Indian Ocean.

The ultimate prize, a practical route to and from the rich trade of Asia, lay almost within da Gama's grasp. He and his men resorted to piracy and the kidnapping of local pilots to help them find their way. On the shore of what is now Kenya they found a pilot who showed them the easiest route to **Calicut**, a trading city on the coast of India, where the Portuguese hoped to find—as one of da Gama's captains put it—Christians and spices.

The Portuguese expedition under da Gama had two main goals. The Portuguese Crown hoped to win glory, papal favor, and some practical political advantage by finding Christian allies somewhere in the Indian Ocean world, friends who would help in struggles against Muslim states of North Africa and Southwest Asia. The Crown also hoped to boost its finances by trading in spices,

peppers, cloves, nutmeg, and more, items that were plentiful in India but scarce and expensive in Europe. Some Italian traders had done well in the spice trade, linking Venetian markets, through Egypt or Syria, with sources of supply in India and even further afield in Southeast Asia. The Portuguese hoped to help themselves to a share of this trade by sailing around Africa and going directly to the source of spices. Da Gama encountered no politically useful Christians in Calicut, but he found plenty of spice traders.

Da Gama and his crew did not linger long in India. The trade goods they had brought with them didn't interest the merchants of Calicut. The local prince wanted da Gama to pay customs fees like any trader, whereas da Gama regarded himself as a royal emissary and above such things. After three disappointing months the Portuguese left, kidnapping a few Indians and sailing back toward Africa. Portuguese–Indian relations were off to a rocky start.

Da Gama left in a huff, pointing his prows into the teeth of the summer monsoon. The route that had taken three weeks with the winds at his back now took him four

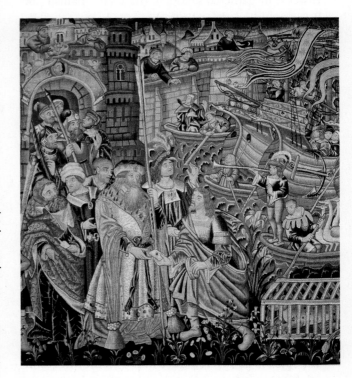

Vasco da Gama A sixteenth-century Flemish tapestry illustrates the moment of encounter between da Gama and his men and the people of the Indian trading port of Calicut—which actually looked much less like a European fortified city than this artist imagined.

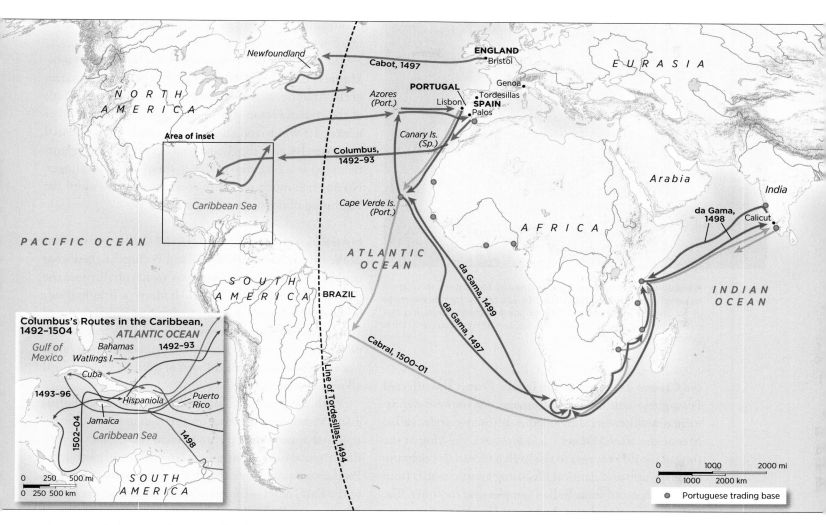

Navigation in the Atlantic and Indian Oceans, 1492–1500 This map shows the new routes pioneered by Columbus, Cabot, da Gama, and Cabral, which began the process of tying together the coasts of Europe, the Americas, Africa, and South Asia. The Line of Tordesillas, established in 1494, divided all "new" lands between Portugal and Spain.

months on the return. Half the crew died before they reached Africa, and only 55 remained alive when da Gama returned to Lisbon more than two years after departing. He had sailed more than 25,000 miles (40,000 km), equal to the circumference of the Earth. He had confirmed the understanding of the winds of the South Atlantic and had pioneered a practical, if slow, route between western Europe and South Asia. And he had brought back enough spices to inspire investors, especially the Portuguese Crown, to send him back again.

In subsequent voyages, da Gama helped set up a lasting Portuguese presence in India and East Africa. It consisted of small trading enclaves, always fortified, sometimes under the protection of local rulers and sometimes at odds with them. The rivalries among rulers on the Indian and

African coasts ensured that da Gama, and later Portuguese as well, could always find allies. Da Gama committed remarkable acts of cruelty, especially against Muslims making the pilgrimage to Mecca. He understood his mission to include piracy against Muslim shipping and did not mind making enemies. (He was not beloved by his own men either—at least, not after he ordered them to rinse their mouths with their own urine to combat scurvy, a gum disease resulting from vitamin shortage, one that often beset sailors on long voyages.)

The Portuguese commercial presence did not matter much to Indians and Africans, who continued their business much as before. But to Portugal, a poor kingdom of fewer than a million people, the occasional trading voyage to India meant infusions of riches, especially for

Manueline Architecture The Jerónimos Monastery in Lisbon, on which construction began in 1501, is a characteristic example of Manueline architecture. The braided pattern encircling the midsection of the column at the center of this double arch is intended to evoke ships' ropes.

the Crown. The trade to the Indian Ocean also affected Portuguese culture and self-image. Portuguese monumental architecture developed a distinctive style, called Manueline after Manuel I (r. 1495–1521), the king at the time of the first voyages to the Indian Ocean. It celebrates those voyages and nautical life, using artistic motifs from sailing ships and from Indian temples and mosques. The Portuguese national saga, known as *The Lusiads*, is an epic poem, first printed in 1572. It is modeled on ancient epics, especially the *Iliad*, but based loosely on the experience of da Gama and other sea captains.

One of the voyages to India missed its target. In 1500, on his swing out into the Atlantic in search of the Southern Hemisphere's westerlies, Pedro de Cabral and his fleet of 13 ships accidentally bumped into Brazil. Cabral claimed it for Portugal, despite the fact that people already lived there. After a brief look around, he continued on across the South Atlantic, around Africa, to India. Like da Gama, he ran into trouble in India with Arab merchants unhappy with competition and engaged in a vengeful massacre in Calicut before heading home in 1501.

Sailors such as Columbus, da Gama, and Cabral made the years 1492–1501 as pivotal as any decade in world history. Mariners from Atlantic Europe learned how to ride the winds back and forth between Europe and America, between Africa and America, and between Europe and South Asia. They found viable routes across the open ocean linking coastlines of continents formerly out of touch with one another.

The discovery of the oceans did not stop in the 1490s. Mariners had now solved the mysteries of the wind system of the Atlantic, as they had long ago the monsoon winds of the Indian Ocean. But the broad Pacific was another matter. Its winds and currents were even more essential to master, because the Pacific is so big that sailing against the wind is a sure way to die at sea of thirst or hunger. No one had much reason to cross the Pacific—until the beginning of the sixteenth century.

MAGELLAN CROSSES THE PACIFIC At the end of the fifteenth century, Spain and Portugal signed what could be the most presumptuous treaty of all time, the **Treaty of Tordesillas** (1494). It drew a line halfway between the American lands Columbus had visited and Portuguese territories known as the Cape Verde Islands off the West African coast. Spain claimed all new lands (meaning new to Spaniards) west of the line, and Portugal all new lands to the east.

With the Treaty of Tordesillas in place, once Portuguese vessels were trading on the Indian Ocean, Spain acquired a motive for trying to cross the Pacific: to gain direct access to precious spices. No one knew how big the Pacific was, and many thought the distance from America to the East Indies—the islands of Indonesia where by 1515 Portuguese merchants were buying spices directly—could not be far. The Molucca Islands, in particular, where nutmeg and cloves grew, excited European imaginations as if they were diamond mines. The Treaty of Tordesillas gave Spain claim to lands west of the Americas, which, if the claim extended far enough, would include the spice islands.

A Portuguese adventurer and dreamer named Fernão de Magalhães, or **Ferdinand Magellan**, tried and failed to convince authorities in Lisbon that it would be easier to reach the **Moluccas** by finding a route south of South America and then sailing west to Asia. He imagined that if there really was an ocean to the west of the American landmass, it was a small one. No one in Portugal would listen. So, like Columbus before him, he took his idea to the Spanish court. Eager to claim the Moluccas and their spices, the Spanish Crown encouraged bankers to invest in Magellan's plans.

So in 1519 Magellan sailed out into the Atlantic with five ships, 250 men (about 1 percent the size of Zheng

CONSIDERING THE EVIDENCE

Portuguese Reasoning about Skin Color

As Portuguese ships explored the oceans, they also recorded observations about geography and people that contradicted traditions handed down from classical scholars. The Portuguese sea captain Duarte Pacheco Pereira (1460–1533) discussed some of these contradictions in his manuscript *Esmeraldo de Situ Orbis*. Pereira had voyaged nearly everywhere the Portuguese reached.

He defended Portuguese forts in India, governed Elmina off the coast of West Africa, and captured a French pirate in the Atlantic. He was also the first person to mention Brazil in a navigation book. In the following excerpt, he draws on personal observations to reconsider the classical Greek assumption that skin color was determined by latitude.

[D]uring the many years we have sailed and operated in this part of the Ethiopias of Guinea [i.e., West Africa], experience has taught us how to take the height of the sun and its declination in order to tell the degrees of latitude by which each place is separated from the Equator and one of the poles. And we have found that this promontory lies directly over the Equator, and have discovered that in this place the days and nights throughout the year are equal....

Many of the ancients said that if two lands lie to the east and west of one another, both would have the same degree of sun and would be in all things alike. As to their equal share of the sun this is true, but such is the great variety employed by the majesty of nature in her work of creation and procreation that we find, from experience, that the inhabitants of this promontory of Lopo Gonçalves and of the rest of Guinea are very black, whereas the people who live beyond the Ocean Sea to the west (who have an equal amount of sun with the blacks of Guinea) are brown, and some almost white. These are the people who live in the land of Brazil.... If any want to claim that these are protected from the heat of the sun because there are many trees in that region, I would say that there are also many trees as great and as thick in this land of Guinea on the eastern side of the ocean. And if any should say that they

are black because they go around naked and that the others are white because they go clothed, I would say that both of them...go around just as they were born. So we can say that the sun does not affect one more than the others. Now it only remains to find out if they are both descended from Adam.

Source: "Duarte Pacheco Pereira Tries to Come to Terms with 'Difference,'" in Malyn Newitt, ed., *The Portuguese in West Africa, 1415–1670: A Documentary History* (Cambridge, 2010).

QUESTIONS FOR ANALYSIS

1. What evidence does Pereira rely on to challenge the conclusions of "the ancients"?
2. After dismissing possible explanations for the differences in skin color between people in Africa and those in Brazil, what direction does he suggest for future research?
3. Does this excerpt suggest that the Portuguese of Pereira's time considered people whose skin color differed from theirs to be inferior in any way?

He's crew), and the most fanciful ideas of how to find the spice islands. Magellan's crew mutinied twice before they even got to the Pacific. Then things went south in a hurry. Magellan thought he could cross from South America to the spice islands easily, but he had been on the ocean for 14 weeks, out of food and fresh water, before his men sighted Guam—they had sailed across an ocean with hundreds of inhabited islands and by bad luck had missed them all. One of the crew explained their suffering:

We only ate old biscuit reduced to powder, full of grubs and stinking from the dirt, which the rats had made

on it when eating the good biscuit and we drank water that was yellow and stinking. We also ate the ox hides which were under the main-yard, so that the yard should not break the rigging: they were very hard on account of the sun, rain, and wind, and we left them for four or five days in the sea, and then we put them a little on the embers, and so ate them; also the sawdust of wood, and rats which cost half-a-crown each, moreover enough of them were not to be got.

On Guam, Magellan guessed he was just off the shore of China. He was 2,500 miles (4,000 km) from it. He next blundered into the Philippines, where he got mixed up in a local war and died in battle.

Magellan's surviving crew kept going west, sailing through the islands of Indonesia, where they picked up a cargo of spices, and into the Indian Ocean, around Africa, and home to Spain. The trip had taken three years, and only about 10 percent of the crew survived. They were the first humans to circumnavigate the globe—although they had intended only to find a route to the Moluccas and spices.

It took many decades before anything practical came of Magellan's quixotic quest. Magellan had showed how big the Pacific really was, and that it—like the Atlantic—had trade winds blowing east to west. Some 40 years later, another captain showed how one could cross the Pacific west to east, from Asia to America, by riding the westerlies, found at the same latitudes as those of the Atlantic. By 1570, Atlantic Europeans had deciphered the wind system of the Pacific too.

WEAVING A MARITIME WEB

Every coastline in the world was now more accessible than ever before to those who knew the secrets of the winds. While Magellan sailed the wide Pacific, other mariners in less dramatic fashion brought more of the world into a tighter web of connections. Portuguese captains began to visit China and Japan, following routes that Asian sailors had used for centuries. From the East African coast, Portuguese adventurers pushed inland, developing a previously small-scale trade in slaves and ivory in Mozambique and making contact with fellow Christians in Ethiopia. These Portuguese travels followed the beaten paths of Asian and African traders.

While European sailors were gathering up knowledge of routes and coasts in Africa and Asia, as far as Australia and Japan, others were adding further information from the Americas. Columbus had begun the process, but dozens of others, mainly Spaniards, followed. They sailed the coastlines, probed the river mouths, and, despite language barriers, absorbed what they could from Amerindian informants. By 1520, they had accumulated a good knowledge of the Caribbean and South America coasts. It took much longer for mariners to figure out the coasts of North America, but by 1620 sailors, mainly English and Dutch, had charted the eastern shoreline all the way north to the fogbound and iceberg-strewn coasts of Hudson Bay. To their dismay, they established that here too there was no good route to the riches of Asia. That dream died hard. As late as the 1630s, Jean Nicolet, a French fur trader, walked and canoed through Wisconsin wearing flowing Chinese robes in hopes of meeting someone who knew the way to China.

Gradually, mariners filled in the remaining blank

Namban Screen This six-fold Japanese screen from around 1600 likely illustrates the arrival of a Portuguese merchant ship in Japan. Portuguese sea captains began to visit Japan in 1543, bringing Christianity, guns, and Chinese silks and porcelain. They bought thousands of Japanese slaves to sell in Macao, Goa, or other Portuguese enclaves until the trade ended soon after 1600.

Magellan's Circumnavigation The Genoese cartographer Battista Agnese made this map of the world in 1540, with lines illustrating the route Magellan took across the Pacific and the Indian Ocean. The extent of Portuguese and other European navigation enabled Agnese to produce detailed renderings of the world's coastlines.

spots on the map of the oceans. Dutch and English ship captains sailed around New Zealand and Australia in the seventeenth century, charting the coasts. But finding the Maori unwelcoming and the Aborigines poor, they left these lands alone for another 150 years. In the eighteenth century, European sailors refined their knowledge of Pacific shores and blundered into most of the inhabited Pacific islands, including the remotest outposts of Polynesia in Easter Island and Hawaii. They charted the American coastlines from Alaska to Chile. By 1780, every significant coast of every ocean had been mapped, and every important island located. For all intents and purposes, the discovery of the winds and the oceans was complete.

European mariners failed in their quest to find a direct route from Europe to Asian spices and failed to find powerful Christian allies against Islamic polities. But they succeeded at something they did not consciously attempt, which was to unite the world's coasts and harbors into a single network and to build geographical knowledge so that any competent navigator, with the right equipment and ship, could go anywhere on the sea with a reasonably good idea of where he was and what lay ahead. The

confidence with which merchants had long sailed the South China Sea, the Arabian Gulf, or the Mediterranean, European merchants (and for a long while only European ones) now extended to the deep oceans. The first pulse of true globalization, achieved partly by accident, was accomplished mainly by Europeans—specifically, those from Atlantic Europe.

BIOLOGICAL GLOBALIZATION, 1492–1800

One of the most important consequences of the discovery of the oceans and their winds, and the establishment of regular traffic linking the world's shores, was a surge in **biological globalization**. This process reshuffled the continents' flora and fauna, bringing both searing new epidemics and useful new food crops to many peoples. It changed the world's demographic balance and altered political and economic fortunes. By and large, it eased life for millions in Eurasia and Africa, and ended it prematurely for millions in the Americas and Oceania. It

Waldseemüller World Map Created by German mapmaker Martin Waldseemüller in 1507, this map was the first to encompass the full Western Hemisphere. It was also the first—on the lower portion of South America—to mention the name "America."

provides an excellent example of the fact that in world history major consequences often flow from events in ways that no one intended or foresaw.

As earlier chapters have noted, over the centuries people moved plants, animals, and microbes around the world. Sometimes they did it on purpose, like the first settlers of North America who brought dogs with them, or the Polynesians who ferried crops and animals to uninhabited Pacific islands. Sometimes they did it by accident, like the anonymous people who brought the plague bacillus from northeast Africa to the Byzantine Empire in the time of Justinian. Biological exchange has long been an important part of history, with powerful effects on food supplies and disease burdens.

The pace of biological exchange sped up whenever web connections boosted trade and migration. It slowed down when webs withered. So, for example, when the Roman and Han Empires were at their height, and trans-Eurasian trade and travel reached a temporary peak along the Silk Roads, so did biological exchange. China acquired camels, donkeys, and grapes. Mediterranean peoples added cherries, apricots, and walnuts to their gardens and diets. When commerce quickened in the Arabian Sea after

800 CE, the exchange of crops among India, East Africa, and the Mediterranean picked up speed.

Biologically, as in other respects, the Americas had remained a realm apart from these Old World web exchanges. Aside from the import of the dog (from Siberia about 15,000 years ago) and the export of sweet potato (to Polynesia about 1,000 years ago), the American hemisphere before 1492 exchanged nothing consequential with the wider world. American plants and animals included many unknown elsewhere—tobacco, armadillos, and grizzly bears, for instance. Australia and New Zealand, even more isolated, each hosted flora and fauna—eucalyptus trees, kangaroos, and moas, for example—found nowhere else on Earth.

After the voyages of Columbus, mariners linked almost every nook and cranny of the humanly habitable Earth into a biologically interactive web. The world's oceans no longer served to isolate ecosystems from one another. It became a world without biological borders, as plants, animals, and disease-causing pathogens scattered wherever ecological conditions permitted their spread. They went wherever people took them, and sometimes even further on their own.

Columbus inaugurated regular exchanges across the Atlantic in 1492. On his second voyage, he deliberately brought a ship full of species new to the Americas and brought home to Spain some biological souvenirs. Over the next few centuries, his followers did the same in an ongoing process known to historians as the Columbian Exchange. The most conspicuous result was that Amerindians acquired hundreds of new plants and animals from Eurasia and Africa, as well as a dozen devastating diseases formerly unfamiliar to them. At first, between 1492 and 1700, the spread of diseases was the most important part of biological globalization, mainly because of their horrific impact on the peoples of the Americas.

DEADLY DISEASES

Upon arrival in the Americas, transatlantic travelers coughed and sneezed billions of deadly microbes into the air that Amerindians breathed. Among them were the pathogens (viruses, mainly) that cause smallpox, measles, mumps, whooping cough, and influenza. All of these had become fairly widespread in the Old World web. From West Africa to East Asia, they were usually endemic, childhood diseases, sometimes now called crowd diseases (discussed in Chapter 5), that killed huge numbers of small children. But in the Old World web, most adults were survivors, and either resistant or fully immune to most or all of these viral infections. In addition to the crowd diseases, the Columbian Exchange brought some lethal vector-borne African diseases to the Americas. The two deadliest were yellow fever and falciparum malaria (the worst form of **malaria**), both spread by mosquitos.

In the Americas in 1492, none of the 40 to 70 million people had any prior experience with, and therefore no acquired immunity to, any of these diseases. Their immune systems did not instantly "recognize" and neutralize the exotic pathogens. This vulnerability was compounded by the weakening of their nutrition and health by Atlantic European colonization—which, as we'll see, included loss of farmlands, enslavement, and forced migration.

The cascade of unfamiliar pathogens brought suffering and death on the largest scale. Here is how one Amerindian, in Mexico, recalled it:

The illness was so dreadful that no one could walk or move. The sick were so utterly helpless that they could only lie on their beds like corpses, unable to move their

limbs or even their heads. A great many died from this plague, and many others died of hunger. They would not get up to search for food, and everyone else was too sick to care for them, so they starved to death in their beds.

In many Amerindian communities, the social fabric dissolved under this onslaught. People lost all hope. Few wanted to bring children into a world such as theirs had become, dominated by sickness and pain, and few were healthy enough to do so.

The scale of epidemics and death was gigantic. Between 1492 and 1650, populations in the Americas fell by 70 to 95 percent in one of the two largest-scale demographic disasters in world history. (The other was the Black Death of the fourteenth century in the Old World web.) The sharp decline in population in the Americas had many consequences that we will meet repeatedly in the chapters ahead.

The Amerindians had little in the way of lethal infectious disease that transferred to Africa and Eurasia. The first migrants to arrive in North America had passed through northeastern Siberia and Alaska during an ice age. The brutal cold probably killed off some pathogens. And since they left Siberia when no animals but dogs had been domesticated, the human infections shared with herd animals (e.g., smallpox, measles, influenza) had not yet appeared. Thus the first Amerindians arrived relatively free from infection.

Epidemics in the Americas This illustration of Aztecs suffering and dying from the smallpox brought by Spanish colonists appears in the Florentine Codex, a treatise written by a Spanish missionary in the sixteenth century about the Spanish conquest of Mexico in 1519–1521.

Once in the Americas, Amerindians did not domesticate any herd animals other than alpacas and llamas, which seem, by chance, not to have hosted pathogens that evolved into agents of human disease. If Eurasia and Africa acquired any new diseases from the Americas at all (syphilis is the leading candidate, but the evidence is far from conclusive), they had trivial consequences. So, as regards disease, the Columbian Exchange was a notably one-sided affair.

The one-sidedness of the health consequences of the Columbian Exchange led Europeans who witnessed this devastation to see divine purpose at work. Francisco de Aguilar, who was present when Spaniards and their allies conquered the Aztec capital of Tenochtitlán, wrote: "When the Christians were exhausted from war, God saw fit to send the Indians smallpox, and there was a great pestilence in the city." More than a century later in New England, John Winthrop, the first governor of the Massachusetts Bay Colony, saw the disaster as divine endorsement of the seizure of land: "For the natives, they are neere all dead of small Poxe, so as the Lord hathe cleared our title to what we possess."

USEFUL ANIMALS

The Columbian Exchange was almost as one-sided with respect to domesticated animals. People transported turkeys and guinea pigs from the Americas to other continents, but nowhere did they become important. Alpacas and llamas never prospered outside their native Andes, although scattered populations do exist elsewhere. The Amerindians had little in the way of domesticated animals, and those they had did not travel well.

In contrast, Eurasian and African animal species flourished when transported to the Americas. Cattle, goats, sheep, pigs, and horses were the most important animal immigrants. They all found empty niche space in the Americas, especially cattle and horses on the vast grasslands of both North and South America. The new animals provided surviving Amerindians with new sources of hides, wool, and animal protein. Horses and oxen made plowing feasible in the Americas for the first time, allowed transportation through wheeled vehicles, and, together with donkeys and mules, provided a greater variety of pack animals. Animal-powered transport extended the potential of commerce and economic specialization, which over centuries raised overall production levels considerably.

In addition to economic growth, the new animals brought unwelcome frictions to the Americas. They munched and trampled crops, provoking quarrels between herders and farmers of the sort familiar in Africa and Eurasia but almost unknown in the Americas before 1492. In this respect, the Columbian Exchange helped make the Americas a bit more like the rest of the world, where such quarrels had long been routine.

In North America, the introduction of horses upset the political order. The Amerindians of the prairies, from Texas to Manitoba, acquired horses from newly Spanish Mexico in the seventeenth century, and some of them quickly mastered riding and horse breeding. On horseback, they became far more adept as bison hunters, solving any subsistence problems as long as the bison lasted. Moreover, those with horses easily inflicted military defeats on those without. Amerindian peoples such as the Sioux and Comanche eventually built considerable empires on the basis of mounted warfare, as Mongol and Malian horsemen had recently done in Asia and Africa. In this respect too, the Americas became less distinctive, more like the rest of the world, thanks to the Columbian Exchange and biological globalization.

KEY CROPS

The Columbian Exchange was more even-handed when it came to crops. The Eurasian staples of wheat, rye, barley, and rice flourished in the Americas. Some of the new crops could survive in cold and dry landscapes where the indigenous crops fared poorly: North Dakota and Saskatchewan do better growing wheat than maize. Others, such as rice, transplanted from both Asia and Africa, required heavy labor in order to produce bumper crops. Rice became a plantation crop in the Americas, worked mainly by imported African slave labor. Aside from grains, the Americas also acquired citrus fruits, grapes, and figs from Eurasia, and millets, sorghums, yams, bananas, okra, and watermelon from Africa. So the new crops extended the possibilities of American agriculture somewhat and allowed a more varied diet. But in many places they brought only a small improvement in nutrition, because people in the Americas already had maize or potatoes (or both) and plenty of fruits and vegetables.

New drug crops changed the Americas at least as profoundly as the new food crops. Sugar, originally from New Guinea but a commercial crop in South Asia, China, and the Mediterranean, came to Brazil and the Caribbean in the sixteenth and seventeenth centuries. Both a mild drug and a food, it became, as we shall see, the mainstay of a plantation economy based on African slave labor. Coffee, from Ethiopia and Arabia, also became a plantation crop in the eighteenth century. We will see the full importance of these crops in a later chapter when we encounter the plantation system in the Americas.

The Americas' contributions to global cuisine included the staples maize, potatoes, sweet potatoes, and cassava, together with tomatoes, cacao, peanuts, pumpkins, squashes, pineapples, and a handful of other food crops. Some of these crops had revolutionary consequences in sizeable regions of Africa and Eurasia. Potatoes, for example, which nicely suited soil and climate conditions from Ireland to Russia, led to a spurt of population growth in northern Europe after 1730.

MAIZE This staple had a broader impact than potatoes. It did well in conditions as varied as those of southern Europe, southern and central China, and much of Africa. **Maize** allowed new lands to be brought under cultivation, because it prospered where grains and tubers would not. It soon undergirded population growth and famine resistance in China and southern Europe. But nowhere was it more influential than in Africa, where today it remains the single most important food crop. In the two centuries after 1550, maize became a staple in Atlantic Africa, from Angola to Senegambia. Different maize varieties suited the several different rainfall regimes in Africa and improved African peoples' chances of surviving drought.

While maize helped feed generations of Africans, it had bleaker consequences too. Maize stores much better than millets, sorghums, or tubers, the traditional crops in most of Africa. It thus allowed chiefs and kings to maximize their power by centralizing the storage and distribution of food. In the West African forest zone, south of the Sahel, maize encouraged the formation of larger states than ever

Maize in Africa This small brass statue, a porcupine making off with a maize cob, was used by the Akan people (in today's country of Ghana) as a counterweight when weighing gold dust. It dates from the seventeenth or eighteenth century, by which time maize was well established in West Africa.

before. The Asante kingdom, for example, embarked on a program of military expansion after the 1670s, spearheaded by maize-eating armies that could carry their food with them on distant campaigns. Maize also served well as a portable food for merchant caravans, which contributed to commercialization in Atlantic Africa, including an expansion of existing slave trades. Slave traders could operate over longer distances if they, and their human property, had an easily portable food supply that stored well. Maize in Africa increased the practicality of the slave trade. As we shall see, it helped make slaving an intercontinental business, linking Europe, Africa, and the Americas.

CASSAVA Also known as manioc, **cassava** was the Americas' other great contribution to African agriculture. A native of Brazil, cassava is admirably suited to drought and poor soils, and resistant to many insect crop pests. It too did well in many parts of Africa, and like maize provided a portable, storable food that underlay state formation and expansion in West Africa and Angola. Cassava, like potatoes, need not be harvested at a particular season but may be left in the ground for weeks or more. So it is an ideal crop for people who might need to run away for their own safety and abandon their fields—for example, people routinely subject to slave raiding. In this respect, it had the opposite effect of maize: it helped peasantries to flee and survive slave raids, while maize helped slavers to conduct raids and wars.

The impact of American food crops on Africa was so great that it makes sense to think of African history, especially Atlantic African history, as divided into pre-Columbian and post-Columbian phases—as is normally done for the Americas. Maize, cassava, and a cornucopia of other crops from the Americas, including peanuts, pineapple, chili peppers, sweet potato, avocado, cacao, and a dozen others, gradually re-fashioned African cuisine and agriculture. This was the second time in African history that imported crops made a big difference—recall the impact of bananas, acquired from Southeast Asia, many centuries before.

African farmers took to the new American crops eagerly, seeing them as either useful additions or even replacements for their old ones. The greater variety of food crops provided a form of insurance against crop failure due to insect pests or bad weather. Maize had the further attraction that birds usually find it too much trouble to

THE HUMAN WEB

The Columbian Exchange

1492–1800

horses

potatoes

EUROPE

Danube R.

maize

maize

NORTH AMERICA

Rocky Mts.

Colorado R.

Mississippi R.

Appalachian Mts.

grains

cotton

coffee
sugar

Mexico

sugar

influenza, measles, mumps,
smallpox, whooping cough
cattle, goats, horses, pigs, sheep
barley, oats, rye, wheat,
citrus, cotton, figs, grapes
sugar

syphilis?
cassava, maize, potatoes, avocadoes, cacao, chili peppers,
peanuts, pineapples, pumpkins, squashes, sweet potatoes, tomatoes
tobacco

horses

malaria, yellow fever
rice, millets, sorghums, bananas,
cotton, okra, watermelon, yams
coffee

Senegambia

Nile R.

Arabia

Niger R.

AFRICA

Ethiopia

cassava
maize

coffee
sugar

PACIFIC
OCEAN

Andes Mts.

Amazon R.

Brazil

ATLANTIC
OCEAN

sugar

Congo R.

cassava
maize

Angola

sugar

SOUTH
AMERICA

Paraná R.

Zambezi R.

▼ Argentina,
wagon caravan
and herd of cattle
crossing a swamp,
1818.

coffee
sugar

Andes Mts.

horses

▲ Dakota Sioux, painted bison hide depicting horsemen and a buffalo, ca. 1850.

ASIA

potatoes

Huang He

maize

Yangzi R.

Himalaya Mts.

potatoes

Ganges R.

China

potatoes

Mekong R.

India

PACIFIC

OCEAN

Philippines

Guam

INDIAN

OCEAN

New
Guinea

▼ West Indies sugar plantation, seventeenth century.

"

THERE WAS THEN NO SICKNESS; THEY HAD NO ACHING BONES; THEY HAD THEN NO HIGH FEVER; THEY HAD THEN NO SMALLPOX; AT THAT TIME THE COURSE OF HUMANITY WAS ORDERLY. THE FOREIGNERS MADE IT OTHERWISE WHEN THEY ARRIVED HERE.

"

THE BOOK OF CHILAM BALAM OF CHUMAYEL, CA. 1530–1550

BETWEEN 1492 AND 1800, mariners tied together the shores of the Atlantic into an especially vibrant part of the emerging Global web. Their voyages created an Atlantic world, similar in many respects to the Indian Ocean world, another lively part of a larger web, built long before. But in one respect—the Columbian Exchange—the Atlantic world had no true parallels in world history.

The Columbian Exchange of plants, animals, and lethal pathogens was the biggest pulse of biological exchange in world history. Anytime that webs extended across vast distances, people—intentionally and accidentally—carried some species to new homes. When the Silk Roads opened, for example, China acquired grapes, sorghum, donkeys, and camels from Southwest Asia. But no other such episode approaches the Columbian Exchange which suddenly united biological communities that had been separate for 50 million years.

The impacts of the Columbian Exchange included drastic changes in population, agriculture, and the economies of the Americas, Africa, and Europe. For some people, such as Amerindians, the Columbian Exchange brought disaster in the form of new diseases. For others, such as southern Europeans or southern Africans, it brought a new, high-energy food crop: maize. The introduction of maize and cassava to African agriculture and diet was so important that for Atlantic Africa at least, it makes sense to think in terms of pre-Columbian and post-Columbian phases, just as scholars routinely do for the Americas.

Questions for Analysis

Based on this feature and your chapter reading, consider the following questions:

1. Why did some peoples suffer and some peoples benefit from the Columbian Exchange?

2. What regions within the Atlantic world felt the strongest impacts of the Columbian Exchange?

Le Manyoc

Cassava in Africa This illustration of the cassava plant appears in a French book about Caribbean plants from 1688. Originating in the Americas, cassava became an even more successful crop in West Africa and Angola, where it was well suited to the climate, soils, and the needs of farming communities.

poke through the husks to get at the grain. Birds don't bother with cassava either. Ripe millet and sorghum, in contrast, provide tempting targets for birds, and people must defend these crops day and night if they wish to enjoy a harvest. The American crops undergirded a slow expansion of farming, state making, and perhaps even population growth in Africa after 1650—despite the demographic effects of the transatlantic slave trade.

BIOLOGICAL GLOBALIZATION IN THE PACIFIC

The **Columbian Exchange** was the largest-scale, fastest, and most important set of intercontinental biological transfers in world history. But it was only part of the

surge in biological globalization that followed upon the navigational exploits of Columbus's generation. A modest transpacific exchange resulted from traffic that followed Magellan's voyages, at first affecting chiefly the Philippines. That exchange intensified in the wake of later sea captains' travels throughout the world's largest ocean. The Pacific islands themselves, rather than the ocean's rim, felt the greatest effects, and as in the Americas the most striking result was sharp depopulation in the wake of repeated epidemics.

Guam, for example, in the seventeenth century became a Spanish outpost on the route between the Philippines and the Americas. Its indigenous population, the Chamorro, fell by about 90 percent within a century—mainly from the impact of smallpox, measles, tuberculosis, and other new diseases, although violence and loss of lands raised the Chamorros' vulnerability to infections. Guam also acquired many new plants and animals, such as cattle, hogs, chickens, rice, citrus trees, and a Mexican shrub tree called Tangantangan. The latter grew quickly on Guam, especially in lands no longer farmed because of the population disaster.

Later on, other Pacific islands experienced similar biological disruptions when put into sustained contact with the wider world. In every case, the demographic consequences overshadowed all others. Population declines of roughly 90 percent befell many archipelagoes, primarily a result of newly introduced diseases. A similar grim history befell aboriginal Australians after 1788 when contact with the wider world became routine. But this was a story of the eighteenth and nineteenth centuries, one that belongs to a later chapter.

THE IMPACT OF BIOLOGICAL EXCHANGE

Taken together, the whirlwind of intercontinental biological exchange in the centuries between 1492 and 1800 brought astounding changes around the world. It led to long-lasting demographic catastrophes among peoples unfamiliar with the crowd diseases. In the Americas and Oceania, indigenous population size typically fell for about six or seven generations before bottoming out and beginning to recover. This rate of recovery was slow compared to the experience of Eurasian populations in the face of most epidemics. That is testimony to the terrible impact of multiple infections assaulting peoples in the

Americas and Oceania in repeated hammer blows. It also reflects the significance of loss of the best lands, enslavement, and forced migration in escalating mortality and suppressing fertility. The population disasters were a part of biological globalization, but they were not just biological processes: they arose from the interaction of biological and social processes. They represent a penalty of isolation from the bigger webs of world history, a theme we have encountered before.

The surge in biological exchange eventually improved the quantity and reliability of food supplies almost everywhere. This process slowly reduced the frequency of starvation and the toll of epidemics (because well-fed people survive most diseases better than malnourished ones). The world's population almost doubled between 1500 and 1800, from about 500 million to about 950 million, and a big reason was improved nutrition thanks to food-crop globalization.

One agreeable way of thinking about the whole (admittedly often grim) subject of biological globalization in the wake of Columbus is to contemplate food. Can you imagine Italian food without tomatoes? Or Polish cuisine without potatoes? What would the South African diet be without mealie maize, or West Africa's without peanuts? Argentina's without beef? New Zealand's or southern China's without sweet potatoes? What would Korean kimchi taste like without chili peppers? If we are what we eat, then the Columbian Exchange and biological globalization not only shaped empires and demography but also helped to make us what we are.

THE BEGINNINGS OF A GLOBAL WEB

The oceanic voyaging of the fifteenth and sixteenth centuries united continents into a single global web for the first time in human history. The web-making process—at work from the very earliest human settlements onward—had developed an extended, multilayered fabric of connections across Eurasia and North Africa. Significant webs had developed also in the Americas, and smaller, local ones elsewhere. But for thousands of years before 1492, the Americas had largely stood apart from Africa and Eurasia, notwithstanding the brief Viking and Polynesian visits. Now the history of the Americas unfolded in continuing

connection with the Old World web. Similarly, after the secrets of oceanic navigation spread and mariners sailed regularly among all the world's inhabited shores, the islands of the Pacific, the coastlands of South Africa, and a few other spots around the world became linked as never before to the new, global web now in formation.

The oceanic voyaging also tightened linkages within the Old World web. In some cases, the tighter links proved temporary, as with Zheng He's voyages to India and East Africa between 1405 and 1433. But in others they endured much longer, as with Portuguese ties to African coasts, India, and the spice islands of Southeast Asia. So the three centuries after the 1490s saw a sudden spurt in web building, one that transformed human history and inaugurated a global age in which we still live.

The spinning of the first truly global web had many consequences. The most enduring and important of these was the biological globalization that reshuffled the distribution of economically significant plants and animals around the world and brought devastating infections to the Americas and Oceania. Another important consequence flowed from the fact that it was mainly Atlantic Europeans—not Chinese, Africans, Polynesians, or anyone else—who first fully deciphered the oceanic winds and currents. As a result, they were the first to sail the seven seas and learn of new long-distance trade possibilities. They also found new opportunities to conquer peoples less militarily formidable than themselves. The role of Europeans, especially seafaring Atlantic Europeans, in influencing world history rose to new levels. Over the prior millennia, only rarely could such a small minority of humankind exercise such outsized influence upon world history as Atlantic Europeans would wield in the three or four centuries to come.

The penalties of isolation for societies with few or no connections to the Old World web were now felt as never before. These societies typically hosted a narrower range of infectious diseases than did peoples in the web that enveloped Eurasia and North Africa, leaving them vulnerable to shattering epidemics when European ships arrived with new pathogens. They typically possessed a less formidable array of weaponry than existed in China, India, or Europe, using less metal, no firearms, and no horses. These societies had not needed or developed institutions and technologies that equipped them to deal with the challenges posed by seafaring, horse-riding, disease-bearing, well-armed strangers.

The spinning of the first truly global web proved transformational in other respects too. It continued the long-standing process by which cultural diversity narrowed. The major religions, especially Christianity and Islam, spread to new ground. They became slightly more diverse themselves as a result, because in every case they adopted some local features; but they reduced the overall diversity of religion with their conversions in Asia, Africa, the Americas, and Oceania. The spread of Arabic, Spanish, and English also, on balance, reduced the variety of languages spoken around the world, even if the English spoken in Australia or Barbados was not the same as that spoken in London. Many languages would gradually go extinct in the centuries after oceanic voyaging linked up the world. The next few chapters will detail the formation of the global web and how it affected political, economic, and cultural life throughout the world.

CONCLUSION

The world in 1400 included one big web and several smaller ones. The Old World web was the big one, containing the majority of humankind and stretching across Eurasia and North Africa from Senegal to Japan. A smaller one existed in the Americas, and local ones existed in several places around the world. In the course of the fifteenth century, however, this longstanding pattern underwent a major reorganization.

Beginning early in the fifteenth century, Chinese and Atlantic European mariners undertook oceanic voyages that brought the world together as never before. The most decisive changes came with the European, mainly Iberian, voyaging. From 1460 onward, this voyaging brought an increasing number of African maritime ports (e.g.,

Elmina) into direct contact with communities of the Old World web. From 1492 onward, it brought the Americas and the Old World web together on a sustained basis. From the early sixteenth century onward, it brought an increasing number of Pacific islands into enduring touch with the Old World web. Thus those mariners, in seeking fortune and glory for themselves and their monarchs, created the first truly global web.

Biological globalization in some respects was the deepest of all the global web's consequences, affecting as it did the life and death of hundreds of millions of people during the sixteenth and seventeenth centuries. Exchanges of food crops resulted in changes to agriculture and diets and, in more cases than not, improvements in nutrition. People in Africa and Eurasia acquired maize and potatoes from the Americas, while those in the Americas acquired wheat, rye, barley, and new varieties of rice. Exchanges of domesticated animals brought horses, cattle, pigs, sheep, and goats (to name only the most significant) to the Americas. These plant and animal exchanges were important in the sixteenth century and remain so today.

The other major component of biological globalization was the exchange of disease pathogens. It was extremely one-sided—and extremely costly to peoples of the Americas and Oceania. Its toll varied from case to case, but generally was on the order of one-half to nine-tenths of populations affected. The population catastrophe, made more costly by violence, loss of lands, and other stresses, generally lasted for the first 150 years after sustained contact with peoples of the Old World web.

The oceanic voyaging of the fifteenth through the seventeenth centuries did not start biological globalization, which can be traced back many thousands of years. But it launched the biggest and most consequential spurt of it in world history.

CHAPTER REVIEW

KEY TERMS

Zheng He (p. 461)
Ming voyages (p. 462)
Reconquista (p. 464)
Guanches (p. 464)
Christopher Columbus (p. 466)

Vasco da Gama (p. 468)
Calicut (p. 468)
Treaty of Tordesillas (p. 470)
Ferdinand Magellan (p. 470)
Moluccas (p. 470)

biological globalization (p. 473)
malaria (p. 475)
maize (p. 477)
cassava (p. 477)
Columbian Exchange (p. 480)

Go to INQUIZITIVE to see what you've learned—and learn what you've missed—with personalized feedback along the way.

REVIEW QUESTIONS

1. What were the main trading routes in Eurasia and North Africa in the fifteenth century?

2. What were the other three, smaller trade networks that existed apart from the main Eurasian and North African trading routes?

3. In what two ways were the Ming voyages exceptional?

4. Identify the three main reasons European explorers sailed west into the Atlantic Ocean during this period.

5. Why was knowledge of the Atlantic Ocean's wind patterns essential for sailors?

6. What was Columbus looking for when he journeyed across the Atlantic?

7. How did the Treaty of Tordesillas spur Spanish exploration of the Pacific Ocean?

8. Why was the transfer of malaria and yellow fever to the Americas so deadly?

9. How did prairie Amerindians, such as the Sioux and the Comanche, use horses to build empires?

10. Which crops that were indigenous to the Old World web became significant plantation crops in the Americas?

11. How did maize support the growth of larger states in West Africa?

12. In what two ways did the global exchange of crops improve food supply around the world?

13. Explain the major consequences of biological globalization in the sixteenth and seventeenth centuries.

FURTHER READING

John Logan ALLEN, ed., *A New World Disclosed* (1997). A detailed account of European voyaging to, and into, North America from the Vikings to about 1680.

Judith CARNEY, *Black Rice* (2002). A detailed study of how African rice got to the Americas.

Alfred CROSBY, *The Columbian Exchange: Biological and Cultural Consequences of 1492* (1972). A classic analysis that essentially invented the idea of the Columbian exchange of plants and animals.

Edward DREYER, *Zheng He: China and the Oceans in the Early Ming Dynasty, 1405–1433* (2007). The best general treatment of the Ming voyages.

Felipe FERNÁNDEZ-ARMESTO, *Pathfinders* (2006). A general (and well-written) history of exploration, with several chapters on European maritime efforts from 1400 through 1800.

Linda NEWSOM, *Conquest and Pestilence in the Early Spanish Philippines* (2009). A careful analysis of how some of this chapter's themes worked out in one archipelago.

CHRONOLOGY

1441
Portuguese begin selling
Africans as slaves

1462
Portuguese mariners
establish Elmina in
West Africa

1519
Hernán Cortés attacks
Tenochtitlán

1519–ca. 1860
The transatlantic slave trade

1524
Waves of epidemics
begin in the Andes

1532
Francisco Pizarro
overthrows Inka
emperor

ca. 1600–1694
Palmares maroon community
in Brazil

1580s
Yermak spearheads
fur trade in Siberia

1652
Dutch East India
Company founds
outpost at Cape of
Good Hope

**Pueblo kill or expel all Spanish
from what is now New Mexico**

1680

1713
Smallpox epidemic kills
up to 90 percent of Khoi

1689
Russian and Chinese Empires
sign treaty dividing Siberian
and East Asian spaces

ca. 1780–1810
King Hamehamea
unites Hawaii

1788–1868
Britain sends convict
settlers to Australia

Disruption

AFRICA, THE AMERICAS, SIBERIA, AND OCEANIA

1492 to 1850

1807–1845
Musket Wars in New Zealand

1840
Treaty of Waitangi

1898
United States
annexes Hawaii

1845–1872
Intermittent
land wars
between Maori
and *pakeha*

1876
Trucanini
dies

T rucanini, who died in 1876, was one of the last of the Tasmanians. She was witness to a grim and frequent process in world history.

Tasmania is an island 150 miles (240 km) off the southern coast of Australia. People first arrived there about 40,000 years ago, when lower sea levels allowed them to walk from Australia. When rising sea levels divided Tasmania from the Australian mainland around 6000 BCE, the Tasmanians were cut off. For nearly 8,000 years, until a few centuries ago, they had no known contacts with the rest of humankind. They gradually lost the skills to catch fish, make bone tools, and even to make fire. Their technological decay is striking evidence of the costs of isolation in small groups.

In 1642, a Dutch sea captain, Abel Tasman, sighted the island that bears his name but did not disembark. British whalers began to use it as a base in 1798, ending the long isolation of Tasmania, and in 1803 British authorities decided to locate a penal colony there. At that time, there were about 5,000

A Linen Market with a Linen-stall and Vegetable Seller in the West Indies, **ca. 1780** Agostino Brunias's finely detailed paintings of Caribbean market scenes capture the social gradations of Creole society through the clothing worn by his subjects. Whites and free persons of color wear fine European styles with African accents such as colorful head wraps. Enslaved people wear almost nothing. The textiles for sale at these weekly markets drew buyers and sellers into the Global web of trade.

FOCUS QUESTIONS

1. What were the major effects in Africa of joining the Global web?

2. What were the major effects in the Americas of joining the Global web?

3. What major changes came to Siberia once it was integrated into the Old World web?

4. How did entry into the Global web affect Oceania and Australia?

to 15,000 Tasmanians in existence. By 1830, only some 300 remained. The British prisoners and their keepers had brought new diseases, casual attitudes to murderous violence, and weaponry far superior to what the Tasmanians could muster. Most of Trucanini's family was abducted, enslaved, or killed. She became an outlaw in her 20s, was shot in the head and imprisoned, but lived into her 60s. Meanwhile, British officials gathered the last of the Tasmanians together with the stated intent of protecting them, but influenza and other infections continued to wreak deadly havoc. With the death of Trucanini, a 40,000-year-old language and culture died as well, after a mere three-quarters of a century of contact with the outside world.

This chapter presents the ways in which peoples previously outside the Old World web found themselves rapidly enmeshed in the Global web in its formative centuries. The processes behind these new connections were simultaneously political and military, economic and technological, religious and cultural, biological and demographic. In most cases, they involved episodes of great brutality. The focus here is on sub-Saharan Africa, the Americas, Siberia, and Oceania and Australia. Later chapters will take up the story of how this globalizing, web-expanding

process played out within the former Old World web itself—that is, within Eurasia and North Africa.

Entry into the expanding global web for peoples long isolated was always hard, and sometimes fully as disastrous as for Tasmanians. Most peoples suffered demographic losses due to **disease disasters**, violence, and declines in fertility. Most also experienced wrenching cultural and political changes, and yet somehow made the adjustments necessary to survive in their new worlds as participants in the Global web. They had a lot to learn about operating in new and larger economic and political contexts, and the people who knew most about global contexts often preferred to kill or enslave them rather than instruct them.

The opening of the oceans to navigation, and the sudden spread of information, diseases, migrants, and much else, reshuffled fortunes dramatically. Just about everyone sought to take advantage of the new situation, including the peoples of Africa, the Americas, Oceania, and Siberia, although they were rarely well placed to do so. The people best positioned to seize the opportunities of the globalizing world were those who had the fullest information about routes, goods, prices, technologies, languages, and religions. These were the people who traveled the seas for themselves—mainly but not exclusively Atlantic Europeans.

European sailors, soldiers, settlers, merchants, and missionaries often knew, or knew how to find out, roughly how much a pound of pepper would fetch in Lisbon markets or whether customers in Calicut preferred pearls over ponies. This enabled them to trade more profitably than others could. They also knew, or could make educated guesses, whether or not their weapons would give them an edge against peoples around the world, and thus whether attacking them might be foolish or not. There was of course much they did not know, and they made many miscalculations. But on average they had a more global perspective than anyone else, and they took advantage of that where they could.

The Last Tasmanians In the mid-nineteenth century, British authorities took this studio photograph of four of the last surviving Tasmanians, dressed in British fashions. Trucanini is seated on the far right.

Atlantic Europeans were only the latest example of people in position to exploit the information advantages of web connections. Ancient Carthaginians usually knew more about distant markets and new technologies than anyone in Spain, and they too took advantage of that when they could. The same was true of the Chola merchants and kings in south India in their relations with landlocked neighbors, or of Arabs with respect to East Africans living inland from the Swahili coast. The difference here is one of scale: the Atlantic Europeans enjoyed information advantages over many peoples around the world and could harvest information from every continent.

And information advantages were only part of their edge. Atlantic European mariners were in effect the Mongols of the sea. Like horse nomads, they didn't always have military advantages over potential rivals, but thanks to their mobility they could choose when and where they might wish to fight, when and where they preferred to flee. With their big shipboard cannon, they could attack enemies from

a safe distance, as horse nomads could with their bows. Like the mobile Mongols, they could, when it suited them, engage in acts of unspeakable cruelty, knowing they could get away safely, never to return and face the consequences. This is not to suggest that either Mongols or sea-going Europeans were by nature crueler than anyone else; only that they could indulge in cruelty and escape retribution more easily than others who lacked superior mobility. And, like the Mongols, Atlantic Europeans' conquests, massacres, co-optations, and absorptions of other peoples helped prepare the way for unprecedented consolidation of webs of economic, cultural, and biological interaction.

It is important to recognize that this process of globalization, even if on balance it led to European domination of large parts of the world, reshuffled fortunes in complicated ways. In Africa and the Americas especially, some rulers, clans, and peoples found ways to turn the linkages presented by European seafaring to their advantage. Some, for example, monopolized European trade goods and got rich. Others managed to control access to firearms and became more powerful. Still others translated support from Christian missionaries into prestige and power. And some, such as the kings of Kongo in West Central Africa, did all of the above, if only for a while. Trucanini and the Tasmanians, mainly because of the penalties of isolation in small groups, did none of the above.

AFRICA AND THE GLOBAL WEB

Sub-Saharan Africa in 1400 already had considerable links to the Old World web, across the Sahara and via the sailing routes of the Indian Ocean. Only the southernmost reaches, and a few pockets here and there, may be said to have been truly isolated from the wider world. However, after 1450, as trans-Saharan travel became more common and Portuguese mariners began to visit its coasts, nearly every part of Africa tightened its connections to what was rapidly becoming a global web. The process, as usual, was a rough one, featuring war, empire building, epidemics, and enslavement, as well as heightened trade and cultural exchange. The main components of the process were, first, the gradual and ongoing spread of Islam through the northern half of Africa, which in places was coupled with wider use of the Arabic language. Second, in a few locations, small colonies of European settlers took root, creating altogether new societies. Third, Africans, especially those living near the coasts, became increasingly active in maritime trade circuits, not only of the Indian Ocean (which had been going on for centuries) but also of the Atlantic. The largest part of this commerce was the transatlantic slave trade.

ISLAM IN AFRICA

Islam, as we have seen, spread from its Arabian homeland into North Africa, largely by conquest, during the seventh century. It subsequently seeped into sub-Saharan Africa along two main paths: by sea to the Swahili coast and across the desert into the western and central Sahel (the southern edge of the Sahara). In both cases, Islam's spread usually occurred not by conquest but through efforts of merchants, rulers, and missionaries—categories that overlapped in many cases.

Merchants from North Africa and Arabia brought their varieties of Islam with them when visiting Sahelian towns or Swahili ports. Since they generally stayed for months and interacted daily with locals, they had plenty of opportunity to demonstrate the attractions of Islam to urban Africans. Merchants in Africa, as in South, Southeast, and Central Asia, often found it both agreeable and convenient to adopt Islam. Many were naturally curious about an unfamiliar religion and welcomed instruction. For many, Islam's tenets held genuine appeal. The Qur'an portrays commerce and merchants (Muhammad was one, after all) in a favorable light. It spells out suitable practices with respect to contracts, money lending, and other business procedures. In addition, treating visiting Muslims and Islam with respect was good for business. Converting to Islam was even better, as it smoothed relations by binding all parties together with the same concepts of law spelled out in shari'a.

Rulers, too, often found advantage in becoming Muslim and proclaiming themselves sultan or emir. They too, no doubt, embraced Islam out of genuine conviction. But doing so could also improve their political position, providing prestige through connections to distant centers of power and learning. Having literate people around was always helpful to monarchs, so Muslim scholars often found employment at African courts. Islam also suited rulers, as all durable religions do, by offering justification (or spiritual compensation) for hierarchy and inequality. Kings and chiefs needed less raw power or personal charisma if their subjects believed it was normal, natural, and divine will that they should be subjects.

The experiences of East and West Africa illustrate the economic and political factors at work in the spread of Islam. In East Africa, the influence of Islam was already widespread before 1400. After 1500, the Portuguese incursions on the Swahili coast that began with Vasco da Gama inadvertently helped to promote Islam, which provided a rallying point for resistance to Portuguese attacks. By the seventeenth century, growing trade links with Oman tightened Swahili cultural connections to the Arabian

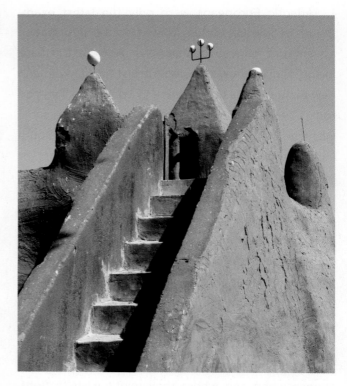

Islam in Africa This eighteenth-century Bambara kingdom mosque in present-day Mali shows how African kingdoms that adopted Islam built mosques reflecting local architectural traditions.

Peninsula. Swahili and Omani forces drove the Portuguese out of East African coastal cities between 1650 and 1730, opening the door to a wave of immigrants from southern Arabia. Omani merchants, generally trading cloth for ivory and slaves, took up residence on the coast, especially its off-shore islands such as Zanzibar. Clerics and holy men, often Sufi mystics, came too. The Omanis gradually extended their operations into the East African interior. Everywhere they went, they interested locals in their religion.

In West Africa, Muslim traders crossing the Sahara had found a welcome reception since at least the eighth century, as we have seen in the history of Ghana and Mali. The Songhai Empire, a successor to Mali that took shape in the 1460s and 1470s, became an active promoter of Islam. Its founder, Sunni Ali, based his new state at Gao and soon conquered the other Niger River trading cities including Timbuktu and Jenne. By most accounts, he practiced multiple religions, was an indifferent Muslim, and clashed with the Islamic scholars of Timbuktu. But under his rule, and especially that of a later king, Askia Muhammad (r. 1493–1528), Songhai used all available means to spread Islam. A firm Muslim, Askia Muhammad supported Islamic scholars, built mosques, and encouraged conversion. He launched wars against infidels wherever they might be found. His success helped to spread Islam widely in the West African Sahel and to revive Timbuktu as a major center of Islamic learning. A Moroccan army, invading across the Sahara, ended the Songhai Empire in 1591, but smaller successor states continued to promote Islam in West Africa.

To the east, in the central Sudan, other, smaller, Muslim states, most notably Bornu in the sixteenth through the eighteenth centuries, promoted Islam much as Songhai had done. South of the Sahel, in West Africa's forest zone, Muslim traders (called Dyula or Juula in West Africa) served as informal ambassadors of Islam. Muslim communities developed along the trade routes. Where trade and states did not figure prominently, Islam had less impact in West Africa before 1800.

Merchants and rulers both, when accepting Islam, did not necessarily renounce their former ways. From their point of view, Islam was one of several spiritual options. Many continued to celebrate feasts; venerate stars, sun, moon, and ancestors; or call upon spirits long familiar to them. Like Sunni Ali, rulers especially might find it politically prudent to become bicultural, both Islamic and non-Islamic, for different audiences and occasions.

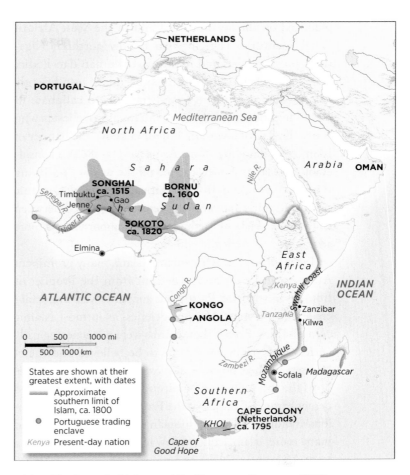

Africa: The Spread of Islam and the European Presence, 1450–1800 Connections between Africa and other parts of the world strengthened in the centuries after 1450. Many Africans along the Swahili Coast and across the Sahel embraced Islam, typically modifying its practices to suit their own traditions. Meanwhile, European mariners, especially Portuguese and Dutch, set up fortified trading posts (and in the Dutch case, an entire colony) in places along coastal Africa.

Wherever Islam spread in Africa, it acquired local characteristics: just as parts of Africa were Islamized, Islam was in those places Africanized. African Muslims built mosques out of mud brick in the western Sahel or of coral on the Swahili coast. Muslim African women rarely dressed as modestly as women did in Islam's heartlands. In what is now northern Nigeria, African Muslims designated some non-Muslim Africans as "people of the book," a category that previously in Islam was used only for Jews, Christians, and Zoroastrians, and in India for Hindus and Buddhists.

Such adjustments to Islam offended purists. Ibn Battuta, the great world traveler, was one of many outsiders irritated by the unorthodox, Africanized versions of Islam practiced on the Swahili coast and in the West African Sahel. Centuries later in what is now northern Nigeria, a poet, scholar, and reformer, Uthuman dan Fodio, launched a rebellion against rulers he judged insufficiently Islamic and went on to found the Sokoto caliphate in 1804. He condemned the local sultans as unbelievers who "raise the flag of a worldly kingdom above the banner of Islam." His daughter, Nana Asma'u (1793–1864), a considerable scholar and poet, carried on the work of purifying the practice of Islam in West Africa, organizing Qur'anic schools for girls and women. Tensions persisted between champions of Islamic orthodoxy and supporters of a more adaptable and Africanized Islam.

In the process of Africanizing Islam, many prominent African Muslims claimed descent from the Prophet or from his inner circle. Prestigious ancestors were important credentials in most African societies, as in most Islamic communities. Even if these claims were not genealogically correct, over time some came to be believed and therefore served their purpose. For example, the ruling house of Mali, the sprawling empire in West Africa, claimed descent from Bilal, one of the Prophet's faithful companions and originally an Ethiopian slave. In these ways and many more, Islam acquired new forms and features drawn from African traditions and practices.

EUROPEAN AND CHRISTIAN INFLUENCES ON COASTAL AFRICA

While Islamic and Arab influence trickled into both East and West Africa, after 1440 Portuguese and then Dutch influence crashed into coastal Africa. In 1462, Portuguese mariners established a fortified post called Elmina on West Africa's coast. Their impact was greater still farther south, in the region of Kongo and Angola, and on the Indian Ocean coasts of Mozambique. Dutch involvement in Africa focused on the area around the Cape of Good Hope.

KONGO AND ANGOLA Just south of the mammoth Congo (or Zaire) River's mouth, Portuguese seagoing expeditions encountered a welcoming king, whom they called the *manicongo*. He ruled over half a million people in a kingdom that had been founded late in the fourteenth century. In the 1490s, Portuguese missionaries convinced a *manicongo* to convert to Catholicism. His son learned to speak, read, and write Portuguese, adopted European dress, and took the name Afonso. The Portuguese helped Afonso to seize the throne in conflicts with his brothers. Subsequently, **King Afonso** (r. 1506–1543) prospered with their continuing help, using Portuguese advisors, military officers, and muskets against neighboring peoples whose weaponry did not include firearms.

Part of the Portuguese interest in Kongo was religious, and in King Afonso they had an eager partner. While Askia Muhammad was using his power in Songhai to spread Islam in West Africa, King Afonso made Catholicism the state religion in Kongo, using it to bolster his legitimacy as ruler. By the 1520s the Pope named King Afonso's son Henrique, who had studied theology in Portugal, bishop of Kongo. Thereafter missionaries from Portugal poured into the kingdom, although most of them quickly died from malaria, yellow fever, or other unfamiliar diseases. Catholicism gradually blended with local traditions and became the dominant religion.

Eventually the kings of Kongo and Portugal fell out, and Portuguese interest in West Central Africa shifted south to Angola. Here too Portugal allied with a local king, called the *ngola*, which became the name for the country. Portuguese helped him in his political struggles and in exchange won the right to preach Catholicism and conduct trade. Soon several local leaders accepted baptism, although they often kept their old ways as well, to the dismay of Catholic missionaries. Rumors of vast silver mines proved unfounded, and efforts to establish Portuguese immigrants as farmers failed miserably, mainly the result of the disease environment.

So in Angola, as in Kongo, the Portuguese turned to the economic activity that yielded the most reliable profit: slaving. They encouraged wars and slave raids among peoples in Kongo and Angola. Local kings (and one

Christianity in West Central Africa A bronze crucifix from sixteenth- or seventeenth-century Kongo demonstrates how Christianity had become an integral part of Kongolese artistic and cultural tradition.

CONSIDERING THE EVIDENCE

The Perils of Trade in Kongo

After Afonso I defeated his half-brother to gain control of Kongo, he emulated the Catholic king of Portugal. Though Kongolese, Afonso appointed officials with Portuguese titles, corresponded with the Pope, and requested priests to conduct Christian Mass with wine and grain imported from Portugal. He also bolstered his prestige by distributing merchandise imported from Portugal that he paid for with ivory, copper, and enslaved men and women who had followed his political rivals. Although Afonso initially benefited from the slave trade, the following letters between him and King João III of Portugal show that he had reservations about the trade. In the end, Afonso agreed with King João III that the slave trade should be continued, but he appointed officials to witness every sale in an effort to ensure that merchants would not capture and sell his own subjects.

Letter of the King of Kongo to [King of Portugal] Dom João III, 1526

[O]ur kingdom is being lost in so many ways...; this is caused by the boldness your... officials give to the... merchants who come to this kingdom to set up shops with merchandise... that we forbid, which they spread... in so great abundance that many vassals that we held in our obedience elevate themselves [i.e., are no longer obedient] by obtaining those things in greater quantities than we possess. With those things we had kept them content, and subjected under our vassalage and jurisdiction, so now there is great damage to the service of God as well as for the security and orderliness of our kingdoms and state.

And we cannot reckon how great this damage is, since these same merchants each day take our native people, sons of the land and sons of our nobles and vassals, and our relatives, because the thieves... steal them with the desire to have the things and merchandise of this kingdom that they covet.... [O]ur lands are entirely depopulated.... [W]e do not need... merchandise, other than wine and bread for the holy sacrament. For this we are asking of Your Highness... not to send either merchants or merchandise, because our will is that in these kingdoms there is no trade in slaves nor outlet for them.

Letter of Dom João III to the King of Kongo, 1529

You say in your letters that you do not want there to be any slave trade in your kingdom because it is depopulating your land.... I am told of the great size of Kongo and how it is so populated that it appears that not a single slave has left it. They also tell me that you send to buy them [slaves] outside [the country] and that you marry them and make them Christian....

If... as you request,... there shall not be any trade in slaves in your kingdom, I will still want to provide wheat and wine for use at Mass, and for this only one caravel [ship] a year will be necessary.... However,... it would be more praiseworthy to draw each year from the Kongo 10,000 slaves and 10,000 *manilhas* [copper bracelets] and as many tusks of ivory.... If you do not want anyone to bring merchandise to Kongo, this would be against the custom of every country.... [A]nd if a *fidalgo* [noble] of yours rebels against you and receives merchandise from Portugal, where will be your power and greatness....

Sources: "Letter of the King of Kongo to [King of Portugal] Dom João III, 6 July 1526," trans. Jared Staller, in *Converging on Cannibals: Terrors of Slaving in Atlantic Africa, 1509–1670* (Athens, OH: 2019); "The Slave Trade Is Good for the Kongo, Extract from a letter of Dom João III to the King of Kongo, 1529," trans. Malyn Newitt, in *The Portuguese in West Africa, 1415–1670* (Cambridge: 2010).

QUESTIONS FOR ANALYSIS

1. How did trade in merchandise, as well as enslaved people, threaten Afonso I's rule?
2. What arguments did the king of Portugal use to convince the king of Kongo to continue trading?
3. Do these letters indicate that these kings dealt with each other as equals?

---

highly successful queen, known as Nzinga or Njinga), seeking Portuguese support and military expertise, eagerly enslaved their enemies. They sold war captives to Afro-Portuguese slave traders, the sons of Portuguese men and African women. As we shall see, Angola became one of the biggest sources of slaves sent to the Americas. Kongo too became a major exporter. By 1660, half the population of Kongo were slaves captured from neighboring peoples.

The Portuguese also brought new strains of smallpox to Kongo and Angola. Sub-Saharan Africans had long experience with the virus, and many peoples regularly used inoculation (the practice of deliberately infecting bodies with weak strains of a pathogen in hopes of triggering immunity without a serious case of disease). But apparently mariners brought a new variety, for major epidemics struck the region in the years 1625–1628 and 1655–1660. Some evidence suggests that tuberculosis and a form of pneumonia also hit Angola in the seventeenth century. For Kongo and Angola, inclusion into the Global web meant new diseases, one additional religion, and much more trade, enslavement, and warfare.

MOZAMBIQUE The Portuguese also took a strong interest in Mozambique. Unlike Angola or Kongo, Mozambique—located in southeastern Africa—had a history of involvement in maritime trade circuits. When da Gama passed by in 1498, its seaborne trade was in the hands of Swahili, Arab, and Indian merchants based at Sofala and Kilwa. Sea power enabled Portuguese merchants to convert Sofala into their own trade enclave, exporting gold and ivory and importing Indian cloth. The Portuguese occasionally sent military missions inland, hoping to seize the goldfields, but these efforts always met with disaster in the form of African armed resistance and deadly disease.

The Portuguese Crown issued land grants to Portuguese settlers who made themselves into local lords and merchants. Their connections to India and Europe—market knowledge and military hardware proved most useful—gave them an edge in dealing with African populations. Unlike Kongo and Angola, Mozambique's commerce consisted mainly of gold and ivory until after 1700, when demand for slaves in the Americas led to a growing slave trade in Mozambique. Meanwhile, Christian conversion made little headway there, and indeed many Portuguese and Afro-Portuguese abandoned Catholicism for either Islam or local African religious culture.

THE CAPE OF GOOD HOPE From the 1620s onward, the Portuguese had a seafaring rival, the Dutch, seeking toeholds in southern Africa. They conquered, and briefly held, some Portuguese coastal outposts in the 1630s and 1640s. But in 1652 the Dutch East India Company—a quasi-governmental trading company known by its Dutch initials as the VOC—founded a base near the southern tip of Africa, at the Cape of Good Hope. It originated as a way station for ships headed from Dutch ports to the East Indies (mainly Java), supplying water, fresh fruit, vegetables, wine, and meat to desperate crews—the death rate on these long voyages ran at 15 to 20 percent. The Cape grew into a full-fledged colony of settlement. Here, unlike

in most of tropical Africa, there was no malaria or yellow fever, and foreigners could flourish. While Portuguese traders and missionaries frequently died soon after arrival in Kongo or Mozambique—mainly from mosquito-borne diseases—Dutch settlers at the Cape survived about as well as their relatives at home.

The Africans who lived at the Cape, hunters and cattle keepers called the **Khoi**, numbered perhaps 50,000 to 100,000 in 1652. At first, the Khoi and the Dutch found they could coexist: the Dutch would buy any extra cattle the Khoi could raise and would pay the Khoi to work on their farms. But soon the Dutch were claiming more land and seeking more labor. The Khoi recognized the threat and attacked the Dutch in 1659 and 1673—unsuccessfully.

The Dutch began to import slaves, mainly from Madagascar, Indonesia, and India in the seventeenth century, and from Mozambique in the eighteenth. This arrangement set the Cape on the path toward a sharply stratified society in which concepts of race mattered fundamentally. By 1700, the colony officially contained some 4,000 people—not including the Khoi, whom officials didn't bother to count. During the next century, population surged because of slave imports, immigration from Europe (often French or German), and social norms of early marriage and big families. With European women scarce, marriage often crossed racial lines, making the Cape not just racially stratified but also racially complex. By the mid-eighteenth century, the whites came to call themselves Afrikaners.

For the Khoi, despite new goods and opportunities, the Dutch colony proved a disaster. They lost control of the best lands to the newcomers. They lost their autonomy if they integrated themselves into Dutch society as laborers. In 1713, a large proportion of them lost their lives in a smallpox epidemic. Within weeks the virus killed a quarter of the Dutch colonists, many of whom had enjoyed rural childhoods without exposure to smallpox and thus remained vulnerable as adults. All the Khoi were equally vulnerable, and as many as 90 percent died in the epidemic of 1713–1714, a mortality rate possible only because of widespread malnutrition. Further epidemics in 1755, 1767, and the 1780s burned through the remaining Khoi population. Little of their way of life survived, and Dutch settlers moved into the interior of South Africa with less resistance than ever before. They also imported more slaves to do the work the Khoi no longer could: as in the Caribbean, the disastrous decline of indigenous population inspired an expanded slave trade. By 1800, the Cape region contained about 20,000 settlers, maybe 25,000 slaves, and very few Khoi. In the taverns of Cape Town, which one VOC official described as the "mother of all scandalous practices," one might hear Malay, Tamil, Arabic, Portuguese, German, Dutch, and a dozen other languages. But one was unlikely to hear Khoi. The Cape settlement was an island of cosmopolitan, globalized society, now thoroughly enmeshed in the Global web.

THE TRANSATLANTIC SLAVE TRADE

The most visible, and for world history the most important, way in which large parts of Africa joined the Global web was through the slave trade. As in most lands, slavery had been a fact of life in Africa long before 1400. In Africa, people became slaves if captured by slave raiders or in war, if they couldn't pay their debts, or if their family or lineage gave them away as compensation for harm done to another family or lineage. In some societies, enslavement was also punishment for certain crimes. Most children of slaves were legally free (a big difference from many other slave systems), but these children could perform useful labor for slave owners, their families, and their communities. Slave owners in Africa preferred women and children for working in the fields, tending animals, making cloth, and doing domestic chores. Above all, they valued young women for reproduction. Only in a few places were male slaves more valued than females, such as the salt mines of the Sahara.

African slave exports to the Mediterranean world, Southwest Asia, and India had a long history. Ancient Egypt had imported African slaves. During the eighth and ninth centuries, many thousands of African slaves had been sold to landowners in Abbasid Iraq. Between 1400 and 1900, perhaps 5 to 6 million Africans were enslaved for sale to these markets.

DIMENSIONS OF THE TRADE The size and significance of African slave exports changed when European mariners connected Africa's coasts to the Americas. Portuguese sailors seized Africans beginning in 1441 and sold some of them on islands such as Madeira—500 miles (800 km) west of Morocco—where sugar plantations were developing. Meanwhile, Moroccan entrepreneurs organized sugar-and-slave plantations supplied with labor by trans-Saharan slave caravans. The success

of sugar plantations worked by enslaved Africans in Morocco and Madeira inspired larger-scale imitation, first on the island of São Tomé off the coast of Kongo.

Then, in 1518, a king of Spain authorized the first direct slave trading voyages from Africa to the Americas. The first recorded voyage arrived in Puerto Rico in 1519, and others to Caribbean islands followed. The population catastrophe in the Caribbean that we saw in the previous chapters was already well under way. The Spanish interest in transatlantic slaving arose from concern that mines and agricultural estates in the Caribbean might languish for lack of labor. In this way, the misfortune of the Americas became the misfortune of Africa.

The first transatlantic slaving voyages to Brazil's sugar plantations began in 1534. Thereafter, the size of the transatlantic trade began to grow rapidly. Before long, the African coast from Senegal to

Abdul Rahaman ibn Sori A prince in what is now Guinea, in West Africa, Abdul Rahaman was captured in a local war in 1788. His captors sold him to British slave traders, who sold him to the owner of a Mississippi plantation, where Rahaman worked for 38 years. He was freed at age 67, through the intervention of a Moroccan Sultan and the U.S. president, on the condition that he return to Africa, which he did shortly before his death.

Slavery and Sugar Enslaved Africans work a sugar mill in the Dutch Caribbean in the seventeenth century. The grinding mill shown was a dangerous machine that could easily injure or kill its operators.

The Middle Passage The conditions aboard slave ships on the Middle Passage are evident in these two illustrations: a diagram prepared by British antislavery activists in 1808, and a watercolor made in 1846 by a British naval officer who assisted in the capture of an illegal slave ship. Both show enslaved men and women packed together in inhumane conditions.

Angola was exporting slaves across the Atlantic, and by the late seventeenth century the coasts of Mozambique and Madagascar were as well.

The **transatlantic slave trade**, the largest forced migration in world history, lasted until about 1860. In all, some 12 to 14 million slaves departed Africa's shores, of whom about 85 to 88 percent—10 to 11 million—survived what is called the **Middle Passage** across the Atlantic. The survival rate improved over the centuries, but the voyage remained hazardous to the end, especially lengthy crossings. The average trip required about two months at sea, after which food and fresh water often ran short. A three- or four-month trip usually killed a large proportion of both slaves and crew. Slaves were kept below decks, usually naked, packed like "books on a shelf" as one observer put it. Men were often kept in chains for most of the voyage, women usually not. Sanitation was negligible. Dysentery was the foremost killer on the Middle Passage, but violence and other diseases took their toll as well.

Slaves attempted uprisings on perhaps as many as one in ten slave ships. Ottobah Cugoano, born in what is now Ghana, survived the Middle Passage in 1770 en route to the Caribbean and remembered a planned uprising: "And when we found ourselves at last taken away, death was more preferable than life, and a plan was concerted amongst us, that we might burn and blow up the ship, and to perish all together in the flames; but we were betrayed by one of our own countrywomen, who slept with some of the head men of the ship, for it was common for the dirty filthy sailors to take the African women and lie upon their bodies; but the men were chained and pent up in holes." Successful uprisings were rare.

Of the 10 to 11 million Africans who survived the Middle Passage, about 44 percent landed in Brazil, another 40 percent in the Caribbean, and 4 percent in what would become the United States. The remainder were scattered among Mexico, Colombia, and other parts of mainland Spanish America. Among slaves sold across the Atlantic, about two-thirds were male and one-third female. Children constituted one-fifth to one-quarter.

The transatlantic traffic peaked in the 1780s at nearly 87,000 slaves per year. It gradually became illegal, outlawed by various countries beginning in 1807, but a secondary peak occurred in the 1820s at 86,000 annually. During the seventeenth century, the transatlantic trade outstripped the size of the combined trans-Saharan, Red Sea, and Indian Ocean slave trades, and cumulatively between 1400 and 1900 was twice as large.

THE SLAVING BUSINESS The transatlantic slave trade was big business. In 1750, about one-third of the British merchant fleet took part, and for Portugal it was even bigger. In West African states such as Oyo or Dahomey, capturing and selling slaves was the main source of mercantile wealth. European slavers, with their newfound global reach, had much to offer African dealers. Cloth from India became the chief West African import, supplemented by iron, copper, guns, tobacco, liquor, and cowrie shells collected in the Indian Ocean. Ottobah Cugoano, enslaved at age 13, recalled that he was sold for "a gun, a piece of cloth, and some lead." A slaver visiting the coast of what is now Nigeria in about 1680 noted that one could buy a male slave for about the same price as 40 baskets of plantains. Cowrie shells came to serve as money in parts of West Africa, and by 1720 about one-third of slaves bought on West Africa's coasts were purchased for cowries. To acquire the cloth and cowries from the Indian Ocean world, European merchants generally sold silver mined in the Americas. Thus the slave trade evolved into a large-scale business linked to trade circuits spanning three oceans and all continents except Australia and Antarctica.

The cloth, cowries, and other items on offer provided reason enough for African rulers and entrepreneurs to capture and enslave as many people as possible. In Africa, as we saw in Chapter 9, ambitious men normally sought prosperity in the form of people—wives, children, servants, slaves—as was typical of places where land was abundant and people scarce. Accumulating large numbers of dependent followers meant status, power, wealth, and security. To achieve such a following, paradoxically, it made sense to sell slaves, especially males. Women and children were usually more useful as slaves within Africa, and less likely to try to escape. If an African entrepreneur could accumulate slaves cheaply through capture or could buy them at a good price and then sell them for guns, iron, cloth, cowries, or horses, then he could use these goods to attract more followers and either purchase or raid more effectively for more slaves. He could reinvest in his business with little risk of diminishing returns because European slavers, and American markets, maintained a voracious demand for ever more slaves. And he could use his growing wealth to support more wives, father more children, and build his retinue and status: in short, he could sell people in order to accumulate more useful people.

African slave traders were overwhelmingly men, but women also took part in the business. European slavers visiting West Africa often formed alliances with local merchant families by "marrying" into them, if only temporarily in most cases. The French called women in these marriages *signares*; the English called them wives of the coast. As European slavers died or moved away, wives of the coast found replacements, new European men, who needed the business connections these women and their families provided. Most wives of the coast were content to remain informal wives or married according to local practices. But some insisted that representatives of a Christian church recognize their marriages.

Two men who knew the slave trade inside out were Little Ephraim Robin John and his nephew Ancona Robin Robin John. They were elite men of the Efik people, living at the mouth of the Cross River (in today's Nigeria). They made a fine living seizing and buying Africans, usually Igbo-speakers, and selling them to English ship captains. They spoke, wrote, and read English, and when dealing with English slavers they dressed as English gentlemen and followed English manners and customs. In 1767, to

ESTIMATED VOLUME OF THE SLAVE TRADES FROM AFRICA, 1400–1900

	1400–1599	1600–1699	1700–1799	1800–1899	TOTAL
TRANS-ATLANTIC	199,000	1,523,000	5,610,000	3,371,000	10,703,000
TRANS-SAHARAN	675,000	450,000	900,000	1,099,000	3,124,000
RED SEA	400,000	200,000	200,000	505,000	1,305,000
INDIAN OCEAN	200,000	100,000	260,000	380,000	940,000
TOTAL	1,474,000	2,273,000	6,970,000	5,355,000	16,072,000

Sources: Nathan Nunn, "The Long-Term Effects of Africa's Slave Trades" (2007), Data Appendix, http://scholar.harvard.edu/files/nunn/files/empirical_slavery_appendix.pdf; and the Slave Trade Database maintained by David Eltis: https://www.slavevoyages.org/voyage/database

Note: The reliability of the transatlantic estimates is much greater than that for the other slave trades. These figures represent disembarkations: those who arrived alive.

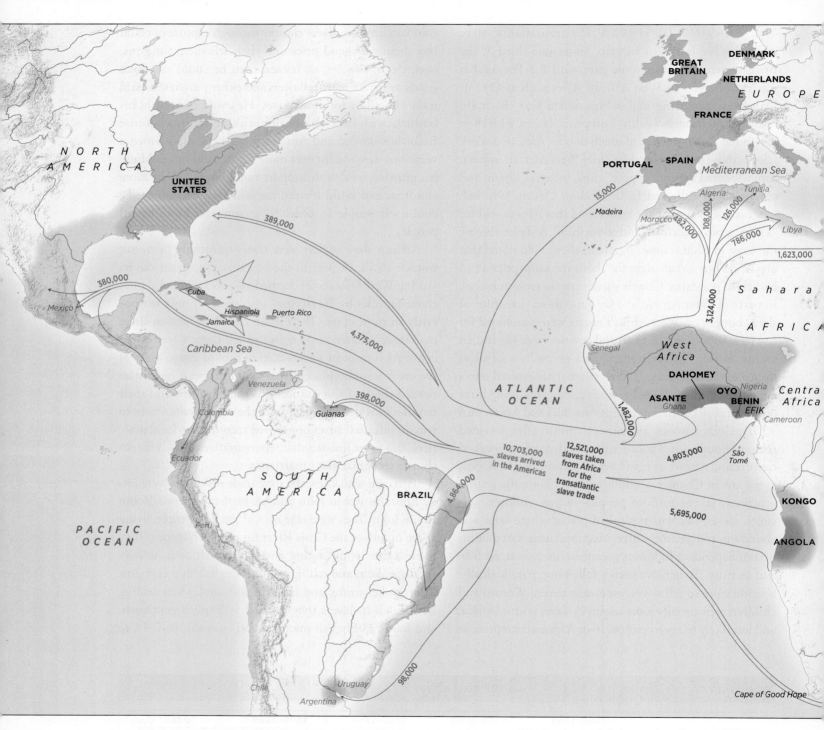

African Slave Trades, 1400–1900 Over these 500 years, roughly 16 million sub-Saharan Africans were enslaved and exported. Brazil, the Caribbean, and Egypt purchased the most Africans. West Central and West Africa supplied the most. The width of the arrows in this map is proportional to the number of people sold on each route.

their horror, an English captain seized them, crossed the Atlantic, and sold them to a French doctor in the Caribbean. They soon escaped, but instead of freedom they found themselves sold again, this time in Virginia. After

further misadventures brought them to England, a judge ruled them free men. They took ship back home to Cross River, where, well acquainted with the horrors of American slavery, they returned to their old business and sold

Slave trade route
1,482,000 Number of slaves shipped from origins in Africa
389,000 Number of slaves arriving at destinations
Area affected by the slave trade (darkness indicates degree of impact)
Sources of slaves
Approximate distribution of slaves
Nation involved in the transatlantic shipping of slaves
Ghana Present-day nation

subject among historians. In the 1780s, at the height of the trade, 87,000 slaves crossed the Atlantic annually—roughly 1/1,000 (or 0.1 percent) of Africa's estimated population of 75 to 125 million. However, for each slave who stepped off a ship in the Americas, two Africans had been enslaved, and one had died en route to the African coast or on the Middle Passage. So on account of the transatlantic slave trade, Africans in the worst years stood a 1/500 chance of being enslaved. On a continental basis, the transatlantic slave trade probably did not have much impact on the size of Africa's population; but at certain times and places, such as Angola between 1750 and 1850, the demographic effects were substantial.

The transatlantic slave trade also spurred the growth of slavery within Africa. During the centuries of the slave trade, far more enslaved Africans lived out their lives within Africa than were transported across the Atlantic. The typical fate of an enslaved African was to be traded (or given to someone) somewhere else within Africa. But the scale of slavery within Africa grew as a result of the export trade, which provided strong incentives for slavers to build their businesses in order to reap economies of scale. The more slaves became available in Africa, the more uses were found for them.

The transatlantic slave trade had other major impacts on Africa. Politically, it encouraged the development of larger and more militaristic states. Stateless societies with weak defenses, such as the Igbo of what is now southeastern Nigeria, suffered as a result. Igbo farmers had to take weapons with them into their fields and lock children in fortified places at night. Predatory states prospered, such as Asante (Ashante) and Dahomey in West Africa, which specialized in seizing people from less militarily adept neighbors. One state that refused to export male slaves, the Kingdom of Benin after 1516, built up a slave army to defend itself.

Signares *Signares* were the African wives of French traders on the West African coast. Many *signares* owned houses and operated businesses in their own right, and they often established independent households when their husbands died or returned to France. This elegant *signare* was painted in the 1840s by Abbé David Boilat of Senegal, who was himself the son of a *signare*.

thousands more Africans into the Atlantic slave trade. There was no surer way to sustain elite status on the West African coast than to deal in slaves.

CONSEQUENCES IN AFRICA The impact of the slave trade on the population of Africa is a controversial

Economically, the slave trade encouraged predatory people—African warlord-entrepreneurs who invested in guns, horses, and violence. This diverted effort and investment from other endeavors that might have proven more socially useful than slaving. It also promoted commercialization, adding traffic to long-distance trade routes. As we have seen, the slave trade also affected African agriculture, making both maize and manioc more appealing crops.

Culturally, the slave trade hastened the spread of Islam in Africa. By law, Muslims may not enslave fellow Muslims, so in those areas where slave raiders were mainly Muslims, such as the western and central Sahel, people fearing enslavement had strong incentives to become Muslim themselves. Socially, the slave trade was divisive. Some people became extremely rich and powerful by conducting it; ordinary people who didn't became more fearful and mistrustful. To this day in many parts of Africa, people remember whose ancestors were slave traders and whose were slaves.

The effects of the slave trade were geographically uneven, as the map on pages 496–97 shows. Peoples within reach of armed horsemen, as in the Sahelian regions, were at great risk. The region most affected was Atlantic Africa, from Angola to Senegal—and within that, Angola itself and West Africa from what is now Ghana across to Cameroon. People living deep in central African rain forests remained almost fully out of reach.

The growth in maritime trade and the spread of Islam helped tighten Africa's connections to the Global web after 1450. Both developments brought some regions that had formerly been remarkably isolated, such as the zone around the Cape of Good Hope, into sustained contact with the wider world. The new maritime links undercut the Sahelian empires that had for centuries enjoyed a stranglehold on the trans-Saharan gold, salt, horse, and slave trades. After Songhai's demise at the end of the sixteenth century, no great Sahelian empire arose again. Instead, many smaller kingdoms emerged, competing for influence, subjects, and control over trade.

For Atlantic Africa, the slave trade stood at the center of tightening webs of interaction. Together with the importance of American food crops explained in Chapter 16, the slave trade's impacts make it sensible to think of pre-Columbian and post-Columbian periods in African history (which Africanists do not typically do) as well as in the history of the Americas (as is commonly done).

THE AMERICAS JOIN THE GLOBAL WEB

Millions of African slaves experienced the brutal rigors of the Middle Passage because in the wake of Columbus the newly transformed economies of the Americas needed labor. The European discovery of sea routes, and the subsequent surge in globalization, disrupted the Americas much more than Africa. The first stage, following upon Columbus's voyages, involved wave after wave of lethal epidemics in tandem with military conquests led by small bands of Spaniards, Portuguese, French, Dutch, and British.

DISEASE AND DEPOPULATION: REGIONAL VARIATIONS

As we saw in Chapter 16, the crowd diseases brought to the Americas by European mariners proved extremely lethal to native populations, who had no prior exposure for protection. Here we will take a closer look at the post-Columbian catastrophe, considering some of the regional variations in the Americas and the role of factors outside of biology.

THE CARIBBEAN The severity of the calamity varied considerably across the Americas. People in the warm coastlands of the Caribbean had the worst of it. The more densely populated islands, such as Hispaniola, where pathogens could most easily find new bodies to infect, suffered losses of more than 99 percent within three generations. Before Columbus arrived in 1492, the **Taíno** (as the Amerindians of this part of the Caribbean are called) on Hispaniola numbered several hundred thousand, perhaps a million or more. By 1514, an attempt to count them recorded only 26,000. By 1550, when malaria inadvertently brought from Africa had joined the crowd diseases, perhaps 5,000 Taíno remained.

Spanish violence and enslavement of the Taíno added to the deadly effect of unfamiliar diseases. Some Spaniards would stop at nothing in their efforts to find gold or seize farmland. Others, meanwhile, tried to convert Taíno to Christianity, which caused divisions within Taíno communities. Their social structures fell apart. Death of spouses, separations, and demoralization led birth rates to plummet. Young Taíno women became wives or concubines of Spaniards. The net effect of the Spanish efforts to make money on Hispaniola and save Taíno souls was to compound the disease disaster and hasten the demographic decline. On Hispaniola and several other islands, Taíno society, language, culture, and identity virtually disappeared—much as would happen later to the Tasmanians with whom this chapter began.

Immigrants from Europe and slaves from Africa came to dominate Hispaniola demographically, and its culture—religion, language, food, dress—evolved, like so many others, as a blended, or creole, culture. Pottery shows how rapid this process was on Hispaniola: in 1515, most pots bore the marks of Taíno potters. By 1530, none did, and the island's pottery was made by Africans. The demographic story on other big Caribbean islands such as Cuba, Jamaica, and Puerto Rico was broadly similar.

MESOAMERICA AND THE ANDES The major centers of Amerindian population—Mesoamerica and the Andes—suffered smaller losses in proportional terms than the Caribbean, but in absolute terms they lost more population than anywhere else in the Americas. Repeated battering from epidemics and disruption of family routines, village life, and the political order cost each region roughly 70 to 90 percent of its population. In Mesoamerica, where perhaps 15 to 20 million people lived in 1492, the disaster began in 1519 when a Spanish adventurer, Hernán Cortés, and a band of a few hundred Spaniards rallied some of the subject peoples of the Aztec Empire in an assault on Tenochtitlán. A raging smallpox epidemic scythed down millions of Amerindians but left Spaniards—normally survivors of childhood bouts with the virus—unscathed. Epidemics recurred time and again, birth rates fell, and by 1620 Mesoamerica held fewer than a million people.

In the Andes, waves of epidemics began in 1524, preceding the arrival of Spaniards. A civil war over succession to the throne divided the Inka Empire when in 1532 a distant kinsman of Cortés named Francisco Pizarro led a band of 168 men into the Andes. The combined effect of epidemic and civil war enabled Pizarro to engineer a coup d'état, overthrowing the Inka Empire. For a hundred years after Pizarro, native population continued to plummet, from perhaps 12 to 15 million in 1532 to under 1 million by 1630.

The demographic disaster in the Americas was least severe in those regions where people were few and

Cortés and the Aztecs A pictographic Aztec chronicle recorded the events of the conquest of Tenochtitlán. In the illustration, Cortés—shown on horseback carrying a large cross—and his troops arrive in the Aztec capital and slaughter the local inhabitants.

pathogens could not easily find new bodies to infect. The Arctic is one such example, where the toll of disease was smaller (closer to 50 percent) and came later, in the eighteenth and nineteenth centuries. The Mapuche of southern Chile, whose armies kept Spanish conquistadores at bay, as they had done with the Inka before, also seemed to have survived better than most.

ECOLOGICAL, SOCIAL, AND ECONOMIC FACTORS The demographic catastrophe varied in its intensity from place to place partly for ecological reasons. Malaria, a warm-weather disease carried by mosquitos and introduced from Africa, became entrenched in some parts of the Americas but not others. Higher elevations and higher latitudes, which are colder than lower ones, hosted fewer mosquitos and less malaria.

The variability of the population catastrophe also had to do with social factors. In some cases, the ravages of introduced diseases began before European conquerors or settlers turned up, as in the Andes. In New England, in the years 1616–1619, epidemics took a terrible toll before the first English settlement at Plymouth Rock (1620). More often, however, social chaos created by European settlement compounded the effects of epidemics, as in Hispaniola during the early sixteenth century.

Warfare, loss of lands, and enslavement magnified the population losses. Wars of conquest, as in Mexico and Peru, were widespread. Although small in scale, these wars often involved Amerindians on both sides. In addition, Amerindian peoples when hit by epidemics often sought to recover their losses by seizing people, normally women and children, from their neighbors. The Iroquois, for example, who began to suffer heavily from epidemics in 1645, launched attacks on the Huron starting in 1648 partly to replenish their own numbers.

Almost everywhere in the Americas, sooner or later, Amerindians lost their best farmland to encroaching Europeans. That created additional problems of food supply and brought the demoralization that people typically experience when forced from their homes. Hunger and demoralization both can weaken disease resistance.

In many parts of the Americas, forced labor and enslavement added to the toll. Recent estimates suggest that between 1500 and 1800, some 2 to 4 million Amerindians were enslaved. Although slavery had existed in the Americas for millennia, its scale increased just when the population of the Americas was collapsing. This was no accident: population collapse created intense demand for labor, filled by both the transatlantic slave trade from Africa and the enslavement of Amerindians.

In particular, the newly developing mining and plantation economies (of which more below) relied on forced labor, both African and Amerindian. Spanish rule in South America continued the Inka practice of the *mita*, the forced labor draft imposed on Andean peoples, using it to provide workers for silver mines—where high mortality prevailed. Silver mines in Mexico, pearl fisheries off the coast of Venezuela, and early plantations in what would become the southeast of the United States also drew upon enslaved Amerindians. Charleston, South Carolina, in the seventeenth century even exported Amerindian slaves to plantations on the Caribbean island of Barbados.

Enslavement of Amerindians was repeatedly prohibited by European authorities. The Spanish did so throughout their empire early in the sixteenth century, but with important exceptions—for peoples judged cannibals, such as the Caribs (of the eastern Caribbean), or for those like the Mapuche of Chile, whose resistance to Spanish rule was especially fierce. Spanish law also permitted slavery for everyone already enslaved. This created incentives for Amerindians to capture their neighbors and sell them to Spanish mining or plantation enterprises.

Forced Labor in the Americas Across the Americas, European settlers enslaved indigenous people as well as importing enslaved people from Africa. In this 1522 Spanish illustration, enslaved indigenous people are being forced to lay the foundations for the Spanish capital of Mexico City.

Where Spanish authorities tried hardest to save Amerindians' souls, death rates were especially high. Catholic missions throughout Spanish America clustered Amerindians together in agricultural villages to hasten their conversion to Christianity. Clustering, however, sped the transmission of most infectious diseases. The California missions begun in 1769, for example, suffered population losses that exceeded 90 percent over 50 years. Here too, few babies were born to take the place of the dead and dying.

EFFECT ON CLIMATE All in all, the fate of Amerindians after 1492 was among the most dismal chapters in world history. The experience of depopulation and displacement was shared with Tasmanians, the Khoi of southern Africa, and several other peoples around the world. But the scale of the population disaster was larger in the Americas than anywhere else—large enough, perhaps, to affect the Earth's climate.

The loss of population in the Americas from 1492 to 1700 may have deepened the chill of the Little Ice Age. Where some 40 to 70 million people had once lived, in

1700 fewer than 5 million remained. Former farmland became forest over broad patches of the Americas. As the forests grew, they absorbed carbon dioxide from the atmosphere, lowering its concentration and weakening (ever so slightly) the greenhouse effect. This (along with big volcanic eruptions and reduced energy output from the sun) probably helps to explain why the coldest spells in the Little Ice Age occurred between 1590 and 1710.

NEW EMPIRES

The arrival of Europeans and the disastrous depopulation in the Americas had political consequences that varied from place to place. Where large empires had existed, as in the Andes and Mesoamerica, new, Spanish-led ones instantly replaced them. Where smaller-scale political structures had existed, as in most of the Americas, guerilla resistance was more common and European control took far longer to establish.

The largest-scale conquests took place in Mexico and Peru. In both cases, small bands of conquistadores allied with big armies of Amerindians, such as the Tlaxcalans who joined Cortés. Locals often out-numbered Spaniards in the armies of conquest by 100:1. So, in effect, Mesoamaerican conquerors used Cortés and his men to overthrow a hated Aztec Empire. Indeed, Tlaxcalans in the mid-sixteenth century considered that they, not Spaniards, had conquered the Aztecs. Similarly, in Peru, Spanish conquistadores made common cause with dissident subjects of the Inkas. When "Spanish" conquerors later marched into Chile, their armies consisted mainly of former Inka soldiers; and when Spaniards led armies into Guatemala or fought the Chichimecs in northern Mexico, it was mainly Aztecs and Tlaxcalans who followed.

In Mesoamerica, when Cortés and his allies overthrew the Aztec state (1519–1521), he and his followers proclaimed the Viceroyalty of New Spain. Pizarro created a Viceroyalty of Peru. In some ways, these Spanish colonial states were just the latest successors in native imperial traditions that stretched back centuries. The Spanish in Peru, for example, not only continued the Inka forced labor system, but they also maintained the reciprocal exchange networks among lineages that had underpinned Andean society under the Inkas, and before them the Moche. They fought on the same frontiers that the Inkas had a century before, using mainly Inka soldiers.

In Mexico, the Spanish re-built an empire on the foundations they seized from the Aztecs. Tribute payments from surrounding districts, formerly sent to Aztec Tenochtitlán, now went to Spanish Mexico City. The Spanish governed together with indigenous elites, splitting the resulting revenues and other perks of power. They did not exact tribute from the Tlaxcalans, their co-conquerors. In Mexico, as in Peru, the Spanish were too few to conquer and govern alone. Spaniards supplied superior armament and global knowledge; indigenous elites supplied local knowledge and manpower. Together, Spanish and local elites could rule the rapidly declining mass of the population.

Where Amerindian polities were small or absent, Europeans encountered more enduring resistance to their rule. The Mapuche of southern Chile and the Maya of Mexico's Yucatán Peninsula, for example, who did not have much in the way of states, fought long and hard against Spanish control. Unlike the populations of Peru and central Mexico, they had no tradition of deference to any imperial authority. For centuries they succeeded in keeping themselves independent in most respects; and when they failed they often mounted rebellions, especially the Mapuche. In general, Amerindian revolts happened more often in northern New Spain and in the southern Andes. In what is now New Mexico in 1680, the Pueblo, an Amerindian people, rose up against Spanish authority and either killed or expelled all Spaniards from their area for the next 12 years. The biggest Amerindian uprising, however, took place in the heart of the Andes, around Cuzco in 1781–1783, led by a descendant of the Inka royal family, Túpac Amaru II. It failed, at a cost of more than 100,000 lives. Nonetheless, the Spanish Empire in America was a patchy one with firm control only in a few centers.

The other European empires in the Americas were smaller than the Spanish. Portugal claimed Brazil but controlled only stretches of coastline and their hinterlands as late as 1600. When the Dutch decided to take a bit of Brazil for themselves in 1618, Portugal could not prevent it. Almost all of Brazil remained Amerindian country into the eighteenth century, when gold and diamond strikes brought a wave of European immigrants. The Dutch Empire was smaller still, confined to a few small Caribbean islands, a tiny settlement of New Netherlands (now New York), and for 30 years a corner of Brazil. And the Dutch surrendered New Netherlands to English rule in 1667.

Like the Spanish and Dutch, both the French and

European Presence in the Americas, ca. 1750 By 1750, most of the land in the Americas was claimed by one or another European state. However, the degree to which they actually controlled American territory varied greatly. Where Amerindians remained numerically dominant, as in the heart of North America, they often exercised economic and territorial power and European claims carried little weight. The new export economy of furs had a longer reach and was a collaboration of Amerindians and Europeans.

British claimed some Caribbean territories. They founded colonies on several small islands and some of the big ones, such as Jamaica, that Spain could not hold. In North America, they took gradual control of the eastern seaboard from the dwindling Amerindian populations. The French settled at Quebec after 1608 but struggled to populate their colony, called New France, with farmers. By 1750, New France had about 50,000 people. British settlement began in 1607 in Virginia and 1620 in Massachusetts, and soon spread everywhere from Georgia to Nova Scotia. These colonies grew quickly, expanding to the Appalachian Mountains by 1750, at which time they held a population of perhaps 2 million. In economic and strategic terms, Caribbean islands such as Jamaica and even tiny Martinique were worth a lot more than the North American colonies—because of the money made selling sugar from slave plantations.

SETTLEMENT AND TRANSOCEANIC ECONOMIES

The sudden loss of native population in the Americas played havoc with economic life and increased the scale of slavery. Labor grew ever scarcer, and ambitious businessmen despaired over how to mine ores or raise crops without sufficient labor. The main motive behind both the African and Amerindian slave trades was to provide cheap labor for the economies of the Americas. European laborers crossed the Atlantic too, a few as slaves, many as indentured servants—meaning they had to work for no wages for a set period, often seven years. But up to 1820, roughly four enslaved Africans had come to the Americas for each European migrant whether indentured or free. It wouldn't be until 1880 that the cumulative number of European arrivals in the Americas equaled the number of enslaved Africans who survived the Middle Passage.

With African and European migrants joining the Amerindian populations, building a new economy in the Americas became possible. The new connections to transatlantic markets, and in some cases new crops or technologies, presented novel opportunities. All the European powers hoped to find precious metals, as the Spanish did in great quantities. Where that failed, the new empires sought other ways to realize the economic potential of the Americas.

FISHERIES AND FURS One opportunity lay in the world's richest cod fisheries, from Cape Cod to Newfoundland. From the 1520s onward, British, French, and Basque (and eventually American and Canadian) fishermen, free men working for wages, caught thousands of tons of cod annually. Most of it was salted or dried and shipped to Europe for sale. On the mainland of North America, at least its northern half, beaver fur offered another way to make money. Amerindians had long hunted and trapped fur-bearing animals. An export trade began around 1630, funneled through Montreal and New Amsterdam (New York after 1667) to Europe. Amerindians still did most of the trapping, but they now sold most of their fur harvest to French, Dutch, or British merchants. Agents for European fur merchants eventually ranged far into the interior of North America—especially those based in New France, often marrying into Amerindian communities in arrangements broadly parallel to those with wives of the coast in the African slave trade. By 1800, the North American fur trade extended as far west as the Rocky Mountains.

THE PLANTATION ZONE Another transatlantic economy, even more lucrative than the fishery or fur trade, took root in the warmer regions from the Chesapeake south to Brazil. This became the **plantation zone** of the Americas, the destination of the great majority of enslaved Africans shipped across the Atlantic. In the Chesapeake, where

Cod Fisheries Fishermen process cod on Newfoundland in this eighteenth-century illustration. After bringing the fish ashore, they gut and dry them, and pack them in salt to preserve them for the journey to other parts of North America and Europe.

English settlement began in 1607, the money-making crop was tobacco. In South Carolina and Georgia, a rice plantation economy flourished after 1690, also based on slave labor and to some extent slave know-how in rice cultivation: some slaves came from rice-growing regions of West Africa and brought their techniques of irrigation and planting with them.

The heart of the plantation zone lay in the Caribbean and northeastern Brazil. Sugar became the most rewarding plantation crop. Unlike fishing, fur trapping, or even tobacco farming, sugar cultivation only made sense on a large scale. Sugarcane juice has to be crystallized within days after the cane is cut, which required elaborate machinery to press juice out of the cane and boiling houses to convert the cane juice to sugar crystals. Because it called for hefty capital investment, sugar production became a business dominated by big planters with connections to European merchant houses. Dozens of Caribbean islands, including British Barbados and Jamaica, Spanish Cuba, and French Saint-Domingue (part of Hispaniola), produced sugar, as did Portuguese Brazil. From 1650 to 1800, sugar islands were the second-most valuable possessions in the Americas. Sugar plantation workers suffered the highest mortality rates of slaves anywhere in the plantation zone. Millions of Africans died on these plantations. Planters bought millions more to take their places.

SILVER Precious metals formed the most valuable transatlantic economy. Cortés and Pizarro sought gold and silver, and found both in envy-provoking quantities. They and their successors used all the tools they had—imagination, guile, technology, brutality—to coax more gold and silver out of Mexico and Peru. Spanish authorities organized large-scale silver mining in Zacatecas, Mexico, and at **Potosí** in the Andes. Potosí alone yielded 40,000 tons of silver between the 1540s and 1780s. Potosí temporarily became one of the world's largest cities, despite an elevation of more than 13,000 feet (4,000 meters).

By 1600, some 20,000 Amerindians—both wage workers and mita forced laborers—mined, processed, and minted silver into coins. Wage workers were well paid by local standards but their lives were brutal and short on account of harsh conditions, frequent accidents, and poisoning from mercury used in the refining process. Laborers in the Potosí mines performed heavy work in darkness relieved only by candlelight. They breathed air laced with dust that over time brought on silicosis and other lung

Silver Mines The Flemish engraver Theodor de Bry had never been to the Americas, but his depiction of silver mining at Potosí indicates the difficult physical conditions that Amerindian forced laborers endured there.

diseases. Many of them spent their shifts carrying 55lb (25-kilo) sacks of ore up rickety ladders, climbing more than 650 feet (200 meters)—no wonder they wouldn't work without a wad of coca leaves in their cheek to dull their pain, hunger, thirst, and minds.

Additional unfree Amerindian workers were dragooned from as much as 350 miles (600 kilometers) away to replace the sick, maimed, and killed. Andean peasant communities held the equivalent of funerals for men drafted for the mita, knowing what lay ahead.

By 1608 the mita could no longer deliver enough workers, and mine-owners bought African slaves for work at Potosí. They generally toiled above ground in transport or refining. Life expectancies were so short for miners, and slaves so expensive, that employers preferred to see mita recruits do the lethal work below ground. One Spanish friar wrote in 1628, "Every peso coin minted in Potosí has cost the lives of ten Indians who died in the depths of the mines." This exaggerated the toll but underlines the human cost of the silver business.

Mule caravans and coastal shipping carried most Mexican and Andean silver to port cities for transport through the Caribbean to Spain. Some went directly from Mexico to Manila in the Philippines. Much of the silver that Spain extracted from the Americas eventually found its way to China or India, as we shall see in a later chapter.

AGRICULTURE But people couldn't eat furs or silver: agriculture fed almost everyone from French Quebec to

Spanish Chile. Amerindian peoples everywhere grew their own food when they could avoid being dragged off to plantations, mines, or missions. They took up the raising of livestock with newly introduced species such as sheep, goats, and cattle. In seventeenth-century New Mexico, for example, the Navajo economy combined sheep herding with farming and raiding. Amerindians sometimes added Old World crops to their gardens too. Settlers from Pennsylvania to New England to Quebec also raised their own food, often planting American maize alongside European varieties of wheat. Farther south, in the plantation zone, the richer European settlers obliged slaves to do all farm work. Poor families in the plantation zone, whatever their racial identity, worked the land themselves. In Spanish America, settlers created big agricultural estates (*haciendas*), and the Crown granted them the right (an ***encomienda***) to conscript Amerindians as unpaid laborers.

By and large, everyone ate local food. But by 1750, locally raised food might well consist of crops and animals that had been introduced from other continents in the Columbian Exchange and integrated into the farms and fields of the Americas.

HYBRID SOCIETIES

With lucrative transatlantic (and in cases transpacific) export economies linking the Americas to Africa, Asia, and Europe, the Americas developed creole societies and cultures that blended elements from these distant places. The changing languages of the Americas were a good measure of broader social and cultural change.

CREOLE LANGUAGES AND CULTURES Many Amerindian tongues spoken in 1492 gradually died out as the number of speakers dwindled. By 1800, perhaps one-third of the roughly 25 million people living in the Americas spoke an Amerindian language. Maybe one-tenth—generally, people born in Africa—spoke an African language. The great majority spoke a European language, although sometimes not as a native tongue. In the plantation zone especially, new, creole languages developed that typically combined features from European and African tongues. (Most people in the Caribbean today speak one or more creole languages.) Haitian Creole combined mainly French vocabulary with grammar based on West African languages such as Fon. Papiamento, spoken

in Aruba, Bonaire, and Curaçao, is a blend of Portuguese, Spanish, Dutch, and indigenous Amerindian languages.

Similar blending took place in religious beliefs and practices. Most people in the Americas practiced one or another form of Christianity, but in ways that might have raised eyebrows in Christianity's homelands. European colonization in the Americas included substantial efforts at conversion and religious education, especially in lands controlled by Catholic kingdoms such as Portugal, Spain, or France. They tended to entrust religion to one or several orders of the Catholic Church, such as the Jesuits, Franciscans, or Dominicans. Missionaries of these orders often accepted great hardship and suffered high on-the-job mortality rates: in New Mexico over the course of the seventeenth century, about 40 percent of Franciscans were killed by the people they were trying to convert, the Pueblo. Members of these orders built missions in French Canada, Portuguese Brazil, and throughout Spanish America, especially in frontier regions: Texas had 30 missions and California 21. Priests and friars, more than officials of the state, brokered the relations between Amerindian and European societies in the Catholic domains. In lands controlled by the mainly Protestant British and Dutch, Christianization of the indigenous population carried a far lower priority.

Missionaries This eighteenth-century manuscript illustration celebrates Spanish Dominican friars for their missionary efforts among Amerindian people. At top a friar gathers his congregants in a church away from attacking demons.

Amerindians who were attracted to Christianity generally preferred to meld the old with the new, to adopt Christian forms and belief selectively and mix them with their own practices—as Africans did with Islam or Chinese with Buddhism.

In the plantation zone, African religions entered the mix and often dominated it. Vodun, a polytheistic religion with a prominent role for female deities, was imported by enslaved Fon- and Ewe-speakers from West Africa. It took root in the Caribbean, Brazil, and Louisiana, acquiring new features, often from Catholicism, in each locale. Slaves (and former slaves) created new religions, such as Santería in the Spanish Caribbean or Candomblé in Brazil, based on West African spiritual practices but with components adapted from Christianity or Amerindian traditions. Yoruba religion played an especially large role in shaping religious practice in the plantation zone. Its tradition of orishas—spirits that guide people to live properly and help win favor from Olorun, the Yoruba creator god—blended fluidly with Catholicism's emphasis on saints. Slaves and former slaves adjusted their spiritual lives to fit the challenges of plantation society.

SHIFTING SOCIAL HIERARCHIES The social structures of colonial societies in the Americas were complex and shifting hierarchies. Status depended on a long roster

New Social Hierarchies Another eighteenth-century portrait by Brunias, *Free Women of Color with their Children and Servants in a Landscape* (ca. 1764–1796), depicts a group of wealthy mixed-race women—*gens de couleur libre*—surrounded by their children and a large retinue of enslaved people of African descent. Both the enslaved people's unfree status and their darker skin color marked them as being of lower status in the complex social hierarchy of the Caribbean.

of variables. Gender and age mattered here much as everywhere else. Legal status (i.e., slave or free) and wealth mattered a lot in the Americas, as almost everywhere else. Skin color and presumed ancestry mattered more here than almost anywhere else because the Americas was one of the few places (the Dutch settlement at the Cape of Good Hope was another) where people from multiple continents and with notably different superficial characteristics (e.g., skin color) coexisted.

But every place calculated social status differently because so many variables were involved. For example, in the eighteenth century in the French plantation colony of Saint-Domingue (Haiti today), the social pyramid featured slaves—roughly 90 percent of the population—at the bottom. Above them stood free blacks of African birth; free blacks of Caribbean birth; *gens de couleur libre,* or free people of mixed African and European ancestry; poor whites; and at the top, prosperous whites. However, in some contexts wealthy *gens de couleur libre* might outrank poor whites. A lengthy vocabulary existed to distinguish among people depending on ancestry.

In Brazil, Mexico, or Peru, even more complex hierarchies existed, because—unlike in Saint-Domingue—Amerindians survived in large numbers. Many people had African, Amerindian, and European ancestors in every imaginable proportion, all captured in a correspondingly detailed vocabulary. In all three of these societies, slaves were on the bottom and wealthy Europeans on top of the social pyramid, but what lay in between was more complicated, and more fluid, than in Saint-Domingue.

New France and New England had different social hierarchies from the rest of the Americas. In 1750, New England had about 350,000 people, of whom roughly 330,000 were free, Christian, and of European descent. About 13,000 were of African descent, slave or free, and fewer were Amerindian. Social distinctions beyond those of age and gender rested mainly on wealth, the prestige of one's ancestry, and one's religious sect. But in New France and farther west, around the Great Lakes, there were only 70,000 French people in 1750 and about 1,200 of African descent. Amerindians outnumbered everyone else until about 1830. Many Amerindian groups retained their old social structures with hierarchies based on age, gender, and achievement. But increasingly they took part in market transactions with frontier settlers—providing furs and hides, for example—and as a result became part of larger societies in which they occupied subordinate roles.

INDEPENDENT GROUPS Some peoples in the Americas managed to keep their distance from the new European empires. The Mapuche and Maya, and the so-called Plains Indians of North America, successfully resisted encroaching empires until the nineteenth century, as did the peoples of the Northwest coast. But even these groups experienced some rearrangements of their social hierarchies. With war and trade more common, specialists in these pursuits could more easily gain status. Many Amerindian tribes in Amazonia evaded contact with outsiders altogether for centuries (some of them even until this day) and probably underwent no sharp changes in their social structures.

Communities of runaway slaves, called maroons in the English-speaking colonies, secured their freedom for decades, often in mountains or jungles. Brazil had many such communities, usually short-lived. The largest, Palmares, was home to 30,000 former slaves and lasted from about 1600 until 1694, when Portuguese forces overwhelmed it in an artillery assault. Other such communities were much smaller, mostly composed of young men eking out a living hunting, fishing, and sometimes raiding plantations from which they had escaped.

Maroons were not the only ones who temporarily escaped the reach of the new empires. Until about 1730, many coastlands of the Americas hosted pirates who operated on the margins of the new empires, preying on merchant ships and occasionally on settlements. Most were Europeans themselves, usually runaway sailors fleeing the harsh discipline of naval or merchant vessels, but perhaps one in three were African or of partly African descent. In general, piracy flourishes when a lucrative maritime trade springs up without powerful naval states nearby. The spurt of seaborne trade in the wake of Columbus and da Gama provided such an opportunity, and pirates multiplied in the Caribbean, the Mediterranean, the Indian Ocean, and in East Asian waters. Pirates in the Caribbean enjoyed considerable success from the 1570s until the 1720s, by which time European navies became too large and efficient for piracy to flourish.

The entanglement of the Americas in the growing Global web was an extremely disruptive process. It entailed the dismantling of the pre-Columbian American webs of interaction—mainly through the massive loss of native populations, but also through compulsory labor, forced migration, and other hardships visited upon Amerindians. Meanwhile, merchants, migrants, missionaries, and others forged new linkages both within the Americas and between the Americas and the wider world of Atlantic Europe, Atlantic Africa, and East Asia. A true global web was spun in the centuries after Columbus, for the first time in the history of the world. The newly refashioned Americas provided much of the thread in the form of silver, sugar, furs, fish, and other commodities traded far and wide.

SIBERIA ABSORBED

Expansion of the Old World web proceeded by land as well as sea. One of the largest territorial expansions took place in Siberia. Nearly the size of South America, Siberia (now Russian territory) lies between the Arctic Ocean to the north and the steppe of Central Asia and Mongolia to the south. It is stunningly cold during its long winter. In 1500, most of it was tall forest or shrubby, coniferous, and often swampy forest called taiga. Getting around within Siberia was a challenge, and getting anything useful out of it was no easier. A strong motive would be required to tempt outsiders to tackle Siberia.

The people of Siberia, some of whose ancestors had been the first migrants to the Americas 15,000 to 20,000 years before, numbered only a few hundred thousand in 1500. They were divided into about a hundred linguistic groups, and most followed a variety of shamanistic religions. Some, in southern Siberia, were Buddhist or at least influenced by Buddhist beliefs acquired from Mongols, whose empire had included parts of southernmost Siberia. Siberians drew their living from the forest: fishing, hunting, trapping, and reindeer herding. In southern Siberia they also raised what crops they could in the brief growing season and traded occasionally with the steppe peoples to their south.

FUR: A LUCRATIVE EXPORT

The main thing outsiders wanted from Siberia was fur. Several million foxes, ermine, squirrels, and sables, all with thick pelts, wandered the woods and swamps. For centuries, a tiny proportion of those pelts were traded to China, the steppe peoples, or the Baltic

Siberian Fur The large fur piece decorating the crown of the tsar Ivan V from the seventeenth century is indicative of the growing status of Siberian fur as a luxury commodity and a symbol of Russian power.

Muscovy, Russia, and Siberia, 1400–1800 The expansion of Muscovy and Russia included the incorporation of Siberia, beginning with the incursions of the Cossacks and Russians led by Yermak starting around 1580. Motivated by a quest for furs, by 1640 Russians had built scattered forts across Siberia to the Pacific shores. By 1730, Russians had crossed the Bering Strait and extended their fur trade to Alaska.

lands and Russia. In the sixteenth century, as more people in those lands became more prosperous, demand for Siberian furs grew. Eventually this demand provoked a growing export trade, providing the motive for outsiders to try to control Siberia.

The outsiders who took this step were Russians and Cossacks. Russians were Slavic-speakers who in 1480 had won independence from the Mongol Golden Horde and formed a state called Muscovy, centered on Moscow. Muscovy grew as Mongol power waned, and its leaders aimed to "gather all the Russias" into a larger empire at the expense of neighbors. The aptly named Ivan the Terrible (r. 1553–1584 as Ivan IV) championed this enterprise, never missing an opportunity to flay or boil an enemy alive. By the late sixteenth century, Muscovy's princes called themselves tsars (derived from the word *Caesar*), or emperors

of Russia, and ruled 8 to 12 million people. Most of those were unfree peasants, called serfs, bound to landed estates and in effect owned by landlords.

Cossacks were mainly serfs (or their descendants) who managed to run away from their owners in what is now Russia and Ukraine. They settled in the river valleys of the steppes north and east of the Black Sea, forming their own self-governing communities beginning in the fifteenth and sixteenth centuries. They were roughly analogous to the escaped former slaves known as maroons in the plantation zone of the Americas. Cossacks lived by farming, raiding, and piracy on rivers and the Black Sea, or by hiring themselves out as mercenaries. In the sixteenth century, Cossacks were often enemies of the Russian state, but sometimes protectors of Russian frontiers against Tatar raiders from the steppe. At all times they were military specialists. Their population was probably no more than 100,000 in 1600.

The spearhead of the process by which Siberia joined the Global web, and the Russian Empire, was a Cossack named **Yermak**. He was successful as a river pirate, but about 1580 he became the equivalent of a conquistador. It was not silver that drew him into Siberia, but fur. An entrepreneurial family with close ties to the tsars, the Stroganovs, hired Yermak to expand their fur trade from Siberia. To do so he had to battle through a Tatar khanate in southwestern Siberia, a legacy of Mongol rule. With a band of about 800—just a few more than the number of Spaniards Cortés led in his assault on Mexico—Yermak defeated the Tatars, thanks to guns and riverboats provided by the Stroganovs. Within a couple of years, Yermak and his roughnecks had reached the Ob River. They sent back enough furs to please the Stroganovs and Tsar Ivan, who—sensing a business opportunity—removed the price he had put on Yermak's head and became his biggest supporter.

Yermak died in 1585 in a scrap with Tatars, but his success inspired a stream of Cossacks and Russians to flow into Siberia. By 1640, they had built wooden forts at key portages and river junctions across Siberia all the way to the Pacific shores. The conquest of Siberia paid handsome rewards for Russia. Soon one-tenth to one-third of the tsar's revenues came from the sale of furs. Yermak became a hero in Russia, memorialized over time with postage stamps and public statues.

Like Spain's conquistadores, Yermak and his successors enjoyed the advantages of living inside the world's biggest web. They had the latest military technologies, thanks to the Stroganovs and the tsars. They knew how to build boats that could operate on Siberia's rivers, and how to put small cannon on their boats. They knew the market price of trade goods—tobacco, alcohol, flour—as well as that of furs. At least some of them could read and write, enabling them to communicate and coordinate the actions of scattered parties over vast distances. And by virtue of childhood exposure, they carried immunities to the standard crowd diseases, which indigenous Siberians generally did not.

THE RUSSIFICATION OF SIBERIA

The Russian conquest carried hard consequences for the native populations of Siberia. In 1600, they numbered over 300,000 people, with 120 languages among them. Like Amerindians, many Siberians died from exposure to unfamiliar diseases. One group, the Yukaghirs in eastern Siberia, lost two-thirds of their population to disease, probably smallpox in the main. By 1700, the Yakut and Tunguz peoples had lost 80 percent of their population of a century before. As in the Americas, brutal treatment compounded the effects of diseases. Cossacks, following Yermak's lead, demanded tribute in the form of furs from all adult males (an arrangement

Yermak Timofeyevich A portrait from the eighteenth century shows Yermak bearing the weapons that helped him to assume control over the fur trade in Siberia.

with no parallel in the North American fur trade). As the Siberian population fell, Cossacks and Russians required more tribute from each man. Many Siberians resisted Cossack and Russian demands, and countless ambushes, skirmishes, and battles resulted. The patriarch of Moscow, the top religious official of the Russian Orthodox Church, complained in 1662 that Russian men were neglecting their Christian duties, mistreating native Siberian women, even buying and selling them. In the end, a few thousand Cossacks and Russians subdued a few hundred thousand Siberians, over 5 million square miles of forest and taiga. Together, they trapped and skinned millions of sables, ermines, and foxes—and helped make the Russian tsars richer and more powerful than ever before.

Over time, Siberia entered the Global web and became increasingly Russian. Military and political control came first. Creole versions of Russian gradually developed and occasionally took the place of indigenous languages. Russian Orthodoxy joined the several forms of shamanism formerly practiced, creating blended religious practices as in the Americas. Siberia in the seventeenth and eighteenth centuries was creating new hybrid cultures, with ever stronger Russian components. By 1795, population surpassed 1 million, mostly Russian in language and culture. Many Siberian women took Russian (or Cossack) husbands, and their children often preferred the identity of their fathers, which conferred more advantages in life. And in later centuries, mainly after 1860, millions of Russians migrated to Siberia, swamping what remained of the indigenous peoples, their languages, and religion, so that Siberian culture became highly Russified.

Russians and Cossacks pushed farther eastward. Clashes with China led to a 1689 treaty that divided vast uncharted Siberian and East Asian spaces between the Russian and Chinese Empires. By 1730, Russians were seeking furs in Alaska. Within decades, they mobilized Alaskan natives—Aleuts, mainly—to hunt fur seals along the Pacific coast from the Aleutian Islands south to San Francisco Bay. These shores of North America, like Siberia, also joined the world's web in part through Russian enterprise.

OCEANIA AND AUSTRALIA ENMESHED

Probably the most isolated peoples in the world in the years between 1500 and 1750 were those living on the continent of Australia and the islands of Remote Oceania. In Australia, as we have seen, people had arrived at least 50,000 years ago and learned to manage a challenging environment. The archeological evidence suggests that by 1750 they numbered 500,000 to 1 million. The islands of Remote Oceania acquired human population as early as 6,000 years ago in some cases and as recently as 750 years ago in others. The most populated archipelagoes, as of 1750, were Hawaii and New Caledonia, each with perhaps 400,000 people, Fiji with 150,000, and Tahiti and New Zealand, each with maybe 100,000. Taken together, the population of Australia plus all the Pacific Islands in 1750 came to less than 4 million people.

ANOTHER DISEASE DISASTER

Except for some island chains of Near Oceania (meaning New Guinea, the Bismarck Archipelago, and the Solomon Islands) where malaria lurked, Pacific islands, like Australia, harbored few infectious diseases. By global standards, people lived unusually healthy lives. That did not mean they lived especially long: droughts, storms, tsunamis, and other natural hazards took a considerable toll. The islanders' minimal experience with infectious disease had long been a blessing, but in the late eighteenth century it became a curse.

In the 1760s, European mariners, especially British and French, began to sail the Pacific more frequently. They increasingly found commodities that, with their knowledge of distant markets, they could sell: sealskins, whale oil, sea cucumber (a delicacy in China), and sandalwood (a luxury in China). Sustained contact between Pacific Island populations and Europeans began between 1767 and 1778 in most cases, and in Australia in 1788.

In every case, the contact brought demographic catastrophe. Unfamiliar diseases had the same effect as in the Americas, Siberia, and among the Khoi of South Africa. The precise scale of these disasters is uncertain, but it appears that the Marquesas Islands were among the hardest hit, losing about 96 percent of their population between roughly 1770 and 1920. Small archipelagoes, where everyone was in regular contact with everyone else, allowed killer diseases to spread quickly. Epidemics hit again and again, sometimes killing a quarter or a third of an island's people each time. As late as 1875, a measles outbreak in Fiji carried off one-third of all remaining Fijians.

Larger archipelagoes, with more dispersed populations, fared somewhat better but still suffered disastrous losses. New Zealand lost about half its Maori population between 1769 and 1870. Australia probably lost more than half of its Aboriginal people between 1788 and 1900. No one had much in the way of useful medicine to combat the epidemics.

Part of the demographic catastrophe, in the Pacific as in the Americas, resulted from falling birth rates. This too had something to do with disease. The arrival of European (and after 1780, American) sailors spurred a sex trade that spread venereal diseases far and wide from Hawaii to New Zealand. These infections made many women infertile. Sometimes women voluntarily took sailors as lovers while a ship anchored offshore, receiving gifts they valued and, as they saw it, enhancing their *mana*, or spiritual prestige, through sex with powerful strangers. Sometimes they did so under duress, compelled by fathers, brothers, or husbands to trade sex for iron nails, liquor, guns, or other items. In New Zealand by the 1820s, Maori clans fought wars to capture and enslave women. Their captors then sold these women's favors to visiting sailors for guns to fight rival clans more effectively.

Just about everywhere in the Pacific, as in Siberia and the Americas, indigenous populations fell for about 150 years after the onset of first contact with the wider world.

Then they stabilized and slowly began to grow. Despite this recovery, in many cases, most notably Australia, New Zealand, and Hawaii, immigrant peoples came to outnumber indigenous populations.

CHRISTIANITY AND TRADE GOODS

Contact with the wider world brought much more than disease and disaster to Oceania and Australia. Christianity was a popular import. Catholic and Protestant missionaries flocked to many Pacific islands, and although easily horrified by local attitudes to clothing (too little) and sex (too much), in time they proved highly successful in making converts. Missionaries had invisible allies in the murderous microbes they and others brought with them: everyone could see that newcomers suffered far less from disease, and many islanders concluded that the Christian God offered better protection than their own deities could. Missionaries had highly visible, if inadvertent, allies in the sailors and whalers who vividly illustrated some of Christianity's seven deadly sins. Within a century of contact, almost all Pacific Islanders and Australian Aborigines had accepted Christianity, although they adapted their new religion to their own traditions and circumstances, as converts normally do.

Trade goods and introduced plants and animals proved as popular as Christianity. European mariners brought such useful novelties as iron fishhooks and farming tools, guns, cattle, horses, goats, and sheep. Pacific peoples traded for these goods and increasingly worked specifically to get them. The new goods increased the economic potential of island (and Australian) landscapes.

AUSTRALIA

In Australia during the eighteenth century, the Aboriginal population of half a million to 1 million divided into roughly 250 groups, each with its own language. According to one of the first foreigners ever to meet them, Captain James Cook in 1770, "They may appear to some to be the most wretched people on earth, but in reality they are far happier than we Europeans. They live in a tranquility which is not disturbed by the inequality in condition: the earth and the sea of their own accord furnish them with all things necessary for life." Cook may have

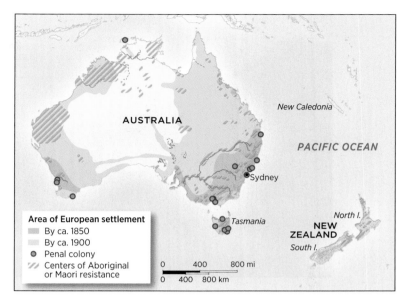

Australia and New Zealand, ca. 1770–1900 Aboriginal Australians had to adjust to British settlement from 1788 onward, as did Maori in New Zealand from about 1800. They often found trade goods attractive, and Christianity too. But like Amerindians, native Siberians, and the Khoi in South Africa, they suffered greatly from imported diseases and attacks by better-armed newcomers. Within a century, both lands were demographically dominated by the newcomers and were securely part of the British Empire.

failed to recognize social inequalities among Aboriginal Australians, which surely existed, even if muted by the standards Cook knew from his native Scotland. Protocols governed inter-group behavior, usually keeping conflict under control.

However, no protocols could protect Aboriginal Australians from what came their way in 1788: a fleet of 11 ships bearing more than 1,000 settlers backed by the British government. Most of the settlers were convicts. Transportation of convicts continued until 1868, totaling 160,000 in all, of whom about 15 percent were women. Once in Australia, a few were freed, and one rose to become a magistrate. Free migrants—mostly English, but one-quarter of them Irish—came in larger numbers by the 1820s, and population spilled out of the original settlements near Sydney onto the tablelands of the interior. Squatters, as Australians who helped themselves to land were called, pushed Aboriginals off the best lands, often violently.

Over the next century, skirmishes and wars between settlers and Aborigines claimed about 27,000 lives, 90

Cook's Voyages This watercolor appeared as an illustration in James Cook's account of his voyages. It shows his ship, the *Endeavour*, anchored on the east coast of Australia on his first voyage in 1770.

percent of them Aboriginal. The Aboriginal Australians fought with spears and shields; the newcomers had muskets and, soon, artillery. Scattered guerilla wars flared up now and again, but the tide flowed in favor of the settlers. As in Siberia, South Africa's Cape, and the Americas, the toll of disease and advantages in military technology made the difference.

By 1850, the rising population of Euro-Australians outnumbered the falling one of Aboriginal Australians among the continent's half million residents. Aborigines increasingly lived in the dryer or more tropical parts of the country that the immigrants did not want. Having lost the best lands, many Aborigines made their peace with the settlers and worked as cooks or stockmen (cowboys) on cattle or sheep stations (ranches). Aboriginal women often married (often informally) immigrant men, especially in the early years of settlement when European women were scarce. Australia now had sprawling wheat fields, millions of sheep and cattle, and a prosperous wool export trade. All this seemed right to most Euro-Australians: as one settler asked in 1845, "which has the better right—the savage, born in a country, which he runs over but can scarcely be said to occupy . . . or the civilized man, who comes to introduce into this . . . unproductive country, the industry which supports life . . . ?" By 1850, the southern continent had undergone a radical transformation, similar in its broad outlines to the fate of the Americas and Siberia, if different in the particulars.

NEW ZEALAND

In New Zealand, the entry into the Global web also came suddenly and wrenchingly. As we've seen, Maori—Polynesians who settled New Zealand about 1250—lived as farmers, fishers, foragers, and hunters, in groups that since 1500 or so had become more competitive and often warlike. They had had no significant interactions with peoples from outside New Zealand and its neighboring small islands for many centuries. In 1642, the Dutch sea captain Abel Tasman sighted New Zealand, stayed for a few hours, and was driven away by Maori. In 1769, two European ships visited. Settlers began to dig in about 1800, at first living among, and more or less as, Maori. But by 1840 organized colonization was under way, and the *pakeha* (as people of European origin are termed in New Zealand) population ballooned to half a million by 1885. Maori population continued to fall due to introduced diseases and violence until about 1890.

As in the Americas, Siberia, and Australia, the local population in New Zealand alternately welcomed and resisted the settler presence. Some Maori went to work on sailing ships to see the wider world. Many more traded eagerly for exotic goods such as iron nails (useful as chisels for the Maori tradition of wood carving), blankets, and guns. Maori also adopted pig raising and potato farming, markedly improving their nutrition by making new animals and plants their own.

Maori Culture A nineteenth-century illustration of a Maori warrior carrying a musket is suggestive of the destructive impact that European firearms had on Maori society.

Maori took up firearms with both enthusiasm and desperation. Martial prowess had long been important to male Maori. Now their internal wars became deadlier. As in Africa during the time of the Atlantic slave trade, it often became necessary to acquire guns to defend oneself against others already equipped with them. In the early nineteenth century, Maori with guns terrorized Maori without guns, until the point came when all surviving Maori peoples had guns. In the process, 20,000 to 40,000 were killed in the so-called Musket Wars (1807–1845), and many thousand women and children captured and enslaved. Women captives, as noted above, could be put to use in the sex trade to acquire more guns. Maori also turned their weapons on visiting whalers and sealers. On one occasion in 1821, they captured six Americans and forced some to eat others (according to Joseph Price of Wilmington, Delaware, who survived this ordeal, his shipmates "tasted very much like roasted pork").

It comes as no surprise that Maori did not often welcome newcomers. For half a century after contact in 1769, Maori exposure to the wider world came mainly via two sorts of men: Australian convicts eager to shed their pasts and gamble on a rough life skinning seals on New Zealand's shores, and sex-starved British, Australian, and American whalers.

But over time, as the newcomers came to include more and more missionaries and even families, Maori found more to welcome. They embraced Christianity with remarkable gusto from the 1830s. Missionaries' Christian messages made sense to many Maori, who witnessed the conspicuous sinfulness of visiting whalers and sealers.

In 1840, in the **Treaty of Waitangi**, most Maori chiefs agreed to put down their weapons and become British subjects in return for guarantees of their land. Large-scale British settlement soon followed; and treaty or no treaty, Maori and *pakeha* engaged in intermittent land wars (1845–1872), which ultimately ended Maori independence and confirmed New Zealand's future as a British settler colony. Epidemics, warfare, and dispossession: the entry of New Zealand into the Global web bore a family resemblance to the experience of Australia, Siberia, and the Americas.

HAWAII

Before contact, Hawaii's roughly 400,000 people lived—mainly on a diet of taro, yams, sweet potatoes, and fish—in a handful of small and competitive kingdoms long isolated from the rest of the world. When Captain Cook and British sailors turned up in 1778, Hawaiian kings sought to exploit the opportunity presented by the strangers' tools and weapons. One king, Kamehameha, scored a brilliant success when he murdered all but one of a ship's crew and invited the sole survivor to instruct his warriors in the arts of using firearms and sailing European vessels. His soldiers learned well, and between the 1780s and 1810 he defeated all his rivals and unified Hawaii as a single monarchy. Unlike the chiefs of New Zealand's rival clans, **King Kamehameha** managed to keep tight control over imported weaponry and thus could vault himself into supreme power over his fellow Hawaiians. He ruled as an autocrat, made a fortune on sandalwood exports, banned human sacrifice, and imposed peace.

Despite the peace, his subjects diminished in number. Whalers, traders, and sailors brought the same infections to Hawaii that ravaged the rest of the Pacific. Venereal disease, previously unknown, spread widely and lowered birth rates. The native Hawaiian population plunged to about 75,000 in 1850 and 40,000 in 1890. As this demographic catastrophe unfolded, many Hawaiians came to wonder whether their old ways were best and whether their familiar gods could still protect them.

After King Kamehameha died in 1819, missionaries arrived in force and met with much success. The most politically ambitious of the deceased king's 22 wives, Ka'ahumanu, adopted a Protestant faith. She served as regent for her son, King Kamehameha II, and did her best to suppress both Hawaiian religion and Catholicism until her death in 1832.

Settlers came late to Hawaii—mainly after 1850—but by 1870 they outnumbered Polynesian (native) Hawaiians.

Hawaiian Monarchy An official portrait recorded Queen Liliʻuoka-lani sitting on her throne in 1892, shortly before Americans deposed her monarchy.

They brought cattle, sugarcane, and a new export economy that bound Hawaii mainly to U.S. markets. Sugarcane in particular required labor, which came in the form of nearly 50,000 Chinese and tens of thousands more Japanese, Koreans, Filipinos, and Portuguese. Hawaii too became a hybrid society and culture. Newspapers in Chinese appeared in 1881. The quintessential Hawaiian musical instrument, the ukulele, was first made about 1880 by Portuguese immigrants. In the 1890s, American businessmen resident in Hawaii deposed the reigning monarch, Queen Liliʻuokalani, and ended the Hawaiian monarchy. The United States annexed the islands in 1898.

Between the 1760s and 1850, the Global web ensnared the Pacific world from Australia to Hawaii. Formerly isolated peoples now found themselves in regular contact with the wider world, thanks to European mariners often seeking goods for Chinese, European, or U.S. markets. The roughly 4 million people affected entered a new epidemiological world full of dangerous new diseases. They entered a new cultural world dominated by European outlooks, languages, and Christianity, to which many Pacific peoples were strongly attracted. They also entered a political realm in which their small numbers, limited state organization, and stone- and wood-based military technologies put them at an acute disadvantage. Even those most determined to fight domination, such as New Zealand's Maori, were vanquished.

CONCLUSION

When people from Eurasia crossed the seas to the Americas, southern Africa, Australia, and Oceania and pierced the forests into the interior of Siberia, they created the first truly global web. In demographic and political terms, this process proved a disaster for indigenous peoples. In cultural terms, it was a disaster for people who preferred the old, familiar ways. Introduced crowd diseases wrought havoc for five or six generations. People lost hope and

initiative. Social networks, institutions, collective memory, and expertise were all eroded or entirely lost. Some peoples—like the Tasmanians with whom this chapter began—were effectively wiped out, and stray survivors attached themselves to new families, tribes, and groups.

In most cases in the Americas and Siberia, the creation of the Global web entailed the destruction of political orders. Empires such as those of the Aztecs and Inkas crumbled. New polities took their place, usually dominated by Europeans, as in the Americas, Siberia, and South Africa's Cape, but sometimes run by opportunistic locals, such as Hawaii's King Kamehameha.

In Africa north of the Cape settlement, the new links to oceanic trade and the Global web had political consequences too, but less radical ones. States rose and fell, and on balance more militaristic states prospered in the new situation, which brought with it the risks and opportunities of the expanded slave trade. But basic political formats held up better than elsewhere. So did population. In most of Africa, as in most of Eurasia, crowd diseases were familiar childhood diseases that rarely caused massive epidemics.

Vast cultural changes resulted from the formation of a globalizing web. These normally led to hybrid, **creole cultures**, with varying mixtures of traditions from Europe and from local populations. In the plantation zone of the Americas, the mix also included a large share of African culture—religion, languages, foodways—carried across the Atlantic by slaves. And in Hawaii it included strong infusions of East Asian cultures, carried across the Pacific mainly by immigrant laborers.

The economies that underpinned all the societies in question also underwent radical restructuring. Oceanic trade reached almost every coast and navigable river, inspiring stepped-up (or altogether new) production or extraction of furs in Siberia and North America, slaves and ivory in Africa, wool in Australia, sealskins in New Zealand, whale oil throughout Polynesian waters, fish from the northwest Atlantic, sugar from the plantation zone of the Americas and Hawaii, and silver from the Andes and Mexico—just to name a few. The growing scale, scope, and pace of commerce created opportunities for survivors, at the same time that unprecedented demographic disasters were unfolding.

Such demographic, political, cultural, and economic tumult around the globe added fuel to the dynamics of change in the heartlands of Eurasia, to which we turn next.

CHAPTER REVIEW

KEY TERMS

disease disasters (p. 486)

King Afonso (p. 490)

Khoi (p. 492)

transatlantic slave trade (p. 494)

Middle Passage (p. 494)

Taíno (p. 498)

mita (p. 500)

plantation zone (p. 503)

Potosí (p. 504)

encomienda (p. 505)

Yermak (p. 509)

Treaty of Waitangi (p. 513)

King Kamehameha (p. 513)

creole cultures (p. 514)

 Go to INQUIZITIVE to see what you've learned—and learn what you've missed—with personalized feedback along the way.

REVIEW QUESTIONS

1. Why were Atlantic Europeans in the best position to take advantage of the opportunities that the globalizing world offered?

2. Identify the three main components of the process of globalization in Africa.

3. What motivated merchants and rulers in East and West Africa to convert to Islam?

4. How did the Portuguese economic and religious presence in Angola and Kongo differ from that in Mozambique?

5. Explain the major political, economic, cultural, and social impacts of the slave trade in Africa.

6. What interrelated factors contributed to demographic catastrophes in the Americas?

7. Compare and contrast the Spanish conquest in the Americas in large empires versus smaller polities.

8. How did silver grease the wheels of global commerce?

9. What happened to the native Siberian population after becoming part of the Russian Empire and the world's largest web, and why?

10. What caused birth rates in the Pacific to plummet following sustained contact with Europeans?

11. How did European military technology affect Maori and Hawaiian society and politics?

12. What were the overarching cultural and economic changes that globalization caused?

FURTHER READING

James BELICH, *Making Peoples* (1996). The first several chapters recount Polynesian and contact-era history of New Zealand with insight, wit, and verve.

J. H. ELLIOTT, *Empires of the Atlantic World* (2006). A work by a master historian on the Spanish and British Empires in the three centuries after Columbus.

David ELTIS and David RICHARDSON (2010). *Atlas of the Transatlantic Slave Trade*. The authoritative source on the size, sources, and destinations of the slave trade. See also the website based on the same research: http://www.slavevoyages.org/

Janet HARTLEY, *Siberia: A History of the People* (2014). A readable overview of that vast land, with good chapters on the Russian absorption of Siberia.

Andrés RESÉNDEZ, *The Other Slavery: The Uncovered Story of Indian Enslavement in America* (2016). The author shines a spotlight on a neglected aspect of the history of the Caribbean, Mexico, and the U.S. Southwest.

John RICHARDS, *The Unending Frontier* (2003). A massive study of environmental change around the period 1450–1800.

Randy SPARKS, *The Two Princes of Calabar* (2004). A true story that explores how the Atlantic slave trade worked in the late eighteenth century.

John K. THORNTON, *A Cultural History of the Atlantic World, 1250–1820* (2012). An excellent transatlantic history, with a broad sense of what counts as "cultural."

CHRONOLOGY

1430–1450
Johannes Gutenberg develops
moveable type and printing press

1517
Martin Luther writes Ninety-Five Theses

1618–1648
Thirty Years War

1542
Re-establishment
of the Inquisition

1608
Invention of
the telescope

1501
Ismail establishes a
Safavid state in Iran

1603
First academy
of science is
founded in
Rome

ca. 1450
Safavis embrace
Shi'a Islam

ca. 1580
Reaction against
Wang Yingming's
followers

1469–1539
Lifetime of Nanak

1540
Founding of the
order of Jesuits

1587–1629
Reign of Shah Abbas I

ca. 1620
Peak of
European
witch
hunts

1472–1529
Lifetime of Wang Yangming

1555
Treaty of Amasya;
Peace of Augsburg

1597
Christianity is banned
in Japan

1514
Nicolas Copernicus writes
down his heliocentric system

1606
Sikhs abandon pacifism and begin military tradition

18

Cultural Upheavals

RELIGIOUS AND INTELLECTUAL MOVEMENTS

1500 to 1750

About 1545, a Japanese samurai named Anjirō killed someone in a brawl. His remorse led to the introduction of Christianity into Japan. Although sorry for his deed, Anjirō chose to flee and live as an outlaw. In 1547 he met a Portuguese sea captain in the port of Kagoshima on Japan's southern island of Kyushu—Portuguese sailors had recently started looking for trade opportunities in Japan. The sea captain suggested that Anjirō might feel better about his crime if he consulted a priest, specifically a Spanish Jesuit named Francis Xavier. The **Jesuits** were a newly founded (1540) order of priests within the Catholic Church dedicated to evangelizing non-Catholics and to rigorous education.

Francis Xavier worked as a missionary throughout the Portuguese Empire in Asia. Anjirō met him in 1547 at Malacca, the cosmopolitan city on the Malayan Peninsula where shipping passed between the Indian Ocean and the South China Sea. While Xavier explained to him the merits of Catholicism, Anjirō—in broken Portuguese—convinced Xavier that the people of Japan

Religious Conflict Dozens of Christians are beheaded and burned at the stake during a backlash against European Christian missionaries in sixteenth-century Japan. The period saw religious upheaval around the world, as new sectarian movements and stronger global connections caused different traditions to come into contact—and conflict—for the first time.

FOCUS QUESTIONS

1. Why was this a period of intellectual upheaval?

2. How were the Renaissance, the Reformation, and the Scientific Revolution disruptions of European culture and society?

3. How did the Safavids enable Shi'a Islam to triumph in Iran?

4. What factors led to the rise of Sikhism in India?

5. How did China's Confucian traditions undergo change in the sixteenth century?

6. How did ruling elites attempt to roll back new religious and intellectual movements?

7. Why was the intellectual upheaval of the period uneven across Eurasia?

might be willing to try a new religion. Together they went to Goa, the Portuguese enclave in India, where Anjirō studied Catholic theology and the Portuguese language at a Jesuit college. In 1548 he was baptized a Christian. Then they returned to Malacca, boarded a Chinese pirate ship (the only one they could find heading to Japan), and arrived at Kagoshima in 1549, intending to convert Japan to Catholicism.

Japan was fragmented politically and religiously at the time. Buddhism was the primary spiritual path, and several different Buddhist sects competed for followers. They also competed with ritual-rich Shinto, Japan's oldest religion. Xavier and Anjirō drew crowds in Kagoshima. Anjirō translated the Christian concept of God as *Dainichi*, one of the Japanese terms for the Buddha. That and the fact that they had come from India, the home of the Buddha, added to the interest Japanese took in their preaching. The Japanese

at first understood Catholicism as another version of Buddhism coming straight from the Buddha's homeland.

Xavier and Anjirō met with a warm reception from the local authorities until, two years into their mission work, Xavier concluded that Anjirō's translation did not convey the true nature of God. He started using the Latin word *Deus* instead and began to denounce Dainichi as a creature of the devil. His reception in Kagoshima cooled quickly.

Xavier left Kagoshima for the capital city of Kyoto, where he hoped to convert the emperor. But he never received an imperial audience, and in 1552 was recalled by the Jesuits to Goa. He died en route. Anjirō, meanwhile, lost most of his following in Kagoshima and returned to a life of crime, taking up piracy. He died at sea.

Nonetheless, his followers won many converts, and by 1579 some 130,000 Japanese came to call themselves Christians. The oceanic voyaging of the Portuguese, together with Anjirō's remorse and Xavier's ambition, brought new ideas to Japan, shaking up its spiritual and political order.

Forging the Global web was a disruptive and destructive process, but also a creative one. As we saw in Chapter 17, joining the web wrought havoc on peoples in Africa, the Americas, Siberia, and Oceania, but in time generated new, hybrid societies and cultures. Within the Old World web, the process was disruptive and creative too, not least in the realm of ideas. During the centuries from 1500 to 1750, the convergence of the webs helped to drive major challenges to established patterns of thought, leading to new religions, schisms in old religions, new paths within old philosophies—and to the beginnings of modern science. These are the subjects of this chapter.

INFORMATION FLOWS AND INTELLECTUAL FERMENTS

With the advent of oceanic voyaging, and the simultaneous quickening of commerce, information moved farther and faster than ever before. Although shipping had carried ideas and information around for millennia, the linking of formerly separate worlds after the 1490s enabled Confucian and Daoist thought to filter (faintly) into Europe, Christianity to take root in China, and Islam to reach Brazil and coastal South Carolina. Sometimes these exchanges were the work of elites operating at the highest rungs of society, such as the Jesuits who brought European cartography and cannon-making skills to the Ming imperial court in China. In other cases, they involved humbler folk, such as the enslaved West Africans who carried Islam to the Americas.

This swirl of new information from around the globe challenged existing systems of thought. In one important realm, astronomy, new and disruptive information also came from well beyond the far corners of the Earth. When glasses-makers in northern Europe invented telescopes, starting around 1608, it soon became possible to see the craters of the moon and the rings of Saturn. Heavenly bodies, it turned out, were rather different from what people had long imagined. By 1625 microscopes were also in use in northwestern Europe. Soon people could see all sorts of unexpected things, such as corpuscles in blood, crystals in frost, and cells in plant tissues (named cells because they reminded their discoverer of monastic quarters). Telescopes and microscopes, like the Americas and the coasts of Africa, furnished Europeans with unfamiliar observations in every realm from astronomy to zoology. Wherever it came from, new information often proved difficult to fit into prevailing religions and philosophies. That inspired great intellectual effort to resolve the new data with the old systems, sometimes convincing, sometimes not.

In this situation, the authority of existing intellectual traditions, religions included, weakened. New versions of truth had an opening. The odds of a new religion, a new wrinkle in moral philosophy, or a new paradigm in science attracting a following improved sharply. This intellectual and cultural ferment took place in several places around the world, but in Europe more than anywhere else. As we've seen, Atlantic Europeans were the ones who completed the linking up of the world's shorelines through oceanic navigation and so came into possession of wider knowledge of the world sooner than others. And they were the ones who first developed the telescope and the microscope, bringing knowledge of worlds unknown to anyone else.

Two other developments, one global and one mainly European, helped create widespread intellectual ferment during these centuries. The first was faster urbanization. As we have seen at many points already, cities served as hothouses for ideas because people could interact so easily with so many others. Between 1500 and 1750, commerce (among other things) drove the growth of cities, especially port cities, almost everywhere. Here people could rub shoulders with strangers from other continents and exchange their understandings of medicine, metallurgy, morality, and everything else. Most of the time, no doubt, language barriers and preference for familiar ideas prevented meaningful exchange. But every now and then they did not. The second development was entirely new, and its impact for centuries focused within Europe: the **printing press**.

INFORMATION TECHNOLOGY: THE PRINTING PRESS

Around the years 1430–1450, a few people including Johannes Gutenberg, a goldsmith and gem cutter in the German town of Mainz, started work on casting metal type for use in printing. At that time printing involved the use of wood blocks, painstakingly carved by skilled woodworkers. Gutenberg gradually developed movable and reusable type, better ink, and a better press. His invention, one of the most consequential in world history and one of the first for whom we know the name of the primary inventor, made possible the ever-cheaper transmission of information.

Gutenberg was not the first to come up with moveable metal type. Chinese in the Song dynasty had used bronze plates to print paper money. Similar technology filtered into Korea in the thirteenth century. But metal type was not a useful advance over woodblock printing when writing in Chinese, because one needs to make thousands of characters to create a text. When Korea introduced an alphabet with only 24 letters in the 1430s, it made more sense to use moveable metal type. That led to a small flurry of publishing there. But literacy was rare in Korea, and some of the elite resisted the new alphabet, preferring the traditional Chinese characters. So even with moveable type, Korea experienced no revolution in reading, publishing, or the circulation of information: the prior invention of moveable metal type in East Asia had none of the consequences that Gutenberg's did. Given the trans-Eurasian traffic in the wake of the Mongols, it's conceivable that Gutenberg was inspired to experiment with casting type after hearing of the Korean innovation—but there is no evidence for that. This case is a reminder that it is not always the first invention of something that matters.

In Europe, conditions different from Korea's led to an explosion in printing once Gutenberg had shown the way. By 1500, 236 towns in Europe had printing presses, and on those presses hundreds or thousands of copies of over 30,000 different books had been printed. This came to about 20 million books in all, in at least a dozen languages. Venice alone had 417 printers. The first presses

using the Cyrillic (for Russian and some other Slavic languages) alphabet debuted in 1483, and in 1501 the first ones using Greek. Regular newspapers appeared by 1605, specializing in business news. The first women's magazine started publication in 1693 (in England), and the first daily newspaper in 1702. By 1753, British readers bought 20,000 newspapers daily, each one probably read by several people. By 1800, European presses had released some 2 million different book titles.

Europeans carried this new device overseas. (The typical press, made of wood, was 6 to 8 feet high and weighed several hundred pounds.) Spanish Mexico acquired a press by 1539, Portuguese Goa (where Anjirō studied) had one by the 1550s, and the Spanish Philippines by 1593. Jesuits brought one to Japan in 1590. The first in English North America was set up by Elizabeth Glover, a widow with five children, in 1638 upon her arrival in Massachusetts.

At first, even printed books were expensive. Gutenberg's printed Bible, published in 1455, cost about a year's wages for an ordinary laborer. But gradual improvements in the alloys of lead used, in the oil-based ink, and cheaper

Moveable Type Sets of metal type like that at left—from Korea in the fourteenth century—had been developed to print text in Chinese as early as the late thirteenth century. But moveable type was more transformative in Europe, where it enhanced the efficiency of producing and distributing texts like the Bible. At right is a page from a fifteenth-century Bible, printed and subsequently hand-illuminated.

paper kept pushing the price of printed material downward. Cheaper books raised the demand for education: literacy rates began to climb.

In Gutenberg's time, only 5 to 15 percent of adult Europeans could read. Two-thirds or more of those were male. By 1500, however, the literacy rate had begun to climb, and by 1650 it reached about 25 to 50 percent. In the Netherlands and Britain, and in New England too, it was slightly above 50 percent; in Sweden and Italy, just below 25 percent. The gender gap remained wide until the twentieth century. The market for books and pamphlets ranged from the Bible (easily the best seller) and texts of Christian instruction such as catechisms, to manuals of farming and mining and light entertainments of every sort.

Scribes and manuscripts did not disappear. They coexisted with print technology for a few centuries. Yet printing was truly revolutionary, lowering the costs of information while improving its accuracy by reducing copying errors.

For centuries, the printing revolution encompassed only Europe and European outposts. The great states of Asia preferred to rely on scribes and hand copying of texts. For written languages that used thousands of ideographic characters rather than alphabets, such as Chinese, moveable type did not seem an advantage. Muslim authorities until the eighteenth century generally thought that the sacred language of the Qur'an should only be copied by hand, that printing it would amount to desecration. In many settings, scribes and literate elites regarded printing as a challenge to their position. Rulers feared that printers would be harder to keep under watch and control than scribes—and they could not have been more correct. Printing made ideas harder to control.

EUROPE: EXTREME TURBULENCE

As we've seen in previous chapters, it was primarily Atlantic Europeans who made the voyages that forged the Global web. So it was primarily in European societies that the global harvest of new information arrived first, sped forward by the printing press. These circumstances colored three great disruptions in the intellectual sphere in early-modern Europe, major developments that we now call the Renaissance, the Protestant Reformation, and the Scientific Revolution. The first deeply affected European thought but did not travel well beyond Europe's shores. The second involved far more people than the others, brought fierce conflict, and motivated spasms of violence. The third involved only a tiny few but brought far larger, and more global, consequences in the long run.

THE RENAISSANCE

In an earlier chapter we saw how exposure to Arab and Byzantine Greek learning helped to stimulate new thinking in twelfth- and thirteenth-century Europe, especially challenges to longstanding Christian dogmas within the newly invented institution of the university. Knowledge of Arabic and Greek gave access to bodies of thought from the ancient world that were otherwise out of reach.

Renaissance Art The Italian artist Carlo Crivelli made this painting of the Annunciation for a church altarpiece in 1486. The painting includes artistic motifs such as the use of perspective as well as small scenes of everyday life, both hallmarks of Renaissance art.

Cathedral of the Dormition Built by the Italian architect Aristotele Fioravanti in the years 1475–1479, this Moscow cathedral was one of many magnificent buildings that Italian architects designed and constructed across Europe during the Renaissance.

Political and military pressure on the waning Byzantine Empire motivated many learned Greeks to seek safe spaces in Italian universities in the early fifteenth century, bringing perspectives, and manuscripts, previously unknown there. The growing fascination with ancient Greek and Roman wisdom brought what historians since the nineteenth century have called the Renaissance, meaning a re-birth of ancient learning. Of course, ancient learning was never dead. It was alive and well in Greek and Arab lands. But in western Europe much had vanished, and it is from that perspective that the term *Renaissance* makes sense.

The heart of the Renaissance was a re-engagement with the literatures, histories, philosophies, and art of the ancient Greeks and Romans. Their emphasis on human affairs and human achievement—as opposed to more spiritual matters—found a ready audience among the literate classes and their wealthy patrons. Plato and Cicero came back into style. Translations of the histories of Herodotus and Thucydides appeared, as did the work of ancient Greek playwrights. Sculptors imitated the ancients' marble statuary, with its emphasis on accurate human form.

The **Renaissance** began in Italy, especially in the city-state of Florence. The political fragmentation of northern Italy probably helped the movement along because local dukes and princes supported artists, architects, and scholars in their competition for political prestige. By the mid-fifteenth century, Italian architects and scholars were in demand elsewhere in Europe too. In Hungary, Poland, and even Russia, rulers hired Italians to build magnificent buildings, such as the Cathedral of the Dormition in Moscow's Kremlin. Aided in part by the printing press, Renaissance texts—literature, history, philosophy—circulated swiftly in sixteenth- and seventeenth-century Europe. Renaissance art, using geometry to achieve perspective and depicting everyday life as well as traditional subjects such as Bible scenes and stories of saints, spread almost as quickly.

Renaissance ideals, especially humanism—the view that human affairs were worthy of careful study and suitable themes for art and literature—also took root in the Netherlands, the German lands, France, England, and beyond. Erasmus of Rotterdam, educated and employed at universities in Paris, Cambridge, Turin, Oxford, and Leuven (now in Belgium), used his extraordinary talents in ancient languages and well-honed powers of reason to produce more coherent translations of the New Testament and to call the Catholic Church to account on some of its inconsistencies. Even the study of politics took on a humanistic tone as writers such as Niccolò Machiavelli, a diplomat in Florence in the early sixteenth century, sought to depict political life as it really was rather than in relation to ideal worlds. The Renaissance affected European elites strongly, especially those who read Latin, and to some extent those in lands elsewhere controlled by Europeans. It did not resonate deeply anywhere else—unlike the upheavals in Christianity, which had more widespread repercussions.

RELIGION: PROTESTANT AND CATHOLIC REFORMATIONS

By 1500, the Catholic Church in Europe had met and mastered many challenges. Since the so-called Great Schism in 1054, when the Church of Rome and the Orthodox Church parted ways, Catholicism had spawned many innovations. The church authorities regarded most of these innovations as heresies. It almost invariably succeeded in stamping them out or confining them to remote mountain districts, often using armed force provided by secular rulers. However, in 1517 Martin Luther (1483–1546) launched a new heresy that proved too popular to uproot. It evolved into a new branch of Christianity, called Protestantism.

LUTHER AND PROTESTANTISM Luther was born to middle-class parents. His father leased and operated mines in a part of Germany known as Saxony. His parents' ambitions for young Martin extended to sending him to the University of Erfurt. He completed his degree by age 21 and entered law school at his father's insistence. He hated it, dropped out, and seeking deeper truths, decided to become an Augustinian friar. His father was outraged, considering that path a waste of a good university education. Martin, however, recalled the University of Erfurt as "a beer hall and whorehouse" and preferred to devote himself to confession, prayer, and pilgrimage.

But Luther was not done with education. His Augustinian mentors encouraged him to study theology, and after acquiring a few university degrees, Luther joined the theology faculty at the newly founded University of Wittenberg just before his thirtieth birthday. He remained employed there all his life.

In his schooling, writings, preaching, and teaching, Luther developed two main ideas. One was the primacy of scripture over the traditions of the church. So, for example, Luther noted that celibacy for priests has no basis in the Bible (it became required practice in the late fourth century CE). Nor, he argued, did the ritual of confession, or the concept of purgatory—in Catholic theology, an anteroom to heaven in which all but the sinless souls must linger for as long as it takes to burn away their sins. He came to regard these (and much else) as obstacles to the proper practice of Christianity. Rather than follow traditions unsanctioned in the Bible, believers should, Luther said, read scripture themselves and decide for themselves just what it meant. To make that easier, he translated the Bible into German, finishing in 1534. In effect, said Luther, Christians should be their own priests.

The second idea is known as justification by faith alone. This meant that salvation of one's soul could result only from a full embrace of the Christian faith and the gift of divine mercy. For Luther, true Christianity was an inward commitment. He took issue with the church's

position that one could ensure salvation through "good works," such as donating money to the church, although he thought that people who had that inward commitment would likely want to perform good works. Luther held fast to these two ideas, arguing for his beliefs with both skill and ferocity.

Martin Luther Luther's friend Lucas Cranach painted this portrait of him in his friar's habit in 1533, when the Protestant movement was becoming increasingly widespread across Europe.

Earlier reformers had foreshadowed some of Luther's ideas. Jan Hus, a university rector in Prague (in today's Czech Republic), challenged the privileges of the clergy and the church's quests for money. Hus also preached a more intimate, personal commitment as the core of Christianity. In 1415, he was burned at the stake at the command of a bishop. Hus and his followers had drawn much of their outlook from John Wycliffe, who preached, taught, and wrote mainly at Oxford University. He oversaw the first translation of the Bible into English, completed in 1382. Wycliffe railed at the wealth and power of the clergy and Papacy, recommending a more personal Christianity and the primacy of scripture over church and tradition. The Pope denounced him, and the head of Oxford University had him imprisoned for his views. Wycliffe died of natural causes in England in 1384, but in 1431 a pope ordered that his corpse be dug up and burned, as befitted a heretic.

Luther found it particularly offensive that the church, in need of money to pay for the building of St. Peter's Basilica in Rome, had sent churchmen around Europe offering promises of expedited salvation in exchange for donations. This practice, not so different from the deals forged between holy men and the Gupta kings in India (noted in Chapter 13), was called the sale of indulgences. The practice was invented in the 1090s to persuade people to join the Crusades. It was never official policy, but it had become routine procedure by Luther's time. In effect, the gates of heaven were treated like a tollbooth. Sinners who paid could escape a painful term in purgatory. The most successful salesmen of indulgences promised that even the most unspeakable sins could be wiped away for a suitable fee.

Luther wrote up his objections, in Latin, in a document now called his Ninety-five Theses. This was not

Reformation The Oude Kerk ("Old Church") in Amsterdam became Calvinist after the Reformation reached the Netherlands in 1578. This seventeenth-century painting indicates some of the Protestant characteristics of the decor, including a relative lack of ornamentation and a prominent raised pulpit at the left of the nave.

quite the undertaking it might seem: most of his theses were only a sentence long. He did not seek to challenge the church directly, but the implications of some of his theses aroused the ire of Rome. Number 86, for example, which he described as a shrewd question of lay people, read: "Why does the Pope, whose wealth today is greater than the wealth of the richest Crassus, build the basilica of St. Peter with the money of poor believers rather than with his own money?"

Legend has it that Luther nailed his theses to the door of the cathedral at Wittenberg in 1517. The door often served as a bulletin board. Whether the story is true or not (it probably is not), he did allow friends to translate his text into German and print it in early 1518 as a pamphlet. By 1519, it had circulated all over Europe.

Here it is important to note the political landscape surrounding Luther and his ideas. Germany was not a unified state but a mosaic of dozens of small states, most of them offering a cautious allegiance to the Holy Roman Empire. The Holy Roman Empire was nominally the successor to Charlemagne's kingdom of the ninth century, but in fact it was a loose and weak collection of duchies and principalities whose rulers enjoyed great autonomy. It

also comprised about 100 self-governing "free cities," not subject to any duke or prince. The Holy Roman Empire's territory had been shrinking for centuries (and would continue to do so until it was wiped off the map in 1806). It was, however, usually the political force most inclined to serve the interests of the Pope. The political fragmentation of Germany made it hard for authorities to do anything, such as executing Luther, unless every prince, duke, and free city agreed.

By Luther's day, the Papacy had plenty of experience in handling upstarts and heretics. It gave Luther a few chances to recant his positions, which he refused, most dramatically in 1521 at the Diet of Worms (not a college meal plan, but an assembly of officials of the Holy Roman Empire held in the town of Worms). Luther stood his ground, and soon the Pope excommunicated him from the church, calling Luther a "wild boar in the vineyards of the Lord." The Pope's political allies called for Luther's murder. Luther responded to efforts to muzzle him by taking more radical positions, including denying the legitimacy of the Papacy altogether and calling the Pope the antichrist and "servant of the devil." He denounced several important church rituals as unchristian. This was a quarrel that could not be patched up.

Despite having enemies in high places, Luther lived on, in effect an outlaw protected by German princes who liked his ideas, and by his university. He produced his German-language edition of the Bible, wrote many hymns and pamphlets, read a translation of the Qur'an and supported its publication (on the grounds that its errors should be held to scrutiny), and in his last years wrote violent screeds against Jews, few of whom he had ever seen. Always bull-headed, by the end of his life he zealously courted controversy and confrontation.

The printing press and spreading literacy, discussed above, made it more difficult for the church to extinguish an appealing heresy. Luther's many pamphlets found receptive readers all over Europe, and he became a celebrity professor. Even an organization as vast and staffed with talent as the church could not keep Luther's ideas in check.

Variations on Luther's themes soon appeared in Swiss cities. In Zurich, a Catholic priest, Ulrich Zwingli, preached a message similar to Luther's and won over the town leaders. In Geneva, John Calvin took up Luther's cause and gave it his own spin based on the gloomy idea that everyone's fate—heaven or hell—was predestined

Religious Geography of Europe, 1555–1650 Beginning in the early sixteenth century, the Protestant Reformation added new Christian sects that by 1555 (main map) had acquired millions of followers in western and central Europe. But, as the inset shows, by 1650 the Catholic Reformation, supported by powerful rulers such as the Habsburgs and the kings of France, had won back certain populations. Some lands remained thereafter a patchwork of religions, with multiple Christian minority sects.

and no amount of good behavior (or donations to the church) could improve one's odds of salvation. Bad behavior such as blasphemy, witchcraft, adultery, or heresy, in contrast, brought a parade of executions by drowning, beheading, and burning in Calvin's Geneva after 1536. Calvin's uncompromising formula, much influenced by St. Augustine, claimed to be the sole authentic form of Christianity. It spread further than Lutheranism in the sixteenth century, taking root in parts of Switzerland, France, Britain, Germany, and the Low Countries. Emigrants from these lands carried it to South Africa and North America in the seventeenth century.

Various groups of Protestants (the term was in use by 1530) formed in pockets across Europe. Those who embraced it tended to be more urban and literate than average. Cities with printing presses were particularly likely to turn Protestant. But village peasants too, especially in Germany, often found **Protestantism** appealing. They felt its emphasis on "God's law" justified their revolt in 1524–1525 against taxes and levies imposed by princes and the church. Luther disavowed the revolt, and it was crushed.

In general, Protestants shared the view that salvation rested on personal commitment to God and that the

Catholic Church had grown stale, stolid, and corrupt, standing as a barrier between individuals and God. Several rulers embraced this new creed, finding it appealing in its own right and often advantageous in political terms—it provided grounds for confiscating church and monastic property, a tempting target. Many German princes had chosen Protestantism by 1530. By 1560, the rulers of Denmark, Sweden, England, and Scotland had become Protestant and encouraged or obliged their subjects to follow suit. In France maybe 10 to 20 percent of the population was Protestant, and in German lands closer to 80 percent. Most of the German speakers in Poland—a sizeable minority there—were as well. Protestantism in the mid-sixteenth century seemed an unstoppable force in Europe north of Italy, Spain, and Portugal.

THE CATHOLIC REFORMATION Yet between 1550 and 1620 the Catholic Church did manage to check the spread of Protestantism. Indeed, the church and its allies regained some lost ground, winning back people in the southern part of the Netherlands (now Belgium) and a good share of Germans. The Catholic Church nearly stamped out Protestantism in Poland and France, and it crushed the followers of Jan Hus in Bohemia (now part of the Czech Republic). Part of its success came through war. The Pope had armies in those days, and so did the house of Habsburg, a firmly Catholic family that held the Spanish and Austrian thrones, as well as a few other duchies and provinces.

The Protestants could not unify their resistance. Splinter sects popped up constantly, much to the annoyance of Luther and Calvin, none more hated than those Anabaptists who regarded polygamy, pacifism, and communal property (as opposed to private property) as acceptable. Protestant sects and princes quarreled fiercely among themselves over fine points of doctrine and over political advantage, which made it harder to fight effectively against Catholic powers. Struggles abated somewhat after an agreement of 1555, the Peace of Augsburg, in which Catholic and Lutheran rulers in central Europe agreed on the principle that rulers should be free to require either Catholicism or Lutheranism of their populations.

The church also undertook major reforms in response to the Protestant Reformation. Beginning in the 1540s, in a movement called the **Catholic Reformation** (or the Counter-Reformation), the church cleaned up its act

considerably. No more libertine popes, living in luxury, fathering children and making a mockery of Christian morals. Bishops and abbots cut back on high living. The church grew more centralized and standardized, settling on a single required script for mass, for example. Popes became more powerful over bishops and priests, abbots and monks. The Papacy re-established its Inquisition (1542), an office tasked with rooting out heresy, and created the so-called Index of banned books (1559). The Index stopped work in 1966.

The church also went global. While Luther and Calvin were diverting souls in Europe from Catholicism, missionaries found fertile fields for the salvation of different souls overseas. In the first half of the sixteenth century, Catholic priests ventured to the Americas, Africa, India, China, Japan, and almost everywhere in between. Religious orders such as Augustinians, Dominicans, and Franciscans came to specialize in converting unbelievers around the world, usually focusing their efforts on the poor. The Jesuits also took to evangelical work, generally working from the top down, trying to convert rulers and courts. They led the rollback of Protestantism in Poland, helped lead it in Germany, brought Catholicism to Japan, and were especially active in China.

By 1620, the Catholic Church had revitalized itself and stopped the Protestant surge. Divisions in Europe—intellectual, cultural, political—became more entrenched. Vicious religious wars only deepened cleavages and resentments, culminating in the Thirty Years War (1618–1648) in western and central Europe, which reduced population there by as much as one-third. As the French mathematician and philosopher Blaise Pascal noted in the 1650s, people "never do so much harm so happily as when they do it through religious conviction." The convulsions in religious life in sixteenth-century Europe created divisions and sectarian identities that live on to this day—less lethally—in Europe itself, wherever European migrants have settled and wherever Christian missionaries made converts.

All durable religions develop schisms and rival sects that get tangled up in struggles for wealth and power. Islam's two largest factions broke apart soon after Muhammad's death, and both Sunni and Shi'a communities subsequently fragmented into many sub-groups. Buddhism's two leading forms, Theravada and Mahayana, also fragmented into smaller sects. Christianity splintered into several churches early in its history. While every schism and sect is different, the human capacity for religious innovation, and reform, makes the process commonplace.

WITCH HUNTS The competition between Catholicism and Protestantism proved Pascal's point in another respect. It fueled a craze for witch trials. Accusations of witchcraft—typically understood as working with the devil to obtain supernatural powers to use against neighbors or family—had been rare in Europe until 1550, by which time they reached a few hundred annually. The next century, however, brought a flurry of accusations, trials, and executions, reaching a peak about 1620 with more than 5,000 trials and 2,000 executions annually. In total, between 1500 and 1700, about 40,000 to 60,000 people were hanged, drowned, or burned as witches, often after confessions extracted with torture. Of these, 75 to 80 percent were women, usually over 40 years of age; although in parts of northernmost Europe—Iceland, Finland, Estonia, and Russia—the majority of those accused and killed were men.

Historians still struggle to explain why the **witch hunts** arose and why they stopped. Nearly nine-tenths of the executions took place in Germany (about 42 percent), Switzerland (35 percent), or France (10 percent), mainly in areas where Protestants and Catholics were vigorously competing for allegiance. One way a ruler could demonstrate the logic of accepting his (or, in rare cases, her) preferred religion was to encourage trials and convictions of witches, so as to appear committed to defending the people against the devil's mischief. King James VI of Scotland personally oversaw some cases and published a book in 1597 about witchcraft, which explained the justice of persecuting witches in a Christian community. (Shakespeare borrowed liberally from this book in writing *Macbeth*). Countries with little Catholic-Protestant rivalry saw far fewer cases. Staunchly Catholic Portugal, Spain, and Italy together accounted for only 6 percent of witchcraft executions.

The fact that the majority of victims were women, in Protestant and Catholic lands alike, requires a different explanation, one anchored in demography. A rise in the proportion of unmarried women likely played a big role. Unmarried women, especially those not under the authority of an adult male, seemed a threat to the sanctioned social order. But the ongoing religious struggles contributed to the visibility of unmarried women: Protestant

Witch Hunts A 1555 German leaflet included this vivid woodcut of three witches—one of whom is evidently possessed by a demon—being burned at the stake, perhaps to elicit sympathy for the witch-hunting cause.

rulers often seized convents' property and pushed nuns out into society at large.

THE SCIENTIFIC REVOLUTION

While both the Renaissance and the Reformation were gathering pace, shaking up the European intellectual landscape, the **Scientific Revolution** began. The term itself is controversial among experts, some of whom see the gradual pace of change in scientific thinking as reason to avoid the term *revolution*. But if significance rather than pace is the key criterion, then the term is warranted.

Two deep principles underlay the Scientific Revolution. The first was accepting that religious scripture and ancient texts did not contain everything worth knowing after all. The logic of accepting this principle strengthened as unfamiliar and baffling information arrived from overseas. Neither scripture nor the ancients had said anything about the existence of manatees and llamas, or hurricanes and typhoons. The second deep principle was the embrace of mathematics and a quantitative culture. In most fields of scientific endeavor, the book of nature was written in the language of mathematics, as the Italian astronomer Galileo put it.

The Scientific Revolution began roughly around 1500, although it is possible to find evidence of new directions in science before that. It too began mainly in northern Italy, like the Renaissance, but quickly leapfrogged to towns, especially university towns, all over Europe. Again, urbanization, universities, printing, and the challenge of new information from overseas helped to create and sustain the Scientific Revolution. So did political fragmentation, in the sense that it was hard for anyone to crush ideas they didn't like when people could easily move to another city or duchy. In addition, the widespread use of Latin helped advance the Scientific Revolution because scholars all over Europe, whatever their native tongue, wrote and read the language.

Historians sometimes say the Scientific Revolution ended around 1700, because many of the fundamental principles of modern science had by then been articulated. But in one sense the Scientific Revolution has never stopped, because its core procedures and deep principles have remained behind scientific inquiry ever since.

One final factor behind the Scientific Revolution deserves emphasis. European scientists in 1500 had no great body of wisdom to protect against new ideas and information. In this they were like the Arab intellectuals after the early Islamic conquests of the seventh and eighth centuries who suddenly came into possession of philosophy and science from India, Persia, and the Greek and Jewish worlds. This situation had led to daring new syntheses, as Arab thinkers tried to reconcile discordant ideas and data and fit them to their own religion. Their emirs and sultans had not felt required to quash this new thinking, because it offered no threat to them or their supporters. Something similar happened in Europe after 1500. Novel ideas, some of them very ancient but new to Europeans, jostled together. New observations from distant continents, and even some from distant planets, challenged old wisdom. But European intellectuals and rulers rarely felt they needed to protect existing ideas (at least, scientific ones) from competitors. And thanks to political fragmentation, intellectual protectionism, when tried, did not fully succeed.

Systematic observation and experimentation lay at the heart of the Scientific Revolution. Scientifically minded men (and a few women) increasingly sought to find the true essence of things by careful study and designed experiments, rather than relying on the theories of Aristotle and his interpreters. They sought, like many before them, to understand the workings of the heavens, the nature of matter, the secret of human health—but with different methods.

The Scientific Revolution was not anti-religion. Every one of its prominent figures considered himself a Christian. Many of them were priests. Most of them sought to reveal God's glory by revealing the perfection of creation in the precise, regular, harmonious workings of the universe. They aimed to read the book of nature alongside the book of scripture, as early Christian writers had put it. The seventeenth-century English scientist Robert Boyle regarded the study of God's creation as a form of religious worship and enjoyed conducting experiments on Sundays. Boyle's father was the second-richest man in England, so Robert could afford to study chemistry and physics every day of the week.

Since the early nineteenth century we have divided science into fields called disciplines, but no one did that in the sixteenth and seventeenth centuries. Many thinkers ranged across fields, considering all of science to be one. But to see its long-term impact, it is helpful to look at a few particular fields before returning to the whole.

ASTRONOMY AND HELIOCENTRISM Let's begin with astronomy. In 1500, most people supposed that the sun moved around the Earth because that's what their eyes told them every day. Ancient Greek philosophers, notably Ptolemy, had explained how and why that was so (although one or two ancient Greeks had suggested the Earth might move around the sun instead). Careful observation of the movements of planets and stars raised questions about Ptolemy's system. One of those puzzled by discordant observations was a Polish-German student in northern Italy, known by his Latinized name as Nicholas Copernicus (1473–1543). He knew Latin and Greek, as well as Polish, German, and Italian, giving him access to a wide intellectual heritage. In 1514, he wrote up an alternative explanation based on a **heliocentric system** in which planets spin around the sun. He tinkered with it for decades, while working in Poland as a cathedral administrator. Just before his death he overcame his fears of persecution and his perfectionist tendencies and published his work in 1543. In it he cited both ancient and recent Islamic astronomers and was clearly influenced by both.

Copernicus's heliocentric system did not catch on quickly. It violated common sense as well as the wisdom of the ancients. Nor did it arouse the ire of the church, as Copernicus had feared. It was useful for astrologers because it simplified calculations about future positions of the planets. Astrology was a prestigious branch of science

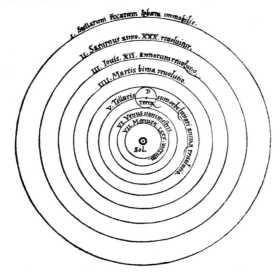

net, in quo terram cum orbe lunari tanquam epicyclo contineri diximus. Quinto loco Venus nono menſe reducitur. Sextum deniꝗ locum Mercurius tenet, octuaginta dierum ſpacio circū currens, In medio uero omnium reſidet Sol. Quis enim in hoc

pulcherrimo templolampadem hanc in alio uel meliori loco po neret, quàm unde totum ſimul poſsit illuminare? Siquidem non inepte quidam lucernam mundi, alij mentem, alij rectorem uo‑ cant. Trimegiſtus uiſibilem Deum, Sophoclis Electra intuentē omnia. Ita profecto tanquam in ſolio regali Sol reſidens circum agentem gubernat Aſtrorum familiam. Tellus quoꝗ minime fraudatur lunari miniſterio, ſed ut Ariſtoteles de animalibus ait, maximā Luna cū terra cognationē habet. Concipit interea à Sole terra, & impregnatur annuo partu. Inuenimus igitur ſub hac

Astronomical Revolution In his 1543 book *On the Revolution of the Spheres*, Copernicus published his theory of a solar system in which (as this diagram indicates) the planets revolved around the sun.

in those days. When Elizabeth I of England chose a day for her coronation, she consulted a mathematician and an astrologer. So did the Pope when choosing an auspicious day for laying the cornerstone of the Basilica of St. Peter's in Rome in 1506. It took some 200 years, and many further observations and refinements of Copernicus's system, before all serious students of the heavens had abandoned Ptolemaic astronomy.

The three scientists whose work did the most to confirm Copernicus's heliocentric view were Johannes Kepler (1571–1630), Galileo Galilei (1564–1642), and Isaac Newton (1643–1727). Kepler, whose major works were published between 1609 and 1627, used careful mathematics to show that planets revolved around the sun in elliptical, not circular, orbits. That helped resolve some discrepancies between observations and Copernicus's theories, although

it took decades to become accepted. Kepler lived in German cities and, although he considered himself a proper Christian, had to overcome occasional persecution at the hands of Lutheran churchmen, Catholic authorities, and political leaders alike. His mother, Katharina Guldemann, was tried for witchcraft.

Kepler's contemporary, Galileo, lived in northern Italy and provided detailed observations of the planets using homemade telescopes. In 1615 Catholic officials warned him to stop writing in favor of the heliocentric view, and in 1632 they put him on trial. He officially recanted when faced with the prospect of torture. His works were banned by the church, but this did not stop their spread. The church abandoned its objections to heliocentrism in 1835.

Two generations later, Isaac Newton, a professor of mathematics at Cambridge University, clinched the case for heliocentrism. In the 1660s and 1670s he formulated his laws of motion and gravity, accounting in detailed mathematical proofs for the movement of planets, comets, the tides, and much else. He too considered himself a devout Christian and maintained that his work, published by 1687, laid out the elegance and beauty of God's creation as revealed by mathematics. The official Anglican Church did not bother trying to dispute or suppress his work. The scientific battle launched by Copernicus in 1543 was over, and heliocentrists had won.

CHEMISTRY AND EXPERIMENTATION As astrology was to astronomy, so was alchemy to chemistry. The greatest motivation behind experiments and new thinking in chemistry during the Scientific Revolution was the hope that cheap metals could be transformed into valuable ones—for example, lead into gold. Boyle dabbled in alchemy and claimed to have seen base metals changed into gold. Alchemy, unlike astrology, did not carry much prestige and was often scorned at universities, although Newton, at Cambridge, was fascinated by it. It had no classical pedigree from ancient Greeks or Romans, it was messy, and its practitioners had reputations as con men.

But, working on their own, sometimes in their own kitchens, sixteenth- and seventeenth-century chemists developed a tradition of experimentation and precise recording of results. We now consider most of the ideas they advanced to be wrong, but their methods proved enduringly useful. One prominent chemist, physician, and astrologer was the Swiss-born Philippus Aureolus Theophrastus Bombastus von Hohenheim, who, understandably, preferred to go by the name Paracelsus (1493–1541). He entered and quickly exited six universities before earning a degree at Ferrara, in northern Italy, in 1516. Along the way he developed the view that all disease results from too much of either sulfur, mercury, or salt, three chemicals that he considered central to all matter. Disdaining tradition in favor of experimentation, he claimed that "my shoe buckles are more learned than Galen and Avicenna [Ibn Sina]." Although often wrong in his conclusions, his insistence on experimentation to show the medical uses of chemicals and minerals helped establish genuinely scientific methods. More than any other branch of science, it was in chemistry that the methodology of experimentation evolved.

MEDICINE Unlike chemistry, medicine was among the prestigious subjects and professions. It too underwent major revision, in both methods and concepts. The most important new methods paralleled changes everywhere in science: greater reliance on observation and experiment, and less deference to ancient authors. The most significant new concept was the principle of the circulation of the blood, detailed by the Englishman William Harvey.

Harvey (1578–1657), the son of a small-town mayor, entered Cambridge University at age 15. After studying medicine for six years, he moved on to northern Italy (like Copernicus and Paracelsus before him), where he learned the fine points of dissection of human cadavers and live animals. In 1628, now a prosperous physician in

Anatomical Innovation William Harvey's 1628 book *The Motion of the Heart and Blood in Living Beings* was accompanied by detailed diagrams illustrating how the heart pumped blood throughout the body.

London, Harvey published his book on the circulation of the blood, showing that the heart pumped blood through arteries into capillaries, and that veins returned the same blood to the heart. Like Copernicus, Harvey showed what others had earlier guessed—notably, Ibn al-Nafis in thirteenth-century Cairo. He built on assertions made by medical men in Italy and Egypt, using systematic observation, in this case based on dissections. In his work, as in Copernicus's, we can see the circulation of knowledge between the Islamic and Christian worlds, made possible by the longstanding connections of the Old World web.

INSTITUTIONS AND CONNECTIONS Every field of science, from astronomy to zoology, experienced some upheaval during the Scientific Revolution. Those most influenced by the global harvest of information and ideas were probably botany and zoology, due to the large number of strange species attested to in distant lands. Ideas and principles from China, India, and the Islamic world, as well as observations made elsewhere, brought challenges to received wisdom in Europe.

The links between science and technology were weaker in those days than ours, but nonetheless the new scientific outlook filtered into fields such as mining, cartography, navigation, and clock making. In particular, more precise mathematics and a culture of quantification helped these fields develop. Technical advances in these fields helped, in turn, to promote commerce and connections within Europe and between Europe and other lands, contributing to the tightening of the Global web.

The Scientific Revolution was a permanent revolution: it continues to this day. Part of the reason for that is the institutionalization of scientific inquiry that began in the late seventeenth century. Academies of science sprouted first in Italy. An 18-year-old from a wealthy family in Rome founded the first one in 1603, but it folded in 1630 upon his death. More durable academies, enjoying royal support, were created in London (1662) and Paris (1666). Others followed in the eighteenth century in Uppsala (Sweden), Berlin, St. Petersburg, and Philadelphia. Networks of scientists solidified, based on correspondence and travel from one city or university town to another, and eased by the shared use of Latin. Carl Linnaeus, the eighteenth-century Swedish botanist who developed a system for naming, ranking, and classifying organisms, maintained a correspondence with nearly a thousand people. Such networks, combined with print technology,

Mining Technology This woodcut, from a mining manual published in Switzerland in 1556, illustrates the technological sophistication developing in sixteenth-century Europe. It shows an overshot waterwheel turning the camshaft of a stamping mill, used to crush rock and extract minerals. Considerable engineering expertise and practical geometry went into building these machines. Such technology, adopted in Spanish America, facilitated silver-mining booms in Mexico and the Andes.

prepared the way for publication of scientific journals, the first of which appeared in England in 1665 and is still going strong. These academies, networks, and journals helped to entrench the Scientific Revolution in European thought and society by 1700. In later centuries similar institutions would underpin science around the world, helping to make modern science a global undertaking.

THE WORLD OF ISLAM: A SHI'A REFORMATION

The intellectual world of Islam, like that of India and China, underwent less turbulence than Europe in the centuries between 1500 and 1700. Its cities were less affected by newly forged links to distant lands than Seville or Amsterdam were. Its religious and scientific establishments by now had a great deal of established belief, practice, and knowledge to protect from novelty. But nonetheless, human creativity, the rise of commerce,

and the advance of urbanization helped bring about some intellectual realignments in Islamdom. The most important of these was the success of the Shi'a branch of Islam in Iran.

SHI'ISM

Shi'ism is almost as old as Islam itself. Its followers regard descendants of Muhammad through his daughter Fatima and his son-in-law Ali to be especially endowed with religious and political authority. Only members of Muhammad's lineage could provide proper earthly guidance.

In the early years of Islam, Sunni caliphs crushed Shi'a factions in battle, and they survived only as a tiny minority. For 800 years Shi'ism suffered frequent persecution from Sunni rulers, who regarded it as heresy, and its followers often kept their convictions secret. Many Shi'a felt disdain for power, authority, and sometimes wealth, seeing virtue in humility and commitment to justice. The most important dynasties to embrace Shi'ism were the Fatimids in Egypt (909–1171) and the Buyids in southern Iran and Iraq (934–1048), but they did not impose it upon their populations. Iran in 1450 had very few Shi'a Muslims.

Shi'a Islam triumphed in Iran for political reasons. In the chaotic conditions of the late fourteenth century, following the decline of Il-Khanid Mongol overlords in northern Iran, charismatic religious leaders competed for influence. They won followers through demonstrations of religious power and military success. Most of them were Sufis.

Sufism (see Chapter 14) is an umbrella term for philosophical, theological, and literary traditions within Islam that emphasize a mystical, intense, and personal engagement with God. Sufi leaders, who usually called themselves sheiks, did not need much formal education in Islamic theology or law. They attracted followers by convincing people that they had a special connection to God. They flourished in regions where states, law, and the *ulema* (the learned interpreters of Islam) were weak. They built solidarity with their followers through rituals involving dance and music—attractions that had no place in more formal versions of Islam. They sometimes added distinctive practices in order to stand out from the competition. As from time to time with various sects in Christianity, Jainism, and Buddhism, these practices could include extreme self-denial and the acceptance of self-inflicted pain. The Riffaiyya, a Sufi sect whose followers lived mainly in Egypt and Syria, felt they could improve their relationship with God by biting the heads off living snakes, thrusting iron spikes into their own bodies, and climbing into hot ovens. Theirs was probably the most eccentric set of practices among hundreds of Sufi brotherhoods. Sufi sheikhs usually required unquestioning obedience among their followers, so Sufi organizations were very hierarchical.

As Iran (and neighboring parts of Anatolia and the Caucasus) became more chaotic in the fourteenth and fifteenth centuries, Sufi movements increasingly coalesced into orders or brotherhoods, often for self-protection. To

Sufi Warriors A history book from seventeenth-century Iran shows Safavi soldiers (with their distinctive red headgear) fighting Sunni troops, as part of the conflict that saw Ismail and his descendants assume control over Iran.

the extent they could provide protection, they attracted more followers. The most successful, by 1450, were the Safavis, a Sunni and Sufi brotherhood. They organized herders, former soldiers, and anyone else willing to pledge loyalty into a formidable warrior band, distinguished by their red headgear, which earned them the name *kizilbash* ("red head").

SAFAVIDS AND SHI'ISM IN IRAN

At some point after 1450, the leader of the Safavis decided to embrace Shi'a Islam, perhaps to mark his leadership off from all the competition. He began to claim descent from Ali. His grandson Ismail—at age 14—led *kizilbash* warriors to several victories and in 1501 established a dynastic state with the northwestern Iranian city of Tabriz as its capital. By 1510 Ismail had taken over all of Iran and much of Iraq as well. He declared himself the Hidden Imam—in Shi'a theology, the messiah who will return at the right moment to bring justice to humankind. Ismail sought to cloak himself in the mantle of prestigious religious and political figures to enhance his legitimacy as ruler:

> My name is Shah Ismail.
> I am on God's side, the leader of warriors.
> My mother is Fatima, my father Ali.
> I too am one of the twelve Imams. . . .
> Know that I am the true coin of Haidar [i.e., Ali]
> Ever-living Khezer, and Jesus son of Mary.
> I am the Alexander of the people of this era.

Before he died in 1524, Ismail set about converting the entire population to Shi'a Islam, something prior Shi'a rulers had not attempted. He had to import scholars from afar because Iran had so few Shi'a. His son, Tahmasp, who ruled for 52 years (r. 1524–1576), took this program further. He closed brothels, taverns, and gambling dens and forbade shaving beards. He banned music from his court. The **Safavids** (Safavis as a Sufi brotherhood, Safavids as a ruling dynasty) executed or exiled Muslims who overtly resisted their religious program and instituted harsh penalties for rule-breakers—a bit like Calvin's Geneva, but on a larger scale.

As with many an embattled theocracy, relations with hostile neighbors made the Safavids sterner at home. They faced a powerful foe in the Ottoman Empire to the west, a champion of Sunni orthodoxy with whom they fought for most of the first half of the sixteenth century. They also fought another Sunni polity to their northeast, the Uzbeks. Despite a difficult military situation, the Safavids obtained a peace treaty with the Ottomans that recognized them as Shi'a Muslims rather than heretics or unbelievers. The Treaty of Amasya, signed in 1555, also secured the right of shahs in Iran to enforce the religion of their choice within their domain—coincidentally, the same year as the Peace of Augsburg that cemented similar rights for central European rulers. Both agreements soothed half a century of deadly religious rivalry by granting opponents legitimacy and allowing monarchs to impose their religions upon their subjects. The Safavids eventually endorsed forced conversion of Jews, Zoroastrians, and most Christians in their quest for uniform religious purity—and political security. The Safavids even turned on Sufis and massacred thousands.

SHI'ISM UNDER THE SAFAVIDS Under Safavid rule, Iran experienced a philosophical and religious reorientation. State power was at the center of it. The most effective of Safavid rulers, Shah Abbas I (r. 1587–1629), enjoyed great economic and military success, and supported artists and thinkers, at least of the sort he preferred—not Sufi sheikhs, whom he preferred to execute. He built a new capital at Isfahan, in west-central Iran, with lavish mosques and palaces. He supported painters, especially the miniaturists who became all the rage in Iran and northern India (Shah Tahmasp had been trained to paint in this tradition). Shah Abbas I also encouraged Shi'a theologians, who worked out a new religious orthodoxy that provided some much-needed glue for Safavid society and equally needed legitimacy for the state.

The most prominent of these theologians was Ṣadr ad-Dīn Muḥammad Shīrāzī (or **Mulla Sadra**, 1571–1640). He was born to a courtly family and moved to the capital of Isfahan for study as a young man. He developed unorthodox ideas that resulted in many years of exile to a village, where he began his writing career, trying to reconcile Sufi emotion and intuition with a more reasoned and intellectual Islam. A provincial governor who liked Mulla Sadra's message installed him as the head of a school in Shiraz, in southwestern Iran, where he built an arts and sciences curriculum. An English traveler who passed through in 1629 wrote: "Shyraz has a colledge wherein is read Philosophy, Astrology, Physick, Chemistry and the Mathematicks; so as 'tis the more famoused through Persia."

Safavid Iran, 1500–1630 The Safavid dynasty, originally from the southwestern shores of the Caspian Sea, imposed its Shi'a form of Islam as thoroughly as it could within its domain. This sharpened conflicts with Sunni rulers on its borders—notably the Ottomans and Uzbeks, with whom the Safavids warred frequently. The Treaty of Amasya (1555) reduced tensions with the Ottomans.

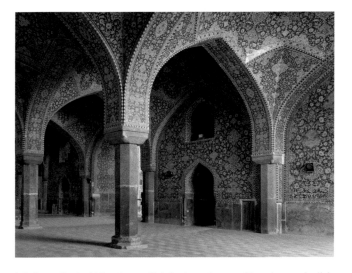

Isfahan Shah Abbas's capital featured magnificent new buildings like this mosque, known as the Shah Mosque, on which construction began in 1611. It remains famous for its extraordinary decorative tilework.

Mulla Sadra wrote prolifically on deep metaphysical and theological issues, squaring mystical Sufi impulses with the thought of earlier Muslim philosophers such as Ibn Sina (Avicenna). He leaned toward a personal, reflective engagement with the world and with God, and taught that one must live by the principles one's philosophy reveals. He died in Basra while en route to Mecca to perform his seventh hajj. He may fairly be considered the most influential Shi'a philosopher and, despite his early troubles with the authorities, the most important intellectual of Safavid Iran.

THE WIDER ISLAMIC WORLD The reformulation of Shi'a belief and its adoption as the state religion in Iran was the most important intellectual current within the Islamic world in these centuries, but it was far from the only one. Iranian refugees from Safavid persecution brought many new wrinkles in philosophy, art, and literature to northern India, including the tradition of miniatures in painting. Scholars in Timbuktu, which had some 150 Qur'anic schools in the sixteenth century, brought

West African Scholarship Scholars in Timbuktu in the sixteenth and seventeenth centuries created tens of thousands of manuscripts that recorded knowledge from across the Islamic world. This page is from a sixteenth-century Qur'an.

ideas and practices from Egypt to West Africa, often when returning from a hajj to Mecca. The annual practice of pilgrimage drew pious Muslims from West Africa to Southeast Asia together in Mecca, where they mingled for weeks or months, prayed together, and debated the fine points of religion. Muslim traders traveled far and wide, bringing their particular beliefs in their saddlebags. The quickening of commerce and the growth of cities, especially port and caravan cities, led to faster circulation of ideas and more friction among faiths and sects. Political turmoil in the Islamic world, as we will see in the next chapter, encouraged rulers to embrace legitimating ideologies, including religion above all, as the Safavids did when embracing Shi'a Islam.

SIKHISM IN INDIA: THE BIRTH OF A NEW RELIGION

New information and ideas from afar affected intellectual life in South Asia too, but not as disruptively as in lands to the west. The greatest departure came in the form of a new religion, now called **Sikhism**. It is a blend of Hindu and Islamic traditions with several innovative twists all its own.

Islam had first come to India in the eighth century. By the end of the tenth century it emerged a powerful political force, the religion of conquerors and rulers from Central Asia. Thereafter its followers jostled with India's more numerous followers of Hinduism, sometimes congenially, sometimes violently. Some thinkers emphasized the compatible features of the two religions to try to achieve a synthesis. This became a little easier with the rise of Sufism within Islam. Sufi sheikhs acquired saint-like status and their tombs attracted worshippers, similar to the shrines of the many Hindu gods. In the fifteenth century, a few thinkers arose in northwestern India claiming that Hinduism and Islam were two approaches to the same sacred truth.

NANAK'S TEACHINGS

The most influential of these was Nanak (1469–1539). He was born in a Hindu family of a merchant caste near Lahore, in Punjab, in today's Pakistan. He had a Muslim teacher, however, and showed keen interest as a youth in theology, philosophy, and poetry. He learned Sanskrit, the ancient language of the Hindu Vedas, as well as Arabic and Persian, giving him access to vast learning—not so different from his contemporary, Copernicus. His father tried to install him in positions as an accountant, his own line of work, but Nanak found keeping track of money tedious compared to the timeless questions of religion, righteousness, and truth. So, like Luther, he disappointed his father and sought elusive truths rather than a safe career. At age 27 he experienced a vision in which God told him that he, Nanak, was to be the prophet of the true religion. Nanak summarized his new message in the phrase "there is no Muslim, there is no Hindu." He left a wife and children to begin a long journey that purportedly took him all over India, to Tibet and Arabia. Everywhere he discussed the big questions about truth, existence, reality, and divinity, refining his message as he went.

Nanak's followers became known as Sikhs ("disciples" in the Punjabi language). They accepted his message that Hindusim and Islam are really one, and several other tenets that gave Sikhism a special character. Sikhs, like Muslims, accepted that there is but one God, the creator of all things. In contrast to most Indian religions, Sikhism held that God's supreme creation is humankind, and other living creatures are lesser beings. So Sikhs have no problem with eating meat, which followers of other Indian religions often avoid. Sikhism did accept reincarnation, more or less along the lines of Hinduism's principle of karma.

Nanak explicitly rejected the elaborate ceremonies of both Hinduism and Islam, just as Protestants scrapped much Catholic ritual. He preferred a more ascetic, personal, plain approach to God, without priests and their arcane knowledge. He regarded religious commitment as something one accepted as an adult, which Sikhs mark with a simple ceremony, rather than something one is born into—again, like some branches of Protestantism. Nanak rejected caste as well and preached an egalitarian creed in which the same moral codes applied to all regardless of birth, family, and status. He extended this to gender, claiming men and women were equal before God. Nanak also preached a strict pacifism, in line with some strains of Hindusim and a few sects of Protestantism. The parallels with Protestantism are not mere coincidence. Nanak and Luther both reacted against religions that seemed to them too ornate, remote, attentive to worldly concerns, and devoted to the self-interest of priests and officials.

THE DEVELOPMENT OF SIKHISM

Nanak Guru (meaning "leader" to Sikhs) died in 1539, but his religion lived on. He left behind an enormous number of hymns, which with a few additions are collectively called the *Adi Granth* (meaning "the first book"), the scripture for Sikhs. It is written mainly in Punjabi, not Sanskrit, and so was accessible to most any literate person in Nanak's part of India, rather as the translations of the Bible by Wycliffe and Luther made Christian scripture accessible to people who had not studied Latin, Greek, or Hebrew.

Subsequent gurus modified Nanak's teachings, most notably in response to persecution of Sikhs by Muslim princes in the early seventeenth century. After one guru was tortured to death in 1606, his son, Guru Har Gobind, the sixth guru, abandoned pacifism and started a Sikh military tradition that survives to this day. Any Sikh male of any background could become a member of a warrior class, called *singhs* ("lions"). They became famous for their valor in battle, which ensured the survival of Sikhism against many threats. Soon Sikh warriors were working as mercenaries here and there throughout South Asia.

Sikhism survived and flourished in north India. It held special attraction for women and low-caste Hindus, for whom it promised some degree of liberation. It also

Adi Granth A copy of the Sikh scripture from around the years 1660–1675 is illuminated with a simple geometric and floral pattern. Written in the vernacular language Punjabi, it was widely accessible to literate people in northwestern India.

Golden Temple Constructed in the 1570s, the Golden Temple at Amritsar became the most important site of worship for Sikhs. An anonymous Indian artist painted this watercolor of the temple around 1840.

appealed to cosmopolitan urban and merchant groups, who had some exposure to the diversity of religion in the Indian subcontinent and Indian Ocean world. It made a sufficiently good impression on the most powerful Muslim ruler of India, the Mughal emperor Akbar (r. 1556–1605), that he donated land for what would become the most important Sikh shrine, the Golden Temple in Amritsar, in the 1570s.

Ideas and information from the Americas or Oceania contributed nothing to the ferment from which Sikhism evolved. Instead, it represents an innovation favored by the tightening of the existing Old World web, rather than its expansion. Increased trade and urbanization created a social milieu in which Sikhism prospered. The constant frictions between Islam and Hindusim provided the spark that inspired Nanak to his quest for reconciliation.

CHINA AND JAPAN: CONFUCIAN REFORMATION AND IMPORTED CHRISTIANITY

In East Asia, as in India, Iran, and Europe, intellectual life had a long and refined formal tradition. Here too the new linkages of the sixteenth century jolted established ideas.

WANG YANGMING

In China since the late Song dynasty (960–1279), a coherent ideology held sway among the intellectual elite, one historians now call **neo-Confucianism**. It built on the ancient sages, Confucius and Mencius, but added an even stronger emphasis on self-cultivation and study in the quest for moral rectitude. It formed the core of the civil service examination, so every ambitious young man sought to master this philosophy in hopes of winning a prestigious place in the bureaucracy. Neo-Confucianism survived the downfall of the Song, the Mongol invasion of China, and the Yuan dynasty set up by the Mongols (1279–1368), and it was flourishing under the Ming dynasty (1368–1644).

But in the early sixteenth century, just when Luther and Nanak were shaking up Europe and India, a Chinese philosopher, **Wang Yangming**, mounted a challenge to the reigning ideology. He did not seek to repudiate Confucianism, but to improve upon it, so he too is called a neo-Confucian thinker.

Wang Yangming (1472–1529) was born to a family of the bureaucratic and intellectual class. His father had come in first in the civil service examinations in 1481, and Wang himself did well too, earning degrees at age 19 and 26 when many other men studied into their thirties trying to pass the examinations. He served in the imperial government in middling roles until he offended the palace eunuchs in 1506 (an offense his father had committed in his day as well). For his transgressions, Wang was publicly flogged and banished far from the capital.

Exile and isolation proved productive for Wang, as it would for Mulla Sadra in Iran. During his three-year banishment, Wang developed his distinctive brand of neo-Confucian thought. His fortunes revived and he won government appointments in southern China, where he distinguished himself by crushing rebellions. He still maintained an active scholarly career while holding official posts and holding forth to many admiring students.

Wang Yangming rejected one of the main tenets of the neo-Confucianism of his youth, which treated knowledge as available only through dedicated study. Although himself a champion at book learning, Wang began to argue that true knowledge could not be separated from action and experience. Indeed, he maintained, one did not need book learning to understand truth and morality. Ordinary people, Wang claimed, could as readily obtain wisdom and

CONSIDERING THE EVIDENCE

A Hymn by Kabir in the *Adi Granth*

India had no shortage of holy men when Guru Nanak founded the community that would become the Sikh religion. *Pirs, bhagats, mullahs, sants, qazis, swami*s, *brahmins, pandits*, and *gurus*; these devotees all defended their doctrine and practices with arguments from the Hindu Vedas and the Muslim Qur'an, just as Protestants and Catholics turned to the Bible for support in their debates. Yet, both Hinduism and Islam also inspired mystics who tired of orthodox religion and the sectarian squabbling it inspired. They rejected rational arguments and the external rituals of fasting, prayer, and pilgrimage as being inferior to an intense, internal devotion to God. Kabir, for instance, was a weaver born in the early fifteenth century to Muslim parents who became the disciples of a Hindu holy man. He lived hundreds of miles away and decades before Guru Nanak; but the Sikh gurus who compiled the *Adi Granth* as their faith's scripture decided to include over 500 of Kabir's songs alongside their own teachings. As shown in the following hymn, Kabir taught that both Hinduism and Islam point to the same God, but everyone needs a personal guru to awaken them to the presence of God in their own hearts.

If Allah lives in a mosque,
to whom belongs the rest of the land?
Hindus say His name dwells in an idol:
I see the truth in neither.

Allah, Ram, I live by Your name.
Be merciful, O Sain. (Rest)

The south is Hari's abode; Allah's camp
is in the west. Look inside your own heart—
inside your heart of hearts—
there is His abode, His camp.

Brahmins fast twice a month twenty-four times;
qazis fast in the month of Ramadan:
Neglecting the remaining eleven months,
they search for treasure in one month.

Why go and bathe in Orissa?
Why bow heads in a mosque?
You're a thug at heart.
Why pray and go on a *hajj* to the Ka'aba.

All these men and women—
they are Your forms.

Kabir is the infant of Ram-Allah;
everyone is my guru, my *pir*.

Kabir says, "Listen, O men and women,
seek only one shelter:
Repeat His name, O mortals.
Only then will you swim across."

Source: Nirmal Dass, *Songs of Kabir from the Adi Granth* (Albany, 1991), pp. 251–252.

QUESTIONS FOR ANALYSIS

1. Does Kabir want Hindus and Muslims to stop praying or fasting, or is he more concerned about their intentions during worship?
2. How do Kabir's critiques of both Hindus and Muslims help him find the common ground of both faiths?
3. Which lines in Kabir's hymn would have appealed to the Sikh gurus who compiled the *Adi Granth*?

act ethically as the most learned of scholars. He believed "the nature of all humans is good" and that anyone, however humble, has innate knowledge and could attain moral perfection. All that stood between people and moral perfection was selfish desire, so freeing oneself from that was key. One can see undertones of Buddhist philosophy, familiar to many Chinese intellectuals, in his logic.

This viewpoint was revolutionary in the context of the Confucian tradition and made Wang in effect a traitor to his class. His confidence in ordinary folk led him to maintain that "all the people filling the street are sages"—a heretical thought in China. His philosophy bore some resemblance to Lutheranism or Sikhism, which held that people could achieve spiritual perfection on their own without guidance from priests.

Wang's philosophy attracted many adherents during the sixteenth century, and in retrospect he stands among the most influential thinkers in the Confucian tradition.

Young strivers of modest means found his message liberating. Wang Yangming study groups proliferated for decades after his death. His philosophy won admirers in Japan too.

Wang Yangming's revision to neo-Confucianism was only one strand in the tapestry of Chinese thought and belief, but it was the most influential and enduring. Other developments included a Buddhist revival among elites that spread in the late sixteenth century with support from an empress, and the arrival of Christianity, brought by missionaries beginning in 1583.

CHRISTIANITY IN CHINA AND JAPAN

In China, Christianity came mainly with the Jesuits, of whom about 900 made the perilous trip from Europe. In the early seventeenth century they met with some success, converting three high officials and thereby acquiring some protection. The Jesuits generally concentrated on the top rungs, the high literati, of Chinese society and used technical knowledge to get a hearing. At the Ming court, Jesuit skills in map making and cannon casting were of particular interest.

In general, however, Christianity was a hard sell to the Confucian literati. They had spent decades mastering a philosophical-religious system that carried immense prestige in China and had no need to exchange it for another. As a practical matter, Christian morality was often a sticking point, as many Chinese literati had concubines in their households. At a maximum, Christianity won over about 1 percent of the Chinese population, and the proportion fell after the late seventeenth century when the Jesuits tried to embrace a new dynasty of conquerors from Manchuria, the Qing. The Jesuits achieved some success with the Qing imperial household, especially that of the great emperor Kangxi (r. 1661–1722), but they never found broad adherence among the Chinese elite.

Christianity also took root in Japan, as we saw at the start of this chapter. Europeans first arrived, shipwrecked on southern islands, in 1543, and missionaries, mainly Spanish and Portuguese, arrived in 1549 beginning with Francis Xavier and Anjirō. As in China, missionaries in Japan focused first on the upper classes, especially the great landowners called *daimyo* who in the sixteenth century dominated the country. Francis Xavier considered the

Japanese to be "of very good manners, good in general and not malicious." Most Japanese, however, regarded missionaries, and other Europeans, as "southern barbarians" and wanted little to do with them except perhaps trade. Missionaries found it convenient to double as importers of exotic goods. Japan was among the world's most urbanized societies, which made the business of conversion a little easier because missionaries could reach bigger audiences in cities. Japan's political divisions also helped the missionaries by preventing any single authority from banning the southern barbarians.

Mission efforts—staffed mainly by Japanese who had already embraced Christianity—converted some 2 to 3 percent of Japan's population, or 200,00 to 300,000 people, by 1590. Christians lived in every province. Hundreds of churches opened. Even some of Christianity's less appealing practices caught on, such as self-flagellation

Christianity in China A sixteenth-century engraving shows the Jesuit missionary Matteo Ricci (left) and Xu Guangqi, a Chinese scholar who converted to Christianity. The two men are depicted in a church, illustrated with a mix of Chinese and Jesuit iconography.

with whips as a way to compensate for sin. But after 1590, rulers of an increasingly unified Japan, including men who had formerly shown some interest in Christianity, tried to prevent conversion. Eager to minimize foreign influence, the government officially banned Christianity in 1597 and again, more effectively, in 1614. Churches were torn down, missionaries expelled, Christian communities conquered by force of arms, and roughly 4,000 converts executed. By 1640, Christianity in Japan was on the edge of extinction, surviving only as an underground religion.

REPRESSION AND PERSECUTION

Reactions against novel religious and intellectual movements, like the suppression of Christianity in Japan, were routine among elites and rulers wedded to existing ideologies. The most secure rulers, however, showed great interest in diverse religions—rather like the Mongol court in the thirteenth century. Among these were Shah Abbas I in Safavid Iran, and two whom we'll see more of in the next chapter—Akbar the Great in Mughal India and Mehmet the Conqueror in the Ottoman Empire. But their successors, often feeling less secure in their power, generally organized clampdowns and persecutions. In Europe, Catholic authorities revitalized the Inquisition in the sixteenth century and supported religious wars against Protestants, and Protestant kings did their best to reciprocate. In Iran, the Safavids eventually attacked just about all religious groups and movements other than their preferred version of Shi'a Islam. Sunni Muslims, Sufis, Christians, Jews, and Zoroastrians all felt the consequences. In India in the early seventeenth century, the Sikhs went from being pacifists to militarists in response to assaults from Muslim princes.

In China, by 1580 a concerted reaction against Wang Yangming's followers took shape, and many were imprisoned or executed. Catholicism in China also provoked official reaction. The Jesuits backed a losing candidate in an imperial succession struggle, and the winner, the Yongzheng Emperor, banned Christianity in China in 1724.

The Scientific Revolution, compared to the several religious movements discussed in this chapter, provoked

Anti-Christian Reaction Dozens of Christians—including several European missionaries—are beheaded and burned at the stake in this seventeenth-century Japanese illustration of the turn against Christianity in unified Japan that started in 1597.

less official reaction. Galileo and Kepler both met with hostility from church authorities, but Galileo had initially found support from the Pope and the Jesuits when attacked by the Inquisition. Only after he went to some lengths to offend the Pope was he forced to renounce his views and confined to house arrest. But most of the new science did not trouble the church, and indeed much of it was conducted by churchmen or devout Christians like Boyle and Newton. About half the mathematics professors in seventeenth-century Europe were Jesuits.

In any case, the political divisions within Europe made clampdowns on new ideas ineffective in comparison with comparable efforts in China after 1580 or Japan after 1590. Religious disunity flourished in Europe, as in India, as did rival schools of scientific thought, and no prince, however determined, could change that. In Europe, unlike in India, easy access to information, a result of the spread of the printing press and the shared use of Latin among scholars, also made it hard for authorities to clamp down.

INTELLECTUAL UPHEAVAL: PARALLELS AND CONTRASTS

The entire process of intellectual upheaval in Eurasia was uneven in three main respects. First, as we have seen, it was geographically uneven, affecting Europe more than the rest of Eurasia, and within Europe some parts more than others. Part of the unevenness within Eurasia had to do with Europe's political fragmentation and Atlantic Europe's greater involvement in global circuits than anywhere else. Much of the unevenness within Europe had to do with local circumstances such as the fact that Calvin took refuge in Geneva rather than somewhere else.

Second, everywhere the intellectual upheaval affected cities and especially trading cities, more—or at least sooner—than the countryside. Remote mountain villages in Asia were less likely to be buffeted by the currents of

Sikhism or neo-Confucianism than were the cities, where new ideas arrived more frequently and were likelier to win followers.

Third, intellectual upheaval was socially uneven. Although the religious transformations of the Reformation(s) and the conversion of Iran to Shi'ism rippled through all levels of society, and the spread of Sikhism touched the lower classes first and foremost, much of this turbulence shook only the elite. Chinese peasants, with the rarest of exceptions, did not know that Wang Yangming and his followers considered them equally as capable of moral perfection as the most learned Confucian scholar. Polish peasants remained entirely unaware that Copernicus was charting a new map of the heavens. English peasants did not know that Newton was formulating an elegantly precise mathematical account of the force of gravity. They and their counterparts, 90 percent of the population of Eurasia, had hungry children, sick

Women Intellectuals The German entomologist and botanist Maria Sibylla Merian, shown here in a 1679 portrait alongside one of her detailed color paintings of butterflies and caterpillars, was one of the women whose work contributed to the Scientific Revolution and other early modern intellectual movements.

babies, tired muscles, fickle weather, ravenous tax collectors, and a hundred other things on their minds every day. Although they worried about what might follow upon death, whether or not to do what priests told them to do, and even contemplated the mysteries of divinity, they generally could not spare much time for moral philosophy or mathematical equations.

There is a fourth respect in which the intellectual and religious turbulence of these centuries was uneven, but consistently so across Eurasia. None of the great religious reformers, philosophers, or scientists mentioned in this chapter were women. Some European women did make contributions to scientific work, such as Margaret Cavendish (1623–1673), an English duchess who wrote poetry, plays, and several works on moral philosophy. She undertook scientific experiments and was once—controversially—permitted to attend a meeting of the Royal Society. Maria Sibylla Merian (1647–1717) was a German entomologist and botanist who published the first detailed work on caterpillars and their metamorphosis into butterflies. She also undertook a self-funded scientific expedition to South America and produced a landmark study of the insects of Surinam.

But the truth is none of them were anywhere near as influential as Copernicus, Galileo, Harvey, or Newton. No women in Iran, India, or China had anything like the impact on religion or philosophy of Mulla Sadra, Nanak, or Wang Yangming. We can be sure that some women were just as interested in truth, the heavens, health, alchemy, morality, divinity, as any man—as the record of more recent centuries shows. But fewer women than men could act upon an interest in these and other intellectual matters. Women were less likely to be able to read than were men, and in most places far less likely. They were much more likely to face discouragement from family and society if they showed inclination toward deep thinking. A French aristocrat, Martine Berterau, who published a book on mining engineering, was charged with witchcraft, as was her husband.

Women were often forbidden to be members of universities, madrasas, and academies. When in 1678 the University of Padua awarded a PhD to Elena Cornaro, a Venetian noblewoman, the university promptly revised its statutes to prevent women from taking degrees. The Swedish aristocrat Eva Ekeblad in 1748 was elected to the Swedish Royal Academy of Sciences for her successful distillation of alcohol from potatoes. But in 1751 she was demoted to honorary membership, on the principle that full academicians should be men. The rare exception was Laura Bassi, the second woman anywhere to earn a doctorate, which she did in 1732 at age 20 from the University of Bologna in Italy. That same year she was appointed there as a chaired professor of physics. She taught science for the next 45 years and conducted experiments in electricity—meanwhile bearing 12 children. But by and large, women could not and did not hold positions like Bassi's; and whatever their inclinations and talents, they did not influence intellectual agendas and paths in major ways. So the religious schisms and revivals, the philosophical twists and turns, the Scientific Revolution—as well as all the efforts to suppress these novelties—were overwhelmingly the work of men.

CONCLUSION

The Eurasian landmass in the sixteenth and seventeenth centuries experienced unusual intellectual and religious turbulence. Ideas, ideologies, and religions are of course changing all the time. But sometimes they change faster and more radically, and this was such a time. This turbulence always had important local causes bound up in the politics and social changes of particular places, such as the demographic trends that underlay the witch craze or the fragmentation of Japan that gave Christian missionaries an opening. But it also had larger, looser causes connected to both the expansion and the consolidation of what was becoming the Global web.

Those general causes included the difficulty of making sense of new data within old systems of thought. Observations from distant continents after 1492, and distant planets after 1608 (the date of the invention of the telescope), called old wisdom into question and set curious minds to work. This particular source of intellectual turbulence was strongest in Europe, because Europe was much more involved in overseas linkages to hitherto isolated lands than was anywhere else in Eurasia. And the telescope and microscope were European inventions.

At the same time that new information was flooding into the minds of Europeans, the flow of ideas and information more generally sped up. In Europe, the printing press played a big role in that. But everywhere in the sixteenth and seventeenth centuries, even in those parts of Eurasia least affected by seaborne commerce to the Americas, the pace of trade, travel, and urbanization crept upward. More people came into more frequent contact with strangers bearing exotic notions. While new ideas were usually shunned, from time to time they appealed to people, who explored them and sometimes adopted them. Or, more often, adapted them into their prior schemes of religion and thought, and in so doing altered those schemes.

Despite their local causes and distinctive characters, these new intellectual and religious movements—many of them—shared some common features. In most of them one can find an emphasis on personal responsibility and personal approaches to truth or God, with minimal mediation from priests, as in Lutheranism, Sikhism, and to some extent the Shi'a movement in Iran. One can find an appeal to the value of experience, as in Wang Yangming's thought and the Scientific Revolution. These common threads reflect not so much interaction among these movements, but similar reactions to dissatisfaction with the entrenched, institutionalized, stolid religions and ideologies, all of them seemingly slow to adapt to changing times.

Most of these intellectual and religious innovations survived into the twenty-first century. Today, in retrospect, we can say that the most important among them was the Scientific Revolution, as it laid the foundations for the technological transformations that distinguish modern times. At the time, however, the religious upheavals seemed most important. They meant more to more people. And they helped to animate the political struggles of the early modern centuries, to which we turn in the next chapter.

CHAPTER REVIEW

KEY TERMS

Jesuits (p. 517)
printing press (p. 519)
Renaissance (p. 522)
Protestantism (p. 525)
Catholic Reformation (p. 526)

witch hunts (p. 527)
Scientific Revolution (p. 527)
heliocentric system (p. 528)
Shi'a Islam (p. 531)
Safavids (p. 532)

Mulla Sadra (p. 533)
Sikhism (p. 534)
Adi Granth (p. 535)
neo-Confucianism (p. 536)
Wang Yangming (p. 536)

Go to INQUIZITIVE to see what you've learned—and learn what you've missed—with personalized feedback along the way.

REVIEW QUESTIONS

1. How did new geographic and scientific discoveries lead to the weakening of existing intellectual traditions?

2. Why was the printing revolution mainly confined to Europe and European colonies for many centuries?

3. What was the source and the main emphasis of the Renaissance?

4. What political and technological conditions helped Luther and his ideas evade Catholic persecution?

5. What principles formed the basis of the Scientific Revolution, and what procedures were at its heart?

6. What measures did the Safavids introduce to transform Iran into a Shi'a theocracy?

7. Whom did Sikhism attract, and why?

8. Why was conversion to Christianity unpopular in China and Japan?

9. Why was it more difficult for authorities to clamp down on new ideas in Europe than it was in China, Japan, and India?

10. What were the three main ways in which intellectual upheaval in Eurasia was uneven?

11. What common features did new intellectual and religious movements share, and what widespread trends did these commonalities reflect?

FURTHER READING

Rula Jurdi ABISAAB, *Converting Persia: Religion and Power in the Safavid Empire* (2015). A work that focuses on the Shi'a clerics imported into Iran by the Safavids.

Daniel BAYS, *A New History of Christianity in China* (2011). Chapter 2 discusses the Jesuits in the sixteenth century.

H. Floris COHEN, *The Rise of Modern Science Explained: A Comparative History* (2015). An excellent and readable study.

Carlos EIRE, *Reformations: The Early Modern World, 1450–1650* (2016). A massive, insightful work with a focus on Europe.

Philip IVANHOE, *Ethics in the Confucian Tradition: The Thought of Mengzi and Wang Yangming* (2002). A dense but thorough exploration of Wang's ideas.

Gurinder Singh MANN, *The Sikhs* (2004). A basic primer on Sikh history and belief.

Colin MITCHELL, *The Practice of Politics in Safavid Iran: Power, Religion and Rhetoric* (2011). A work of serious scholarship rather than an introductory text, but the author contextualizes religion well through the time of Shah Abbas I.

Lawrence PRINCIPE, *The Scientific Revolution: A Very Short Introduction* (2011). A perceptive look into the mindset of the time.

Lyndal ROPER, *Martin Luther: Renegade and Prophet* (2017). The 500th anniversary of Luther's 95 theses inspired several new biographies, of which this serious but readable account might be the best.

CHRONOLOGY

1453
Ottomans besiege Constantinople

1508–1519
Emperor Maximilian I's reign

ca. 1490
Very large cannon introduced

1520–1566
Suleiman's reign

1516–1517
Ottomans defeat Mamluks and conquer Egypt and the Hejaz

Chinese ship brings Portuguese guns to Japan

1526
Mughals conquer sultanate of Delhi

1543

1547–1584
Ivan the Terrible's reign

1556–1605
Akbar's reign

1550s
Habsburgs acquire windfall of silver from Americas

ca. 1590
Introduction of disciplined and drilled standing armies

1591
Saadians conquer Songhai in West Africa

1592–1598
Toyotomi Hideyoshi's Korea campaign

1638
Manchus conquer Korea

ca. 1620–1680
Zheng family flourishes

ca. 1600
Japan is unified; start of Tokugawa shogunate

1644
End of Ming dynasty and start of Qing dynasty

1682–1725
Peter the Great's reign

1662–1722
Kangxi emperor's reign

1658–1707
Aurangzeb's reign

1694
National banks invented

University of War

EMPIRES AND POWER

1450 to 1800

Z heng Zhilong and his son were the most successful pirates in world history. Zheng the elder was born to a Chinese gentry family. In 1622, at age 18, unhappy with his schooling, he ran off to Macao (a Portuguese trading post in southern China), where he had an uncle. He learned Portuguese, was baptized a Christian, and soon took up trade and piracy. Sent by his uncle to Japan, he married a Japanese woman, Tagawa Matsu. Their son, Zheng Chenggong (1624–1662), although born and raised in Japan, was sent to study in a Chinese Confucian academy in hopes that he would qualify for the Ming dynasty's bureaucratic elite. But Zheng Chenggong (also known as Koxinga or Coxinga) eventually joined the family business.

Active along the southeastern coasts of China, from Nanjing to Macao, the Zheng family ran an international trade and piracy operation. In 1628, they captured nearly half of the recorded Chinese ships returning from the Philippines laden with silver. A Chinese governor explained why:

> The Zheng pirate gang is very clever and tricky, and good at sea fighting. Their pirate troops...consist mainly of Chinese bandits, with some Japanese

1719–1722
Bartholomew Roberts captures 400 ships in the Atlantic and Caribbean

ca. 1750
Qing crush Zunghars

1735–1796
Qianlong emperor's reign

Military Prowess The early Mughal ruler Babur leads his forces in besieging a city—one of the early conquests that enabled the Mughals to accumulate a land empire in Central Asia. Babur's army includes war elephants and cavalry, but also guns and cannon. Innovations from technology to tactics transformed warfare across the world during the early modern period.

FOCUS QUESTIONS

1. What general conditions contributed to the growth of empires in the early modern period?

2. What were the most important components of the military revolution during this period?

3. What role did firearms play in the consolidation of power in Japan?

4. Why was the Qing dynasty so effective over its first century and a half?

5. How were the Mughals able to create a multireligious empire in India?

6. What policies helped in the expansion of Ottoman rule during this period?

7. What initiatives of Ivan III and Peter the Great strengthened the power of the Russian state?

8. How did the Habsburgs become rulers of the first global empire?

9. What was the "university of war," and how did it strengthen European states?

10. How did smaller states adapt to the changes wrought by the military revolution?

11. How did nomads and pirates fare during this period of growing state power?

and Europeans. Their war ships and weapons are manufactured by the distant barbarians [i.e., the Dutch]. Their ships are tall and solid, and their cannon can hit targets miles away.

From the late 1620s to the 1680s, no one could trade safely on the southeast China coast without permission from the Zheng family. In the 1650s, they employed some 400,000 sailors and soldiers, mostly Chinese and Japanese, but also some Europeans and a 300-man East African bodyguard. Their fleets included 5,000 ships.

The Zhengs and their sea captains raided and traded far and wide in East Asian waters. When the Chinese Empire tried to deny him supplies and bases on the mainland, Zheng Chenggong conquered the island of Taiwan, then held by the Dutch East India Company. His captains controlled 80 percent of the trade to Japan, carried cargoes from Cambodia and Thailand, and raided as far afield as the Philippines. He organized his own bank and minted coins.

The Zhengs were in effect building their own maritime state when Zheng Chenggong died, probably of malaria, at age 39 in 1662. They used all the resources at hand in their quest for power and wealth: Dutch and Chinese shipbuilding skills; Dutch and Portuguese cannon; Chinese and Japanese manpower; their own wide knowledge of East Asian coasts, islands, and waters; and their deep fund of daring. They ultimately lost, crushed by China's improving military in the early 1680s.

The Zhengs were among many such losers in the centuries between 1450 and 1800, often called the early modern period. Pirates, nomads, and the rulers of hundreds of small states, few of them as powerful as the Zheng clan at its height, lost out to larger, imperial states. These empires flourished as they grew more successful at winning over subject people's loyalties, more skilled at tax collection, and above all, more effective in using new technologies and techniques of violence.

This chapter deals with political, military, and economic history in an age of imperial consolidation. It explains how a handful of great powers arose, how they sometimes competed with one another, and how they shared (often unwillingly) technologies and techniques useful to states. In particular, it focuses on Tokugawa Japan, Qing China, Mughal India, the Ottoman Empire, Russia, and the Habsburg Empire. It includes more about military matters than any previous chapter, because in these centuries military innovations came thick and fast, spread throughout the Global web, and carried greater consequences for the global distribution of wealth and power than ever before.

These imperial powers used their improved skills and technologies to destroy hundreds of smaller states, crush pirates like the Zhengs, suppress bandits, and overwhelm tribal peoples—anyone who stood in their way. They took over lands formerly filled with peoples living in principalities, city-states, tribal confederations, or in no state whatsoever. In political terms, the big got bigger. The small polities and the peoples without states became fewer, surviving mainly in nooks and crannies of world politics such as high mountains, barren deserts, or unhealthy swamps—outside the nodes and threads of the Global web. The variety of political formats in which people lived became smaller—another example of how the globalizing web-building process reduced diversity.

EARLY MODERN EMPIRE IN GLOBAL PERSPECTIVE

The main reason that the big political fish gobbled up the small fish in the early modern period is that the economics of power evolved in ways that favored big fish. In almost every part of the world, the costs of projecting power rose, especially the technologies and techniques of warfare. Big states could bear those costs with less difficulty than small ones.

The history of empire gives us a valuable perspective on these developments. Today, there are very few states conventionally called empires, so it is easy to regard them as abnormal. But between Sargon of Akkad and today—and especially since the formation of the Roman and Han empires roughly 2,000 years ago—most of the world's people most of the time lived in empires. Most empires came and went quickly, even powerful ones such as those of Alexander the Great or Genghis Khan. Only a few endured, such as the Chinese, dynasty after dynasty—and even it experienced interludes of chaos and disunity.

World history shows two main periods when big

	GLOBAL	PROPORTION LIVING IN THE
DATE	POPULATION	SIX MOST POPULOUS STATES
1500	438 million	36% (China, Muscovy/Russia, Aztec Empire, Inka Empire, France, Ottoman Empire)
1600	556 million	55% (China, Russia, Japan, Mughal India, Ottoman Empire, Habsburg Empire)
1700	603 million	60% (China, Russia, Japan, Mughal India, Ottoman Empire, Habsburg Empire)
1800	950 million	57% (China, Russia, Japan, Mughal India, Ottoman Empire, France)

PROPORTION OF GLOBAL POPULATION IN THE MOST POPULOUS STATES, 1500–1800

Sources: Colin McEvedy and Richard Jones, *Atlas of World Population History* (1978), 55–60, 78–82, 137, 166–75, 179–89; Angus Maddison, *The World Economy* (2001), 241–43; Max Roser's website Our World in Data: https://ourworldindata.org/world-population-growth.

empires grew bigger. The first occurred between about 600 BCE and 100 CE, when Achaemenid Persia, Mauryan India, Rome, and Han China emerged and expanded. For the first time, single states controlled big territories, including all the most populous parts of the world. The second period was the one under consideration in this chapter, roughly the period 1450–1800.

Seen within a single national or imperial tradition, these surges in empire may appear to be accidental or the work of extraordinarily great leaders. Seen in world-historical perspective, they appear as parallel processes with some connections uniting them. In the first era of imperial growth and consolidation (600 BCE–100 CE), the challenge of steppe warriors helped inspire people to band together into larger and larger agrarian states in places such as Persia and China.

In the second era (1450–1800 CE), as we shall soon see, the parallels and connections were even stronger, showing the Global web in action. Empires learned military and fiscal techniques from one another, adopted technologies used effectively by others, and in the process came to resemble one another more as time went on. Improved printing technology sped the flow of information generally, including manuals on naval shipbuilding, army maneuvers, and other military topics. The mobility of experts, especially military architects and shipwrights, promoted the spread of information as well. Although rulers in possession of the best military technologies and expertise generally tried to keep it for themselves, by 1600 it had become harder than ever to keep useful secrets of power from one's neighbors.

Population figures help illustrate the growth of big states (see table on page 547). In 1500, about 36 percent of the global population lived in the six most populous states; by 1700, by which time the roster of most populous states had changed, that proportion was 60 percent. Two main developments underlay this trend: the Inka and Aztec empires had disappeared from the list of most populous states, to be replaced by the Habsburg Empire and Japan; and the big states in Eurasia had gotten bigger.

Military Revolution A sixteenth-century Dutch etching, "The Battle of the Moneybags and the Strongboxes," satirizes the fact that the military revolution was only available to monarchs with treasuries large enough to bankroll it.

WARFARE AND ITS PRICE: THE MILITARY REVOLUTION

Every state and society conducted war in its own way, shaped by its own culture, traditions, and constraints. Societies without horses—as in the pre-Columbian Americas, for example—fought on foot. Mongols and other steppe peoples fought on horseback. South Asians often used war elephants. Some states had navies, but most did not. The reasons for war also differed, and often went no deeper than a monarch's quest for glory. But states also fought in the name of religion—or at least their ruler's religion. Most wars were also fought for control over land or people, and the wealth and prestige that control might bring. Vikings and the kings of Kongo often fought to acquire slaves for sale. And, as we've seen, the Aztecs fought to acquire captives for sacrifice.

All these approaches to warfare had proven effective in their specific settings. Now, however, with the formation of the Global web, several new and useful technologies and techniques of fighting spread widely, replacing some of the local variations. War elephants and big armored horses, for example, gradually became obsolete.

In the years between 1450 and 1800, war grew more expensive and complex just about everywhere. Historians call this development the **military revolution**. It happened at different times, and at different paces, in different places. Many trends underpinned the military revolution. Here we will touch on six.

BIGGER BATTALIONS, HIGHER TAXES

In the seventeenth century French soldiers had a saying: "God is on the side of the bigger battalions." The first reason warfare became so costly was the expansion of the scale of military operations, with larger armies and, in some cases, navies. In the sixteenth and seventeenth centuries, big empires spent 60 to 90 percent of their state budgets on their armed forces. (Today, the U.S. government spends about 15 to 20 percent of its budget on its military.) By 1700, several states around the world had learned how to organize, equip, and field armies of more than 100,000 men, and a few, mostly Atlantic European states of modest size, boasted battle fleets of dozens of large ships each studded with 40, 50, even 100 heavy cannon.

A second trend was the availability of greater funding for war. It was both a cause and a consequence of the trend toward bigger and costlier militaries. More money supported more expensive forms of warfare for kings, but costlier forms of warfare also required monarchs to find more funding. Usually, this entailed making taxation more efficient. It often also involved financial practices that made it easier for states to borrow money, either through the invention of national banks (beginning in 1694), the courting of private bankers, or the practice of

Oceanic Navies States that built ocean-going fleets in the early seventeenth century included Japan (left) and the Ottoman Empire (right), whose galleys were better suited to the quieter waters of the Mediterranean.

tax farming—an arrangement in which an entrepreneur advanced money to a ruler in exchange for permission to extract taxes in the future.

The vast expansion of commerce around the world beginning in the sixteenth century enlarged the tax base for monarchs. It also made it feasible for kings and emperors to demand taxes in the form of money, rather than in rice, maize, or labor. The monetization of taxes enabled rulers to pay more professional soldiers and buy more equipment.

Despite these innovations and opportunities, most successful monarchs teetered on the edge of bankruptcy in wartime. They had to negotiate, often in a hurry, with anyone who had vast wealth, in hopes of getting cash quickly in order to pay troops. This financial desperation proved a consistent check on monarchs' power, and it gave people with ready cash, such as big merchants and bankers, great leverage with which to pursue their own interests. In short, the rise of trade and finance—again, the Global web in action—made the military revolution affordable for a fortunate few monarchs, with the effect of often putting rulers at the mercy of bankers.

NAVIES AND ARTILLERY

A third trend of the military revolution that made war more complex and expensive was the emergence of oceanic navies. Local navies operating close to home had existed for more than 2,000 years, but oceanic navies were novel. As we saw in Chapter 16, Ming China built one beginning in 1405 but abandoned it after 1433. Over the next four

centuries, China's navy stayed close to home, patrolling rivers, canals, and inshore waters, battling pirates such as the Zhengs but not sailing the open sea. Atlantic European states, however, began to build ocean-going navies and kept expanding and improving them.

Their main innovation was to build ships big and sturdy enough to serve as gun platforms for heavy cannon. Building such ships was expensive and took great expertise. The workhorse of the British Royal Navy in 1780, the 74-gun ship, cost ten times as much to build as the largest factory in Britain. But such ships allowed monarchs to project power—through bombardments—anywhere on Earth within reach of the sea. This capacity more than anything else accounts for the rise to global power of five small Atlantic European states: Portugal, Spain, France, the Netherlands, and Britain.

Other Eurasian and North African states built navies too, but usually with galleys and small craft, not ocean-going cannon platforms. An exception was Japan between about 1600 and 1635: it built a few hundred armed merchant vessels that each carried about six or eight cannon, used mainly in trading with Southeast Asia. But these ships were small and unsuited to naval warfare, and in any case in 1635 Japan stopped making them.

Most rulers preferred not to compete at sea and to focus their efforts on land. An English doctor wrote of Aurangzeb, the last of the powerful emperors of Mughal India, in the 1670s, "if the King's Fleet be but ordinary, considering so great a Monarch . . . , it is because he minds it not; he [is] contenting himself in the enjoyment of the *continent* [India], and styles the Christians Lions of the Sea; saying that God has allotted that Unstable Element for their Rule." Heavy cannon mounted on sturdy ships enabled "Christians"—more precisely, Atlantic Europeans—to become the lions of the sea.

A fourth trend was the development of **field artillery and fortification**. Beginning in the early fifteenth century, armies lugged cannon into battle. By the 1490s, they used cannon so large that teams of horses or oxen, or a couple of elephants, might be needed to haul them around. To counter the power of such weapons, military architects built new kinds of fortresses with thick walls—those at the fortress of Kumbharlgarh in northwest India, built in the fifteenth century, were 15 feet (4.5 m) thick. The new fortresses had to be big, bristling with artillery, and designed according to geometric principles. It often took 20 years to construct one. In Italy, both Michelangelo and Leonardo da Vinci used their architectural skills designing fortresses before succeeding as artists. The new fortresses also needed garrisons, supplies, and plenty of cannon of their own, all of which made them extremely costly. But the cost of not building them, if one's neighbors had capable field artillery, was surrender.

STANDING ARMIES

A fifth trend came later, in the 1590s: the formation of disciplined and drilled standing armies. Most monarchs before 1590 recruited men for fighting only when they needed them. They paid military entrepreneurs to raise armies of mercenaries. When there was no war brewing, monarchs didn't want to pay for an army. From the 1590s onward, this system began to give way to one of standing, professional armies that rulers had to pay in times of both war and peace.

The main reason for this change was the effectiveness of drilled and disciplined infantry armed with reasonably accurate muskets—long, smoothbore guns developed in the sixteenth century. Dutch and Ottoman war captains pioneered drill, apparently independently of one another. They found, as had Japanese and others, that musket fire was devastatingly effective in volleys. They arranged musketeers in parallel lines (ranks) and taught them to fire, reload, and fire on command. While one rank fired, another was busy reloading. To do this quickly, without injuring one's fellows, and while one's closest comrades were being wounded and killed, required iron discipline.

Ottoman Drill A painting shows Ottoman troops from the era of the sixteenth-century sultan Suleiman in battle. It took years of drilling to achieve coordination among the ranks of artillery, infantry, and cavalry attacking in formation.

To achieve it, Dutch captains obliged their troops to drill endlessly on parade grounds until their choreographed motions were second nature. Close-order drill took years to master, so men had to be housed, fed, and clothed in peacetime at government expense. If unpaid, these men could turn their violent skills against civilians or kings. So wherever armies adopted drill, and therefore became standing armies, monarchs had to pay soldiers in peacetime and wartime alike to avoid chaos.

A sixth trend underlying the military revolution was the development of a more sophisticated logistical apparatus. With bigger armies and navies, someone had to come up with more horses, oxen, mules, camels, elephants, and their food; and more iron, steel, bronze, tin, wood, leather, and saltpeter (used in gunpowder) to be made into weapons and other war materiel. More men had to right places at the right times, and

be transported to the right places at the right times, and in the right proportions of infantry to cavalry to artillerymen, not to mention cooks, gunsmiths, engineers, and muleteers, camel drivers, or elephant handlers. All these animals, supplies, and people had to get across rivers, over mountains, or through deserts on schedule. Creating, maintaining, and deploying a big military machine required a military bureaucracy, made up of literate and numerate people with desk skills usually despised by men at arms.

To summarize, the innovations that made up the military revolution consisted of a hardware package of ships, cannon, muskets, gunpowder, and fortification, and a software package of improved financial systems, military engineering, infantry drill, and logistical bureaucracy. Rulers adopted those innovations that they could afford and that addressed the threats they faced.

Let's look at a few examples of states that to one degree or another adopted the innovations of the military revolution to become more powerful. This approach focuses on the winners in military competition. Some of the many losers are mentioned along the way, but there were many more that aren't.

THE TOKUGAWA CONSOLIDATION OF POWER IN JAPAN

An archipelago of perhaps 12 to 18 million people in 1500, Japan was politically fragmented. Any semblance of unity had vanished by the late fifteenth century, and thereafter numerous warlords fought one another for territory, resources, influence, and glory. None could count on the allegiance of, or extract taxes from, more than a couple of million people. But within 140 years Japan became a unified country. The process was bloody.

Locked in ruthless competition, Japan's warlords were open to innovations that might give them an edge. After 1500 their armies grew in size, and they turned increasingly to unskilled foot soldiers—ordinary peasants with no training or socialization in military culture. Warlords learned to integrate massed infantry into battle tactics. Sieges and elaborate fortification became the rule. Samurai

(an elite warrior class that took shape in the twelfth century) infantry and horsemen, formerly the cutting edge of Japanese warfare, now played smaller roles.

THE INTRODUCTION OF FIREARMS

In 1543, a Chinese pirate ship introduced Portuguese guns to Japan's vortex of violence. Guns required little training or skill to use, and so were well suited to the ordinary infantryman. Soon there were hundreds of thousands of firearms in Japan, and every warlord had to have plenty of them and figure out how to integrate them into his tactics.

In order to obtain guns, many warlords sold slaves. Chinese, Japanese, and Korean pirates had been enslaving coastal villagers off and on for centuries and selling them far from home. Now, Japanese warlords turned to slave exports, especially of young women, to Portuguese merchants, who in turn sold them in China or in Portuguese trading posts such as Macao or Goa. The Portuguese slave trade from Japan probably involved a few hundred people annually until the trade was outlawed soon after 1600. Many more slaves remained in Japan. As in West Africa and New Zealand, in Japan more guns meant more enslavement.

NOBUNAGA AND HIDEYOSHI

The most successful warlord at exploiting the political potential of guns was **Oda Nobunaga**, whose battlefield successes unified the southern half of Japan by 1580. He arranged his gunmen in tight formations to maximize their firepower, and perhaps—accounts are unclear on this—invented the tactic of volley fire. Nobunaga and his successors unified Japan by mobilizing hundreds of thousands of peasants and giving them guns manufactured by Japanese smiths. For a few decades, Japan made more guns than any other country in the world. A great change was taking place in Japan, a country where formerly only exquisitely trained warriors—samurai—could win battles. This change in the social foundation of war loosely resembled the transition in the ancient world from aristocratic warriors armed with bronze armor and weapons to mass armies using iron.

Oda Nobunaga's career exemplifies a pattern that would become increasingly common after 1500. As the Global web connected distant regions, ambitious rulers

Japan Invades Korea This painting shows an assault on a defensive position held by Hideyoshi's army in Korea in the 1590s. When Ming forces entered the war in Korea, Hideyoshi had to retreat to Japan.

time and again borrowed useful techniques and technologies from afar. They mastered them, modified them as needed, integrated them into local culture, and used them to smash or enslave rivals and neighbors, and build empires. The pattern was not new: the adoption of horses or iron in earlier times sometimes had had similar effects. From the sixteenth century onward, the adoption of guns produced this result in many cases around the world, including, as we saw, with King Kamehameha in Hawaii.

Upon Nobunaga's death in 1582, a former foot soldier and servant, **Toyotomi Hideyoshi**, out-maneuvered all rivals to succeed Nobunaga. In 1592, he decided to invade Korea and then China with 160,000 soldiers, a quarter of them gunmen. Japanese armies succeeded in Korea, where guns remained rare. Hideyoshi, who had tried to restrict the export of Japanese slaves in 1587, now eagerly enslaved and sold thousands of Koreans to Japanese and Portuguese buyers. In the end, China sent an army to Korea, and it became clear that Japan's sea power was not up to the task of supplying an overseas army against a large force. In 1598, Hideyoshi's Korea campaign ended in retreat.

At the same time that his soldiers ravaged Korea, Hideyoshi was defeating rival warlords in Japan. By his death in 1598, he had just about unified the country. That task was completed by his successor, a samurai, Tokugawa Ieyasu, who crushed rival forces loyal to Hideyoshi's young son. Only the sparsely populated northern island, Hokkaido, remained outside his realm.

ESTABLISHING THE TOKUGAWA SHOGUNATE

By 1600, Tokugawa Ieyasu stood supreme over a unified Japan. In 1603 he acquired the title of shogun (roughly: top general), which meant he was the de facto ruler of Japan. His descendants continued in that role until 1868 in a dynasty called the **Tokugawa shogunate**. With the country unified after 1600, and peace imposed (except on Hokkaido), Japan ceased to be a center of military innovation. Hideyoshi, despite his common origins, had begun the process of restoring samurai to their former status by banning peasants from owning weapons in 1588. Under the Tokugawa, that became entrenched policy, and only samurai could own and use weapons. The shoguns with their new military policy after 1600 reversed a social, democratizing—but bloody—revolution that helped bring them to power.

The process of consolidation continued into southernmost Hokkaido. There an indigenous population

The Unification of Tokugawa Japan, 1580–1603 The Japanese archipelago was politically fragmented for most of its history. But in the late sixteenth century, local leaders or warlords found ways to use guns effectively, destroy rivals, and create—by 1603—a politically unified Japan in the heavily populated islands of Honshu and Kyushu. The northernmost island, Hokkaido, became part of Japan only later.

Tokugawa Shogunate A painting on silk from the seventeenth century illustrates the importance of the samurai to supporting and legitimating the Tokugawa shoguns' rule. It shows the shogun at court, surrounded by samurai from the 16 most noble families.

called the Ainu, who had only rudimentary technology by Japanese standards, resisted centralized control off and on until about 1700. War and newly introduced diseases reduced their numbers to about 25,000 by 1800, and eventually ethnic Japanese from the southern islands colonized Hokkaido, swamping the Ainu demographically.

The Tokugawa shoguns consolidated their power before 1600 by using new technologies and techniques of war. After 1600 they kept the peace, and kept themselves in power, by time-honored tactics including threats of force and keeping regional elites either content or cowed. Successful monarchs elsewhere did similar things.

THE QING CONSOLIDATION IN CHINA

China's Ming dynasty (1368–1644) ruled over a quarter of the world's population, perhaps 175 million people, by 1600. As we have seen in earlier chapters, it launched great oceanic voyages under the command of Zheng He and presided over a buzzing hive of intellectual activity, including the neo-Confucian revival associated with Wang Yangming. The Ming also found ways to profit from international trade opportunities (see Chapter 20) brought by European sailing ships. Sales of silk and porcelain for

silver from Japan and Mexico fueled an economic expansion that extended from 1520 to 1580. In general, despite droughts, rebellions, and frontier struggles with pastoral peoples to the north, the Ming governed well enough to remain in power for 200 years.

THE FALL OF THE MING

But by the end of the sixteenth century, their troubles mounted. The Ming's campaign against Hideyoshi in Korea in the 1590s depleted the treasury. Adverse climate change—long spells of drought and cold of the Little Ice Age—brought more famines and lowered state revenues. When an emperor granted palace eunuchs the right to collect taxes, he precipitated a crisis between the eunuchs and the gentry. His successor allowed the eunuchs free rein in the early seventeenth century, provoking determined hostility from the gentry. At the same time, the overseas supplies of silver dried up when mining output in Spanish America and Japan fell, starving Chinese commerce of its medium of exchange and making it harder for anyone to pay their taxes—which by law had to be paid in silver. By the 1630s, China was fracturing and civil war loomed.

Then things went from bad to worse for the Ming: an enterprising steppe leader from Manchuria, Nurhaci, and his son, Hong Taiji, united many of the tribes of the eastern steppe, forged a new ethnic identity (called Manchu), built an efficient army in ways that recalled Genghis Khan, conquered Korea (1638), and threatened China. When one faction in China's civil war invited the Manchus to help, they helped themselves, occupying Beijing and refusing to leave. The last Ming emperor hanged himself from a garden tree in 1644, an ignominious end for one of China's great dynasties.

THE QING CONQUEST

The Manchu elite renamed themselves the Qing, ruling China as the **Qing dynasty** until 1911. But first they had to consolidate their power, eliminating pockets of Ming loyalists in battle. Then they had to win over elite Chinese, the literati, without whom routine administration and tax collection was next to impossible. The literati, who admired elegant handwriting more than good horsemanship, normally found the Qing foreign barbarians with undistinguished ancestry and strange customs. Male

The Qing Empire, ca. 1600–1800 From their homeland in eastern Manchuria, the Manchu expanded militarily in the steppe and woodlands of northeastern Asia. They intervened in a power struggle in China's declining Ming Empire, and between 1644 and 1683 they took over most of the Ming territory. As rulers of China they took the name Qing, and for another century proved effective in war and diplomacy, expanding their empire westward.

Qing shaved the front part of the top of their heads and wore a long braid, a style they made a legal requirement for all Han Chinese men. It took most literati families several generations to overcome their resentment of Qing rule.

The Qing faced two main military challenges during their first century in power. One was the naval power of the pirate king and Ming loyalist Zheng Chenggong and his clan, with which this chapter began. The Qing finished them off by 1683. The other was the perennial problem of Chinese dynasties: confederations of steppe nomads to the north. In the late seventeenth and early eighteenth centuries, a subset of the Mongols, the Zunghars, forged large confederacies, threatening the security of northern China. At the same time, Tibetans to the southwest showed signs of hostility to the Qing and supported their fellow Buddhists in Mongolia.

The Qing's answer to the challenge from the steppe came in the form of army campaigns to the north and west, which, combined with smallpox epidemics, decisively broke Mongol power in the 1750s. Soon thereafter they added more territory, including the desert and oasis lands in the far northwest now known as Xinjiang, and the high plateau of Tibet. The Qing campaigns doubled the territorial size of their empire and secured their frontiers. They also made their empire more multicultural, multilingual, and multiethnic than the Ming or most previous Chinese empires. By 1800 it counted some 350 million people, roughly a third of the global population.

Kangxi as Sage A 1699 portrait of the Kangxi emperor emphasizes his classical learning. It was important to the Qing, a foreign dynasty, to gain the support of Chinese intellectuals.

The Qing also fought expansionist campaigns in the south, against Burma and Vietnam, but with no success. Mountain terrain and rain forest hamstrung the Qing cavalry. Malaria killed many thousand Qing soldiers. Combined with stern resistance, these factors—after multiple failed campaigns—persuaded the Qing that southern expansion was not worth the cost.

The Qing were led by two long-lived, vigorous, conscientious, clever, and ruthless emperors, conventionally reckoned among the greatest in Chinese history. The Kangxi emperor, who reigned for some sixty years (r. 1662–1722), was the first Qing emperor born and raised on Chinese soil rather than in Manchuria. His grandson, the Qianlong emperor, reigned from 1735 to 1796, abdicating at age 85 in order not to outdo his grandfather. Of the 265 years of Qing dynastic rule, about 125 took place under these two men. They were both cultivated, multilingual, highly literate political wizards—and mercilessly brutal when it suited them. The Kangxi emperor, for example, welcomed foreign Jesuits to his court, but he also obliged the people of Fujian province to evacuate the entire coastal district in his effort to undermine the Zheng family. The Qianlong emperor spoke six languages, took a deep interest in Tibetan Buddhism, and hired Italian and French Jesuits to build palaces—but also ordered the extermination of Zunghar Mongols as a people in 1755.

STATECRAFT AND MILITARY INNOVATION

The Qing consolidation of power and expansion of empire owed something to the Eurasian military revolution, but much less than the Tokugawa did. The Ming had already used guns and adapted them into their military system—gunpowder was a Chinese invention, after all. As early as 1400, about 10 percent of Ming soldiers used firearms.

Jesuits in China Jesuit missionaries capitalized on the Kangxi emperor's scholarly interests, using astronomy as an entrée to his court. The German Jesuit Adam Schall (right), shown in this 1667 portrait with his astronomical instruments, spent most of his life at the Qing court. A Jesuit colleague of Schall refitted the observatory on Peking's eastern wall (left) with a sextant, quadrant, and other instruments.

Qing Military Strategy A large eighteenth-century scroll painting illustrates a scene from the imperial hunt, a ritualized court event. Here athletes train in a circle at the center of the camp, as the emperor and numerous spectators look on. Such activities allowed the Qing army to practice the logistical competence and military readiness for which it was renowned.

By the time of the war against Japan in Korea (1590s), the Ming had a formidable field artillery force.

Yet guns and artillery mattered much less in China than in Japan. Siege artillery did not work well in China, because cities typically had earthen walls thick enough to stop cannonballs. Neither guns nor artillery were much use against China's main enemies, the Mongols, whose ponies enabled them to scamper out of range quickly. So although firearms were invented in China, and used by both the Ming and the Qing, the Chinese did not always keep pace with other states in firearm quality. In 1644, when the Qing took power, the best muskets, according to the Chinese, were Ottoman, and the best cannon were Portuguese. The Qing military sometimes imitated the best technologies, and in some cases made small improvements upon them. Like the Ming before them, they studied cannon making with Jesuit teachers skilled in European casting techniques. But they did not rely on firearms to the extent that other early modern empires did.

The Qing's military secret sauce, more than new technology, was new technique. Even before they came to power, Nurhaci and Hong Taiji had organized their steppe warriors into units, called banners, that cut across kin lines and strengthened centralized command—just as Genghis Khan had done with Mongol tribes 400 years

before. In their campaigns in China, the Qing effectively integrated cavalry, their own strong suit, with infantry, artillery, and siege skills. They learned, from the Ming, to conduct naval warfare along the rivers and coasts. And when they chose to attack the Zunghar Mongols in the eighteenth century, they combined canny diplomacy that divided their enemy together with brilliant logistics that enabled them to campaign out on the steppe grasslands without running out of food and water.

The Qing emphasized military virtues in their efforts to influence Chinese culture. They boosted military spending and highlighted military achievements in art and architecture to a degree unusual in China, where cultured people tended to regard military men as uncouth. The Qianlong emperor in his first year on the throne (1736) stressed the importance of military preparedness even in peacetime.

Keeping the military paid was a high priority for the Qing. They knew their own rise to power rested in part on disaffected Ming army units rising in rebellion. So they boosted the military's budget, even while lowering taxes overall. They improved the efficiency of tax collection. They also encouraged "voluntary" contributions of silver from big merchants, who knew better than to refuse. And they encouraged the military to go into business for itself to bolster its finances.

All these initiatives, more than new technologies, helped the Qing consolidate their power and expand their empire. They did not disdain foreign military technology. But their most effective statecraft and military innovations came locally, from within China and the Qing homeland of the eastern steppe, and not from contact with the wider world. This was unique among the great powers in the early modern centuries.

Qing Rule This portrait of the emperor Qianlong (r. 1735–1796) illustrates the military technologies that enabled the Qing to consolidate their power: horses and archery, rather than firearms, organized into strong centralized units.

THE MUGHAL EMPIRE IN INDIA

The Mughal Empire took shape in the early sixteenth century in northern India. Its Muslim founders came from Central Asia and identified with the Turkic and Mongol (hence "Mughal") warriors of the steppe. After taking a beating from an Uzbek emir in Central Asian warfare, they invaded northern India and, after four failed attempts, conquered the much-decayed Delhi sultanate in 1526. A forceful emperor, Abu'l-Fath Jalal ud-din Muhammad Akbar (usually just called **Akbar**, which in Arabic means "the great one"), stabilized the Mughal state and launched it on a path to expansion. He took power as a teenager in 1556 and reigned to his death in 1605, almost as long as Kangxi or Qianlong. Soon the Mughal Empire controlled, although loosely, most of South Asia—like the Mauryans (fourth to second centuries BCE) and the Gupta (fourth to sixth centuries CE) before them.

No state in a thousand years had been able to unify as much of South Asia as the Mughals. Akbar ruled over perhaps 60 million people. A century of geographical expansion later, his great-grandson, Aurangzeb, ruled about 120 million, about 20 percent of the world's total. At its height the Mughal Empire was the second most populous state in the world, trailing only China, and controlled all but southernmost India.

MUGHAL MIGHT

Mughal success rested in part on military innovations. Like the Qing, they found effective combinations of old and new. Warfare in India for five centuries before the Mughals had hinged on foot soldiers, mounted archers, war elephants, and sieges. Indians also used bamboo rockets fired from iron tubes. Guns first arrived, via Central Asia and Iran, about 1450, but were not yet effective enough to catch on widely. Then, in the 1520s, the Mughals introduced larger quantities of guns and cannon in their North India campaigns, and figured out how to combine these new weapons with cavalry archers. Akbar recruited skilled gunsmiths from the Ottoman Empire and Europe to improve the quality of his weaponry, and soon Mughal smiths and guncasters were making excellent muskets and cannon. Now firearms spread widely in

Mughal Conquests The Mughal emperor Akbar owed his military success in part to the combination of old and new technologies: on the one hand, war elephants and horses, seen here (left) crossing the Ganges in a 1600 manuscript; on the other, advanced siege artillery, shown here (right) being used to attack a hill fort in central India in 1568.

India, including among enemies of the Mughals. To maintain a military edge, the Mughals also had to ensure access to horse-producing regions in Central Asia—and deny it to enemies. Lacking enough good grassland, India itself could not raise enough horses. The Mughals imported up to 16,000 annually via Afghanistan. By 1560, in the early years of Akbar's reign, the Mughals had perfected the combination of horses and guns—cavalry, infantry, and artillery—and added to that a mastery of both siegecraft and fortification.

The Mughals also learned to use the navigable rivers, especially the Ganges and Indus, to move their military machinery around. In the watery landscapes of Bengal, which in the monsoon season could become a maze of swampy creeks and ponds, they conducted warfare from boats. On rivers and inshore seas, they used gunboats in support of their army. They never built a navy capable of projecting power on the high seas—recall Aurangzeb's willingness to concede the oceans to the "lions of the sea." At all times, the Mughal navy was subordinate to their army in importance and in prestige within Mughal society.

Malik Ambar An anonymous artist made this portrait of the Ethiopian slave-turned-military-leader near the end of his life, in about 1620.

The careful integration of infantry with firearms together with cavalry, field artillery, siege-craft, and armed river boats made the Mughals more formidable at war than any South Asian rival. In Akbar's time, and through-out the seventeenth century, the Mughals generally crushed those who resisted them. They met stern resistance from some Indian rulers, however, such as those of the sultanate of Ahmadnagar in west-central India. In the late 1590s, its armies were led by a female regent, Chand Bibi, who beat back Mughal attacks on her capital for four years. Despite the Mughal conquest of Ahmadnagar city, resistance continued under the leadership of an Ethiopian slave, Malik Ambar. Born in Africa, sold by his impov-erished parents to Arabs, shipped to Iraq, Arabia, and finally India, Malik Ambar became a slave soldier and through skill and guile rose to be the leading minister of Ahmadnagar by 1607. He masterminded guerilla resis-tance to Mughal expansion for two decades before his suc-cessors succumbed to the superior power of the Mughals. Just about everyone else in South Asia also bowed before Mughal power sooner or later.

MUGHAL CONSOLIDATION

The Mughals needed all the raw power they could amass because, as Muslim invaders in an overwhelmingly Hindu land, they faced a legitimacy problem. Akbar addressed this not only with military force, but with a tolerant reli-gious policy as well. Although illiterate himself, Akbar supported scholars and libraries and seems to have been genuinely curious about and tolerant of multiple religions, like some of the Mongol khans and the Kangxi emperor in China. He enjoyed discussions with Sufis, Jesuits, Jains, and Buddhists. When the Mughals had first arrived in South Asia in the 1520s, they allowed only Muslims to serve in their military. Akbar recruited Hindus too, and relaxed other forms of religious discrimination. He sus-pended the normal Islamic policy of taxing non-Muslims

at higher rates, allowed Hindu landowners to hold high office, welcomed Hindus at his court, celebrated Hindu holidays such as Diwali, and married a Hindu woman, Mariam-uz-Zamani (one of his 14 wives). The Mughal religious policy, with a few adjustments in favor of Islamic orthodoxy, remained in effect until the time of Aurangzeb (r. 1658–1707).

Like every early modern state, the Mughals needed huge sums to pay for their military. Like every success-ful early modern state, the Mughals made tax collection more efficient. They also raised money by negotiation with, and occasional intimidation of, local elites, typi-cally landowners who took a share of what the toiling peasantry produced. Under Akbar they also encouraged foreign trade and benefited from custom duties. As they conquered new territories, they used the plunder to lower

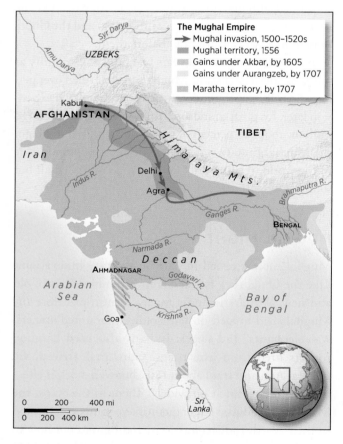

The Mughal Empire, ca. 1500–1707 The Mughal dynasty, origi-nally from Central Asia, became one of the great powers of the early modern world. Once they dominated the fertile Ganges basin, they had the resources to bring most of South Asia under their control. By 1600, their territorial success rivaled that of the Gupta Empire a thousand years earlier. But by 1700, other poli-ties, such as the Maratha states, were adapting to the Mughals' technologies and techniques, and their empire was in retreat.

tax rates and win their subjects' loyalty. They could dole out conquered lands to reliable followers, who gave a share of their income to the Mughals.

As long as new conquests kept coming, this system worked admirably—as a similar one had worked for the Roman Republic and Empire long before. The early Mughals rarely lacked for money, and this underwrote their military and political success. Shah Jahan, who ruled from 1627 to 1658, was able to field an army of a million men and pay for a glorious mausoleum, the Taj Mahal, built to honor his favorite wife, Mumtaz Mahal, who died while giving birth to her fourteenth child in 1631. When Emperor Aurangzeb (the sixth of Mumtaz Mahal's children) went on campaign in Afghanistan in the 1670s, he brought 300 camels carrying gold and silver to cover his expenses.

MUGHAL DECLINE

In Aurangzeb's later years, the Mughal Empire weakened. Having imprisoned his father and defeated his brothers on the battlefield, he took the throne at age 29. Aurangzeb sought legitimacy by burnishing his credentials as a Muslim ruler. By all accounts he was pious and knew the Qur'an by heart. His religious devotion—and misguided political calculation—led him to adopt a policy that emphasized Sunni orthodoxy and instituted Islamic law (shari'a) throughout his empire. He forbade construction of new Hindu temples, permitted destruction of some existing ones, and imposed higher taxes on non-Muslims. This departure from Mughal tradition alienated Hindus, Sikhs, Jains, Shi'a Muslims—as well as everyone who enjoyed music, dancing, drinking, and gambling.

As a result, the Mughal state faced more frequent rebellions and tax revolts. Eventually it could not control its southern frontiers. In a region called the Deccan, Hindu warriors known as Marathas gradually rolled back Mughal control. Starting in the 1660s, a successful guerilla captain, Shivaji Bhonsle, built up a Maratha state, including a navy. His state building was a rough equivalent to that of the Zheng family on the southeast coasts of China. But whereas the Qing ultimately vanquished the upstart Zhengs, the Mughals could not overcome the Marathas, despite the efforts of Aurangzeb, who personally campaigned against them for 25 years. By 1770, the Marathas controlled half of India. Aurangzeb's absence from the empire's heartlands in north India led elites

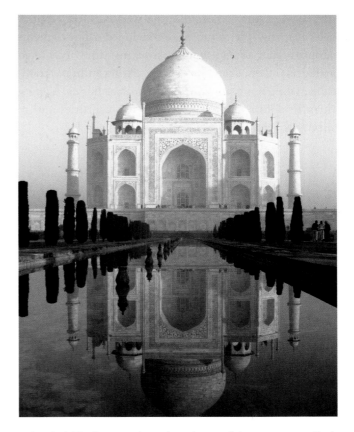

Taj Mahal The huge scale and opulence of the monument Shah Jahan built for his favorite wife indicates what a large treasury he and other Mughal rulers amassed through conquest and taxation.

there to experiment with keeping bigger chunks of revenue for themselves, and central control, never very strong, weakened.

After Aurangzeb's death in 1707, with the empire under less able successors, the Mughal retreat gathered pace. Princes and warlords broke free and carved out their own states. In 1739, Nader Shah, a former slave from northeastern Iran who had just overthrown the Safavid dynasty and made himself shah of Iran, sacked Delhi. He massacred tens of thousands, looted the city, and carried off the Mughals' peacock throne. India became more politically fragmented, and the Mughals held only small parts of the country until their final collapse in 1857.

Like the Qing in China, the Mughals were originally foreign invaders who built a formidable multiethnic and multireligious empire within 40 years. Also like the Qing, they focused their efforts on their landward frontiers, leaving the sea to others, and took advantage of innovations in the military sphere to expand their territory. But unlike the Qing—more like the warlord Oda Nobunaga in Japan—their innovations included major elements adopted from abroad, notably firearms. They integrated artillery and muskets into their existing military traditions, while monopolizing the import of horses, helping them to dominate South Asia for two centuries and to survive for three.

THE OTTOMAN EMPIRE

While the Mughals lasted some 300 years, the Ottomans, another Turkic and Muslim dynasty that traced its origins to Central Asia, lasted over 600. Their success rested on factors important to the Mughals as well: canny integration of new weaponry into existing military culture, liberal religious policy, and healthy finances.

The Ottomans began as a community of Turkish-speaking mobile pastoralists, followers of a tribal chieftain named Osman. They began to enjoy military success in northwest Anatolia against Byzantine Greeks in the fourteenth century. They may have benefited politically from the bubonic plague pandemic of 1346–1351 which probably killed urban and agrarian populations faster than it did pastoralists. In any case, the Ottomans gradually expanded their domain in Anatolia and the Balkans at the expense of the Byzantine Empire and several smaller polities. By 1453, under a 21-year-old sultan known as Mehmet the Conqueror, they successfully besieged Constantinople, the best-fortified city in all Europe. That brought the Byzantine Empire to its knees, and within eight years its last remnants disappeared.

The Ottomans made Constantinople, also called **Istanbul**, their capital and exploited its geographic location astride the straits connecting the Black and Mediterranean Seas. They now controlled one of the world's most lucrative trade routes. Their conquests continued after 1453, notably in the Balkans and along the Black Sea coasts.

OTTOMAN EXPANSION

Then between 1514 and 1526 Ottoman good fortune multiplied. Battlefield victories stabilized their eastern frontier with the Safavids of Iran, the Shi'a dynasty with whom the Sunni Ottomans competed for power and prestige. With that frontier secured, in 1517 they conquered Egypt and the Hejaz, the strip of Arabia where Mecca and Medina lie. This was a double windfall for the Ottomans. Egypt yielded reliable surpluses of grain and revenue. The Ottomans used Egypt, as Achaemenids, Romans, Byzantines, and others had before them, as a means to feed their armies and cities, and to help finance wars and administration. By some calculations, conquering Egypt doubled the revenues of the Ottoman state. On top of that, when drought afflicted the eastern Mediterranean region and crops failed, those of Egypt did not—because the Nile flowed from the mountains of Ethiopia, where rain is more reliable and determined by different weather systems. So Egypt not only provided grain and revenue, it also provided insurance against the droughts common in the other lands of the Ottoman Empire.

Taking over the holy places, Mecca and Medina, might have doubled the prestige of the Ottomans. Soon Ottoman sultans (as their leaders were called) took the title of caliph, proclaiming themselves the successors of the Prophet Muhammad and the spiritual leaders of all Muslims. Not all Muslims agreed. But nonetheless, most Sunni Muslims—always a majority within Islamdom—regarded the Ottoman caliphs as the guardians of the Islamic community. This prestige won considerable cooperation and deference.

Moreover, a long spell of good rains in the Ottoman heartland of Anatolia, around the years 1520–1590, boosted livestock herds, grain harvests, population, and imperial revenues. Whereas both the Qing and the Mughals had to import horses, the Ottoman lands produced all the horses, grain, timber, and important mineral ores that the empire's population and military might need.

These circumstances contributed to the notable success of the empire's longest-reigning sultan, Suleiman (r. 1520–1566), who consolidated Ottoman control over vast territories and added several more—most importantly, Iran and Hungary. Both yielded grain surpluses in most years, and Hungary also provided great herds of horses and cattle. Controlling Hungary meant the Ottomans could use the Danube River as a transport artery to tighten their hold on southeastern Europe. Controlling the Tigris and Euphrates rivers enabled them to move troops and supplies easily along their eastern frontier with Iran.

The Ottoman Empire reached its territorial peak in the late sixteenth and seventeenth centuries. Stretching from

The Expansion of the Ottoman Empire, ca. 1320s–1683 From their beginnings in northwest Anatolia early in the fourteenth century, the followers of Osman—the Ottomans—expanded their domain for three centuries into southeastern Europe, Southwest Asia, and North Africa. Under sultans such as Mehmet and Suleiman, the Ottomans wielded the techniques and technologies of power effectively, becoming one of the great powers of Eurasia.

Iraq to Algeria and from Yemen to Hungary, it contained nearly 30 million people, about 7 percent of humankind.

OTTOMAN CONSOLIDATION

Like that of the Mughals, Ottoman political success rested on military, financial, and religious power. Like the Qing and the Mughals, the Ottomans integrated firearms into their military culture. They used guns as early as the 1390s and artillery by the 1420s. They quickly mastered the fine points of siege warfare and fortification, demonstrated in the capture and rebuilding of Istanbul in 1453. They recruited an elite infantry force, called the janissaries, from Christian communities of the western Balkans. The **janissaries** were taken from their homes as boys, trained in the arts of war and administration, and deployed, nominally as slaves of the sultans, in the army or bureaucracy. Although slaves, many of them rose to powerful positions.

As gun-wielding infantry (by 1560 more than half of the janissaries carried firearms), they played a key role in many battlefield triumphs, such as the defeat of the Safavid army, which did not yet use guns, in 1514. Most states equipped their least skilled soldiers with guns, because they did not take much practice to learn to use. The Ottomans did the reverse, arming their elite and best-trained soldiers with muskets. By the 1560s, the janissaries had developed the technique of volley fire with muskets, like Hideyoshi's troops. To equip their forces, the Ottomans built up military industries and produced high-quality artillery and small arms. They blended all their military innovations with cavalry, their traditional strength.

The Ottoman military machine grew bigger as well as more efficient. During the reign of Suleiman, the artillery corps tripled in size. Until the 1690s, the Ottomans could usually put more men, horses, and weapons in the field than any of their enemies. They also built a big navy

Ottoman Conquest A sixteenth-century account of the sultan Suleiman's military victories shows his ranks of cannon and infantry besieging a Christian fortress. Through such military precision the Ottomans swiftly expanded their empire.

of galleys propelled by oarsmen, suited to the conditions of the Mediterranean and Black Seas, but also active in the Indian Ocean, at times as far afield as Mombasa and Malacca. As everywhere, fielding such an expanded and well-equipped military was extremely expensive.

THE TAX SYSTEM

Like every other empire, the Ottomans sought to tighten up their tax system. Mehmet the Conqueror (r. 1451–1481) attempted to centralize taxation and bureaucracy, and to take a bigger chunk of the revenues of provincial elites. He even tried to impose fixed prices on items bought and sold in the markets, which proved hard to enforce. The local elites, often quite different from one province to another, proved resilient. With the scale and cost of warfare expanding so quickly during the sixteenth century, Mehmet and his successors had to strike bargains with them.

The fiscal windfall of expansion, especially the conquest of Egypt, helped. But the state also turned increasingly to tax farming—selling to private entrepreneurs the right to collect taxes from Ottoman subjects. And the Ottomans in the sixteenth century encouraged the monetization and commercialization of the economy, which enabled them to collect more revenue in cash rather than in produce—always preferable for governments. After territorial expansion and plunder stopped, the sultans had to become more efficient to keep solvent.

THE MILLET SYSTEM Ottoman religious policy helped reduce the costs of ruling. From the beginning, the sultans happily recruited Christians into their military and bureaucracy. They valued loyalty wherever they found it. They welcomed tens of thousands of Jewish refugees from Spain, expelled in 1492 by Ferdinand and Isabella. Mehmet the Conqueror was genuinely curious, like Akbar, about religions other than Islam and at times tried to present himself as a worthy successor to Byzantine (Christian) emperors. Although they taxed non-Muslims at higher rates, the Ottomans by and large left Christian and Jewish communities to adjudicate their own affairs until the nineteenth century. Sometimes called the **millet system**, this tolerant religious policy, like Akbar's, made the empire a bit easier to govern.

With these measures, the Ottomans managed to stay afloat, to field and finance a military equal to foreign challenges and internal rebellions through the end of the seventeenth century. After a defeat by the combined forces of the Habsburg Empire and Poland-Lithuania in 1683, their position relative to their neighbors and rivals weakened, and after the 1770s the tide was running against them. They could not keep up with their neighbors, especially Russia and the Habsburgs, and their neighbors more often formed coalitions against them. The empire shrank after every lost war. But the Ottomans, like the Qing, lasted into the early twentieth century. So did the Russian Empire.

IMPERIAL CONSOLIDATION IN RUSSIA

Russia is another case of **imperial consolidation** and territorial expansion at the expense of weaker neighbors. In earlier chapters we saw how the original Russian state emerged on trade routes linking the Baltic and Black Seas,

CONSIDERING THE EVIDENCE

An Ottoman Register in Ukraine

In addition to training janissaries to run its war machine, the Ottoman Empire hired thousands of scribes and tax farmers to keep money flowing. Census takers (*muharrir*) determined tax levels by interviewing farmers, traders, herders, bakers, ferrymen, and even alcohol distillers to estimate what they produced in a normal year. Then they wrote everything in duplicate registers: one for the imperial archive in Istanbul and one for local officials to reference. The excerpt below is from a register for the Ukrainian province of Kamaniçe near the Black Sea, which the Ottoman Empire took from the Polish-Lithuanian Commonwealth in 1672. The imperial government wanted to protect its productive settlements on the nearby Black Sea.

The introduction to the register begins with two lists. The first list describes collections from tax farmers reserved for the Ottoman sultan: poll taxes from Christian and Jewish immigrants, fees from a boat toll, and pre-paid taxes on fishponds. The second list, shown below, summarizes the collections from tax farmers that the *beylerbeyi*—the governor—would retain. Although additional taxes pushed annual revenue to over 5 million silver coins (*akçe*), this amount was not nearly enough to pay the 6,000 soldiers garrisoned in the border province. So, each year, the empire subsidized military salaries with nearly 13 million *akçe* from the central treasury in Istanbul until it abandoned Kamaniçe in 1699.

The domains of the *beylerbeyi* [governor] of the province of Kamaniçe

[Tax collections] from market dues on horses, mules, oxen, sheep, goats, and others in Kamaniçe ... Žvanec', and ... Mohyliv: yearly 54,000 [silver coins]

[and] from weighing and measuring fees in Kamaniçe, except for the rent of the buildings [where the weighing and measuring was done]: yearly 42,000

[and] income from coffee-roasting in Kamaniçe: yearly 19,000

[and] from market tolls, coffee-houses, candle works, slaughterhouses, sheep [herders], eating houses, cook-shops with dye-houses and others in Kamaniçe and from the fair-brokers' fees in Žvanec': yearly 52,200

[and] from the head-broker's fee in the "black" market ... [and the] head-broker's fee in the horse and cattle [market] in Kamaniçe ...: yearly [scribe did not record amount]

[and] from the fees of the [drivers] of oxen, sheep, goats and with the pasturage and passage fee [collected] from the [drivers] in Žvanec': yearly 25,300

[and] from the [unclaimed] property devolved upon the imperial treasury, left by ordinary subjects and state servants except for *janissaries,* ... and from the property of missing and absent persons, stray and run-away [slaves, arrested and sold in auction] in [Kamaniçe] with the fee from the [wineries] and distillery kettles and with the cask fee in Žvanec' and ... Mohyliv: yearly 50,000

Source: Dariusz Kołodziejczyk, trans., "Appendix 1: Translation of the Beginning of the *Defter*," The Ottoman Survey Register of Podolia (ca. 1681), *Defter-i Mufassal-i Eyalet-i Kamaniçe* (Cambridge, MA: Harvard Ukrainian Research Institute, 2004).

QUESTIONS FOR ANALYSIS

1. What products and activities did the Ottoman Empire tax?
2. Besides adding a new revenue stream, what could have motivated the Ottoman Empire to tax coffee and alcohol production?
3. Why would the Ottoman Empire conquer territory that provided less revenue than it cost to maintain?

---

how the Muscovite princes served as clients of Mongol khans for a while, and how, in the sixteenth century, the Russian state sponsored expansion into Siberia. The conquest of Siberia and its fur trade bolstered Russian state revenues almost as much as the conquest of Egypt helped Ottoman finances. By 1600, Russia was a large

and—in ethnic and religious terms—highly diverse state, an empire in all but name. It was, however, sparsely settled, with a population of only 10 million.

While the princes of Moscow, who after 1547 took the title **tsar**, were underwriting Siberian expansion, they also took large parts of Ukraine and the Muslim lands of the lower Volga. These were more fertile than their home region around Moscow. This territorial expansion helped boost the population to about 14 million in 1700. During the next century, natural increase helped propel it to 40 million. By 1800, the tsars ruled about 5 percent of the global population.

The early tsars faced difficult conditions—the harsh climate of the Little Ice Age, frequent famines and rebellions, and formidable neighbors such as Poland-Lithuania to the west and Muslim khanates to the east and south. Their response was to grab all the power they could. That meant forcing regional elites, mainly landed aristocrats called *boyars*, to knuckle under to the tsars. The tsars drew upon their revenues from the fur trade, the plunder from newly conquered lands, politically astute marriages, and the legitimacy conferred by the Russian Orthodox Church to build a remarkably centralized state over their sprawling domain.

IVAN IV

Much of that was the work of Ivan IV, called Ivan the Terrible (although Ivan the Tough might be a better translation of *groznyi*). He reigned for nearly four decades (r. 1547–1584) and more than anyone else brought the nobility to heel and gave imperial Russia its political character. He oversaw conquests (and defeats), required military service of his population, wrapped himself in the mantle of the Russian Orthodox Church, married eight

St. Petersburg The Summer Palace in St. Petersburg, built in the early eighteenth century on the banks of the Neva River where it flows into the Baltic Sea, suggests the grandeur that Peter the Great imagined for his new imperial capital.

or nine times, killed his son and heir in a tantrum, spent lavishly on war and monumental architecture—following in many ways the age-old emperor's playbook.

But Ivan the Terrible was also an innovator. He helped set up the first printing press in Russia. He sought overseas contacts, especially with England. Most important in the context of this chapter, he built up a huge army and an armaments industry to match. His engineers and craftsmen manufactured countless guns and cannon, and his officers (selected for talent rather than ancestry) refined the blending of infantry, cavalry, and artillery into a cohesive force. Russian engineers even invented mobile fortifications, made of wood, which could be dragged or floated here or there as needed, like a set of giant Lincoln logs. In conquering the lower Volga, Ivan made that great river into a Russian transport artery, like the Danube in the Ottoman Empire. It gave Russia easy access to the Caspian Sea and trade with Iran. After he died—while playing chess—Russia almost fell apart.

PETER THE GREAT

A later tsar, Peter the Great (r. 1682–1725), was equally innovative. After surviving murderous power struggles within the imperial family, now the Romanovs, Peter inherited an unstable country as a 17-year-old. He had studied military matters, mathematics, and navigation keenly as a teenager, grew to be 6′8″ (2.03 m) tall, and scorned the soft, courtly life. After becoming tsar, he took the extraordinary step of visiting western Europe, and at one point he worked as an apprentice carpenter in a Dutch shipyard to learn the ins and outs of shipbuilding. As an English politician of the seventeenth century so brilliantly put it, "A prince who will not undergo the difficulty of understanding must undergo the danger of trusting." Peter studied hard, undergoing the difficulty of understanding, fearing there were few he could trust.

Like Ivan the Terrible, Peter felt the need to make Russia strong lest its enemies destroy it. Like Ivan, his reforms put Russia through great stress, but left the country more formidable than before. He too put the *boyars* on a short leash, modernized the military, and nourished military industries. (He also killed one of his sons, like Ivan.) Like the Qianlong emperor in China, he encouraged a military culture especially among the elite of society. He built Russia's first real navy and introduced drill into the army.

He reined in the power of the Orthodox Church, which had grown politically powerful under weaker tsars, winning for himself the right to appoint bishops. In building a new capital on the Baltic, called St. Petersburg, he gave Russia an outlet to the Baltic Sea as Ivan's conquests had given Russia an outlet on the Caspian Sea. Access to the Baltic brought better trade connections with all of northern Europe and enabled the use of the navy in wars with Russia's Baltic neighbors such as Sweden. Reveling in his conquests, Peter formally declared Russia to be an empire, which indeed it was.

Despite initially controlling little in the way of natural resources beyond timber and furs, the Russian state flourished politically under the tsars. The dedicated and energetic ones found ways to mobilize the population and resources of the country, increase tax revenues, control regional elites, and integrate military innovation—especially guns, cannon, army drill, and ships—into the cultural fabric of Russia, all in the service of their own power.

THE HABSBURG EMPIRE: THE FIRST GLOBAL POWER

The **Habsburgs**, a clan of modest nobles from southwest Germany and Switzerland, managed to join the winner's circle of Eurasian empires through their mastery of the new technologies and techniques of power. In the thirteenth century, good fortune in war added Austria to their domains. Silver from mines in the Austrian Alps helped finance their ambitions. In the fourteenth century, through war and strategic marriages, they garnered new territories here and there in central Europe, creating a patchwork empire with Vienna as its capital. Between 1477 and 1526 they enjoyed a run of excellent political marriages, which brought them Burgundy (a sizeable piece of France), territories in the Low Countries (today's Belgium and the Netherlands), northern Hungary, and Bohemia (the Czech lands). These were comparatively productive provinces. Through another marriage they inherited the kingdom of Spain, a comparatively poor land with about 6 million people.

With Spain came its overseas empire in the Americas and the Philippines. This was worth little at first, but in the 1550s silver began to cascade out of Mexico and the

Habsburg Patrons Habsburg Archduke Leopold Wilhelm (in hat) appears in this 1647 painting in his own art gallery, surrounded by artists and their works. Habsburg patronage of the arts helped burnish their prestige.

Andes. The windfall was analogous to what the Ottomans enjoyed after taking Egypt with its vast surpluses of grain. By the mid-sixteenth century, the Habsburgs were the strongest dynasty in Europe and a power on the global stage. With territories in Europe, the Americas, and Asia (the Philippines), the Habsburgs count as the first true global power in history, the first empire on which the sun never set.

SOFT POWER

The Habsburgs became justly famous for finding marriage partners for their eligible princes and princesses that brought new territories to the empire. An irritated king of Hungary wrote of them, "What kingdoms Mars gives to others, Venus gives to thee." The grandmaster of strategic matchmaking was Emperor Maximilian I (r. 1508–1519), who used marriages—his own, his children's, and his grandchildren's—to add Spain, Bohemia, and northern Hungary, and a few other useful slivers of Europe to the Habsburg collection. He would have been especially pleased with his daughter-in-law Anna, who bore 15 children, potential political assets all, before she died at age 44.

In addition to marriages, the Habsburgs used image-making to good effect. As rulers of a hodge-podge of territories, they had to work hard to win their subjects'

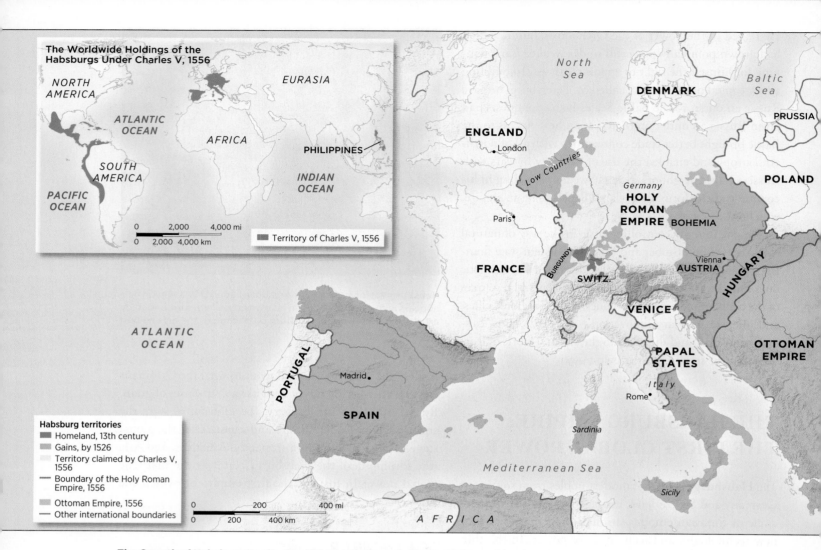

The Growth of Habsburg Territories, Thirteenth through Sixteenth Centuries The Habsburgs built an unusual empire consisting of scattered territories throughout central Europe, soon supplemented in the sixteenth century by others in western Europe, the Americas, and the Philippines. The Habsburgs, like the other great powers of the early modern world, adopted most of the innovations of the Eurasian military revolution to acquire their new lands and defend a stable frontier against their great rival, the Ottomans.

loyalty. They became champions of the Roman Catholic faith, sometimes militantly so. They paid painters, sculptors, architects, and composers to create art that boosted the reputation of the dynasty. Patronage of the arts was expected of rulers in Europe, as in India or China, and the Habsburgs cannily played that role. In another effort to amass prestige, several of them contrived to be elected as Holy Roman Emperor, linking themselves to the legacy of Charlemagne, who ruled much of Europe and was the first to hold this office. They used every form of soft power to try to burnish their image, inspire loyalty or awe, and thereby reduce their reliance upon brute force to rule.

HARD POWER

But they could not neglect hard power. They were full participants in the military revolution of Eurasia. The Spanish branch of the Habsburgs built an oceanic navy in the sixteenth century and took part in all the innovations of marine warfare. They also oversaw the creation of infantry units called *tercios* that combined musketeers and pikemen to become Europe's most feared soldiers. Pikemen wielded long spears and were effective in protecting musketeers from cavalry charges. In the Austrian domains, Maximilian took a special interest in developing a formidable body of infantry, the *Landsknechte*, German mercenaries who fought in most central European Habsburg campaigns. Until about 1650, the Habsburg army still consisted largely of units recruited by private entrepreneurs and rented out to monarchs. The Habsburgs, like the Ottomans and the Mughals, fielded larger and larger armies. Habsburg military architects and commanders mastered the expensive business of building fortresses and the use of field artillery. Their many wars with the Ottomans, France, and other powers ensured that they kept up to date on military technology and technique.

The Habsburgs needed all the military power and money they could get to wage war. There were rebellions to stamp out. There were religious wars to fight, against Protestants and against Muslims, to protect the interests of Catholicism. And there were dynastic wars to fight in the interest of the Habsburg family. Through the sixteenth century, these wars more often than not went well for the Habsburgs. After 1620 or so they went less well and the dynasty reeled from crisis to crisis, almost collapsing a few times. But fortunately for the Habsburgs, their most formidable neighbor, the Ottomans, also faced many crises after 1620.

A PATCHWORK EMPIRE

The patchwork character of most of their empire made the Habsburgs more dependent than most rulers upon the consent of their elites. They could not easily launch aggressive wars, unlike the Ottoman sultans or Qing emperors. They could rally all the many kings, princes, dukes, and counts—nominally their subjects—for defensive wars and could often build coalitions among neighbors to resist the Ottomans or France when it became powerful. After the 1520s, the Spanish and the Austrian parts of the dynasty ruled their domains separately, more allies than a single state. The Habsburgs never achieved the cohesion within their empire that smaller European states, or the Qing, the Ottomans, or Russia's Romanovs, managed.

Nonetheless, between the 1530s and 1556, Charles V, both king of Spain and Holy Roman Emperor, almost became emperor of all Europe. Several of the world's other big concentrations of population were undergoing violent unification in the sixteenth century: Japan, India, and, under the Ottomans, the eastern Mediterranean. China remained unified, and when it fragmented in the early

seventeenth century the Qing soon put it back together again. The Habsburgs made a bid to be the unifiers of Europe. They tried to crush Protestant princes in Germany, drive the Ottomans back in southeastern Europe, and defeat a rival dynasty, the Valois, in France. Charles V financed, directed, and in cases personally fought in these campaigns. In the end, his enemies made common cause against him, and he could not pull it off. He abdicated his thrones in 1556 and died three years later. The Habsburgs remained a major power in Europe until 1918, but never again could they realistically consider creating a pan-European empire.

THE UNIVERSITY OF WAR AND THE RISE OF EUROPE

Nor could anyone else create a pan-European empire. Europe remained a cockpit of pitiless political competition. It was, as one Dutch observer put it, a "**university of war**." In this respect it resembled China of the Warring States period (771–256 BCE) before its first unification, or, on a much smaller scale, the independent, rivalrous Greek city-states of the fifth century BCE. These were terrible circumstances in which to live. War, rapine, and epidemics (many of them associated with armies at war) flourished in Europe.

MILITARY COMPETITION AND STATE POWER

One result of this constant military competition was a gradual growth in the power of surviving European states. Many small ones disappeared, absorbed by the Habsburgs, the Ottomans, the French, the English, the Swedes, the Prussians, or the Russians. But, despite Charles V's best efforts, none of these successful states could destroy all others, establish an empire across the entire region, enforce peace at home, and confine warfare to its frontiers, as did the Qing in East Asia, the Mughals in South Asia, and the Ottomans in the lands around the eastern Mediterranean. Europe, in the sixteenth through the eighteenth centuries, was out of step with the other major population centers of Eurasia because competition among near equals prevailed.

The Costs of Conflict The sixteenth-century painter Pieter Breughel the Younger made this painting of impoverished peasants paying tithes to the lords on whose land they lived—which would in turn be used to fund rulers' military campaigns.

This university of war provided strong incentives for every ruler to maximize the efficiency of revenue collection and military operations. Those who were not successful in these tasks were typically crushed by their neighbors. So European states were forced to get better and better at taxing their subjects and fighting their neighbors. This brutal pressure lasted for centuries—unlike the situation for the Qing and the Mughals, whose success at unification and expansion meant they no longer had to compete with equals. By 1750, this unusual circumstance enabled a handful of European states—Spain, France, the Netherlands, Prussia, Habsburg Austria, and Britain—to attain world-class efficiency in taxing and fighting.

POLITICAL FRAGMENTATION AND GLOBAL REACH

As we've seen, world history includes several examples of regions divided politically and engulfed in ceaseless warfare. But early modern Europe was unique in the combination of political fragmentation with global reach, global knowledge, and low information costs because of printing. Their maritime prowess and their role in weaving the first Global web gave Europeans access to information from all over the world. They quickly learned of best practices in use elsewhere. If Italian architects showed

there was a better way to build a fortress, other Europeans learned about it quickly. If Ottoman commanders showed there was a better way to combine light cavalry, field artillery, and disciplined infantry, Europeans learned about it quickly. The terrible experience of incessant war and chaos in Europe during the sixteenth through the eighteenth centuries provided states strong incentives to learn and adapt. These early modern advances helped set the stage for European global power in the nineteenth and twentieth centuries.

THE RISE OF BIG STATES: LEADERSHIP OR CIRCUMSTANCE?

The early modern centuries raise a question that has long divided historians: how much importance to give to individuals in shaping history. It may seem that the big empires prospered because they had a run of great emperors—Kangxi and Qianlong, Ivan the Terrible and Peter the Great, Akbar and Aurangzeb, Mehmet and Suleiman, Maximilian I and Charles V—all men of intellect, vision, ambition, and political savvy. Seen from the perspective of a single state or empire, that conclusion appears hard to dispute.

But if one steps back and takes a world history perspective, another possibility appears: it could be that the greatness of these emperors was owing mainly to the situations of their rule. They all came to power when circumstances, especially those connected to the exercise of military power, favored big states. They could expand at the expense of little states more easily than at most times in history. While conquests lasted, these emperors had the prestige, revenue, land, and armed power to keep their subjects in line and negotiate with regional elites through strength—and generosity if they wished. So the extraordinary longevity and political success of an Akbar, Suleiman, or Kangxi can in part be explained by the circumstances of their historical moment.

RESPONSES OF THE SMALLER POWERS

While the Qing, the Mughals, the Ottomans, the Russians, and the Habsburgs became the biggest of the big fish, they did not devour all the little fish. Smaller states could survive by playing the great powers off against one another, although this was a hazardous game that required skill and luck. To succeed, the small fish had to embrace at least parts of the military revolution—streamlining tax collection and improving their bureaucracies and militaries. Let's look briefly at some that did—and some that didn't.

IRAN AND SOUTHEAST ASIA

Some were successful. The Safavids in Iran, sandwiched uncomfortably between the Ottomans and the Mughals, faced enormous pressure to keep up with their neighbors' military innovations. They had to transition from a strictly cavalry-based military (defeated by the gun-using Ottomans in 1514) to one that used the full arsenal of the military revolution: gun-wielding infantry, field artillery, fortresses, as well as cavalry. And they had to raise all the money they could to finance campaigns, which they accomplished in part by promoting and taxing long-distance trade in silks, silver, and porcelain through their territory. The Safavids survived in power until 1736.

Smaller powers elsewhere survived, and often grew larger and more powerful, by modernizing their militaries and boosting their revenues. In Southeast Asia, Vietnam, after suffering invasion by the forces of Ming China early in the fifteenth century, adopted firearms and used them effectively against its neighbors. Other small kingdoms such as Burma and Thailand took shape and prospered at the expense of their immediate neighbors. In Burma, firearms and centralization of taxation helped to build the Toungoo dynasty (1510–1752) into the largest empire in the history of Southeast Asia for a few decades (ca. 1540–1580). In the late seventeenth century, a kingdom in Thailand briefly attained similar success after imitating Burmese military methods and securing access to weaponry from European merchants trading in the Indian Ocean.

KONGO AND MOROCCO

In Africa, a few states such as Kongo or Morocco took advantage of new opportunities presented by firearms to build their power. Kongo, as we've seen, was a major participant in the transatlantic slave trade. Through contacts with Europeans, mainly Portuguese, the kings of Kongo

maintained a privileged position (not quite a monopoly) on imported guns. That gave them the power to attack and enslave neighboring peoples and to make their kingdom the most powerful in southern Africa in the seventeenth century.

In Morocco in the sixteenth century, ambitious dynasts called the **Saadians** used revenues from trans-Saharan trade and sugar plantations to build their power. They studied Ottoman military tactics and acquired firearms and, from England, cannon. They demolished a Portuguese assault in 1578, and in 1591 sent an expedition across the Sahara to the Middle Niger to crush the last of the great West African Sahel states, called Songhai. The Songhai Empire had ruled for about a century, had centralized its bureaucracy and military, but did not adopt firearms. Gunpowder weapons were decisive in the encounter between the Saadian army and Songhai.

The Moroccans, aware of their military advantages, were probably aiming to control the West African goldfields, and perhaps to create a caliphate to rival the Ottomans. They achieved neither. Moroccan troops died quickly of diseases along the Niger; and although they held the cities for many years, they could not end resistance and never came close to the goldfields. One Saadian ruler, al-Mansur, in 1601 proposed to England's Queen Elizabeth I that they should join forces and divide Spain's American empire between them. Unable to corner West Africa's gold, he set his sights on Spanish America's silver. His plan came to nothing. Mastery of firearms enabled

Moroccan Battles A seventeenth-century engraving shows Moroccan troops (right) facing off against Portuguese opponents (left) during the unsuccessful 1578 Portuguese invasion.

the Saadians to unify Morocco, destroy enemies across the Sahara, and dream of greater conquests—but firearms alone could not guarantee that those dreams would come true.

NORTH AMERICA AND HAWAII

In North America, several Amerindian peoples exploited the potential of firearms to strengthen themselves and assault their neighbors. The most successful examples came in the nineteenth century, when Plains Indians confederacies, the Comanche and the Lakota Sioux, for example, built up power through access to guns and horses. As we saw in Chapter 17, in Hawaii King Kamehameha forged his kingdom with the help of a monopoly on imported firearms.

From Hawaii to Morocco to Burma, the same broad pattern prevailed. Local states were created or expanded through prudent adoption of new technologies and techniques of warfare. An edge, even if temporary, in military formidability enabled ambitious rulers to extend their domains. Obtaining such an edge was much easier in times of flux, when technologies and techniques were changing faster than usual. The resulting states and empires were often fleeting, as neighbors formed coalitions or adopted new and effective military techniques and technologies themselves.

The broad pattern was a smaller-scale version of the pattern among the great Eurasian powers from the Qing to the Habsburgs: the big got bigger because they were better able to realize the potential of expensive new technologies and techniques. Kamehameha I was not a big chief in global terms, but he was in his own neighborhood of the Hawaiian Islands. And he used the opportunity that presented, once firearms were introduced, to get bigger, make himself a king, and dominate the archipelago, as Oda Nobunaga and Hideyoshi did in the Japanese islands and the Mughals in their (larger) neighborhood, or the Ottomans in theirs.

THE COSTS OF MAINTAINING TRADITION: POLAND AND EGYPT'S MAMLUK SULTANATE

The costs of not following the trend are illustrated by the case of the Polish-Lithuanian Commonwealth (Poland for short). Poland took shape in the fifteenth century, officially merged with the Grand Duchy of Lithuania in 1569, and enjoyed its greatest power in the mid-seventeenth century. Its kings were elected by members of the nobility, who tenaciously guarded their liberties from central control. The Polish military relied on cavalry composed chiefly of nobles, which proved effective against Muscovy, Sweden, and the Ottomans, if less so against Tatar raiders. The Polish nobility kept alive traditions of chivalry long after other states had built up large infantries composed of peasants and had invested in fortresses, artillery, and navies. The Polish elite long resisted these trends: it did not wish to help pay for fortresses and ships, nor did it want to see common foot soldiers or the architects of fortresses siphon off any prestige or glory. One Polish nobleman dismissed siege warfare as "mole's work." The nobles particularly did not wish to see the king equipped with a standing army, rightly fearing that kings with armies would trample upon the nobility's liberties.

Unfortunately for the liberty-loving Polish elite, by 1690 their military did not match, in size or technique, that of Russia or the Habsburgs, and gallant cavalry charges could not make up for that. Their decentralized, consensual political system prevented the military and fiscal reforms that might have preserved their state. Between 1772 and 1795, Poland's neighbors—Russia, Prussia, and Habsburg Austria—partitioned it three times.

The Polish nobility was not alone in clinging to cherished traditions. Slave soldiers of the Mamluk sultanate, based in Egypt, did so too with similar consequences. In the thirteenth century, Mamluk forces had defeated the Mongols (1260) and become the most powerful military in the Islamic world. The sultans' soldiers mastered archery, swordsmanship, and horsemanship. But their commitment to, and success with, these skills and weapons led them to scorn firearms. When one sultan organized a corps of infantry with muskets in 1498, the slave soldiers attacked it. In 1516–1517, Ottoman armies using all manner of firearms crushed the Mamluks and took Egypt.

The Mamluk and Polish-Lithuanian cases show the dangers of disdaining military modernization in a time of rapid change. In both, elites—whether nobles or slave soldiers—prized their identity as skilled horsemen and the status that conferred, and could not contemplate adjusting to the times.

NOMADS AND PIRATES IN A WORLD OF EXPANDING STATES

The broad pattern of centralization and expansion of state power through fiscal and military reform was hard on smaller states, but harder still on nomads and pirates. On the world's grasslands and seas, nomad confederations and pirate gangs were for many centuries important political and military forces. But between 1650 and 1890, their power was decisively broken by the armies and navies of agrarian states. Nomads and pirates still existed afterward, but never again exercised much influence in history.

NOMAD POWER

Nomads—or more properly, mobile pastoralists—had operated on the grassy steppes of Asia and North Africa for millennia, and as we have seen time and again, they interacted both peacefully and violently with settled, agrarian populations and states. They often enjoyed considerable political and military power, thanks to their mobility and their capacities for surprise attack and tactical retreat. They could, when unified, defeat great empires. During the tenth through the thirteenth centuries, steppe pastoralists took over China, North India, and Iran, and North African pastoralists did roughly the same in Morocco and Egypt.

But by the seventeenth and eighteenth centuries, settled agrarian states were re-inventing themselves and the nomads could not follow suit. Mobile peoples could not develop more efficient tax collection, manufacture cannon, build elaborate fortifications, or add navies to their arsenals. They became increasingly dependent upon agrarian empires and less menacing to them. Their fighters more often served kings and emperors as auxiliary cavalry in exchange for cash, cloth, food, or weaponry. The Russians and Ottomans, for example, made good use of steppe peoples such as the Tatars. The Ming and the Qing hired Mongols to do some of their fighting for them. But the steppe warriors sometimes proved disobedient and dangerous allies, leading decision makers in Beijing or Istanbul to conclude that it would be wiser to crush pastoralists than to continue to risk keeping them in service and supplied with weaponry.

So, roughly between 1700 and 1850, hundreds of campaigns, small and large, took place from Manchuria to Morocco in which emperors and kings sent their armies against pastoralists and nomads. They built strings of forts in the steppes and deserts. Their armies at times managed to surround or trap a group of nomads and disarm them, slaughter them, or sell them into slavery. Guns played a role in this—although nomads often had guns too—but logistics, money, and manpower played larger ones. The Saadians, Ottomans, Russians, Safavids, Mughals, and Qing all mounted intermittent wars against nomads and pastoralists. The last large-scale confederacy of nomads was that of the Zunghars in Mongolia, about 750,000 people, which was crushed militarily and then slaughtered by the Qing in the 1750s.

On a smaller scale, and in a compressed time frame, a

Nomads (Left) A large-scale painting executed collaboratively by Chinese and European painters shows Qing forces decisively defeating the nomadic Zunghars in their camp. (Right) In the United States, in 1876 Lakota Sioux, Cheyenne, and Arapaho forces defeated U.S. troops at the Battle of Little Bighorn, as this 1900 image by Lakota artist Amos Bad Heart Buffalo records—but they ultimately lost the war.

similar saga played out in the Americas. With the introduction of horses and guns, after 1800 peoples such as the Comanche and Lakota Sioux created mobile and militarized ways of life that bore some resemblance to that of steppe peoples in Asia. The Comanche and Lakota Sioux were not pastoralists on any scale; they did not keep livestock except horses. They lived more by hunting than stock raising. But they became a political force in North America and terrorized settled, farming peoples—mainly other Amerindians—with frequent brutal raids.

In South America, horse cultures arose in northern Patagonia during the seventeenth and eighteenth centuries among peoples such as the Tehuelche. They took to hunting guanacos (close relatives of llamas) and rheas (big flightless birds), raising cattle and sheep, and raiding neighboring settlements. They used lances, guns, and a weapon called the bolo, two stones tied together with a hide rope, in hunting and warfare. The basis of their newfound power, as for the Comanche and Lakota Sioux, was the mobility conferred by horses.

The age of nomad (or semi-nomad) power in the Americas came late compared to Asia and North Africa, beginning only in the eighteenth or nineteenth century. It ended in the second half of the nineteenth century, when the armies of settled agrarian societies—Argentina, Chile, Mexico, the United States, Canada—crushed the last remnants of nomad power in world history. This after-echo of the Qing obliteration of Zunghar power brought to a close a 3,000-year epoch in world history in which nomads and mobile pastoralists were a force to be reckoned with.

The relentless competition among agrarian states, their swift exchange (often unwilling) of information about the technologies and techniques of warfare, and their growth in size and capacity—all directly or indirectly resulting from the tightening of the Global web—spelled the end for nomads. They could not keep up with their agrarian neighbors, and their courage, horsemanship, and marksmanship no longer mattered.

PIRATES

Pirates played a far smaller role in world history. They probably existed even earlier than mobile pastoralists, from soon after the beginning of waterborne trade. Conditions generally suited pirates best when and where long-distance seaborne trade flourished, navies were weak, and at least a few good bays or inlets with minimal population could serve as bases. Access to markets was also important for piracy: when pirates grabbed a cargo of porcelain or sugar, they couldn't use much of it themselves and needed to sell it for money or swap it for what they wanted.

The early centuries of the Global web were a golden age for pirates. The linking up of the world's coastlines by European mariners led to a vast expansion in long-distance maritime trade. Port cities everywhere did a thriving business, and stolen cargoes could find ready buyers. Navies remained too small to patrol the world's oceans, leaving extensive safe space for pirates. Navies were so weak that in wartime they often inadvertently created pirates by recruiting sailors to assault enemy shipping—they were called privateers. In peacetime privateers were out of work, and many chose to stay afloat as pirates. The distinctions between pirate and privateer were sometimes fuzzy.

THE CARIBBEAN AND INDIAN OCEAN Although pirates might roam anywhere, they preferred certain locations. The Caribbean met their requirements nicely, and from the 1550s to the 1720s it was a hotbed of piracy and privateering. Spanish ships bearing silver exports from Mexico passed through the Caribbean, attracting pirates and privateers such as the Dutch privateer Piet Heyn, who captured a silver fleet off of Cuba's coast in 1628. Bartholomew Roberts, a Welsh-born pirate, captured 400 merchant ships in the Atlantic and Caribbean between 1719 and 1722. In the early eighteenth century, about one-third of pirates were Africans or of African descent, and at least two—Mary Read and Anne Bonny—were women.

The Indian Ocean, from the Red Sea to the Straits of Malacca, also presented pirates with splendid opportunities. These were exploited both by interlopers from the Atlantic, such as the Scottish-born Captain Kidd who built a base in Madagascar, and by locals, such as the Arakan (or Magh) pirates based on the shores of Burma who feasted on Bengali shipping and coastal settlements. Even better hunting grounds for pirates lay in the South and East China seas. The largest-scale pirate operation was that of the Zheng family on the southeastern coasts of China from Nanjing to Macao, the story of which began this chapter.

Barbary Pirates A sizable Barbary fleet appears off the coast of Nice, in the western Mediterranean, in this 1558 illustration. As was typical for Barbary fleets, its commander was an Ottoman *bey*: Hayreddin Barbarossa. He was responsible for many naval victories against Spain.

THE BARBARY PIRATES Other large operations were based in the North African cities of Algiers, Tunis, and Tripoli from the sixteenth century onward. The Mediterranean suited pirates because of its abundant shipping and lively slave markets where captives could be sold. With Ottoman encouragement, local officials, called *beys*, organized pirate/privateer forces to prey on shipping and coastal settlements mainly in Spain and Italy. The Barbary pirates, as they are known, sought cargoes and Christian captives to sell in North African markets. By one estimate, over the years from 1500 to 1800 they seized and enslaved about 1 million captives. On occasion they ventured farther afield, raiding Iceland in 1627, Ireland in 1631, and even the coast of Argentina in 1720. The Barbary pirates were at the height of their power in the early and mid-seventeenth century. Moroccan rulers offered similar support for pirates/privateers operating in eastern Atlantic waters from their base in Salé.

Christian kingdoms such as Spain and France encouraged European piracy and privateering against North African shipping and ports, and by 1630 used their navies against the Barbary pirates with some effect. But they did not yet have the power to close them down. Piracy flared up in the 1780s and 1790s, and now the targets included American merchant ships in the Mediterranean. For several years, the U.S. government paid protection money to get the pirates to desist—as much as 20 percent of the U.S. federal budget in 1800. The United States launched attacks in 1805 and 1815, and a British-Dutch force bombarded North African ports in 1816. By 1830 the naval power of their foes had become too great and the Barbary pirates were just about out of business.

The same fate befell pirates elsewhere. The Mughals routed pirates from their coastal lairs, mainly in Bengal and Burma, in the seventeenth century. British naval power largely eliminated pirates in the Caribbean by 1730. Everywhere around the world, from Taiwan to Jamaica, pirates were hunted down and piracy declined. It did not entirely disappear—indeed, a few pirates are active today in the Arabian Sea and Southeast Asian waters—but they never again attained anything like the power and wealth of the Zhengs or the *beys* of North Africa. Like the mobile pastoralists, the pirates of the world ran afoul of the ever-growing power of big empires.

CONCLUSION

The turmoil of the early modern centuries may seem a confusing blur of wars won and lost, dynasties rising and falling, states and empires appearing and vanishing, but there is a general pattern behind it. If one steps back from the details, it is possible to see a brutal political shakeout in which a few polities prospered and many disappeared. This pattern showed up more strongly in Eurasia than elsewhere, but it can also be found on smaller scales in places such as Hawaii and Morocco. As the technologies and techniques of war and power grew more complex and costly, the big got bigger, usually at the expense of the small. A handful of empires dominated Eurasia, and increasingly—a development without precedent in world history—the whole world.

The history of war and empire in these centuries reveals two other significant developments. First is the eccentricity of Europe. Despite the Habsburgs' best efforts, no state could build a pan-European empire. The other great centers of population in Eurasia—China, North India, and the Ottoman lands—all became the seats of gigantic empires far stronger than most of their frontier neighbors. Europe's eccentricity led to relentless competition—the university of war—and, in the long run, to stronger, more efficient, more formidable states. It also led to exceedingly difficult times for ordinary people caught up in the maelstrom. This peculiarity, combined with the access Atlantic Europeans had to information and commercial opportunity all over the world, helps to explain the rise of European power, specifically the Atlantic European powers, in the global political arena.

The second notable development was the destruction of nomad power and the marginalization of piracy. In the eighteenth and early nineteenth centuries, the big states developed sufficient capacity—logistics more than firepower—to abandon their at times cozy relations with nomads and pirates and to turn forcefully against them.

This simplified international politics, by reducing the role of non-state actors and leaving the stage, increasingly, to a smaller number of bigger players.

Part of the reason for the general pattern of consolidation of power around the world came from a quickening of world trade in the early modern centuries. Ships and caravans carried valuable goods and money—often, silver from the Americas or Japan. Any ruler could take a cut, and those located at choke points on long-distance routes could take big ones. In the next chapter we will see how this came to pass by turning to the new global economy made possible by the formation of a truly global web.

CHAPTER REVIEW

KEY TERMS

military revolution
(p. 548)

field artillery and
fortification (p. 550)

Oda Nobunaga (p. 551)

Toyotomi Hideyoshi
(p. 552)

Tokugawa shogunate
(p. 552)

Qing dynasty (p. 553)

Akbar (p. 557)

Istanbul (p. 560)

janissaries (p. 561)

millet system (p. 562)

imperial consolidation
(p. 562)

tsar (p. 563)

Habsburgs (p. 565)

university of war (p. 567)

Saadians (p. 569)

pirates (p. 572)

Go to INQUIZITIVE
to see what you've
learned—and learn what
you've missed—with
personalized feedback
along the way.

REVIEW QUESTIONS

1. What is the main reason that large imperial states were able to destroy hundreds of smaller states during the early modern period?

2. What six trends making up the military revolution caused warfare to become more complex and expensive?

3. How did Oda Nobunaga and his successors use guns to unify Japan?

4. Identify the Qing's most successful military innovations, and explain what was unique about these initiatives.

5. What military, religious, and economic techniques did the Mughals employ to consolidate power?

6. Describe how Istanbul, Egypt, the Hejaz, Mesopotamia, and Hungary contributed to Ottoman power.

7. What social, political, and military reforms did Ivan the Terrible and Peter the Great introduce in Russia?

8. What were the main forms of soft power the Habsburgs employed to expand their power in Europe?

9. How did constant political competition in Europe affect successful European states?

10. Explain the main technologies and techniques that small states adopted in order to survive.

11. What was the contribution of the elite class to the downfall of Poland and the Mamluk sultanate?

12. Why did the relationship between nomads and agrarian states change during the early modern period?

13. What was the chief reason for the loss of power among pirates?

14. What two significant developments does the history of war and empire in the early modern period reveal?

FURTHER READING

Jos GOMMANS, *Mughal Warfare* (2002). This remains the most careful assessment of the military revolution in India.

Xing HANG, *Conflict and Commerce in Maritime East Asia* (2015). The standard work on the Zheng family enterprise.

Peter LORGE, *The Asian Military Revolution* (2008). A handy summary of cases in South, Southeast, and East Asia. Especially good on China.

Alfred RIEBER, *The Struggle for the Eurasian Borderlands: From the Rise of Early Modern Empires to the End of the First World War* (2014). One of a few comparative studies of multiple empires—the Qing, Mughal, Safavid, Ottoman, Russian, and Habsburg.

Brian SANDBERG, *War and Conflict in the Early Modern World, 1500–1700* (2016). A work that is attentive to questions of organization and culture as well as technology.

Douglas STREUSAND, *Islamic Gunpowder Empires: Ottomans, Safavids, and Mughals* (2011). An accessible summary of its subject.

Joanna WALEY-COHEN, *The Culture of War in China: Empire and the Military under the Qing Dynasty* (2006). A very readable and compact study, emphasizing cultural sides of the Qing military buildup.

CHRONOLOGY

1490s
Portuguese mariners
settle São Tomé

1511
Portugese defeat
the Muslim sultanate
of Malacca

1520s–1540s
Silver strikes in Japan

1530s
Portuguese introduce
sugar plantations in
northeastern Brazil

1545–1558
Silver strikes
in Mexico

1555
English Muscovy
Company founded

1570s
Ming China requires
everyone to pay
taxes in silver

1560s
Ming China rescinds
foreign trade band

1550s
Sultan of Aceh begins to compete with Portuguese spice merchants

1590s
Brazil leads world's sugar production

1602–1799
Dutch East India
Company (VOC)

1621
Japanese silver production peaks

1609
Bank of Amsterdam founded

1684–1715
Shipping from south
China to Manila triples

By 1640s
Sugar and slavery are
booming in Caribbean

The First Global Economy

1500 to 1800

JAKOB FUGGER (1459–1525) and Virji Vora (ca. 1590–1670) knew how to make money. When Fugger died, his net worth was equivalent to about 2 percent of Europe's total annual economic output. Vora's trading partners reckoned he was the richest man in the world. Both men had acquired the knowledge and contacts to take full advantage of two recent changes that came with the formation of a truly global web: rulers' growing need to borrow money for wars (discussed in Chapter 19) and the expanding scale of long-distance trade.

Fugger was the tenth of eleven children in a merchant family in Augsburg in southern Germany. At age 14 he was sent to represent his family's business in Venice, and he ended up living there for 14 years. Most of his older brothers died young, and he took over the family business, shifting its focus from textiles to mining. He invested in copper and silver mines all over central Europe and traded copper to markets as far away as Russia and India. He also invested in a successful voyage from Portugal to India that returned with cargoes of spices. But his core business was mining, and he eventually controlled most of Europe's copper output.

Global Trade Set within the Dutch East India Company's fort in its capital, Batavia (present-day Jakarta, Indonesia), this 1661 painting by a Dutch artist shows a market of global goods. Merchants from China, Bengal, Europe, and Batavia itself meet to buy and sell—just one of countless instances in which trade knitted the Global web closer together.

1720
British Parliament forbids the wearing and use of imported calico cloth

1760
Tacky's War in Jamaica threatens plantation regime

ca. 1750
China has enough silver in circulation to satisfy demand

1750–1800
Laborers' wages in Beijing, Delhi, and Florence bottom out

FOCUS QUESTIONS

1. What broad factors drove the increases in world population and economic growth between 1500 and 1800?

2. What evidence is there that economic growth in this period mainly benefited elites?

3. How did the spice, cotton, and silver trades help integrate the global economy?

4. What was the significance of the new business formats that emerged during this period?

5. Which world regions experienced commercial revolutions, and why?

Banking became another core business for Fugger. He made loans to dukes, emperors, and popes. He financed the rise of the House of Habsburg. He paid for the Pope's Swiss guards. Fugger earned interest on his loans and also the cooperation of the powerful, which he used to win control over more mines throughout Habsburg Europe. Mining, banking, and political influence underlay Fugger's success.

A similar formula worked for Virji Vora a century and a half later. Trade, banking, and political influence underpinned his prosperity. He was probably a Jain and lived in Surat, in northwest India. He first appears in the written record in 1619 and for the next half-century figured prominently in Indian commerce of almost every variety. Commodity trading was a core business for Vora. Documents record him either buying or selling cloth, silver, gold, mercury, lead, pearls, diamonds, rubies, ivory, tea, opium, indigo, coral, and many kinds of spices. His agents had offices in eight Indian cities and as far afield as the shores of the Persian Gulf, the Red Sea, and Malacca in Southeast Asia. He was a master of cornering a market—buying up the entire supply of a certain good and then re-selling it on his own terms. He dominated trade with English, Dutch, and French merchants, who often complained of his business tactics.

Like Fugger, Vora was also a banker. He lent money to aristocrats of the Mughal court and to Mughal governors. He lent to European traders, even while he competed with them. Like Fugger, he translated his banking role into favors from politically powerful people, both Mughal officials and those of the English East India Company.

Both Fugger and Vora became immensely rich at a time when—as we shall see—most people around them were poor and getting poorer. These men exploited their knowledge of distant markets and prices and their connections with rising political powers, taking advantage of opportunities presented by changes in the world economy.

This chapter takes up economic history in the sixteenth to the eighteenth centuries. It begins with some data about global population, economic growth, and welfare. It emphasizes the big changes—for example, the rise of long-distance trades in spices, cotton, and silver. It also emphasizes the innovative features of the world's economy, including business and financial organizations such as large-scale slave plantations, joint-stock companies, and banks. In focusing on long-distance trade and innovation, the chapter tilts toward the European experience, because Europeans, mainly Atlantic Europeans, specialized in intercontinental trade and in innovative business organizations. This was no accident: long-distance trade encouraged novel business formats, and novel business formats eased long-distance trade.

For all this economic history to make sense, we need to remember three points in particular. First, that for several millennia before 1500, Southwest Asia was the region most connected to the world's largest web—the Old World web. That region stood at the center of connections among the northern half of Africa, South and Southeast Asia, Europe, and the Mediterranean. It lay close to the steppe corridor of

Eurasia. The least well connected regions in the Old World web were probably Siberia, the interior of sub-Saharan Africa, and the European subcontinent. But after the 1490s, as we've seen, all that changed and Atlantic Europe became the best-connected place on Earth.

The second point to remember is that Atlantic European mariners and merchants had forged most of the intercontinental connections after 1490. This gave them an information edge that translated into more available technologies for adoption, and more opportunities for profit based on knowledge of prices in different markets. This information edge, combined with the military advantage of shipboard cannon, goes far toward explaining the rising prominence of Atlantic European societies and states in global economic history after 1500. Atlantic Europeans were not richer than everyone else in 1500. But they, more than anyone else, changed the course of economic history in the three centuries after 1500. And, very gradually, their societies began to grow richer faster than others around the world. To put this another way, Atlantic Europeans took the lead in forming the Global web and knitting it together with trade. They derived greater wealth and power from it than anyone else between 1500 and 1800.

The third point to remember is that despite the long-distance trade and economic innovations, most people between 1500 and 1800 lived much as their ancestors had for centuries. Whether in China, Russia, West Africa, Scotland, or Peru, most people lived in villages, farmed for a living, ate most of what they produced, and rarely ventured far from home. Their economic existence—indeed, their entire existence—was precarious. It depended on the weather and the harvest, as well as the health of their animals (if they had any) and of the able-bodied members of their families. If they were free people, as most were, they turned over a bit of what their hard work produced to landlords or tax collectors, or both. The unfree—whether slaves, serfs, indentured laborers, or in some other bonded status—turned over most of what their work produced to lords and masters. Some of these people, both free and unfree, did additional work on the side, especially in the slack seasons of the farming year, perhaps making cloth or cutting timber. Few of them used money regularly, knew about the business empires of men like Fugger or Vora, or were aware of the commercial webs spanning the globe.

Of course, most people's lives were not exactly the same as their ancestors'. They might raise different crops or animals, perhaps ones newly introduced via the Columbian Exchange. Some technological improvements took place on farms during these three centuries—perhaps most important, in the means of draining swampland. A slightly larger proportion of farming families sold some of their harvest or even all of it. A few million people worked to produce spices, cotton, silk, sugar, tea, tobacco, or some other agricultural commodity that someone else traded to distant markets, a way of life rare among their ancestors. And a small but growing proportion did no farmwork and specialized in other tasks, such as spinning cotton or mining silver. But for most people alive before 1800, the routines of life changed little and slowly and remained centered on farming. Nonetheless, this chapter will focus on the new developments in economic life that changed the course of world history.

WORLD POPULATION AND THE GLOBAL ECONOMY

Despite some terrible demographic catastrophes, in the three centuries between 1500 and 1800 global population more than doubled. Although slow by the standards of our time, this growth was faster than in any previous era of world history. Improvements in agriculture and food supply helped spark the **population surge**. The Columbian Exchange enabled farmers to raise crops well suited to their local environments that had not been available before, such as maize in Africa or wheat in the Americas. Minor improvements in agricultural technology or practice in some parts of the world also helped. But there were no transformative technical breakthroughs in food production anywhere.

A second reason for the surge was what one historian has called the "microbial unification of the world." As travelers spread pathogens around the globe, the resulting diseases at first had terrible consequences, most notably in the Americas. But over time, populations developed resistance to a wider array of infections than before. More infections became childhood diseases, endemic in communities and only rarely sparking epidemics. No one understood it at the time, but this process of biological adjustment was speeding up by 1700 or 1750.

As more infections became endemic, they killed children without immunities even if antibodies now protected more disease-experienced adults. As before, families had to expect about half their children would die of disease before reaching adulthood. So they did their best to produce plenty of them, and fertility rates stayed high in most societies. Globally, mortality diminished slightly between 1500 and 1800. Before 1800, medical improvements remained trivial everywhere in their demographic impact.

The table above gives a rough idea of the trajectory of world population growth over these three centuries. Bear in mind the figures are educated guesswork.

The sixteenth century, as we have seen, was catastrophic for many Amerindian peoples. But elsewhere, as best we can judge, populations grew despite repeated epidemics and famines. In Europe and China, where the estimates are more reliable than elsewhere, that was clearly true. Population levels recovered from the losses of the fourteenth-century plague pandemic and kept growing briskly.

But the seventeenth century saw slower growth due mainly to enormous disasters. In the Americas, the effects of imported and unfamiliar diseases such as smallpox, measles, influenza, and malaria were still making themselves felt. More broadly, the seventeenth century brought the chilliest and driest years of the Little Ice Age. The years between 1618 and 1697 were ones of recurrent crisis in food supplies, the result mainly of a cluster of volcanic eruptions and their "dust veils." Sharp cold snaps and repeated droughts led to crop failures and starvation,

GLOBAL POPULATION GROWTH, 1500–1800		
DATE	GLOBAL POPULATION	AVERAGE ANNUAL GROWTH RATE (ROUNDED)
1500	438 million	
1600	556 million	0.25% (1500–1600)
1700	603 million	0.1% (1600–1700)
1800	950 million	0.6% (1700–1800)

Source: Angus Maddison, *The World Economy: Historical Statistics* (2003), 256.

resulting in more epidemics (worsened by malnutrition) and more warfare than normal. Political violence spiked in China, where the invading Manchus battled the collapsing Ming dynasty; in Ottoman lands, unsettled by internal rebellions; and in Europe, with its bloody religious wars and rebellions. In Gujarat and the Deccan, in India, an official Mughal chronicle described severe famines:

> . . . [A] perfect drought prevailed. . . . [H]igh and low were clamouring for their bread and dying from sheer exhaustion. . . . the streets and marketplaces were so thronged by the immense number of corpses that [one] could scarcely make [one's] way through them.

More broadly, infanticide and suicide apparently peaked in several societies around the world during the seventeenth century. On a global basis, the 1640s were probably the worst decade for humankind since the plague pandemic of the 1340s.

A POPULATION LANDMARK

The eighteenth century, in contrast, brought faster population growth than our species had ever before experienced. China more than doubled its population, a result partly of the spread of American food crops such as sweet potatoes and maize, but also of a reduction in deadly epidemics and political violence. In the Americas, the ravages of introduced diseases abated and millions of immigrants—mostly enslaved Africans—arrived. Europe's population increased by roughly 50 percent, with Ireland's growing the fastest. It more than doubled to about 5 million, fueled by the introduction of the potato from the Americas, a crop that suited Irish conditions well and allowed a family to survive—in poverty—on a small patch of land. The populations of India, Southwest Asia, and Africa grew more slowly—in Africa's case, probably by very little compared to China, the Americas, and Europe. Nobody knew it at the time, but in the eighteenth century the world began its modern rise of population that is still ongoing. From about 1750, if not a decade or two before, growth rates tilted upward at steeper and steeper rates through the late twentieth century, as we will see.

THE SIZE OF THE WORLD ECONOMY

The size of the world economy, the total value of goods and services produced, is called the **gross world product**, or GWP. We have only educated guesses of GWP, but by 1500 those estimates become more reliable.

So let's look at the numbers. The table below uses index numbers, with GWP in 1500 set at 100. (GWP in later years is presented relative to GWP in 1500—so a value of 150 in the year 1700 means the economy was half again as large as in 1500.) In today's money, the size of the world economy in 1500 was about U.S. $250 billion, equivalent to that of Louisiana or Finland or Bangladesh in 2018.

The world economy more than doubled in size between 1500 and 1800. It grew by about one-third in the sixteenth century, probably a record at that time. The seventeenth century, marked by crop failures, epidemics, and mass violence, posted a far weaker rate, but the eighteenth century showed resurgent growth.

The growth rates in global population resemble those of GWP, as they should: most economic growth was merely the result of more people living and working. But some of it derived from small technical advances in farming, and from more important ones in textile manufacturing, mining, and other arenas. A larger spur to economic growth came from the efficiencies of specialization and exchange, whereby more people than before were doing what they did best and trading the fruits of their labor

GROSS WORLD PRODUCT, 1500–1800

DATE	SIZE	AVERAGE ANNUAL GROWTH RATE (ROUNDED)	
1500	100		
1600	133	0.3%	(1500–1600)
1700	150	0.1%	(1600–1700)
1800	250	0.7%	(1700–1800)

Source: Elaborated from Angus Maddison, *The World Economy: Historical Statistics* (2003), 259.

for goods that others produced. After 1500, long-distance trade flourished as never before, quickened by the gradual extension of the Global web into almost every nook and cranny of the globe.

THE DISTRIBUTION OF ECONOMIC BENEFITS

But the gains from expansion of trade and technical improvements mainly benefited a fortunate few. There are several ways to estimate how well off people were in the past. Two of the better methods use data on people's heights and incomes. They suggest that although societies in the aggregate grew slightly richer between 1500 and 1800, most people did not.

INCREDIBLE SHRINKING HUMANS

Changes in the average heights of populations are a good indication of changes in the childhood nutrition and disease burden in a society. Well-fed and healthy children reach their genetic height potential. Malnourished ones ravaged by chronic disease don't. The raw data on stature generally come from archeology (skeletons) or, more often, records of military recruits. Let's consider some data from around the world on average heights.

The largest sample available comes from northern Europe: Scandinavia, the Netherlands, and Britain. These data in the table on page 582 show that on average northern Europeans shrank from medieval times until the late eighteenth century by nearly 3 inches (7.5 cm), with the fastest declines in the seventeenth through the eighteenth centuries. By 1800, northern Europeans were smaller than at any time before or since. This loss of stature is extreme in the annals of human height history. Populations in southern Germany (Bavaria), the Habsburg Empire, and northern Italy also shrank a bit between 1730 and 1780. We don't have earlier data for them.

In Russia, matters were apparently similar. The average height of military recruits, most of whom would not have come up to Peter the Great's armpit, fell during the eighteenth century by 2 inches (5 cm). These were glorious times for Russia's rulers and its elites, who managed to corral the benefits of a growing economy and territorial expansion, but times of grinding hunger and

AVERAGE MALE HEIGHTS IN SAMPLES FROM NORTHERN EUROPE	
PERIOD	**AVERAGE HEIGHT**
9th to 11th century	173.4 centimeters (just under 5′7″)
12th to 14th century	171.5 cm
17th to 18th century	167.5 cm
18th century	166.2 cm (or 5′4½″)

Source: Richard Steckel, "Health and Nutrition in the Pre-Industrial Era: Insights from a Millennium of Average Heights in Northern Europe," in *Living Standards in the Past: New Perspectives on Well-Being in Asia and Europe*, eds. R. C. Allen, T. Bengtsson, and M. Dribe (2005), 242.

Note: 1 inch = 2.54 cm

economic hardship for regular people. Russia, like many other places, grew richer in the aggregate and on average, yet at the same time more miserable for most people.

In Mexico, data on army recruits suggest the male population was shorter in 1840 than in 1740 by an average of 1.6 inches (4 cm). Argentine male heights shrank by about half as much in the same years. In both countries, the population and economy grew while stature declined.

In Korea, the only East Asian society for which we have data prior to 1800, army recruits on average grew taller through the sixteenth century and the beginning of the seventeenth, despite the devastating Japanese invasion of Korea in the 1590s. But during the late seventeenth and early eighteenth centuries, recruits lost 1.6 inches (4 cm) in height on average.

All these cases of declining average heights reflect poorer nutrition and heavier burdens of stunting diseases. The main reason for these trends was probably lower protein supply for children. Urbanization may also have played a role: city folk everywhere averaged an inch or two shorter than their country cousins, again a reflection of nutrition and disease.

Army recruit records only pertain to men. If we had more data for women, they would probably show just as much, or even more, loss of stature during the period from 1500 to 1800. In most cultures, when families were short of food, they usually gave more to boys than to girls—as remains true today where food is scarce.

In British North America, the history of stature tells a different and happier story about nutrition and welfare. The population of European descent grew taller on average between 1710 and 1810, by about 0.8 inches (2 cm). British army recruits born and raised in North American colonies towered over their cousins born in Britain, by about 3 to 5 inches (8 to 12 cm) on average, an indication of the superior nutrition and health in the lands that would become the United States and Canada. Enslaved people's average heights fell slightly before 1800 in the United States, but from 1800 to 1840 average male slave heights climbed 1.5 inches (4 cm) to 5′8½″, suggesting they benefited from improving nutrition in those decades.

Meanwhile, the nutrition experience of Amerindians in North America was mixed. Skeletons show that the Iroquois, Cherokee, Delaware, and Ottawa all grew taller, by about 2 to 3 inches (4 to 7 cm), between 1650 and 1800. President Thomas Jefferson in 1804, upon meeting a delegation of Osage from the Kansas plains, wrote that they were "certainly the most gigantic men we have ever seen." While it is hard to imagine this reflected better nutrition, given the rough fate of Amerindians in these years, it is either that or else short people (and their genes) were ruthlessly weeded out by violence, hunger, and disease, which over a mere 150 years is unlikely.

Probably improved protein supply played a role. To judge by their skeletons, the equestrian buffalo hunters of the plains were the tallest and healthiest Amerindian populations anywhere in the Americas. Indeed, by the mid-nineteenth century, Plains Indians were the tallest people in the world for whom data exist, probably a reflection of a meat-rich diet. In contrast, Amerindians who clustered around Spanish missions in California shrank, especially males. That probably registers a change of boys' diet toward cereals and away from meat. Just as human

Stature and Nutrition North American Plains Indians owed their tall stature to a protein-rich diet centered on game like buffalo. They were known for their height as well as their nomadic hunting lifestyle, as this nineteenth-century romanticized painting by a German American artist suggests.

populations in the deeper past shrank when they transitioned from hunting and foraging to farming, so, perhaps, the buffalo hunters of the plains grew in stature from an increasingly protein-rich diet.

While we don't have data yet for Africa, China, and India before the nineteenth century, it appears that the global trend—to which North America was an exception—was that people grew smaller even as economies grew larger. The benefits of expanding economies (outside of North America) seem to have flowed overwhelmingly to elites while the standard of living for most people fell between 1500 and 1800.

FALLING INCOMES FOR WAGE LABORERS

The evidence on incomes for ordinary city folk supports this discouraging conclusion. In Beijing, Delhi, London, Amsterdam, and Florence, laborers' real incomes climbed during the fourteenth and fifteenth centuries. The plague pandemic of the 1340s had had one silver lining for survivors: the resulting scarcity of people drove wages up. Unskilled laborers earned three to four times what they required for subsistence in 1450, which meant each one could support a small family. But in the late fifteenth century, laborers' incomes began a long slide, which in Beijing, Delhi, and Florence bottomed out around the years 1750–1800. At that point, a laborer barely earned enough to feed one mouth, which meant in families everyone had to work. In Amsterdam and London, laborers' incomes slipped rather less; they climbed a bit in the seventeenth century, before falling again in the eighteenth. Everywhere, the constraints of an economy based on human and animal muscle meant that the great majority of people lived close to subsistence levels. Britain's North American colonies, again, were an exception to the dismal trend. In the mid-eighteenth century, unskilled free laborers in Boston and Philadelphia earned four or five times what they needed for subsistence, more than anywhere else in the world for which data exist.

Why did ordinary people grow poorer while economies grew faster than ever before? At any time of large-scale economic reorganization, some people are better situated to benefit from change than others. Most of the economic growth from 1500 to 1800 created rewards for those involved in trade, finance, and government. Ordinary peasants and laborers, outside of a few favored locations

The Laboring Poor Peasants and laborers—ordinary people—were hit hardest by major environmental, demographic, and economic shifts. A seventeenth-century French painting depicts the realities of subsistence life for a peasant family: ragged clothing and a few basic dishes empty of food.

such as eastern North America, saw their economic position weaken as their numbers grew.

TRADE

The burst of oceanic voyaging after the 1490s linked markets as never before. This created opportunities for buying cheap in one market and selling dear in another. To do this optimally, one needs more market knowledge than competitors have—exactly what the people who made the voyages acquired. These voyagers were mainly Atlantic Europeans, not the maritime traders of the East China Sea or the Indian Ocean, nor the caravan merchants of Iran or Central Asia, who by and large did not go global.

Certain trades, such as cotton, rewarded market knowledge more than others. You needed to know a lot in order not to lose your shirt in the cotton business. On the production side, some varieties of cotton plants produced better fiber than others. Spinners and weavers had several techniques for making yarns and cloths of different quality and cost. Different dyestuffs and printing methods produced an array of colors and patterns. And at every stage, spinners, weavers, and other workers had varying skill levels. So "cotton" amounted to dozens of different products.

On the demand side, communities of consumers had particular preferences, and these might change over time.

Cotton Production Technological advances and market know-how enabled Europeans to begin to compete in the global cotton trade. In this painting, mid-seventeenth-century French peasants spin cotton on a spinning wheel and weave it into cloth on a large frame loom within their own cottage—the typical form of cotton production at the time.

During the early modern centuries, most Chinese markets valued plain white cotton. West African markets preferred vivid hues, while Latin American consumers paid more for floral motifs. But beneath these generalizations, specific villages and individuals had different preferences. Knowledge of these complexities helped people make money in the long-distance cotton trade. This favored literate people and those who actually did the voyaging and trading: they accumulated broader knowledge faster.

Atlantic Europeans had another important edge in long-distance trade, noted in the previous chapter. Their sturdy ships, built to withstand Atlantic gales, accommodated heavy cannon. European merchants active in oceanic trade almost always carried serious armament. They could fight back against pirates and hope to prevail. They could engage in piracy themselves when it suited them, attacking, say, Bengali or Malay ships and seizing their cargoes. They could threaten to bombard port cities until local princes and merchants offered their goods at lower prices. Well-armed ship captains could sell "protection" to the less well armed, allowing them to live in peace for a price. These twin advantages, in information and seaborne firepower, went a long way toward enriching Atlantic Europe's merchant classes.

Before 1500, the Indian Ocean world, from China to Egypt, was the central arena of long-distance seaborne trade. The sea lanes of the Atlantic, the Baltic Sea, North Sea, and the coasts as far south as Senegal were busy too, but not on the same scale. Regular transatlantic traffic began in the wake of Columbus, and the slave trade extended it to African coasts as far south as Angola and Mozambique. Almost all Atlantic trade took place in ships owned and operated by Atlantic Europeans. By the 1550s, this burgeoning Atlantic trade was increasingly linked to the Indian Ocean commerce. European merchants gradually got involved in the trade circuits of Indian Ocean and East Asian waters, although never outstripping Asian trading communities.

Three commodities accounted for a sizeable chunk of world trade during the early modern centuries: spices, cotton, and silver. While many other things (as well as millions of people) were traded, these three played central roles in tightening the commercial webs of the world, integrating far-flung regions in particular.

SPICES AND THE SPICE TRADE

Cooks have flavored food with spices for several thousand years. When people thought that good health rested on a proper balance of hot and cold influences, spices such as pepper, ginger, and cinnamon acquired reputations as health foods. (In fact, many spices are rich in micronutrients and antioxidants.) The lands that produced the most spices were the islands of Southeast Asia. Spices featured prominently in local diets, but more than 2,000 years ago they also became staples in long-distance trade to both India and China. Ancient Rome imported spices too, as did, later on, the Muslim caliphates based in Damascus and Baghdad, and Byzantine markets in Constantinople. Eventually, spices, especially peppers, were grown in south India as well as Southeast Asia. In addition to peppers, the most marketable spices included nutmeg, cinnamon, and cloves, valued for their flavor and purported medicinal value. The port cities of the Indian Ocean world, from Malacca to Basra, all had spice bazaars.

In 1400, China and India remained the chief markets for spices. Europe's supply, maybe 2,000 tons annually, came mainly via Egypt to Venice. Vasco da Gama sought a route to the Indian Ocean around Africa in the 1490s, with the backing of the Portuguese Crown, in part to cut out the middlemen in the **spice trade** and get to the

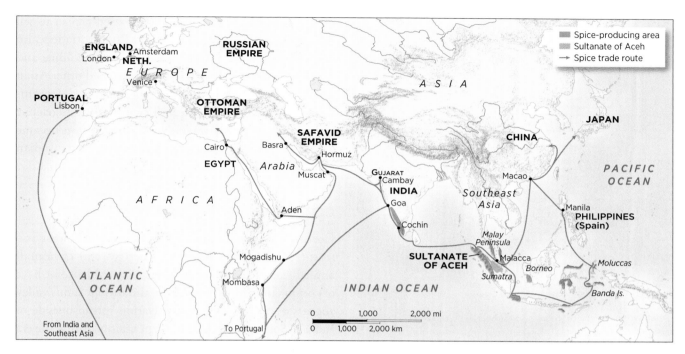

The Spice Trade, ca. 1600 The spice trade had flowed along the maritime routes of the Indian Ocean world for millennia. The main production zones were Southeast Asian islands such as the Moluccas and Bandas, and eventually southwestern India. The biggest markets by 1600 were China, India, Southwest Asia, and Europe. Before the Portuguese voyages around the southern tip of Africa, spices had arrived in Europe overland via Ottoman territories. By 1600, the Ottomans were losing that trade to seagoing European merchants. The sultans of Aceh kept their grip on the trade passing west from the spice islands through the Straits of Malacca until 1600.

source—Southeast Asia and India. An all-sea route lowered the price of spices in Europe, boosting demand. After da Gama's return in 1498, Lisbon soon became one of the world's great spice markets.

The best spices grew wild on islands such as the Moluccas and the Bandas, now parts of Indonesia. Much of the trade flowed through the port of Malacca, a great trading city with perhaps 100,000 people by 1500. Superior firepower enabled the Portuguese to defeat the Muslim sultanate of Malacca in 1511 with a force of only 1,200 men. This strategic conquest was the most important step in the Portuguese quest for a commanding position in the spice trade. Tomé Pires, a Portuguese who visited Malacca in 1511, wrote that one could hear 84 languages spoken on its streets on any given day. Its connections with northwest India were so strong that Pires wrote: "Melaka cannot survive without Cambay, nor Cambay without Melaka." Portuguese merchants now carried increasing shares of the trade not only to Lisbon, but also to markets in India and China. The Portuguese language became the lingua franca of the spice trade. Superior market knowledge and

naval firepower permitted tiny Portugal to play this outsized role.

The spice trade initially brought spectacular profits for merchants who survived the dangers of long sea voyages. When da Gama first arrived in India, the market price of pepper there was 4 percent of the price in Europe. In the Moluccas, spices could be had for 1/700 the Lisbon price. In the years from 1500 to 1630, an average of seven Portuguese ships set out each year for Asian spice markets. Storms, shipwrecks, and pirates claimed an average of three, but the surviving four brought magnificent profits.

The quantities of spices going to China, India, and Islamic lands remained greater than that headed to Europe. In the pepper trade perhaps a quarter or a third went to Lisbon, while the rest found its way to Asian markets, often in Portuguese ships. For cloves, more expensive and profitable than pepper, the proportion (for the sixteenth century) was roughly 90 percent to Asia and 10 percent to Europe.

After 1550, the sultan of Aceh (on the northern end of Sumatra) sought to control the spice trade. With allies

Women in the Marketplace An engraving from a Dutch book of the late seventeenth century shows women involved in market transactions on the island of Java. In Southeast Asia, women often took part in market trading.

in Gujarati traders and even Ottoman sultans, Aceh's sultan became a formidable competitor for Portuguese merchants after 1550. They acquired more competitors after 1590 when the Dutch, and soon English traders too, tried to get a share of the spice trade. By 1620, the Dutch and English between them sent about ten ships laden with spices back to Europe annually, more than twice what Portugal managed. The more competitive market meant less profit for everyone, but Dutch data show the spice trade returned an annual profit averaging 27 percent from 1602 to 1650. By the late seventeenth century, Amsterdam prices were only about 5 times Malacca prices for pepper, and 15 times for cloves. The fabulous profits of the early years of the spice trade were gone forever. But more people were able to enjoy spices' flavors and healthful effects.

With their market knowledge and shipboard cannon, Portuguese, Dutch, and English merchants won a large share of the world's spice trade after 1511. They cut Egyptian and Venetian middlemen out of the trade to Europe. By 1615, English merchants were trading pepper to Ottoman markets in the eastern Mediterranean, where

a century before Venetians had purchased pepper to sell in Europe. Portuguese, Dutch, and English traders also carried spices from Southeast Asia to Japan, China, and India, competing with Malay, Gujarati, and other Asian merchants on their home turf. The spice trade continued to grow into the eighteenth century. But its relative importance in global trade dwindled as cotton became the staple of the long-distance trade between the Indian Ocean world and the Atlantic.

COTTON AND THE COTTON TRADE

Cotton grows only in lands where there are at least 200 frost-free days and either 20 inches (50 cm) of rainfall annually or irrigation water. The earliest evidence we have of cotton cultivation comes from the ancient Indus valley about 5,000 years ago. Its cultivation spread outside of India to Southwest Asia and Egypt mainly during the era of Islamic expansion, the eighth through the tenth centuries. But world production remained centered on India. Chinese farmers in the southeastern province of Fujian grew cotton too. When the Ming decided to accept cotton as a means of paying taxes in the fourteenth century, the crop spread widely in southern China.

Before 1450, cotton was raised, spun, and woven into cloth, and traded chiefly in India and China. It was grown mainly on small farms, spun into thread by women and children in villages, and woven into cloth usually by men in village workshops. During the fifteenth through the seventeenth centuries, India's cotton farming and manufacturing was concentrated in the regions of Gujarat and Punjab, in northwest India, which specialized in cheap cottons; and in Coromandel, in the southeast; and Bengal, in the northeast, both of which specialized in fine muslins and high-quality printed cloth such as calicoes and chintzes.

High-quality cotton, like silk, was well suited for long-distance trade. It was lightweight and durable, and it could be folded or rolled into nearly any shape. In the fifteenth century it was valued from Japan to Spain to East Africa. Merchants traded it by land and sea, including along caravan routes of Asia, many of which were "cotton roads" as much as "silk roads." In the mid-seventeenth century, Iran imported 25 to 30 thousand camel loads of cotton annually from India.

As with spices, it was European oceanic merchants who most conspicuously expanded the scope of the world

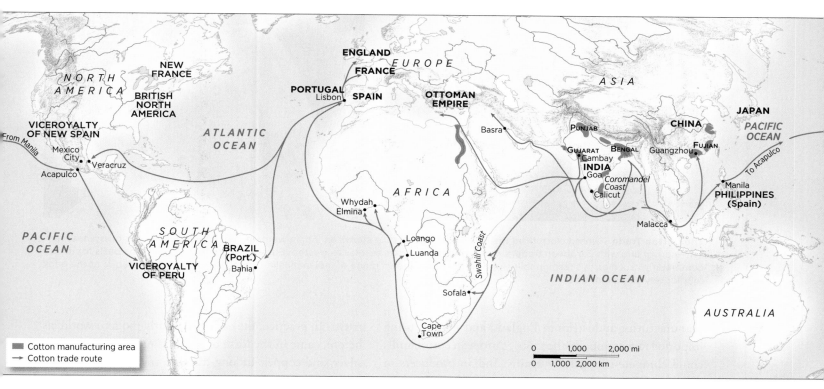

The Cotton Trade, ca. 1700 Cotton grew well in several zones around the world in 1700, but India was the biggest producer. With markets almost everywhere, cotton was one of the first truly global trade commodities. The seaborne circuits shown here include both transatlantic and transpacific routes to markets in the Americas. Southeast Asia, both East and West Africa, the Ottoman lands, and Atlantic Europe were also major importers of cotton.

cotton trade. They carried it to new markets in Africa, Europe, and the Americas. They also competed with Asian traders carrying cotton from one Asian port to another.

In the course of the sixteenth century, the Atlantic slave trade came to involve cotton. West Africans already had a taste for Indian cottons, available at considerable cost via trans-Saharan routes from North Africa and Egypt. Between 1500 and 1800, some 50 to 60 percent of African imports in the slave trade were Indian cloth offered by Portuguese, Dutch, or English merchants. Of the roughly 8 million Africans bought for shipment to the Americas in those centuries, over 4 million were purchased with Indian textiles.

People in the Americas also bought Indian cotton goods. Cotton cloth, like Chinese silk and porcelain, crossed the Pacific to Spanish America via Manila and Acapulco. But it also came through Spain's ports and across the Atlantic. Women in Mexico City wore fine calicoes from India. According to one eighteenth-century account, even slave women in Veracruz (Mexico) wore

skirts of embroidered muslin. Portuguese merchants sold Indian cotton cloth in Brazil.

European markets eventually bought more Asian cottons than did either Africa or the Americas. The Portuguese trade to Indian Ocean ports had initially focused on spices, but by 1620 textiles—mainly cotton—made up 60 percent of it (by value). In 1708, the English man of letters Daniel Defoe (author of *Robinson Crusoe*) complained that imported cotton had "crept into our Houses, our Closets and Bed Chambers, Curtains, Cushions, Chairs, and at last Beds themselves were nothing but Calicoes or Indian stuffs." Indian cotton was sufficiently good and cheap that it menaced Europe's wool and linen business and put thousands of weavers out of work. Responding to weavers' riots and complaints voiced by men such as Defoe, France and Britain enacted tariffs and outright bans on Indian cloth imports, starting in the 1680s. In 1720, the British Parliament passed a law forbidding the use or wearing of imported calico cloth.

These protectionist measures spurred domestic cotton

The Cotton Trade Painted cloth from the Madras region of India shows an Indian woman (center)—perhaps a cotton-spinner herself—conversing with European traders. Traders shipped Indian textiles to western Europe, where they became the basis for luxury commodities such as this fashionable eighteenth-century gown made of Indian muslin. The pleated, floor-length fabric at the back falls loosely as a slight train.

manufacturing industries in England and France, using imported raw cotton. By the 1760s, European cotton mills could compete successfully against Indian producers in African and American markets. Cotton was now a global business—one that, as much as anything else, brought the Indian Ocean and Atlantic Ocean into a unified trading world, providing a strong strand in the Global web.

SILVER AND THE SILVER TRADE

Silver became another of the first global trade commodities, but with a difference. It served primarily as money, whereas cotton was most often used for clothing and only occasionally as money. There were two main reasons for silver's expanded role. First, governments, always in need of revenue, found it advantageous to demand that taxes be paid in silver as opposed to grain, cotton, livestock, labor, or anything else. Silver gave them the flexibility to pay for weapons, soldiers, or whatever else they might need on short notice. The Mughals gradually put tax payments in India on a silver basis. The Ming did the same in China, where tax had previously come most often in the form of rice. In the 1570s they changed the laws to require everyone, even peasant families, to pay taxes in silver. A huge proportion of the world's population now needed silver.

The second reason for the rise of silver as a global commodity was that it solved a problem of mistrust that hampered long-distance trade. When people don't know and trust one another, they need money that everyone trusts. In practice, the cash of the early modern world, as before, came in the form of precious metals such as gold, silver, and copper. In long-distance trade, silver emerged as the best option because copper wasn't valued enough, gold was too rare, and paper money or promises of future payment were unreliable.

The silver needed to keep governments going and long-distance trade humming came mainly from Spanish America, central Europe, and Japan. New silver strikes

Silver Production An illustration of the *patio* process shows workers at a mine in Mexico refining silver on an industrial scale—producing the pure silver that was increasingly fueling the global economy. Transmission of the most efficient mining and ore-refining technologies of the day boost silver output around the world.

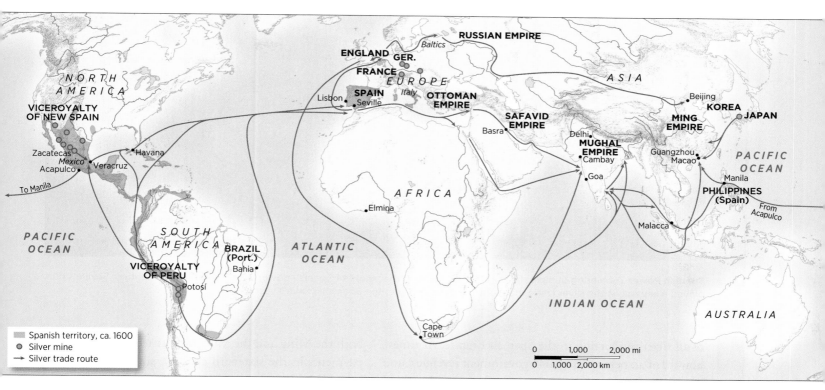

The Silver Trade, ca. 1600 Silver became a truly global commodity in the sixteenth century. The main silver-mining zones were in Japan, central Europe, and Spanish America—especially in Zacatecas, Mexico, and Potosí. Silver was crucial to the Spanish Empire's finances. However, it commanded a higher price in India and China than anywhere else, so silver flowed across land and sea to the Mughal and Ming empires. Silver was so prized in China that it could bear the high transport costs across the length of Asia by overland caravan.

took place in Japan in the 1520s through the 1540s, in Mexico during the years 1545 through 1558, and the biggest of all—as we've seen—at Potosí (in today's Bolivia) high in the Andes, in 1545. In Japan, Chinese and Korean mining technology adopted in the 1550s improved the yield of silver veins. In the Americas, the latest German technology was applied in Mexico in the 1550s and at Potosí in the 1570s. Japan's mines adopted it, via Mexico, by 1580, leading to a peak in production from 1602 to 1630.

These technologies, especially the so-called ***patío process*** in Spanish America, made it easier to separate silver from its surrounding rock, so lower-grade ores became worth mining. Japan in the sixteenth century mined about 30 percent of the world's silver, and in the seventeenth century about 15 percent. Spanish American mines produced a good deal more, and Potosí alone accounted for 60 percent of world silver production between 1550 and 1650. Thus the transmission of technology along international circuits helped advance a silver mining boom on three continents. The effects enabled some monarchs to spend

as never before and tightened the Global web through the enhanced use of silver in global trade.

FINANCING THE SPANISH AND JAPANESE STATES The rising tide of silver production floated the Spanish and Japanese states and tempted them to overreach. Despite Spain's small population (about 7 million) and poverty of natural resources, it became a great power in Europe and controlled much of the Americas and the Philippines after the mid-sixteenth century. In Europe, the Spanish Crown—a branch of the Habsburg dynasty from 1519 to 1700—used its silver bonanza to fight endless wars and champion the Catholic effort to roll back Protestantism. Spanish monarchs also committed to continual warfare against the Ottomans (and Muslims more generally) in the Mediterranean. A Spanish friar writing in 1638 put it this way: "Potosí lives in order to serve the imposing aspirations of Spain: it serves to chastise the Turk, humble the Moor, make Flanders tremble and terrify England." By law, the Crown was entitled to one-fifth

Spanish Power A painting depicts the port city of Seville at the height of Spanish power in the late sixteenth century. Seville's port played a key role in the silver trade that contributed mightily to the Spanish Crown's vast wealth.

of all silver production in the Spanish Empire. At times, upward of 40 percent of Spain's government revenue came from Potosí alone.

The silver mountain's bounty peaked in the 1590s and slipped sharply after about 1640. Spanish kings managed to spend all the silver that crossed the Atlantic on royal account and then some. When pinched for funds after production started to fall, they sometimes grabbed private traders' silver as it came ashore. Felipe IV (r. 1621–1665) said, "Nothing do I regret more than having to seize silver." But he did it anyway to fight wars.

Similarly, in Japan, the military entrepreneurs who unified the country—Oda Nobunaga (1534–1582), Toyotomi Hideyoshi (ca. 1536–1598), and Tokugawa Ieyasu (1543–1616)—financed their campaigns against rival warlords with silver. They converted the mines into a state monopoly exploiting convict labor. Silver revenues also helped pay for Hideyoshi's unsuccessful invasion of Korea in the 1590s. Like Habsburg Spain (and, for that matter, like Athens of the fifth century BCE), Tokugawa Japan's hard power rested largely on military force supported by the yields of silver mines while they lasted. By 1640, Japan's silver production had shrunk to half its peak levels of 1621.

PROMOTING ECONOMIC GROWTH IN CHINA AND INDIA The silver that was mined in Spanish America and Japan traveled around the world. Most of it eventually went to China or India, where it served to promote commerce and underpin economic growth. When both the Ming and the Mughals insisted on silver for tax payments in the sixteenth century, silver became more valuable in those lands than anywhere else. People could exchange silver for more goods, or more gold, in India and China than elsewhere. Anyone who could survive the risks of trading across the seas could do well exchanging silver for Indian cotton cloth and pepper, or Chinese silk and porcelain. As a Portuguese official in Macau, Manuel de Comara de Noronha, put it in 1630, "When the Chinese smell silver, they will bring mountains of merchandise." In the same year, He Qiaoyuan, a Ming scholar and official, remarked that silver acquired through foreign trade resulted in massive exports, thereby ensuring "employment for weavers, potters, and merchants, whose waxing affluence augured higher standards of living for all." The ceramic kilns at the southern town of Jingdezhen employed more than 10,000 workers during the late Ming. Silver flows helped to bolster both the Chinese economy and world trade.

Merchants sent Japanese silver to China, often in Dutch or Portuguese ships because Japanese were officially forbidden to trade with foreigners. American silver flowed along many pathways. Some bullion crossed the Pacific via Acapulco to Manila in the Philippines, and on to China from there. In this way, Chinese silk and ceramics entered markets in Mexico and Spanish America generally. The bulk of American silver crossed the Atlantic, usually via Cuba's main port of Havana, to Seville in Spain. But it did not rest there long. Some of Spain's incoming silver went

Chinese Ceramics The export of Chinese luxury goods, like this intricate Ming-era painted and enameled porcelain box, brought the silver needed for coinage and tax payments in China.

to repay loans from Italian and German bankers, including the house of Fugger. After the 1560s, plenty of it went to finance Spain's army, which was at war with the Dutch. Once delivered to bankers or the Spanish army, American silver flowed through Otto-man lands, the Baltic, and Russia, or traveled in European ships sailing around Africa, always heading for India and China, as if pulled by a magnetic attraction.

For two centuries nothing produced in the rest of the world, except at times European cannon, interested Chinese and Indian merchants as much as silver. But by 1750 or so, China had enough silver in circulation to satisfy demand and reduce its price to about the same as the world price. Silver flows slowed and no longer quickened global commerce.

Silver, cotton, and spices: they could be produced only in some places but were in demand everywhere. They formed the lifeblood of global trade between 1500 and 1750, and they exemplify the process by which merchants connected far-flung markets in a global commercial web. Tea, sugar, silk, gold, ivory, and many other items—even dried fish—were traded across the oceans as well. So were millions of slaves. At any given time after 1550, hundreds of ships were sailing on well-traveled routes, linking ports such as Guangzhou, Manila, Cambay, Goa, Basra, Cape Town, Elmina, Seville, Amsterdam, London, Bahia, Havana, Acapulco, and many others. Year after year ships and cargoes sailed, tightening the web of global commerce.

NEW BUSINESS FORMATS: PLANTATIONS, COMPANIES, BANKS

The quickening pace of global commerce invited creative entrepreneurs to invent or refine the institutions through which they did business. Three of the most important in the early modern centuries were plantations, trading companies, and banks.

PLANTATIONS

A seventeenth-century Barbadian slave was quoted in 1676 as saying, "The devil was in the Englishman that he makes everything work; he makes the Negro work, he makes the horse work, the ass work, the wood work, the water work and the wind work." But it was not the devil that inspired Englishmen on Barbados to try to force everyone and everything to make sugar. It was the opportunity to get rich by selling sugar grown, harvested, and processed by enslaved labor on plantations.

Plantations are large-scale commercial farming operations with labor forces of dozens or hundreds of people—sometimes free wage workers, sometimes unfree laborers, and often both. They have existed here and there since ancient times. But the interconnected commercial world that developed after the 1490s improved the economic logic of plantations. When many markets were within reach, the rewards to large-scale production (known as **economies of scale**) multiplied. Nothing worked better as a plantation crop than sugar.

Sugar is a grass native to Southeast Asia. It will grow in tropical and subtropical latitudes where temperatures are warm for most of the year. It needs either abundant rain or irrigation, and fertile soils. In the harvest season,

Sugar Plantations In this early nineteenth-century scene representing a sugar plantation in Antigua, a British Caribbean colony, enslaved men and women prepare the ground for planting. The world's sugar trade rested on the plantation system and slave labor. The windmill provided the power that squeezed cane juice from harvested sugarcane.

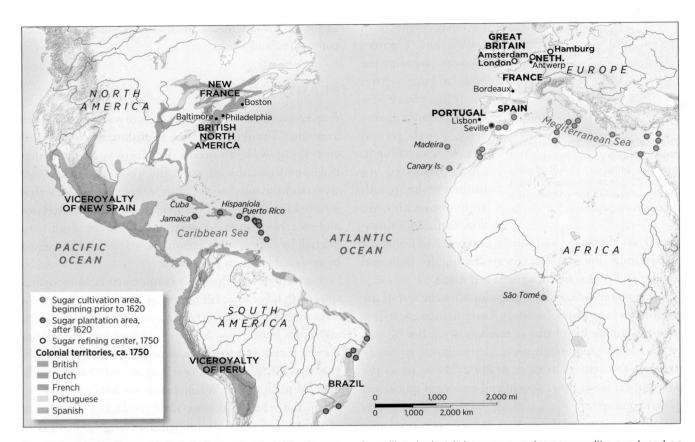

The Sugar Industry, ca. 1750 People had been cultivating sugar for millennia, but it became a major commodity, produced on plantations with slave labor, in the Mediterranean world around 1000 CE. In the sixteenth century, Portuguese and Spanish entrepreneurs brought sugar plantations into the Atlantic world, first to islands such as Madeira, the Canaries, and São Tomé, then across the ocean to the Caribbean and coastal Brazil. Sugar refining was concentrated in Hamburg, Amsterdam, and London, with smaller centers elsewhere in Europe and in British North America, especially Boston and Philadelphia.

it needs a burst of labor. Its economies of scale came in the processes of milling and refining, in which juice is squeezed by rollers from sugar cane and then boiled into a goopy mass that dries into crystals. To make sugar pay, one needed to make big investments in land, labor, machinery, buildings, and other infrastructure. Sugar is rarely a small farmer's crop, and for the last thousand years it has been mainly a plantation crop.

Sugar was grown on a modest scale in China and India in ancient times. By 650 CE it had appeared in Iraq and Egypt. By 800 its cultivation had spread to several Mediterranean islands, southern (Islamic) Spain, and river valleys of Morocco. In the Muslim lands of the Mediterranean, slaves—mainly captives from Christian Europe—formed the backbone of the sugar labor force. In Morocco by 1450, entrepreneurs and emirs imported African slaves across the Sahara to work on sugar plantations. Portuguese

and Spaniards did the same on Atlantic islands such as Madeira, the Canaries, and São Tomé.

THE SPREAD OF THE SUGAR PLANTATION São Tomé, in the Gulf of Guinea, pointed the way toward a large-scale slave-and-sugar complex. Portuguese mariners settled the formerly uninhabited island in the 1490s. Its volcanic, nutrient-rich soils and rainy climate proved ideal for sugar. By the 1550s, the island's economy focused so tightly on sugar that it raised too little food for its population. Merchants brought food from Portugal, a month away by sail. The plantations required a constant influx of people—slaves from Kongo on the mainland of Africa, and settlers, often unwilling migrants, mostly from the communities of Portuguese Jews, debtors, and criminals, and other populations the Portuguese Crown was happy to deport. For nearly half a century, São Tomé served as the leading example of a new business format, the large-scale slave plantation.

In the 1530s, Portuguese businessmen took the plantation format to the northeast of Brazil. There they found good soils and climate for sugar cultivation, but a shortage of labor. They tried enslaving the Amerindian population, but extremely high death rates from disease and maltreatment convinced them that the answer to their problem was massive imports of African slaves. By the 1590s, Brazil led the world in sugar production. By the 1640s, the tandem of sugar and slavery was booming in the Caribbean too, where planters on Spanish, French, British, and Dutch islands all raised cane in quantity. Some Caribbean planters at first tried using enslaved Scots and Irish, but too few could be found. Next came indentured European laborers, who were bound to work for a fixed number of years in exchange for free passage across the Atlantic. But too few volunteered (or could be kidnapped), and once in the Caribbean they died fast from diseases. So, as in Brazil, Caribbean planters turned to Atlantic Africa, where local merchants offered slaves in great numbers at advantageous prices. Thereafter, for 200 years, Brazil and the Caribbean led the world in sugar exports and slave imports.

The **slave-and-sugar plantations** in Brazil and the Caribbean were a novel form of enterprise, far larger and more efficient than their predecessors in São Tomé or the Mediterranean. The plantations, at least on the smaller islands of the Caribbean such as Barbados, imported most of their food from afar, as had São Tomé—so they could specialize on one product, sugar. Plantations usually held between 100 and 500 slaves, and sugar districts supported the densest rural populations anywhere in the Americas. They were all located near the seacoasts because sugar was an export crop, destined for European markets in Lisbon, Seville, Bordeaux, Antwerp, Amsterdam, or London— and after 1730 or so also North American ones such as Baltimore, Philadelphia, or Boston. They were often enormously profitable for planters.

SUGAR AND PLANTATION SLAVERY Sugar profits rested on a double exploitation. Sugar monoculture depleted soil nutrients, so planters periodically had to move to virgin fields, usually to forested land. In time, often about 50 to 75 years, plantations on smaller Caribbean islands became unprofitable due to nutrient loss,

and the sugar industry gradually shifted to bigger islands such as Jamaica, Hispaniola, and Cuba. The big islands had more land and forests that, when burned, released in their ash a pulse of nutrients to the soil from which a bumper crop could spring for a few years.

The exploitation of people was more consequential. From 1550 to 1850, about half of the nearly 11 million Africans shipped across the Atlantic went to sugar plantations in Brazil and the Caribbean. The majority were field slaves who worked long hours in labor gangs overseen by armed men. During the harvest and milling seasons, men, women, and children worked around the clock with scant rest. A combination of strenuous work, brutality, and a lethal disease environment made sugar plantations notoriously unhealthy and contributed to the short life expectancy of slaves on these plantations: shorter than anywhere else in the Americas, averaging about 10 years after arrival for those born in Africa. (Free blacks' life expectancy was marginally longer, indentured Europeans' slightly shorter.) Among slaves on sugar plantations, deaths outstripped births until the nineteenth century. So, after more than two centuries of continuous slave imports, the population on sugar plantations in the Americas in 1790 stood at about 2 million people, 90 to 95 percent of them slaves.

Brutality stood at the core of sugar plantation society. Masters and overseers resorted to violence and the threat of violence as the chief means of enforcing discipline among the labor force. Thomas Thistlewood, an overseer on a Jamaican plantation starting in 1750, left a diary in which he detailed the various punishments and tortures he inflicted on slaves. His diary also recounts his sex life with slave women, showing him to be a sexual predator and a rapist. Thistlewood's conduct was not unusual for overseers and slavemasters. Their brutalities were calculated to make slaves choose obedience over defiance. That calculation worked most but not all of the time. Slaves defied Thistlewood on occasion, for which he made them suffer.

Slaves from time to time risked everything on attempts to run away or rebel. In 1760, some 1,500 slaves, led by Akan-speakers from what is now Ghana, tried to take over the island of Jamaica. **Tacky's War**, as it is called, lasted a few months and shook the foundations of the plantation regime on that island. As we've seen, in northeast Brazil a community of runaway slaves, Palmares, managed to defend its independence from 1605 to the 1690s. The greatest of all slave risings took place in the 1790s in the French sugar colony of St. Domingue, as we will see in Chapter 21. By and large, slaves on the smaller islands were less likely to try to run away because recapture was more likely there than on bigger islands or in Brazil, where sparsely populated forests beckoned slaves yearning to escape the plantation.

Sugar was not quite the global commodity that silver or cotton was. Because it does not keep as well as silver or cotton, and could be grown widely, it was not traded from the Atlantic basin into the Indian Ocean or Pacific on any scale. The primary significance of sugar for the global economy was that it demonstrated the viability of the large-scale slave plantation.

Other crops in the Americas, notably tobacco, cotton, rice, and indigo, would also be produced on the plantation model. The particulars varied from place to place and from crop to crop. But plantation owners all used slave labor, relied heavily on terror for labor discipline, systematically sought economies of scale, and filled distant markets with their products. By the mid-eighteenth century, some of the richest men in the world made their money this way.

CHARTERED JOINT-STOCK COMPANIES

The commercial opportunities of the Global web offered economies of scale in long-distance trade as well as in cash-crop production. Just as the slave plantation brought new levels of efficiency, human suffering, and profit to the business of sugar production, so the joint-stock company did for oceanic trade.

Intercontinental shipping was risky business. Storms, pirates, disease outbreaks, and other hazards could ruin any voyage. To make business sense, ventures needed to be big: big enough to fight off pirates, negotiate bulk discounts on trade goods, and ensure that *some* ships would surely survive a storm. Sending several ships together made sense, and sending a fleet was better still.

To achieve economies of scale in long-distance trade, merchants found ways to cooperate and pool their resources. Traders and businessmen had done this for millennia, usually with family members or close friends because mutual trust was crucial. These kin-based concerns could be gigantic, like the Zheng family operations

Stock Exchanges The Dutch painter Emanuel de Witte made this painting of the Beurs, or Amsterdam stock exchange, in 1653. Investors met in this busy courtyard to trade shares in increasingly popular and profitable joint-stock companies.

along the coast of China or the merchant empire of Virji Vora in India.

ORIGINS During the sixteenth century, more anonymous forms of partnership developed to spread and share the risks of long-distance trade. Some were chartered companies, granted monopoly rights over certain trades by governments. Others were joint-stock companies in which hundreds or thousands of investors might own shares, as in modern corporations. Some were both, such as the English Muscovy Company, founded in 1555, or the Levant Company, chartered by England's Queen Elizabeth in 1581 to conduct trade with Ottoman lands. All had professional managers. This was a business model that could expand to indefinite size more readily than the kin-based business empires of the Zhengs or Virji Vora.

The English pioneered **chartered joint-stock companies**. France and the Netherlands soon followed, and during the eighteenth century Spain, Denmark, and others did too. One of these, the Hudson's Bay Company, begun in 1670 to handle the fur trade in Canada, still exists, albeit in much different form. The gold standard of chartered joint-stock trading companies was the **Dutch**

East India Company, the VOC, founded in 1602, which we've already encountered in South Africa and in East Asian waters.

THE DUTCH EAST INDIA COMPANY (VOC) The VOC was a chartered joint-stock company, formed to share the risk of voyages to the spice islands of Indonesia. Voyages in the seventeenth century from Amsterdam to Indonesia and back typically took 200 to 300 days outbound, and more than 300 on the return. About 3 to 5 percent never returned, better than the 40 percent rate for Portuguese ships in the sixteenth century.

The VOC proved a spectacular success for nearly 200 years. Between 1602 and 1796, the company sent nearly 5,000 ships around Africa to the Indian Ocean. They brought back some 2.5 million tons of trade goods and exchanged countless cargoes between Asian ports. Detailed records for a 300-ton ship, the *Ceulen*, which sailed from Java to Amsterdam in 1697, reveal something of the business: in addition to a crew of 105 seamen and 30 soldiers, it carried a cargo of Japanese copper, tin from Thailand, ceramics from China, aromatic wood, saltpeter, tea, ginger, nutmeg, cloves, cardamom (another spice), bird's nests, cotton, silk yarn—and black pepper equal to the ship's weight. The *Ceulen* was small as VOC East Indies ships went, less than one-third the size of a typical East Indiaman, as the biggest ships were called. The VOC's most lucrative trade was buying Indian cloth and selling it for spices destined for European or Chinese markets.

As part of its strategy, the VOC captured port cities, many such as Malacca in 1641 taken from the Portuguese, and built others, such as Cape Town, founded in 1652. It held dozens of fortified posts and at times had as many as 100 hundred heavily armed merchant ships cruising Indian Ocean waters. By 1669 it had 50,000 employees, 10,000 soldiers, and a navy of 40 warships. It constituted a privately funded, state-sanctioned, maritime empire devoted to commercial gain, a smaller version of the Zheng family business empire but with more global reach and governmental support.

The VOC captains enjoyed a military edge in the Indonesian archipelago. VOC forces were frequently outnumbered, but rarely outgunned. Wherever they could maneuver their big floating fortresses, they could concentrate firepower enough to destroy a city in hours. In order to found their center of operations on Java, they destroyed

VOC Conquests This detail of an illustration of VOC forces assaulting a local sultanate in the spice islands (part of Indonesia today) indicates the typically violent methods that the VOC used to establish a foothold in lucrative trading locations.

a local town and rebuilt it as Batavia in 1619. In an effort to monopolize the clove and nutmeg trades in the 1620s, they attempted to kill the entire population of the Banda Islands and replace them with loyal settlers. They tried to burn all pepper vines and clove or nutmeg trees not under their control to undermine their competition. They took part in a slave trade in Southeast Asia that specialized in the sale of women from the island of Bali.

In general, the VOC's business model consisted of using force or the threat of force to extract favorable terms of trade—preferably a monopoly—from local rulers and merchants. The approach was backed up with merciless punishment of anyone who traded with rivals. The centrality of violence to their business is captured in a letter from the governor general of the Dutch East Indies, Jan Pieterszoon Coen, in 1614 to the directors of the VOC. Coen, the man later responsible for the effort to exterminate the Banda Islanders, wrote: "You gentlemen ought to know from experience that trade in Asia should be conducted and maintained under the protection and with the aid of your own weapons, and those weapons must be wielded with the profits gained by the trade. So trade cannot be maintained without war, nor war without trade." Violence half a world away was part of the price for adding a pinch of nutmeg to millions of cakes, sauces, and glasses of cider.

This business strategy worked brilliantly for Coen and the VOC. Before it was liquidated amid a morass of corruption in 1799, the VOC averaged roughly 18 percent

Dutch Colonists Some merchants settled down in VOC colonies—such as the Dutch merchant Pieter Cnoll, who managed trade in Batavia, the capital of the Dutch East Indies. Cnoll is shown here with his half-Dutch, half-Japanese wife, their children, and their servants.

annual profit on the totality of its business. Other companies imitated its formula, most notably the English East India Company (EIC). But in its entire career, 1600 to 1857, the EIC managed to carry only about one-fifth the goods traded by the VOC.

BANKS

As long-distance trade grew in volume and reach, businesses more often needed to finance their operations by borrowing money. They borrowed to mount large trading ventures that could realize economies of scale. They also borrowed to cover the period between their purchase of goods and the subsequent sale of those goods, which might be years in trade between Europe and Southeast Asia or China. So the demand for private finance grew dramatically after 1500.

New institutions evolved quickly in response to this demand and governments' constant need for cash to pay military expenses. Most notable among these institutions were modern banks, bond markets (in which people traded governments' debt), and stock exchanges (in which people traded shares of companies). All these institutions helped both governments and merchants get cash when they needed it and earn a return on their money when they didn't need cash.

LENDING AT INTEREST Of these, the most important were banks. To have a flourishing banking sector, societies

first had to discard the idea that lending money at interest was immoral. Hindu, Buddhist, Islamic, and Christian scripture and tradition include objections to the practice of charging interest, or too much interest, for loans. Jewish law prohibits lending at interest to fellow Jews, although not to others. Plato, Aristotle, Cicero, the Buddha, Jesus, Muhammad, and Aquinas all denounced lending at interest, and Confucius disdained money-grubbing of all sorts. Luther got his start railing against usury, and early Protestants generally regarded lending at interest as sinful. So robust banking required cultural change.

In Europe the moral objections and legal prohibitions against lending at interest weakened in places such as northern Italy, where small family banks emerged as early as the thirteenth century, and Barcelona (northeastern Spain), where a city-owned bank appeared by 1381. Elsewhere in Europe, those objections eroded during the sixteenth and seventeenth centuries. The intellectual climate in which old truths were subject to renewed questioning, combined with economic changes that heightened the demand for finance, probably both contributed to this cultural trend. Lending at interest gradually lost its taint among Protestants, and eventually Catholics as well, despite repeated papal pronouncements about the evils of usury.

The Bank of Amsterdam, founded in 1609, was the first modern bank. It attracted depositors, cleared debts, offered quick transactions, and maintained public trust

Banking The Bank of Amsterdam, the first modern bank, was originally located inside the Amsterdam town hall—shown here in a 1672 painting.

CONSIDERING THE EVIDENCE

On the Circulation of Blood and Money

Usually, the value of a commodity drops when more of it is in circulation. However, as the gold and silver mined in the Americas became more plentiful in Europe, their value increased because more people demanded cold hard cash instead of accepting bartered goods. Some people even began shaving small slivers of metal off of coins before passing them on. Bankers and loan sharks simply lent the money they had in return for a larger amount of money later. Today that difference is known as interest, but European theologians and politicians saw interest as a euphemism for the sin of usury (i.e., lending at interest) that should be banned, or at least regulated. It seemed right to be paid for a hard day's work or a risky investment in overseas trade, but making money from money struck Christians, Jews, and Muslims alike as immoral.

For the Italian scholar Bernardo Davanzati, usury was just one of the mischiefs people could make with money. In a 1588 lecture on coins, he described money as the lifeblood of states to illustrate why money must circulate to retain its value. Although a scientific description of blood circulation eluded Europeans until William Harvey published his research on the subject in 1628, it was commonly understood that blood moved through the heart and lungs to nourish the rest of the body. Over a century after Davanzati delivered his lecture, a British philosopher named John Toland translated it into English, introducing Davanzati's ideas to a new generation of thinkers and bankers on the other side of the continent. As the center of banking moved from Italy to England, so did the demand for ideas about how to deal with money problems.

Some grave and famous Authors have call'd Money the Sinews of War and Government; but, in my Opinion, it may be more properly stil'd the Second Blood thereof. [F]or as Blood, which is the Juice and Substance of Meat in the natural Body, does, by circulating out of the greater into the lesser Vessels, moisten all the Flesh, which drinks it up as parch'd Ground soaks Rain Water; so it nourishes and restores as much of it as was dri'd up and evaporated by the natural Heat: In like manner, Money, . . . does, by circulating out of the richer Purses into the poorer, furnish all the Nation. . . . From the poorer it returns again into the richer Purses; and thus circulating without Intermission, it preserves alive the Civil Body of the Common-wealth. Hence . . . every State must have a quantity of Money, as every Body a quantity of Blood to circulate therein. But as the Blood stopping in the Head or the larger Vessels puts the Body naturally into a Consumption, Dropsy, or Apoplexy, etc. so [if] all the Money be only in a few Hands, as in those of the rich for Example, the State falls unavoidably into Convulsions, and other dangerous Distempers. . . . We ought therefore to set a high Value upon the living Member of the Common-wealth, and to preserve it from those Mischiefs which usually befal it, when not carefully look'd after; such as Counterfeiting, Monopolizing, Simony [buying religious privileges], Usury, and the like, already decri'd, and known every where. But, . . . I shall now confine my Discourse only to . . . debasing of Coin.

Source: Bernardo Davanzati, *A Discourse upon Coins,* trans. John Toland (London: 1696).

> ### QUESTIONS FOR ANALYSIS
>
> 1. How is the circulation of money in a state like the circulation of blood in a body?
> 2. Why does Davanzati think that concentrating money in a few hands is dangerous?
> 3. In what ways did ideas about how to manage money, and money problems, circulate in Europe?

---

by reliably allowing anyone to withdraw a deposit on demand. In 1609, at least 800 different coins circulated in Amsterdam, including copper, silver, and gold coins from dozens of countries as far away as Japan. Doing business amid this diversity of money—like conducting conversations in 800 languages—was enormously inefficient. The city council of Amsterdam sought to solve this problem by creating a new bank that kept accounts of merchants' deposits and converted them to a single standard, at first a tally of who owed whom how much of an abstract accounting unit, called bank money. This practice reduced transaction costs and attracted yet more business to Amsterdam. The city required merchants to use the bank for all big transactions. Soon the bank routinely

Financial Power A detail of an illustration of Jacob Fugger's lavishly decorated house in Augsburg shows visitors bowing before the powerful merchant. Fugger is a key example of someone who leveraged the opportunities presented by long-distance trade and rulers' need for loans to amass vast wealth.

lent out more money than it held, a practice typical of modern banks called **fractional reserve banking**. This innovative, expansive practice had the effect of creating money in the form of credit; although if all depositors demanded their money at the same time, the bank would be unable to pay. To avoid this problem, any bank engaged in this practice had to maintain a solid reputation, as the Bank of Amsterdam did for nearly 200 years. Fractional reserve banking helped lubricate the wheels of commerce by making credit more easily available to merchants.

BANK NOTES AND CREDIT Bank notes boosted commerce too. The Bank of Amsterdam did not issue paper money. Other banks had tried and found customers mistrustful, often rightly so. Banks sometimes would print too many notes and then refuse to honor them. But the Bank of Sweden in the 1670s, and then the Bank of England, founded in 1694, managed to win public trust in bank notes. They successfully lobbied for government monopoly rights on printing bank notes and issued them only in modest quantity. Both fractional reserve banking and the use of paper money—if trusted—expanded the amount of money in circulation and reduced the transaction costs of commerce.

Banks often found that their best customers were kings. As we've seen, the spiraling costs of warfare, navies, and standing armies put pressure on royal treasuries. Borrowing was one of the few solutions monarchs could find. If the costs of, say, five years of campaigning could be spread out over the next 50 years, then the need to raise taxes would not be so sharp, making tax revolts less likely. Early modern monarchs had every reason to wish to see healthy banking systems in their countries. The Habsburgs had relied heavily on the banking house of Fugger to attain and retain power.

In practice, northwestern European monarchs, and the Dutch Republic, had the most extensive banking systems to draw upon. Creditworthiness became a strategic asset for states: in the eighteenth century, bankers lent the British government money at half the rate they charged the French Crown. Indeed, the British government's reputation for repaying debts enabled it to spend as much on war as could the far larger Qing empire: it could borrow at low rates and the Qing could not borrow at all. Banks kept kings and governments solvent, and kings and governments, if they paid their debts, helped keep banks profitable. Governments without access to banks, or deemed poor credit risks by bankers, struggled financially.

Large-scale plantations, joint-stock companies, and banks were among the new business formats that developed in response to the opportunities and challenges presented by the Global web. Partnerships and family-run businesses survived, of course. But they could not take full advantage of potential economies of scale in production, commerce, and finance that resulted from the newly global reach of ships, the connections among far-flung markets, and the frequent need for ready cash on the part of kings and merchants.

GLOBAL LINKS AND COMMERCIAL REVOLUTIONS

In eastern Canada about 1680, a Mi'kmaq told a French priest, "In truth, my friend, the beaver does everything to perfection. He makes for us kettles, axes, swords, knives, and gives us drink and food without the trouble of cultivating the ground." By trapping beaver and selling fur, Mi'kmaqs and other Amerindians could buy an array of useful goods produced across the Atlantic in Europe. A Khoisan raising cattle in South Africa or a Dayak in

Chinese Commercial Revolution In this 1696 painting, a peasant and a water buffalo prepare the soil for rice planting. The poem in the upper left praises the farm tool depicted, which flattens the ground. New, intensive agricultural practices enabled late Ming and Qing China to become more commercialized.

Borneo gathering sandalwood might have said much the same thing. They all found advantages in taking part in global commerce, selling something they were good at producing in order to buy other things they could not easily produce. People had taken part in such exchanges for millennia before 1500. But now more people did so more often, and over longer distances.

During the early modern centuries (1500–1800) the world's trade networks fused into one giant, but patchy, commercial web. Regular shipping linked places that had previously been isolated, such as Caribbean islands or southernmost Africa. Strong links emerged across the Atlantic where none had existed before, such as the trade routes between Mexico and Spain, or Angola and Brazil. New routes also spanned the Pacific between Acapulco and Manila. Strong links also developed where only weak ones had existed before, such as between south China and the Philippines or between Atlantic Europe and West Africa.

These links and shifts to a more commercial orientation touched some places more than others. The commercial transformation ran deepest in coastal China and Atlantic Europe, at the two ends of the Eurasian landmass.

CHINA

Between 1550 and 1800, China underwent a second **commercial revolution**. The first one had occurred during the Song dynasty (960–1279). This second one, under the late Ming and then the Qing, was something of an economic miracle. China doubled its population without impoverishing it. This was achieved partly by conquest of new lands, not only in Mongolia and Tibet (economically not all that helpful) but also in western Sichuan and other southwestern lands populated by non-Han minorities. China absorbed, killed off, or pushed out these peoples and put their lands to more intensive use with state-of-the-art agricultural technologies. This resulted in more rice paddies and millet fields, and less swampland, forestland, and grassland—hence a bigger economy and more tax receipts for the emperors.

But even more than frontier conquest and territorial expansion, China built its economy through increased commercialization of both agriculture and manufacturing. Regions came to specialize more in certain products, such as tea or cotton, and to import their food from elsewhere in China or even Vietnam. Most of this specialization and exchange took place within China. But some of it linked up to foreign markets, especially for silk and porcelain.

The Ming and Qing governments had ambivalent views about foreign trade. Sometimes they tried to ban it, and sometimes they encouraged it. In the 1560s the

Chinese Manufacturing Chinese goods manufactured in large industrial workshops, such as those in the town of Guangzhou, could be traded worldwide. Guangzhou's manufacturing district is shown here in an 1807 painting.

Ming rescinded an earlier ban, helping to create a surge in foreign trade. Restrictions returned, but under the Qing between the 1680s and 1760s foreign trade again generally met with official approval and grew apace. Shipping from south China to Manila tripled from 1684 to 1715, to some 20 ships per year. Silver imports increased by nearly sixfold between 1728 and 1800, and exports increased by a similar proportion. By 1800, some 10 percent of Chinese grain, 25 percent of cotton, 90 percent of silk, and 95 percent of tea was produced for markets, whether domestic or foreign. Only a few other spots in the world matched this degree of commercialization.

ATLANTIC EUROPE

One was Atlantic Europe, which also underwent a commercial revolution. Here, as in China, frontier expansion played a role. Some settlement and agricultural expansion took place in drained wetlands in Europe, especially in England, the Netherlands, and along Baltic shores. But the main thrust came overseas. The plantation zones of Brazil and the Caribbean were under the control of Atlantic Europeans. By the 1690s, smaller plantation regions were taking shape in South Carolina (rice) and around the shores of the Chesapeake (tobacco). Most of the wealth squeezed from plantations enriched Atlantic Europeans.

But, as in China, the heart of the commercial revolution in Atlantic Europe took place at home. Ever-larger shares of agricultural harvests went to nearby markets. Wool and cotton textile businesses expanded. In Atlantic Europe as a whole, the proportion of people working the land in 1500 was about 75 to 80 percent—less in the Netherlands, more in Iberia. By 1750 that proportion had fallen to about 60 percent, and in England and the Netherlands was well under half. Manufacturing and services made up the rest, both attuned almost entirely to market production. Market towns sprouted and financial centers, such as Antwerp, Amsterdam, and London, flourished. By 1600, even bulk items were traded over long distances, such as grain from Poland to Amsterdam or to north Italian cities.

This slow but steady march toward market societies in China and Atlantic Europe distinguished them from the rest of the world. Elsewhere, except in the plantation zones and India's cotton districts, markets and commercial production existed in pockets but did not pervade societies. This did not mean ordinary people in Atlantic Europe and coastal China were better off than those elsewhere. By

and large they were not. But their societies were richer and included more prosperous families, generally merchant families and owners of agricultural estates. In Atlantic Europe, but less so in China, rulers became more responsive to the wishes of commercial elites, nowhere more so than the Dutch Republic, where the rulers and the commercial elite were the same people.

OTHER REGIONS IN THE GLOBAL ECONOMY

India's connections also expanded after 1500, thanks above all to the cotton trade. They now reached to the Americas and West Africa, although rather thinly. The older links to Southeast Asia, East Africa, and Southwest Asia only strengthened, although some of the actual connecting was now done by European merchants, including the VOC. In general, India's position with respect to the world's webs changed less than coastal China's or Atlantic Europe's: it had long been tightly linked throughout the Indian Ocean trading world, by foreigners—Malays, Persians, and Arabs mainly—as much as by Indian merchants, and that remained true after 1500, although the foreigners involved now sometimes included Europeans. Those parts of India where cotton growing, spinning, and weaving were concentrated—Gujarat and Bengal especially—became yet more commercial in orientation. So did Kerala, in the southwest, where peasants and landowners found that raising peppers for export and buying food was a preferable strategy to subsistence food production.

Europe east of the Elbe River also underwent a shift to a more commercial economy after 1500 or 1550. Landowners in Prussia, Poland-Lithuania, and Russia developed big grain-producing estates and sold their harvests to cities around the Baltic and in Atlantic Europe. Like the plantations of the Americas, these estates relied on forced labor. Peasants—called **serfs** because they were legally tied to the land and not free to leave—increasingly were required to work several days a week on their landlord's estate. In Russia, serfs could also be bought and sold, and their status differed little from that of slaves in Brazil or the Caribbean. Landlords also monopolized the right to make alcohol from excess grain and sell it. Commercialization in eastern Europe was agrarian: it did not lead to rapid urban growth but to the proliferation of big estates, each one a world unto itself but with ties to ports and through them to overseas urban markets—again like the plantations of the Americas.

Southwest Asia before the 1490s had stood at the center of the Old World web, a crossroads of trade, travel, and information. Under Ottoman control by 1550, this region together with Egypt had long been among the most commercialized in the world—since the cloth workshops of ancient Sumer. By 1800, it was still closely linked to neighboring lands, and by sea to the Indian Ocean's ports. But the biggest flows of world trade now passed it by. The relative importance of caravan trade across the steppe lands of Asia declined, even if absolute quantities did not. Trade and information flows elsewhere in the world—across the Atlantic, for example, or between China and Southeast Asia—grew far faster than anything involving Southwest Asia. Its economic importance in the world dwindled, and its former advantages in access to information about distant markets and foreign technologies disappeared. In a sense, Atlantic Europe dethroned Southwest Asia between 1500 and 1800.

One indication of that change is the connections in which Africa was enmeshed. Before 1500, Africa's strongest linkages, by far, were with Southwest Asia, both by land via Egypt and by sea. But in the course of the next few centuries, while these connections persisted, stronger ones developed linking Africa to Atlantic Europe and to India, mainly in the form of the slave and cotton trades.

Nonetheless, the bulk of Africa's economies, devoted to farming and pastoralism, bore little connection to the outside world except for the gradual spread of American food crops. Most families produced for themselves. Few sought to maximize production in the ways that Chinese or Indian cotton-producing peasants did in response to market incentives. The African entrepreneurs attuned to distant markets were mainly slave traders or in the elephant-hunting and ivory export business. They were just as ruthless profit-maximizers as Dutch VOC traders or Gujarati cotton merchants, but this culture of commercialism was a rarity in Africa. Where the violence and commercial opportunities of the slave trade did not intrude, African economic life was more stable, less dynamic and disruptive, and less market oriented than in either coastal China or Atlantic Europe.

The Americas, in contrast, became much more powerfully, and disruptively, connected to the wider world between 1500 and 1800. The plantation zones, the mining regions, and the northern lands devoted to the fur trade

The Fur Trade An 1845 watercolor depicts a white trapper and his Amerindian family navigating the waters of interior North America. Mixed families like this worked at the source of what was a transatlantic trade in furs.

were thoroughly enmeshed in the commercial web that now spanned the globe. By 1800 even some small-farming districts, such as those of southern New England, were substantially market oriented and took part in a transatlantic economy that extended not only to Atlantic Europe but to the Caribbean and West Africa too. Many of the Amerindian peoples had also linked up to market economies, whether through the mines of the Spanish Empire, the fur trade of French North America, or a deerskin trade that thrived in the Carolinas in the eighteenth century. Only a few people in 1800, maybe 2 to 4 million in all the Americas, conducted their economic lives locally without reference to distant markets.

This patchiness of the global economic web carried consequences that we will return to in later chapters. The most momentous of them flowed from the fact that by the late eighteenth century the most connected place of all—not the happiest, not the most just, not the best in any moral sense, but the most connected—was Atlantic Europe.

CONCLUSION

In the three centuries after 1500, a true global economy developed for the first time in world history. Like all economic shifts, it benefited some and hurt others.

During these centuries, world population and the world economy more than doubled in size. Some people, like Jakob Fugger and Virji Vora, became unimaginably rich by taking advantage of new opportunities in trade and banking. Most people, however, grew poorer over these centuries, as evidenced by data on both shrinking average heights and falling wages.

The most dramatic economic change in these centuries was the rise of transoceanic trading in commodities such as spices, cotton, and silver. All three had existed for many centuries on smaller scales, but now all three expanded in size and scope, flowing along the new circuits of global commerce. New business formats arose in response to the globalizing economy and to the growing financial distress of rulers. Plantations, joint-stock companies, and modern banks all fit the new realities. They could mobilize resources on a scale unavailable to most family businesses and partnerships.

The new global economy rewarded those people who could gather the most information about conditions, prices, and politics around the world. Such people could buy cheap and sell dear in different markets. Or they could lend money wisely—rather than to a prince about to be defeated or a merchant about to go broke. Such people might live almost anywhere, including in Augsburg and Surat, like Fugger and Vora. But, increasingly, they were likelier to be found in Atlantic Europe. Flows of information and goods combined to make Atlantic Europe's economy, by 1800 and probably by 1750 if not 1700, more innovative, dynamic, and disruptive than that anywhere else, including the other parts of Europe. The next century and a half of world history, from roughly 1750 until 1918, may be seen in many ways. But one of those ways is as an age of Atlantic European pre-eminence.

CHAPTER REVIEW

KEY TERMS

population surge (p. 579)
gross world product (GWP) (p. 581)
spice trade (p. 584)
cotton (p. 586)
silver trade (p. 588)
patío **process** (p. 589)

economies of scale (p. 591)
slave-and-sugar plantations (p. 593)
Tacky's War (p. 593)
chartered joint-stock companies (p. 594)

Dutch East India Company (VOC) (p. 594)
fractional reserve banking (p. 598)
commercial revolution (p. 599)
serfs (p. 600)

Go to **INQUIZITIVE** to see what you've learned—and learn what you've missed—with personalized feedback along the way.

REVIEW QUESTIONS

1. What accounts for the rising prominence of Atlantic European societies in global economic history after 1500?

2. Why did global population more than double between 1500 and 1800?

3. What spurred the massive growth of the world economy between 1500 and 1800?

4. Why did most ordinary people around the world grow smaller in stature while economies grew faster than ever before?

5. In what ways did European oceanic merchants change the scope of the spice and cotton trades?

6. Explain the two main reasons for silver's expanded role.

7. How and why did sugar profits rest on the exploitation of environments and people?

8. Describe the novel tactics merchants used to reduce the risks of long-distance trade beginning in the sixteenth century.

9. Who relied heavily on banks, and why?

10. What were the similarities and differences between the commercial revolutions in China and those in Atlantic Europe?

11. Compare how the global economic connections of India, eastern Europe, Southwest Asia, Africa, and the Americas changed after 1500.

12. What was the most dramatic economic change between 1500 and 1800?

FURTHER READING

Robert C. ALLEN, Tommy BENGTSSON, and Martin DRIBE, eds., *Living Standards in the Past: New Perspectives on Well-Being in Asia and Europe* (2005). A good source of information about consumption, wages, nutrition, and height for Eurasian populations.

Femme GAASTRA, *The Dutch East India Company: Expansion and Decline* (2003). Perhaps the best of several histories of the VOC.

Arturo GIRALDEZ, *The Manila Galleons and the Dawn of the Global Economy* (2015). An accessible account of world trade, and especially good on silver.

Geoffrey GUNN, *History without Borders: The Making of an Asian World Region, 1000–1800* (2011). A seriously scholarly economic history of the connections among Japan, China, and Southeast Asia.

Wim KLOOSTER, *The Dutch Moment: War, Trade, and Settlement in the Seventeenth-Century Dutch Atlantic* (2016). A general study of the Dutch activities in North America, Brazil, and Africa with plenty on the economy.

Lodewijk PETRAM, *The World's First Stock Exchange* (2014). Explains how Amsterdam developed modern financial institutions in the seventeenth century.

Marjorie SHAFFER, *Pepper: A History of the World's Most Influential Spice* (2013). An enjoyable popular history of the early modern spice trade.

Zheng YANGWEN, *China on the Sea: How the Maritime World Shaped Modern China* (2012). The early chapters deal with the Ming and Qing regulation of overseas trade.

PART 5

REVOLUTIONS

1640 TO 1920

The weaving of the Global web between 1450 and 1800, the subject of Part 4, had several revolutionary consequences. Some of them, such as the formation of a global economy and the advance of commercialization, were part of the process of web building itself. Others, no less revolutionary, were not. Part 5, which includes Chapters 21 through 25 and deals with the years 1640 to 1920, takes up some major transformations that followed—and to some degree, resulted from—the spinning of the Global web. They were all interconnected and overlapping.

Destruction of the Roehampton Estate, January 1832 An episode in the Jamaican slave revolt of 1831–1832, when some 60,000 slaves rose up against local planters and the British Army.

TRANSFORMATIONS: POLITICAL, ECONOMIC, SOCIAL

The first of these major transformations involved politics and violence. Several political revolutions reverberated throughout the world during these centuries, rearranging hierarchies but never—revolutionary rhetoric notwithstanding—eliminating them. The most consequential of these political revolutions took place around the shores of the Atlantic Ocean, in West Central Africa, western Europe, eastern North America, and Spanish America. They all shared some general features, although they led to different outcomes. Together, they established ambitions for self-rule that have reverberated around the world ever since. They are the subject of Chapter 21.

The second transformation was, and remains, the most important: the industrial revolutions, the first of which took place in England. Several more followed, all of which changed the ways things were made, affected living conditions and health, reshuffled geopolitical relationships, and brought new impacts on the environment. At the heart of this economic transformation was a shift in energy regime—specifically, the widespread adoption of fossil fuels beginning with coal. Industrialization included important changes in transport and communications, such as railroads, that sped up connections in the Global web. This transformation is the focus of Chapter 22.

The third transformation partly flowed from the second: it was a pair of liberations helped along by industrialization. The first of these, a partial liberation from disease and early death, translated into giant improvements in human health and life expectancy between 1750 and 1950. The other liberation was the abolition of legal slavery and serfdom, which began in the late eighteenth century. For thousands of years, most societies had recognized forced labor systems such as slavery or serfdom as legal and just. Then, from about 1780 to 1920, almost every society changed its laws on this. Some came to regard slavery or serfdom as immoral or a sign of backwardness. Others, such as the southern states of the United States, abandoned slavery only by force, after losing a war over it. But one way or another, slavery and serfdom were abolished, a dramatic departure from the patterns of the deeper past. In a sense it is as if history was speeding up. Social changes—and big ones fundamental to the human condition such as health and freedom—were now coming thick and fast, as Chapter 23 shows.

Chapter 24 considers nationalism and imperialism between 1800 and 1920. Both of these major developments were also helped along by industrialization. Nationalism, which is at root a sense of shared identity among the people of a nation-state, or people hoping to create one, was rare or non-existent before 1600. After 1790, however, it emerged in several settings, and by 1900 was felt strongly by hundreds of millions of people around the world. Its emergence strengthened some countries such as Japan but weakened ethnically diverse empires such as the Ottoman Empire. Nationalism together with industrialization made some societies far more formidable than others in economic and military terms. The strong took advantage of the weak, acquiring new territories and incorporating them as subordinate colonies in a political system that is often called modern imperialism. The Global web came to include ever more direct political relationships, as the most industrialized states—including Britain, France, and other European states, the United States, and Japan—built overseas empires in Asia, Africa, and the islands of the Pacific.

Empires provoked resistance. So did nationalism when it seemed to trample on other forms of identity. Several kinds of resistance, especially rebellions and political revolutions, reverberated around the world between 1850 and 1920—the subject of Chapter 25. It first considers several uprisings against imperial power in the nineteenth century, from small-scale examples in the U.S. West and the Brazilian backcountry to giant struggles such as the Taiping Rebellion, the Indian Rebellion, and the U.S. Civil War. The chapter moves on to a threesome of large-scale political and social revolutions in the early twentieth century, in China, Mexico, and Russia.

In Part 5 we see some of the indirect effects of the formation of the Global web. Old certainties, such as the acceptability of slavery or of monarchical rule, came in for questioning. Old hierarchies and social orders sometimes now seemed unjust—or merely unfavorable to new coalitions of people who were acquiring the wealth, power, and ambition to change them. Meanwhile, industrialization and changes in health and labor regimes profoundly affected millions of people worldwide. Social and economic changes, such as the rise of commercial classes or the formation of an urban working class, were coming faster than ever. The foundations of longstanding political orders shook and often crumbled as a result, opening the door to new kinds of politics. That crumbling began in the Atlantic world.

CHRONOLOGY

1576
Establishment of
Portuguese trading
colony at Luanda

1649–1660
Commonwealth
and Protectorate
in Britain

1641–1649
British Civil Wars

1641–1660
Garcia II reigns
in Kongo

1661–1685
British Restoration

1665–1709
Fragmentation of
power in Kongo

1707
Union of Scotland
and England

ca. 1684–1706
Lifetime of
Beatriz Kimpa
Vita

1688–1689
Glorious Revolution

ca. 1743–1803
Lifetime of
Toussaint
L'Ouverture

1756–1763
Seven Years' War

Bourbon Reforms begin in Spanish America

1767

1764
Britain imposes new
taxes on American
colonies

1763–1765
Pontiac's War

Continental Congress assembles

1774

1775–1781
American
Revolution

1780–1783
Revolt in Andes led
by Túpac Amaru

Slave uprising in St. Domingue

1790

1793–1798
British troops fight Haitian revolutionaries

1789–1799
French
Revolution

1787–1789
American
Constitution
drafted and
adopted

1791–1804
Haitian
Revolution

1793
Jacobins end
elections; French
royal family is executed

1799–1815
Napoleon Bonaparte heads French government, becomes emperor

1807–1814
Napoleon Bonaparte occupies Spain

1815
Spanish king sends large armies to Colombia and Venezuela

1825
Formal recognition of Brazilian independence

1826
Spain's American empire is reduced to two islands

The Best and Worst of Times

ATLANTIC REVOLUTIONS

1640 to 1830

O n July 14, 1789, a crowd of 900 artisans and workers attacked a 400-year-old prison in eastern Paris. The Bastille, as it was known, had once held important political prisoners, including aristocratic enemies of French kings such as the satirical author Voltaire. As prisons went, it was a nice place, complete with a library—it held 389 books in 1787—a garden, and curtained windows in most cells. In the eighteenth century, the French Crown used the Bastille in its attempts to control unruly publishers—as a place to store books it had banned and printing presses it had seized. The Bastille had acquired public notoriety in part through banned, and therefore prized, memoirs of prisoners such as Henri Latude, a soldier and mathematics student who had done time for, among other things, sending a box of poison to the mistress of King Louis XV. But by the summer of 1789, the Bastille's best days were behind it: the expense of keeping it up seemed too great to those in charge of French finance, who hoped to close it. Its 82-man garrison guarded only four counterfeiters, two madmen, one nobleman accused by his family of sexual depravity—and 250 barrels of gunpowder. It was the gunpowder the crowd of 900 was after.

Atlantic Revolutions Haitian revolutionary leader Toussaint L'Ouverture leads a group of guerilla fighters in a battle against French troops. The Haitian Revolution was one of a wave of revolutions that swept the Atlantic world in the late eighteenth century.

FOCUS QUESTIONS

1. In what ways was the Atlantic world becoming more densely connected after 1600?

2. What were the key similarities between the revolutions in Kongo and Britain in the seventeenth century?

3. What tensions between Britain and its American colonies led to the American Revolution?

4. What were the major outcomes of the French Revolution?

5. In what ways was the Haitian Revolution a distinctively Atlantic revolution?

6. What tensions contributed to the wave of revolutions in Spanish America?

7. What features did all of these Atlantic revolutions share?

At the cost of several dozen deaths, the crowd fought its way into the Bastille, killed its governor (prison warden), liberated its surprised prisoners, and seized the gunpowder—igniting an urban uprising in Paris. The uprising grew into a revolution, and its opening act, the storming of the Bastille, became the pre-eminent symbol of liberation in France. A sharp-eyed businessman got permission to tear down the prison and sell its fragments, which then were taken on tours of France as icons of the toppling of an unjust despotism. July 14, Bastille Day, has been France's national holiday for over 120 years. But the Bastille was only one of several symbols, and the French Revolution only one of several Atlantic revolutions. Something was afoot around the shores of the Atlantic. This chapter explores six revolutions around the Atlantic and tries to explain both what they shared and each one's particular elements.

THE ATLANTIC WORLD IN GLOBAL PERSPECTIVE

As we've seen in recent chapters, a Global web formed in the centuries after 1500 as oceanic trade, travel, and biological and intellectual exchanges knitted the world together as never before. The process affected coastal communities, especially port cities, more than anywhere else. But it touched every society and every state involved in oceanic links.

The Atlantic world was forging new connections faster than anywhere else after 1600. New circuits of Atlantic trade reshuffled fortunes and misfortunes. Men and some women of modest origins became rich by trading slaves, sugar, cottons, indigo, wine, fish, and other goods. Those lifted by the new commerce wanted liberty to make more money faster than before, liberty in some cases to practice minority religions, and liberty in the form of guarantees against arbitrary measures by old political elites. To secure these liberties they sought a greater political voice. Many of them, ironically, were slaveowners or slave traders who would never consider liberty for slaves.

The quests for new liberties developed alongside new political ideas. These ideas, often about freedom, sovereignty, and the sharing of power, spread with ships, sailors, and merchants from port to port. Coffee houses and taverns, custom houses and dockyards witnessed arguments about tyranny and liberty. Where people could read, cheap pamphlets and newspapers, as well as word of mouth, served to spread the new political principles. Even if merchants, sailors, cobblers, peasants, and slaves did not agree on just what liberty or freedom might mean, increasing numbers of them felt that they had a right to more of it.

Outside the Atlantic world, the new oceanic connections proved less politically disruptive, for several reasons. In some cases, such as in Qing China or Mughal India, oceanic trade accounted for a smaller proportion of the economy as a whole than in most Atlantic societies. Some merchants grew rich in these lands, as we saw in Chapter 20; but overall they were few and weak compared to the thousands of landlords living off of rents paid by peasants, and the ruling elites living off of taxes or war loot. As long as these landlords could control their laborers and in turn supported the state, the basic arrangements of political life endured. Newly rich merchants had a tough time banding together as an interest group against such well-entrenched incumbents—landowners, bureaucrats, military castes, and imperial courts. Instead, they gradually joined the old elites, if they did not come from those groups to begin with.

In general, merchants around the Indian Ocean and the South China Sea were already plugged in to the circuits of power, the result of centuries-long negotiations with kings, sultans, emperors, and their bureaucrats. They had mastered the arts of securing political favors through generous gifts to rulers and savvy marriages of their daughters to princelings. They could reach their goals within the system and rarely wished to overthrow it.

Although they faced many challenges, the ruling elites in Tokugawa Japan, Qing China, Mughal India, and the Ottoman, Russian (Romanov), and Habsburg empires proved adept enough at adjusting to a globalizing world to avoid revolutions before 1850. In these places, the underlying principle of monarchical rule survived intact. These ruling elites contained, co-opted, or destroyed rival coalitions of power in their own domains more successfully than did several of the old elites in the Atlantic world.

In some Atlantic societies, the new pressures and opportunities coming from the new circuits of commerce and ideas proved enough to spark revolution. In others, they didn't. To understand why, let's zoom in on specific Atlantic societies.

KONGO AND BRITAIN, 1640–1709

In the decades after 1640, the kingdom of Kongo in West Central Africa and the British kingdoms of England and Scotland experienced revolutions. After costly civil wars and eras of religious strife, by 1710 merchant elites in both settings had sharply reduced royal power and expanded their own.

CIVIL WAR AND REVOLUTION IN KONGO, 1640–1709

Kongo, as we've seen, was an African kingdom formed in the fourteenth and fifteenth centuries and centered on the south bank of the Congo River. Its subjects were mainly from an ethno-linguistic group called Bakongo and spoke a language called Kikongo. After 1483, its kings forged ties with Portuguese mariners to bolster their royal power. That led to sustained trade links, Christianization of the royal lineage, expansionary warfare, and occasional reliance on Portuguese military power. It also led to one of the best-documented histories anywhere in sub-Saharan Africa before 1800. The Kongo elite left Portuguese-language documents from about 1520 onward, and European missionaries and traders who learned local languages, and took part in Kongo life, wrote down their observations and experiences beginning about 1580, giving us a richer understanding of history here than in most places in Africa.

MONARCHY AND THE SLAVE TRADE Kongo kings maintained diplomatic relations with Catholic countries of Europe and with the Papacy. Their power rested on their ability to use Portuguese trade goods, including firearms, to maintain a military, win prestige, and buy and raid for slaves. The Kongo state also controlled other exports such as ivory and copper, and it maintained the firm loyalty of lineage heads who themselves controlled, at least loosely, the labor of the common people. Most of those people farmed cassava and maize, American food crops first acquired via Atlantic trade. The geographic base of royal power was the fertile, productive, and densely populated vicinity of the capital, São Salvador. It was, by African standards, an unusually centralized state, thanks to the concentrated resources and population around the capital.

The **Kongo monarchy** was not hereditary but, in theory, elective. In practice, each time a king died a power struggle took place, often bringing brief civil wars, the winner of which became king. To stay alive and in power, kings had to negotiate a challenging diplomatic

The Kingdom of Kongo, ca. 1640 One of many African kingdoms, Kongo took shape in the fourteenth and fifteenth centuries. Its rulers strengthened their grip through participation in Atlantic trade, especially by acquiring firearms from Portugal. When Portugal established a base at Luanda in 1576 and expanded its slave trade to Brazil, it gradually destabilized Kongo.

Portuguese Kongo By the late seventeenth century, the Portuguese colony based in Luanda in northern Kongo was itself a large planned city, as this image from the period suggests. Figures in the foreground highlight the centrality of the slave trade to the city's economy.

and military landscape. They faced problems of internal cohesion, as in any kingdom; border troubles, mainly to the east and south; and after the 1570s, the presence of a Portuguese colony based in the northern Angolan city of Luanda.

One particular responsibility of Kongo's kings was to protect their subjects from enslavement. A large part of the kings' legitimacy and support depended on it. One king in the 1580s went so far as to ransom some of his subjects who had been enslaved and shipped to the offshore Portuguese sugar island of São Tomé. In Kongo society, subjects explicitly expected kings to protect them; if kings could not, their authority collapsed.

In this regard, the establishment in 1576 of a Portuguese trading colony just south of Kongo, at Luanda, created an enduring problem for Kongo kings. The Portuguese eagerly traded in slaves and would happily buy anyone, including subjects of Kongo. To protect their Kongo subjects, the kings needed income, weapons, and loyal followers—and to get all that, they had to continue to trade slaves on their own account. They tried hard to get them from neighboring societies or from the ranks of rebels within Kongo, and not from their own loyal subjects. They had succeeded in this while Kongo was expanding at the expense of neighbors; but by the 1590s, when expansion slowed and then ceased, kings of Kongo found it harder to get slaves to sell for weapons.

After 1590, most royal reigns in Kongo were short and

many more Kongo subjects were captured in civil wars or rebellions and enslaved. Then a particularly skilled and lucky king, Garcia II, took over in 1641. When he acceded to the throne, his subjects spelled out their expectations: "You shall be king, be no thief, neither covetous nor revengeful, but be a friend of the poor: You shall also give alms for the release of prisoners or slaves." He ruled over roughly half a million people, most of them speakers of the Kikongo language. Garcia, a graduate of a Jesuit school in the capital city of São Salvador (today's M'banza-Kongo in northernmost Angola), took power by force and constantly had to fight rebels to maintain his kingdom. His success represented a high point in the history of the Kongo monarchy. The stability of his reign allowed trade to prosper, boosting the fortunes of some of his lieutenants and supporters. Part of that trade was in slaves, generally captured or purchased on the frontiers of the kingdom. Like earlier kings of Kongo, Garcia II traded in slaves himself. On one occasion, he sold 700 slaves to the Dutch in exchange for an attack on Portugal's Luanda colony.

FRAGMENTATION OF POWER Things fell apart for Kongo soon after the death of Garcia II in 1660. His successor renewed war with Portuguese forces—made up mainly of African soldiers serving the Portuguese colonial governor in Luanda—and was killed together with most of his high-ranking followers in 1665. Various contenders for power emerged, many of them men who had become empowered and enriched by trade during Garcia's reign. For decades none could vanquish all rivals, and Kongo fell into civil war. Neighboring states took advantage of the chaos to try to put their puppets on the throne. São

Garcia II of Kongo An engraving from nineteenth-century Europe imagines the successful Kongolese king seated in his throne room while receiving a delegation from the Netherlands. Garcia depended on successful trade agreements with European merchants and politicians to secure his power in the region.

Kongo and the Atlantic This portrait of Kongolese diplomat Miguel de Castro shows him wearing Dutch garb. The portrait speaks to Kongo's embeddedness within the Atlantic world during the period.

Salvador was sacked several times.

The fragmentation of power had something to do with Kongo's Atlantic connections. Rival factions competed for alliances with the Portuguese and briefly with the Dutch. They tried to use European missionaries to bolster their authority. They struggled to win advantageous positions in the trade for foreign goods such as cloth, iron, and guns. That inspired them to try to monopolize exports of slaves, ivory, and copper. During the violent decades of fragmentation (1665–1709), the volume of slaves exported from Kongo increased sharply, and Kongo warlord-entrepreneurs increasingly financed their quests for political power by capturing and selling their fellow Bakongo—which had rarely happened before the kingdom fell apart. In 1701, one Kongo warlord wrote a letter to the Pope asking permission to sell Kongo Catholics so he could afford to defend his territory. (There is no record of any papal response.) At this point, the old prohibition in Kongo against enslaving subjects of the kingdom had vanished, and all were at risk.

BEATRIZ KIMPA VITA'S MOVEMENT FOR RE-UNIFICATION A young woman inspired by a Christian saint tried to bring the chaos in Kongo to an end. **Beatriz Kimpa Vita**, born about 1684 to a prominent Kongo family, sought to re-unite the kingdom. Women had long played behind-the-scenes roles in Kongo politics, and after the breakdown of the kingdom following 1665, some took more direct parts in the ensuing power struggles. Beatriz was apparently a high-spirited youth who preferred to think for herself. Two early marriages did not work out, and in her late teenage years she became more interested in faith than husbands. She had some training in local religious traditions, but by 1700 or so felt more attracted by Catholicism. She soon felt possessed by the spirit of St. Anthony, a medieval Portuguese priest and the patron saint for the recovery of lost goods or people.

She believed that Christ was unhappy with the fragmentation of Kongo and preached that it must be re-united. She approached two claimants to the throne, one after the other, but both declined her help. So she decided to do it herself.

She convinced thousands that God spoke through her and that all should work for the re-unification of Kongo. She took the unorthodox view that Jesus, Mary, and other central figures in Christianity were all Bakongo, which offended European missionaries but won supporters in Kongo. By 1705, she and her followers had taken up residence among the ruins of São Salvador, where she established herself in the wreckage of the cathedral. One rival sent an army against her, but she converted its commander and the wife of the would-be king who sent it. She had become a major force in Kongo politics by age 21, commanding strong loyalties among masses of poor people and an increasing number of prosperous ones.

Beatriz Kimpa Vita did not, however, command much of an army. Her movement threatened all other aspirants to power in Kongo, and in 1706 one of them launched his forces against her. She was captured, declared a witch and a heretic, and burned at the stake. Her followers were defeated in battle, and 30,000 of them sold into the Atlantic slave trade. By 1709, a much weaker Kongo was nominally under the control of a new king. In reality, the king had little authority and local rulers held sway. Kongo became a highly decentralized polity with power residing in provincial families and warlords, not in the court or the king in São Salvador. Civil war, partly a routine power struggle and partly an outgrowth of changes brought on by Kongo's participation in the Atlantic world, especially the slave trade, destroyed the old kingdom of the Kongo and gave rise, after decades of violent anarchy, to a new, different, and weaker state. This was a revolution that constrained royal authority sharply and shifted power to local elites.

The old political principle undergirding the legitimacy of kings, one that obliged them to see to the security and welfare of their Bakongo subjects, was gone. After 1665, no one was secure, and

Beatriz Kimpa Vita and St. Anthony This brass pendant of St. Anthony of Padua was cast by a Kongo artist around the time that Beatriz Kimpa Vita sought to re-unite the Kongo kingdom. St. Anthony was one of the most popular saints in the Catholic kingdom of Kongo, and he inspired Beatriz Kimpa Vita's re-unification movement.

anyone in Kongo might be enslaved. The political contract between ruler and ruled had changed. Kongo's troubles had loose parallels elsewhere.

THE BRITISH CIVIL WARS AND REVOLUTION, 1640–1707

Another land beset by religious strife and civil war was England. Here again a **rising class of merchants** enriched by Atlantic trade were at the center of events. And here again they and their allies upset the structures of power, weakened kingly authority, and in the process put their country through a bloodbath. A charismatic religious zealot tried to unite the country—and briefly succeeded rather better than Beatriz Kimpa Vita in Kongo.

These events are traditionally called the English Civil War (or Civil Wars), lasting from 1641 to 1649, followed by the Commonwealth and Protectorate (1649–1660), the Restoration (1660–1685), and the Glorious Revolution (1688–1689). But because Scotland and Ireland took such a large part in these struggles, it makes more sense to see them as British Civil Wars or a British Revolution. At issue was how much power monarchs should have, whether there should be monarchs at all, and how much religious liberty to allow Britons, as well as the proper relation of Scotland and Ireland to England.

England and Wales in 1600 counted about 4 million inhabitants, mostly Protestant in religion. Both were ruled by a long-lived queen, Elizabeth I, who reigned with a strong hand, although not quite the iron fist favored by her father, Henry VIII. She consolidated the position of the Protestant religion in England, giving rise to what would become the Church of England (Anglicanism), headed by herself. Elizabeth lasted 44 years on the throne, providing stability. But she died, unmarried and childless, in 1603, the last monarch of the Tudor dynasty.

Her throne passed to her cousin James, a Scottish king from the Stuart dynasty, long in power in Scotland. James had keenly awaited this moment, because Scotland was a small kingdom with under a million inhabitants, most of them dirt-poor, and most of them Protestants of a Calvinist sort, called Presbyterians. As James I of England, he would rule a much larger and richer kingdom. Ireland came with his inheritance. Ireland was also poor, with a population of 2 million, almost all Catholics. The three kingdoms had long histories of warfare among them, and many of their subjects had long memories and strong attachments to their preferred sect of Christianity.

James balanced the interests of his three kingdoms reasonably successfully for a while, although a Catholic conspiracy tried to blow him up in 1605. In his later years, when he was drinking heavily and his health slipping, he indulged his taste for arbitrary rule and alienated some of the elite who felt entitled to a larger voice in political matters. He was a learned man, conversant in Latin and French, and liked to lecture everyone within earshot on the "absolute prerogative of kings." And in fact his legal authority, like that of the Tudor monarchs before him, was close to absolute. His biggest problem was finance: he needed the consent of **Parliament**—a legislative assembly partly elected by property owners (House of Commons) and partly composed of hereditary nobles (House of Lords)—to raise enough revenue. In 1625 James died, and his son Charles took the throne with a firm belief in the right of kings to rule as they pleased.

KING VERSUS PARLIAMENT   Charles I (r. 1625–1649) came to power at age 24 and had not learned to play well with others. He quarreled with Parliament, which in 1628 officially forbade taxation without its consent. No one was willing to lend to the Crown. Desperate for money, Charles resorted to seizing property and selling it. To many of his subjects, he appeared too sympathetic to Catholics—his wife, a French princess, was one. He was

Elizabeth I of England   Painted in 1588 at the height of her reign, this portrait depicts Elizabeth I surrounded by symbols of her country's rising naval power and its supremacy over its rival, Spain.

Sectarian Warfare in Ireland English anti-Catholic sentiment led to propaganda like this image, which suggested that Irish Catholics were routinely massacring Protestants—including women—at the instigation of their priests.

less popular than his father, who had been less popular than Elizabeth. The monarchy's stock fell further when Charles tried to force the Scots Presbyterian Church to adopt a new prayer book based on Anglican tradition. Many Scots rose in rebellion. Now in urgent need of armies and money, Charles I could no longer ignore Parliament.

His timing could hardly have been worse. The entire seventeenth century in Britain was marked by rising prices and stagnant standards of living. Fuelwood and coal prices climbed especially fast. And the 1640s was one of the coldest decades of the Little Ice Age in Britain, with bad harvests and pervasive hunger. Ordinary people had plenty to complain about.

So did the more comfortable ones elected to Parliament. A torrent of complaints, mainly about royal overreach, flooded the body when it met in 1640. Many in Parliament were Puritans, zealous Protestants who felt that bishops and royal power over the church were illegitimate. Compromise did not come easily to them. When an Irish rebellion flared up in 1641 and the king needed even more money and men, he could not get the cooperation he wanted. Soon both he and members of Parliament were recruiting their own armies, and by 1642 they were at war. The king set up his headquarters in a college of Oxford University.

Warfare now ravaged England as well as Ireland and Scotland. Allegiances were chaotic. Every county had its own civil war. But in general English Catholics sided with the king, and Puritans with Parliament. The people of London, and the urban middle classes, tended to support Parliament. Royalists, as those loyal to the Crown were called, seemed to be getting the upper hand in the early 1640s, but Scottish armies helping the forces of Parliament turned the tide. King Charles was captured, and in 1649

tried for treason and publicly beheaded, maintaining to the end the right of kings to rule unhindered and that no court could try a king for any crime.

THE COMMONWEALTH The victors set up a republic called the Commonwealth of England. It soon slid into military dictatorship, ruled by Oliver Cromwell. Cromwell, a parliamentarian and Puritan, distinguished himself in warfare against the royalists. Confident that God endorsed his every move, he was among those who signed the death warrant of King Charles. He led a brutal suppression of Ireland in 1649–1650 and managed to subdue Scotland by 1653. By force of arms he had achieved what kings could not: a unified Britain under the near-absolute power of one man. But his religious zealotry alienated all those who did not share his Puritanism. His persecution of Catholics in Ireland and Scotland bordered on genocide. After a while, many who had opposed Charles I and welcomed a republic began to think kings weren't so bad after all. The wars and their attendant epidemics and famines, between 1639 and 1653, cost England about 4 percent of its population, Scotland 6 percent, and Ireland a staggering 40 percent.

Death Warrant of Charles I A detail of the death warrant that was signed by representatives of Parliament in 1648. Oliver Cromwell was among the signatories.

When Cromwell died of malaria in 1658, the republic gradually fell apart. After an interval of chaos, Parliament invited the son of the beheaded king to rule over England, Scotland, and Ireland. Charles II ascended the throne in 1661. His followers dug up Cromwell's body and beheaded it on the anniversary of the beheading of Charles I. Cromwell's severed head remained on display in London until 1685.

THE RESTORATION The principle of monarchy was restored and endures to this day in Britain. But Parliament and the propertied classes it represented—landowners, merchants, lawyers, and others—had successfully asserted their privileges. The monarchy henceforth was weaker than it had been in Elizabeth's time, and it would weaken further. Cromwell's political revolution had been overturned, but the result was a decentralization of power. As in Kongo, the British Civil Wars weakened central authority; unlike Kongo, Britain restored internal peace—and exported only a few thousand of its people to the Americas as forced laborers, mostly Irish and Scottish vagrants and rebels.

King Charles II lived until 1685, devoting at least as much attention to his mistresses as to affairs of state. He sought to reduce discrimination against Catholics and lost a war with the Dutch, provoking his own struggles with Parliament. His younger brother, James II, was a Catholic, and his succession brought a new crisis. Once on the throne, James showed signs of trying to re-establish a more centralized monarchy and of treating religious minorities, chiefly Catholics, with toleration. But Protestant elites, fearful of what James might do, invited a Dutch aristocrat, William of Orange (who was married to James II's eldest daughter, Mary), to invade the country. Eager to improve the Dutch position against France in European geopolitics, William accepted the invitation, overthrowing his father-in-law in 1688–1689.

THE GLORIOUS REVOLUTION William's English allies, members of the Protestant elite, intended to prevent James II from solidifying royal power at their expense. In effect, they wanted to preserve the principles established in the wars between Parliament and king in the 1640s. Their remarkable act of conspiracy and treason became known as the **Glorious Revolution**. Almost bloodless, in sharp contrast to the wars of four decades before, it consolidated the position of Protestants in England and Scotland and the strength of Parliament with respect to monarchs. Parliament made it illegal for Catholics to ascend the throne, a law not changed until 2013. Partly to ensure that no Catholic could come to power in Scotland, Parliament in 1707 undertook the union of Scotland and England, ruled ever since by a single government seated in London.

The British Revolution, spanning the period 1640–1707, ultimately established the principle that Parliament ruled over England and Scotland. Kings and queens increasingly became symbols, sovereign only in name, while their ministers and the people's representatives in Parliament governed. The British Revolution resulted in the triumph of both mercantile elites and landed gentry, but above all of Protestants, especially Anglicans, at the expense of Catholics, who were denied the right to serve in Parliament or as officers in the military. These arrangements at first inspired some rebellions, especially among Catholics in Scotland, which ended in 1746. The settlement of 1707 provided the basis for a stable polity in Great Britain for centuries to come.

NORTH AMERICA, 1750–1790

The British Civil Wars and Revolution left most British subjects with the impression that property-owning adult males should enjoy some political rights, and that government should be based on consent of the governed. Many who left Britain for North America brought these convictions with them. The literate and best connected among them also kept in touch with friends and relatives in Britain, and a few, mostly merchants, had ties with other lands as well. As a result, they knew something of the political struggles ongoing in Europe over the proper forms of government and the extent of royal power.

North America in 1750 remained home to a substantial, if falling, Amerindian population, almost all of whom lived west of the Appalachians. These lands were claimed by Britain or France, but not yet occupied by either power except for a few wooden forts. The Amerindians, however, had long been fighting losing battles for their land—indeed, since the first English and French settlements in 1607 (Virginia) and 1608 (Quebec).

By 1750, North America's eastern seaboard was dominated demographically by European immigrant settlers and their slaves, all but a few of whom were at least partly of African descent. It was dominated politically by Great Britain and included 14 British colonies stretching from Georgia to Nova Scotia. The colonies' population was about 1.3 million—but growing fast. Migrants kept pouring in from Britain, and to a lesser extent, Germany and elsewhere. Land was cheap, and free people, usually with enough to eat, were remarkably healthy. Families with 6 to 10 children were common. Even the most downtrodden, the slave population of the plantation colonies (South Carolina and Virginia chief among them), was growing through natural increase, reaching about 230,000 in 1750. French settlements along the St. Lawrence River, called Quebec or Canada, counted about 60,000 people, also growing quickly. An even smaller population existed in Spanish outposts in Florida and along the Gulf Coast. Virginia was the biggest of all these colonies, with nearly half a million people in 1750, 40 percent of whom were slaves.

In 1750, no one supposed that any of these colonies would soon become independent. None of the mainland colonies, not even Virginia, was as important to Britain as Jamaica or even tiny Barbados, with their profitable sugar plantations. The North American colonies were squabbling constantly. But within a quarter-century, 13 of them would be fighting for freedom from British rule.

GROWING TENSIONS WITH BRITAIN

Broad economic and social changes would lead some Americans to aspire to independence from Britain. Many of these changes came from Atlantic connections. Not only did colonists share in some of the political ideas in circulation in Britain, but trade links created prosperous elites with ambitions. In the southern colonies, rice and tobacco plantations, based on slave labor, supported a class of rich planters who considered themselves every bit as good as English aristocrats. In New England, New York, and Pennsylvania, successful merchants and professionals, including some whose fortunes came from slave trading, increasingly thought of themselves as equal to their counterparts in England and deserving of the same political rights.

That situation alone probably would not have led to anything much, but in 1754 a 22-year-old Virginian unintentionally started what would become the first global war. In the summer of that year, authorities in London instructed the colonies in North America to coordinate

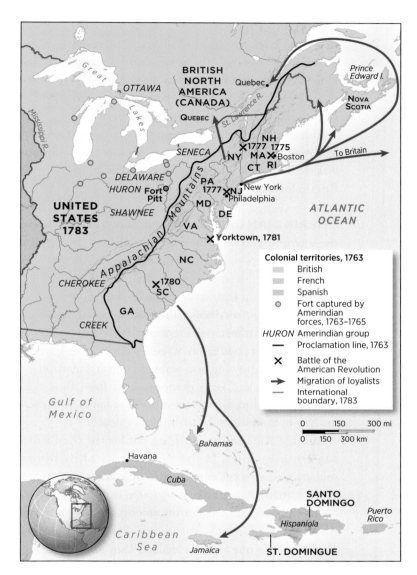

North America, 1750–1783 The peace settlement of the Seven Years' War (1756–1763) left Britain in nominal control of all eastern North America. France ceded all its territorial claims there, and Spain traded Florida for the return of Havana in Cuba and Manila in the Philippines. Amerindian populations, most of them west of the Appalachian Mountains, had no voice in the settlement. The grievances of American colonists grew steadily during the late 1760s and led to the American Revolution, which effectively ended with the siege of Yorktown. Thirteen of the British mainland colonies became independent as the United States. Spain recovered Florida for another 35 years, and thousands of loyalists fled the United States for British colonies in Canada or the Caribbean.

an effort to check French expansion west of the Appalachians. The colonial assembly in Virginia decided to send its militia, commanded by a youthful George Washington, into what is now western Pennsylvania. After he attacked a French post, Britain and France declared war on one another, and eventually fought on three continents and the high seas in the Seven Years' War (1756–63, sometimes called the French and Indian War in the United States). Britain's superior sea power and better state finance enabled it to prevail, acquiring nominal title to lands west of the Appalachians from France.

But British victory led to new tensions in North America. Most of the British colonies soon felt that Britain was treating them unfairly. The colonials' irritation with Britain focused on two main issues.

AMERINDIAN LANDS First was access to the lands in the interior of North America. Now claimed by Britain, these lands were populated by Amerindians. Authorities in London tried to control that vast space from the Gulf Coast to Canada with some 500 soldiers, whose conduct alienated many Amerindian chiefs accustomed to reasonably smooth relations with French traders. Meanwhile, the Euro-American population of the eastern seaboard, whose numbers were growing fast, wanted to push Amerindians off their lands and farm them or profit from their sale. Britain wanted to reserve most of those lands for Amerindians in the interest of maintaining peace.

A large Amerindian uprising confirmed the British concern over unrest in the region. Irritated by British soldiers, and in some cases fearful of losing their land to settlers, many Amerindians—groups from the Ottawa, Delaware, Seneca, and Huron among them—joined in what is called Pontiac's War in 1763. Pontiac, an Ottawa chief, was only one of many leaders. They took eight British forts around the Great Lakes during the years 1763–1764 in a loosely coordinated set of campaigns. Their assaults on colonial settlements in Pennsylvania and Virginia brought counterattacks on Amerindian villages. A few thousand people were killed, many in grotesque ways. British tactics included deliberately trying to infect Amerindians with smallpox at Fort Pitt (now Pittsburgh) and paying a bounty for scalps of any Amerindians over age 10, a response to the scalping of white children by Amerindian war parties.

Militarily it was a standoff, but politically Pontiac and his followers won a significant victory. In the early months of the struggle, the British issued a proclamation that designated North America, from the Appalachians to the Mississippi River and from Florida to Quebec, as an "Indian reserve." Negotiations ended **Pontiac's War**

in 1764–1765, confirming Amerindian rights to lands west of the Appalachians.

For many colonists, especially in Virginia, Pennsylvania, and New York, the settlement seemed a betrayal of their rights and interests by a distant king. The Crown, as they saw it, had taken the side of savages who had massacred hundreds of colonists, rather than allow British subjects to occupy western lands. The king, or at least his ministers, had larger strategic interests to consider, and those were incompatible with colonial expansion sure to inflame Amerindian resentment.

BRITISH TAXES The second issue was taxes. The British government in 1764 began to impose new taxes on the American colonies in order to help pay debts incurred in winning the Seven Years' War. After all, their armies and navy had protected the colonists from assaults by the French and their Amerindian allies. Many colonials, however, saw the matter differently. After 1763, there was no French threat anymore. With no further need for British protection, the colonists didn't want to pay for it, especially considering that they had no representation in the British Parliament that decided upon taxes. This irritation at new taxes was gradually framed as a matter of principle: British subjects in North America should have the same rights as British subjects in Britain, and therefore should be taxed only by their consent, by representative assemblies of their own choosing. "No taxation without representation" became a popular slogan.

Colonial Americans organized boycotts of sugar, official documents, and tea—items on which Britain hoped to collect new taxes. Some proclaimed that they would be no better than slaves if they permitted themselves to be taxed with no say in the matter. In Boston especially they rioted now and again, on one occasion dumping valuable cargoes of tea into the harbor in what became known as the Boston Tea Party. In 1768, the British government chose to send two army regiments to Boston to keep the peace. Ben Franklin, the Boston-born, Philadelphia-based printer and all-purpose intellectual, warned that this was as prudent as "setting up a smith's forge in a magazine of gunpowder." And so it was.

Frictions in Boston flared up into violence in the early 1770s. On the coasts, the British Royal Navy fell into conflict with merchants and fishermen. British governors tried to keep colonists out of the Indian reserve, but with little success. Virginia's governor, Lord Dunmore, complained that he could not "restrain the Americans [who] do and will [move west] as their avidity and restlessness incite them." Farmers in North Carolina, who called themselves the Regulators, refused to recognize British courts and tried to establish their own system of justice. From Massachusetts to Georgia, colonists who before 1763 could agree on nothing now agreed that they deserved the full "rights of Englishmen" and should not be taxed without their consent.

In 1774, their representatives came together in a new assembly called the Continental Congress. They petitioned Parliament to reconsider several of its policies. But fighting broke out around Boston in the spring of 1775 between local militias and British regiments, leading to six years of warfare.

THE AMERICAN REVOLUTION

The **American Revolution** (1775–1781) was a revolutionary war and a civil war. It was a revolutionary war in that the American forces—mainly poor men—were led by elites who sought fundamental political changes. In the summer of 1776, representatives of 13 colonies gathered in Philadelphia as the Second Continental Congress. The representatives cited grievances going back to 1764 and principles that separated just government, with the consent of the governed, from "absolute despotism." The second sentence of their Declaration of Independence read:

Revolution in North America In this French engraving, New Yorkers tear down a statue of King George III following approval of the Declaration of Independence in July 1776.

Declaration of Independence An early draft of the Declaration of Independence, handwritten by Thomas Jefferson.

"We hold these truths to be self-evident, that all men are created equal, that they are endowed by their Creator with certain unalienable Rights, that among these are Life, Liberty and the pursuit of Happiness." The author of these words, Thomas Jefferson, ironically was a Virginia slaveowner.

The American Revolution was a civil war in that about 15 to 20 percent of Americans were loyalists who wanted to remain within the British Empire. Rebels and loyalists occasionally indulged in bloodbaths, especially in the Carolinas. It was an unpopular war in Britain, where most of the population wanted peace and favored making concessions to get it—as Britain had done in Pontiac's War.

KEYS TO AMERICAN VICTORY The war was a close contest. The Americans won because the fighting was an ocean away from Britain, and because France, Spain, and the Netherlands all joined in against Britain. They provided the Americans with much of the money, weaponry, and engineering expertise they needed, and almost all the naval power. Their entry sapped political support for the war in Britain. There the Crown was mainly concerned about preserving its colonies in the Caribbean, its position in India, and its naval superiority in the waters close to Britain. The rebellious lands from Georgia to Massachusetts just weren't worth that much in comparison.

The Americans also won because their leaders, in particular George Washington, had the good sense to fight a patient war. He avoided major battles, which, as he knew, the better-trained, better-armed, and better-disciplined British Army was almost sure to win. When he did get trapped into giving battle, he normally lost. His volunteer army sometimes threatened to melt away. Most of his foot soldiers had signed on for a cash enlistment bonus or the promise of land after the war, and not for principles of representative government. Keeping them together as an army was a remarkable feat. In 1781, Washington had to shoot the ringleaders of mutinous New Jersey troops, who were owed money that Congress could not pay.

Washington also had the wisdom to require inoculation against smallpox for every man in the Continental Army when an epidemic was threatening to destroy it. Diseases killed about 10 times as many men as did combat in the war, and so reducing losses to infection made a big impact.

Major combat operations ended in 1781. The French navy coordinated with both the French and the Continental armies to pin the bulk of the British forces in a swampy, malarial spot at Yorktown, Virginia, where they surrendered. When a peace treaty was negotiated confirming American independence in 1783, some of Washington's followers urged him to declare himself king and establish a monarchy. Instead, Washington resigned his commission and retired to his Virginia plantation.

Only thirteen British colonies had joined the war. The Caribbean island colonies, such as Jamaica and Barbados, and the northernmost—Nova Scotia, Prince Edward Island, and Quebec—chose to remain British. Seventy thousand loyalists fled during and after the war, mainly north to what would become Canada. They took about 2,000 slaves with them.

OUTCOMES OF THE REVOLUTION

Those who remained in the newly independent United States had many differences among them. It took years of politicking before Americans could agree on the principles underlying their new country, formalized in a constitution drafted in 1787 and adopted in 1789. Based on the belief that just government required the consent of the governed, it established a federal structure balancing the authority of a central government against that of constituent states. It also carefully divided power among three branches of government: a judiciary, a legislature, and an executive—a president, the first of whom would be Washington, coaxed from retirement. Its first ten amendments,

called the Bill of Rights, added in 1791, guaranteed certain liberties for citizens, such as the freedom of religion, of speech, to bear arms, and to a jury trial. Voting rights were left up to the states, most of which allowed only property-owning adult white males, about 6 percent of the population, to vote.

WOMEN'S RIGHTS Political rights for women hardly crossed men's minds. In early 1776, while her husband John was away in Philadelphia hatching plans for rebellion from Britain, Abigail Adams tried to alert him to an oversight. She wrote to him:

> I long to hear you have delivered [independence]—and by the way in the new Code of Laws which I suppose it will be necessary for you to make I desire you would remember the Ladies and be more generous and favourable to them than your ancestors. Do not put such unlimited power into the hands of Husbands. Remember all Men would be tyrants if they could.

When her husband replied and dismissed her concerns, in another letter (with the inconsistent capitalization normal in the eighteenth century) she added:

> I cannot say that I think you are very generous to the Ladies, for whilst you are proclaiming peace and goodwill to Men, Emancipating all Nations, you insist upon retaining absolute power over Wives. But you must remember that Arbitrary power is like most other things which are very hard, very liable to be broken.

Neither the Declaration of Independence nor the Constitution reflected any of Abigail Adams's views. In general, the American Revolution left the matter of women's political rights untouched, despite the participation of women in the boycotts of the 1770s and

Abigail Adams Born in 1744, Abigail Adams was one of the revolutionary era's most influential women. In a letter to her husband, John Adams, she urged the Continental Congress to "put it out of the power of husbands to use us as they will."

the support they gave the Continental Army as cooks, nurses, and washerwomen—indeed, a few had even managed to serve as soldiers by disguising themselves as men.

COMPROMISING ON SLAVERY The Revolution was no more revolutionary on the issue of slavery, although it came in for more discussion. After much debate, and difficult compromise, the framers of the Constitution decided to permit slavery where it already existed and to allow the continuation of the Atlantic slave trade until 1808. States, however, were free to make their own rules, and Vermont and Massachusetts, which had relatively few slaves, soon passed laws making slavery illegal. But the states where most of the Republic's half a million slaves lived passed no such laws, and those states' political strength ensured that the federal government could not either. Jefferson in 1782 had written that slavery was an "unremitting despotism" and that "I tremble for my country when I reflect that God is just." But he did not even free his own slaves. Ironically, slavery lasted in the United States until 1865, long after it had ended in the British Empire against which Americans had fought for freedom.

FRANCE, 1780–1815

The **French Revolution** led to the formation of another republic at the expense of another monarch. It led to deeper changes in France than had the American Revolution in the United States. The revolutionaries in France overthrew the principle of monarchy, proclaimed the sovereignty of the people, established a secular republic, killed a king, seized most of the property of the Catholic Church, abolished slavery throughout the French Empire, abolished all they could of feudalism, legalized divorce, established freedom of religion, and even instituted a new calendar. The French did all this, and then undid most of it.

ORIGINS OF THE FRENCH REVOLUTION

The origins of the French Revolution make up one of historians' favorite puzzles. Like all the revolutions considered in this chapter, the French Revolution had deep and tangled roots. Some of them were intellectual, anchored in what is called the Enlightenment. Some

were socioeconomic, based in slow changes in French society. Other, shallower, roots were financial, and even climatic.

THE ENLIGHTENMENT The European Enlightenment took shape in the early eighteenth century. Its center lay in France, but participants lived in most parts of Europe, from Poland to Spain and from Italy to Scotland. It was, in essence, an intellectual movement involving a few thousand well-educated people, although to some extent their ideas affected others, even people who could not read or write—the majority everywhere. In France, its chief targets for reform—or perhaps for elimination—were the twin

Salons In this engraving from the eighteenth century, Suzanne Necker is shown seated with her daughter at one of her famous Parisian salons, listening to a writer read his work aloud. The spaces created by *salonnières* such as Necker helped Enlightenment ideas to develop and spread.

institutions of monarchy and church. To supporters of the Enlightenment, both seemed out of date and obstacles to human progress. The ideals of the Enlightenment included reliance on reason and science, wider political liberty, and religious toleration for Christians of all sorts and often for Jews. Its exponents were thinkers such as François-Marie Arouet (1694–1778), who mocked the institutions and traditions of France under the pen name Voltaire; Denis Diderot (1713–1784), who tried to compile all knowledge in a 28-volume encyclopedia, published between 1751 and 1778; and Immanuel Kant (1724–1804), a German philosopher who claimed that morality derives from reason. Its sponsors were mainly wealthy patrons, often women who organized "salons" dedicated to discussion of political questions as well as to art and literature. The most prominent was Suzanne Necker (ca. 1737–1794), a Swiss Protestant of modest origins. An intellectual in her own right, she was particularly interested in hospital reform and the question of whether divorce should be legal. She married a successful financier and ran a Paris salon in the 1770s and 1780s that attracted the most active thinkers, writers, and artists.

SOCIOECONOMIC CHANGES The intellectual currents of the Enlightenment flowed together with socioeconomic changes in France. In the late eighteenth century, the French, like other Europeans, divided their society legally, politically, and culturally into three "estates." The clergy constituted the First Estate, about 0.5 percent of the population of 28 million as of 1789. It owned 10 percent of the farmland and pastureland in France and had the right to impose taxes (tithes) on peasants. The nobility made up the Second Estate, about 1 to 2 percent of the French public. They owned about 25 percent of the productive land and enjoyed exemption from most taxes. The Third Estate included everybody else—except the landless poor, who were outside this system altogether. Peasant farmers made up most of the Third Estate, which paid almost all the taxes and had the least political influence in France. They owned at most 40 percent of the useful land in France, usually in small plots. Urban artisans and professionals were also in the Third Estate; many urban families owned farmland too. There was little social mobility in this system: only rarely did anyone change their status as a member of one or another estate. This system of social and political hierarchy, all subject to the authority of the French king, is often called the Old Regime.

Over the course of the eighteenth century, France became more urbanized. Atlantic trade played some role in this shift, especially in western France. Cities such as Bordeaux and Nantes rose to prominence on Atlantic trade, including the slave trade. Merchant and professional classes grew in number, strength, and ambition. They resented the grip on social status and political influence held by the nobility. For many in these classes, monarchy and church seemed hostile to their ambitions.

Meanwhile, the French aristocratic elite—the nobility and the top ranks of the clergy—began to divide against itself by 1770. Like all elites, it had always had its lines of fracture. But now some came to share doubts about the Old Regime system, particularly about the efficiency of the monarchy, which wasted money, employed incompetent bunglers, and lost most wars. Voltaire recommended following the Chinese example and staffing government offices not with well-connected aristocrats but with smart young men selected by examination. Many among the elite thought the Catholic Church suffocated society and culture. Others thought that aristocratic lords (often, their own friends and relatives) did the same to agriculture and the economy by resisting innovations, whether in crop rotations or technologies.

Food Riots One of the catalysts of the French Revolution was a poor harvest and astronomically high food prices. The price of bread impelled hundreds of women of all social classes to march on the royal palace of Versailles in 1789, as illustrated in this engraving.

OTHER PRESSURES Other pressures were slowly building in the lower echelons of society. France's population grew from 20 million to 28 million between 1700 and 1789. Unlike the situation in the colonies in North America, where land was plentiful, in France population growth did not enhance prosperity for ordinary folk. Land was growing scarce, and much of it was already owned by nobles and the church. Population growth did not mean expansion so much as overcrowding. The prospects for poor peasants were getting bleaker.

All of this might have come to nothing without short-term financial and climatic stresses. The French Crown, like most monarchies, had perpetual money problems worsened by the heavy costs of war. After 1778, French involvement in the American Revolution drained what was left in the French treasury, now deep in debt. Neither bankers, nobles, nor the Catholic Church would lend money to the king except at the most exorbitant interest rates. In France, the body with the authority to vote taxes was the Estates-General. No French king had consulted it for over 170 years. When the king, desperate for revenue, summoned the Estates-General in 1789, he ignited a political wildfire, blown this way and that by swirling winds beyond anyone's control.

To add to the pressures, in the 1780s bad weather brought meager harvests and widespread hunger. An Icelandic volcano erupted in 1783–1784, spewing dust into the atmosphere and blocking sunlight. Its effect lasted two or three years, reducing harvests and raising grain prices in northern Europe. In 1788, drought hit France—and then a cold winter. Ordinary people normally spent about half their income on food, but by 1789 that was up to 90 percent. Now people who had never heard of Voltaire or discussed ideas of sovereignty rioted over bread prices and clamored for lower taxes—the last thing King Louis XVI wanted. The food crisis brought poor people—men and women—together as nothing else could, and briefly made them a political force in France.

THE EARLY REVOLUTION

The French Revolution began when the Estates-General, composed of representatives of the three estates, met in 1789. Its members understood that they, like England's Parliament in 1641, had bargaining power because the king needed money desperately. Soon the Third Estate declared itself to be a National Assembly, embodying the will of the people. Some clergymen joined it. The king tried offering some concessions, but in the summer of 1789 he fired his most reform-minded ministers, a signal that he hoped to face down the Third Estate. Then the poor artisans, clerks, and petty shopkeepers of Paris stormed the Bastille, hungry people rioted in other cities, and peasants began to attack the property of their landlords and the church. The Revolution was under way, and no one knew where it would lead.

THE DECLARATION OF THE RIGHTS OF MAN AND CITIZEN
In August 1789, the National Assembly decided to abolish the feudal privileges of the clergy and nobility. All citizens of France would henceforth be legally equal. No more tax exemptions for the nobility. No more dues owed by peasants to nobles or tithes to the church. The Assembly adopted an extraordinary document entitled The Declaration of the Rights of Man and Citizen, which borrowed from Enlightenment thought and from the American Declaration of Independence. The first of its 17 Articles proclaimed that "Men are born and remain free and equal in rights." The third stated that "The principle of sovereignty resides essentially in the nation," which meant adult males.

Some French women objected to being excluded. In the fall of 1789, one group wrote a pamphlet intended for the National Assembly asking why 13 million females should be the slaves of 13 million males (they underestimated the national population slightly). In 1791, Olympe de Gouges, a woman of modest origins from the southwest of France who had moved to Paris and become a playwright, a political intellectual, and a fierce opponent of the enslavement of Africans, wrote a counterblast that she called Declaration of the Rights of Woman and Citizen. Although de Gouges won little popular support among either men or women in her call for equality, women soon achieved the right to divorce husbands and to equality in matters of inheritance. But not to vote or hold office.

Men did a little better with political rights in the first years of the Revolution. At first only men over age 25 who paid taxes were allowed to vote—about 4 to 5 million Frenchmen, around 15 to 18 percent of the population. By 1792, almost all males over age 21 could vote. But in 1793 they elected representatives, most of them young men, who allowed no further elections.

TARGETING CHURCH AND MONARCHY
Securing political rights was only one part of the Revolution. In the late fall of 1789, the National Assembly confiscated most of the lands and buildings of the Catholic Church and sold them. It forced most clergy to retire and made the others employees of the state. It made Protestants and Jews equal citizens with Catholics. The church in France eventually recovered some of its property, but never the power it lost in 1789.

From 1789 to 1791, the National Assembly ruled France in uneasy harness with King Louis XVI. But the king, sensing his position weakening, attempted to flee the country. He was caught, eventually put on trial, and executed. This earned the revolutionaries many enemies within France and in Europe. The French royal family had kinship ties with royalty in Austria. Kings everywhere felt

Execution of the King A key element of the radical phase of the French Revolution was the formal execution of the deposed king, Louis XVI, at the guillotine, in early 1793.

threatened. By early 1792, revolutionary France was at war with the monarchs of Austria and Prussia.

A RADICAL TURN

Now the Revolution entered a much more radical and violent phase. The wars against foreign monarchies required unity among the French. But unity could not be achieved by consensus, as many sympathized with the dead king and the dispossessed church, especially in the provinces. So the revolutionaries sought unity through compulsion. The executive machinery of government (called a Legislative Assembly in 1791–1792 and the National Convention in 1792–1795) was increasingly dominated by men called **Jacobins**, mostly middle-class, many of them lawyers, who were prepared to take drastic measures to prevent the Revolution from collapsing. They often allied with the urban poor, usually called *sans-culottes* because they wore trousers rather than the more fashionable knee-breeches. The Jacobins ended elections in 1793 and ruled with an iron hand.

JACOBIN REFORMS Jacobin members of the revolutionary government sought to change almost everything. Sometimes they aimed to improve the human condition, sometimes to save the Revolution from its enemies, sometimes to destroy one another in their competition for power. One of them, Louis Antoine de Saint-Just, a 26-year-old law school dropout and poet, declared that "everything that is not new in a time of innovation is pernicious." The Jacobins instituted a tax reform whereby the wealthier paid more, a popular move. They created a mass army through conscription, an unpopular one. They tried to create a new religion, sometimes called the Cult of the Supreme Being, based on concepts of civic virtue and an abstract God who preferred reason to faith. They promulgated a new calendar in which the beginning of the Republic in fall 1792 became Year I. It divided years into 12 months, each of three 10-day weeks. No longer would ordinary people get one day in seven off; the calendar was never popular. Days were divided into 10 hours, and hours into 100 minutes of 100 seconds, part of an effort to replace tradition with reason. The Jacobins instituted the metric system of weights and measures. They banned aristocratic fashions such as men's powdered wigs and women's velvet dresses. They abolished slavery in France and French colonies. They encouraged people to destroy statues of kings and bishops and melt them down to be turned into weapons for the army. And they made it clear they would tolerate no dissent. By late 1793, citizens who did not have a "certificate of public virtue" issued by the state could be arrested on sight. The unfortunate Madame de Gouges, suspected of disloyalty to the Revolution, was among those guillotined in Paris.

THE COMMITTEE OF PUBLIC SAFETY The Revolution now reached a stage that historians call the Terror. The government, dominated by a so-called Committee of Public Safety, itself soon dominated by a 34-year-old lawyer, Maximilien Robespierre, found enemies everywhere. Robespierre, who liked to be called "The Incorruptible," was a man of principle at any cost. In early 1794, he wrote that "the spring of government during a revolution is virtue combined with terror: virtue, without which terror is destructive; terror, without which virtue is impotent. Terror is only justice prompt, severe and inflexible; it is . . . a natural consequence of the general principle of democracy, applied to the most pressing wants of the country." Saint-Just told the deputies of the Convention that "a nation creates itself only upon heaps of corpses."

He and Robespierre did their part to build those heaps. The Committee of Public Safety ordered the arrest of half a million people and had some 20,000 executed. Everyone now lived in fear. Some 150,000 people, mostly nobles and clergy, fled France, many of them for America. Rebellions in the countryside, prompted by conscription as much as anything else, cost tens of thousands of lives. Ambitious revolutionaries denounced one another, hoping to climb the slippery pole of political power at one another's expense. Robespierre turned on his friends and comrades at the slightest suspicion of dissent. As one observer put it, "Like Saturn [of ancient Greek mythology] the revolution devours its children." In the summer of 1794, the Terror reached a climax with public executions in Paris averaging about two dozen daily.

Unfortunately for Robespierre, Saint-Just, and the Committee of Public Safety, the military situation for France improved, weakening their main justification for relentless execution of their political enemies. In a few dramatic days, they lost much of their support in the Convention and, together with their closest supporters, lost their heads at the guillotine in late July 1794.

The Convention created a new government called the Directory (1795–1799), which excluded men under age 30

Napoleon Rising A painting from the period shows the young Napoleon, surrounded by both supporters and detractors, at the center of the 1799 coup that ultimately brought him to absolute power over France.

from office. It faced many challenges, from hunger riots to coup d'état conspiracies to rampant inflation. Political turmoil declined but did not disappear. The Directory re-instituted elections but was appalled when royalists won. Some of its members in 1799 mounted a coup against their own government. They installed a military man, **Napoleon Bonaparte**, who gradually made himself a dictator—in the name of liberty and equality.

NAPOLEON BONAPARTE: EXPANSION AND OVERREACH

Bonaparte (1769–1821), who had served in France's revolutionary army, rose from obscurity through talent and ambition. He made his name by crushing a royalist rebellion in Paris in 1795 and became a general at age 26. He won a string of astounding victories against foreign armies beginning in 1796.

The revolutionary republic had been at war since 1792. While fighting for its life against reactionary foreign monarchs, it was nonetheless pursuing traditional French foreign policy, conquering and occupying the same neighboring lands that French kings had previously tried to subdue. Under Bonaparte, however, the French

army roamed farther afield and with startling success, especially in Italy, Austria, and Germany. Everywhere it went, Bonaparte's army tried to set up new governments. They were supposedly embodiments of universal principles proclaimed by the Revolution, but in practice mainly puppets of Napoleon, sometimes ruled by his relatives. They always found local people who joined them enthusiastically against their own kings and princes. Thus Bonaparte's armies and agents re-wove the fabric of European politics, spreading some of the ideals and practices of the French Revolution.

Bonaparte's military success was part genius and part system. He knew his business well and was especially effective in coordinating field artillery with infantry and cavalry. Thanks to conscription and the size of the French population, he usually had a bigger army than his enemies. Big armies were hard to feed, but Bonaparte found that his could live off the land, buying or stealing food from farms and villages. This worked well as long as the army kept moving and operated in the agriculturally richer parts of Europe that produced enough surplus food.

Bonaparte's system failed when his armies entered poorer lands without much surplus food. Unfortunately for him, for France, and for the Revolution, Bonaparte could not stop attacking other countries, even poor ones with slender surplus. He had a bottomless need for glory. And he rightly feared what would happen, to him and

Napoleon's Russian Campaign A dramatic 1808 painting depicts the bleak aftermath of the 1807 Battle of Eylau in East Prussia, which Napoleon's forces lost. Napoleon appears at the center on horseback, while bodies lie piled in the snow and farms and villages burn in the distance.

From French Revolution to French Empire, 1789–1814 The government guiding the French Revolution declared war on Austria and Prussia in April 1792, igniting more than two decades of warfare. Under Napoleon Bonaparte, the French set up sympathetic rulers in Italy, Germany, Spain, and Poland, but none survived his downfall. The inset shows the location of key sites in revolutionary Paris.

to France, if he discharged a million men with military skills. When he attacked Spain in 1807, his army became bogged down in endless anti-guerilla operations. When he attacked Russia in 1812 and occupied much of the country, his army of 600,000 dwindled to 25,000 within months through starvation, typhus and other diseases, and an unexpectedly stiff resistance from Russians. As the French novelist Victor Hugo put it, Bonaparte was "conquered by his conquests."

These and other disasters undermined his political support at home, and by 1814 he had to abdicate the imperial throne he had earlier awarded himself. In France, the nobility soon recovered most of its former lands, and the monarchy and church returned atop society, although less powerful than before 1789. Some changes, such as the Napoleonic law code, remained in force. In Europe, all the revolutionary governments installed by Bonaparte's army were overthrown, and monarchs across Europe climbed back onto thrones—even in France in 1815. But in most cases they had to share power with legislatures.

The Revolution was dead, politically and militarily defeated, but it lived on in the hearts and minds of millions of people in Europe. The ideas it unleashed, however imperfectly brought into practice, retained some of their appeal. Revolutions and republics since 1789 have drawn inspiration from the French experience. And the stated political principles, like those of the American Revolution, remain compelling to billions of people today who cherish freedom, justice, and equality before the law—even if everyone understands these concepts differently.

HAITI, 1780–1804

The French Revolution proved inspirational in the French colony of St. Domingue (today's Haiti), where a revolution exploded in 1791. Like the French Revolution, the Haitian Revolution attacked a hierarchical social and political order. But, in contrast to the French revolution, race and slavery were at the center in Haiti.

A PLANTATION COLONY: SUGAR, COFFEE, SLAVES

Acquired in war from Spain in 1697, St. Domingue soon became France's most valuable colony. Its lowland plains proved excellent for raising sugar, and its hills equally good for less profitable crops such as coffee. By the 1780s, St. Domingue had 8,000 plantations. It produced nearly half the sugar and coffee harvested in the Atlantic world. Thirty ships a week used its ports, carrying its products to France and bringing in human cargoes from Africa.

Its population, about 550,000 in all, was nearly 90 percent slaves, two-thirds of whom were born in Africa. In the 1780s, some 30,000 slaves arrived annually, largely from Kongo. Two-thirds were male. They worked mainly on the plantations. About 5 percent of St. Domingue's people were free blacks or people of mixed African and European ancestry, called *gens de couleur*. Some of them were rich planters and slaveholders—indeed, they owned one-quarter of the colony's slaves—but most were artisans, petty merchants, or laborers. Another roughly 5 percent of the total population were whites, mainly born in France, 80 percent of whom were men. Some were rich planters, others wage laborers. All whites enjoyed legal privileges based on skin color, such as the right to bear arms or to hold political office. Almost all hoped to get rich and get back to France. Few succeeded.

St. Domingue was a tinderbox of unfulfilled ambitions. Whites wanted political representation in Paris, much as in British North America colonists a few years earlier had wanted representation in London. They wanted to be free to trade their sugar and coffee anywhere, not just to France. The *gens de couleur* wanted equality with whites. Slaves wanted freedom. Word of the revolution unfolding in France in 1789 provided a spark. The first uprising involved the *gens de couleur* in 1790, led by one of the richest men in the colony. Colonial authorities crushed it.

TOUSSAINT AND THE HAITIAN REVOLUTION

A far bigger one, involving at its outset about 100,000 slaves, erupted in the summer of 1791. It took the whites and *gens de couleur* by surprise. Most slave risings in the Americas failed before they started because someone betrayed the plans in advance. Somehow this one, the biggest of all, was kept secret.

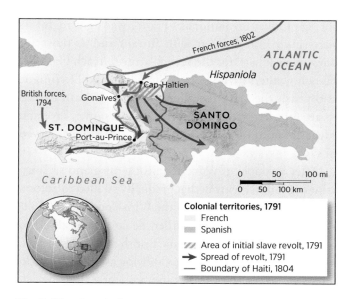

The Haitian Revolution, 1791–1804 Enslaved Africans, and others of African descent, engineered the largest slave revolt in world history beginning in 1791, turning the French sugar colony of St. Domingue into a new country, Haiti, by 1804. The uprising began on sugar plantations in the north and prospered especially in difficult, mountainous terrain where guerilla warfare was practical. French armies, arriving in force in 1802, controlled the ports but could not crush the revolution in the countryside. What little remained of them departed in 1804.

Toussaint L'Ouverture The leader of the Haitian Revolution appears in uniform on horseback—cast in the role of a heroic general—in a French engraving from the period.

The primary leader of the revolution, **Toussaint L'Ouverture**, was born a slave in the north of St. Domingue, probably in 1743. He grew up handling animals and became an expert horseman. He also learned the healing arts. His master freed him when Toussaint was about 30, and as a free man he sometimes owned slaves himself. He spoke French, Ewe (the West African language of his father), and the French-based creole (*kreyol*) that was the lingua franca of St. Domingue. He was a practicing Catholic and learned to read and write as an adult. It turned out that as a middle-aged man he had remarkable physical stamina, courage in the face of death, and the smarts and flexible principles of a master politician. By 1792, he was one of the top commanders of the slave insurrection.

French planters in St. Domingue could not get much help from France against the uprising. Many Jacobins sympathized with the slave insurrection. And by the spring of 1792, revolutionary France was fighting for its survival in Europe. War with Britain and its powerful navy made it hard for the French army to reach Haiti. So French planters invited Britain to occupy St. Domingue and crush the slave insurgency, which Britain agreed to attempt lest the uprising spread to its own slave and sugar colonies in the Caribbean. British troops arrived in 1793.

After a couple of years of shifting allegiances, Toussaint organized an army that gradually swelled to 20,000 poorly equipped men to fight the British occupation. Like Washington a generation earlier, he could not afford to fight set-piece battles against the British army and knew it. He fought a guerilla campaign, moving as needed, attacking when he saw an opening, and prudently allowing yellow fever to scythe down his enemy.

Toussaint recognized that he had an ally in yellow fever. Most of his men had acquired immunity to the lethal disease either in Africa or in St. Domingue, where just about everyone faced it in childhood. Virtually no one in the British Army had ever encountered it. Two-thirds of the British soldiers who landed in St. Domingue died of it. Those who survived left in 1798.

FRENCH INTERVENTION The French then tried to undo the revolution in St. Domingue. A peace treaty with Britain opened the seas to French navigation in 1802, and soon Bonaparte's brother-in-law, leading an army about 65,000 strong, arrived. Bonaparte gave instructions to defeat the insurgents, then re-install the plantation system and slavery, less than a decade after France's revolutionary government had abolished it. Things went well at first for the French. But Toussaint and his ragtag army ("naked as earthworms," as he put it) had other ideas and knew time was on their side. He drew inspiration from the slave revolt of Spartacus two thousand years before (Toussaint owned books on Roman history). The army of former slaves, many of whom had prior military experience in Africa, tried to pin the French down in the unhealthy lowlands while keeping the mountains to themselves. Although Toussaint was captured in 1802 and died the following year in a French prison, his strategy worked again.

Toussaint's followers stunned France and the world by winning their revolutionary war against an army—Bonaparte's—that had humbled the kings of Europe. The French had spared no effort and still lost. Once again, the Haitians used their ally, yellow fever, which killed about 75 percent of the French army. The Haitians lost many as well, to combat, disease, and massacres (of which there were many on all sides). But they could recruit from the local population, which the French found difficult to do after it was revealed that Napoleon had re-legalized slavery in the French Caribbean.

AFTERMATH The **Haitian Revolution** triumphed by 1804. It ended both French colonial rule and legal slavery in Haiti. It was, perhaps more than any other, an Atlantic revolution. Some of its animating ideas came from the revolutions in America and France. Nearly a thousand *gens de couleur* had fought in the American Revolution against Britain. Between 1789 and 1804, events in Haiti and France directly affected one another. Some of the Haitian Revolution's soldiers came from the civil wars in Kongo, via the slave trade. And its victors would soon give advice and arms to revolutionaries in what is now Venezuela.

Haitian Revolution A French engraving dramatizes the uprising of enslaved people against their masters at the center of the Haitian Revolution. Enslaved people are shown killing their masters, burning houses and fields, and fleeing the plantations.

The Haitian Revolution, like the French, devoured its children. Toussaint's most prominent lieutenant, Jean-Jacques Dessalines, organized massacres of the remaining French and of his political rivals—and declared himself emperor. His own troops killed him in 1806. His successors, also leaders of the revolution, fought one another in civil wars, created regional despotisms, and, without calling it slavery, re-established forced labor on plantations where they could.

Toussaint and his followers had pulled off the largest slave rebellion in history, won wars against two of Europe's great powers, and established the second independent country in the Americas. But the Haitian Revolution still left the great majority of Haitians poor and powerless.

SPANISH AMERICA, 1765–1825

Spanish America underwent a set of revolutions in the early nineteenth century. They were anti-colonial, like the American and Haitian revolutions, and resulted in several new republics. They led to abolitions of slavery and in places a degree of popular rule. But in most cases, they resulted in unstable autocracies or military rule.

A DIVERSE SOCIETY

At the end of the eighteenth century, Spanish America included most of South America, Central and North America as far north as Texas and California, plus several Caribbean islands. Social and economic conditions were extremely diverse over this vast terrain. Some 13 to 15 million people lived there. About 5 million lived in the Viceroyalty of New Spain (today's Mexico), with smaller centers of population elsewhere.

Ever since the conquests of the sixteenth century, people of Spanish birth (*peninsulares*) or Spanish descent (*criollos*, or creoles) dominated Spanish American society politically and economically. They held all public offices, filled the officer corps of the military, and staffed the top positions in the Catholic Church. They made up most, though not all, of the merchant class. Most parts of Spanish America included in their populations Amerindians—usually the demographic majority except in the Caribbean—slaves, free blacks, as well as large and growing communities of mixed descent. *Mestizos* were of Spanish and Amerindian ancestry; *mulattos* of African and European descent; *zambos* of African and Amerindian parentage. These groupings were fluid around the edges, and to some extent people could claim whatever status they wanted if they could make others believe it. These designations mattered, partly because of social prejudices and partly because of law: various privileges were reserved for *peninsulares* and *criollos*, and various legal handicaps for people of African descent, whether free or enslaved.

By 1760, the Spanish Empire in America was about 250 years old. This empire was essential to Spain's standing in Europe and the world, the source of about a quarter of its revenues. From Spain's viewpoint, its American empire had two great vulnerabilities. First, it was threatened by rising British military power. Second, its merchants objected to a monopoly trade system that required them to trade only with Spain. They wanted to trade with foreigners too. The rise of Atlantic commerce tempted them with opportunities they were legally forbidden to take.

Race in Spanish America Intermarriage between people of Amerindian, European, and African heritage in Spanish America created new categories of racial difference and hierarchy. Many images from the period show families of mixed racial heritage, such as these eighteenth-century paintings of families in everyday scenes.

THE BOURBON REFORMS

Spain's anxiety about British power, and its failures in the Seven Years' War (1756–1763), including a defeat at its major port of Havana, led to reforms coming from Madrid beginning in 1767. Known as the **Bourbon Reforms**, after the name of the ruling family in Spain, these were intended to strengthen the empire. Their backers had read Enlightenment thinkers and preferred reason to tradition as a guide to action. They were, in effect, technocrats, convinced they could make Spain's rule more efficient and productive, but in cases also idealists, hoping to improve human welfare. Under these reformist influences, the Crown allowed more cities to trade with Spain but cracked down on illegal trade with other empires. It reserved a larger proportion of political appointments for Spaniards at the expense of *criollos*. And it tried to curtail the power of the Catholic Church, most notably by expelling all Jesuits from the Americas in 1767. With these reforms, the Crown hoped in particular to strengthen colonial defenses, pump up the economy, and increase the wealth flowing to Spain through new taxes and other means. The Bourbon Reforms, like most dynamic reform programs, pleased some and irritated many—rather like the reforms Britain enacted (new taxes and restrictions on westward migration) in the wake of the Seven Years' War.

TÚPAC AMARU'S REVOLT Almost nobody liked the higher taxes. In 1780, a giant tax revolt broke out in the Andes. It was led by an elite, Jesuit-educated *mestizo*, **Túpac Amaru II**, a descendant of the Inka Empire's ruling family. He proposed a return to the supposedly good old days of the Inka Empire. He promised justice, an end to oppression of Amerindians and *mestizos* by Spaniards, and the elimination of all distinctions based on ethnicity. He also called for fully free trade. His wife, Micaela Bastidas, was one of several Amerindian women who helped organize the rebellion. She took charge of military logistics.

This revolutionary agenda provoked firm and at times ruthlessly violent responses from Spanish authorities, which in turn made Túpac Amaru and his followers more radical still. Many of them concluded that the only route to justice involved full independence from Spain and the murder of all Spaniards. The revolt lasted until 1783 and cost the Viceroyalty of Peru about 10 percent of its population. It was suppressed with maximal cruelty, including a gruesome public execution of Túpac Amaru.

Túpac Amaru's Failed Revolution
The revolutionary leader Túpac Amaru was memorialized on Peruvian currency in the late twentieth century. Although his revolution failed in the 1780s, it became a part of later conceptions of Peruvian national identity.

Of the 73 leaders killed by Spanish authorities, 32 were women. Like many smaller revolts of Amerindians and *mestizos* before, it failed militarily but its memory lived on, among both those who welcomed it and those who defeated it.

Túpac Amaru's failed revolution frightened everyone committed to the future of the Spanish Empire in the Americas. It had almost deprived Spain of the wealth of the Andean silver mines. Ministers in Madrid, and their agents in the colonies, trembling with relief, redoubled their commitment to reform.

Amerindians generally found little to like in the Bourbon Reforms. They lost some legal protections. The Crown's efforts to unshackle the economy led to new opportunities for entrepreneurs, especially on the frontiers such as northern Mexico. To exploit those opportunities businessmen needed laborers, and they found ways to require Amerindians (among others) to work for them in mines, on ranches, and on farming estates. Debt peonage was one such technique, whereby poor people were encouraged to borrow money and obliged to pay off their debts through labor.

The reforms also increased the scope for slavery in Spanish America. In the 1770s, the Crown opened the Atlantic slave trade to all merchants. For three decades, the traffic boomed and over a million slaves were sold to the mines of Mexico, the plantations of the Caribbean, and elsewhere in Spanish America. An internal document of the Spanish government from 1802 acknowledged that "the opulence of [Spanish] America…could not exist without the slave trade."

The *criollo,* or creole, elites found plenty to dislike in the Bourbon Reforms too. They lost access to many political offices, which henceforth were open only to men born in Spain. Those creoles who had enjoyed privileged positions in the old monopoly trade system—the merchant guilds of Lima, Mexico City, and Havana, for example—lost out when the Crown permitted more free trade.

TENSIONS OVER TRADE The Crown's experiment with freer trade was perhaps its most destabilizing step. Formerly only a few merchant guilds in the Americas were allowed to conduct transatlantic trade, and only with the merchant guild in Cadiz, a city in southwestern Spain. These rules, although widely flouted by smugglers, severely constrained the chances to make money in commerce. Beginning in 1765, the rules grew looser.

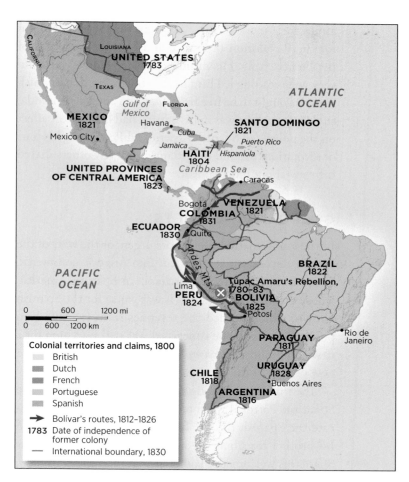

Spanish America, 1800–1830 In 1800, most of the American hemisphere was claimed by European powers, the greater part of it by Spain. Nevertheless, Amerindian peoples actually controlled sizeable parts of both continents; moreover, the United States was already an independent country, and Haiti would soon be. Spanish rule was shaken by the revolt led by Túpac Amaru in the Andes in the 1780s, and further uprisings against Spanish rule began in 1808, centered on what is now Mexico, Venezuela, Colombia, and Peru. By 1826, 17 new republics had emerged from the ruins of the Spanish Empire in the Americas.

By 1789, nine Spanish cities were allowed to trade with almost anyone in Spanish America, but no one was permitted to trade with foreigners. This program worked, but in a sense too well. Some creole merchants prospered mightily but grew ever more frustrated by their reduced political voice.

Thus, as in Haiti, few in Spanish America found political arrangements to their liking by the end of the 1780s. All sorts of suggestions arose for reworking relations with Madrid. A very few thought that independence from Spain was the best course. One such was Francisco Miranda (1750–1816), from what is now Venezuela. He had fought with Spanish forces in Florida against Britain in the American Revolution. In the 1790s, he fought for the Revolution in France and became a marshal of the French army. His military service, wide travels, and very wide reading led him to the conclusion that Spanish America ought to be free from Madrid's control. Miranda, tireless though he was in his efforts, had little direct effect on the politics of Spanish America while making his tour of revolutions around the Atlantic, and few others shared his view about independence.

GEOPOLITICAL SHIFTS

In the 1790s, matters grew more urgent as the wars of the French Revolution at times cut into Atlantic commerce. This was bad for creole merchants in Spanish America, whose discontent deepened. It was worse for the Spanish Crown, which needed the revenues from its American possessions. Everyone concerned was still searching for a new compromise between Spain and Spanish America, a new version of the empire.

Then in 1807–1808 Bonaparte's armies marched into Spain and Portugal and forced King Fernando VII to abdicate the Spanish throne. Bonaparte eventually installed his brother Joseph as the new king of Spain, which few Spaniards welcomed. Having lost St. Domingue in 1804, Bonaparte might have had his eye on the silver mines of Spanish America. He got, instead, six years of vicious guerilla war in Spain.

Now Spain and Spanish America were cut off from one another more than ever. This created a power vacuum in Spanish America, giving rise to countless factions. In cities such as Caracas, Bogotá, and Buenos Aires, local elites began to debate politics with the vigor of Jacobin clubs in Paris. Many wanted liberties of the sort Bonaparte often promised and rarely delivered, such as freedom from censorship, and fully free trade—in this case meaning trade outside the Spanish Empire, with Britain and the United States, for instance. From 1808 to 1814 the situation was fluid, although few yet thought in terms of independence.

In 1814, Bonaparte's army left Spain in defeat. King Fernando VII returned to power and immediately tried to restore Spain's hold over Spanish America. He hoped to turn back the clock. Many of the elites in Spanish America, now accustomed to greater liberties, especially in foreign trade, objected to the king's plans and embraced independence as a goal. Others, however, remained loyal to Spain. Civil wars soon erupted between revolutionaries and loyalists. As in North America in the 1770s, clumsy royal policy brought matters to a head quickly, converting reformists into revolutionaries.

Spain's efforts to bring its American colonies back into

South American Revolutionary Movements Representatives in a new revolutionary assembly voting in July 1816 to declare Argentina's independence from Spanish rule.

the fold failed spectacularly. In 1815, the king sent a large army to what is now Colombia and Venezuela, where, like the European armies in Haiti, it suffered epidemics of yellow fever and malaria. More than 90 percent of the army never came home. This was the only place where sizeable armies fought. Combat took place also in Mexico, Peru, and Chile, and around the city of Buenos Aires, but it involved small armies of a few thousand.

BOLÍVAR AND THE SPANISH AMERICAN REPUBLICS

Revolutionary leaders, such as **Simón Bolívar** (1783–1830), a wealthy, aristocratic creole from Venezuela, forged coalitions of creole elites, free blacks, and *mestizos*. Bolívar was educated in Spain and France in his youth and admired Enlightenment ideas as well as the French and American revolutions. He supported women's political rights and made one woman, Manuela Sáenz, a general in his army. During a period of exile, he went to Haiti and learned about the revolution there. Bolívar and other revolutionaries often promised slaves freedom if they joined their forces.

Spain had little power to deploy in the Americas. Loyalists in Spanish America, although numerous in the upper ranks of society, could not drum up much support among the common people. Bolívar's and other ragtag revolutionary armies trudged far and wide across Spanish America, showing a determination that Spain's troops lacked. In addition, the revolutionaries enjoyed British support. The Royal Navy made it difficult for Spain to carry men and supplies across the Atlantic. Fighting waned after 1826, and soon Spain gave up entirely. Only Cuba and Puerto Rico remained of Spain's American empire.

Bolívar was hoping to achieve a united states of South America. Instead, seventeen new republics were born from the ruins of the Spanish Empire in America—a greater number than the leaders of the revolutions had hoped for. Confederations in Central America, in northern South America, and between Argentina and Uruguay fell apart a few years after independence. Bolívar expressed his disappointment with this fragmentation when he wrote that all who had served the revolution had only "plowed the sea."

In most of the newly independent republics, creole factions feuded for power. In most cases the new rulers reduced the sway of the church, leaving the military often as the only institution with any prestige. Military dictatorships were frequent. Only Chile managed some measure of stability in the coming decades. Amerindians generally found the revolutions did nothing for them. But the republics, whether dictatorships or not, abolished slavery within a few years or decades—whereas it lasted until 1874 in Puerto Rico and 1886 in Cuba. Spain, exhausted by recurrent warfare and with its American empire reduced to two islands, was finished as a world power and even as a great power within Europe.

Simón Bolívar A contemporaneous portrait of the Venezuelan creole revolutionary depicts him clad in military dress.

THE ATLANTIC REVOLUTIONS IN BROADER PERSPECTIVE

Other Atlantic societies, such as Portugal, Spain, and Brazil, also underwent revolutionary changes. Bonaparte as we've seen invaded Spain and Portugal in 1808, creating conditions that led not only to independence across the Atlantic, but to struggles in Iberia. Absolutists supported restoration of monarchical rule, while liberals sought either republics or constitutional monarchies with representative legislatures. By the 1830s, after 20 years of instability, both Spain and Portugal emerged as constitutional monarchies. Brazil won its independence from Portugal when in 1807 the Portuguese Crown and court moved from Lisbon to Rio de Janeiro and governed the Portuguese Empire from that Brazilian city. When the king and court returned to Lisbon in 1822, they lacked the power to keep Brazil under their control. A prince, Dom Pedro I, defied his father and declared Brazil an independent monarchy, with constitutional limits upon royal power. After a few small battles, the Portuguese gave up, confirming the independence of Brazil in 1825.

A Revolutionary's Letter from Jamaica

The revolutions in North America, France, and Haiti inspired revolutionaries in Spanish America, including Simón Bolívar (1783–1830). Bolívar was Spanish by descent, but his birth in South America made him part of the creole class that the Spanish Empire excluded from political offices after the Bourbon Reforms of 1767. For Bolívar, who had studied Enlightenment writings in Europe as a young man, the tyranny of imperial rule was distressing, but he also found it attractive because it commanded respect. He felt that if Americans like him could rule, instead of distant Spain, they could build a better future by unifying the provinces of South America. While living as an exile in Jamaica in 1815, he set down his reasons for revolting against Spain in a letter to a British gentleman.

We are still in a position lower than slavery, and therefore it is more difficult for us to rise to the enjoyment of freedom. ...A people is therefore enslaved when the government... usurps the rights of the citizen or subject. Applying these principles, we find that [Spanish] America was denied not only its freedom but even an active and effective tyranny. Let me explain. Under absolutism there are no recognized limits to the exercise of governmental powers. The will of the great sultan [is] carried out more or less arbitrarily by the lesser pashas, khans, and satraps of Turkey and Persia. ...But...the rulers of Ispahan are Persians; the viziers of the Grand Turk are Turks....

How different is our situation! We have been...kept... in a sort of permanent infancy with regard to public affairs. If we could at least have managed our domestic affairs... [w]e should also have enjoyed...unconscious respect from the people, which is so necessary to preserve amidst revolutions. That is why I say we have even been deprived of an active tyranny, since we have not been permitted to exercise its functions.

Americans...who live within the Spanish system occupy a position in society no better than...serfs destined for labor, or at best...that of mere consumers. Yet even this status is surrounded with galling restrictions, such as being forbidden to grow European crops, or to store products which are royal monopolies, or to establish factories of a type the Peninsula [Spain] itself does not possess. To this add the exclusive trading privileges [of merchants favored by Spain]...and the barriers between American provinces. ...[D]o you wish to know what our future held?—simply the cultivation of [cash crops]; cattle raising on the broad plains; hunting wild game in the jungles; digging in the earth to mine its gold—but even these limitations could never satisfy the greed of Spain....Is it not an outrage and a violation of human rights to expect a land so...vast, rich, and populous, to remain merely passive?

Source: Harold A. Bierck Jr., ed., *Selected Writings of Bolívar, Vol. 1: 1810–1822*, trans. Lewis Bertrand (New York: 1951).

QUESTIONS FOR ANALYSIS

1. For Bolívar, what restrictions in the Spanish system justified revolution?
2. What reason does Bolívar give for asserting that Americans, instead of the government in Spain, should exercise "active tyranny"?
3. How do Bolívar's references to rights, slavery, and commercial restrictions reflect the influence of earlier revolutions?

ATLANTIC CONNECTIONS

All of these revolutions, from Kongo and Britain in the late seventeenth century to Spanish America and Brazil in the early nineteenth, had their own local causes. At the same time, they all shared Atlantic roots: the reshuffling of fortunes resulting from expanding Atlantic commerce proved destabilizing almost everywhere around the ocean's shores. Rising merchant classes increasingly objected to the monopoly on state power held by monarchs and their traditional allies.

By and large, the Atlantic revolutions brought **political decentralization** of two sorts. First, they undermined highly centralized kingdoms such as Kongo and England before 1640, and France before 1789. Second, they dissolved some of the bonds of transatlantic empires by giving birth to newly independent countries in the Americas. In Kongo and England, the revolutions were in effect national, reducing royal authority and empowering commercial elites. In France, the revolution began that way, but it became international when Bonaparte invaded much of Europe and St. Domingue as well. In the Americas, the revolutions were anti-imperial, with the effect of creating newly independent countries, generally republics in place of colonies subject to European monarchs.

This pan-Atlantic movement did not sweep all before it. Many West African polities, even some deeply involved in Atlantic trade, managed to survive—partly because they were not so centralized to begin with. Several Caribbean colonies such as Jamaica and Barbados, as well as Cuba and Puerto Rico, remained colonies long after the era of Atlantic revolutions. So did the British colonies that are now in eastern Canada.

Nonetheless, the Atlantic record of revolution after revolution, establishing new principles of sovereignty, contrasts sharply with most of the rest of the world, where older polities and older principles held up better. In the big centers of population, such as China, north India, or Southwest Asia, the effects of oceanic commerce were less sudden and disruptive. Existing institutions and elites withstood better whatever revolutionary pressures bubbled up, even if specific dynasties came and went. Not so around the Atlantic.

This Atlantic taproot was not the only element that all these revolutions had in common. They also had direct links in the form of mobile ideas and personnel, and interlocking events. The ideas of limited royal sovereignty that animated the British Revolution filtered into British North America, France, and at least indirectly into St. Domingue and Spanish America. Similarly, the principles embodied in the American Declaration of Independence and France's Declaration of the Rights of Man and Citizen were prominent in the revolutions in Haiti and Spanish America.

People such as Francisco Miranda moved from revolution to revolution. Many of the fighters in Toussaint's armies in Haiti came from Kongo, bringing not only military skills but ideas about proper exercise of power. Similarly, thousands of Frenchmen fought in the American Revolution, and many of them just a few years later took part in the French Revolution. And a few thousand veterans of the wars of the French Revolution fought for independence in Spanish America.

In some cases, the events of the Atlantic revolutions were interlinked. The French and the Haitian revolutions, overlapping in time and both involving the French Empire, directly affected one another's course. The French Revolution, via Bonaparte's invasion of Spain in 1808, opened the political vacuum in Spanish America that ultimately brought independence there. And French involvement in the American Revolution deepened debts that pushed the

Liberty in the Atlantic World This 1792 painting uses an Atlantic world setting—including a globe, a liberty cap, and trading ships—to convey its message of freedom and the abolition of slavery.

French king to summon the Estates-General, setting in motion events he would regret.

DIFFERENT OUTCOMES

For all their common roots and interconnections, the Atlantic revolutions produced differing results. Some decentralization occurred everywhere, but beyond that each situation had its own character. Kongo became more unstable, violent, and enmeshed in the slave trade. Britain achieved considerable stability after 1689. So, too, the United States after a rocky start, although the issue of slavery would bring on a civil war a few decades later—as we shall see. In France, the revolution collapsed into dictatorship, and in 1815 a restoration of royal power followed Bonaparte's exile. Haiti also collapsed into dictatorship and then a very unstable republic. In Spanish America, unstable republics alternating with intervals of military dictatorship became the norm.

The Atlantic revolutions also brought different results for the most disenfranchised members of society. In Kongo, the United States, and France, women took part in various ways, and some of them hoped that revolution would usher in a new age for women. In Britain, Haiti, and Spanish America, the evidence for women's involvement is thinner. None of the revolutions immediately changed the political circumstances of women, although in New Jersey the state constitution allowed unmarried women who owned property to vote between 1797 and 1807. After that New Jersey restricted voting rights, as in most U.S. states, to adult white males. In France, Bonaparte actually restricted women's rights more narrowly than before 1789.

Slaves also played a part in several of these revolutions, most prominently in Haiti and Kongo, but also in the birth of the United States and in Spanish America. The revolutions produced abolition of slavery in Haiti and most parts of Spanish America. In the United States, some northern states abolished slavery after the revolution, but it took the Civil War to achieve this on the national scale. France abolished slavery but then Bonaparte reinstated it, and it lasted until 1848 in the French Empire. In Kongo, slavery survived until the kingdom ended in the 1850s.

The American Revolution and those in Spanish America also had important implications for Amerindians. Both Britain by 1763, and Spain long before, had imposed constraints on the exploitation of Amerindians, in particular checking the seizure of Amerindian lands. The revolutions lifted most of those constraints, inviting the displacement of Amerindians by settlers of European descent. In the Unites States, settlers poured westward into the Midwest and, after 1810 or so, into the Deep South—sometimes bringing slaves as well. In Mexico and most of South America, for half a century (ca. 1820–1870) the newly independent states were too weak militarily to impose their laws on most Amerindian communities, but by the late nineteenth century the legacy of the revolutions in Spanish America and Brazil proved deeply unfortunate for surviving Amerindian communities.

The Atlantic revolutions helped to reshuffle fortunes in a geopolitical sense too. The big winners eventually proved to be Britain, France, and the United States, which in the nineteenth and twentieth centuries would play enlarged roles in international politics. The biggest losers were Spain and Kongo, both of which emerged weaker than before.

REVOLUTIONS AS EXPERIENCE

The Atlantic revolutions, like most revolutions, had two more important things in common. First, the outcomes just described were never inevitable, and they rarely resembled what revolutionaries intended. They all took place in fluid situations in which old beliefs, customs, institutions—and usually treasuries and armies—grew weaker. People began to imagine new futures of all sorts, but not necessarily the futures they got. In Kongo, Beatriz Kimpa Vita did not get a united Kongo but a weakened one. Abigail Adams and Olympe de Gouges hoped for political rights for women, but did not get them. Bolívar wanted a united South America, not a handful of unstable republics.

The Atlantic revolutions were also miserable experiences for most people. Although many people felt hope, liberation, and exhilaration, many also felt fear, anxiety, betrayal, and worse. Mass executions, massacres, torture, as well as the more routine sufferings of war, famine, and disease, abounded. While history is rightly concerned with causes and consequences of major events, it is well to remember, at least from time to time, what it was like to live through them.

CONCLUSION

From 1640 to 1830, the Atlantic world took a new and different path. It experienced an especially rapid expansion of commerce, faster than it had before and faster than anywhere else in the world at the time. This change brought new pressures from new social groups that upset political arrangements all around the Atlantic. Every revolution had its own particular causes, of course, but they all owed something to the economic and social changes common around the Atlantic.

In Britain, the United States, and Spanish America, these revolutions led to a decentralization or disappearance of royal power, greater self-rule, and more representative political institutions such as legislatures or parliaments. Even where such formal institutions did not develop, as in Kongo, royal power weakened and merchant groups, typically Kongolese slave traders, won greater political voice. In France and Haiti, the revolutions brought a temporary decentralization of power, followed by dictatorship.

The extension of self-rule in the Atlantic revolutions did not go so far as to include women; nor Amerindians in their homelands. The revolutions in Spanish America led to the abolition of slavery, but former slaves remained marginal citizens with limited, if any, political rights. And in the United States, slavery long outlasted the revolution.

In the long run, however, the trend established by the ideas, principles, and rhetoric of the Atlantic revolutions led to more open, equal, and democratic societies, both around the Atlantic and eventually in many countries around the world. In cases it took centuries before women, Amerindians, and people of African descent in the Americas enjoyed legal equality with other citizens. That it happened at all is testament to the strength of ideals voiced by the makers of revolution in Kongo, Britain, the United States, France, Haiti, and Spanish America.

CHAPTER REVIEW

KEY TERMS

Kongo monarchy (p. 609)

Beatriz Kimpa Vita (p. 611)

rising merchant classes (p. 612)

Parliament (p. 612)

Glorious Revolution (p. 614)

Pontiac's War (p. 616)

American Revolution (p. 617)

French Revolution (p. 619)

Jacobins (p. 622)

Napoleon Bonaparte (p. 623)

Toussaint L'Ouverture (p. 626)

Haitian Revolution (p. 626)

Bourbon Reforms (p. 628)

Túpac Amaru II (p. 628)

Simón Bolívar (p. 631)

political decentralization (p. 632)

Go to INQUIZITIVE to see what you've learned—and learn what you've missed—with personalized feedback along the way.

REVIEW QUESTIONS

1. What liberties did the rising merchant classes seek during this period?

2. On what principle did the legitimacy and power of Kongo kings rest?

3. In what ways was the fragmentation of power in Kongo linked to its Atlantic connections?

4. What were the main sources of conflict between Charles I and Parliament?

5. What political and religious arrangements did the British Civil Wars and Revolution cement?

6. Describe the disagreements between American colonists and the British government over land access and taxes.

7. What principles did the American Constitution include, and whose rights did it exclude?

8. Explain the intellectual and socioeconomic changes that contributed to the start of the French Revolution.

9. Why and how did the French Revolution enter a violent phase?

10. What features did the Haitian Revolution share with the American and French Revolutions, and what feature was different?

11. How did Toussaint L'Ouverture fend off British and French armies during the Haitian Revolution?

12. Whom did the Bourbon Reforms irritate, and why?

13. How did Napoleon Bonaparte's takeover of Spain contribute to Spain's loss of control over most of its colonies in the Americas?

14. What were the common roots and interconnections of the Atlantic revolutions?

15. What were the effects of the Atlantic revolutions for women, slaves, and Amerindians?

FURTHER READING

Jeremy ADELMAN, *Sovereignty and Revolution in the Iberian Atlantic* (2006). An insightful and thorough study of the Spanish American revolutions.

Robert ALLISON, *The American Revolution: A Very Short Introduction* (2015). Just what the title suggests, and very readable.

John CHASTEEN, *Americanos* (2008). A readable narrative of Spanish American revolutions.

Laurent DUBOIS, *Avengers of the New World: The Story of the Haitian Revolution* (2005). A crisp narrative by one of the top historians of the subject.

Brian HAMNETT, *The End of Iberian Rule on the American Continent, 1770–1830* (2017). A handy synthesis of independence in Brazil and Spanish America.

Anne HILTON, *The Kingdom of the Kongo* (1985). This remains one of the key books on Kongo.

Wim KLOOSTER, *Revolutions in the Atlantic World: A Comparative Perspective* (2009). Provides brief narratives together with an analysis that emphasizes Atlantic dimensions.

Peter McPHEE, *Liberty or Death* (2016). A general summary of the French Revolution, unusually sympathetic to Robespierre.

Janet POLASKY, *Revolutions without Borders* (2015). Explores the circulation of ideas among revolutionary societies.

CHRONOLOGY

1733
"Flying shuttle" is introduced in Britain

1769–1785
James Watt registers six patents on steam engines

Cotton mill makes use of steam engine for first time in Britain

1790

1780s
Water-powered loom is developed

1770s
First steamships are built in France

1791
Alexander Hamilton writes tract supporting tariffs

1804
First locomotives go into use in coal mines in Britain

1794
Cotton gin is patented

1825
First railway carrying passengers and general freight operates in Britain

1838
Steam-powered vessels begin scheduled Atlantic crossings

1840s
Long-distance telegraph is patented

1848
Worker uprisings in Milan, Berlin, Vienna; *Communist Manifesto* is published

1853
American fleet invades Japan; Lowell girls successfully lobby for shorter work day

1853–1856
Crimean War

1867–1868
Meiji Restoration

1871
German unification

1872
Compulsory education for girls and boys is introduced in Japan

1875
German Social Democratic Party is founded

1879
French socialist party is founded; Canada launches National Policy to promote industry

1882
Japan's first modern cotton mill is set up

1886
Canada's first transcontinental railway opens

1889
Hull House is set up in Chicago

Fossil Fuels and Mass Production

INDUSTRIAL REVOLUTIONS AROUND THE WORLD

1780 to 1914

The world is too much with us; late and soon,
Getting and spending, we lay waste our powers;—
Little we see in Nature that is ours;
We have given our hearts away, a sordid boon!

—William Wordsworth, ca. 1802

[The steam engine] has armed the feeble hand of man with a power to which no limits can be assigned; completed the dominion of mind over the most refractory qualities of matter; and laid a sure foundation for all those future miracles of mechanical power which are to aid and reward the labours of after generations.

—Sir John Sinclair, 1825

The first four lines of Wordsworth's sonnet express regret about the changes brought by Britain's **Industrial Revolution**. He felt people had become overly concerned with money and had spoiled nature's beauty. Sinclair, in contrast,

1894–1895
Sino-Japanese War

1903
Trans-Siberian Railway opens

1901
Japanese Social Democratic Party is founded

1900
British Labour Party is founded

1905
Revolution of 1905 in Russia

Industrial Britain This print depicts a scene at the heart of the Industrial Revolution, in the town of Stockport in Britain's West Midlands region ca. 1845. Chimneys belch coal smoke into the air, large factory buildings are visible in the background, and a steam train from London crosses a viaduct above the town.

FOCUS QUESTIONS

1. In what ways was the Industrial Revolution an energy revolution?

2. Why did England experience the first Industrial Revolution?

3. How did the aims and technologies of industrialization spread across the globe?

4. What were the important global effects of the industrial revolutions?

praised the potential of industrial technology and brimmed with confidence in benefits to come. Wordsworth (1770–1850) and Sinclair (1754–1835) were contemporaries and lived only a few miles apart—the former in England and the latter in Scotland. Together, they capture some of the key features of the British Industrial Revolution: it shattered longstanding limits on production and wealth, while fundamentally changing society and nature. It was the most significant revolution in modern history.

The term *Industrial Revolution* entered the English language in the 1880s and refers to two main changes in manufacturing methods. The first was the transition from muscle and hand tools to machinery driven by inanimate power—at first water power and then coal-burning steam engines. The second change was the transition from household- or workshop-scale production to factory-scale production. What made these transitions truly revolutionary was steam power, which vastly expanded the levels of production and consumption a society could achieve. What made steam power work was the energy locked up in coal.

The Industrial Revolution began in the eighteenth century, roughly 250 years ago, and is still under way. No other 250-year period in world history can rival this one for the scale and scope of the transformations it has brought. In the process of transforming many parts of the world, the Industrial Revolution tightened many of the connections of the Global web.

The term *Industrial Revolution* is sometimes used only for the first century or so, from about 1770 to about 1870, and sometimes only for the case of Britain. This chapter, however, deals with the origins and course of industrial revolutions globally up to 1914, emphasizing in particular the experiences of Britain, Germany, the United States, Russia, and Japan. In following the story to 1914, this chapter includes what historians sometimes call the Second Industrial Revolution. In some cases—notably the United States, Britain, and Germany—after 1870 new industrial techniques dramatically improved the efficiency and scale of production of steel, chemicals, oil, and electricity. This surge of technological change relied more heavily on science and educated engineers than did the early Industrial Revolution. A large proportion of the important technologies of today—automobiles, aircraft, turbines—made their debut between 1870 and 1914 in the Second Industrial Revolution.

The Industrial Revolution began in Britain; but as it spread, it had global consequences. It transformed economies through the production of cheap, mass-produced goods, and it vaulted Britain, a small island nation, to the first rank of economic powers for the entire nineteenth century. It transformed societies through the formation of a new urban class of factory workers and the expansion of a middle class of accountants, lawyers, teachers, secretaries, and factory managers. It transformed politics by creating a newly rich class of entrepreneurs who eventually claimed a share of political power in accordance with their wealth. It also led to groups of workers claiming a share of power through union activism and politics, although that happened more slowly. It transformed the environment too, by generating unprecedented quantities of air and water pollution from its factories, and by equipping people with powerful new tools that made it more profitable than ever before to dig new mines, turn forests into cotton fields, or kill 30 million North American bison for their hides.

The Industrial Revolution was the most momentous change in human history since the Neolithic Revolution some 10,000 years ago. The Neolithic Revolution—the domestication of plants and animals and the advent of farming—opened the way to dense settled populations, cities, hierarchical societies, and eventually states. The Industrial Revolution opened the way to a high-energy society based on fossil fuels such as coal or oil. Over decades, the use of fossil fuels in industry and transport boosted economic growth so that it usually outpaced population growth, enriching at least a segment of every society around the world. It opened the way to greater inequality, as some people could now amass wealth on a scale unavailable even to pharaohs and emperors in previous times. It opened the way to fossil-fuel combustion and carbon emissions to the atmosphere in quantities sufficient to change the Earth's climate. And it opened the way to outcomes we haven't yet seen or imagined, because industrialization is still ongoing.

Although both the Neolithic Revolution and the Industrial Revolution were momentous turning points in world history, they were very different. For one thing, people independently transitioned from hunting and foraging to farming in at least seven places around the globe, and with different sets of crops and animals in each case. In contrast, there was only one independent transition from agrarian to industrial society, in Britain. Every subsequent transition has drawn directly or indirectly upon the British experience. By the time of the Industrial Revolution, unlike the situation in 9000 BCE, the world was so bound together by the connections of the Global web that one transition was enough: sooner or later, the example of the British Industrial Revolution influenced every corner of the world.

Compared to the Neolithic Revolution, industrialization spread at a lightning pace. What germinated in British soil could not, however, simply be transplanted to other lands. In every case geography, culture, legal systems, and much else were different from Britain's. Rather, the ambition to imitate Britain's Industrial Revolution spread to many other peoples, some of whom managed to pull off their own industrial revolutions.

The interconnectedness of the Global web made the ambition to imitate Britain an urgent one from a business point of view. Once Britain could mass-produce inexpensive goods, the increasingly unified world economy created ruthless competition for businesses everywhere else. They needed to modernize and mechanize quickly to survive. There was a geopolitical urgency to industrialization too. As British society and the British state quickly grew in wealth and power after 1800, some people in other societies recognized that they needed to follow suit to avoid domination. This recognition created enormous internal stresses within societies and states, as reformers eagerly sought to industrialize their societies while traditionalists fought to preserve the old ways that, as they saw it, had served their societies so well for so long.

The circuits of the Global web proved highly efficient in transmitting the desire to industrialize. They proved reasonably efficient in transmitting specific technologies, whether power looms or locomotives, from one setting to another. But the underlying knowledge of how to build and maintain machinery, or how to manage a factory and a supply chain, traveled less well. And the interlocking social, political, economic, and technological systems that enabled industrialization to develop, grow, and survive amid the social tensions it provoked—those systems developed only here and there. Some countries, such as the United States or Japan, built such interlocking systems fairly quickly and rode the wave of industrialization with a success that surprised all observers. Other countries, such as Egypt, tried and failed. A few countries, mainly those with minimal traditions of formal education and meager natural resources, did not try at all.

The industrial revolutions changed the nature of older global linkages, especially in terms of economic specializations and economic power. More than ever before, some regions specialized in raw material production—cotton, iron ore, leather—while others concentrated on making these raw materials into shirts, ships, and shoes. By and large, those regions focused on raw material production found themselves poor and weak in relation to those that performed the more skilled, complex, and profitable tasks of industrial production.

So the industrial revolutions of the period 1780–1914 created a more differentiated world, but also a more unified one. It became more differentiated because social inequality within societies, and economic and military gaps between societies, grew spectacularly, and they continue to grow to this day. But it also became more unified because the connections among people, institutions, and societies grew thicker than ever before, thanks to new technologies of transport and communications, new market linkages, and much else brought about by industrialization, patchy though it was.

AN ENERGY REVOLUTION

In every case around the world, industrial revolutions featured textiles and metallurgy above all else. In most societies, spinning thread and weaving cloth had long occupied many peasant women and girls. Men also wove, especially in the slack months of the agricultural calendar. Other handicrafts, such as leather working or furniture making, were typically male pursuits, followed both in village households and in town workshops. This local, small-scale manufacturing was conducted with muscle power or occasionally with help from a watermill or windmill. Many of these businesses—leather working or beer brewing, for example—could not scale up to factory mass production easily.

But **textiles and metallurgy** could scale up. Mills, forges, and factories, in which relatively unskilled laborers worked at machines powered by flowing water or by steam engines, suited the tasks of making cloth and iron. So these industries were in the vanguard of industrialization. By 1870, with the Second Industrial Revolution, factory-scale production was successfully applied to a wider range of activities, creating new key industries such as steel, chemicals, and electricity. To scale up, almost every industry required inputs of energy far beyond what human and animal muscle could provide. So underlying the newly mechanized industries lay a special resource vital to the British Industrial Revolution and important to all of them: coal.

COAL AND STEAM

At its heart, the Industrial Revolution was an energy revolution. At first, the textile industry in Britain scaled up to factory production with waterwheels that conveyed the energy of flowing water to power looms. Steam engines weren't efficient enough yet. But over time, the best riverside locations for siting water-powered mills were taken and steam engines improved. So by the 1830s, new mills typically used steam power.

Steam power came from **coal**. The central feature of the energy revolution was the development of new ways to use the chemical energy contained in coal and, later, in other fossil fuels such as oil or natural gas. The use of

Water Power Harnessing the energy of flowing water made possible factory-scale textile production in Britain. An illustration of an early textile mill from eighteenth-century England emphasizes the large waterwheel necessary to power the mill's machinery.

fossil fuels for heat energy wasn't new. In north China during the Song dynasty (960–1279), for example, coal had fueled a metallurgical industry that flourished for over a century. In the Dutch lands from the fourteenth century onward, people used peat (semi-fossilized remains of bog moss) to fuel brewing, salt making, sugar refining, and other energy-intensive pursuits. From the sixteenth century, Londoners used coal for home heating and for enterprises such as glass making that needed heat energy.

STEAM POWER Steam engines, however, could convert the chemical energy of fossil fuels into mechanical energy rather than simply into heat energy. They used coal fires to heat water into steam. The expansion of hot steam, and its contraction as it cooled, served as the motor force behind pistons, shafts, and belts that carried power to looms, pumps, or wheels. Coal worked its transformations only because of steam engines.

For centuries, people in Ptolemaic Egypt, the Ottoman Empire, Italy, France, and possibly China as well, had experimented with rudimentary steam engines, but they were only curiosities. In eighteenth-century Britain, which had a developed coal industry already, steam engines proved more useful. The first steam engines built there were so fuel-hungry that they could only be used at the mines themselves, where scraps of coal lay around unused. Only Britain had enough coal mines, and a strong enough market for coal, to make it worthwhile to improve steam engines. Between 1712, when Thomas Newcomen revealed an early model, and 1812, steam engines mainly worked to pump water out of coal pits. That made mining easier and coal cheaper, and in turn motivated people to tinker with steam engines. During those same years, engineers introduced many small improvements to steam engines, making them 10 times more fuel efficient.

The most famous of these engineers was **James Watt** (1736–1819), a Scot born into an educated family and trained to make mathematical instruments. While employed to maintain instruments at the University of Glasgow, he registered six patents on steam engines between 1769 and 1785. Watt had no head for business, but he found partners who did. Together, they designed, built, and marketed much more efficient steam engines starting in the 1780s. They also sued everyone else who built good steam engines until their key patent ran out in 1800.

The first cotton mill to make use of a steam engine

Steam Engines James Watt's new, more efficient steam engine, depicted here in a technical illustration, used the pressure generated from steam to drive a series of pistons and shafts, which in turn could operate machines in factories and mines.

opened in Manchester, England, in 1790. Water power still remained more efficient for most factories until the 1830s, but by 1870 steam engines reigned supreme and water power was effectively extinct in British manufacturing.

THE POWER OF FOSSIL FUELS

This shift in Britain represented the beginning of a global energy transition to fossil fuels. The Neolithic Revolution had allowed people to harvest perhaps 10 to 100 times as much energy, in the form of edible plants, as they could when foraging and hunting. Farming allowed more people to exist, but most of them had to work harder to get enough to eat than did hunters and foragers. Despite the expanded energy harvest, energy regimes based on the annual conversion of sunshine into plant tissues kept almost everyone poor. But coal, and fossil fuels generally, made it possible for the first time ever for more than a tiny fraction of people to avoid poverty.

Coal is the residue of ancient plants, the equivalent of solid sunshine. Burning it provided access to accumulated stocks of energy, the bounty of about 500 million years of photosynthesis. Machines that could transform coal's energy into motor power burst the boundaries of the old economy, permitting the creation and accumulation of previously unimaginable wealth—as Sinclair foresaw.

Since about 1870, humankind has obtained more energy annually from coal than all the green plants on Earth could capture from the sun through photosynthesis.

In short, fossil fuels, combined with machinery and know-how, enabled industrial production far faster and far greater than even the hardest workers could manage using only human or animal muscle. This ended the necessity of mass poverty, to which all previous societies were condemned. That was the most important social consequence of the Industrial Revolution.

But the energy in coal scarcely made everyone rich. The wealth created by burning vast quantities of fossil fuels in order to make goods more efficiently normally went only to some people, especially in the early decades of industrialization. So a second major consequence of the adoption of coal, and of the industrial revolutions more generally, was an expansion of inequality. This combination—simultaneous increases in both wealth and inequality—is routine in world economic history, but rarely did it come so suddenly as during the Industrial Revolution.

THE INDUSTRIAL REVOLUTION IN BRITAIN

England, specifically the north of England, was the birthplace of the Industrial Revolution. Why not in Europe's centers of textile manufacturing such as Flanders (in today's Belgium) or northern Italy? Or the textile districts of India, such as Gujarat or Bengal? Or Ottoman Egypt? Or China's manufacturing heartlands? England in the seventeenth century was still a backwater within Europe. It was among the least urbanized lands, and innovations in its economy often required importing Dutch or Italian expertise. Why was England the site of this economic revolution?

WHY ENGLAND?

A short answer is: a fateful coincidence. England by 1700 had cheap coal and expensive labor. So it made more economic sense in England than anywhere else to find ways to use less labor and more coal in order to create goods. A fuller answer involves trends in English agriculture, urbanization, transport, and public policy—and it begins with farming.

England underwent a gradual agricultural modernization after 1650. Technical improvements doubled cereal yields per acre between 1650 and 1900. By the 1750s, England was exporting about 7 percent of its grain harvest. More efficient farming also fed urbanization. Fewer people were needed as farmworkers. In human terms, this often led to underemployment and hunger in villages. In economic terms, it meant labor was freed to work in non-agricultural sectors. Young people streamed from farms into cities, seeking work. England was urbanizing faster than anywhere else in the world for two centuries after 1650. Industrialization did not launch England's spurt in urbanization; it sped up a trend already in motion.

Urbanization and industrialization each promoted the other. Cities, as always, served as hothouses of information exchange and innovation. Industrialization rested on technical advances in machinery, and those happened more often when mechanically inclined people with restless minds could easily find one another, share ideas, and either work together or compete with one another. Industrialization fostered urbanization, but the connectivity of city life also fostered industrialization.

IMPROVED TRANSPORTATION INFRASTRUCTURE Improvements in rural transport also spurred industrialization. The growth of towns and the increase in farm production required better roads and canals to move more food to cities. Firewood, bales of wool, and other bulky items could find bigger markets if better transport links existed. So landowners and merchants saw it in their interest to pay people to build and maintain roads and canals. Coal use also provided incentive to dig canals: if moved in carts pulled by animals, coal's price doubled within 10 miles, even on the best roads.

Before 1750, Britain had few good roads. In 1703, the ruts and potholes along a 50-mile stretch of road out of London caused the horse-drawn carriage of future Habsburg emperor Charles VI, at that time merely a king of Spain, to overturn 12 times. The young king survived.

After 1750, British and immigrant Irish laborers constructed thousands of miles of new canals and roads. Between 1750 and 1850, they quadrupled the extent of Britain's navigable inland waterways. By 1770, Britain had 15,000 miles (25,000 km) of turnpikes, or privately maintained roads, and almost everyone lived within a day's walk of one. What had been a four-day ride between London and Holyhead before 1787 took little more than

Water Transportation A nineteenth-century painting shows construction of a canal in southwest England. Canals joined Britain's inland waterways into a single system, enabling raw materials, manufactured goods, and people to travel much more efficiently around the country.

one day by 1837. This infrastructure development, roughly analogous to what Song China (960–1279) had done with its canals, dramatically increased the connectivity of Britain. It became one of the most internally integrated parts of the Global web—as Song China had been within the Old World web. By 1820, even before railroads, the dense transport network moved people, goods, and information more swiftly around Great Britain than almost anywhere else.

The government showed unusual enthusiasm for spending on infrastructure. After the British Revolution (1640–1689), the English nobility and merchant elite who dominated Parliament gradually grew accustomed to taxing itself and empowering government ministers to attend to the national interest. That occasionally included building a turnpike or a canal across landowners' property against their wishes. Moreover, in an effort to pacify rebellious Scots, the British government invested in military road and bridge building throughout Scotland in the 1730s and 1740s.

PROTECTIONIST TARIFFS The British state took other steps that contributed to the Industrial Revolution, if sometimes in unforeseen ways. Parliament imposed tariffs on imported cloth from India and erected other tariff barriers to protect British manufacturers. The government clarified property rights and patent laws. After the 1790s, innovators could patent not just new inventions but also improvements to existing ones. In addition, during decades of warfare against revolutionary France (1793–1815), the government became an important customer for large-scale production runs of certain manufactures, such as military uniforms and weaponry. James Watt drew on changes in cannon design to make key improvements in steam engines. So British government policy on transport infrastructure, tariffs, intellectual property rights, and patent law—and its frequent wars—helped promote the Industrial Revolution without the intention of revolutionizing anything.

LABOR COSTS AND TECHNOLOGICAL CHANGE
None of these changes would have brought on the Industrial Revolution had it not been for low-lying coal and high wages. After 1680, wages in England climbed, then stagnated from 1700 to 1740, then climbed again. By 1780, wage labor in England was more expensive than just about anywhere else in Europe—or the world. High labor costs created persistent incentives for employers to find ways to substitute machinery for labor.

As a result, almost every manufacturing process in England underwent labor-saving technological changes, which often, in turn, inspired more technological change. The textile industry provides the best examples. The "flying shuttle," introduced in 1733, doubled the productivity of weavers, who now wanted more cotton yarn than hand-spinners could make. This created pressure to invent a more efficient spinning process, which happened in the 1760s with the "spinning jenny" and in the 1770s with the "spinning mule." One person operating a "mule" in 1830 could spin as much cotton into thread as 350 skilled women working by hand with spinning wheels. With spinning machines churning out yarn and thread by the mile, incentives now grew to make weaving even more efficient. Tinkerers developed a water-powered loom in the 1780s, and despite active opposition from skilled weavers, by 1800 some 2,000 power looms were installed in Britain. By 1857, there were 250,000 of them—weaving more cloth than tens of millions of hand-weavers could make.

Other industries, from iron making to lens grinding, underwent technological change, motivated by the entrepreneurial desire to save on labor costs. Thousands of men, and some women, learned the intricacies of the new machinery, tinkered with it, and found ways to make improvements.

Textile Machinery The "spinning jenny" *(left)* sped up the process of making yarn or cotton thread. The "spinning mule" *(right)* accelerated production far more by using water to power hundreds of spindles at once. Substituting machinery for labor was central to the British Industrial Revolution.

This blend of circumstances and policies might have been enough to start the Industrial Revolution in Britain, but only coal kept it alive. Many places had coal, but Britain had large quantities of cheap, transportable coal that lay near riverbanks and natural harbors.

BRITISH COAL

As we've seen, the first important industrial use of coal was in the mines themselves. Once the easiest surface deposits of coal had been exploited, what remained lay underground in pits where water collected rapidly unless pumps outworked the rain. Coal-powered steam pumps working night and day prevented the Industrial Revolution from drowning in infancy. This was the only major technical improvement in mining between 1780 and 1914. It remained hard labor throughout. A vigorous coal miner scraped 200 to 300 tons per year from the earth.

Coal enabled British manufacturing to escape its former constraints. By 1700 if not before, brewing, glass making, brick making, metal smelting, and tile making had all switched from firewood to coal except in a few remaining well-wooded parts of Britain. Half of England's energy use came from coal, a situation unique in the world. After 1700, British coal use rose briskly, from 3 million tons annually to 30 million in 1830.

Using coal enabled Britain to keep less land in forest. The 5 million tons of coal burned in 1750 took the place of fuelwood that would have required forests covering one-third of Britain's surface area. By 1820, if all the British Isles had been forested, it would have yielded fuelwood energy equal to that year's coal use. Several Britains covered in forest could not have yielded as much fuelwood energy as the 125 million tons of coal burned in 1870. Britain's coal deposits were in effect a subterranean forest, providing a resource equivalent to extra land.

Coal substituted for labor as well as for wood. In 1840, steam engines in Britain did the work of about 1 million adult men. In 1880, the energy obtained from the coal they produced performed work equal to that of 100 million adult men. At the time, Britain's total population was 34 million, of whom maybe 8 million were adult men. It took about half a million men, women, and children to dig out the necessary coal.

Until the 1830s, few recognized what coal was doing to Britain. The brilliant economists Adam Smith, Thomas Malthus, and David Ricardo all supposed that economic growth could never last long because the supply of natural resources (they termed it *land*) was limited. By the 1860s, however, everyone could see what was happening. As the economist W. S. Jevons put it in 1865: "Coal in truth stands not beside, but entirely above, all other commodities. It is the material source of the energy of the country—the universal aid—the factor in everything we do. With coal almost any feat is possible; without it we are thrown back into the laborious poverty of early times."

Jevons put his finger on it. Coal, and the ability to convert its energy into motion that could do work and make things, lay at the heart of Britain's Industrial Revolution.

BRITISH INDUSTRIES

The power of coal and steam engines transformed almost every part of British industry in the decades after 1830. Of these, the most important to British history, and to world history, were cotton, iron, and transport—specifically, the advent of railroads and steamships.

COTTON A large part of the work that coal did was powering machines that made cotton cloth. In 1700, Britain hardly spun any cotton and imported finished cloth from India. British cotton was uncompetitive with India's because British wages were too high and skills too low, and because raw cotton had to be imported since the plant would not grow in Britain's climate. British weavers, who made mainly woolens and linens, objected to the foreign cotton cloth. To protect the woolen industry and its weavers, Parliament restricted the import of Indian woven cotton cloth, although not raw cotton. That policy inadvertently helped English cotton manufacturers by eliminating Indian competition.

The tariff gave entrepreneurs an incentive to find ways to weave more cotton in Britain and to adopt the new devices—flying shuttle, power loom—that would reduce labor costs. In a few decades, British cotton manufacturing became internationally competitive: by 1810, cotton cloth accounted for nearly half of British exports. By 1830, cotton mills employed nearly half a million workers in Britain and accounted for about 8 percent of the national economy. Overall, between 1770 and 1840, British imports of raw cotton climbed 100-fold and the cost of cotton clothing fell by 85 percent. The cotton industry became increasingly steam-powered after 1830 and continued to occupy a central place in Britain's industrial landscape.

IRON The energy in coal had an even greater impact on the iron industry, which became as important as cotton to Britain's economy and far more important to British military power. Iron making was fuel-intensive. It took 10 acres (4 hectares) of English woodland to make enough fuel to make a ton of iron in the eighteenth century. Fuel constraints made the industry uncompetitive

British Iron Shipbuilding, with its reliance on high-quality iron, was one of the industries that coal power revolutionized. An 1854 illustration shows dozens of metalworkers forging an iron ship's hull at a London dockyard that built ships for the Royal Navy.

against imported iron from Sweden and Russia, where fuelwood was far cheaper. Coal, together with some technical improvements that made it easier to remove impurities in the iron-making process, revolutionized the British iron industry.

In the century after 1788, British iron production climbed 130-fold, and Britain, instead of importing iron, became Europe's largest producer and the world's largest exporter. Massive iron foundries sprang up near coalfields. Iron replaced wood as the key material in construction of everything from tools to bridges to ships. By 1815, with its flourishing iron industry, Britain produced millions of guns annually and all the cannon needed for the world's biggest navy. By 1890, British shipyards built naval vessels for several countries and some 80 percent of the world's seagoing ships of all sorts.

RAILWAYS The iron and coal industries gave rise to locomotives and **railways**, another key sector of the British Industrial Revolution. The first locomotives were used underground in coal mines, in 1804. The first railway to carry passengers and general freight opened in 1825. A railway line between the port of Liverpool and the cotton-manufacturing center of Manchester opened in 1830. Newspapers reported in detail on this maiden voyage, not least because the first train to make the journey ran over a member of Parliament, killing him. Despite this inauspicious debut, the Liverpool and Manchester railway quickly proved a commercial bonanza, carrying half a million passengers in its first full year of operation,

Railways Spectators cheer in this 1829 illustration as a steam locomotive designed by inventor Robert Stephenson wins a race against another engine. "Stephenson's Rocket," which could travel at the astonishing speed of 30 miles per hour, was ultimately chosen to power the Liverpool–Manchester railway.

and many thousands of tons of cotton and coal. A frenzy of railway construction followed, undertaken by private companies employing tens of thousands of poor men with picks, hammers, and shovels, so that Britain quadrupled its total railway track between 1850 and 1880. Railways linked the country together more thoroughly than canals ever could, making Britain the world's most interconnected country, the thickest patch of the Global web.

STEAMSHIPS   Meanwhile, seaborne navigation tightened Britain's links to the rest of the world. Steamships were first built in France in the 1770s. The first to become a commercial success plied North American waters—the Hudson River in 1807 and the St. Lawrence in 1809. In the next few decades, steamships came to rival and then replace most sailing ships on rivers and in coastal waters.

Oceanic steam navigation took longer to take hold because it required carrying so much coal. Scheduled Atlantic crossings with steam-powered vessels began in 1838. Sailing vessels still dominated the routes between Britain and Asia until the opening of the Suez Canal (in Egypt) in 1869, because steaming around Africa required too much expenditure on coal. The Suez Canal shortened the route between Britain and India by about 4,000 miles (6,400 km), making it practical for steamships. By 1870, new ocean-going ships were usually steam-powered. Only

on the longest routes—between Britain and China, for example—did sailing ships still out-compete steam vessels into the 1890s.

Steamships lowered freight rates at sea, as railways did on land. Between 1840 and 1910, British seaborne freight costs fell by 70 percent, the result mainly of the switch to steamships and continuing technical improvements such as the screw propeller, in regular use by the 1860s. Railways and steamships, built of iron—iron that was made with coal—knitted Britain together and tied it ever tighter to the rest of the world.

BRITISH SOCIETY

Industrialization brought a social revolution to Britain. In 1750, most of the work done in Britain, as in most societies, was farm work, and most people lived in villages. By 1850, half the British population of 27 million lived in cities and millions worked in coal mines, textile mills, iron foundries, or factories.

The conditions of life and work in the new industrial cities took a toll on the health of factory workers. Titus Rowbotham, for example, went to work in Manchester's cotton mills at age 18. In 1801, looking back on his life, he said of textile mill workers like himself: "Their intellect is enfeebled. . . . They are more like grown up children. . . . The long hours of labour, the high temperatures of the factories, produce lassitude and excessive exhaustion. The operatives . . . seek to sustain life by the excitement of drink."

Labor in coal mines made factory work look like leisure. Child labor was commonplace in the tight spaces underground. Sally Fletcher, age 8, testified to a government committee in 1841 that she had worked in a coal pit since age 5 and had never been to school. "I cannot read or write. . . . I go to work between six and seven o'clock in the morning. . . . I sometimes go home at three o'clock. Sometimes six." Her job was pushing small wagonloads of coal along a 400-yard underground passage. Most mine work was done by people younger than 30. Few miners could still work by age 40. On-the-job accidents and lung diseases from the long-term effects of breathing coal dust ended many a working life. One flood in a coal mine in 1838 drowned 26 mineworkers, the eldest of whom was 17 and the youngest 7 years old.

THE WORKING CLASSES   The new forms of work in mines and factories created new social classes in Britain.

Child Labor As an 1844 lithograph demonstrates, British mine owners relied on the small bodies of children to transport coal through extremely narrow tunnels underground. Children could spend as many as 12 hours a day, 6 days a week, underground.

Over a generation or two, millions who toiled at looms and lathes, or worked as household servants, gradually came to see themselves as members of a vast "**working class**," amounting to about 40 to 45 percent of the English population by 1850. Unlike farmworkers, they worked shifts defined by the clock, not the light of the sun. At work they were subject to the discipline of bosses, not their parents or older siblings. The din, drudgery, and danger of factory or mine work dominated their lives for 10, 12, or 14 hours a day. They lived and worked in crowds. Manchester in the 1840s had a population density higher than any big city in the world today except Dhaka (Bangladesh). Its working-class districts were a warren of dingy alleys and open sewers.

The term *working class* might better be *working classes* because a person's condition and prospects could vary. Fortunate working-class men learned a skill that ensured employment and a wage sufficient to support a family. With luck, some could rise to positions of management, overseeing the work of others. Women typically held poorer-paying jobs with fewer prospects of advancement. The most common job for women in nineteenth-century Britain was domestic service, doing housework and child care for someone else, but many worked in factories or mines too. Daughters expected to contribute their wages to their parents' household. If they married, they might quit factory work. If they became mothers, they usually did quit.

The least fortunate members of the working classes rarely found work and lived on city streets, slept under bridges, dressed in rags, and scrounged for food. In London, thousands of sharp-eyed, nimble-fingered, hungry children, called mudlarks, lived by scavenging buttons, nails, and other saleable items from city sewers and the muddy banks of the river Thames. Orphans and widows often could survive only by stealing or by selling their bodies for sex.

Britain's working classes lived and worked on the verge of disaster. If they annoyed an overseer, they might lose their job—which meant going hungry. Their jobs were dangerous. Thousands lost fingers, hands, or limbs to power machinery or mine accidents, ending their working lives. Many others, especially miners, lost their lives on the job in explosions, cave-ins, or floods. Like everyone, rich or poor, they also worried about lethal diseases—much more dangerous than anything else in their lives.

You might wonder why anyone agreed to work in factories or mines in industrial Britain. The answer is that millions of young people had no better option. Farms now needed fewer workers. Spinning and weaving within the home was hopeless in the face of factory competition. Teenage girls could become domestic servants; boys could join the army or the navy. They could gamble on life in Canada, Jamaica, or Australia as indentured servants. But these and other options looked no better to most young people than a hard life in the factories or mines.

THE MIDDLE CLASSES A notch above the working classes in industrial Britain's evolving social hierarchy stood a lower middle class, also growing, some 10 to 15 percent of the population by 1850. Its members were shop clerks, nurses, teachers, pharmacists—jobs for which at least some education was required. Their work included little dirt or danger, but their wages remained modest. Women in these jobs usually quit upon marriage or motherhood. These families typically rented rather than owned their homes but might have books and even a piano in them.

Industrial Britain also generated a more prosperous upper middle class. Factories and mines, if large enough, required managers and professionals. Accountants, engineers, purchasing agents, lawyers—these and other growing professions permitted hundreds of thousands of men (and a few thousand women) to earn enough for a comfortable life in the new industrial society. These men could expect to own their homes, pay fees to educate their children, support small-scale charities, and enjoy deference, at least outwardly, from members of the working classes. Their wives did not need paid work. They could expect to manage a house with domestic servants and might devote their time to civic causes, music and art, their church and their children—unless they assigned all child care to servants. The prosperous middle classes also included middling entrepreneurs, who might own a single mill or small factory. They rejoiced in a good year and feared bankruptcy in a bad one. These middling entrepreneurs were usually but not always men: about 10 percent of British businesses were owned by women between 1780 and 1850. That figure included widows who took over the business affairs of dead husbands, and women who owned small bakeries or butcher shops rather than mills or factories.

INDUSTRIALISTS Higher up the social pyramid of industrial Britain stood a new class of rich factory and mine owners. Some came from modest origins, such as John Rylands (1801–1888), born in a village near Manchester and recipient of a grade school education. He learned the weaver's trade and soon founded a textile manufacturing company with his brother and father. Rylands, who allegedly worked 19-hour days, became the first cotton millionaire in Manchester and, despite giving substantial sums to charities, died very rich. Wealth did not insulate him from personal tragedy, though: he buried all of his seven children. Manchester was an unhealthy city, even for its richest citizens. More typical of this new class—in his social origins—was Joseph Chamberlain (1836–1914). His father was a businessman who could afford to educate his son to age 16, at which point Joseph became an apprentice in his father's warehouses. But at age 18 he moved to Birmingham, started work in his uncle's brass screw–manufacturing business, became a partner, and at age 37 retired immensely wealthy and launched a career in politics, fighting for social reforms.

The traditional uppermost elite in British society, the landed aristocracy, often resented the wealth of industrialists such as Rylands or Chamberlain. But times were changing, and new money was slowly taking over. Aristocrats who found themselves strapped for money often chose to marry a son or daughter into a prosperous industrial family to restore their fortunes.

FAMILY LIFE Industrialization changed family life as well as social structure in Britain, particularly the condition of young people. In 1820, more than half of Britain's cotton workers were teenagers. In 1842, one-third of mineworkers were teenagers. Factory and mine bosses preferred young workers, who were easier to train and—in most cases—easier to control. Some textile work required fine motor skills and small hands, for which employers preferred girls. When young people went to work in factories and mines, they partly escaped the authority of their parents. During working hours they became subject to the authority of male bosses, which women sometimes found hazardous. In their scant free time, young industrial workers became freer from parental supervision than village youths could expect to be.

If they held a job, people could marry young. Age at first marriage for British men dipped to about 26, and for women fell from about 26 in the early eighteenth century to about 23 in the mid-nineteenth, and lower still in the industrial cities. Despite younger marriage, out-of-wedlock births became far more common in the industrial towns than in rural villages—a reflection of the greater independence of industrial youth from parental supervision.

ENVIRONMENTAL IMPACTS AND HEALTH

In 1837, the German chemist Justus von Liebig visited England. He described the country between Leeds and Manchester as "one big smoking chimney." Soot and cinder blanketed the iron-making region north of Birmingham by 1840, earning it the name "the black country." In London, a million chimneys spewed sulfur dioxide and soot into the air. In Manchester in 1900, the pH of rain averaged 3.5—somewhere between the acidity of tomato juice and that of wine. A perpetual haze of coal smoke enveloped all the industrial towns. Just as the sun famously never set on the British Empire, it never really rose on countless alleys and tenements. Lung diseases became common complaints, especially among miners and millworkers who breathed coal or cotton dust day and night. By one modern estimate, health problems provoked by air pollution around 1900 reduced Britain's total economic output by one-quarter.

Water quality was no better. Rivers and canals everywhere served as industrial sewers. The water of the river

Calder made a "tolerably good ink" in 1864, according to a government commission. Another commission, in 1869, described a river flowing through Manchester as:

> ... caked over with a thick scum of dirty froth, looking like a solid, sooty crusted surface. ... Wherever a yard or two of the scum was cleared away, the whole surface was seen simmering and sparkling with a continual effervescence of smaller bubbles ... showing that the whole river was fermenting and generating gas. The air was filled with the stench of this gaseous emanation many yards away. The temperature of the water was 76 F, and that of the air 54 F.

For a few generations, industrialization had catastrophic effects on British health. In the "black country," average life expectancy fell by six years between 1820 and 1840. While the industrial working classes grew in number, they shrank in stature. Between 1800 and 1850, army recruits and prisoners—the only populations systematically measured—lost an average of 1 inch in height. The average male in 1850 stood 5′4″ (163 cm) and the average female 5′0″ (152 cm). The shortest came from industrial cities, and the tallest from the counties farthest from the centers of industry. Some combination of poor nutrition, heavy work, and frequent disease accounted for the stunted stature of industrial workers.

After 1850, these grim conditions gradually improved. Industrial workers' wages began to inch upward. Life expectancy in Britain lengthened, and after 1870 it never again dipped below 40 years. Health improved more quickly after 1890 through improved medical understanding of infectious disease. By 1900, the Industrial Revolution had clearly improved the average health and well-being of the British population, now 38 million, nearly four times its size in 1800. Twenty-year-old army recruits in 1900 averaged nearly 5′6″ in height (167 cm) and 130 lbs (60 kg).

The Industrial Revolution enriched and empowered Britain. It made Britain the "workshop of the world." Britain's manufacturing exports in 1840 stood at about 50 times their level as of 1700. Efficient production of coal, cotton, or iron underpinned hundreds of huge personal fortunes. And the Industrial Revolution enabled Britain to construct a military machine that helped make a little island into a great power. The rest of the world took notice.

Air Pollution The toxic smoke of copper foundries fills the sky of the copper-producing region of Cornwall in southwest England in this late-nineteenth-century engraving. Air pollution was a feature of life throughout industrial Britain, leading to widespread respiratory illness and other health problems.

INDUSTRIAL REVOLUTIONS AROUND THE GLOBE

Britain strove to keep the Industrial Revolution to itself. Parliament passed laws making it illegal for people who knew industrial secrets to go abroad. Authorities vigorously hunted down foreign industrial spies, hundreds of whom prowled British factory towns. The government tried hard to enforce intellectual property rules. But nothing worked. Industrial secrets leapt to the European continent and beyond.

The technologies and organizational techniques of industrialization first escaped to continental Europe. Thousands of European towns had supported small-scale handicraft production of textiles since medieval times. As in Britain, by 1800 water power provided the primary energy source for new mills and factories on the Continent. Clusters of textile mills sprang up where ambitious entrepreneurs found suitable rivers for water power, undercutting household-scale spinning and weaving.

But quickly coal became king in much of continental Europe as it had in Britain. A long carboniferous crescent, as important for the early industrial age as the

Fertile Crescent had been for the early history of agriculture, underlay parts of Britain, northern France, Belgium, Germany, the Czech lands (Bohemia), and what is now southern Poland (Silesia). By 1820, northern France and Belgium had developed steam-powered textile mills and metallurgical industries. Businessmen soon brought coal-fired industry to coalfields farther east, such as those in Germany's Ruhr region. It also sprouted in port cities, or in cities astride rivers where ships and barges could bring coal at low cost: Hamburg, Rotterdam, Vienna, and Bilbao, for example. Germany's Industrial Revolution eventually outstripped all others in continental Europe.

GERMANY

Germany, as we shall see, was a country cobbled together from a welter of small and middling states. Upon unification in 1871, its population was about 40 million—and rising fast. It was still mainly an agrarian nation, but with an industrial sector poised for rapid growth.

The first steam engine in German lands had fired up in 1789. The first railroads opened in the late 1830s, using British locomotives. But industrial production remained tiny for decades, most of it in textiles and rarely using steam power. Some obstacles had to be addressed first. German agriculture needed to provide enough surplus to feed big urban populations. States had to enact social and political reforms that allowed peasants freedom to migrate to cities and fill industrial jobs. But by the 1850s, these and other obstacles were sufficiently overcome that the high-quality coal of the Ruhr in Germany was fueling a flourishing metallurgical industry. Workers flocked to the Ruhr for jobs, making it a European melting pot. Berlin was also rapidly developing textile and metallurgical industries.

STATE SUPPORT Germany's Industrial Revolution was more of a conscious effort than Britain's, partly because the British example inspired urgent imitation. By 1850, anyone could see that without industrialization no society could rival Britain. Efficient British firms would drive German spinners, weavers, and smiths out of business—just as they were doing in Britain. Several German political leaders hoped to use state power to do something about it.

Friedrich List (1789–1846) gave German politicians an intellectual blueprint for using the power of the state

The Global Impact of Industrialization, ca. 1914 Industrialization gave rise to a global economy that was both more geographically differentiated than before—into zones of industrial production and zones of raw material production—and also more tightly knitted together through long-distance trade. Cotton mills, steel mills, and factories as of 1914 were concentrated in Japan, Europe (including Britain), and eastern North America, but the raw materials necessary for industrial production were scattered among all the continents. Railroads, ports, and ocean-going ships handled enormous quantities of raw materials to keep factories and mills supplied. In Europe's case, one crucial raw material—coal—came from one of the world's giant coalfields, the carboniferous crescent, stretching from Scotland to Silesia.

to industrialize. List was German by birth, an accountant, professor, and political prisoner before emigrating to Pennsylvania in 1825. There he became an American citizen, a landowner, newspaper editor, coal merchant, and author of a book praising the protectionist trade policies of the U.S. government. Returning to Germany in 1833, List wrote newspaper articles and books urging that German states form a customs union, protect their industries against foreign competition, and build railroads. List's ideas proved one of the world's most influential guides on how to industrialize a country.

The German state after unification in 1871 made strong contributions to the country's rapid industrialization. It invested in technical education. It funded research institutes, especially in physics and chemistry, to bolster the science behind industry. By 1900, this expenditure had repaid the investment handsomely, and by many accounts Germany led the world in scientific research and the application of science to industry. Germany also put up tariffs from the early 1870s to keep out foreign competition. It built transport infrastructure—mainly railways (partly state-owned), ports, roads, and a few new canals—helping to create a unified national market. In 1850, Berlin had still imported its coal by ship and canal-barge from Britain. By 1880, the city's coal all came from Silesia by rail.

BISMARCK AND LABOR POLITICS Like other industrializing countries, Germany developed a working class and a labor movement representing their interests. German labor unions at first represented workers from single industries, such as the cigar-workers union that formed in 1865. The unions joined their efforts to support industrial workers in a political party known by its German initials, the SPD (Social Democratic Party), born in 1875. More radical workers—a tiny minority of the whole—supported the revolutionary ideals of the German journalist Karl Marx, whose powerful pamphlet, the ***Communist Manifesto***, co-authored with Friedrich Engels, was published in 1848. Presenting class struggle as the motor of history, Marx and Engels called on the workers of all countries to unite to overthrow the ruling class of entrepreneurs and their allies in government and the professions. The idea of communist revolution remained unpopular until the 1870s, attaining major importance only with the Russian Revolution of 1917. But the strength of the SPD worried the German chancellor and aristocrat Otto von Bismarck.

German Industrialization Workers in the Krupp factory in Essen ca. 1900 inspect the steel train wheels that the factory manufactured. The steel industry and the expansion of the German railway network allowed it to rival Britain for industrial dominance.

Under Bismarck, the German state used carrot and stick to promote labor peace in pursuit of industrial strength. The state provided, or obliged employers to provide, pensions, health insurance, and unemployment benefits for workers—the first country in the world to do so. Bismarck also encouraged employers to compromise with laborers on wages and working conditions. Employers at first complained that such compromises would undermine their international competitiveness, but time and protective tariffs soothed their fears. At the same time, Bismarck banned the SPD and labor union activity in his anti-socialist laws of 1878. As a result, the German labor movement remained modest until the 1890s, when the anti-socialist laws were repealed and unionization skyrocketed. By 1904, fully 1 million German workers had joined unions, and by 1913, some 2.5 million—the metalworkers union alone had half a million members.

Bismarck's program of state-supported industrialization worked. Between 1850 and 1913, the per capita size of the economy in the German lands tripled, while industrial growth quintupled. Cities sprouted from next to nothing. Essen, in the Ruhr, was a big village of 3,000 people in 1831, and in 1913 an industrial city of 300,000. The major surge in German industrialization came after unification in 1871, with heavy industry in the vanguard. Iron ore production jumped ninefold between 1870 and 1913, while coal output quintupled. Germany's total railway mileage, still smaller than Britain's in 1870, was double its rival's by 1910. The growth of railways created a huge and reliable market for Germany's iron and steel industries.

The German version of industrial revolution favored giant firms. In 1870, almost all German industrial workers still toiled in tiny enterprises, no bigger than a family. But soon large firms came to account for nearly half of industrial employment. By 1913, Krupp, an iron, steel, and weapons manufacturer in Essen, employed 77,000 people. Siemens, an engineering firm based in Berlin and Nuremberg, employed 57,000 people.

THE UNITED STATES AND CANADA

The United States at its birth was an agrarian country, with 95 percent of its population living on the land. Many of its leaders preferred it that way, but not **Alexander Hamilton** (ca. 1755–1804). As secretary of the Treasury in 1791, Hamilton wrote a tract advising that the new nation should protect its small and inefficient manufacturers from foreign—mainly British—competition. Tariffs would, he claimed, enable American manufacturers to survive and grow, taking advantage of an ever-larger domestic market. Hamilton's vision served as the chief inspiration for U.S. trade policy for more than a century, during which time the United States became an industrial powerhouse. Hamilton's program also served as an inspiration for Friedrich List's ideas.

A nation of only small-scale industry in 1790, the United States had, as Hamilton saw, strong growth potential. It had plentiful timber, good soil, coal, iron ores, and other minerals. Its population was among the fastest-growing in the world: from 4 million in 1790, it leapt to 17 million in 1840 and 63 million by 1890.

High wages (by international standards of the time) throughout the U.S. economy strengthened the economic logic of both slavery, prevalent in the southern states, and labor-saving machinery. To get labor-saving technology, American businesses and officials tried to lure British craftsmen versed in the secrets of the textile and iron-working industries to break British law and bring their knowledge to America. Samuel Slater had worked in the textile business for years when he left England for Rhode Island in 1789. Rather than risk arrest for carrying plans of the latest textile mill technology, he committed it all to memory. He set up a cotton mill for the merchant family that had founded Brown University but felt ill-treated and soon set up his own. In the following

decades, thousands of others emigrating to the United States brought British industrial technology with them.

American entrepreneurs such as Francis Cabot Lowell also went to Britain to learn what they could. A Bostonian with an inherited fortune, he traveled to Manchester and Scotland in search of the secrets of cotton manufacturing. He learned enough—how to build a power loom using water or steam power—to set up a large-scale cotton mill in Waltham, Massachusetts.

Not all of the imported expertise for U.S. industrialization came from Britain. One of the nation's first large-scale factories was the gunpowder works established by refugees from the French Revolution, the du Pont family. Pierre du Pont, a watchmaker's son, had done stints in Parisian prisons in the 1790s. Du Pont fled revolutionary France with his family, emigrating to the United States in 1799. One of his sons founded a gunpowder factory in 1803 using water power from Delaware's Brandywine River and chemistry expertise he brought from France.

THE AMERICAN SYSTEM The U.S. weapons industry was especially important to world history. Together with clock making, the arms industry developed the practice of manufacturing with interchangeable parts. Instead of a single craftsman making an entire musket or grandfather clock, this system relied on semi-skilled workers using machine tools to mass-produce components that other workers could assemble into a final product. This method, pioneered in British naval shipbuilding, required less skill, lowered production costs, and—crucially for weapons—eased repair. All musket triggers, for example, were so close to identical that a musket with a broken trigger was not junk; it just needed a new trigger. The virtues of the system of interchangeable parts in weapons manufacture became clear during the War of 1812 with Britain, and the principle was widely followed throughout U.S. industries by 1850. Guns and clocks, and eventually almost everything else, were not designed to last, but instead to be cheap to make and easy to fix. The use of interchangeable parts in mechanized production was often called "the American system" of manufacturing.

SOUTHERN COTTON, NORTHERN TEXTILES, AND AMERICAN SLAVERY Americans also developed technologies beyond those they acquired from overseas. Perhaps most important were the cotton gin and the telegraph. The **cotton gin** (short for "engine"), patented

U.S. Cotton Enslaved people work a cotton gin on a plantation in the American South. The raw cotton that enslaved people grew and processed on southern plantations was spun and woven into cloth in factories in the northern United States and Britain.

in 1794, was a device that helped remove the seeds from cotton fiber, making it ready to spin. It eliminated a bottleneck in cotton manufacture and was crucial for the rise of mechanized cotton production in the United States as well as in Britain. It was equally crucial in spreading cotton cultivation and slavery in the U.S. South—the cotton industry could not flourish without abundant raw cotton. Samuel Morse patented the long-distance telegraph in the 1840s. It helped tie the country together by sending information at the speed of electricity from telegraph office to telegraph office. Such near-instant communication suited the needs of railroads and eventually became an important military technology as well. In the 1850s alone, Americans registered 28,000 patents for inventions.

By 1830, the United States had a robust textile industry based in New England. Francis Cabot Lowell had opened his first mill in Waltham in 1814, followed by several more in Lowell, Massachusetts, outside of Boston. At first the American textile industry relied on water power, but, like Britain's, it gradually shifted to coal and steam. Also like Britain's, it relied heavily on female labor, and on cotton grown—before the Civil War—on slave plantations in the southern states. In 1860, about 70 percent of the 4 million enslaved African Americans worked on cotton plantations producing the raw material for New England's—and Europe's—cotton industry.

INDUSTRY AND GOVERNMENT SUPPORT Meanwhile, the U.S. metallurgical industry churned out rails, locomotives, and guns, among other goods. The iron industry began to take off in the 1840s in Pennsylvania, where high-quality coal was abundant. Coal output jumped 13-fold and iron ore 16-fold between 1870 and 1913. Immigrants from Europe flocked to American coal mines, iron foundries, and by 1880 big steel mills in cities such as Pittsburgh and Cleveland. Led by iron, steel, and railroads, total U.S. industrial output leapt 8-fold in the years 1870–1913. The United States and Germany were the tigers of the world economy in those decades, fed by their industrial revolutions.

The U.S. government took deliberate steps to advance its Industrial Revolution, although not as directly as the state in Bismarck's Germany. Tariffs protected young and inefficient industries from foreign competition. Cotton cloth, for example, received tariff protection in 1816. The patent system and legal system rewarded innovation and investment—as in Britain. The law provided for a limited liability corporation, widespread among U.S. states by 1860, which enabled investors to pool their resources without fear of becoming liable for a company's debts. The Congress and the Patent Office supported Morse financially while he was improving the telegraph. The federal government gave millions of acres of public land to railroad companies and, beginning in 1862, to the states to encourage the creation of agricultural, technical, and engineering colleges and universities.

ECONOMIES OF SCALE The most distinctive feature of the American Industrial Revolution was its exploitation of economies of scale. After the Erie Canal opened in 1825 and railroads crisscrossed the country by 1870, the United States was sufficiently connected that it essentially formed one big, fast-growing national market. U.S. industries got very good at mass production of cheap goods. Several million American families could afford to buy clothing, furniture, and tools made in factories. That prosperity, a result of both high wages by the standards of the time and a thriving middle class, helped to enlarge the market and reward manufacturers in their quests for economies of scale.

The size of the U.S. market and the scale of production also favored bigger business organizations. American entrepreneurs, like their counterparts in Germany and Japan, created gigantic companies and conglomerates that employed tens of thousands of people. At one point in nineteenth century, the DuPont company employed 10 percent of the population of the state of Delaware. By 1890, the United States had surpassed Britain in total industrial production to become the global leader, the result mainly of the size of its domestic market.

CANADA Industrialization came more slowly to Canada than to the United States. For most of the nineteenth century, Canadians imported most of their industrial goods from either the United States or Britain. Until Confederation in 1867, Canada was a set of British colonies largely governed from London. Britain sought to keep its edge in industrial production, and so Canada had few manufacturing enterprises. But after 1867, Canada—with about 3.5 million people and abundant natural resources—acquired more authority over its own affairs. It soon launched a **National Policy** (1879) intended to promote industry. Tariffs on foreign goods boosted enterprises such as textiles, shoemaking, pulp and paper, meatpacking, and steel, mainly in Quebec and Ontario. Nova Scotia also developed coal, steel, and shipbuilding. A political emphasis on railroad building—Canada's first transcontinental railroad opened in 1886—helped inspire rail and locomotive works, as well as iron ore and coal mining.

A growing labor supply, as well as abundant raw materials and prudent national policy, also helped Canada to industrialize. By 1890, its population was climbing fast, the result of slowed emigration of Canadians to the

Chinese Labor in Canada Chinese workers build the tracks of the Canadian Pacific Railway. In 1882 alone some six thousand Chinese arrived to work on the Canadian Pacific in British Columbia.

United States combined with booming immigration from Britain, continental Europe, and—to British Columbia—from China. Many immigrants settled in industrial centers, as did many native-born farm youths. By 1910, when the national population reached about 7 million, some 3 million lived in cities and towns, and half a million worked in industry. Many Canadian industries exported to the much larger market in the United States; some were branch plants of U.S.-owned firms. Canada was well on its way to becoming an industrial society, deeply integrated with the United States as well as Britain.

RUSSIA

Like the United States and Canada, Russia had natural resources well suited to launching an industrial revolution. It had abundant coal and iron. During the nineteenth century, it conquered Central Asian lands that would prove suitable for growing cotton. Russia's social base, however, was less promising. Part of Russia's elite was attuned to western European trends and accustomed to borrowing ideas from abroad. But the rest of the population was poorly prepared to support industrialization— partly because it was too poor to buy much. Unlike in Britain or the United States, the middle class, and the market for anything beyond basic goods, was small.

As of 1860, some two-thirds of Russia's roughly 70 million people were serfs, some owned by the state and others bound to lands owned by the nobility. Most had only rudimentary education, if any. Few were legally free to migrate to cities or jobs. Russia's largest industrial cluster was around the city of Łódź (pronounced Woodge) in Russian-controlled Poland. The city hosted hundreds of small textile mills in 1850, most of them owned by German businessmen. At that time, almost no one imagined that a Russian Industrial Revolution was either possible or desirable.

Russia's existing industrial plant was old and small. The weapons industry, developed originally under Ivan the Terrible and Peter the Great, was antiquated by the 1850s. The country had only one real railroad line, opened in 1851 between Moscow and St. Petersburg. Despite long-standing efforts to import technology and expertise from abroad, which included an offer to James Watt to move to Russia, the Russian Empire in 1850 remained overwhelmingly agrarian.

Then Russia lost a war in humiliating fashion. Russia's military performed embarrassingly in the Crimean War (1853–1856) against the Ottoman Empire, France, and Britain. The defeat clarified matters for Russian elites: they needed to reform and strengthen their country in a hurry. Their anxieties made more of them sympathetic to new ideas such as the abolition of serfdom (see Chapter 23) and the industrialization of Russia.

The ambition to industrialize faced many obstacles. Before 1880, the country lacked engineers, compared to Britain or Germany, and technical training was rare. The legal system made it awkward to create businesses. Transport infrastructure was creaky. By 1880, it still had only about 13,000 miles (21,000 km) of railroad—about one-seventh the U.S. total. But in the 1880s and especially the 1890s, Russian industrialization gathered steam. Industrial output expanded at 8 percent per year in the 1890s, and the rail network more than doubled between 1880 and 1905. Russia was late getting started by the standards of Germany or the United States, let alone Britain, but it made up ground fast. From low levels in 1870, Russian coal output climbed 40-fold by 1913 and industrial production 9-fold.

The crowning achievement of Russia's Industrial Revolution was the opening of the **Trans-Siberian Railway** in 1903, financed mainly by the state. Construction began in 1891 and required 90,000 laborers, many of them convicts, army conscripts, or migrants from Korea and China.

When finished, the iron road crossed bogs, mountains, and hundreds of rivers over about 5,700 miles (9,000 km) from Moscow to the Pacific Ocean. The railroad opened much of Siberia and its natural resources to Russian settlement and use.

GOVERNMENT SUPPORT The Russian Industrial Revolution was very much a revolution from above. It could scarcely have succeeded without determined government support, stronger than that in the United States or Germany. That support resulted largely from the efforts of **Sergei Witte** (1849–1915). Born into a noble family, Witte aspired to an academic career in mathematics. Instead, he made his early mark in railroad management and entered government service in 1888. In a political career spanning nearly three decades, and inspired in part by Friedrich List's ideas, Witte promoted railroad building and the creation of technical schools, together with tariffs to protect Russian industry. Guided by Witte, the Russian government welcomed foreign investment (except on the Trans-Siberian project) and technical experts, financed the sale of Russian industrial goods to neighboring countries without much industry (such as China and Iran), and fostered heavy industry by purchasing locomotives, rails, and military hardware. No one else in Russia—or for that matter in Germany, Japan, the United States, or Britain—played a larger role in advancing industrialization than Witte.

JAPAN

Japan blazed its own trail to industrialization. It involved more labor and less machinery, because in Japan labor was cheap and, initially, machines and mechanical expertise were scarce. As much or more than the Russian, American, and German cases, the Japanese Industrial Revolution was nourished by state support.

Like Russia, Japan in 1850 seemed an unlikely candidate for industrialization. Its economy remained agrarian, although Japan was unusually urbanized: perhaps 10 percent of Japanese lived in cities in 1700, and 20 percent—of about 34 million—by 1870. With its countryside crowded after 1720 or so, couples tried hard to limit their family size, and population growth proceeded slowly for about five generations. Japan had some accessible coal, but not much iron ore. Japan seemed to lack the incentive and most of the wherewithal for an industrial

Trans-Siberian Railway Like Canada's transcontinental railroad, the Trans-Siberian Railway was a feat of engineering that connected widely separated regions of a vast territory. A photographer recorded the railway's first locomotive traveling along the shores of Lake Baikal in 1900.

revolution, although its highly productive agriculture could feed cities.

MEIJI REFORMS But in 1853 Japan received a shock when a well-armed American fleet steamed into Edo (Tokyo) Bay and demanded diplomatic relations, a commercial treaty, and the rights to build a coaling station. The government—the Tokugawa shoguns in power since 1603—had for 200 years sought to minimize contact with the rest of the world. Now some of the elite realized that their national security was at risk and Japan's power inadequate. This provided motivation for reforms, just as the defeat in the Crimean War did for Russia. The efforts of the Tokugawa deepened divisions, and a civil war in 1867–1868 brought the **Meiji Restoration**, which reinstated rule by emperors. A new elite took power in Meiji Japan (1868–1912) that was committed to pursuing the knowledge and technologies that made foreigners so threatening. Occasional bombardments of Japanese ports by British, French, Dutch, and American naval ships seeking better trade deals emphasized to the leaders of Meiji Japan the urgency of strengthening the country.

Japan's population was unusually literate and accustomed to hierarchy, group loyalty, and discipline. Millions of women were used to long hours spinning thread in their homes. Japan had the makings of a productive working class. But it needed efficient technology, which the government set out to acquire. Japan's coastal shipping routes and longstanding commercial traditions allowed the makings of a national market by 1868. That appealed to ambitious entrepreneurs who were eager to build industrial enterprises.

No one was more ambitious than **Eiichi Shibusawa**. He was born in 1840 to a prosperous farm family and studied Confucian classics. After an eye-opening trip to view efficient, modern factories in France, he came home during the chaotic fall of the Tokugawa. Called to government service in the Ministry of Finance, he used his office to help start hundreds of companies in textiles, shipping, sugar refining, beer brewing, paper manufacture, hotels, banking, insurance, and railroads. Shibusawa moved among elite businessmen and high government officials who showed remarkable determination to bring an industrial revolution to Japan. They sometimes differed on the means, but rarely on the end: a prosperous, strong, industrial Japan. Most also hoped to get richer in the process.

TEXTILES AND HEAVY INDUSTRY As in Britain, Germany, and the United States, textiles led the way in Japanese industrialization. In 1870, Japan was importing vast amounts of cloth from British factories, which produced cheaper and better cottons than could Japanese households. Then in 1877 a Japanese student at the University of London agreed to the suggestion from a total stranger—Shibusawa—that for the sake of Japan he should abandon his study of economics and instead learn the cotton business. So Takeo Yamanobe headed to Manchester, learned all he could, and in 1882 came home to help Shibusawa set up Japan's first modern cotton mill, in Osaka. It soon prospered, drawing imitators into the business. By 1890, Japan was producing almost all its cloth in its own factories and had begun exporting to neighboring countries. Its factories generally worked differently from those in Europe, often using human muscle to power machinery instead of steam engines—because labor was cheap.

The biggest industrial sector in Meiji Japan by employment was textiles, but Japan's place in the world depended more on heavy industry. Meiji reformers regarded iron, steel, shipbuilding, chemicals, mining, and railroads as too important to be left to the private sector. The state guided, and often initiated, the industrial revolution in these sectors, while leaving textiles to the market.

Acquiring industrial expertise became a top priority. At any given time in the 1870s and 1880s, some 2,000 foreign engineers, mechanics, or technicians were working in Japan, sharing their knowledge. Japan also sent students overseas to learn, as Yamanobe had done in London and Manchester. Between 1868 and 1900, some 11,000 Japanese students, almost all male— the first large-scale study-abroad initiative in world history—went to the United States, Germany, and Britain, mainly to master the latest industrial techniques and technologies. Japan also imported foreign technology directly and encouraged engineers to build similar, perhaps better, models, adapted to Japanese conditions.

Japanese Textiles By the end of the nineteenth century, industrial methods of textile production overtook traditional Japanese methods. An 1872 illustration depicts the spinning floor in a silk factory, combining the methods of manual and machine labor.

The Metallic Web

1800–1920

IN 1800, THE FASTEST ANYONE could move was atop a galloping horse at about 30 mph (48 kph)—and that only for a couple of minutes. Horse travel averaged about 5 mph (8 kph). Boats or ships traveled at the speed the wind propelled them, which at times meant no movement at all. It might take 6 to 18 months for messages to get back and forth between Java and Amsterdam.

Between 1800 and 1844, three new technologies sped up global movement: the railway, steamship, and telegraph. Metallic webs soon spanned the globe: steel railway track, copper telegraph wires and undersea cables, and iron steamships. Telegraph messages from Java to Amsterdam and back took a few hours. Overland journeys from New York to San Francisco in 1850 took 6 months, but by 1870 only one week by rail. Transatlantic crossings by sail in 1800 had taken about a month on average; by 1880, steamships took a week.

The metallic web made the world feel smaller. The isochronic areas shaded on the map show, for instance, the broad swathe of Eurasia reachable from London in five days. Even those millions around the world who as late as 1900 had never seen a locomotive, steamship, or telegraph wire—mainly villagers in the areas shaded purple in South America, Africa, and Asia—found their lives changed by people, businesses, and governments who used these technologies every day.

KEY

— Railway

▨ Shipping lane

— Undersea cable

• 20 largest cities

○ Other city

Lima ○ Port

Questions for Analysis

Based on this feature and your chapter reading, consider the following questions:

1. What parts of the world remained least globally connected in 1900, to judge by the isochronic regions and the railway networks?

2. Within Africa and Asia, South Africa and India had unusually dense rail networks. Why?

> **THE WHOLE SURFACE OF THIS COUNTRY [WILL SOON] BE CHANNELED FOR THOSE NERVES WHICH ARE TO DIFFUSE, WITH THE SPEED OF THOUGHT, A KNOWLEDGE OF ALL THAT IS OCCURRING THROUGHOUT THE LAND, MAKING, IN FACT, ONE NEIGHBORHOOD OF THE WHOLE COUNTRY.**

SAMUEL F. B. MORSE, 1914

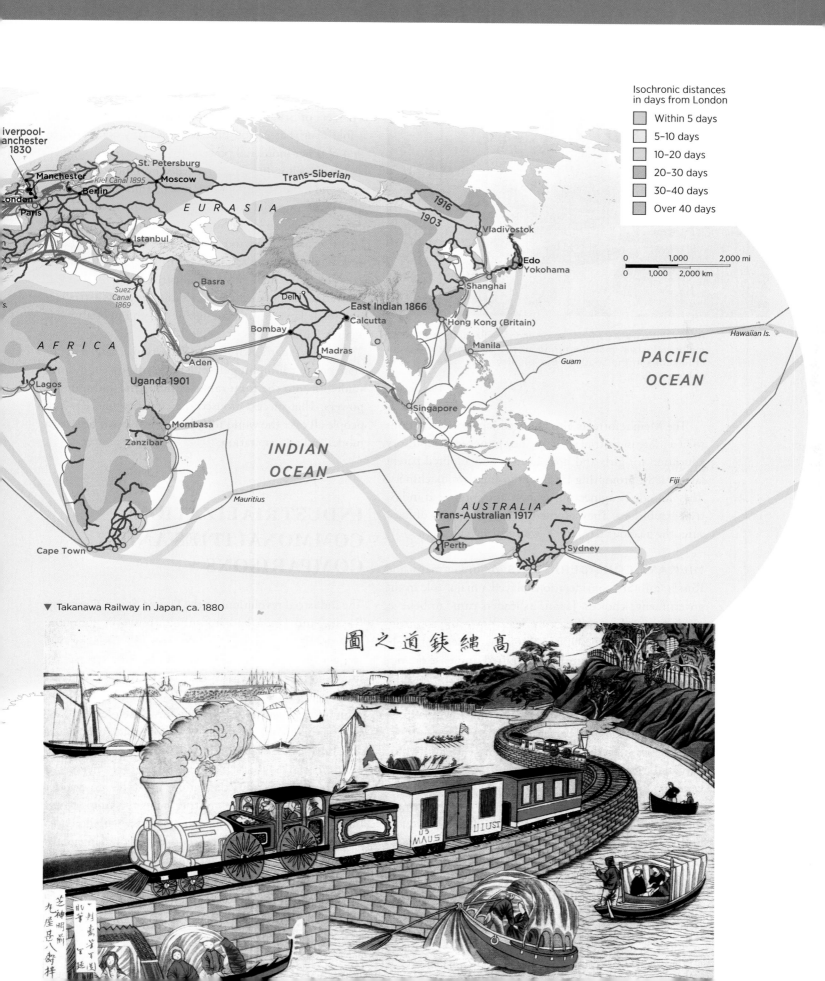

▼ Takanawa Railway in Japan, ca. 1880

Heavy Industry As Japan rapidly industrialized, the state built major industrial manufacturing works—like this steel plant in Fukuoka in the south of the country, seen here in a 1910 photograph.

The Meiji reformers also changed Japanese conditions to fit a more industrial society. They imposed compulsory education for girls and boys in 1872 and adopted patent law in 1885, prompting inventors to improve machinery. They founded engineering schools and sponsored industrial exhibitions. They adopted the metric system of measure, the 24-hour day, and a Westernized calendar.

MILITARY CONSIDERATIONS As in Germany and Russia, military considerations played a major role in the government's choices. Japan, its leaders came to believe, needed a modern military to deter powerful countries such as Britain or the United States that otherwise might conquer it. A modern military required immense quantities of iron and steel. The Meiji state supported shipbuilding, mines, railroads, steel, and armaments with subsidies, credit, and tax breaks. At times it also unleashed police or army violence against disgruntled laborers and peasants—whose taxes helped finance industrialization and whose irrigated ricefields increasingly suffered from deadly water pollution. Firms nurtured their political connections to get their share of state support, an arrangement that favored big businesses like Mitsubishi and Kawasaki, both originally shipping and shipbuilding companies. By 1890, both were giant conglomerates owning mines, steel mills, and factories.

The results of these efforts pleased Meiji reformers. Japan's total industrial production climbed 6-fold between 1870 and 1913. Coal output, close to zero in 1868, climbed 20-fold from 1883 to 1913, reaching 21 million tons (about 8 percent of Britain's total). Iron ore production increased 4-fold over that period but remained tiny compared to that of other industrial powers.

Japan, as it industrialized, needed ever more materials, and nature hadn't given it much. Thus the Meiji state undertook imperial conquests at the expense of China, defeated by Japan in the Sino-Japanese War of 1894–1895. Japan secured access to coal and iron ore in Manchuria and sought to promote cotton farming in Taiwan. Shortages of key raw materials put industrial Japan on the road to overseas imperialism; at the same time, industrialization made Japan strong enough to win an imperialist war against China.

By 1914, Japan's swift industrialization, a case of deliberate policy triumphing despite unpromising conditions, vaulted it into the front ranks of industrial and military powers. That success aroused the curiosity, and envy, of people all over the world for whom Meiji Japan became a model and an inspiration.

INDUSTRIALIZATION: COMMONALITIES AND COMPARISONS

The industrial revolutions in the United States, Germany, Russia, and Japan had important things in common. Information flowed easily through the Global web by 1850, so it was easy to learn from the prior British example. All four countries rejected free trade and a fully free market in favor of protection of their industries and government promotion of transport infrastructure. Their leaders were well acquainted with the ideas of Alexander Hamilton and Friedrich List, and adapted them to their own circumstances. The Russian and Japanese governments, late to start pushing industrialization, took the most active roles. Each of the four countries benefited from a large domestic market, providing manufacturers with potential economies of scale. Good transport systems and integrated national markets were a requirement for large-scale industrialization. And it helped to have additional accessible markets—for example, in the form of overseas empire or neighbors with few efficient industries of their own.

COAL OUTPUT, 1820–1900 (IN MILLION TONS)

	BRITAIN	GERMANY	FRANCE	RUSSIA	JAPAN	UNITED STATES	CANADA
1820	~25	1	1	n/a	n/a	0.3	n/a
1840	43	4	3	n/a	n/a	2	n/a
1860	88	19	8	0.3	n/a	18	0.3
1880	149	59	19	3	0.8	72	1
1900	229	150	33	16	7	245	5

Sources: B. R. Mitchell, *International Historical Statistics: Europe, 1750–2005* (2007), 464–66; *Africa, Asia & Oceania, 1750–2005* (2007), 375; *The Americas, 1750–2005* (2007), 327–28.

IRON ORE OUTPUT, 1840–1900 (IN MILLION TONS)

	BRITAIN	GERMANY	FRANCE	RUSSIA	JAPAN	UNITED STATES	CANADA
1840	n/a	0.4	1	n/a	n/a	n/a	n/a
1860	8	1	3	n/a	n/a	n/a	n/a
1880	18	5	3	n/a	0.2	7	n/a
1900	14	13	5	6	0.3	28	0.1

Sources: B. R. Mitchell, *International Historical Statistics: Europe, 1750–2005* (2007), 490–91; *Africa, Asia & Oceania, 1750–2005* (2007), 397; *The Americas, 1750–2005* (2007), 341.

All four countries also shared a reliance on military industry. The first large-scale industrial system of interchangeable parts came in American armories charged with military production during the War of 1812. The first high-precision mass production took place in Portsmouth, England, in a factory designed during the Napoleonic Wars to produce hundreds of thousands of standardized pulleys for naval ships. What motivated the Englishman Henry Bessemer to find a new way to make steel in the 1850s was the problem of making big artillery pieces more durable. German steel making, especially that undertaken by Krupp's firm, was first devoted to tableware but by 1865 to weaponry. The programs of industrialization in Russia and Japan, at least the large sectors devoted to metallurgy, were calculated to make their countries militarily strong.

The tables above show the growth of heavy industry in various countries worldwide. Note the early start but modest growth in France; the surge in the United States after 1860 and in Russia after 1880; and the general dominance of the United States, Britain, and Germany.

DE-INDUSTRIALIZATION

All these industrial revolutions sparked a related process: **de-industrialization**, the disappearance of old handicraft industries that could not compete for long with mechanized production. It too began in Britain. Hand-weavers, for example, working at home, eventually had to find other work after steam-powered textile mills were up and running. Village smiths, whose hoes and horseshoes could not compete with those churned out by iron foundries in Birmingham, had to do the same. Industrial cities put village industries out of business. This also happened in France, Belgium, and Germany after factory systems took root there, taking decades in each case.

Soon de-industrialization was a near-global trend. By 1830, millions of spinners, weavers, and metalsmiths working in China, India, Iran, or Algeria were feeling the impact of British factory competition. A Bengali widow in 1828 reported that she had taken up spinning when her husband died but her business quickly evaporated. She said that previously:

> . . . weavers would come to my doorstep to buy the yarn . . . and they would immediately advance as much cash money as I wanted. As a result, we did not have any anxiety about food and clothing. . . . Now . . . the weavers have stopped coming to my doorstep to buy my yarn, [and] even when I send it to the [market] they will not buy it at one-fourth the former price. . . . I . . . have learned that the weavers are using English yarn now. . . . When I examined the yarn I found it better than mine.

Handicraft Industry A mid-nineteenth-century watercolor shows a South Asian woman spinning thread by hand, one of the traditional crafts that was threatened worldwide by industrialization.

She was not alone in her misfortune. In 1835, the governor-general of British India wrote: "the bones of the cotton weavers are bleaching the plains of India."

Misfortune befell spinners and hand-weavers wherever factory cloth could be sold. Isfahan, in Iran, in 1890 had only 10 percent as many silk looms as in 1830 because British cotton took market share from Iranian silk. Spinners and weavers from China to Chile faced similar challenges. The table below shows some of the geographical relocation of industry in the nineteenth century.

By the mid-nineteenth century, Britain's factories produced so much so cheaply—and often of such good quality—that handicraft industries worldwide met the same fate as Indian and Iranian textiles. British-made iron, steel, pottery, and even coal were competitive on every continent. The innovations of the Industrial Revolution conferred an enormous advantage on British industries, especially those that were energy- or knowledge-intensive. By 1870, industries in the United States and continental Europe came to share that advantage, contributing to more de-industrialization. Industrialization not only changed peasants into workers in Britain, Germany, Russia, or Japan; in much of the world it changed handicraft workers into peasants or paupers.

ECONOMIC SHIFTS AND POLITICAL POWER IN THE GLOBAL WEB

The efficiency of modern industrial production and transport launched a geographical reorganization of the world's economy. Lands with limited prospects for industrialization came to specialize more in primary products, mainly food and fiber crops. The slave states in the U.S. South before the Civil War, for example, deepened their commitment to cotton production in response to the demand for raw cotton from British and New England mills. After the Civil War, despite the abolition of slavery, the trend toward cotton strengthened in the southern states. Egypt, India, and China by 1900 produced more raw cotton and less cotton cloth than they had in 1800. Australia and Argentina found niches producing wheat, wool, and leather, although each developed some light industry too. The advent of refrigerated shipping in the 1870s enabled the North American plains, the Argentine pampas, and other grasslands to specialize in beef, transported by rail and ship to distant markets.

The rails and steam that stood at the center of the industrial revolutions helped to knit the world economy into a tighter web than ever before. In the early modern centuries, as we've seen, certain goods such as silver, spices, and sugar were traded across oceans. Bulk goods, with few exceptions, did not reward the cost of long-distance transport. But by the 1840s that was changing fast. Cheap cloth, grain, timber, and coal could now yield profit if carried by steam-propelled trains or ships. Ever-larger spaces functioned more or less as single markets—where tariffs permitted.

Industrialization also changed the distribution of military and political power around the world. Britain, already on its way to becoming a great power before its

APPROXIMATE SHARE OF GLOBAL INDUSTRIAL PRODUCTION, 1800–1900		
	BRITAIN + EUROPE	**CHINA + INDIA**
1800	25%	50%
1850	37%	30%
1900	60%	12%

Source: Elaborated from Kaoru Sugihara, "Global Industrialization: A Multipolar Perspective," in *The Cambridge World History*, eds. J. R. McNeill and Kenneth Pomeranz, Vol. 7 (2015), 123.

CONSIDERING THE EVIDENCE

Rage against the Machines

The capitalists who owned textile mills and the laborers who worked in them often disagreed about the benefits of steam power. Capitalists claimed the machines made life easier for workers by saving them from the time and labor of monotonous tasks; workers focused on how machines reduced the number of available jobs. Great Britain and other states initially defended the interests of the less numerous capitalists against the demands of the much larger population of workers. Without a sympathetic ear in government, some workers organized violent riots to destroy the machines that threatened their livelihoods. In the following excerpt from a newspaper in Leeds (near Manchester, England), an anonymous contributor describes a confrontation in 1812 between a "furious mob" and mill owners who had recently adopted steam power.

Middleton, April 22, 1812.

On Monday...afternoon, the Mills of Messrs. Daniel Burton and Sons...about five miles from Manchester, were attacked by a furious mob, not from any dislike personally to the proprietors,...but from using a species of looms worked by *power*, as it is called, that is by steam, and by the use of which manual labour is materially diminished.... Mr. Emanuel Burton and [about 50] men...posted themselves in the works, determined to resist any attacks.... After breaking the windows, the mob fired several shots into the Factory, and endeavoured to force an entrance; in this they did not succeed, and Mr. Burton and his party fired about 50 blank cartridges...to intimidate and disperse [the mob]...; but [they] found [it] necessary to fire upon them with ball, when five of the rioters were shot dead, and a number were desperately wounded, two...have died of their wounds. Seeing their companions fall around them, the assailants became panic-struck, and...they dispersed.

...Early on Tuesday morning a much more numerous mob...assembled....Finding that a detachment of the Scotch Grevs [a cavalry regiment of the British Army] had been brought to protect the works, the mob...burnt [Mr. Emanuel Burton's mansion] to the ground.

Encouraged by their success, they repaired to [the mill], when an engagement between the mob and the cavalry took place, [four rioters were] shot dead upon the field, besides a great number wounded, and 17 of the most active of the insurgents taken prisoners.... It was observed that all the rioters were strangers at Middleton, and that [Middleton's] labouring classes...took no part in the engagements.... This simple narrative of facts cannot be read without mixed emotions of horror and regret. For many years the military of this country have been solely employed against our foreign enemies; but now, unfortunately, they are under the necessity of acting against their own misled countrymen, and the tranquillity of the country is only imperfectly preserved even at the point of the bayonet!

Source: "Riots," *Leeds Mercury*, 25 Apr. 1812, in *British Library Newspapers*.

QUESTIONS FOR ANALYSIS

1. Why do you think the narrator needed to explain what "steam power" was and why it made people angry in 1812?
2. Does the narrator seem to have more sympathy for the "labouring classes" or the mill owners?
3. Why would the British government give a military regiment (which was accustomed to fighting foreign wars) an assignment to defend the private property of a mill owner?

Industrial Revolution, became the world's strongest power by 1840. It used its leverage to force weaker countries to lower tariffs on British goods and to expand its overseas empire. Germany too, after unification (1871), emerged as a great power within Europe and, by the late 1880s, as an imperial power in Africa and the Pacific. France, although early to begin industrialization, could not keep pace with Britain and Germany, and by the 1870s no longer matched them in military power. The United States and Russia accelerated their overland expansions with their newfound industrial might, and in the U.S. case took up overseas empire after 1898 as well. As we've seen, Japan's Industrial Revolution thrust that nation into the East Asian mainland as an imperial power from the 1890s.

Meanwhile, Mughal India vanished and Qing China languished. Their militaries, still formidable in the mid-eighteenth century, by 1840 proved helpless in the face of British gunboats and artillery. Britain controlled India by 1860 and, together with other industrial powers, parts of China as well. After 1870, peoples without industrial weaponry generally soon lost their independence—and some disappeared altogether. Rarely in world history had so much political and military power concentrated in so few spots. Now, in the nineteenth century, those who had pulled off industrial revolutions found themselves far more formidable than those who hadn't, and usually converted their advantages into conquest and empire. We will examine this theme more closely in Chapter 24.

SOCIAL CONTRACTS AND INDUSTRIAL SOCIETY

The energy revolution and economic transformation that industrial societies experienced deepened their inequalities. This cast new doubt on the social contracts on which those societies had formerly operated. Social contracts—the phrase was popularized by the French Enlightenment thinker Jean-Jacques Rousseau—are not real contracts. They are shared understandings of what is fair in terms of the distribution of wealth, income, and opportunity. They always reflect the distribution of political power and are reinforced by laws, customs, and policies.

The social contract of industrial society had to incorporate the new urban and professional upper middle classes into ruling elites that formerly had comprised aristocrats, landowners, and big merchants. Between 1830 and 1900 in every industrialized country, the upper middle classes obtained rights to vote and hold public office, to join prestigious schools and clubs—in short, to acquire substantial political power and social standing.

It was harder for industrializing societies to agree on the proper standing of the working classes. The older elites included a few people who sympathized with workers, but most people in the upper classes were reluctant to share power, or even the right to vote, with people they considered their social and cultural inferiors. Also, workers could never unify behind a single set of aims. Some advocated for individual self-improvement, emphasizing the virtues of sobriety, hard work, and thrift. Others despaired of achieving improvement in this world and placed their hopes in a better life to come in the next. Many, however, came to think that political action provided their best hope.

REFORM In political terms, workers were divided on the question of reform or revolution. Reform, meaning working within established institutions to achieve gradual improvements in working conditions and political rights, rested on the belief that progress was possible. In Europe, this outlook drew strength from Enlightenment ideology. Some of the poor, and as we've seen some middle-class observers such as Marx and Engels, rejected reform as a strategy for workers and advocated revolution. Workers' resentments sometimes boiled over into riots or rebellions. French workers took major roles in uprisings in 1830, 1848, and 1871. Workers in Milan, Berlin, Vienna, and other cities joined in revolutions in 1848—chaotic events that involved unstable coalitions with many agendas. In Russia, urban workers played a central role in an insurrection called the Revolution of 1905. But most attempts at revolution failed, sometimes in rivers of blood, and none managed to put the working class in power.

Reform efforts were more successful than revolution in renegotiating social contracts to the advantage of the working classes. There were several keys to the success of labor reform movements: the level of organization, the strength of alliances with the middle classes, and the continuing threat of revolution or economic disruption.

LABOR ACTIVISM The most important key to the success of working-class reform was organization. Where they created labor unions, workers could negotiate more effectively with employers and put pressure on politicians. In 1824, the British Parliament repealed the Combination

Trade Unions Speakers rally a crowd of striking mineworkers in Ludlow, Colorado, in 1914. By joining a union, workers could collectively demand better working conditions. But governments often opposed unionization: the National Guard violently broke up this particular strike, resulting in the deaths of 21 people.

Acts that prohibited unions and strikes. In the ensuing decades, trade unions successfully drove parliamentary reforms of working conditions and the use of child labor. The unions also supported efforts to expand suffrage to all adult males.

The main weapon available to workers was the threat of a strike. In certain industries, such as coal or railroads, workers had particular power. In 1877, for example, U.S. railroad workers went on strike in response to reduced wages. State governors called out militias and violence broke out in several cities, obliging the federal government to send in the army. The strikers returned to work, but the railroad companies soon offered pensions and better wages in hopes of preventing further strikes. On a much larger scale, in 1912 nearly 1 million British coal miners struck for a minimum wage. Because factories, railroads, and the navy could not operate without coal, the miners had real power; after 37 days, the national government intervened and the miners got a minimum wage.

ALLIANCES Another key to the success of labor reform was alliances with sympathetic members of the ruling elites or middle-class reformers. Every industrial country included people who were appalled at the squalor of urban working-class neighborhoods and the greed of many factory owners. In Britain, for example, Joseph Chamberlain, the industrial millionaire who turned to politics, became mayor of Birmingham and worked to deliver better schools, public libraries, clean water, streetlights, and other improvements to the entire city, including its working-class tenements. Others, such as the intellectuals Beatrice Webb and Sidney Webb and their colleagues in the Fabian Society (est. 1884), supported public education, shorter working hours, a minimum wage, and nationalized health care. Bismarck, as we've seen, agreed to provide health insurance and other benefits to German workers.

In Chicago, Jane Addams and other educated, well-to-do women set up Hull House in 1889 as a center for research into the plight of the city's poor, especially women and children, and advocated for improved education, housing, health care, and working conditions. By 1913, the United States had 413 **settlement houses**, as these institutions were called. In Japan, middle-class reformers such as the professor Kanai En called attention to the widening social gulf, lamenting that "since the coming of factory organization . . . there is an estrangement between managers and workers." They supported

Settlement Houses Chicago children pose for a photograph outside Jane Addams's Hull House in 1908. Settlement houses like Hull House pioneered new methods of social work among the urban poor.

legislation, passed in 1911, that outlawed labor for those under age 12 and shortened the working day to 12 hours for women and children over age 12. These reform efforts were all linked to one another. Bismarck's program influenced the Fabian Society. Hull House, based on a London settlement house called Toynbee Hall, was itself the model for a settlement house in Tokyo set up by American and Japanese women in 1919. Russian reformers established a settlement house in Moscow in 1905.

EXPANDING SUFFRAGE Some of these allies of the working class, and many workers too, called themselves liberals or socialists. Roughly speaking, liberals favored individual freedoms, constitutional checks on rulers, and often some legal protections for society's most vulnerable members. At the core of liberal movements and political parties were the urban middle classes. **Socialists** placed stronger emphasis on empowering the working classes—in some cases through cooperatives and unions, in others through workers' ownership of factories, farms, and mines. Both liberals and socialists generally wanted to end aristocratic privileges, curtail religion in public life, and broaden political participation. Most sought to reform, rather than smash, existing political systems.

An important focus of political reform was expanding the right to vote. Workers in the early decades of industrialization were not allowed to vote. But through the allied efforts of workers and middle-class liberals, universal male franchise became law in France in 1848, in Germany in

1871, and in Japan in 1925. In Britain it came in steps between 1868 and 1918. In the United States, adult white males could generally vote by 1856, with exceptions in particular states. African American men generally could not vote until ratification of a constitutional amendment in 1868; even then, their voting rights were often denied in the southern states for another century.

Everywhere that workers were winning the right to vote, they and their middle-class allies formed new political parties focused on advancing the welfare of the working classes. The German Social Democratic Party (SPD) was founded in 1875, the French socialist party in 1879, the British Labour Party in 1900, and a Japanese Social Democratic Party in 1901. By 1910, they were all important forces in the day-to-day politics of their countries, part of the political system. The United States, in contrast, never developed a successful political party explicitly devoted to the interests of workers. The main workers' party in Russia, the Russian Social Democratic Workers' Party, founded in 1898, did not seek reform within the Russian political system but, instead, strove to overthrow it.

WOMEN AND YOUTH In Britain, the United States, and elsewhere, women launched suffrage movements in the nineteenth century, but they achieved few political rights until the twentieth. But with industrialization, wage work in factories set apart from the home altered the fabric of women's lives. They now had a little money to spend, and sometimes a wider network of friends in their co-workers, usually other women much like themselves, to whom they could turn in time of need. Women also organized to advance their own interests in response to new pressures brought by industrialization. In the early years in Lowell's mills, for example, young women made what for the time were good wages and were offered free evening educational classes. By the late 1830s, however, Lowell's mills slashed wages to match competition from other entrepreneurs. The Lowell girls, as they were known, resisted by going on strike and organizing a union. By 1853, they managed to convince the mill owners to reduce the work day to 11 hours.

In Japan, teenage girls made up most of the labor force in textile mills and worked in miserable conditions. They often lived in dingy dormitories and labored long hours for little pay. Women coal miners, usually older and married to male miners, fared worse. One observer

Young Women Workers An engraving shows young women working at weaving machines in the textile mills of Lowell, Massachusetts. Factory work increasingly became a sector that employed young, unmarried women, which gave them access to independent income and a new form of social independence away from home.

commented: "Returning black and grimy from a day's work in the pits with their husbands, they immediately had to start preparing meals . . . [and] nursing their babies. . . . [N]o man would be found helping with what were designated as women's tasks."

In the early Meiji years, activists sought a new social contract for women. They argued that the new Japan needed educated, independent women in order to compete in the international arena. Their main impact came in 1872, when four years of compulsory education was required for girls as well as boys. But by the 1890s, the Meiji state had banned women from all political activity and passed new legislation confining them to traditional roles, summarized in the slogan "good wife, wise mother." The most successful women's organization in Meiji Japan, the Patriotic Women's Society established by Okumura Ioko, which had half a million members by 1905, worked to prepare soldiers for overseas deployments and console families whose sons never returned from war. That suited the Meiji state perfectly.

For working-class teenagers and children of both sexes, the industrial revolutions brought more independence from family supervision and, for some, the first formal schooling. They spent more of their time with other youths, whether on the streets, in cotton mills, or in schools. In every industrial city, unemployed children roamed the streets while their parents toiled in factories. Many children worked long hours in mills or mines. Increasingly, some attended school. Industrial societies from France to Japan to Canada created systems of public education between 1830 and 1880, changing the nature of childhood. In many cases, education for girls came later than for boys. In most Catholic countries, girls' education was entrusted to nuns rather than public employees. In addition to reading, writing, and arithmetic, schools taught the young to accept adult discipline, preparing them for life in the workplace.

More time spent together with their age-mates led the young in industrial cities to create their own culture—and led dismayed adults to try to shape it. British boys in growing numbers turned to sports such as soccer. In nineteenth-century Britain, and other countries too, young men in many working-class trades—masons, carpenters, smiths, tailors—regularly took to the road, tramping from town to town, looking for work, singing songs, forging bonds of youth before settling into full adulthood. In many cities teenage gangs sprang up. Concerned adults organized wholesome organizations and clubs, such as the YMCA and YWCA, founded in London in 1844 and 1855, respectively, or the Girls Club Union, begun in London in 1880. Churches of every denomination began creating youth groups starting in the 1880s. The industrial revolutions forced renegotiation of social contracts between generations and within families as well as within societies.

INDUSTRIALIZATION AND THE GLOBAL ENVIRONMENT

The industrial revolutions altered nature as well as human society. In the industrialized lands, the sharpest impacts came in the form of air and water pollution, as we saw in Britain. The iron and steel centers of the Ruhr or Pittsburgh or Osaka (Japan), and hundreds of other cities, were also enveloped in smoky haze day and night. Their rivers became toxic currents contaminated by chemicals from dyeworks, bacteria from meatpacking plants, and coal soot raining down from chimneys and smokestacks. Efforts at pollution control remained rare until the twentieth century, although filtration, which turned dirty water into drinkable water, made considerable progress in industrial cities between 1850 and 1920 and sharply reduced the burden of disease.

The environmental impacts of the industrial revolutions were not confined to industrialized landscapes. They were global, transmitted via long-distance trade in commodities. The fibers, minerals, and lubricants needed for industry often came from far afield. Demand for whale oil, a good lubricant for machinery, inspired a global hunt that by 1870 had brought sperm whales and right whales to the edge of extinction. The suitability of bison hide as leather belting in textile mills helped drive the North American bison hunt that reduced herds of 30 million to a total of about 1,000 animals between the 1830s and 1880s. Farmers in New Zealand burned ancient forests to make room for sheep pasture to provide wool for Britain's textile mills. To feed cotton mills, huge swathes of forest in the U.S. South were converted into cotton plantations. To provide lead for British industries, Spanish miners gouged ore from mountains in the southeastern province of Almería. These were all ecological changes brought about by industrialization and its long-distance commodity trade links.

Last, but perhaps most important in the long run, the burning of hundreds of millions of tons of coal added more greenhouse gases to the atmosphere. This had no discernible effect on climate during the nineteenth century, and no one was concerned by it at the time. But these greenhouse gas emissions began, in a small way, the process of destabilizing climate that is still ongoing today. Some of the carbon dioxide from the chimneys of early coal-burning factories in 1830 remains in the atmosphere nearly 200 years later, warming the Earth. Some of it is now in the oceans, raising their acidity.

CONCLUSION

Here's an indication of how extraordinary the British Industrial Revolution was: in 1845, raw cotton grown in India was carried by ox-carts to ports, put on ships to sail around Africa to Britain, there spun into thread, woven into cloth, put back onto ships to sail around Africa again to ports in India, off-loaded and carried to Indian markets—and that cloth would be better and cheaper than cloth made in Indian villages.

The industrial revolutions in Europe, North America, and Japan shook up the world in several ways. They freed societies from the old constraints and near-universal poverty of an energy regime based on muscle and wood, as steam engines enabled conversion of the chemical energy in coal into motion and power. They re-ordered social relations by creating industrial working classes and expanding the middle classes. The industrial revolutions altered family dynamics. They created new inequalities of unprecedented size within societies. They also reshuffled international relations, creating a handful of great powers in Europe, North America, and Japan out of formerly small or peripheral states. And they recast the ongoing relationships between human societies and the natural world, accelerating the use of resources such as iron, lead, or copper ores and fibers such as cotton or wool, and pouring out pollution—including greenhouse gases such as carbon dioxide.

All these changes are still with us. By 1900, they shaped the lives of almost everyone in industrial countries, affecting work, consumption, social groupings, travel habits, and much else. Today, lives everywhere, even in remote villages, are shaped by the industrial revolutions of the years 1780–1914.

CHAPTER REVIEW

KEY TERMS

Industrial Revolution (p. 637)

textiles and metallurgy (p. 640)

coal (p. 640)

steam engine (p. 641)

James Watt (p. 641)

railways (p. 645)

working class (p. 647)

Friedrich List (p. 650)

Communist Manifesto (p. 652)

Alexander Hamilton (p. 653)

cotton gin (p. 653)

National Policy (p. 655)

Trans-Siberian Railway (p. 656)

Sergei Witte (p. 656)

Meiji Restoration (p. 657)

Eiichi Shibusawa (p. 657)

de-industrialization (p. 661)

settlement houses (p. 665)

socialists (p. 665)

Go to INQUIZITIVE to see what you've learned—and learn what you've missed—with personalized feedback along the way.

REVIEW QUESTIONS

1. What two main changes in manufacturing methods define the Industrial Revolution?

2. What were the key industries of the Industrial Revolution, and why were they well suited to new manufacturing methods?

3. What combination of fuel and technology made up the energy revolution at the heart of the Industrial Revolution?

4. How did expensive labor and plentiful coal in Britain contribute to the start of the Industrial Revolution?

5. How did energy from coal change the cotton and iron industries in Britain?

6. Describe each tier of the social hierarchy of industrial Britain.

7. What measures did the German state introduce to spur industrialization?

8. Why was the U.S. weapons industry especially important to world history?

9. What obstacles to industrialization did Russia face, and how did it overcome them?

10. What was the role of the Meiji government in Japan's industrialization?

11. Why, after transport and communication technologies changed slowly for millennia, did the technologies of the metallic web come in a cluster between 1800 and 1850?

12. Compare and contrast the level of state involvement in industrialization in Britain, the United States, Germany, Russia, and Japan.

13. What important features did the industrial revolutions in the United States, Germany, Russia, and Japan have in common?

14. How did the Industrial Revolution lead to de-industrialization among handicraft industries?

15. In what ways did industrialization change military and political power around the world?

16. What were the most important keys to working-class labor reform, and what was the main alternative to reform?

17. Identify and describe the main environmental impacts of industrialization and long-distance commodity trade.

FURTHER READING

Robert C. ALLEN, *The British Industrial Revolution in Global Perspective* (2009). A summary statement by one of the foremost economic historians.

Gareth AUSTIN and Kaoru SUGIHARA, eds., *Labour-Intensive Industrialization in Global History* (2013). The best way to get access to Sugihara's important take on industrialization in East Asia.

Emma GRIFFIN, *A Short History of the British Industrial Revolution* (2010). A very handy summary of the story and the controversies among earlier historians.

Toni PIERENKEMPER and Richard TILLY, *The German Economy during the Nineteenth Century* (2004). A basic survey with a focus on industrialization.

Eiichi SHIBUSAWA, *The Autobiography of Shibusawa Eiichi: From Peasant to Entrepreneur*, translated by Teruko Craig (1994). The life story of the "father of Japanese capitalism."

Robert C. H. SWEENY, *Why Did We Choose to Industrialize? Montreal 1819–1849* (2015). A detailed study of one city contextualized in the world history of industrialization.

Barrie TRINDER, *Britain's Industrial Revolution: The Making of a Manufacturing People* (2013). A thorough examination of the subject with endless interesting detail.

Peer VRIES, *Averting a Great Divergence: State and Economy in Japan, 1868–1937* (2019). An analysis of the state's role in Japanese industrialization.

Richard WHITE, *The Republic for Which It Stands: The United States during Reconstruction and the Gilded Age, 1865–1896* (2019). A general history with a lot on industrialization and its consequences.

E. A. WRIGLEY, *Energy and the English Industrial Revolution* (2010). The most accessible version of the ideas of this master historian.

CHRONOLOGY

1670s
Objections to slavery arise in Quaker community in Barbados

late 17th century
Kangxi emperor requires smallpox inoculation in imperial lineage

1758
Philadelphia chapter of Quakers formally denounces slavery

1773–1774
Emelian Pugachev's rebellion in Russia

1787
Thomas Clarkson, Quakers, and evangelicals form abolitionist committee in Britain

1798
Edward Jenner publishes account of cowpox experiment

1800–1860
Slave population in American South quintuples

1801
Toussaint L'Ouverture abolishes slavery in Haiti

1802–1805
Spanish Empire establishes vaccination program

1807
Britain bans slave trade; Prussia ends serfdom

1808
United States bans slave trade

1812
José Aponte leads slave revolt in Cuba

1817
Cholera begins to spread worldwide; Spain bans slave trade

1823
Jack Gladstone leads Demerara revolt; Anti-Slavery Society forms in Britain

1831
Samuel Sharpe leads slave revolt in Jamaica; autobiography of Mary Prince is published

1834
Britain abolishes slavery

1835
Malê revolt in Brazil

1845–1847
Famine kills 12 to 15 percent of Ireland's population

ca. 1850
Germ theory of disease develops; sanitation reform begins

1850–1880
Migrant flows of indentured labor peak

1853
Britain requires smallpox vaccination for all children

1848
France's final abolition of slavery

Cattle disease kills almost all herds in East and southern Africa

1861
Emancipation of serfs in Russia

1865
United States abolishes slavery

1870s
Slave imports peak in Egypt

1873
Puerto Rico abolishes slavery

1886
Cuba abolishes slavery

1888
Brazil abolishes slavery

1890s

Two Liberations

THE VITAL REVOLUTION AND THE
ABOLITIONS OF SLAVERY AND SERFDOM

1750 to 1950

1902–1904
Cholera kills 200,000 people
in the Philippines

1910
China abolishes slavery

1924
Turkish Republic
abolishes slavery

1918
Flu pandemic kills
50 to 100 million people

1928
Iran abolishes
slavery

Christine of Mecklenburg-Güstrow was born in 1663, one of 11 children, to a noble family in a reasonably healthy part of Germany. The daughter of a duke, she married a count when she was 19 and gave birth to twins almost exactly 8 months later. Both twins died the day they were born. Over the next 22 years, Christine bore 21 more children (she had four pairs of twins). Of her 23 children, 12 died before age 5. Of those who made it to age 5, all survived to age 38 and four saw their 70th birthdays. Christine herself succumbed in 1749 at age 85. Seventeen of her children had already died.

Christine was unusual for her time. She was a noblewoman, she married young, she lived long, and she bore about four times as many children as the average woman of that era. But she was far from unique. England's Queen Anne, born two years after Christine, made every effort to provide the realm with an heir. She had 18 pregnancies that led to 5 births. Only one of her babies reached age 2, and the survivor died at age 19. She had the benefit of the best diet and medical care available in her era—as did Christine.

Even though she was unusual in some ways, Christine's career as a mother tells us a few things about health history in her day. Despite being prosperous and reliably well fed, more than half of her children died young, probably all

Destruction of the Roehampton Estate, January 1832 An episode in the Jamaican slave revolt of 1831–1832, when some 60,000 slaves rose up against local planters and the British Army.

671

FOCUS QUESTIONS

1. What made the Vital Revolution such a dramatic departure in human history?

2. What major developments contributed to the abolition of slavery in the nineteenth century?

3. How did the abolition of serfdom come about?

4. What brought the use of indentured labor to an end?

victims of disease. Even a family as comfortable as hers could not consistently keep children healthy and alive. That was equally true in Mecklenburg, Mozambique, and Mongolia—and the London of Queen Anne. In most of the world, just as it took two adults to generate a birth, it took on average two births to make an adult.

Christine's family story also shows us that people who made it past age 5 had a good chance of making it to 40. After age 40, life grew more precarious quickly. Even though life expectancy at birth was only about 25 or 30 years, people age 10 to 40 stood the lowest risk of dying—on average. Warfare and childbirth could raise the risk of death for people in the prime of life. But in general, death stalked the very young and those over age 40.

A lot has changed since Christine's day. Consider this: for the first 10,000 generations in human history, the average life expectancy of *Homo sapiens* populations was about 25 years. In the last 10 generations since Christine's death (1749), it has nearly tripled. It now stands a little above 72 years—slightly higher for women and lower for men. Japanese people can expect to live the longest, on average about 85 years, and people in the Central African Republic the shortest, about 53 years. This lengthening of life expectancy has brought a new inequality around the world. In Christine's day, life expectancy in the least

healthy lands might have stood around 25, and in the healthiest around 35. Now the gap between richest and poorest countries is 32 years of life expectancy, three times longer—although in percentage terms the gap remains about 40 percent. The gaps between the richest and poorest within societies today are much smaller—roughly 2 to 10 years, depending on the country and the particular measure. Whether these gaps have grown or shrunk since Christine's day is unclear.

So industrialization, the focus of the previous chapter, was far from the only process at work changing the world after 1750. This chapter takes up two broad themes, each of which had some links to industrialization but both of which were, in their own right, major historical forces shaping the modern world.

The first of these is sometimes called the Vital Revolution, because it deals with basic biological facts of life such as disease, health, and longevity. On average, human health and life expectancy improved steadily after 1750. For ordinary people, this change might have been the most important revolution of them all, even if at the time no one noticed it—because it was slow and incremental. It is a curious paradox that the most important processes changing the lives of ordinary people might go unnoticed. It is also testimony to the advantages of hindsight—of historical perspective.

The second of these important historical shifts was the decline of forced labor—a broad category. Forced labor ranged from chattel slavery, a lifetime status as human property in which people were bought and sold and their children were slaves by birth, to milder forms of bonded status that were temporary and not heritable. In some systems of forced labor, especially in Africa, the Islamic world, and Brazil, manumission—the granting of freedom—was more common than in others. In eastern Europe, serfs were bound to labor for the lords who owned the land they worked; serfs could also be their masters' legal property. In some cases, such as in the Americas and the Arab lands, forced labor carried with it a strong racial component, as we will see. In the rest of the world, that was less often the case. This chapter will focus on slaves and serfs, but even these categories were broad and variable: there could be a world of difference between the lives of a slave cutting Cuba's sugar cane and another weaving Central Asia's carpets.

Between the 1790s and 1920s, slavery as a legal institution in all its variety almost disappeared around the world. And between 1800 and 1870, the eastern European practice of serfdom vanished, and other forms of forced labor elsewhere waned. New labor arrangements and new hierarchies took the place of slavery and serfdom. Unlike the Vital Revolution, this historical shift was easily visible to contemporaries—because it was sudden, controversial, and contested.

These two fundamental changes help mark the modern world off from what came before. Until 1750, for all of human history, life expectancy at birth in every society was less than 30 years, and a third or a half of all babies born did not make it to their fifth birthday. That was the normal human condition. But in the nineteenth century, and more conspicuously in the twentieth, that changed. More people survived infancy and more lived to ripe old age. In broad terms, since 1750 life expectancy has tripled in the healthiest societies and doubled in the least healthy.

Until recently, forced labor was also a normal part of the human condition, although perhaps only for the last 5,000 years or so. Just about every agricultural society had one or another form of forced labor. Just about every agrarian culture regarded forced labor as acceptable, natural, and normal. Then, at the end of the eighteenth century, that attitude began to change. People who were held in bondage increasingly found allies elsewhere who opposed slavery or serfdom, and together they forced an end to legal forced labor—even if illegal forced labor survives in the shadows of the world economy to this day.

One can judge the improvements in health and

Justifications for Slavery Europeans who wanted to defend chattel slavery often relied on images of Africans as childlike, savage, or otherwise mentally and psychologically unfit for freedom—as in this 1833 American cartoon, which is critical of abolitionists.

longevity, and the abolition of forced labor, as human triumphs and important examples of progress in modern world history. One can also judge the remaining inequalities in health and longevity, and the lingering legacies of slavery and serfdom, as continuing injustices. The study of world history enables each of us to assess these issues and arrive at informed conclusions.

THE VITAL REVOLUTION

Like the Industrial Revolution, the **Vital Revolution** was a gradual development with no clear starting date. It began earlier in some places (such as France and Sweden) than in others (such as China and Japan). It could be temporarily reversed: in many cities of Britain, as we've seen, health worsened with industrialization. But whenever it began, within a century it brought a giant change in the human condition.

Just as the Old Regime preceded the French Revolution, what we can call a **biological old regime** preceded the Vital Revolution. It was broadly similar around the world. For most people, life was nasty, sickly, and short. Rich and poor alike were preoccupied with their health and, particularly in the case of women, with the health of their families. And there was a lot to fret about. Poor people had to worry about not getting enough to eat, and everyone had to face the risks of many dangerous diseases, few of which anyone could prevent or treat effectively. It is hard for those of us who have grown up with vaccines, antibiotics, and other powerful tools of modern medicine to imagine the insecurity of life and health under the biological old regime. But let's try.

THE BIOLOGICAL OLD REGIME: HEALTH AND NUTRITION BEFORE 1800

Before 1800, everywhere from China to Chile and Iceland to India, most people were sick much of the time. The crowd diseases, such as smallpox, measles, or mumps, were the most dangerous. They all had spread widely around the world by 1700. Wherever populations were dense enough and large enough to sustain them, they appeared as endemic diseases, always present and afflicting mainly babies and toddlers. Older people had already

Childhood Illness A Chinese painting from around 1800 shows a little girl covered in the distinctive sores of smallpox, one of the common crowd diseases often contracted in infancy or early childhood.

encountered and survived them, developing disease resistance in the process. Sometimes, however, such as in more isolated places, the crowd diseases appeared as epidemics, which arrived suddenly, from afar, and could affect people of all ages. Smallpox and measles were the worst of the crowd diseases. Both were breath-borne and spread easily from person to person. Both were extremely dangerous to people who had never had them before. In Iceland in 1707, for example, smallpox returned after a 35-year absence and killed about 30 percent of the population—most of them younger than age 35. Other important crowd diseases, although less lethal than smallpox or measles, included influenza and whooping cough (pertussis).

Many other infections besides the crowd diseases caused misery.

Gastrointestinal infections raged wherever people lived in settled communities, and these illnesses were often fatal to babies. Typhoid was one such disease, usually spread by bacteria in contaminated water. In warm weather—and in many places it was always warm enough for typhoid—it could rip through a community, killing up to 10 percent. Cholera, another mainly water-borne disease, was more deadly. Before 1800 it probably existed only in South Asia, but after the 1810s cholera occasionally attacked communities around the world. Where wastewater and drinking water were not carefully kept apart, which before 1800 was almost everywhere, water-borne diseases took a dreadful toll.

AT-RISK POPULATIONS Cities were especially unhealthy. In 1608 a Chinese observer described Beijing, then the world's biggest city, writing:

> The houses in the capital are so closely crowded together that there is no spare space, and in the markets there is much excrement and filth. People...live together in disorderly confusion, and there are many flies and gnats. Whenever it becomes hot it is almost intolerable. A little steady rain has only to fall and there is trouble from flooding. Therefore malarial fevers, diarrhea and epidemics follow each other without stopping.

European cities were no better. In the early eighteenth century, Tsar Peter the Great's family lived mainly in Moscow and the new city of St. Petersburg. Of his 14 children, 11 died before age seven. London between 1550 and 1800 recorded more deaths than births every year. Only a steady inflow of thousands of migrants each year kept the city going. Every sizeable city had a similar murderous effect due to its intense disease environment. As a German physician put it in 1796, cities were the "open graves of humankind." Before 1800, only about 3 percent of humankind lived in cities. The proportion could not have been much higher without the human race dwindling toward extinction—because urban conditions before 1850 inflicted such a harsh penalty.

Children whose immune systems had not yet been strengthened by surviving infections faced particularly daunting risks, as Christine's misfortunes in motherhood attest. The most dangerous age for babies began the day they were weaned of breast milk, which carried some immunity protection loaned, so to speak, by mothers. Children were also especially likely to suffer from diarrhea and gastrointestinal ailments, as they are today. The wide range of lethal diseases was the main reason that 35 to 50 percent of children around the world did not live to age five.

In some cultures, the risks babies faced also included infanticide. Unwed mothers often abandoned or drowned their babies. Families sometimes did the same when they judged that the addition of a new child was disadvantageous. The best-documented case is probably Qing China, where in the eighteenth-century infanticide (already practiced for more than 1,500 years in China) was commonplace. In some parts of the country, such as the lower and middle Yangzi, infanticide claimed about half of all newborns. Girls were especially vulnerable. Across the empire, roughly 20 to 25 percent of baby girls were deliberately killed before their first birthday. Even the imperial lineage, among the most prosperous segments in Qing society, killed about 10 percent of their baby girls. In Chinese families, elders decided when young people should marry, when they should have children, how many children there should be, and whether or not to kill unexpected babies. They left less to chance than families in most other parts of the world.

Adult women faced at least one health danger that children and men did not: childbirth. The evolution long ago of our big brains and big heads came at a price that mothers pay. Before 1800, about 1 to 3 percent (reliable figures are scarce) of births killed the mother via hemorrhage or infection. By 1880, the risks of childbirth began to diminish in Finland, the country for which we have the earliest systematic data, and by 1940 just about everywhere else. The biggest cause of this improvement was the recognition that those assisting with births—midwives, nurses, and doctors—should wash their hands. Today, worldwide, about 0.2 percent of births are fatal to mothers, but in Africa it is 0.5 percent while in Australia and New Zealand about 0.007 percent.

MALNUTRITION AND FAMINE The health risks of the biological old regime included malnutrition and starvation. As we have seen, during the worst decades of the Little Ice Age in the seventeenth century, cold and drought ruined many a harvest. Even in less challenging times, bad weather sometimes destroyed crops. In India, where a bad monsoon meant crop failure, a drought during the years 1630–1632 cost at least 3 million lives in the area around Gujarat. Over the next 200 years, sizeable killing famines appeared somewhere in India about once a

Dangers of Childbirth In this 1882 engraving, a Swiss doctor applies an early blood transfusion technique to treat the hemorrhage of a woman who has just delivered twins. Though very risky at the time, transfusions became one of the medical discoveries that decreased the rate of women dying in childbirth.

decade, on average. As late as 1845–1847, a famine killed 12 to 15 percent of Ireland's population. Because most people around the world lived close to the bone, even modest shortfalls—the sort that came one in every three or five years—usually brought hunger.

Peoples who lived from herding, or otherwise depended on animals, suffered hunger and malnutrition too. When drought dried up pastures, then cattle, sheep, and other grazing animals died in droves, depriving people of milk, cheese, and meat. Without animals, herders found it difficult to trade for other foodstuffs. Animal epidemics (called epizootics) could have the same deadly effect as drought. Where farming involved plows pulled by oxen, horses, or water buffalo, as in most of Eurasia, the loss of animal traction paralyzed plowing. The worst episode we know about came in the 1890s, when a cattle disease wiped out 80 to 95 percent of the herds in East and southern Africa. The result was starvation that killed as much as one-third of the population of Ethiopia and twice that proportion among the cattle-keeping Maasai of East Africa.

Famine meant different things for different people, of course. The rich and powerful could usually find a way to get the food they needed—by buying or seizing it. Ordinary families had to ration food, which brought painful decisions. All else equal, women survive food deprivation slightly better than men, but all else was often not equal within families. In most cultures, parents preferred to feed boys over girls when they could not feed everyone.

In Africa and China, where the prestige of the elderly was high, grandparents might eat more and younger people less when there was not enough for everyone. Babies and toddlers were often the first to suffer malnutrition. Parents knew that their older children were more valuable, not only because they were already more useful around the home but also because they were likelier to survive. So if families faced the cruel choice of feeding only some children, it made sense to feed the older ones.

Malnourished people suffered more from diseases because a consistently poor diet had weakened their immune systems. So, in the biological old regime, disease and hunger often went hand-in-hand, and death was front and center in life.

IMPROVING GLOBAL HEALTH

After 1750 or so, health started to improve and life spans lengthened. To understand how this happened, let's first review the facts on the macro scale, beginning with global population. As the table below shows, global population grew just about everywhere after 1650. The increase started slowly at less than 0.1 percent per year; but by 1750 in some places, such as China, it had gathered pace. Between 1850 and 1950, global population doubled, meaning it had achieved an annual growth rate of 0.7 percent.

DECLINING MORTALITY Global population was increasing because people lived longer as death rates fell. The largest component of the drop in death rates was declining infant and child mortality. Crisis mortality (from famines or epidemics) also fell sharply, although this happy trend contributed less to the bigger demographic picture. A still smaller reason behind the overall trend was that fertility rates in some places increased a bit, mainly because people married a year or two younger.

Overall mortality, and especially infant and child mortality, fell in part because of better nutrition. That improvement came to some degree from the Columbian Exchange, in which people brought crops from one continent to another. Potatoes in northern Europe, maize in Atlantic Africa, and wheat in Canada or Argentina: each of these introduced crops, well suited to their new locations, raised farming output. Refined techniques, such as the adoption of crop rotations that restored nitrogen to soils, boosted farm yields in western Europe and elsewhere. Moreover, the worst of the Little Ice Age had passed by 1750, so bad weather brought killer famines less often. Last, the distribution of food improved in many places, thanks to better transport networks and in Qing China to government policies. The Qing maintained state granaries, which absorbed roughly 5 percent of their empire's annual harvest. These enabled the government to distribute grain wherever it might be needed. All these developments helped to check the ravages of hunger and reduce the frequency of starvation after 1750.

The death toll from disease began to fall after about 1730. Better nutrition and healthier immune systems contributed to this outcome, but a larger factor was an accidental by-product of the microbial unification of the world, an effect of the interactions in the Global web. After a few centuries of more frequent contact among the various parts of the world (ca. 1500–1750), pathogens had gotten pretty much everywhere they could easily go and had become endemic just about everywhere they could. As a result, big epidemics—and crisis mortality—gradually became less common. In northern Europe, for example, between 1680 and 1780 mortality crises almost disappeared—a big change in what people could expect in life. Plague disappeared from Europe, making its final appearance in Russia in the 1770s. Other diseases that formerly had killed adults and children alike as epidemics

ESTIMATED WORLD POPULATION, 1650–1950

YEAR	GLOBAL POPULATION	URBAN POPULATION	PERCENTAGE OF GLOBAL POPULATION IN EURASIA	PERCENTAGE IN AFRICA	PERCENTAGE IN AMERICAS	LIFE EXPECTANCY AT BIRTH (GLOBAL AVERAGE IN YEARS)
1650	630 million	15 million	80%	16%	1–2%	[no data]
1750	770 million	20 million	83%	13%	2–3%	approx. 27
1850	1.2 billion	100 million	84%	8%	5%	[no data]
1950	2.5 billion	800 million	77%	9%	13%	approx. 45

Smallpox Inoculation Chinese doctors pioneered a technique for inoculating patients against smallpox from the sixteenth century. They used a needle to expose patients to a small sample of a smallpox scab, as illustrated in this undated Chinese print.

Jenner's Smallpox Vaccine European anti-vaccination sentiment is evident in this British cartoon from 1802, which found absurd the notion that anything found in cattle could give patients immunity to a human disease.

became endemic and only killed small children. The average life got a little healthier and longer.

CONTROL OF SMALLPOX Some of the reduced burden of disease was not accidental but the result of conscious efforts such as **smallpox inoculation**: deliberately putting a tiny bit of infected scab into a cut or scratch on the skin. In most cases, inoculation brought on a mild case of smallpox yet conferred lifetime immunity. In about 2 percent of cases, inoculation proved fatal; but those odds easily beat taking one's chances with the disease. The earliest good evidence for inoculation comes from sixteenth-century China. In the late seventeenth century, one of the Qing rulers, the Kangxi emperor, began to require inoculation against smallpox in the imperial lineage. When inoculation became routine in the imperial families, infant and child mortality fell from about 40 percent (before 1740) to about 10 percent (by 1830). Smallpox inoculation grew in popularity among ordinary people too, helping to account for the doubling of the Qing Empire's population between about 1720 and 1820.

By the mid-eighteenth century, many people in Eurasia and Africa had learned about inoculation. It was practiced in Mughal India and the Ottoman Empire, although to what extent is unclear. Some Africans inoculated against smallpox too. In early eighteenth-century Boston, an enslaved African named Onesimus explained to his legal owner, the prominent Puritan preacher Cotton Mather, that he had undergone inoculation and that many Africans did so. In Mather's version of Onesimus's words, "People take Juice of Small-Pox; and Cutty-skin, and Putt in a Drop." By 1800, smallpox inoculation of babies helped to lengthen lives, reduce mortality, and raise population in many lands. The interconnectedness

of the world after 1500 helped smallpox inoculation to spread widely.

After 1796, an even better method of smallpox control came to light. In that year an English dairymaid, Sarah Nelmes, consulted a country doctor, Edward Jenner, about a rash on her hands. Jenner, a university graduate trained in medicine, thought she had cowpox, a mild cattle disease. He had heard that people who milked cows rarely got smallpox, and Sarah Nelmes's hands gave him the opportunity to conduct an experiment. He scraped pus from her rash and put a drop into two scratches he made on an eight-year-old boy. The boy felt poorly for a couple of days, then recovered quickly. Jenner, himself a smallpox survivor, next infected the boy with smallpox and exulted when no symptoms appeared. Jenner repeated the experiment on others and then in 1798 published an account of his work. Today, Jenner's medical ethics would earn a prison sentence, but the British government in 1802 awarded him a princely sum for his experiment.

Jenner's experiment gave rise to the first vaccination programs in history. Vaccination, using cowpox virus, was less risky than inoculation, which used real smallpox virus. In 1853, Britain made vaccination against smallpox mandatory for all children.

The spread of inoculation and then vaccination spelled the beginning of the end for the smallpox virus, the greatest killer of human beings ever known. The growing interconnectedness of the Global web spread vaccination around the world faster than inoculation had done. In the Spanish Empire between 1802 and 1805—only a few years

Why Do Humans Live So Long?

Three hundred years ago, average human life expectancy around the world was 25 to 30 years, similar to that of our closest cousins, chimpanzees. It was the same 3,000 years ago and 30,000 years ago. But over the last 300 years, something unprecedented happened in human history and probably in the history of life on Earth. Our lives—on average—got longer, slowly at first, but amazingly fast after 1920 or so. Global human life expectancy now is 73 years.

How can we account for this startling change? Demographic, medical, and agricultural historians disagree, but some patterns are clear. A huge part of modern longevity, maybe half of it, comes from the reduction in child mortality, which is defined as death before age five. In the bad old days, nearly half of all deaths were among children under age five. By 1990, that had fallen to one-quarter, and today it is 10 percent.

More reliable food supplies played a big role in boosting longevity from the eighteenth century onward. Today, killing famine strikes far less often than centuries ago, mainly because of higher farm yields and better food transport and storage. Improved sanitation helped after about 1880, slashing the toll from water-borne diseases such as typhoid, especially in cities. Medical care improved beginning around the same time, and it improved dramatically after the introduction of antibiotics in the 1930s. Vaccination checked many viral infections, most important being the eradication of smallpox by 1980. It also seems that violent death—from warfare, murder, and accident—is a smaller risk today than in centuries past, although that has had a much weaker effect on longevity than disease control and changes in nutrition. Nowadays heart disease, stroke, and cancer are major killers. Three centuries ago, far fewer people lived long enough to suffer these diseases.

How long might the trend continue? On average, Japanese people live 12 years longer than the global average, so there is still room for improvement. But we are unlikely ever to match Greenland sharks and bowhead whales, each of which has a life expectancy of around 200 years.

QUESTIONS FOR DISCUSSION

1. How might family life, especially relationships between parents and children, have been different in a world in which nearly half of all children died before age five?
2. What major differences would the jump in longevity have made in our lives, from planning for an education to health care?

---

after Jenner published his results—authorities established a vaccination program that saved millions of lives. The decline of smallpox between 1750 and 1900 played a large role in lengthening life expectancy and reducing the fear of disease in general. In 1978, smallpox was eradicated, the first such success in human history.

SANITATION REFORM Sanitary improvements after 1850 had a parallel effect to the spread of smallpox vaccination. In cities especially, clean water had always been scarce, and dirty water killed millions. By the second half of the nineteenth century, scientists and doctors in western Europe figured out the role of bacteria in many infections, developing what is sometimes called the **germ theory of disease**, and successfully lobbied for waterworks that carefully separated wastewater from drinking water. These measures were expensive, and public officials often resisted on the grounds of cost. But the results, in the form of reduced death and illness from typhoid and cholera between 1880 and 1930, were so spectacular that the news spread almost everywhere. Chicago, for example, lost 6 percent of its population to cholera in 1854 and suffered repeated typhoid epidemics in the 1880s. But by 1920, water-borne disease killed almost no one in Chicago. Just about every city in western Europe, the United States, Canada, and Japan paid the price for cleaner water in money so as no longer to pay the price of dirty water in lives.

Sanitation reform did not spread uniformly. Some cities continued to run the risks of water-borne disease, partly for reasons of cost. Cities without access to banks and lenders simply could not pay for waterworks. In addition, many people did not subscribe to the novel germ theory of disease, without which there is no obvious logic

Sanitation Reform An 1880 diagram illustrates a design for an elaborate new water supply and waste management system under the streets of Paris. By increasing access to fresh drinking water and separating fresh water from wastewater, it dramatically reduced deaths from water-borne illnesses.

pandemics—worldwide epidemics—which now spread faster and farther than ever before.

CHOLERA Cholera escaped South Asia in 1817. It is a bacterium, transmitted from person to person via contaminated water or, more rarely, food. Untreated, it can kill half of those who contract it. Its course is swift, with only a few hours between first symptoms and death. This speed, combined with gruesome symptoms, inspired particular dread. People fled at the rumor of cholera. Authorities put up quarantines, forbidding entry into cities or countries, when they suspected cholera among travelers. But in 1817 cholera made it to Russia and in 1820 to southern China and Java. In the following decades it traveled all over the world, killing tens of millions and hitting cities especially hard.

to paying for sanitary measures and waterworks. So the spread of effective sanitation around the world took more than a century—and indeed is still incomplete.

The control of smallpox and the emergence of sanitation were the most important steps in checking the ravages of disease between 1750 and 1950. But there were many more. The germ theory opened the door to research on the specific organisms—pathogens—behind infections. Medical research and public health programs after 1890 led to successes in reducing the impact of tuberculosis, yellow fever, polio, and several other killers (1885–1960). All these developments saved lives, improved health, and set the stage for a golden age of health and longevity after 1950—a subject for a later chapter.

COUNTER-TRENDS: CHOLERA AND THE 1918 FLU

Two great exceptions bucked this happy trend. One was the globalization of cholera after 1817, and the other was the great influenza pandemic of 1918. Both show how the tightening of the Global web brought hardships as well as benefits in health. That tightening converted many infections into endemic, childhood diseases through the microbial unification of the world, which on balance was an improvement for humankind. But it also unleashed searing

Cholera Epidemics An 1883 illustration from a British newspaper shows inhabitants fleeing a Cairo neighborhood during a cholera outbreak. Fear of the disease was such that even news of an outbreak was enough to inspire unrest.

Faster and more frequent travel changed cholera from a local to a global scourge. It was an occasional companion of South Asian Muslims making the annual *hajj* in the nineteenth century; in 1863, it killed 30,000 pilgrims in Mecca. Once British soldiers took control of parts of India in the 1760s, they carried cholera to ports around the British Empire. For example, Quebec City, in British Canada, suffered frequent cholera epidemics between 1832 and 1854 generally brought by soldiers and sailors re-located from India. After 1850, cholera gradually came under control wherever efficient sanitation was practiced. But elsewhere its destruction continued, claiming 270,000 in Russia in 1892 and 200,000 in the Philippines in the years 1902–1904. By 1925, however, public health authorities and sanitation infrastructure had cholera in check. At the same time that faster transport was spreading cholera to all inhabited continents, better water sanitation—wherever such expensive investments were made—was stopping its ravages.

INFLUENZA Influenza was harder to control. It is a virus, or a series of viruses, in circulation among pigs, birds, humans, and a few other species. It spreads via coughs, sneezes, and contact. Usually, the flu was an inconvenience and killed well under 0.1 percent of those who contracted it. But it mutates quickly, and from time to time produces a new and deadly strain. This is what happened in 1918.

In late 1917 a new strain evolved somewhere, perhaps on the farms of the American Midwest, perhaps in China, perhaps near the battlefields of World War I in western Europe—there is as yet no clear evidence for its origin. Unlike most forms of the flu, the **1918 flu pandemic** was most severe among people in the prime of life. It killed primarily people between ages 15 and 40, and so it was especially dangerous in communities such as universities and armies. Pregnant women were the most vulnerable of all.

When millions of soldiers dispersed in late 1918 at the end of World War I, they carried the flu all over the world. About 500 million people suffered from it, and 50 to 100 million died—roughly 3 to 6 percent of the global population. In India alone it killed about 15 million, about 5 percent of the total population. On some Pacific islands, it killed 10 percent or more. In Samoa, for example, it killed 22 percent of the population within two months. It killed a little under 1 percent of the people in the United States (some 675,000) and Canada (50,000). Japan imposed rigorous quarantines and kept mortality to 390,000 (about 0.7 percent of the population). After peaking in late 1918, the flu died out within months for reasons that remain unclear.

Cholera outbreaks and the 1918 flu pandemic were deadly exceptions to the general rule. They were both diseases of globalization in the sense that improved transport and stronger interconnections eased their spread. But the stronger trend was the Vital Revolution, in which mortality fell and lives lengthened. The Vital Revolution, too, spread around the world, through the Global web's circuits of information about crops, inoculation, vaccination, sanitation, and other practices that either improved nutrition or limited the toll of infectious diseases. That is the main reason why people on average now live nearly three times as long as their ancestors did before 1800.

THE ABOLITIONS OF SLAVERY AND SERFDOM

Forced labor is an old human tradition. Legal codes designating some people as the property of others go back to ancient Mesopotamia. The Greek philosopher Aristotle thought that some people are by nature slaves and others free. Ibn Sina (Avicenna), the great physician and philosopher of eleventh-century Persia, held a similar

Influenza in 1918 Volunteer nurses tend invalids in a makeshift flu ward at a concert hall in Oakland, California, in 1918. So many people worldwide contracted the illness that it was not possible to care for them in standard medical facilities.

view, extolling the wisdom of God (Allah) who had "placed, in regions of great heat or great cold, peoples who were by their very nature slaves, and incapable of higher things—for there must be masters and slaves." The English philosopher-statesman Thomas More, imagining the ideal society in his novel *Utopia* (published in 1515), depicted each family with two slaves. Slavery and other forms of bondage were widespread until 250 years ago, and few people viewed slavery as immoral or unnatural. Strange as it may seem today, many former slaves worked on slaving ships transporting fellow Africans to plantations in the Americas. In the Caribbean, many former slaves owned slaves themselves. In Russia, serfs who had escaped to freedom sometimes bought serfs. In some societies, forced labor was rare. In others, including those in Korea, Southeast Asia, Central Asia, the Ottoman lands, Russia, West Africa, Brazil, the Caribbean, and the United States, among many others, slavery or other forms of unfree labor were common.

In some places, slavery was a racial institution. In the Americas after 1492, slaves were almost all of African or Amerindian descent, or at least partly so, and slaveholders usually of European descent. There were also many free blacks in Brazil, the Caribbean, and the United States, but they were often subject to discriminations derived from prevailing concepts connecting race and slavery. A similar racial outlook had taken hold even earlier in North Africa and Southwest Asia. As we've seen, Arabs imported slaves from sub-Saharan Africa and came to associate black skin with slavery, notwithstanding the presence in these lands of slaves imported from southern and eastern Europe. But elsewhere slavery and other forced labor regimes had little or nothing to do with concepts of race. In Russia, both masters and serfs were normally Russian. In Korea, both slaves and masters were Korean. And in sub-Saharan Africa, slaves and slave owners were equally African.

Masters and slaves in Africa and Asia often came from different ethnic or religious groups. In Central Asia, slave owners were generally Muslims and speakers of Turkic languages, while many if not most slaves were Hindus from India. In China, slaves often came from Muslim groups in Central Asia or from Vietnam. In maritime Southeast Asia, slaves were usually taken on one island and sold on another, so masters and slaves often differed in language or religion. In nineteenth-century Ethiopia, Christians generally enslaved Muslim war captives, and Muslims typically enslaved Christians. These differences—in ethnicity, language, religion, or race—helped slave owners and their supporters to believe that slavery was part of the natural order of things. But in Russia and Korea, where such differences between master and serf or slave did not exist, the commitment of both society and state to forced labor was no weaker.

Unfree labor and its abolition bore a complex relationship to the processes of globalization and industrialization. Recall that globalization both extended the ravages of some diseases and at the same time encouraged the spread of practices that led to longer and healthier lives—the Vital Revolution. A similar paradox exists with slavery: the Global web eased the spread of the trade in human beings, but then it also propelled ideas, information, attitudes, and practices that curtailed slavery. To make sense of the paradox, we need to zoom in.

THE EXPANSION OF SLAVERY AND FORCED LABOR, 1750–1850

Industrialization, as we saw in Chapter 22, quickened the demand for fibers, ores, and lubricants needed in factories. Clever entrepreneurs saw reward in expanding operations in the mines, forests, and plantations that produced cotton, copper, palm oil, and a hundred other raw

African Chattel Slavery There were 4 million enslaved people of African descent living in the states of the American South before the U.S. Civil War. A mid-nineteenth-century photograph shows enslaved men, women, and children picking cotton on a plantation.

materials. To do so they usually needed more labor, which they sometimes hired for wages and in other cases bought in the form of slaves. During the first roughly 75 years of industrialization, until about 1850, market-savvy land-owners and businessmen had strong incentives to deepen their reliance on forced labor.

THE AMERICAS In the American South, between 1800 and 1860 the slave population quintupled to 4 million. This was the largest enslaved population in any single polity in modern world history, although much smaller than that of the Roman Empire. Slaves accounted for about 12 percent of the U.S. population in 1860, and for about 45 percent in the South. While slaves worked in many different trades, the biggest reason for the expansion of U.S. slavery lay in the growing appetite for raw cotton in the textile mills of New England and Britain. Slave labor also underpinned the production of tobacco in Virginia and Maryland, rice in South Carolina and Georgia, and sugar in Louisiana. But cotton, grown from Georgia to Texas, stood at the heart of the slave economy of the United States.

Elsewhere in the Americas, a similar expansion of slavery took place after 1780. Sugar, tobacco, cotton, and coffee were the main plantation crops in the Caribbean and Brazil. As we saw in Chapter 21, the French colony of St. Domingue had nearly half a million slaves in 1790. The British Caribbean colonies—Jamaica, Barbados, and several others—by 1830 had 1.5 million slaves. In Cuba, the enslaved population grew from 30,000 to 290,000 between 1750 and 1870. In 1840, more than 2.5 million Brazilians, about 20 percent of the total population, were slaves. As in the United States, they were almost all African or of at least partially African descent. They worked in every sphere from whaling to mining and on plantations. They also worked in cities—cooking, washing clothes, laying bricks, tanning leather, and at other tasks, many of them dirty or dangerous. In contrast to the United States, where the sex ratio in the slave population was about even by the nineteenth century, it remained primarily male in the Caribbean and Brazil, where imports rather than natural increase accounted for growth, and slave purchasers selected males specifically for plantation work.

OTHER REGIONS The eighteenth- and nineteenth-century expansion of forced labor was no less remarkable outside the Americas. In Southeast Asia, growers of sugar,

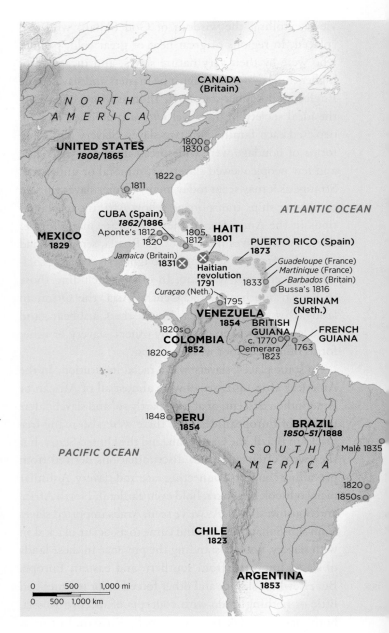

peppers, and other goods used slave labor on an expanding scale, contributing to a boom in slave raiding and slave trading in the islands of Indonesia between 1770 and 1840. Slavery surged on several Indian Ocean islands, such as Mauritius and Réunion, where after 1780 French planters increasingly bought slaves from East Africa for newly created sugar and cotton plantations. Unfree labor, long commonplace in Africa, expanded after 1780 as powerful men took advantage of new opportunities, first in South Africa and then, by 1850 or so, in West and East Africa too. In both latter regions, new plantation economies emerged

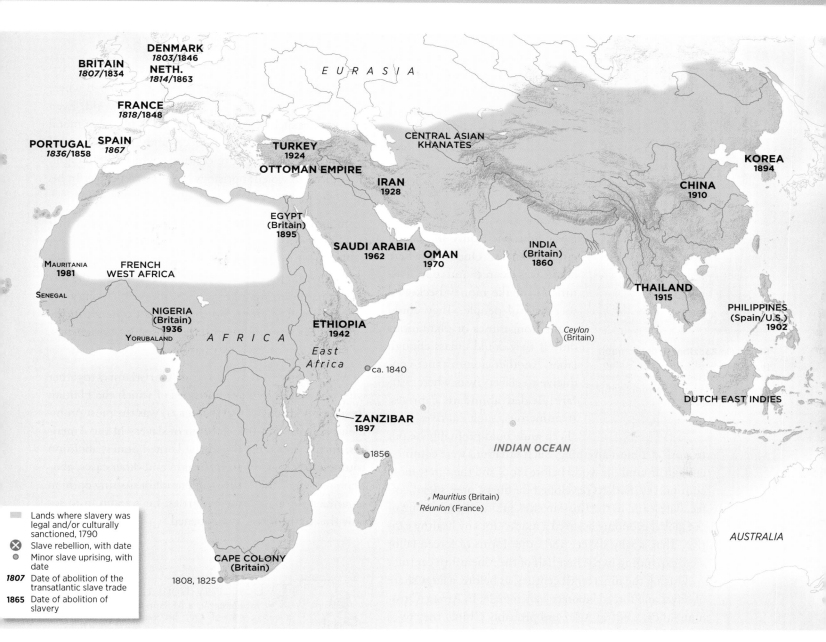

Resistance to Slavery and Abolition of Slavery, ca. 1750–1950 Slavery was legal and commonplace across much of the world in 1750. In the Atlantic world, slave uprisings became more frequent after the rebellion in Haiti (1791–1804), weakening the support for slavery in Europe and the Americas. Beginning with Denmark in 1803, the European nations whose merchants—together with those of Brazil, Cuba, and the United States—conducted the transatlantic slave trade, made it illegal. The abolition of legal slavery began soon after in the Atlantic world and was complete by 1888. Partly through pressures applied by Britain, legal slavery was abolished throughout Asia and Africa later in the nineteenth and twentieth centuries.

using slave labor, notably for palm oil in the Niger delta and cloves in Zanzibar. On the Arabian shores of the Persian Gulf as well, slavery increased sharply after 1820. Here the rise of export industries of dried dates and pearls led to heightened demand for slaves, most of whom came from East Africa on ships owned by merchants based in Oman or Zanzibar. Egypt, which turned to cotton production

increasingly after 1805, experienced an upsurge in slavery too; its slave imports peaked in the 1870s. Precise numbers are lacking for Southeast Asia, the Indian Ocean islands, and Africa, but a reasonable guess is that among them the enslaved population reached 10 to 15 million as of 1850.

Slavery or bonded labor as a legal category and common practice existed elsewhere in the nineteenth century

Slavery in Zanzibar A photograph of an enslaved boy in the Sultanate of Zanzibar ca. 1890. Potent images such as this furthered the cause of abolition.

too—in Central Asian khanates, the Ottoman Empire, India, and on a modest scale in China and Korea. In the Russian Empire, the numbers of serfs also increased as a result of population growth. As we shall see, Russia's forced laborers numbered about 50 million in 1860, some 70 percent of the total population.

By and large, slavery and forced labor flourished only in certain circumstances. One was where labor was scarce and opportunities to make money beckoned to powerful people. They could profit from mines or plantations only if they could amass enough labor. Another circumstance conducive to slavery was where warfare yielded abundant captives. If numerous, such captives were cheap and could profitably be put to work at almost anything. Such situations were common enough around the world before 1800, and they grew more common as markets developed for fibers, ores, sugar, coffee, dates, and in the Russian case, grain. The evolution of the global economy ensured a market for any healthy captive. That is why slavery and other forms of forced labor were expanding in the first half of the nineteenth century.

During the nineteenth century, as before, a large share of slaves and forced laborers were female. In Africa, Ottoman lands, Central Asia, and probably China, they were the majority. Their labors included household chores such as cooking, cleaning, and caring for children, as well as spinning and other textile work. And, as was typically the case for women slaves and serfs throughout history, their duties often included sex with their masters.

Even as slavery, serfdom, and forced labor expanded around the world between 1750 and 1850, they came under attack as never before. In retrospect, this may seem inevitable, normal, and proper. But at the time it was extraordinary. A practice that had seemed to almost everyone for millennia moral, appropriate, and sanctioned by religious and political authority almost overnight became increasingly seen as immoral, impractical, and contrary to divine will. How did this happen?

ABOLITION OF THE SLAVE TRADE IN THE ATLANTIC WORLD

Systematic moral objections to slavery originated where the practice was strongest, in the Atlantic world. Even slave owners such as Thomas Jefferson could harbor moral objections to slavery. He most certainly feared the consequences of allowing it to continue, which, he thought, might lead to violent uprisings by enslaved people. In his *Notes on the State of Virginia* (1785), he wrote:

> Indeed I tremble for my country when I reflect that God is just: that his justice cannot sleep for ever.... The spirit of the master is abating, that of the slave rising from the dust, his condition mollifying, the way I hope preparing, under the auspices of heaven, for a total emancipation, and that this is disposed, in the order of events, to be with the consent of the masters, rather than by their extirpation.

Moral objections anchored in Christianity, together with fear stirred by slave uprisings of which the Haitian Revolution (discussed in Chapter 21) was the most prominent, help explain the abolition of slavery in the Americas. In two cases, Haiti and the United States, abolition triumphed through war. In Britain and other cases, abolition prevailed politically—as a result of shifting opinion organized through political parties. Let's zoom in to see how this transformation happened.

RUN away from the subscriber in *Albemarle*, a Mulatto slave called *Sandy*, about 35 years of age, his stature is rather low, inclining to corpulence, and his complexion light; he is a shoemaker by trade, in which he uses his left hand principally, can do coarse carpenters work, and is something of a horse jockey; he is greatly addicted to drink, and when drunk is insolent and disorderly, in his conversation he swears much, and in his behaviour is artful and knavish. He took with him a white horse, much scarred with traces, of which it is expected he will endeavour to dispose; he also carried his shoemakers tools, and will probably endeavour to get employment that way. Whoever conveys the said slave to me, in *Albemarle*, shall have 40 s. reward, if taken up within the county, 4 l. if elsewhere within the colony, and 10 l. if in any other colony. from
THOMAS JEFFERSON.

American Slave Owners Many of the United States' founders owned large numbers of enslaved people despite their stated moral opposition to the institution of slavery. Thomas Jefferson, who owned over 600 enslaved people throughout his life, circulated this advertisement for a runaway slave in colonial Virginia.

The first movements for abolition came in lands where slavery was not central to society: the northern United States, Britain, and France. But in all three of those lands, profits from slavery and the transatlantic slave trade were economically significant and supported a segment of society with much to lose if slavery vanished. And in all three, information about the horrors of the slave trade and slavery was readily available by 1750. Antislavery activists in Britain and America, and to a lesser extent those in France and elsewhere, were regularly in touch with one another through correspondence, by reading one another's published writings, and occasionally in person. They were all familiar with the arguments against slavery voiced by thinkers of the Enlightenment, such as the Baron de Montesquieu, who extolled liberty and condemned slavery as bad both for slaves and for slave owners.

QUAKER OPPOSITION

The organized antislavery movement began among **Quakers**, a small Protestant sect originating in seventeenth-century England. Quakers defied social convention, avoided alcohol and fine clothes, refused military service, and were regarded as peculiar by everyone else. Many Quakers, like other religious minorities, were conspicuously successful in business. Before 1750, many of them in North America owned slaves and some were slave traders. But within the Quaker community religious and moral objection to slavery

emerged, first in Barbados in the 1670s, and more prominently in England and colonial America by the 1750s. Quakers regarded all warfare as immoral, and so trading or owning slaves captured in African wars ran contrary to their principles. Moreover, their interpretation of Christianity stressed humility, simplicity, and the fundamental equality of all human beings. This view of the moral duties of Quakers gradually won out among the Philadelphia chapter—by far the biggest in North America—which

Quaker Abolitionists John Woolman, shown here in an anonymous and undated portrait, was a Quaker abolitionist who in 1758 persuaded his fellow American Quakers to oppose slavery.

formally denounced slavery in 1758. Several Philadelphia Quakers visited London to convince their brethren of the Christian duty to end slave trading and slavery. By 1774, all Quaker meetings (as their communities are called) in Britain and North America had agreed that one could not both be a Quaker and also own slaves. In 1790, Quakers petitioned Congress—in vain—for an end to slavery throughout the United States.

BRITISH ABOLITION OF THE SLAVE TRADE

Quakers and their allies proved more effective in Britain. Although Britain had few slaves, it was deeply invested in slavery. British merchants ran the biggest slave trade in the world in the late eighteenth century. Britain's empire included Caribbean slave plantation colonies—Barbados, Jamaica, and others—exports from which were worth five times those of all British North American colonies combined in 1773. The Church of England owned slaves in the Caribbean. Adam Smith, author of *The Wealth of Nations*—a defense of free markets—lamented in 1763 that although wage labor would be more efficient, "the love of dominion and authority over others will probably make [slavery] perpetuall." Smith was wrong on both counts as regards the British Empire: slavery remained more efficient than wage labor until abolished, and it proved anything but perpetual.

CLARKSON AND WILBERFORCE

Quakers started the British antislavery movement. Barred from serving in Parliament because they were not Anglicans, to change any laws they needed allies and spokesmen from within the Anglican elite. They found one in **Thomas Clarkson**, who in 1785, as a 25-year-old fresh out of Cambridge University, entered a Latin essay contest with no loftier intention than winning a prize. But the contest's question was about the justice of slavery, and Clarkson, a good student, read everything he could find on the subject, won the prize, and in the process came to the conclusion that slavery was un-Christian. From the evangelical wing of the Anglican

British Abolitionism The abolitionist ceramics entrepreneur Josiah Wedgwood manufactured medallions bearing an image of a manacled enslaved man and the phrase "Am I Not a Man and a Brother?" This iconography became closely associated with the abolitionist cause in Britain and the United States.

Church himself, Clarkson became a tireless pamphleteer, researcher, and activist in the cause, sometimes risking his life on the docks of port towns to gather information about the British slave trade. Clarkson and friends, mostly Quakers and evangelicals, formed an abolitionist committee in 1787 and decided to focus their efforts on legal reform, in Parliament, and to target the slave trade first, leaving slavery itself for later.

Clarkson helped recruit a sitting member of Parliament to the cause in 1787. William Wilberforce was sickly and half blind, but rich and well connected. He also had attended Cambridge University, where he specialized in gambling and drinking before becoming an evangelical Christian. At Cambridge he became close friends with William Pitt, who in 1783—at age 24—had become prime minister. Wilberforce, the same age as Pitt and a year older than Clarkson, became the parliamentary voice of antislavery, denouncing the slave trade as contrary to God's will and a source of moral corruption. By some accounts, including Pitt's, he was the silkiest public speaker in Britain.

The movement organized by Clarkson, Wilberforce, and their colleagues took shape in the late 1780s. With zeal and stamina, they documented and publicized both the cruelties of the slave trade and the debauchery of slave traders and their crews.

CUGOANO AND EQUIANO Former slaves such as Ottobah Cugoano and Olaudah Equiano added their voices to the anti–slave trade movement at the same time. About a dozen of them formed the **Sons of Africa**, an abolitionist committee in London closely allied with that of Clarkson and Wilberforce. Cugoano had been born in West Africa, captured as a young teenager, and shipped to the British Caribbean, where he worked on a plantation for two years before a master brought him to England. While it is unclear whether or not Equiano was born in West Africa (as he wrote in his autobiography), he worked as an enslaved and later as a free man, traveling all over the Atlantic world as a sailor before

Olaudah Equiano A detail of the frontispiece of Olaudah Equiano's eighteenth-century account of his life. Equiano's antislavery activism as a freedman in the Atlantic world played an important role in rallying support for abolitionism.

settling in England. Both men wrote detailed accounts of their experiences, helping to convince readers of the moral depravity and injustice of slavery and especially the slave trade. Their descriptions of slave ordeals had an air of authenticity about them that the youthful, privileged, and white-skinned Wilberforce and Clarkson could never provide.

ACTION IN PARLIAMENT In 1787, both the antislavery and proslavery factions in Parliament held about 40 seats. They debated the humanity of Africans, whether slavery was supported in the Bible, and the economic value of the institution. Opponents of the slave trade published reams of moral argument and statistical data, distributed pamphlets, organized mass petitions to Parliament, and raised funds. They penned plays, novels, and especially poems against the slave trade. They presented more than 100 petitions against the slave trade to Parliament, signed by about 12 percent of Britain's population. They persuaded Pitt, as prime minister, to denounce the slave trade in Parliament. They pointed out that Denmark ended its slave trade in 1803. Within two decades they achieved a shift in public opinion against the slave trade. All this was necessary, but it was not enough: every attempt to pass a law banning the slave trade failed—until 1807.

Then Wilberforce, by now a veteran of 23 years of parliamentary intrigues, took advantage of changed political circumstances to press for abolition of the slave trade. A weak, coalition government that needed abolitionist votes took office in 1806. With the help of its topmost ministers, Wilberforce framed abolition of the slave trade as a patriotic measure that would hurt Napoleon Bonaparte's effort to re-establish profitable French Caribbean colonies after the Haitian Revolution. In 1807 he shepherded an abolition bill through Parliament, carrying the House of Commons by a vote of 283–16.

Banning the British slave trade was a dramatic beginning of the end for slavery. By this time in the Caribbean, except on Barbados, the slave population did not reproduce itself biologically, so without the transatlantic slave trade slavery could not long continue there. Wilberforce and his colleagues expected that with their legislative victory, slavery in the British realm would fade away.

OTHER SLAVE TRADE ABOLITIONS Other countries around the Atlantic soon followed the British example. The U.S. government made slave imports illegal in

1808, the first year permitted by the Constitution. That act carried different implications, however, because it did not endanger slavery in the United States. Slave populations in the United States since about 1730 had grown by natural increase (more births than deaths), which meant that slavery could persist there without the transatlantic slave trade. Indeed, as we saw above, the enslaved population expanded for 50 years after 1808 in the United States.

Nevertheless, the British abolition established a precedent. In the next 20 years, the Netherlands—a minor participant in the slave trade—and France both prohibited slave trading. Spain announced abolition of its slave trade in 1817 but did not enforce it until 1867. Britain began to use its navy, the world's largest, to intercept slave ships on the high seas and return captives to Africa, usually to Sierra Leone, a British colony established largely for this purpose. Some 100,000 Africans disembarked in Sierra Leone this way. The re-captives, as they were called, had come from all over Atlantic Africa, spoke dozens of different languages, and had to forge a new society in Sierra Leone. The tiny Haitian navy between 1811 and 1819 also captured three slave ships and liberated more than 800 people.

The strength of the slave markets in Cuba and Brazil kept the slave trade alive after 1830. Both markets still imported thousands of Africans annually—in Brazil's case, up to 60,000. A large share of these came from Yorubaland in West Africa, where frequent warfare during the decline of the Oyo Empire resulted in streams of captives sold into the Atlantic trade. This surge in the slave trade, however, helped lead to its demise.

The large and growing concentrations of Yoruba-speakers in both Cuba and Brazil led to an upsurge in slave revolts. One, in Cuba in 1812, was led by **José Aponte**, a Yoruba-speaking free black, an artist, and a former militia officer whose scrapbook, found by police, contained homages to both Toussaint L'Ouverture and George Washington. After 1825, Cuban elites increasingly questioned the slave trade, alarmed by the frequency of revolts. They also feared the introduction of epidemics from Africa, the "Africanization" of Cuba's population, and the patrols of the British Royal Navy. Spanish slavers and some Cuban planters resisted for a while, but Cuba's slave trade wound down in the 1850s and became illegal in 1867.

In Brazil, where the scale of the slave trade was much larger than in Cuba, it ended sooner, in the years 1850–1851. Uprisings averaged about one per year from 1810 to

Abolition of the Slave Trade British Royal Navy sailors are shown chasing and capturing a slaving ship off the coast of East Africa in this 1877 painting. After deciding to support the abolitionist cause, the British state began to actively combat the slave trade.

1830, and climaxed in the Malê revolt in 1835, involving some 600 slaves—mostly Yoruba speakers. Fear of further revolts played a role in shifting elite opinion. So did attacks on Brazilian and Portuguese slavers by the British Royal Navy. As in Cuba, intellectual and political elites gradually became convinced that the slave trade was bad business and banned it. Like Wilberforce, they anticipated that without the slave trade, slavery would die out.

ABOLITION OF SLAVERY IN THE ATLANTIC WORLD, TO 1832

The abolition of slavery in the Atlantic world, as opposed to the slave trade, came later and involved not only legislation but two major wars. The first of these, the Haitian Revolution of 1791–1804 (see Chapter 21), brought the first large-scale abolition of slavery and raised hopes for abolition throughout the Atlantic world. The second, the American Civil War (1861–1865), put an end to slavery in the largest slave society of the Atlantic—and made it clear to all that slavery's days were numbered.

Even before the Haitian Revolution, movements for the abolition of slavery met with some minor successes in the Atlantic world. Since 1606, it had been legal in Scotland for mine owners to hold miners—fellow Scots—in lifelong bondage. If they ran away, they were subject to "torture in the irons provided only for colliers and witches and notorious malefactors." But in 1775, Scotland banned enslavement of new recruits to the coal mines. In 1777, during the American Revolution, Vermont banned slavery, and Massachusetts did so in 1783. Other New England states followed suit. In 1780, Pennsylvania enacted a gradual abolition that finally brought slavery to an end in the state in 1847. These acts of abolition did not resonate loudly because none of these places had many slaves.

SLAVE UPRISINGS AND THEIR POLITICAL CONSEQUENCES St. Domingue, in contrast, had nearly half a million slaves when the Haitian Revolution erupted in 1791. Toussaint L'Ouverture, who had been both a slave and a slave owner himself, formally abolished slavery in 1801. The destruction of slavery in Haiti showed slaves throughout the Atlantic that they could conceivably free themselves. It convinced slave owners everywhere that they courted economic ruin and vengeful massacres if slavery ended through revolution rather than legal abolition. The Haitian Revolution, because of its scale and violence, resonated throughout the circuits of the Atlantic world, an inspiration to some and a terror to others.

While former slaves were ending slavery in Haiti, the revolutionary French government in Paris decided in 1794 to end the institution everywhere in the French Empire. French antislavery activism, a modest movement compared to that in Britain, had less to do with the 1794 abolition than did fears that the uprising in Haiti might spread to nearby French colonies such as Guadeloupe, Martinique, and French Guiana. But principle supported political calculation: slavery, after all, was clearly incompatible with the "rights of man" and other ideals of the French Revolution. The 1794 abolition, however, proved incomplete and fleeting. It was never implemented in Martinique, Senegal, or France's Indian Ocean colonies. And in 1802, Bonaparte reinstated slavery throughout the French Empire and would have restored it to Haiti had his army there not been defeated. He restored slavery, using force where necessary, to prevent French Caribbean planters from surrendering their islands to Britain, his archenemy, which they seemed ready to do in order to preserve slavery. And he did it to please his wife, Josephine, and her family, who were slave owners from Martinique.

Bonaparte could not stop the momentum of Atlantic abolition. The Haitian Revolution inspired slaves elsewhere to test their chains in a series of uprisings. In addition to the revolts in Cuba and Brazil—word of which

also ricocheted around the Atlantic—several broke out in British slave colonies. One took place in 1816 on Barbados, led by an enslaved African known as Bussa. A larger one occurred at Demerara, in British Guiana, a sugar colony, acquired from the Dutch in 1814. For a few days in 1823, some 10,000 slaves there resisted their masters, following the call to freedom issued by one **Jack Gladstone**. Gladstone and his father, an African-born slave named Quamina, had learned of discussions of emancipation in Britain. Both were literate and, as carpenters and coopers, relatively privileged slaves. Quamina was a deacon in the local church and by all accounts deeply pious. Jack Gladstone (his surname was that of his master, the father of a future British prime minister, William Gladstone) believed that legal abolition had already passed in London and that the Demerara planters were conspiring to hide the fact. This conviction lay behind his call to freedom and what was until then the largest slave revolt in the British Empire.

A still larger revolt caught fire in Jamaica in 1831, involving perhaps 60,000 slaves, one-fifth of Jamaica's total. It too was led by a slave preacher, Samuel Sharpe, a deacon in the Baptist church; thus the revolt is sometimes called the Baptist War. Sharpe's lieutenants were mainly from the slave elite—smiths, masons, coopers, and coachmen. They were all born in the West Indies. As at Demerara, rumors of emancipation swirled around Jamaica, leading to the false belief that London's Parliament had already voted for slavery's abolition. Sharpe called for a slave strike

Slave Revolts A lithograph shows a Jamaican plantation set on fire during the major slave revolt that Samuel Sharpe led in the British colony in the years 1831–1832.

during the sugar harvest season, which led to widespread burning of the crop. In sporadic violence, 14 whites and several hundred slaves were killed. Planters managed to suppress the rising with decisive help from maroons—former slaves who had escaped to Jamaica's mountains—and the Jamaica garrisons of the British Army.

The growing frequency and size of slave revolts in the British West Indies quickened the debate on abolition of slavery in Britain. The planter lobby wished to see the activities of missionaries curtailed, because rebel leaders in Demerara and Jamaica were educated Christians, schooled by missionaries. In Jamaica, proslavery factions attacked missionaries and burned several mission churches. The effect was to reduce political support for slavery within Britain. The fact that very few whites had been killed in these uprisings, unlike in Haiti, supported the argument of abolitionists that freed slaves would be capable of restraint and would not massacre their former tormentors. They were proved right.

ABOLITIONS OF ATLANTIC SLAVERY, 1833–1888

The first truly large legislated abolition of slavery came in the British Empire. The groups that had lobbied for abolition of the slave trade mostly disbanded after 1807. Few favored a swift end to slavery. Even Wilberforce in 1807 wrote that slaves were unready for freedom and "To grant it to them immediately, would be to insure not only their masters ruin but their own." Instead, Wilberforce and his circle thought slavemasters should improve conditions on plantations and provide Christian instruction to prepare for an eventual end to slavery, which in the absence of the slave trade time alone would bring.

Once again, events changed opinion. The Demerara revolt in 1823 in British Guiana created new support for the immediate abolition of British slavery. Over the next eight years, abolitionists, once again led by religious minorities such as Methodists, Congregationalists, Baptists, and Quakers, printed and circulated nearly 3 million antislavery tracts. They—Clarkson, Wilberforce, and a younger generation more inclined to push for immediate abolition—formed the Anti-Slavery Society in 1823 and beginning in 1825 sponsored a monthly periodical, *The Anti-Slavery Reporter*. They helped prepare and publish, in 1831, the autobiography of Mary Prince, born into slavery in Bermuda and sold several times in the British

Abolitionist Propaganda A 1791 cartoon illustrating one of William Wilberforce's antislavery speeches in Parliament brought to life some of the most gruesome horrors of slavery in the West Indies. It shows an overseer murdering an enslaved person in a vat of boiling sugar cane juice.

Caribbean. The book sold out three printings in its first year. In the years 1828–1830, some 5,000 petitions asked Parliament to end slavery. Over 98 percent of Britain's 233,000 Methodists signed at least one. News of the 1831–1832 slave revolt in Jamaica (the Baptist War) and the proslavery attacks on churches there strengthened support for immediate abolition. About 20 percent of Britain's entire adult male population signed the petitions of 1833. The petitions also included one that was half a mile long with the names of 350,000 women on it. Women could not vote in Britain, but they could sign petitions.

The antislavery faction in the House of Commons expanded when non-Anglicans became eligible to sit in Parliament in 1828. Two years later, an election brought to power the Whig Party, keen on reforms of many sorts, including abolition. In 1832, the Whigs succeeded in broadening the franchise to include some of the upper middle class, and then won a large majority in another election. They used the victory to pass the **Slavery Abolition Act**, which took effect in 1834. As with the abolition of Britain's slave trade in 1807, sustained agitation, a shift in public opinion pushed along by slave uprisings, and a political realignment in Parliament combined to bring about the legislation that ended slavery in the British Empire.

The terms of slavery's abolition included a large payment to slave owners by their government. Moreover, the abolition would be gradual. Until 1838, former slaves still owed services to their former masters, which left many former slaves disappointed. But as of 1838, all slaves in the

Frederick Douglass Douglass, who escaped slavery in Maryland, became one of the most influential advocates of abolition in the United States.

British West Indies, Mauritius, and British territories elsewhere (except India, Ceylon, and the tiny South Atlantic island of St. Helena) were free, a little under 1 million people. British India officially ended slavery in 1860.

Abolition within the British Empire inspired abolitionists elsewhere. In the northern United States, abolition gathered momentum in the 1830s, at the same time that slavery was growing entrenched in the cotton South. An antislavery society formed in 1833. Abolitionists such as William Lloyd Garrison offered moral, religious, and economic arguments in countless lectures, pamphlets, and editorials, drawing freely on the works of British abolitionists. Former slaves such as Frederick Douglass did the same, with the added weight of firsthand knowledge of slavery's grim realities as he had lived them in Maryland before his escape to freedom in 1838. The 1852 publication of Harriet Beecher Stowe's melodramatic novel *Uncle Tom's Cabin*, which sold more copies in the United States than any book other than the Bible, won sympathy for slaves—and support for abolition. The formation of the Republican Party in 1854 was motivated by opposition to the expansion of slavery into the western territories. Abolitionists and slave owners both realized that if freedom was the rule in the new states entering the union, then over time Congress would become more antislavery and abolition would prevail. The new party won the 1860 election, putting Abraham Lincoln in the White House without carrying any southern states. Abolitionism in the United States proved influential enough to threaten restrictions on slavery that seemed, to slaveholders and their supporters, dangerous to the institution and their prosperity.

In the end, it required an all-consuming war between North and South to end slavery in the United States. When 11 southern states seceded in the wake of Lincoln's election, the president resolved to go to war to keep the union intact. In the Civil War (1861–1865), the North enjoyed a preponderance of resources and military manpower, and after four years of grinding combat, prevailed. Meanwhile, hundreds of thousands of slaves ran off either to the North or to the Union Army encampments, in effect liberating themselves. Lincoln in 1863 issued the Emancipation Proclamation, a military order that declared slaves in rebel-held territory free. Complete abolition came only with the war's conclusion and the **Thirteenth Amendment** to the Constitution, both in 1865. Altogether, some 600,000 soldiers died in the Civil War, liberating 4 million people—the single largest slave emancipation in world history.

The end was now near for Atlantic slavery, which remained mainly in some Caribbean sugar islands and Brazil. The success of beet sugar—5 percent of the world's sugar market in 1840 and 50 percent in 1880—weakened sugarcane planters everywhere by cutting their sales. Dutch Caribbean colonies—Surinam and Curaçao the largest—abolished slavery in 1863. An abolition society formed in 1858 in Puerto Rico, still a Spanish colony. An uprising there in 1868 included abolition among its goals. Shifts in Spanish politics led to the abolition of slavery in Puerto Rico in 1873, freeing 30,000 people over the next three years. Cuba, which had some 370,000 slaves (27 percent of the island's population), did the same in 1886, ending the long history of slavery in the Spanish Empire.

Brazil was the second-largest slave society in the Americas after the United States. By 1800, slaves worked in many economic sectors, including mines, manufacturing, and domestic services as well as on plantations. So a broad coalition of slave owners defended slavery. But by 1850, rapid immigration of poor Europeans was making wage labor increasingly practical for slave owners. It made business sense to manumit (grant freedom to) their slaves, especially the old, sick, or injured, and to hire labor instead. So by the 1880s they put up little resistance to abolition, which finally arrived in Brazil in 1888, freeing about 1.7 million slaves, or 17 percent of the overall population.

ABOLITIONS OF SLAVERY BEYOND THE ATLANTIC

The Atlantic world by the late eighteenth century was by headcount the world capital of slavery and slaving, but it was not the only region where bonded labor, after prevailing for centuries, now came under assault. Abolitionism went global, an example of an idea spreading around the web, crossing cultures, and effecting changes on every continent.

In many cases, the abolition of slavery struck local elites as desirable, even necessary, to make their countries modern and competitive. The example of abolition by Britain, the world's most powerful country by 1850, was highly influential. In cases such as Cuba and Brazil, the rapid growth of population, which reduced labor shortages and thereby undercut the economic logic of slavery, swayed elites. With enough potential laborers, wages would be low enough to keep mines and plantations profitable. In this way, the trends of the Vital Revolution, outlined in the first section of this chapter, helped to advance the cause of abolition.

Slavery was abolished on the Pacific coasts of Spanish America beginning in newly independent Chile, which had very few slaves, in 1823. Peru, where African slavery had been important in mining and agriculture for more than two centuries, enacted abolition in 1854. France re-abolished slavery in its empire in 1848, within weeks after a revolution overthrew a monarchy and established a republic led by reformers hostile to slavery. Some 250,000 people in the Caribbean, Senegal, and the Indian Ocean sugar islands gained their freedom, but not all instantly. As in the British and Dutch cases, liberation in the French Empire came gradually, and some legal labor obligations to former masters remained in effect for a few years. In East Asia, Korea—where slavery had once been a major institution—joined the trend in 1894. China, where slavery had existed for many centuries but was never important, officially abolished it in 1910. Thailand did so in 1915.

In the Ottoman Empire, slavery had long been a crucial social institution. The status of slave is recognized in the Qu'ran and Islamic law, which stipulates that slave status cannot be inherited and Muslims cannot be enslaved. Outside pressure made a difference here. After about 1850, Britain in particular used its influence to induce the Ottoman sultans to restrict the import of slaves, most of whom were women—concubines, servants, or textile workers. The Royal Navy intercepted slave ships sailing from East Africa, reducing slave imports and slave populations in Ottoman lands. The Ottoman sultans could not, however, formally abolish slavery. As caliphs—successors to the Prophet Muhammad—they had the duty to prevent revisions to the divine word of Allah. After the fall of the Ottoman Empire, the Turkish Republic formally banned slavery in 1924. In Iran, rulers responding to British pressure abolished slavery in 1928.

In Africa, European pressure was even more direct. African slavery had expanded notably after 1850: British suppression of the Atlantic slave trade lowered slave prices within Africa, as we've seen, and made it economically attractive to African entrepreneurs to create new plantations, raising peanuts, cloves, or palm oil using slave labor. In the West African Sahel, a series of wars launched by Muslim reformers, who felt that African rulers did not fully abide by the rules of Islam, generated streams of captives. The enslavement of many thousands of these captives, in places such as what is now northern Nigeria, raised the slave proportion of the total population to a third or a half. By some estimates, after 1850 there were more slaves in Africa than in all the Americas, which then had about 7 to 8 million.

In the next few decades, as we shall see in Chapter 24, almost all of Africa fell under European colonial rule. Christian missionaries flocked in and, as in the British West Indies early in the nineteenth century, began to agitate against the evils of slavery and slave trades. This agitation normally struck African elites as unwelcome, presumptuous, and culturally ignorant. For them, as for so many people for so long, slavery was normal and

Ottoman Slavery This engraving by a British artist depicts a nineteenth-century Ottoman domestic scene with several domestic workers and concubines who were likely to have been enslaved.

CONSIDERING THE EVIDENCE

Demanding Freedom and Dignity in West Africa

After abolition, enslaved men and women often had to take the initiative to demand their freedom. For example, Abina Mansah gained her freedom by leaving the household where she was enslaved in the Gold Coast Protectorate of Great Britain (now part of Ghana). She had been captured as a young girl during a war between her people and the Asante kingdom. A few years later, a man named Yowahwah bought her to be his wife. When they visited the Gold Coast together on business in 1876, Yowahwah secretly sold her to a man named Quamina Eddoo. Abina only became aware that she had been sold after Eddoo demanded that she marry one of his other dependents. This deception and disregard for her dignity as a married woman convinced her to flee and seek assistance from British colonial courts. Leaving Eddoo's household freed her from those who treated her as a slave; but she also decided to press charges against Eddoo for purchasing her. The trial transcript reveals what slavery and freedom meant to her and other enslaved women in West Africa as they asserted their new status after abolition.

Yowahwah brought me [to Gold Coast] from [Asante]. I was his wife.... [H]e handed me over to [be with Eddoo], and said that he was going back and would return.

About ten days after, [Eddoo] gave me two cloths and told me that he had given me in marriage to one of his house people.... I asked him how ... he had given me in marriage to one of his people. On this I thought that I had been sold and I ran away.... The defendant [Eddoo] said that if I did not consent to be married ... he would tie me up and flog me. ... If the defendant had not given me in marriage, I could not have formed any idea that he had purchased me.... I thought I was a slave, because when I went for water or firewood I was not paid.

. . .

I did not know that I was free.... I heard that [the colonial government] had said we were all free. Yet I had been sold and I had no will of my own and I could not look after my body and health: that I am a slave and I would therefore come and complain.

. . .

If [Eddoo's sister] said to me "go for firewood" and I said "I won't go," she said "If you don't you will be tied and flogged," and I said "Now all are free. I also am free. I claim freedom." That was why I ran away.... [Eddoo's sister said:] "You are your master's slave." [W]hen she said this I sat down and said I did not like this and I made up my mind to come away.

Source: Trevor Getz, *Abina and the Important Men*, 2nd ed. (Oxford, England, 2015).

QUESTIONS FOR ANALYSIS

1. What are the different reasons Abina Mansah gives for why she ran away?
2. Why did Abina equate freedom with the ability to "look after my body and health"?
3. How did people who had been enslaved assert their dignity, despite the servile status that slaveholders and others forced upon them?

---

natural. In the early decades of colonialism in Africa, European authorities often went along with slavery, even if they did not like it and missionaries hated it. In most parts of the continent, they could only rule with the help of Africa's slave-owning elites, and the continuation of slavery was one of the prices they were willing to pay for that cooperation. Moreover, colonial authorities often judged that slavery within Africa was not so oppressive—an argument advanced by African slave traders and slave owners themselves. In any case, the authorities made an uneasy truce with slavery for a while.

Enslaved Africans, however, often took a different view. Many sought to liberate themselves by running away, often to Christian missions. In the 1890s, this movement became a torrent in West Africa. Their escapes, in some respects parallel to the actions of southern slaves fleeing to Union Army camps during the American Civil War, weakened the elites on whom colonial authorities intended to rely. So, making a calculated decision that went hand-in-hand with their moral views, both British and French colonial rulers changed their allegiances and began to support former slaves, especially those who

FORMAL ABOLITIONS OF SLAVERY

JURISDICTION	DATE
Vermont	1777
Massachusetts	1783
Chile	1823
New York	1827
Mexico	1829
British Empire	1834
Danish West Indies	1846
French Empire	1848
Colombia	1852
Argentina	1853
Peru	1854
Venezuela	1854
Portuguese Empire	1858
Dutch Empire	1863
United States	1865
Cuba	1886
Brazil	1888
Korea	1894
Zanzibar	1897
China	1910
Thailand	1915
Iran	1928
Northern Nigeria	1936
Ethiopia	1942
Saudi Arabia	1962
Mauritania	1981

Note: These represent final, formal abolitions. In some cases, such as the French Empire, slavery was abolished, reinstated, and abolished again. In many cases, abolition was a drawn-out process involving gradual steps.

abolished it again in 1981. The table at left indicates the date of legal abolition in 26 jurisdictions around the world.

The largest abolition took place in the United States, freeing 4 million slaves. The next largest was Ethiopia and then either northern Nigeria or Brazil—the numbers are too unreliable to be sure. In total, the many acts of abolition of slavery freed about 15 to 25 million people.

ABOLITION OF SERFDOM

The largest of all labor liberations took place in Russia. In 1861 and the years following, the Russian state freed 23 million serfs held by landlords, 25 million state peasants owned by the imperial government, and nearly 2 million crown peasants owned by the tsar's family. Together, they accounted for more than two-thirds of Russia's population

embraced Christianity, and to pressure African elites to abandon slavery. This was a case of simultaneous abolition from below and above. Formal, legal abolitions began in 1905. The biggest took place in northern Nigeria in 1936, where about 1 to 2 million slaves became officially free; and in Ethiopia in 1942, when roughly 3 million were liberated.

As everywhere, the passing of laws did not instantly end an age-old institution. Slavery persisted illegally in many parts of Africa. It was abolished in what is now Mauritania when that was officially French territory but survived well enough that independent Mauritania

The Abolition of Serfdom in Eastern Europe and Russia, ca. 1800–1861 The abolition of serfdom freed tens of millions of peasants, beginning in German lands and moving eastward to Russia and Romania. The largest of all abolitions of legal forced labor in world history occurred in Russia.

of roughly 74 million people. This momentous event followed on prior abolitions of serfdom in central and eastern Europe, all much smaller than Russia's.

SERFDOM AND REFORM IN EASTERN EUROPE AND RUSSIA

Serfdom in Europe had a long history, existing in one form or another for 1,500 years. In Europe east of the Elbe River, it became widespread in the fifteenth and sixteenth centuries, when markets for grain developed and landlords wanted to secure labor for their expanding agricultural estates. Serfdom consisted of a package of legal obligations that peasants—serfs—were by law and custom obliged to furnish to lords. The package usually included obligatory labor on the lords' estates, and often delivery of produce to lords' households, fees for using the lords' grinding mills, and permission from lords to marry, leave an estate, or take up a trade. In many cases, serfs were in effect owned by lords. In others, serfs were legally bound to land owned by lords, which for serfs amounted to much the same thing. In some cases, serfs paid money in place of furnishing labor to lords.

By and large, forms of serfdom were milder in the Habsburg lands and Prussia, and harsher in Poland-Lithuania and Russia. Serfs in the latter lands had no legal recourse against exploitation, were subject to brutal punishments, and differed little in status from chattel slaves. Individuals or families could be bought and sold—whole villages of serfs could be bought and sold. Lords routinely used enserfed women for sex. In fact, in Russia, serfs differed from slaves mainly in that serfs were required to pay taxes and serve in the army. That inspired some of them to sell themselves into slavery until, in 1723, slavery was abolished in Russia to prevent that escape route from serfdom. In Prussia, the Habsburg lands, Poland, and Russia, the landlord class, church, and state all supported serfdom until at least 1750; and while they did, there was little serfs could do to improve their condition, let alone end serfdom.

THE IMPACT OF THE ENLIGHTENMENT AND FRENCH REVOLUTION In the late eighteenth century, the ideals of the Enlightenment undermined the agreement of lords, church, and state about serfdom. Voltaire, Kant, Adam Smith, and other influential writers denounced the institution as inhumane, contrary to the principle of liberty, and inefficient besides. Monarchs in Prussia, the Habsburg Empire, and Russia by 1780 tended to agree with the intellectual challenge to serfdom and changed their minds about its legitimacy. But they did little about it, bowing instead to the interests of landlords.

The Enlightenment changed some minds, but it took the French Revolution to change the politics of serfdom in eastern Europe. French armies under Bonaparte proclaimed an end to serfdom wherever they found it. In the case of Prussia, disastrous defeats at the hands of Bonaparte's free peasant armies in 1807 inspired the king to abolish serfdom in hopes of modernizing his country—and converting Prussia's serfs into more motivated peasant soldiers. Some 25 tiny German principalities abolished serfdom between 1807 and 1852. The Habsburg lands did so between 1848 and 1853.

RUSSIA In Russia, the morality and utility of serfdom had also come into question. In her memoirs, the tsarina Catherine the Great (r. 1762–1796) wrote that serfdom was both immoral and inefficient, even while she extended its domain by awarding serfs to loyal nobles. By the 1790s, a few courageous intellectuals such as Aleksandr Radischev had begun to denounce it (he likened serfdom to Caribbean slavery), risking exile or prison. Like their counterparts elsewhere, educated Russians absorbed Enlightenment ideals of liberty and equality, and gradually came to see serfdom as a backward institution that

Serfdom An eighteenth-century Russian engraving shows Cossacks brutally abusing enserfed farm laborers, who had no protection from such maltreatment.

dragged their country down. But landowners usually did not see how they could manage their estates without it: they considered serfdom an inevitable evil. As with slavery, moral opposition was necessary for the abolition of serfdom, but far from sufficient to get it done.

The Russian reformers were aware of the ongoing saga of abolition of forced labor in the Atlantic world. Some, like Radischev, saw resemblances between serfdom and slavery. In the early nineteenth century, Russian emperors often used the word for slave (*rab*) to describe serfs. The novelist Ivan Turgenev referred to serfs, whom he often depicted in a favorable light in his short stories, as "our own blacks." Many in Russia's elite were moved by the gripping scenes in Harriet Beecher Stowe's *Uncle Tom's Cabin* (1852), which was translated into Russian in 1857 and struck a chord with many readers. The Atlantic examples of abolition, often in the background of debate, did not make the issue of emancipation any easier for Russians, but perhaps made it a little more urgent.

As often happens, war made matters more urgent still. Back in 1812, Russia's army, with help from winter and typhus, had expelled Bonaparte's army of 600,000 soldiers. In contrast, during the Crimean War (1853–1856), Russia could not defeat 60,000 British and French soldiers encamped on the Crimean Peninsula (which juts into the Black Sea). The great Russian novelist Leo Tolstoy, who served as an officer in the Crimea, wrote that Russia did "not have an army but a mob of oppressed disciplined slaves." Defeat in the Crimea and the performance of an army composed mainly of serfs convinced Tolstoy and thousands of others that his country was administratively, technologically, and economically backward compared to Britain and France.

ALEXANDER II AND MEMORIES OF PUGACHEV

A new tsar, **Alexander II**, came to power in 1855 determined to enact reforms that would modernize Russia and restore it to the first rank of European powers. Among his top priorities was military reform—in particular, providing the army with more educated, patriotic conscripts than could be found among the serf population. He especially wanted a reserve system such as several European countries had devised, in which soldiers in peacetime would go home but could be called up quickly when war broke out. This was far cheaper than maintaining a full-size standing army in peace and war. But no Russian

Pugachev's Rebellion Chaos unfolds in a dramatic large-scale painting of the Battle of Kazan, fought between Pugachev's forces and the Imperial Russian Army in July 1774. Pugachev himself appears at the center, facing off against a frightened nobleman.

tsar wanted serfs with military skills on the loose in their home villages, and for good reason. To get a cheaper and better army, Alexander would have to get rid of serfdom.

Alexander and Russian reformers rightly feared serfs with military skills. Just as in the Atlantic world, uprisings of the oppressed in Russia caused shudders among the elite. Just as every slaveholder in the early nineteenth-century Atlantic world knew of the Haitian Revolution and its furious violence, so every Russian lord was aware of the vast rising in the years 1773–1774 led by a Cossack named Emelian Pugachev. In the middle of a war against the Ottoman Empire, Pugachev, a low-ranking army officer, led a ragtag rebel army of tens of thousands of Cossacks and serfs on a sustained rampage. They looted estates and took important cities such as Kazan on the Volga River, promising freedom to all serfs and death to landlords—of whom they killed about 3,000. It took all that the Russian state could do to defeat Pugachev, who was betrayed by associates and executed in 1775.

Fears of another Pugachev were stoked every year by news of serf uprisings somewhere in Russia. The office responsible for Russia's internal security recorded 712 revolts between 1826 and 1854, or roughly one every two weeks. As with the abolition of slavery in the Caribbean, fear of uprisings provided a strong motive for abolition of serfdom.

THE POLITICS OF RUSSIAN ABOLITION

For Alexander II and reform-minded Russians, the problem of abolition was practical: how to enact it without alienating either the serf owners or the serfs. In this respect as well, the situation paralleled that of the abolition of slavery. Even those masters who wanted to do away with serfdom felt they were riding the tiger: it was dangerous either to stay on or to get off.

In 1856, Alexander II convened a committee of serf owners, men from the landholding elite, to craft a program of **emancipation for serfs**. Invoking the ghost of Pugachev, he stated in his instructions that "the existing condition of owning souls [serfs] cannot remain unchanged. It is better to begin to destroy serfdom from above than to wait until that time when it begins to destroy itself from below. I ask you, gentlemen, to figure out how all this can be carried to completion." After five years, the committee produced recommendations that underlay the 1861 statute of emancipation of the serfs, a 360-page small-print document. The tsar was so worried that the terms of liberation might disappoint the serfs that he arranged for it to be read out on the first day of Lent, when Orthodox Christians are expected to abstain from alcohol. In theory, it allowed former serfs to own property, engage in trade, move freely, marry as they pleased, sue in courts, and vote in newly created local elections.

But the landlords who crafted the statute had not neglected their own interests. The government paid them handsomely for the loss of their serfs and some of their land. The emancipation provided former serfs with some land but required them to pay for it—except the few who accepted tiny plots called paupers' allotments. Since they had no money, serfs in effect had to buy land on credit from the state by paying a "redemption tax" over the next 50 years. Until they met their payments, former serfs faced many restrictions on their freedom and often remained tied to their village. In many cases, the restrictions lasted the rest of their lives. The landlords kept about two-thirds of the land—usually, the best. As with the abolitions of slavery, the fine print in the deal did not live up to the

Emancipation of the Serfs Alexander II's proclamation announcing the emancipation of the serfs was read aloud in churches throughout Russia in March 1861. This illustration shows a crowd listening to the proclamation at the Dormition Cathedral in Moscow.

hopes of those liberated, because legal constraints and obligations lingered on for many years. Peasant unrest remained a feature of Russian rural life in the decades following the abolition of serfdom.

But the mere fact of liberation, of slaves and serfs—some 60 to 80 million people in all, most of them Russian, but many either African or of African ancestry—carries world-historical importance. Thousands of years after forced labor became widespread, enshrined in law codes, and routinely judged normal, natural, and divinely sanctioned, it was prohibited almost everywhere.

INDENTURED LABOR

Temporary labor bondage, however, persisted. In 1840, shortly after the abolition of slavery in the British Empire, a future prime minister, Lord John Russell, wrote that the growing business of **indentured labor** was in danger of becoming "a new system of slavery." Indentured labor systems had existed for a long time. In the Atlantic world from the seventeenth century through to the 1830s, some 450,000 indentured laborers came from Europe to work in the Americas. Some early ones worked on sugar plantations in the Caribbean, until replaced by African slaves. Others worked as domestics, artisans, or farm laborers. A second and larger stream of indentured laborers, mainly from India and China, arose in the nineteenth century. It began as a trickle in response to the end of the slave trade and rose to a torrent with the end of slavery.

Russell's remark notwithstanding, the legal terms of indentured labor were not the same as those of slavery. The main differences were that indenture was a voluntary arrangement and applied for a fixed number of years, usually between two and eight. But often trickery or coercion lay behind an indenture contract. Unworldly villagers in India or China fell for sunny promises made by labor recruiters. And until their contract expired, indentured laborers often faced some of the same hardships that slaves or serfs endured: they could not leave their employment, or marry, without permission from their employers, and they often faced corporal punishment if

they failed to satisfy their bosses. Indentured laborers, unlike almost all slaves or serfs, drew a wage, although a lower one than planters or mining companies would have had to pay without indenture—which is why the system existed.

INDENTURED MIGRANTS

Between 1830 and 1920, about 2 million indentured laborers left India and China for hard work as plantation laborers or miners in the Caribbean, Peru, Hawaii, Mauritius, South Africa, or Southeast Asia. Smaller flows came from Japan, several Pacific islands, and parts of Africa. Some Europeans, mainly Portuguese, also signed up as indentured laborers. Indians accounted for the majority, about 1.4 million—much more than that if one adds in more local migrations to nearby Ceylon, Burma, or Malaya. Chinese indentured migrants numbered about 500,000. Pacific Islanders and Africans each accounted for about 100,000. Most of the Africans were taken from the re-captives in Sierra Leone. Some of them, in fact, never made it to Sierra Leone, but were rescued from a slave ship in the Atlantic only to be indentured for labor in the Caribbean. Japanese indentured migrants numbered about 85,000; and Europeans 56,000. The flows,

Indentured Labor After the abolition of slavery, unfree labor still contributed to the global movement of peoples—such as these Indian indentured workers in British Jamaica (left) and Chinese indentured workers in Spanish Cuba (right).

boosted by each famine or war in Asia, peaked between 1850 and 1880.

The chief destinations for Indians were sugar plantations in Mauritius, the Caribbean, South Africa, and Fiji (the Pacific archipelago) and for Chinese, the plantations of Cuba or the mines of Peru. For Japanese, the likeliest destinations were plantations in Hawaii and Peru.

Most indentured laborers were men, about 95 percent in the case of Chinese, maybe 75 percent for Indians. The first indentured Japanese in Peru, a shipload of 790 who arrived in 1899, were all men, destined for sugar cane plantations. Single men, if they stayed after their indenture expired, usually married local women if they married at all.

Crossing the oceans in sailing ships with hundreds of other labor migrants was risky. Voyages typically took from one to six months. The death rate for the roughly 150,000 Chinese shipped to Cuba (1847–1873) averaged about 3 percent. For Indians sailing to the Caribbean, it was about 2 percent. Meanwhile, during the last decades of the transatlantic slave trade (1811–1867), mortality in the Middle Passage was 6 percent. (For reference, the death rate for free people traveling from Britain to New York in these decades was 1 percent, and the annual risk of death on the roads of the United States today is about 0.01 percent.) All the death rates for indentured migrant voyages fell with time, so that after 1880 all averaged under 1 percent.

Indian Laborers in Trinidad Between 1847 and 1917, nearly 150,000 Indians went to Trinidad as indentured laborers, and 90 percent remained there all their lives. Most were men in their 20s from northern India, destined for sugar plantations and bonded for five years. Here we see Indian families, which accounted for a small minority of indentured migrants.

Many of these indentured migrant laborers, especially the Indians, returned home. About one-third of Indians who went to Jamaica, Surinam, or Mauritius went home after their term was up. And more than two-thirds of those who went to Thailand or Malaya did so. Many indenture contracts included promise of a return trip. But even for those whose arrangements did not include that promise, it was often possible eventually to earn enough money for the passage home. By the late nineteenth century, information about global travel was more abundant than before, and its price lower, making return voyages for indentured laborers likelier.

THE END OF INDENTURED LABOR

Indentured labor, although not the same as slavery, served the same purpose. It kept the plantations and mines formerly worked by slaves in business. It disappeared, gradually, because mines and plantations could increasingly find enough cheap labor on the free market. After 1870, tens of millions of free people—Europeans, Indians, and Chinese predominantly—left home to cross the oceans in search of employment. Accelerating population growth brought more youths into labor markets. Their sheer numbers reduced labor shortages and lowered free-market wages to the point where indentured labor no longer made economic sense for anyone even in the less thickly populated regions. By 1914 it was, for all intents and purposes, finished. And with it, a long era in human history in which unfree labor was legal and commonplace came—almost—to an end.

Unfortunately, one has to include "almost." Legal slavery lasted in a few countries—Saudi Arabia, Ethiopia, Mauritania, for example—well into the twentieth century. Colonial rulers in Africa—the same ones who had legally abolished slavery in many cases—in the 1920s and 1930s organized temporary forced labor brigades for work in mines, plantations, or on railroads. Certain totalitarian regimes—Nazi Germany, Soviet Russia, among others—re-established slave labor by other names for a few years or decades. As we will see, about 18 million people worked in Soviet forced labor camps between 1929 and 1953. North Korea uses 200,000 slave laborers in its manufacturing and agricultural economy today. And various forms of illegal slavery persist, involving millions of people. Dozens of countries traffic in sex slaves, typically young women lured by false promises of good wages far from home.

CONCLUSION

Over the period 1750–1950, humankind underwent two great liberations. The first liberation was from a biological old regime that had featured frequent disease, famine, and early death. As a result of scientific advances, deliberate policies, and some good fortune, the biological old regime was banished in a Vital Revolution that saw life expectancy lengthen and child mortality shrink dramatically. By 1950, far fewer parents had to bury most of their children as Charlotte of Mecklenburg, Queen Anne, Peter the Great—and millions of anonymous mothers and fathers—had done. For the fabric of ordinary people's lives, this stands among the biggest changes in modern history, although the benefits of the Vital Revolution remain unequally distributed. The revolution might continue, but it might also prove reversible: there is no guarantee we can always keep infectious diseases in check.

The second great liberation involved less fortune and more human will. The various abolitions of slavery and serfdom around the world, from 1777 to 1981, represent another sea change. Serfdom had existed for centuries, and slavery for millennia. Until the end of the eighteenth century, few voices objected to forced labor, even if many slaves and serfs objected vehemently to their own exploitation. In some cases, former slaves became slave owners themselves. But then, starting in the 1770s and 1780s, a groundswell of dissent began to build. It rose up in eastern Europe against serfdom as it was mounting in the Atlantic world against slavery. Slavery's abolition rested in part on the skill and commitment of antislavery activists. But it also rested on the actions of slaves themselves, who launched rebellions that in one case—Haiti—directly forced the end of slavery and in others such as Brazil, Cuba, and the British Caribbean, helped tip the political balance against slavery. Serfs too, with their frequent uprisings, hastened the abolition of serfdom in Russia.

Looking more deeply, one can see other forces at work in the end of forced labor. One was the general rise in population that gathered pace after 1750, the result of the early stages of the Vital Revolution. Forced labor in most contexts made economic sense when and where labor was scarce and therefore, in a free market situation, expensive. Slavery and serfdom kept labor costs low. At great cost in human suffering, they made plantations and other enterprises profitable. When population grew, labor at free market prices grew cheaper, undermining the economic logic of forced labor. Bear in mind this was not central in some important cases, such as the British West Indies, where population was not growing and slavery remained, up to the day of abolition, economically rewarding for employers. Nor was it relevant in the United States, where slavery remained profitable and a massive war was required to abolish it.

A second force at work was intellectual. Enlightenment thinkers after 1750 increasingly advanced ideals of liberty and attacked slavery and serfdom as unjust and inefficient. Their ideas won many followers in influential circles from Brazil to Britain to Russia. At the same time, religious thinking shifted against slavery—less so against serfdom. While for centuries established churches had supported slavery, in the eighteenth century a few branches of Protestantism came to see slavery as a moral evil and repugnant to God. Quakers, Methodists, and evangelical Anglicans stood in the forefront of antislavery in Britain and the United States, and used their networks to promote abolition.

Another influential force was the prestige of British example. In the nineteenth century, thanks mainly to the power conferred on it by the Industrial Revolution, Britain enjoyed an influence all out of proportion to its size. When it threw its weight behind antislavery, that commitment reverberated around the world. The tightened webs—which British steamships, railroads, and telegraph lines helped tighten even more—ensured that millions on every continent knew the moral and economic arguments against slavery. Many of them gradually found themselves persuaded. Others, whose minds were less susceptible to gentle suasion, knew by 1820 that the British Royal Navy would punish them for slave trading and, by about 1870, that British foreign policy would penalize them for maintaining slavery.

All these broad currents—population growth, shifting intellectual currents, and the weight of British example—depended on the tightening links in the Global web forged over the course of the eighteenth through the nineteenth centuries. The spread of inoculation, sanitation, and vaccination occurred as speedily as it did only because millions learned quickly about the success of these practices and changed their behavior accordingly. So too with the spread of ideas opposed to slavery and serfdom, and for that matter, of information about slave or serf uprisings. Globalization has its dark sides, many of them noted in this book. But globalization also contributed to the Vital Revolution and the decline of regimes of forced labor.

The twin liberations were linked, momentous, and simultaneous. The growth of population resulting from the Vital Revolution reduced the economic logic of forced labor. The end of the deliberate deprivations of slavery and serfdom helped improve health and longevity for tens of millions. The two liberations were part of a new era of revolutions in which big changes happened faster and more globally. The Industrial Revolution, Vital Revolution, and abolition of forced labor took a century or two to affect the whole world—a blink of the eye compared to the spread of domestication, cities, writing, or gunpowder in previous eras.

CHAPTER REVIEW

KEY TERMS

Vital Revolution (p. 673)
biological old regime (p. 673)
smallpox inoculation (p. 677)
germ theory of disease (p. 678)

1918 flu pandemic (p. 680)
Quakers (p. 685)
Thomas Clarkson (p. 685)
Sons of Africa (p. 686)
José Aponte (p. 687)
Jack Gladstone (p. 688)

Slavery Abolition Act (p. 689)
Thirteenth Amendment (p. 690)
Alexander II (p. 695)
emancipation for serfs (p. 696)
indentured labor (p. 697)

Go to INQUIZITIVE to see what you've learned—and learn what you've missed—with personalized feedback along the way.

REVIEW QUESTIONS

1. What health risks, including specific risks for women and children, characterized the biological old regime?
2. What accidental and deliberate changes caused the death toll from disease to drop after 1750 or so?
3. What do cholera and the 1918 flu pandemic demonstrate about globalization and disease?
4. Explain the link between race and slavery, and discuss where this connection was most prominent.
5. Why and where did slavery expand between 1750 and 1850?
6. Why did the 1807 British ban of the slave trade endanger slavery more than the 1808 U.S. ban?
7. Describe the key driving forces of the abolition of the slave trade in Britain, the United States, Cuba, and Brazil.
8. What was the broader impact of the Haitian Revolution on abolishing slavery?

9. Compare and contrast the main reasons for the abolition of slavery in the British Empire, the United States, the Caribbean sugar islands, and Brazil.
10. Why did elites outside of the Atlantic world find the abolition of slavery appealing?
11. Why did African slavery expand after 1850?
12. Identify the links among the Crimean War, Alexander II's military reforms, and the emancipation of the serfs.
13. What did the abolition of serfdom mean for former serfs?
14. Who constituted the second and larger stream of indentured laborers, and where were they mainly working?
15. Explain the chief forces that caused the decline of forced labor during this period.
16. Identify the links between the Vital Revolution and the decline of forced labor.

FURTHER READING

Matt CHILDS, *The 1812 Aponte Rebellion in Cuba and the Struggle against Atlantic Slavery* (2006). On the risings in eastern Cuba and their connections to antislavery activities elsewhere.

David Brion DAVIS, *Inhuman Bondage: The Rise and Fall of Slavery in the New World* (2006). An overview by one of the most prominent historians of slavery; includes historiographical context providing a sense of what others have had to say.

Dale GRADEN, *Disease, Resistance, and Lies: The Demise of the Transatlantic Slave Trade to Brazil and Cuba* (2014). Emphasizes the role of slave revolts and pressure from the British navy in changing elite opinion against the slave trade.

Adam HOCHSCHILD, *Bury the Chains: The British Struggle to Abolish Slavery* (2005). A lively popular history, with excellent sketches of the principal actors.

Peter KOLCHIN, *Unfree Labor: American Slavery and Russian Serfdom* (1987). Still the only extended study that puts both these systems of forced labor in direct comparison.

David NORTHRUP, *Indentured Labor in the Age of Imperialism, 1834-1922* (1995). The best overview of the subject.

James RILEY, *Rising Life Expectancy: A Global History* (2001). A handy synthesis of the Vital Revolution.

Manisha SINHA, *The Slave's Cause: A History of Abolition* (2016). A comprehensive history of abolition in the United States, with some attention to Britain, and due recognition of slaves' roles.

Emilia Viotta da COSTA, *Crowns of Glory, Tears of Blood: The Demerara Slave Rebellion of 1823* (1994). A classic in-depth study of one of the key revolts.

EUROPE FOR 1870
Prepared by, in Paris.
HADOL
Published by L. Prang & Cº.
Chromo Publishing House
BOSTON. MASS

BRITAIN
IRELAND
NORTH SEA
NORWAY
SWEDEN
BALTIC SEA
DENMARK
HOLLAND
HOLSTEIN
BELGIUM
PRUSSIA
ATLANTIC OCEAN
FRANCE
SWITZERLAND
AUSTRIA
PORTUGAL
SPAIN
CORSICA
SARDINIA
ITALY
ADRIATIC SEA
TURKEY IN EUROPE

CHRONOLOGY

1795
France makes *La Marseillaise* its national anthem

1818
Hongi Hika begins importing guns and potatoes to New Zealand

1819
British found Singapore

1829
Establishment of Serbia

1830s
Abdelkadir leads Algerian uprising

1832
Establishment of Greece

1847
French capture and exile Abdelkadir

ca. 1840
Peak of Comanche Empire's economic and military strength

1858
Start of the British Raj

1859
Charles Darwin publishes *The Origin of Species*

1860s
Italian unification

1867
Canadian Confederation; Kingdom of Hungary is granted limited independence

1871
Algerian uprising

1876–1878
Major famine in India

1878
Establishment of Romania and Bulgaria

1884–1885
Berlin Conference partitions Africa

1888–1892
Drought and famine in Ethiopia kill half of population

1889
Adoption of Meiji constitution; rinderpest arrives in East Africa

1894–1895
Japan defeats China in war and takes Taiwan

1896
Menelik II's army defeats Italians at Adowa

24

Nationalism and Imperialism

TIGHTENING THE GLOBAL WEB

1800 to 1930

In 1890, on the Makonde plateau in what is now southern Tanzania, in East Africa, there lived a merchant-prince and slave trader named Machemba. Leader of a people known as the Yao, he was among a handful of African and Afro-Arab warlords prospering from a growing trade in slaves and ivory that linked the East African hinterland to its seacoast and beyond to distant markets in Arabia, India, and Europe. Germany had just laid claim to a big slice of East Africa—Tanganyika—and needed cooperative African leaders who would support German authority. Hermann von Wissman, a distinguished German army officer who had spent several years in Africa, invited Machemba to do so. Machemba had his own ideas:

> I have listened to your words but can find no reason why I should obey you. I would rather die first.... If it should be friendship that you desire, then I am ready for it, today and always; but to be your subject, that I cannot be. If it should be war you desire, then I am ready, but never to be your subject. I do not fall at your feet, for you are God's creature just as I am.... I am Sultan

A Satirical Map of Europe, 1870 Drawn from a French perspective, this satirical view of the geopolitical situation in Europe in 1870 uses stereotypes to represent nations and their relationships. Britain holds Ireland on a leash, Prussia kneels on Austria, and France draws a sword to defend itself against Prussia, an allusion to the Franco-Prussian War of 1870–1871. The map reflects the view that nations had shared cultural or ethnic identities—a view that flourished in an era of rising nationalisms.

1898
Spanish-American War; United States takes Spain's colonies and annexes Hawaii

1899
Rudyard Kipling publishes "The White Man's Burden"

1900
Australian Federation

By 1910
All local Indonesian rulers submit to the Dutch

1918
Collapse of Habsburg Empire; Aladura churches in Nigeria take shape

1910
Japan annexes Korea

1912
Italy takes Libya from Ottoman Empire

1930s
Development of Yamato race theory

FOCUS QUESTIONS

1. In what ways did nationalism prove a powerful force in the modern world?

2. What made imperialism such a powerful force in the nineteenth and twentieth centuries?

3. What were the most important land empires during this period?

4. What global effects did nationalism and imperialism have?

here in my land. You are Sultan there in yours. Yet listen, I do not say that you should obey me: for I know that you are a free man. As for me, I will not come to you, and if you are strong enough, then come and fetch me.

Disappointed but not surprised, von Wissman came to fetch Machemba. The Germans assembled an army of Africans, some from as far away as Zululand (South Africa) and Sudan, trained and equipped by German veterans of European wars. It took nine years to defeat Machemba and a few more to subdue all of Tanganyika.

Machemba, in his defiance, had not appreciated that von Wissman had behind him the resources of an industrialized country of 50 million people. Even when he learned the full measure of German power, there was little he could do to preserve his own independence. For his part, von Wissman didn't know much about Machemba and the Yao, who proved to be resourceful guerrilla fighters. But when he learned, there was plenty he could do to them.

Encounters of this sort, featuring unequal levels of knowledge about the world and unequal resources, became especially frequent in the nineteenth century. Thanks mainly to industrialization, some societies and states, including Germany, were in a position to use overwhelming power thousands of miles from home. It proved a temptation hard to resist.

Between 1826 and 1919, about a quarter of the Earth's land surface changed hands politically. People inspired by the ideologies of **nationalism** and imperialism, and in most cases empowered by industrialization, helped to re-draw the political map of the world through violence and negotiation. These ideologies, in effect, made some peoples and states stronger and others weaker, rearranging the world political order.

Nationalism and imperialism were the most powerful ideologies changing world politics between 1800 and 1930. Other important political ideas, such as democracy, socialism, or pan-Islamism (the belief that Islam should be politically unified), had less global consequences. Nationalism and imperialism loomed so large because they traveled well from one cultural setting to the next. People on every continent found the idea of nationhood appealing. And most people in powerful societies approved of imperialism too.

This chapter begins with an assessment of nationalism, explaining the concept, where it mattered, why it arose when it did, and what difference it made. It then considers imperialism, outlining why it reached such heights during the nineteenth century, what forms it took, and where it mattered most. As we shall see, nationalism and imperialism sometimes overlapped in mutually reinforcing ways, and sometimes worked at cross purposes. Both encouraged people to emphasize their differences, but both brought peoples into closer interactions and tighter webs.

NATIONALISM AND NATION-STATES

Nationalism—perhaps the single most powerful ideological force in modern centuries—is stubbornly difficult to define. It is a set of ideas, beliefs, and attitudes that exalts the virtues of a community claiming distinctive characteristics and, in most cases, a bounded territory.

The characteristics that provide solidarity can be shared language and culture, shared ethnicity and ancestry, or shared political and civic values—or some combination of them.

Scholars often distinguish between ethnic nationalism and civic nationalism. The first refers to groups, such as Japanese, that get their sense of solidarity from a common language, ethnic identity, or ancestry. The claim to common ancestry can be, and usually is, fanciful. But if people believe it, the effect is the same as if it were true. The second, civic nationalism, refers to nations whose sense of solidarity comes instead from common acceptance of a set of institutions and political values. The United States is a good example: the ideals articulated in the Declaration of Independence and the U.S. Constitution, though never fully realized in American society, remain an inspiration and a source of identity for the nation. In practice, ethnic nationalism and civic nationalism often overlap.

Nationalism begins with human biology but doesn't end there. A craving to belong to a group is one of the deepest human desires. Our fellow apes seem to feel it too. In the long hominin and human career, this desire conferred strong advantages. People could forage, hunt, and defend themselves better as groups than as lone individuals. Over hundreds of thousands of years, our brains evolved to make us long to belong to groups.

But human biology has no bearing on just which groups we wish to belong to. It could be a hunter-forager band, a high school debate team, or the community of Green Bay Packer fans known as Cheeseheads. Membership in all these groups and millions of others, however large or small and whatever their practical advantages, delivers psychic rewards. For some people at least, nationalism offers a satisfying sense of solidarity with a large community, enabling people to feel part of something greater than their family or village. We humans are pre-adapted to be receptive to group identities such as nationalism.

Modern nationalism, especially ethnic nationalism, has a strange relationship to history. It rests on simplifying myths. Nationalists typically emphasize glorious, ancient, and unified pasts—air-brushed pasts. Modern Mongolian nationalism harkens back to the Eurasian conqueror Genghis Khan, overlooking his gory massacres. Mexican nationalism invokes the Aztecs, overlooking their ruthless rule over the ancestors of millions of today's Mexicans. As the French scholar Ernst Renan wrote in 1882,

"Forgetting, I would go so far as to say historical error, is a crucial factor in the creation of a nation."

Nationalism prospered in some circumstances more than others. Ethnic nationalism arose most easily where ethnic, linguistic, cultural, and religious diversity was minimal and a unified state already existed. Nineteenth-century Japan is a good example. Nationalism also developed where ethnic minorities in multiethnic states felt persecuted: Poles in the Russian Empire or Afrikaners in South Africa. The idea—whether accurate or not—of a peasantry deeply rooted in the ancestral soil, as in modern Korea or France, also helped foster ethnic nationalism. People who felt their nation was specially chosen for some divine purpose or that their nation was unfairly victimized—or both—also found nationalism appealing.

Another circumstance that favored the development of nationalism was urbanization. As we've seen, cities grew larger and more numerous during the nineteenth century, especially in industrializing countries. Tens of millions of people uprooted from villages felt the need to belong to a community, and so were all the more receptive to nationalistic messages. Those messages might take the form of journalism, heroic novels, poetry, or painting—or stirring patriotic music adopted as national anthems. France in 1795 designated *La Marseillaise* as a national anthem, launching an international trend. Vietnam chose one in 1802, Argentina in 1813, Peru in 1821, and Japan in 1888. The United States adopted its national anthem in 1931. City populations, because clustered together, were easier to reach with nationalist music, art, or journalism.

Nationalism's adherents generally wanted a state whose borders matched those of an ethnic or linguistic group, whether Germans or Koreans or Bengalis. They often claimed that any state with borders that did not correspond to a nation—a multinational state—was illegitimate. Their ambitions almost always required some political re-engineering: nationalism served to unite peoples into a single nation-state in some cases and in others to grind multicultural empires into pieces. Let's look at some examples.

FRANCE

Many scholars think France provides the earliest example of genuine nationalism. While France became a kingdom over the span of many centuries, only its elite felt French before

French Nationalism An 1880 lithograph shows the Place de la Bastille in central Paris decorated with French flags in honor of France's July 14 national holiday. A national day, imagery connected with a national flag, and national history grounded in pivotal founding events such as the storming of the Bastille are all characteristic nationalist symbols.

the 1790s. The masses generally felt attachments to their family, village, region, religion, and perhaps to their king. But in the course of the French Revolution and especially Napoleon Bonaparte's foreign wars, more and more people within France came to feel increasingly French. Some were moved by the ideals of the Revolution—liberty, equality, and fraternity (perhaps better translated as solidarity). When the French established a republic that supposedly represented the will of the people, many of them felt they had laid the foundation for a better political community.

In the 1790s, leaders of the French Revolution tried to drum a sense of French-ness into the uneducated peasantry—80 percent of the population. One tactic was requiring the use of standard (Parisian) French throughout the country, a policy employed off and on ever after. Another tactic, used only in the desperate 1790s, was killing people who declined to identify themselves with the French nation.

Two decades of warfare, from 1792 to 1815, helped forge a French nation. Military service in a national army made soldiers feel French. Supporters of the Revolution and Bonaparte devised symbols, ceremonies, and rituals to convey the meaning of French identity to people who could not read: a national flag to match the anthem, for example, or parades and funerals for heroes of the French nation. Army service exposed young men to standard French, no matter which tongue they spoke at home.

After the final defeat of Bonaparte in 1815, subsequent rulers of France, even monarchists who hated everything else about the French Revolution, cultivated nationalism. Throughout the nineteenth century, French elites hammered home the nationalist message, using the newly created countrywide public school system, the army, and the press to deepen the popular sense of French national identity. After 1871, the government, now called the Third Republic, tried again to impose a standard French language on the country. Ordinary French citizens learned to feel that theirs was a special nation, committed to political ideals such as liberty and equality. They were also taught to consider themselves blood descendants of the formidable ancient Gauls, in whom various admirable traits were conveniently found. At the same time, they identified with the glorious legacies of the Romans and Charlemagne, and the more recent glory of Bonaparte. French nationalism was, and is, mainly civic nationalism, based on the ideals of the French Revolution; but it also has had, and still has, an ethnic basis for many French people.

JAPAN

Japanese nationalism was based mainly on a sense of ethnic solidarity. It had deep roots, but it matured in the late nineteenth century when Japanese leaders worried, with ample reason, that their country might be overrun and colonized by Britain or another industrial power. They made a concerted effort to industrialize, as we've seen, and to foster nationalism and a sense of Japanese exceptionalism. They calculated that these efforts would rally the masses to make sacrifices for the state, which they believed was essential to Japan's continued independence.

Around 1875, Japanese leaders started promoting the fiction of common ancestry among all Japanese. By the 1930s it had developed as **Yamato race theory**, according to which the Japanese were descended from an ancient ancestral people and were different from, and better than, Koreans, Chinese, and other neighbors. Japanese nationalism also had a strong religious component: the elite in Japan typically embraced the ancient Japanese rituals called Shinto in preference to imported religions such as Buddhism. The state supported Shinto shrines and encouraged worship of the emperor as divine. The Meiji constitution, adopted in 1889, instructed Japanese people that their first allegiance was to the state. Japan's nationalists emphasized the respects in which the country was

Japanese Nationalism Japanese efforts to support Shinto as the national religion resulted in the persecution of Buddhists. An 1874 illustration shows Shinto priests burning Buddhist scriptures, over the tears and protests of a Buddhist monk.

unique, and especially how it was different from—and, as they saw it, more disciplined, energetic, and warlike than—China.

As elsewhere, public education in Japan helped get the message to the masses. After 1870, an older tradition of Confucian learning taught to a few was replaced by a more practical, and nationalistic, curriculum, and by 1900 almost every Japanese boy and girl attended school. University students had to swear an oath promising to "offer [myself] courageously to the state." Urbanization and increasing literacy also helped nationalism to take root.

Japan's nationalism emphasized military virtues. By 1890, sailors and soldiers were instructed to see Japan as a "sacred nation protected by the gods." Civilians were encouraged to revere the armed forces as embodiments of the warrior spirit of the Yamato race. As we will see, after Japan's defeat in World War II, the character of its nationalism underwent a radical makeover, dropping militarism in favor of a narrative of victimization and pride in economic progress.

CANADA

Canadian nationalism, in contrast, had (and has) no ethnic basis and little military emphasis. In 1800, what is now Canada was a handful of British colonies with two distinct ethnic and religious populations. In Quebec, especially in the countryside, almost everyone spoke French and followed the Catholic religion, a consequence of French colonization and settlement dating back to 1608. In what are now the Maritime provinces and Ontario, people mainly spoke English and were mainly Protestants. The process of building a Canadian identity and nation took shape with Confederation in 1867, the fusing of the various colonies into a self-governing country through negotiations and an act of the British Parliament. The British North America Act reserved Canadian military and foreign affairs for Britain to control but left domestic matters to Canadians.

FIRST NATIONS AND ASSIMILATION The biggest challenge in creating a Canadian nation was reconciling differences between the Anglophone and Francophone communities—something Canada is still working on. Few Canadians had any intention of including First Nations, as the indigenous Amerindians of Canada are now called, in their political community—unless the First Nations first abandoned their culture. For two centuries after European settlement, Canada's First Nations had slowly lost land in the east but lived alongside Euro-Canadians as trading partners. Wars between France and Britain in North America, especially between 1756 and 1815, featured Amerindian involvement, which in every case turned out badly for Canada's First Nations. After those wars ceased, First Nations seemed more like obstacles to expanded Euro-Canadian settlement than potential allies and trading partners.

By 1870, Amerindian numbers in Canada had been reduced to a few tens of thousands through loss of land, searing epidemics in the 1780s and 1830s, and the near extinction of the buffalo, a major food source in western Canada. Through treaties in the 1870s, Canada confined the lands available to First Nations to "reserves" that usually did not include good farmland. First Nations leaders accepted these treaties, in effect making them wards of the Canadian state, in order to obtain medicines, manufactured goods, and education for the young. A program of residential schools, often run by Catholic or Protestant churches, aimed to assimilate First Nations into Canadian Anglophone or Francophone culture. Many members of First Nations did assimilate; 6,000 volunteered for the armed forces in World War I. Those who didn't assimilate remained, in effect, outside the Canadian nation.

The great champion of Confederation and Canadian nationalism was a Scottish-born lawyer, John A. MacDonald, who after 1867 served 19 years as prime minister.

Despite a weakness for whiskey and bribes, he energetically sought to forge a nation from the newly confederated parts of Canada. He encouraged railroad building on a transcontinental scale and pursued a form of economic nationalism, trying to keep American imports to a minimum, to build a truly national economy. He favored the settlement of western farmlands as far as the Pacific. When some 350 Métis—French-speaking people of partly Amerindian descent in Manitoba and Saskatchewan—decided they didn't want to be part of Canada, in what is called the North-West Rebellion (1885), MacDonald sent Canadian militia to crush them. He then insisted on the execution of Louis Riel, the charismatic Métis leader. By 1905, western and prairie regions had been organized into Canadian provinces, and the country stretched from the Atlantic to the Pacific.

CANADIAN NATIONALISM AND FOREIGN RELATIONS

The unintentional help of the colossus to the south helped make the idea of Canada work. Part of nationalism's appeal rested on popular fears that the United States might try to conquer Canada, using the giant army that had won the U.S. Civil War in 1865. Ragtag bands of Irish Americans called Fenians, mainly Civil War veterans, burned to right the wrongs Britain had done to Ireland: they invaded British Canada twice in 1866 and killed several Canadian militiamen. The U.S. purchase of Alaska (1867) only added to Canadian concerns. Invasion fears subsided after 1871, when a hapless

group of 35 Fenians misjudged the location of the border and attacked northern Minnesota by mistake.

But realistic anxieties about American economic and cultural power persisted, strengthening a sense of national solidarity among Canadians. In addition, many Canadians, Francophones especially, resented the power—in military and foreign relations—that politicians in London still exercised over them after Confederation. So Canadian nationalism was—paradoxically enough—based on fears and resentments directed at the United States and Britain, Canada's closest cultural cousins and political allies. It was and is for the most part a civic nationalism crafted to overcome the ethnic and religious diversity characteristic of Canada from the outset.

GERMANY

German nationalism, like Canadian, served to weld together a country. German nationalists fused many smaller political units together to make a new country, but at the same time they set Germany off from the larger cultural unit of German-speakers. Most Austrians and Swiss also spoke varieties of German, but they remained outside of Germany.

Like Japanese nationalism, German nationalism emphasized ethnic and linguistic solidarity. The notion of a common language involved more wishful thinking than it did in Japan. In the eighteenth century, despite a common literary language, the many varieties of spoken German were often mutually unintelligible. As late as 1800, few people thought there should be a country called Germany.

But when Bonaparte destroyed the Holy Roman Empire in 1806, he united several little German duchies and principalities into a rickety political structure called the Confederation of the Rhine. He then demanded soldiers and taxes from them, arousing fierce resentment and helping German-speakers to see their collective interest and identity more clearly. Parallel efforts following conquests by Bonaparte in Spain, Italy, the Netherlands, and elsewhere helped to inspire nationalisms elsewhere in Europe. After Bonaparte's final defeat in 1815, some Germans tried and failed to unite Germany politically. But they did manage to establish a customs union called the *zollverein*—basically a free-trade zone—that gradually tightened the economic bonds among its members.

Canadian Nationalism Native students attend class at a Catholic residential school in the Northwest Territories in northern Canada. The forced assimilation of First Nations people through the residential schools weakened First Nations communities and cultures, with effects that persist to the present day.

German Nationalism Philipp Veit's *Germania* (1848) imagined the German nation in the form of a beautiful woman in supposed medieval dress—appealing to a myth of a common ethnic German identity that stretched back centuries.

German cultural nationalism prospered too. Literature, music, and painting extolled the supposed special merits of German-ness, such as the canvas by Philipp Veit that presents Germany in the form of a medieval woman. German scholars and schoolmasters found inspiration in the hardihood and virtue of the wild Germanic tribes described by the ancient Roman author Tacitus, and they encouraged modern Germans to see themselves as a single people, descendants of the ancient tribes. As in Japan, in Germany some nationalists by 1880 understood German ethnicity as a matter of race. They argued that Germans stood superior to all other "races"—a view that, as we shall see, attracted more followers after 1918.

BISMARCK AND GERMAN UNIFICATION The development of German nationalism and the political unification of Germany went hand in hand. Uprisings against princes and kings in 1848 briefly led to an all-German parliament and an effort by some of the urban middle classes to create a united German republic or at least a constitutional monarchy. Although the revolution failed and the principalities, dukedoms, and kingdoms of the German Confederation survived, the prospect of a united German nation proved inspirational. Soon the chancellor of Prussia (a kingdom and the biggest part of Germany) saw a way to make nationalism serve his ends. In a series of small wars and one-sided negotiations from Prussia's position of strength, the Prussian aristocrat Otto von Bismarck fused patches of predominantly German-speaking lands to Prussia, creating a politically unified country by 1871. Bismarck deliberately left German-speaking Austria out of this union to ensure that his Prussia would dominate Germany. Ironically, in the process of unification

Germany acquired minority populations who spoke Polish, Lithuanian, Danish, or French. They did not feel at all German, although with time many of their children did.

At every step, Bismarck encouraged the development of a German national identity, using the same tools—schools, army, press—as in France or Japan. As in Japan, industrialization and urbanization helped put more people within reach of messages urging them to think of themselves as German rather than as, for example, Swabian or Silesian. Bismarck's version of German nationalism emphasized military virtues and promoted the army and navy as symbols of national strength. He and his successors encouraged Germans to think in terms of national greatness and geopolitical strength, which many Germans eagerly embraced until it brought their country to ruin in two world wars.

NATIONALISM AS A SOURCE OF STATE POWER

As these four examples show, there were many routes to nationalism and to a nation-state. Where ethnic, linguistic, and religious divisions were weak, and where a unified state already existed, as in Japan, nationalism was an easier project than in France, where nationalism was born of revolution and war. In Germany and Canada, deep Catholic-Protestant divisions proved an obstacle, and nationalist leaders such as Bismarck and MacDonald had to deploy formidable political skills to create a nation-state out of smaller units.

Nationalism could confer great power upon states. If people accepted the notion that they were, say, French, then a government of the French people could get tax revenues and military conscripts with less resistance than if people did not agree they were French. Nationalism helped justify bigger military budgets. Nationalism could discourage workers from calling strikes that would weaken the state. It could prepare people psychologically to let the state manage schooling of the young or use private property for railroad-building programs—both of which (schools and railroads) helped governments foster nationalism even more. Nationalism, in short, could make states much stronger, both with respect to their own citizens and with respect to foreign countries. It reduced the difficulties of governing—as long as the state's citizens felt that they belonged to one nation and that the state championed the interests of the nation.

NATIONALISM AND MULTIETHNIC EMPIRES

Nationalism could also weaken states. The best examples were big multiethnic polities of the nineteenth century such as the Habsburg, Russian, or Ottoman empires. These **multiethnic empires** all included many linguistic and religious groups, as well as millions of people who might be just as comfortable speaking Czech as German or equally comfortable in Turkish and Greek. Nationalists, although often educated and multilingual themselves, wanted people to declare themselves as members of one or another nation, and wanted separate states for each nation—or at least a state for their own nation.

THE HABSBURG EMPIRE The Habsburg Empire, dominated by German-speaking Austrians, comprised many ethnic minorities, including Hungarians, Czechs, Slovaks, Poles, Italians, Romanians, Serbs, and Croats, among others. Its multiethnic character made it especially vulnerable to nationalist divisions. After 1815, many members of these groups gradually concluded that they should be recognized as nations. They did not necessarily want to be fully independent but sought autonomy within the Habsburg framework, which the rulers—themselves mostly German-speaking Austrians—were slow to offer. So the minorities increasingly considered the imperial state an unjust yoke. Nationalist uprisings peppered the empire from 1848 onward. The Habsburgs responded with repression and attempts to impose the German language in schools and for all official business, provoking more unrest.

Eventually, the Habsburgs relented and allowed more cultural expression and some political autonomy among certain minorities. In 1867, the historic Kingdom of Hungary was granted independence except in military matters and foreign policy—a similar status to the one Canada achieved within the British Empire in the same year. The arrangement for Hungary incited other minorities who felt their nationality was just as worthy of special status. To compound matters, once Hungarians acquired power over their internal affairs, they ruthlessly repressed Romanians, Croats, and other minorities in their part of the empire. Until its collapse in 1918, the Habsburg Empire struggled to contain minority nationalisms.

THE RUSSIAN EMPIRE The Russian Empire faced a similar problem. Although most of its subjects spoke

Nationalism in the Russian Empire A Polish painter depicts Polish nationalist rebels fighting Russian troops at an arsenal in Warsaw in November 1830, during the central battle of the Polish nationalist uprising of 1830–1831.

Russian and adhered to the Russian Orthodox faith, it had a dozen or more sizeable ethno-linguistic groups and some religious minorities. Poland, as we have seen, was partitioned during the eighteenth century among Prussia, the Habsburg Empire, and Russia, leaving Poles with no country of their own. That circumstance led to a robust nationalism, at least among urban and educated Poles, creating a recurrent problem for Russia. Bonaparte's armies had established a short-lived puppet Polish state, the Duchy of Warsaw. With Bonaparte's defeat, most of it was taken over by Russia. Polish nationalism inspired major rebellions in the years 1830–1831 and 1863–1864. Russian authorities tried to prevent the rise of Polish, Lithuanian, Ukrainian, and other nationalisms, often forbidding the use of these languages. Such repressive measures, part of a general program of Russification, typically inflamed minority nationalist sentiment still further.

In Russia, religious divisions often strengthened minority nationalisms. In the first census (1897), some 70 percent of the tsar's subjects were counted as Russian Orthodox, which left roughly 40 million followers of minority religions. For most Poles, Catholicism was a sacred point of pride. In Finland and the Baltic provinces, Lutheranism was woven into people's sense of identity, as was the Armenian Apostolic Church for Armenians. In the western parts of the empire, the census showed Russia with more than 5 million Jews, few of whom identified strongly with the empire. The Caucasus and Central Asia were home to 14 million Muslims, who firmly resisted efforts at conversion to Russian Orthodoxy. The Russian Empire's promotion of Orthodoxy, which included banning several other religions, added to the irritation of religious minorities, providing them another reason to feel Polish or Estonian or Armenian. As in the Habsburg Empire, in Russia the imperial state never found a way to subdue surging minority nationalisms.

THE OTTOMAN EMPIRE The multicultural and multiethnic Ottoman Empire also suffered from the rise of nationalisms. As in Russia, religious identities and national ones often bolstered one another. Muslims accounted for the great majority of Ottoman subjects—about 75 percent in 1906, the first year for which good census data exist. Some 14 percent were officially Greek Orthodox in religion, although not necessarily Greek in language or nationality. In the nineteenth century, Greeks, Serbs, Romanians, Bulgarians, and other linguistic and religious minorities of the empire grew more restive, convinced that they constituted nations. They each had their own increasingly national form of Orthodox Christianity, with priests and bishops who occasionally stirred up nationalist

Nationalism in the Ottoman Empire An evocative painting by the French Romantic artist Eugène Delacroix shows Greek rebels—including women and children—being massacred by Ottoman troops during the Greek War of Independence. The pathos of the image invites the viewer to sympathize with the Greek nationalist cause.

sentiments. From the beginning of the nineteenth century, the Ottomans faced one rebellion after another in the Balkans, often led by university graduates who had lived in France or Germany and who pined for national independence.

Although nationalist consciousness was mainly an elite concern, armed rebellions helped establish new nation-states such as Serbia (1829), Greece (1832), Romania (1878), and Bulgaria (1878). All were mainly Orthodox in religion, but with substantial Muslim minorities. All were keenly nationalistic at birth, eager to expand their territories so as to embrace all their "unredeemed brethren"—to use the language of the time. Arab nationalism was a worrisome sleeping giant for Ottoman authorities, because so much Ottoman territory—the Levant, the Arabian Peninsula, and much of what is now Iraq—was inhabited by Arabic-speakers. But into the early twentieth century, only a few intellectuals and merchants had developed much sense of Arab national identity.

In the early twentieth century, the Ottoman state increasingly turned to a policy of Turkification, broadly parallel to Russification. All branches of government were increasingly required to use only the Turkish language. Muslim minorities, such as Arabs and Kurds, were urged to consider themselves Turks. (Kurds were an ethno-linguistic group living in what is now southeastern Turkey, northeastern Syria, northern Iraq, and northwestern Iran.) Christian minorities, such as Armenians and Greeks living in Ottoman lands, were encouraged to convert to Islam and speak Turkish. Turkification brought scanty results and irritated many of those who were its targets—again, roughly parallel to Russification.

MINORITY NATIONALISMS The Russian and Ottoman empires became masters at meddling in one another's affairs by means of minority nationalism. Russia encouraged Greek, Serbian, and Bulgarian nationalisms, supporting publications, welcoming exiles, or supplying weapons for uprisings. To some extent, this policy rested on a shared Orthodox Christianity, but often it emerged from Russian geopolitical calculation. Russia's leaders hoped that vigorous minority nationalisms would weaken their historical foe. In turn, the Ottomans, especially after 1908, promoted nationalisms, and Muslim identity, among peoples of the Russian Empire in the Caucasus region and Central Asia. Britain and France, and eventually Germany too, meddled in Ottoman and Russian ethnic politics, at times encouraging nationalism among minorities. Nationalism provided a new weapon for geopolitical struggles, one that undermined multinational empires but not nation-states.

Minority nationalisms also made it difficult for multinational empires to allow subjects more political voice. The emperors and elites in the Habsburg, Russian, and Ottoman empires feared—quite reasonably—that permitting more representative institutions would inflame ethnic passions and weaken their own grip on power. So they experimented with political reform, but only tentatively, and overall held fast to the principle of autocracy. Nation-states, in contrast, could, and did, enhance their popularity and legitimacy by allowing more citizen representation in politics—for example, by allowing more people to vote. In this way too, nationalism strengthened the hand of the state in Germany, France, and Japan, but weakened it in the multinational empires.

IMPERIALISM

Empire were once widespread and widely regarded as normal and natural. They go back at least 44 centuries to Sargon of Akkad in ancient Mesopotamia. For most of those millennia, empires were built mainly by land. They could be large, like the fourteenth-century Mongol or the fifteenth-century Inka empires, but they usually comprised contiguous territories. Only a few, like South India's Chola kingdom in the eleventh century, also had a significant seaborne element.

But in the sixteenth and seventeenth centuries, as we have seen, truly oceanic empires emerged with the Iberian conquests in the Americas. By 1700, the Atlantic European states—Portugal, Spain, France, the Netherlands, and Britain—all had substantial seaborne empires, held together by commerce and naval power. This marked the beginning of a new era in the long history of empire, one in which naval power and commercial dominance mattered as much as armies.

European overseas empires in 1830 covered about 6 percent of the Earth's land surface and held about 18 percent of its population. Over the next century, a surge of imperialism, mainly on the part of western Europeans and Japanese, changed the world's map as well as its politics,

economy, and much else. By 1914, European and Japanese overseas empires controlled about 39 percent of the Earth's land surface and about 33 percent of its population.

While empire was common enough before 1800, by 1900 it reached almost everywhere. Seaborne empires on which the sun never set now spanned the globe. Imperialism after 1870 was so pervasive, and different enough from what had come before, that historians often call it the **new imperialism**. They might better call it industrial-strength imperialism, because what made it so pervasive and different was, first and foremost, the industrialization of some parts of the world—western Europe, Japan, the United States—but not others. That created huge gaps in power and wealth, a situation that invited imperialist attitudes and actions.

TECHNOLOGIES AND IMPERIALISM

Just as the Americas were breaking free of European control (1776–1830), several European states, Britain and France foremost among them, were growing more powerful through the effects of industrialization and nationalism.

Industrial societies developed new technologies useful for building empires. Steamships, at first small, shallow-draft gunboats, proved excellent at projecting military power on coasts and up navigable rivers. They first saw duty putting down rebellions along the St. Lawrence River in Canada in 1837. Over the next 50 years, others chugged up and down rivers such as the Niger, Ganges, Mekong, and Yangzi, helping Europeans to trade and negotiate treaties on favorable terms. Steam-powered gunboats on the Waikato River gave British forces a major advantage in wars with Maori that led to the entrenchment of British rule in New Zealand. Big steam-powered ocean-going ships became practical in the 1870s, which cut transport times and permitted "sailing" routes independent of prevailing winds. That made it much easier for industrial powers to project military force overseas.

At least as important as industrial sea power were new, improved, and cheaper guns. Over the course of the nineteenth century, European and U.S. gun manufacturers multiplied the killing power of their products, ranging from pocket-sized pistols to large artillery pieces. This opened a chasm between the effectiveness of their armies and those of peoples without modern guns. While the

Industrial Empire An 1890 illustration advertises a steam-powered British gunboat, designed for use on the inland waterways of southeast Africa. New technologies such as steamships aided European empires' efforts to forcibly consolidate power and protect trade routes in overseas colonies.

Zulu of South Africa, the Maori of New Zealand, or the Lakota Sioux in North America could trade for guns, and learned to repair them, they did not have the capacity to mass-produce them. They could win occasional battles against industrial states, but not wars. As the British writer Hilaire Belloc put it in 1898, referring to an early version of a machine gun:

> Whatever happens, we have got
> The Maxim gun, and they have not.

The couplet captured the gulf in military technology between the armies of imperialists and the forces arrayed against them in Africa or Asia.

Other new technologies further widened that gulf. The telegraph, in use from the 1840s, radically cut the time needed to transmit messages over long distance. After 1870, the British government could exchange messages with its representatives in India in five hours instead of five months. Over the next 30 years, Britain laid submarine telegraph cables across the world's oceans, linking its empire in a communications web far superior to anything available to anyone else. Aspiring imperial powers tried to imitate Britain's network. For military and commercial purposes, the telegraph was a crucial tool of imperialism.

So was a growing ability to check the ravages of malaria through the mass production of a drug, quinine. Use of quinine, extracted from the bark of a tropical tree called cinchona, dates back centuries. Malaria had long menaced

people from malaria-free zones who tried to visit, let alone conquer and occupy, most of Africa, South Asia, and Southeast Asia. People born and raised in malarial lands usually carried strong resistance to the disease. But quinine, mass-produced by the 1850s, could make anyone resistant. Chemical industries capable of mass-producing quinine, together with ships, guns, and telegraph networks, were all part of the surge in power that industrialization afforded to a handful of societies in the nineteenth century.

Military Technology British Marines stationed in South Africa at the end of the nineteenth century demonstrate the use of a state-of-the-art Maxim machine gun, which proved effective in wars of imperial conquest in Africa, including Hermann von Wissman's campaign to establish German rule in East Africa.

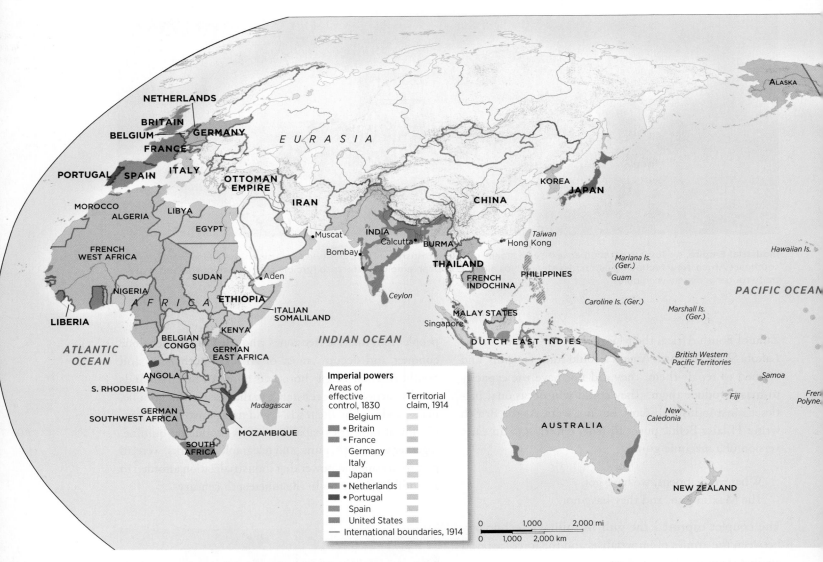

Colonial Empires in 1830 and 1914 Between 1830 and 1914, European powers, the United States, and Japan acquired the capacity to extend or create colonial empires. That capacity depended largely on industrial strength and the ability to mass-produce weaponry, steamships, quinine, and other tools of empire. Africa and both South and Southeast Asia were colonized by European powers. Japan took Korea and Taiwan, while the United States acquired Alaska, Hawaii, Puerto Rico, and the Philippines.

NATIONALISM IN SUPPORT OF IMPERIALISM

If industrialization provided new hardware suited to empire building, nationalism offered new popular support. Nationalism contributed to the capacity of states such as Britain, France, Japan, and Germany to indulge in imperialism. The same held for Italy, unified by committed nationalists by 1870, and eagerly imperialist by the 1890s. All cases of imperialism enabled by modern industry were supported by populations fired by nationalism.

This support often took the form of an ideology that explicitly justified imperialism. The French developed the *mission civilisatrice* ("civilizing mission") according to which it was France's special destiny to bring civilization— Christianity, sanitation, antislavery, self-discipline, and so forth—to peoples of the world who lacked it. Such an outlook helped to legitimize the human and financial costs of conquests. Every other imperial power created some version of the same self-serving ideology, according to which their nation must shoulder the moral obligation— rarely met in practice—to lift up downtrodden and often strong in the case of Germany, which had no tradition of overseas empire when Bismarck came to power over the newly unified state in 1871. By the 1880s, Germany, pushed by nationalistic lobbies, competed for influence and territory in Africa and the Pacific, plunging into imperial ventures for fear that its rivals were getting ahead. Russia and Britain waded deeper into Central Asia after 1870 mainly to prevent the other from dominating it.

CULTURES OF IMPERIALISM

Nationalism and imperialism fed off each other. Nationalistic feeling made it easier for people to support imperialism; but at the same time, successful imperialism made many people feel more nationalistic. The British in particular developed a sense of themselves as an imperial people, fit to rule over others, and gradually wove that self-image into their culture. In the later nineteenth century and well into the twentieth, they created celebratory literature, theater, music, public ceremonies, honors, and medals—in short, a **culture of imperialism**. It helped them feel more British, as opposed to merely English, Scottish, Welsh, or Irish. It helped them take pride in their country, as opposed to focusing on their social class or religion. And it helped them to support a more nationalistic British policy.

In the 1870s, the British even invented a new word for a particularly pushy foreign policy based on faith in one's own superiority: jingoism. It came from a popular ditty sung in pubs, the refrain to which went:

> We don't want to fight but by Jingo if we do
> We've got the ships, we've got the men, we've got the
>   money too...

Rudyard Kipling was an influential exponent of this British culture of imperialism. His poetry, short stories, and novels were extremely popular in his day, and are still read—and made into movies—more than a century later. Kipling, who was born in India and spent much of his life there, wholeheartedly endorsed British imperialism. He emphasized the duty of racially superior peoples (as he saw it) to rule the rest in his 1899 poem "The White Man's Burden," which begins this way:

> Take up the White Man's burden—
> Send forth the best ye breed—
> Go bind your sons to exile
> To serve your captives' need

darker-skinned masses in Africa or Asia through imperial rule.

Nationalism bolstered imperialism in another important way: through the geopolitical logic of imperial rivalry. From about 1500 onward, European states had competed with one another overseas, mainly in the Americas. Now, in the nineteenth century, with growing global connections, they did so everywhere else—in Africa, Asia, and the archipelagoes of the Pacific. European statesmen came to think in terms of global competition. With nationalistic journalists, business lobbies, and religious establishments all urging action lest their country be left behind, governments sometimes leapt into imperial ventures without much idea of what they were getting into.

This particular motive, geopolitical rivalry, proved

To wait in heavy harness
On fluttered folk and wild—
Your new-caught, sullen peoples,
Half devil and half child.

The culture of imperialism and confidence in national fitness to rule over others developed as strongly in Britain as anywhere. But to a lesser extent it existed by the 1880s in the United States, France, Germany, Italy—and was developing rapidly in Japan.

SOCIAL DARWINISM AND PSEUDO-SCIENTIFIC RACISM

The European, U.S., and to some extent Japanese cultures of imperialism drew strength from three particular late-nineteenth-century trends. One was pseudo-scientific racism. In 1859, Charles Darwin published his masterwork on biological evolution through natural selection, *The Origin of Species,* with its emphasis on competition and the survival of the fittest. Others soon extended his concepts to subsets of the human species in a doctrine now called **social Darwinism**, which held that some people—usually either nationalities or "races," but sometimes socioeconomic classes—were more fit, in Darwin's sense, than others. If Europeans, and their biological descendants in North America, South America, South Africa, Australia, and New Zealand, were economically and militarily successful, the thinking ran, it was ultimately because they were a superior breed of human, fit and foreordained to rule over the world. Sometimes Europeans, and their descendants around the world, applied this notion to white people in general, understood as an inherently superior "race." But especially in Germany and Britain, the notion of a superior breed of human suited for imperial rule was often applied to a nationality understood to be a "race." Cecil Rhodes, the English business magnate and politician who made a fortune in South Africa, put it confidently in 1877:

> I contend that we are the finest race in the world and that the more of the world we inhabit the better it is for the human race. . . . Africa is still lying ready for us it is our duty to take it. . . . It is our duty to seize every opportunity of acquiring more territory and we should keep this one idea steadily before our eyes that more territory simply means more of the Anglo-Saxon race, more of the best, the most human, most honorable race the world possesses.

The social Darwinist perspective and pseudo-scientific racism proved especially popular in Germany, the United States, Britain, and the British dominions of Australia, New Zealand, South Africa, and Canada. The supposedly unfit breeds of humankind included all Africans, Asians, and Amerindians, and usually several sorts of Europeans as well, such as the Irish, Slavs, Greeks, Italians, Spaniards, and Jews, among others.

At the same time, Japanese intellectuals developed their own version of social Darwinism. A prolific professor and colonial official, Nitobe Inazo, who had studied at U.S. and German universities, justified Japanese imperialism by arguing that Koreans were not suited to self-government and it was Japan's responsibility to bring modern civilization to Korea. Japanese intellectuals adapted social Darwinism to encourage the belief that the

The first step towards lightening

The White Man's Burden

is through teaching the virtues of cleanliness.

Pears' Soap

Popular Imperialism Late-nineteenth-century British advertising and popular culture often appealed to imperialist and nationalist imagery. This advertisement references Kipling's poem "The White Man's Burden" and the idea of the civilizing mission in order to sell soap.

Japanese were a distinct biological race, inherently superior to Koreans and Chinese—if not everyone else too.

Disdain for other peoples is of course routine in world history. Chinese and Mongols typically considered one another inferior, as did French and Germans. Rival religious groups regularly vilified one another. What was different about social Darwinism was its resort to science for supposed proof of the notion that humankind is composed of biologically distinct races, of which some are better than others. That gave pseudo-scientific racism an impressive intellectual basis for nearly a century, but in the end made it brittle because it was susceptible to scientific disproof via genetics. Racism flourishes on every continent today, but it no longer appeals to science.

CONCEPTS OF MANLINESS AND MUSCULAR CHRISTIANITY

Beyond social Darwinism, the culture of imperialism also drew upon anxieties about manliness. In industrializing and urbanizing societies such as Japan, Britain, Germany, France, and the United States, some people came to think men were growing soft, losing their resourcefulness and hardihood. It seemed less worrisome if women lacked these qualities because they were not considered suitably feminine virtues. Physically challenging duties in the great outdoors might prevent the enfeeblement of males, and so conquest and empire were, so to speak, a cure for this societal disease. The U.S. president Theodore Roosevelt was among the more eloquent spokesmen for this anxious view, and he dedicated himself to restoring to American men a suitable vigor and valor.

Curing a loss of manliness could go hand in hand with advancing the cause of one's preferred religion. The culture of imperialism also drew upon developments within European and North American Christianity in the nineteenth century—specifically, the advent of what was called muscular Christianity. The phrase became commonplace by the 1870s, embraced by Protestants and Catholics alike as an ideal. Roosevelt was one among many advocates in the United States. Britons, Germans, and French had their own versions. The best places to exhibit muscular Christianity were in distant, physically challenging lands such as Africa, where, amid hardships, certain disciplined, forceful, and energetic men might spread the gospel. Christian missionary societies enjoyed unprecedented support in the late nineteenth century, typically working within the frameworks of one or another empire. New ones, such as France's Pères Blancs ("White Fathers"), were founded to

Muscular Christianity A 1900 photograph records a member of the French Pères Blancs missionary order preaching to an audience in what is now present-day Mali.

focus on Africa. Muscular Christianity wasn't confined to missionaries. Soldiers could exemplify it too. A British author in 1901 delighted in "the Englishman going through the world with rifle in one hand and Bible in the other."

SOME INTELLECTUAL RESPONSES

The culture of imperialism provoked a variety of intellectual responses in Africa and Asia, including everything from self-doubt to defiance. An anti-colonial politician from the Dutch East Indies, E.F.E. Douwes Dekker (also known as Setyabudi), noted the psychological impacts of the culture of imperialism in 1912: "There is nothing we need so much as self-assurance . . . we must feel . . . a strong sense of our own worth, a realization that we are not inferior to anybody." In an assessment of imperialism written in 1950, Aimé Césaire, a poet and essayist from Martinique, wrote of colonized people around the world: "I am talking about millions of men in whom fear has been cunningly instilled, who have been taught to have an inferiority complex, to tremble, kneel, despair." As we shall see in Chapter 28, colonized peoples in the course of the twentieth century rebuked the culture of imperialism in winning independence.

Industrialization, nationalism, and cultures of imperialism, in varying mixtures, created strong coalitions in favor of imperialism in western Europe and Japan, and a modest one in the United States. But the main incentive for the so-called new imperialism was simply that by 1870, for a handful of countries, Britain first and foremost, industrialization made imperialism increasingly cheap and easy. Thus it was both more practical and tempting.

THE BRITISH IN INDIA, 1818–1914

Britain, with its former American colonies having become an independent nation by 1783, focused its imperial efforts primarily on South Asia—all of which was generally called India. British influence in India remained largely in the hands of the East India Company, or EIC, which held a monopoly on external trade and maintained its own armed forces. The EIC had conquered small parts of India beginning in the 1750s, even before Britain's Industrial Revolution. In the early nineteenth century, it acquired much more territory and power through war and diplomacy, leaving it in control of most of India by 1818. Meanwhile, the British Crown took Ceylon in 1815 and parts of Burma starting in 1824, among other territories. Then, after a major uprising and civil war in India in 1857–1858 (discussed in the next chapter), the British state terminated the once-mighty Mughal Empire and the EIC, and in 1858 claimed control over most of India. Nearly 600 "princely states" remained, which had formerly paid tribute to either the Mughals or the EIC. They were all militarily weak, and their rulers had to bend to British wishes on every important matter, even though Britain did not rule them directly.

The princes, variously called *rajputs, maharajas, nawabs, sultans,* or *emirs,* were part of the local elite through which Britain ruled. In 1880, the ratio of Briton to Indian in India was only about 1:250,000. The large standing army of British India consisted overwhelmingly of Indians, called *sepoys,* who enforced British rule and fought overseas for the British. So, of necessity, British rule relied on the cooperation of Indian elites, including princes, big landowners, and the religious authorities of both Hinduism and Islam. For these men (and they were all men), British rule—sometimes called the **British Raj**—offered many advantages, helping to firm up their authority, including the property rights of landowners. But it brought frustrations too, as when, despite their distinguished ancestry, great wealth, or deep learning, they were treated as inferior beings by—as they saw it— ignorant commoners without princely blood whose only distinction was being British.

British Rule in India Sikh infantrymen in the British Army pose for a portrait during the Indian Rebellion of 1857–1858. Sikhs remained loyal to Britain during the rebellion—one of the many divisions between minority ethnic and religious groups that Britain exploited in order to consolidate power in India.

IMPERIAL STRATEGY: DIVIDE AND RULE In addition to finding willing partners among the elite, British rule relied on divisions in South Asian societies. All imperial states practiced the policy of divide and rule; five aspects of India's diversity made this policy especially effective there. First, India had been politically fragmented since the decline of the Mughal Empire in the early eighteenth century. Second, India, although mainly Hindu in religion, had large Muslim, Buddhist, and Sikh minorities. Third, within the Hindu majority, longstanding caste identities discouraged people from making common cause. Fourth, Indians spoke hundreds of different languages and wrote in several different scripts. And fifth, British authorities recognized certain groups in India as "martial races," such as Sikhs or the hill peoples of Nepal called Gurkhas, suitable for army and police work. Men from the "martial races" were encouraged to see themselves as better than others and to sign up for duty controlling other Indians on behalf of the British Raj. Only by exploiting these divisions could Britain rule some 250 million Indians.

ECONOMIC EFFECTS British rule in India had modest economic effect on the bulk of the people. Roughly 80 percent raised rice or wheat for their families and village markets. Their yields were among the world's lowest; their risk of crop failure and famine, usually from droughts, among the world's highest. British rule affected their routines only rarely before 1914. The biggest exception came during a major famine in the years 1876–1878, when colonial policy prioritized grain exports over relief efforts, contributing to the death of 5 to 6 million Indians.

British rule made a much bigger difference for those Indians in cities, or connected to export agriculture, and for the long-term direction of India's economy as a whole. Beginning in the 1840s, British engineers laid out thousands of miles of railroads and upgraded port facilities. The new infrastructure helped to extend the domain of market relations into Indian society. Together with British efforts to standardize law throughout India, and the spread of English as a common language, the new infrastructure promoted market integration within India and the integration of Indian markets with those elsewhere in the British Empire. Many Indian merchants and landowners took advantage of these market opportunities. The politician Jawaharlal Nehru expressed the ambivalence that many other Indians felt about the infrastructure acquired under the Raj: "I am all in favor of . . . the latest methods of transport, but . . . as I rushed across the Indian plains, the railway, that life-giver, has almost seemed to me like iron bands confining and imprisoning India." Overall, the Indian economy grew slowly under British rule.

The biggest change in economic life under the Raj came as a result of the policy of free trade, both within the empire and with the world at large. That proved devastating in the short run for Indian weavers and cloth manufacturers, who could not compete against the mass production of British factories. For decades, India's economy shifted in the direction of raw material production, typically of fibers such as cotton and jute—jute fiber is used to make burlap bags for transporting commodities such as rice and cotton. By the 1870s, however, Indian and British businessmen in the leading cities of Bombay and Calcutta (now Mumbai and Kolkata) began to build textile mills; and for a while, until the rise of the Japanese cotton industry by 1900, they did very well selling to China. Jamsetji Tata, for example, from the Parsi religious minority in Gujarat, made a fortune in cotton exports, and in 1907 his descendants started India's most successful steel business. This pattern, in which some found ways to profit handsomely from the changes brought by imperialism while the bulk of the population did not, proved characteristic of modern empires as a whole.

For its economic contributions, its military manpower,

and its strategic position in the Indian Ocean world, India remained the jewel in the crown of the British Empire. How Indians responded politically to British rule, and ultimately overthrew it in 1947, is a story taken up in Chapters 25 and 28.

THE FRENCH IN ALGERIA, 1830–1914

Algeria was as important to France as India was to Britain. Located in the Maghreb region of North Africa, Algeria was overwhelmingly Sunni Muslim in religion and mainly Arabic-speaking. It had been a loosely governed part of the Ottoman Empire since the sixteenth century, dominated by local authorities called *deys*. Several of the *deys* practiced piracy and the ransoming of Christian captives, attracting attention from French officials. Disputes over debts and ransoms, and an alleged insult to a French diplomat in Algiers, triggered a French assault on Algeria beginning in 1830. In the coming decades, Algeria became—officially—part of France, although in all but name it was a colony. Boatloads of European settlers, Italian and Spanish as well as French, flooded in. The French army pushed the locals off the best lands, sometimes with ruthless violence, turning them over to settlers—called *colons* in French North Africa. The big cities, such as Algiers and Oran, soon had more *colons* than Muslim Algerians. The indigenous Algerian population, only about 1.5 million in 1830, fell during the early years of French rule, the result of dispossession, disease,

French Algeria A French painting imagines the scene of the Algerian rebel leader Abdelkadir surrendering to the French governor of Algeria following the unsuccessful uprising of 1847—the moment that solidified French colonial rule there.

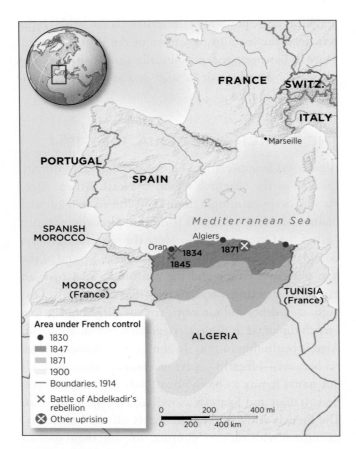

French Expansion in North Africa, 1830–1914 Beginning in 1830, Algeria was conquered by France and became its most important overseas possession. Algerians resisted militarily in the 1830s and 1840s, and again in an uprising in 1871. But French power advanced steadily southward, extending well into the Sahara desert by 1900.

and violence. It recovered, to about 3 million in 1862 and 4 million in 1900. The *colons* numbered 650,000 by 1900.

The French conquest initially provoked violent rebellions. The biggest, led by a Sufi scholar named **Abdelkadir**, took control of most of Algeria in the 1830s. But when the full force of the French military was brought to bear, Abdelkadir's uprising ended in his capture and exile in 1847. Another rebellion in 1871 lasted a few months, after which French rule remained secure, although punctuated by small-scale violence, until the 1950s.

COLONS **AND FRENCH RULE** With hundreds of thousands of *colons* living in the cities and on the best lands, French rule relied less on a cooperative indigenous elite than did British control in India. Nevertheless, cultivating cooperation was a useful imperial strategy everywhere, and the French worked hard at it. They claimed to

be civilizing Algeria and encouraged Algerians to embrace French language and culture, and to accept Christianity. Those who did so could become French citizens. Many learned French, but only about 3,000 abandoned Islam to take this path.

Like every other imperial power, the French in Algeria followed the strategy of divide and rule. Dealing with an overwhelmingly Muslim population, the French exploited distinctions based on language between Arabic-speakers (about 75 percent) and Berber-speakers (25 percent). Berber is a language, or set of languages, long spoken in North Africa, but since the arrival of Arabs in the eighth century mainly confined to mountainous areas. The French also played up more local tribal identities among both Arabs and Berbers, and, like the British in India, recruited some groups reputed to be warlike—such as the highlanders known as Zwawa or Zouaves—for army and police duty. This strategy of divide and rule helped France to maintain control until 1962.

ECONOMIC IMPACT The economic impact of French imperialism in Algeria was considerable. The *colons* by and large did better than they could have hoped for had they stayed in Europe. A few Algerians who worked with the French also found rewarding niches in the new imperial economy. The majority of Algerians found little or no economic benefit in French rule, especially the peasants and herders who lost their land and the textile producers suddenly put in direct competition with power looms in French industrial cities. The size of Algeria's economy grew considerably under French rule, but the redistribution of land and wealth away from Muslim Algerians and toward *colons* was more conspicuous—and accounts for the vigor of Abdelkadir's resistance and Algerians' later efforts to overthrow colonial rule, discussed in Chapter 28.

FORMS OF IMPERIALISM: SETTLER COLONIES

Algeria and India exemplify an important contrast in modern imperialism: colonies with settlers and those without. Algeria was a **settler colony**. Its European population varied between 10 percent and 30 percent of the total. French policy put settler interests foremost, but not always fully to their satisfaction. The *colons* often wanted yet more land and more restrictions placed on Muslim Algerians. The authorities in Paris, and French officials in Algeria, did not always agree with the *colons*. The situation resembled that in British North America before the American Revolution, when colonists wanted to take more Amerindian land and officials in London did not fully cooperate. Settler colonies always featured conflicts over land, and consequently more violence, than those without settlers. In addition to Algeria, the best examples of settler colonies—after the independence of the Americas—include Australia, New Zealand, South Africa, and to a lesser extent Morocco, Kenya, and Southern Rhodesia (now Zimbabwe). Japan's colonial empire, discussed below, also featured partial settler colonies.

Australia, New Zealand, and Canada were settler colonies, but with a big difference. Unlike the situation in Africa or East Asia, in these lands the indigenous populations were, as we've seen, drastically reduced in numbers by disease and violence. They were driven off not just the best lands, but almost all productive lands, and in the nineteenth century they were swamped demographically by European settlers. With such a small proportion of indigenous people left in the population in these colonies, almost everyone, except the French in Quebec, traced their ancestry to Britain and had kinfolk there. These ties enabled Australia, New Zealand and Canada to negotiate more and more self-government and autonomy, beginning in the 1840s. Canada, as we saw earlier in this chapter, won substantial independence at Confederation in 1867. Australia achieved much the same in 1900, when several colonies united in what Australians call Federation. Both Canada and Australia became fully self-governing in 1931. New Zealand's transition from colony to nation had many little steps, spanning the period 1852–1947, and nothing comparable to Confederation or Federation. These were settler colonies that, in the heyday of imperialism, stopped being colonies—but only because their populations had become predominantly British and therefore were judged capable of self-rule by British authorities in London.

India, in contrast, attracted very few European settlers. Malaria and other dangerous diseases discouraged migration, and so did the absence of free land. Other destinations, especially North America, appealed more to potential migrants. The British presence in India, therefore, was mainly administrative and military. Almost no expropriation of land took place. During the period of industrial imperialism, roughly 1850–1960, the majority of colonies around the world were, like India, exploited economically but scarcely settled by colonizing populations.

After 1870, the European powers extended their imperial reach in Africa and Asia. Their motives included the hope they might grab territory with minerals or other resources useful to industry, the geopolitical ambition to seize colonies so as to deny them to their rivals, and the desire to spread what they regarded as the best culture and religion—their own—to other peoples. Colonization often happened quickly, without much knowledge about the peoples or lands in question, especially in Africa.

THE PARTITION AND CONQUEST OF AFRICA, 1874–1914

In 1870, sub-Saharan Africa remained extremely diverse politically. Many people lived in kin groups without any state ruling them. Some lived in small statelets, others in full-blown states with kings, taxes, and armies. A few lived in small imperial states, such as the Zulu kingdom in South Africa. The only places not under African control were southernmost South Africa, British since 1815; the thinly administered Portuguese colonies of Angola and Mozambique; and a few small coastal outposts.

THE BERLIN CONFERENCE Between 1874 and 1890, six European powers carried out the **partition of Africa** among themselves. At first it was a haphazard process in which European states would unilaterally claim chunks of African territory, often merely to prevent a rival from seizing it. But in the years 1884–1885 at Bismarck's insistence, European diplomats gathered at the so-called Berlin Conference and agreed on who should get which territories. They also agreed to ban trading in slaves, guns, and alcohol in their territories. The first agreement held up better than the second.

MILITARY CONQUEST AND CATTLE DISEASE Once these six powers had carved up Africa on the map, they set about conquering it on the ground. For centuries African militaries, combined with a lethal disease environment, had kept outsiders at bay except in the far north and far south of the continent. From the 1870s, however, armies working for European states increasingly fared well in battle in Africa. Improved medicine and guns—and in the case of Britain, the availability of Indian troops—all helped to change the military balance. The bigger African states might win major battles now and again, as the Zulu kingdom (1879) and Ethiopia (1896) did, but the tide had

Berlin Conference An 1885 French cartoon shows delegates to the Berlin Conference expressing surprise as the German chancellor, Otto von Bismarck, slices a cake—representing the cavalier way in which Bismarck proposed to carve up the continent of Africa among the European powers.

turned very quickly in favor of Europe's armies. Those armies were led, trained, and equipped by Europeans. The rank-and-file soldiers were overwhelmingly Africans. So, in a sense, African soldiers in the service of European states conquered Africa. It took until about 1914.

As in the conquest of the Americas centuries before, European imperialists in late nineteenth-century Africa had an extraordinarily powerful ally in the form of disease—in this case, a cattle disease. Rinderpest broke loose in Asia in the 1860s and 1870s and arrived in East Africa from India in 1889. Over the next 12 to 15 years, in many regions it killed as much as 95 percent of the cattle and goats, sheep, and wildlife too. The plague extended from the savannas of East and southern Africa to the Sahel in West Africa. Cattle were the main form of wealth in these lands and a major source of food. Millions of Africans starved to death in the 1890s. In the pastoral and farming societies of East and southern Africa, men had to accumulate cattle before they could hope to marry. With rinderpest rippling throughout the continent, this became a forlorn hope. For some young men, serving as a soldier and helping to conquer Africa on behalf of colonial armies was the best remaining option.

The rinderpest plague stands among the greatest

disasters in modern African history. It made European conquest much easier, as Lord Frederick Lugard, a leading British empire builder, recognized: "[Rinderpest] has favored our enterprise. Powerful and warlike as the pastoral tribes are, their pride has been humbled and our progress facilitated by this awful visitation." Indeed, one wonders: Would European societies have willingly paid the price in blood and treasure for colonization that African resistance—without rinderpest—would have exacted?

Even as rinderpest sapped the will and capacity of Africans to resist conquest, armed resistance and rebellions flickered on and off for two decades. In the West African Sahel, local rulers fought off French authority until 1898. In what is now Zimbabwe, armed resistance to British rule lasted until 1897. In German Southwest Africa (Namibia today) in the years 1904–1905, rebellion brought especially vicious responses—sometimes labeled genocide—almost obliterating a people called the Herero. As we will see, in Ethiopia, African armies succeeded in fending off colonialism. Elsewhere in Africa, however, by 1914, armed resistance had faded away, and opposition to colonialism took other forms.

COLONIAL AFRICA TO 1930

These victorious powers set up cheap and flimsy colonial states in Africa. Governments in Europe did not wish to invest in infrastructure, education, or almost anything else for Africans. Neither did private businesses, except

Conquest and Disease South African settler colonists stand in a field strewn with cattle carcasses in 1897 at the height of the rinderpest outbreak. They have shot the infected animals in an effort to prevent transmission of the disease, whose economic effects were felt much more harshly by native South African farmers than by settlers.

where mining was involved. So, until the late 1940s, African colonies did not get much in the way of roads or railroads, except lines connecting mines to ports. They got only rudimentary schools, generally run by missionaries. At times, colonial officials restricted the educational work of missionaries, fearing it would raise the hopes and skills of Africans so much that they would become harder to rule. The colonial court systems were also threadbare, with the administration of justice entrusted to favored African elders.

Imperial power in colonial Africa worked through local elites. The strategy was generally to find cooperative Africans and enhance their authority. This normally meant empowering male elders, making them responsible for organizing labor brigades, tax collection, and military conscription, and rewarding them when they did so. Machemba, the Yao leader in Tanganyika with whom this chapter began, refused just such an offer.

Colonial rule also relied on large lineage and language groups, labeled tribes. By assigning tribal identity to everyone, whether or not they considered themselves Xhosa, Masai, Hausa, and so forth, colonial administrators emphasized social divisions, making colonial rule easier. Such identities existed to some extent before colonial rule in Africa; but because they suited administrative needs, colonial rulers tried and generally succeeded in strengthening them. In particular, colonial authorities found it useful to recruit soldiers and police from among those groups they regarded as "martial tribes," such as Bambara-speakers in what is now Mali or Kamba in east-central Kenya. This recruitment policy encouraged some—males, at least—to prize their distinction from non-martial, lesser peoples.

ECONOMIC EXPLOITATION The economic approach of the imperial powers, at least until the 1930s, was ruthlessly extractive. They intended to make money from mining or commercial agriculture. Each colony was to pay for its own administration and ideally contribute revenue to its colonizer. Monetized, taxable economic activity such as commercial farming helped attain this goal; subsistence farming or herding did not. In West Africa, colonial rulers encouraged cocoa, palm oil, peanuts, cotton, and other cash crops. In South Africa and the copper belt of central Africa, colonial authorities invited private companies to develop mining and offered to provide migrant workers for the mines by organizing labor recruitment drives. In

Imperial Economies A photograph from the 1920s shows workers laboring in a tin mine in British Nigeria. Mining was one of the extractive industries in which European colonial powers tapped African natural resources for their own economic gain.

South Africa, that sometimes required recruiting young men from hundreds of miles away, housing them in barracks, and policing them carefully.

In the Congo, where Belgium's King Leopold II claimed a personal fiefdom, economic extraction took a notoriously brutal form. Private companies paid the king for the right to harvest rubber from the forests, with no constraints on how they did it. They relied on forced labor and created a police force encouraged to kill men who refused to collect rubber. Sometimes they held women hostage until their husbands brought in enough rubber. In one case, 55 women were hanged because their husbands did not meet a production quota. The Belgian parliament considered the abuses sufficient to take control of the Congo away from the king in 1908.

Supporters of imperialism cloaked this economic exploitation in altruism. Confident in the righteousness of their religion and the superiority of their culture, colonial rulers convinced themselves and their publics back home that imperialism was good for Africans and Asians. Britain's Secretary of State for Colonies in 1897, Joseph Chamberlain (the former Birmingham industrialist we encountered earlier), gave voice to this conviction: "We now feel that our rule over these territories [British colonies in Africa and Asia] can only be justified if we can show that it adds to the happiness and prosperity of the people, and I maintain that our rule does." Chamberlain, and tens of millions of others in Europe, sincerely believed in the uplifting effect of colonial rule. A minority of Africans agreed.

CHRISTIANITY IN AFRICA   Many Europeans counted Christianity as a blessing conferred by colonial rule. As we've seen, Christianity had ancient roots in Ethiopia and won many converts in Portuguese-influenced Angola after 1500. But elsewhere in Africa it figured little, if at all. In 1900, about 6 to 9 million Africans, of a total population of 80 to 90 million, considered themselves Christians. By 1930, missionary work and the spread of hundreds of independent African churches had boosted the Christian population to about 20 million. (Today, African Christians number about 400 million.)

By 1910, some 10,000 Christian missionaries—Catholics and at least 10 varieties of Protestants—were at work in Africa. Their most lasting impact came through mission schools, which appealed to many Africans who wanted to learn to read and write, and perhaps get a post in the colonial bureaucracy. Instruction in literacy came with instruction in Christianity. Slaves, women, poor men, refugees from wars, and the young were especially likely to embrace Christianity. In most African societies, young men had to prove themselves before they could hope to marry and take fully adult roles, while older and richer men could marry several women. Christian missionaries denounced polygamy and, through literacy, offered the hope of rapid advancement to younger men. For young women who preferred to marry someone of their own generation, it offered hope too. In some respects, the success of mission Christianity was a youth revolt against the authority of African male elders.

Many Africans joined independent churches outside of missionary control. Interactions with missionaries under colonialism inspired novel versions of Christianity. Some independent churches accepted polygamy, which mission churches never could. Some promised to counter the evils of witchcraft and sorcery, in which most Africans believed, whereas mission churches denied such malevolent powers existed. Some offered rewarding roles for women as spiritual leaders and faith healers. And all emphasized certain sides of the Christian tradition that spoke to millions of Africans, such as healing the sick. In some respects, the success of independent churches was

Missionaries in Africa   A German nun teaches reading and writing to children enrolled at a mission school in South Africa in this 1912 photo. Mission schools were one of the most visible presences of Christianity—and of European power and cultural influence—in colonial Africa.

a revolt against missionary control over Christianity and against colonialism in general. The most successful independent churches developed in Nigeria, South Africa, and the Belgian Congo.

The Aladura churches in Nigeria took shape during the 1918 influenza epidemic. A young Anglican schoolteacher, Sophie Odunlami, had a vision in which God told her that faith alone could heal the sick. She and others began to preach against traditional African religions, polygamy, and European medicine, claiming healing powers through God and blessed water. Within a decade, they gathered disciples and thousands of followers who set up churches.

In South Africa, the most popular independent churches were those called Zionist. They followed the teachings of faith healers from Zion, Illinois (a northern suburb of Chicago), notably John Lake. Lake moved to South Africa in 1908 to escape the wrath of parishioners after an attempted exorcism left two dead. His preaching skills brought him followers who quickly organized several Zionist churches. Migrant workers in South Africa's mines carried African Zionist faith and practices back to their home villages all over southern Africa.

The most enduring of the independent African churches arose in the Belgian Congo. **Simon Kimbangu**, raised at a Baptist mission in western Congo, felt called as a prophet in 1921, and followers credited him with many healing miracles at a time when epidemics were ravaging central Africa. His popular preaching quickly aroused suspicions among Belgian authorities, who imprisoned him for the last 30 years of his life. But disciples spread his message of faith healing, non-violence, monogamy, and sobriety—and added the notions of Kimbangu's divinity and the injustice of Belgian rule. By the end of the colonial era in 1960, half a million people had embraced Kimbanguism (as do roughly 20 million today). Independent churches—the Africanization of Christianity in the context of the partial Christianization of Africa—constituted the most important and enduring cultural response to colonialism in Africa.

ISLAM IN AFRICA Islam, like Christianity, prospered as a result of colonial rule. As we've seen, Islam also had deep roots in the northern half of Africa. Colonial rulers often found prestigious Muslim clerics useful in their efforts to control subject populations. French authorities in Senegal supported Malik Sy, who in 1902 set up a *zawiya* (as Islamic schools are called in West Africa) and urged his fellow Muslims to accept French rule and to serve in the French army. Colonial rule inadvertently promoted Islam. Village families often could not pay taxes demanded by colonial authorities and sent their young men to towns, mines, or plantations where they could earn a wage. In these new and unfamiliar settings, Islamic brotherhoods often offered these youths community and hospitality. Muslim clerics in West Africa who needed workers for their peanut farms employed many such young men, who often became disciples as well as laborers. They brought back Islamic practices with them when they returned to their native villages. In these ways, colonial rulers, although intending nothing of the sort, expanded the domain of Islam especially in West Africa.

Colonial rule changed African religious life as much or more than it did African economic life. While Africans had long been receptive to innovation in spiritual matters, now they had a wider range of examples to choose from. Selective borrowing led to great creativity and novelty, as well as to the spread of established forms of both Christianity and Islam.

EUROPEAN IMPERIALISM IN SOUTHEAST ASIA AND THE PACIFIC

Europe's imperial powers fastened colonial rule on Southeast Asia and the Pacific Islands at the same time that they partitioned Africa. The Dutch East India Company (VOC) had dominated island Southeast Asia since the sixteenth century. The trading company went bankrupt by 1800. The Dutch monarchy then stepped in and tried to tighten its grip on the archipelago (now Indonesia). That required repeated warfare from the 1820s to 1910, by which time all local Indonesian (the term came into use in the 1880s) rulers had submitted to the Dutch. Export trade in spices and plantation crops formed the basis of the Dutch colonial economy. Meanwhile, in 1819 the British founded Singapore, a port at the southern tip of the Malay Peninsula. They gradually took over large parts of Malaya, which had the world's best tin deposits and was well suited to rubber tree plantations—both tin and rubber were important to British industrial production. Islam had been the majority religion in these lands since the sixteenth century; neither the Dutch nor the British tried hard to convert Indonesians or Malays to Christianity.

The French conquered much of mainland Southeast Asia starting in 1858. Initially intending only to protect French Catholic missionaries from persecution by Vietnam's Nguyễn dynasty, French armies, with gunboats and industrial weaponry, soon claimed the kingdoms of Vietnam, Cambodia, and Laos—all formerly in the orbit of China. Vietnam became a principal rice exporter and eventually home to rubber plantations too. Many of its elite families, who had long served Vietnamese monarchs, nimbly pivoted to work with French authorities. Few French migrated to Southeast Asia; in 1913 in Vietnam, the French were outnumbered about 700:1 by locals.

Most Vietnamese were Buddhists. The Catholic Church, which had been present for 200 years and the spiritual home of perhaps 3 to 5 percent of Vietnamese, proved a valuable ally: most Vietnamese Catholics welcomed French rule. France rewarded them, and the Church, with land grants and other favors. In mainland Southeast Asia, only Thailand (or Siam, as it was then) remained outside of European empires. Its kings carefully played off the French against the British and preserved a precarious independence.

In the Pacific, the French, Germans, and British claimed several archipelagoes in the late nineteenth century. Islanders could not resist effectively. Their populations were too small and, in most cases, falling fast due to introduced infections. Their stone and wood weapons, supplemented by a few imported muskets, were no match for what European navies could bring to bear. So European rule came swiftly. France used New Caledonia as a dumping ground for convicts and political prisoners after 1864. British Fiji and German Samoa became plantation islands. None of these islands mattered economically to their colonizers. But in an age when navies needed coal to power their warships, Pacific ports carried strategic value as **coaling stations**. Whatever their value, the cost of controlling Pacific islands was so low by European standards that using them to park coal or grow coconuts was reason enough to keep them. Missionaries met greater success here winning converts to Christianity than they had in Southeast Asia, partly because there was no Islam to contend with.

IMPERIAL LATECOMERS: ITALY, JAPAN, AND THE UNITED STATES

Italy, unified only in the 1860s, was a latecomer to overseas imperialism. By the 1880s, boatloads of poor Italians migrated every year to the United States, Brazil, or Argentina. Italian nationalists hoped to build an empire of settlement in Africa, where Italian emigrants could contribute to Italy's strength. Ambitious statesmen found it irresistible to bring up the Roman Empire as an example to follow, and to exhort Italians to greatness through conquest. Italy first tried to get hold of Tunisia in North Africa but lost out to France. It did manage to obtain part of Somalia in the 1880s.

But that hardly signaled greatness worthy of descendants of the Caesars. Taking advantage of drought, rinderpest, and a resulting famine that killed about half of Ethiopia's 7 million people (1888–1892), Italy launched an invasion of Ethiopia in 1896. At the Battle of Adowa, Ethiopian armies killed or captured three-quarters of the Italian force, securing Ethiopia's independence for the next 40 years. Italy managed to take Libya from the Ottoman Empire in 1912 with the help of the first aerial bombing campaigns in world history. Italy's empire was small, thinly populated, of little economic value, and controversial within Italy.

Japan and the United States were also latecomers to overseas empire. Both had some background in territorial expansion. Japan in the eighteenth and nineteenth centuries had conquered and settled the northern island of Hokkaido, at the expense of the indigenous Ainu people. The United States from its inception had expanded westward across the continent, at the expense of Amerindians. Both had become industrial powers with modern weaponry, increasingly nationalistic populations, and vocal lobbies eager for imperial ventures. In the 1890s, both

Russo-Japanese War A Japanese illustration celebrates a Japanese military victory against Russian opponents in 1904. Winning the Russo-Japanese War enabled Japan to consolidate its presence as an empire in the Pacific.

became seaborne empires, although on far smaller scales than Britain or France, exploiting the regional military superiority they enjoyed by industrializing earlier than their neighbors.

Japanese imperialists began calling for expansion in the mid-1870s, believing that to fend off foreign imperialists Japan had to become imperialist itself. Their opportunity came when Japan defeated China in war in the years 1894–1895, took over Taiwan, and began to play a larger role in Korea. Japan's expansion brought on the 1904–1905 Russo-Japanese War, which ended with the Russian navy at the bottom of the sea. When Japan fully annexed Korea in 1910, it ruled a seaborne empire with a population only somewhat smaller than that of the home islands.

Japan's government encouraged emigration to its colonies. Taiwan, under Japanese rule until 1945, was partly a settler colony: some 5 to 10 percent of the total population was Japanese. Only a few hundred thousand Japanese moved to Korea, accounting for roughly 1 percent of the peninsula's population. But Japanese settlers took over half the farmland by the 1930s and obliged Korean farmers to work as tenants, giving Korea a key feature of settler colonies. Japan also resorted freely to deadly military force to suppress political resistance in Korea, especially in the years 1919–1920.

The United States became an overseas imperialist power in 1898. Ever since the Monroe Doctrine in 1823, the United States had tried to discourage European imperial powers from extending their sway in the hemisphere. In 1898, it intervened in a Cuban nationalist rebellion against Spain, which expanded into the Spanish-American War. Victorious, the United States took over Spain's colonies in the Philippines, Puerto Rico, Guam, and—briefly—Cuba, meanwhile annexing the Hawaiian Islands, partly to secure the ocean route to the Philippines. The newly acquired territories and populations were small compared to the continental United States and, in the Philippines, where a nationalist guerrilla resistance lasted until 1903, cost considerable blood and treasure to keep. Suppressing the Filipino insurrection cost the U.S. army 10 times as many lives as did the Spanish-American War. Overseas imperialism delivered no conspicuous advantages to the United States except naval outposts, and as in Italy it was controversial domestically. The new overseas empire thrust the United States into world affairs as never before.

LAND EMPIRES

It is customary to use the word *imperialism* in modern history for empires that stretched overseas, but empires existed on land as well. One could use the term *empire* for nineteenth-century Canada, the United States, Brazil, and Argentina: they were all new countries, and they used industrial technologies and nationalist ideologies to support westward extension of their rule over Amerindian peoples. Indeed, even an Amerindian people, the Comanche, used rifles, an industrial technology, to help build a **land empire** in North America. In Africa, Ethiopians used modern firearms, combined with a growing sense of nationalism, to create a land empire of their own. The biggest land empire was Russia's.

RUSSIA: THE WORLD'S BIGGEST LAND EMPIRE

Through war or diplomacy in the eighteenth century, Russia had already acquired what are now called the Baltic States—Estonia, Latvia, Lithuania—as well as Crimea, parts of Poland, and Ukraine. In 1809, it acquired Finland in a peace treaty. Emerging victorious in war against Napoleon Bonaparte, Russia accelerated its territorial expansion. Between 1812 and 1864, it conquered territories in the Caucasus—the region between the Black Sea

and Caspian Sea—populated by diverse ethnic groups such as Georgians, Armenians, Circassians, and Chechens. In the Baltics, Poland, and the Caucasus, the Russian state tried hard to spread Russian language, culture, and the Russian Orthodox religion—policies called Russification. It banned the use of Polish, for example, in schools and offices, and converted some Catholic churches into Russian Orthodox ones. Growing Russian nationalism spurred the belief, in elite circles, that it was Russia's destiny to rule over lesser peoples on its periphery.

Between 1860 and 1885, the tsar's armies also conquered vast swathes of steppe and desert in Central Asia. Like other imperialists, they exploited advantages conferred by modern rifles, telegraph systems, and a growing railroad network. Dotted by oases, the region was inhabited by Muslim and mainly Turkic-speaking groups such as Uzbeks and Kazakhs. Russia also tightened its grip on Siberia with the construction of the Trans-Siberian Railway beginning in the 1890s and added territories along the Pacific coast northeast of Manchuria. It gave up on overseas empire when it sold Alaska to the United States in 1867.

Russia acquired both headaches and assets in the process of extending its land empire. Its expansion, and Russification attempts, inflamed nationalism among minorities and inspired repeated uprisings in Poland and Islamist rebellions in the Caucasus. Outside the Caucasus, Russia managed to find Muslim clerics willing to operate under Russian authority. They took care of meting out justice and family matters, while encouraging the empire's 14 million Muslims (as of 1897) to accept Russian rule and pay their taxes—as Malik Sy did with French rule in Senegal. The state also continued its efforts to get nomads to settle down and become reliable taxpayers. It invested in irrigation in Central Asia, hoping to create a viable cotton industry. Despite all its internal tensions and military defeats in the Crimean War (1853–1856) and the Russo-Japanese War (1904–1905), Russia built the world's largest land empire—after 1880 enabled by its industrialization.

SECONDARY EMPIRES: COMANCHE TEXAS AND ETHIOPIA

Any state with weaker neighbors could take up imperial expansion. In the nineteenth century, the advent of mass-produced weaponry made it easier for a king or chief to monopolize military power in his neighborhood

Russia's Land Empire, 1800–1900 Russia had built an empire in thinly populated Siberia beginning in the sixteenth century. During the nineteenth century, it began to use the tools of industrial imperialism to expand into the Caucasus region and Central Asia at the expense mainly of Islamic khanates. This brought millions of Muslim subjects into the Russian Empire. As the Trans-Siberian Railway progressed eastward, Russia was also able to tighten its hold on southern Siberia and eventually the Pacific coast, which in the years 1904–1905 brought conflict with Japan.

and use it to build a regional empire. The phenomenon is sometimes known as secondary empire, because a key source of power undergirding this imperialism was not internal, but acquired from abroad—usually from armaments factories in Europe or the United States.

COMANCHE TEXAS, 1730–1870 Between 1730 and 1850, a Comanche empire flourished on what is now the southern plains of the United States—roughly central and west Texas, plus bits of Oklahoma, Kansas, Colorado, and New Mexico. The Comanche, one of many Amerindian peoples called Plains Indians, based their political power on access to horses and guns. They were recent migrants to the plains, having arrived in the seventeenth century from what is now Utah and western Colorado at more or less the same time that horses galloped onto the scene. Horses had revolutionized North American plains life starting around 1680. Spanish traders introduced horses via New Mexico, and the Comanche quickly mastered the arts of riding and

raising horses. With the mobility that horses gave them, the Comanche became more efficient bison hunters—and more effective fighters against their neighbors.

The Comanche numbered about 40,000 people in 1780, with herds of about 300,000 horses. Smallpox in the period 1779–1782 halved their number, but they rebounded quickly by capturing women and children from neighboring Amerindian peoples and assimilating them into Comanche society. Although few in number by the standards of imperial peoples, the Comanche were lords of the vast grassland of the southern plains.

The **Comanche Empire**'s political success rested on guns as well as horses. Spanish authorities in Mexico prohibited the trade of guns northward to Amerindian peoples, but the French based in Louisiana did not; nor did the Americans who bought Louisiana from France in 1803. The Comanche secured a near-monopoly position in the gun trade on the southern plains, allowing them to exert military power unmatched in their neighborhood.

They seized captives from the agricultural peoples in New Mexico. After 1820, when Mexico was becoming independent from Spain, the Comanche raided deep into Mexico, taking horses, mules, and women and children to keep or sell as slaves.

Successful raiding over broad territories enabled the Comanche to trade profitably. They sold people, horses, and mules from Mexico to Amerindians of the central plains (today's Kansas and Nebraska) or to white Americans in the Louisiana Territory. The Comanche traders came to know which markets preferred which kinds of horses and who would pay the most for captives. They exploited their mobility to acquire broader market knowledge and prospered as a result.

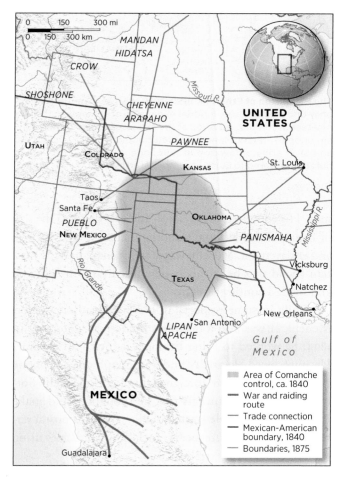

The Comanche Empire, ca. 1800–1850 After 1780, horses and guns gave the Comanche advantages over their neighbors. They mounted raids deep into Mexico, especially during the period 1820–1845, and maintained long-distance trade with several other Amerindian peoples and with white Americans along the Mississippi River. The Comanche way of life ended between 1850 and 1875, defeated by U.S. forces and repeated epidemics.

They occasionally captured white children and raised them as Comanche. In 1836 in east Texas, Comanche raiders seized 10-year-old Cynthia Ann Parker, who gradually became Comanche. She married Peta Nocona, leader of the Nokoni band and one of the most successful of Comanche war captains in the 1850s. Among their children was the last independent Comanche leader, Quanah Parker.

Comanche economic and military strength peaked around 1840. They demanded tribute and attacked anyone who did not pay. Most people gave the Comanche what they wanted most of the time. By 1840, 10 to 25 percent of Comanche people had been kidnapped from Mexico and assimilated as adopted children, wives, or slaves. In 1846, the Mexican authorities in the northern state of Chihuahua complained of the Comanche: "We travel the roads...at their whim; we cultivate the land where they wish and in the amount they wish." Comanche attacks in the years preceding the Mexican-American War (1846–1848) made it easier for U.S. forces to drive deep into Mexico and win that war. The resulting treaty cost Mexico nearly half its territory and put the Comanche lands fully inside the United States—a great misfortune for them.

Quanah Parker The last independent Comanche leader was photographed in 1892. He is seen standing outside his house with his wife, Tonasa.

The Comanche Empire came to an end for several reasons, the most important being the arrival on the southern plains after 1848 of the U.S. army backed by an industrial economy and the largest population in North America. Suffering from repeated smallpox, measles, and cholera epidemics and military defeats, the Comanche population slipped to about 20,000 by 1850. The Comanche struggled against U.S. forces and emboldened Amerindian enemies such as the Osage. After the U.S. Civil War (1861–1865), the U.S. army, battle hardened and well supplied, reduced the Comanche to a shadow of their former glory. In 1875, the last of the remaining 3,000 Comanche straggled onto Indian reservations in Oklahoma, led by Quanah Parker.

ETHIOPIA, 1870–1913 Ethiopia, a land of mountains and deserts in northeastern Africa, is another example of a secondary land empire built on monopoly access to imported weaponry. It was home to a mainly Christian population with a literate elite aware of Ethiopia's ancient heritage as the land of Aksum, an empire of the fourth century CE. For centuries before 1850, however, Ethiopia had been disunited, and its various peoples fought among themselves and against Muslim sultanates in neighboring lands. External threats, especially from Egypt, helped Ethiopians unite across linguistic and cultural lines from the late 1850s, a process begun by a warlord who united much of Ethiopia by force. Calling himself Tewodros II, he and his successors sought to prevent foreign encroachments and make their country more formidable—much as Japan's leaders were doing after the Meiji Restoration. The surest route, in Ethiopia as in Japan, was judicious borrowing of techniques and technologies of power from elsewhere. In the 1870s, a successor of Tewodros managed to get large quantities of modern British weapons, which he used to subdue all rivals within Ethiopia, fend off an Egyptian attack, and assault his nearest neighbors. Ethiopia was becoming an empire.

The master empire builder of Ethiopia was **Menelik II**. He took the throne in 1889 when the reigning emperor was killed in battle. Menelik claimed descent from King Solomon and the Queen of Sheba (of Old Testament fame) and maintained he was the rightful heir of the ancient emperors of Aksum. Through diplomacy and force, he increasingly brought the various peoples in and around Ethiopia (Amharic- and Oromo-speakers were the biggest groups) into a single imperial state. Aware of the **partition of Africa** under way in the late 1880s, he was determined to keep newly enlarged Ethiopia under Ethiopian—and his—rule.

Menelik adapted foreign techniques and technologies that bolstered his own power. In the early 1890s, as rinderpest was ravaging the pastoral societies in and around Ethiopia—Menelik himself lost 250,000 head of cattle—he forged a friendship with a Russian cavalry officer sent by the tsar to build a Russian-Ethiopian bond. Nikolai Leontiev brought advisors and weapons for Menelik's army, including 30,000 modern rifles and a few dozen artillery pieces. Menelik's army even acquired a few machine guns. With this armament, Menelik's forces sliced to ribbons the Italian army of 18,000 men at Adowa in 1896.

Menelik continued to exploit his access to foreign weaponry and skills after scattering the Italians. He campaigned against any neighbor bold enough to resist his armies, which now numbered a few hundred thousand

The Expansion of Ethiopia, 1850–1910 Access to modern weaponry underpinned the imperial expansion of Ethiopia in the late nineteenth century, achieved at the expense of neighboring Muslim peoples. Under Menelik II, the Ethiopian military destroyed an Italian army of invasion in 1896, one of the few resounding defeats delivered to European imperial armies during this period.

men. His conquests to the south and east doubled the size of Ethiopia and left longstanding memories of atrocities and enslavement. Menelik was grateful enough to his Russian friend that he created a new titled rank in Ethiopia and made Leontiev a count.

While in some respects an old-fashioned conqueror, Menelik II was also a relentless modernizer. Starting in 1894, he worked to bring Ethiopia its first railroad line. He introduced electricity and a telegraph and telephone system. In addition to foreign technologies, Menelik borrowed foreign institutions that he thought would make Ethiopia stronger. He started public schools, a postal service, and a formal bureaucracy including a judiciary using the principle of jury trials.

By the time of Menelik's death in 1913, Ethiopia stood alone as a fully independent polity in Africa. He had ruled for a quarter-century over an empire the size of Texas, made possible by the judicious introduction of foreign technologies and skills.

CONSIDERING THE EVIDENCE

Ethiopian Imperialism through Russian Eyes

Alexander Bulatovich first arrived in Ethiopia in 1896, as part of the Russian Red Cross. The medical mission was charged with offering aid during the conflict between Italians and Ethiopians that culminated in the Battle of Adowa. When the rest of the delegation left, Bulatovich stayed to explore the western regions that Ethiopia had recently conquered and to record the customs of the Oromo people who lived there. When he returned to Ethiopia again the following year as part of Russia's diplomatic delegation, he joined several thousand Ethiopian soldiers on a military expedition to claim territory between the Nile River and the Red Sea. Emperor Menelik had claimed this region to preempt British and French claims, but it was much farther than Ethiopia had previously extended its reach. In Bulatovich's journal of the expedition, published in 1900, he wrote the following introduction to justify Ethiopia's conquests.

Menelik is only carrying out the traditional mission of Ethiopia as the propagator of culture and the unifier of all the inhabitants of the Ethiopian Mountains and of the related tribes in their neighborhood, and only makes a new step toward consolidating and developing the power of the black empire....

[W]e Russians cannot help sympathizing with his intentions, not only because of political considerations, but also for purely human reasons. It is well known to what consequences conquests of wild tribes by Europeans lead. Too great a difference in the degree of culture between the conquered people and their conquerors has always led to the enslavement, corruption, and degeneration of the weaker race. The natives of America degenerated and have almost ceased to exist. The natives of India were corrupted and deprived of individuality. The black tribes of Africa became the slaves of the whites.

Clashes between nations more or less close to one another in culture bring completely different results.

For the Abyssinians [Ethiopians], the Egyptian, Arab, and, finally, European civilization which they have gradually adopted has not been pernicious: borrowing the fruits of these civilizations, and in turn conquering and annexing neighboring tribes and passing on to them her culture, Abyssinia [Ethiopia] did not obliterate from the face of the earth, did not destroy the uniqueness of any one of the conquered tribes, but rather gave them all the possibility of preserving their individual characteristics.

Thus Christian Abyssinia [Ethiopia] plays an important role in world progress as a transmission point of European civilization to wild central African peoples.

The high civilizing mission of Abyssinia [Ethiopia], its centuries-old, almost uninterrupted struggle for faith and freedom against the surrounding Moslems [Muslims], the nearness of her people to the Russian people in creed, won for her the favor of the Russian people.

Source: Alexander Bulatovich, *Ethiopia through Russian Eyes: Country in Transition*, trans. Richard Seltzer (Lawrenceville, NJ, 2000). Published in print by Red Sea Press.

QUESTIONS FOR ANALYSIS

1. What "political considerations" and "human reasons" motivated the Russians to support Ethiopia's imperial expansion?
2. Why does Bulatovich think Ethiopians are better than Europeans at transmitting "European civilization" to Africans?
3. How does Bulatovich's description of Ethiopia's "role in world progress" reveal European stereotypes about Africa?

OTHER SECONDARY EMPIRES

Secondary empires of the sort built in Ethiopia and Texas were many but fleeting. The Maori leader Hongi Hika in New Zealand studied European military and agricultural methods before importing guns and potatoes to New Zealand's North Island in 1818. He used the guns to defeat rivals who had none, capturing slaves whom he put to work raising potatoes for his armies. For a decade, he ruled a secondary empire. On a larger scale, the Albanian Mehmet Ali created a secondary empire in Egypt, wresting it from Ottoman control in the early nineteenth century and using European weaponry and military technique to extend Egyptian power south into Sudan.

Secondary empires of a sort had existed long before the nineteenth century, but with industrialization they became easier to create. The gap in formidability between those with modern guns and those without was huge, and modern guns came from only a few places. The Global web enabled transfers of guns and relevant military skills from Britain and Russia to Ethiopia or from French Louisiana and the United States to Comanche Texas. But the world was not yet so well connected that everybody in and around Ethiopia and Texas had similar access to the tools of power. So ambitious, skilled, and lucky warlords could monopolize that access in their own neighborhoods and build secondary empires—at least for a while. Most secondary empires vanished within years or decades, destroyed by their neighbors, by internal rifts, or swallowed up by larger empires.

NATIONALISM, IMPERIALISM, AND THE GLOBAL WEB

Nationalism and imperialism further tightened the Global web. Nationalism, often sparked by conflict, was infectious and spread along the circuits of the Global web. Its emergence thickened the web—for example, by inspiring people in Japan to pay more attention to military practices in Germany.

Imperialism, for its part, contributed to the more rapid exchange of goods, and the extension of market relations, into places such as central Africa or Samoa, where they had been weak. It helped spread versions of Christianity in colonized lands. And in parts of Africa and Southeast Asia, it—unintentionally—helped extend the realm of Islam, the religion that appealed most to people who opposed European empire. Most conspicuously, imperialism brought political consolidation. Its forces crushed hundreds of smaller polities around the world, replacing them with a few empires. Imperialism and nationalism made the world a smaller, more tightly interactive, place.

While nationalism and imperialism brought the world into tighter interaction, they also deepened the differences among peoples in two respects. The first was economic status. The imperial powers, already growing rich through industrialization, enriched themselves further through the economic policies of imperialism—although by just how much is controversial among scholars.

Second, imperialism and nationalism emphasized differences among peoples and religions. As ideologies, nationalism sometimes and imperialism always supported racialist outlooks that divided humankind into several "races" arranged in hierarchies based on either skin color or ethnicity. In racial hierarchies, whites deemed darker-skinned people to be inherently inferior. Imperial strategy fostered division to make subject populations easier to rule, underscoring distinctions, perhaps inventing them. Nationalism had contradictory effects: nationalists invited people to bury their class or religious differences and to prize solidarity as a Japanese, Canadian, or Italian nation; but at the same time, they divided humankind into hundreds of nationalities and often claimed these were biological categories and unchangeable. With respect to religion, both nationalism and imperialism showed contradictory effects: while helping to spread Christianity and Islam, they also helped to splinter both religions. Christianity in Nigeria or Vietnam took on local flavoring. Local religion and culture colored Islam too, as it spread in West Africa or Indonesia under European imperial rule. So nationalism and imperialism bound the world more tightly into a global web; but at the same time, they both emphasized differences within the human species.

CONCLUSION

The ideas and practices of both nationalism and imperialism reshaped the world between 1800 and 1930. Nationalism took root first in revolutionary France but spread easily to other lands. It helped to forge nation-states and to weaken multiethnic empires. Together with industrialization, it combined to make some countries, such as Britain, France, Germany, Japan, and the United States, much stronger. They used that strength to expand, or to create, overseas empires at the expense of less powerful societies in Africa, Asia, and the Pacific.

Sometimes imperialism took the form of settler colonies in which migrants from Europe or Japan put down roots in conquered lands, as in Algeria or Taiwan. But more often settlers were few and colonial rule more narrowly focused on economic extraction and religious conversion. The empires of the nineteenth and early twentieth centuries often had profound economic and cultural effects. Among the unintended effects was the emergence of many new examples of nationalism among the colonized peoples. Their political ambitions, as later chapters will explain, made imperialism too costly to sustain.

CHAPTER REVIEW

KEY TERMS

nationalism (p. 704)
La Marseillaise (p. 705)
Yamato race theory (p. 706)
multiethnic empires (p. 710)
new imperialism (p. 712)

culture of imperialism (p. 715)
social Darwinism (p. 716)
British Raj (p. 718)
Abdelkadir (p. 720)
settler colony (p. 720)
partition of Africa (p. 721)

Simon Kimbangu (p. 724)
coaling stations (p. 726)
land empire (p. 727)
Comanche Empire (p. 728)
Menelik II (p. 730)

Go to INQUIZITIVE to see what you've learned—and learn what you've missed—with personalized feedback along the way.

REVIEW QUESTIONS

1. Identify the circumstances that contributed to the rise of nationalism, and explain the difference between ethnic nationalism and civic nationalism.

2. Compare and contrast the emphases of French, Japanese, Canadian, and German nationalisms.

3. In what ways did nationalism confer power upon states?

4. How did nationalism contribute to the weakening of the Habsburg, Russian, and Ottoman empires?

5. What were the key reasons that imperialism after 1870 was so pervasive and different from the empire building that came before?

6. Name the industrial technologies that contributed to the rise of the new imperialism, and describe their contributions.

7. On what three trends did Europe, the United States, and Japan base their cultures of imperialism?

8. Identify the similarities between British control in India and French rule in Algeria, and explain the main difference between the two.

9. What was the main difference between settler colonialism in Australia, Canada, and New Zealand and that in Africa and East Asia?

10. How did rinderpest facilitate the European conquest of Africa?

11. In what ways did colonial rule in Africa rely on local elites and the assignment of tribal identities?

12. To whom did missionary Christianity appeal in Africa, and why?

13. What products formed the basis of the Dutch, British, and French colonial economies in Southeast Asia?

14. Discuss the main reasons for Italian, Japanese, and U.S. late imperial expansion.

15. On what techniques and technologies did the political success of the Comanche and Ethiopian empires depend?

16. In what significant ways did nationalism and imperialism tighten global connections, and in what ways did they deepen global divisions?

FURTHER READING

David ABERNETHY, *The Dynamics of Global Dominance* (2000). A political scientist's systematic and comprehensive history of European imperialism.

Alexander BULATOVICH, *Ethiopia through Russian Eyes* (2000). The 1897—1898 diary of a Russian soldier serving under Menelik II in Ethiopia. A fascinating document.

Pekka HAMALAINEN, *Comanche Empire* (2008). A masterpiece of research and analysis.

E. J. HOBSBAWM, *Nations and Nationalism since 1780* (2012). A readable and excellent work on languages and their links to nationalisms.

Adam HOCHSCHILD, *King Leopold's Ghost* (1999). A detailed narrative of the Belgian king's pillaging of the Congo.

Heather STREETS-SALTER and Trevor GETZ, *Empires and Colonies in the Modern World* (2016). A broad overview, thematic in structure.

CHRONOLOGY

1813
British state strips
East India Company
of its trade monopoly

1821
Mexico wins
independence
from Spain

1839–1842
First Opium War

1842
Treaty of Nanjing

1848
Mexico loses territory
to the United States

1850–1864
Taiping Rebellion

1856–1860
Second
Opium War

1857–1858
Indian
Rebellion

1869–1870
Development of Ghost
Dance among northern
Nevada Paiute

1876–1910
Porfiriato

1877–1878
Drought in Brazil;
famine in China

1879
Japan takes
Ryukyu Islands

1885
French
seize
Vietnam

1887
Dawes Act opens
Amerindian land
to white settlers

1889
Wovoka has first prophetic vision;
Brazil becomes a republic

1890
Massacre of Wounded Knee

1894–1895
Sino-Japanese
War

1897
Brazilian army
defeats Canudos
rebellion

1899–1900
Boxer Rebellion in northern China

1899–1902
Boer War in South Africa

25

Making the Modern World

CONFRONTING INDUSTRIALIZATION, NATIONALISM, AND IMPERIALISM

1850 to 1920

1913
Yuan Shikai forces
Sun Yatsen
into exile

1905
Revolution of 1905 in Russia
1905–1911
Revolution in Iran

1910–1911
Chinese Revolution

1908
Cixi and Guangxu die;
Young Turk Revolution

I n April 1856 a teenage girl named Nongqawuse, of the Xhosa people in South Africa, was on duty chasing birds from maize fields down by the Gxarha River. As she explained it, she saw two strangers who instructed her to tell her people they must kill all their cattle and destroy all their crops. The cattle and crops were impure, the strangers said, having been raised by the Xhosa people, who practiced witchcraft. She also heard them say that if the Xhosa did this, new cattle would spring up from the Earth, fresh maize would burst forth, and the ancestors of the Xhosa would return from the dead. Joy and justice would prevail in the land.

It was a difficult time for the Xhosa. They were engaged in frequent wars with their neighbors, including the British-run Cape Colony, which was swelling daily with new settlers from Britain. The Xhosa leader, Sarhili, a man of considerable diplomatic talents and now at the height of his powers, was hard-pressed to maintain Xhosa independence. To make matters worse, a terrible cattle plague had struck—a disaster for a cattle-keeping people like the

Civil War in China A battle scene from the Taiping Rebellion, a massive uprising against the Qing dynasty in the mid-nineteenth century.

FOCUS QUESTIONS

1. How were millenarian movements responses to the pressures of state power?

2. How did the Taiping and Indian rebellions reflect the impact of global connections?

3. What mix of global and local forces fueled the Chinese and Mexican revolutions?

Xhosa. Many of them were desperate for relief and eager for good news.

At first no one believed Nongqawuse, even though for the Xhosa it was not unusual for spirits to appear from time to time and offer prophecies. Young girls' words did not count for much in Xhosaland. But she told her uncle, Mhlakaza, who went with her to meet the strangers and heard their message for himself. Mhlakaza had once worked for an Anglican archdeacon, and he embraced Anglican ideas of redemption and resurrection. Now he convinced King Sarhili to visit the Gxarha. The king heard the voices, accepted the prophecy, and arranged for the slaughter of his vast herds of cattle. He instructed his followers, some of whom had also gone to hear the strangers' voices, to do the same. Most of them did so, and then keenly awaited the day when the new cattle would come and their ancestors would arise.

Over the next two years, the Xhosa killed about 400,000 of their cattle. They dug up their maize crop. And then they starved. No replacement cattle came, no new maize sprouted, and the ancestors did not return to help them oust their enemies. The Xhosa population fell from about 105,000 to 27,000. They lost much of their land too. The Cape Colony's governor, the brilliant and ruthless Sir George Grey, urged British settlers to help themselves to Xhosa

land, spelling the end of Xhosa independence. After 1858, they were a subject people in British South Africa.

The Xhosa were one of many peoples in the nineteenth century struggling to make sense of a confusing world. For many, as for the Xhosa, the extraordinary power of modern imperialism cost them land and liberty. For others, the newly unleashed force of nationalism upset their lives, making them feel like foreigners in their own land. For still others, the overnight economic changes brought on by industrialization and new competition turned their worlds upside down and dimmed their future prospects.

All these forces, and others too, worked together to confuse, irritate, and arouse millions of people around the world. Old truths came into question. Old ways no longer worked. Young people tuned out the old, seeking new opportunities and new forms of truth. The disruption, disorientation, and dissatisfaction drove many of the millions to seek spiritual solutions, like the Xhosa. Others took up arms. Some did both at once. Some wished to embrace nationalism and industrialization—in short, to compete with the imperial powers at their own game. Others rejected such a course, hoping instead to strengthen their communities without imitating foreign ways. The growing power of industrial societies made these choices increasingly urgent after 1850.

This chapter explores several responses to the pressures people came to feel during the nineteenth century. First, we'll consider a pair of small-scale **millenarian movements**—religious movements in which people expect spiritual or divine intervention to bring about a better world. We'll see how some Amerindians in the United States tried to cope with their problems by calling for spiritual aid through the Ghost Dance. Then we'll move to Brazil, to the town of Canudos, where destitute people tried to set up their own new community according to Catholic principles as they understood them. These were religious responses with political meanings, involving tens of thousands of people.

Next we'll turn to a pair of giant rebellions that involved tens of millions of people. The Taiping Rebellion (1850–1864), also a millenarian movement in some respects, shook Qing China to its foundations, a cataclysm from which the dynasty never recovered. The Indian Rebellion (1857–1858) destroyed both the Mughal Empire and the East India Company, brought more direct British rule over more of the subcontinent, and stimulated the first stirrings of Indian nationalism.

Finally, we'll look at a pair of revolutions that occurred between 1910 and 1920, one in China and the other in Mexico. Both of these succeeded in overthrowing a ruling elite in the name of liberty and justice, and of creating nations strong enough to resist foreign encroachments.

Millenarian movements, rebellions, and revolutions happen from time to time. This book has touched on several already. But they came thicker and faster in the late nineteenth and early twentieth centuries, because the pace and prevalence of change was so great, and because the changes so unsettled populations across the globe. These three pairs of millenarian movements, rebellions, and revolutions represent a sampling of ways in which peoples confronted, and participated in, the disruptive changes of the period from 1850 to 1920.

MILLENARIAN VISIONS: THE GHOST DANCE AND CANUDOS

Among the many responses to the pressures of imperialism and intrusive state power were efforts to enlist spiritual forces against unwelcome change. These efforts took many forms, but a common one was millenarian movements.

THE GHOST DANCE IN THE WESTERN UNITED STATES

The nineteenth century brought hard and bewildering times to the Amerindian peoples of North America. They were defeated in wars by the U.S. Army and decimated by disease. In the first half of the century, native peoples of the eastern United States were pushed westward or confined to small reservations.

After 1850, those of the western part of the country met similar fates. On their home ground in the Great Plains, Rocky Mountains, and the Great Basin, Amerindians had to deal with vast disruptions to their ways of life. Fur traders offered access to novel goods such as guns and hard liquor. Epidemics raged as never before. Hunters—including many who were Amerindians themselves—obliterated the once vast bison herds in order to sell hides, leaving the Plains Indians without their main source of food and clothing. The U.S. government kept breaking promises and treaties, turning over more and more Amerindian land to white American settlers. After the end of the U.S. Civil War in 1865, these disorienting trends grew stronger. In 1887, the Dawes Act opened the vast preponderance of remaining Amerindian land to white settlers. Amerindians had to face more soldiers, settlers, and railroads; restriction to reservations; and efforts by the federal government to "Americanize" their children through special schools and conversion to Christianity.

The disruptions of Amerindian life invited intellectual and religious creativity in response. The Amerindians of the Great Basin and northern Rockies had long had a prophetic tradition which, from the 1830s onward, acquired some Christian overtones through contact with white Americans and Iroquois missionaries from upstate New York.

This prophetic tradition took a new direction among the Paiute in northern Nevada in the years 1869–1870. In a vision, a prophet sometimes known as Wodziwob ("Gray-hair") foresaw that if people followed certain ceremonies, spirits would respond: the vanished game would return, and the recently departed (of whom there were many after an 1867 typhoid epidemic) would return to life amid joy and plenty. By some accounts, his vision included the idea that the Earth would swallow up the whites whose arrival had brought such misery.

The **Ghost Dance**, as this spiritual movement is called,

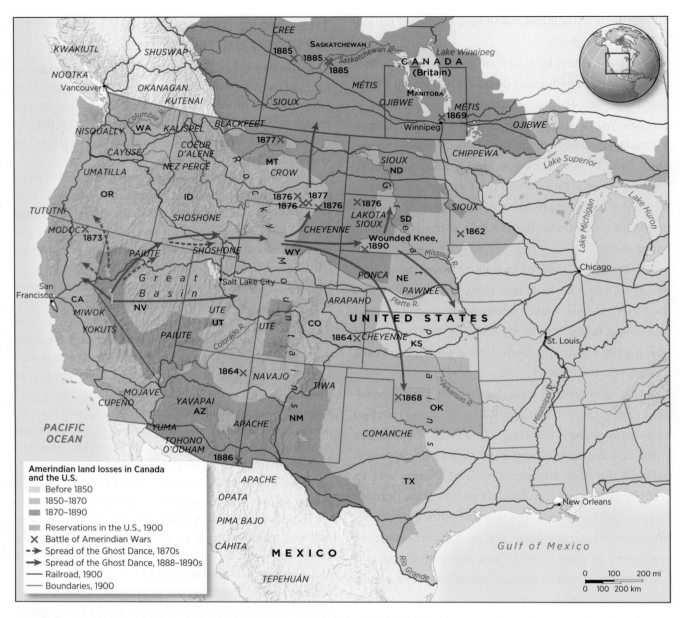

Amerindian North America: Devastation and Response, 1850–1900 The centuries-long displacement and destruction of Amerindian communities continued during the late nineteenth century in the United States and Canada. Land losses accelerated, as Amerindians lacked the military and demographic power to fight off the U.S. Army and prevent further expansion by land-hungry American settlers, whose numbers swelled, especially along railroad lines. The popularity of the Ghost Dance among several Amerindian peoples reflects the desperate position they shared.

featured a ceremony built around a circular dance common among Amerindians of the West. Men, women, and children held hands, sang, and sidestep-shuffled gently clockwise to a drumbeat. They performed this spirit dance at night, for long hours, five nights in a row, to invoke the help of powerful spirits. The ritual dance spread to nearby California and Oregon. But the prophecy failed to come true, and the preaching and spirit dancing died out in

these lands by 1873. It survived and spread in southern Idaho and Utah, where Mormon influence reinforced the prophetic tradition of local Amerindians.

Mormons had migrated westward to Utah in the 1840s, bringing a religion that emphasized prophecy. Mormon belief had a special role for Amerindian prophecy: as Mormons saw it, one of the lost tribes of ancient Israel had come to North America, and Amerindians were

Ghost Dance In 1890, the leading American magazine, *Harper's Weekly*, published artist Frederic Remington's impression of Lakota Sioux people from the Dakota Territory performing the circle dance ritual that was central to the Ghost Dance movement. Remington based his drawing on sketches from firsthand observers, but he never saw the Ghost Dance himself.

their descendants. Parts of Mormon doctrine appealed to many Amerindians, and the Ghost Dance prophecies resonated with many Mormons who also looked forward to the restoration of justice and faith. Both groups felt, with justification, persecuted by the U.S. government. Although almost hidden from view, the Ghost Dance survived through the 1870s and 1880s, mainly among Amerindians in touch with Mormon communities.

WOVOKA'S PROPHECY Then in 1889 Wovoka, a Paiute like Wodziwob, had his first prophetic vision. Having lived for 20 years with a white ranching family of devout Presbyterians, his visions had strong overtones of messianic Christianity. Wovoka believed he had gone to heaven, where everyone he saw was healthy and forever young, enjoying their favorite pastimes. His reputation as a healer and spiritual specialist who could end droughts helped earn Wovoka an audience. In the years 1889–1890, he preached that if Amerindians conducted themselves peacefully and honestly, and performed the spirit dance, then the joyful prophecy would come true.

Wovoka's prophecy passed from one people to another. In some versions of the prophecy, white people would be swallowed up by the Earth or drowned in a flood. In others, they and Amerindians would live together in peace and health. At some point, Wovoka added the promise that Jesus Christ would return in 1892 to oversee peace on Earth, working through the American president and through Wovoka himself.

Everywhere, the prophecy included the instruction to perform the circle dance for five days and nights. The community dance helped people feel that they were doing something constructive to heal their broken world. It also expressed a growing sense of Indian-ness across tribal lines, a new—we might say nationalist—identity for thousands of people who had formerly seen themselves as Paiute, Shoshone, Ute, Blackfeet, Arapaho, and so forth. The common experience of catastrophic disease, loss of land, and other misfortunes helped the various Amerindian peoples of the West feel more "Indian." The spirit dance expressed this growing new identity.

WOUNDED KNEE Among the peoples attracted by Wovoka's prophecy were the Lakota Sioux of the Dakota Territory. Their devotion to the spirit dance worried some local U.S. officials, who called it the Ghost Dance. They summoned support from the U.S. Army. A confrontation just after Christmas in 1890 turned violent, resulting in the deaths of 25 members of the U.S. 7th cavalry and 153 Lakota Sioux, most of whom were women and children. The event, known as the massacre of Wounded Knee, came just short of two years after Wovoka's original vision. It cast a dark shadow over the Ghost Dance movement.

But the Ghost Dance did not die in 1890. It continued to appeal to some Amerindians as a means of meeting up with their dead friends and kin, and as a means of expressing their Indian-ness in an increasingly white world. Amerindians from Oklahoma to Saskatchewan continued to practice the faith and its rituals well into the twentieth century, often secretly. They were trying to revitalize their vanished world.

CANUDOS IN NORTHEASTERN BRAZIL

While the Ghost Dance movement was sweeping the U.S. West, another religious revitalization movement was washing over the northeast of Brazil. It flourished in the thinly populated backcountry called the Sertão, a scrubby land of cattle ranches and erratic rainfall. Its leader was Antônio Maciel.

Maciel was born in 1830 to a moderately prosperous family. But his mother died young, his father took to the bottle, and Antônio left home to live with his grandfather, a schoolteacher. While in his twenties he married and began work as a teacher. In his mid-thirties, his marriage

CONSIDERING THE EVIDENCE

Messengers of the Ghost Dance

In November 1889, a Cheyenne Amerindian named Porcupine traveled by railway, wagon, and foot to "meet other Indians and see other countries." Beginning near Fort Washakie in Wyoming, he passed through Indian and Mormon communities in Utah before reaching Pyramid Lake in western Nevada, where he stayed with the Paiute communities who had started the Ghost Dance movement. After returning home, Porcupine related the following account of his journey to Major Carroll of the U.S. Army, who transmitted a transcription to the Indian Office. Porcupine's description of meeting Christ may refer to an actual meeting with Wovoka, the prophet of the Ghost Dance movement who lived near Pyramid Lake. However, it also resembles a story from the Book of Mormon that claims Jesus Christ visited America after his death. Regardless, Porcupine's account emphasizes the diversity of Amerindians who embraced the Ghost Dance movement and became its messengers.

All the Indians from the Bannock agency [in Wyoming] down to where I finally stopped [in Nevada] danced this dance.... [T]he whites and Indians danced together.... The people there seemed all to be good. I never saw any drinking or fighting or bad conduct among them. They treated me well on the [railway] cars, without pay. They gave me food without charge, and I found that this was a habit among them toward their neighbors.... I and my people have been living in ignorance until I went and found out the truth. All the whites and Indians are brothers, I was told there. I never knew this before....

The Fish-eaters [Paiute] near Pyramid Lake told me that Christ had appeared on earth again.... [T]hat was why unconsciously I took my journey.... Christ had summoned myself and others from ... fifteen or sixteen different tribes. There were more different languages than I ever heard before and I did not understand any of them....

Just after dark some of the Indians told me that the Christ ... was arrived.... [H]e commenced our dance, everybody joining in, the Christ singing while we danced....

He told us also that all our dead were to be resurrected ...; that we must tell all the people we meet about these things. He spoke to us about fighting, and said that was bad, and we must keep from it; ... and we must all be friends with one another. He said that in the fall of the year the youth of all the good people would be renewed, so that nobody would be more than 40 years old.... He said if we were all good he would send people [to] heal all our wounds and sickness by mere touch, and that we would live forever. He told us not to quarrel, or fight, nor strike each other, nor shoot one another; that the whites and Indians were to be all one people. He said if any man disobeyed what he ordered, his tribe would be wiped from the face of the earth.

Source: "Porcupine's Account of the Messiah," in James Mooney, "The Ghost Dance Religion and the Sioux Outbreak of 1890" in J. W. Powell, ed., 14th Annual Report Part II, Bureau of Ethnology, Smithsonian Institution (Washington, DC, 1896).

QUESTIONS FOR ANALYSIS

1. What did Porcupine find appealing about the Ghost Dance movement?
2. How did the teachings of the Ghost Dance movement, as described above, promote a shared Amerindian identity?
3. What features did the Ghost Dance movement share with other millenarian movements discussed in this chapter?

---

failed, his career fizzled, and he began to wander the countryside. He dressed in a simple robe, wore a beard and long hair, and reminded some people of paintings of Jesus Christ. Everywhere he went, he repaired churches and cemetery walls.

Gradually he became known for his soaring sermons. Listeners felt as if they were "flying up to the clouds" when he spoke about the path to redemption and salvation. He emphasized that the correct path was one of frugality, sobriety, and modesty. People began to call him Antônio Conselheiro ("Anthony the Counselor") for the sage advice he dispensed. Listeners started to follow him from village to village.

ANTÔNIO CONSELHEIRO'S QUEST FOR JUSTICE

In 1877 and 1878, northeastern Brazil was hit by a searing drought caused by one of the biggest El Niños in recent centuries. (El Niños are periodic shifts in Pacific equatorial currents associated with both droughts and floods around the world.) Several hundred thousand people died of starvation as crops failed and livestock died. Antônio Conselheiro attracted still more followers among the destitute refugees, who were drawn to his message of social justice and salvation for the righteous poor. His preaching came to include attacks on Protestantism, which was rare in Brazil, alcohol and prostitution, and the evils of slavery. The drought led many slave owners in northeastern Brazil to free their slaves, turning them loose in desperate times with no means of support. A large proportion of Antônio Conselheiro's followers came from their ranks.

In 1893, after 20 years of wandering, Antônio Conselheiro settled down. He chose a mud-hut town, Canudos, in the middle of nowhere. Brazil had abolished slavery (1888) and become a republic (1889). The new state was anti-clerical and claimed the right to recognize civil (as opposed to church) marriages. Antônio Conselheiro took vigorous exception to this claim and started to denounce the injustice of the state prominently in his outdoor sermons. He tossed tax edicts onto a bonfire. He encouraged his followers—by 1897 some 20,000 people, mainly women—to form a just community, unconstrained by the new godless laws. He wanted to withdraw from the world of injustice and corruption, but in so doing he was now challenging the Brazilian state. He also promised his admirers that in 1900 Jesus Christ would return to bring about the Kingdom of Heaven on Earth.

The Brazilian Army attacked Canudos three times, and three times it failed. Former slaves, servants, and hungry farmworkers with rusty weaponry and no training defended Canudos against three assaults. But in 1897, on a fourth attempt, made with tens of thousands of soldiers, machine guns, and field artillery, the army prevailed. All those captured were promptly killed. Antônio Conselheiro had already died—of dysentery.

Tens of thousands of poor, hungry, illiterate Brazilians, hammered by drought, found hope in the message of Antônio Conselheiro, just as thousands of Amerindians in the U.S. West put their faith in the Ghost Dance. For both groups, as for the Xhosa in South Africa, the world in the late nineteenth century seemed to be spinning out of control. Nature seemed especially unruly. Powerful people seemed to be conspiring against them. They needed something powerful of their own to restore justice to the world and make life more rewarding. Millenarian faith answered their needs, even if, in the end, it could not protect them against modern armies with industrial weaponry.

Antônio Conselheiro's Followers Dozens of Conselheiro's destitute followers who settled in Canudos huddle together under the gaze of a photographer's lens. In the background of the photo, a line of the rebel soldiers who defended Canudos watches over the group of mostly women and children.

Movements such as these cropped up around the world during the age of industrial imperialism in Africa, South Asia, New Zealand, and elsewhere. In hundreds of cases, including the Lakota Sioux, prophets encouraged people to believe that spiritual forces—talismans, amulets, tattoos—could protect them against bullets. They knew they could not match the material power of their enemies. If they were not to give up all hope, they had to place their faith in spiritual power. Yet, whatever its merits, that power could not stop the advances of imperial and national states backed by artillery, machine guns, and railroad networks.

GIANT REBELLIONS, 1850–1864: CHINA AND INDIA

The millenarian prophets who judged that the tide was running against their people could only mobilize a few thousand followers. Far bigger rebellions, involving tens of millions of people, also broke out in the middle of the nineteenth century in China and India. Both rebellions showed the growing impact of global connections, although in different ways, shaped by specific cultures, religions, institutions, and personalities.

THE TAIPING REBELLION, 1850–1864

China in the mid-nineteenth century was ruled by the Qing dynasty, which had taken power from the Ming 200 years before. The Qing had doubled the size of their empire during the eighteenth century and benefited from the stability provided by effective and long-lived emperors. The last of these, the Qianlong emperor, died in 1799. In the years that followed, the sprawling Qing Empire—with its far-flung territories in Mongolia, Central Asia, and Tibet; its numerous religions, languages, and ethnic groups—became increasingly unsettled.

THE PLIGHT OF THE QING At the time of Qianlong's death, the Qing governed lightly. Tax rates were about a quarter of those in Europe. Most revenues (60

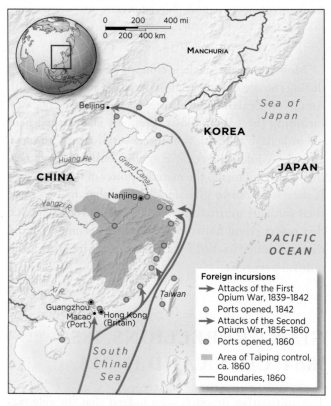

Foreign Incursions and the Taiping Rebellion, 1842–1860 Qing China suffered great disruptions in the middle of the nineteenth century. In the First Opium War, Britain used superior naval forces to force the Qing to open many seaports to foreign trade and made Hong Kong a British colony (1842). In the Second Opium War, Britain and France obliged the Qing to open many more seaports and riverports to foreign commerce. Meanwhile, in central and southeastern China, the Taiping Rebellion brought violence and destruction on a staggering scale. The Qing never fully recovered.

to 70 percent) went to the army, which nonetheless was under-paid and under-equipped. The Qing bureaucracy was thin, with roughly 10,000 paid officials, and relied on the goodwill of local landlords for routine administration. That left the state vulnerable to corruption, which flourished, particularly in the 1790s. It also contributed to the development of a large pool of talented men who had passed the civil service exams but could not get a job in government. Many of them became critics of Qing incompetence and corruption, both of which were displayed when a rural revolt, the White Lotus Rebellion (1796–1804), began in central China. At first a largely Buddhist uprising against state corruption, it ended with Qing army units fighting one another in order to continue to draw pay. That drained the Qing treasury dry.

Economic problems facing the Qing worsened early in the nineteenth century. For most of Chinese history, population growth had raised total output and strengthened states because peasants had carved out new farmland from swamps and mountainsides. But now too little land suitable for farming remained. Farm acreage per capita fell by almost half from 1753 to 1812, and continued population growth led only to hunger. In addition, the highly commercial Chinese economy, which had grown accustomed to large infusions of silver for coinage, suffered when the supply of silver diminished in the early nineteenth century. With the wars of independence in Latin America (1808–1830), world silver production fell by about half. After 1810, silver was flowing out of China to pay for imports. Upkeep of canals, dams, roads, and bridges ebbed. By the 1820s, dredging of silt in the Grand Canal was so neglected that the annual supplies of grain from the south to the capital at Beijing rarely arrived. Military morale sagged as Qing revenues plummeted and corruption soared.

Widespread use of opium compounded the Qing plight. An addictive drug that had been introduced by Arab traders a millennium before, opium had been illegal in China since 1729. But its use climbed sharply after about 1820. The British East India Company served as the major supplier, cultivating and purchasing the drug in Bengal and selling it cheaply in southern China. Aware of the growing addiction problem and the resulting outflow of silver to foreign merchants, Chinese officials tried to restrict opium imports in 1838. The British regarded this as an unjust restriction on free trade and used their navy to defeat China in the First Opium War (1839–1842).

Foreign Influence in China French, American, British, and Dutch flags fly over trading posts belonging to those countries in mid-nineteenth-century Canton. The treaty system established after the Opium Wars allowed foreign powers unprecedented levels of influence within China.

The harsh terms of the Treaty of Nanjing ending the war opened several Chinese ports to British trade, obliged China to pay a large cash indemnity to Britain, and ceded Hong Kong "in perpetuity"—among other concessions. The defeat shocked China, and the terms of the treaty outraged most Chinese who learned of them. The prestige and finances of the Qing were nearing rock bottom. Many Chinese concluded that in order for their country to restore its fortunes, the Qing would have to go.

JESUS'S YOUNGER BROTHER Things soon got a lot worse thanks to Hong Xiuquan. Hong (1814–1864) came from a gentry family that had fallen a few rungs. His great-grandfather had been a Qing official and landowner in the southern coastal region of Guangzhou. His family, part of an ethnic minority in south China called the Hakka ("Guest Families"), still owned land. But Hong needed the support of many relatives and neighbors while he pursued that venerable ambition: to pass the civil service exam and pursue a career in government. After many years of study, Hong, now in his mid-twenties, failed the examination three times.

Such failures were common, but Hong's reaction to disappointment was unique. He read Christian missionary pamphlets and, after a stint as a schoolteacher in his home village, began to study Christian doctrines with an American Baptist missionary, Issachar Roberts, in the port city of Guangzhou. Under Roberts's tutelage, and the influence of dreams, Hong in 1843 concluded that he was a son of God, the younger brother of Jesus, and responsible for realizing the Kingdom of Heaven on Earth. Prominent among his instructions was to rid China of corrupt,

foreign rulers—that is, the Qing dynasty, which was originally from Manchuria. Roberts refused to baptize his imaginative pupil, so Hong did it himself.

Hong began to preach a version of Christianity blended with popular spiritual beliefs. He found an audience in the poorest parts of the population—at first, mainly among his fellow Hakka. The economic decline of China and the humiliation of the First Opium War played into his hands. Before long he had inspired a social movement, tinged with Christian lore, dedicated to the overthrow of the Qing, whom he branded as foreign devils. Hong's agenda included the extermination of demon-worship, by which he meant Buddhism and Confucianism. Persecuted by Qing authorities, Hong raised the flag of rebellion in 1850 during a local famine in south China.

REBELLION By 1853, his army had taken cities in the Yangzi valley, the commercial highway of China. They made Nanjing (which means "Southern Capital") their base. Northern thrusts toward Beijing ("Northern Capital") proved unsuccessful—by and large, northerners found Hong's message, soaked as it was in southern culture, unappealing. But for 10 years the Taiping (meaning "Great Peace") controlled much of the Yangzi valley and parts of southern China.

The Taiping had a distinctive program that in ordinary times would have repelled most Chinese. On the social front, they assaulted the traditions of the Chinese family. They proclaimed that women were equal to men, and they banned prostitution, adultery, concubinage, and indeed all sex outside of marriage. Until 1855, they tried to enforce segregation of the sexes. They proscribed alcohol, opium, and tobacco. On the political side, they invited, and soon compelled, peasants to reject private property and contribute all their possessions to a central Taiping treasury. They instructed everyone to regard Qing officials as foreign devils and southerners, Taiping rebels especially, as the only uncorrupted Chinese. As for religion and culture, Hong and his followers preached that Christianity was not an import from abroad but had been born in China. They took a militant line against rival faiths, destroying Buddhist and Confucian temples and texts, and killing priests and sages. They were gentler with Islam, a minor religion in the areas they controlled. They disdained the refinement and learning of Chinese elites.

Despite their puritanical principles, the Taiping leaders indulged in the looting, forced sex, and gratuitous

The Taiping Rebellion A massive battle between Taiping and Qing forces in the region of Nanjing, the Heavenly Capital of the Taiping leader, Hong Xiuquan. Qing forces prevailed over the Taiping in part through the effectiveness of regional militia organized by talented leaders such as Zeng Guofan (right).

violence of conquest. Taiping leaders organized the kidnapping of women for sex duty. They amassed personal fortunes in looted goods, apparently including solid-gold chamber pots. They readily executed those who disagreed with them, and massacred millions whose loyalties displeased them.

At first, the Qing armies offered scant resistance. In 1856, Britain and France invaded north China, attacked Beijing, and burned the emperor's summer palace. They wanted still greater trading privileges in China and the legalization of opium, which was of considerable importance to Britain's commercial prosperity. Meanwhile, three or four other significant rebellions broke out. Amazingly, the dynasty limped on.

In 1860, Britain and France got the trade concessions they wanted from the Qing, and yet more indemnities, and threw their support behind the dynasty. The Taiping, after all, had banned opium and preached a faith that looked like heresy to European Christians. So Qing armies trained and led by American and British officers began to attack the Taiping. At the same time, local gentry leaders such as Zeng Guofan in Hunan raised effective anti-Taiping armies. Now the momentum switched, and the Taiping leaders' quarrels, already murderous, became large-scale purges. Hong died, either from illness or from poison, in 1864. A few months later the Hunan army finally finished off his diehard supporters, massacring the population of Nanjing in 1864.

When after 14 years it was all over, at least 30 million of China's 350 to 400 million people, some 7 to 9 percent of the population, were dead. As usual, epidemics and starvation killed more than combat did. Some

provinces along the middle and lower Yangzi lost 70 to 90 percent of their population to death and flight. The Qing survived, tottering, until 1910.

The **Taiping Rebellion** shows the interplay of internal and external forces in China. Many of its underlying causes were linked to China's changing place in the Global web. The sources of Qing economic weakness involved its dependency on imported Latin American silver and its people's growing addiction to opium from British India. Hong's ideology, a curious mix of local beliefs and Christianity imported from the United States, was as persuasive to downtrodden people eager for hope as the prophecies of Nongqawuse, Wokova, or Antônio Conselheiro. Defeat by a distant nation they disdained as barbarian also undercut the legitimacy of the Qing—before 1839, few Chinese officials had a proper appreciation of the power of Britain's Royal Navy and its modern weaponry. The Qing's failings with respect to the economy, opium, and foreign powers made them all the more vulnerable to nationalistic charges that they were not proper Chinese. China, of course, has always had rebellions. But the character and magnitude of the Taiping Rebellion had everything to do with the global processes corroding the Qing Empire.

THE INDIAN REBELLION, 1857–1858

The **Indian Rebellion**—also known as the First War of Independence, Indian Mutiny, Sepoy Rebellion, or Great Rebellion—also showed the impacts of global connections, most obviously of British rule. Before 1857, British rule in India was mainly company rule. Since the 1750s, the British East India Company (EIC) had acquired growing authority in parts of India, especially Bengal in the northeast. The Mughal Empire still nominally ruled north India, but increasingly it served as a façade behind which stood agents of the EIC. By 1803, the EIC—some 600 British merchants and officials protected by an army of 200,000 Indian soldiers—had outmaneuvered or defeated all indigenous powers in India and stood supreme in most of the subcontinent. Until 1813, the company enjoyed a monopoly on trade with India and tried hard to keep interlopers, including missionaries, out. But in 1813, the British state, bending to the wishes of merchant and evangelical groups at home, stripped the EIC of its trade monopoly and lifted the ban on missionaries. The British government took an ever-larger role in India and directly controlled about two-thirds of it by 1857, with the rest either under Company control or under local independent Indian rulers.

GRIEVANCES The British—both the EIC and the Crown—enacted reforms that deeply aggrieved the Indian elite through whom Britain governed the country. Among these were changes to the trade and tariff regime that opened up India to foreign competition, including the efficient cotton mills of England. As we've seen, this undercut the business of Indian merchants as well as village spinners and weavers. Reform to the patchwork tax regime awarded the Company most of the revenues from Indian lands and required some landlords to pay tax on lands that had formerly been exempt. A political reform (called the doctrine of lapse) stipulated that any principality without a biological son as heir would henceforth fall to British rule, which meant that sooner or later all of India would be British. In addition, the EIC by means fair and foul annexed chunks of India, leading many princes to suspect that they might be next. In 1856, the Company took over a prosperous polity, Oudh (also spelled Awadh), on the grounds that its ruler was inept and corrupt.

Religion also provided grounds for Indian anxiety and grievance. Christian missionaries proved a particular source of irritation to Indians, all out of proportion to their tiny success in converting Hindus, Muslims, Sikhs, or Jains. Moreover, the EIC army, made up overwhelmingly of Indians, grew restive over call-ups for overseas duty in the Crimean War, Persia, and Burma. High-caste Hindus, who could not cook according to ritual requirements on shipboard, risked their caste status as a result of these deployments. In general, elite Muslims and Hindus felt that they—not Christian foreigners—should rule India.

The spark that ignited the Indian Rebellion came in 1857 in the form of new rifle cartridges introduced in the Bengal Army, the largest of the three separate Indian armies run by the EIC. Annoyed by overseas duty and reductions in pay, the Indian soldiers, called *sepoys*, were

The Indian Rebellion, 1857–1858 Large-scale uprisings against British authority took place in the years 1857–1858 in the Ganges plain and in central India. The British-led Indian Army defeated the uprisings militarily, leading to the end of EIC rule and the creation of a British Crown colony of India in 1858. Those states that remained nominally independent had to bow to British wishes on all important matters.

already on edge. The Enfield rifle, a big upgrade over the muskets in use before, required cartridges that would slide down the gun barrel for loading. Rumors spread that the grease used for this purpose was animal fat from both pigs and cows. Since soldiers had to bite off the tip of a cartridge before inserting it in their rifle barrel, Muslims feared defilement by pig fat and Hindus feared breaking taboo against beef. In the spring of 1857, soldiers who resisted orders to use these new cartridges were hanged by EIC military officers, setting off a rebellion.

REBELLION The Indian Rebellion of 1857–1858 was an army mutiny combined with a series of local and regional rebellions. It was never a unified movement under a single command. Several garrisons in northern and central India rose in revolt, joined by about a quarter of the Bengal Army. At its height, the rebels controlled much of the Ganges plain for more than a year, and pockets elsewhere in India.

British Atrocities A painting by a British military artist shows East India Company officers ordering the brutal execution of Indian soldiers who refused to use new rifle cartridges. The soldiers were tied to the muzzles of cannons and killed by cannonballs at point-blank range.

The main goals of the rebellion were the destruction of British rule in India and the restoration of various old regimes. For Muslims, that generally meant returning to the glory days of Mughal power through the person of Bahadur Shah II, the 82-year-old figurehead emperor. Bahadur Shah, who preferred poetry to politics, reluctantly sided with the uprising. For Hindus, the goal was to restore earlier golden ages, when one or another Hindu leader had ruled wisely. Followers of minority religions generally chose not to rebel. Sikhs, for example, proved staunchly loyal to the EIC, preferring it to the prospect of Hindu or Muslim rule.

Local princes were divided too. Several took the opportunity to try to reclaim lost power. One of these was **Lakshmibai**, known as the Queen of Jhansi, a city in north-central India. Married at age 13, she was a widow when the EIC invoked the doctrine of lapse, which she regarded as an unjust seizure of her throne. Age 29 when the rebellion came, she gambled on its success and for a few months ruled Jhansi in defiance of the EIC armies. But soon her capital was under siege, her kingdom captured, and her life lost in combat. She has since become a national hero in India, portrayed in movies, TV shows, and video games.

The Indian Rebellion failed because too many Indians, and especially army units, resisted the call to revolt and stayed loyal to EIC army commanders. Had the armies united in revolt, they would easily have driven the British from India. The rebels hoped in vain that Britain's rivals, France or Russia, might come to their aid.

AFTERMATH The rebellion and its aftermath featured all the butchery and gore that are customary in warfare. In one notorious episode, an Indian commander, Nana Sahib, an aristocrat well educated in English and French literature, arranged for 200 British women and children to be chopped up and stuffed down a well in Kanpur—the event is famous in Britain as the massacre of Cawnpore. British officers oversaw vengeful reprisals against Indians, killing men, women, and children indiscriminately. These slaughters continued after the rebellion ceased. The greatest legacy of the rebellion was bitterness on all sides.

The casualties included 11,000 British (most of whom died of disease), several hundred thousand Indians, the Mughal Empire, and the EIC. The rebellion made clear that everything would have to change if Britain were to continue to rule India. India became a Crown colony, and back in Britain Queen Victoria added the title Empress of India. Now Parliament and the India Office in London, represented in India by a viceroy, would rule the country. Hundreds of princely states remained, but all stood subservient to the viceroy. What little remained of the Mughal Empire now vanished into British India, and Bahadur Shah, the last of a line that included great emperors such as Akbar and Aurangzeb, lived out his final years in exile. The EIC lost all its remaining authority. The British Crown took all its assets and liquidated what was left of it in 1874.

Indians often refer to the rebellion as the First War of Independence, emphasizing the attempt to throw off foreign rule and the first stirrings of Indian nationalism. Although Indians fought one another furiously during the rebellion, thereafter the violence, bitterness, and continuing resentments against foreign rule helped them see their common condition more clearly.

Lakshmibai The Queen of Jhansi is portrayed wearing white and riding on a white horse, crowned and carrying a crop. All these symbols indicate her status as a hero in the eyes of many Indians for her support of the Indian Rebellion.

British India Students at a school for girls in India during the early twentieth century. The British Raj put schools and other social institutions in place across India, enabling it to consolidate its control over the subcontinent.

In the aftermath, British rule in India, known as the Raj, changed its character in ways that hastened the development of nationalism in India. British authority became more bureaucratic and less personalized. It gave more attention to public works, especially railroads, education, and irrigation. It tried harder to regulate justice and health, and it created an India-wide post and telegraph system. It rewarded the many princes who had stayed loyal by allowing them to exercise modest authority and collect enough tax revenue to live in splendor. In general, the Raj made the experience of being ruled more uniform and less localized. In the long run this helped Indians feel more Indian, as opposed to feeling strictly Muslim or Hindu, or strictly Tamil, Bengali, or Punjabi.

The Indian Rebellion reflected deep distress on the part of many Indians with their situation in the 1850s. The rebels' grievances were different from those that lay behind the Taiping Rebellion in China, and the loss of life far smaller, but at root they had some things in common. One was economic distress resulting from the disruptive impacts of international trade, an example of the blowback from economic globalization. Another was the unintended consequences of Christian missionary activity. A third was resentment against foreign rule.

Resentment against foreign rule took different forms in India and China, but both involved the EIC. Muslim and Hindu elites in India objected to their loss of authority and to the rapid encroachments of the EIC over the

previous 100 years. The Taiping resented the foreign origins of China's Qing rulers, in power for 200 years. But part of what led them to despise the Qing was the dynasty's inability to cope with British aggression—specifically, in the First Opium War, which was fought mainly to preserve the Chinese opium market of the EIC. The business interests of the EIC, and the military adventures it inspired, played a role in both of these giant rebellions.

REBELLIONS AS GLOBAL AND LOCAL

The great rebellions in China and India drew on powerful combinations of macro trends—including nationalism, imperialism, and industrialization—and local institutions, cultures, and leaders. The growing connectivity of the Global web ensured that these were not the only disruptions shaped by the combustible interaction of global and local forces. Pressures from Europe and the United States, as we've seen, helped spur the revolution in Japan known as the Meiji Restoration (1866–1868). Foreign examples of liberal and anti-clerical government helped inspire civil wars in Mexico (1857–1867), in which France intervened. Doctrines of nationalism played central roles in wars of unification of Italy and Germany in the 1860s, and in the deadliest war in South America's history, in which Brazil, Argentina, and Uruguay pummeled Paraguay (1865–1870).

Even the U.S. Civil War (1861–1865), another momentous rebellion, reflected a combination of global trends, in this case including abolitionism, and local causes. The westward—imperial—expansion of the United States provoked the war over slavery. As we've seen, slaveholders and their supporters understood that as new free (non-slave) states joined the Union, they would eventually tip the political balance in Congress in favor of abolition. To counter the effect of expansion into the West, proslavery forces urged imperial expansion into the Caribbean and twice raised private armies in hopes of adding islands such as Cuba as additional slave states. The industrial power and railroad network of the North helped decide the war, keeping the Union intact—at the cost of about 625,000 lives, some 2 percent of the U.S. population. The aftermath of the war featured a more powerful, activist, and nationalist federal government. It amended the Constitution to abolish slavery and extend full political rights to former slaves—although after 1877 most southern states nevertheless sharply curtailed civil and political rights for African Americans. The federal government applied its power to accelerating territorial expansion, including the purchase of Alaska from Russia in 1867; speeding the domination and assimilation of Amerindian peoples; supporting the industrialization of the country; and—by 1898—undertaking overseas imperialism in both the Caribbean and the Pacific.

Meanwhile, the global forces of nationalism, imperialism, and industrialization grew still more influential. Technological advance continued to tighten the world's connections. The first transatlantic telegraph cable came in 1866. The Suez Canal in Egypt, which connected the Indian Ocean world to the Mediterranean Sea, and the first U.S. transcontinental railroad both opened for business in 1869. The flows of information, goods, and people would only quicken. And so social struggles, although as always largely about local concerns, increasingly reflected international and global influences too.

A common pattern emerged in the societies under pressure from Britain and the world's other leading powers. Some reformers in these societies wanted to strengthen their countries by imitating the most powerful foreign examples, while others thought the way to withstand foreign power was to hold tight to their traditions. In Russia, for example, there were so-called Westernizers such as Sergei Witte who, as we've seen, wanted to make Russia strong by adopting techniques and technologies from industrial western Europe. But at the same time so-called Slavophiles, such as the novelist Fyodor Dostoevsky, argued that Russia's strength lay in its unique

Suez Canal Steamships line up to enter the Suez Canal at around 1890. The canal connecting the Indian Ocean with the Mediterranean Sea was an engineering marvel and a major step toward further tightening of the Global web.

traditions and culture, especially the Russian Orthodox Church. Japan faced similar divisions from the 1850s onward, although there the groups that were inclined to adapt foreign examples won decisively in the policy arena. Muslim states such as Egypt or Iran confronted the same issue in their own ways: should they seek to industrialize and encourage a national identity among their populations, or should they try to strengthen their countries by rallying behind the banners of Islam? These divisions fractured many societies and focused political attention on religion, education, economic policy, technology, and other areas that might help peoples and states become stronger in the face of the challenges of the late nineteenth century.

REVOLUTIONS, 1870s–1920: CHINA AND MEXICO

The military defeat of the rebellions in China and India did not resolve the grievances that underlay them. To the contrary, anger and disappointment over the failings of rulers existed widely around the world, particularly wherever imperialism, nationalism, or the difficulty of competing against industrial production affected poor families. In places as different as China, Mexico, Russia, and the Ottoman Empire, millions despaired over their prospects in life and came to resent their governments' failings. For peasants, the main issue was land. Population growth everywhere reduced the land available per family. In some countries, especially those where governments were attempting reform programs, the peasants' tax burdens grew too. Among the educated middle classes, frustration developed at ruling elites that seemed unable to address rising challenges such as the suffering of the peasantry, the lack of opportunity for educated youth, and the growing threat from industrialized and imperialistic states. Observant reformers around the world were concerned by—and often inspired by—the mounting power of Britain, Germany, the United States, or Japan. They wanted their own governments to match that power— typically, by means of military modernization, industrialization, expulsion of foreign missionaries or businesses, and expansion of education. If complacent and corrupt rulers would not rise to the challenge, then the only course was to replace them through revolution.

THE CHINESE REVOLUTION, 1880s–1910s

After the Taiping Rebellion ended in 1864, matters improved—a little—in China. The intense fighting had laid waste to cities and countryside so that, as one eyewitness put it, "weeds and jungle cover[ed] the land." China's population in 1864, perhaps 350 to 400 million strong, was on average poorer than it had been a century before. In the south and southeast of China, millions gave up on life at home and emigrated to Southeast Asia, the Pacific Islands, and the Americas.

PRESSURES AND GRIEVANCES The Qing government never fully recovered its authority. Without much prestige or money, it could not control the provinces, which gave local officials leeway to pursue their own programs. Governors and provincial officials increasingly used the taxes they raised to build their own military forces and undertake their own reform initiatives in education, infrastructure, industry, and military matters.

These efforts in the provinces are sometimes known as China's self-strengthening movement. It owed little to the Qing court, and much to provincial governors. They typically focused on military industries. In Jiangnan province (around Shanghai) and in Wuhan along the central Yangzi River, officials worked with private entrepreneurs to set up iron, steel, and weapons industries. Li Hongzhang, who had made his reputation helping to defeat the Taiping Rebellion, built arsenals, shipyards, a steamship company, a telegraph network, and military academies in eastern China's Hebei province.

These provincial officials were trying to provide the Qing Empire—and themselves—with the tools of modern state power. They saw themselves as following an old saying that originated with Chinese struggles against steppe raiders: "using the barbarians' ways to defend against the barbarians." Now the "barbarians" were not Mongol but European, American, or Japanese. These reformers often wanted to retain Confucian ethics and ideology, or "essence" as they put it, but also acquire the hardware of industrial power.

An illustrative initiative was Li Hongzhang's study abroad program. On the advice of Yung Wing, a Christian convert and the first Chinese graduate of an American university (Yale, Class of 1854), Li sent 113 promising boys to high schools in New England to prepare them for administrative posts in his province—a radically different approach from training them in the Confucian classics. They studied those subjects that fit them for high responsibility: science, technology, engineering, math, languages—and, of course, history. In 1881 the program was discontinued when it appeared the boys had grown too Americanized, taking up baseball among other undignified pursuits. To some Qing officials, it seemed that they were losing their Confucian essence in their effort to acquire foreign practical knowledge.

The urgency of self-strengthening grew with time. For sophisticated Chinese, aware of the antiquity of their culture and the majestic power of earlier dynasties, the role of foreign influence in the late nineteenth century was especially irksome. The treaties signed in 1842 and 1860 after the two Opium Wars gave foreigners special rights, called extra-territoriality, which included exemption from Chinese law. Foreign missionaries roamed the country. Foreign businessmen ran new mines, railroads, and factories. Foreigners controlled the maritime customs houses. Foreign gunboats slithered up and down the Yangzi River, enforcing the privileges of foreigners. In 1879 Japan took the Ryukyu Islands, which Qing rulers regarded as their own. In 1885 the French seized control of Vietnam, which the Qing considered to be under their protection. By the 1880s, it seemed that at any time Britons, French, Germans, Americans—and, increasingly, Japanese and Russians—might carve up China, as imperialist powers were doing in Africa and Southeast Asia.

The foreign presence was only part of the discouraging situation that set the stage for the **Chinese Revolution**. Opium addiction continued to plague all levels of Chinese society. A terrible famine in the years 1877–1878, caused by the same giant El Niño that brought killing drought to Brazil, cost millions of lives. Japanese silk and Indian tea competed all too well against the Chinese products, undercutting important export trades. More fundamentally, the population kept growing while the available land did not. New crops—maize and sweet potatoes from the Americas—helped somewhat by raising production in areas ill-suited to rice, millet, or wheat. But population growth mainly caused families to grow poorer, more desperate, and more likely to kill their infant girls. Poverty, poor prospects, and a shortage of potential brides encouraged young men to consider radical choices such as banditry, emigration, or rebellion.

The Chinese Revolution, 1905–1911 Foreign pressures exacerbated internal weaknesses, speeding the decline of the Qing Empire and bringing its final collapse. Foreign powers including Russia, France, and Japan exploited the vacuum of power created by Qing weakness, seizing territories that had long been under Qing sway or even part of the Qing state. Qing subjects in Mongolia and Tibet broke away. Qing failings inspired ethnic Chinese increasingly to see their rulers as incompetent foreigners and led many to support the Chinese Revolution that began in Wuhan in 1910 and ended two and a half centuries of Qing rule by 1911.

The Qing showed few signs of addressing these challenges. Huge indemnities from lost wars and the cost of suppressing rebellions kept their finances in a desperate state. They sometimes supported, but often opposed, the initiatives taken by talented provincial governors such as Li Hongzhang. In any case, the treaties forced upon them in 1842 and 1860 had deprived the Qing of some of the tools—such as tariffs—used by other countries, including Japan and the United States, to help them industrialize.

Patriotic Chinese did not agree on what to do about these pressing problems. For the self-strengtheners such as Li, China needed to adopt modern weaponry, telegraphs, steamships, and railroads. But it became clear that this approach required engineering experts, trained managers, bankers, an industrial labor force, and an educational system to match. You could not get the teeth—modern military might—without the tail of a socially and culturally transformed society, one that undercut the authority of fathers, reduced the subservience of women, de-emphasized family ties, and compromised Confucian principles. For most Chinese, even the keen reformers, that was a painful prospect.

An alternative approach, always popular in difficult times in societies with glorious pasts, was to try to return to tried and true ways. Conservatives recommended banning all things foreign and purifying the commitment to Confucian principles. In most of China, and most of the time at the Qing court, this view prevailed.

FOREIGN PRESSURE AND INTERNAL REVOLT

The contrast with Japan brought Chinese observers further discomfort. As we have seen, Japan responded to the shock of foreign aggression with an internal revolution that put in power an elite dedicated to strengthening the nation. With brisk energy and judicious borrowing from foreigners, they had created an industrial economy, a modernized military, and a reformed educational system, and embarked on a program of imperialism. Japan, almost overnight, had become both an inspiring example and a direct threat to China. The Chinese view of Japan as a lesser culture, derivative of China, made Japan's ascendance even more painful.

As Chinese elites struggled with their choices, the urgency of the situation grew. Japan's imperialist actions led Koreans to appeal to China for help, which brought on the Sino-Japanese War (1894–1895). China was trounced, its newly built navy sunk. Humiliated, it had to cede Taiwan to Japan and pay yet another large indemnity. The emperor at the time, 24-year-old Guangxu—the only Chinese emperor to learn English—in practice shared power with his aunt, Cixi, known as the Empress Dowager. In 1898, he embarked on a bold program of reforms. His advisors, inspired by Japan's history, proposed new universities, railroads, and even a constitutional government. But Cixi, an ardent reformer in her younger days, was now a fierce and formidable conservative and a veteran of court intrigue. She engineered a palace coup, confined her nephew to house arrest, and executed reformers who could not escape China.

In the years 1899–1900, an anti-foreign, anti-Christian, and initially anti-Qing uprising by nationalist youths, who called themselves the Righteous and Harmonious Fists, boiled over. Known to foreigners as the Boxers because of their interest in martial arts, they originated during a time of drought and hunger in the northeastern province of Shandong. Their xenophobic movement had a millenarian tinge to it, including a belief that their rituals could make them invulnerable to bullets. They killed Chinese Christians and foreign missionaries. They looted churches and foreign property throughout northern China and killed the German ambassador. After foreign troops guarding embassies and legations killed several Boxers, Cixi in 1900 declared war on all foreign nations involved in China. Within months an international force of eight nations, made up mostly of Japanese and Russian soldiers and ships—and partly funded by overseas Chinese eager to end Qing rule—invaded China. Twenty thousand foreign troops crushed the Boxers and Qing forces, and imposed yet another heavy indemnity on China. Russia occupied Manchuria, the homeland of the Qing. Cixi and her nephew Guangzu fled Beijing.

The Qing, it seemed in 1901, could sink no further. The futility of fighting foreign ways became clearer after the Boxers' defeat. Advisers convinced even Cixi that radical reform was required if the dynasty—indeed, China—were to survive. Her government sent thousands of students to Japan to observe its modernizing reforms. China abolished the 1,300-year-old civil service examination system, established new schools, including ones for girls, and routed major investment toward military industries.

Empress Dowager Cixi The elderly Empress Dowager at court in the 1890s.

Boxer Rebellion Boxer soldiers stand at attention flanking some of the leaders of the movement, in a photograph taken at the height of their uprising in 1900.

But it was too little, too late for the Qing. Their incompetence in the face of China's humiliations turned many of their most talented subjects, such as **Sun Yatsen**, into revolutionaries. Sun was born in 1866 to a peasant family in Guangdong. At age 13 he followed an older brother to Hawaii, where he received an English-language education at the same school from which President Obama graduated a century later. Having had little exposure to Confucian study, Sun was fully open to the teachings on offer in Hawaii. He was the most notable of the many young Chinese who were concluding that the Qing could not spearhead reform, and that to save China from foreign domination and enduring weakness required overthrowing the Qing.

SUN YATSEN, REVOLUTIONARY After his schooling in Hawaii, Sun moved to Hong Kong, a British colony, where he studied with missionaries, was baptized an Anglican, and earned a medical degree. Disappointed by Qing weakness, Sun wanted, as he put it in 1894, to see China "do what the Europeans could do." He "tried especially to learn how these countries had grown rich and strong and how they had civilized their people." He thought it especially admirable that in Western countries "the interests of the state and those of commerce flourish together." Building railroads and battleships would not suffice, he thought. China needed to modernize its education system, its agriculture, and its commerce, to address the root of its weakness. His efforts to energize reform by Qing officials, and to gain employment with the government, were rebuffed in 1894. If Qing officials refused to embark on suitably thorough reforms, Sun maintained, it was time for a revolution. He left China in 1895 when the Qing put a price on his head, and did not return for 17 years. Throughout the 1890s and early 1900s, Sun traveled to Southeast Asia, Britain, Canada, the United States, and elsewhere, organizing opposition to Qing rule among overseas Chinese and looking for ideas he could mix into his program for reforming China.

Sun Yatsen Pictured here at age 17, Sun concluded early on that China's advance required overthrow of the Qing.

Sun devised a revolutionary credo, his Three Principles. The first was a Chinese nationalist position: the Qing—those Manchu barbarians—must go, and real Chinese must rule China. The second principle was that the imperial monarchy must be replaced by a constitutional republic. This drew on the examples Sun had seen abroad; nothing in Chinese tradition supported this principle. The third was the social principle—influenced by his exposure to European socialism—that everyone should have enough to eat, economic justice should prevail, and peasants should get an education and have a chance to apply their talents. Sun hoped that a China recast along these lines would both recover its proper place in the world and alleviate the suffering of the masses.

For 15 years Sun's efforts at revolution brought only failures. He raised money and recruits, often collaborating with Chinese students in Japan, for rebellions in Guangzhou in 1895, 1900, 1907, and early 1911. All fizzled. But later in 1911, army officers inflamed by nationalist ideas sparked a mutiny in the central city of Wuhan (Hubei province). The uprising spread, and many provinces declared themselves independent of Qing rule. Sun Yatsen, however, was on a fundraising trip in Denver. Now middle-aged, he sensed this was the best chance he would get to change China, and after visiting Europe in hopes of enlisting support, he returned home.

REVOLUTION AND REPUBLIC, 1911–1916 Sun's assessment was correct. Both Cixi and Guangxu had died in 1908. She had designated a three-year-old boy as successor to the throne, so power passed to a handful of princes. To suppress the army mutiny, the princes chose a talented general named Yuan Shikai. He saw more promise in the mutineers than in the princes.

An ambitious youth from a distinguished family, Yuan had failed the civil service exams twice, then joined the army. In the 1880s he made his mark serving the Qing in Korea. As Qing power waned, he built his own army in the 1890s, trained by German officers. His Beiyang ("Northern") army quickly became China's most effective military force. At Yuan's command, it loyally massacred thousands of hardline Boxers when they rejected Qing authority. In the coming years, Yuan honed the Beiyang Army and helped implement educational and military reforms.

Once given full command to suppress the 1911 mutiny,

Yuan decided to join forces with Sun Yatsen and other revolutionaries, and they forced the last Qing emperor, still a child, to abdicate. (A gardener for most of his life, the last emperor—after 2,000 years of imperial rule in China—died in 1967.) Sun was elected president of a new constitutional republic in December 1911. He hoped to reform China along the lines of his Three Principles. Yuan, however, thought a new dynasty would be more agreeable—with himself as emperor. Yuan tossed aside a constitution Sun had written; suppressed Sun's new political party, the Guomindang; arranged for the assassination of many of Sun's associates; and in 1913 drove Sun into exile, in Japan. Various liberations and reforms of 1911 and 1912, including press freedom and representative assemblies, were quickly rescinded. Yuan began to govern like an emperor.

Power in China soon fragmented. Japan made new demands on China in 1915, to which Yuan agreed in return for support of his dynastic dreams. That sparked renewed nationalist outrage and provincial uprisings. Several of Yuan's own Beiyang Army disciples deserted him, and when he died of disease in 1916 at age 56, central rule collapsed. While the republic officially survived in the hands of the Guomindang, China was now fragmented, with dozens of regional warlords competing for power, revenues, and personal survival. Sun Yatsen struggled to unite the country from his base in Guangdong, but he died of disease in 1925 at age 58. Internal warfare continued to plague China for the next 25 years.

The Qing, in power since 1644, had entered a long death-spiral in the 1790s and were finally undone by military defeat and revolution during the years 1895–1912. Confucian ideology, which had provided a compelling vision of the proper relations among heaven, ruler, and ruled, now stood at a low ebb. Much of the old Qing elite and the Chinese gentry threw their support to the revolution, seeing it as the best bet for the restoration of order and the reconstruction of China. This stood in contrast to elite behavior during the Taiping uprising, when their grandfathers had stood by the dynasty. But in the intervening half-century, the Qing had lost the loyalty of those they most needed.

In the end, the combination of two main challenges undermined the Qing. Population growth and increasing poverty among the peasantry was one, if always slow-moving and rarely commanding urgent official attention. The second challenge was the mounting economic and military strength, and aggression, of industrialized societies, especially Britain, Russia, and Japan. That one was easier to identify and did command urgent attention at the Qing court. But responding to it seemed to require such drastic changes not merely to the state, but to society and family as well, that the Qing policy elite could not agree upon any sustained course of reform. They feared, probably rightly, that enacting radical reforms as the most energetic and imaginative self-strengtheners recommended would provoke widespread rebellion and only hasten the end of the dynasty.

Anti-Qing Rebellion A barber cuts off a boy's queue, or braid, following the overthrow of the Qing dynasty in 1911. The Qing had required all men to wear their hair in a long braid, on pain of death. Cutting off the braids came to be seen as a symbol of liberation.

THE MEXICAN REVOLUTION, 1870s–1920

Similar challenges—peasant poverty and unrest combined with inability to fend off foreign power—fueled the **Mexican Revolution**. Like the Chinese Revolution, it was decades in the making. Mexico had won independence from Spain in 1821 but lost the northern third of its territory to the United States in 1848, the result of the Mexican-American War. After independence, its chaotic political life included repeated bouts of civil war, Comanche raids, and in the 1860s a French invasion. After 1876, its politics stabilized owing to the authoritarian rule of Porfirio Díaz. His decades in power, 1876–1910, are called the **Porfiriato**.

THE PORFIRIATO, 1876–1910 Díaz, a theology school dropout from a poor family in Oaxaca, fought in the Mexican-American War as a youth and became a hero of the anti-French struggle in the 1860s. He converted his military prestige into a political career and in 1876 came to power by means of a coup. He stayed in power through intimidation, army support, and rigged elections. His policy consisted of three main initiatives beyond doing whatever was necessary to keep power. First, he restored to the Catholic Church some of the lands

Mexican Grievances A 1910 poster celebrates one of the factions opposed to Díaz's rule. It shows (top) Liberal Party members being rounded up by government troops, and (bottom) the same members distributing newspapers and speaking at a rally for factory workers oppressed by Díaz's exploitative policies.

and privileges it had lost in recent decades when anti-clerical factions had ruled Mexico. Second, he recruited foreign investment in Mexico, mainly from the United States, Britain, Germany, and France. He awarded tax breaks and other incentives to firms that would own and operate mines, railroads, plantations, and other big enterprises. Third, he endorsed the dispossession of poor peasants whose self-sufficient ways did not contribute to national economic growth, and whose small, communal landholdings got in the way of bigger, more efficient, businesses.

Díaz presided over a rapid growth of inequality in Mexico. On his watch, Mexico's economy grew fast and its richest people prospered mightily. So did many of the foreign firms he invited in. Foreign trade increased ninefold during the Porfiriato, and foreign companies—British, French, and American—built 7,500 miles (12,000 km) of railroads. Investment in mining skyrocketed after Díaz offered tax breaks to foreign companies. It was a good time to be an investor or business leader. But the Porfiriato was a bad time to be poor in Mexico. The standard of living and nutrition for average Mexicans in 1910 was probably lower than in 1810. Wages in the foreign-owned businesses stayed low, and Díaz used armed force to defeat strikes and discourage negotiations for better working conditions.

Peasants, the majority of the population, found less and less land available to them. That trend resulted partly from a rise in population from 9 to 15 million between 1876 and 1910. But mainly it came from land concentration: by 1910, about 80 to 90 percent of Mexican land was owned by 1 percent of the population, mostly of Spanish descent and proud of it. The same elite controlled most irrigation water, which in some arid regions was more precious than land. Education did not provide an exit from poverty: most peasants received little or none, and 70 to 80 percent of the population remained illiterate. Most of them were Amerindians, called *Indios* in Mexico, and

spoke indigenous languages such as Mayan or Zapotec rather than Spanish.

The vast and widening social inequality, particularly with respect to land, was the primary grievance behind the Mexican Revolution. Waves of labor strikes and peasant rioting after 1905 demonstrated the levels of discontent. A secondary grievance was nationalist irritation at the generous deals offered to foreign businesses in Mexico. The loss of the north in 1848 and the ejection of the French in the 1860s had bolstered Mexican nationalism. So did awareness among the educated classes of the rising tide of nationalism in Europe and the United States. While Díaz did his best to wrap himself in the cloak of nationalism, and he was skilled at such things, he gave away too much to foreign companies to suit many Mexicans and thus became—like late Qing emperors in China—an object of nationalist frustration and disdain. These two threads, quests for social justice and Mexican nationalism, ran through the Revolution.

REVOLUTION, 1910–1920 The Mexican Revolution started when Díaz said he would retire and scheduled a presidential election for 1910. When various candidates emerged, he changed his mind and jailed the most promising one, Francisco Madero. A previously apolitical northerner, Madero emerged from a wealthy family with interests in ranching, mining, and cotton. He had ties to Díaz's inner circle. But his education in Paris and at the University of California-Berkeley had persuaded him that a less autocratic system would be better for Mexico—similar to the impact of study abroad in Sun Yatsen's career. After landing in jail, Madero wrote up his political vision, escaped to the United States, and decided to call for the overthrow of the Porfiriato. Insurgencies bubbled up all over Mexico. Díaz, now age 80, chose comfortable exile in Paris.

Those insurgencies included two larger ones driven by grievances of inequality. In Morelos, just south of Mexico City, a peasant, Emiliano Zapata, had been helping villagers retain their land against encroaching sugar plantations. He organized an effective guerrilla war against the big landholders and attracted a large following. Meanwhile, in the ranchlands of the far north, Pancho Villa led another uprising made up mainly of cowboys and bandits like himself, at home on horseback. Villa was a tactical magician at organizing cavalry raids, so much so that the U.S. Army studied his techniques. He also had a fine public relations instinct and made a deal with Hollywood producers to have his exploits filmed. He was well connected with gun runners in the United States who kept his forces supplied. Zapata and Villa both promised land and work to their followers—if they won.

Other insurgent factions were led by urban, middle-class men less flamboyant than Zapata or Villa. But Venustiano Carranza, a politician with a medical education, and Álvaro Obregón, a prosperous chickpea farmer with no education, were the equal of anyone when it came to political guile. They represented more moderate factions, not interested in major redistribution of land or wealth. They favored constitutional government—and focused on crushing their rivals.

Mainly through the backing of Zapata's peasant army, Madero, not yet 38 years old, became president late in 1911. But one of his supporters, Victoriano Huerta, a former military officer, engineered a coup. Huerta arranged for Madero's murder and established a military dictatorship that lasted about a year. But his forces lost out to other factions, and he took the road of exile.

In the coming years, the various factions fought, joined forces, quarreled, and fought again. Their leaders became warlords, leading private armies, making their own rules, enforcing their will where they could. It became hard to tell the revolutionaries from the bandits and vice versa. Rival armies marched this way and that, carrying off food and livestock. The contest was a multisided civil war

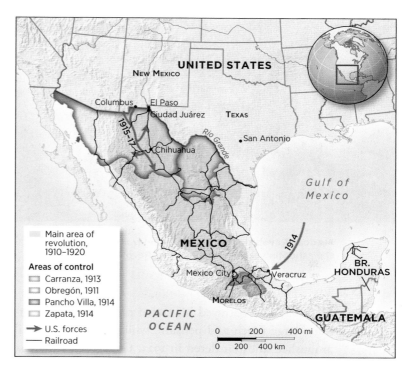

The Mexican Revolution, 1910–1920 Under the rule of Porfirio Díaz, the average Mexican became poorer. Millions lost control of their farmlands, often to foreign companies that Díaz welcomed. Mexico exploded into revolution and multi-sided civil war in 1910, and the main factions built up regional bases either in the north along the U.S. border or in the highlands south of Mexico City. The largest of the U.S. interventions came first by sea in 1914 and second over land from U.S. states that before 1848 had been part of Mexico.

Francisco Madero A mural in present-day Mexico City celebrates the revolutionary leader. Madero appears seated on a horse and carrying a large Mexican flag, surrounded by supporters ranging from peasants to middle-class professionals.

fought by amateur soldiers with modern armaments. The United States intervened twice, once in Veracruz to help pressure Huerta into resigning, and once in the north to punish Pancho Villa for a raid on a New Mexico town. Germany also got involved, negotiating with most of the warlord factions at one point or another between 1914 and 1918. In early 1917, Germany, wanting the United States too distracted to enter World War I, offered to pay Carranza's government if Mexico would make war on the United States. Mexico turned down the offer.

OUTCOME AND AFTERMATH By 1920, when the fighting calmed, more than a million Mexicans—6 percent of the population—had been killed. In proportional terms, this came to three times the death toll of the U.S. Civil War. If anyone may be said to have won, it would be the Constitutionalist faction of Carranza and Obregón. They drove out Huerta, murdered Zapata, and bought

Mexican Revolution A group of rebel women and girls practice their shooting skills for the Mexican Revolution in 1911.

off Villa, who betrayed his stated principles by accepting a large ranch and pension, which he enjoyed until ambushed and murdered in 1923. Obregón, as the last man standing after Carranza's assassination, became president in 1920, crushed the last Zapata loyalists, and ruled Mexico directly or through a loyal subordinate until assassinated in 1928.

The Revolution remade Mexico. It adopted a new constitution that brought some land reform; more would come in the 1930s. Big estates were broken up and parceled out to indigenous communities, a radical step that resonated throughout the Americas wherever *Indio* and *mestizo* populations were in the majority—for example, in Central America and the Andes. New labor laws provided for a minimum wage, maximum hours, and—astonishing at the time—paid maternity leave for mothers. The new state stripped the Catholic Church of its lands and privileges, converted churches into public property, and even forbade clerics from wearing their ecclesiastic garb in public. Education was taken from the church and put in the hands of the state. These broad social and economic changes amounted to a fair chunk of the agenda that the followers of Zapata and Villa wanted.

Politically, the constitution and the agreements that ended the fighting guaranteed universal male suffrage and the formal equality of male citizens regardless of wealth or ancestry. It also sharply reduced the economic rights of foreigners, claiming for the state all rights to minerals, oil, and other natural resources. There wasn't much the revolutionary factions could agree on after ousting Díaz,

but undermining the church and foreign businesses met with widespread approval.

The Mexican Revolution was both a social and a national revolution. It took until the 1930s before several of the provisions of the new Constitution were put into effect, but eventually the old landed elite lost most of its grip on the country and peasants won access to more land. Although Mexico became a one-party state, its politics after the Revolution included more segments of the population and more representation than during the Porfiriato. The mobilization for revolution and civil war, and anti-foreign sentiments resulting from the two U.S. interventions and Germany's meddling, all sharpened Mexican nationalism. That found expression in popular culture—food, folk dress, songs—and in economic policy, largely directed against the United States. Many Mexicans in 1920 agreed with the statement attributed to the former theology student Porfirio Díaz: "Poor Mexico! So far from God and so close to the United States."

So, although fundamentally about land, the Mexican Revolution became something more than that. It was a succession struggle among warlords, similar to what happened in China after 1911. (Indeed, one might say Mexico had its revolution and warlord period all at once, whereas China did it in stages.) It was a national struggle to reassert the independence of Mexico from foreign influence. It was an anti-clerical struggle to free the country from the grip of the Catholic Church. And, from the point of view of most ordinary people, it was a terrifying, chaotic bloodbath.

REVOLUTIONS AND GLOBAL FORCES, 1900–1920

The great revolutions in China and Mexico early in the twentieth century were accompanied by several others that resulted from the macro-scale forces of nationalism, imperialism, and the uneven effects of industrialization. In South Africa between 1899 and 1902, the Boer War, a keenly nationalist uprising against British rule by the Boers—Afrikaans-speaking whites descended from Dutch settlers—led to a settlement in 1910 that, while not called a revolution, in some respects was one. It conceded much more local control and representative government to white South Africans, who quickly stripped black Africans of the right to own most farmland. In

Boer War Taking up arms against the British Empire's hold in South Africa, Boer soldiers guard an outpost against British forces during the Boer War, which lasted from 1899 to 1902. The British would gain the upper hand over the Boers in late 1900, though Boer guerrilla warfare continued until the parties agreed on a peace treaty that promised the Boers self-government.

Iran, revolutionaries led by the merchant classes imposed a constitution, parliament, and elections upon the ruling shahs of the Qajar dynasty between 1905 and 1911. The Qajars had seemed unable to resist Russian and British influence. They were all too willing to grant monopolies to foreign companies, concede control of their finances to foreign bankers, and squander the tax revenue they collected from the commercial classes.

In the neighboring Ottoman Empire, nationalist army officers engineered a coup d'état in 1908 called the **Young Turk Revolution**. The Young Turks considered the imperial government incapable of facing up to foreign encroachments on Ottoman territory. As in Iran, they too constrained a monarch with a constitution. In Russia, frustration with the tsar's inability or unwillingness to address mass poverty and permit wider political participation led to street demonstrations against the government. Although bloodily suppressed, the demonstrations led to constitutional constraints in what is known as the Revolution of 1905. We will return to the Ottoman and Russian cases in the next chapter, because their stories are inseparable from that of World War I.

Each of these revolutions was unique, with its own grievances, coalitions, personalities, and train of events. The Chinese and Mexican revolutions were bigger and bloodier than that of the Young Turks or the Iranian merchants. Yet they all represent the disruptive impacts of nationalism, imperialism, and industrial power upon agrarian peoples.

CONCLUSION

All of the movements, uprisings, and revolutions in this chapter form important parts of national histories in the United States, Brazil, China, India, Mexico, and South Africa. They occurred in very different settings. They were triggered by things as different as greased rifle cartridges and a young Xhosa girl's prophetic vision. But they all took place within the span of a human lifetime (1856–1920) and shared a few overlapping features.

In a general way, all of them resulted from widespread anxieties about ongoing trends. Changes seemed to be coming too thick and fast. People outside the handful of industrialized countries found reason to fear new technologies and new weapons, powerful strangers from afar, and missionaries with new religions. Economic competition from the other side of the world ruined what had once seemed secure livelihoods. Familiar ways, institutions, and rulers no longer seemed up to the challenges of safeguarding their subjects, keeping order, and preventing hunger. In short, the forces of economic globalization, imperialism, and nationalism, circulating through the Global web, were shaking things up in confusing and threatening ways.

In most cases (Brazil was an exception), the perceived threats to a cherished way of life came in part from foreigners. Sometimes those foreigners were settlers, as in the U.S. West. Sometimes they were Christian missionaries, as in India and China. Sometimes they were representatives of encroaching imperial powers and foreign businesses, as in India, China, and Mexico. The degree to which international influences affected daily life and domestic politics was on the increase, a result of tightening travel, trade, financial, and intellectual links within the Global web.

In many cases, the causes for which so many people died took on religious hues. The followers of prophets such as Nongqawuse, Antônio Conselheiro, Wovoka, or Hong Xiuquan found in their faiths an answer to their fears. Many of the Indian rebels of 1857 couched their battles in terms of Hindu or Islamic revivals. Even the revolution of Sun Yatsen carried religious tinges. Sun's program for nationalist China was inflected by his Christian education. The Mexican Revolution was an exception (on the surface), a case in which the revolutionaries considered the church among their targets. But at the same time the appeal of Zapata and Villa to peasants, servants, and ranch-hands was of a better world to come, a concept that their Catholic upbringing prepared most Mexicans to embrace.

The great rebellions and revolutions heralded an onrushing era of mass politics and mass mobilizations around the world. The forces of nationalism, imperialism, and industrialization—transmitted along the pathways of the Global web—would affect more lives more forcefully, as the next chapter will show.

CHAPTER REVIEW

KEY TERMS

millenarian movements
(p. 736)

Ghost Dance (p. 737)

Antônio Conselheiro
(p. 740)

Taiping Rebellion
(p. 744)

Indian Rebellion (p. 744)

Lakshmibai (p. 746)

Chinese Revolution
(p. 749)

Sun Yatsen (p. 752)

Mexican Revolution
(p. 753)

Porfiriato (p. 753)

Young Turk Revolution
(p. 757)

Go to INQUIZITIVE
to see what you've
learned—and learn what
you've missed—with
personalized feedback
along the way.

REVIEW QUESTIONS

1. Describe the feelings and ideas that the Ghost Dance helped Amerindians to express.

2. Who was drawn to Antônio Conselheiro's message, and why?

3. What shared experiences caused the Xhosa, Amerindians, and Antônio Conselheiro's followers to put their faith in millenarian movements?

4. Explain the external forces that contributed to the Taiping Rebellion.

5. What economic, political, and religious grievances did Indians under British rule have?

6. How did the British Raj change after the Indian Rebellion, and what were the long-term effects of this shift?

7. What common pattern emerged among reformers in societies under pressure from the world's leading powers?

8. During this period, what were the main grievances of peasants and the educated middle classes around the world?

9. Who led the self-strengthening movement in China, and what were its focuses?

10. Identify and discuss the two challenges that ultimately undermined the Qing.

11. What were Porfirio Díaz's three main policy initiatives, who benefited from them, and which groups did they disadvantage?

12. In what ways did Mexico change socially, economically, and politically after the Mexican Revolution?

13. Compare and contrast the aims and frustrations of rebels in South Africa, Iran, the Ottoman Empire, and Russia.

14. What widespread anxieties and changes contributed to revolutions and rebellions around the world during this time?

FURTHER READING

Michael ADAS, *Prophets of Rebellion: Millenarian Protest Movements against the European Colonial Order* (1979). A work on millenarian movements in East Africa, South and Southeast Asia, and New Zealand.

C. A. BAYLY, *The Birth of the Modern World, 1789–1914* (2004). A very imaginative and thoughtful take on connections around the world.

Man-houng LIN, *China Upside Down: Currencies, Society, and Ideologies, 1808–1856* (2006). An in-depth account of China's struggles before the Taiping Rebellion.

Jürgen OSTERHAMMEL, *The Transformation of the World: A Global History of the Nineteenth Century* (2014). A gigantic

book with lots of insight about globalization, imperialism, nationalism. His main emphases are on China and Europe.

Gungwu WANG, *Anglo-Chinese Encounters since 1800* (2003). A readable and slender book emphasizing intellectual and technological transfers from Britain to China, mainly through overseas Chinese.

Louis WARREN, *God's Red Son: The Ghost Dance Religion and the Making of Modern America* (2017). An authoritative and accessible study.

O. Arne WESTAD, *Restless Empire: China and the World since 1750* (2012). A highly readable book, and strong on the international dimensions of the decline of the Qing.

THE GLOBAL WEB

SINCE 1870

The web of connections among societies that helped bring about the revolutions and rebellions discussed in Part 5, grew tighter after 1870. The main engine behind this process was continuing technological change, which sped up and cheapened communication and transport. But several other trends contributed to the growth of the Global web after 1870, such as ideologies that claimed global relevance, the alliance systems of international politics, and the steady march of the English language to its current status as a common world language. All these processes, and others as well, made the

Arab Spring With flags upraised, Egyptians rejoice in Tahrir Square following the 2011 resignation of President Hosni Mubarak. Between 2010 and 2012, a series of protests in Arab countries brought about changes in government.

contemporary world more interactive than ever before—but in fits and starts rather than at a regular pace.

THE PACE OF GLOBAL INTEGRATION

The irregular pace of modern globalization consisted broadly of three phases. The first, from 1870 to 1914, saw rapid extension of links driven above all by new technologies such as railroads, steamships, and telegraphs. The second phase, from 1914 to 1945, showed a mixed record. New technologies such as radio and air travel emerged, speeding flows of information and people. But two world wars and a worldwide economic depression drove several societies to turn inward, fall back on their own resources, and try to be self-sufficient. In economic terms, global integration retreated as flows of international trade and finance slowed. In political and cultural terms, however, there was no retreat. Societies took one another increasingly into account in shaping their own policies and preferences, whether in military matters or music. The third phase, from 1945 to the present, again saw an intensification of the process of globalization, with louder objections to it than ever before. The pace, scale, and scope of international interactions came to exceed those of any previous era especially after about 1980, when computerization and digitization began to take hold.

KEY THEMES

The next four chapters—Part 6 of the book looks closely at three main themes. First is the prominence of international politics and war. Ordinary people increasingly could not escape involvement in the affairs of states, especially the many states that took part in major wars. These chapters explore World Wars I and II, and the Cold War, the primary conflicts that re-fashioned political, social, and economic life after 1914.

Second is a shift in world power away from Europe. Beginning in the 1490s, Atlantic Europe had slowly attained unusual wealth and power by global standards. With industrialization in the nineteenth century, Europe, North America, and Japan had rapidly attained still greater power expressed in overseas empires. Between 1945 and 1991, the empires of Japan and the European

states—including the USSR—crumbled sooner and faster than almost anyone expected. A general re-balancing of world wealth and power took place, and indeed is still in motion. The formerly colonized peoples of Africa and Asia won their independence, and those in several Asian countries—first Japan, but then South Korea, Singapore, Taiwan, and to some extent China—became rich almost overnight. This rise of East Asia is the fastest and most dramatic re-arrangement of the global economy in world history.

The third general theme is the recurrent backlash against global integration. Immediately after World War I, political and ideological movements—fascism and Soviet communism—arose that intensified nationalism and encouraged economies built on self-sufficiency rather than international trade. The global economy became still more protectionist and fragmented during the Great Depression of the 1930s. While international linkages were repaired after World War II, and economic and cultural globalization galloped ahead in the following decades, once again it produced discontent. Politics based on sectarian religion made a comeback, for example, and after about 2010 xenophobic nationalism did too. Many millions also blamed economic globalization for rising inequalities in wealth and income.

Chapter 26 takes up international politics, specifically World War I and its aftermath. It emphasizes not only the war itself, but also some of the political and ideological movements created or advanced by revulsion at the war and its peace settlements: fascism, communism, and anti-colonialism. The chapter also presents suffragism, the campaign to win the vote for women, in the general context of World War I. Chapter 27 continues with the broad political patterns formed during World War II (1937–1945) and the Cold War (1945–1991), explaining the origins, course, and results of both. Chapter 28 focuses on decolonization between 1945 and 1980, and on the extraordinary economic rise of East Asia from about 1950 to the present. These twin developments amount to another basic shift in the geography of power in the global system.

Chapter 29 considers the—equally extraordinary—acceleration of almost every form of globalization since 1980, including international migrations and financial flows. It emphasizes the economy, environment, popular culture, and health and disease, and shows some of the political backlash against globalization. The chapter also explores some unintentional effects of the tight Global web, such as the faster spread of emerging diseases including HIV/AIDS, Ebola, SARS, and COVID-19.

CHRONOLOGY

1869
The Subjection of Women is published; Wyoming allows women to vote

1893
New Zealand allows women to vote in national elections

June 28, 1914
Gavrilo Princip kills Austrian archduke

July 1914
Start of World War I

1915
Italy enters World War I; Japan issues The Twenty-one Demands

1915–1916
Gallipoli campaign

Feb.–Dec. 1916
Battle of Verdun

July 1916
Battle of the Somme

Mar. 1917
Tsar Nicholas II abdicates

Apr. 1917
United States enters World War I

Nov. 7–8, 1917
Bolshevik Revolution

1918–1919
Global influenza pandemic

1918–1921
Russian Civil War

Mar. 1918
Treaty of Brest-Litovsk

Nov. 1918
World War I ends

Apr. 1919
Amritsar massacre

1919
Treaty of Versailles is signed; Weimar Republic is established

May 1919
May Fourth Movement

1920
League of Nations opens

1921
Kronstadt rebellion; Hitler becomes head of Nazi Party; formation of Chinese Communist party

1922
Start of Mussolini's rule

International Politics

WAR, PEACE, AND IDEOLOGIES

1870 to 1940

> If you could hear, at every jolt, the blood
> Come gargling from the froth-corrupted lungs,
> Obscene as cancer, bitter as the cud
> Of vile, incurable sores on innocent tongues,—
> My friend, you would not tell with such high zest
> To children ardent for some desperate glory,
> The old Lie: *Dulce et decorum est*
> *Pro patria mori.*

1927–1928
Stalin consolidates power

1939
Germany attacks Poland

1933
Hitler becomes
chancellor of
Germany

1929
Start of Great
Depression

1930
Gandhi leads
salt march

1935
Hitler
introduces
Nuremberg
Laws

Wilfred Owen wrote the poem "Dulce et Decorum Est" during the last months of World War I. An infantry officer in the British Army, Owen had witnessed up close the final agonies of soldiers dying from poison gas attacks. Twice wounded and decorated for valor, Owen was killed in action one week before an armistice ended the war in November 1918. In quoting Horace, an ancient Roman poet, whose message he calls "The old Lie," Owen expresses his disillusionment with the war and his resentment of its proponents. "Pro Patria Mori" was inscribed on the chapel wall of Sandhurst, Britain's foremost military

The Western Front New technologies intensified the brutality of warfare. The American painter John Singer Sargent painted *Gassed* in 1919, after spending several months embedded with British and American troops in France. A line of wounded soldiers, blinded by mustard gas, gropes in search of medical treatment while casualties lie piled around them.

1. In what ways was World War I a global event?

2. How did fascism and communism advance in the 1920s and 1930s?

3. Why did anti-colonial movements gain strength after World War I?

academy, and familiar to Britain's educated classes. The quotation translates as: "How sweet and suitable it is to die for one's country."

Among the many strands of global politics in modern times, one that stands out is the extreme violence of modern war. The warfare that characterized both world wars (I: 1914–1918, and II: 1937–1945) involved complete mobilizations of the resources and populations of the combatant countries, as well as deadly new technologies, including poison gas in **World War I** and the atomic bomb in World War II. The thorough destruction and mobilization brought by these wars is sometimes called total war.

A second strand is the global scale of politics. The ancient Romans, Mauryans, or Olmecs never worried about peoples on the other side of the world. For them, all politics was local or regional. By the early twentieth century, however, policy makers took into account circumstances and events on distant continents as a matter of course. The interconnectedness of the Global web had reached a point at which decisions made in Paris could quickly trigger uprisings in China.

A third is the increased impact of international politics on ordinary people. Centuries ago, millions of people lived beyond the reach of tax collectors and military recruiters, and they had few dealings with any state. No longer. Since 1914, almost no one has lived free from the demands of states. If your country got into a big war, your life would change, whether you served on the front lines or remained on a family farm. Total war was not the sport of kings, but the concern of all.

A fourth strand is the rise of mass ideological and political movements, including those considered here: fascism, communism, anti-colonialism, and suffragism—the effort to secure voting rights for women. Such movements were not strictly new in the twentieth century, but they became much more common than before. This was the result partly of disillusionment with established authorities brought on by World War I, partly of new media such as radio that connected audiences with charismatic politicians as never before, and partly of longer-term trends in urbanization and globalization that reached new heights in the twentieth century. Monarchies and empires fell; traditions and certainties melted into air. People everywhere, whether frightened or inspired by the crumbling of old regimes, searched for a new basis for politics. World War I and the peace settlement that followed shaped all of these developments, so that's where this chapter will begin.

WORLD WAR I AND ITS LEGACIES

World War I, despite its name, was mainly a European war, but its repercussions reached every continent. Its unprecedented butchery and unsatisfactory peace settlement gave rise to resentments and ambitions that shaped life for decades—indeed, to this day.

THE GREAT POWERS, 1870–1914

Great powers are great because they have more people, money, military force, and unity of purpose than lesser powers. In the nineteenth century, industrialization and the emergence of nationalism created a handful of new great powers, several of them mid-sized European states such as Germany, France, and Britain. They joined multicultural empires such as the Ottoman, Russian, and Habsburg—longstanding great powers—atop the greasy pole of international politics. In the years 1914–1918, these powers went to war with one another. Before wading into World War I, let's look briefly at the major participants.

In 1914, the most powerful polity on Earth was the British Empire, thanks to its industry and its navy. Britain's industrial production stood third in the world behind that of the United States and Germany; but counting the industry of the empire—Canada, India, South Africa, Australia—it easily surpassed Germany. Britain's army was tiny, but the British navy was the largest and probably most effective in the world. The British Isles in 1914 had 42 million people, and with the dominions of Canada, Australia, and New Zealand, the empire included 57 million more—most of them British immigrants or their descendants. To some extent, Britain could also rely on the manpower of British India, another 252 million people. Britain's population was, by and large, reliably patriotic, although in the Empire many resented British rule.

By 1914, the United States had the potential to become the world's second most powerful state. Its population of some 100 million was growing fast—by about 2 percent per year. Although about one in every six Americans in 1914 had been born overseas, their loyalty to the state proved reliable when war came. The country produced two-thirds of the world's oil and led the world in coal, iron, and steel production. It had a tiny overseas empire consisting mainly of the Philippines, Hawaii, and Puerto Rico, as well as a small and inexperienced army, but a sizeable and growing navy. Its political elites generally did not like to think of the United States as a great power but rather as a hemispheric power in the Americas. So the United States had the capacity but not the will to function as a great power in 1914.

If the United States was not the second most powerful state in 1914, then Germany was. Its population of about 67 million was growing by 1.2 percent annually. The majority were enthusiastically patriotic. The sharp divisions between Protestants and Catholics, or among social classes, did not appreciably weaken loyalties to the German fatherland. Its coal, iron, and steel output trailed only that of the United States. Its technological and scientific sophistication was second to none. It had an overseas empire, in Africa and the Pacific, but that added next to nothing to German power. Germany's army and navy

British Imperial Might A fleet of British battleships maneuvers through the Atlantic in 1914. A new class of battleships called dreadnoughts constituted perhaps the strongest weapon in the British Empire's arsenal, contributing to its status as the world's greatest power at the start of World War I.

were large, well trained, and well equipped, probably the best and second best, respectively, in the world.

A notch below these three, in terms of strength in international politics, stood France and Russia. France had 40 million people and a bit more manpower and resources available in its overseas empire. Its industrial production and its navy came well behind Britain's or Germany's. Russia's strength lay mainly in its size. It had 175 million people and the resources of a giant territory. Its industrial production was growing rapidly, and the recently completed Trans-Siberian Railway gave access to some of the vast mineral supplies of Siberia. But the loyalty of its minority populations was shaky. Russia's Poles, for example, still prized their Polish identity long after the eighteenth-century partitions of their country placed them inside the Russian Empire. Russia's army was big but poorly trained and equipped. Its navy was no better.

A notch below France and Russia stood Austria-Hungary and the Ottoman Empire. Austria-Hungary, as the Habsburg Empire was generally known after 1867, had 48 million people in 1914, but many of them belonged to ethnic or religious minorities and their allegiance to the state was tempered. The table below gives some idea of the ethnic diversity of Austria-Hungary's army. Industrial production was modest—lots of textiles, but not much iron and steel. Austria-Hungary had no overseas empire and virtually no navy, but an effective army despite its mix of languages. The Ottoman Empire in 1914 had recently lost

LANGUAGES OF THE ARMY IN AUSTRIA-HUNGARY, 1914	
German	25%
Hungarian	18%
Czech	13%
Serbian and Croatian	11%
Polish	9%
Ukrainian	6%
Romanian	6%
Slovak	4%
Slovenian	2%
Italian	2%

Note: Another 4 percent of army recruits spoke other languages.

Source: David Reynolds, *The Long Shadow: The Legacies of the Great War in the Twentieth Century* (2015), 7.

a lot of territory in little wars in the Balkans and North Africa. It had about 19 million people, some 4 million of whom were ethno-religious minorities—mainly Armenians, Arabs, and Greeks, whose loyalty Ottoman elites often rightly distrusted. Ottoman industry produced little military materiel. The army, however, was substantial and partly trained by German officers.

ORIGINS OF THE WAR

For more than a century, the question of the origins of World War I has fascinated historians, who still don't agree on an answer. The controversies swirl around the whys of the war, and less around what happened. For the sequence of events to make sense, we have to understand that by 1914 Europe's international system, long in flux, was divided into two big **alliance networks**. One, the Triple Alliance anchored by Germany, included Austria-Hungary and Italy. The other, the Triple Entente, enrolled France, Russia, and Great Britain. The purpose of these alliance networks was to extend Europe's long peace, concluded in 1815 in the aftermath of the Napoleonic Wars. Instead, the alliances drew states into a long, devastating war.

On June 28, 1914, a 20-year-old Serbian nationalist, Gavrilo Princip, shot and killed an Austrian archduke on the streets of Sarajevo. Princip was a member of underground Serbian nationalist organizations eager to liberate Serbs (and other "south Slavs," or "Yugoslavs") from Austro-Hungarian rule. The assassination led to an ultimatum from Austria-Hungary: Serbia must surrender much of its independence or face war. Confident of support from Russia—fellow Slavs who had championed Serbia before—the Serbian government chose war.

In preparing to fight on Serbia's behalf at the end of July 1914, Russia mobilized its vast army against both Austria-Hungary and Germany. Germany, in keeping with its war plans, mobilized its army to attack both Russia to the east and France to the west. When Germany did attack, Great Britain joined the war. By August 4, the two alliance systems—minus Italy, which at first kept out—were at war. In late 1914, the Ottoman Empire joined on the German side; and in 1915, Italy entered the war against Germany and Austria-Hungary despite its treaty commitments to those powers. As wartime coalitions, these two blocs became known as the Central Powers (Germany, Austria-Hungary, the Ottoman Empire) and the Entente or Allied Powers (France, Russia, Britain, Italy). Many smaller nations in Europe joined in too.

So why did the conflict between Serbia and Austria-Hungary bring on a general European war? A short answer includes the cultural climate of nationalism, the political influence of armies in most of the great powers, the rigidity of war plans, and the alliances that bound countries to go to war on one another's behalf. It would also include, more specifically, some key decisions—two above all.

First was the choice made by German diplomats to support whatever Austria-Hungary elected to do against Serbia. That made Austria-Hungary's leaders more willing to accept the risk of war with Russia, which they knew might result if they attacked Serbia. Second was Russia's choice to mobilize its army in support of Serbia, which was not a treaty obligation, and, as part of that strategy, to mobilize against Germany and Austria-Hungary. Russian war plans called for such a broad mobilization, but they might have been overridden by a more forceful, attentive, and imaginative tsar. (Nicholas II once described himself as "without will and without character.") These and other fateful decisions might well have been made differently if diplomats and emperors had understood that in the circumstances of 1914, war would bring little glory and much gore.

European Alliance Systems and the Ottoman Empire, 1914 Before World War I, the great powers of Europe organized two major alliance systems. One included France, Britain, and Russia. The other enrolled Germany, Austria-Hungary, and Italy. The Ottoman Empire, which lost most of its territories in southeastern Europe between 1830 and 1913, was neutral. When the war began in August 1914, Italy proclaimed neutrality despite its alliances. And by November, the Ottoman Empire, despite its former neutrality, joined with Germany and Austria-Hungary, forming the Central Powers. In 1915, Italy would join the Allies.

THE COURSE OF THE WAR

Fighting began in August 1914 and continued until November 1918, and in a few places beyond that. Declarations of war were welcomed in some cities by cheering crowds and provoked mass enlistments in most of the countries involved. But joy evaporated fast. In the first months of the war, armies sprinted after one another. Where they met, they discovered the pitiless violence of modern combat. The effect of machine guns on infantry became evident on August 22, 1914, when a French attack against German positions led to the deaths of 27,000 Frenchmen in a matter of hours.

By early 1915, the armies on the western front had settled into lines of trenches. Occasional offensives required men to run across no-man's-land toward enemy trenches amid a hail of bullets and, if all went well, fall upon the enemy. More often, they fell in no-man's-land. On the eastern front, attacks sometimes won a little more ground; but nonetheless the war became one of stalemate and attrition, in which both sides were losing soldiers faster than they could recruit new ones.

Weaponry as well as soldiers soon ran short. Of the combatants in 1914, only Germany, Britain, and France had military-industrial complexes equal to the situation. Mines and munition factories everywhere hummed

Trench Warfare In a 1916 photograph, British Army soldiers hole up in captured German dugouts to shelter from the fighting of the Somme offensive. Trench warfare became characteristic across Europe during World War I.

Munitions Factories A photograph of the factory floor at the German Krupp factory in 1917 shows many women workers. Women even operate heavy machinery, which would have been unusual before the war.

around the clock to meet the demand for weapons and explosives. Labor supply became a bottleneck. With millions of men in the armed forces, women filled the munitions factories. Germany's Krupp armaments factories employed almost no women in 1914, but by 1917 nearly 30 percent of its workforce of 175,000 was female. The enormous industrial capacity of the United States, despite its official neutrality until 1917, helped ease the situation for the Allies. In general, the Allies had a strong advantage in industrial production, food production, and military manpower.

World War I's chief theaters were in Europe; but from the start, small-scale campaigns took place in Africa among rival colonies. British forces launched bigger campaigns against Ottoman armies in Palestine and Mesopotamia, using mainly Indian troops. Naval actions occurred in the Pacific and off of Argentina, as well as in European waters.

For four years, all efforts to break the stalemate failed. In 1915, the Allies tried to knock the Ottoman Empire out of the war with an attack in Turkey, at Gallipoli, but they succeeded only in opening a new stalemated front. The Allies abandoned the front within a year—a major setback. In 1916, the Germans decided to "bleed France white" with a sustained offensive at Verdun in eastern France. It gained nothing of note and cost both countries rivers of blood. To relieve the pressure at Verdun, the British and French launched an offensive along the

Somme River in northern France in July 1916. It cost Britain 20,000 dead on the first day—more Britons than had died in 15 years of wars against Bonaparte.

By 1917, the gambles grew more desperate. Naval power enabled the Allies to blockade the Central Powers. All could see that Germany and Austria-Hungary would slowly starve, because they did not grow enough food—Germany had imported about one-quarter of its calories before 1914. Meanwhile, Britain, which produced only one-third of its food, relied on supplies from the United States, Canada, and Argentina. This situation led the German High Command to open unrestricted submarine warfare everywhere in the Atlantic, attacking neutral shipping in order to starve Britain. Sustained submarine warfare, new with World War I, sank nearly 4 million tons of merchant shipping within six months, from February through July 1917. German leaders understood that submarine attacks would bring the Americans, with all their men and industrial capacity, into the war against them; but they hoped the attacks would weaken Britain fast enough that the Central Powers could win before American forces tipped the balance. But the gamble failed: the attacks drove the United States into the war against the Central Powers in April 1917.

The Russian Revolution of 1917 (see below) gave Germans new reason to hope. By the fall of that year, Russia had stopped fighting. In March 1918, Russia agreed to the Treaty of Brest-Litovsk, surrendering to

World War I, 1914–1918 World War I was fought mainly in Europe and Ottoman lands in the Middle East, with smaller campaigns on the high seas and in German overseas holdings in Africa, New Guinea, and China. The western front stretched between Switzerland and the shore of the North Sea. The eastern front extended from the Baltic Sea to the Black Sea. Fighting also took place along the Caucasus front, in Ottoman Mesopotamia and Palestine, and in the Balkans. The Allied blockade of the Central Powers, and the German U-boat (submarine) campaigns against Allied and neutral shipping, led to food shortages for civilians behind the lines.

the Central Powers its 16 westernmost provinces, including 34 percent of its population, half its industry, and 89 percent of its coal mines. The German army now moved 50 divisions to the western front and used its

numerical superiority to mount one more gigantic offensive. It almost worked—Britain and France were tottering. But they drew strength from the American forces pouring into Europe in early 1918. The prospect of far

WAR CASUALTIES, 1914–1918

COUNTRY	TOTAL MOBILIZED FORCES	KILLED	WOUNDED	PRISONERS AND MISSING	TOTAL CASUALTIES	CASUALTIES AS PERCENTAGE OF FORCES
ALLIED AND ASSOCIATED POWERS						
Russia	12,000,000	1,700,000	4,950,000	2,500,000	9,150,000	76.3
British Empire	8,904,467	908,371	2,090,212	191,652	3,190,235	35.8
France	8,410,000	1,357,800	4,266,000	537,000	6,160,800	73.3
Italy	5,615,000	650,000	947,000	600,000	2,197,000	39.1
United States	4,355,000	116,516	204,002	4,500	325,018	7.1
CENTRAL POWERS						
Germany	11,000,000	1,773,700	4,216,058	1,152,800	7,142,558	64.9
Austria-Hungary	7,800,000	1,200,000	3,620,000	2,200,000	7,020,000	90.0
Ottoman Turkey	2,850,000	325,000	400,000	250,000	975,000	34.2

Source: https://www.pbs.org/greatwar/resources/casdeath_pop.html

more Americans yet to come sapped German morale, as did the Allies' blockade: by 1918, German city-dwellers were living on 1,000 calories a day, half of what an adult body needs to maintain itself. Talk of revolution swirled in the cafés, classrooms, and factory floors of Berlin and Vienna. Strikes broke out. In November, the German top military leadership, aware of the worsening odds against them, decided to quit and negotiated an armistice, ending the war.

THE HUMAN COST

In 51 months of war, the combatants lost about 10 million dead and 21 million wounded, of whom 7 million were maimed for life. On average, about 6,000 men were killed per day. Half of France's male population age 18 to 40 was either killed or wounded. In Austria-Hungary, 90 percent of those mobilized were either killed or wounded. The United States lost 53,000 killed in battle and another 63,000 to disease—some 0.4 percent of males of military age. Canada lost 54,000 killed in combat and a few thousand more to disease—roughly 3 percent of males 18 to 40 years old. The table shows the human cost to the major combatants.

Most World War I armies included units drawn from specific regions, so villages and counties could lose almost all their young men in one bloodbath. The Royal Newfoundland Regiment, for example, lost 90 percent of its men (killed or wounded) in a matter of minutes in the Battle of the Somme.

The slaughter broke the morale of the best-trained armies in the world. All except Germany's army mutinied within 35 months. (The American army experienced only six months of combat and did not mutiny.) French soldiers in 1917 baa-ed like sheep going to the slaughter when ordered into an attack. Millions of soldiers suffered mental breakdowns. Few could keep their composure after years living for weeks on end among rats, lice, and mud, regularly enduring artillery bombardments, and, most terrifying of all, occasionally going "over-the-top" into a fusillade of bullets. Since armies were among the most revered institutions in Europe in 1914, the evaporation of military discipline left many soldiers and civilians feeling unmoored.

A cruel irony maximized the carnage. In prior wars, infectious disease had prevented soldiers from massing in their millions long enough to butcher one another on such a scale. By 1914, advances in military medicine enabled armies to stay healthy enough for long enough to kill one another wholesale. In another cruel irony, a global influenza pandemic broke out at the war's end, killing some 50 million people in the years 1918–1919.

The horrors of war extended to civilian populations. In Lebanon, dependent on food imports, one-third of

Armenian Genocide Armenian refugees—including several children—flee Ottoman persecution around 1916. The Ottoman state systematically starved or murdered about 1.5 million Armenians during World War I.

the population starved to death in 1915 when the war interrupted shipping. The Ottoman Turks, suspicious of Armenian loyalties, starved, shot, or bayoneted 1 to 2 million Armenians in 1915–1916 in a genocidal campaign. In German East Africa (today's Tanzania), the war reduced population by 20 percent, mainly through starvation and disease. Atrocities on scales large and small occurred wherever armies occupied enemy territory, as in eastern France or western Russia.

Life on the home fronts grew ever grimmer as the war dragged on. Food ran short in Russia, Germany, and Austria-Hungary in particular. Civilians had to work long hours in mines, factories, fields, offices, and hospitals. In many countries, currency inflation ate into workers' wages, leading to hardship and strikes.

Women did the work of men in addition to their own. In Britain, 1.4 million women joined the paid labor force between 1914 and 1917. In Austria-Hungary by 1918, 1 million women had done so. Most of the women laboring in armaments and heavy industry during the war had already been workers before 1914, but now they shifted from textile mills to munitions plants. This was especially true in France and Germany, where total female employment climbed the least during the period 1914–1918. Most of the extra work that women shouldered was on farms. Some armies let some soldiers go on leave during harvest season. But in Germany, France, Austria-Hungary, Serbia, and other countries where almost all able-bodied men and horses were at war, women, children, and the elderly had to assume even the heaviest farm work.

Hundreds of thousands of women volunteered as nurses—some 120,000 in France and 92,000 in Germany. In the United States, about 22,000 did; and 3,000 in Canada. Vera Brittain, a middle-class Englishwoman, put her Oxford education on hold at age 21 to serve as a nurse. Before she returned to her studies, she had spent three hard years amid splintered bodies and shattered minds. She lost her only brother, her fiancé, and her two closest male friends to the war.

German, Austro-Hungarian, and French armies recruited thousands of female prostitutes for regulated army brothels. Unregulated brothels and the demand for prostitutes in general flourished during the war, as millions of men and women were away from the constraints of family and village.

On a small scale, women also served in combat. Bulgaria, Romania, Serbia, and Russia allowed women soldiers to fight. Milunka Savić, who took her brother's place in the Serbian Army, was wounded several times, won a handful of decorations for valor, and on one occasion captured 23 Bulgarian soldiers by herself. In Russia in the summer of 1917, a call for volunteers resulted in 5,000 women joining special battalions, the original purpose of which was to try to shame male soldiers into fighting harder. But two of the women's battalions took part in an offensive in July 1917; and one, the so-called Women's Battalion of Death, led by Maria Bochkareva, a 27-year-old of peasant origins, stormed a German trench line successfully.

The mobilization of women for war work was controversial everywhere. It ran counter to prevailing notions of femininity. Skeptics feared that driving ambulances, doing police work, selling train tickets, or building tanks alongside men would corrupt women's morals. After the war, most of the women who had taken on men's roles left their wartime jobs to return to their former lives.

Women at War Maria Bochkareva, posing with medals she earned for bravery in combat in the Russian army. She was wounded several times but survived the war.

THE RUSSIAN REVOLUTION OF 1917

In addition to the human casualties, World War I destroyed most of the political structures of Europe and the Middle East. The defeated Central Powers—Germany, Austria-Hungary, and the Ottoman Empire—all crumbled. So did one of the Allies, Russia. The experience of war stoked Europe's nationalisms and made these multicultural and multinational empires less popular than ever. The experience of defeat—which Russia shared with the Central Powers—destroyed them.

The **Russian Revolution of 1917** stands among the largest political legacies of World War I, partly because Russia was a big country but mainly because it featured an ideology that inspired imitation far and wide. Although it was triggered by World War I, and probably would not have happened without it, the Russian Revolution, like those in China and Mexico discussed in the previous chapter, had deep roots.

GRIEVANCES AND REFORMS After the abolition of serfdom in 1861, Russia remained an agrarian country of 75 million. By 1914, its population had grown to 175 million. For the peasantry, freedom from serfdom did not bring freedom from hunger and hard work. For many educated Russians, the conspicuous strengthening of Britain, France, and Germany as industrial and imperial states led, around the period 1860–1900, to worries that their country was falling behind.

What to do? The answers came down to two broad choices. One, that of the conservatives called Slavophiles, was to return to true Russian ways and shun innovations and reforms. Novelties such as representative government and factories were not suited to Russia, they thought, and would corrode the social cement of Russian Orthodoxy, faith in tsars, and village solidarity. According to others, often called Westernizers, autocracy and the power of the Orthodox Church held Russia back.

These debates grew more urgent in 1881 when a group that called itself The People's Will assassinated Tsar Alexander II. They were one of several tiny groups who sought solutions to Russia's ills through revolution, spurning the path of reform. After his father's assassination, Tsar Alexander III outlawed public discussion of many political topics and drove the revolutionaries underground.

Russia's revolutionaries, although few in number and divided among themselves, figured time was on their side.

Some put their faith in the peasantry, noting the egalitarian custom in many Russian villages of periodically re-distributing land, animals, and tools according to every family's needs. Others, under the influence of the ideas of Karl Marx, thought that real revolution could only come from the industrial working class—or as Marxists put it, the proletariat.

The hour seemed to strike in 1905. The government, now headed by Tsar Nicholas II, unleashed the army on unarmed demonstrators in the capital of St. Petersburg, killing more than 100. Instead of being intimidated, workers, peasants, and dissident middle-class groups known as the intelligentsia became more vocal. Demands rang out for more schools, legislative assemblies, and land for peasants. Peasants themselves wanted reduced rents or ownership of the land they worked. Workers wanted better wages and a voice in factory management. Urban workers invented new, city-wide workers' councils, called soviets.

These events, sometimes called the 1905 Revolution, led Nicholas—reluctantly—to make concessions, including an empire-wide legislative assembly, called the Duma, whose members would be elected. The first Duma met in 1906 and called for a radical land reform. To the tsar and his aristocratic landowning counselors, land redistribution seemed to strike at the heart of Russia's political system.

The tsar called upon a brilliant bureaucrat, aristocrat, and scholar of agriculture, Pyotr Stolypin, to manage the Duma's demands. Stolypin tried to stave off peasant resentment with, as he put it, the "wager on the strong." His reforms favored richer peasants, easing their route to greater prosperity and property ownership. He wanted to establish a peasant bulwark against revolution. But a young revolutionary who also worked for the secret police assassinated him in 1911, leaving Russia in less capable hands. Even the most capable hands would have been full, given the pressures facing Russia after the outbreak of World War I.

WAR, DEFEAT, AND REVOLUTION From the start of the war in 1914, Germany hammered the Russian army. Russia's economy proved unable to produce enough ammunition, artillery, locomotives—even shoes—for the war effort. Russia's soldiers, justifiably, began to think their government was failing them, treating them as mere cannon fodder, while profiteers grew fat from government contracts. Russia mobilized 12 million men, of whom 1.7

Bolshevik Revolution Russian soldiers rebelling against the tsar's authority in early 1917 march through the streets of St. Petersburg, carrying a banner that reads "Liberty, Equality, Fraternity" in homage to the French revolutionary slogan.

million were killed, 5 million wounded, and 2.5 million missing or captured. Only Austria-Hungary's casualty rate was worse.

In this time of crisis, Tsar Nicholas II showed all his many weaknesses. He could not control bickering generals. In late 1915, the tsar went to the front to supervise the conduct of the war personally. That invited Russians to hold him directly responsible for military misfortunes. He ignored mounting economic problems on the home front—notably, inflation of food and fuel prices. The tsar's authority melted away.

Mass demonstrations took place in March 1917 (February by the calendar then in use in Russia). Troops called out to tame the riotous crowds refused to fire. Generals and Duma politicians, agreeing that the tsar had become a liability, forced him to abdicate in favor of his brother, who refused the throne. Russia now had no tsar. The Romanov dynasty, in power for 300 years, was no more.

A handful of Duma politicians now formed a Provisional Government that represented mainly the privileged segments of Russian society. In the capital, now called Petrograd, workers and revolutionaries organized into a soviet and claimed authority. Russia had, in effect, two governments, and thus no government.

Through the spring and summer of 1917, the Provisional Government, headed by the moderate socialist lawyer Alexander Kerensky, made two big mistakes. First,

it chose to continue fighting, even ordering an offensive in June that became another retreat by July. Second, it postponed land reform. Millions of peasants took matters into their own hands, seizing control of estates, ousting and sometimes killing landlords. Soldiers from peasant families deserted the battlefront in droves so as not to miss re-distributions of land. Critics of the Provisional Government promised peace, land, and bread—none of which Kerensky could provide.

LENIN Into this chaotic situation came **Vladimir Lenin**. Born in 1870 to a prosperous provincial family, Lenin became a dedicated revolutionary in his teens after the shock of seeing his brother hanged for trying to build an assassin's bomb. An excellent student interested in physics and math, and a fine chess player, Lenin studied law at university but was expelled for taking part in a demonstration. He responded by studying revolutionary writers, especially Marx, on his own. Thanks to his mother's intervention, he was allowed to take university examinations in 1890, despite not having been a student for years. He passed brilliantly and became a provincial lawyer, while devoting every spare minute to preparing for revolution. His activities earned him banishment to Siberia in 1897 and then exile, where he wrote political treatises. He was in Switzerland in early 1917 when the High Command of the German Army decided to provide him with a special train to neutral Finland. From there, he could take his revolutionary skills to Petrograd and undermine the teetering Russian war effort.

Lenin in 1917 was a middle-aged man in a hurry. He belonged to a minority faction of a Marxist party called the Bolsheviks, and because of his theoretical writings and his forceful personality he stood high among them. Most Bolsheviks hoped to take power soon, some of them optimistic it could happen through elections. Lenin wanted revolution now, by whatever means necessary, using the slogan "all power to the soviets." Within those soviets, the Bolshevik faction prevailed, thanks to tight organization and the fervor of its members.

THE OCTOBER REVOLUTION AND EARLY BOLSHEVIK RULE Lenin ordered an armed insurrection. The Bolshevik Revolution was a coup d'état on November 7–8, 1917 (but sometimes called the October Revolution because of the different Russian calendar). Within 10 days, the Bolsheviks controlled Petrograd and

Moscow and had begun to squeeze out other revolutionary factions. Within three months, they were governing alone and had set up a secret police and revolutionary courts to identify, and then imprison or murder, those insufficiently loyal to their party.

Their policies, however, won them the loyalty of many Russians. The Bolsheviks made peace with the Central Powers early in 1918. They ratified the peasants' seizures of land. They stripped away the civil rights of priests, landlords, bankers, and others whom they deemed exploiters.

Lenin and many Bolsheviks believed that the Duma, and all democracy, was a sham. The appropriate government for Russia was what they called the dictatorship of the proletariat. In practice, that meant a one-party state led not by proletarian workers but by people like Lenin: long-time professional revolutionaries, some of them brilliant intellectuals, well schooled—if self-educated—in German philosophy, British political economy, and the history of the French Revolution. They saw themselves as "the vanguard of the proletariat" and were so convinced of their historical mission that at times they used armed force against workers and peasants in whose name they claimed to rule. They thought they were "building communism," a social and political system first outlined by Marx that, in theory, was without private property, without exploitation, and in some versions (not Lenin's) without a state.

It took four difficult years for Lenin to consolidate power. In the Russian Civil War (1918–1921), the Bolsheviks—officially called communists by March 1918—created an improvised army to fight opponents of their revolution. Lenin assigned this task to Leon Trotsky, who had planned the coup of 1917. Despite having no military experience, Trotsky built an effective military in the terrible conditions of 1918. He imposed conscription on a war-weary population and hired officers from the old tsarist army against the wishes of almost every Bolshevik. His Red Army prevailed against a loose coalition of counter-revolutionaries backed by foreign powers, including troops from France, Britain, the United States, and—by far the largest contingent—Japan.

By early 1921, Lenin and the Bolsheviks ruled a shattered, bankrupt, and impoverished country now called the Union of Soviet Socialist Republics (USSR). Some 8 to 13 million people had died of violence or disease in the turmoil of the years 1917–1921. Another 2 million emigrated. Industrial production stood at 20 percent of 1914 levels. Hunger stalked the streets. The Bolsheviks concluded that they could not let workers run the factories after all, so they imposed hierarchical management. They requisitioned all the grain they could from the peasantry, who responded with strikes. In March 1921, sailors at a naval base, Kronstadt, renowned for its revolutionary ardor against the tsars, rebelled against Bolshevik rule. The Red Army crushed them at the cost of many thousand lives, demonstrating—for those who needed convincing—that the Bolsheviks would brook no dissent. In the years to come, they would try to destroy the surviving elites of pre-revolutionary Russia, spread their ideology abroad, and make the USSR a powerhouse in world politics.

VERSAILLES AND POST-WAR PARTITIONS

In 1919, representatives of the victorious powers gathered at Versailles outside Paris to hammer out a set of peace treaties. The Allies excluded the defeated Central Powers and communist Russia, which had announced it would not pay the tsars' debts. Edith Wilson, the wife of the American president, Woodrow Wilson, told her husband that the assembled diplomats poring over their maps looked like so many little boys playing a game. The president assured her theirs was a serious business. They were re-drawing the map of east-central Europe and Southwest Asia, dividing up territories, creating countries, marking borders, and defining peoples. In short, they were doing roughly what an earlier generation of European diplomats had done to Africa at the Berlin Conference of 1884–1885.

Vladimir Lenin Speaking in Moscow in 1920, Lenin addresses a crowd of Red Army soldiers about to go to war against counter-revolutionaries in Poland.

A New Political Geography: Europe, the Middle East, and Africa, 1922 The treaties signed in 1919 and 1920 concluding World War I re-drew the boundaries of Europe, European colonies, and the Ottoman Middle East. New countries arose in east-central Europe and in former Russian, Austro-Hungarian, and German territories. New de facto colonies, as well as the new country of Turkey, were created in former Ottoman lands in the Middle East. The Allied powers devising this new political geography tried to respect ethnic identities in Europe, but not in the Middle East or Africa.

RE-MAKING EUROPE The European powers had carried out the partition of Africa in ignorance, but they undertook the partition of the territories of the Central Powers in a mood of vengeance. French diplomats especially wanted to cripple Germany. The deal imposed on Germany, the **Treaty of Versailles**, explicitly blamed Germany for the outbreak of the war, required Germany to pay huge sums (called reparations) to the victors, and turned some 13 percent of German territory over to either France or newly re-created Poland. It put strict limits on the size of Germany's armed forces. Other treaties, equally

vengeful, were signed with Austria, Hungary, Bulgaria, and the Ottoman Empire.

The treaties reflected two other ambitions aside from vengeance. The first was **self-determination**, to use Wilson's preferred phrase. The American president thought that each European nationality ought to rule itself. This would, he hoped, remove an important cause of discontent, helping to ensure future peace. Wilson did not consider Africans and Asians capable of self-rule. Racism of this sort was commonplace in 1919.

The second ambition behind the treaties was, in

Wilson's phrase, collective security. He hoped that international institutions might restrain the militarism and nationalism that underlay World War I. So the Allies designed an international body, the League of Nations, to prevent war through arbitration. Based in Geneva, Switzerland, the League opened for business in 1920 and enjoyed modest success in settling international disputes during the 1920s. But in the 1930s it proved helpless in the face of renewed militarism—as we shall see. In a bitter rebuke to Wilson, the U.S. Senate refused to ratify U.S. membership in the League.

World War I and its peace treaties left legacies more durable than the League of Nations. The Romanovs in Russia were not the only longstanding dynasty destroyed. In Germany, when the emperor, Kaiser Wilhelm II, fled the country late in 1918, it ended the reign of the House of Hohenzollern, emperors of Germany since 1871 and kings of Prussia since 1701. In the absence of the monarchy, political factions battled in the streets. In Berlin, a communist uprising was crushed. In Munich, a Soviet-style government briefly came to power. In August 1919, after nine months' painful gestation, Germany brought forth a republic, soon called the Weimar Republic after the town where its first constitutional assembly took place. It struggled to gain legitimacy among Germans. The economy careened from hyperinflation of the currency in 1923 and 1924 to economic depression in 1931. The rise of Adolf Hitler to power in Germany, in 1933, described below, reflected the inadequacies of the Weimar Republic and stands as one of the legacies of World War I.

In Austria-Hungary, the House of Habsburg also lost its throne after 400 years as a major force in Europe. As in Germany, revolution followed defeat in 1918. Reorganization followed along lines set forth in the treaties negotiated in Paris in 1919, which created a series of new countries in place of the multinational Habsburg state. Austria and Hungary became independent countries. Poland was re-created from Habsburg, German, and Russian territory. Another republic, Czechoslovakia, was cobbled together from Habsburg provinces. The southern Slavs were gathered into a new kingdom, Yugoslavia, ruled by a Serbian dynasty. All of these countries were small and comparatively weak. Their borders did not perfectly match ethnic geography—no borders could. Most of them soon became nationalist and authoritarian in character.

RE-MAKING THE MIDDLE EAST After 600 years as the ruling family of the Ottoman Empire, the House of Osman also lost its empire as a result of World War I. The result was a dramatic transformation of the Middle East—a term that came into occasional use in the late nineteenth century and became common after 1918. Its precise meaning varies, but in this book it refers to Southwest Asia and Egypt.

After weathering all manner of challenges for centuries, the Ottoman state proved unequal to the demands of industrial warfare in the years 1914–1918. The treaty its representatives signed with the Allies in 1919 amounted to the partition of most of the empire among Britain, France, Italy, and Greece. This outraged many Turks, sparking a nationalist revolution led by an army hero, **Mustafa Kemal**, who as we've seen had played a role in the Young Turk Revolution of 1908. Between 1919 and 1924, Kemal's forces defeated all rivals, repelled a Greek invasion, expelled millions of non-Turks from Anatolia, replaced the Ottoman state with a new Turkish republic, and, most radical of all, abolished the Islamic caliphate.

For more than 1,200 years, caliphs, the earthly leaders of the Islamic faith and the official successors of Muhammad, had guided Muslims. Since 1517, every Ottoman sultan had claimed the mantle of caliph; and for most Sunni Muslims, and therefore most Muslims, the Ottoman claim was legitimate. So it came as a great shock when Kemal's government eliminated the caliphate in 1924.

Kemal and his followers drew the lesson from defeat in World War I that the Ottoman Empire had been backward and inefficient, held down by an antiquated culture steeped in Islamic tradition. So he pushed through reforms in education and law that secularized Turkey, closing Islamic schools and courts. Religious symbols and garb were banned in public. Sisters' inheritances now equaled their brothers', contrary to normal practice under Islamic law. Women acquired more legal rights as individuals rather than as wards of their fathers or husbands. Polygamy was banned and women could initiate divorce. From 1930, women could vote and hold office. The Latin alphabet replaced the Arabic.

This package, often known as the Atatürk Reforms after Kemal's adopted name of Atatürk ("father of the Turks"), was part of a century-long process of reform in Ottoman lands. It was also a legacy of World War I. Kemal's main motivation was to strengthen Turkey as the

Secularized Turkey A photograph of a Turkish classroom dated to around 1930 shows women students being taught to read and write in the Latin alphabet. Most of the women wear Western dress, and many have their hair uncovered: characteristic signs of Atatürk's program of reform.

Meiji reformers had done in Japan. To achieve this, he drew upon the law, culture, and technology of the most formidable states of the day—those of western Europe. Kemal's military record and his success in rallying Turks against foreign invasion gave him the prestige and power to enact far-reaching reforms and harness the nationalism of ethnic Turks.

The territory of the Turkish republic was a mere remnant of the Ottoman Empire. The mainly Arab provinces of the defunct empire, now officially called Mandated Territories of the League of Nations, became de facto colonies of Britain and France. The French got Syria and Lebanon; the British took Palestine, Jordan, and Iraq.

That arrangement stored up trouble for the future. During the war, the British government had promised unspecified land in Ottoman Palestine to Zionist Jews, persuaded by Chaim Weizmann, a Russian immigrant and Zionist leader. A nationalist movement of the Jewish people, Zionism grew up partly in response to anti-Semitism in Europe in the late nineteenth century. Another early organizer, Theodor Herzl, a journalist from Budapest, gave the movement its ideological foundation. The Zionist movement aimed to create a Jewish homeland centered on Jerusalem, despite the presence of tens of thousands of Muslim and Christian Arabs who themselves considered Palestine home. British diplomats had also promised independence to Arabs if they rebelled against the Ottomans. And other British diplomats cut a deal with France, promising to divide the Arab provinces of the Ottoman Empire between them. So when the peacemakers in Paris in 1919

re-drew the map of the Middle East, just about everyone felt betrayed. Their descendants often still do.

The diplomats in Paris re-arranged the political geography of Africa and the Pacific as well as the Middle East. Germany's former African colonies, such as Tanganyika, Togo, Southwest Africa, and others, became League of Nations Mandated Territories administered by Britain, France, Belgium, or South Africa. In the Pacific, former German colonies went to Japan, Britain, Australia, or New Zealand. The local populations in Samoa or New Guinea or Togo were not consulted.

SUFFRAGISM TO 1939

While the peacemakers at Versailles were discussing the fine points of the right of self-determination of peoples, women reminded them that the female half of humankind did not enjoy that right. As we've seen, Olympe de Gouges, Abigail Adams, and others had advocated women's political rights in the late eighteenth century with little success. Winning the vote—the goal of **suffragism**—and taking part in the direction of one's country was an essential step in women's quest for political equality. It happened in a rush, like the abolitions of slavery, and World War I provided a big push.

PRE-WAR SUFFRAGE MOVEMENTS As of 1850, voting was a male preserve in the few countries that permitted it at all. Many voices challenged this arrangement. Their arguments included the notion that denying women the vote was inherently unjust; that women's influence in politics would reduce corruption and war; and, in some cases such as the United States, that woman suffrage, if confined to a preferred class or race, would reduce the influence of poor people, immigrants, or racial minorities who, if they did not already vote, might do so one day.

During the nineteenth century, women in the United Kingdom and the United States built social movements aimed at winning the vote, often allied with supporters

Women's Suffrage On May 21, 1914, British suffrage activist Emmeline Pankhurst was arrested outside Buckingham Palace in London, England.

of moral causes such as banning prostitution or alcohol. Women in other countries took note: suffragism, like abolitionism, was an international movement, coursing through the Global web. Many who took up the suffragist cause in the United States were abolitionists or Quakers—including Lucretia Mott and Elizabeth Cady Stanton, who in 1848 organized a women's rights gathering in upstate New York, the Seneca Falls Convention. Stanton held that only the vote would make woman "free as man is free." The convention concluded by issuing a Declaration of Sentiments modeled on the Declaration of Independence. The most influential suffragist publication was John Stuart Mill's *The Subjection of Women* (1869), likely written with substantial input from his wife, Harriet Taylor Mill, who had published on suffragism in 1851. The book was translated into dozens of languages and read by suffragists all over the world.

By 1890, suffragists and other reformers in a few countries had achieved some important goals such as limits on working hours or the sale of alcohol, improved city lighting or sanitation, more girls' schools, and a woman's right to own property in her own name. But, despite sustained effort and support from many male politicians, they were not significantly closer to securing women's right to vote in national elections.

In Britain, the movement took on an especially militant character between 1909 and 1914. Suffragists, frustrated with 70 years of meager results, tried mass demonstrations, hunger strikes, and sabotage. They even exploded a bomb at a prime minister's residence. These efforts, organized by a minority wing of British suffragists led by Emmeline Pankhurst and her daughters, failed in their purpose as of 1914.

EARLY SUFFRAGE When World War I began, about 2 million of the world's roughly 400 million voting-age women could vote, all of them in four small countries. Not counting places such as the state of New Jersey that had provided women the vote and then quickly took it away, the first jurisdiction in the world where women could vote was Wyoming. It was a U.S. territory with only 8,000 people in 1869 when one activist—Esther Hobart Morris—convinced the legislature that women would exert a civilizing influence upon the politics of a wild west territory. Utah followed suit in 1870 when the federal government threatened to ban polygamy, a common practice in the Mormon-dominated territory. Utah's polygamous

men granted women the vote to show that the women of Utah were not oppressed. By 1914, women had won the right to vote in state elections in most other western U.S. states.

New Zealand was the first country to pass nationwide legislation enfranchising women. The foremost leader of the suffrage movement in New Zealand was Kate

Kate Sheppard The influential New Zealand women's suffrage activist posed for this portrait around 1910.

Sheppard, a Scottish immigrant, wife, mother, and formidable organizer in anti-alcohol campaigns. She published persuasive arguments in the same vein as Taylor and Mill, adding the idea that expanding the electorate would reduce vote buying and other forms of corruption. Sheppard presented New Zealand legislators with a petition in favor of enfranchising women signed by a goodly share of the country's adult population. She and her allies, who included several of New Zealand's leading politicians, prevailed in 1893. By 1902, Australia had followed suit. Both New Zealand and Australia were composed substantially of immigrants, with men handily outnumbering women. This made woman suffrage less threatening to them than it did in most other countries. And, as in Wyoming, many men thought women voters might raise the moral tone of public life.

Finland in 1906 and Norway in 1913 allowed women to vote as a result of nationalist campaigns. Finland, part of the Russian Empire since 1815, won substantial autonomy in 1906, including a legislature. To maximize the Finnish voice within what remained a Russian territory, Finnish men agreed that Finnish women should vote. In Norway, the nationalist quest was for independence from Sweden, and once again women's votes seemed politically useful to men hoping to strengthen Norway's claims for independence. These four countries, all small in population, overwhelmingly rural, and far from the centers of world power and intellectual ferment, were the only ones anywhere that allowed women to vote in national elections before World War I.

Elsewhere, resistance to suffragism was too strong. In Catholic countries of southern Europe, for example, and in Islamic countries such as Iran or those of the Ottoman Empire (where few men could vote), the dominant culture led people to suppose that the position of women in society was divinely ordained rather than politically negotiable. Resistance was also entrenched where men—some men, at least—had long ago won voting rights, as in France, the Netherlands, the United States, and the United Kingdom. Political participation had become a ritual of manhood, one that most men felt would undermine feminine virtues if shared with women. In Britain, one of the most active and effective opponents was Mary Augusta Ward, founder in 1908 of the Anti-Suffrage Society. Mrs Humphry Ward, as she preferred to be known, showed astute political skills while arguing—paradoxically—that women were unfit for politics.

SUFFRAGE AND THE WORLD WAR In the end, it required major social upheavals—war, invasion, revolution—to splinter the opposition to enfranchising women. World War I provided an opening for suffragist movements, one they were by 1914 fully capable of exploiting.

Between 1914 and 1920, women won the vote in 19 countries, including big and populous ones such as Russia, Poland, Germany, the United Kingdom, Canada, and the United States. Some restrictions applied—so, for example, in the United Kingdom only women over age 30 could vote until 1928, and in the United States the southern states quickly found ways to disenfranchise black women. In Russia, now becoming the communist USSR, women from privileged backgrounds were denied the vote. In Canada, women of Asian or Amerindian (First Nations) background could not vote. But, taken together, more than 100 million women acquired the vote in these seven years. The following table shows the significance of the era of World War I in the history of women's suffrage up to 1940.

In some countries, including the United Kingdom and the United States, the political winds shifted because women's patriotism and sacrifices for the war effort won them enough goodwill—and undermined notions of their unfitness for public life—to get enfranchisement bills over the top in all-male legislatures. In others, such as Germany, Austria, and Russia, when the collapse of autocracy in the years 1917–1918 opened the way to a democratization

WHEN WOMEN WON THE VOTE (NATIONAL ELECTIONS)	
1893	New Zealand
1902	Australia
1906	Finland
1913	Norway
1915	Denmark, Iceland
1917	Russia
1918	Austria, Canada, Germany, Hungary, Latvia, Lithuania, Poland, United Kingdom
1919	Belgium, Luxembourg, Netherlands (and white women in colonial Kenya, Rhodesia)
1920	Albania, Czechoslovakia, United States
1921	Sweden
1922	Ireland
1923	Burma
1924	Mongolia
1928	Guiana
1929	Ecuador
1930	South Africa (white women only)
1931	Spain (revoked 1939)
1932	Brazil, Uruguay, Thailand
1934	Cuba, Turkey
1937	Philippines (U.S. territory)
1938	Bolivia
1939	El Salvador

Source: Jad Adams, *Women and the Vote* (2014), 437-38.

of politics in general, opposition to women's voting—never organized—quickly crumbled. In all combatant countries, where almost all young men were away from wives and families for months or years, moral reformers hoped that enfranchising women would check the spread of drunkenness and prostitution. In Canada in 1917, a prime minister trying to build support for military conscription pushed through a law allowing the vote to women who were wives, mothers, daughters, or sisters of men in uniform. His reasoning, which proved correct, was that they would favor conscription of other men to join their relatives in the Canadian Army in the trenches of France and Belgium.

So among the legacies of World War I was a giant stride toward the political emancipation of women. By 1920, of countries with constitutional government that allowed regular elections, only France and Italy denied the vote

Arguments for Suffrage A California poster in support of women's suffrage from around 1910 suggests that women should be given the vote because they are ready to "clean up" politics by combating bribery, corruption, and social problems.

to women. (These countries granted women full suffrage in the 1940s.) Overall, suffragism in the era of World War I was a success. In the coming decades, it would prevail almost everywhere.

THE RISE OF THE UNITED STATES

In addition to sparking revolutions, shattering empires, and accelerating social and political movements, World War I permanently shifted the global balance of power. In broad terms, it weakened Europe and bolstered the United States. This shift showed up in many spheres, from the size of navies to the pace of industrial innovation. It was most obvious in finance. Britain and France had borrowed heavily from New York bankers and the U.S. government. Anyone seeking big loans in the 1920s now first thought of New York rather than London, Amsterdam, Paris, or Berlin. As the American theologian Reinhold Neibuhr put it in 1930, "We are the first empire of the world to establish our sway without legions. Our legions are dollars."

Bankers aside, Americans proved reluctant to take on the role of the world's leading power. The United States retreated into isolationism in the 1920s, refusing to join the League of Nations, for example. It remained active in the American hemisphere, using its military power freely to intervene in Haiti, Nicaragua, and elsewhere. It kept a world-class navy, equal in size to Britain's. But most Americans preferred to stay out of the world's trouble spots and rely upon broad oceans for U.S. security.

American power—or more precisely, potential power—rested in part on the fact that the United States pumped two-thirds of the world's oil. The centrality of oil to world politics was another legacy of World War I. By the end of the war, trucks, tanks, aircraft, and submarines had become important instruments of military power, and all used oil derivatives as fuel. So did an increasing proportion of surface ships. At the war's end, Lord Curzon, a prominent member of Britain's War Cabinet, said the "Allies floated to victory on a wave of oil." Oil had become essential to modern warfare and a strategic good of the utmost importance—as it remains today.

A further political legacy of World War I was the changed relationship between governments and the governed in many societies. The war dealt a setback to the ideal of restrained government. None of the combatant states trusted the market to provide enough war materiel. All of them relied on government to organize war production to some extent. The German war economy, entirely improvised but carefully controlled by the military, worked miracles in munitions factories, even if it could not adequately feed the civilian population. It made such a favorable impression on Lenin that he used it as his model for Russia once he took power. The combatants only partly demobilized their economies after 1918, keeping government regulation of markets in effect in different ways. World War I advanced a long-term trend, one with several subsequent ebbs and flows, toward bigger government.

American Industry A 1912 photograph of an oil refinery in Richmond, California, the largest in the United States at the time. The refinery belonged to John D. Rockefeller's Standard Oil Company.

THE GREAT DEPRESSION

Government direction of economic life surged again in response to the Great Depression of the 1930s, which in some ways was also a legacy of World War I. The Depression began in 1929 with a stock market collapse in the United States. It spread quickly, faster than any previous economic downturn, because of the speed with which information and money now flowed. People tried to pull their money out of banks, many of which failed. Global economic output fell by 15 percent from 1929 to 1932. Agricultural prices fell by as much as 60 percent, and international trade shrank by half. It was the worst economic contraction in twentieth-century world history, by a large margin.

Countries deeply tied into international circuits of finance or dependent on exports were especially hard hit. Unemployment in Germany, which owed large sums in reparations from World War I, reached between 30 and 33 percent; and in the United States and Canada, about 25 percent. Australia and New Zealand, dependent on farm exports, suffered heavily. So did countries relying on mining exports, such as South Africa, Peru, Bolivia, and above all Chile, where total economic output fell by half.

In contrast, countries less tied in to the international circuits and more structured around peasant food production felt far less distress. China, India, and Japan weathered the crisis comparatively well outside of small export sectors. Japan's economic contraction was about 8 percent, India's less, and China's less still. The USSR scarcely took part in international trade or financial flows and thus was unscathed by the Great Depression, although, as we'll see below, it underwent its own homemade economic crisis in the early 1930s—collectivization.

In the hard-hit countries, families were thrown back on their own resources. Farm families could at least feed themselves. Urban families whose breadwinner lost a job struggled more, selling what they had, scratching out livings as day laborers, peddlers, beggars, or thieves. Families also cut back on reproduction: the global birth rate fell by 5 to 10 percent between 1930 and 1935.

Governments did not know what to do to ease the crisis. The record of successful economic management during World War I made it impossible for them to do nothing, as had been normal in previous—much smaller—global depressions of 1893 or 1873. Some tried to boost their own

Great Depression Unemployed men wait for a hot meal outside a Chicago soup kitchen. In the United States, unemployment during the Depression reached about 25 percent.

economies by imposing tariffs on imported goods, which, when many countries did it, only deepened the Depression. Some tried rigorously to balance budgets in hopes of winning reputations for responsible public finance and inspiring investors. The most effective response was increasing public spending, even if it deepened national debt and ran counter to the wisdom of most 1930s economists. At the center of this response was re-armament. Germany and Italy pioneered this path, under leaders who looked forward to a new war that would undo the result of World War I.

FASCISM AND COMMUNISM, 1919–1939

The return to peacetime conditions did not mean the end of turmoil around the world. In 1919, political chaos boiled over in cities throughout Europe and from Winnipeg to Sydney, Buenos Aires to Beijing. New ideologies simmered almost everywhere, with fascism, communism, and anti-colonialism the most important. All were radical in the sense that their followers wished to see thorough changes in the political order. All thrived upon either disgust at the mass butchery of war or the sordid compromises of the 1919 peace—or both.

FASCISM TO 1939

Fascism was born in Italy during World War I. Italy had joined the war in 1915 on what became the winning side, lured by promises of territory. But in the peace settlement, Italy got precious little and lost some of what was promised by treaty to Kemal's nationalist revolution in Turkey.

To many Italians, this outcome was an outrageous betrayal of the more than 2 million killed, wounded, or missing in the war. They blamed, among others, a weak government, parliamentary institutions, and cultural and business elites. They wanted an Italian state that would be more forceful, nationalistic, imperialistic, and unified—and less hobbled by debate, division, and deliberation. They wanted action, not words. People who saw matters this way found the fascist movement to their taste.

Fascism, whether in Italy or elsewhere, had certain distinctive features. First among them was militant nationalism. Fascists idolized vigor, power, ruthlessness, and war. Their nationalism included a call for regeneration and purification of the nation. Many fascists felt only violence could cleanse their nation of impure elements, which usually included ethnic minorities and immigrants. Fascism also emphasized the cult of the dynamic leader, the man (never a woman) who took bold action and rejected political bickering and backroom deals. Fascists scorned multi-party politics and preferred a one-party state—like Lenin and the Bolsheviks.

Fascist movements tried to make a display of national solidarity and strength through theatrical marches and rallies. They adopted uniforms for party members: blackshirts in Italy, blueshirts in Ireland, brownshirts in Germany. Fascists had their own salutes and catch phrases. Their rallies, often dramatic, emotional affairs, extolled strength and exuded menace toward people judged not genuinely part of the nation. The parties always included youth movements, because the cult of action, vigor, and renewal required young faces.

On the home front, fascists wanted men to wield authority in families and women to keep house and raise strong children. The growing independence of women under wartime conditions often annoyed men—and many women too—who preferred that families live under the authority of an adult male. Fascists wanted men to re-assert that domestic authority. Fascist gender politics was an extreme version of a commonplace outlook around the world in the early twentieth century.

Fascists usually offered an economic program that was critical of both capitalism and communism, proclaiming a third way, sometimes called corporatism, involving substantial state direction but mainly private ownership of property. In any case, they claimed to provide an economy that served all the people, not just bosses or workers. Religious policy differed greatly among fascists. Some were scornful of organized religion. Others allied themselves with the Catholic or Orthodox Church. Fascism never amounted to much outside of Christendom, although Chinese nationalists borrowed some of its elements.

ITALIAN FASCISM AND MUSSOLINI The mainspring behind Italian fascism was **Benito Mussolini**, born in 1883 in a provincial town. His father was a blacksmith with socialist politics, his mother a pious Catholic and former schoolteacher. Benito did well in school and was certified as an elementary school teacher. But in 1902 he left Italy for Switzerland to avoid army service. He read widely, especially in political philosophy, took part in socialist organizations and strikes, and was arrested now and again in both Switzerland and Italy. He thought of himself as an intellectual, and as of age 30 there was nothing about him to suggest he would become Italy's dictator.

Then came World War I. Unlike most socialists, Mussolini eventually argued for Italy's entry into the bloodbath. He decided that national identity was more important, more natural, than class identity. He volunteered for the army and spent nine months near the trenches, where an accidental explosion left shrapnel in his body. The war years gave Mussolini credentials for political leadership and an audience he otherwise could not have had. In 1919, he formed a paramilitary group in the northern city of Milan that embraced the term *fascist*.

Italy in 1919 was in disarray. Class conflict boiled over into violence between workers and bosses—or thugs hired by bosses—and between peasants and landlords. Fascists claimed to offer a solution, one based on national unity, discipline, and authority. They denounced deliberation and compromise as weakness. In practice they advocated suppressing communists, building up the military, entrusting power to a fascist party elite, and grabbing territory from supposed racial inferiors, specifically Slavs in what is now Slovenia and Croatia, and Africans. In 1922, some 30,000 fascists marched on Rome threatening a coup d'état. The king, afraid of civil war, asked Mussolini to form a government.

Mussolini The Italian fascist leader addresses an enormous crowd in May 1936, delivering a speech in which he proclaims a new Italian empire following Italy's invasion of Ethiopia.

Mussolini ruled Italy for more than 20 years in an increasingly authoritarian fashion. He excelled at manipulating mass media, including print journalism, his former profession, but also radio and film. He appealed to all those worried about communism, which included most employers. In this respect, the Bolshevik Revolution was indispensable to the rise of Mussolini. He made an effort to appeal to the church and Catholics, and to those upset by women's autonomy—he presented the memory of his pious mother as the ideal for Italian womanhood. Above all, he appealed to the sentiment of Italian nationalism. After 1922, he squashed or co-opted all opposition and increasingly ruled as dictator, through the Fascist Party.

The anxieties that made Mussolini and fascism attractive to millions of Italians existed elsewhere too. Italy's example—a purposeful government that promoted deeds, not bickering—appealed broadly. Mussolini's propagandists did their best to bolster that appeal, trumpeting decisive actions such as draining marshes or building highways and dams.

By 1933, fascist movements had arisen in a dozen or more countries, mainly in Europe. Even countries with longstanding traditions of representative government, such as France and Britain, had fascist movements. The British Union of Fascists claimed tens of thousands of members in the early 1930s, although it never did well in elections. Nor did fascist groups in France. Fascists came to power in Hungary in 1932 and Spain (after winning a bloody civil war) in 1939. Movements that, while not genuinely fascist, found inspiration in Mussolini's Italy took power in Romania, Poland, Greece, and Portugal. Small fascist movements took shape in some Latin American countries such as Chile and Brazil.

GERMAN FASCISM AND HITLER By far the most important case was Germany, where a fascist party emerged in the 1920s and took power in 1933. They were called National Socialists, or Nazis for short. The Nazi Party emerged from the chaotic and violent world of post-war Germany. The Versailles treaty, particularly its war guilt clause and reparations, seemed deeply unjust to most Germans, who felt they had neither caused nor lost World War I. Many found it comforting to believe in the "stab in the back," the idea that traitorous politicians working for Jews or communists or both had sacrificed Germany. One who admired such thinking was the Austrian **Adolf Hitler**.

Hitler was born in 1889 to a modest family—one of six children, three of whom died in infancy. His father was a customs inspector and beekeeper in various small towns along the border between Austria-Hungary and Germany. Hitler's younger brother died in 1900, leaving Hitler sullen and uncooperative, a reaction not so different from Lenin's to the death of his older brother. He quit school at age 16 and went to Vienna, where he was twice rejected for art school. For the next seven years, he eked out a living selling watercolor paintings and sleeping in homeless shelters. In 1913, he moved to Munich in Germany. When World War I began, he volunteered for

Adolf Hitler Hitler giving a campaign speech in a beer garden tent in Munich. The banner urges voters to elect Hitler and the National Socialists, or Nazis, whose party headquarters were in Munich.

the German army and served with distinction, chiefly as a messenger, winning an Iron Cross, for which a Jewish officer recommended him. He was wounded in 1916 and temporarily blinded by mustard gas late in 1918. Hitler loved the camaraderie and commitment, and the acceptance, he found in the army.

Outraged by the Versailles treaty, Hitler drifted into politics in 1919 in Munich. He joined a fringe group, the National Socialist Party, one of many hyper-nationalist organizations in Germany. By 1921 he was its leader. He honed a gift for oratory, practicing poses and turns of phrase in front of a mirror. He encouraged the anger and resentment of common people, especially those who felt Germany had been wronged at Versailles. Hitler urged them to believe that Germany's future depended on ridding the country of Jews and communists, and that he alone embodied the will of the people. He promised action, not words—a renewal of German greatness, rather than the squabbling of democracy.

He had a strange charisma, with his frenzied gestures, theatrical poses, and absurd hyperbole. He was a peculiar politician, living simply, avoiding tobacco, alcohol, meat, and the pleasures of the flesh. He was lazy and undisciplined in his work habits, although he went to lengths to project an image of vigor and stamina. For millions of struggling Germans, he seemed like the savior they needed. His early efforts to seize power landed him in jail, and for most of the 1920s he remained a marginal figure in German politics.

Hitler rode to power on a wave of anxiety and anger that grew with Germany's economic setbacks. Hyper-inflation wiped out the value of the currency in the years 1923–1924, so that one needed a wheelbarrow full of banknotes to buy a loaf of bread. Then in 1931 the global depression hit Germany hard.

The Nazi Party started doing well, winning 18 percent of the vote in 1930 and 37 percent in early 1932. Germany's veteran politicians, mainly educated men often from aristocratic backgrounds, thought little of Hitler, a mere Austrian corporal and school dropout. They calculated that they could control him if he became chancellor (more or less prime minister). In early 1933 he took power—because it was offered to him.

In the next few years, he outmaneuvered both the old politicians and all rivals within his party. He co-opted the military, which shared Hitler's contempt for the Versailles treaty restrictions. He gradually purged all institutions of

Hyper-Inflation Amid the hyper-inflation crisis that hit the Weimar Republic in 1923 and 1924, banknotes became so worthless that children used bundles of them as building blocks.

people with insufficient loyalty to himself. He installed Nazis atop all universities, professional societies, and courts, while banning labor unions and political parties other than his own. He was building a totalitarian state—one in which all aspects of life were politicized and displays of loyalty to a dictator and his party were required. It was similar in some respects to what Lenin and his successors had done after the Bolshevik Revolution. But Hitler's consolidation of power was a means to a set of ends very different from Lenin's.

Hitler wanted absolute power in order to return Germany and Germans to great power status. As a first step, that required unshackling the German military from the terms of the Versailles treaty, and Hitler moved to covertly expand the army and create an air force. It also meant gathering into a larger Germany all of the German-speaking peoples, whether they lived in Austria, the Sudetenland (part of Czechoslovakia), or East Prussia (mostly Lithuania at the time). Hitler wanted to purify what he imagined as the German race, which meant killing or exiling those who in German were called *untermenschen*—people he considered lower racial types, such as Jews, Slavs, and Roma (Gypsies). Last, he wanted to smash Bolshevism, which he connected with Jews. He hoped for another great war, one that Germany would win and set terms for the rest of the world. Like most fringe ideologues, he nurtured revenge fantasies.

None of these ambitions were original with Hitler. Most of them were in circulation in Munich, where he settled in 1919, and some of them in the Vienna of his youth. But Hitler gave them both a modest coherence as a political program and an extreme, toxic, and murderous character. In the early and mid-1920s, his views struck most Germans as too crazy for consideration. But by 1932, as we've seen, 37 percent of German voters supported him.

After Hitler became chancellor in 1933, his popular support strengthened. He undertook a large-scale public works and re-armament campaign, which boosted the economy quickly. Workers found jobs more easily—unemployment was eliminated by 1938—and businessmen made bigger profits. Given the frequent hardship Germans had experienced since 1914, Hitler's economic successes won over millions. Most Germans preferred greater prosperity and renewed national pride to the political liberties Hitler took from them. The segments of society that lent him the strongest support were small farmers, artisans, shopkeepers, university students, and youth in general. As long as the economy flourished, most Germans were content with Hitler, and many of them were enraptured by his charisma, accepting his claim to be the authentic voice of the German people.

The business elite adjusted quickly to Hitler and Nazism. Many large industrial firms, such as Krupp and I. G. Farben, looked forward to re-armament or massive public works projects, and donated generously to the Nazi Party. Most employers welcomed Nazi destruction of labor unions. Even some of the refined cultural elite embraced Hitler after he became chancellor. Germany's most distinguished philosopher, Martin Heidegger, joined the Nazi Party in 1933, and as rector (more or less president) of Freiburg University he lavished praise on Hitler. A famous dancer and film star, Leni Riefenstahl, also gushed about Hitler's greatness and made skillful propaganda movies for the Nazi Party.

Despite his genuine popularity among Germans, Hitler and the Nazi Party had plenty of detractors. Most of the political left—socialists and communists—despised him. Many of the more religious Germans, Catholics and Protestants alike, found him too unchristian in his conduct. Some of the old elites regarded him as an uncouth, uneducated upstart who was unfit for the chancellor's office. Hitler ruthlessly repressed his opponents, some of whom were murdered and many more imprisoned.

Hitler ruled for six and a half years before unleashing World War II in Europe. His social program, extremely important to him, included building a classless national German community. He thought it had to be purely German to be strong, which meant purging those deemed un-German. This view lay behind various racial purification efforts such as the Nuremberg Laws of 1935, which deprived German Jews of citizenship and political rights, banned marriage—and sex—between Jews and Germans, and defined Jewish identity as a matter of ancestry, not religion. Hitler also felt strongly that women ought not

German Fascism The filmmaker Leni Riefenstahl played a pivotal role in constructing the iconography of Nazism. Her 1935 propaganda film *Triumph of the Will* featured speeches by Hitler and other Nazi leaders and aerial photography of mass rallies.

to compete with men for jobs but should focus on home-making and child rearing. His laws limited women to 10 percent of the places in universities and offered incentives to marriage and motherhood for women considered truly German. Every marrying couple received as a gift a copy of Hitler's political and philosophical ramblings, dictated from prison in the 1920s and published as *Mein Kampf* (*My Struggle*). Nonetheless, many young women found a career and an escape from humdrum village life by joining the Nazi Party and training as a secretary or a nurse.

In his first six years in power, Hitler delivered on many of his economic promises. He failed, however, in his ambition to make Germany self-sufficient in food and fuel, which contributed to his decision to seek more *lebensraum* ("living space") for Germans in 1939—by launching an expansionist war.

COMMUNISM TO 1939

Communists took their cues from Marx and his most influential follower, Lenin. They wanted a political order without private property or capitalism. They entrusted their hopes to hierarchical, disciplined parties that promised revolution and a bright future of equality, harmony, and prosperity. Marx and Lenin touted imagined laws of history assuring the inevitability of such a future. For people raised to believe in a second coming and the arrival of the kingdom of heaven on Earth, **communism** had some familiar features.

As we've seen, Lenin and the Bolsheviks took over Russia during the period 1917–1921, which inspired some people and frightened others around the world. Once the Bolsheviks had consolidated their hold on Russia, they set about spreading communist revolution to other countries, actively supporting tiny communist parties in Europe, China, British India, the United States, and elsewhere. They financed and dominated the Comintern, an international union of communist parties. Thanks in large part to economic downturns, communists in Italy, Germany, Hungary, and elsewhere in Europe attracted followings in the 1920s and 1930s, arousing fears that fed fascism. And to a lesser extent, the success of fascism in Italy, Germany, and elsewhere fed fears that inspired people to join communist parties. Both movements, although enemies, benefited from the other's existence.

Communist and fascist movements typically shared certain elements: a militant and hierarchical party organization, a cult of the leader, a willingness to use violence in politics, an emphasis on youth and the future, for example. Most ominous, both shared the commitment that life would be permanently improved if certain class enemies or national enemies were destroyed.

They differed in important respects too. Communists typically proclaimed equality of the sexes, even if practice was another thing altogether, while fascists claimed either nature or God had subordinated women to men. Fascists could coexist cheerfully with capitalist business and private property, which communists reviled as the root of all evil. Fascism extolled the virtues of war and the solidarity of the nation, whereas communism extolled the virtues of class struggle—specifically of workers against owners and bosses—and the solidarity of the international working class. Fascism found it possible to co-opt churches and coexist with organized religion, whereas communists normally treated religion as an enemy.

Their fortunes differed too. Fascism was an important political movement for a little more than two decades, mainly in Europe. Communism held wider appeal and for a longer period. For 70 years after the Russian Revolution, communism remained an occasional political force in many countries and enjoyed a monopoly on power in a few, the most important of which was the USSR.

SOVIET COMMUNISM AND STALIN In the USSR, the revolutionary regime at first wobbled from crisis to crisis. A power struggle followed Lenin's death in 1924, won by **Josef Stalin** (1878–1953). He was a Georgian from the Caucasus, the son of a hard-drinking cobbler father and a deeply religious mother. A fine student at seminary school, he dropped out and took up radical politics as a teenager. He played small roles in the 1917 revolution. But he caught Lenin's eye as a useful, unflinchingly loyal communist, willing to take on any task. He also had real administrative and organizational gifts. Unlike Hitler and Mussolini, Stalin was hardworking and self-disciplined.

Upon consolidating power in the years 1927–1928 (which involved exiling or murdering senior Bolsheviks), Stalin set to transforming the USSR. He intended to make it—as all communists wanted—a more industrialized country. He wanted a workers' paradise but also a militarily formidable state. Neither goal was easy to attain. To advance these priorities, he put Soviet support for revolution abroad on the back burner. He promoted

Soviet Reforms A 1921 Soviet propaganda poster uses a quotation from the Russian poet Pushkin—"Long live the sun!"—to celebrate the expanded education system bringing knowledge and social mobility to people from peasant backgrounds across the Soviet Union.

a "socialism in one country" policy that sat uneasily with the Marxist theory he and all communists had studied. His most revolutionary act came in agriculture.

To squeeze out the investment funds for industrialization, Stalin pushed through collectivization of agriculture from 1929. His agents forcibly gathered private landholdings into huge farms, run either as collectives or as state farms. The collectives had to turn over quotas of food to the state, which sold it cheaply to industrial workers. Collectivization amounted to taking peasants' land, forcing them into collectives, and seizing much of their grain. Peasants resisted by eating their livestock, destroying machinery, and hiding grain.

Stalin's innovations were more revolutionary than the Russian Revolution of 1917. Let's look first at two areas beyond agriculture: the industrial economy and education. Stalin instituted formal planning of the national economy in 1928. Millions of peasants migrated, some involuntarily, to mines and factories to produce vast quantities of coal, iron, steel, locomotives, and weaponry. In 1931, Stalin proclaimed—correctly, as it happened—that the USSR had only 10 years to become strong enough to defend itself from foreign attack. He spared no effort to build up the armaments industry. After 1934, the economy grew quickly owing to forced industrialization. By the late 1930s, the USSR was the world's third largest industrial economy, after the United States and Germany, an astonishing achievement given its overwhelmingly agrarian

character in the late 1920s and the disaster that collectivization brought to agriculture.

Thanks to state schools for all children, social mobility became commonplace in Stalin's USSR. The children of peasants routinely became engineers and doctors, army officers and professors. The number of children in school doubled between 1928 and 1933, despite chaos in parts of the country. The number of high school students climbed from 2 million in 1927 to 12 million in 1939. Stalin intended to create a "proletarian intelligentsia," an educated cohort of peasant or worker background—and he did. They proved his most loyal backers.

At the same time, Stalin's program relied on brutal coercion. It did not begin with him. Lenin had unleashed terror without qualms when in power (1918–1922). Ten years later, when peasants resisted collectivization, Stalin ordered the "liquidation" of *kulaks* ("fists," the term used in the USSR to describe prosperous peasants). About 8 million farmers were either killed or sent to forced labor in Siberia in the gulag, a system of slave labor camps scattered in cold and remote parts of the USSR. In 1932 and 1933, poor harvests combined with pitiless requisition of grain led to famines that killed 5 to 7 million peasants, mostly in Ukraine and Kazakhstan.

Stalin responded to these and other misfortunes by unleashing state terror. His secret police, the NKVD, arrested and killed millions. He purged the ranks of the Communist Party and the army, and targeted ethnic Poles and Germans. He murdered most of the remaining heroes of the 1917 revolution and anyone who might supplant

Gulags *Kulaks* (prosperous peasants) perform heavy manual labor in a Soviet prison camp in 1930. Millions of *kulaks* died in the forced labor camps that Stalin instituted.

him. People whose class origins—children of bankers or aristocrats, for example—made them suspected of disloyalty to the "workers' paradise" were shipped to the gulag. So were people who made jokes about Stalin, people who were denounced by jealous neighbors or by jilted lovers, people who were late to work three times or who stole a hammer from a collective farm. Stalin's terror had a random quality to it. The terror also had a bureaucratic quality. Officials kept records of those whom they shot. In 1937 and 1938, Stalin issued quotas, by district, of the numbers to be shot.

In the gulag, malnutrition, overwork, disease, and brutality had few limits. In all, between 1929 and Stalin's death in 1953, perhaps 18 million people passed through the 500 camps of the gulag, and 1 to 3 million died there. More were released when on death's door and died within days or weeks after regaining freedom. In all, Stalin's peacetime policies killed about 10 to 12 million Soviet citizens between 1928 and 1941. Part of the reason behind Stalin's enthusiasm for educating millions of peasant children was that so many doctors, engineers, and accountants had been killed or imprisoned.

Soviet communism—like Italian fascism and German Nazism—both attracted and repelled people around the world. The overnight industrialization struck many observers as a model path to wealth and power. But rumors of famine, purges, and state terror leaked out, despite the best efforts of Stalin's loyalists to conceal the truth. As of 1939, communism had come to power only in the USSR.

ANTI-COLONIALISM TO 1939

Another important political movement that gathered pace after World War I was **anti-colonialism**. Asians and Africans, almost all of them subjects of one or another colonial empire, created new ideologies and social movements that helped them focus their resistance. Their experience of World War I, as participants or observers, generally lowered their estimate of their colonial masters. Fewer than ever now accepted British or French claims to represent a higher civilization. The cynicism and duplicity of the peace settlement invited further contempt for the colonial powers. Thus movements arose calling for self-rule and the end to colonial empires. In most cases it took decades, and

another world war, for these movements to bear fruit, but they first came of age during the tumult of World War I and its aftermath.

CHINA AND THE MAY FOURTH MOVEMENT

In China, as we've seen, the Qing dynasty had collapsed during the years 1910–1911. World War I, when it came, at first seemed distant. But in 1915 Japan exploited the European powers' preoccupation with the war to issue an ultimatum, The Twenty-one Demands, calling, in effect, for China to become a de facto colony of Japan.

Many Chinese students and intellectuals responded with defiance. But negotiations between China and Japan resulted in an agreement signed in 1915 by Yuan Shikai—the military man running most of China at this point. The agreement focused popular anger upon the government of China as much as upon Japanese imperialism. Nationalistic intellectuals re-doubled their questioning of China's policies and traditions in the New Culture Movement. Hundreds of new publishing houses and journals sprang up in which debates raged about how best to reform China. An example was the magazine *New Youth*, edited by a dean of Beijing University, Chen Duxiu. In a soul-searching essay, "Our Final Awakening" (1916), Chen wrote:

> We ... must ask ourselves what is the level of our national strength and our civilization. This is the final awakening. ... [I]f we open our eyes and take a hard look at the situation within our country and abroad, what place does our country and our people occupy, and what actions should we take?

At the same time that Chen and others were searching for a new basis for Chinese society, the existing government entered World War I in 1917 against Germany. Its leaders hoped to recover the German territorial concessions established in 1898 in Tianjin, a port near Beijing. Some 600,000 Chinese men served the Allied cause in Europe as laborers, most of them in Russia, and more than 30,000 died—almost all in Russia.

In the spring of 1919, the Chinese learned, to their shock, that the Versailles treaty had transferred German concessions in China to Japan. Britain, France, and Italy had made a secret deal, offering Japan the German holdings, to secure its wartime support for the Allies. The diplomats in Paris had ignored the principle of

May Fourth Movement Students join a demonstration outside the seat of Chinese government in Beijing's Forbidden City in 1919. The May Fourth movement, sparked by discontent with the terms of the Versailles treaty, launched a broad examination of Chinese culture and politics.

self-determination and instead supported Japanese imperialism. They had ignored the Chinese contribution to the Allied war effort. As in the Arab Middle East, they had made incompatible promises, justified to themselves by the urgency of winning the war.

That spring, university students in Beijing led protests against Japan, the Versailles treaty, the diplomatic missions of the Allies, and the Chinese government that seemed inclined to accept humiliation. Boycotts and demonstrations swept across the country in the May Fourth Movement, named for the day of the first big protests in Beijing. Police arrested over 1,000 students, but thousands more joined strikes and protests. The government soon concluded it could not endorse the Versailles treaty and would have to risk standing up to Japan.

The insulting terms of the Versailles treaty did much to strengthen the cause of anti-imperialism in China. The treaty's support for Japanese imperialism undermined the appeal of European ways and examples, although one European idea, Marxism, rose in the balance. Many young, educated Chinese in the years 1919–1921 admired the Bolsheviks' swift seizure of power in Russia and their dedication to re-making society. They formed the Chinese Communist Party in 1921—of which more in the next chapter.

INDIA

In India, World War I and its aftermath strengthened another nascent anti-colonial movement. After the uprisings of the years 1857–1858, British rule had fastened more

tightly upon India. Although many Indians resented British power, they knew that the Indian Army, trained and commanded by British officers, would smash any rebellion. But in the 1880s, elite, educated Indians, mostly Hindus, came together to form the Indian National Congress. At first a group that lobbied for a larger Indian role in government, Congress, as it was called, gradually came to function as a political party, at first with British approval. Meanwhile, educated Muslims created their own political organizations, such as the All-India Muslim League formalized in 1906 and soon led by a brilliant London-trained lawyer, Muhammad Ali Jinnah, also a Congress member. The leaders of Congress were products of schools and colleges established by the British to create a class of men—no women—competent to handle the lower rungs of officialdom. The schools also created a cadre of fluent English speakers well acquainted with

The Indian Independence Movement, 1915–1935 The Indian independence movement, the world's largest decolonization campaign, involved a mixture of peaceful protests and violent insurgency. Gandhi and his followers mounted non-violent actions designed to undermine colonial British authorities, such as the salt march he led in 1930 from Ahmedabad to the sea. But other Indians clashed with imperial forces, such as those involved in a failed insurrection in Chittagong—also in 1930. By 1935 India was on the road to self-rule.

British traditions, law, literature—and the merits of representative self-government.

Most of these educated Indians expected that India would one day become ready for self-government—perhaps in 50 or 100 years. World War I reduced their patience. Some 1.2 million Indians served the armies of the British Empire, mainly in campaigns against the Ottomans. About 62,000 died in the war. Indian businessmen and landowners contributed a lot of money to the British war effort. They did so in the expectation that in exchange for its blood and treasure, India would win something akin to the self-governing dominion status within the British Empire already accorded to Canada, New Zealand, Australia, and South Africa. Like the Chinese who expected a reward for their contributions to the Allies in World War I, these Indians were soon keenly disappointed.

After the war's end, British authorities showed no eagerness to extend self-rule to India. It was not the Versailles peace settlement that disappointed Indians. Indeed, India was allowed to send its own delegation to the talks. But early in 1919, when the British government of India extended its own wartime powers preventing freedom of speech and assembly, Indian nationalists reacted with outrage. Demonstrations dotted the country. That April, a demonstration in the holy city of Sikhs, Amritsar, ended in bloodshed. A British general ordered his Indian troops to fire into an unarmed crowd, killing some 400 demonstrators and wounding 1,000. Afterward, the general who gave the order was commended by the British House of Lords. To many Indians, the Amritsar massacre showed that Britain would never allow India to enjoy dominion status but would try to rule the country indefinitely.

GANDHI The anti-colonial movement in India was already growing more impatient when **Mohandas K. Gandhi** returned to India in 1915 and joined Congress. He came from a middle-class family, and despite a mediocre school record went to study law in London at age 20. Starting in 1893, he spent 21 years in British South Africa defending the rights of the Indian community there. He suffered various slights at the hands of white South Africans but remained a loyal subject of the British Empire, even winning a medal for his work organizing Indian medics for the Boer War (1899–1902).

In South Africa, he developed the political tactic called *satyagraha* (translated as "truth force" or "soul force"),

Gandhi Followers of Gandhi's civil disobedience movement join him on the 1930 salt march. Gandhi's shaved head and traditional attire signal his public commitment to a life of simplicity.

which amounted to the practice of non-violent civil disobedience in the face of unjust treatment. It drew upon Hindu, Jain, and Christian religious traditions. Gandhi also learned from the writings of the American author Henry David Thoreau and the Russian novelist and philosopher Leo Tolstoy, with whom he corresponded. The South African compound where he trained people in *satyagraha* was called Tolstoy Farm. Gandhi's thought combined many influences, a reflection of the growing interconnectedness of the world in his day.

When he arrived in India in 1915, Gandhi encouraged Indians to join the British armed forces, hoping that by showing loyalty Indians would win political independence after World War I ended. His fellow Congress members found him strange. He had abandoned his lawyer's suit and tie for the *dhoti* worn by poor Indians. He ate sparingly and flaunted his frail physique. The Bombay (Mumbai) police considered him "a psychological case." But in 1919, he more than anyone else converted Indian anti-colonial nationalism from an elite affair into a mass movement.

The spur was the massacre at Amritsar. Gandhi now proclaimed there could be no cooperation with the British "satanic regime." Since armed resistance to British rule was futile, Gandhi, with his non-violent tactics honed in South Africa, became the most effective and prestigious leader of anti-colonialism in India. He pioneered mass politics, rousing illiterate peasants to the cause of self-rule. Congress chose him as its president in 1920.

Gandhi's program baffled most other Indian nationalists. He argued for a self-sufficient peasant economy and

Satyagraha: Gandhi's Strategy of Resistance

Before Gandhi returned to India in 1915, he had already spent two decades in South Africa, where he led Indian settlers in protests against laws that limited their rights because of their color of their skin. It was there that he first distinguished *satyagraha* from the campaigns of suffragists and other political movements that he associated with violence. Gandhi taught his followers to disobey unjust laws without resorting to physical force—instead, they dared the British governments in South Africa and India to commit violence against them. Through such suffering, they hoped to shame the British Empire into living up to the principles of justice that Gandhi had studied as a law student in London.

The suffragists had no franchise rights. They were weak in numbers as well as in physical force.... The suffragist movement did not eschew the use of physical force. Some suffragists fired buildings and even assaulted men. I do not think they ever intended to kill any one. But they did intend to thrash people when an opportunity occurred....

But brute force had absolutely no place in the Indian movement in any circumstance,... no matter how badly they suffered, the *satyagrahis* never used physical force. *Satyagraha* is soul force pure and simple, and whenever ... there is room for the use of arms or physical force or brute force, there and to that extent is there so much less possibility for soul force. These are purely antagonistic forces....

[Yet] even a generous friend like Mr. Hosken [an English supporter of Gandhi in South Africa] imagined us to be weak. The power of suggestion is such that a man at last becomes what he believes himself to be. If we continue to believe ... we are weak ... our resistance would never make us strong.... On the other hand, if we ... offer *satyagraha*, believing us to be strong,... we grow stronger and stronger every day....

Satyagraha and brute force, being each a negation of the other, can never go together.... In *satyagraha* there is not the remotest idea of injuring the opponent. *Satyagraha* postulates the conquest of the adversary by suffering in one's own person.

Source: M. K. Gandhi, *Satyagraha in South Africa*, trans. Valji Govindji Desai. (Madras, 1928).

QUESTIONS FOR ANALYSIS

1. Why did Gandhi reject the idea that *satyagraha* was weak?
2. How did the woman suffrage movement affect Gandhi's approach to anti-colonial resistance?
3. Contrast Gandhi's anti-colonial movement with the fascist and communist movements in Italy, Germany, and Russia.

against factories and industrialization. He claimed that British education, of which he was a product, corrupted India and prevented its liberation. He particularly disliked modern science and technology, preferring Hindu traditions. Yet he was no respecter of caste, campaigning for the rights of the lowest of the low in India's caste system, people called *dalits* ("untouchables"). Gandhi embraced all Indians, Muslim and Hindu alike, and Christians, Jains, and Buddhists too. He spoke out against child marriage, dowry, and the Muslim custom of seclusion of women. He felt India's strength could come from piety and moral righteousness, not factories and armies. He regarded women as natural champions of this cause: "If by strength is meant moral power, then woman is immeasurably man's superior."

His methods included deft use of the weapons of the weak. He lived simply, all the better to be an Indian David against a British Goliath. He went on well-publicized hunger strikes. He and his colleagues in Congress organized marches involving thousands of poor Indians who were trained not to resist violence but to suffer it—in order to seize the moral high ground and undercut British claims to superiority.

To succeed, he had to know his adversary well, and three years of legal education in London helped in that regard. And he required an adversary that was vulnerable to public shaming and moral truth—the weapons of the weak—one that would not be willing to repeat the massacre of Amritsar time and time again.

Gandhi's classic act of civil disobedience was the salt

march of 1930. By law, the sale of salt was a government monopoly, and Indians had to pay a salt tax. Gandhi exploited this by organizing a 24-day march from his base near Ahmedabad, in western India, to the coasts of the Arabian Sea in order to scoop up natural sea salt in defiance of the law. Tens of thousands of Indians joined him, and several journalists too. As he expected, Gandhi's act of civil disobedience earned him a jail sentence. Some 80,000 others were arrested. The British authorities undermined their own legitimacy in India, Britain, and around the world by arresting so many poor people over salt—just as Gandhi intended. By 1935, Britain had passed new legislation turning many governmental functions over to Indians. India was on the road to self-rule.

European rule in India had begun in the sixteenth century as a result of a quest for valuable peppers, and it would end in 1947 as a result—in part—of Gandhi's salt march. He was able to make the struggle for self-rule a mass movement after 1919, parallel in this respect, but different in every other, to what Mussolini did with fascism in Italy in 1919. He re-cast a political movement based on novel tactics that fit India's circumstances far better than violent resistance. He made non-violent civil disobedience into a potent political force.

AFRICA, THE CARIBBEAN, AND PAN-AFRICANISM

In Africa and the Caribbean, anti-colonial movements also drew strength from the disillusionment that came with World War I and the peace settlement. Recall that in 1914, Africa was almost entirely colonized by European powers, chiefly Britain and France. The Caribbean too was a patchwork of European colonies, with a population mainly descended from Africans brought to the region in the transatlantic slave trade.

In World War I, several hundred thousand Africans and a few thousand West Indians—as people from the Caribbean are known—served in European armies. Some 400,000 black volunteers and conscripts fought for the French Army on the western front and often were assigned the most dangerous tasks. The president of France, Georges Clemenceau, made his views clear in 1918: "We are going to offer civilization to the Blacks. They will have to pay for that. . . . I would prefer that ten Blacks are killed rather than one Frenchman." Some

30,000 to 70,000 Africans died in the French Army in Europe in World War I. The British refused to use African troops in Europe. But, like the French and Germans, they employed large numbers in the campaigns fought in East and West Africa, and a few thousand, as laborers, in the Middle Eastern theater.

Almost all soldiers and laborers came from the lower ranks of African societies. They volunteered, often encouraged by those chiefs and kings who now supported colonial rule, in hopes of improving their status. Chiefs and kings hoped that African contributions to the war effort would win political concessions from France and Britain in the form of more autonomy, political rights, and power for chiefs and kings. These hopes, like Gandhi's during World War I, were to be disappointed. Policy makers in France and Britain believed Africans needed centuries of tutelage to become ready for self-rule.

Soldiers and their sponsors were not the only ones to be disappointed. Africa by 1918 included a small population of men—and far fewer women—equipped with European formal education and a cosmopolitan knowledge of the world. They liked the sound of President Wilson's emphasis on self-determination, until it became clear that neither Wilson nor any of the peacemakers of 1919 intended to apply it to Africa.

PAN-AFRICANISM Many of them found hope in **pan-Africanism**, an idea that had not won much attention before 1914. The war seemed to present new opportunities. African American intellectuals from the Caribbean and the United States, including the Harvard-trained historian and sociologist W.E.B. Du Bois, called for unified political action among Africans and people of African descent. Many saw anti-colonialism in terms of race. In an essay appearing in 1915, Du Bois, after calling for the extension of the "democratic ideal to the yellow, brown, and black peoples," wrote apocalyptically: "The colored peoples still will not always submit to foreign domination. . . . These nations and races, composing as they do the vast majority of humanity, are going to endure their treatment as long as they must and not a moment longer. Then they are going to fight and the war of the Color Line will outdo in savage inhumanity any war this world has yet seen." To avoid this grim prospect, Du Bois concluded, would require an end to racism and colonialism.

Other pan-Africanists looked forward to the imminent

Pan-Africanism The pan-African movement leader Marcus Garvey pictured here in a New York City parade in 1922.

liberation of Africa. Marcus Garvey, a Jamaican who lived in London and later New York, organized a political and cultural movement that celebrated black identity. He wanted educated people of African descent to return to their ancestral homeland and "assist in civilizing the backward tribes of Africa." In 1920, he proposed to "organize the 400 million Negroes of the world into a vast organization and plant the banner of freedom on the great continent of Africa."

Several Francophone pan-Africanists shared Garvey's emphasis on culture and identity. In the late 1930s, a black poet from Martinique, Aimé Césaire, and his friend and fellow-poet from Senegal (West Africa), Léopold Senghor, developed a cultural philosophy they called Négritude (literally: "blackness"). They extolled the qualities of black people, among which they counted generosity, warmth, spontaneity, and honesty. In their own way, which featured literature as much as politics, they too endorsed the notion of solidarity among people of African background both as an end in itself and as a means to end colonial rule. Both men became leading politicians in later decades.

Pan-Africanism had a strong literary and cultural component. Garvey, Senghor, and others shared the view of Chinese intellectuals of the New Culture Movement: a revitalization of culture was required before political independence could be achieved. Theirs was an elite movement, with no equivalent to Gandhi's outreach to the illiterate masses.

To give pan-Africanism political weight, Du Bois and others organized pan-African Congresses in 1919 and 1921, held in Europe. Another took place in New York in 1927. Scores of educated men—no women—from the African diaspora and Africa itself attended. They specifically challenged the continuation of colonial rule in Africa and called for an Africa for Africans.

ANTI-COLONIALISM AND THE GLOBAL WEB

Within Africa itself, anti-colonialism consisted of more than pan-Africanism. Every colony had its own groups working toward greater political voice for Africans. In most cases, those groups imagined that one day they would replace the colonial masters themselves and rule independent countries. Indeed, in time this vision—rather than the pan-African ideal of African unification—would come to pass.

All these movements, in China, India, and Africa (and the African diaspora), had local grievances and causes. But they all shared some commonalities too, first and foremost their anti-colonialism. In each case, World War I and the disappointing peace settlement contributed mightily to a sense of disillusionment—and to a sense of new possibilities. The war and the peace showed conspicuously that Europeans were not the morally superior beings they had claimed to be. The rhetoric of self-determination rang hollow when followed by renewed imperialism.

These movements also shared a reliance on European-educated elites. In Africa, as in India, the key to the formation of effective anti-colonial groups was colonial education. In the 1920s and 1930s, a new generation with more formal education arrived on the scene in Africa. A symbol of the ongoing change occurred in Gabon (West Central Africa), where a people called the Fang altered one of their rituals: where once spears were dipped in the water in which baby boys took their first bath, now their parents dipped pencils in the bathwater. Education, they foresaw, was the key to power and status.

In every case, anti-colonial leadership came substantially from young men educated in European schools—often, mission schools. While colonial authorities generally wanted the colonized peoples to confine their educations to job training—such as rudimentary office skills—Africans and Indians wanted to study subjects that, as they saw it, fit people for leadership, such as law, philosophy, and history.

There are two lessons here. One is the irony of colonial rulers creating institutions that contributed to the downfall of colonial rule. The other is the power of the swirl of ideas in the decades after 1914. Growing literacy, and then the advent of radio after 1920, made it easier for Wilson's and Lenin's ideas to reach Chinese students,

Tolstoy's ideas to reach Gandhi, or Garvey's ideas to reach black people in Lagos or London. The interconnections of the Global web were now better than ever at spreading ideas and ideologies, offering people everywhere new choices with which to try to fashion their futures. The Global web, which had helped to form and strengthen colonial empires in the nineteenth century, now began to undermine them through the flow of ideas, ideals, and ambitions for self-rule.

CONCLUSION

World War I wasn't all that worldwide as a war. The combat took place mainly in Europe and the Ottoman lands of Southwest Asia. But as a political event, World War I was truly global. It inspired the mobilization of people and resources on every inhabited continent. More enduringly, the war's horror and destruction posed strong challenges to existing authority in every sphere. If the leaders and institutions of Europe permitted the slaughter of 10 million soldiers, what argument could there be to leave such leaders and institutions in place? Millions thought it must be better to try something new and different, such as fascism or communism. The peace settlement, with its evident hypocrisies, multiplied the challenges to existing authorities by dashing hopes and breaking promises, especially in Asia and Africa. How could such leaders and institutions

be permitted to rule over most of the world's population through colonial empires? Millions thought it must be better to end colonial rule as soon as possible. Considering that men—and only men—had directed a brutal war and an unsatisfactory peace, what argument remained for excluding women from politics? Millions found no convincing argument and agreed that women should vote.

Like the influenza virus in 1918 and 1919, the intellectual and political repercussions of the war and the resulting peace spread quickly around the world—but news and ideas traveled even faster than pathogens. The peace settlement in Versailles gave rise to events in China almost instantaneously in 1919.

Of all the meanings and legacies of World War I and its peace settlement, perhaps the greatest was one that took decades to work itself out: the decline of western Europe in world affairs. It is not that European states necessarily grew weaker as a result of the war and its aftermath, although some did. Rather, the United States and soon the USSR grew much stronger, as did, if less obviously, the enemies of empire in Asia and Africa. The growing strength of the United States and the USSR came mainly in the form of material power such as industrial capacity. The enemies of empire in Asia and Africa gained strength through organization, education, and determination. Their material resources were scant—wholly inadequate for a military challenge to colonial rule. But, as Gandhi showed, sometimes the weapons of the weak are enough to change history.

CHAPTER REVIEW

KEY TERMS

World War I (p. 764)

alliance networks (p. 766)

Russian Revolution of 1917 (p. 772)

Vladimir Lenin (p. 773)

Treaty of Versailles (p. 775)

self-determination (p. 775)

Mustafa Kemal (p. 776)

suffragism (p. 777)

fascism (p. 782)

Benito Mussolini (p. 782)

Adolf Hitler (p. 783)

communism (p. 786)

Josef Stalin (p. 786)

anti-colonialism (p. 788)

Mohandas K. Gandhi (p. 790)

pan-Africanism (p. 792)

Go to INQUIZITIVE to see what you've learned—and learn what you've missed—with personalized feedback along the way.

REVIEW QUESTIONS

1. What are the four main strands of global politics in modern times?

2. In order of strength, who were the great powers in 1914, and to which alliance network did each belong?

3. Discuss the two key decisions that contributed to the start of World War I.

4. Why did the German High Command begin unrestricted submarine warfare in the Atlantic, and what effect did it have on the war?

5. Describe the various roles that women filled during World War I, and explain what happened to these positions when the war ended.

6. Compare and contrast the policies of the Provisional Government in spring and summer 1917, the Bolsheviks in 1918, and the Bolsheviks in 1921.

7. What were the chief ambitions behind the post-war peace treaties?

8. What longstanding dynasties did World War I destroy, and what governing structures replaced each one?

9. How did World War I lead to the extension of the vote to women in several large and populous countries?

10. Why did Mussolini's fascism seem an attractive choice to millions of Italians after World War I?

11. What were Hitler's ambitions, and what economic and cultural policies did he introduce after 1933 to achieve them?

12. Identify the significant elements that communist and fascist movements shared, and explain their important differences.

13. What agricultural, economic, and educational policies did Stalin advance?

14. How did World War I contribute to the rise of anti-colonialism as a mass movement?

15. What elements did anti-colonial movements in China, India, Africa, and the Caribbean share?

16. Explore the global aspects of World War I as a political event.

FURTHER READING

Volker BERGHAHN, *Europe in the Era of Two World Wars* (2006). A brief overview of European affairs, with useful sketches of fascism and communism.

Laura ENGELSTEIN, *Russia in Flames: War, Revolution, and Civil War* (2018). A massive narrative of momentous events, with many insights along the way.

Adrian GREGORY, *A War of Peoples, 1914–1919* (2014). A short overview of World War I, with a chapter on how historians have presented it for the last hundred years.

Erez MANELA, *The Wilsonian Moment* (2009). A study of the reception of the 1919 peace agreement in Egypt, India, China, and Korea.

David REYNOLDS, *The Long Shadow: The Legacies of the Great War in the Twentieth Century* (2015). A readable and insightful study of the meanings of World War I.

Vladimir TISMANEANU, *The Devil in History: Communism, Fascism and Some Lessons of the Twentieth Century* (2012). A thoughtful reflection on the origins and character of communism and fascism, mainly in the USSR, post-1945 Eastern Europe, and Germany.

IRLANDE
DUBLIN
OCÉAN ATLANTIQUE
ANGLETERRE
LONDRES
MANCHE
MER DU NORD
OSLO
STOCKHOLM
COPENHAGUE
DANEMARK
MER BALTIQUE
Königsb
BERLIN
Vistule
AMSTERDAM
PAYS-BAS
BRUXELLES
BELGIQUE
PARIS
ALLEMAGNE
PRAGUE
SLOVAQUIE
VIENNE
BUDA-PEST
FRANCE
MUNICH
BERNE
SUISSE
HONGR
MER

CHRONOLOGY

1949
Stalin acquires nuclear weapons; NATO is formed;
Mao Zedong establishes People's Republic of China

Nov. 1942–Mar. 1943
Battle of Stalingrad

Aug. 1945
United States drops
atomic bombs on
Hiroshima and Nagasaki;
Japan surrenders

1965–1975
Vietnam War

1937
Japan attacks China;
World War II in Asia begins

June 1942
Battle of Midway

1954
Vietnam is
divided
between
north and
south

June 1941
Operation Barbarossa;
war on eastern front begins

June 1944
Normandy
landings

1961
Start of
construction of
Berlin Wall

Sept. 1939
Germany invades Poland;
World War II in Europe
begins

Dec. 1941
Japan attacks United
States, British Malaya,
Philippines;
Pacific War begins

May 1945
Germany surrenders

1948
Berlin
airlift

1956
Uprisings in
Poland and
Hungary

Oct. 1962
Cuban missile
crisis

Sept. 1943
Italy surrenders

1945
Start of Cold War

1945–1949
Chinese Civil War

1950–1953
Korean War

World War II and the Cold War

1937 to 1991

We rely upon the loyalty and courage of Our subjects in Our confident expectation that the task bequeathed by Our forefathers will be carried forward and that the sources of the evil will be speedily eradicated and an enduring peace immutably established in East Asia, preserving thereby the glory of Our Empire.

With these words the high command of the Japanese armed forces concluded its public declaration of war, issued in the name of Japan's emperor, against the United States and the British Empire on December 8, 1941. Attacks proceeded against American bases at Pearl Harbor (where it was December 7) and the Philippines, and against British positions in Hong Kong, Malaya, and Singapore. In 1941, Japan was a colonial power in East Asia, controlling Korea, Taiwan, Manchuria, and most of eastern China. The leadership appealed to ordinary Japanese citizens to continue the overseas expansion under way since 1895, and to expel European and American colonial powers from East and Southeast Asia, thereby leaving Japan unrivaled in the region. Confidence in the loyalty and courage of the emperor's subjects proved well placed, but Japan lacked

"Crusade against Bolshevism" A poster from Vichy France announcing Operation Barbarossa, Germany's invasion of the Soviet Union in June 1941. The symbols on the arrows indicate the multinational composition of the German Army.

1975 Start of Angolan Civil War
1991 Collapse of USSR
1986 Chernobyl disaster
1979–1989 Soviet-Afghan War
1989 Fall of Berlin Wall

FOCUS QUESTIONS

1. What factors had the biggest impact on the outcomes of World War II?

2. Why was the Cold War a hot one in some parts of the world?

the economic resources to defeat its foes. Rather than preserve the glory of Japan's empire, these attacks sealed its doom, which came in August 1945 after 43 months of pitiless combat.

This chapter explores the titanic political battles and unspeakable violence of World War II (1937–1945) and the Cold War (1945–1991). Both were truly global contests, much more so than World War I or any previous struggles. The Global web had grown so strong that politics spilled across boundaries and oceans with ease. In World War II, combat took place on three continents and three oceans. During the Cold War, the United States chose to fight wars in Korea (1950–1953) and Vietnam (1965–1975), whereas it had previously avoided wars in Asia. And the USSR, which had previously had minimal interests in the American hemisphere, chose to support Cuba beginning in 1960.

Three main themes predominate in this chapter. First, these conflicts featured violence on astonishing scales. The technologies of war had grown so efficient that death and suffering outstripped even the carnage of World War I. Ordinary civilians could not keep out of harm's way in World War II, or in the hotspots of the Cold War such as Vietnam or Angola. This marked a return to an older pattern of warfare in which the distinction between military and civilian was often blurry. As a result, the violence of these wars affected women and children at home more often than in World War I. These were hard and dangerous times, none harder than the years between

1937 and 1952—especially if you were Chinese, Japanese, Korean, German, Italian, Greek, or any kind of eastern European, but above all Jewish.

Second, ferocious ideological hatreds sharpened these conflicts. Sometimes these were ethnic or "racial," as in the case of Hitler and his supporters. Such hatreds had long been commonplace, but in World War II they became extreme. During the Cold War, ideological hatreds were based on differing conceptions of how best to organize societies and economies.

Third, this chapter tries to explain why the winners won and the losers lost in both World War II and the Cold War. These struggles, and especially their results, shaped the international political system we live in today, and fundamentally affect all our lives. It is important to grasp why they turned out as they did.

WORLD WAR II, 1937–1945

By any measure except duration, **World War II** was the biggest war in history. It ranged over more terrain, mobilized more resources, and killed more people than any other war. It also re-configured world politics dramatically, as had World War I. Sometimes scholars like to lump the two world wars together as one extended conflict (1914–1945). In the European context this makes some sense, because in both wars Germany and its allies fought against a coalition including Russia, Britain, France, and the United States. But whereas World War I took place mainly in Europe, World War II involved major theaters of combat in China and the Pacific, and another in North Africa. From the perspective of world history as opposed to European history, it makes sense to treat the world wars separately.

ORIGINS

The origins of World War II are not as complex, accidental, or contested as those of World War I. Most historians agree that its causes lay in the expansionist ambitions of Japan, Germany, and to a lesser extent Italy. Those powers formed a loose alliance in the late 1930s known as the **Axis**. Each was run by an authoritarian clique hostile to pluralist democracy and rule of law. Each felt shortchanged by the international status quo. Each eagerly ran the risks of provoking large-scale warfare in order to acquire more territory and resources. Indeed, many in their governing elites regarded war as something to be sought rather than avoided, because, they thought, it was good for a nation to be tested in blood. The fact that almost no one thinks such things anymore is in large part a consequence of the many horrors of World War II.

As we've seen, both Italy and Germany by the 1930s had fallen under fascist dictatorships, led by Mussolini and Hitler, respectively. Each had consolidated his grip on power by 1935 or before, muzzling the press, squashing legislatures, and filling the court system, the military, and key government ministries with reliable fascists. Outraged by the terms of the Treaty of Versailles, both leaders felt that their country should not shrink from launching wars to achieve a more glorious future for the Italian or German people. Germans and Italians were peppered with messages, in schools and state-run media, encouraging them to embrace nationalism and militarism as solutions to almost all problems.

Both Mussolini and Hitler envisioned futures based on nationalistic fantasies. For Mussolini, that glorious future entailed re-creating the grandeur of ancient Rome. He wanted Italy to dominate the Mediterranean, as the Romans had done, and to acquire colonies in Africa. For Hitler, overseas colonies were not a priority. Instead, he wanted what he called *lebensraum* ("living space") for Germans in Europe. He wanted to unite all Germans, including millions living in Poland, Austria, Czechoslovakia, Ukraine, Russia, and elsewhere, into a greater Germany. His understanding of U.S. history, which relied heavily on adventure stories by the popular German author Karl May, suggested to him that Germans could displace or kill Slavs and Jews in eastern Europe and take it for themselves—as Americans had pushed Amerindians off their lands in the nineteenth century. He was convinced that the German people faced a mortal threat and could survive only by means of expansion at the expense of neighbors—specifically, the Slavs and Jews whom he held responsible for all the misfortunes Germans experienced. Both Mussolini and Hitler concocted mythical pasts to try to justify their future plans.

Italy was poorly positioned for expansionist warfare.

In the late 1930s, it had about 43 million people, most of them undernourished peasants. It had almost no coal and only a small military-industrial complex, and it depended on imports for vital goods. Its armed forces were sizeable but neither well trained—one-third of army recruits could not read—nor abundantly supplied, although the quality of their equipment was good.

Germany included about 67 million people. In 1938, Hitler absorbed his native Austria into the German Third Reich (*Reich* means "empire"), raising the population closer to 80 million. The Versailles treaty had officially limited the size of Germany's armed forces; but since coming to power in 1933, Hitler had been building up the military in secret. By the late 1930s, Germany had a formidable and technologically modern military.

The third Axis power was Japan. Since the Meiji Restoration (1868), Japan had industrialized its economy and modernized its state administration and armed forces with astonishing speed, despite a comparative lack of raw materials. It had defeated China (1895) and Russia (1905) in war and had acquired Taiwan and Korea as colonies. In 1919, it took over some former German possessions in the Pacific through the Versailles treaty. The Japanese people increasingly came to see themselves as a special nationality—indeed, a "race," better than their neighbors if not everyone else. Their leaders, like those in Italy and Germany, used schooling and media to hammer home messages of Japanese racial superiority and victimization by foreigners.

JAPANESE AGGRESSION IN ASIA Like Italy and Germany, Japan wanted to revise the international system. It aimed to expand its imperial power. But it was thwarted mainly by the United Kingdom and the United States, neither of which wished to see Japan or any other nation become pre-eminent in East Asia. A treaty of 1922 limited the size of Japan's navy to 60 percent of that of either the American or British fleets. Japanese military officers grew impatient with these constraints, and in 1931 they manufactured an incident in Manchuria (in northeast China) to justify seizing it. Rich in natural resources such as coal and iron ore, Manchuria could strengthen Japan's heavy industry, including its weapons industry.

By the mid-1930s, Japan's population stood at about 70 million and was growing rapidly. Its navy was the world's third largest; its army was six times the size of the American army. Japan's rulers felt their nation needed more space and resources. They envisioned Japan leading the peoples of East Asia in throwing off the shackles of European rule. They offered an anti-colonial ideology but in reality intended to make all of East Asia subordinate to Japan. By the late 1930s, the European colonial rulers of Southeast Asia—Britain, France, and the Netherlands—were becoming increasingly anxious about the rising power of Germany in Europe and less inclined to devote military resources to Asia. Japan took advantage of that to attack China in 1937.

China made a tempting target for Japan. Its 511 million people—as of 1937—were politically divided. The central government, run by the Guomindang, a party that had evolved out of Sun Yatsen's 1910 revolution, was famous for corruption and unloved by the masses. It controlled only parts of the country. It had virtually no navy and a poorly equipped army. China was a peasant land, with little industry. Yet it had plenty of raw materials, especially ores and coal, that Japan wanted. Japan's assault on China in 1937 was the beginning of World War II in Asia.

GERMAN AGGRESSION IN EUROPE The war in Europe began in 1939 when Germany invaded Poland. France and Britain, the other great powers in Europe, offered no effective response to German expansion. At the Munich Conference in 1938, they signed over the Sudetenland, a mainly German-speaking region of Czechoslovakia, to Hitler in exchange for a promise that he would seek no more territory. A few months later, in March 1939, Hitler seized the rest of Czechoslovakia anyway.

France and Britain proved feeble adversaries in the diplomacy of the late 1930s. Both were haunted by the human losses of World War I and eager to avoid another war at almost any cost. They had a population of 90 million between them, plus reserves of military manpower and resources in their overseas empires. They also had enormous manufacturing capacity but, compared to Germany, poorly equipped armies and air forces. After the seizure of Czechoslovakia early in 1939, their leaders realized that they could not check Hitler's Germany short of going to war.

In August 1939, Hitler's diplomats negotiated a non-aggression pact with the Soviet Union, a stunning reversal of both German and Soviet foreign policy. The agreement reduced Germany's risk of a two-front war against both Soviet Russia and the western allies, a lesson from World War I. Stalin signed it in order to buy time to

Aggressions in Europe, 1936–1939 Germany, under Hitler from 1933, sought to undo the settlement established in the Treaty of Versailles. Among his early violations of the treaty was the stationing of military units in the Rhineland near the French and Belgian border. He followed with territorial annexations of Austria and parts of Czechoslovakia. In 1939, Italy's fascist dictatorship under Mussolini annexed Albania after a brief battle. When World War II in Europe began in 1939, military aggression became much more violent with the German and Soviet invasions of Poland.

build up his military, which had suffered greatly from his own purges of top commanders. The agreement included secret protocols for yet another partition of Poland—there had been three during the eighteenth century. The German Army invaded Poland on September 1, the start of World War II in Europe. France and Britain agreed that they could not allow Germany to gobble up the remainder of Europe, so they declared war against Germany. Two weeks later, the Soviet Red Army invaded Poland too, seizing the share promised to it in the Nazi-Soviet pact.

FOUR THEATERS World War II in effect consisted of four overlapping wars in four different theaters. They

Nazi Aggression A cartoon published in August 1939 depicts the Nazi threat to Poland. Germany invaded Poland within weeks.

began at different times, but all ended in 1945. The first to break out was that between Japan and China in 1937. Most of the fighting took place in China. The second was Germany's and Italy's war against Poland, Britain, France, and most of the rest of Europe, begun in 1939. Fought in Europe, North Africa, and on the waters of the North Atlantic, by the end of 1941 it included the United States aligned against the Axis powers. The third began in June 1941, when Germany attacked the USSR despite the recent Nazi-Soviet pact. It was fought in the lands between Berlin and Moscow. The last was Japan's war against the United States, the United Kingdom, and Australia in the Pacific and Southeast Asia, begun in December 1941. The United States, the Soviet Union, and Britain formed the major Allied forces, or **Allies**, opposing the Axis of Germany, Japan, and Italy.

New technologies such as tanks and long-range aircraft enabled armies and air forces to roam widely, unlike in World War I, and inflict terrible brutalities on civilians especially in China and eastern Europe. Many more civilians than soldiers lost their lives during the course of the war, partly through aerial bombing campaigns and partly because they could not escape rapidly moving invading armies. Millions of women and girls who fell into the hands of marauding soldiers were raped, especially in China, eastern Europe, and Germany.

THE COURSE OF THE WAR

Until mid-1942, the Axis—Japan, Germany, and Italy—went from strength to strength. Japan inflicted huge losses on China and took the richest parts of the country. In late 1940, it conquered French Indochina (now Vietnam, Laos, and Cambodia) and reduced Thailand to the status of a dependent ally. Part of Japan's interest in mainland Southeast Asia lay in its rubber and tin supplies, important for military production. Japan's aggression inspired a joint response from the United States, Britain, and the Netherlands, whose colonies in Southeast Asia were now threatened: in August 1941, these countries stopped all oil and steel exports to Japan. They hoped to force Japan to give up expansionist warfare.

JAPANESE ADVANCES IN SOUTHEAST ASIA AND THE PACIFIC The policy backfired. The Japanese leadership, mainly military elites, gambled on a surprise attack on British Malaya, the U.S. colony of the Philippines, and the American naval base at Pearl Harbor in Hawaii. The attacks, in December 1941, were intended to cripple American and British naval power, giving Japan a chance to seize oilfields in the Dutch East Indies

Pearl Harbor The USS *West Virginia* was badly damaged in the Japanese attack on Pearl Harbor, December 7, 1941. The battleship was repaired and later re-entered the war in the Pacific.

Japanese Expansion and World War II in Asia and the Pacific, 1931–1945 Japan focused its war effort on campaigns in China, beginning with the seizure of Manchuria in 1931. After Japan's attacks of December 7–8, 1941, on Pearl Harbor, the U.S. bases in the Philippines, and British bases in Malaya, the Japanese war widened to include vast spaces of the Pacific, from the Aleutian Islands to Australia. This became a war of movement, fought with ships and aircraft, and therefore a war of oil—which Japan lacked. By late 1942, American forces had begun to turn the tide and were island-hopping toward Japan. By mid-1944, U.S. bombers were pounding Japan relentlessly, ending with the two atomic blasts of August 1945.

(Indonesia today) and time to win its war in China. Once Japan had firmed up its positions in East and Southeast Asia, the thinking went, the United States and the United Kingdom would acquiesce. The Japanese leaders knew the United States had twice the population of Japan and far more industrial might, but they hoped, and many believed, that Americans were too soft and undisciplined to pay the price of war with Japan. President Franklin Roosevelt responded to the December 7 attack on Pearl

Harbor by asking Congress to declare war, which it did on December 8, 1941. The Pacific War, as this part of World War II is often called, was under way.

The United States in 1941 was a sleeping giant. It had retreated from international politics after World War I. Its armed forces had shrunk, and its military equipment was obsolete. Its economy was slowly emerging from the Great Depression. But it had the largest industrial capacity of any country in the world. And it had more than 130 million people, who turned out not to be as soft as the Japanese hoped.

Nonetheless, Japanese armed forces thrashed the United States in the first six months after Pearl Harbor. They drove U.S. forces out of the Philippines. They seized Britain's colonies of Malaya and Singapore, as well as the Dutch colony of Indonesia, and bombed northernmost Australia. Their navy sank British battleships, shelled Australia's Sydney suburbs, and attacked two Alaskan islands. By mid-1942, they had won dominion over almost all of Southeast Asia and the western Pacific.

AXIS ADVANCES IN EUROPE Meanwhile in Europe, the Germans also fared well early on. After conquering Poland in late 1939, in the spring of 1940 they overran France, Belgium, the Netherlands, Denmark, and Norway. Only Britain continued to resist. Many in Britain thought it wise to reach a deal with Hitler. But the new prime minister, Winston Churchill, in office since May 1940, refused to consider it. Churchill was an elderly career politician, nationalistic, imperialist, and stubborn as a man can be. He had an American mother, an aristocratic politician father, a fondness for reading history, and a burning desire to make it. He also had an eloquence that inspired the British public when they needed it most.

Britain withstood a sustained German air attack—the Battle of Britain—in the summer and fall of 1940. Londoners called this the blitz. They crowded into underground (subway) stations night after night to avoid the worst of German bombing. Industrial workers in munitions factories worked long shifts amid the bomb blasts. Fighter pilots of the Royal Air Force took a sufficient toll upon the German Air Force that Hitler abandoned plans of an invasion of Britain. Churchill famously said of the

Winston Churchill British prime minister Winston Churchill displays a "V for Victory" during the Battle of Britain in 1940. Churchill's effectiveness as a political and military leader won him widespread popular support during the war.

pilots, "Never in the field of human conflict was so much owed by so many to so few." Meanwhile, late in 1940 Italy attacked Greece. To nearly everyone's surprise, the Greek Hellenic Army bested Mussolini's legions. But the German Army made short work of Greece in the spring of 1941, leaving the Axis supreme on the European continent. Romania and Bulgaria both joined forces with the Axis. Then Hitler made an epic blunder.

OPERATION BARBAROSSA AND STALINGRAD
On June 22, 1941, in Operation Barbarossa—named for a medieval German emperor—Germany attacked the Soviet Union. Hitler believed its mostly Slavic population was sub-human, inferior to Germans, and therefore ripe for conquest—despite Napoleon Bonaparte's experiences in Russia in 1812. The population of the USSR in 1941 was about 195 million people, many of whom were fervently devoted to its ruler, the dictator Josef Stalin. Many more passively endured Stalinism. Soviet industry was considerable, growing by leaps and bounds, and by the late 1930s oriented toward military production. The Soviet military had just undergone a political purge in which Stalin ordered many of the best officers killed. But the army was still large and well equipped. The Soviet Union's vast spaces and few roads made movement difficult for attackers. Its stoic population, accustomed to harsh conditions, proved Hitler's low estimation wrong.

Hitler intended to destroy the USSR and settle its western regions with German families. The Nazi-Soviet pact of 1939 had bought him time to conquer western Europe first so he would not have to fight on two fronts. Now, in June 1941, he felt the time had come to complete his life's

Battle of Stalingrad The bodies of German soldiers, as well as broken-down trucks, lie abandoned in the snow near Stalingrad, following the decisive German defeat in the winter of 1942–1943.

▮	Axis Powers, 1939
▮	Axis allies, June 1941
▮	Axis occupied, May 1941
▯	Axis gains, Operation Barbarossa, June 1941–Nov. 1942
▯	Axis controlled, Nov. 1942
▯	Allied Powers
▯	Neutral nations
→	Axis offensive
→	Allied offensive
✕	Battle
⛏	Oil production
—	Boundaries, 1939

World War II in Europe, Africa, and the Middle East, 1940–1945 Roughly three-quarters of the German war effort was devoted to the eastern front against the Soviet Union. The German drive eastward was stopped at Stalingrad, after which the Soviet Red Army, using great quantities of American equipment, pushed the Germans back to Berlin. In North Africa, the tide turned against the Axis in 1942 at El Alamein in Egypt, which was followed by the Allied invasion of Italy launched from Tunisia in 1943. In the final year of the war in Europe, another major front opened in France with the Allies' D-Day invasion.

ambition by shattering the USSR, destroying communism, and—of fundamental importance to him—killing the millions of Jews who lived in eastern Europe and the USSR.

Stalin—surprisingly—was taken by surprise. It is remarkable that anyone as cynical and calculating as Stalin could have been unprepared for Hitler's double-dealing. But he was. He went into hiding for a couple of weeks

while the Soviet army was in full retreat. For 16 months the German Army pushed eastward, inflicting tremendous damage along the way. In October 1941, Hitler declared victory, claiming the war was over. But the Soviet state, the Soviet economy, the Soviet people, and the Soviet Red Army did not break. They summoned grim determination, withdrew to the east, and, as their ancestors had done with Bonaparte's legions in 1812, pulled the Germans

The Eastern Front A Soviet propaganda poster from 1943 depicts the German army as a tiger, whom the Soviet army might destroy with one well-placed spear. The caption reads, "Beat the German beasts! The destruction of Hitler's army must be done."

deeper and deeper into Russia. Late in 1942, they checked the German advance.

The epic **Battle of Stalingrad** was one of the war's turning points. The city, on the banks of the Volga River in Russia's southwest, had both strategic and symbolic importance. With control of Stalingrad, the Germans could prevent oil barges from the Caspian region from chugging upstream on the Volga to supply the Soviet forces around Moscow. Stalingrad carried additional psychological importance because Stalin had named it for himself. Aware that the war's outcome might be decided there, huge German and Soviet armies clashed at Stalingrad between November 1942 and March 1943. In the end, the Soviets encircled and captured the Axis armies, which Hitler had unwisely forbidden to retreat. The Axis lost about 800,000 men. After Stalingrad, Soviet forces began slowly to drive the Germans out of the USSR.

The eastern front, as the Soviet-German war is called, was the scene of unremitting horror before, during, and after Stalingrad. The Soviet army here consisted of 6 to 9 million men and thousands of women. The Axis forces, about 80 percent German, included Finns, Romanians, Hungarians, and Italians, and by 1942 added hundreds of thousands of Soviet citizens—Russians, Ukrainians, Lithuanians—who saw the German invasion as their liberation from communism. At its mid-1943 maximum, the Axis forces on the eastern front counted 4 million. This was the decisive theater of the war in Europe, and the largest in world history. Four-fifths of German war dead fell here, and more than half of the total Axis casualties in all theaters. In total, about 15 million soldiers of all nationalities died on the eastern front, and another 15 million

civilians; another 25 million were homeless because of wartime destruction by 1945.

In each major theater except China, the Axis suffered defeats that turned the tide against them. In the Pacific, at the Battle of Midway (June 1942), U.S. naval aircraft destroyed a large chunk of Japan's fleet. In North Africa, where the Germans were driving toward British bases in Egypt and the strategic prize of the Suez Canal, the key moment came in October–November 1942 at El Alamein, in the desert of northwestern Egypt, when the British turned back a German-led attack—most of the foot soldiers were Italians. At El Alamein the Axis lost about 50,000 men, or 6 percent of the toll at Stalingrad.

THE WAR IN CHINA The war in China (1937–1945) cost about 15 to 20 million lives, 80 percent of them Chinese. Japan by the end of 1938 occupied most of north and eastern China, and by mid-1942 all of the major ports. Chinese armies lacked military materiel, and once the Japanese occupied the coastal regions, aid from the Allies had to come over the Himalayas to the southwest. Little arrived. Here there was no major turning point, only deadly stalemate. Japanese forces bombed Chinese cities at will. Tens of millions of refugees streamed to the west and south, hoping to escape the Japanese. Hunger, disease, and currency inflation were rampant. China could not counter-attack; it could only hope to outlast the Japanese in a war of attrition.

After 1940, Chinese strategists learned to avoid big

Chinese Leaders Mao Zedong (left) and Chiang Kai-shek (right) were leaders of the Chinese Communist Party and the Guomindang, respectively. Each led an army against the Japanese, with Mao's guerilla forces proving effective in mobilizing resistance to the invasion.

D-Day An embedded U.S. Coast Guard photographer took this picture of American soldiers wading ashore onto Omaha Beach during the D-Day landings on the Normandy coast on June 6, 1944.

Hiroshima A trade exhibition hall was the only building left standing near the epicenter of the atomic bomb's explosion over Hiroshima on August 6, 1945. Today the building's ruins are the site of a memorial park.

battles in favor of smaller operations in Japanese-occupied areas. They remained divided between forces fielded by the Chinese Communist Party headed by Mao Zedong and the far larger—but often less effective—armies loyal to the Guomindang now led by Chiang Kai-shek. After Pearl Harbor, both expected Japan would ultimately lose, which undercut their ability to cooperate as each one intended to rule China after the war. They fought one another frequently after 1938, and as Japanese defeat seemed more certain by late 1944, they prepared for all-out civil war.

THE FINAL YEARS In 1943, without any key battle, the Allies also prevailed over Germany on the seas of the North Atlantic. The U.S., U.K., and Canadian navies learned how to protect shipping and hunt submarines effectively. That enabled millions of tons of North American food, fuel, weapons, munitions, and other supplies to reach Britain and the USSR safely. After these turning points—Stalingrad, Midway, El Alamein, and the Atlantic—the Axis powers remained on the defensive, their now-slim chances of victory waning with each passing month.

The war dragged on for two and a half more years. Italy quit in 1943, leaving Germany and Japan to fight on. Both fought tenaciously, even after all rational hope was lost. Their forces had committed countless atrocities

on foreign soil, and they feared payback if and when the fighting reached their own countries. But desperate tenacity was not enough. Over the course of 1943 and 1944, the Soviets pushed the Germans out of the USSR. On June 6, 1944—D-Day—the British, Canadians, and Americans landed the largest amphibious invasion force in world history on the beaches of Normandy, in northwestern France, and pushed Hitler's armies back toward Germany. Meanwhile, the Americans island-hopped across the South Pacific, driving the Japanese back toward their home islands.

The end came at last in 1945. In Europe, the Red Army slugged its way into Germany and took Berlin (April 1945), while the Americans and British fought their way into the western half of Germany in early 1945. The Germans were running low on men, fuel, and the will to combat. Relentless bombing campaigns hampered their war production and especially their movement, as rails, roads, bridges, and tunnels were by late 1944 bombed constantly. They surrendered in May 1945 shortly after Hitler committed suicide.

In the Pacific, the Americans pushed the Japanese back, island by island. The fiercest combat took place on Guadalcanal, in the Solomon Islands, and on Iwo Jima and Okinawa, islands close to Japan. In the summer of 1945, the Americans prepared to invade Japan, which they expected would cost a quarter-million American lives—and many more Japanese. But before they embarked on that mission, in early August 1945, the United States dropped an atomic bomb on each of two mid-size cities, **Hiroshima and Nagasaki**. The explosions instantly killed about 105,000 people, 90 percent of them civilians. Radiation poisoning soon killed roughly an equal number. In the same week, the USSR declared war on Japan. The Japanese high command chose to surrender in mid-August 1945.

WHY THE ALLIES WON

The Axis won almost every encounter in the years 1937–1941. But time was not on its side. The only realistic chance it had was a quick victory, before the Allies could bring to bear their enormous advantages in manpower and materiel. Until 1941, the Axis held an edge in military manpower and the quantity and quality of weaponry. But after the Axis attacked the USSR and the United States, it was heavily out-numbered and soon out-gunned. Its chances of winning shrank, slowly at first and more quickly after Midway and Stalingrad.

COALITION WAR The Axis was also out-managed. Germany, Japan, and Italy scarcely cooperated at all and, in the case of Germany and Italy, often worked at cross-purposes. When Hitler occupied Romania in 1940 he did not tell Mussolini, and Mussolini returned the favor when Italy invaded Greece months later. The Italian Fascist Party included Jews until 1938 and did not round up Jews for extermination. The Italian Army protected Jews in areas under its control, which confirmed Hitler's sense of Italian softness. When Italy surrendered to the Allies in 1943, the Germans captured hundreds of thousands of Italian soldiers and took them as slave laborers to Germany. Cooperation between Japan and its Axis partners amounted to little beside information sharing, because their theaters of operations were so distant.

In contrast, the Allies cooperated—not smoothly, but effectively. This was a remarkable achievement, given the ideological chasm between Stalin on one side and Roosevelt and Churchill on the other. Churchill had long been a vocal anti-communist; but after the German invasion of the Soviet Union in 1941, he concluded a pact with Stalin. He justified his position by saying, "If Hitler invaded hell I would make at least a favorable reference to the devil in the House of Commons." The United States provided vast quantities of war materiel to Britain and, despite the U.S. government's disdain for communism, the USSR.

The United States and Britain frequently shared secret intelligence with each other, and from time to time shared it with Stalin, who rarely reciprocated.

The biggest tensions in the alliance arose over the American and British caution in opening a second front against Germany. With German armies deep in Soviet territory, Stalin wanted his allies to invade France in 1942. But U.S. and U.K. commanders did not feel ready to mount an amphibious assault on France, and they sent armies to Axis-occupied North Africa instead. Churchill was keen to defend Britain's position in Egypt and the Suez Canal, the lifeline to British India. Stalin suspected his allies were content to see his army bear the brunt of German firepower, and they probably were. But the shaky performance of the U.S. Army against German forces in North Africa in 1942 and 1943 strongly suggested it was not prepared for an invasion of German-occupied Europe. These tensions pitting the USSR against the United States and the United Kingdom, as we will see, helped break the wartime alliance and usher in the Cold War. But holding the alliance together until victory in 1945, across an ideological chasm, was the supreme achievement of Roosevelt, Churchill, and Stalin. It enabled them to make full use of their inherent advantages.

ECONOMIC WAR The biggest advantage the Allies enjoyed was their economic strength. In population, the Allies outnumbered the Axis by 2 to 1, if one counts only the major combatants (the USSR, United States, United Kingdom and its dominions of Canada, Australia, New Zealand, and South Africa on one side; and Germany, Italy, and Japan on the other). If one includes India and China among the Allies, the ratio swells to close to 7:1. The combined economies of the Allies was 2.1 times as large as that of the Axis in 1940—before the United States and the USSR entered the war—and 5 times larger by 1945. In the core years of the war, 1942 through 1944, total Allied military production outstripped that of the Axis by ratios between 3:1 and 10:1. The imbalance came in part from the success of the U.S. and U.K. navies in maintaining access to international trade flows, while the Axis had to rely on its own resources and those of the lands it conquered. Japan in 1940 had adequate supplies of only 2 of the 32 raw materials its high command deemed essential to warfare—graphite and sulfur. By and large, the Axis enjoyed an advantage in the quality of its military goods, but suffered an enormous disadvantage in quantity, partly from shortages of raw materials.

The Allies controlled almost all the world's oil, a crucial advantage. The most effective weapons systems in the 1940s—tanks, ships, and airplanes—all ran on oil. Fighting without oil meant moving men and equipment by rail or draft animal, in effect fighting with one hand tied behind your back. In particular, there was no way to fight an air war without oil. As it happened, most of the world's oil production in 1940 took place in the United States, the USSR, Mexico, Venezuela, and parts of the Middle East mainly under British control. The Axis produced almost none. Japan's initial conquests included oilfields in the Dutch East Indies (now Indonesia), and the Germans took over an oil patch in Romania. They targeted the Soviet oilfields near Baku on the Caspian Sea, but after Stalingrad they had no hope of adding to their oil supplies. Late in the war, the German Air Force could not fly for lack of fuel. Oil was the most important economic resource in warfare, and the Allies had almost all of it. American oilfields pumped 86 percent of the oil used by the Allies.

Economic culture mattered too. For different reasons, both the American and Soviet economies could change almost overnight into effective war economies. The mobilization of the American economy was stunning. Soon after the United States entered the war, one of Hitler's closest comrades, Air Marshall Hermann Goering,

American Manufacturing Workers on the assembly line at a Chrysler factory in Michigan manufacture tanks in 1942. Theirs was one of many American auto plants that mobilized to produce war materiel.

scoffed that the Americans were only good at producing razor blades. But in fact the U.S. economy was good at producing mass quantities of anything.

The Detroit area was the center of the world's automobile industry, which had been using electrified assembly lines for decades. This production technique worked superbly for the mass production of tanks, aircraft, jeeps, and trucks. The U.S. auto industry stopped making cars in 1942 to focus entirely on military vehicles and aircraft. The Ford Motor Company alone out-produced Italy during the war. By 1944, Ford workers could assemble a B-24 bomber every 63 minutes. Their counterparts in U.S. shipyards could weld together big cargo ships in 8 days. The United States launched 16 warships for each one Japan could build. As President Roosevelt put it, the United States had a "genius . . . for mass-production."

The United States also had the resources to pay for, and found the labor to undertake, a giant war effort. The government sold billions of dollars of bonds to ordinary Americans and raised taxes across the board—the richest Americans paid a 94 percent income tax. As men left for war, American women streamed into war work in factories, offices, and on farms as well. Five million women joined the paid labor force between 1940 and 1945. By 1943, the majority of workers assembling airplanes were women. Thousands of women, including chemists and physicists, worked to create atomic bombs. Some 350,000 women joined the U.S. armed forces, driving trucks, serving as nurses, or handling paperwork. But overall, women made up a smaller proportion—27 to 29 percent—of the American industrial labor force during the war than in the United Kingdom (27 to 32 percent), Germany (27 to 32 percent), or the USSR (about 60 percent). Labor was less of a constraint on the war effort in the United States than it was for other major combatants.

The Soviet economy also performed miracles during the war. Since 1918 it had been a command economy in which the government, not market forces, made most major decisions. Since 1929 it had used five-year plans to run the economy and specialized in heroic mobilization—building a new steel mill in weeks or a factory in days. This helps to explain why the Soviet economy did not collapse in the years 1941–1942 while the Germans hammered ever deeper into the country, occupying lands that formerly had accounted for one-third of Soviet economic output. Soviet factory workers packed up everything they could, took it east, behind the Ural Mountains, and put their factories back together again. Everyone not in uniform or producing food—teenagers, the elderly, political prisoners—was recruited for armaments production. The Soviet economy already made widespread use of female labor before 1941 and, unlike the United States, had no great reserve of labor to mobilize. Nevertheless, the Soviet economy, despite losing many of its most industrialized regions to Hitler's armies and much of its male workforce to active military duty, produced more military materiel than Germany in every year of the war.

Both the Americans and the Soviets relied on mass production of simple designs built with interchangeable parts, which made it easier to maintain and repair machinery. Neither the Americans nor the Soviets made high-quality military goods, at least not until 1944. But they could make much more, much faster than anyone else. The United States was able to ship about 17 percent of its military output to either Britain or the USSR in a program called Lend-Lease, in which the U.S. government "lent" food, fuel, trucks, and aircraft to its allies with little expectation of repayment. When the Red Army marched to Berlin in 1945, it rode in Dodge and Studebaker trucks made in the American Midwest. The top Soviet general, Marshall Georgy Zhukov, said afterward that without the American equipment the USSR could not have continued to fight.

The contrast with the German and Japanese war economies was sharp. Both had strong industrial traditions of skilled craftsmen. They built excellent tanks and airplanes; but lacking electrified assembly lines, they could not make them quickly, and repair was difficult. American jeeps were easy to maintain, but it took prolonged training to maintain German or Japanese high-quality equipment. Skilled labor shortages became a bottleneck in the German and Japanese war economies.

Indeed, labor of any kind became a bottleneck for the Axis economies. They mobilized almost all young men for military service from the outset of war. By 1943 they were conscripting middle-aged men, and by 1945 they were putting 15-year-olds in uniform. For ideological reasons, they—the Japanese especially—did not want women in factories. Women were supposed to stay at home and provide a wholesome environment for children, or perhaps work as teachers and nurses. Half a million German women went to work, mainly as nurses, in occupied

Women at Work Women aeronautics workers assemble the fuselage of a B-17F bomber at a California factory in 1942. They were some of the millions of women in Allied countries who joined the paid workforce to aid the war effort.

territories. The proportion of women in Japan's industrial workforce was about half of Germany's, which in turn was about half that in the USSR. Meanwhile, both Germany and Japan enslaved millions of men from countries they occupied and dragged them into war production. Thus Germany and Japan relied on legions of forced laborers, who if not constantly intimidated would slow production or even sabotage it.

BRAINPOWER WAR The enormous economic advantages of the Allies told in the long run. But as the war dragged on, the Allies acquired another advantage too. They harnessed the brainpower of their populations more effectively than did the Axis powers.

Part of the Allies' success resulted from the flight of scientists from Germany and Europe as the Nazi threat took shape. Before the rise of the Nazis, Germany had, by far, the world's most advanced centers of physics. Several great physicists, such as Albert Einstein, were Jewish and left Europe to escape from Nazism. A dozen or more worked on the U.S. atomic bomb project. Enrico Fermi oversaw the first self-sustaining nuclear reaction, which took place in 1942 under the stadium stands at the University of Chicago. He had left Italy in 1938 because his wife was Jewish. Refugees from Nazism contributed significantly to scientific war work in the United States and the United Kingdom.

Manhattan Project Members of an all-female engineering team operate equipment at a uranium enrichment facility in Oak Ridge, Tennessee, in 1944. Laboratories and other facilities around the United States were dedicated to the effort to develop a nuclear bomb.

Moreover, the United States and the United Kingdom converted their industrial laboratories, engineering works, and universities to war work. This strategy paid dividends in the form of weaponry, radar, better bombsights, and much else that helped win the war. The most famous example is the Manhattan Project, the secret project to build an atomic bomb that, starting in 1941, tapped scientists and engineers from several American, British, and Canadian universities and U.S. corporations. Together with hundreds of thousands of laborers, they built the engineering and weapons complex that developed the bombs used to destroy Hiroshima and Nagasaki.

Another important example of war-related technological development was miniaturized radar. The Allies needed to ferry millions of tons of fuel, food, and munitions across the Atlantic, from North America to Britain and the USSR, running a gauntlet of German submarines. To do so successfully, they needed radar devices small enough to fit on airplanes. Two British physicists at the University of Birmingham—one of them, Harry Boot, only 22 years old—developed miniaturized radar technology (used today in microwave ovens), and American factories built the needed devices. Before they had them, the Allies were losing ships to German submarines faster than they could build new ones. After they started using micro-radar in airplanes, they could hunt down and destroy submarines faster than the Germans could

build new ones. That enabled North American farms and factories to keep Britain and the USSR supplied by sea.

In addition to engineering improvements in military hardware, the Allies put to use extraordinary advances in medicine. A good example is the use of DDT, a chemical compound that kills insects. (It was later banned in many countries because of its toxic effects on wildlife.) The Americans mass-produced it and sprayed their troops with it to protect them from lice, which can carry typhus, and mosquitoes, which can carry malaria. In the South Pacific and New Guinea campaigns, where malaria was far more deadly than combat, abundant supplies of DDT gave American and Australian troops a major advantage over the Japanese, who had none. The Allies also had an edge in anti-bacterial drugs such as penicillin, which saved countless soldiers from dying from infected wounds.

More generally, the United States and the United Kingdom, and to a lesser extent the USSR, proved better at learning from mistakes than did the Axis powers. Both the United States and the United Kingdom were more open societies, in which information flowed more freely than in Germany or Japan—although this was not true of the USSR. The first requirement of learning from mistakes is admitting them and studying them. Much went wrong for the United States, the United Kingdom, and especially the USSR early in the war, and they could not pretend to themselves they knew how to fight as well as the Germans and Japanese. They had urgent reason to study their failures and improve their performance. After some disastrous experiences, the Americans got very good at amphibious landings on Pacific islands. After costly disasters, the Soviet army learned how to fight tank battles. The Axis proved less able to improve combat performance by learning from failure. The Japanese navy even concealed its loss of one-third of its aircraft carriers at Midway from civilian leaders and the army, which for several months forged its strategy in the false belief that 12 carriers were still available.

Finally, the Allies did much better than the Axis in codebreaking. With the help of Polish mathematicians and intelligence officers, the British learned the secrets to German encoding machines before the war even began. As the Germans changed their codes through the course of the war, British codebreakers, many of them mathematicians, got better at deciphering them. The Germans and Italians broke some of the Allies' codes too, which helped them considerably in the years 1940–1942. The Germans, with Italian help, were reading coded dispatches on Allied plans sent by an American army officer in Cairo. The legendary German general Erwin Rommel, known as the "desert fox," could read these messages within hours. But the Germans and Italians could not keep up with periodic changes in the Allies' codes, and by 1943 were usually operating in the dark.

In the Pacific War, codebreaking was also crucial. The Americans could read the main Japanese diplomatic and naval codes throughout the war. Convinced that their code was too complex to decipher, the Japanese made only small changes that did not baffle codebreakers for long. The Japanese failed to break any important American codes.

THE HUMAN COST

The death toll of World War II reached 60 million, more than any previous war and about 3 percent of humankind. In addition to those killed, many millions more suffered bodily or psychological harm that lasted all their lives. The death and destruction were greatest in eastern Europe and China. The USSR, Poland, Yugoslavia, and Greece lost large proportions of their population. The United States, which made huge contributions in terms of war materiel, paid the lowest human cost of any major combatant—partly because it joined the war later than most, but mainly because after Pearl Harbor no combat took place on American soil. The table above reduces the grisly tragedy to numbers and percentages.

WAR CRIMES War crimes took place on an unprecedented scale. Outside of combat, Germans and their accomplices murdered 10 to 14 million people, including nearly 6 million Jews (see below). Stalin's henchmen killed at least 1.2 million and perhaps as many as 7 million—the figures are highly controversial. They killed anyone suspected of favoring the Germans, which included many Ukrainians and Poles, among others within the USSR. In addition, they tried to kill all educated people and military officers in the parts of Poland they controlled. Japanese forces murdered or deliberately starved millions more, most notoriously in the Nanjing Massacre of 1937–1938 in which perhaps 200,000 Chinese civilians were slaughtered and 20,000 women and girls raped. In north

THE HUMAN COST OF WORLD WAR II

	War dead (in millions)	1940 population (in millions)	War dead as a percentage of 1940 population
USSR	25–29	194	13–16%
China	15–20	520	3–4%
Germany	6.9–7.4	70	8–9%
Poland	6	35	17%
Dutch East Indies	3–4	70	4.3–5.7%
Japan	2.5–3.1	72	3.5–4.3%
Yugoslavia	1.0–1.7	16	7–11%
Greece	0.5–0.8	7.2	7–11%
France	0.6	42	1.4%
Italy	0.5	45	1%
United Kingdom	0.5	48	1%
United States	0.4	132	0.3%
Canada	0.04	11.3	0.4%
Australia	0.04	7	0.6%
WORLD	60	2,300	3%

Sources: Gerhard Weinberg, *World at Arms* (1995), 894, and https://en.wikipedia.org/wiki/World_War_II_casualties#Total_deaths_by_country

China in 1941, the Japanese implemented a policy known as the Three Alls: kill all, loot all, burn all. That resulted in nearly 3 million civilian deaths. Of the 30 million prisoners of war, perhaps 6 to 10 million died of starvation and disease, most commonly those held by the USSR, Germany, or Japan.

BOMBING OF CITIES Aerial bombing of cities, regarded by some as a war crime, killed several hundred thousand civilians in Europe and Japan. War strategists thought, incorrectly, that they could break civilian morale by bombing cities and terrorizing populations. But the bombing only hardened the popular will to resist. Worst hit were Britain in 1940–1941, Germany in 1943–1945, and Japan in 1944–1945. Squadrons of bombers burned whole cities to the ground. In Tokyo in March 1945, one American air raid killed about 100,000 civilians. In February 1945, British and American bombing of Dresden, in Germany, killed about 25,000.

As we have seen, in August 1945 the United States dropped two atomic bombs, one each on the Japanese cities of Hiroshima and Nagasaki. Counting lingering deaths from radiation exposure, the bombs killed roughly 200,000 people. These were the first and, thus far, the last uses of nuclear weapons in warfare. They succeeded in their immediate purpose: to force a Japanese surrender without the heavy losses expected in an invasion of Japan's home islands. President Truman's decision to use them was welcomed by the Allies at the time, but later became highly controversial because of the uniquely devastating power of atomic weapons.

THE HOLOCAUST The horrific human cost of the war included the near destruction of European Jewry. Hitler intended to kill Europe's entire population of 9 to 10 million Jews. Sporadic murders of Jews in Germany, of whom there were more than 400,000, began before the war. In 1939, when the Germans conquered half of Poland, they murdered many more Jews and tried to collect all the rest into ghettoes—in effect, urban prison camps. Larger-scale systematic murder, carried out by specialized death squads called *Einsatzgruppen*, began with the German invasion of the USSR in June 1941.

Hitler intended to win the war quickly and afterward finish off the Jews, but he realized that the war would drag on after two events in December 1941: the first Soviet army counter-attack against German forces, and the Japanese attack on Pearl Harbor, which brought the United States into the war. He decided to kill all of Europe's Jews while the war was still under way, and his underlings convened a conference in early 1942 outside of Berlin at Wannsee to plan what they called "The Final Solution to the Jewish question."

At the Wannsee Conference 15 Nazi officials, nearly half of whom held doctorates in law, worked out the broad outlines of the plan. Even after the tide of battle had turned against them in 1943, the Germans devoted manpower and rail cars to the transport of Jews from all over Europe to dozens of concentration camps—both labor camps and extermination camps. The extermination camp names are synonyms for the deepest abyss in the annals of human morality: Treblinka, Sobibor, Auschwitz. In all, the Germans and their helpers murdered between 5.6 million and 6 million Jews, the vast majority from eastern Europe. Some they worked to death, some they starved to death, some they shot, and most they gassed in specially built death chambers. A quarter of the victims were children. In Poland, as in Germany, most

Holocaust Emaciated survivors of the Buchenwald concentration camp in eastern Germany were photographed shortly after U.S. troops liberated the camp in April 1945.

Christians had a pretty good idea of what was happening to their Jewish neighbors, but judged it was safest for themselves to do and say nothing. In western Europe, where Jews were comparatively few, puppet governments such as the so-called Vichy regime that governed most of France collaborated with the Nazi genocide. German executioners often had eager assistants, especially among those Croats, Ukrainians, Romanians, Hungarians, and Poles who willingly took part in the murders. Croatian fascists even set up their own death camp.

Occasionally Europe's Jews had courageous defenders. Led by a Protestant pastor, one village in the south of France, Chambon-sur-Lignon, hid a thousand or more Jews and helped others escape from France. A Dutch village, Nieuwlande, also inspired by a Protestant clergyman, did much the same. In 1943, when German authorities ordered the mayor of the Greek island of Zakynthos to provide a list of the island's Jews and their property, they received a list with two names: the mayor's and that of the island's bishop. Islanders helped all 275 Jews on Zakynthos to hide, and all survived the Nazi occupation. So, improbably, did the mayor and the bishop. The Swedish diplomat Raoul Wallenberg, posted to Budapest, saved thousands of Hungarian Jews by issuing them documents providing the legal protection of neutral Sweden. (The Soviet army seized Wallenberg when it captured Hungary in 1945, and he perished not long after, probably in a Soviet prison.) The Polish diplomat Jan Karski snuck into the Warsaw ghetto twice, and a Jewish transport camp once, in order to bring authentic information of the fate of Poland's Jews to the attention of the outside world. He went to London and Washington to explain what he knew, but with little result. Churchill and Roosevelt thought the best way to save lives, whether Jewish or not, was to win the war fast.

A few tens of thousands of Jews fought back against Hitler's extermination campaign. Some managed to join Polish or Ukrainian guerillas in the forests and swamps of eastern Europe. Some rose in rebellion in the ghettoes. The largest such rising took place in the Warsaw ghetto, which had once held 400,000 Jews. Less than a quarter remained by January 1943, when renewed deportations to the extermination camps were met with violent resistance by a few hundred poorly armed Jews who had smuggled in weapons over the previous months. They held off German units for 27 days before being overwhelmed.

The mass murder of the Jews was the biggest part of a larger Nazi extermination project. Hitler also regarded Roma (Gypsies) and the mentally ill as unworthy to live in the expanded and racially purified Germany. His supporters murdered roughly 200,000 to 500,000 Roma, most of them in the same camps as the Jews. That amounted to about 20 to 50 percent of Europe's Roma population. Some 300,000 people judged by doctors to have mental or physical disabilities were also killed in Hitler's efforts to safeguard the German "race."

Hitler also regarded all Slavs as sub-human. German soldiers, police, and other units killed millions of Poles, Ukrainians, and Russians. They particularly sought to kill anyone with an education, except those who could

The Holocaust, 1939–1945 This map shows a landscape of death and despair. Beginning in 1933, the Nazi Party set up a system of concentration camps, also called labor camps, which held about 21,000 people when World War II began in Europe in 1939. They held 715,000 at their height in early 1945. A parallel system of seven extermination camps opened in 1942. (Auschwitz, opened in 1940, was both a labor camp and an extermination camp.) Some 800,000 people died in the labor camps of starvation, disease, and brutality. About 3.1 million died in the extermination camps—most of them Jews. Another 2.6 to 2.9 million Jews were murdered outside the camp systems.

Warsaw Ghetto After defeating the uprising of 1943, German soldiers round up Jewish residents of the Warsaw ghetto—including many children—for deportation to extermination camps.

be recruited into the German war effort. Of 5.7 million Soviet prisoners of war in German hands, 3.3 million died from starvation, disease, or violence.

Hitler was one of few extreme racists ever to hold sufficient power to put his views into practice. He thought a pure German race existed and deserved to thrive, while Slavs, Roma, and Jews were obstacles to German greatness. He wanted to kill, starve, or enslave them all. German voters, politicians, and military men had put him in a position to realize much of his murderous agenda.

HOME FRONTS

World War II reached into lives far from the many battle zones. Total war required the involvement of all citizens, whether on the front lines or at home.

GERMANY In Germany, all was quiet on the home front until 1943. Remembering the privations of World War I, German authorities reserved plenty of food and other necessities for civilians until late in the war when they no longer could. Domestic support for Hitler remained strong, and organized resistance to his regime—extremely dangerous for anyone—was minimal. The most famous anti-Nazi movement was a non-violent and ineffective student group in Munich called the White Rose, almost all of whom were executed in 1943. Three times military officers organized assassination plots against Hitler: all three narrowly failed.

By 1943, the veneer of normalcy in Germany was challenged by growing knowledge of the death camps, the presence of 10 to 12 million slave laborers dragged from occupied territories, and Allied bombing of German cities. Most Germans eventually knew that Jews were disappearing, many knew they were being killed, but almost no one objected publicly. Either they approved of the mass murder, or they feared—with good reason—for their own position and safety. In 1944 and 1945, any appearance of normalcy disappeared. Allied bombing intensified. Shortages of food and supplies became common. A dark joke at the time went like this: "Enjoy the war, because the peace will be horrible." Anxiety about what was to come when the Red Army entered German lands was commonplace, and well founded: Soviet soldiers raped about 20 percent of the German women they encountered in 1944 and 1945.

JAPAN AND ITALY Japan's home front was also quiet into 1943. The military exercised tight control and kept any discouraging information, such as the fate of the Japanese fleet at Midway, from the public. They also suppressed all information about the atrocities at Nanjing. Support for the emperor and the war stayed high. By 1944, the strain hit home. Amidst growing shortages, the government asked women to work in war industries, and half a million "volunteered" before the war's end—they could be fined if they didn't. Hiroko Nakamato, whose Hiroshima high school closed in 1943, went to work in an unheated airplane factory where she toiled long hours, slept on the premises, and got little to eat. Heavy aerial bombing began late in 1944 and intensified thereafter, making the last months of the war a living hell for Japanese. Even then, there was no serious resistance to the imperial government or the war.

In Italy, the war was never popular outside of committed fascist circles. Many Italians thought they were fighting on the wrong side, a conviction deepened by witnessing German atrocities in North Africa and eastern Europe. A steady diet of military defeats sapped morale. In the summer of 1943, when Allied armies invaded Italy's southernmost island of Sicily, Mussolini's hold on the country crumbled, the Fascist Party turned on him, and Italy quit the war. In 1944 and 1945, Italian factions were fighting one another while the Allies occupied the southern part of the country and the Germans the north.

THE SOVIET UNION In the Allied countries, governments were able to demand greater sacrifices sooner from their populations. In the USSR, Stalin had no choice because the war started so badly. Total and immediate mobilization of manpower, womanpower, and all resources followed quickly upon the German invasion and the sudden loss of millions killed or taken prisoner. Women took over most of the farm work and much of the factory work. Nearly a million women served in the armed forces, including in combat roles such as tank commander, infantry sniper, or fighter pilot. Food shortages were widespread and strict rationing imposed. In Leningrad, which the Germans besieged for nearly 900 days, one-third of the population (800,000 people) starved to death.

And yet the Soviet home front did not collapse. Soviet citizens were accustomed

Soviet Mobilization In the Soviet army, it was relatively common for women to serve in combat roles. The highly decorated Soviet fighter pilot Lydia Litvyak, posing here with her plane, was shot down in the Battle of Kursk in 1943, at age 22.

CONSIDERING THE EVIDENCE

Propaganda for the Japanese Home Front

During World War II, the Japanese government produced films, leaflets, plays, radio broadcasts, and posters to unify the home front. But some of the most effective propaganda was *kamishibai*—that is, one-person performances accompanied by 10 to 30 hand-painted illustrations presented in sequence. Before the war, *kamishibai* artists and writers worked under the direction of managers who rented the illustrations, scripts, and bicycles to performers, who made their money by selling candy. The performers visited the same neighborhoods every day, captivating their young audiences with serialized melodramas and adventure stories. After Japan seized Manchuria from China in 1931, government agencies began writing and sponsoring official *kamishibai* performances at factories, farming collectives, and schools to promote the idea that Japan was liberating, rather than conquering, the rest of East Asia. The *kamishibai* also encouraged adults to support wartime policies—for example, by depositing the money saved by rationing into the country's banks. In the following excerpt, members of a group that grows vegetables together speak with their leader, named Sakuta, about the best way to spend the profits from their sales.

Scene 12

Troop member: "Troop Commander, sir! I have run out of face cream; may I purchase some, sir?"

Sakuta: "What? You want to buy face cream? Outrageous! Don't you know that 'Luxury is the Enemy'? Huh?"

Another troop member: "Troop Commander, I would like to buy a pair of socks."... "I would like to eat some bread." ... "I am out of tissues."...

Scene 13

Sakuta: "Stop yelling 'Troop Commander' in my ear! 'I need to buy this, I want that'—you sound like a bunch of whining babies. I am about to make a speech, so listen up."...

Scene 15

Sakuta continues: "...what Japan needs now is not just money; we also have to use goods as carefully as possible. Buying things just because you have some money...weakens our nation."...

Scene 16

Sakuta continues: "The money that you keep in hand belongs just to the person who has it, but...putting money into savings is an expression of loyalty to the nation....

"What would you do if you had children? Would you eat those adorable little kids?

"Or, instead, would you loyally offer them up to the service of the nation? Hmm? It's just the same with money."...

Scene 17

Sakuta continues: "If you don't understand something as simple as this, even children will laugh at you. In fact, the reason I am making this speech is that I heard it from my son who is in elementary school. These days even children understand the importance of savings."

Source: Sharalyn Orbaugh, "Record of the Cheerful Troop," in *Propaganda Performed: Kamishibai in Japan's Fifteen Year War* (Boston, 2015).

> ## QUESTIONS FOR ANALYSIS
>
> 1. Which parts of the script suggest that this *kamishibai* was intended for adults instead of children?
> 2. How did the writers of this *kamishibai* use references to children to persuade adults that they should contribute to the war effort?
> 3. Why was it important to Japan and other countries for their people to ration resources, save money, and invest in war bonds?

to stoic endurance. Many truly idolized Stalin and were prepared to sacrifice for him and their country. His appeals to patriotism helped, which extended to enlisting the Russian Orthodox Church in the war effort, reversing two decades of official atheism and ruthless Soviet persecution of the church. Well-publicized German brutality made it clear to almost everyone that the lesser of the evils available was to work as hard as possible for victory. And for those who doubted it, Stalin's network of informers and secret police stood ready to execute anyone suspected of defeatism, sympathy for the enemy, or just insufficient admiration of Stalin.

THE UNITED KINGDOM In the United Kingdom, thorough home-front mobilization was also the rule. Strict rationing prevailed and made everyday life drab—except during German bombing raids, when it was terrifying. Morale at times was shaky, despite Churchill's charismatic leadership. Petty crime spiked during air raid blackouts. In 1940 and early 1941, when Britain suffered defeat after defeat, many thought—and some said—that making peace with Germany made sense. Women worked long hours in armaments factories, entrusting their children to relatives and friends. In 1941, they were required to register for national—not military—service, working wherever the government judged they would be most useful. The entry into the war of the USSR and then the United States, and stepped-up deliveries of American and Canadian food, fuel, and other supplies, brightened the outlook by late 1943, as did the improving prospect of victory.

THE UNITED STATES The United States instituted rationing too but experienced no serious deprivations, nor any serious bombing after Pearl Harbor. Most citizens accepted the necessity for sacrifices, and little compulsion was needed. The government worked with business leaders to mobilize the economy for war production. As we've seen, millions of women took on war work in offices, factories, and the armed forces—but not in combat roles. Hundreds of thousands of African Americans and poor whites left the rural South for armaments factories in the Midwest or California. The war against the most uncompromising racists in world history drew heightened attention to racial inequalities at home. Whereas in 1941 only 4,000 African Americans were in uniform, by 1945 about 1.2 million had served, albeit in segregated units and usually in non-combat roles. But the so-called Tuskegee Airmen, fighter pilots who flew out of bases in Italy in 1944 and 1945,

Tuskegee Airmen African American fighter pilots, who belonged to the U.S. Air Force's segregated 332nd Fighter Group, pose in front of their plane in 1944.

Japanese Internment The American photographer Dorothea Lange took this photograph of the Mochida family of Hayward, California, preparing for their removal to an internment camp in May 1942.

were in particular demand by bomber crews who wanted the best fighter escorts they could get for air raids over Nazi-controlled Europe. The United States de-segregated its armed forces in 1948.

The United States and Canada both treated citizens of Japanese ancestry as potential enemies. Most of the Japanese American population on the West Coast, about 110,000 people, was rounded up in 1942 and kept in internment camps for the duration of the war. This was Roosevelt's decision, upheld by the Supreme Court in the *Korematsu* decision of 1944. In contrast, almost none of the larger Japanese Hawaiian population was interned. German Americans were sometimes kept under surveillance, and some 11,000 were interned. Almost all Japanese Canadians, about 22,000 people, most of whom were born in Canada, were put into camps and their property sold to help pay for the war.

Racialist thinking shaped—and often weakened—the war effort of most major combatants. Britain recruited only from Indian and African populations deemed "martial races." South Africa refused to use black Africans, the vast majority of the population, in military roles, until losses of white troops left it no choice. New Zealand was slow to mobilize Maori. The USSR initially refused to use men from non-Slavic minorities as combat troops, until the death toll obliged the army to pour Tajiks, Uzbeks, Turkmen, and others into battle. It also deported about 2 million people from Muslim minorities in the Crimea and the Caucasus to Siberia or Central Asia on the grounds—often well founded—that they preferred the Germans to Stalin.

OCCUPATIONS

Lands occupied by Axis troops in Europe or East Asia suffered grievously. In German-occupied western Europe, conditions were grim; in eastern Europe, they were horrific. Food, fuel, and other supplies went first to the Germans; everyone else had to make do with what remained. Germans found willing collaborators, especially early on when it seemed likely they would win. Collaborators throughout Nazi-occupied Europe helped to organize German war production, labor drafts, and the deportation of Jews to death camps.

Occupation also incited resistance, which was strongest in Yugoslavia and the conquered parts of the USSR, but present on some scale everywhere. None of it had much effect until the years 1944–1945, and even then it was far from decisive. Yugoslav partisans operating in mountains and forests at times kept two German Army divisions tied up. Partisans operating in the woods and swamps of eastern Europe, and, late in the war, in the mountains of Italy and France, also gave the Germans trouble. But acts of resistance in German-occupied and Italian-occupied Europe provoked terrible reprisals, typically featuring the murder of dozens or hundreds of civilians taken at random. As a consequence, civilians in occupied Europe often resented resistance fighters as much as those who collaborated with the Germans.

In the parts of China, Southeast Asia, or the Pacific Islands occupied by Japanese forces, the war years were also exceedingly grim. In occupied China, millions collaborated with the Japanese and millions resisted them. Japanese racial ideology encouraged extremely harsh treatment of Chinese, which over time nourished resistance. Both the Guomindang and the Chinese Communist Party (CCP) mounted military resistance in occupied China, generally in small-scale guerilla actions. The Guomindang confined itself to guerilla operations after 1943, but on balance proved less successful at them than the CCP, which did a better job of winning over peasant support and dodging Japanese reprisals.

Throughout China and Southeast Asia, food often ran short, and the Japanese took what they wanted. Epidemics raged. With ship and rail transport serving mainly military purposes, it became next to impossible to transport food or medicine. In Indonesia, 1 million people starved in the years 1944–1945. In the Philippines, where resistance was widespread during the Japanese occupation (1941–1945), some 330,000 starved and another 140,000 were massacred—most famously in the so-called Bataan death march in 1942, when about 9,000 captured Filipino soldiers and 1,000 Americans lost their lives. Millions of men and women were forced into slave labor for the Japanese war effort, most notoriously in 1943 on a railway-building project linking Burma and Thailand, on which 90,000 Southeast Asians—and 12,000 Allied prisoners of war—died.

In another grievous wartime abuse, the Japanese army seized hundreds of thousands of young women in Korea, China, the Philippines, and elsewhere and forced them to work throughout occupied Asia as sex slaves. Only about one-quarter of these **comfort women** survived the abuse meted out to them. A few survivors, such as Maria Rosa Luna Henson, a Filipina who was 15 years old when first raped by Japanese soldiers, wrote harrowing memoirs of their sufferings.

AFTERMATH

The war's end left much of Europe and East Asia in ruins. Millions of war refugees wandered in search of safety, food, and shelter. Allied troops liberated the remaining Nazi death camps and the shockingly emaciated survivors. Millions of Japanese struggled to get home from China. Millions of Germans who had trudged westward to get away from the Soviet Red Army huddled in camps all over Germany, dependent on Allied charity. Violent clashes continued, as people settled scores with those they had come to resent for personal or political reasons. Many thousands who had collaborated with the Germans or Japanese were casually killed. The Allies formally charged 24 top-ranking Nazis and 28 Japanese political and military leaders with war crimes and conducted trials at Nuremberg (1945–1946) and Tokyo (1946–1948). Almost all were found guilty and sentenced to death or prison.

HUMAN RIGHTS Sorrow and anger at the atrocities and crimes of World War II led to a surge of interest in ways to prevent anyone, governments especially, from doing such things again. One form this took was renewed discussion of individual human rights, usually understood to include

PUZZLES IN WORLD HISTORY

How Much Do People of Prominence Influence World History?

You can find prominent people throughout this book, but the revolutions and world wars discussed in recent chapters afford an especially good opportunity to weigh the question of how much these people matter to the course of history. For example, without Kate Sheppard's leadership of its suffrage movement, would New Zealand still have launched the international trend of granting women the vote in national elections?

We can't know with certainty the answers to such hypothetical questions. Thinking about them, however, helps us understand why history and, for that matter, current events unfold as they do. Historians today use the word *agency* when talking about how individuals and groups of people act to advance their interests and ideals on the historical stage. At times, actions like these can push history in one direction or another; in other cases, history is influenced more by larger economic or social structures that are the collective outcomes of countless daily routines of living and working.

With the Global web tying movements and peoples together around the world, the question of agency applies globally as well as locally. Kate Sheppard was part of an international community of advocates for women's suffrage as well as an organizer of New Zealand women—a key human node at the intersection of global and local networks. At the same time, larger structures have demonstrated global effects: for example, the economic productivity of the Allied Powers made a clear difference in the outcome of World War II. How can we weigh the impact of economic power against the strategic decisions made by leaders like Churchill, Roosevelt, Hitler, and Stalin?

QUESTIONS FOR DISCUSSION

1. Using an example, how do you weigh the importance of individual decisions and actions in history?
2. In today's globally connected world, do individual actions have more influence or less? Explain the reasoning behind your response.

---

at a minimum the right to life, freedom of expression, and equality before the law. The concept had deep roots in western Europe and its offshoots in North America—despite their histories of imperialism, slavery, and disenfranchisement of women. Most cultural traditions in world history, in contrast, understood rights not as held by individuals, but as shared by groups such as clans or tribes. Nonetheless, the principle of human rights held broad appeal—not least in the colonized world, where it lent moral support to independence movements. When the victorious Allies met in San Francisco in 1945 to establish an international body charged with keeping the world at peace, the United Nations, they set up a commission for human rights.

Chaired by Eleanor Roosevelt, widow of the late president, the commission issued a Universal Declaration of Human Rights in 1948, the preamble of which included these words: "[R]ecognition of the inherent dignity and of the equal and inalienable rights of all members of the human family is the foundation of freedom, justice, and peace in the world." All UN member nations voted to adopt the Declaration as a statement of principles—with the exception of the USSR and those eastern European countries under its control; Saudi Arabia, where slavery was still legal; and South Africa, which had just passed racist laws denying basic rights to its black majority.

The new emphasis on human rights was subsequently expressed in UN agreements on the rights of refugees (1951), women (1979), children (1989), and other conventions. The World War II tradition of tribunals—temporary courts—for war criminals, such as at Nuremberg and Tokyo, led to the establishment in 2002 of the International Criminal Court (ICC), based in The Hague. The ICC has opened 12 prosecutions, 10 of them of African rulers. The ICC and the UN's human rights regime generally are ongoing responses to one of the saddest legacies of World War II and its more recent echoes.

THE POST-WAR PERIOD Over time, a new normal settled in. Tens of millions of soldiers and sailors went home, shedding uniforms for civilian garb. Millions of women gave up factory or office jobs and returned to domestic roles, some willingly, some only because they were fired in favor of ex-soldiers. In some countries, including France and Italy, the wartime contributions of women translated into political rights in the form of suffrage; the United States during its post-war occupation of Japan imposed a new constitution providing for female suffrage. Food and fuel shortages eased in most countries—but slowly. Starvation stalked the USSR in 1946 and 1947; rationing of some items in the United Kingdom lasted into the 1950s.

In terms of international politics, the new normal was very different from the pre-war world. Two former great powers, Germany and Japan, were defeated, partially destroyed, and now under military occupation. The United Kingdom, although victorious, was financially ruined and dependent on the United States. Its empire—as we shall see—was more unstable than ever. The USSR, also triumphant, was exhausted, hungry, and now without the supplies formerly shipped from North America. Soviet forces remained in most of the lands they had taken from the Germans and soon created communist governments to rule them. China remained at war after the Japanese left, as the Guomindang and the CCP fought to control the ravaged country.

The United States, in contrast, with only 7 percent of the world's population, now accounted for half of its industrial production and a quarter of the global economy. It had the only nuclear weapons in the world, and the biggest air and naval forces by far. It produced most of the world's surplus food and much of its oil. Its science and technology communities, buoyed by the arrival of refugees, were the world's most dynamic and creative. Never before or since has the United States been as dominant in world politics as in late 1945. Never in the history of the world had any single state exercised greater power relative to all others. It could not last.

THE COLD WAR, 1945–1991

The **Cold War** was an ideological and strategic struggle principally between the United States and the USSR. It dominated international politics between 1945 and 1991. Its tensest moments are the closest the human race has yet come to self-destruction. Within societies, it helped

support Stalin's continuing dictatorship in the USSR and brought harsh divisions and increased regimentation to life in the United States. It divided Korea and Germany, and it added a dangerous combustibility to conflicts and civil wars in countries such as Greece, China, Korea, Vietnam, Mozambique, Angola, Ethiopia, Somalia, Chile, Guatemala, and Nicaragua. It was a genuinely global struggle. The international system no longer featured multiple great powers but became a "bipolar system," with two superpowers more formidable than all the rest: the United States and the USSR.

ORIGINS: FRACTURES IN THE ALLIANCE

In some respects, the Cold War began before World War II ended. The politics of the Allied coalition, although on balance highly successful, showed strains from early on. The biggest strategic differences, noted above, were what Stalin considered the delayed opening of a second front in Europe and, much less important, the late opening, from the American perspective, of a Soviet front against Japan in Manchuria.

SOVIET SECURITY AND EASTERN EUROPE

Other problems also helped to fracture the wartime alliance. When the war ended, the Soviet army occupied the eastern half of Europe and the eastern one-third of Germany. Stalin had no intention of leaving all this territory to its own citizens. In 1945, Stalin's strongest commitment in foreign policy was that the USSR should never again be traumatized by invasion. He wanted all of eastern Europe, including what was to become East Germany, as a buffer under his control.

Stalin's position, although partly a result of his long-standing paranoia, had a rational basis to it. The USSR had lost about 18,000 to 20,000 citizens daily during World War II, albeit many of them from Stalin's own brutalities. In mortality terms, this amounted to the equivalent of a Pearl Harbor every three hours for the duration of the war. Aware of massive invasions by Bonaparte's forces in 1812 and by Germany in 1914 and 1941, most Soviet citizens would have agreed with Stalin: it was wise to control eastern Europe so any future invasions could be challenged before reaching Soviet soil.

In 1945, Stalin annexed to the USSR small slices of Romania and Czechoslovakia to go with the Baltic countries—Latvia, Lithuania, and Estonia—and the eastern half of Poland annexed in 1940–41. In the years 1945–1948, he found willing puppets—or, in his view, loyal and reliable communists—to govern Poland, Czechoslovakia, Hungary, Romania, Bulgaria, and East Germany. He shipped huge amounts of machinery and other goods from eastern Europe, and especially from East Germany, to the USSR.

COLLECTIVE SECURITY The American leadership, however, preferred a different vision of international security. The United States, in comparison to the USSR, had suffered lightly in World War II. Led now by Harry Truman, who became president when Roosevelt died in April 1945, the U.S. government favored a system of collective security anchored by the United Nations, founded in 1945 as an improved version of the League of Nations. That and the American monopoly on nuclear weapons would theoretically ensure international security.

These incompatible visions defeated any hopes of prolonging Allied wartime cooperation. At a conference in February 1945, held at Yalta in the Soviet Crimea, Stalin, Roosevelt, and Churchill agreed to divide Germany when the war ended and to give the USSR part of the Japanese island of Sakhalin. They formally agreed on free elections in the eastern European countries controlled by the Soviet army, but in fact Stalin had no intention of permitting elections that would not return governments subservient to him. The wartime Allies continued discussions in July 1945 at Potsdam outside Berlin, but they could agree on little aside from details of the treatment of a defeated Germany and the requirement of absolute surrender from Japan. The fate of eastern Europe was the biggest unresolved issue: the United States and the United Kingdom wanted free elections rather than communist rule, but were not prepared to force the Soviet army out of the region in a new war.

Even the United States and the United Kingdom, which had collaborated effectively during the war, discovered that they had postponed some important disagreements. The greatest of those was the future of the British Empire, which Churchill dearly wished to protect but Roosevelt and Truman did not. In need of American money, food, and oil, Britain had to bow to American wishes. Churchill decisively lost a national election in July 1945, and his successors did not share his imperialist bent.

The British Empire, as we will see, would soon dwindle to insignificance.

Truman and Stalin also clashed over China's future. After Japan's defeat, China's warring factions—the communists of Mao Zedong and the nationalists, or Guomindang—stepped up their fighting in what is known as the **Chinese Civil War** (1945–1949), the final chapter in their decades-long competition for power. Each side appealed for outside help and received it, one from the USSR and the other from the United States. So the security ambitions of the two greatest powers were fundamentally at odds in eastern Europe and China.

THE WORLD ECONOMY In addition, the United States and the USSR held incompatible ambitions for the world economy. Both self-interest and ideology stood behind these ambitions. The United States emerged from the war with the world's most competitive industries and healthiest financial sector. Its leadership supported an international economy with free trade and free flows of capital, lightly regulated by international institutions such as the International Monetary Fund and what would become the World Bank. These institutions anchored the Bretton Woods system, named for the resort in New Hampshire where a conference in 1944 hammered out agreements to manage monetary policy, currency rates, and debt, with the aim of preventing a return of the Great Depression.

This capitalist vision did not suit Stalin and the USSR. Soviet ideology regarded capitalism as exploitative and as a regrettably necessary stage of history to be replaced as soon as possible by communism. Moreover, the Soviet economy was uncompetitive internationally. Its remarkable growth since 1929 had derived from the enormous, inefficient use of raw materials and the ruthless exploitation of labor. Stalin preferred to shield his economy from the pitiless competition of the market and divide the world into spheres of control, much as the Germans and Japanese had wished to do in the 1930s. Divergent self-interest and ideologies made for incompatible visions of the global economy between the United States and the USSR.

Once the Axis menace disappeared, there was nothing to bind the United States and the United Kingdom to the USSR and much to divide them. So within months after the peace settlements with Germany and Japan, the victorious Allies were allies no longer. They resigned themselves to grim competition and tried to keep it from erupting into outright war.

THE CHARACTER AND COURSE OF THE COLD WAR

Although the United States and the USSR never engaged each other in actual combat during the Cold War, except on a tiny scale, they competed fiercely. Their guiding Cold War strategies were similar: to outlast their opponents rather than to destroy them militarily. The American version of this strategy, called containment, was formulated in 1946 by George Kennan, a diplomat and student of Russian history. The **containment strategy** rested on the faith that Soviet communism would ultimately collapse if the United States prevented communism from expanding elsewhere. It reflected the confidence that people everywhere would prefer greater political freedom and material prosperity than the Soviet system seemed likely to provide. The Soviet version rested on a supposed law of history according to Marxism: that capitalism would inevitably collapse under the weight of its own contradictions—specifically, the rise of a militant, alienated working class that would recognize that its true interest required a revolution to usher in communism. Not everyone believed this doctrine in the USSR, but everyone pursuing a political career had to pretend to believe it. So although ideologically at odds, both the United States and the USSR pursued strategies of patience.

Rather than strike militarily, both tried in several ways to hasten the—theoretically inevitable—collapse of their foe. They built up their armed forces, including nuclear arsenals, in readiness for actual war. They mounted propaganda campaigns aimed at their own citizens and people all over the world. They competed for influence, especially in Europe and East Asia. And they fueled **proxy wars** in which they supported rival factions in local conflicts around the world. The most dangerous of all these undertakings was their nuclear arms race.

NUCLEAR WEAPONS Both the United States and the USSR invested heavily in their armed forces during the Cold War. The most distinctive, expensive, and risky part of this buildup was in their nuclear arsenals. From 1945 to 1949, the United States enjoyed a nuclear weapons monopoly. Then, thanks to good spies and better physicists, Stalin acquired atomic weapons in 1949. Thereafter, the United States and the USSR built thousands of nuclear bombs and missiles, enough to wipe out the human race and perhaps all life on Earth. Before long, Britain (1952), France (1960), and China (1964) were testing nuclear weapons too, although they never built arsenals anywhere near the size of the Soviet or American ones. Of the roughly 2,000 nuclear tests conducted during the Cold War, about 1,000 were American, 700 Soviet, 200 French, 45 British, and 45 Chinese. Until a treaty banned atmospheric testing in 1963, most tests—about 500—involved nuclear explosions that sprinkled toxic radiation downwind of test sites.

Nuclear weapons reinforced the Cold War strategies of patience. Everyone knew that all-out nuclear war would annihilate a large share of the human race. The superpowers did not go to war in part because their leaders understood that neither country could survive nuclear war. Once armed with nuclear weapons, neither side had any incentive to disarm or to use nuclear weapons. Their value lay in what was called deterrence. Paradoxically, both superpowers felt it was vital to their security to have giant arsenals of nuclear weapons and equally vital that the arsenals should never be used.

Nonetheless, at times, the world was a whisker away from self-annihilation. A close call came during the Cuban missile crisis of October 1962. In 1959, a revolution led by Fidel Castro succeeded in ousting a corrupt, pro-American military government in Cuba. After a failed U.S.-backed attempt to overthrow the Castro regime in 1961, the Soviets shipped some nuclear missiles to Cuba, only 90 miles from Florida. When U.S. president John Kennedy insisted on the removal of the missiles, two anxious weeks followed in which the world faced the very real possibility of a nuclear exchange. In the end, the Soviets chose to avoid the worst and removed their missiles, averting nuclear war.

Several even closer calls came as a result of malfunctions in weapons systems. In 1966, a U.S. Air Force plane accidentally dropped four hydrogen bombs—each one many times more powerful than mere atomic bombs—on the coast of southeastern Spain. None exploded. At least five times during the years 1979–1983, leaders of either the United States or the USSR were briefly convinced that enemy missiles had already launched, and they prepared to unleash a devastating counter-attack. Despite these brushes with planetary disaster, nuclear arms races continued amid occasional arms-reduction talks.

The fear of obliteration became part of everyday life during the Cold War. It gave rise to civil defense systems in North America, Europe, and the USSR, intended to improve survival chances in the event of nuclear war. These ranged from extra-deep subway systems built after 1950 in the USSR and eastern Europe to "duck-and-cover" drills for schoolchildren in the United States, adopted in the early 1950s. By the 1960s, several societies had built bomb shelters in public buildings and stocked them with food and water. Switzerland required all citizens to maintain bomb shelters in their homes.

PROPAGANDA Propaganda competition was also a regular feature of the Cold War. The United States sought to portray itself as a shining city on a hill, often using that biblical phrase, in which democracy, freedom, justice, and prosperity prevailed in the land of opportunity. The government underwrote hundreds of documentary films illustrating the merits of U.S. technology or democratic governance. It did its best to emphasize the many dark parts of Soviet life, such as the vast network of prison camps for political dissenters, the routine surveillance of citizens, the lack of political rights and economic opportunity. The U.S. government created offices specifically charged with spreading these messages, and radio stations such as Radio Free Europe that broadcast news to communist countries. They did not need to bend the truth to make life in the USSR or eastern Europe look grim, although they often did so anyway.

For its part, the USSR's propaganda machinery tried to paint communism as the wave of the future. The USSR was, or would shortly be, a workers' paradise in which equality triumphed, the exploitation normal in capitalism was banished, and everyone was content and well fed. Given actual conditions in the USSR and eastern Europe, this required routine dishonesty. The obvious gap between daily realities and official pronouncements provided citizens in communist countries with endless opportunities for sarcastic humor and, in the long run, undermined what confidence they might have had in official information.

A DIVIDED EUROPE The big prizes of the Cold War lay in Europe and East Asia. In Europe, as Stalin was

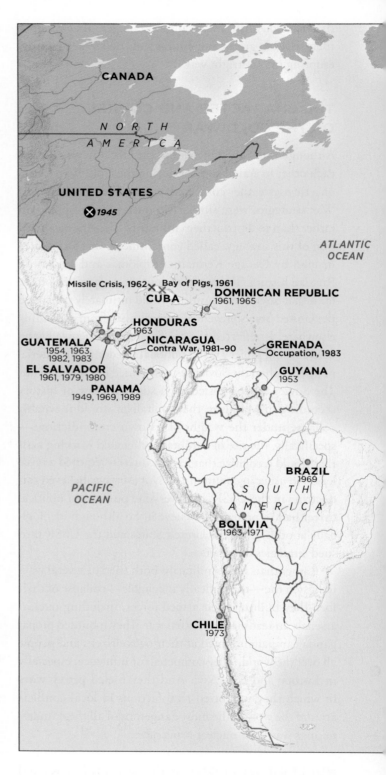

consolidating power in eastern Europe in the years 1945–1948, the new American president, Harry Truman, countered what he and most Americans regarded as Soviet aggression. He made security guarantees to Turkey and

The Cold War World, 1946–1991 The Cold War was a global contest in which the world's superpowers—the United States and the Soviet Union—asserted their power repeatedly in Africa, Asia, and Latin America. The Cold War was particularly tense in Europe, most notably Berlin, and particularly violent in East Asia, most notably Korea and Vietnam. The map shows the most important of the superpowers' military or political interventions, backing one or another faction in civil wars, coups d'état, or other forms of political struggle, with arms, money, intelligence, or training.

Greece in the Truman Doctrine announced in 1946, and helped Greek nationalists defeat an insurgent communist army in the Greek Civil War that ended in 1949. He delivered large flows of economic aid to western Europe through the Marshall Plan, begun in 1947. He offered Marshall Plan funds to countries in eastern Europe; Stalin told them to refuse it. The U.S. government also led the formation of the North Atlantic Treaty Organization (NATO, 1949), a military alliance binding the United States, Canada, and most of western Europe, intended to check Soviet ambitions.

By the end of 1948, the lines were clearly drawn. Eastern and western Europe were divided politically, ideologically, and militarily by what Winston Churchill called the iron curtain, running from the head of the Adriatic to the shores of the Baltic, and right through Germany. The one exception was Berlin, well within the Soviet zone, which by agreement was a divided city with its eastern half under Soviet control and the western half occupied by American, British, and French forces. Cold War Europe was tense, occasionally marked by crises, but generally stable, after 1948.

CRISES IN BERLIN AND EASTERN EUROPE The biggest crises in Cold War Europe were sparked by tensions in Berlin or by uprisings of East European populations against Soviet domination. The first Berlin crisis began in 1948 when Stalin, alarmed by the Marshall Plan, ordered a blockade of West Berlin, leaving 2.5 million Germans with no sources of food, fuel, or electricity. The United States and the United Kingdom responded

Berlin Airlift Boys from West Berlin cheer a U.S. cargo plane arriving with supplies during the Soviet blockade of West Berlin in summer 1948. Heavily bombed in the war, much of the city was still in rubble.

Berlin Wall Children walk along a street in Kreuzberg, West Berlin, in the 1960s. The street was divided in half by the Berlin Wall, construction on which began in 1961.

with the Berlin Airlift, flying 270,000 loads of supplies into West Berlin over 11 months until Stalin lifted the blockade.

The second Berlin crisis arose in August 1961, when East Germans at Soviet direction began to erect a wall dividing East and West Berlin, to prevent the escape of East German citizens—one-fifth of whom had already fled to West Germany and 1,500 of whom were leaving every day in Berlin. For the next several weeks, incidents at the boundary between East and West Berlin took place almost daily, and a shooting war seemed likely to break out. But cool heads prevailed, and a new reality took hold in Berlin, dominated by a wall that divided families and symbolized the imprisonment of Eastern Europeans within a political system most of them did not want. The two Berlin crises were moments of high anxiety but not violence.

Violence flared when Eastern Europeans tried to loosen the Soviet grip on their countries. The first major uprising came in East Germany in 1953. In the 24 largest cities, industrial workers led demonstrations against pay cuts and in favor of free elections. Several hundred thousand people took to the streets and in East Berlin almost toppled the government before Soviet military forces intervened, killing dozens before restoring order. In Poland in 1956, a factory workers' uprising met with a similar response and ended with 50 to 80 people dead.

A larger revolt followed later that year in Hungary.

Police fired on anti-Soviet demonstrators, leading to wider protests and an effort by the Hungarian communist government to enact reforms and loosen its ties to the USSR. That brought a full-scale invasion by the Soviet army, resisted by units of the Hungarian military and civilian militias. Some 2,500 Hungarians were killed and another 22,000 imprisoned, while 200,000 escaped to other countries. Many Hungarians expected support from the United Nations or the United States, not least because Radio Free Europe broadcasts told them it would come. It did not, because American leaders feared nuclear war.

Czechoslovak efforts at reform in 1968 prompted another Soviet invasion. The communist government in Prague, in response to citizen unrest, promised what it called socialism with a human face. In practice, that mainly meant less censorship and more personal and press freedom. That opening, sometimes called the **Prague Spring**, unleashed a torrent of public criticism of the communist system and Soviet domination. The Soviet leadership responded with troops and tanks, killing between 70 and 140 people, despite mostly passive resistance from Czechs and Slovaks.

The brutal suppression of reform efforts in Hungary and Czechoslovakia divided communist parties around the world. The French, Italian, and Finnish communist parties denounced the Soviet invasion of Czechoslovakia. The Chinese foreign minister, Zhou Enlai, called it great-power chauvinism and compared it to Hitler's

Prague Spring Massed demonstrators block Soviet tanks from moving through the streets of Prague in August 1968, during the Prague Spring uprising against Soviet control.

invasion of Czechoslovakia in 1939. The USSR never recovered the prestige it sacrificed in 1956 and 1968 by invading its allies.

MAO AND THE COMMUNIST VICTORY IN CHINA

In East and Southeast Asia the Cold War began hot, with the military victory of the Chinese Communist Party (CCP) over its Guomindang foes in the years 1945–1949. During the war with Japan (1937–1945), as we've seen, both factions fought one another as well as the Japanese. When the Japanese left, the Chinese Civil War grew fiercer.

Mao Zedong (1893–1976), one of the most consequential leaders of the twentieth century, helped organize communist guerilla forces during World War II and rose to the top of the CCP. The son of prosperous peasants from the south-central province of Hunan, he had played a small role in Sun Yatsen's revolution. While working as a grade-school history teacher in Hunan and as an assistant librarian at Peking University, he had become interested in socialism, Marxism, and revolution, and he joined the newly formed CCP in 1921.

During the war against Japan and the Chinese Civil War, the CCP offered a program shaped by Mao and calculated to appeal to China's 400 million peasants. It resembled the Taiping program of a century before: peasants should take farmland from landlords; social equality should replace Confucian hierarchy; women should live free from male oppression; discipline and morality should replace corruption and decadence; and foreigners should go home. Unlike the Taiping, the CCP program had no Christian components, but it used a different foreign idea, Marxism, to lend it prestige and coherence. Mao's main innovation within Marxism was the argument that peasants could lead a communist revolution, whereas Marx and Lenin had believed only industrial workers could do so.

The message worked: peasants increasingly supported the CCP after 1945, and its armies swelled with recruits. By the end of 1949, with some help from Stalin, the communist forces had driven the Guomindang army to the offshore island of Taiwan. China was now in the hands of Mao and his lieutenants, and was aligned with the USSR as the People's Republic of China (or PRC). The Cold War had become more complex, with two major communist powers, the USSR and the PRC, both anti-American and anti-capitalist, but neither fully trusting the other.

WAR IN KOREA Once China had joined the communist camp in 1949, the United States deepened its involvement in East Asia. The first challenge came in Korea. With Japan's defeat in 1945, the status of its former colony was thrown into doubt. By agreement between the superpowers, American forces took control south of the 38th parallel and Soviet soldiers occupied the north. Each supported a government that claimed sovereignty over all Korea and denied the legitimacy of the other. That arrangement hardened as the Cold War got chillier. Then, in 1950, with Soviet and Chinese encouragement, the North Koreans launched an invasion across the 38th parallel, starting the **Korean War**.

The UN resolved to defend South Korea and sent a joint force in July 1950. That UN army, 88 percent of which was American, drove the North Koreans back north, which prompted Mao to send in his battle-hardened infantry with Soviet air support. It drove the UN forces back south. For the U.S. Army, this retreat, costing many thousands of lives, was its worst defeat since the American Civil War. The remainder of the Korean War was one of attrition until, with Stalin's death, Soviet leaders decided to end the war, overruling Mao and the North Koreans who still hoped to win, and a cease-fire was agreed on in 1953. No peace treaty was ever signed, so North and South Korea still officially remain at war today.

Korea suffered tremendous damage as armies rampaged up and down the peninsula. The U.S. Air Force bombed North Korea relentlessly. By 1952, no significant buildings remained upright in North Korea. The war killed about 10 percent of Koreans, roughly 3 million people, mostly civilians. Some 35,000 Americans lost their lives, and perhaps 250,000 Chinese.

The Korean War hardened Cold War divisions in East Asia and indeed worldwide. The United States emerged more concerned about China as a regional threat. China, the USSR, and North Korea, now painfully well informed about the American capacity for bomber offensives, emerged more concerned about what they saw as "imperialist" military superiority. The Korean War boosted economic recovery in Japan, which served as a base for American operations, and brought the United States and Japan closer politically. Last, the Korean War showed that there were limits to U.S. power, including its reluctance to use nuclear weapons—which encouraged Mao to consider the United States a "paper tiger." The extraordinarily powerful position in world affairs that the United States had occupied at the end of World War II was already eroding.

WAR IN VIETNAM Over the course of the next 25 years it would erode further, for many reasons including American defeat in the **Vietnam War**. Vietnam had been colonized by France late in the nineteenth century and occupied by Japan during World War II. After the war, France tried to reassert its colonial rule, but in 1954 a Vietnamese force—with Chinese army participation—delivered a crushing defeat of the French at Dien Bien Phu. Negotiations followed, and the Geneva Accords of 1954 left Vietnam divided into a communist-nationalist government in the north, aligned with China and the Soviet Union, and an anti-communist state in the south, aligned with the United States. From the mid-1950s onward, the United States crept deeper and deeper into Vietnamese politics and its emerging civil war, trying to support the corrupt government in South Vietnam and prevent communists from taking over the country.

In 1964, after North Vietnamese torpedo boats and a U.S. naval ship clashed off the Vietnam coast, President Lyndon Johnson chose to escalate the struggle. By late 1967, half a million American troops were in Vietnam. The justification was the so-called **domino theory**: Johnson was concerned that if Vietnam went communist, the rest of Southeast Asia would soon follow. As in the

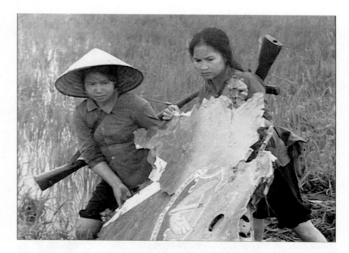

Vietnam War Two North Vietnamese fighters salvage wreckage from a downed American jet during the Vietnam War in 1968. The United States dropped countless bombs and chemical weapons on Vietnam.

Korean War, the United States did most of its damage from the air: it dropped more than three times as much bomb tonnage on Vietnam as it had used in all of World War II. The United States also used chemical defoliants such as Agent Orange on the forests of Vietnam, killing about 10 percent of the country's vegetation. Nevertheless, the United States and its allies, including the ineffective South Vietnamese government, could not prevail on the ground against determined forces employing guerilla tactics. The war became unpopular in the United States, especially among young people subject to the draft. The Americans consequently sought an acceptable way out starting in 1968 but could not find one despite years of peace negotiations. In 1975, as U.S. forces left Saigon, the capital of South Vietnam, communist forces took control of the entire country. The victors put some 250,000 South Vietnamese who had sided with the Americans into labor camps.

Roughly 1.5 million Vietnamese died in the war between 1965 and 1975, as did 59,000 Americans. No further dominoes fell, but the war cost the United States dearly in prestige and popularity around the world: it seemed a contest between David and Goliath, with the North Vietnamese showing enormous courage standing up to a superpower. The war also fueled intense political divisions in the United States.

After 1975, the Cold War in East Asia stabilized. Crises flared up, sometimes between Taiwan and the PRC, sometimes on the Korean Peninsula. But none escalated into serious fighting, and none changed the balance of power significantly.

WAR IN ANGOLA The Cold War reached from Europe and East Asia to every continent. The U.S. and Soviet governments backed rival factions in at least 50 local struggles and civil wars, providing weapons, money, training, and other support. The goal was to show resolve and win an ally or at least prevent the enemy from winning one.

Angola, a Portuguese colony for nearly 500 years, became Africa's biggest cauldron of Cold War competition. During the 1960s, several rival parties and militias eager to oust Portuguese rule emerged. But they found cooperation difficult for two reasons: one of these parties, UNITA, mainly represented the Ovimbundu people of central Angola, and other Angolans feared Ovimbundu domination; the other obstacle was the involvement of

foreign powers, whose support enabled groups to fight on even if their popularity within Angola was small. Angola's substantial oil reserve, discovered in 1955, heightened the interest of foreigners.

When a revolution in Portugal in 1974 led to the sudden end of colonial rule in Angola and the departure of 500,000 Portuguese citizens, fighting among anti-colonial factions stepped up. UNITA's main rival was a faction called the MPLA, whose leaders had proclaimed themselves communists. Angola seemed up for grabs. South Africa, Israel, and the United States supported UNITA with weapons, money, and training, while the USSR, several East European governments, and Cuba backed the MPLA. Cuba sent 40,000 soldiers in the mid-1980s to bolster the MPLA. But in 1990 and 1991, as the USSR was coming apart, the MPLA's position weakened, bringing peace talks. The local war continued, at lower intensity, even after Soviet, East European, and Cuban aid ceased. In all, about half a million—of 8 million Angolans—were killed, and another 2 to 4 million became refugees.

War in Angola A poster for the MPLA shows a young mother carrying an automatic rifle—signifying the devotion the faction called for ordinary citizens to show to the cause. Supported by the USSR, the MPLA became caught up in a proxy war against the U.S.-backed UNITA.

WAR IN AFGHANISTAN The USSR, with less capacity to fight proxy wars than the United States, used its own troops sparingly in combat except in Afghanistan. The Soviet-Afghan War (1979–1989) ranks with Korea and Vietnam as the deadliest of Cold War contests. Afghanistan, on the USSR's southern border, was an extremely poor, mainly Muslim country of 13 million in 1978 when the Afghan Communist Party staged a successful coup. Communist rule provoked widespread rebellion, particularly among committed Muslims called mujahideen ("those who follow jihad," or Islamic struggle). When they appeared likely to topple the government, the Soviet leadership, without consulting its allies, sent in the Red Army in December 1979. The invasion brought wide condemnation.

Soviet forces fought several bands of mujahideen, most

of which enjoyed support from Pakistan, Iran, China, Saudi Arabia, the United Kingdom, or the United States. Over a 10-year span, combat and massacres killed about 1.5 million, 90 percent of them Afghan civilians. In addition, about 5 to 6 million Afghans fled the violence, becoming refugees in neighboring Iran or Pakistan. After losing nearly 15,000 soldiers, the Soviets withdrew in 1989, leaving Afghanistan in turmoil.

OTHER PROXY WARS Smaller proxy wars smoldered in Latin America. For more than a century, the United States had considered Latin America its own backyard and had often intervened, especially in the Caribbean, to support or create friendly governments. After Cuba's alignment with the USSR in 1960 and 1961, the Cold War in Latin America intensified. The U.S. government supported coups and often brutal military dictatorships in Brazil, Argentina, Chile, Guatemala, the Dominican Republic, and elsewhere, as long as their leaders convincingly claimed to be anti-communist. The most sustained combat took place in Central America during the 1980s, where Nicaragua and El Salvador descended into civil wars in which the United States became deeply involved. The loss of life in Cold War conflicts in Latin America, even if one includes political murders in addition to combat, remained far smaller than in Africa or Asia.

When the Americans or Soviets committed large numbers of their soldiers, as in Korea, Vietnam, and Afghanistan, these ventures became costly and unpopular at home. But when they didn't, the costs of backing factions in conflicts in Africa, Asia, or Latin America were low, and therefore the temptation to do so was high. Governments and rebels around the world grew adept at posing as ardent communists or ardent anti-communists in order to receive flows of money and weapons. In this way, while avoiding direct conflict between themselves, the United States and the USSR inflamed conflicts in the poorer parts of the world.

THE DECLINE AND COLLAPSE OF THE USSR

In the end, the Cold War was won and lost at home. The United States survived the Cold War's pressures but suffered deep divisions over domestic campaigns in the 1950s to purge the army, the State Department, the media,

and universities of suspected communists and communist sympathizers. Divisions over the U.S. intervention in Vietnam also left lasting effects. The USSR, however, came apart under Cold War pressures. The Soviet regime collapsed during the years 1989–1991, leaving Russia and 14 smaller countries. Among the reasons the USSR crumbled were the cost of nuclear competition, the implausibility of its propaganda, and the toll of war in Afghanistan. But the biggest reasons were the USSR's failure to construct an international economy to rival the American-led one, and the tensions with China that led to an open split.

After World War II the Soviet planned economy, with few incentives for innovation, stagnated technologically except in weapons production. Its growth rate sagged after the 1960s. Soviet agriculture, handicapped by collectivization, could not reliably feed the population by the 1970s. Soviet international economic linkages, such as loans to India or bartering oil for Cuba's sugar, proved a net drain on Soviet resources. At the same time that its economy sputtered, the military commitments of the USSR expanded.

THE SINO-SOVIET RIFT The first big problem to arise was the Sino-Soviet rift. In the late 1950s, cracks began to appear between the two communist powers. Mao resented his treatment by the Soviets as a junior partner and preferred his own version of communist ideology. Mao maintained that peasants, of which China had many, could spearhead a communist transformation, whereas Soviet ideology reserved that role for industrial workers, of which China had few.

Mao also came to see Stalin's successors as disappointingly soft on capitalism. When in the years 1959–1961 Soviet premier Nikita Khrushchev tried to reduce Cold War tensions by meeting with American presidents, Mao sensed treasonous compromise. He began to compete with the USSR for influence and admiration among communists worldwide. Chinese and Soviet leaders started denouncing one another at international communist congresses. Whereas in 1956 Mao had strongly supported the Soviet invasion of Hungary, in 1968 he denounced the invasion of Czechoslovakia. By 1969, their armies were shooting at one another at points along their border.

The Sino-Soviet rift cost the USSR dearly. It had to park roughly 20 percent of its military on the long Chinese border, far from the food and supplies it needed and therefore expensive to sustain. Moreover, in 1972 when the U.S. government wanted Chinese help to make an exit from the Vietnam War, Mao saw an opportunity to bolster his position against the USSR. China suddenly welcomed warmer relations with the United States, adding new strains for the Soviets.

During the 1970s, however, an economic windfall bolstered the USSR. The production of its giant Siberian oil fields spurted in time for spikes in the world price of oil in 1973 and 1979. For a few years, the USSR could afford to import new technology, food, and other goods. But in 1985 and 1986, world oil prices—and Soviet revenues—plummeted. Moscow had grown accustomed to oil money and had no substitute when it dried up. The legitimacy of the Soviet state, long shaky, was crumbling.

GORBACHEV'S REFORMS In 1985, a vigorous new leader, **Mikhail Gorbachev**, age 54, came to power in Moscow. Gorbachev's response to the challenges facing the Soviet Union was to gamble on radical reforms. In some respects, his approach resembled those taken by self-strengtheners in the nineteenth century who recognized that their countries could not compete with the industrial powers, that time was not on their side, and that only radical economic development could stave off political defeat.

Gorbachev's version of self-strengthening featured twinned policies called *perestroika* ("restructuring") and *glasnost* ("openness"). With *glasnost*, he permitted much more free circulation of information, hoping to breathe life into a re-structured Soviet economy through innovation and technological advances. He aligned his foreign policy with these goals and sought to relax tensions with the United States and NATO, and he negotiated arms reductions treaties with President Ronald Reagan. He was trying to buy the USSR some time to reform. But his gamble did not work: the medicine killed the patient.

The Soviet system, without a vibrant economy, could not survive a freer flow of information. In 1986, at Chernobyl (in today's Ukraine), a nuclear reactor blew up, spreading lethal radiation far and wide. At first, ignoring *glasnost*, Soviet authorities tried to cover it up. But the accident was too big to hide. For Ukrainians especially, the Chernobyl meltdown and cover-up underscored the technological backwardness of the USSR and the untrustworthiness of the government.

Gorbachev's *glasnost* also allowed the expression of hopes and ambitions that did not fit with the Soviet system. It let the genie of ethnic nationalism out of the bottle. The USSR contained dozens of ethnicities, some with strong but long-underground nationalist traditions. Now Ukrainians, Lithuanians, Armenians, Georgians, and others found ways to express their national identities and—within limits—denounce Soviet oppression.

By the mid-1980s, keeping the lid on in Eastern Europe was getting harder, especially in Poland. Poles, East Germans, Czechs, and Hungarians had grown more restive, showing their frustration at

End of the Cold War Demonstrators take sledgehammers to the Berlin Wall, which fell on November 9, 1989. Soldiers watch from atop the wall, but do not intervene to stop the protesters.

stagnant living standards, acute environmental pollution, and the ever-present surveillance state. The more they learned about life in Western Europe, the more they resented their own lack of freedoms and comforts.

In 1989, Gorbachev decided to take the lid off before the pot boiled over. He signaled, gradually, that Eastern Europe's communist rulers could not count on the USSR's army to suppress demonstrations calling for greater freedoms. East Germans began to flee to West Germany, Czechs into Austria, and Gorbachev did not send in tanks. Soon the Berlin Wall, symbol of the imprisonment—as many saw it—of East European populations, was crumbling. The security forces watched the wall fall on November 9 and did not shoot. By 1991, the USSR itself dissolved. The Russian component declared itself independent of the USSR, and soon the others followed suit. A once-mighty superpower went out with a whimper, not a bang.

The Cold War ended because the strategy of containment worked. The U.S.-led international economy outpaced the Soviet one, and the material comforts and relative freedom of capitalist liberal democracy, for all its flaws, held more appeal to more people than any variant of communism did. The Cold War ended *peacefully* because Gorbachev undertook his desperate gamble to save the USSR from itself, and because he was prepared to let Eastern Europe go. He recognized that in an age of intercontinental missiles, holding Eastern Europe did not actually provide much of a buffer against enemies. Sometimes a single person makes a big difference—especially in autocratic systems.

CONCLUSION

World War II (1937–1945) and then the Cold War (1945–1991) took about 75 million lives and imperiled many more. Humankind came closer than ever before, or since, to destroying itself.

The half-century between 1937 and 1991 was defined by genuinely global struggles. The world had become a smaller place. Great powers could meddle across oceans with ease. Any small conflict had the potential to blow up. Power struggles in poor places, such as Vietnam or Angola, now attracted superpower support. All the interconnections of the Global web, and the technological and economic power they created, made international politics more unstable, unpredictable, and unsafe than before.

In particular, the uneven prosperity of the globalizing economy, combined with resentments caused largely by the settlement of World War I, encouraged the advent of nationalist regimes. Three of these, in Germany, Italy, and Japan, developed expansionist ambitions that other great powers resisted. World War II was in part a struggle over the future political and economic organization of the globe: spheres of influence dominated by nationalist states, as the Axis hoped; a more open international economy, as the United States wished; or the spread of communism, as Soviet ideologists dreamed.

After the Allies won in 1945, the world fractured along different lines. The Cold War too was a battle over the future organization of the world. Once again, in that contest, the forces favoring internationalism and globalization of the world economy won out. Bonaparte once had said that God is on the side with the bigger battalions, by which he meant bigger armies usually win. In the great political struggles of the twentieth century, the bigger, more productive, more connected economies could field bigger battalions. They could make more of whatever was needed to prevail in international politics, whether oil, tanks, and aircraft, or just plentiful ordinary consumer goods—such as the razor blades that Goering mocked.

CHAPTER REVIEW

KEY TERMS

World War II (p. 798)
Axis (p. 799)
Allies (p. 801)
Battle of Stalingrad
(p. 805)
Hiroshima and Nagasaki
(p. 806)

Holocaust (p. 812)
comfort women (p. 817)
Cold War (p. 819)
Chinese Civil War
(p. 820)
containment strategy
(p. 821)
proxy wars (p. 821)

Prague Spring (p. 825)
Mao Zedong (p. 825)
Korean War (p. 826)
Vietnam War (p. 826)
domino theory (p. 826)
Mikhail Gorbachev
(p. 829)

Go to INQUIZITIVE
to see what you've
learned—and learn what
you've missed—with
personalized feedback
along the way.

REVIEW QUESTIONS

1. Describe the shared ambitions and beliefs behind Germany, Italy, and Japan's expansionist pursuits.

2. What four overlapping wars and four theaters made up World War II?

3. What key moments caused the tide of the war to turn against the Axis powers?

4. Compare and contrast the cooperation among the Allied powers with the cooperation among the Axis powers.

5. What economic, natural resource, and labor advantages did the Allies have over the Axis powers during World War II?

6. Which groups did Hitler's extermination program target, and why?

7. Compare and contrast the level of home-front mobilization in Germany, Japan, the Soviet Union, the United Kingdom, and the United States.

8. Explain what happened to people of Japanese ancestry living in the United States and Canada during World War II.

9. In terms of international politics, what was different about the post-war world?

10. Discuss the competing U.S. and Soviet visions of international security after World War II.

11. What were the guiding Cold War strategies of the United States and the USSR?

12. In which cities or countries did the biggest crises in Cold War Europe erupt, and why?

13. What was Mao Zedong's program during the Chinese Civil War, and to whom did it appeal?

14. What were the main international consequences of the Korean War?

15. Whom did the Soviets support with their invasion of Afghanistan, and who supported their enemies, the mujahideen?

16. Why did the Cold War end, and why did it end peacefully?

FURTHER READING

Svetlana ALEXIEVICH, *The Unwomanly Face of War* (2017). Narratives of the lives of women who served in the Soviet armed forces during World War II.

Anonymous, *A Woman in Berlin* (2016). First published in the early 1950s, this diary details the grim experiences of a young woman in the weeks after the Soviet army marched into Berlin.

Pierre ASSELIN, *Vietnam's American War* (2017). A well-researched account of how North Vietnam prevailed over the United States in the Vietnam War.

Paul KENNEDY, *Engineers of Victory* (2013). A very clear analysis of how the Allies learned to do things better during the course of World War II.

Xiaobing LI, *The Cold War in East Asia* (2017). A synthesis ... on the Chinese role.

Richard OVERY, *Why the Allies Won* (1995). A readable and insightful analysis of World War II.

S.C.M. PAINE, *The Japanese Empire: Grand Strategy from the Meiji Restoration to the Pacific War* (2017). A brief narrative and analysis of Japan's rise and overreach.

Peipei QIU, *Chinese Comfort Women: Testimonies from Imperial Japan's Sex Slaves* (2013). A study based on recent and disturbing interviews of women who survived terrible ordeals.

O. Arne WESTAD, *The Cold War: A World History* (2017). A massive and detailed work by a dean of Cold War historians.

Vladislav ZUBOK, *A Failed Empire* (2007). A good study of the USSR during the Cold War.

CHRONOLOGY

Decolonization and the Rise of East Asia

1945 to 1991

> It doesn't matter whether the cat is black or white,
>   as long as it catches mice.
>
> —Deng Xiaoping (1962)

Deng Xiaoping, the leader of communist China from 1978 to about 1995, was a practical man. His reference to cats (above) was an assertion that ideological stripes matter less than effectiveness. What he wanted to effect was a transformation of China into a global power, and he did more than anyone else to achieve that. Deng and his allies within the Chinese Communist Party (CCP) revolutionized China by emphasizing practicality. The resulting changes in East Asia were as great as any since the Qing conquests of the seventeenth century. The changes to the global balance of power were as great as any since the Industrial Revolution in the nineteenth century and the rise of Britain, Germany, and the United States.

1989
Tiananmen Square massacre

1992
China's stock exchange re-opens

The Rise of East Asia This 2016 streetscape in Shanghai, China, shows the ongoing transformation of East Asia's major cities as the region experienced rapid economic growth.

833

FOCUS QUESTIONS

1. What broad factors opened the way to decolonization in the decades after World War II?

2. Why did East Asian nations experience strong economic advances in the late decades of the twentieth century?

3. How did the economic rise of East Asia shift the balance of the Global web?

Usually, shifts in the global distribution of wealth and power are gradual and work themselves out over centuries. But not always. This chapter concerns two sudden shifts in world balances of power under way since World War II—and still afoot today. Just when the United States and the USSR were emerging as Cold War superpowers in the 1940s, colonial empires around the world began to crumble. Asians and Africans found new ways to challenge imperial rule. They succeeded in raising its costs beyond the thresholds that imperial peoples and governments were willing to pay. That brought a spurt of decolonization starting in 1947, a scramble from empire every bit as hasty as the scrambles for empire of the late nineteenth century. Roughly 100 new countries emerged within three decades.

Decolonization opened the door to the second sudden shift, what we might call the rise of the East. Historians for generations have wrestled with what they sometimes call the rise of the West, referring to the accumulation of wealth and power by Atlantic European countries and eventually the United States, Canada, and Australia—a process that began in the sixteenth century and accelerated with industrialization in the nineteenth. Since 1960 or so, a rebalancing of global wealth and power has been under way, led by the rise of East Asia. The centerpiece was the

tremendous economic growth in Japan, South Korea, Taiwan, Singapore, and Hong Kong—the "Asian tigers," as journalists and economists called them—and, after 1980, in China.

Just as colonization of much of the world was important in the rise of the West between 1500 and 1914, so decolonization was a crucial pre-condition to the rise of the East. The first step came with the destruction of Japan's empire in World War II. Liberation from Japanese colonial rule was necessary before South Korea and Taiwan could transform themselves into rich countries. Likewise, Singapore shed British rule before becoming a "tiger." Hong Kong, however, became rich while still a British colony—a unique case and the exception that proves the rule.

In the story of the rise of East Asia, China takes center stage. From the 1840s to 1931, foreigners exploited its resources and menaced its independence but never formally colonized the country. Then in Manchuria starting in 1931 and much of the rest of China beginning in 1937, Japan conquered and in effect ruled most of the country. After Japan's empire collapsed in 1945, China could begin its remarkable self-transformation from a weak and divided country to a great power. That process started under Mao Zedong, who led the CCP's re-unification of China in 1949. But the major advances in China's wealth and power came after Mao's death, when Deng Xiaoping took the helm by 1980.

As in the heyday of the Tang and Song dynasties (roughly the seventh through the twelfth centuries), East Asia now became an interconnected space. After 1980 it was the most dynamic part of the global economy, exchanging goods, technologies, and ideas at a feverish pace, thanks to new connections both within East Asia and between the region and the wider world. And its engine, China, engineered the largest shift in global power politics so far in the twenty-first century.

DECOLONIZATION AS A GLOBAL MOVEMENT

With the formation of a truly global web in the sixteenth century, overseas empires became easier to create and therefore more numerous. But they were not always easy to keep: there were four pulses of decolonization in recent centuries, all of them linked to major international conflicts.

THE LONG ARC OF DECOLONIZATION, 1776–1991

The first pulse of decolonization came between 1776 and 1826 with the liberation of the Americas from European imperial rule during the Atlantic revolutions (see Chapter 21). This burst of decolonization led to the creation of roughly 20 new countries in the Americas. The term *decolonization* can also be applied to the demise of the Habsburg, Ottoman, and Romanov (Russian) empires during the years 1917–1923, brought on by the intense pressures of World War I. As we've seen, this led to the creation of eight new countries in east-central Europe and to an independent Turkey. In Russia's empire, decolonization resulting from the Romanov dynasty's collapse in 1917 was temporary: by 1925, Lenin and his successors put most of the empire back together again as the USSR. The financial and manpower demands of World War I also contributed mightily to the creation of the Irish Free State (Eire) in 1922. After three years of guerilla war and civil disobedience between 1918 and 1921, Irish revolutionaries negotiated independence from an exhausted United Kingdom. In these two pulses of decolonization, during the periods 1776–1826 and 1917–1923, big wars put events into motion. They put pressures on imperial powers, giving anti-imperial forces opportunities they seized.

The third—and biggest—pulse of decolonization came between 1945 and 1975, and it is the focus here. Colonized peoples took advantage of the material pressures that World War II and the Cold War placed on several more empires, notably the Japanese, British, French, Dutch, and Portuguese. This time about 100 new countries emerged, mainly in Africa, Asia, and the Caribbean.

The fall of the USSR was a Cold War story more than a decolonization story. But the USSR too was a vast empire, and when it lost its grip on Eastern Europe in 1989 and then dissolved in 1991, roughly 20 countries acquired independence. Poland, Czechoslovakia, Hungary, Romania, and Bulgaria were officially independent already, but in reality they were controlled by the USSR in all important matters between the late 1940s and the late 1980s. So the destruction of the Soviet empire, during the years 1989–1991, constitutes the fourth great pulse of decolonization.

THE BIG PULSE, 1947–1975

Empires of one sort or another had been commonplace around the world for millennia; but in the twentieth century, empire suddenly—at least on the time scale of millennia—seemed less inevitable and more illegitimate. The mobilizing rhetoric of the Allies in the World Wars—self-determination of peoples—had something to do with this change in perspective. So did the sorry record of colonial rule on the ground in Africa, Asia, and the Caribbean. In 1960, the United Nations declared colonialism a violation of human rights.

The moral legitimacy of empire was slipping after 1945, but more important were the shifts in power relations between colonized and colonizers. Within many colonies, those people who chafed most under colonial rule organized themselves into political parties or guerilla bands. Anti-colonial movements sometimes made common cause across borders, sharing expertise, weapons, or money. Many future leaders of anti-colonial movements learned about fighting wars during World War II. Others learned about law, politics, and culture as students in British or French universities, and they used their new knowledge to advance the cause of independence. All this gave anti-colonial movements more tools than they had wielded before 1940. Over time, more and more colonized peoples raised the costs of continued empire to colonizers.

For example, anti-colonial leaders seized upon the Allies' rhetoric of liberation from tyranny in World War II, embodied in the Atlantic Charter of 1941 signed by Roosevelt and Churchill. Its third clause endorsed the principle that all peoples should be free to choose their form of government. Although Churchill did not intend that to apply to colonized peoples of the British Empire, the text makes no exceptions, and people in Asian and African colonies logically argued that it should apply to them too.

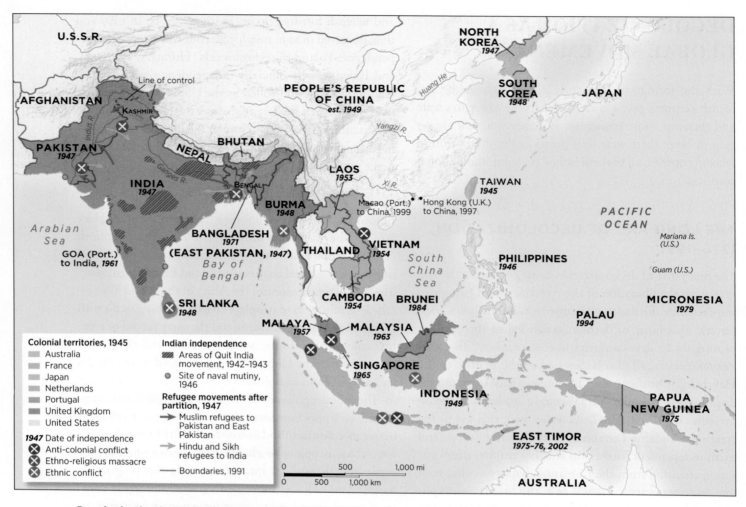

Decolonization in South and Southeast Asia The third pulse of decolonization got under way in the late 1940s and began in Asia. Anti-colonial movements in Indonesia and Vietnam won independence by militarily facing down the colonial powers—the Netherlands and France, respectively. Britain's exit from South Asia was negotiated, but the formation of India as primarily Hindu and of Pakistan as primarily Muslim brought intense violence and massive refugee movements. Independence for East Timor and Bangladesh required victory first over European colonial powers and then over rival local powers.

And while colonized peoples were getting stronger, better organized, and more committed to ending empires, imperial powers were struggling with resources and resolve. World War II had drained the manpower and treasuries of most of the combatants. Defeat in 1945 destroyed Japan's empire. Meanwhile, the effort required for victory in 1945 exhausted Britain and France both. They began to lose the determination necessary to maintain empires, partly because they were strapped for military manpower and money, but mainly because colonized peoples were raising the costs of continued empire. Public support for imperialism faded.

Beyond the impacts of World War II, two other aspects of the Global web of the mid-twentieth century,

one economic and the other both technological and cultural, also propelled the **third pulse of decolonization**. Colonial rule depended financially on mines and plantations. The sale of gold, diamonds, and mineral ores, and crops such as cotton or jute, made the money that supported colonial governments. Those ores and crops normally traveled by rail to seaports for export. Asian and African railway workers and dock workers thus acquired power over colonial economies: if they refused to work, exports and revenues would both cease. By the late 1940s, strikes among rail and dock workers became increasingly common—undermining the finances of colonial rule.

In addition, the speed with which information now traveled helped spur the process of decolonization. By the 1920s, newspapers used the telegraph networks to report on important events within hours of their occurrence. During the 1930s and 1940s, radio and newsreels—short films of current events—carried news around the world quickly and reached the great majority who could not read. By the 1960s, television added to the flows of information—and of inspiration. When Indians achieved independence in 1947, Indonesians—and many others—were watching. When Algeria won an independence war (1956–1962), everyone was watching. Images of anti-colonial successes coursed through the pathways of the Global web, hurrying the end of empire. Let's look at a few examples.

ASIA: INDIA AND INDONESIA

The movements for decolonization in Asia, Africa, and the Caribbean were all connected. Many activists had studied together in their youth in Lisbon or London. Some had attended the same pan-African congresses or other international gatherings. After 1945 they offered what support they could to one another, as they recognized a common struggle against imperial rule. Everyone keen on ending colonialism paid attention to India, the most populous of all the world's colonies.

INDIA At midnight on August 14, 1947, some 400 million people cast off British colonial rule for independence as the countries of India and Pakistan. Ceylon and Burma, longtime British colonies administratively linked to British India, became independent in 1948. (Ceylon changed its name to Sri Lanka in 1972, and Burma changed to Myanmar in 1989.)

As we've seen, anti-colonial nationalism had a deep tradition in British India. After 1919, Gandhi and the Indian National Congress made it a mass movement. After 1935, British legislation put Indians in more and more government posts and set colonial India on a path toward independence. World War II shortened that path.

India contributed mightily to Britain's efforts in World War II. Several million Indians volunteered for military service, and 87,000 of them died in the war. In summer 1945, Britain's Indian Army counted 2.5 million men, the largest all-volunteer army in world history. Most of them fought against the Japanese in Southeast Asia, some against German and Italian forces in North Africa, and a few in Europe.

At the same time that millions of Indians volunteered to fight for the British Empire, World War II sharpened opposition to British rule in India. Some 40,000 Indians captured by the Japanese chose to switch sides and fight for Japan, or—as they saw it—against the British Empire in Asia. One independence leader, Subhas Chandra Bose, visited Axis leaders in Berlin and Tokyo, and organized Indian forces against Britain. To the British, he was a traitor; to many Indians, a national hero. Most leaders of the Indian National Congress—now operating as a political party—refused to cooperate with the war effort from late 1942 on. Following Gandhi and the British-trained lawyer **Jawaharlal Nehru**, who since the late 1920s had emerged as the second most important figure in Congress, they demanded immediate independence as the price of their cooperation. Britain's viceroy agreed to promise liberation only after the war. Gandhi called that promise "a post-dated cheque on a crumbling bank," not to be trusted.

Indian Independence Residents gather en masse in central Delhi to celebrate the declaration of Indian independence on August 15, 1947.

Instead, Gandhi called for Britain to "quit India" immediately, despite the risk of Japanese invasion. Britain's wartime prime minister, Churchill, who had served in India as a young man, was determined that India should remain British. Relying on loyal police and Indian Army units, the British responded to the Quit India movement by arresting over 100,000 Indians in 1942 and 1943, including Gandhi, Nehru, and all the top leadership of the Congress Party. At the same time, British authorities did little to address a famine in Bengal that killed 2 to 3 million Indians in 1943 and 1944. British rule in India was now more unpopular than ever.

As the war wound down, everyone attentive to politics knew independence was coming, especially when Churchill was voted out of office in July 1945. The Congress Party tried to represent all Indians, not just Hindus, but many Muslims regarded it as deaf to their interests. Muslims, who formed about a quarter of India's population in 1941, had taken the opportunity to fill many administrative positions open by 1943 as a result of the imprisonment of so many Congress Party

Gandhi and Jinnah Gandhi, leader of the Quit India movement, and Jinnah, leader of the Muslim League, pose together for a photograph at talks in Mumbai in 1944. But Gandhi's and Jinnah's efforts at cooperation could not avert the violence of partition.

Partition Conflict between Hindus and Muslims over the partition of India led to widespread violence and upheaval. Here police in Calcutta use tear gas to suppress rioters attempting to set fire to a Hindu temple in 1948.

members. This deepened the divide between the Muslim and Hindu communities. The **Muslim League**, headed by the cosmopolitan and wealthy lawyer Muhammad Ali Jinnah, grew increasingly committed to the idea of a divided post-colonial India with a Muslim state and a Hindu one.

Jinnah and South Asia's Muslims generally feared they would be oppressed by the Hindu majority if independence yielded a united India. Most of them wanted their own state, where they could be in the majority. Many Sikhs (about 3 percent of India's population) wanted their own state too. Many Hindus, however, objected to the idea of a fragmented India and opposed Muslim and Sikh ambitions. Almost everyone wanted independence, but they couldn't agree on how to define the nation.

By this point, most British politicians were almost as eager for Indian independence as Indians were. Indians had succeeded in making India ungovernable for Britain. This became clear in early 1946, when a mutiny among Indian naval units showed that Britain could no longer rely on the loyalty of Indian military manpower. Without it, Britain could not continue as an imperial power in South Asia. Soon the government in London appointed a lawyer who had never been to India to draw a line on the map, based on religious identities, as a border between what were to become two countries.

The lawyer was given a month to draw the line: getting it done fast was more important to all parties than getting it done well. No line, however well drawn, could have

tidily divided Hindu from Muslim from Sikh in India. On August 14–15, 1947, India and Pakistan were born. Nehru, whose appetite for politics far exceeded Gandhi's, became prime minister of India, while Jinnah led Pakistan. Gandhi, the pacifist, was murdered in 1948 by an assassin who considered him too sympathetic to Muslims and Sikhs.

The partition of British India into two countries provoked a bloodbath. Roughly 1 million people died in violent clashes. Another 10 to 17 million became refugees, fleeing to one or another side of the new borders to avoid persecution or worse. India and Pakistan quickly became lasting enemies, fighting three wars since 1947 and perpetually skirmishing over Kashmir, a majority Muslim region claimed by India. Pakistan was born in two parts, one in the Indus valley and one in East Bengal, an arrangement that Bengalis often likened to colonial rule. In 1971, Pakistan's Bengalis seceded, fought a brief independence war with India's help, and created their own country, Bangladesh.

Independence in Burma and Sri Lanka brought conflicts too. It plunged Burma into a brief civil war among factions hoping to rule the new country. Sri Lanka suffered from ethnic division between Sinhalese and Tamil groups—the Tamils mainly descended from Indian immigrants. That rivalry escalated into civil war in the 1980s.

INDONESIA Indonesia's path to independence was no less rocky than India's. The Dutch had acquired a foothold on this sprawling archipelago of 13,000 islands in the seventeenth century. By 1940, the Dutch East Indies had 70 million people divided by religion, language, and ethnicity—among other things. Muslims were the most numerous religious community, maybe three-quarters of the population; but many Indonesians were Hindu, Buddhist, Christian, or followers of one of several indigenous faiths. Indonesia was then and is now one of the most diverse places in the world, with hundreds of languages spoken and some 600 ethnicities. Nationalism and unity did not come easily there.

Early anti-colonial groups had formed in the 1920s. These included an Islamic group, a communist organization, the Congress of Indonesian Women, and a nationalist political party, the PNI (or Partai Nasional Indonesia). The PNI mainly represented traditional landed elites on the most populous island, Java, but claimed to speak for all Indonesians. Its founder and moving spirit was **Sukarno**, who like most Javanese went by a single name.

Sukarno came from an aristocratic Javanese Muslim family on his father's side, but one that had fallen on hard times. His mother was from a high-caste Hindu family. Sukarno trained as an architect and spoke four Indonesian languages as well as Dutch, English, French, Arabic, and Japanese. His greatest talent, though, was political flexibility.

Sukarno's agitation for independence in the late 1920s earned him a prison term. He collaborated eagerly with the Japanese occupation (1941–1945), helping recruit millions of Indonesians as essentially slave laborers for work on railroads, bridges, and airfields throughout Japanese-occupied Southeast Asia. He also helped Japan secure access to Indonesia's natural resources, notably bauxite, from which aluminum is made, and oil. In return, the Japanese helped Sukarno to denounce Dutch colonialism and to spread his version of Indonesian nationalism—together with his own fame and prestige.

The Japanese occupation took a heavy toll on Indonesia. Malaria flared up, and food requisitioning for Japan's army led to starvation. Thousands of Indonesian women, and dozens of Dutch women, were forced into sex slavery as comfort women for Japanese troops. In 1944 and 1945, roughly a million Indonesians died from these and other hardships. The Japanese departed hastily in the summer of 1945, leaving Sukarno and other prominent collaborators in a tight spot.

With the Japanese going and the Dutch not yet returning, some Indonesian nationalists thought the moment of liberation had come. Sukarno was unsure; but after one night held hostage by a fervently nationalist youth group, he agreed to declare independence. He also declared himself president.

In September 1945, the Dutch returned, intending to restore colonial rule. They negotiated with many different groups, following the old strategy of divide-and-rule. They succeeded in rallying people in the outer islands against Javanese domination, Sukarno, and the PNI. Indonesia in the next few years was racked by political violence.

In 1948, the Dutch deployed 150,000 soldiers to try

Indonesian Independence (Left) Sukarno, as president of an independent Indonesia, addresses a crowd of demonstrators in 1950. (Right) Peasants from rural parts of Indonesia—photographed here being trained as guerilla fighters in 1947—were a key component of the opposition to Dutch colonial rule.

to impose their will. Sukarno and the PNI responded with guerilla warfare. Both the UN and the United States denounced the Dutch action and called for a cease-fire. The U.S. government threatened to stop delivering food and fuel to the Netherlands under the Marshall Plan. The Dutch government was too poor and too indebted to defy that threat.

The Dutch could not turn back the clock in Indonesia without American approval. In 1946, the United States had cautiously supported the Dutch attempt to restore colonial power in Indonesia. But by 1949, with communists about to take over China, American policy makers judged that the best bet for resisting communism—the dominant consideration in Washington—was a resolutely non-communist independent country. The PNI and Sukarno, despite his wartime collaboration with the Japanese, fit the bill. Once the Americans made it clear they preferred Sukarno to continued Dutch colonialism, the Dutch gave up and negotiated a quick exit from Indonesia.

So in 1949 Indonesia acquired the independence the PNI had claimed since 1945, thanks to the disruptions of World War II, the persistence and opportunism of Sukarno and the PNI, the weakness of the Netherlands, and the intervention of the United States. The PNI and Sukarno now undertook an ambitious experiment in democracy in an ethno-linguistic patchwork of a country. Indonesian nationalism proved too weak to overcome the country's diversity. By 1957, the democratic experiment was on hold and the country was an autocracy, with Sukarno and the army in charge.

AFRICA: GHANA AND ALGERIA

In a broad sense, the story of independence in Africa followed the same lines as in Asia. African anti-colonial nationalists found ways to band together and use what tools they had either to negotiate or to fight their way to freedom. In the late 1940s, France and Britain still intended to keep their African colonies and develop them to strengthen their empires. But by 1956 or 1957, Africans had persuaded them to change their plans.

Let's look at a couple of examples: Ghana and Algeria. Ghana was among the first African countries to achieve independence and among those that took the most peaceful of roads. Algeria was among the last, and it took the most violent road of all.

GHANA The West African peoples of the Gold Coast, as Ghana was called in colonial times, mainly spoke languages of the same group, called Akan. But they did not think of themselves as Akan, or Gold Coasters, or Africans. More local identities, based on clan and village, prevailed. As in Indonesia, national identity did not come easily here.

The British had colonized the Gold Coast beginning in the 1870s and controlled it by 1900. By the 1920s, the Gold Coast economy hinged largely on cocoa production. It became Britain's most prosperous African colony—indeed, Britain's model African colony.

For the Gold Coast, World War II was a lot farther away than for India or Indonesia, but it nonetheless provided a catalyst for independence. Tens of thousands of volunteers from the Gold Coast fought in British armies. To secure fuller cooperation in wartime, British authorities created an advisory body of Gold Coast Africans called the Legislative Council. Its members worked with the British rulers on a new constitution that would delegate some authority to Africans. Almost everyone still thought British rule in the Gold Coast would last far into the future.

But as the war ended, the Gold Coast came to simmer with discontent. The colonial government infuriated peasant farmers when it killed over 2 million cocoa trees to try to stop a crop disease. Many former soldiers, of whom the Gold Coast counted about 63,000, felt dissatisfied with the reward for their military service in World War II on behalf of the British Empire—they wanted bigger pensions. School graduates also stewed with resentments. The Gold Coast in 1950 enrolled 44 percent of school-age children in school, an extraordinarily high percentage for colonial Africa. But schooling raised hopes for jobs and careers that in the late 1940s too often went unfulfilled. Unemployment climbed. Riots broke out in several towns and cities, particularly the capital of Accra.

Broad discontent led in 1947 to the formation of a new political party, the United Gold Coast Convention (UGCC), the first in Africa to adopt independence as its stated goal. Its members were British-educated elites, eager to negotiate better terms within colonial structures, eventually leading to self-rule—not unlike the Indian National Congress in its early decades.

The UGCC's gradualist ambitions did not suit one of its members, **Kwame Nkrumah**, who did not wish to wait for freedom. Nkrumah looms large over Ghana's history. Born in 1909, he came from a poor and illiterate family in a seaside village in the southwest of the Gold Coast. He excelled in Catholic schools and in the late 1920s became a schoolteacher himself. But his intellectual gifts caught the attention of other West Africans who recommended that he go overseas for further education. With money from relatives, Nkrumah enrolled at Lincoln University near Philadelphia. There he grew interested in pan-African ideas in circulation among the African American intelligentsia and came to envision an Africa united and free from foreign rule. In late 1945, having gone to London for PhD work in anthropology, he organized a pan-African congress in England, where he met many prominent African and Caribbean politicians and intellectuals. He gave up his studies for politics, hoping to liberate Africa—beginning with his homeland.

Nkrumah returned to the Gold Coast in 1947 after 12 years abroad. He instantly joined the UGCC and almost as quickly grew impatient with its gradualism. He founded a rival party, the Convention People's Party, to demand independence "now." He sought to appeal not to the intellectuals and well-to-do of the Gold Coast, but to former soldiers, dock workers, students, market women (as the women who dominate West African open-air markets are called), and other groups he thought he could organize politically. He knew how threadbare Britain was in 1947, and he understood the opportunity that presented.

Nkrumah had studied the arts of political organization, particularly the examples from India, and developed his own program of non-violent agitation—demonstrations, strikes, boycotts—that he called Positive Action. His talents as a political orator and organizer had few rivals within the Gold Coast. Even though the British jailed him, he and his party easily won an election in 1951, the first in African history open to adult male franchise. At this point, the British authorities either had to work with Nkrumah or face massive unrest in their model African colony.

They released Nkrumah from prison and invited him to form a cabinet. In effect, he led a colonial government for the next several years. He and his supporters negotiated an orderly transition to independence, officially achieved in 1957. British policy makers judged it too difficult to hold on to the Gold Coast. A constitutional handover of power suited them—if power could be handed to someone willing to maintain business and military ties with Britain. Nkrumah could seem such a person when he wished.

Kwame Nkrumah Officials of the newly independent Ghanaian government carry its new prime minister, Nkrumah, on their shoulders in celebration in 1957.

Ghana—the name was chosen to honor West Africa's ancient kingdom—was the first sub-Saharan African country to slip the bonds of colonial rule. Thanks to the pressure groups organized by Nkrumah and his colleagues, and thanks to British willingness to withdraw, the process happened peacefully with few disturbances of any size after 1951. A wave of hope and optimism splashed over Ghana and indeed all Africa. As Nkrumah put it in a speech to a big crowd at the moment of Ghanaian independence, "We are going to demonstrate to the world, to the other nations, that we are prepared to lay our own foundation. . . . We are going to create our own African personality and identity. It is the only way we can show the world that we are ready for our own battles."

The aftermath proved disappointing. Nkrumah hoped the liberation of Ghana would be only the first step toward the independence of all Africa and the formation of a unified African federation: a united states of Africa. Unity proved elusive, though, even within Ghana. Soon Nkrumah was detaining political opponents and censoring newspapers. Cocoa prices nosedived, and unrest bubbled up. By the early 1960s, Nkrumah banned all but his own party and had himself declared "president for life." Unhappy army officers ousted him in a coup d'état in 1966.

The discouraging record of Ghana between 1957 and 1966 was partly a matter of Nkrumah demonstrating the truth of the old saying that "power corrupts." It was also

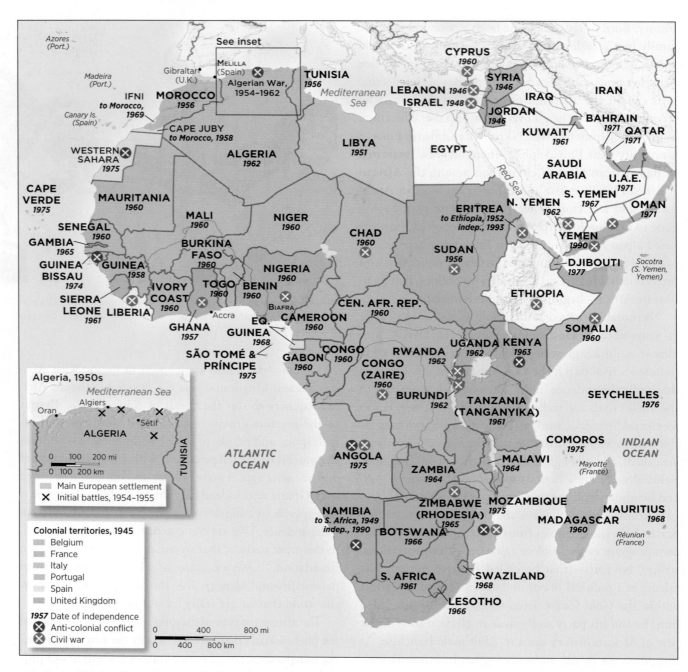

Decolonization in Africa and the Middle East The third pulse of decolonization created almost 50 new countries between 1956 and 1975. Independence involved warfare—particularly in former Portuguese colonies, but also in Algeria and Madagascar and, on a smaller scale, Kenya. Political conflicts with ethnic or religious components were widespread in Africa's newly independent countries, and exploded into warfare most lethally in Nigeria, Angola, and Mozambique.

something else: African nationalists—indeed, Asian ones too—promised too much when rallying people against colonial rule. As a motivational tool it made sense to claim that independence would bring peace, justice, and prosperity. But it set up post-colonial rulers for failure, whether in Ghana or Indonesia, when ordinary people

found that independence would not necessarily enable them to get jobs or feed their families.

ALGERIA Algeria's independence struggle took a different, darker form than Ghana's. French armies had claimed Algeria beginning in 1830. Thousands of French,

Spanish, and Italians crossed the Mediterranean to settle in Algeria. They often benefited from the colonial government's efforts to push native Algerians off their land. As we've seen, Algeria became a settler colony, and by the 1950s settlers accounted for 10 percent of the population of 10 million. Settlers, known as *pieds-noirs* ("black feet" in French), owned a quarter of the land—including all the best farmland.

Algeria's indigenous population was overwhelmingly Muslim and mainly Arabic-speaking. Large numbers of them learned French, and some tried to advance within the confines of the colonial system. But French Algeria held limited promise for Algerians. Still, few agitated for independence until after World War II.

Once again, the war proved galvanizing. There was no heavy fighting in Algeria, but the rhetoric of the Allies—including the right of all peoples to self-determination—was widely heard. At least 200,000 Algerians served with French armies in the years 1943–1945, fighting in Italy and in the liberation of France from German occupation. Their experiences pushed many of them to think hard about how to liberate Algeria from France.

In May 1945, news of Hitler's defeat prompted a celebration in the eastern Algerian city of Sétif. Somehow—accounts differ—shooting broke out and about 100 *pieds-noirs* were killed. Local police and vigilantes reacted by killing several thousand Muslim Algerians, the great majority of whom had done nothing more than celebrate the Allies' triumph over Nazism.

As the news of Sétif spread, millions of Algerians changed their minds about French rule. Liberation organizations sprouted. In 1954 one of them, known as the FLN (short for "national liberation front" in French), declared a war for independence—a few months after French armies, made up substantially of Algerian soldiers, were crushed at Dien Bien Phu in Vietnam. In Algeria and throughout the French Empire, people followed the news from Vietnam and recognized French weakness.

The **Algerian war for independence** lasted from 1954 to 1962 and cost a million lives. France fought hard to keep Algeria, the most important part of the French Empire. The French fought to protect the *pieds-noirs,* who were in legal fact French citizens, and to preserve its strong business and economic ties to Algeria. The forces of the FLN proved equally committed and just as ruthless.

The French Army—bolstered by tens of thousands of Muslim Algerians, known as *harkis,* who fought against

Algerian War Guards of the French Foreign Legion capturing FLN fighters during the Algerian war for independence. The controversial and bloody war lasted for eight years, with the tenacity of the FLN ultimately achieving independence.

Algerian independence—fared well in combat. But the FLN would not quit. They outlasted the French, who by 1962 had already given up in Vietnam, and conceded independence to all their African colonies, including Algeria's neighbors, Morocco and Tunisia. Fighting on in Algeria was very controversial in France and led to a constitutional crisis and almost to civil war. In the end, a French leader with strong imperialist and nationalist leanings, Charles de Gaulle, decided to quit Algeria in order to save France. The FLN and Algerians had successfully made it clear that the costs to France of continued war would outweigh the benefits of protecting the *pieds-noirs* and preserving French Algeria.

The gruesome war had a gruesome aftermath. Some 800,000 of the million *pieds-noirs,* told to choose between "a suitcase and a coffin" by the FLN, left Algeria for France. France under de Gaulle refused entry to *harkis,* leaving them to the mercy of the FLN, whose supporters murdered about 70,000 and brutalized many more, often by cutting off their noses.

VIOLENCE AND LEGACIES OF DECOLONIZATION

Between 1945 and 1975, the process of decolonization swept away the Japanese and European colonial empires. Japan lost its empire in East and Southeast Asia by losing World War II. For the other imperial powers, the fundamental story was that anti-colonial nationalists found ways to raise the costs of continued colonialism above the

CONSIDERING THE EVIDENCE

Sankara Condemns Neo-Colonialism

In 1983, a 33-year-old military officer named Thomas Sankara launched a successful coup against the president of Upper Volta in West Africa, whom he condemned as a French puppet. He promptly re-named the country Burkina Faso, or "Land of Incorruptible People." While the first generation of African nationalists had declared political independence from European colonialism, Sankara and others of his generation sought economic independence from neo-colonialism—the control exercised by the United States, the Soviet Union, and other nations through trade regulations, monetary policy, foreign aid, and loans. Under Sankara's leadership, Burkina Faso supported other countries from Asia, Latin America, and Africa in the Movement of Non-Aligned Countries, which refused to take sides in the Cold War and lobbied for their own interests as members of what was considered an underdeveloped "third world" in the General Assembly of the United Nations. In the following speech to the UN, Sankara expresses support for liberation movements in Palestine, South Africa, Ireland, East Timor, Grenada, Nicaragua, and Afghanistan and decries the exploitation of an international economic order that continues the legacies of colonialism.

I do not intend to enunciate dogmas here. I am neither a messiah nor a prophet. I possess no truths. My only ambition is to . . . express . . . the feelings of that mass of people who are disinherited—those who belong to that world maliciously dubbed "the third world"—and to state, even if I cannot make them understood, the reasons that have led us to rise up. . . .

Nobody will be surprised to hear us associate . . . Burkina Faso with that despised rag-bag, the third world, which the other worlds [i.e., the United States and Europe, and the Soviet Union] invented at the time of our independence in order better to ensure our intellectual, cultural, economic and political alienation. We want to fit in there without at all . . . accepting that we are a backward world left behind by the West. Rather, we do so to affirm, . . . as one of the non-aligned countries, our deeply felt conviction that a special solidarity unites the three continents of Asia, Latin America and Africa . . . [against] political traffickers and economic exploiters.

. . .

There must be no more deceit. The new international economic order . . . can be achieved only if we manage to do away with the old order, which completely ignores us, only if we insist on the place which is ours in the political organization of the world, only if we realize our importance in the world and obtain the right to decision-making with respect to the machinery governing trade, economic and monetary affairs at the world level.

The new international economic order is simply one among all the other rights of peoples . . . it is a right which can be gained only through the struggle of the peoples. It will never be obtained by any act of generosity by any Power whatsoever.

Source: Transcript of Thomas Sankara's Address to the United Nations General Assembly, 20th plenary meeting, Thursday, October 4, 1984, New York.

QUESTIONS FOR ANALYSIS

1. According to Sankara, what "special solidarity" unites the three continents of Asia, Latin America, and Africa?
2. What parts of Sankara's speech would be appealing to "third world" countries but concerning to other countries?
3. How is Sankara's critique of neo-colonialism similar to or different from the grievances that motivated the earlier independence movements in Ghana and Algeria?

threshold that populations and politicians in Europe were prepared to pay.

Decolonization proved a violent process especially in colonies with sizable settler communities, such as Algeria, Kenya, or Mozambique. Madagascar's independence from France also came with a high price in blood, exacted by African troops under French command who suppressed a revolt in 1947 and 1948. The table shows the size of the military commitments in a few cases of violent decolonization.

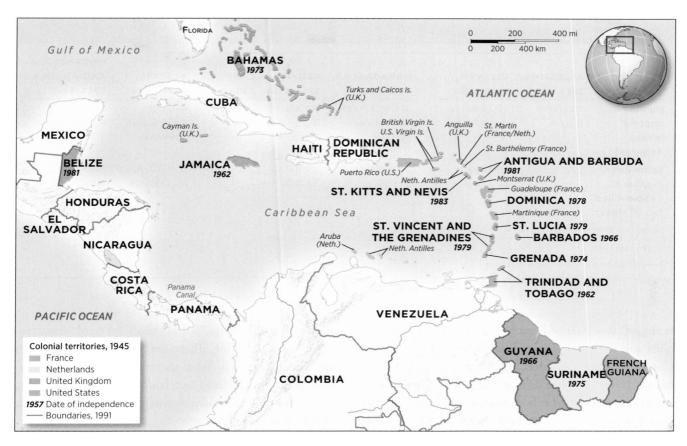

Decolonization in the Greater Caribbean Region The third pulse of decolonization reached the Caribbean in 1962 when Jamaica, and Trinidad and Tobago, won independence. Thirteen new countries emerged, counting the mainland territories of Belize, Guyana, and Suriname. Unlike decolonization in Asia or Africa, in the greater Caribbean no major violence took place. Several territories remain in effect colonies today, such as Puerto Rico, French Guiana, and the Netherlands Antilles (Aruba, Bonaire, and Curaçao).

In far more cases, decolonization came reasonably peacefully, as in Ghana. This was true in the Philippines and everywhere in the Caribbean. But part of the reason colonial powers did not fight to keep every colony is because they saw—in Vietnam, Kenya, Algeria, and elsewhere—the high price of fighting to hold on.

With few exceptions, former colonies kept their colonial borders when becoming independent countries. In most cases, the borders did not fit snugly around any ethnic or language group, ensuring cultural diversity within almost every former colony. In many countries, diversity produced divisions that led to internal strife. Nigeria, for example, suffered through a secessionist war when the southeastern part of the country proclaimed independence as Biafra in 1967. Biafra collapsed in 1970 amid a famine that killed 2 million, and Nigeria—unlike British India—held together. Only a handful of secession movements have succeeded; Bangladesh is by far the largest.

Brief experiments with federations were also tried, uniting Egypt and Syria, for example, in the United Arab Republic, during the years 1958–1961. None lasted, and the borders of the colonial world largely remain in place.

Decolonization remains incomplete. A small number of colonies still exist, relics of earlier empires. They are generally little islands or enclaves, economically subsidized by their colonizers. Examples include Spanish Melilla on the coast of Morocco, British Gibraltar, French Martinique and Guadeloupe (officially a *département* in the Caribbean), and the U.S. territories of Guam and Puerto Rico.

Decolonization remains incomplete from another point of view as well. Nkrumah and others scorned what they called flag independence, referring to former colonies that were formally independent but still economically and politically dependent on their former imperial masters—a situation sometimes called neo-colonialism. Chad, for

CASUALTIES OF DECOLONIZATION, 1945–1975

	PALESTINE, 1945–1948	VIETNAM, 1946–1954	MADAGASCAR, 1947–1960	KENYA, 1953–1963	CYPRUS, 1954–1959	ALGERIA, 1954–1962	MOZAMBIQUE AND ANGOLA, 1961–1975
Number of imperial troops deployed	100,000 British	190,000 French and Africans	30,000 French and Africans	10,000 British and Africans	20,000 British	470,000 French and Africans‡	125,000 Portuguese
Estimated number of people killed (on all sides)	500*	500,000 to 800,000†	30,000 to 50,000	15,000 to 30,000	300	500,000 to up to 1 million	80,000 to 100,000

*and another 15,000 to 20,000 killed in a 1948 war between Arabs and Israelis
†This refers to the Vietnamese war against France. The war with the United States, 1962–1975, is discussed in Chapter 27.
‡not including *harkis*

Sources: Data drawn by author from various sources.

example, once part of French Central Africa, still maintains strong ties to France. French companies dominate Chad's economy, and the French military still props up or overthrows Chadian leaders as it pleases. French armed forces have intervened at least 20 times since 1962 in countries that are former French colonies in Africa.

THE RISE OF EAST ASIA

At least as momentous as decolonization was the rise of East Asia—the economic "miracles" of Japan, South Korea, Singapore, Hong Kong, Taiwan, and mainland China. They all managed sustained economic growth, as measured by GDP, at rates rarely if ever achieved in world history. (GDP—gross domestic product—measures the total monetary value of all goods and services produced annually by a country.) Together, the success of the **Asian tiger economies** amounted to the most rapid large-scale economic transformation in world history. Each case had national features, as sections below explain, but they also had some important common characteristics.

SOURCES OF ECONOMIC GROWTH

East Asians often explain the astonishing economic record of several East Asian countries as a result of culture and values. Singapore's first prime minister, Lee Kuan Yew,

never tired of touting "Asian values" of hard work, frugality, and discipline. There may be some truth in that argument, but East Asian societies with "Asian values" were poor for centuries and condemned by necessity to hard work and frugality. Something more is needed to explain their modern rise.

An important pre-condition was peace. Revolutions, civil wars, and international wars ravaged much of East Asia on and off before 1945. China suffered from civil war between 1946 and 1949, and Korea from a civil war that quickly became an international war between 1950 and 1953. But after 1953, with tiny exceptions, peace prevailed in East Asia, although not in Vietnam and elsewhere in Southeast Asia. As we'll see, warfare in Vietnam actually helped the economies of East Asia.

DEMOGRAPHIC CHANGE Another factor common to the economic success of East Asia was a gigantic **demographic dividend**. The key to a demographic dividend is a fertility transition that offers a window of time highly favorable for economic growth and development. Under the old biological regime, with high fertility and big families, adults—women especially—devoted great effort to child care. When fertility falls, the age structure changes: the ratio of people of prime working age to children and the elderly rises. That shift makes economic growth and development likelier. In addition, with fewer children to support, families find it easier to pay for education. In short, fertility transitions deliver demographic dividends in the form of economic growth, and nowhere—so far—has this happened faster than in East Asia after 1950.

The demographic dividend in East Asia was in some cases partly a result of government policy encouraging lower birth rates, as we will see. But since it happened everywhere at almost the same speed, and close to the same time, regardless of policy, it is likely that the effect of choices made by hundreds of millions of couples through-out East Asia was more fundamental than policy. As for-mal education became more important to securing one's future, couples increasingly preferred to invest more heav-ily in fewer children.

TECHNOLOGY AND THE OPEN ECONOMY

Another factor contributing to the economic rise of East Asia came from technical changes to shipping, the biggest of which was **containerization**. Before the 1950s, ports were the bottlenecks in maritime shipping. Longshore-men filled and emptied ships, which might take weeks. Beginning in the United States in the late 1950s, entre-preneurs started to use shipping containers—enormous metal boxes—to hold freight. Containers could go on ships, trains, or trucks, and no one had to "break down" the cargo first. Big cranes plucked containers from ships to shore or vice versa. Containerization cut the costs of maritime shipping between the 1950s and 1990s by one-third. Labor costs plunged as longshoremen were let go. Trans-oceanic shipping times fell by nearly 90 per-cent. The risk of broken or stolen goods declined, and longshoremen's strikes no longer delayed transport. Ship-ping times became so reliable that companies—led by the Japanese carmaker Toyota—began what is now known as "just-in-time delivery" of product parts. With no invento-ries sitting around, production costs declined.

The container revolution was global, but East Asia ben-efited most. Containerization put the big consumer mar-kets of North America and Europe within reach of the East Asian economies. Export-oriented growth strategies became much more practical when shipping costs and times were plummeting and more predictable.

Another general factor contributing to the East Asian economic rise is connected to containerization's success: the comparative openness of the world economy, or at least a big slice of it, since 1950. All of the successful East Asian economies prospered on the basis of exports—the

The Rise of East Asia The "tiger" economies of Japan, South Korea, Taiwan, Hong Kong, and Singapore formed the leading edge of the East Asian economic explosion. China's economic transformation, begun under Deng Xiaoping, was of greater magnitude and global impact, even if uneven across China's interior regions.

imports of other countries. The United States, historically a protectionist country, by 1950 encouraged free trade and low tariffs everywhere around the world. It had the power to persuade many countries in Western Europe and Latin America to lower trade barriers. This opened the door for export-led growth of the sort the East Asian tigers pursued.

Cheap labor was another important factor. Just as Meiji Japan's industrialization at the end of the nineteenth century took advantage of low labor costs, so it was with all of the East Asian tigers in the late twentieth century. Hundreds of millions of very poor people were willing to work for paltry wages. If they asked for higher pay or

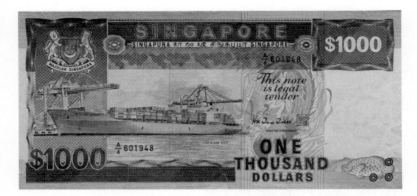

Containerization A 1980s Singaporean banknote displays an image of a freighter filled with shipping containers. The innovation of containerization contributed to immense economic growth in post-war Singapore and other East Asian economies.

better working conditions, their bosses—at least in South Korea, Japan, and China—could easily find eager replacement workers in rural villages. Hong Kong and Singapore did not have masses of poor villagers, but they could draw on cheap immigrant labor from China or Malaysia.

Let's now look more closely at the examples of Japan, South Korea, and China. The story of Taiwan is equally remarkable but similar to South Korea's. Hong Kong and Singapore also engineered economic surges, but on the smaller scale of city-states. North Korea missed out entirely. Its leadership did not choose export-led industrial growth as its guiding strategy. It preferred to rely on its own meager resources rather than integrate into the international economy. North Korea suffered mass starvation in the 1990s and remains very poor today. Its record shows, among other things, the economic penalty of isolation from the commercial circuitry of the Global web. Self-reliance, in a global economy, has often proved disastrous.

JAPAN

Japan's post-1945 economic miracle was its second. It had pulled one off after the Meiji Restoration of 1868. That one featured rapid industrialization, beginning with textiles and shifting to heavy industry. It continued into the 1930s, little troubled by the Great Depression, with a new emphasis on military production and planning.

Bombing during World War II obliterated about one-quarter of Japan's buildings and infrastructure and slashed its GDP in half (1940–1945). In the immediate post-war years, most people were hungry and some starved

to death. Malnutrition caused the average heights of children to decline. Japan's currency lost almost all value to inflation in the years 1945–1949. But Japan had expertise, traditions, and institutions that, with a few tweaks, could support another economic surge when conditions improved—as they did markedly in the 1950s.

THE U.S. OCCUPATION AND STRATEGIC SUPPORT From 1945 to 1952, the Allies—mainly the U.S. military—occupied Japan and directed its high-level policy. American army officers wrote a new constitution for Japan, adopted in 1947. Their goals were to eradicate militarism and ensure a stable, democratic, and pro-American Japan. They pushed through land reform that ended the domination of the countryside by big landlords and made Japan into a country of small farmers, a key step on the road to economic transformation.

The new constitution provided for the equality of men and women in articles written by Beate Sirota, a 23-year-old American of Ukrainian parentage. She had grown up in Japan and was working for the occupation authorities as a translator when invited to help draft the constitution. Equality of the sexes was a revolutionary concept in Japan and helped bring about a fertility transition and demographic dividend.

Once communists took over China (1949) and the Korean War broke out (1950), U.S. policy toward Japan shifted. Engineering social change seemed less urgent than re-building Japan as a bulwark against communist expansion in East Asia. After some missteps, the Americans came to understand that on economic policy they needed to work within Japan's cultural traditions, one of which included cooperation between business elites and government bureaucrats to craft national economic and industrial strategies. After 1949, a new ministry for international trade and industry (MITI) took primary responsibility for creating these strategies. It sponsored research and directed investment funds toward chosen industries. Like the leaders of the Meiji era, post-war Japan's government did not trust the free market to make the best economic decisions for Japan.

One important factor sustaining the Japanese economic miracle was its role in supplying the U.S. military during the Korean and Vietnam wars. These war efforts needed vast quantities of supplies, and Japan was close to the war zones, especially to Korea. A Japanese prime

JAPANESE PER CAPITA GDP, 1950–2020 (INDEXED TO 1950)	
YEAR	GDP (1950 = 100)
1950	100
1955	144
1960	208
1965	309
1970	506
1975	591
1980	701
1985	803
1990	980
1995	1043
2000	1069
2005	1125
2010	1145
2015	1144
2020	1151 (estimated)

Source: Maddison Project, https://www.rug.nl/ggdc/historicaldevelopment/maddison/releases/maddison-project-database-2018

Note: Per capita GDP refers to the national GDP divided by the national population.

minister referred to the Korean War, a bit callously, as "a gift of the gods."

In 1950, Japan's economy, halved by war's ravages, was smaller than that of Colombia, Costa Rica, or Morocco. Its per capita annual growth after 1950 averaged about 8 percent to 1973, a sustained rate never seen anywhere before, and more than twice the global average of those years. During the 1970s, a tough decade for the world economy because of oil price hikes, Japan's economy still grew rapidly, and by 1980 was the third largest in the world. Prosperity—in the form of cars, TVs, washing machines, and the like—reached into the villages and formerly poor neighborhoods of big cities. The expansion slowed in the 1990s and beyond. These trends are evident in the table above.

Some of the general factors discussed above help explain Japan's economic takeoff. It benefited from a demographic dividend, containerization, and easy access to the U.S. market. At first, its industrial competitiveness also benefited from cheap labor. But under the Allies' occupation Japanese workers had been encouraged to unionize, which led to rising wages by the mid-1950s. In addition, the supply of poor villagers willing to work for low wages dried up by about 1960, so Japan could not profit for long on the basis of cheap export manufactures such as textiles and toys.

ZAIBATSU AND KEIRETSU Japanese business organizations, especially large, integrated corporate conglomerates, proved especially nimble at exploiting the opportunities of the post-war years. These conglomerates had existed in Japan since the late nineteenth century, when they were called *zaibatsu*. They brought together banks, trading companies, and industries all under the same leaders, often from one family. They had led industrialization in late nineteenth-century Japan, when they emphasized iron, steel, and ship building, and during the years 1937–1945, when they organized war production. The *zaibatsu* tradition was woven into the fabric of Japanese society, culture, and politics.

The Americans had at first tried to break up the *zaibatsu* during the post-war occupation, but the effort withered as U.S. policy shifted to building up Japan to counter communism in East Asia. Called **keiretsu** after 1945, the conglomerates re-grouped and led a new campaign, aimed at capturing foreign markets in select industries. Their success in some areas was stunning: in 1965, nearly two-thirds of the world's new ships were built in Japan.

Like the *zaibatsu* of the Meiji era, the *keiretsu* proved successful at technological innovation, especially adapting foreign technology to Japanese contexts. The rising wages of Japanese workers in the 1950s tempted companies to give up on labor-intensive approaches. With the encouragement of MITI, they shared research costs and pooled resources to buy licenses for foreign technology. They sent people abroad to study the latest production techniques—as Japan had done during the Meiji era. In the 1950s and 1960s, the U.S. government eagerly assisted in transferring industrial technology to Japan. Japanese engineers worked small wonders inventing or improving cameras, computers, printers, electronic keyboards, automated teller machines, and hundreds of other common devices.

The *keiretsu* and other Japanese firms entrenched assembly-line production in Japan and found ways to ensure better quality control than the Americans, the originators of the assembly line. In the 1950s, they succeeded mainly because they made cheaper goods than industry elsewhere could manage; but by the 1970s they did it with high-quality goods: better steel, ships, cars, audio equipment, and TVs than companies elsewhere could make. The *keiretsu* and smaller firms also pioneered miniaturization. Post-war Japan was crowded. Its urban apartments were small and its streets narrow. Japanese industry responded with small TVs, refrigerators, and cars that fit Japanese spaces—and similarly crowded societies elsewhere. In pursuing miniaturization, they developed skills and technologies that proved useful in markets such as personal computers, mobile phones, and robotics.

The Japanese economic spurt lasted into the 1970s and made Japan an industrial powerhouse and one of the richest societies in the world. Its growth rates slowed from a sprint to a trot during the 1970s and 1980s, and after 1995 to a crawl. Among the reasons for its economic stagnation was an ageing population, the price Japan pays for its rapid reduction in birth rates between 1950 and 1970. The public and politicians have resisted immigration—which skews young—leaving Japan since 1990 with the world's oldest population. By 2020, 28 percent of Japanese were age 65 or older, and in no other country was the proportion above 23 percent. Japan's total population has been falling since about 2010. In addition, since the 1980s, Japan has also enjoyed less cooperation from the United States, whose automobile and other businesses came to feel threatened by Japan's. And Japan's export sector faced growing competition from South Korea, Taiwan, Singapore, and, by 1990, China.

SOUTH KOREA

South Korea engineered an economic miracle even more extraordinary than Japan's. Whereas Japan already had decades as an industrial society behind it in the 1950s, South Korea had next to nothing. Its few modern industries had been built to serve the interests of Korea's colonial master, Japan, which siphoned all the wealth and resources that it could from Korea between 1910 and 1945. In the Korean War (1950–1953), Korean, Chinese, and American armies blasted the peninsula into tatters and left it divided in two. South Korea in the late 1950s had virtually no natural resources, and per capita incomes were lower than those of newly independent Ghana—and of communist North Korea. Yet by 1990 South Korea was well on its way to becoming one of the world's best-educated and richest populations. Between 1960 and 2017, its GDP per capita grew roughly 300-fold. How could a former colony ruled so harshly pull off such a self-transformation?

Although harsh, Japanese colonial rule (1910–1945) in Korea left a few useful legacies. The Japanese built the foundations of a modern educational system. They also built a transportation infrastructure, although most of that needed re-building after the Korean War. And they trained some Koreans in industrial skills, both as workers and as managers.

American military occupation of the south beginning in 1945 left another helpful legacy: **land reform**. In 1948, most South Koreans were peasants, renting land from aristocratic landowners called *yangban* who made all important decisions about farming. But by 1956, South Korean peasants owned most of the farmland, grew whatever they liked, and sold as much of their harvest as they wished. Land reform, undertaken under pressure from the U.S. government, was the foundational act of South Korea's economic miracle.

A second step was building a universal education system for both boys and girls. In the 1950s, South Korea's

Economic Miracle Consumer goods and electronics helped to fuel Japan's economic revolution in the mid-twentieth century. During the 1970s, the Nissan factory near Yokohama could turn out three cars per minute for worldwide export. Workers in a 1960s Tokyo factory assemble components of color television sets, which became commonplace even in poorer Japanese households as prosperity increased.

government began an enduring investment in primary and secondary school education that paid off in the decades ahead. In the mid-1950s, school lessons were often held in tents and teachers had to cope with classes of as many as 100 students. By 1960, almost every child over five years of age spent long hours in newly built schools. Soon South Korea's literacy rates were among the highest in the world. By 1980, its workforce was among the world's most educated.

INDUSTRIAL POLICY AND U.S. SUPPORT Government policy helped in other ways too. In the early 1960s, South Korea's rulers embarked on a series of five-year plans featuring government direction of economic policy but private ownership of most business enterprises. In the latter respect, it was crucially different from communist five-year plans followed in the USSR or China. The government's industrial policy rewarded companies that exported goods. It protected South Korean industry behind tariff barriers. It also increasingly welcomed foreign investment, which came mainly from the United States and Japan.

The United States regarded South Korea, like Japan, as an important Cold War bulwark against communism in Asia. During the 1950s, the U.S. government paid about 80 percent of South Korea's government budget. From 1946 to 1976, the United States gave twice as much aid money to South Korea as it did to all of Africa. The Vietnam War provided South Korean industry, especially construction firms, with an opportunity to win contracts from the U.S. military—as it did for Japanese firms. And most important of all, the United States opened its market to South Korean exports. For decades, it was the main customer for South Korean manufactures.

ECONOMIC AND SOCIAL CHANGE At first, those manufacturing exports were mainly textiles and shoes. Then, in the 1970s, the South Korean government—ignoring advice from U.S. economists—decided to leave textiles behind and invest in heavy industry such as steel, ship building, automobiles, and chemicals, following the Japanese route. By this time, South Korean schools and universities had trained enough scientists and engineers to staff such industries. This gamble on heavy industry worked well, as it had for Japan.

South Korea's leaders were no angels. They had studied the experiences of Meiji Japan and Atatürk's

Turkey—both of which fended off foreign domination and used threats, detention, and violence against their own citizens. In 1980, South Korea's military government unleashed the army on peaceful pro-democracy protesters, killing hundreds in the city of Gwangju. Until the late 1980s, South Korea's rulers were authoritarian nationalists, whose aim was to strengthen South Korea economically and to cast off dependence on the United States.

Throughout the decades of its economic surge (1960–1990), South Korea underwent social change that boosted economic growth. The land reform enabled peasants to save enough to educate their children in hopes of upward social mobility. Millions moved from farm to city. And like much of the rest of East Asia in these years, South Korea underwent a lightning-fast fertility transition. In the 1950s, South Korean families averaged more than 5 children. In the decades that followed, partly as a result of government support for birth control, South Korean women changed their ambitions and their lives. Mothers' clubs in thousands of villages spread knowledge of birth control methods, which were eagerly taken up by South Korean women. In 1975, they averaged under 3 children each; and in 2005, only 1.2. This social change delivered a huge demographic dividend to the economy as the proportion of people in the prime of life climbed. In addition, during these decades women took up jobs in offices and factories in unprecedented numbers.

South Korea transformed itself from a poor peasant country to a rich industrial one within a generation. Its economy grew by 8 to 10 percent annually from 1960 to 1985, and in the late 1980s it led the world with annual growth rates of up to 12 percent. The explanation for this spurt lies in shrewd industrial and educational policy; a quick fertility transition and big demographic dividend; and the opportunities presented by U.S. strategic support such as massive aid, access to U.S. markets and technology, and U.S. guarantees of security that made South Korea an attractive destination for investment.

CHINA

China's economic rise is the most miraculous of all. It has lifted several hundred million people out of grinding poverty. It has taken place under the rule of an authoritarian and often brutal Communist Party that has embraced capitalism and the unabashed pursuit of private gain. And it has achieved all this without the support from the United States that helped Japan and South Korea.

In longer historical perspective, China's economic transformation is not so miraculous. Chinese society and culture had deep-seated traditions of entrepreneurship and technological innovation. China—as we've seen—was the first market society, dating back to the Song dynasty (960–1279 CE). Chinese culture was suited to competition in a global economy. But first China's economy had to survive a century of imperialist exploitation, revolution, war, and Maoist rule.

Concerted efforts to modernize and industrialize China began in the late nineteenth century under the wobbling Qing dynasty. These efforts continued after the revolution of 1910 under Guomindang rule, but the results were modest: in 1936, factories accounted for only 3 percent of China's economic output—compared to 25 percent in Japan. Textiles in the area around Shanghai made up most of that industrial output. The only other industrial cluster in the 1930s was in Manchuria, which was under Japanese control after 1931.

As we've seen, World War II (1937–1945) and the Chinese Civil War (1946–1949) took a terrible toll on China. Violence, disease, and starvation killed about 7 to 8 percent of the population in those 12 years. The standard of living fell to levels of the early nineteenth century. In 1945 and 1946, hyperinflation reduced the currency to near worthlessness. China was among the poorest countries in the world when Mao Zedong and the Chinese Communist Party came to power in 1949. It remained overwhelmingly rural with only small pockets of industry.

THE ECONOMY UNDER MAOISM Mao Zedong ruled China from 1949 until his death in 1976. His economic policies were ambitious and erratic. He thrived on chaos and used sudden reversals in policy as a political tool to destroy rivals. Given the economic history of China's neighbors since 1950, and that of China itself since Mao's death, it is tempting to conclude that the main impact of Mao and Maoism was to slow the economic rise of China by 30 years.

In the early years of the People's Republic of China (PRC), Mao and his fellow communists aimed to make China stronger, richer, and fairer. Their reforms drew on Chinese precedents and, despite their frictions, the record of Stalin's USSR, which had stood the test of

Chinese Collectivization A 1960 propaganda poster shows farm workers prospering under collectivization. The poster associates collectivization with modern technology: electricity, tractors and other farm machinery, and a factory in the background.

World War II. So they tried to build a hierarchical communist party, a one-party state, a robust military, and a highly regulated society. They shared the standard communist faith in five-year plans and heavy industry, which they hoped would make China economically and militarily strong and give it a proletariat with which to build communist society. They began with collectivization of agriculture, as Stalin had done.

Collectivization began with the murder of a few million landlords in the early 1950s and the intimidation of the rest. Once the power and authority of the landed gentry was eliminated, the CCP re-organized peasants into communal "work units" that shared land, tools, and animals. Party-appointed leaders of work units decided almost everything for peasant families, including who could marry and who could have children. Peasant families were allowed to keep about 10 percent of the farmland for themselves. Collectivization in China proved unpopular with peasants, as it had in the USSR. In the far south, many slipped over borders to the British colony of Hong Kong or to Burma. The hundreds of millions who remained usually worked much harder on their own tiny plots than on the communal fields—if they could get away with it.

In Japan and South Korea, breaking the hold of land-holding elites and turning land over to peasants was a crucial step in launching their economic upsurges. In China, crushing the landlords and turning land over to communal work units was a disaster. At Mao's death in 1976, agricultural efficiency, measured in yields per hectare or per acre, were lower than in 1956. The tiny private plots were the only exceptions: their yields were 5 to 10 times higher than those on collectively farmed land. China became a food importer from 1961 to 1996, despite Mao's ambitions for self-reliance.

In embracing heavy industry as a path to growth, Mao was also following in Stalin's footsteps. In what could be the most massive technology transfer in world history, China imported industrial machinery from the USSR and Eastern (Sovietized) Europe in the 1950s. By 1955, two-thirds of China's foreign trade was with the USSR, and Moscow paid for one-third of the projects undertaken in China's first five-year plan (1953–1957). Thousands of Soviet experts flocked to China, giving advice on factory construction, mining, dam building, and much else. Millions of Chinese peasants now became factory workers. In sheer quantitative terms, Mao's program of industrialization was a success. Starting from a very low base, it achieved roughly 11 percent annual growth in industrial output between 1952 and 1978. But the growth in output came only from using more labor, coal, ores, and other raw materials. Chinese industry remained inefficient, wasting energy and raw materials. The quality of goods remained shoddy.

The most spectacularly inefficient—and tragic—of Mao's policies was the **Great Leap Forward** of 1958 through 1961. To strengthen his hand in domestic politics, Mao decided to make a massive economic push involving both industry and agriculture. Instead of building modern steel mills, for which China did not have the capital or expertise, he required the work units to produce steel in a million "backyard furnaces." For Mao, steel had a

Great Leap Forward Workers manufacture steel in the "backyard furnaces" mandated by Mao's Great Leap Forward economic policy of the period 1958–1961.

symbolic value. He wanted to outstrip British and American production levels and show that he could build a steel industry from scratch even faster than Stalin. Even students and faculty at China's elite Peking University had to meet steel quotas. Through heroic effort, China doubled its steel output, melting down doorknobs, bedsprings, bicycle frames, and cooking pots. But steel made this way was usually brittle and useless, a waste of vast quantities of coal, charcoal, and labor, not to mention bikes, beds, and pots.

The Great Leap Forward also featured fiascoes in agriculture. Skeptical of scientific expertise, Mao maintained that seeds of the same species even if planted close together would not compete for nutrients and water. When food ran short, he demanded that the village work units hand over more grain for the cities, the army—and even for export. Fearing the consequences if they did not deliver, party workers took so much grain that peasants starved. Estimates vary greatly, but between 1958 and 1961 some 20 to 50 million Chinese starved to death—3 to 8 percent of the population of 650 to 700 million. It was by far the worst self-inflicted famine in world history. The Great Leap Forward coincided with a rupture in Sino-Soviet relations, resulting in the expulsion of Soviet advisers and the isolation of China.

THE CULTURAL REVOLUTION Mao's reliance on political mobilization campaigns continued to hamper China's economy. The biggest of these was the Great Proletarian Cultural Revolution (1966–1976), an effort to re-kindle revolutionary spirit and oust some of Mao's critics within the CCP. He shut down schools and universities, urging young people to organize themselves as Red Guards and to assault everything old. The Red Guards destroyed temples and texts, and attacked elders from teachers to party cadres to their own parents. They beat up foreigners, including Soviet and East German diplomats. They targeted ethnic minorities, killing thousands, especially Mongolians and Tibetans. They inflicted public humiliations on their targets, exhibiting them to jeering crowds. One Red Guard recalled: "We were told that we needed to use violence to destroy a class, spiritually and physically. That was justification enough for torturing someone. They weren't considered human anymore. If they were the enemy, they deserved to be strangled to death, and they deserved to be tortured. This was the education we received."

Cultural Revolution Red Guards humiliate victims—forcing them to wear dunce caps proclaiming their crimes—as crowds look on. Humiliation tactics were characteristic of the ideological warfare of the Cultural Revolution.

In 1967 and 1968, Mao called out the army, in some cases to tame the Red Guards and in others to support them. The Cultural Revolution was now virtually a civil war with 1 to 2 million killed by either the Red Guards or the army. It was also an economic disaster, costing the country about 7 to 8 percent of its GDP in each of 1967 and 1968—a more severe decline than any two-year period of the Great Depression in any major country. By keeping young people out of school for several years, and by encouraging them to memorize the quotations of Chairman Mao rather than learn to read and write, it cost China in the longer run too. As the economic growth surge swept the rest of East Asia in the 1960s, Mao's policies, whatever their motives, kept China poor and, after the Sino-Soviet split, isolated.

At the same time, however, Mao laid a foundation for future economic growth. He and the CCP re-unified China in the 1940s and then, despite domestic turmoil, kept it together as one country. He succeeded where Gandhi, Nehru, and Jinnah in India failed. In effect, he established a new dynasty—not of a family or lineage as in China's past, but of the CCP. National unity would help vault China's economy upward after his death.

Also, in obliterating the landlord class, Mao achieved through murder and brutality what American-imposed land reform achieved in South Korea and Japan. When collectivized agriculture ended after Mao's death, land did not revert to landlords but went to the peasants in long-term leases. His reliance on Soviet machinery and expertise in the 1950s trained a few million Chinese in how to handle machine tools, truck engines, and other useful skills. And as we've seen, Mao thawed relations with the United States in the early 1970s, setting the stage for the full participation of China in the international economy. But it took Mao's death in 1976, and a few other favorable developments, for China to embark on its epic rise.

DENG XIAOPING In the years following Mao's death, **Deng Xiaoping** emerged as China's supreme leader—head of the party, the government, and the army. His re-orientation of Chinese economic policy led to a genuine great leap forward and a real cultural revolution.

Deng was born in the southwestern province of Sichuan in 1904 to a family of middling gentry status. His father had attended university and played a local role in Sun Yatsen's nationalist revolution. As a schoolboy Deng became an ardent nationalist, eager to rescue China from weakness, poverty, and humiliation. As a teenager he joined a work-study program in France, where over a six-year stay (1920–1926) he worked in factories and joined the European branch of the Chinese Communist Party. Like several young Chinese, he saw communism as a way to make China strong. In 1926, Deng went to Moscow to study at a university set up by the Soviets to train Chinese revolutionaries. A year later, he returned to China and began political work.

For the next several decades, Deng rose through the ranks of the CCP. He worked as an ideological enforcer in the CCP's army units during the long struggles against Japan and Chiang Kai-shek's Guomindang party. After the CCP took power in 1949, he served as mayor of a major city, Chongqing, and in many central government posts in the 1950s and 1960s. By and large he supported Mao's policies, but he occasionally ran afoul of Mao anyway and was stripped of his posts more than once. During the Cultural Revolution he and his family were attacked by Red Guards, and his son thrown out of a fourth-story window (he survived as a paraplegic).

Patience and shrewdness were among Deng's hallmarks. He weathered all the storms of Mao's rule and the power struggles after Mao's death. When he took power beginning in 1978, Deng was well over 70 years old and about to embark on a world-changing program of reform to make China strong again.

In 1978, Deng visited Japan and Singapore. At the time, China was poor and

Deng Xiaoping A meeting in 1959 between Deng (right) and Mao. Deng's careful negotiation of politics during the period of Mao's rule enabled him finally to assume power himself in 1978.

technologically backward—its per capita income was less than half of sub-Saharan Africa's. Singapore dazzled Deng with a shiny vision of wealth combined with one-party rule and an orderly society—and all overseen by a local population of ethnic Chinese. Thousands of CCP officials visited Singapore after 1978, and Singapore's autocratic leader, Lee Kuan Yew, traveled to China many times. Lee's Singapore had the prosperity of Western countries and all the advantages of an open, technologically modern economy, but no political opposition, no litter or graffiti, and almost no drugs or decadence. Why couldn't China be more like Singapore?

In fact, it could. Deng cautiously allowed the profit motive to operate within limits prescribed by the Communist Party and called it "socialism with Chinese characteristics." In fact, he was dismantling Maoist socialism and gradually replacing it with capitalism—with Chinese characteristics. Deng's economic reforms unleashed the rise of contemporary China while keeping the CCP's monopoly on political power intact.

DENG'S ECONOMIC REFORMS Deng's first task was replacing the Maoist economy. He allowed peasant families to lease farmland long-term, ending the commune work-unit system. Agricultural production skyrocketed. Between 1978 and 1990, the average Chinese calorie intake doubled, and by 1991 China no longer needed to import food. Between 1979 and 1988, Deng, working with provincial party bosses, created several "special economic zones," at first next door to Hong Kong and across from Taiwan, and invited foreign investment and trade in these zones. Small businesses, such as textile workshops, sprouted alongside the older state-owned factories built under Mao. China's stock exchange, closed since 1949, re-opened in 1992.

Whereas Mao had tried to raise production by means of political exhortation and threat, Deng let economic incentives do that work. He allowed local governments to make most of their own decisions about how to invest, produce, and trade. Following the path blazed by the East Asian tigers, he encouraged export-oriented industry and welcomed foreign technology and factory management techniques. Deng unchained the profit motive, claiming that in China markets and socialism were compatible. He translated his earlier remark—that the color of a cat doesn't matter, only that it catches mice—into action: economic growth mattered more than ideological purity.

Chinese Industry A young woman assembles a machine component in a factory in Sichuan in 2012. By the early twenty-first century, China was producing a large share of the world's consumer goods.

His pragmatic policies sparked an industrial revolution in China, focused on textiles and consumer electronics—just as in South Korea and Taiwan. Deng retired in the early 1990s and died in 1997, but his successors steered China along the same path.

Deng was no democrat. He ordered mass executions to encourage obedience and reduce corruption. He maintained oppressive policies toward ethnic minorities such as Uighurs and Tibetans. Whereas Gorbachev in 1989 declined to use the Soviet army to crush East Europeans' efforts to win greater freedom, Deng in 1989 called out the army against peaceful democracy protesters at Tiananmen Square in the heart of Beijing, leading to a massacre much larger than the one South Korea's army perpetrated in Gwangju in 1980. His commitment to one-party rule was as firm as Mao's.

His ruthless authoritarian streak did not interfere with his liberalization of the economy, the results of which were of world historical importance. By 2004, China was receiving more foreign investment than any other country in the world. Between 1980 and 2020, the economy grew 50-fold, posting annual growth rates of 8 to 11 percent. No big country had ever done this before, or even come close. The United States achieved such rates only during World War II.

Comparison between the world's two most populous countries helps show how extraordinary China's economic trajectory was. China and India between 1950 and 1990 were twins in poverty. In both countries, most people barely had enough to eat. After 1990 both got richer; but

Tiananmen Square An Associated Press photojournalist took this iconic photo of a single Chinese man attempting to block tanks on their way to Tiananmen Square to crush peaceful pro-democracy protests on June 5, 1989. As many as several thousand protesters may have been killed by the Chinese military during the protests.

uninhabited islands in the South China Sea into military bases. It became a major arms dealer, especially to Pakistan. It offered loans to many governments in Asia and Africa, in exchange for control of commercial ports and military bases around the Indian Ocean. It purchased long-term leases on farmland in Africa. Some 10,000 Chinese companies were active in Africa as of 2020, creating new factories, mines, and plantations, and building roads, bridges, dams, and hotels. Outside of Lagos, Nigeria, for example, a Guangdong-based firm opened a new industrial zone, which its Chinese manager said was "like managing a country. We have our own customs, our own police, our own operations." There is irony in the resemblance of these quasi-imperial arrangements to the autonomous commercial compounds run in the nineteenth century by Europeans in Guangzhou, the capital of today's Guangdong. By the early twenty-first century, the Chinese state had become a major force not only in East Asia but in global politics as well.

China did so far faster, so that in 2020 its per capita GDP was roughly five times that of India.

ECONOMIC EFFECTS AND GLOBAL REACH
The Chinese government and some Chinese citizens were getting rich. By 2000, government revenues were about 30 times the level of Mao's last years and rising fast. The wealth of the central and provincial governments allowed tremendous investment in infrastructure: China built 54 new airports between 2000 and 2010 and a network of bullet trains covering much of the country. Millionaire and billionaire entrepreneurs sprouted up. According to World Bank figures, about 800 million Chinese climbed out of poverty between 1990 and 2020. This represents the largest and fastest escape from mass poverty in world history.

By 2015, China was the workshop of the world—as Britain was called in the mid-nineteenth century. It was the world's largest carmaker, having overtaken the United States in 2009. It built 90 percent of the world's personal computers and mobile phones, 80 percent of the air conditioners, 70 percent of the solar panels, and 65 percent of the shoes. Its biggest cities—Beijing, Shanghai, Guangzhou—became nodes of the Global web.

Economic prosperity also brought China international prestige and power. By the mid-1990s, China was doubling its military budget every few years and converting

SOURCES OF CHINA'S ECONOMIC SURGE
Deng's economic reforms took advantage of several favorable circumstances with roots in the Mao period. The diplomatic opening to the United States that Mao had engineered in the early 1970s enabled China's return to the global economy. It joined the World Trade Organization (WTO) in 2001, symbolizing its economic re-integration. The Chinese economy also benefited from the millions of overseas Chinese living in Singapore, Hong Kong, Taiwan, and scattered throughout Southeast Asia. These communities included bankers and entrepreneurs who spoke Chinese, understood Chinese cultural contexts, and were willing to trade with and invest in Deng's China. For the first two decades after Deng's reforms, the majority of investment in China came from overseas Chinese and from South Korea.

Education was another source of China's economic surge. When the CCP took power in 1949, only about 20 percent of Chinese could read. By 1964, thanks to intensive efforts in primary education, about 65 percent could. The Cultural Revolution (1966–1976) slowed progress, so that the figure remained about the same in 1980—and women were still much less likely to be literate than men. But by 2018, fully 97 percent of Chinese could read, and the gender gap had almost vanished. By 2020, 8 million Chinese graduated from universities each year, and another 400,000 were studying in U.S. universities.

Additionally, Deng and his successors inherited a growing demographic dividend. During the 1950s and 1960s, Mao urged Chinese to have big families on the theory that a country's strength lies in its people and there could never be too many Chinese. In 1967, Chinese women averaged six births over their lifetime. By 1978, the average had dropped to only three. As the graph to the right shows, it took the United Kingdom 95 years (1815–1910) to reduce fertility from six to three births per woman over her lifetime. The United States took 82 years (1844–1926). China did it in 11—and did not stop there.

In the years 1978–1980, with the birth rate already falling rapidly, the CCP abandoned Mao's position on population and imposed a "one-child rule" that penalized families with two or more children. Birth rates continued to slide; by 1990 the average fell to two children per woman. It is likely that urbanization and the education of females had more to do with this fall in fertility than did the government restriction. But whatever the causes, it delivered an enormous demographic dividend. Some economists credit this factor alone with one-quarter of China's economic growth since 1980. Today, China's birth rate is a little over one child per woman—the lowest fertility rate in the world. Faced with a rapidly aging population, China abandoned the one-child policy in 2016.

So Deng, his allies, and his successors took advantage

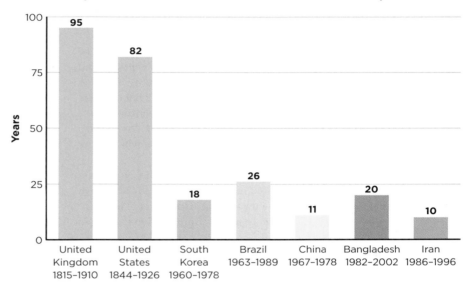

Fertility Declines from More Than 6 to Fewer Than 3 Children per Woman

This bar graph shows the timing and pace of fertility transitions in seven countries. The earlier transitions—in the United Kingdom and the United States—were slower. Those occurring from 1960 on were far faster. Fast transitions created an age structure—lots of people in the prime of life and fewer who were very old and very young—that sped up economic growth for a few decades. China and Iran were among the countries with the fastest fertility transitions in world history.

Source: OurWorldinData.org (data from Gapminder fertility dataset, version 6, and World Bank World Development Indicators).

of some favorable circumstances that, combined with shrewd policies, ignited an era of economic growth in China that fit the earlier regional pattern. While Japan launched the economic rise of East Asia, and South Korea, Taiwan, Singapore, and Hong Kong confirmed it, China—because of its size—completed it.

ENVIRONMENTAL AND SOCIAL PROBLEMS

Economic growth spurts usually come at a price. In the East Asian cases, that price included heavy pollution loads affecting air, water, and human health. Environmental protection carried a low priority in East Asia while countries were trying to industrialize and escape poverty. Japan suffered many episodes of acute pollution in the 1950s and 1960s. The most famous of these was so-called **Minamata disease**, referring to a seaside bay teeming with mercury from a nearby chemical plant. Many people who ate seafood from Minamata developed nerve damage, and their babies often had horrible birth defects. By the 1970s and 1980s, Japan got around to addressing its environmental health. South Korea and Taiwan followed a similar

One-Child Rule A billboard with the caption "one pair of husband and wife delivers one child," promotes the one-child policy of the Chinese government, in place from 1980 to 2016.

PUZZLES IN WORLD HISTORY

How Many Children per Family?

Most cultures, and all those reliant on agriculture, have long encouraged big families. Until the nineteenth century, and in many places well into the twentieth, so many children died young that it made sense to have several. That ensured enough hands for the countless tasks in a farming household, as well as help for its elderly members. The world's major religions, all of which emerged in times when many children died young, all endorse big families.

Kings and emperors agreed that big families were best for everyone. They wanted more taxpayers and soldiers in order to expand their own revenues and power. They generally encouraged people to marry young and discouraged any form of birth control.

In 1800, the average woman in Japan or France had 4 children over her lifetime, and in Russia and the United States about 7. Since then, parents have increasingly come to see family size differently. More families sought to limit the number of children they had, either because they expected more to survive or perhaps because they lived in a city and didn't need children to tend chickens, pick berries, or weed fields. By 1970, the average had fallen to 2.5 in the United States and France, and to about 2 in Japan and Russia; by 2010, it was 2 or fewer in all four countries.

Most kings, emperors, and other rulers in the nineteenth and twentieth centuries still promoted big families because they still wanted large populations. Fascist Italy, Nazi Germany, and several communist countries awarded women medals for having many children. Several other countries offered "baby bonuses" or tax incentives to encourage parents to have more children.

Along with its economic reforms, China took the opposite position on family size between 1978 and 2016. Its rulers discouraged families from having more than one child through various rewards and punishments. The policy yielded an enormous demographic dividend; but then in 2016, when its leadership grew concerned with the aging population distribution, China abandoned that policy. Likewise, Iran in the 1990s aggressively promoted family planning and cut its birth rate in half within 15 years; but in 2012 its Supreme Leader, Ali Khameini, proclaimed that birth control was wrong and that Iran needed more Iranians. Japan, South Korea, and Taiwan, which decades ago promoted birth control, now have financial incentives to encourage bigger families.

Families and rulers used to agree that big families were best. In recent history, their views on the ideal number of children often diverge—and often change.

QUESTIONS FOR DISCUSSION

1. Why did parents change their view of family size after 1800?
2. Why has family size long been a concern of rulers?

---

trajectory. China today is trying to address monumental pollution problems, but air and water pollution still kill a few million Chinese annually.

East Asia's concentrated economic growth also produced the frictions and resentments of social inequality. Some people got very rich while others did not. Japan suffered less strife from this cause than South Korea or China. Today, China is—depending how you measure it—among the most spectacularly unequal societies in the world. In 1978, its top 1 percent of earners took in 6 percent of national income, but by 2015 they received 15 percent. One-quarter of its population remains dirt-poor, and in the interior, away from the more prosperous coasts, the proportion is much higher.

A demographic inequality affected China as well, one that empowers young women and deprives tens of millions of Chinese men of a chance to marry and raise families. Chinese families for centuries have had a strong preference for boys, and in difficult times had often sold or killed girl babies. When ultrasound technology became available around 1990, and the government permitted most families only one child, many couples turned to selective abortion in their effort to ensure that they got a boy. As a result, China's population in recent decades developed a shortage of females. The ratio of boys to girls among newborns peaked at 1.22 to 1.0 in 2008, by far the highest in the world. Today, Chinese women of marriageable age are in short supply and consequently enjoy unprecedented

Minamata Disease A mother in the village of Minamata in southern Japan holds her 12-year-old daughter, who was born with severe nerve damage due to exposure to the mercury that polluted Minamata Bay.

choice in selecting partners. Their good fortune came at the expense of tens of millions aborted because they were female, and tens of millions of men unhappily unmarried.

Economic development also brought corruption. Where governments take a strong role in the economy, as in every East Asian economic surge, officials have countless opportunities to accept bribes and kickbacks. Hong Kong and Singapore minimized this problem, partly because they are small and easy to monitor, but also because those in charge chose to suppress corruption rather than revel in it. Japan tackled the problem and today ranks with Singapore and Hong Kong among the least corrupt societies when it comes to business practices. China, however, has suffered from widespread corruption that, despite occasional crackdowns, often involves top government officials and their families.

Despite these and other dark clouds, almost no one in East Asia regrets the economic transformation of the past two generations. Their full meaning, of course, is impossible to assess because the process is still under way.

REBALANCING IN THE GLOBAL WEB

By the second half of the twentieth century, the Global web was no longer expanding much. It had drawn in just about every population on Earth. But, as always, the web of connections was changing shape, with some pathways carrying more traffic and others slowing down. And just what those circuits carried—political ideas, trade goods, investment funds, cultural fashions, human migrants, and microbes—also evolved.

Decolonization and the rise of East Asia both re-shaped the Global web. At warp speed they reversed the long-standing process whereby Atlantic Europe had accumulated wealth and power and had established imperial rule over much of the world. Colonization and the rise of the West had taken several centuries; decolonization and the rise of East Asia took several decades. The difference in the pace of change is rooted in the densely connected world of the mid- and late twentieth century: the end of empire in India could instantly inspire people in Indonesia or the Gold Coast, and the prosperity of Singapore could inspire reformers in Beijing.

East Asia became one of the Global web's most interactive zones. During the 1930s and 1940s, Japan had tried to unify most of East Asia within an imperial system that it called the Greater East Asian Co-Prosperity Sphere. It collapsed with Japan's defeat in 1945. But a more successful version soon followed, held together by modern communications and container shipping. Sometimes called Asia-Pacific, this tightly integrated space centered on the humming economies of China and the neighboring Asian tigers. Overseas Chinese, often bilingual in English, played crucial roles bringing this integration to East Asia; but students, entrepreneurs, diplomats, and others from Chinese-speaking lands, and from Japan and South Korea as well, took part.

East Asia also became firmly linked—economically, culturally, and politically—to the United States and to some extent almost everywhere else. Japanese businesses built links to companies based on the Pacific coasts of Canada, the United States, and South America by the 1960s. China and Brazil had had almost nothing to do with each other before 1980, but by 2009 China was Brazil's biggest trade partner, importing soybeans and ores and building new ports and railroads in South America. Flows of investment, joint research ventures, diplomatic visits by heads of state, and much else bound them together. South Korea developed strong business connections to the Persian Gulf, pioneering another new strand of the Global web.

CONCLUSION

Decolonization resulted from the weakening of the imperial powers and the rising strength of colonized populations. The big colonial empires teetered under the impacts of World War II. Whether defeated in war or merely enfeebled by it, Japan, France, Britain, and the Netherlands could not easily continue as colonial powers after 1945. Colonial populations made it too hard to continue by building better political organizations and in some cases acquiring new military skills. During the third big pulse of decolonization in modern history, between 1945 and 1975, some 100 new countries were born.

Decolonization prepared the way for the rise of East Asia. The defeat of Japan's empire enabled it to integrate into the global economy, and gave South Korea and Taiwan their chance to engineer their own economic miracles. Singapore remained a poor and ragged place when it acquired independence in 1965, but it achieved a similar economic surge soon thereafter. China's economic transformation owed much to the examples of Singapore, Taiwan, and South Korea, and at least as much to the end of empire and the subsequent liberalization of global trade and investment flows. Without decolonization, the rise of East Asia would have come much more slowly, if at all.

A new architecture of the international system, shaped by the outcomes of World War II and the ongoing Cold War, also favored the rise of East Asia. First, peace prevailed in the region after 1953. Second, the United States provided a security umbrella for Japan, South Korea, and Taiwan, and most of the time they happily accepted it. The U.S. government underwrote a liberal economic order in which the East Asian tigers could export to American markets even if their own markets were protected. Third, after Mao and Nixon defrosted China-U.S. relations in the early 1970s, even communist China could, and shortly did, enter the liberal economic order. These developments proved highly favorable for trade and investment flows in and out of East Asia.

Decolonization and the rise of East Asia are much more significant for the early twenty-first century than the rise or fall of any single state or empire since 1960—even the fall of the USSR. They represent fundamental shifts in the international order and the distribution of wealth and power around the world.

CHAPTER REVIEW

KEY TERMS

third pulse of
   decolonization
   (p. 836)
Jawaharlal Nehru
   (p. 837)
Muslim League (p. 838)
Sukarno (p. 839)

Kwame Nkrumah (p. 840)
Algerian war for
   independence (p. 843)
Asian tiger economies
   (p. 846)
demographic dividend
   (p. 846)
containerization (p. 847)

keiretsu (p. 849)
land reform (p. 850)
Great Leap Forward
   (p. 853)
Deng Xiaoping (p. 854)
Minamata disease
   (p. 857)

Go to INQUIZITIVE
to see what you've
learned—and learn what
you've missed—with
personalized feedback
along the way.

REVIEW QUESTIONS

1. What two sudden shifts in world balances of power emerged after World War II?

2. How and why did power relations between the colonized and colonizers change after World War II?

3. What were the short- and long-term outcomes of the partition of British India?

4. How and why did the United States support Sukarno and Indonesian independence?

5. Explain why Ghana's transition to independence was peaceful.

6. Why did Charles de Gaulle decide to quit the Algerian war for independence?

7. What was the consequence of former colonies keeping colonial borders?

8. Identify the common demographic, technological, and global economic factors that led to the economic success of East Asia.

9. How did the *keiretsu* contribute to the Japanese economic miracle?

10. What social changes facilitated South Korea's economic surge?

11. Discuss the economic consequences of the Great Proletarian Cultural Revolution.

12. What chief agricultural and economic policies did Deng Xiaoping introduce?

13. Identify and explain the main environmental and social problems associated with rapid industrialization.

14. What international developments favored the rise of East Asia?

FURTHER READING

Kent DENG, *China's Political Economy in Modern Times* (2012). A work presenting lots of data not easily available elsewhere.

Barry EICHENGREEN, Dwight PERKINS, and Kwanho SHIN, *From Miracle to Maturity: The Growth of the Korean Economy* (2012). An authoritative and readable book on South Korea's economic transformation.

Dane KENNEDY, *Decolonization: A Very Short Introduction* (2016). A thematic study and the quickest way to get a good general picture.

Yasmin KHAN, *The Great Partition* (2007). A mix of analysis and personal stories from the saga of Indian independence and partition.

Robert MCMAHON, *Colonialism and Cold War: The United States and the Struggle for Indonesian Independence, 1945–49* (2011). A detailed study of the evolution of U.S. policy.

Tessa MORRIS-SUZUKI, *The Technological Transformation of Japan* (1994). A compelling analysis, strong on how Japanese traditions proved favorable for its post-war surge.

Kwame NKRUMAH, *I Speak of Freedom: A Statement of African Ideology* (1961). The leader of Ghana's independence movement in his own words.

Martin THOMAS, *Fight or Flight: Britain, France, and Their Roads from Empire* (2014). An authoritative comparative study, strong on international context and the stories of Algeria, Madagascar, India, Kenya, and Malaysia.

Ezra VOGEL, *Deng Xiaoping and the Transformation of China* (2011). A detailed assessment arguing that Deng stands among the titans of twentieth-century history.

CHRONOLOGY

1961
Amnesty International
is founded

1964
Beginning of worldwide
TV broadcasts of Olympics

1970s
Eradication of smallpox

1971
Médecins Sans Frontières
(Doctors without Borders)
is founded

1973
End of Bretton Woods system of
currency and debt management

1977
Likud Party
rises to power
in Israel

1979
Iranian Revolution

1980s
HIV/AIDS pandemic begins

1986
Overthrow of
Ferdinand Marcos

1988
Intergovernmental Panel on
Climate Change is founded;
Osama bin Laden founds
al-Qaeda

1991
Launch of Women's World Cup of soccer

1992
Hindu extremists
destroy Babri mosque

1994
South
Africa
ends
apartheid

1996
Rise of the
Taliban

1997
Kyoto
Protocol

1998
Indonesia ends
military rule

2001
Vladimir Putin ends democracy in Russia

Sept. 11, 2001
Terrorist attacks in New York, Virginia, and Pennsylvania

2002
Islamist party in Turkey
wins election

2003
U.S. invasion of Iraq

A Shrinking World

GLOBALIZATION SINCE 1980

2006
Shakira and Wyclef Jean record best-selling song (to date) of twenty-first century

2011
Arab Spring

2019
Covid-19 pandemic begins

2016
Paris Agreement

2007–2009
Great Recession

Wangari Maathai was persistent. Born in 1940 in a farming village in the central highlands of Kenya, a British colony at the time, she started school at age eight. A good student, she mastered English, won a scholarship to attend high school, and was selected in 1960 as one of 300 young Kenyans to study in the United States. After studying biology at a small Catholic women's college in Kansas, she won another scholarship for graduate work at the University of Pittsburgh, where she grew interested in grassroots movements to combat the Steel City's notorious air pollution. After further study in Germany and at the University of Nairobi, in 1971 she became the first woman in the history of East Africa to earn a PhD.

Maathai embarked on an academic career in Nairobi while raising a family, but she was drawn to grassroots environmental activism. In her analysis, environmental problems such as soil erosion and water contamination underlay Kenya's economic and social ills. She established the Green Belt Movement in 1976, which encouraged women to stand up for their rights and for the environment. She objected when Kenya's autocratic president proposed to build a skyscraper with a giant statue of himself in a public park. Police beat and arrested her more than once. The president said she should behave like a proper African woman, respect men, and be quiet. But she persisted.

Coronavirus Pandemic A Palestinian artist drawing a COVID-19 awareness mural, Gaza, March 28, 2020. The Arabic writing at top reads #StayInYourHome.

FOCUS QUESTIONS

1. What major environmental changes have become evident in recent decades?

2. How have population trends and public health interacted since 1980?

3. What major developments have occurred in global politics since 1980?

4. What major changes has the global economy undergone since 1980?

5. How have music and sports reflected the intense globalization of the period?

6. What limits to global integration have become evident in recent decades?

The Green Belt Movement eventually planted 30 million trees in Kenya. A figure of national and international prominence, **Wangari Maathai** was elected to Kenya's parliament in 2002, and two years later she was awarded the Nobel Peace Prize. Before her death in 2011, she had garnered 15 honorary degrees and nearly 50 public service awards in 11 countries. She raised funds all over the world for the Green Belt Movement and for women's rights in Africa. Wangari Maathai operated—skillfully and persistently—within a Global web of educational, environmental, and fundraising communities.

The main themes in this chapter are the scale and pace of contemporary environmental change, the ongoing—but imperiled—golden age of human health and longevity,

Wangari Maathai The successful leader of the Green Belt Movement was also a strong proponent of women's rights in Africa.

and the meanings of globalization for politics, economics, and culture. In many respects, the strands of the Global web since 1980 have grown thicker and stronger, carrying more goods, ideas, data, and microbes than ever before—and at faster speeds. That is a shared human experience, but everyone lived it—and lives it—differently.

Some 400 years ago, the English adventurer, politician, and historian Sir Walter Raleigh observed that "Whosoever is writing a modern History, shall follow truth too neare the heeles, it may haply strike out his teeth." This chapter enters the treacherous terrain of contemporary history. It is easy to know what happened in recent decades but hard to know what it means. The Bantu migration, the rise of the Mughal Empire, and the Meiji Restoration happened long enough ago that their consequences have worked themselves out. With a little effort, we can hope to know what they meant and mean for today. But we can't yet know the full significance of recent events or how ongoing trends will unfold. What seems important now may seem superficial in years to come, and what now seems trivial might loom large. Treacherous terrain indeed, but no reason to shy away from trying to understand the human experience.

ENVIRONMENTAL CHANGE: INTO THE ANTHROPOCENE?

According to geologists, the Earth for the last 11,700 years has been in an epoch called the Holocene (from the ancient Greek for "wholly recent"). But since 2000, increasing numbers of scientists have argued that the Holocene is over and a new interval of geological time has begun. They call it the **Anthropocene**, to highlight the role of humankind (*anthropos* in Greek) in changing big natural systems, including global climate. Most earth scientists who embrace the concept of the Anthropocene think it began in the middle of the twentieth century.

It is important to bear two points in mind here. First, the Earth's natural systems have always been changing. So, for example, the Earth's climate over the past 3 billion years has undergone ice ages that come and go as a result of regular changes in the Earth's orbit. So the mere fact of change to the Earth's natural systems is nothing new. What is new, as we shall see, is the scale and pace of change in the recent past, and what lies behind it.

Second, humans have been causing major environmental changes mainly by accident. The concept of the Anthropocene does not mean that humans now control the global environment. Far from it. We influence the global environment, now more than ever, but mainly in ways no one intends and no one fully understands. The Anthropocene is an age of unintended consequences.

CLIMATE CHANGE AND CLIMATE POLITICS

Earth's climate is affected by many variables, including changes in the Earth's orbit, how much energy the sun emits, and how well the atmosphere traps heat. Climate has never been changeless. But in the past 30 to 40 years it has been changing faster than at any other time in human history.

The main reason for the current pulse of **climate change** is that the atmosphere now traps heat from the sun more efficiently than it has for the last 3 million years. That is a consequence of rising concentrations of the gases that do the trapping, called greenhouse gases, the most important of which is **carbon dioxide** (CO_2). Air bubbles trapped in polar icecaps show that for the entire human career—some 300,000 years—carbon dioxide levels in the atmosphere have ranged between 180 and 280 parts per million (ppm). For the past 12,000 years, carbon dioxide concentrations fluctuated a little bit on either side of 280 ppm. That made for unusually stable climate by the standards of the last few million years.

After 1840 or so, CO_2 concentrations slowly climbed above 280 ppm. The causes lay in the Industrial Revolution and the burning of fossil fuels and, to a lesser extent, the extension of agriculture and the burning of forests. For a century, the impact on climate was tiny.

Then, after 1950 or so, fossil fuel combustion around the world took off. By 1960, the CO_2 level had climbed to 315 ppm and by 2020 it topped 417 ppm (see the graph below), a level not previously touched in 3 million years and not consistently topped in 16 million years. At 2 ppm per year, the current rate of increase in atmospheric CO_2 levels is roughly 10 times faster than ever before—as far as we know. But there have been times in the deep past (about 500 million years ago, long before any mammals existed) when CO_2 levels stood much higher than today's, and the Earth was a lot hotter. We know about CO_2 concentrations in the past from measurements taken since 1958 on Mauna Loa, a Hawaiian mountain, and before that from air bubbles trapped in ice cores taken from Greenland and Antarctica.

Burning billions of tons of carbon every year amounts to a gigantic unintentional experiment on the planet. It has helped power machinery that allowed billions of people to enjoy more comfortable lives. But together with

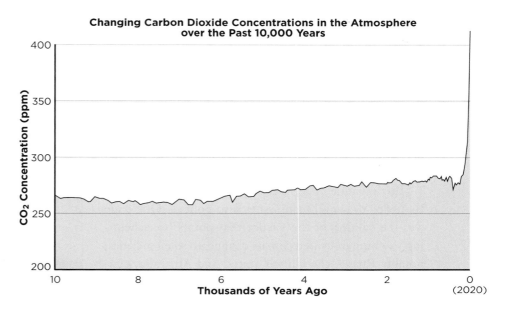

Through most of human history, the amount of atmospheric CO_2—the main greenhouse gas that helps to regulate climate—was fairly stable. The Industrial Revolution in the nineteenth century and the widespread adoption of fossil fuels in the twentieth ended that age of stability. Since 1950 or so, the atmosphere has been changing faster than at any time in many millions of years.

Source: Scripps Institution of Oceanography and NOAA.

Changes in Global Average Surface Temperature, 1850–2018

This chart of global average surface temperature shows a strong warming trend from the 1850s to the present, especially pronounced since 1980. This warming trend is occurring far faster than any known in the deeper past. The main cause of the warming measured here is the atmospheric carbon dioxide trend shown in the figure on page 865.

Source: Land data prepared by Berkeley Earth and combined with ocean data adapted from the UK Hadley Centre.

other greenhouse gases, the added carbon in the atmosphere has also raised average temperatures on Earth by about 2 degrees Fahrenheit (1.1 degree Celsius) since widespread temperature measurement began in the 1880s. As is evident in the graph above, most of that warming took place after 1980. It has also raised sea level by about 11 inches (28 cm) since 1880, because warmer air temperatures melt glacial ice and warmer sea temperatures expand the oceans' volume. The extra carbon also seeps into seawater, making it more acidic—about 30 percent more since 1800. Over the last 500 million years, oceans have grown notably more acidic about 30 times. On four of these occasions, more than 75 percent of marine animal species went extinct.

This gigantic experiment upon the Earth has since the 1980s drawn climate issues into politics. One issue was the validity of the science that points overwhelmingly to human-caused climate change. In some societies, notably Russia, the United States, and Australia, constituencies developed that encouraged some politicians either to deny the existence of climate change or, if they accepted it, to deny that humans had a role in it. In most of the world, however, these arguments got nowhere in the face of strong evidence and near-unanimous consensus among scientists. Only in countries where the fossil fuel industry was politically powerful did the existence of rapid climate change become controversial.

The second focus of climate politics was on what to do internationally about rising temperatures and greenhouse gas levels. Most nations contended that others should burn less carbon. Chinese diplomats, for example, noted correctly that the United States and Europe had burned more fossil fuels over the past 200 years than anyone else, and, the Chinese argued, should therefore reduce their carbon emissions first. American diplomats noted, also correctly, that Chinese CO_2 emissions (as of about 2013) were the highest in the world, and they argued that China should curtail its emissions. Poorer countries argued that they needed to burn more fossil fuel energy in order to escape poverty and should be exempt from any reductions in carbon emissions. Such differences proved hard to reconcile, resulting in the trends shown in the graphs above. The major international agreements that sought to slow climate change—the Kyoto Protocol of 1997 and the Paris Agreement of 2016—had no visible effect on carbon dioxide levels. The U.S. government chose not to ratify Kyoto and withdrew from the Paris Agreement, refusing to accept restrictions on its

Climate Change A polar bear leaps over melting ice in Svalbard, at the northern tip of Norway. Arctic regions have warmed disproportionately quickly, with profound consequences for animals adapted to life in cold, icy conditions.

Climate Change: Emissions and Sea Level Rise, 1751–2016 The international politics of climate change is complicated by the fact that the countries most responsible over centuries for the buildup of greenhouse gases—carbon dioxide being the most important—are not necessarily the same as those now emitting the most greenhouse gases. The United States now releases far less greenhouse gas than China, but over time has emitted far more. In addition, the countries most likely to suffer from ongoing climate change are often those with low emissions such as Egypt, Bangladesh, Mozambique, Vietnam, or the Maldives—all of which have densely populated areas just above sea level. The key to the future of climate change lies in South, Southeast, and East Asia, where half of humankind lives, tens of millions are at risk of sea level rise, and greenhouse gas emissions are rising rapidly.

greenhouse gas emissions—a position that undermined both agreements.

ENVIRONMENTAL TURBULENCE

Climate change was only one of several global environmental concerns that emerged in the late twentieth century. Biologists documented rapidly accelerating rates of animal and plant extinctions. Over the long history of life on Earth, on average about one in every million species has gone extinct each year. By the early twenty-first century, that annual rate had climbed to several hundred, perhaps several thousand, suggesting that life on Earth was entering a sixth spasm of mass extinction. The

previous one, about 66 million years ago, led to the disappearance of dinosaurs. The sixth one, if it is indeed that, is in its early stages and its consequences thus far remain modest. The driving force behind the acceleration of extinction is destruction of habitat, notably tropical forests, which are rich in species diversity. Vigorous efforts at species conservation dating from the 1960s have rescued some creatures, such as whooping cranes, California condors, and grizzly bears—at least for now.

Other acute environmental issues affected people more directly than the loss of species. For example, after the 1980s over-fishing brought several of the world's economically important fisheries, such as the North Atlantic cod or Atlantic bluefin tuna, to the point of collapse,

CO₂ Emissions A Chinese city enveloped by the dense smog that coal-fired power stations and home coal fires cause in cities across China. Particles emitted from burning coal fill the sky beyond, giving it a hazy appearance.

depriving fisherfolk of their livelihoods. Air pollution in hundreds of cities reached levels sufficient to kill millions of people every year, especially in India, China, and elsewhere that people breathed too much coal soot into their lungs.

Most of these environmental issues were more difficult to address politically than technologically. Reducing air pollution, for example, proved feasible in cities in Western Europe, Japan, and North America once citizen activism, between 1965 and 1980, produced enough political will to nudge public policy toward tighter regulations. But in many cases, political will remained weak. Some environmental problems, such as climate change or the accumulation of plastics in the oceans' food webs, were slow-brewing, so that ignoring them for another year or two seemed unlikely to make matters much worse. Moreover, the economic activities behind environmental problems produced winners as well as losers, and winners fought to preserve their gains. Thus coal miners and coal companies checked regulation of carbon emissions. Fishermen fought regulations on fishing—even if it meant their catch would shrink with each passing year.

Although it is hard to say what all this global environmental flux may mean in the long run, we can be sure of a few things. First, while human-caused environmental change is not new, the pace, scale, and scope of it in the last couple of human generations are unique. Second, global averages, whether of temperature, biodiversity loss, or the reduction in fish stocks, don't reveal much about

specific places. Arctic regions, for example, have warmed far more than the tropics in the past 30 years. The collapse of the Atlantic cod fishery in the early 1990s brought bitter consequences for people living in Newfoundland, while the global marine fish catch has held steady since 1980 at about 75 million tons annually. Hundreds of millions of people within reach of tropical storms in places such as the Philippines, Bangladesh, or the Caribbean had to face more frequent and larger typhoons, cyclones, and hurricanes. Meanwhile, the hundreds of thousands of people who live in northern Siberia, Scandinavia, Greenland, Canada, and Alaska experienced longer growing seasons and much milder winters.

Just why the world became so environmentally turbulent over the last 70 years is easy to explain. Many factors contributed, among them culture. Most people around the world clung to, or adopted, a culture of consumption, preferring more clothes, more furniture, more travel—more of just about everything. Cultural traditions such as Buddhism or Christianity, which historically had associated virtue and godliness with poverty and asceticism, proved extremely flexible in this regard. So did the Chinese Communist Party, which in the 1950s had trumpeted poor peasants as the most admirable of classes, but after 1980, as we've seen, converted to the gospel of wealth. In India, Gandhi's emphasis on simplicity lost out to a political culture that idolized industry, wealth, and power. Bhutan, a tiny kingdom high in the Himalaya, formed an exception: there the government since 2008 tried to measure, and to maximize, gross national happiness rather than gross national product.

Politics reinforced the impact of culture. Neither elected officials nor dictators thought asking anyone to consume less was good politics. Moreover, leaders concerned with national security normally thought a

	WORLD	United States	China	Japan	India	Egypt
1975	5,762	1,698	337	329	82	10
1995	8,545	2,117	917	489	236	38
2015	13,105	2,276	3,006	446	685	87

ENERGY USE SINCE 1975 (IN MILLIONS OF TONS OF OIL EQUIVALENT)

Source: BP Statistical Review of World Energy, various years.

wealthier society would help fund a bigger military, which would make everyone safer. Rulers for 5,000 years had thought the same way. But now the consequences were different.

At the same time as these notions of consumption and security prevailed, an enormous expansion in energy use made mass consumption much easier. We last looked at energy in the chapter on the Industrial Revolution, which emphasized the transition to fossil fuels. As late as 1960, however, that transition was mainly confined to North America, Europe, and Japan. Since then, the continuing rise of energy-intensive activities, such as motor vehicle use or the production of nitrogen-based fertilizer, has changed the picture. The world's vehicle fleet (cars, buses, trucks), for example, grew from 250 million in 1970 to 1.2 billion by 2015. Nitrogen fertilizer use rose sevenfold between 1961 and 2020. As the table on page 868 shows, the total quantity of energy used globally more than doubled between 1975 and 2015. China, India, and Egypt by 2015 used eight or nine times their 1975 totals.

About 80 percent of this surge in energy use came in the form of fossil fuels. So this global trend led to considerable increases in urban air pollution, especially in India and China. It also led to more oil spills—notably in the oilfields of Siberia and Nigeria, and in the world's shipping lanes, where tankers occasionally ran aground or broke up in storms. And, as noted above, the increased use of fossil fuels elevated CO_2 concentrations in the atmosphere, warming the Earth.

POPULATION TRENDS SINCE 1950

Population growth was another powerful driving force behind environmental change and much else in recent decades. We last looked at the subject in Chapter 23 in the context of the Vital Revolution, which carried the story up to 1950.

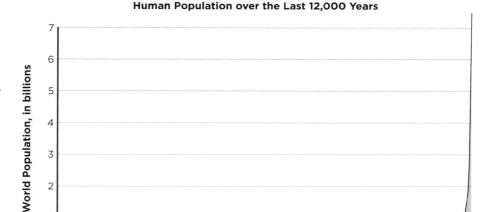

Human Population over the Last 12,000 Years

This chart shows the size of the human population over the past 12,000 years. It reached 1 billion around 1820 and 2 billion by 1930. Since 1960, it has grown by 1 billion every 12 or 15 years. Although the rate of growth is now slowing, the record of the recent past through to the present is an extreme departure from the pattern of the longer past.

Source: World Population Data from the United Nations, the U.S. Census Bureau, and others, found at https://en.wikipedia.org/wiki/Estimates_of_historical_world_population#/media/File:Population_curve.svg

POPULATION AND PUBLIC HEALTH

The population history of planet Earth since 1950 is unique, although almost everyone alive has known nothing else and so considers it normal. In the span of one human lifetime (1950–2020), global population more than tripled, from 2.5 billion to 7.8 billion, growing at well over 1 percent per year. For the previous 10,000 years, the annual rate was closer to 0.05 percent. Put another way, two-thirds of the population growth in all 300,000 years of human history took place after 1950. We now outnumber any other large mammal on Earth, and we account for about 5 percent of the globe's animal biomass (although ants easily outweigh us—because there are so many of them). The graph above shows how peculiar the last few decades are in light of longer patterns.

The key to this unique development has been better public health programs since 1945. One way to think of it is that humankind invented and adopted effective "death control" measures before we adopted much birth control. It began in the nineteenth century but took a giant stride forward in World War II when medical personnel figured out how to administer vaccines and antibiotics to large military populations. After 1945, similar techniques applied more broadly reduced mortality, especially for infants and children, especially in Asia, Africa, and Latin America. A glorious landmark came in the late 1970s, when international health teams wiped out smallpox, ridding the human race of one of its greatest killers. Even when we count deaths caused by the COVID-19 pandemic, the global death rate in 2020 stood at less than half the 1950 rate, mainly through reductions in infectious diseases such as measles, smallpox, and typhoid. Average life expectancy around the world exceeded 71 years. In almost every country except India, women outlived men.

The surge in life expectancy—one of the signal social changes of recent history—was a global phenomenon achieved mainly by the quick spread of new vaccines, anti-bacterial drugs, and public health measures. But improved nutrition and a rollback of famines also helped. More fertilizers and irrigation, better crop breeding and weather forecasting, and a host of other changes to agriculture enabled the global food supply to grow even faster than global population. In addition, better transport enabled people to move food faster to places where it was in short supply. All these changes reduced the frequency and size of killing famines. While hundreds of millions of people remained persistently malnourished, after the 1980s mass starvation occurred only in war zones and the hermit country of North Korea.

The consequences of improved public health and food supply played out differently around the world. Richer, more stable countries could provide the means of death control more thoroughly than could poorer or unstable countries, as the table below suggests. Lives are briefest in Africa, which accounts for 32 of the 33 countries with the shortest life expectancy. Even the poorest and most unstable countries, however, now have life expectancies almost twice as long as the richest places in the world two centuries ago.

COUNTER-CURRENTS IN PUBLIC HEALTH: EMERGING DISEASES

Recognition of this golden age of human health and longevity should not overshadow some grim exceptions. In the former Soviet Union, especially Russia and Ukraine, life expectancy fell in the 1990s mainly because of illnesses associated with alcohol and smoking. It has rebounded since. In the United States, where overall life expectancy crept upward after 2000, it fell for the middle-aged white male population through suicides, alcoholism, and drug overdoses—so-called deaths of despair. It has not yet rebounded.

New infectious diseases also imperiled the golden age of human health. The viruses that caused AIDS in the 1980s, SARS in 2003, MERS in 2012, and COVID-19 beginning in 2019 all mutated and leapt successfully from animal to human populations. As more people brushed up against wild and domestic animals more frequently, they gave viruses more opportunity to evolve so as to survive in human bodies. **HIV/AIDS**, genomic evidence tells us, was an infection of chimpanzees until the 1940s, when it first became a human infection. It did not spread much until the 1980s, when growing connectivity within Africa enabled it to travel farther and faster, igniting a global pandemic that took some 30 million lives as of 2020. HIV/AIDS was much worse in Africa than elsewhere. In South Africa, for example, it shortened average life expectancy by about 10 years from 1990 to 2005. (It has rebounded, thanks to medical interventions.) SARS and MERS had killed fewer than 1,000 each as of 2020.

The so-called novel coronavirus (SARS CoV-2), which causes the disease COVID-19, apparently lived only in bat colonies until late in 2019. It mutated into a human pathogen in or near Wuhan in central China and spread quickly around the world, causing another global pandemic and killing hundreds of thousands. To prevent far

ESTIMATED LIFE EXPECTANCY IN 2020			
	YEARS		**YEARS**
Japan	85	Mexico	75
Switzerland	83	Egypt	72
Australia	83	Russia	72
New Zealand	82	Indonesia	72
Greece	82	India	69
United Kingdom	81	Pakistan	67
United States	79	Haiti	64
China	77	South Africa	64
Vietnam	76	Uganda	63
Brazil	76	Nigeria	54
Jamaica	75	Central African Republic	53

Source: United Nations Development Program data, found at https://en.wikipedia.org/wiki/List_of_countries_by_life_expectancy

greater death tolls, people worldwide adopted social distancing to slow the virus's spread, which seriously damaged the inter-connected world economy.

The devastating health impact of **COVID-19** was the result of four conditions. First, the pathogen itself is easily transmitted from human to human. For days before showing symptoms, infected people shed virus with every breath, cough, or sneeze. Normal gatherings, such as weddings, concerts, or religious services, could create clusters of infection anywhere. Second, nobody carried any resistance or immunity to the disease, because it was new to humans. Third, air travel moved so many people so far and so fast that they carried the virus out of central China to every other country within two months. About 13 million people flew in airplanes every day in 2019—about 16 times the daily air traffic in 1970. And fourth, the world's public health systems were—like individual immune systems—unprepared for what hit them. The main exceptions were effectively governed countries such as Costa Rica, South Korea, Vietnam, New Zealand, Germany, and Iceland. Partly because of their experience of either SARS or MERS, South Korea, Singapore, and Hong Kong took COVID-19 seriously weeks or months sooner than other countries, and they escaped the first wave with minimal mortality. National leaders in China, Western Europe, Brazil, and the United States, in contrast, reacted only after the virus had already spread widely within their countries, and their populations—indeed, the entire human population—paid a price for that.

Whether or not these newly emerging infectious diseases mark the end of the golden age of human health, or a temporary setback, it is too soon to say. None of them equaled the 1918 influenza, which killed perhaps 50 million people worldwide. But more new diseases are sure to come, because humans so frequently are in contact with animals such as bats and rodents that harbor an immense variety of viruses. And when new diseases are highly infectious, even in people showing no symptoms, as with COVID-19, they will spread around the world in days or weeks, because air travelers course throughout the Global web every day.

FERTILITY DECLINES

Regardless of the impact of emerging diseases, the anomalous moment of supercharged population growth after

Viral Epidemics COVID-19 patients fill a temporary hospital erected in a sports center in Wuhan, China, in February 2020. Wuhan was at the center of the first outbreak of COVID-19, when the virus that causes the illness made the jump from bats to humans.

1950 is now slowing because birth control is catching up to death control. The rate of population growth reached its maximum in the 1960s, briefly exceeding 2 percent per year. It now stands at 1.1 percent per year, because birth rates have fallen almost everywhere. By 2019, roughly three out of every four women of reproductive age around the world used some form of birth control. About 140 million babies were born that year (and about 55 million people died).

The main reasons behind the downward fertility trend were urbanization and the spread of formal education for females. On average, women with more education prefer not to have large families, and couples living in cities want smaller families than do their country cousins. The places where fertility did not fall much—Afghanistan and parts of Africa, mainly—are places where urbanization and formal education for females made little headway in the past 70 years.

The **declines in fertility** around the world amount to an enormous change in the lives of families and women in particular. Adult women came to spend far less of their lives pregnant, and a good deal less time attending to the needs of small children than their mothers and grandmothers had done. Instead, they spent much more time in school and working in factories and offices. Each trend—lower fertility and time spent outside the home—reinforced the other.

FROM MIDNIGHT TONIGHT WE BUNKER DOWN FOR FOUR WEEKS
TO TRY AND STOP THE VIRUS IN ITS TRACKS. . . . EVERY MOVE YOU
THEN MAKE IS A RISK TO SOMEONE ELSE. THAT IS HOW WE MUST ALL
COLLECTIVELY THINK. THAT'S WHY THE JOY OF PHYSICALLY VISITING
OTHER FAMILY, CHILDREN, GRANDCHILDREN, FRIENDS, NEIGHBORS, IS
ON HOLD. BECAUSE WE'RE ALL NOW PUTTING EACH OTHER FIRST. **"**

JACINDA ARDERN   MARCH 18, 2020
PRIME MINISTER OF NEW ZEALAND

Europe

**UNITED
KINGDOM**
44.0

GERMANY

BELGIUM
9.8

FRANCE
29.8   Milan

SPAIN
28.4

ITALY
34.8

0   200   400 mi
0   200   400 km

See inset

RUSSIA
9.5

E U R A S I A

Milan

To New York City

TURKEY

IRAN
11.0

PAKISTAN

CHINA

Beijing

Seoul

JAPAN

Wuhan

EGYPT

SAUDI
ARABIA

INDIA
17.4

TAIWAN

A F R I C A

Bangkok

PACIFIC OCEAN

ATLANTIC
OCEAN

INDIAN OCEAN

AUSTRALIA

SOUTH
AFRICA

NEW ZEALAND

**Reported cases and deaths, by July 1,
2020**
Number of reported cases, by country

2,600,000
1,400,000
650,000
85,000
200

34.8 12 countries with the highest
number reported of deaths, in
thousands

29.5 10 states of the United States
with the highest number of
reported deaths, in thousands

KEY

Initial spread of infection from
Wuhan, China, January 1–31,
2020. Arrow thickness indicates
approximate number of travellers.

• City with recorded outbreak, by
January 31, 2020

**Stay-at-home requirements in place, by
March 24, 2020**

Required, with virtually no exceptions

Required, except for daily exercise,
food shopping, and essential trips

Recommended

None

No data

0   1000   2000 mi
0   1000   2000 km

The COVID-19 Pandemic

► COVID-19 testing site, Wuhan, China, May 2020.

CANADA

NORTH AMERICA

ILLINOIS 7.1

Seattle

MICHIGAN 6.2

MASSACHUSETTS 8.1
From Italy

UNITED STATES 125.2

New York

CONNECTICUT 4.3
NEW YORK 29.5
NEW JERSEY 15.0
PENNSYLVANIA 6.6

CALIFORNIA 6.0

FLORIDA 3.7

LOUISIANA 3.2

ATLANTIC OCEAN

MEXICO 27.8

BRAZIL 59.6

PERU 9.7

SOUTH AMERICA

CHILE

Questions for Analysis

Based on this feature and your chapter reading, consider the following questions:

1. How did the COVID-19 pandemic reveal connections between your life and the Global web?

2. Did the public health emergency of COVID-19 show the need for stronger national and global coordination of response measures or more local autonomy? Explain your response.

LATE IN 2019, A CORONAVIRUS new to humans burst upon the world, causing a disease called COVID-19 in those infected. The outbreak began in Wuhan, a provincial capital in central China, and spread rapidly within the country aided by travel at the Chinese New Year. The virus then spread around the world and grew to pandemic proportions. By July 1, 2020, global agencies had recorded about 10 million confirmed cases and half a million deaths from COVID-19, with the numbers continuing to rise. The stay-at-home and shut-down orders adopted in many countries and large cities shook the global economy.

The pandemic was entangled in the Global web in three main ways. First, the virus itself moved along every pathway of the Global web. It spread by jet from China to the hubs of the world's airline systems in cities such as Milan, London, and New York. From the hubs it eventually traveled out to every city and town of any size everywhere in the world.

Second, information about the virus and how to combat it spread at electronic speed throughout the Global web. The virus was formally identified in China on January 7, 2020, and its genome was published on the Internet on January 10. Scientists around the world collaborated in the effort to find effective drugs and a vaccine. Strategies for slowing the virus, such as social distancing, stay-at-home requirements, and the use of face coverings, also spread almost instantly, although authorities often delayed implementation at the cost of many thousands of lives.

Finally, the necessary measures to slow the virus resulted in economic hardship wherever web connections were strong. Tens of millions of people lost jobs and billions lost income. The COVID-19 pandemic led to more economic pain than the far deadlier 1918 flu pandemic because economic globalization was stronger in 2020 than in 1918. The world economy in 2020 was built on dense and active international supply chains, trade, and travel. These strong global connections made the world economy more vulnerable to interruption than at any earlier time in world history.

Humans grew bigger as well as more numerous after 1950. The greatest changes came in East Asia, southern Europe, and the Baltic countries. South Koreans topped the list, growing 7 to 9 inches (18–23 cm) taller on average between 1950 and 2015, an indication of better diets especially among the poor. A few populations, mainly in Africa, have not grown taller since 1950. Egyptians and Ugandans, because of malnutrition, have been shrinking since 1990.

On average, people grew heavier as well as taller. More sedentary lifestyles and more food have caused the average person to gain weight in just about every country since 1980. In the United States, the average adult in 2015 weighed 15 lbs. (7 kg) more than in 1990. Taking both height and weight together, the average human has expanded in size far faster in the past 50 years than ever before.

Urbanization Residents throng the streets of Mumbai, one of the world's largest cities. In 2020, Mumbai had a population of over 20 million.

URBANIZATION IN OVERDRIVE

While humans have been growing more numerous, and on average bigger, we have also become primarily urban animals. For most of the last 10,000 years, the typical human habitat was the farming village. A century ago, only about 10 to 15 percent of the world's people lived in cities. By 1950 that figure reached 29 percent, and by 2020 some 55 percent of people were city-dwellers, about 4.2 billion in all.

Big cities got bigger. In 1800, only one, Beijing, had more than 1 million inhabitants. By 1950, there were about 70, led by New York, London, Tokyo, and Moscow. By 2015, some 540 cities reached the 1 million threshold, and 39 of those had more than 10 million people. The biggest were in Asia: Tokyo, Jakarta, Seoul, Karachi, Shanghai, and Manila all counted more than 24 million in their metro areas.

Two trends drove this spurt of accelerating urbanization. First, city life stopped killing people quite so fast. Until about 1880, cities everywhere were so unhealthy that their residents died at faster rates than new ones were born. Cities survived only because villagers moved in looking for better lives. Between 1880 and about 1950, cities around the world became healthy enough that their birth rates came to exceed their death rates. That happy trend grew stronger after 1950. Meanwhile, streams of migration from the countryside swelled to torrents: population growth and land shortages in the villages drove young people to seek their futures in cities. The largest

and fastest urbanization in world history took place in China after 1980.

Migrants from village to city rarely had it easy. Carolina María de Jesus moved from a Brazilian village to the metropolis of São Paulo and lived in its shantytowns (called *favelas* in Brazil) for several decades. She had only a second-grade education and struggled to make a living as a single mother, protect her three children from violence, and avoid falling into the despair that claimed so many of her neighbors. She kept a diary, translated as *Child of the Dark*, which gives an unsparing picture of *favela* life in the late 1950s with its daily fare of domestic violence, alcoholism, jealous gossip, and the constant struggle to put food on the table—which she did by selling paper she scavenged from garbage heaps. Hundreds of millions of women around the world lived similar lives after leaving their native villages for the slums of Bangkok, Nairobi, or Lima.

Another who went to the big city to better himself is the uncle of one of my students. Alim (not his real name) was born in 1960 in a village in what was then East Pakistan, now Bangladesh. He spent his early years in a corrugated tin hut. His life changed when he was sent to live with a relative whose village had a school. He loved school, did well in it, and began to win scholarships—as Wangari Maathai did. He kept winning them and studied electrical engineering at a polytechnic institute. That allowed Alim to get a job helping the government build an electrical grid in rural Bangladesh. In the 1980s he tried his hand at business, distributing fertilizer, but ended up in

Favelas Houses built from scrap wood line a hillside in 1950s Rio de Janeiro. *Favelas*, or shantytowns, became sites of poverty and over-crowding in rapidly urbanizing Brazil.

debt. In the 1990s he moved to the capital, Dhaka, seeking better opportunities because he now had a family to feed. They stayed in the countryside while Alim, feeling lonely and economically insecure, worked in Dhaka. Hundreds of millions of men around the world found themselves in similar predicaments, able to make a better living in the big city than in their native village but unable to support their families comfortably.

In Australia, Argentina, Japan, and a few smaller countries, more than 90 percent of people live in cities. In the United States, 82 percent do. But in South Asia and sub-Saharan Africa, only a third of the people live in cities, although cities there are growing fast. Across the globe, urban population is growing at about twice the rate of total population, a little above 2 percent annually.

It is still too soon to tell the full meaning of this overnight urbanization of the human species. It has contributed to lowering fertility—a social revolution in and of itself. It has also helped raise levels of education, because providing such services is easier where people are close together. On average, it has made people slightly richer. But it surely has also made them more acutely aware of inequality, as rich and poor live close together. And it has created opportunities for infectious diseases, such as COVID-19, to flourish in tightly packed neighborhoods.

INTERNATIONAL MIGRATION

The movement of hundreds of millions from village to city was not the only important migratory flow in recent decades. In 1980, some 100 million people lived in a country other than where they were born. In 2019, roughly 270 million people, or 3.5 percent of humankind, did so. About 10 percent were officially refugees who fled war or persecution. The table below shows the five biggest population groups living abroad in 2019.

In 2019, some 51 million **international migrants** lived in the United States, with the next largest totals in Germany and Saudi Arabia, with 13 million each. In 2012, a Gallup poll concluded that 640 million people *wanted* to migrate to another country but couldn't. International migration remains highly restricted. Much of it goes uncounted. Each year since 2010, about 8 to 16 million people have migrated internationally, of whom about one-quarter were going back home.

This surge of migration is best understood in longer context. Between 1840 and 1940, inexpensive, steam-powered transport enabled over 170 million people, mostly young men, to move to another country. They left home for factories in Detroit and Dortmund, for mines in Manchuria and Minnesota, for plantations in Thailand and Trinidad. The number of international migrants peaked in 1913 and again in the late 1920s at a little more than 3 million per year.

Broadly speaking, there were three main currents of migration in the century before 1940. One involved 55 to 60 million people moving to the Americas from Europe and the Middle East. The British Isles, Germany, Italy, Poland, and Russia provided the most emigrants, two-thirds of whom went to the United States and most of the others to Canada, Argentina, or Brazil. A second current featured 45 to 55 million Indians and southern Chinese going to Southeast Asia and other rimlands of the Indian Ocean such as Burma and Ceylon (now Sri Lanka). A third current took 45 to 55 million northern Chinese, Koreans, and Russians to Manchuria or Central

LARGEST POPULATIONS LIVING ABROAD, 2019	
Indians	18 million
Mexicans	12 million
Chinese	11 million
Russians	10 million
Syrians	8 million

Source: United Nations Department of Social and Economic Affairs, www.un.org/development/desa/en/news/population/international-migrant-stock-2019.html

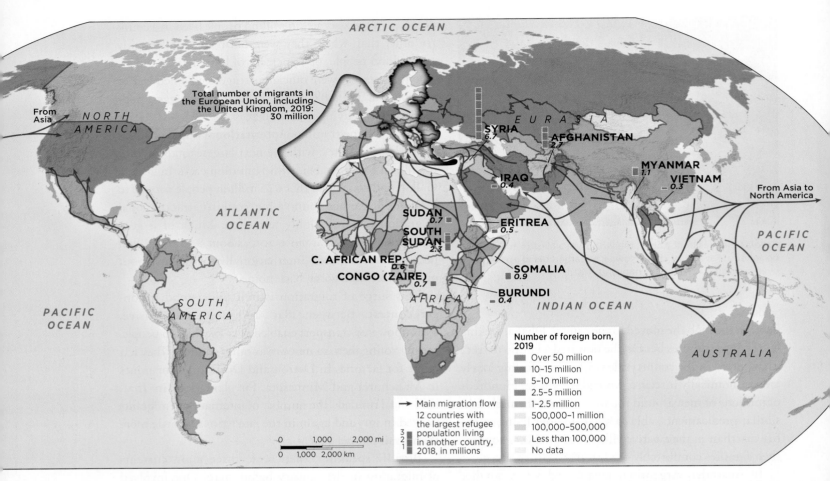

International Migration and Refugee Flows, ca. 2015–2020 The broadest pattern in recent migration history is movement from poor countries to richer ones. Several million people migrated every year in the 2010s, mainly to North America, Europe, the Persian Gulf region, and Australia. Latin Americans went chiefly to the United States; Africans to Europe; East and Southeast Asians to both North America and Australia. Refugees left war-torn lands, especially Syria, Afghanistan, and several countries of central and eastern Africa. Those leaving Myanmar fled religious persecution rather than war.

Asia. But there were smaller flows too, such as the 2 to 3 million Canadians who migrated to industrial cities in the United States, and a few million from all over southern Africa who went to the mines of South Africa.

After a downturn during the Great Depression and World War II, international migration revived in 1945. The first pulse came in the form of perhaps 10 million war refugees in Europe and East Asia. Then came the flows provoked by decolonization, such as the 10 to 17 million Muslims and Hindus who were uprooted because of the 1947 partition of India.

A more sustained pulse began in the 1960s. Northern European countries, especially West Germany, began to recruit large numbers of supposedly temporary workers from southern Europe and Turkey. Called guest workers,

many of them wound up staying for life. Meanwhile the United States, Canada, and Australia changed their immigration rules, which had been overtly racist, opening doors for more migrants from Asia, the Caribbean, and Latin America. And in the 1970s, an oil boom attracted millions of migrants to the Arabian Peninsula, mainly the tiny countries of the Gulf. Most came from South Asia and the Philippines. So, since the 1970s, the main destinations for migrants have been Western Europe, North America, and the Gulf. The numbers of migrants increased a bit after 1990. The dissolution of the USSR led to migrations of ethnic Russians out of several formerly Soviet territories. The booming U.S. economy of the 1990s attracted many job seekers from Mexico and the rest of Latin America.

The share of migrants in the world population in the quarter-century 1990–2015 was about the same as that in 1890–1915. But there were two big differences in the makeup of the migrant populations. In 1890–1915, the great majority of migrants were men, the normal pattern until recently. Since 1990, however, nearly half of all international migrants have been women, mainly because families are likelier to migrate together. In many European countries, a small majority of immigrants are women.

The other big difference is education. Before 1940, the overwhelming majority of migrants were uneducated. Their skill set was usually confined to what they learned growing up in farming villages. Since 1990, in contrast, roughly 20 percent of migrants brought with them university educations and professional training. This change reflects immigration policy, especially in the United States, Australia, and Canada, which gave preference to people with skills expected to be economically useful. It also results from the more globalized world of multinational corporations, in which business managers from Italy or India might work a few years in Hong Kong, then a few in London or Rio de Janeiro. There is, then, in addition to a majority of migrants who are poor (as before), a sizeable share who are among the world's richest 1 percent.

Migration contributed powerfully to the recent spurt of globalization. Although uneven in impact from place to place, the net effect was to tie the Global web a little tighter, bringing more people into more frequent contact with strangers from afar.

Guest Workers Migrant mineworkers from Turkey disembark from a plane in Düsseldorf, Germany, in 1961. In the 1960s Germany recruited thousands of guest workers, many of whom made their homes in the country long-term.

POLITICS AND THE GLOBAL WEB

In the decades since the end of the Cold War (1989), the most important political trends were the rise of China (discussed in Chapter 28), the growing role of international institutions, a revival of religious politics, and a cresting wave of democratization.

INTERNATIONAL INSTITUTIONS

Many of the powerful **international institutions** still with us were created in the 1940s as leaders sought to avoid future crises of the sort that had brought on the Great Depression and World War II. The most important were the United Nations and the pair tasked with looking after the world economy—the International Monetary Fund and the World Bank. Some others are a little older, such as Interpol, founded in 1923, which facilitates cooperation among law enforcement agencies around the world. Some are more recent, such as the Intergovernmental Panel on Climate Change, formed in 1988 under the authority of the UN, which reports periodically on all aspects of global climate.

With the rise of problems and challenges that are global in scale, such as international drug trades, human trafficking, and climate change, states around the world came together more often to create such institutions and to rely on them to an unprecedented extent. The United Nations grew particularly active after the end of the Cold War, for example, mounting far more peacekeeping operations than previously, helping to end 21 civil wars between 1991 and 2017.

The UN's peacekeeping record, however, was mixed. UN forces grew from about 20,000 in 1990 to about 100,000, in 2010, mainly provided by the armed forces of South Asian and African countries. While its interventions in Cambodia (1991–1993) and El Salvador (1989–1995) contributed to lasting peace, it failed to prevent genocide in Rwanda, in East Africa, in 1994, or massacres in Bosnia (part of the former Yugoslavia) in 1995. As of 2020, it maintained 14 peacekeeping operations, half of them in Africa. Since the UN, like other international institutions, had no armies, its authority ultimately came from the support of countries—only some of which consistently proved supportive. This problem limited the impact of the UN and at times made people and politicians skeptical of its value.

Also over the last half-century, an increasing number of international non-governmental organizations emerged to play larger and larger roles. Médecins Sans Frontières (Doctors without Borders) took shape in 1971 as a volunteer group of medical professionals who donated their services, particularly in war-torn areas. Amnesty International, formed in 1961, sought to protect people against governmental abuses. Such outfits, and many like them, gradually became part of the fabric of international affairs. So too (less happily) did criminal cartels, which also responded to global opportunities by internationalizing their businesses—for example, moving cocaine from Peru and Bolivia to high-priced markets in the United States and Europe. In some cases, such as the Russian mafia since the 1990s, international criminal cartels were informally allied with governments. All these organizations and groups arose in response to a more globalized world and by their actions helped to globalize it further.

REVIVALS OF RELIGIOUS POLITICS

A second powerful trend around the world was a revival of religious politics. Most societies throughout world history blended political and religious authority together. Religious politics are as old as religion itself. But during the nineteenth and twentieth centuries many states had distanced themselves from formal religion, following a tradition born in the French and American revolutions, both of which put barriers between church and state. Most communist states, including the USSR, China, and Cuba, were officially atheist. But in the 1970s, religious politics made a comeback.

POLITICAL ISLAM The most conspicuous case is the rise of political Islam. Religion had always mattered in the politics of Muslim societies—both Shi'a, who predominated in Iran and Iraq, and Sunni, the majority almost everywhere else. But between the 1920s and 1960s, it mattered less and national and class identities mattered more. Nationalist regimes, often run by military men, held sway in several countries such as Turkey from the 1920s, Egypt from the 1950s, and Algeria after independence in 1962.

By the 1970s, the governments of most Muslim societies struck their citizens as corrupt and ineffective. Despite decades in office, they had failed to live up to promises of social justice or national wealth and power. Religious leaders called for more virtuous, godly, and efficient rule. In Iran, mullahs—meaning Muslims learned in Islamic law and tradition—seized power in a revolution in 1979. They overthrew a monarch whom they regarded, with justification, as corrupt and subservient to foreign powers. They installed an Islamic republic, enforcing a Muslim law code and imposing rules about personal conduct and dress—mainly for women—that they deemed consistent with their religious heritage.

The dominant form of Islamic political revival was party politics. Muslims, like everyone else, had been adapting to electoral systems for decades when the revolution in Iran added to the inspiration of a new generation of politically active Muslims. In Turkey, an Islamic party grew prominent in the 1990s and started winning elections in 2002. It gradually re-asserted the authority of religion in Turkish society, undoing some of the Atatürk revolution of the 1920s that, as we've seen, had built a secular state in Turkey. Islamic parties did well in elections in Algeria, Tunisia, Bangladesh, Indonesia, and elsewhere. They typically promised a more just and godly society, and in particular an end to corruption. They proved adept at providing social services such as food kitchens and support for widows and orphans. They funded school systems intended to instill the teachings of Islam in the young.

In some cases, Islamic politics took extremist, intolerant forms. Religious parties often struggle with notions of compromise and negotiation, because some believers consider any compromise with divine will to be immoral. Several factions claiming to represent the will of Allah in the politics of Islamic societies resorted to terrorist violence. The Taliban in Afghanistan, active since 1996, are a leading example, but many others arose across the Islamic world from Mali to the Philippines. In places where repressive monarchs or military rule quashed all forms of opposition, terrorist tactics seemed—to those who adopted them—the only weapon at their disposal. Most Muslim societies by 2010 had some experience with terrorist factions operating in the name of Islam. The proportion of civil wars around the world that involved an Islamist faction was below 10 percent in the decades before 1990, but thereafter climbed to about 40 percent, where it remains in 2020.

A small proportion of these factions flourished internationally. The most successful was **al-Qaeda** (its name means "the base" in Arabic), begun in 1988 by a

Al-Qaeda Rescue workers remove casualties from the wreckage of the U.S. Embassy in Nairobi, Kenya, following a 1998 al-Qaeda attack that killed more than 200 people. The Nairobi bombing was one of several international terrorist attacks that Osama bin Laden orchestrated in the 1990s and 2000s.

charismatic and wealthy Saudi Arabian and Sunni zealot, Osama bin Laden. He acquired his prestige helping to defeat the Soviet army in its war in Afghanistan from 1979 to 1989. He based his ideology of militant jihad—as warfare in the name of Islam is often called—on his selective interpretation of the Qur'an. He promoted the notion of a restored Islamic caliphate and sanctioned violence against Shi'a Muslims and other minorities within Islam, as well as against non-Muslims.

In the 1990s, after the Soviets left Afghanistan, bin Laden turned his sights on new enemies, especially the United States. At that time, the United States had troops stationed in bin Laden's home country. He regarded foreign armies in Saudi Arabia as an intolerable affront and organized anti-American terrorist assaults. He was the paymaster behind the terrorist attacks of September 11, 2001, that killed nearly 3,000 people in New York, in Arlington, Virginia, and in Shanksville, Pennsylvania. Al-Qaeda also flourished in Iraq after an American invasion of that country in 2003, undertaken in the mistaken belief that Iraq had weapons of mass destruction, left it in chaos. Offshoots of al-Qaeda engaged in terrorism, usually targeting other Muslims, in several countries such as Somalia, Syria, and Yemen. American forces killed bin Laden in Pakistan in 2011, but al-Qaeda lived on. Its franchises and affiliates continued to operate in at least 20 countries, sharing funding, training, and propaganda using international banks, air travel, the Internet, and other sinews of the Global web.

OTHER RELIGIONS Like Islam, other major religious traditions after the 1970s served as fuel for political ideologies. In India, for example, organizations promoting various versions of Hindu values grew more active. A political party (the Bharatiya Janata Party, or BJP) devoted to making India more authentically Hindu took shape in the 1980s. Since the 1990s, the BJP has been in and out of power, and always one of the two biggest parties in Indian politics. Its leaders wanted to see India become more forceful in international affairs, especially in its stance toward its Muslim neighbor Pakistan. Many of its members wished to stop Muslim immigrants from entering India. In 1992, Hindu extremists destroyed the old Babri mosque in Ayodhya, in northern India, with the aim of building a temple to the Hindu god Rama on the site. Deadly riots followed. Various Hindu terrorist cells stood behind bombings of mosques, attacks on Christian missionaries, and assaults on representatives of India's secular state. But, as with other cases of religious politics, the primary expression of Hindu political revival was in Indian party politics.

Christianity, especially its Protestant evangelical forms, has also been increasingly enlisted in political struggles since the 1970s. Evangelical Christians in the United States, often motivated by social issues such as the legality of abortion, overcame their traditional distaste for politics. Evangelical Protestantism became a political force in several Latin American countries, such as Brazil and Guatemala, from the 1980s onward. In 1960, the Protestant population of Latin America was tiny, but by 2015 some

Hindu Militancy A photograph of the Babri mosque in northern India in 1992, shortly before Hindu extremists destroyed it with the intention of building a Hindu temple on the site.

15 to 20 percent of Latin Americans considered themselves Protestants, usually Pentecostalists. They typically pressed their governments to restrict abortion and gay marriage. In Africa too, evangelical Protestant faiths acquired many recruits after 1980, and by 2015 they accounted for perhaps 20 to 25 percent of all African Christians. Both Kenya and Zambia elected presidents who identified as evangelical Protestants, and Zambia's, Frederick Chiluba, officially declared his country a Christian nation in the 1990s.

Buddhism too acquired a new political edge. Since 2000, in majority-Buddhist countries such as Thailand, Burma, and Sri Lanka, small groups, sometimes called Buddhist fundamentalists, have organized militant wings that target Muslims and Christians. Many Buddhists in these countries felt that their religion and culture were under threat from foreign values, including those of Islam, Christianity, and the marketplace. They appealed to their governments for laws that would ban uncomplimentary remarks about the Buddha or make it illegal for Buddhist women in Burma to marry anyone of another faith.

Israel, the only country with a Jewish majority, also developed a more religious politics after the 1970s. Officially a Jewish state since its foundation in 1948, its central political issue was that it claimed land—the land of the ancient Hebrews—that Palestinian Arabs regarded as their own. So Israelis had to choose whether to try to co-exist with Palestinians or dominate them, a dilemma complicated by Israel's vulnerability to the often hostile Arab states surrounding it. In its early decades, Israel was led by secular Jews of European background. But in 1977, several religious factions, calling for a more observant society and less compromise with Palestinians, helped put the nationalistic Likud Party in power. Thereafter, religious groups provided crucial support for nationalist parties that consistently did well in elections. What unified them was the wish for a more aggressive policy toward Palestinians and the so-called West Bank, land that the Israeli army conquered in 1967 but that Palestinians—and most of the world—considered theirs. Governments in Israel encouraged Jews to settle in the West Bank, guaranteeing frictions with Palestinians, and used those frictions to justify stricter controls on Palestinians.

Everywhere, globalization created problems that people hoped religion would solve. Some of those problems were economic, and some cultural. The sudden ups and downs of a globalized economy cost many people their economic security. When in distress, they felt grateful for the charity and social support that religious groups typically provided. The rapid urbanization in Latin America and parts of Africa and South Asia uprooted people from their communities, leaving emotional and psychological voids in their lives. Religious groups offered comfort and companionship for those in need. Religion also offered an affirmation of identity and community for those who felt their culture was under siege by strangers with alien values.

DEMOCRACY RISING

One of the signal trends of world politics in the late twentieth century was the **spread of democracy**. In 1974, the world had twice as many authoritarian states as liberal democracies. Then, in the mid-1970s, dictatorships in Portugal, Spain, and Greece fell in near-bloodless revolutions that led to durable parliamentary democracies. Between 1978 and 1990, military dictatorships in 11 Latin American countries collapsed and were replaced by democracies. The Iranian Revolution, mentioned above, also replaced an authoritarian monarchy with a parliamentary system. In the Philippines, a popular revolution overthrew a dictator in the late 1980s. In 1989 and 1990, Eastern Europe's communist regimes tumbled down with the Berlin Wall, giving way to much more democratic states. Communist Yugoslavia fragmented in the late 1980s, giving rise to six new republics, two of which, Slovenia and Croatia, built more or less democratic political systems by the late 1990s. In Mexico, what was essentially a one-party system became a more pluralistic multi-party one in the 1990s. South Korea and Taiwan replaced authoritarian regimes with more democratic ones in the 1980s and 1990s. Indonesia ended military rule in 1998. In Africa, where authoritarian rule had become the norm after independence, 13 one-party dictatorships fell in the early 1990s. South Africa in 1994 ended decades of *apartheid* ("separateness"), a political system of democracy for whites only that excluded nearly 90 percent of South Africans. The result—thanks in large part to the commitment of Nelson Mandela, a longtime foe of racial politics who had spent 26 years as a political prisoner—was a more inclusive and pluralist system.

By 2010, the world had twice as many democracies as authoritarian regimes—a remarkable turnaround since 1974. Durable dictatorships, such as those of Fidel Castro in Cuba, Hosni Mubarak in Egypt, Robert Mugabe in

Zimbabwe—or the Communist Party in China—now were the exception.

CONTRIBUTING CONDITIONS Three forces, all connected to late twentieth-century globalization, help explain this worldwide upsurge of democracy. First, in Latin America and Eastern Europe especially, governments with large amounts of debt ran into trouble in the early 1980s when interest rates spiked. New loans became expensive, and governments had to impose austerity on their populations. This cost them what little legitimacy they had and strengthened dissent.

Second, the end of the Cold War proved bad news for dictators. Not only did the end of the USSR mean the end of Soviet support for communist dictatorships, but it normally meant the end of American support for anti-communist dictatorships. During the Cold War, the U.S. government had propped up dozens of brutal military rulers because they were anti-communist, but after 1991 the United States lost interest. Most of these dictators could not survive in power without the weapons and money that had formerly flowed from Washington.

Third, the power of example helped propel the spread of democracy. The case of Argentina, which in the years 1982–1983 overthrew a brutal military regime, was inspirational throughout Latin America. The "people power" on display in the Philippines in 1986, when Ferdinand Marcos was overthrown, resonated in Southeast Asia. The well-televised scenes of ordinary Germans hacking apart the Berlin Wall in 1989 struck chords everywhere, as did the courage, in a losing battle, of Chinese protesters at

Arab Spring Citizens celebrate in Tahrir Square in Cairo in 2011, following protests that led to the resignation of President Hosni Mubarak. However, democratic government in Egypt lasted only two years.

Tiananmen Square. Modern communications, especially television news, spread sound and image of these events far and wide, helping to motivate and mobilize people who had for years grudgingly accepted their life under authoritarian rule. They accepted it no longer.

AUTHORITARIAN RESPONSES Some autocrats withstood the global wave of democratization. In China, as we have seen, the communist leadership crushed a democratization movement in 1989 and retained its monopoly on politics. In Central Asian countries such as Uzbekistan or Turkmenistan, the end of Soviet rule led merely to new dictatorships run by men who had formerly served Moscow's will. Some dictators such as Mugabe or Castro managed to out-maneuver and outlast their enemies until feeble with age.

In several countries, experiments with democracy left many citizens unsatisfied. Ambitious authoritarian politicians learned how to rig elections, intimidate the opposition, use social media for propaganda purposes, and cut deals with billionaires who owned media empires. These tactics enabled them to undermine democracy even while preserving its outward forms. In Russia, Vladimir Putin proved a master of this general strategy. In 2001, he ended a chaotic flirtation with democracy and thereafter ruled Russia with the help of billionaire oligarchs whose businesses he protected.

In the so-called Arab Spring in 2011, democracy protesters challenged several longstanding dictatorships, and in Tunisia and Egypt overthrew them. But only in Tunisia

Mothers of the Plaza de Mayo A 1987 demonstration in Buenos Aires by mothers whose children had been "disappeared" by the Argentine dictatorship.

CONSIDERING THE EVIDENCE

Social Media in the Arab Spring

On January 25, 2011, over 50,000 Egyptians marched into Tahrir Square in downtown Cairo to demand the resignation of their president, Hosni Mubarak. They accused him of corruption and negligence, but they were also angry at his plans to pass the presidency to his own son in the next election. The protesters overwhelmed police who assaulted them with tear gas, rubber bullets, and water cannons. To keep the protest going, organizers throughout Egypt used social media to announce and organize events, communicate with one another, and share news independently of the state media. When the government responded by shutting down the Internet and cell phone networks, the protests gained even more support. By February 11, when the president resigned, the crowds in Tahrir Square alone had swelled to over 250,000 people. As Adel Abdel Ghafar writes in his recollection of the protest, organizing on Facebook could never compensate for getting people out onto the streets.

Revolutions are not hatched in smoke-filled rooms or by activists armed with Twitter and Facebook accounts; rather, revolutions are made by everyday people who are no longer afraid. That is the profound change that happened in Egypt on January 25. Egyptians, who had bowed down to their pharaohs for seven thousand years, simply said, no more.

As the riot police approached us with their armor and batons raised high, they noticed that we were not moving, something they had never seen before. The line of soldiers started to slow down until they abruptly stopped a few meters in front of us. For a moment, both crowds stared at each other, polar opposites on an urban battlefield. That moment will be etched in my memory forever; time almost seemed to stand still.

Then the most incredible thing happened. The riot police turned back and started running for their lives. We chased them, captured a few, hit them, and took away their weapons and helmets. They ran back to their lines, psychologically broken. Although they would still fight us in the coming days, we all knew that something profound had just taken place. There was a raised collective consciousness among us. A realization. An epiphany. Simply that we will no longer be afraid. We drew strength, courage, and resolve from one another, from our numbers, and from our conviction. Our small group right there reached that conclusion, just as other Egyptians had reached it across the country that day. And in that moment, the Mubarak regime had lost its most significant weapon: fear. Eighteen days later, the tyrant stepped down.

Source: Adel Abdel Ghafar, "The Moment the Barrier of Fear Broke Down," in *Voices of the Arab Spring: Personal Stories from the Arab Revolutions*, ed. Asaad al-Saleh (New York, 2015).

QUESTIONS FOR ANALYSIS

1. According to Adel Abdel Ghafar, why were the protesters successful this time?
2. How did the Internet help protesters organize support on the streets during the Arab Spring?
3. How were the actions taken by the protesters in Egypt similar to or different from the methods promoted by Gandhi as *satyagraha*?

---

did democracy endure. In Egypt and Bahrain authoritarian rulers recovered, and in Syria, Libya, and Yemen civil wars resulted from popular efforts to topple dictators. Meanwhile, Turkey, the Philippines, Venezuela, Uganda, Hungary, Poland, Brazil, South Africa, and several other countries drifted toward more authoritarian rule in the early twenty-first century.

Two main factors lay behind this revitalization of authoritarianism. One was the rise of China, the best example of an undemocratic state that achieved wealth and power rapidly. China also provided economic support for rulers without imposing conditions about human rights or democracy. Another factor was the frequent failure of democracies to protect their citizens from the economic dislocations of globalization. Millions who lost their jobs after a major economic downturn in 2007 and 2008 also lost their faith in their system of government. And in 2020 the COVID-19 pandemic enabled many governments to claim emergency powers, which in India, Sri Lanka, Cambodia, Bolivia, Hungary, and elsewhere they used to detain political opponents illegally.

THE ROLE OF SOCIAL MEDIA Twenty-first-century politics was also shaped by the rise of the Internet, and by social media in particular. Social media are online platforms designed for communication and for sharing, via computers and mobile devices, information including images, videos, news, stories, and opinions. They include social networking sites such as Facebook, launched in 2004; microblogging platforms such as Twitter (2006) and Tumblr (2007); and platforms used mainly for image and video sharing such as YouTube (2005), Instagram (2010), and Snapchat (2011). The most frequented social media networks in 2020 were offered by either American or Chinese companies. Facebook had more than 2.5 billion users, YouTube and WhatsApp (owned by Facebook) both around 2 billion. Approximately 3.8 billion people—half the human race—used social media in 2020, and some 4.5 billion used the Internet.

The Internet has been used for political purposes practically since its inception, and by the late 2000s pro-democracy movements around the globe were using social media to advance their agendas. As one Egyptian activist of the Arab Spring tweeted in 2011, "We use Facebook to schedule the protests, Twitter to coordinate, and YouTube to tell the world." Popular protests in Turkey, Iran, Russia, the United States, Hong Kong, and many other places did so as well.

At first governments were outflanked, less by the technology itself than by the online tactics of young, technologically savvy activists. But within a few short years, authoritarian governments began to restrict unwelcome online content and block social media platforms or users. They also arrested people who organized dissent through social media, and they used the platforms themselves to create and spread lies designed to discredit their critics. Their security services used data collected from online communications companies and social media platforms to monitor citizens, improving the efficiency of surveillance operations. In 2017 in Myanmar, the military used Facebook to incite violence against a Muslim minority population, the Rohingya.

States found that they could use social media at minimal expense to influence political opinions in other countries as well as their own, and undertook to sway elections or even incite riots abroad. Meanwhile, terrorist organizations such as ISIS (the Islamic State of Iraq and Syria, or Daesh) also found that social media served their ambitions, especially for recruiting volunteers, spreading propaganda, and coordinating attacks. Every new communications technology in world history—writing,

printing, telegraph, radio, TV—carried political consequences, sometimes empowering states, sometimes weakening them. Often the new technologies at first weakened states by enabling subjects and citizens to share information more rapidly and cheaply, but states eventually learned how to exploit the new tools for their own purposes.

THE GLOBAL ECONOMY SINCE 1980

As usual, political changes were tightly bound up with economic ones. Other than the rise of East Asia, which we have seen, the major developments in economic history since the 1980s are a surge in global connectedness and the increase of inequality within most countries. To see the significance of the recent tightening of economic integration, it helps to look backward first.

The international economy before 1914 had been knitting itself together rapidly. But with world wars and the Great Depression, the decades between 1914 and 1945 were a time of economic de-globalization. International trade and investment flows fell to levels below those of 1880. So did labor migration. After 1945, the global economy resumed its integration, limited by the Cold War. Indeed, it might be better to say that two rival processes of economic integration began—a communist one under Soviet leadership, and a capitalist one anchored by the United States. In the years 1989–1991, the end of the Cold War gave globalization another boost by opening the former Soviet bloc to stronger connections with the capitalist world. The two most important features of this entire process—integration, disintegration, re-integration—were trade and finance.

THE GROWTH OF INTERNATIONAL TRADE

In 1913, about 20 to 25 percent of the world's goods were traded internationally. During the 1930s and 1940s, that fell to about 10 percent. The proportion recovered to 20 to 25 percent by 1980, and then it skyrocketed. In the decade between 2008 and 2017, it reached a plateau at about 55 to 60 percent. Machinery, consumer electronics, and oil have lately topped the list of goods traded across borders.

Why this sudden change since 1980? Part of the explanation is illusion: there are more countries than before. Shoes exported from Russia to Ukraine in 1980 were not international trade; but after 1991 and the breakup of the USSR, they were. However, the fuller explanation involves basic changes in the organization of the global economy, the result of several shifts in ideas, policy, business organization, and technology.

FREE TRADE POLICY In the realm of ideas and policy, the 1980s marked a major shift in favor of **free trade**. It was led by the United States and the United Kingdom, in particular by President Ronald Reagan and Prime Minister Margaret Thatcher, who spearheaded efforts to get other countries to liberalize trade. Most big American businesses by now had abandoned their support for high import tariffs because much of their own production took place overseas. Since the United States remained by far the biggest national economy and the most powerful country in the world, especially after the collapse of the USSR, its ideas, policies, and preferences carried considerable weight internationally in the 1990s.

A second key policy shift was the effort to reduce barriers to trade within Europe, which dated back to the 1950s. The main idea then was to make Western Europe stronger and richer through cooperation and integration, so it would not be eclipsed by the Cold War superpowers. But the biggest steps toward free trade in Europe took place in the early 1990s, with the formation of the European Union (EU), symbolized by the adoption of a common currency, the euro, which replaced more than a dozen national currencies. Between 2004 and 2013, the EU expanded to include almost all the countries of the former Soviet bloc, creating a highly integrated trade zone accounting for about 22 percent of the world economy.

As the policies of free trade spread around the world, multinational corporations got bigger and better at scattering parts of their operations in several countries. For labor-intensive jobs, they chose low-wage countries. Reagan and Thatcher regarded labor unions as obstacles to the economic changes they wished to see, and both succeeded in reducing the power of unions—making it easier for firms to move manufacturing jobs from the United States or the United Kingdom to Mexico, India, or China. Meanwhile, firms put technology-intensive work in countries with a highly educated labor force. They located their pollution-intensive operations in countries with minimal environmental regulation. This trend accelerated after 1980, in part owing to the trade liberalization pushed by Reagan and Thatcher. So by 2015, a Ford truck might be designed in Michigan, have a transmission built in China, an engine from Brazil, and be assembled in Kentucky. Most big companies in the auto, petrochemical, pharmaceutical, electronics, and computer industries found ways to cut costs by globalizing their supply chains. When big companies did this, they "traded" internationally with themselves to prepare finished products for market. By 2015, roughly 80 percent of international trade took place within such global firms.

INFORMATION TECHNOLOGY Much of the success of globalized firms came from new technology, some of which we've seen with containerization. **Information technology** (IT)—the use of computers to store, transmit, and process data—did at least as much to enable firms to conduct global operations. Together, these innovations reduced the cost of transporting goods from factory to customer by about 95 percent between 1980 and 2015, making global supply chains much cheaper than any alternative.

The keys to the impact of IT were cheaper computing power and the Internet. In 1946 there were 10 computers in the world, and in 1960 about 5,000. By 2020 there were 2 billion laptops and desktops, each one more than 100 billion times more efficient than the computers of 1946. And there were 3.5 billion smartphones, each one with more computing power than NASA could wield in 1969 when it put men on the moon. In the 1990s, the Internet connected computers into one vast network, enabling

Early Computing A Bell Labs mainframe computer, developed for the U.S. Army, 1946.

each one to access an almost infinite quantity of digitized information.

With the advent of this digital revolution, a firm could learn the preferences of its customers from their web-browsing habits and almost instantly revise production schedules for everything from shoes to cars. With quick and reliable shipping, it could move components anywhere at minimal cost, reduce inventories in warehouses, and rely on so-called just-in-time delivery both at assembly plants and at retail shops. This system, sometimes called lean production, rested on IT, free trade, and container shipping. Firms also increasingly enticed consumers to buy goods online with vast selection, secure ordering, and quick delivery. In 2019, consumers spent some $3.5 trillion online globally, roughly 16 percent of total retail sales for the year. Many brick-and-mortar stores that did not adjust to the new model were forced to close.

Lean production and globalized supply chains relied fundamentally on peace and health. During the twentieth century, world wars interrupted international flows of goods in a much less globalized economy, bringing shortages, rationing, and hunger. In 2020, the vulnerabilities of a much more globalized economy, especially firms reliant on just-in-time delivery, were laid bare by the COVID-19 pandemic, which threw sand in the gears of supply chains everywhere. So the enormous expansion of international trade after 1980 carried risks as well as rewards.

By 2020, businesses also found that social media could boost their global profiles and profits. Some platforms allowed advertising—which could potentially reach billions of people. Other platforms did not, but clever marketers could achieve the same effect by creating messages that went viral—or by encouraging satisfied customers to do so for them. Businesses also purchased data about potential customers harvested from social media platforms to learn how best to target their marketing efforts. New firms with limited brand awareness were especially likely to turn to social media to expand their global customer base.

GLOBAL FINANCE

While world trade was booming, international financial flows were gushing. Finance is basically the business of pooling savings and investing them in other businesses expected over time to become profitable. Before 1980, it

was done mainly by banks. Once again, it helps to take a brief backward glance.

International financial flows flourished during the 1870–1913 surge in economic integration. Like trade, financial flows then dropped with the world wars and Great Depression. As World War II ended, the victors (except the USSR) re-built the world's banking systems with tight restrictions on capital flows and fixed exchange rates for currencies.

In 1973, the so-called Bretton Woods system came apart when the currency inflation of the Vietnam War era caused the U.S. government to withdraw its support. In the following decade, the international financial system underwent major reforms, most of which reduced regulations and eased international capital flows.

Financiers responded with investment innovations that opened the floodgates of finance. New communications and information technology sped the movement of money. In the mid-1970s, employees of the investment bank Goldman Sachs in New York would send faxes of the *Wall Street Journal*'s page on stocks to British colleagues so they could begin their day in London knowing where New York markets closed the day before. By 1990, new digital technology instantly alerted investors in London, New York, and Tokyo to every shift in interest rates and stock prices.

Finance now became far more lucrative than trade or manufacturing. Tiny differences in the value of a currency from one market to the next would cause an overnight stampede of billions of dollars. By the late 1990s, foreign exchange markets every week handled more money than the annual GNP of the United States, and by 2016 they did so every three days.

DE-REGULATION AND ECONOMIC INSTABILITY
The **financialization** of the world economy (as it came to be called) meant money could flow easily and instantly to wherever it might earn the best return on investment. De-regulation meant that insurance companies, hedge funds, and pension funds could all get into the finance business. The brave new world of de-regulated finance attracted reckless speculators. In 1995, a 28-year-old financier working in Singapore, because his ethical lapses had barred him from employment in England, lost every penny entrusted by customers to Baring Brothers, a 233-year-old bank.

The boom in finance brought much more economic

instability. During the period 1870–1913, most international capital supported building durable enterprises such as railroads or mines that investors hoped would pay off for them over decades. After 1990, the sums that traders could move around the world with a few keystrokes exceeded the value of the entire economy of a mid-sized country. So governments in Argentina or Thailand had to obey the preferences of international investors with respect to their budgets, currencies, and banking regulations, or risk a massive withdrawal of money. Governments occasionally chose not to obey financial pressures because they did not wish to face the political consequences of firing thousands of government workers or cutting the military budget.

THE GREAT RECESSION The ease with which big investors could withdraw vast sums made major financial crises more common in the 1990s. The biggest came in Mexico in 1994, Southeast Asia in 1997, and Russia in 1998. These crises all became more or less global, although none reached the proportions of the 2007 financial crisis that originated in the housing market and financial system of the United States. That one rippled throughout the world, causing massive bankruptcies, layoffs, and dis-investment in the Great Recession of 2007–2009. The U.S. Treasury bailed out the biggest banks, insurance companies, and investment firms, including European ones, to keep the crash from getting worse. Countries with big debt problems, such as Greece and Ireland, needed foreign bankers to bail them out too, and with those bailouts came brutal austerity in the form of higher taxes and slashed public services. Tens of millions of people around the world lost their jobs or homes. Street protests in the United States and Europe lasted for months, and citizens voted out existing governments in favor of more radical parties. Countries with no debt loads, and those least linked to the world's financial system—China, India, Indonesia, Australia, and several African nations—managed to weather the crisis comparatively well.

The financialization of the world economy thus led to a spike in economic volatility. It amounted to a rising tide that lifted some boats but swamped others. It added to the hunger felt around the world for economic stability and security, especially among older citizens who remembered less volatile times and who had more in the way of savings or property to lose. Politicians capitalized on this hunger, winning support with promises of a return to stable jobs and economic security, which none of them could deliver.

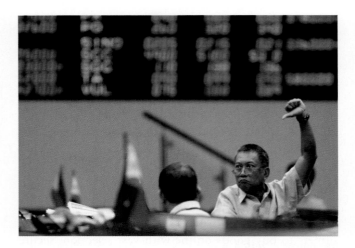

Global Financial Crisis A trader on the Philippine Stock Exchange shows his disgust as red deficit figures fill up a screen behind him. The collapse of the U.S. investment bank Lehman Brothers in September 2008 led to economic shocks worldwide.

HEIGHTENED INEQUALITY

Like every earlier surge in economic globalization, the rapid one after 1980 created winners and losers. Globally there were more winners than losers. In poor countries, roughly 500 to 700 million people with few options found new opportunities in the years between 1980 and 2015. They left their villages to accept low wages and sometimes dangerous working conditions in new factories. They may not have won much, but they were the bulk of the winners from economic globalization. Most of the winnings—a different thing—went to the few people who had the education, skill, connections, and luck to profit from either the growth in finance or the migration of manufacturing from high-wage to low-wage countries. This profit flowed to a few million people around the world, most of whom became super-rich.

One of those was the Mexican business magnate Carlos Slim, born in 1940. He was a first-generation Mexican whose ancestors hailed from Lebanon. He parlayed a modest inheritance into diverse business holdings in Mexico, the rest of Latin America, the United States, and Europe. He became one of the world's 10 richest people in the 1990s, thanks in part to the growth of several manufacturing businesses he owned in Mexico, most of which exported goods to the newly open U.S. market. He owned Latin America's biggest mobile phone company when mobile phones took off. As of 2015, he owned about 200 companies. Slim took full advantage of de-regulation

De-industrialization A woman walks past an abandoned steel plant in western Pennsylvania in 2008. As well-paid industrial jobs disappeared in developed countries like the United States, income inequality widened dramatically.

of telecoms, insurance, and financial industries, as well as the reduction in barriers to transactions among Mexico, the United States, and other countries. He is among the biggest beneficiaries of economic globalization (and says his favorite subject in high school was history).

The losers from globalization included the tens of millions of people in high-wage countries who saw the market for their skills disappear. In the 1970s, it was possible for a Seattle steelworker to support a family by himself, to own a home and a car, and take foreign vacations. But as steel production migrated to South Korea, Mexico, and elsewhere, high-paying jobs of this sort gradually disappeared in the United States, much of Europe, and Japan. Secure industrial jobs also disappeared in Russia and Eastern Europe after 1989 as communist-era factories could not compete internationally. Automation of factory work also replaced high-wage laborers everywhere. In the United States, the proportion of the economy that went to wages and salaries peaked at around 50 to 52 percent between 1945 and 1970, and it fell thereafter as a result of global competition and automation in American factories. By 2020, it had slid to 42 percent. Wage earners struggled to keep what they regarded as decent jobs in the globalized economy.

All this re-shuffling of income as a result of economic globalization changed patterns of inequality in the world. On most measures, **income inequality** of the global population declined after 1990. Rising wages in China and to a lesser degree India accounted for most of that change. Apart from these cases, there was very little reduction in global inequality. By and large, Africa did not close any gaps.

Income inequality within—as opposed to among—countries was a simpler story. Throughout the twentieth century up to about 1980, a strong trend toward greater equality had prevailed just about everywhere. Then, in the 1970s through the 1980s, that trend leveled off in Europe. In the United States, the United Kingdom, Canada, and Australia it reversed direction sharply. Those societies developed mega-rich classes, known colloquially after 2008 as "the one percent." In the United States in 2017, the top 1 percent got 18 percent of all national income—up from 8 percent in 1970. Most of the countries with the greatest income inequality were poor countries with super-rich elites such as South Africa, Botswana, and Panama. Those with the least income inequality were mainly in Europe.

Measured by wealth—what people owned, rather than their incomes—inequality widened even more sharply after 1990. By 2015, the richest eight individuals on Earth owned as much as the poorest 3.7 billion people.

All of these post-1980 economic trends—the growth in international trade, the power of finance, and heightened inequality—were jolted by the consequences of the COVID-19 pandemic beginning in 2020. The need for social distancing to reduce the loss of life proved disastrous for business sectors that required either international transport or crowds. International trade fell abruptly. Tourism and professional sports halted almost overnight. Auto manufacturers could not get parts for assembly, and customers put off purchases. Many sectors, including education and finance, shifted on the fly to tele-working. Countries that struggled to mount a coherent pandemic response or relied heavily on global trade suffered the greatest economic dislocation. In the United States, for example, unemployment skyrocketed to levels experienced only during the depths of the Great Depression. Canada suffered a smaller spike in unemployment. Outside of North America, job losses remained minimal, but global economic output in 2020 slumped by about 4 percent.

CULTURAL GLOBALIZATION

Recent decades witnessed globalization in the realm of culture as well as economics. Thanks to technical advances in communication and to the upswing in international migration, people more frequently came in contact with unfamiliar languages, customs, food, and music. This proved unsettling for many people but also sparked a surge of creativity around the world.

Everything from food fusion (such as sushi burritos) to Facebook friendships (15 percent of which were international in 2015) has globalized lately. Here we'll look more carefully at two aspects of the broader cultural trend: music and sport.

MUSIC

Music is one of the cultural forms that travels well through the Global web. People can enjoy it without words, or without understanding the words. Until the 1880s, music was always experienced live. It traveled most easily when musicians traveled, bringing, for example, Celtic ballads (from Ireland and Scotland) to North America in the eighteenth and nineteenth centuries. Religious music traveled wherever religions did. Sufi ceremonial music and dance went everywhere that Sufism went, from Morocco to Mindanao (in the Philippines) and every Islamic land in between.

The globalization of music accelerated with the invention of recording technology beginning in the 1880s and radio in the 1920s. Those technologies took hold first in the richer countries, so in the first half of the twentieth century European and North American music proved the most mobile. Classical music—the symphonies, sonatas, and concertos that Europeans had raised to a high art during the eighteenth and nineteenth centuries—found audiences around the world. Today more people are trained in classical music in East Asia than anywhere else. European musical styles often traveled in the footsteps of European empire.

In the 1950s, a dramatic change in the history of music took place with recordings marketed exclusively to youth—a growing share of the world's population after 1945, owing to the widespread "baby boom." The change began in the United States and proved lucrative. Young people came to define themselves partly by the music they liked, and to mark themselves off from their elders with their musical preferences. This development, combined with cheaper recordings, led to an even faster surge of musical globalization.

The engine room of this musical movement was the American South, the home of jazz and blues. In the late

Fela Kuti The Nigerian musician Fela Kuti with his band in 1980. Fela's music, called Afrobeat, was a blend of American rhythm and blues, jazz, and Yoruba traditions.

1950s, when John Lennon and Paul McCartney were Liverpool teenagers, they eagerly awaited the arrival of American ships because sailors brought records made by black American artists with roots in the South. Lennon and McCartney imitated the music of Chuck Berry and Little Richard, got good at playing it in bars in Germany, and soon became the core of one of the most popular musical acts of all time, the Beatles.

The music they learned, at the time called rhythm and blues in the United States, was itself derived partly from West African traditions, including polyrhythmic drumming used in jazz. Black Americans in the 1950s and 1960s combined those traditions with vocal styles from gospel church choirs. In their lyrics they replaced gospel music's intense longing for salvation with longing for love and sex. This proved a magic formula, generating a youth music—including soul and rock 'n' roll, among others—that exploded on the scene in the 1960s.

In an ironic twist, the wealth and power of the United States by the 1960s helped to spread the cultural influence of its most underprivileged population, black Americans from the South or from the inner cities of Detroit or Chicago. During the Cold War years, the economic and political clout of the United States was at its height. The U.S. State Department sponsored global goodwill tours by American jazz musicians. U.S. soldiers and sailors stationed around the world served as unofficial ambassadors for American popular music. In earlier centuries, the power and wealth of the Roman Empire had helped to spread the tastes and fashions of its aristocrats throughout Europe and North Africa. The prestige of China's Song dynasty had a similar impact in Korea and Southeast Asia. Now the United States wielded even broader influence, but, in music at least, the influence came not from the higher echelons but from the lower rungs of the social hierarchy.

Musicians all over the world developed their own styles blending local and international—often American—influences. Brazilians made bossa nova—a style combining their own tradition of samba and American jazz—internationally popular in the 1960s. The South African singer Miriam Makeba melded a style from Johannesburg's dance halls with American pop to create an international hit in the Xhosa language. Other African musicians—perhaps most notably the Nigerians King Sunny Ade, who sang in Yoruba, and Fela Kuti, who sang in Nigerian English—enjoyed international popularity in the 1980s with styles that incorporated instruments from American popular music such as the pedal steel guitar and synthesizers, but relied on West African drumming traditions. Both were in the forefront of what since 1987 has been called world music, a loose category of popular music made by people outside of North America or Europe but influenced by the popular music traditions of the United States.

American country music also went global, finding audiences especially in Europe and Australia. Bal Kishore Das Loiwal, born to a prosperous family in northern India, learned to play and sing country music from records sent home by an aunt who had moved to Nashville, the mecca of country music. He changed his name to Bobby Cash and after 2005 broke into the Australian market as well as creating a following at home, calling himself the Indian cowboy and dressing the part.

One of the world's most popular musical forms by the 1970s was the Jamaican invention called reggae, a blend of older Caribbean styles with American jazz and rhythm and blues. It was associated with the Rastafarian religion, a Jamaican innovation of the 1930s, which revered the Ethiopian king Haile Selassie as a prophet. Reggae's most successful artist was Bob Marley, a global star from the early 1970s until his death in 1981. By the 1980s, Jamaican reggae was popular everywhere: even Iceland and Japan had their own reggae bands.

Few musicians blended as many global influences as Shakira, whose name means "grateful" in Arabic. Born in Colombia, her ancestors came from Spain, Italy, and Lebanon. By her teenage years she was performing throughout Colombia, singing in Spanish and occasionally in Arabic. She learned from an eclectic mix of music, from Lebanon, Latin America, the United States, and the United Kingdom. Her Lebanese dance style translated well to music video, a genre that became popular in the 1980s. In the early 2000s she began to record in English, expanding her audience. Together with a Haitian American rapper, Wyclef Jean, she recorded the best-selling song of the twenty-first century (so far) in 2006. Asked in 2001 to describe herself, Shakira said: "I'm a fusion between black and white, between pop and rock, between cultures—between my Lebanese father and my mother's Spanish blood, the Colombian folklore and Arab dance I love and American music."

Drake and Rihanna were almost as international in their inspirations as Shakira and even more successful as global stars. Drake, whose Canadian mother had Eastern European Jewish roots and whose father was an African American musician from Tennessee, grew up in Toronto. He helped develop a rap style that proved enormously popular around the world by 2010. Rihanna began singing in outdoor markets in her hometown of Bridgetown, Barbados. She moved to the United States in her late teens and launched a recording career that mixed Caribbean reggae and dancehall styles with American pop, rap, and dance music. By 2020 she stood among the 10 best-selling recording artists ever, and the only one among them born after 1960. Like Drake and Shakira, she became a movie star and entrepreneur with a global following.

Nowadays, thanks to YouTube, Spotify, and their successors, music swirls around the world as never before. Traditions rubbed up against one another, leading to new forms every year. Rap stars from Korea (Psy) could become

Global Popular Culture Fans cluster around the Colombian pop singer Shakira after she opened a childcare center in Cartagena, Colombia, in 2012. Shakira's performances in Spanish, Arabic, and English made her a global sensation.

global celebrities overnight. Opera, whose fans usually expect rigid adherence to tradition, also globalized: one of the most admired sopranos of the last 40 years, Kiri Te Kanawa, who sang in Italian and German, as opera singers normally do, was raised in a Maori family in New Zealand.

SPORT

Modern sport took shape at the end of the nineteenth century with the reincarnation of the ancient Greek Olympic games and the formation of leagues for team sports such as soccer in Britain and baseball in the United States. These became spectacles for crowds as well as competitions for athletes, like chariot racing in the ancient world. All the major global sports developed first in Europe and America, and often spread along the trails of empire. Polo, originating in Iran, is the closest thing to an exception. Cricket became popular in South Asia, Australia, and the Anglophone Caribbean—all regions within the former British Empire. Baseball took root in Mexico and those parts of the Spanish Caribbean with the strongest historical links to the United States such as Puerto Rico, Cuba, the Dominican Republic, and Panama. It acquired a following in those parts of East Asia where the U.S. presence, especially military presence, was strong, such as Japan, Taiwan, and South Korea. Basketball by the 1990s spread far and wide, aided by its minimal need of equipment, unlike ice hockey, a Canadian invention played only in cold and prosperous countries, or American football, which won only minor followings outside North America.

The most global of sports was soccer, which first took shape in Britain during the nineteenth century. Britain's global reach in the nineteenth century brought soccer to every continent. It found especially fertile soil in South America and continental Europe, which to this day produce most of the best male players, lately joined by West Africa. The secret to soccer's global appeal lay in how little one needs to play it: some open space and a ball.

The women's game also originated in Britain, where a public match was played as early as 1895 and one in 1920 drew 53,000 spectators. France and Italy had amateur leagues by the 1930s. But it took until late in the twentieth century before professional women's soccer leagues sprang up in Europe and the United States, aided by the development of girls' sports programs in schools, the launching

Global Sport A member of the U.S. women's national soccer team plays in a match against Sweden during the 2019 Women's World Cup tournament. The world's most popular sport, soccer is today played on every inhabited continent.

of the Women's World Cup in 1991, and the inclusion of women's soccer as an Olympic sport in 1996.

The men's soccer World Cup began in 1930 with only 13 national teams taking part. The first TV broadcasts came in 1954, and soon the World Cup was a global cultural event held every four years. Decolonization led to increased participation, so that by 2006 nearly 200 national teams competed for slots in the 32-team tournament. The World Cup attracted more TV viewers than the Olympics or any other sporting competition. Since 2006, the final match of each tournament has been seen live by 10 to 12 percent of the global population. The Women's World Cup, at first a 12-team tournament, expanded to a 24-team event and between 1999 and 2019 attracted many millions of spectators on TV and major corporate sponsorships.

Sports changed less when traveling than did music. The rules of baseball were very much the same in Korea and Panama as in Kansas and Pennsylvania. Styles of play differed a bit more than rules, but any innovations that brought competitive advantage spread almost instantly, because of modern communications and the intense competition in sport. Stable rules through the decades were important to the public appeal of sports, so fans could enjoy arguing whether Walter Payton was a better football player than Christian McCaffrey (he was), whether Serena Williams was better at tennis than Margaret Court (she was), or whether Pelé was better at soccer than Lionel Messi (he wasn't).

Television helped convert international competitions

such as the World Cup and the Olympics into global cultural phenomena and arenas of peaceful national competition. The modern Olympics began in Europe in 1896 as a gentlemanly competition, mainly in track and field. Women—at first only golfers and tennis players—began to take part in 1900. With the beginning of worldwide TV broadcasts at the Tokyo games in 1964, the Olympics began to attract global audiences. Decolonization increased the number of teams and competitors, and it made the Olympics more interesting to Africans and Asians. The increasing participation of female athletes also increased the popularity of the Olympics. Women runners competed in the 1500-meters beginning in 1972, and the women's marathon debuted in 1984. In the most recent Olympiads, about 42 to 44 percent of athletes were women.

During the Cold War, the Olympics became one of the stages on which the USSR and the United States tried to demonstrate the superiority of their sociopolitical systems. Both supported officially "amateur" athletes for the purpose of winning medals. Sports fans—and politicians too—developed an obsession with medal counts. In East Germany and China, which entered Olympic competition in 1980, all sports organizations were directly under government control, and party leaders went to great lengths to use sport to show the vigor of their brand of communism. East German politicians, desperate to outdo West Germany, encouraged the nation's sports federation to administer performance-enhancing drugs to the best athletes, often without the athletes' consent. Some as young as 10 years of age were fed testosterone, steroids, and amphetamines. They did bring home a bumper crop of Olympic medals—at the price of health problems later in life. The Olympics, which officially admitted professional athletes by 1992, remains one of the most politically meaningful sporting events today even if the intensity of the Cold War years is gone.

The advent of TV in the 1950s and 1960s made many sports into big businesses and enabled some athletes—a few hundred in all—to become exceedingly rich. In most years, all of the top 30 earners among athletes were male. The top women were always tennis players, with Serena Williams recently leading the way. Prize money for men and women in tennis was equalized at major tournaments between 1973 and 2007, though at lesser tournaments around the world women players as of 2020 earned 80 percent as much as men.

IMAGINED GLOBAL COMMUNITY AND ITS LIMITS

Strong as they are in light of the past, all these currents of globalization are much weaker than people think they are. A survey of people in 138 countries undertaken in 2015 revealed that on average, people imagine that international migrants make up 30 percent of the world's population, whereas 3.5 percent is about right. Respondents thought that 22 percent of university students came from abroad; the real figure was 2 percent. They thought foreign trade was twice as large as it was. Across dozens of variables, the survey showed that people around the world imagined globalization was about five times more prevalent than it actually was in 2015.

The fast pace of cultural and economic globalization after 1980 has had its limits. First of all, many people feared globalization as a threat to their livelihood, their identity, or both. Elections in the United States and several European countries after 2012 reflected this sentiment. More fundamentally, there are big and basic obstacles checking globalization. People in Nigeria and Norway have good reason not to dress alike, because it's always warm in Nigeria and often cold in Norway. And it seems most unlikely that anyone other than Icelanders will ever regard fermented shark meat as a delicacy.

The long trend, nevertheless, remains toward greater integration of the Global web. Since its formation in the sixteenth century, it has expanded and tightened despite several setbacks along the way. The COVID-19 pandemic is another setback, but hardly a reversal. The web-building process has been woven into world history since the earliest times, and it has rebounded from shocks, including world wars and pandemics a hundred times more deadly than COVID-19. No one planned it and many people resent its effects, but almost everyone by pursuing their own economic, intellectual, cultural, and religious interests contributes to the ongoing life of the Global web.

CONCLUSION

The post-1980 world at the moment looks like one of tumultuous change. Climate change sped up dramatically. Population growth slowed down with reduced fertility, as women increasingly devoted more time to schooling and paid work and less to child rearing and household chores. Emerging viruses threatened human health on every continent, perhaps heralding a counter-trend to the remarkable centuries-long reduction in the burden of disease. Nevertheless, population growth as of 2020 remained more rapid than at any time in human history before about 1940. Humankind became predominantly urban for the first time ever. Politics evolved so as to become more democratic, more religious, and more influenced by global international institutions—and all three trends sparked smaller counter-trends in the form of authoritarian revivals that fed on anti-globalization sentiment. Cheap travel and cheap communications brought a kaleidoscopic swirl of cultural interaction, vividly expressed in music. The same trends made sport into an international spectacle of immense popularity.

But to people in 50 or 100 years, the world of 1980 to 2020 will look very different from what it seems to any of us now. We are following truth too near the heels to know for sure just where we are.

CHAPTER REVIEW

KEY TERMS

Wangari Maathai (p. 864)
Anthropocene (p. 864)
climate change (p. 865)
carbon dioxide (p. 865)
HIV/AIDS (p. 870)
COVID-19 (p. 871)

declines in fertility (p. 871)
international migrants (p. 875)
al-Qaeda (p. 878)
spread of democracy (p. 880)
free trade (p. 884)

information technology (p. 884)
financialization (p. 885)
income inequality (p. 887)
international institutions (p. 877)

Go to INQUIZITIVE to see what you've learned—and learn what you've missed—with personalized feedback along the way.

REVIEW QUESTIONS

1. What is new about climate change since 1840?
2. Culturally and politically, why did the world become so environmentally turbulent over the last 70 years?
3. What key innovations in medicine and agriculture led to population growth after 1950?
4. What four conditions contributed to the devastating health impact of COVID-19?
5. Explain the main reasons behind the worldwide downward fertility trend since 1960.
6. What two trends drove the spurt of urban growth since 1950?
7. Compare and contrast the characteristics of international migrants in the periods 1890–1915 and 1990–2015.
8. Why have so many international organizations arisen since World War II?
9. What factors caused political Islam to grow in popularity in Muslim societies after 1970?
10. Identify and describe three forces related to late-twentieth-century globalization that help explain the worldwide upsurge of democracy.
11. Why did multinational corporations get bigger and globalize their supply chains?
12. Describe the consequences of the financialization of the world economy.
13. Who were the winners and losers of economic globalization after 1980?
14. Compare how music and sport changed when traveling worldwide.
15. Discuss the long trend of global integration.

FURTHER READING

Richard BALDWIN, *The Great Convergence: Information Technology and the New Globalization* (2016). An economist's take on recent trends, written informally.

Angus DEATON, *The Great Escape: Health, Wealth, and the Origins of Inequality* (2013). A work that's strong on health trends and the economics of globalization.

Edward R. DICKINSON, *The World in the Long Twentieth Century: An Interpretation* (2018). A very useful look at political, economic, and environmental trends.

Wangari MAATHAI, *Unbowed: A Memoir* (2006). An account of her path from a Kenyan village girl to international environmental activist.

J. R. MCNEILL and Peter ENGELKE, *The Great Acceleration* (2016). A brief account of global environmental changes since 1945.

Branko MILANOVICH, *Global Inequality: A New Approach for the Age of Globalization* (2016). A book that's packed with data but highly readable (as economists' prose goes).

GLOSSARY OF KEY TERMS AND PRONUNCIATION GUIDE

AH *a* sound, as in *far*
IH short *i* sound, as in *hit*
OO long *o* sound, as in *snooze*
UH short *u* sound, as in *cup*
A short *a* sound, as in *tap*
EE long *e* sound, as in *sneeze*
OH long *o* sound, as in *bone*
EH short *e* sound, as in *very*
AY long *a* sound, as in *say*
EYE long *i* sound, as in *white*
OW diphthong *o* sound, as in *how*
AW diphthong *a* sound, as in *saw*

Emphasis: Syllables in capital letters receive the emphasis. If there is no syllable in capitals, then all syllables get equal emphasis.

1918 flu pandemic: A flu mutation that spread worldwide after World War I, killing 50 to 100 million people mostly between the ages of 15 and 40. Due to tighter global connections, it spread quickly and widely.

Abbasid caliphate [ah-BAH-sihd KA-lih-fayt]: The Islamic successor state (750–1258) to the Umayyads. Based in Baghdad, the Abbasids consolidated power over most of the Islamic world, profited from widespread trade, supported scholars and artists, and had learned works from Chinese, Sanskrit, Hebrew, Greek, and Latin translated into Arabic and Persian.

Abdelkadir [ab-dehl-KAH-dihr] (1808–1883): A Sufi scholar and the leader of the biggest revolt against French rule in Algeria, which reached its height in the 1830s. The French captured and exiled Abdelkadir in 1847.

aboriginal Australians: Also known as Aborigines, aboriginal Australians were mobile hunter-foragers. They spoke 200 to 250 related languages and shared consistent animist religious beliefs across the continent.

Achaemenids [ak-KEE-muh-nids] (559–330 BCE): A dynasty that came from what is now southwestern Iran. They conquered all major powers from Egypt to northwest India, making their empire unprecedented in size.

Adi Granth [ah-dee GRAHNTH]: The scripture of the Sikhs. Written in Punjabi, it is a collection of Nanak's hymns, or teachings, as well as some additional hymns.

Adolf Hitler (1889–1945): The fascist head of the Nazi Party who became chancellor of Germany in 1933. Wanting to return Germany to great power status, he introduced social and economic reforms, including national purification, which targeted Jews, Slavs, and Roma for elimination.

Ahura Mazda [uh-HOOR-uh MAHZ-duh]: A benevolent, all-knowing god and the preferred deity of the Achaemenid dynasty from Darius onward. A priesthood called the Magi led Ahura Mazda worship, which involved outdoor fire ceremonies and sacrifices.

Akbar [AHK-bah] (r. 1556–1605): A Mughal emperor who spearheaded the unification of most of South Asia. He used a combination of horses, guns, and siege-craft along with tolerant religious policy to assert and maintain power.

Aksum: An African state south of Kush that reached its peak between 300 and 500 CE. It traded African products to Egypt, the Mediterranean world, and Mesopotamia, which enabled it to amass wealth and power.

al-Andalus [al-ANN-duh-luhs] (711–1492): The Muslim-controlled part of Spain that the last Umayyad dynast founded in 711 and the Córdoba caliphate ruled from 929 to 1031. Afterward, it remained fragmented until Christian armies defeated it in 1492.

al-Qaeda: An extremist Islamist political faction begun in 1988 by Osama bin Laden that funded the September 11, 2001, terrorist attacks on the United States. It became powerful in Iraq after 2003, and its offshoots have engaged in terrorism targeting other Muslims in several countries.

Alexander II (1818–1881): The tsar of Russia who emancipated the serfs due in part to his commitment to military reform. He wanted a standing army and hoped the abolition of serfdom would lead to a cheaper and better-educated army without the risk of rebellion.

Alexander Hamilton: An American politician who prescribed tariffs to protect U.S. industry when he was secretary of the Treasury in 1791. His recommendations guided U.S. trade policy for a century and inspired the German economist Friedrich List.

Alexander the Great (356–323 BCE): Born in Macedonia to the king of Macedon, Alexander was one of the most skilled military commanders in history. He continued and completed his father's conquest of the Greek world and claimed the Achaemenid throne, uniting both regions in a vast empire.

Alexandria (founded 331 BCE): A wealthy Mediterranean seaport city during the Hellenistic age that fostered trade linkages among Egypt, Africa, the Mediterranean, and Southwest Asia. It was a center for manufacturing, medicine, mathematics, commerce, and culture.

Algerian war for independence (1954–1962): The conflict between the FLN, Algerian independence fighters, and the French Army, along with its collaborators, over France's colonial presence. It led to Algerian independence; the massacre of Muslim Algerians, known as harkis; and the mass expulsion of French settler-colonists, the pieds-noirs.

alliance networks: Two groups into which the great European powers were divided in order to uphold peace in Europe after the Napoleonic Wars. In 1914, Germany, Austria-Hungary, and Italy belonged to the Triple Alliance; and France, Russia, and Great Britain belonged to the Triple Entente.

Allies: A coalition of countries that fought against the Axis powers in World War II, most prominently the United Kingdom, United States, USSR, and China. The alliance also included many other countries, colonies, and members of the British Commonwealth.

American Revolution (1775–1781): An anti-colonial, revolutionary war between thirteen British colonies in America and the British government. The colonists won and created the United States, an independent country.

Ancestral Pueblo Inhabitants of the high-plateau Four Corners area in today's U.S. Southwest who developed a dispersed agricultural society around the ninth century. Their distinctive architectural style of cliff dwellings and ceremonial spaces called *kivas* is evident at their central settlement of Chaco Canyon. Their settlements declined in the twelfth and thirteenth centuries as a probable result of long-lasting drought cycles. They are also known as the Anasazi, which means "ancestors of our enemies" in the Navajo language.

Anthropocene: The proposed new geological age defined by the influence of humans on big natural systems, such as climate. Around 2000, many scientists started to argue that the Holocene ended in the mid-twentieth century and that we are now living in the Anthropocene.

anti-colonialism: A mass political and social movement that developed after World War I. Supporters, disillusioned with European rulers and post-war peace settlements, advocated for self-rule and the end of colonial empires.

Antônio Conselheiro [kohn-say-YAY-roo] (1830–1897): A traveling preacher in Brazil who eventually settled in Canudos. He attracted many followers with his sermons on salvation, denunciations of the state, and promise of the imminent return of Jesus Christ.

Arabs: At the time of Muhammad's birth, Arabs were a group of polytheistic, loosely connected, mostly nomadic tribes who lived in the Arabian Peninsula and made a living herding, trading, and raiding. In the seventh century, united under Muhammad, they became a formidable military force, conquering lands from India to Spain.

Asian tiger economies: Collective name for the economies of certain East Asian countries—Japan, South Korea, Taiwan, Singapore, Hong Kong, and China—that experienced massive economic growth after World War II.

Assyrian [uh-SEER-ee-uhn] **Empire** (ca. 911–609 BCE): A large and multicultural empire based in northern Mesopotamia; its power rested partly on raising horses and forging iron tools and weapons.

Augustine (354–430): A North African bishop whose prolific moralistic writings influenced the creation of a more uniform Christianity called Catholicism.

Axis: A loose coalition among Germany, Italy, and Japan. The Axis powers instigated World War II through their expansionist aims and fought against the Allies during the conflict.

Bantu [BAN-too]: A language group that originated in the area of the modern-day Cameroon-Nigerian border. It is made up of 600 related languages now spoken in East, central, and southern Africa.

Battle of Stalingrad (1942–1943): A brutal, months-long conflict between Soviet and German armies on the eastern front. The German loss of the battle was a major turning point in World War II and part of a broader Axis decline.

Beatriz Kimpa Vita (ca. 1684–1706): A young woman in Kongo who was drawn to Catholicism, became a preacher, and sought the re-unification of Kongo. She gained thousands of followers by telling them God spoke through her, but her movement threatened other aspirants to power and she was burned at the stake as a witch and heretic.

bell beaker ware: Clay containers shaped like an upside-down bell that became popular across Europe and North Africa between around 2900 and 1800 BCE. Used mainly for beer, their widespread presence points to commercial and cultural connections among elites in Europe.

Benito Mussolini (1883–1945): The fascist and authoritarian ruler of Italy who took power in 1922. He manipulated the media, promoted Italian nationalism, and capitalized on Italians' anxieties, particularly about communism, to build support.

Bhakti [BAHK-tee] **movement**: A popular form of Hinduism that emerged in the seventh century in India and appealed to a broad segment of the population. The religion stressed intense, personal devotion to one god (usually Shiva, Vishnu, or Devi) and used local languages (not Sanskrit) spoken by the common people.

Big Bang: The origin of our universe and the start of time, space, and energy. It occurred about 13.8 billion years ago, and the universe has been cooling and expanding since that time.

biological globalization: A worldwide exchange of plants, animals, and microbes that followed the discovery of the oceans and of which the Columbian Exchange was a part. It led to connections among ecosystems and a change of flora, fauna, and diseases across the world.

biological old regime: Conditions of human health that preceded the Vital Revolution. Deadly crowd diseases, gastrointestinal infections, high infant mortality, malnutrition, and starvation defined it.

bipedalism: The ability to stand upright that evolved 6 million to 4.5 million years ago; a trait that distinguishes hominins from apes and ape-like ancestors.

Bourbon Reforms: Changes reflecting Enlightenment thought that the Spanish Crown introduced in Spanish America to revitalize its empire. They included new taxes, strengthened fortifications, administrative reorganization, and freer trade.

British Raj [rahj] (1858–1947): British colonial rule in India, which relied on the cooperation of local Indian elites and the exploitation of existing societal divisions. It reordered the Indian economy with the introduction of free trade and new infrastructure.

bronze: An alloy, or combination, of the two metals copper and tin; used in many cultures for armor and weapons as well as for ornamentation.

Byzantine [BIHZ-ann-teen] **Empire**: The eastern part of the Roman Empire and all that remained of the empire after 476. At its height in the sixth and seventh centuries, it included Egypt, the Levant, Anatolia, and the Balkans; it lasted until 1453.

cabotage: Port-to-port, local trade links. In the Indian Ocean world, shorter-distance cabotage trade in everyday goods supported long-distance trade in luxuries.

Cahokia [kuh-HOH-kee-uh] (ca. 1000–1350): A large Amerindian city that was located in the floodplain of the Mississippi River in present-day Illinois and home to mostly farming people. Cahokians engaged in coordinated efforts to build ceremonial plazas and over 100 mounds used mostly for sacrifices and burials.

Calicut: An important commercial port city on the southwest coast of India. Its merchants traded various spices that were highly sought by Arab, Persian, and European merchants.

caravanserais: In Eastern countries, inns along major trade routes that accommodated large numbers of traders, their animals, and their wares.

carbon dioxide (CO_2): Released by burning fossil fuels, it is one of the most important greenhouse gases. The rise of fossil fuel use since around 1840—especially since 1950 or so—has contributed to increased concentrations of CO_2 in the atmosphere and, in turn, the current pulse of climate change.

Carolingians (ca. 750–843): A dynasty that ruled a comparatively modest and poor state in western Europe and introduced feudalism. The state became an empire during the reign of Charlemagne (r. 768–814) but fell apart after his death.

Carthage: A Phoenician colony on the Mediterranean Sea's North Africa coast that became a formidable seaborne empire based on commerce. Carthage flourished between approximately 800 and 146 BCE.

cassava [kuh-SAH-vuh]: Native to Brazil, as part of the Columbian Exchange cassava (also called manioc) became a staple food in many parts of Africa. It is drought resistant, does well in poor soils, and remains edible even if left in the ground for long periods of time.

caste system: A hierarchical and hereditary division of society that developed in the Ganges basin. The early caste system split people into four main tiers: Brahmins, Kshatriya, Vaishya, and Sudra.

Catholic Reformation: Also called the Counter-Reformation, a period of major reforms in the Catholic Church undertaken in response to the Protestant Reformation. The Catholic Church became more centralized and standardized; popes, bishops, and abbots cut back on high living; efforts were made to root out heresy and ban certain books.

Celts: A loose grouping of various peoples in Atlantic Europe who spoke similar languages and shared cultural features. They emerged between 1300 and 700 BCE. They migrated south from the Alps and Danube in droves during the fifth to third centuries BCE.

Chaco Canyon: A settlement in northern New Mexico that was likely the center of the broader Ancestral Pueblo (Anasazi) region spread throughout the Four Corners area. All roads built by Ancestral Pueblo led to Chaco Canyon, and it was the home of religious and political elites until its collapse due to drought in the twelfth century.

champa rice: A variety of rice that matures quickly, is drought resistant, and ripens at higher and cooler elevations than other strains. After the Chinese imported it from Vietnam in the eleventh century, it became a reliable food supply that spurred massive population growth.

chariot: A two-wheeled carriage pulled by horses and often used as a weapon of war. Chariots appeared first in western Asia around 2100 BCE and were widespread in Eurasia by 1500 BCE.

chartered joint-stock companies: Companies to which governments grant monopoly rights by charter and in which hundreds or thousands of investors own shares. These innovative measures, developed during the sixteenth century, helped share the risks and increase the scale of long-distance trade.

Chinese Civil War (1945–1949): Conflict between the Chinese Communist Party, led by Mao Zedong, and the nationalist Guomindang. The CCP won and created the People's Republic of China.

Chinese Revolution (1880s–1910s): A long revolution that ultimately overthrew the Qing dynasty. Yuan Shikai, an army general, along with Sun Yatsen and other revolutionaries, took advantage of an army mutiny to force the last Qing emperor to abdicate.

choke point: A narrow route providing strategic, affordable passage from one large body of water to another—such as the Straits of Malacca between Sumatra and the Malay Peninsula, or the strait between India's southern tip and Sri Lanka. Those who controlled choke points often were able to profit economically and politically.

Chola [CHOH-lah] **kingdom** (ca. 970–1300): A state that arose in southeastern India and ultimately controlled Indian Ocean trade passing along south Indian coasts and Sri Lanka. Partly an alliance of merchant trading guilds, the Chola flourished through commercial and naval activity, and even attacked Srivijayan cities while under the expansionary rule of Rajendra I (r. 1012–1044).

Christopher Columbus: Born in Genoa, Italy, Christopher Columbus secured funding from the king and queen of Castile (a powerful state in Spain) to sail west from Europe and find a route to China in 1492. He instead found islands in the Caribbean and inaugurated a new age of global interconnection.

Cimmerians: Horse nomads from the Russian and Ukrainian steppe who began arriving on the Hungarian plain around 900 BCE, bringing with them steppe traditions. Many waves of nomads and semi-nomads followed, migrating from the steppes to eastern Europe in subsequent centuries.

city: A large settlement with elaborate divisions of labor, social hierarchies, tightly packed living spaces, open public areas, and large buildings. Trade, exchange, and markets feature prominently in cities.

civil service examinations: The use of written examinations on Confucian ideology to select public administrators in China (and in Korea while under Tang influence). This system fostered cultural unity and an educated elite.

classic Hinduism (begun ca. 400 BCE): An evolution of Vedic traditions of caste, ritual, and sacrifice. Hindus added several new beliefs to Vedic foundations, including the endless migration of souls based on moral conduct, or *karma*.

climate change: Recent, rapid change in Earth's climate patterns that is unprecedented in human history and largely human-caused. It is due mainly to a significant increase in fossil fuel use in the past 30 to 40 years, which created high concentrations of greenhouse gases in the atmosphere and caused Earth's temperature to rise.

Clovis points (ca. 12,000–11,000 BCE): Stone spearheads used throughout North America; their broad dissemination indicates widespread cultural and technological diffusion across the continent.

coal: A fossil fuel made up of ancient plant remains that can be converted into motor power. Cheap, low-lying coal gave rise to the Industrial Revolution in Britain and fueled industrialization around the world.

coaling stations: Pacific ports where imperial powers' naval ships refueled during the late nineteenth century. European powers seized Pacific islands largely for their strategic use as coaling stations and the low cost of controlling them.

Cold War (1945–1991): An ideological and political struggle, primarily between the United States and the USSR, that led to a proliferation of nuclear weapons and pervasive propaganda campaigns. It also intensified conflicts around the world through the two countries' participation in proxy wars.

Columbian Exchange: The transfer of plants, animals, and microbes among Eurasia, Africa, and the Americas that followed Columbus's initiation of contact.

Comanche [kuh-MAN-shee] **Empire** (1730–1870): The Comanche rule of the southern plains of the present-day United States, resulting from their near monopoly of the regional gun trade and mastery of horses.

comfort women: Hundreds of thousands of women that the Japanese army captured from various places, including Korea, China, and the Philippines, and forced to work as sex slaves in occupied areas.

commercial revolution: The increased commercialization and specialization, coupled with frontier expansion and territorial conquest, that occurred especially in China and Atlantic Europe during the period 1500–1800. In combination, these factors caused the regions' economies to grow and their societies to become richer.

communism: A broadly appealing international movement and political theory based on the ideas of Karl Marx and Vladimir Lenin. Communists opposed capitalism and private property and believed that inevitable revolution would bring about a prosperous, equitable world.

Communist Manifesto (1848): A political pamphlet co-authored by Karl Marx and Friedrich Engels arguing that class struggle propels history. It describes the inevitability of a communist revolution and calls for the working classes around the world to join together in the struggle against the ruling elite.

complex society: A social unit characterized by a large hierarchical society, regulatory institutions, and a complex division of labor. Complex societies often developed states and cities.

Confucius [kuhn-FYOO-shuhs] **(Kong Qiu)** (ca. 551–479 BCE): A *shi* whose followers wrote down his ideas in the book *Analects*, which emphasized ethical conduct, ritual, social hierarchy, and the importance of scholars.

Constantine (r. 306–337 CE): A Roman emperor who established a second Roman capital in Byzantium (modern-day Istanbul), renamed it Constantinople, and split the Roman Empire into two halves. He converted to Christianity, ultimately making it an imperial, state-supported religion.

containerization: The transition to the use of shipping containers for the transport of goods that led to decreased shipping and labor costs as well as shorter shipping times. Containers facilitated the connection between East Asian export economies and large North American markets.

containment strategy: An approach guiding U.S. Cold War policy toward the USSR based on defeating it with patience and endurance rather than military strength. The strategy was based on the belief that Soviet communism would collapse if the United States prevented its spread.

cotton: Lightweight and durable cloth woven from the cotton plant. During the early modern period Atlantic Europeans expanded the trade of cotton to new markets in Africa, Europe, and the Americas, and it became an essential global trade commodity.

cotton gin: A machine, invented in the United States and patented in 1794, that separated cotton seeds from cotton fiber, thereby easing cotton production. It contributed to the rise of cotton manufacturing and the spread of cotton production and slavery in the U.S. South.

COVID-19: An easily transmittable infectious disease caused by the novel coronavirus (SARS CoV-2), which apparently originated in bat colonies before mutating into a human pathogen in or near Wuhan, China, in late 2019. In 2020, COVID-19 quickly spread around the world, causing a global pandemic that killed hundreds of thousands.

creole cultures: Societies in the Americas, particularly in the plantation zone, that blended various features from Africa and Europe to create hybrid cultures, religions, and languages.

crowd diseases: Infections such as smallpox, mumps, or measles that require large populations in order to stay in circulation. In large populations, these pathogens mostly affect children.

Crusades (1096–1231): Waves of small-scale wars and attacks on the Levant that were motivated by both religious and military aims. Over 200 years, Crusaders of mostly French, German, and English origin established small kingdoms that all fell by the thirteenth century.

culture of imperialism: Celebratory literature, theater, music, and public ceremony that supported the belief in the right and duty of one group to rule over others. It was most prominent in Britain but also existed in the United States, France, Germany, Italy, and Japan.

cuneiform: The earliest known form of writing, cuneiform developed in Uruk around 3400 to 3300 BCE and consisted of scratches made on wedges of clay.

Darius (r. 522–486 BCE): A lance-bearer who staged a coup d'état and became an Achaemenid king. He introduced many innovations that helped him effectively manage the vast Achaemenid territory.

dark earth: Human-made patches of nutrient-rich soil in Amazonia. People used these areas to raise crops that supported thousands of settlements.

declines in fertility: The global drop in birth rates since about 1960 due to growing urbanization, the spread of female education, and the increased use of birth control.

de-industrialization: During the Industrial Revolution, the decline of industries that could not compete with the price and quality of factory-made products.

Delhi sultanate (ca. 1206–1400): A military aristocracy established in northern India by Turkic horsemen from Central Asia who fostered an Indo-Islamic culture fusing Indian, Turkic, Persian, and Arabic elements. Its legacy includes palace and mosque architecture, and Urdu poetry—a blend of Hindi and Persian.

demographic dividend: A shift in fertility patterns that aids economic growth and development. Demographic dividends in East Asia after 1950 contributed to the Asian tigers' economic success.

demokratia [day-moh-kra-TEE-uh]: After 508 BCE, a form of government that the Athenian *polis* introduced wherein all citizens directly participated in governance. It was based on an elected ruling council of 500 that was responsible to a larger assembly of all free Athenian men over age 18 who had completed military training.

Deng Xiaoping [DUHNG show-pihng] (1904–1997): The head of China beginning in 1978 and leader of its economic transformation. His economic reforms, which essentially replaced socialism with capitalism, included the end of the commune work-unit system, re-introduction of profit motives, and encouragement of export-oriented industry.

dhows [dows]: Ships used by Arab seafarers in the Indian Ocean. Dhows featured slanting, triangular sails to efficiently capture the wind and hulls sewn with coconut fiber for maximum flexibility.

disease disasters: As a result of entry into the expanding Global web, the introduction of deadly diseases to previously isolated areas of the world that had no experience with them. In combination with violence and declining fertility, these diseases led to devastating demographic collapses in the Americas, Siberia, many Pacific Islands, and parts of southern Africa.

dolmens: Stacks of stones, erected mainly between 1500 and 500 BCE, that mark burial sites and imply growing social stratification. Although they were built in many places in Eurasia, Korea contains almost half the world's dolmens.

domestication: The genetic modification of plants or animals through human selection or breeding. Domestication enables humans to produce food instead of searching for it.

domino theory: Conjecture among U.S. policymakers that if one country fell to communism, then the countries surrounding it would follow. This theory drove U.S. involvement in the Vietnam War because officials feared that if Vietnam became entirely communist, the rest of Southeast Asia would too.

dreamtime: One of the religious beliefs of aboriginal Australians according to which a distant past linked to the birth of the world when supernatural entities crossed Australia, forming the continent and tracing paths that became "songlines."

Dutch East India Company (VOC): A very successful chartered joint-stock company created to control the Dutch spice trade. During the seventeenth and eighteenth centuries, the VOC's heavily armed ships dominated the Indonesian archipelago as the company used force and violence to gain advantageous trade terms.

economies of scale: Economies of scale occur when a producer's costs per unit of output decline as the scale of the enterprise grows. This condition, which exists in only some industries such as sugar production, benefits large-scale enterprises.

Eiichi Shibusawa [ay-EE-chee shih-boo-SOW-ah] (1840–1931): A Japanese government official and businessman who was passionate about bringing industrialization to his country. He set up Japan's first modern cotton mill in Osaka with the help of Takeo Yamanobe.

emancipation for serfs (1861): A labor liberation granted by a statute that, in theory, liberated serfs by granting them freedoms they previously lacked. In practice, it introduced many new legal constraints to which former serfs remained subject.

encomienda [ehn-koh-mee-EHN-dah]: Granted by Spanish rulers to colonizers in Spanish America, the legal right to conscript Amerindians as unpaid laborers.

Epic of Gilgamesh: A long poem written down around 2100 BCE in cuneiform and the oldest surviving epic poem in world history. It is about a legendary Uruk king, Gilgamesh, who lived around 2600 BCE.

Eurasian steppe: A broad grassland that stretches from eastern Europe to East Asia.

fascism: A political movement and ideology that formed the basis of Benito Mussolini and Adolf Hitler's governments. It emphasized militant nationalism, purification of the nation, a cult of the leader, and showy displays of national strength.

Ferdinand Magellan: A Portuguese explorer whom the Spanish Crown funded to find a route to the Moluccas by sailing west from Europe and along the southern coast of South America in 1519. He died in the Philippines after crossing the Pacific, but his crew became the first people to sail around the world and attained knowledge of the vastness of the Pacific Ocean.

field artillery and fortifications: Large and heavy mobile guns and cannon deployed in the field, and the highly engineered structures used to defend against them. These elements increased the cost and intricacy of war during the early modern period.

financialization: The rise in the prominence, prevalence, and profitability of finance worldwide due to de-regulation and digital technology. It has eased the global flow of money and contributed to increased economic volatility.

firestick farming: Intentional burning of landscapes and methodical use of fire that promotes the growth of edible plants and attracts animals for hunting. Aboriginal Australians employed firestick farming to increase their food supply.

flint maize: A form of maize, developed in the American Midwest around the ninth or tenth century, that matured faster than other varieties and with bigger kernels. It boosted food supplies and enabled North American farmers to subsist mainly on agricultural crops and less on hunting and foraging.

Florentine Codex: A comprehensive catalogue of Aztec history and culture, complied between 1545 and 1590 by a Spanish priest and his Aztec students. The *Codex* incorporates about 2,000 illustrations of Aztec daily life along with text in Nahuatl expressed in the Roman alphabet.

fractional reserve banking: The practice of banks lending out more money than they have in their reserves in order to create money in the form of credit. The Bank of Amsterdam pioneered this practice, which promoted commerce by reducing its costs.

free trade: De-regulation of trade beginning in the 1980s that Ronald Reagan and Margaret Thatcher spearheaded. Free trade policy spread around the world, leading to bigger multinational corporations and globalized supply chains.

French Revolution (1789–1799): A political revolution within France aimed at reforming the hierarchical social order. It led to sweeping changes, descended into terror and dictatorship, and was largely reversed when the monarchy was re-established in 1814.

Friedrich List (1789–1846): An economist born in Germany who wrote newspaper articles and books that guided state-sponsored industrialization. He advocated for protectionist policies and the construction of railroads.

Ganges [GAN-jeez] **basin**: Rich alluvial lands surrounding the Ganges River that supported the development of a new Indian culture and complex society starting around 1500 BCE. It is also known as the Gangetic plain.

Genghis Khan (ca. 1165–1227): Born as Temujin, Genghis Khan was the founder

and leader of the Mongol Empire. Under his command, the Mongols conquered territory from China to Ukraine.

germ theory of disease: The scientific theory developed after 1850 that pointed to bacteria's role in infection. It led to sanitation reforms that reduced death and illness from water-borne diseases and paved the way for understanding infections.

Germanic tribes: Groups originating from east of the Danube River and north of the Rhine River in Europe, including Goths, Vandals, and Franks. Beginning in the 370s, the Germanic tribes migrated to Roman territory as they fled from the Huns, or when the Romans hired them to fight against other tribes or to fight for one set of Romans against another in civil wars.

Ghost Dance: A spiritual movement that arose in response to disruptions in Amerindian life during the nineteenth century. Inspired by Wovoka's prophecy, participants performed a community circle dance in hopes that this ceremony would bring the return of peace, joy, and plenty.

Glorious Revolution (1688–1689): The nearly bloodless replacement of James II with William of Orange on the throne of England, organized by Protestant British elites. It cemented the increased power of Parliament in relation to the monarchy.

Göbekli Tepe [goh-behk-LEE teh-peh]: A site in southeastern Turkey; likely a religious temple that a sedentary or semi-sedentary group built around 9000 BCE and abandoned by 7000 BCE.

gracialization: The thinning and shrinking of skeletons through evolution. Humans underwent this process as social groups grew and relied less on their physical strength for survival.

Grand Canal: A massive public works project, started under the Sui dynasty (581–618), that linked north and south China, promoting unity and enabling emperors to move troops and food quickly and easily.

Great Leap Forward (1958–1961): Mao Zedong's massive and disastrous campaign to improve China's industry and agriculture. He called for citizens to produce steel in their own backyards, the output of which proved to be useless, and introduced new agricultural policies that caused a devastating famine.

Great Zimbabwe (ca. 1250–1450): A city and center of power in southern Africa based on cattle wealth and a thriving gold trade. The rulers at Great Zimbabwe had enough authority and wealth to erect great stone buildings beginning in 1275.

gross world product (GWP): The size of the world economy, which is calculated by using the combined value of all goods and services produced worldwide. Between 1500 and 1800, the GWP almost doubled.

Guanches [GWAHNCH-ihz]: Descendants of North African Berbers, the Guanches were inhabitants of the Canary Islands who fought against Spanish conquest and settlement from 1402 to 1496. Spanish weapons technology and the diseases they carried with them eventually led to the defeat of the Guanches.

Gulf Stream: The counterclockwise movement of North Atlantic Ocean currents that warms the climates of western Europe's coastal areas from Portugal to Norway.

Gupta [GOOP-tah] **dynasty** (ca. 330–550): A dynasty that ruled the north of India and supported religious institutions, math, science, and arts. Samudragupta (r. 335–375) and Chandragupta II (r. 375–415) were two successful Gupta kings.

Habsburgs (1282–1918): Originating as Swiss and German nobles, the Habsburgs extended their territory with military force and advantageous political marriages. They built a global empire and became a major European power but were unable to unify Europe.

Haitian Revolution (1791–1804): An anti-colonial, political, and anti-slavery revolution rooted in racial tensions and led primarily by Toussaint L'Ouverture, a former slave. It began with the largest slave rebellion in history and ended in victory, but it left Haiti fractured in its aftermath.

Hammurabi [hahm-uh-RAH-bee] (r. 1792–1750 BCE): A king of Babylon who formed a short-lived empire; he erected a stone monument inscribed with 282 laws that survives today.

Han dynasty (206 BCE–220 CE): Emperor Gaozu founded the Han dynasty following Qin rule. Han rulers expanded Chinese territory and promoted Confucian ideology; under their leadership the economy and population grew, and land and maritime trade flourished.

Hannibal Barca (247–ca. 182 BCE): A member of the Carthaginian Barca clan who transformed Carthage's presence in Spain into an empire there. Hannibal led the fight against Rome in the Second Punic War and gained renown for his skills as a military commander.

Harrapans [hah-RAP-puhnz] (ca. 2600–1700 BCE): The name of the Indus valley populations and culture; its two largest cities were Harappa and Mohenjo Daro.

Hawaiian kings: Between 1450 and 1700, several Hawaiian chiefs responded to shortages of resources and increased competition by making themselves kings, thereby initiating a ruling class, an administrative bureaucracy, and struggles for succession to the throne. Kings and kingdoms were unique in the Pacific world; no other Polynesians outside of Hawaii had them.

heavy cavalry: One of Darius's military innovations. Instead of arming mounted warriors with only light equipment, heavy cavalry rode on large, strong horses with full armor and weaponry.

Heian [HAY-ahn] **Japan** (734–1185): A period of rule in Japan, based at Heian (modern Kyoto), during which Chinese influence waned, indigenous religious traditions (especially Shinto) became dominant, aristocratic social order prevailed, and refined courtly life produced the first substantial body of literature written by women anywhere in world history.

heliocentric system: The idea, which Nicholas Copernicus wrote down in 1514, that planets rotate around the sun as opposed to the idea that the sun moves around the Earth. Johannes Kepler, Galileo Galilei, and Isaac Newton built on this work, and the heliocentric system won acceptance in 1687.

Hellenistic age (323–31 BCE): The age of Greek and Macedonian rule in Greece, Egypt, and Southwest Asia. It began after Alexander died and his generals Ptolemy, Antigonus, and Seleucus divided his empire among themselves.

herders: People who mainly lived off of domesticated grazing animals that they raised in arid and semi-arid grassland and scrubland regions.

hieroglyphs [HEYE-ruh-gliphs]: The primary Egyptian writing system, which eventually contained nearly 1,000 symbols; it developed around 3000 BCE, possibly influenced by Sumerian cuneiforms.

Hiroshima and Nagasaki: Two Japanese cities and centers of military production onto which the United States dropped nuclear weapons in August 1945. The bombs killed 105,000 people immediately and were the first, and so far only, nuclear weapons used in warfare.

HIV/AIDS: The infectious and deadly disease that spread from chimpanzees to humans in the 1940s and caused a global pandemic beginning in the 1980s. Africa was the hardest hit. As of 2020, the disease has killed 30 million people.

Holocaust: The outcome of a Nazi-led effort to racially purify Germany through the mass murder of groups Hitler deemed inferior, particularly Jews. During the Holocaust, Nazis murdered millions of Jews, as well as Roma (Gypsies), the mentally ill, and the physically disabled.

Holocene: The name given to the roughly 11,700-year period beginning with the end of the Younger Dryas and continuing until today.

hominins [HAWM-ih-nihms]: The term used to describe all humans, extinct human branches, and ape-like human ancestors who have lived in the last 7 million years. Fossil hunters have discovered 18 species of hominin so far.

Homo erectus [HOH-MOH ee-REHK-tuhs]: A hominin species that emerged 1.5 million years ago and went extinct 190,000 years ago. *Homo sapiens*, Neanderthals, Denisovans, and Flores Island "Hobbits" are all probably descended from *Homo erectus*.

Homo sapiens [HOH-MOH SAY-pee-uhns]: A type of hominin and the name for our species, human beings. *Homo sapiens* emerged 300,000 to 200,000 years ago in Africa.

Hyksos [HICK-sohs]: A group of people, probably from the area of modern-day Lebanon, who migrated to and invaded Egypt. They ruled Egypt from around 1700 to 1500 BCE.

imperial consolidation: The general trend during the early modern period of empires growing bigger and more powerful at the expense of smaller powers.

income inequality: The growing divergence in incomes beginning in the 1980s. Globalization caused a vast share of the world's wealth to be concentrated in the hands of the few, creating the mega-rich class.

indentured labor: Commitment to a fixed period of bonded labor, usually between two and eight years. Although signing indenture contracts was technically voluntary, labor recruiters often used predatory practices to secure laborers.

Indian Ocean monsoon: Regular and predictable alternating winds that made the Indian Ocean relatively easy to sail.

Indian Rebellion (1857–1858): A rebellion that began with an army mutiny and spread to include many regional revolts. The rebels' aims were to get rid of British rule and restore old regimes; but many Indians remained loyal to Britain, and the rebellion collapsed.

Indus River: A river 2,000 miles (3,000 km) long that runs from the Himalayan glaciers to the Arabian Sea. The Indus was central to agriculture and trade for the complex Indus valley cities.

Industrial Revolution: A monumental switch to factory-scale production using machinery driven by water power and fossil fuels instead of human muscle and hand tools. It began in Britain in the late eighteenth century and spread to other countries and continents, with global consequences.

information technology (IT): Innovations in information storing, processing, and sharing, particularly via the Internet and computers. IT reduces the costs of transportation and production, thus aiding in the growth of globalized supply chains.

Inka (ca. 1300–1532): An empire located in the Andean region with its capital in Cuzco. Using a combination of military force and cultural influence, it quickly became one of the two largest polities in the Americas prior to 1492.

international institutions: Governmental, non-governmental, and illicit organizations that operate internationally due to the rise of challenges, problems, and opportunities that are global in scale. Prominent examples include the United Nations, Amnesty International, and drug cartels.

international migrants: People who live in a country other than that in which they were born. Since the 1970s, the majority of migrants have moved to Western Europe, North America, and the Arabian Gulf; by 2019, international migrants made up about 3.5 percent of the global population.

iron: Made from a relatively common ore, iron was cheaper and better than bronze in many ways. However, it required a lot of fuel to smelt and highly skilled ironsmiths to shape it into useful objects.

iron working: The complex process of transforming a raw material, iron ore, into a metal useful for tools and weapons. It appeared in Europe around 1000 BCE and in Africa at roughly the same time.

irrigation: The process of diverting water from lakes, streams, and rivers and supplying it to fields and gardens to ensure crop growth. Irrigation enabled farmers to cultivate land that was otherwise too dry for growing crops.

Islam: A monotheistic religion established in the seventh century whose followers are called Muslims. Its scripture is the Qur'an, which contains God's revelations to Muhammad.

Islamization: The widespread conversion to, and adoption of, Islam. India underwent Islamization beginning in 1000; coastal East African Islamization mostly occurred between the seventh and thirteenth centuries.

Istanbul [ihs-tan-BOOL]: Formerly named Constantinople, it was the capital of the Ottoman Empire from 1453, after Mehmet the Conqueror seized it from the Byzantine Greeks. Istanbul gave the Ottomans control of profitable trade routes and was a launching point for several successful attacks in the Balkans and along the Black Sea coasts.

Jack Gladstone: A slave in British Guiana who led the Demerara revolt of 1823 with his father, Quamina. Gladstone believed that legal abolition had passed in London and called Guiana's slaves to freedom, causing 10,000 slaves to revolt.

Jacobins: A political faction made up of mostly middle-class lawyers who increasingly dominated the government of revolutionary France. They ended elections in 1793, introduced wide-reaching reforms, and ushered in the Terror—a period of widespread suspicion and public executions.

James Watt (1736–1819): A Scottish-born engineer who designed and built more efficient steam engines. He was among a group of engineers who made steam engines more appealing to and useful for manufacturers.

janissaries [JAN-ih-sehr-eez]: Slave soldiers who formed an elite infantry under the Ottoman sultan and developed volley fire with muskets. They were taken as young boys from Christian homes in the Balkans and trained in warfare and administration.

Jawaharlal Nehru [jah-WAH-hah-lahrl NAY-roo] (1889–1964): Instrumental leader of the Indian independence movement and first prime minister of India. Next to Gandhi, he was the second most important figure in the Indian National Congress.

Jenne: An archeological site in West Africa where either a cluster of villages or a city stood by 450 CE. It offers evidence of long-distance trade along the Niger River.

Jesuits: Founded in 1540 in Spain, an order of priests in the Catholic Church dedicated to evangelizing non-Catholics and to rigorous education. During the sixteenth and seventeenth centuries, Jesuit missionaries worked to counter Protestantism in places as varied as Poland, Germany, Japan, China, India, and the Americas.

Jomon culture: A group that became sedentary around 7000 BCE, mostly along the east-central Pacific coast of Japan.

They lived off of shellfish, fish, acorns, and chestnuts and were among the first inventors of pottery.

José Aponte [HOH-say uh-POHN-tay]: A Yoruba-speaking free black who led a slave revolt in Cuba in 1812. This revolt was part of a rise in resistance in Cuba and Brazil due to the growing number of Yoruba-speaking slaves being shipped to these slave markets.

Josef Stalin (1878–1953): The leader of the USSR who consolidated power in the years 1927–1928. He introduced policies of industrialization and collectivization and headed state-led mass terror and brutal coercion.

Julius Caesar (100–44 BCE): A skilled military commander who gained prominence and the loyalty of legions of soldiers, which he refused to disband when the Roman Senate instructed him to. This decision led to civil war, from which Caesar emerged successful and then ruled as dictator from 49 BCE until his assassination five years later.

Justinian (r. 527–565): A Byzantine emperor who built the famous church Hagia Sophia in Constantinople and sought to reconstitute the old Roman Empire by re-conquering territories the Romans had once controlled. He was militarily successful, but he drained the empire of money and his successors lost many of his gains.

keiretsu [kee-REHT-soo]: Large, often family-based Japanese corporate conglomerates made up of banks, trading companies, and industries. They led Japan's post–World War II economic miracle by spearheading technological innovation, assembly-line production, and miniaturization.

Khazaria [kuh-ZAHR-ee-uh] (ca. 640–ca. 970): A Turkic-speaking, multireligious kingdom located in the grasslands of the North Caucasus. The leaders converted to Judaism in the ninth century.

Khoi [KOH-ay]: African hunters and cattle raisers who lived in the southern tip of Africa and clashed with Dutch colonists. Many Khoi eventually died, and their culture largely disappeared due to dispossession and disease epidemics.

King Afonso (r. 1506–1543): A king in Kongo, West Central Africa, whose father, also a king, had converted to Catholicism. Afonso learned to speak, read, and write Portuguese, and as king he made Catholicism the state religion in Kongo. His power grew with the help of Portuguese advisers and military technology.

King Kamehameha [kah-MAY-hah-MAY-hah] (r. 1782–1819): A ruler who unified

Hawaii as a single kingdom by using imported military and sailing technology that he strictly controlled. His monarchy lasted a century.

Kongo monarchy: Elected rulers of the kingdom of Kongo whose legitimacy and backing largely rested on protecting their subjects from enslavement.

Korean War (1950–1953): A conflict that began when Soviet-backed, communist North Korea invaded U.S.-backed South Korea. Chinese and United Nations forces joined the fight, which became a war of attrition until a cease-fire was agreed to in 1953.

Koryo [KOHR-yoh] (918–1392): A kingdom in Korea that was based on an alliance of aristocratic families known as *yangban*. It was started due to the threat of steppe nomads.

Kwame Nkrumah [KWAH-may n-KROO-mah] (1909–1972): An influential anti-colonial agitator and chief negotiator in the Gold Coast's transition from British colony to the independent country of Ghana. He was Ghana's first leader and ruled in an increasingly authoritarian way until his ouster in 1966.

La Marseillaise [MAHR-say-yehz]: The song chosen as the French national anthem in 1795. It inspired many countries to designate national anthems, which became a part of growing nationalist cultures around the world.

Lakshmibai [lahk-SHMEE-beye]: A local Indian ruler, also known as the Queen of Jhansi, in north-central India who continued to rule in defiance of British East India Company armies until she died in combat. She remains a national hero in India.

land empires: Empires that used industrial technologies and/or nationalist ideas to extend control over large areas of land rather than overseas. These empires included Russia, the United States, Canada, Brazil, and Argentina. The Comanche Empire in North America and the Ethiopian Empire in northeastern Africa were secondary land empires.

land reform: In South Korea, the transition from the majority of peasants renting land from wealthy landowners to the majority owning their own land. Pursued under pressure from the U.S. military during the post–World War II occupation, land reform laid the foundation for South Korea's economic growth.

Lapita: An Oceanic group that sailed out into the Pacific Ocean from the Bismarck Archipelago around 1300 BCE. They settled most of Remote Oceania, including Fiji, Tonga, and Samoa.

latte stones: Large stone pillars erected on several islands of the Marianas that probably formed the bases of buildings. The Chamorro of Guam began to build latte stones around 1000.

League of Peace and Power: An Iroquois confederacy forged sometime before 1450 among the five Iroquois nations; the League united them and stopped them from warring among one another.

Legalism: A political philosophy that emphasized law, punishment, regimentation, and the power of the state. Lord Shang (390–338 BCE), one of Legalism's chief advocates, promoted intimidation as an ideal governing method.

Levant: The eastern Mediterranean coast and its hinterland. It forms the western edge of the Fertile Crescent and is the location of the first strong evidence of farming.

Lucy: Discovered in 1974 in Ethiopia, a fossilized skeleton of a hominin called *Australopithecus afarensis* who lived 4 million to 3 million years ago.

Magdalenian culture: A semi-settled group that lived between Portugal and Poland and intercepted seasonal migrations of reindeer for sustenance. Magdalenians painted the famous cave art at Lascaux and Altamira.

maize [mayz]: A staple food crop indigenous to the Americas; also known as corn. Part of the Columbian Exchange, maize flourished in southern Europe, China, and western and southern Africa.

malaria: A disease originating in Africa that is transmitted by mosquitos and was particularly deadly in warm, humid, and populous locations. Malaria spread widely around the world, including to the Americas, as part of the Columbian Exchange.

Mandate of Heaven: A cultural formula positing the divine authority that allowed kings to rule. It was a provisional legitimacy that rulers had to convince their subjects they maintained.

Manichaeism [man-ih-KEE-iz'm]: A dualistic religion derived from the preachings of Mani around the third century CE. A blend of Christianity, Zoroastrianism, and Buddhism, it emphasized a struggle between good and evil and a code of conduct including non-violence, fasting, and restraint.

Mao Zedong [MOW tsay-TOHN] (1893–1976): Head of the Chinese Communist Party beginning in World War II and founder of the People's Republic of China. He developed a novel perspective on Marxist theory, arguing that peasants, not just industrial workers, could lead a communist revolution.

Maori [mow-ree]: Polynesians who live in New Zealand. They arrived from central or eastern Polynesia around 1280 and experienced two centuries of peace and prosperity until population growth led to scarcity and warfare at the end of the fifteenth century.

Mauryan [MAWR-yuhn] **Empire** (ca. 321–230 BCE): Indian prince Chandragupta Maurya united the Indus and Ganges valleys for the first time and established the Mauryan Empire; it ended after his grandson Ashoka's reign.

Maya [MEYE-uh] (ca. 600 BCE–900 CE): A complex hierarchical Mesoamerican society that was culturally and linguistically united but politically fragmented. Its rulers amassed wealth through the export of products such as salt, jade, and obsidian, and the Mayan glyphs were the most complete Mesoamerican writing system.

Meiji [MAY-jee] **Restoration** (1867–1868): A political revolution in Japan that ended in the reinstatement of rule by emperor and the introduction of a new elite. Meiji reformers were committed to strengthening Japan and promoting its industrialization.

Menelik II [MEHN-eh-lihk] (1844–1913): Architect and ruler of the Ethiopian Empire who used foreign military technology and skills to conquer surrounding lands and defeat Italian forces at the Battle of Adowa. He also introduced foreign technologies and institutions, such as railroads and public schools.

menhirs: Large oblong stones, standing upright, that began appearing in Europe in about 5500 BCE, marking a shift in spiritual practices that spread across the region. One example is Stonehenge, built around 2500 BCE in southern England.

merchant trading guilds: Formal organizations of groups of traders who worked together to facilitate trade and ease the risks associated with it. An alliance of merchant trading guilds formed the foundation of the Chola kingdom's power (ca. 970–1300).

Meroë [MEHR-oh-wee]: A kingdom in Kush located on the Nile between Egypt and sub-Saharan Africa that reached its peak around the first century BCE. It was the center of iron working in Africa and controlled the export of African goods to Egypt.

Mesopotamia: A largely agricultural region in the Tigris and Euphrates river valleys where Sumer, Akkad, Assyria, and Babylon were located.

metallurgy: The process of separating metals from ore—the rock in which they are found—and then fashioning metals into objects.

Mexican Revolution (1910–1920): A social and national revolution that remade Mexico. It began when a succession struggle led to the jailing of presidential candidate Francisco Madero, which sparked insurgencies across the country and led to a decade of fighting.

Middle Passage: The months-long journey of slave ships between Africa and the Americas. Slaves were tightly packed below deck, usually naked and in chains, and many died due to unsanitary conditions and violence.

Mikhail Gorbachev [mihk-HEYEL gohr-bah-CHUHV]: The reform-minded final leader of the USSR who came to power in 1985. He introduced policies of perestroika ("restructuring") and glasnost ("openness"), defused international tensions, and pursued nuclear arms reduction treaties but ultimately could not prevent the collapse of the Soviet Union.

military revolution: An increase in the complexity and expense of war between 1450 and 1800. It comprised several innovations in weaponry, defense, technique, and administration.

millenarian movements: Religious movements whose adherents believe that spiritual or divine intervention will transform the world for the better.

millet system: The Ottoman Empire's tolerant religious policy: the Ottomans taxed non-Muslims at a higher rate than Muslims but also welcomed Christians and Jews and left them alone to oversee their own communities.

Minamata disease: The effects of mercury poisoning that those who ate seafood from the Minamata bay in Japan developed due to pollution from a nearby chemical plant. It was one among many acute pollution disasters in the 1950s and 1960s that arose from East Asia's rapid industrialization.

Ming voyages (1405–1433): Seven large maritime voyages arranged by Zheng He under the Yongle Emperor of China during the Ming dynasty. The extent of the voyages and the size of their wooden ships were unprecedented, and they served to project power as far as East Africa.

mita [MEE-tah]: The forced labor draft imposed on Andean peoples by the Inka. Under Spanish rule in South America, the *mita* provided unfree labor to work in the brutal conditions of the silver mines.

Mohandas K. Gandhi (1869–1948): The Indian anti-colonial activist who developed the practice of non-violent civil disobedience called satyagraha. His activism led to a widespread nationalist movement in India and contributed to the end of British rule in 1947.

Moluccas [moh-LUH-kuhz]: Part of the islands of Indonesia, also known as the East Indies, where nutmeg and cloves grew. Because Europeans placed great value on these spices, trade connections to these islands were very attractive to merchants.

monasticism: A way of life long prominent in Christianity and Buddhism that involves voluntary withdrawal from society, including a rejection of marriage and family, in favor of dedication to rigorous spiritual work.

Mongol western campaigns (1219–1260): A series of campaigns beginning under Genghis Khan and carried on by his grandsons Batu and Hulegu. By 1260, Mongol rule stretched from Russia and the Black Sea to Mongolia.

monotheism [MAW-noh-thee-iz'm]: A religious system that espouses a belief in one god, or the oneness of God. Judaism, Christianity, and Islam are all monotheistic religions.

Muhammad [muh-HAH-mehd] (570–632): The founder of Islam who was born in the city of Mecca in Arabia and had visions at age 40 telling him he was God's prophet. He subsequently gathered a group of followers, called Muslims, and embarked on a successful military campaign in 622, establishing Islam as both a political and a religious movement.

Mulla Sadra [MOO-lah SA-drah] (1571–1640): An influential Shi'a theologian living in Safavid Iran. His writings attempted to reconcile Sufi mysticism with Islamic philosophical traditions and helped create an intellectual foundation for the Safavid theocracy.

multiethnic empire: A polity comprising different linguistic and religious groups and containing many ethnic minorities and multilingual people. The Habsburg, Russian, and Ottoman empires were all multiethnic.

Muslim League: The organization of Muslims in British India that advocated for the division of post-colonial India into a Muslim state and a Hindu state. Muhammad Ali Jinnah, who became the first head of Pakistan, was its leader.

Mustafa Kemal [MUHS-tah-fah kuh-MAHL] (1881–1938): Leader of Turkey's nationalist revolution and its first president. Also known as Atatürk, he introduced a set of educational and legal policies, the Atatürk Reforms, aimed at strengthening and secularizing Turkey.

Nalanda: A Buddhist monastery in northeast India that was a center of learning and science in the Indian Ocean world, reaching its height in the sixth to the ninth centuries. Nalanda was part of the thriving intellectual scene in India between 500 and 1000.

Napoleon Bonaparte (1769–1821): A military man who ascended to power in France in 1799 by way of a coup d'état and became a dictator. He won numerous military victories against foreign armies but abdicated in 1814 after a string of disastrous campaigns.

Narmer: The first ruler of Upper and Lower Egypt who completed unification around 2950 BCE; also known as Menes.

National Policy: A Canadian program that was launched in 1879 to stimulate industrialization. It involved the introduction of tariffs on foreign goods and investment in railroads.

nationalism: A set of beliefs, ideas, and attitudes that provides a sense of solidarity for a group. The group usually occupies a defined territory and claims to share language, culture, ethnicity, ancestry, political values, civic values, or some combination of these.

Natufians (ca. 12,500–9,500 BCE): Sedentary residents of the Levant who showed the earliest known signs of plant cultivation and farming.

natural selection: The process whereby organisms that are better adapted to their environments pass down advantageous genetic traits through generations.

Neanderthals [nee-ANN-duhr-tawls]: An extinct "cousin" of human beings that lived from 400,000 to 40,000 years ago in Europe, Siberia, and southwestern Asia.

neo-Confucianism: An ideology originating in the Song dynasty (960–1279) that emphasized rigorous study and academic learning as the path to morality and righteousness. In the sixteenth century, Wang Yangming—also considered a neo-Confucianist—claimed that book learning was not necessary for obtaining wisdom and acting ethically.

new imperialism: A pervasive and widespread form of empire that arose after 1870 due to the power and wealth gaps that industrialization caused and the popular support that nationalism stirred.

Nile River: A river 4,000 miles (nearly 7,000 km) long that flowed through Nubia and Egypt, bringing precious water and fertile silt.

Norte Chico (ca. 3100–1600 BCE): The collective name for a group of roughly 25 settlements in the Andes. Norte Chico was the earliest complex society in the Andean world, and its elites' power was based on the control of dried fish, a staple in the food supply.

Nubia [NOO-bee-uh]: A region south of Egypt and upriver from it on the Nile. Egypt mostly traded with or ruled over Nubia, but on occasion Nubia asserted control over parts of Egypt.

Oceania: The Southeast Asian region that includes the islands in the Pacific Ocean, including Melanesia, Micronesia, and Polynesia. Near Oceania consists of New Guinea, the Bismarck Archipelago, and the Solomon Islands; Remote Oceania reaches as far as Hawaii and Easter Island.

Octavian (Augustus): Caesar's grand-nephew, adopted son, and heir, who became emperor of Rome and changed his name to Augustus. He was a ruthless emperor who ruled for 40 years, consolidated the Roman state, and built a strong administrative foundation for subsequent emperors.

Oda Nobunaga [oh-DAH noh-boo-NAH-gah] (1534–1582): A Japanese warlord who unified southern Japan and may have invented volley fire. He met his political aims by militarizing peasants and arming them with widely produced Japanese guns.

Olmecs: Concentrated in the urban centers of San Lorenzo (ca. 1600–900 BCE) and La Venta (ca. 900–300 BCE) in southern Mexico, the Olmecs were the first Mesoamerican group to develop complex hierarchical societies. They were builders of giant basalt heads and pioneers of pyramid construction in the Americas.

oracle bone inscriptions: The first evidence of Chinese writing, oracle bone inscriptions are questions posed to the gods written on turtle shells and cattle bones. Diviners heated the bones until they cracked and then interpreted the gods' answers using the fragments.

Paleolithic: The period lasting from 2.6 million years ago to 13,000 years ago; the latter part, the late Paleolithic, saw a profusion of cultural change.

pan-Africanism: The call for Africans and people of African descent to liberate Africa and end racism through unified political action. The movement also supported literary and cultural revitalization. W.E.B. Du Bois and Marcus Garvey were prominent pan-Africanists.

Parliament: A British legislative body comprising elected officials and hereditary nobles. Following the British Civil Wars and Revolution, Parliament became the chief governing authority in Britain.

Parthians (247 BCE–224 CE): Successors of Seleucid rule that emerged from a group of mobile pastoralists. They are particularly notable for successfully cultivating long-distance trade.

partition of Africa: The dividing up of African lands among Britain, France, Germany, Belgium, Spain, and Portugal between 1874 and 1890. It began as an informal process, until the Berlin Conference convened to officially partition the African continent in 1884–1885.

***patío* process**: A technology involving the use of mercury to separate silver from its surrounding rock. This process made the task of silver extraction easier in the sixteenth and seventeenth centuries, thus increasing the value of lower-grade silver ores.

Pax Mongolica (ca. 1260–1350): Meaning "Mongolian Peace," a relatively calm period during which the Mongolian Empire boosted trade along the Silk Road by creating an environment of largely peaceful exchange.

pharaohs [FARE-ohs]: Egyptian kings; there were about 170 pharaohs between around 2950 and 30 BCE.

Phoenicia [fih-NEE-shuh]: The Greek name for the cities on the eastern coast of the Mediterranean, including Tyre. The word *Punic* is derived from *Phoenicia* and is used to describe things Carthaginian.

pirates: Seafaring bandits who took advantage of periods when long-distance trade was widespread and navies were weak. The beginning of global trade was a very lucrative period for pirates such as the Zhengs and those organized by the North African beys.

plague pandemic (1346–1351): A disastrous outbreak of plague that is historically unmatched in its death toll. At the time incurable, plague killed 30 to 50 percent of the Eurasian population and continued to return regularly for centuries.

plantation zone: An area stretching from the Chesapeake to Brazil where the majority of African slaves were used. Plantations grew tobacco, rice, and sugar on a large scale as part of the transatlantic economy.

plebeians [plih-BEE-uhns]: Roman citizens who did not come from elite families. Plebeians were commoners who often performed the same work as slaves, although plebeians were reimbursed for their labor whereas slaves were not.

plow agriculture: The use of large domesticated animals to pull plows—a piece of farm equipment that tills soil. Farmers could cultivate five times more land using plows.

polis [POH-lihs]: A political institution, a type of city-state, developed by the Greeks around 700 BCE, that included governance by magistrates, citizenship for adult males, and required military duties for citizen-soldiers.

political decentralization: The weakening of centralized kingdoms and the diminishing of links among transatlantic empires, all as a result of the Atlantic revolutions.

Pontiac's War (1763–1765): An Amerindian uprising against the British. Named after one of the uprising's leaders, the Ottawa chief Pontiac, it was a military standoff but resulted in the designation of all North American lands between Appalachia and the Mississippi River as an "Indian reserve."

population surge: A nearly twofold growth of the global population in the three centuries between 1500 and 1800.

Porfiriato [POHR-fihr-ee-AH-toh] (1876–1910): The decades of Porfirio Díaz's authoritarian rule in Mexico. During this period the Mexican economy grew rapidly, as did increasing inequality, due to Díaz's encouragement of foreign investment and support of dispossessing poor peasants.

Potosí [poh-toh-SEE]: Site of large-scale, dangerously deadly silver mining in the Andes under Spanish authorities during the sixteenth and seventeenth centuries; laborers were mostly conscripted Amerindians and, later, African slaves who suffered harsh conditions, frequent accidents, and mercury poisoning. Silver was the most valuable transatlantic commodity.

praetorian guard: A select group of 4,500 men that Augustus created in order to protect the emperor. On five occasions, the praetorian guard assassinated emperors deemed ineffectual or corrupt, including Caligula and Elagabalus.

Prague Spring (1968): A Czechoslovak reform effort that called for less censorship and more freedom during post–World War II communist rule. The Soviets repressed it with a violent military invasion, causing widespread criticism of communism and the USSR.

printing press: A device invented by Johannes Gutenberg in the mid-fifteenth century that involved the use of movable metal type. It allowed for easier, faster, and cheaper production and dissemination of written information.

Protestantism: A branch of Christianity, initiated by the monk Martin Luther (1483–1546), that took issue with the

Catholic Church. Luther's writing and preaching emphasized scripture over tradition and salvation by inner faith. Many variations of Protestantism arose, but all denominations generally emphasized the importance of individual relationships with God.

proxy wars: Local conflicts around the world in which the United States and the USSR supported rival factions, with each superpower indirectly engaging the other as part of broader Cold War competition. There were at least 50 proxy wars, including the Korean War, the Vietnam War, the Angolan Civil War, and the Soviet-Afghan War.

Punic Wars (264–241 BCE, 218–201 BCE, 149–146 BCE): A series of three wars between the Romans and the Carthaginians. Rome won all three wars and razed Carthage after the Third Punic War.

pyramids: Monumental tombs, containing provisions for an eternal afterlife, that Old Kingdom pharaohs used conscripted peasants to build. The largest was Khufu's Great Pyramid at Giza.

Qin [chihn] **dynasty** (221–207 BCE): A state, under the ruthless leadership of Shi Huangdi, that conquered the Warring States, expanded to the south, and made unifying reforms that left a legacy of a large and united China.

Qing [chihng] **dynasty** (1644–1911): An imperial dynasty descended from a group of Manchu elite. Using innovative military techniques such as banners (units that cut across kin lines) and improved centralized command, the Qing vastly expanded Chinese territory and power.

Quakers: A Protestant sect originating in England that began the organized anti-slavery movement. Quaker beliefs stress the fundamental equality of all human beings, and their moral objections were instrumental to antislavery efforts in Britain and the United States.

Queen Boudica: A British queen who led an uprising against the Roman Empire in the years 60 to 61 CE. The Roman army ultimately defeated Queen Boudica and her followers.

railways: Transportation infrastructure that was central to industrialization and an outgrowth of the coal and iron industries. Railways and locomotives lowered transportation costs, connected markets, and linked countries together.

raised-field agriculture: A labor-intensive and very productive, early farming technique used in the Americas from today's Bolivia to Mexico. It is a form of amphibious agriculture that involves creating islands in wetlands and raising crops on them.

Reconquista [ray-kohn-KEE-stah]: A centuries-long Christian campaign to retake Iberia from Muslim rulers. Europeans, especially Iberians, viewed sailing expeditions as a way to continue the Reconquista in new lands by spreading Christianity and depriving Muslim states of wealth from trade.

Renaissance: A fascination among European elites with the intellectual and artistic traditions of the ancient Greeks and Romans. Humanism, the focus on human bodies and experiences, was a defining feature of the Renaissance.

rising merchant classes: Those of modest backgrounds who traded goods in the Atlantic world and became wealthy. With their newly accumulated fortune, they sought liberties and political voice to ease their commerce and preserve their position.

Russian Revolution of 1917: The overturning of imperial rule in Russia that started with a coup d'état led by the Bolsheviks, a minority Marxist faction. They eventually seized control of the government and set out to reform Russia based on the ideology of communism.

Saadians [SAHD-ee-ihnz]: Dynasts who successfully used guns and cannon to unify Morocco and defeat the Songhai in West Africa. They ultimately were unsuccessful in further attempts to gain wealth and power.

Safavids [SAH-fah-vihds]: A dynasty that originated as a Sunni-Sufi brotherhood but adopted Shi'a Islam and then conquered Iran and most of Iraq. They made Shi'a Islam the state religion, reformulated its theology, and pursued mass conversions.

Sahel: An area of semi-arid grassland that stretches east to west and is located on the southern edge of the Sahara Desert. The Senegal and Niger rivers are in the western Sahel, and ancient Ghana and Mali were located in their floodplains.

Sargon of Akkad: A king who pioneered the political format of empire and united the city-states of southern and central Mesopotamia around 2340 BCE; he built the first professional army, promoted trade, and reigned for about 56 years.

Sassanid [suh-SAH-nid] **dynasty** (224–651 CE): Successors of the Parthians and leaders of the Sassanian Empire who popularized the term *Iran* to refer to Persia. They built up irrigation works, introduced new agricultural crops, promoted long-distance trade, and made Iran into a great regional power.

schisms [SIH-zuhms]: Formal divisions generally based on opposing beliefs, especially within young religions. Early Christian schisms included Arianism, Nestorianism, and Monophysitism. Islam split into Shi'a and Sunni branches soon after its inception.

Scientific Revolution: The adoption of mathematics, observation, and systematic experimentation to understand the world instead of relying solely on scripture and ancient texts, as had been done previously.

sedentary: A term that describes people who stay in one place and form settlements instead of moving around.

self-determination: U.S. president Woodrow Wilson's idea that every European nationality had the right to its own, self-ruled nation. This concept was an important feature of the post–World War I peace treaties and an inspiration for anti-colonialists.

Seljuk [sahl-JYOOK] **Turks** (ca. 980–1090): A pastoral, Sunni Muslim group that rode into Iran, took Baghdad, and conquered Byzantine territory in Anatolia. They spearheaded the lasting Turkification and Islamization of the eastern Mediterranean.

serfs: Peasants who worked as forced labor on large, grain-producing estates for the gentry in Prussia, Poland-Lithuania, and Russia. Landlords of these estates controlled the movement, economic activity, and personal lives of serfs.

Sergei Witte [SAYR-gay VIHT-tee] (1849–1915): A Russian statesman who was deeply involved in the country's industrialization. He directed the government to build railroads, create technical schools, and introduce protectionist tariffs.

settlement houses: During the Industrial Revolution, institutions that elite and middle-class women set up to research and help improve the conditions in which poor and working-class people lived and labored.

settler colony: A form of imperialism in which migrants from a conquering nation establish colonies in conquered lands. Settlers often seek land and dominance, and settler colonies are more violent than colonies without settlers.

shabti [SHAH-tee]: Miniature figurines buried with pharaohs to aid them in the afterlife. Pharaohs sacrificed humans to be their otherworldly attendants until 2600 BCE, after which the use of *shabti* supplanted this practice.

shamanism [SHAH-mah-niz'm]: A broad set of religious beliefs and practices, including direct communication with the supernatural realm and a belief in the existence of a spirit world where the dead live.

Shang dynasty (ca. 1600–1046 BCE): A highly militarized and hierarchical society based in the lower Huang He basin that worshipped the deity Di. During Shang rule, Chinese writing was invented.

shari'a: Meaning "the path" in Arabic, shari'a is the body of Islamic holy law and ethics that governs every aspect of Muslim life. Originally developed on the basis of the Qur'an and accounts of Muhammad's life, it has evolved to form the basis of several schools of Islamic legal practice today.

shi: A cultural elite that emerged under the Zhou and consolidated much of Chinese culture. During the Warring States period, they transformed from being just scholars, to being both scholars and men of war.

Shi Huangdi [shee HWAHNG-dee] (259–210 BCE): Also known as King Zheng and Qin Shi Huang, Shi Huangdi was a successful military commander who conquered vast amounts of land, put an end to the Warring States period, and began the Qin dynasty. He promoted Chinese unity and created a base of unification for subsequent dynasties.

Shi'a [SHEE-ah] **Islam**: An orthodox branch of Islam that was adopted as the state religion in Iran under the Safavid dynasty in the sixteenth and seventeenth centuries. Followers of Shi'a Islam believe that only members of Muhammad's lineage can hold religious and political authority.

shifting agriculture: A type of farming in which farmers cleared land, farmed it for a few years, and then moved to a new patch of land once soil was depleted; often used in forest zones with poor soils.

Shinto [SHIHN-toh]: Meaning "the way of the gods," Shinto is an indigenous Japanese religion that is animistic and polytheistic. It emphasizes ritual and is based on tradition, folklore, shrines, and monuments.

Siddhartha Gautama [sih-DAHR-tuh GOW-taw-mah]: A Kshatri caste prince, born in the sixth or fifth century BCE, who rejected his privileged background and became the Buddha (the Enlightened One); his followers established the religion known as Buddhism.

Sikhism [SIHK-ihzm]: A religion that developed in India in the sixteenth century based on the teachings of Nanak (1469–1538), who asserted that Hinduism and

Islam were one and the same. Nanak rejected elaborate ceremony and the caste system, promoted pacifism, and stressed the importance of humankind over other living creatures and the equality of all people before God.

Silk Road: Relay trade routes that crossed the steppes and deserts of Asia from China to the shores of the Mediterranean; named after one of the most valuable commodities transported on these routes—Chinese silk.

silkworms: Domesticated caterpillars that provided the raw materials for the silk industry in China. Women and girls produced silk, a lucrative trade item, from the threads that silkworms excreted.

silver trade: The worldwide buying and selling of silver that sustained the global economy and grew increasingly important as more people used silver as money. In particular, governments and merchants sought silver to engage more easily in state spending or long-distance trading.

Simón Bolívar [see-MOHN boh-LEE-vahr] (1783–1830): A Venezuelan creole revolutionary leader who fought the Spanish Crown and hoped to found a united states of South America.

Simon Kimbangu [KIHM-ban-goo] (1887–1951): The Congolese founder and leader of the independent African Kimbanguist Church, whom the Belgians imprisoned for 30 years until his death. He preached faith healing, non-violence, monogamy, and sobriety.

slave soldiers: Slaves used in the military; most had been sold by their families in Central Asia to the armies of caliphs and sultans. A few slave soldiers managed to overthrow their masters and install themselves on thrones. The Ghaznavids and Turkic horsemen who established the Delhi sultanate were slave soldiers, and they spread the practice of slave soldiery into India.

slave-and-sugar plantations: Profitable, extensive commercial sugar farms in Brazil and the Caribbean that were larger and more efficient than their predecessors. They relied on the brutal exploitation of slaves who worked in notoriously unhealthy conditions and faced a life expectancy shorter than that of slaves anywhere else in the Americas.

Slavery Abolition Act (1834): Passed in Britain, the first large abolition of slavery. When the Whig Party took power in British Parliament, it introduced the act with widespread support from petitioners. It inspired abolitionists around the world.

smallpox inoculation: The intentional infection of humans with cowpox to produce an immunity against smallpox. It replaced riskier methods of inoculation, quickly spread around the world, and reduced worldwide deaths from smallpox.

social Darwinism: The pseudo-scientific application of Charles Darwin's ideas to subsets of the human species. Arguing that some humans were more fit than others, social Darwinism appealed to science to support racism and racial hierarchies.

socialists: People who sought to alter social and political institutions with an emphasis on the rights of the working class. They often supported ideas such as strong unions, worker cooperatives, and communal ownership of industry.

Sons of Africa: A London-based abolitionist organization. It was made up of former slaves, including Ottobah Cugoano and Olaudah Equiano, who wrote detailed descriptions of their experiences as slaves to strengthen the anti-slave trade movement.

spice trade: The exchange of spices that became increasingly widespread in the early modern period and acted as a driving force of global trade. Portuguese, English, and Dutch merchants dominated the spice trade after 1511.

spices: The most frequently traded raw materials in the Indian Ocean world. Spices—including nutmeg, cloves, cinnamon, and a variety of peppers—largely came from Southeast Asia and southern India; the greatest importers were China, Egypt, Arabia, and Iran.

spread of democracy: The shift from the world having twice as many authoritarian states as liberal democracies in 1974 to the reverse by 2010 due to a rise in interest rates, the end of the Cold War, and the power of example.

Srivijaya [sree-VIH-juh-yuh] (ca. 670–1300): A Southeast Asian, Buddhist kingdom based in Sumatra that Indian culture influenced. It controlled the Straits of Malacca, gaining income from taxes on Indian and Chinese shipping.

state: A territorial unit and political community with a formal government. States always have bureaucrats, judges, and soldiers, and usually have ideologies.

steam engine: A machine that converts the chemical energy in fossil fuels into mechanical energy, called steam power. Steam engines powered the defining technologies of the Industrial Revolution and vastly expanded production levels.

steppe nomads: Mobile peoples, including Khitans, Jurchens, and Mongols, who came from the steppe grasslands north of China. Often clashing militarily with the Chinese, they conquered north China three times and all of China once.

suffragism: A mass political and ideological movement that sought to give women the right to vote. It originated in the nineteenth century, and World War I greatly facilitated its progress and success.

Sufi [SOO-fee] **movement**: A form of mystical Islam that sprang up in the ninth century in response to official attempts to enforce orthodoxy. Instead of following scholarly traditions, Sufism promoted a more personal relationship with God and incorporated song, poetry, and dance into its rituals.

Sukarno [soo-KAHR-noh] (1901–1970): Javanese aristocrat, Indonesian independence activist, and founder of the nationalist Partai Nasional Indonesia. He became the first president of Indonesia after collaborating with the Japanese during World War II and then fighting off the return of Dutch colonialism.

Sumer [SOO-mehr]: The region and culture of southern Mesopotamia, located in today's southern Iraq; the early cities Ur and Uruk were in Sumer.

Sun Tzu [suhn-zoo]: Attributed author of *The Art of War*, possibly written in the sixth or fifth century BCE. The classic work gives insight on military strategy, diplomacy, statecraft, and espionage.

Sun Yatsen [suhn YAHT-suhn] (1866–1925): A physician and revolutionary who opposed the Qing and wanted to reform China in the image of powerful Western countries. He led the Chinese Revolution and became president of China's new constitutional republic until his ouster and exile to Japan in 1913.

Swahili [swah-HEE-lee] **coast**: The coast of East Africa where Arab and Persian traders interacted with local Africans. A distinct Swahili culture and language rooted in Indian Ocean trade developed along this coast.

Tacky's War (1760): An uprising in Jamaica of nearly 1,500 slaves, led by Akan-speaking slaves from what is now Ghana, that lasted for several months before it was brutally suppressed.

Taíno [TAY-noh]: The indigenous population of the Spanish-controlled Caribbean island of Hispaniola. Disease, violence, and enslavement led to a demographic catastrophe among the Taíno.

Taiping [TEYE-pihng] **Rebellion** (1850–1864): A large rebellion led by Hong Xiuquan and his army, the Taiping. Motivated by political, nationalist, and Christian goals, the Taiping managed to control much of the Yangzi Valley for 10 years until their defeat and Hong's death.

Tenochtitlán [thuh-NOCH-tee-tlahn]: The large, populous capital of the Aztec Empire located on an island in Lake Texcoco in the Basin of Mexico.

textiles and metallurgy: The two main industries at the forefront of industrial revolutions around the world. Both cloth making and iron making were well suited to steam-powered mass production.

third pulse of decolonization: The comparatively rapid emergence of around 100 new countries that occurred between 1945 and 1975, mainly in Africa, Asia, and the Caribbean.

Thirteenth Amendment (1865): Introduced at the end of the Civil War, an amendment to the U.S. Constitution that abolished slavery. It led to the liberation of 4 million people, making it the largest emancipation in world history.

Thomas Clarkson (1760–1846): A member of the Anglican elite and a staunch anti–slave trade and abolitionist activist. He allied with the Quakers to publicize the atrocities of the slave trade and was influential in the British abolition of the slave trade and slavery.

Tibetan Empire (ca. 618–842): Also known as Yarlung, the Tibetan Empire was located north of the Himalaya, and its influence spread from India to Mongolia. It was a formidable competitor to the Tang.

Tigris and Euphrates Rivers: Twin rivers that flow into the Persian Gulf; they supported agriculture and trade in Mesopotamia.

Tiwanaku [tee-wahn-AH-koo] (ca. 100–1100 CE): An Andean city and empire that amassed wealth and power through its control of the supply of llamas. The city was a religious center located near Lake Titicaca in what is now Bolivia; its empire and influence reached as far as northern Chile, lowland Bolivia, and the Peruvian Andes.

Tlacélel [tlah-KAY-luhl] (ca. 1398–1480): A successful and influential Aztec king who fortified the cultural legacy and importance of the Aztecs. He invented a glorious Aztec history and strengthened the Aztecs' religious importance by putting them in charge of sustaining the sun god.

Tokugawa shogunate [TOH-koo-GAH-wah SHOH-guh-nayt] (1600–1868): A ruling dynasty in Japan made up of the descendants of Tokugawa Ieyasu, who completed the task of unifying Japan in 1600.

Toussaint L'Ouverture [TOO-sahn LOO-vehr-toor] (ca. 1743–1803): The main leader of the Haitian Revolution. He was born a slave on St. Domingue but was freed around age 30, after which he led the Haitian slave insurrection and became a successful commander in the Haitian army.

Toyotomi Hideyoshi [tohh-yoh-TOH-mee hee-day-OH-shee] (1537–1598): Oda Nobunaga's successor; a Japanese warlord whose soldiers liberally employed guns and nearly united all of Japan. He invaded Korea, enslaving thousands, but retreated from a failed invasion in China.

transatlantic slave trade (1519–ca. 1860): The transportation by European traders of 12 to 14 million slaves from Africa to the Americas, mainly to work on plantations. This trade constituted the largest forced migration in world history.

transition to agriculture: The switch between human populations finding or cultivating food and settled human populations producing food through domestication. This process occurred in various places independently of one another.

Trans-Siberian Railway: A railway from Moscow to the Pacific Ocean that was completed in 1903. A remarkable feat of engineering and construction, the almost 6,000-mile-long railway built by 9,000 laborers was a defining symbol of the Russian Industrial Revolution.

Treaty of Tordesillas (1494): Spain and Portugal used this agreement to demarcate a line halfway between Columbus's discoveries in the Americas and the Cape Verde islands off the coast of West Africa. It gave all lands west of the line to Spain and all lands east to Portugal.

Treaty of Versailles [vehr-SEYE] (1919): A peace treaty written by the victorious Allies that imposed strict and punitive policies on Germany in the aftermath of World War I. The treaty provoked outrage in Germany due to its reparations and war guilt clauses, as well as among Chinese because it gave German concessions in China to Japan.

Treaty of Waitangi [weye-TANG-ee] (1840): A treaty in which the Maori of New Zealand agreed to become British subjects in exchange for land guarantees. British settlers soon broke this treaty, fought the Maori for land, and ended Maori independence.

tsar [ZAHR]: The title Russian rulers adopted after 1547. The tsars, particularly Ivan the Terrible (r. 1547–1584) and Peter the Great (r. 1682–1725), built an expansive and centralized Russian empire by modernizing the military and asserting control over the Russian elite.

Túpac Amaru II [too-pak ah-MAHR-oo] (1738–1781): A Jesuit-educated mestizo revolutionary descended from the Inka ruling family. He led a tax revolt in the Andes beginning in 1780 and emphasized justice and the end of ethnic oppression.

Tyre: A merchant town that linked the trade of Egypt, northern Mesopotamia, Syria, and Anatolia and specialized in a highly desirable maroon-purple dye. In order to expand their metals trade, Tyre's merchants established Carthage as well as several other colonies along the Mediterranean coast.

Umayyad caliphate [oo-MEYE-ahd KA-lih-fayt]: The first genuine Islamic state (661–750), based in Damascus and led by caliphs ("deputies of God") who claimed to be successors of the prophet Muhammad. They expanded their empire through conquests and exerted "soft power" through monumental architecture such as the Dome of the Rock mosque.

universities: The first opened in Cairo in the tenth century, followed by several in Europe in the twelfth century. European universities, as comparatively free spaces of inquiry and debate, prompted the development of science and art.

university of war: The state of constant military competition and chaos in Europe during the early modern period. These conditions increased the power of successful states and made them skilled in warfare, efficient at tax collection, and able to adapt quickly to innovations.

Vasco da Gama: A low-ranking Portuguese noble who led an expedition in 1497 around the southern tip of Africa and into the Indian Ocean in search of Christian allies and valuable spices for the Portuguese Crown. He helped set up a lasting Portuguese presence in India and East Africa.

Vedas [VAY-duhs]: Four texts, which probably originated as oral traditions, that are the earliest existing examples of literature in Sanskrit and the oldest sacred texts of Hinduism. The culture of the Ganges basin is called Vedic after them.

vertical archipelago: The system by which Andean clans, called *ayllus*, placed people from a given lineage in communities at each elevation level of the mountains in order to exploit the resources of the

different environments. The Inkas did not invent this system, but greatly expanded it.

Vietnam War (1965–1975): A proxy conflict between communist North Vietnam, aligned with China and the USSR, and anti-communist South Vietnam, aligned with the United States. The United States committed hundreds of thousands of troops to the domestically unpopular war, which the North Vietnamese ultimately won.

Vikings: A group of seaborne marauders from Scandinavia that looted, slaved, and conquered nearby territories beginning around 800 CE. They settled land from Russia to Greenland and established several enduring trade links.

Vital Revolution: The steady improvement of human health and life expectancy after 1750. Better nutrition, microbial unification, control of smallpox, and sanitation reform contributed to this shift.

Vladimir Lenin (1870–1924): A Russian-born revolutionary and influential member of the Bolsheviks. He consolidated power by 1921 and was the first leader of the USSR.

Wang Yangming [wang YAHN-mihng] (1472–1529): A Chinese philosopher who challenged prevailing neo-Confucian thought and gained followers by arguing that ordinary people could attain moral perfection through inherent knowledge rather than through book learning.

Wangari Maathai [wahn-GAH-ree MAH-theye] (1940–2011): A prominent political, environmental, and women's rights activist. The first woman in the history of East Africa to earn a PhD, founder of the Green Belt Movement, member of the Kenyan parliament, and Nobel Peace Prize laureate.

witch hunts: The spike in accusations of witchcraft between 1500 and 1700, which resulted in the widespread use of torture and execution of accused witches. Unmarried women over age 40 were the main targets.

working class: A section of society, formed during the Industrial Revolution, that comprised factory and mine workers who performed shift work for wages. Workers' lives at this time were precarious and dangerous, and they were politically divided between seeking reform and inciting revolution.

World War I (1914–1918): A conflict between the Central Powers (Germany, Austria-Hungary, the Ottoman Empire) and the Entente or Allied Powers (France, Russia, Britain, Italy)

fought mainly in Europe. Many smaller European nations joined in, as well as ultimately the United States. The war required mass mobilization of populations and resources and led to unprecedented violence and destruction.

World War II (1937–1945): The most expansive and deadliest war in history, fought between the Axis powers and the Allies. It involved four overlapping wars, fought primarily in Europe, China, the Pacific, and North Africa.

Wu Zetian [woo ZAY-shihn] (624–705): The only woman who both ruled China in her own name and was the most powerful person on Earth when in power. Wu was a controversial ruler who was ruthless toward her enemies, adept at foreign affairs, a great patron of Buddhism, and a supporter of commerce.

Yamato race theory: A fictional idea developed in the 1930s. It held that all Japanese people shared a common ancestry to an ancient race that was superior to other nearby peoples, including Koreans and Chinese.

Yamato region: A state in the southeast of Japan that began to expand its influence in the 600s. It ruled several rice-producing regions, emphasized military skill, adopted Buddhism, and imported cultural ideas from the Tang.

Yangzi [YAHNG-zuh] **River**: A river in China whose valley was home to the second transition to agriculture, which occurred about 7000 BCE and was rice-based.

Yermak [yehr-MAHK]: A Cossack who pioneered the expansion of the Russian fur trade into Siberia during the 1580s. His success also spearheaded the introduction of disease and practices of brutality that ultimately killed many native Siberians.

Yoshinogari [yoh-shih-noh-GAH-ree]: A site on Japan's southern island of Kyushu where evidence of weaving, bronze casting, and other crafts has been found, as well as mainland trade goods such as Korean-made bronze daggers and Chinese bronze mirrors.

Young Turk Revolution (1908): A coup d'état in the Ottoman Empire that nationalist army officers, called the Young Turks, led. They were frustrated with foreign encroachment on Ottoman territory and successfully imposed a constitution.

Younger Dryas (10,700–9,700 BCE): A severe cold and dry period that temporarily reversed the process of slow global warming that occurred after the coldest part of the last ice age.

Yuan [yoo-AHN] **dynasty** (1279–1368): The dynasty established by the Mongols after the defeat of the Song by Khubilai Khan. Despite their rough-edged steppe-nomad nature, the Yuan allowed religious diversity, promoted scientific creativity and cultural exchange, and encouraged trade throughout the many lands they controlled.

Zanj revolt (868–883): A massive uprising of slaves from East Africa who worked on plantations in Iraq. One of the most successful slave rebellions in world history, it dealt an immense blow to southern Iraq and ended the practice of plantation slavery in Iraq for around a millennium.

Zheng He [SHENG-hah]: An admiral and an important ally of the Yongle Emperor. He arranged and led the Ming voyages during the fifteenth century.

Zhou [JOH] **dynasty** (1045–256 BCE): The dynasty that began the process of Chinese unification, developed irrigation, promoted iron farm tools, and began using chariots in war. In 771 BCE, Zhou rulers lost much of their territory; only part of their kingdom, the Eastern Zhou, survived until 256 BCE.

ziggurats [ZIG-uh-rahts]: A pioneering form of monumental architecture, ziggurats are temple-palaces dedicated to local gods.

Zoroastrianism [zohr-oh-ASS-tree-ahn-iz'm]: A monotheistic religion that arose in Persia around the prophecies of Zoroaster sometime between the tenth and sixth centuries BCE. With priests called magi, it emphasized the creator-god Ahura Mazda, human choice between good and evil, and divine judgment.

TEXT CREDITS

CHAPTER 4

(pp. 94–95) Elizabeth Kolbert (trans.); © 2006 "The Curse of Akkad" from *Field Notes from a Catastrophe: Man, Nature, and Climate Change*. With permission from Bloomsbury Publishing Plc.

(p. 95) Republished by Permission of Penn State University Press. From *The Lamentation over the Destruction of Sumer and Ur* by Piotr Michalowski (1998) p 59. Permission conveyed through Copyright Clearance Center, Inc.

(p. 96) Republished by Permission of Princeton University Press. From *The Ancient Near East, Vol. 2: A New Anthology of Texts and Pictures* by James B. Pritchard (Princeton: 1975). pp 99–104. Permission conveyed through Copyright Clearance Center, Inc.

(p. 104) Samuel Noah Kramer (trans.); Excerpt from "The Love Song of Shu-Sin," from *History Begins at Sumer*, (Falcon's Wing Press, 1956), p. 300. All rights reserved. Except for brief quotations used for purposes of scholarly citation, none of this work may be reproduced in any form by any means without written permission from the publisher. For information address the University of Pennsylvania Press, 3905 Spruce Street, Philadelphia, Pennsylvania 19104–4112.

CHAPTER 5

(pp. 115–116) Republished by Permission of University of California Press. From *Ancient Egyptian Literature A Book of Readings; Vol 2: The New Kingdom* by Miriam Lichtheim (U of California Press: 1976). pp 168–172. Permission conveyed through Copyright Clearance Center, Inc.

(p. 134) Brians, Paul, and Mary Gallwey. Michael Myers, Ed. *Reading about the World. Vol. 1.* Orlando, FL: Harcourt College Publishers, 1999. Print. Reprinted by permission of Michael Myers.

CHAPTER 11

(p. 318) Republished by Permission of Princeton University Press. From *A Reader on Classical Islam* by F. E. Peters (Princeton: 1994). pp 118–120. Permission conveyed through Copyright Clearance Center, Inc.

CHAPTER 14

(p. 403) Republished by Hebrew Union College Press. From *The Jew in the Medieval World: A Sourcebook* by Jacob Rader Marcus (New York: 1972). pp 229–230. Permission conveyed through Copyright Clearance Center, Inc.

CHAPTER 15

(p. 433) Arthur J. O. Anderson and Charles E. Dibble (trans.): Excerpt from "Third Chapter," from *Florentine Codex, Book 3: The Origin of the Gods*, 2nd Ed. (School of American Research, 1978). Republished with permission from University of Utah Press.

CHAPTER 16

(p. 471) "Duarte Pacheco Pereira Tries to Come to Terms with 'Difference,'" in Malyn Newitt, ed., *The Portuguese in West Africa, 1415–1670: A Documentary History*. Cambridge, U.K. (Cambridge University Press, © 2010).

CHAPTER 17

(p. 491) "Duarte Pacheco Pereira Tries to Come to Terms with 'Difference,'" in Malyn Newitt, ed., *The Portuguese in West Africa, 1415–1670: A Documentary History*. Cambridge, U.K. (Cambridge University Press, © 2010).

(p. 491) "Letter of the King of Kongo to King of Portugal Dom João III, 1526,'" in *Converging on Cannibals: Terrors of Slaving in Atlantic Africa 1519–1670 (Africa in World History Series)* Jared Staller ed. and trans. Athens, Ohio. (Ohio University Press, © 2019).

CHAPTER 18

(p. 537) "A Hymn from the Kabir," from Dass, Nirmal, *Songs of Kabir from the Adi Granth/translation and introduction by Nirmal Dass*, pp. 251–252. Albany: State University of New York Press, [1991].

CHAPTER 21

(p. 618) ADAMS FAMILY CORRESPONDENCE, VOLUME 1 AND 2: DECEMBER 1761–MARCH 1778, edited by Harold A. Bierck, Jr. Compiled by Vicente Lecuna. Translated by Lewis Bertrand. New York, N.Y.: The Colonial Press Inc. 1951. © 1951 Banco de Venezuela.

(p. 632) "A revolutionary's letter from Jamaica," from *Selected Writings of Bolivar, Vol 1: 1810–1822*, edited by L. H. Butterfield, Cambridge, Mass.: The Belknap Press of Harvard University Press, Copyright © 1963 by the Massachusetts Historical Society.

CHAPTER 22

(p. 662) "Approximate Share of Global Industrial Production, 1800–1900,'" from J. R. McNeill and Kenneth Pomeranz, ed., *The Cambridge World History: Volume 7, Production, Destruction, and Connection, 1750–Present*, p. 122. Cambridge, U.K. (Cambridge University Press, © 2015).

(p. 663) "Riots," Leeds Mercury, 25 Apr. 1812, in *British Library Newspapers*.

CHAPTER 23

(p. 692) Excerpts from the testimony of Abina Mansah in "SCT 5/4/19 *Regina V. Quamina Eddoo, 10 Nov 1876*" from Getz, Trevor R and Liz Clarke *Abina and the Important Men A Graphic History*. pp. 87–89, 92, 94, 97. Oxford, U.K. (Oxford University Press, © 2016).

CHAPTER 24

(p. 731) Excerpts from *Ethiopia Through Russian Eyes, Country in Transition 1896–1898* by Alexander Bulatovich; Richard Seltzer, trans. Reprinted by permission of Richard Seltzer and Red Sea Press.

CHAPTER 27

(p. 815) Excerpts from "Record of the Cheerful Troop," presented by Nippon Kyoiku Kamishibai Kyokai. From *Propaganda Performed: Kamishibai in Japan's Fifteen Year War, 2015,* Sharalyn Orbaugh, ed. pp. 24–25, 27–29. (Copyright © by Koninklijke Brill NV, Leiden), reprinted by permission of Brill.

CHAPTER 29

(p. 882) From "The Moment the Barrier of Fear Broke Down" by Adel Abdel Ghafar in *Voices of the Arab Spring: Personal Stories From the Arab Revolutions*, Asaad Alsaleh, ed. Copyright © 2015 Columbia University Press. Reprinted with permission of Columbia University Press.

PHOTO CREDITS

History/Age Fotostock; p. 183: World History Archive/Alamy Stock Photo; p. 184 (both): Lou-Foto/Alamy Stock Photo; p. 185: Wiliam Perry/Alamy Stock Photo; p. 186 (top): ERIC LAFFORGUE/Alamy Stock Photo; (bottom): Gianni Dagli Orti/Shutterstock; p. 187: Cultural Relics Publishing House (Wenwu), Beijing, China; p. 189: akg-images/Bildarchiv Steffens; p. 190: Science & Society Picture Library/Getty Images; p. 191: Album/Alamy Stock Photo; p. 192 (top): akg-images/Pictures From History; (bottom): Lou-Foto/Alamy Stock Photo; p. 194 (top): age fotostock/Alamy Stock Photo; (bottom): Werner Forman Archive/Bridgeman Images; p. 196: DGP_travel/Alamy Stock Photo; p. 198: The Picture Art Collection/Alamy Stock Photo; p. 199: DeAgostini/Getty Images; p. 201: Werner Forman/Art Resource, NY.

Chapter 8: Page 206: Alinari/Art Resource, NY; p. 209: album/Alamy Stock Photo; p. 211 (top): Robert Preston/Alamy Stock Photo; (bottom left): Musee National de Carthage, Carthage, Tunisia/Bridgeman Images; (bottom right): Peter Horree/Alamy Stock Photo; p. 212 (top): Peter Horree/Alamy Stock Photo; (bottom): EnriquePSans/Alamy Stock Photo; p. 213: Album/Alamy Stock Photo; p. 214: Andrej Privizer/Alamy Stock Photo; p. 215: Scala/Art Resource, NY; p. 217: Alinari/Art Resource, NY; p. 219: eye35.pix/Alamy Stock Photo; p. 220: bpk Bildagentur/Antikensammlung, Staatliche Museen, Berlin/Art Resource; p. 221: Scala/Art Resource, NY; p. 223: Ancient Art and Architecture/Alamy Stock Photo; p. 224: INTERFOTO/Alamy Stock Photo; p. 225 (left): De Agostini/G. Berengo Gardin/Getty Images; (right): Museo della Civilta Romana, Rome, Italy/Bridgeman Images; p. 226 (top): Werner Forman Archive/Bridgeman Images; (bottom): Alinari/Art Resource, NY; p. 230: Album/Alamy Stock Photo; p. 232: Alpineguide/Alamy Stock Photo; p. 233: De Agostini Picture Library/Bridgeman Images; p. 234: Scala/Art Resource, NY; p. 235: akg-images.

Chapter 9: Page 238: Marcin S. Sadurski/Alamy Stock Photo; p. 240: Ashmolean Museum, University of Oxford/Bridgeman Images; p. 243: Akg-images; p. 244: ©Carla Klehm; p. 245: Peter Horree/Alamy Stock Photo; p. 246: ©Olivier Testa 2018; p. 247 (top): De Agostini Picture Library/C. Sappa/Bridgeman Images; (bottom): De Agostini Picture Library/C. Sappa/Bridgeman Images; p. 252 (top): imageBROKER/Alamy Stock Photo; (bottom): Fratelli Alinari/AKG Images; p. 254: PRISMA ARCHIVO/Alamy Stock Photo; p. 255: Album/Alamy Stock Photo; p. 256: Songquan Deng/Alamy Stock Photo; p. 257: Ashmolean Museum, University of Oxford/Bridgeman Images; p. 259: Album/Alamy Stock Photo; p. 260: Album/Alamy Stock Photo; p. 262: HIP/Art Resource, NY.

Chapter 10: Page 266: akg-images/Fototeca Gilardi; p. 270: Department of Anthropology, National Museum of Natural History, Smithsonian Institution, A581650; p. 272: Werner Forman/Universal Images Group/Getty Images; p. 273: Toño Labra/AgeFotostock; p. 275: Indianapolis Museum of Art at Newfields, USA/Gift of Bonnie and David Ross/Bridgeman Images; p. 277: CM Dixon/Print Collector/Getty Images; p. 278 (top): DeAgostini/Getty Images; (bottom): Justin Kerr; p. 280: Werner Forman Archive/Bridgeman Images; p. 282: Erich Lessing/Art Resource,

NY; p. 283 (both): Peter Horree/Alamy Stock Photo; p. 285: Michael Rooney/Alamy Stock Photo; p. 287 (both): DEA/G. DAGLI ORTI/De Agostini/Getty Images; p. 288: Jean-Michel COUREAU/ Gamma-Rapho via Getty Images; p. 291: Suzanne Long/Alamy Stock Photo; p. 293: Douglas Peebles Photography/Alamy Stock Photo.

Chapter 11: Page 296: Heritage Images/Getty Images; p. 297: akg-images/Pictures From History; p. 298: Julie Billingsley; p. 300: akg-images/Rainer Hackenberg; p. 302 (top): Erich Lessing/Art Resource, NY;(bottom): Musee des Antiquites Nationales, St. Germain-en-Laye, France/Bridgeman Images; p. 304: Hemis/Alamy Stock Photo; p. 305: Cultura Creative (RF)/Alamy Stock Photo; p. 309 (left): World History Archive/Alamy Stock Photo; (right): www.BibleLandPictures. com/Alamy Stock Photo; p. 310: GL Archive/Alamy Stock Photo; p. 311: Westend61 GmbH/Alamy Stock Photo; p. 312: Hervé Champollion/akg-images; p. 314: DeAgostini/Getty Images; p. 319 (top): B.O'Kane/Alamy Stock Photo; (bottom): Bridgeman Images; p. 320 (left): akg-images/Bildarchiv Monheim; (right): Umayyad Mosque, Damascus, Syria/Bridgeman Images; p. 323: The British Museum/Trustees of the British Museum; p. 324: Qusayr 'Amra, Jordan/Bridgeman Images.

Chapter 12: Page 328: Wolfgang Kaehler/World Pictures/agefotostock; p. 332: Artokoloro Quint Lox Limited/Alamy Stock Photo; p. 334: Dorling Kindersley ltd/Alamy Stock Photo; p. 337 (top): Album/Alamy Stock Photo; (bottom): Pictures from History/Bridgeman Images; p. 339: Wolfgang Kaehler/LightRocket via Getty Images; p. 342: The Picture Art Collection/Alamy Stock Photo; p. 344: De Agostini Picture Library/De Agostini Editore/agefotostock; p. 345: Daniel Schwen / Pictures From History/Newscom; p. 346: FLHC 16/Alamy Stock Photo; p. 347: akg-images/De Agostini Picture Library; p. 348: De Agostini Picture Library/G. Dagli Orti/Bridgeman Images; p. 349: akg-images/Dirk Radzinski; p. 351: akg-images; p. 353: GRANGER—All rights reserved; p. 355: Marco Secchi/Alamy Stock Photo.

Chapter 13: Page 358: Fine Art Images/Heritage Images/Getty Images; p. 362: pixel shepherd/Alamy Stock Photo; p. 364: Tomas Abad/Alamy Stock Photo; p. 365: Muthuraman Vaithinathan/Alamy Stock Photo; p. 366: imagebrOKER/Alamy Stock Photo; p. 367: SEF/Art Resource, NY; p. 369 (left): robertharding/Alamy Stock Photo; (right): © RMN-Grand Palais/Art Resource, NY; p. 370: Atlantide Phototravel/Corbis Documentary/Getty Images; p. 372: Purchase, Oscar de la Renta Ltd. Gift, 2006, Metropolitan Museum of Art, released into public domain; p. 373 (top): Digital Image © Museum Associates/LACMA. Licensed by Art Resource, NY; (bottom): Photo © Stephen Coyne/Bridgeman Images; p. 374: Christine Osborne Pictures/Alamy Stock Photo; p. 375: Fine Art Images/Heritage Images/Getty Images; p. 377: Art Collection 3/Alamy Stock Photo; p. 378: robertharding/Alamy Stock Photo; p. 381: Heritage Images/Getty Images; p. 382: Photo © Luca Tettoni/Bridgeman Images; p. 383: Jason Gallier/Alamy Stock Photo; p. 385 (left): Christopher Scott/Alamy Stock Photo; (right): Heritage Image Partnership Ltd/Alamy Stock Photo.

Chapter 14: Page 388: Bibliotheque Nationale, Paris, France/Bridgeman Images; p. 392: Album/Alamy Stock Photo; p. 396: mauritius images GmbH/Alamy Stock Photo; p. 398: akg-images/Pictures From History; p. 399: Heritage Image Partnership Ltd/Alamy Stock Photo; p. 400 (top): akg-images/Pictures From History; (bottom): Elizabeth Whiting & Associates/Alamy Stock Photo; p. 402: DEA Picture Library/Getty Images; p. 406: Index Fototeca/Bridgeman Images; p. 407: imageBROKER/Alamy Stock Photo; p. 409: age fotostock/Alamy Stock Photo; p. 411: Roland and Sabrina Michaud/akg-images; p. 412: age fotostock/Alamy Stock Photo ; p. 413: Roland and Sabrina Michaud/akg-images; p. 414: akg-images/Pictures From History; p. 415: akg-images/WHA/World History Archive; p. 416: Art Collection 2/Alamy Stock Photo; p. 417 (top): Werner Forman/Art Resource, NY; (right): British Library, London/Bridgeman Images; p. 418: Gianni Dagli Orti/Shutterstock; p. 420: Pictures from History/Bridgeman Images; p. 422: Bibliotheque Royale de Belgique, Brussels, Belgium/Bridgeman Images.

Chapter 15: Page 424: musée du quai Branly—Jacques Chirac, Dist. RMN-Grand Palais/Art Resource, NY; p. 430 (left): Michele Burgess/Alamy Stock Photo; (right): De Agostini Picture Library/G. Dagli Orti/Bridgeman Images; p. 431: Jesse Kraft/Alamy Stock Photo; p. 434: HIP/Art Resource, NY;p. 435: Bibliotheque Nationale, Paris, France/Bridgeman Images; p. 436: akg-images/Universal Images Group; p. 437 (top): De Agostini Picture Library/G. Dagli Orti/Bridgeman Images; (bottom): akg-images/De Agostini Picture Library; p. 438: INTERFOTO/Alamy Stock Photo; p. 439: akg-images/WHA/World History Archive; p. 440: Ian Dagnall/Alamy Stock Photo; p. 442: Werner Forman Archive/Bridgeman Images; p. 443: Carver Mostardi AgeFotostock; p. 445: Bibliotheque Nationale, Paris, France/Bridgeman Images; p. 448 (top): Universal Images Group North America LLC/DeAgostini/Alamy Stock Photo; (bottom): Alpha Historica/Alamy Stock Photo; p. 450: Douglas Peebles Photography/Alamy Stock Photo.

Chapter 16: Page 452: Alamy Stock Photo; p. 454: age fotostock/Alamy Stock Photo; p. 457 (left): Topkapi Palace Museum, Istanbul, Turkey/Bridgeman Images; (right): Bibliotheque Nationale/De Agostini/Bridgeman Images; p. 458 (left): Thai School/Photo © Luca Tettoni/Bridgeman Images; (right): Michael Runkel/Alamy Stock Photo; p. 461: Gregory A. Harlin/National Geographic Image Collection/Bridgeman Images; p. 462 (top): The Picture Art Collection/Alamy Stock Photo; (bottom): Pictures from History/David Henley/Bridgeman Images; p. 463 (top): Pictures from History/Bridgeman Images; (bottom): Sofia Pereira/StockPhotosArt - Palaces/Alamy Stock Photo; p. 464: G. Dagli Orti/De Agostini Picture Library/Bridgeman Images; p. 465 (top): Art Resource, NY; (bottom): Sabena Jane Blackbird/Alamy Stock Photo; p. 466: Alamy Stock Photo; p. 467: Granger Collection; p. 468: Banco Nacional Ultramarino, Portugal/Bridgeman Images; p. 470: Roman Pesarenko/Alamy Stock Photo; p. 472: Album/Alamy Stock Photo; p. 473: Private Collection/Bridgeman Images; p. 474: The Picture Art Collection/Alamy Stock Photo; p. 475: Granger Collection; p. 477: Photo © Heini

INDEX

WORLD POLITICAL MAP

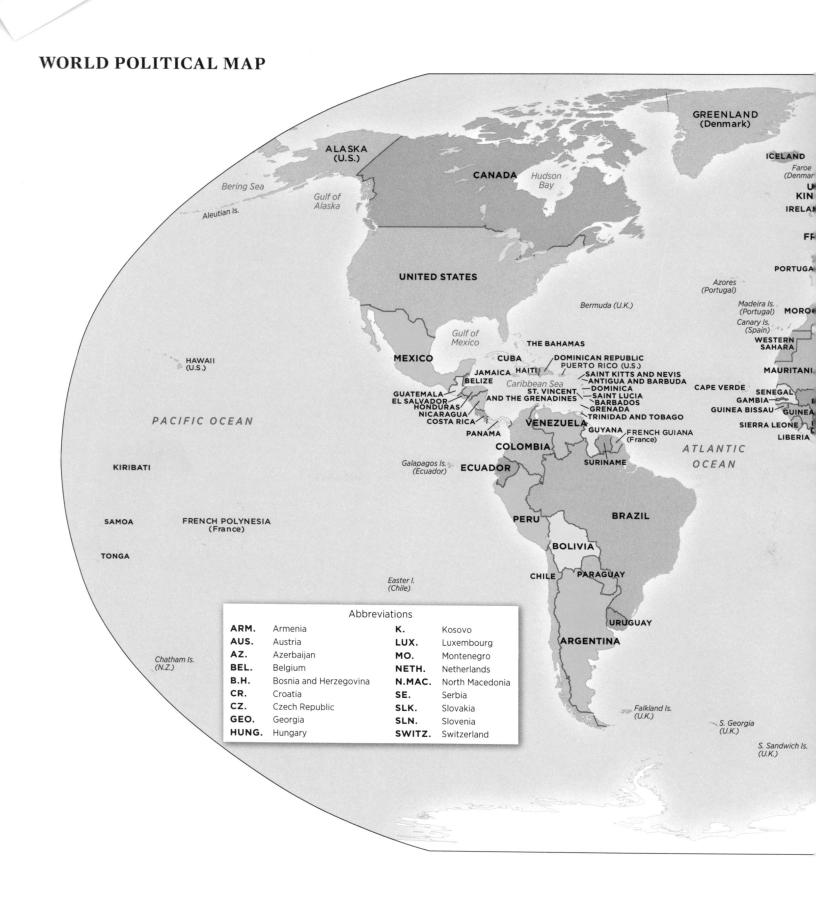

GREENLAND
(Denmark)

ICELAND

Faroe
(Denmar

ALASKA
(U.S.)

CANADA

Hudson
Bay

U
KIN

IRELA

Bering Sea

FR

Gulf of
Alaska

Aleutian Is.

UNITED STATES

PORTUGA

Azores
(Portugal)

Bermuda (U.K.)

Madeira Is.
(Portugal) MORO

HAWAII
(U.S.)

Gulf of
Mexico

THE BAHAMAS

Canary Is.
(Spain)

WESTERN
SAHARA

MEXICO

CUBA

DOMINICAN REPUBLIC
PUERTO RICO (U.S.)

JAMAICA HAITI
BELIZE

SAINT KITTS AND NEVIS
ANTIGUA AND BARBUDA

MAURITANI

CAPE VERDE

GUATEMALA
EL SALVADOR
HONDURAS
NICARAGUA
COSTA RICA

Caribbean Sea

ST. VINCENT
AND THE GRENADINES

DOMINICA
SAINT LUCIA
BARBADOS
GRENADA

TRINIDAD AND TOBAGO

SENEGAL

GAMBIA

GUINEA BISSAU GUINEA

SIERRA LEONE

PACIFIC OCEAN

PANAMA

VENEZUELA

GUYANA

FRENCH GUIANA
(France)

ATLANTIC

LIBERIA

COLOMBIA

OCEAN

KIRIBATI

Galapagos Is.
(Ecuador)

ECUADOR

SURINAME

SAMOA

FRENCH POLYNESIA
(France)

PERU

BRAZIL

TONGA

BOLIVIA

Easter I.
(Chile)

CHILE

PARAGUAY

Chatham Is.
(N.Z.)

URUGUAY

ARGENTINA

Falkland Is.
(U.K.)

S. Georgia
(U.K.)

S. Sandwich Is.
(U.K.)

Abbreviations

ARM.	Armenia	K.	Kosovo
AUS.	Austria	LUX.	Luxembourg
AZ.	Azerbaijan	MO.	Montenegro
BEL.	Belgium	NETH.	Netherlands
B.H.	Bosnia and Herzegovina	N.MAC.	North Macedonia
CR.	Croatia	SE.	Serbia
CZ.	Czech Republic	SLK.	Slovakia
GEO.	Georgia	SLN.	Slovenia
HUNG.	Hungary	SWITZ.	Switzerland